The Federal Legal Directory

A Guide to the Legal Offices and Key Legal Personnel of the U.S. Government

The Federal Legal Directory

A Guide to the Legal Offices and Key Legal Personnel of the U.S. Government

Compiled and edited by
Richard L. Hermann
Linda P. Sutherland
FEDERAL REPORTS INC.

ORYX PRESS
1990

The rare Arabian Oryx is believed to have inspired the myth of the unicorn. This desert antelope became virtually extinct in the early 1960s. At that time several groups of international conservationists arranged to have 9 animals sent to the Phoenix Zoo to be the nucleus of a captive breeding herd. Today the Oryx population is nearly 800, and over 400 have been returned to reserves in the Middle East.

4041 North Central at Indian School Road
Phoenix, Arizona 85012-3397

Published simultaneously in Canada

Printed and Bound in the United States of America

ISBN 0-89774-675-9
ISSN 1052-2832

TABLE OF CONTENTS

INTRODUCTION

Federal laws and regulations, and the Federal lawyers who administer, enforce, and advise policymakers about them, affect every aspect of our daily lives. From prohibiting age discrimination to assigning ZIP Codes, the Federal Government is involved in every arena of interest and endeavor, causing a proliferation of complex laws and regulations, Government attorneys to enforce them, and private-sector attorneys who represent individuals and organizations affected by them.

The maze of Federal law and legal offices and their complex interrelationships can be intimidating both to attorneys and laypeople faced with an issue involving Federal law or regulation. Finding a way through this maze can be a daunting, time-consuming task.

This inaugural edition of the Federal Legal Directory is designed to assist attorneys and other people who are faced with legal issues involving the U.S. Government. It is the first comprehensive compilation of information about the Federal legal establishment--its many legal offices; its key legal personnel; and the major statutes and regulations it administers and under which Federal attorneys operate.

The information is arranged as follows: Executive Branch departments and agencies are presented first (the cabinet departments, then the independent agencies, each in alphabetical order), followed by Legislative Branch agencies and Judicial Branch organizations. Within each agency, the user will generally find the following information:

*Department/agency name and address

*Department/agency description

*Name and telephone numbers of the department/agency head, the key legal personnel in the general counsel's office as well as in all the other legal offices of the organization, and other individuals and offices with whom practicing attorneys must frequently deal, such as the:

*Public affairs or public information office, which is generally responsible for the department/agency public information program

*Procurement information office, which includes department/agency efforts to set aside procurements for small, minority-owned, and women-owned businesses and to assist eligible businesses become Federal contractors

*Central FAX numbers

*Freedom of Information Act (FOIA)/Privacy Act office, which is often the first place an attorney or concerned citizen must turn for information

*Library facilities and their accessibility to the public

*Inspector General office

*Addresses and phone numbers of regional/field counsel offices

*Other department/agency legal offices and key personnel, including Boards of Contract Appeals, Offices of Administrative Law Judges, and other administrative adjudicative bodies, as well as where to find rules of practice and procedure and published decisions for these entities

*Publications and accessible Government databases of interest to attorneys and individuals with a Federal legal problem, question, or interest

*Key legal authorities from which Federal departments and agencies derive their authority and which they administer, including abstracts of key statutes and statutory citations to the United States Code, citations to general agency regulations and regulations implementing these statutes, and relevant Executive orders and treaties. (U.S. Code Cong. Service refers to the United States Code Congressional Service, the predecessor publication to the United States Code Congressional and Administrative News.)

Two appendixes are also included immediately following the department and agency sections:

(1) Annotated Bibliography of Federal Legal Databases and Publications, a comprehensive list of all of the databases and publications described in the department/agency sections of the Directory, as well as additional publications of general interest or government-wide applicability

(2) Detailed description of commercial online databases and document retrieval services available to attorneys and organizations with a need to monitor Federal legal developments

Finally, the Directory also has two indexes to assist users:

(1) Topical Index useful for identifying specific agency legal offices and personnel by their responsibilities

(2) Department and Agency Index.

The editors hope this Directory will assist everyone deal more effectively with the Federal legal establishment. Like every bureaucracy, the Federal Government's structural and functional intricacies can frustrate or even overwhelm those without the key to the maze. How much time--and money--has been spent trying to find the right answer, the right person, or an informed opinion? How many times has it been said that something cannot be done or does not exist? Most people have heard these responses over and over again.

Those who are able to contend successfully in the Federal arena all have one thing in common--access to information. They all know how to work the system in order to represent their interests and concerns most effectively. This Federal Legal Directory is intended to be a tool to locate that information and work the system.

ACKNOWLEDGEMENTS

The Editors would like to thank everyone who has contributed time and effort to this Federal Legal Directory. In particular, the following staff members of Federal Reports: Larissa Brickach, Beth Fishkin, Rita Johnsos, Mark Pompeo, and Jeanette Sobajian. We would also like to acknowledge the special efforts of Joan Davis, Stanley Legum, Gail Rayburn, and Gail Shirley who formed a kind of special task force handling research projects for the Directory, as well as Steve Hendrich, John Husk, and Michael Ray who worked with us as legal interns while they were attending law school.

The Editors would also like to express a general note of thanks to hundreds and hundreds of Federal officials who assisted all of us handling the research and editing responsibilities for this Directory. These individuals include attorneys from all branches of the Government, administrative law judges, law librarians, Freedom of Information Act Officers, the Inspector General staff members, docket clerks, publication and public affairs officials, and regional legal personnel across the country.

We have all made a concerted effort to make this Directory as accurate as possible. However, the Federal Government is in a constant state of flux. Offices reorganize, individuals move to new positions, and phone numbers change. Future updates of this publication will reflect these changes.

MAJOR SOURCES OF FEDERAL LAW

NOTE: Official Government publications listed below for which GPO Stock Numbers are indicated are available from: Superintendent of Documents, U.S. Government Printing Office, Washington, D.C. 20402. Tel: (202) 783-3238.

The Constitution of the United States

The Constitution of the United States of America, Library of Congress, Congressional Research Service, 1987. This 800-plus page annotated volume is augmented biennially with pocket supplements. Each article, section, and clause of the Constitution is immediately followed by analysis and commentary, including a discussion of the most important Supreme Court interpretive decisions. The volume also includes tables of proposed amendments pending before the states, proposed amendments not ratified by the states, and acts of Congress held unconstitutional in whole or in part by the Supreme Court. Price: $70.00. GPO Stock# 052-071-00674-5.

Statutory Materials: Official U.S. Government Compilations

United States Code (U.S.C.). The United States Code is arranged in 50 subject-matter titles. A new edition of the complete set of titles is published every six years, with cumulative supplements, published in separate volumes, issued during the intervening years. The United States Code represents a codification of all sections of the Revised Statutes and Statutes at Large in force. The entire United States Code is not prima facie evidence of the law for legal purposes. Rather, it is being submitted to Congress for enactment into positive law title by title, as revised by the Office of Law Revision Counsel of the U.S. House of Representatives. To date, 25 titles have been so enacted into positive law. It is important when citing the United States Code to determine (as indicated in the introductory material at the beginning of each title) if the title in question has been enacted into positive law. If not, the comparable sections of the Statutes at Large should also be cited, since those titles not enacted are not considered prima facie evidence of the law.

The 1988 edition of the United States Code, containing the general and permanent laws of the United States, in force on January 3, 1989, are:

Volume 1, Title 1 to Title 6. Contains Title 1, General Provisions; Title 2, The Congress; Title 3, The President; Title 4, Flag and Seal, Seat of Government, and the States; Title 5, Government Organization and Employees; and Title 6, Surety Bonds (Repealed). Price: $47.00. GPO Stock# 052-001-00310-1.

Volume 2, Title 7 to Title 9. Contains Title 7, Agriculture; Title 8, Aliens and Nationality; and Title 9, Arbitration. Price: $46.00. GPO Stock# 052-001-00311-0.

Volume 3, Title 10. Contains Title 10, Armed Forces. Price: $49.00. GPO Stock# 052-001-00312-8.

Volume 4, Title 11 to Title 12. Contains Title 11, Bankruptcy; and Title 12, Banks and Banking. Price: $47.00. GPO Stock# 052-001-00313-6.

Volume 5, Title 13 to Title 15. Contains 13, Census; Title 14, Coast Guard; and Title 15, Commerce and Trade. Price: $47.00. GPO Stock# 052-001-00314-4.

Volume 6, Title 16. Contains Title 16, Conservation. Price: $53.00. GPO Stock# 052-001-00315-2.

Volume 7, Title 17 to Tile 19. Contains Title 17, Copyrights; Title 18, Crimes and Criminal Procedure; and Title 19, Custom Duties. Price: $51.00. GPO Stock# 052-001-00316-1.

Volume 8, Title 20 to Title 21. Contains Title 20, Education, and Title 21, Food and Drugs. Price: $50.00. GPO Stock# 052-001-00317-9.

Volume 9, Title 22 to Title 25. Contains Title 22, Foreign Relations and Intercourse; Title 23, Highways; Title 24, Hospitals and Asylums; and Title 25, Indians. Price: $57.00. GPO Stock# 052-001-00318-7.

United States Statutes at Large. Annual. Published by the Office of the Federal Register, National Archives and Records Administration. The Statutes at Large serve as the official legal evidence of Federal laws, concurrent resolutions, Presidential proclamations, and proposed and ratified amendments to the Constitution in all U.S. Federal and state courts. It is sold in sets only.

Volume 99, Parts 1-2. Price: $70.00. GPO Stock# 069-000-00010-0.

Volume 100, Parts 1-5. Price: $132.00. GPO Stock# 069-000-00024-0.

Statutory Materials: Commercial Compilations

United States Code Annotated (U.S.C.A.). Published by West Publishing Company. The U.S.C.A. is very similar to the United States Code Service (see below). Like the United States Code, it has the same, 50 subject-matter title format. The entire set is kept updated by an annual, cumulative, pocket part supplement in the back of each volume or separate, soft-cover volume when the amount of new material requires it. Pamphlets are also issued during the year in order to keep the pocket parts up to date. Each code section is annotated by the inclusion of court decisions which have cited or interpreted the section, Code of Federal Regulations citations when appropriate, amendments to the section, Executive orders, reorganization plans, and citations to the relevant legislative history as reproduced in the United States Code Congressional & Administrative News (see below). The notes following each code section also refer to other West publications where additional cases and discussion may be found. For price and ordering information, contact: West Publishing Company, 50 West Kellogg Blvd., P.O. Box 64833, St. Paul, MN 55164. Tel: (800) 328-9352 or (612) 688-3600 in Minnesota.

United States Code Service, Lawyer's Edition (U.S.C.S.). Published by Lawyers Co-operative Publishing Company. The U.S.C.S. is one of the two primary commercial compilations of the United States Code. It contains detailed annotations for each code section, including case notes, amendments, references to implementing regulations, Executive orders and reorganization plans, cross-references to relevant code sections, and includes a multi-volume index and a multi-volume U.S. Code Guide. It follows the United States Code title arrangement and is published by Lawyers Co-operative Publishing Company in conjunction with the Bancroft-Whitney Company. There is an annual supplement; quarterly supplements which update the cumulative Later Case service (annual supplement); and monthly supplements which are an advance service and update the Later Case service (quarterly supplements). Price: $2,340.00 for a complete set of books and three years of upkeep and all supplements, or $65.00 a month for three years for upkeep and all supplements ("level-charge" program). Discount and variable price information is available from local representatives. Contact Lawyers Co-operative Publishing Company, 50 Broad Street East, Rochester, NY 14694, for the name and telephone number of local representative. Tel: (800) 828-6266.

Legislative Histories

United States Congressional Code and Administrative News (U.S. Code Cong. & Admin. News). Published by West Publishing Company. Monthly. Contains new Public Laws and legislative histories (selected Senate and House committee reports and conference committee reports on bills that have become law). Published first in monthly soft-cover pamphlets and subsequently in bound volumes. Note: The predecessor publication was known as the United States Code Congressional Service and is cited as U.S. Code Cong. Service. Price: $170.00 per year from West Publishing Company, 50 West Kellogg Blvd., PO Box 64833, St. Paul, MN 55164. Tel: (800) 328-9352 or (612) 688-3600 in Minnesota.

Federal Regulations

Federal Register. Published by the Office of the Federal Register, National Archives and Records Administration. This daily document contains all of the proposed and final regulations and significant legal notices and other documents having legal effect, or of public interest, issued by Federal agencies. It also includes Presidential proclamations and Executive orders. Permanent agency regulations are codified annually in the Code of Federal Regulations (see below). Price: Annual subscription is $340.00 domestic; $425.00 foreign. GPO Stock# 769-004-00000-9.

Code of Federal Regulations (C.F.R.). The C.F.R. codifies the general and permanent rules of the Federal Government originally published in the Federal Register by the executive departments and agencies of the Federal Government. The C.F.R. is divided into 50 titles, each covering broad areas subject to Federal regulation. Each title is divided into chapters which generally correspond to the specific Federal agencies that issued the regulations therein. Each chapter is further divided into parts covering specific regulatory areas.

The C.F.R. is kept up to date by the daily issues of the Federal Register. Any amendments issued since the latest revision of a C.F.R. title are cited in the List of CFR Sections Affected (LSA), a monthly issuance, and the "Cumulative List of Parts Affected" in the "Reader Aids" section of each issue of the Federal Register.

Title 3 of the C.F.R. contains a compilation of Presidential documents required to be published in the Federal Register, primarily proclamations and Executive orders, as well as a codification of regulations issued by the Executive Office of the President.

The C.F.R. is revised annually, title-by-title, beginning on January 1 each year. Reference assistance is available from the Director, Office of the Federal Register, National Archives and Records Administration, Washington, D.C. 20408. Tel: (202) 523-5240. Price: Annual subscription is $620.00 domestic; $775.00 foreign. GPO Stock# 869-011-00000-2. Individual titles are also available at varying prices.

Presidential Proclamations and Executive Orders

Codification of Presidential Proclamations and Executive Orders, April 13, 1945 - January 20, 1989. Published by the Office of the Federal Register, National Archives and Records Administration. Provides in one convenient volume proclamations and Executive orders with general applicability and continuing effect. Proclamations and Executive orders issued before April 13, 1945 are included if they were amended or otherwise affected by documents issued during the 1945-1989 period. One of the great benefits of this volume is that it incorporates amendments into the text of each codified proclamation and Executive order. All documents are cited to the Federal Register and Code of Federal Regulations. It also reflects changes made by a document other than a proclamation or Executive order, such as a Public Law or Federal regulation.

The Codification is divided into 50 chapters corresponding to the title designations of the Code of Federal Regulations and the United States Code. There is also a Disposition Table listing all included documents with their amendments and an indication of their current status. Price: $32.00. GPO Stock# 069-000-00018-5.

Weekly Compilation of Presidential Documents. Published every Monday by the Office of the Federal Register, National Archives and Records Administration. This publication contains proclamations, Executive orders, statements, messages, and other Presidential materials released by the White House during the previous week. Price: $55.00 domestic ($96.00 for first class mailing); $68.75 foreign; single copies are $2.00 domestic ($2.50 foreign). GPO Stock# 769-007-00008-8.

Treaties and International Agreements

Treaties in Force. Annual. Published by the U.S. Department of State. This compilation lists all treaties and international agreements by country and subject. Price: $20.00 for January 1, 1989 edition (a new January 1, 1990 edition will soon be available). GPO Stock# 044-000-02257-5.

Treaties and Other International Acts Series (TIAS). This compilation, which begins with Treaty No. 1501, contains all treaties proclaimed during the calendar year to which the United States is a party, as well as all international agreements other than treaties to which the United States is a party, which have been signed, proclaimed, or subjected to any other final formality during the calendar year. TIAS consists of literal prints of single copies of the original treaties and international agreements, published in pamphlet form. Ultimately, the pamphlets are compiled and published in bound volume sets under the title United States Treaties and Other International Agreements (see below). Price: $89.00 domestic; $111.25 foreign. Single copy prices vary. GPO Stock# 844-001-00000-2.

United States Treaties and Other International Agreements (UST). Bound set of TIAS compilations in 29 volumes. The first ten volumes are out of print. Contains the full text of U.S. treaties and agreements. Through Volume 35, the treaties and agreements have been prepared for publication in chronological order. Beginning with Volume 36, the most frequently requested treaties and agreements will be given priority for publication. The volumes are priced individually. The most recently published volumes are:

Volume 34, Part 3, 1982 (published in 1988). Price: $48.00 domestic; $60.00 foreign. GPO Stock# 044-000-02214-1.

Volume 34, Part 4, 1982 (to be published in 1990). No price available. GPO Stock# 044-000-02215-0.

Government-wide Statutes, Executive Orders, and Regulations

A number of very significant administrative laws, Executive orders, and general regulations apply across-the board to every U.S. Government agency. These directives have, for the most part, been implemented by regulations issued by each agency. In the case of government-wide regulations, individual agencies often supplement them by issuing their own, more specific regulations. For the sake of brevity, these laws and Executive orders, and their implementing regulations, and the general regulations, are discussed below rather than in the context of each and every agency section in this Directory.

Agency regulations implementing or supplementing government-wide administrative statutes, Executive orders, and regulations, are generally included in the Code of Federal Regulations sections cited throughout this Directory. While agencies have, as a rule, promulgated similar implementing regulations for each of these statutes, there are often slight differences from agency to agency. For example, there may be differences in the amounts agencies charge for copying documents requested under the Freedom of Information Act.

Some of the most important Federal administrative laws, orders, and regulations applicable to every agency of the U.S. Government are:

Administrative Procedure Act, as amended, 5 U.S.C. 551 et seq.--requires every Federal agency to develop policies and procedures to ensure that private parties having business before the agencies are treated fairly.

Freedom of Information Act (FOIA), as amended, 5 U.S.C. 552--requires every Executive Branch agency to publish or make available to the public:

*methods of operation
*public procedural rules, policies, and precedents
*other matters of official record

Its primary utility is as a vehicle for members of the public to request the release or disclosure of official records. Each agency has a Freedom of Information Officer responsible for determining whether records must be released or withheld from disclosure and is authorized to deny FOIA requests. Agency-implementing regulations contain the procedures for making FOIA requests. For background, see the legislative history of the FOIA at 1974 U.S. Code Cong. & Admin. News 6267.

Privacy Act, as amended, 5 U.S.C. 552a--requires that every Federal agency develop procedures describing how an individual may discover whether such agency maintains a record pertaining to the individual in any of its record systems. The Act also authorizes an individual to inquire as to any requests by other persons for access to his or her record(s) or as to any disclosure. An individual may also request that his or her record(s) be amended or corrected and may appeal any initial adverse determination concerning such requests. For background, see the legislative history of the Privacy Act at 1974 U.S. Code Cong. & Admin. News 6916.

Government in the Sunshine Act of 1976, as amended, 5 U.S.C. 552b--requires that all Federal agency meetings be open to the public. The Act applies to the Federal Election Commission and the U.S. Postal Service, as well as any Federal agency presently covered by the Freedom of Information Act which is headed by a body of two or more members, a majority of whom are appointed by the President. The meetings subject to the Act include not only sessions at which formal actions are taken, but also those at which a quorum of members deliberate agency business. Every portion of every meeting must be open to the public unless it falls under one of the Act's specific exemptions. For background, see the legislative history of the Sunshine Act at 1976 U.S. Code Cong. & Admin. News 2183.

Equal Access to Justice Act, as amended, 5 U.S.C. 504 et seq.--authorizes certain persons (including individuals, businesses, and other organizations) to recover attorney fees, expert witness fees, and other expenses against the U.S. when actions by the U.S. against the person are unjustified. This fairly recent enactment makes it possible for persons to seek review of, or defend against, unjustified Government action despite the expense which, prior to this statute, often deterred such reviews or defenses. Fees and other expenses are awarded by the agency adjudicative officer. For background, see the legislative history of the Act at 1980 U.S. Code Cong. & Admin. News 1984 and 1985 U.S. Code Cong. & Admin. News 132.

Ethics in Government Act of 1978, as amended, 2 U.S.C. 201 et seq.--directs every Federal agency to develop rules and regulations pertaining to conflicts of interests and standards of conduct. The independent Office of Government Ethics administers the Act and approves agency regulations promulgated thereunder. Each agency must designate an Ethics Official (usually the General Counsel) to:

- act as liaison with the Office of Government Ethics
- review financial disclosure reports from employees, consultants, and contractors
- monitor administrative actions and sanctions
- run ethics education and training programs

For background, see the legislative history of the Act at 1978 U.S. Code Cong. & Admin. News 4216.

Age Discrimination Act of 1975, as amended, 42 U.S.C. 6101 et seq.--requires every Federal agency to promulgate regulations prohibiting discrimination on the basis of age in programs or activities receiving Federal financial assistance. For background, see the legislative history of the Act at 1975 U.S. Code Cong. & Admin. News 1252 and 1978 U.S. Code Cong. & Admin. News 3388.

Rehabilitation Act of 1973, Sec. 504, as amended, 29 U.S.C. 794 et seq.--requires each Federal agency to issue regulations to prohibit discrimination on the basis of handicap in agency programs and activities. Such regulations must include the enforcement and hearing procedures the agency has adopted in implementing Title VI of the Civil Rights Act of 1964. For background, see the legislative history of the Rehabilitation Act at 1973 U.S. Code Cong. & Admin. News 2093 and 1978 U.S. Code Cong. & Admin. News 7312.

Public Printing and Documents Act of 1968, as amended, 44 U.S.C. 1901 et seq.--requires that Government publications, except those classified for reasons of national security, administrative, or operational purposes, be made available to the public through depository libraries through the Superintendent of Documents (Government Printing Office). Libraries designated as depositories include:

- all state libraries
- land grant college libraries
- two designated regional libraries in each state
- libraries of Federal executive departments
- service academy libraries

For background, see the legislative history of this Act at 1968 U.S. Code Cong. & Admin. News 4438.

Contracts Disputes Act of 1978, as amended, 41 U.S.C. 601 et seq.--establishes a uniform Federal system and remedies for resolving Government contract claims. The Act encourages the resolution of disputes under Federal contracts through negotiation, but also provides for an administrative litigation procedure through alternative forums designed to adjudicate the different types of disputes that may arise. Agency Boards of Contract Appeals derive their authority from this Act. For background, see the legislative history at 1978 U.S. Code Cong. & Admin. News 5235.

Program Fraud Civil Remedies Act of 1986, 31 U.S.C. 3801 et seq.--provides Federal agencies victimized by false, fictitious, and fraudulent claims and statements with an administrative remedy to compensate them for losses resulting therefrom. For background, see the legislative history at 1986 U.S. Code Cong. & Admin. News 3607.

Federal Acquisition Regulation (FAR) System, codified in Title 48 of the Code of Federal Regulations, contains uniform procurement and contracting policies and procedures followed by all Federal agencies. Each agency may prescribe acquisition regulations not inconsistent with the FAR, and many agencies have done so. These supplemental regulations are also found in Title 48 of the CFR.

Executive Order 12549, 3 C.F.R., 1986 Comp., p. 189--directs that executive departments and agencies participate in a government-wide system of debarment and suspension applicable to non-procurement activities. A participant in a Federal program or activity who is debarred or suspended is excluded from receiving Federal financial and non-financial assistance and benefits. Debarment or suspension by one agency has government-wide effect. Agency implementing regulations must include:

*the programs covered by the debarment and suspension system

*criteria for debarment and suspension

*due process procedures required before debarment or suspension may take effect

*a listing of debarred and suspended participants

*the consequences of debarment, suspension, determination of ineligibility, or voluntary exclusion.

Executive Branch

EXECUTIVE OFFICE OF THE PRESIDENT

1600 Pennsylvania Avenue, N.W.
Washington, D.C. 20503

(Area Code 202)

Office of Counsel to the President
Counsel to the President: C. Boyden Gray 456-2632
Deputy Counsel: John P. Schmitz 456-6611
Associate Counsel to the President:
Brent Hatch 456-7953
Lee Liberman 456-6257
Nelson Lund 456-2896
Fred Nelson 456-2607
Steve Radamaker 395-5026
Amy Schwartz 456-2674

(Area Code 202)

Assistant Counsel to the President:
Jay Bybee 456-2898
Jeff Holmstead 456-7803

President's Intelligence Oversight Board
Counsel to the Board: Seth L. Hurwitz 395-6113

Office of Administration
General Counsel: Robert W. Kelly 395-2273

PUBLICATIONS OF INTEREST

The following publication can be purchased from the U.S. Government Printing Office. Stock number and price for annual subscription is shown below. Submit requests for this publication to: The Superintendent of Documents, U.S. Government Printing Office, Washington, D.C. 20402. Tel: 202/783-3238.

Weekly Compilation of Presidential Documents. Includes transcripts of the President's news conferences, messages to Congress, public speeches and statements, and other presidential materials released by the White House. The Compilation carries a monthly dateline and covers materials released during the preceding week. Each issue carries an index of contents and a cumulative index to prior issues. Separate indices are published quarterly, semiannually, and annually. Other finding aids include lists of laws approved by the President, nominations submitted to the Senate, and a checklist of White House releases. Price: $96.00/year domestic (priority mail) or $55.00/year domestic (non-priority mail); $68.75/year foreign (non-priority mail). Foreign airmail distribution available upon request. GPO Stock#769-007-00000-8.

COUNCIL ON ENVIRONMENTAL QUALITY

722 Jackson Place, N.W.
Washington, D.C. 20503

DESCRIPTION: The Council on Environmental Quality develops and recommends to the President national policies which further environmental quality; performs a continuing analysis of changes or trends in the national environment; reviews and appraises Federal programs to determine their contributions to sound environmental policy; and conducts studies, research, and analyses relating to ecological systems and environmental quality.

(Area Code 202)

Chairman: Michael R. Deland 395-5080
Public Information/Publications 395-5750
Facsimile 395-7329

(Area Code 202)

Freedom of Information Act/Privacy Act Office 395-5754
To obtain rules and procedures see 40 C.F.R. 1515, 1516.

OFFICE OF GENERAL COUNSEL (Second Floor)

The Office of General Counsel handles legal issues related to the National Environmental Policy Act (NEPA), as well as legal responsibilities relating to contracts, procurement, the Freedom of Information Act (FOIA), the Privacy Act, and other administrative issues. Attorneys review and draft comments relating to proposed legislation; respond to requests for information regarding NEPA regulations; assist Federal agencies in fulfilling their NEPA responsibilities; analyze legal issues; review all contracts, requests for proposals, and related documentation; and perform legal research and writing.

(Area Code 202)

General Counsel: Dinah Bear 395-5754
Deputy General Counsel: Lucinda Low Swartz 395-5754
Assistant General Counsel: Edward Yates 395-5754
Assistant General Counsel: Carl Bausch 395-5754

COUNCIL ON ENVIRONMENTAL QUALITY
KEY LEGAL AUTHORITIES

Regulations: 40 U.S.C. Parts 1500-1517 (1989).

National Environmental Policy Act of 1969, as amended, 42 U.S.C. 4321 et seq.--the basic charter for protection of the U.S. environment, it established policy, sets goals, and provides means for policy execution, and also requires that environmental impact statements be prepared in connection with every major Federal action significantly affecting human environmental quality; and established the Council on Environmental Quality.

Legislative History: 1970 U.S. Code Cong. & Admin. News 2751.

NATIONAL SECURITY COUNCIL
Old Executive Bldg, 17th and Pennsylvania Avenue, N.W.
Washington, D.C. 20506

DESCRIPTION: The National Security Council was established by the National Security Act of 1947 as amended (50 U.S.C. 402). Reorganization Plan No. 4 of 1949 (5 U.S.C. App.) placed the Council in the Executive Office of the President. The National Security Council is chaired by the President. Its statutory members, in addition to the President, are the Vice President and the Secretaries of State and Defense. The Chairman of the Joint Chiefs of staff is the statutory military adviser to the Council, and the Director of Central Intelligence is its intelligence adviser.

The statutory function of the Council is to advise the President with respect to the integration of domestic, foreign, and military policies relating to national security.

(Area Code 202)

Members

The President: George Bush 456-1414
The Vice President: Dan Quayle 456-2326
Secretary of State: James A. Baker III 647-4910
Secretary of Defense: Richard B. Cheney 695-5261

Statutory Advisors

Director Central Intelligence Agency:
William H. Webster ....(703) 482-6363
Chairman Joint Chiefs of Staff:
General Colin L. Powell 697-9121
Director Arms Control & Disarmament Agency:
Ronald F. Lehman 647-9610

Staff

Assistant to the President for National Security Affairs:
Brent Scowcroft 456-2255
Assistant to the President and Deputy for National Security Affairs: Robert M. Gates 456-2257

Legal Advisor

Special Assistant to the President and Legal Advisor:
C. Nicholas Rostow 456-6538
Deputy Legal Advisors:
Daniel B. Levin 395-3854
Stephen Rademaker 395-5026

NATIONAL SECURITY COUNCIL
KEY LEGAL AUTHORITIES

Regulations: 32 C.F.R. Parts 2101-2103 (1989); 47 C.F.R. Parts 210-215 (1989).

National Security Act of 1947, as amended, 50 U.S.C. 401 et seq.--provides for the coordination of national security matters and established the National Security Council.

Legislative History: 1947 U.S. Code Cong. Service 1483; 1951 U.S. Code Cong. Service 2250; 1986 U.S. Code Cong. & Admin. News 2186, 5627, & 6413; 1988 U.S. Code Cong. & Admin. News 5937.

Communications Act of 1934, as amended, 47 U.S.C. 606--authorized the President, in the event of war, to direct that certain communications essential to national defense and security, shall have preference or priority.

Legislative History: 1947 U.S. Code Cong. Service 1359; 1951 U.S. Code Cong. Service 2393.

Disaster Relief Act of 1974, 42 U.S.C. 5121 et seq.--provides overall Federal coordination of assistance to state and local governments when there is damage caused by a disaster.

Legislative History: 1974 U.S. Code Cong. & Admin. News 3070; 1988 U.S. Code Cong. & Admin. News 6085.

National Emergencies Act of 1976, 50 U.S.C. 1601--terminated existing declared emergencies and established authority and set forth criteria for declarations of future national emergencies.

Legislative History: 1976 U.S. Code Cong. & Admin. News 2288; 1980 U.S. Code Cong. & Admin. News 6333.

Presidential Memorandum of Aug. 21, 1963, "Establishment of a National Communications System," 3 C.F.R., 1959-1963 Comp., p. 858.

Exec. Order No. 12046, as amended, 3 C.F.R., 1978 Comp., p. 158, "Relating to the Transfer of Telecommunications Functions"--delegated the war powers functions of the President under section 606 of the Communications Act of 1934 to the National Security Council, in part.

Exec. Order No. 12333, 3 C.F.R., 1981 Comp., p. 200, "United States Intelligence Activities"--established guidelines and regulations for the conduct of U.S. intelligence activities by the National Security Council and other agencies within the U.S. intelligence establishment and defined these agencies intelligence roles with respect to each other.

OFFICE OF MANAGEMENT AND BUDGET

Old Executive Bldg, 17th and Pennsylvania Avenue, N.W.
Washington, D.C. 20503

DESCRIPTION: The Office of Management and Budget (OMB) serves as the President's management arm for the Executive Branch. OMB's functions include:

*assisting the President in the preparation of the budget and the formulation of the Government's fiscal program;

*supervising and controlling the administration of the budget;

*reviewing Executive Branch organizational structure and management procedures;

*developing efficient coordinating mechanisms to implement Government activities and to expand interagency cooperation;

*clearing and coordinating departmental advice on proposed legislation and making recommendations to the President as to action on legislative enactments;

*assisting in the development of regulatory reform proposals and paperwork reduction proposals; and

*assisting in the consideration, clearance, and, where necessary, in the preparation of proposed Executive Orders and proclamations.

(Area Code 202)

Director: Richard G. Darman 395-4840
Public Affairs 395-3080
Procurement Information 395-3080
Publications Information 395-7332
Legislative Affairs 395-3192
Facsimile 395-3888

(Area Code 202)

Freedom of Information Act/Privacy Act 395-7250
Requests should be submitted in writing to Mr. Darrell Johnson, Assistant Director for Administration, Office of Management and Budget, Washington, D.C. 20503.

OFFICE OF GENERAL COUNSEL (ROOM 262)

The Office of the General Counsel advises the Director of OMB and the senior staff on all agency legal matters, including fiscal law, regulatory law, and information law issues.

(Area Code 202)

General Counsel: Robert G. Damus (Acting) 395-5044
Deputy General Counsel: Robert Damus 395-5600
Associate General Counsel: Rosalyn Rettman 395-5600
Assistant General Counsel:
Steven Aitken 395-5600
Russell George 395-5600
Mac Reed 395-5600
Karen MacIntyre 395-5600

(Area Code 202)

Office of Federal Procurement Policy
Deputy Associate Administrator for Procurement Law and Legislation: William S. Coleman 395-3501
Deputy Associate General Counsels:
Michael Gerick 395-3501
Richard Ong 395-3501

EXECUTIVE OFFICE OF THE PRESIDENT

STAFF SPECIALISTS

(Area Code 202)

The Judiciary: Frederick W. Zierman 395-3603
Justice and Commerce Departments: Cora P. Beebe 395-3914
Legal Division (Justice): vacant 395-3914
Acquisition Law: William S. Coleman 395-3501
Administrative Procedure Act: Karen MacIntyre 395-5600
Antitrust: vacant 395-3914
Apportionment (Legal Implications): Rosalyn Rettman ...395-5600
Civil Rights (Education): Kathryn Burchard 395-5880
Civil Rights (HHS): Michael Dost 395-4922
Contract Administration: Joseph F. Zimmer 395-6803
Contract Compliance/EEO: Joseph Wire 395-3262
ERISA/Labor: Thomas L. Arthur 395-3262
ERISA/Treasury: James Simpson 395-6156
Ethics/Financial Disclosure/Conflicts of Interest:
Mac Reed 395-5600
Ethics/General Michael Gerick 395-3501
Executive Orders: Mac Reed 395-5600
Export Promotion: Thomas Dorsey 395-4594
Federal Acquisition Regulation: David Baker 395-7207
FOIA: Robert Damus 395-5600
Labor Relations/Federal Government: vacant 395-5090

(Area Code 202)

Labor Relations/General: Maureen Walsh 395-3262
Labor Relations/Mediation and Conciliation:
Joseph Wire 395-3262
Labor Relations: Railroads and Airlines:
Robert B. Rideout 395-3262
Labor Unions: Thomas L. Arthur 395-3262
Law of the Sea: Michael Katsen 395-4580
Legal Opinions/Advice: Robert Damus 395-5044
Legal Services Corporation: Sara Brentlinger 395-4686
Litigation: Robert Damus and Steven Aitkin 395-5600
Medicare Contractors: Chris Nolan 395-4926
Patent Policy and Data Rights: Wayen Leiss 395-3501
Prevention of Waste and Fraud in Procurement:
William S. Coleman 395-3501
Privacy Act: Robert Damus 395-5600
Procurement Policy: Charles Clark 395-6803
Procurement Regulations: David Baker 395-7207
Small Business Procurement: Karen Maris 395-3300
Standards of Conduct in Procurement: Richard Ong 395-3501
Tax Policy: vacant 395-5800
Toxic Waste Clean-up/Superfund: Richard Mertens 395-6827

OFFICE OF MANAGEMENT AND BUDGET

KEY LEGAL AUTHORITIES:

General Agency Regulations: 5 C.F.R. Parts 1300-1320 (1989).

31 U.S.C. 501-522, 1101-1114--established the Office of Management and Budget (OMB), delineates its statutory officers and outlines the Federal budget process.
Legislative History: 1982 U.S. Code Cong. & Admin. News 1895.

Reorganization Plan No. 2 of 1970, 31 U.S.C. 501 note--transferred functions of the Bureau of the Budget to OMB and outlined OMB's responsibilities.

Exec. Order No. 11541, 3 C.F.R., 1966-1970 Comp., p. 939--authorized OMB to issue policy guidelines (normally in the form of circulars) to Federal agencies to promote efficiency and uniformity in Government activities.

Paperwork Reduction Act of 1980, as amended, 44 U.S.C. 3501-3520--seeks to minimize the Federal paperwork burden on individuals, businesses, and other governmental entities and other persons, and establishes the Office of Information and Regulatory Affairs in the Office of Management and Budget to administer the Act; and requires OMB to approve agency information collection requests.
Legislative History: 1980 U.S. Code Cong. & Admin. News 6241.

Exec. Order 12615, 3 C.F.R., 1987 Comp., p. 259, "Performance of Federal Government Commercial Activities"--directs agency heads to ensure that new Federal requirements for commercial activities are provided by the private sector, except where statutes or national security requires that the Government perform the activity or private industry's costs are unreasonable; and directs OMB to issue guidelines to agencies to implement this Order.

OFFICE OF NATIONAL DRUG CONTROL POLICY
Washington, D.C. 20500

DESCRIPTION: The Office of National Drug Control Policy has the following major responsibilities:

* to annually promulgate a national drug control strategy, which is the Federal guide for the war on drugs;
* to coordinate and oversee the implementation of that national strategy by agencies of the Federal Government; and
* to advise the President on anti-drug policy and related issues.

(Area Code 202)

Director: William J. Bennett 673-2520
Chief of Staff: John P. Walters 673-2520

(Area Code 202)

General Counsel: Terence J. Pell 673-2682

OFFICE OF THE U.S. TRADE REPRESENTATIVE
600 Seventeenth Street, N.W.
Washington, D.C. 20506

DESCRIPTION: The Office of the U.S. Trade Representative is charged with administering trade agreements programs under various trade acts and for setting and administering overall trade policy. The Office is headed by the U.S. Trade Representative, a Cabinet-level official with the rank of Ambassador. The U.S. Trade Representative is the chief representative of the United States for all bilateral and multilateral discussions, meetings, and negotiations dealing with tariff and trade issues.

(Area Code 202)
U.S. Trade Representative: Carla A. Hills 395-3204
Public Affairs/Publications 395-3230

(Area Code 202)
Freedom of Information Act/Privacy Act Office 395-3432
Facsimile 395-3911

OFFICE OF GENERAL COUNSEL (ROOM 223)

The Office of the General Counsel advises the U.S. Trade Representative, the Deputy Trade Representatives, and the agency's staff on all areas of international trade law and agency responsibilities. The office is responsible for the following: ensuring that all actions of the U.S. related to trade are analyzed for conformity with U.S. rights and obligations under international agreements affecting trade; developing Administration positions on trade legislation; carrying out dispute settlement proceedings under GATT (General Agreement on Tariffs and Trade); developing and carrying out U.S. antidumping and subsidy/countervailing duty policy; investigating/prosecuting certain cases; reviewing certain unfair import trade cases; and providing advice on questions involving government ethics, conflicts of interest, financial disclosure, and the Freedom of Information Act/Privacy Act issues.

(Area Code 202)
General Counsel: Joshua B. Bolten 395-3150
Deputy General Counsel: A. Jane Bradley 395-3432

(Area Code 202)
Deputy General Counsel: Daniel M. Price 395-6808

UNITED STATES TRADE REPRESENTATIVE
KEY LEGAL AUTHORITIES

General Agency Regulations: 15 C.F.R. Parts 2001-2013 (1989).

Trade Act of 1974, as amended, 19 U.S.C. 2101 et seq.--established the Office of U.S. Trade Representative and outlines the duties and powers of the Trade Representative function.

Legislative History: 1974 U.S. Code Cong. & Admin. News 7186; 1982 U.S. Code Cong. & Admin. News 4405; 1984 U.S. Code Cong. & Admin. News 4910; 1986 U.S. Code Cong. & Admin. News 42, 4075; 1988 U.S. Code Cong. & Admin. News 1547.

Exec. Order No. 12188, 3 C.F.R., 1980 Comp., p. 131, "International Trade Functions"--gives the U.S. Trade Representative primacy in representing the U.S. in international trade negotiations and matters with respect to the General Agreement on Tariffs and Trade (GATT), the Organization for Economic Cooperation and Development (OECD) for trade and commodity issues, the United Nations Conference on Trade and Development and other multilateral organizations for trade and commodity issues, and other bilateral or multilateral negotiations on trade and commodities.

OFFICE OF THE VICE PRESIDENT
Old Executive Bldg, 17th and Pennsylvania Avenue, N.W.
Washington, D.C. 20501

(Area Code 202)
Counsel to the Vice President: Randolph Wilson 456-2816
Deputy Counsel: David McIntosh 456-2816

(Area Code 202)
Deputy Counsel: John Howard 456-2816

DEPARTMENT OF AGRICULTURE

14th and Independence Avenue, S.W.
Washington, D.C. 20250

DESCRIPTION: The U.S. Department of Agriculture (USDA) is a diverse agency with responsibility for a broad range of Government programs. They include agricultural scientific research, price supports, loans to businesses and individuals in rural communities, financing of rural electric and telephone utilities, food stamps, international food aid, food safety, animal and plant disease control, inspection and grading programs for agricultural commodities, and the land management and resource activities of the U.S. Forest Service.

(Area Code 202)

Secretary: Clayton K. Yeutter 447-3631
Office of Operations Procurements Division 447-3037
Small and Disadvantaged Business Utilization 447-7117
Hot Line for Waste, Fraud, and Abuse:
Washington, D.C. Metro Area 472-1388
Outside Washington, D.C. Metro Area ....(800) 424-9121
General Information 447-2791
Publications 447-2791

Freedom of Information/Privacy Act Office 447-8164
The charge for Freedom of Information Act requests is 20 cents per page. The time it takes to fulfill a request varies but one is assured of receiving a response within 10 working days.

(Area Code 202)

Law Library (Room M-1406) 447-7751
The law library is located in the South Agriculture Building. It is open to the public by arrangement. Hours are from 8:30 AM until 5:00 PM Monday through Friday. A government or photo ID is needed for access to the building. Materials may be copied at a cost of 10 cents per page. Arrangements may be made for the loan of materials through the Law Library Society loan program.

National Agriculture Library
10301 Baltimore Boulevard, Beltsville, MD 20705
The National Agriculture Library is open from 8:00 AM until 4:30 PM Monday through Friday. The library is open for public use, but materials may not be taken out. A copying machine is available at a cost of 10 cents per page. Arrangements may be made for the loan of materials through the Interlibrary Loan Program.
Information ....(301) 344-3755
Reference ....(301) 344-4479

THE OFFICE OF THE GENERAL COUNSEL (Room 243-W)

The Office of General Counsel (OGC) attorneys in Washington, D.C. and in regional offices. OGC attorneys litigate and practice administrative, natural resources, environmental, business, and international law, and provide continuing legal advice and legislative interpretation to USDA program agencies. In field offices, attorneys work with agency personnel who manage a wide range of programs, with U.S. Attorneys' offices, with representatives of other Federal/state/local government offices, and with the private sector.

(Area Code 202)

General Counsel: Alan Charles Raul 447-3351
Deputy General Counsel: J. Robert Franks 447-2571
Freedom of Information Act Office 447-5565
Facsimile 447-2550

The Office of the General Counsel is divided into four major sections, each containing several divisions:

The **International Affairs, Commodity Programs and Food Assistance Programs Section** is responsible for all legal work relating to: Foreign Agricultural Service such as Public Law 480, Commodity Credit Corporation export credit and barter programs, Sec. 416 foreign donations, foreign market development, import and export control activities, foreign trade and tariff activities, GATT negotiations, agricultural treaties, and commodity export programs; Agricultural Stabilization and Conservation Service and Commodity Credit Corporation such as price support, production adjustment and payment programs, agricultural conservation and land diversion programs, farm acreage allotment and marketing quota programs, CCC storage operations, U.S. Warehouse Act, farm storage facility loans, procurement activities, supply and foreign purchase operations, Foreign Investment in Land, National Wool Act, and Defense Production Act; and, Federal Crop Insurance Corporation.

(Area Code 202)

Associate General Counsel: Thomas Conway 447-6883
Assistant General Counsel for Food and Nutrition
Division: Ronald W. Hill 447-6181

Assistant General Counsel for International Affairs
& Commodity Programs Division:
Rosina Bullington 447-2432

The **Community Development and Natural Resources Section** includes the **Natural Resources Division**, which represents the Forest Service and the Soil Conservation Service; the Community Development Division, which represents the Farmers Home Administration; and the Electric and Telephone Division, which serves as legal counsel to the Rural Electrification Administration and Rural Telephone Bank.

(Area Code 202)

Associate General Counsel: Richard Fowler 447-5665
Assistant General Counsel for Community Development
Division: Stephen Babcock 447-4591
Assistant General Counsel for Electric and Telephone
Division: Michael Kelly 447-2764
Assistant General Counsel for Natural Resources
Division: James D. Perry 447-7121

The **Regulatory and Marketing Section** includes the following divisions:

The **Regulatory Division**, which is responsible for all legal work relating to approximately 35 regulatory statutes and also handles the legal work of the Animal and Plant Health Inspection Service and the Food Safety and Inspection Service. This Division prepares complaints, motions, and other pleadings, acts as counsel for the Government in administrative hearings, and prepares appeals from decisions of administrative law judges.

The **Marketing Division**, which serves as legal counsel to the Agricultural Marketing Service, the Food Safety and Inspection Service, the Federal Grain Inspection Service, the Agricultural Cooperative Service, the Animal and Plant Health Inspection Service, and the Office of Transportation. Division lawyers typically interpret statutes; draft and review statutes and regulations; participate in formal rulemaking hearings; litigate issues concerning marketing orders and agreements; participate in administrative adjudicatory actions under regulatory statutes; and prepare documentation for referral of criminal actions to the Department of Justice. Finally, the Packers and Stockyards Division serves as legal counsel to the Packers and Stockyards Administration.

(Area Code 202)

Associate General Counsel: John Golden 447-3155
Assistant General Counsel for Marketing Division:
Thomas Walsh 447-5935
Assistant General Counsel for Trade Practices Division:
Kenneth H. Vail 447-5293
Assistant General Counsel for Regulatory Division:
Ronald D. Cipolla 447-5550

The **Legislation, Litigation, Research and Operations Section** contains the **Legislative Division**, which analyzes, interprets, and advises on legislation affecting USDA programs and activities; the **Litigation Division**, which handles the Department's appellate litigation in Federal/state courts and represents the Department in administrative litigation concerning the environment; and the **Research and Operations Division**, which serves as legal counsel for the Economic Research Service, the Statistical Reporting Service, the Agricultural Research Service, the Cooperative State Research Service, the Extension Service, the Office of Governmental and Public Affairs, the Inspector General, and the Assistant Secretary for Administration. This Division also provides legal services relating to USDA's budget, fiscal, and personnel matters, and internal administration. It handles civil rights matters; all legal work concerning patents, trademarks, copyrights, and labor-management activities; and issues arising under the Freedom of Information Act and the Privacy Act.

(Area Code 202)

Associate General Counsel: James Michael Kelly 447-7219
Assistant General Counsel for Legislative Division:
William A. Imhof 447-5354
Assistant General Counsel for Litigation Division:
Raymond W. Fullerton 447-4733
Assistant General Counsel for Research & Operations
Division: Kenneth Cohen 447-5565

REGIONAL OFFICES

The Office of General Counsel Regional Offices are as follows:

Albuquerque
Assistant Regional Attorney: T. Adrian Pedron
U.S. Department of Agriculture, Federal Building, 517 Gold Ave, S.W., Albuquerque, NM 87102. Tel: 505/766-2264. FAX: 505/766-1223.

Atlanta
Regional Attorney: Donald R. Kronenberger
U.S. Department of Agriculture, 1371 Peachtree Street, N.E., Ste 600, Atlanta, GA 30367. Tel: 404/347-4161. FAX: 404/347-0043.

Chicago
Associate Regional Attorney: Edward A. Hoffman
U.S. Department of Agriculture, 230 South Dearborn, Rm 2920, Chicago, IL 60604. Tel: 312/353-5640. FAX: 312/353-8273.

Columbus
Assistant Regional Attorney: Gerald E. Husted
U.S. Department of Agriculture, 200 N. High Street, Rm 209, Columbus, OH 43215. Tel: 614/469-2455. FAX: 614/469-5245.

Denver
Regional Attorney: Lawrence M. Jakub
U.S. Department of Agriculture, 1405 Curtis Street, Ste 1950, Denver, CO 80202. Tel: 303/844-4031. FAX: 303/564-6584.

Harrisburg
Regional Attorney: D. Charles Valsing
U.S. Department of Agriculture, Federal Bldg, 228 Walnut Street, Harrisburg, PA 17108. Tel: 717/782-3713. FAX: 782-3843.

Hato Rey, PR
Assistant Regional Attorney: Francisco R. Davila Vega
U.S. Department of Agriculture, 612 Federal Bldg and U.S. Courthouse, Carlos E. Chardon Ave, Hato Rey, PR 00918. Tel: 809/766-5200. FAX: 809/766-5866.

Jackson
Assistant Regional Attorney: Jerry W. Robertson
U.S. Department of Agriculture, Federal Bldg, Ste 335, 100 West Capitol St, Jackson, MS 39201. Tel: 601/965-4435. FAX: 601/965-5270.

Juneau
Assistant Regional Attorney: Robert A. Maynard
U.S. Department of Agriculture, P.O. Box 1628, Juneau, AK 99802. Tel: 907/586-8826. FAX: 907/586-7251.

Kansas City, MO
Regional Attorney: Robert Purcell
U.S. Department of Agriculture, P.O. Box 419205, Kansas City, MO 64141-0205. Tel: 913/236-3170. FAX: 913/236-3174.

Lincoln
Assistant Regional Attorney: James H. Wood
U.S. Department of Agriculture, 250 Federal Bldg, 100 Centennial Mall North, Lincoln, NE 68508. Tel: 402/437-5296. FAX: 402/437-5068.

Little Rock
Associate Regional Attorney: Claude Skelton
U.S. Department of Agriculture, 3201 Federal Bldg, 700 West Capitol Street, Little Rock, AR 72201. Tel: 501/378-5246. FAX: 501/378-5482.

Milwaukee
Associate Regional Attorney: Michael Danaher
U.S. Department of Agriculture, Henry Reuss Federal Plaza, Ste 200, 310 West Wisconsin Ave, Milwaukee, WI 53203. Tel: 414/297-3774. FAX: 414/297-3763.

Missoula
Assistant Regional Attorney: Mark D. Lodine
U.S. Department of Agriculture, Federal Bldg, 340 North Pattee Street, P.O. Box 7669, Missoula, MT 59807. Tel: 406/329-3066. FAX: 406/329-3064.

Montgomery
Assistant Regional Attorney: Jack Purser
U.S. Department of Agriculture, Aronov Bldg, Rm 227, 474 South Court Street, Montgomery, AL 36104. Tel:205/223-7323. FAX: 205/223-7124.

Ogden
Assistant Regional Attorney: Dean A. Gardner
U.S. Department of Agriculture, 205 Forest Service Bldg, 507 25th Street, Ogden, UT 84401. Tel: 801/625-5441. FAX: 801/625-5465.

DEPARTMENT OF AGRICULTURE

Portland, OR
Associate Regional Attorney: Arno Reifenberg
U.S. Department of Agriculture, 1734 Federal Bldg, 1220 S.W. 3rd Ave, Portland, OR 97204. Tel: 503/326-3115. FAX: 503/326-3807.

Raleigh
Assistant Regional Attorney: David Chambers
U.S. Department of Agriculture, 4505 Falls of Neuse Road, Ste 240, Raleigh, NC 27609. Tel: 919/856-4675. FAX: 919/790-2997.

Richmond
Assistant Regional Attorney: Demetrie L. Augustinos
U.S. Department of Agriculture, 8225 Federal Bldg, 400 North 8th Street, Richmond, VA 23240. Tel: 804/771-2026. FAX: 804/771-2396.

San Francisco
Regional Attorney: Robert Simmons
U.S. Department of Agriculture, 211 Main, Ste 1060, San Francisco, CA 94105-1924. Tel: 415/744-3011. FAX: 415/744-3170.

Stillwater
Assistant Regional Attorney: Robert Bird
U.S. Department of Agriculture, Agricultural Center Bldg, Rm 229, Stillwater, OK 74074. Tel: 405/624-4275. FAX: 405/624-4208.

Temple
Associate Regional Attorney: (vacant)
U.S. Department of Agriculture, W.R. Poage Federal Office Building, Ste 351, 101 South Main, Temple, TX 76501-7686. Tel: 817/774-1204. FAX: 817/774-1209.

THE OFFICE OF THE INSPECTOR GENERAL (Room 248-E)

The Office of the Inspector General (OIG) is responsible for auditing and investigating the programs and operations of the Department of Agriculture in order to prevent and detect fraud, waste, and abuse. In addition, the OIG promotes economy, efficiency, and effectiveness in the Department's programs and reviews existing and proposed regulations and legislation and makes appropriate recommendations. The OIG keeps the Secretary of Agriculture and Congress fully informed of problems and deficiencies relating to the administration of Departmental programs and actions designed to correct such problems and deficiencies. The OIG is composed of an Inspector General, a deputy Inspector General, and three operating units: the Office of Investigation, the Office of Audit, and the Office of Policy Development Resources Management.

(Area Code 202)

Inspector General: Leon Snead (Acting) 447-8001
Deputy Inspector General: Leon Snead 447-8001
Chief Counsel to the Inspector General: Thomas Coogan ..447-8341

(Area Code 202)

Freedom of Information Act Office 447-6915
Facsimile 382-0319

THE BOARD OF CONTRACT APPEALS (Room 2912)

The Board of Contract Appeals decides disputes appealed from the decisions of contracting officers of Agriculture Department agencies, such as the Forest Service, Commodity Credit Corporation, Soil Conservation Service, etc. Under the Contract Disputes Act of 1979, the Board may grant the same relief as the U.S. Claims Court, and Board decisions are final and conclusive within the Department. Appeals from Board decisions are taken to the U.S. Court of Appeals for the Federal Circuit.

Board of Contract Appeals Reporter reports the decisions of the Department of Agriculture Board of Contract Appeals. The monthly publication also includes rulings of other Boards of Contract Appeals. It can be obtained at an annual cost of $760.00 from Commerce Clearing House, Inc., 4025 West Peterson Avenue, Chicago, IL 60646. Tel: 312/583-8500. Or, in Washington, D.C., call 202/626-2200.

To obtain rules of procedure, contact Recorder Elaine Hillard at 202/447-7023 and ask for Rules of Procedure.

(Area Code 202)

Chairman/Administrative Judge: Edward Houry 447-6110
Vice Chairman/Administrative Judge:
Marilynn M. Eaton 475-5710
Recorder: Elaine Hillard 447-7023

(Area Code 202)

Administrative Judge: Sean Doherty 447-7242
Administrative Judge: Elden M. Gish 447-2583
Administrative Judge: Robert M. M. Seto 447-2066
Chief Counsel: Daniel W. Wentzell 475-4772

OFFICE OF ADMINISTRATIVE LAW JUDGES (Room 1055)

The Office of Administrative Law Judges presently consists of a Chief Administrative Law Judge, and four other Administrative Law Judges. The judges conduct both adjudicatory and rulemaking hearings pursuant to more than 30 statutes requiring formal hearings and the issuance of written findings and conclusions under the Administrative Procedure Act. The cases adjudicated by the judges are typically enforcement actions instituted by various agencies of the Department in which civil penalties may be assessed and previously issued licenses may be revoked or suspended. The hearings are held throughout the nation. Decisions of the Administrative Law Judges may be appealed to the Judicial Officer.

Decisions of the Administrative Law Judges and the Judicial Officer are published in Agriculture Decisions, which also contains selected court opinions on issues related to agricultural law from a variety of courts. Although this journal is published monthly, the schedule is running late and the office is currently working on ALJ decisions from 1988. To get on the mailing list for this free publication, contact: Hearing Clerk Unit, Office of Administrative Law Judges, U.S. Department of Agriculture, Room 1081 South Agriculture Building, Washington, D.C. 20250. Tel: 202/447-4443.

To obtain a copy of current decisions, contact the Hearing Clerk's Office at 202/447-4443 or write to: Hearing Clerk Unit, Office of Administrative Law Judges, U.S. Department of Agriculture, Room 1081 South Agriculture Building, Washington, D.C. 20250.

To obtain rules of procedure, contact the Hearing Clerk at 202/447-4443 and ask for the Rules of Practice.

(Area Code 202)

Chief Administrative Law Judge: Victor W. Palmer 447-6645
Administrative Law Judge: Dorothea A. Baker 447-8305
Administrative Law Judge: Edwin Bernstein 447-8161
Administrative Law Judge: James W. Hunt 447-6383
Administrative Law Judge: Paul N. Kane 447-8423
Hearing Clerk: Lydia C. Jones 447-4443

JUDICIAL OFFICER (Room 510-A)

The Judicial Officer decides regulatory appeals.

(Area Code 202)

Judicial Officer: Donald A. Campbell 447-4764
Assistant Judicial Officer: Michael J. Stewart 447-9268

OFFICE OF ADVOCACY AND ENTERPRISE (Room 102-W)

The Office of Advocacy and Enterprise provides leadership, direction, and coordination for the Department's programs for civil rights, equal employment opportunity, small and disadvantaged business, minority research and teaching, and competition advocacy.

(Area Code 202)

Director: Evelyn M. White (Acting) 447-5212
Small and Disadvantaged Business Utilization 447-7117
Public Information Office 382-1150
Freedom of Information Act Office 447-5681

FOOD SAFETY AND INSPECTION SERVICE (Room 331-E)

(Area Code 202)

Administrator: Lester M. Crawford 447-8217

Food Safety Consumer Inquiries:
Washington, D.C. Metro Area ....(202) 447-3333
Outside Washington, D.C. Metro Area ....(800) 535-4555

DATABASES AND PUBLICATIONS OF INTEREST

Databases:

Note: The National Agricultural Library (NAL) provides reference-research services to Government staff and the public. U.S. citizens who have made full use of their local, state, and/or university resources can receive services up to the threshold level without charge. The threshold level is defined as one hour of staff time or $25.00 in computer time. Services beyond the threshold are provided for a fee.

The following databases associated with the USDA are available to the public:

Agriculture Buyer Alert Program. This is a network that provides product publicity to assist American suppliers in introducing their agricultural products to foreign markets. For access information, call either 202/447-7103, or Telex 7400232 Buyer UC. FAX:202/472-4374.

Agricultural Economics. This is a subfile of the **AGRICOLA** database, and covers literature of the US and Canada pertaining to agricultural marketing, agricultural policies and programs, as well as other agricultural information.

One can access **AGRICOLA** through such commercial vendors as BRS and DIALOG or one can perform searches in person at the National Agriculture Library in Beltsville or at the South Building of the USDA in Washington, D.C. For more information call 202/344-4479.

Agricultural Research Results Database contains over 1500 one-page narratives of recent research discoveries that are ready for distribution to farms, ranches, and rural communities. The subject matter covers animal and plant production and protection. Database reports are available nine to 18 months before information becomes available through literature publications.

To obtain complete access to this database one must subscribe to the Dialcom database. However, if one wants a specific piece of information one may get it through the USDA or land grant universities. For further information, contact: Dr. Janet Poley, Extension Services, U.S. Department of Agriculture, 14th and Independence St NW, Room 3329 South, Washington, D.C. 20250. Or call Dr. Poley at 202/447-8155.

Information Services Agricultural Market News Service (MARKET NEWS) is a nationwide network for the gathering and reporting of up-to-the-minute information on the supply, demand, prices, and movement of agricultural products.

To access **MARKET NEWS** contact: Telenet Communications Corporation, 12490 Sunrise Valley Dr, Reston, VA 22096. Or call: 703/689-5700 or 800/835-3638.

DEPARTMENT OF AGRICULTURE

Publications:

How to Get Information from the United States Department of Agriculture. USDA Office of Public Affairs, Office of Programs and Planning, April 1990. Lists sources of information in the Department and its agencies. Contains brief descriptions of the responsibilities of each office and agency. Also includes the names of the various Freedom of Information Act officers. Free. To obtain copies call 202/447-7454.

Federal and State Regulations of Food Product Safety and Quality: A Selected, Partially Annotated Bibliography. USDA Economic Research Service, September, 1988. Available from National Technical Information Service (NTIS), 5285 Port Royal Road, Springfield, VA 22161. Tel: 703/487-4650 or 800/336-4700. Price: $15.00. NTIS Order Number PB90187345.

The following publications can be purchased from the **U.S. Government Printing Office.** Stock numbers and prices for annual subscriptions are shown below. Submit requests for these publications to: The Superintendent of Documents, U.S. Government Printing Office, Washington, D.C. 20402. Tel: 202/783-3238.

Inspection System Guide. The subscription service consists of a basic looseleaf manual and eight supplements over a three year period. Price: $39.00 domestic, $48.75 foreign. GPO Stock# 901-006-00000-8.

Meat and Poultry Inspection Regulations (1986). Consolidated reprint. Contains regulations for slaughter and processing of livestock and poultry, as well as for certain voluntary services and humane slaughter. Subscription service consists of a basic manual and monthly changes for an indeterminate period. In looseleaf form, punched for binder. Price: $133.00 domestic; $166.25 foreign. GPO Stock# 901-005-00000-1.

DEPARTMENT OF AGRICULTURE
KEY LEGAL AUTHORITIES

Food Security Act, 7 U.S.C. 2275(b)--requires the Secretary of Agriculture to consult with the US Trade Representative before relaxing or removing any restriction on agricultural imports.
Legislative History: 1985 U.S. Code Cong. & Admin. News 1103.

Watershed Protection and Flood Prevention Act, as amended, 16 U.S.C. 1001 et seq.--authorizes loans to states and localities for flood prevention and watershed protection.
Legislative History: 1954 U.S. Code Cong. & Admin. News 2897; 1956 U.S. Code Cong. & Admin. News 4502; 1961 U.S. Code Cong. & Admin. News 2404; 1965 U.S. Code Cong. & Admin. News 4212; 1972 U.S. Code Cong. & Admin. News 3147; 1986 U.S. Code Cong. & Admin. News 6639.
Implementing Regulations: 7 C.F.R. 622.1 et seq. (1990).

Consolidated Farm and Rural Development Act, as amended, 7 U.S.C. 1921 et seq.--the basic statute authorizing Farmers Home Administration loan and grant programs. Loans are available to farmers who are unable to obtain credit elsewhere for family farm development, expansion, and operations as well as rural housing Loans are also available for rural business enterprises. An **Emergency Loan** program is available for losses arising from natural or other major disasters.
Legislative History: 1961 U.S. Code Cong. & Admin. News 2243; 1970 U.S. Code Cong. & Admin. News 5749; 1985 U.S. Code Cong. & Admin. News 1103.
Implementing Regulations: 7 C.F.R. Parts 1900 et seq. (1990).

Energy Security Act of 1980, 42 U.S.C. 8811 et seq.--authorizes Department of Agriculture funding for certain biomass energy projects.
Legislative History: 1980 U.S. Code Cong. & Admin. News 1743; 1986 U.S. Code Cong. & Admin. News 1833.
Implementing Regulations: 7 C.F.R. 1990.1 et seq. (1990).

Senior Citizens Housing Act, as amended, 42 U.S.C. 1471 et seq.--institutes a low-rent apartment loan program for senior citizens (age 62 and over) and authorizes loans for recreational facilities.
Legislative History: 1949 U.S. Code Congressional Service 1550; 1962 U.S. Code Cong. & Admin. News 2737; 1977 U.S. Code Cong. & Admin. News 2884.
Implementing Regulations: 7 C.F.R. Parts 1800 & 2003 (1990).

Agricultural Fair Practices Act of 1967, 7 U.S.C. 2301-2306--prohibits unfair agricultural trade practices and procedures, and safeguards farmers' rights to join cooperatives or otherwise organize.
Legislative History: 1968 U.S. Code Cong. & Admin. News 1867.

Plant Variety Protection Act, as amended, 7 U.S.C. 2321-2582--protects the proprietary rights of breeders of novel varieties of sexually reproduced plants.
Legislative History: 1970 U.S. Code Cong. & Admin. News 5082.
Implementing Regulations: 7 C.F.R., Part 180 (1990).

Perishable Agricultural Commodities Act, 7 U.S.C. 499a et seq.--designed to suppress unfair and fraudulent practices in the marketing of perishable agricultural commodities (fruits and vegetables) in interstate and foreign commerce; and to prevent the destruction and dumping of farm produce received in interstate commerce by commission merchants and others; also establishes licensing requirement for dealers, commission merchants, brokers, shippers, and agents dealing with such commodities. Since 1984, there has been a trust fund from the proceeds of sales of perishable agricultural commodities for the benefit of unpaid sellers.
Legislative History: 1962 U.S. Code Cong. & Admin. News 2749.
Implementing Regulations: 7 C.F.R., Parts 46-47 (1989).

Tobacco Inspection Act, as amended, 7 U.S.C. 511--establishes tobacco classification standards and an inspection system.
Legislative History: 1985 U.S. Code Cong. & Admin. News 1103; 1986 U.S. Code Cong. & Admin. News 42.
Implementing Regulations: 7 C.F.R. 29.1 et seq. (1990); 7 C.F.R., Chapts. IX-X (1990).

Agricultural Marketing Agreement Act of 1937, as amended, 7 U.S.C. 671 et seq.--authorizes marketing orders and agreements to regulate the handling of milk and set minimum farmer prices, and regulates certain commodity imports for quality purposes.
Implementing Regulations: 7 C.F.R. 900.1 et seq. (1990).

Agricultural Marketing Act of 1946, as amended, 7 U.S.C. 1621 et seq.--authorizes Federal standards for farm products, grading, inspections, market news services, cooperative agreements, and transportation services.
Legislative History: 1946 U.S. Code Cong. Service 1584; 1955 U.S. Code Cong. & Admin. News 2727; 1977 U.S. Code Cong. & Admin. News 1704; 1985 U.S. Code Cong. & Admin. News 1103.
Implementing Regulations: 7 C.F.R. 2.1. et seq. (1990).

Egg Products Inspection Act, 21 U.S.C. 1031-- establishes an inspection program and standard-setting authority, and also addresses administrative detention, seizure, and condemnation.
Legislative History: 1970 U.S. Code Cong. & Admin. News 5242.
Implementing Regulations: 7 C.F.R. Part 59 (1990).

Federal Seed Act, as amended, 7 U.S.C. 1551 et seq.--requires "truth-in-labeling" and in seed advertising; sets up a seed inspection program; and prohibits importation of poor quality seeds.
Legislative History: 1966 U.S. Code Cong. & Admin. News 3504; 1969 U.S. Code Cong. & Admin. News 1165.
Implementing Regulations: 7 C.F.R. 201.1 et seq. (1990).

U.S. Warehouse Act, as amended, 7 U.S.C. 241-273--regulates agricultural warehouses, including their licensing, and establishes a warehouse inspection system.
Legislative History: 1981 U.S. Code Cong. & Admin. News 396.

Soil Conservation and Domestic Allotment Act, as amended, 16 U.S.C. 590a--authorizes conservation improvement and erosion prevention loans and payments to farmers and others.
Legislative History: 1972 U.S. Code Cong. & Admin. News 3147.
Implementing Regulations: 7 C.F.R. 610.1 et seq. (1990).

Water Bank Act, as amended, 16 U.S.C. 1301 et seq.--authorizes funds for wetlands improvement and maintenance, runoff control, flood control, erosion prevention, and water management.
Legislative History: 1970 U.S. Code Cong. & Admin. News 4974.
Implementing Regulations: 7 C.F.R. 720.1 et seq. (1990).

Animal Welfare Act, as amended, 7 U.S.C. 2131-2157--regulates the transportation, sale, and handling of certain animals in interstate and foreign commerce, provides for licensing of dealers and exhibitors, and requires that animals intended for use in research facilities, for exhibition purposes, or as pets are provided humane care and treatment.
Legislative History: 1966 U.S. Code Cong. & Admin. News 2635; 1970 U.S. Code Cong. & Admin. News 5103; 1976 U.S. Code Cong. & Admin. News 758.
Implementing Regulations: 9 C.F.R. Parts 1-4 (1989).

Plant Quarantine Act, as amended, 7 U.S.C. 151 et seq.--prohibits, or restricts by quarantine or other methods, the importation of certain plants, plant products, plant pests, as well as soil and related products which may be infested or infected by plant pests.
Legislative History: 1947 U.S. Code Cong. Service 1521.
Implementing Regulations: 7 C.F.R. 300.1 et seq. (1990).

Federal Plant Pest Act, as amended, 7 U.S.C. 150aa-jj--regulates the movement of plant pests, earth, stone and quarry products, garbage, and certain other products and articles into or through the U.S.
Legislative History: 1957 U.S. Code Cong. & Admin. News 1184; 1982 U.S. Code Cong. & Admin. News 4426; 1981 U.S. Code Cong. & Admin. News 1877.
Implementing Regulations: 7 C.F.R. 330.1 et seq. (1990).

Act of July 2, 1962, 21 U.S.C. 134--regulates interstate transportation of animals exposed to communicable diseases.

U.S. Grain Standards Act, as amended, 7 U.S.C. 71 et seq.--authorizes the establishment and regulation of official standards for grain.
Legislative History: 1968 U.S. Code Cong. & Admin. News 3341; 1976 U.S. Code Cong. & Admin. News 6522; 1977 U.S. Code Cong. & Admin. News 1704; 1986 U.S. Code Cong. & Admin. News 6005.
Implementing Regulations: 7 C.F.R., Parts 800-802, 810 (1989).

Food Stamp Act of 1964, as amended, 7 U.S.C. 2011-2030--established the food stamp program, which is designed to safeguard the health and well-being of the Nation's population by raising nutrition levels among low-income households. The regulations under this act provide for the submission of applications for approval by retail and wholesale food concerns who wish to accept and redeem coupons under the food stamp program.
Legislative History: 1964 U.S. Code Cong. & Admin. News 3275; 1977 U.S. Code Cong. & Admin. News 1704; 1982 U.S. Code Cong. & Admin. News 1641.
Implementing Regulations: 7 C.F.R., Subch. C (1989).

National School Lunch Act, as amended, 42 U.S.C. 1751-- establishes standards for school lunch programs and eligibility requirements for participating schools and children.
Legislative History: 1962 U.S. Code Cong. & Admin. News 3244; 1968 U.S. Code Cong. & Admin. News 1932.
Implementing Regulations: 7 C.F.R. Parts 210 & 245 (1990).

Poultry Products Inspection Act, as amended, 21 U.S.C. 451-469--establishes a Federal inspection system to ensure that all poultry products are safe, wholesome, and properly labeled.
Legislative History: 1957 U.S. Code Cong. & Admin. News 1630; 1968 U.S. Code Cong. & Admin. News 3426; 1982 U.S. Code Cong. & Admin. News 411; 1986 U.S. Code Cong. & Admin. News 1103.
Implementing Regulations: 9 C.F.R. 381.1 et seq. (1989).

Wholesome Meat Act, as amended, 21 U.S.C. 601 et seq.--establishes a Federal meat inspection system to ensure safety, wholesomeness, proper labeling, and humane methods of slaughter.
Legislative History: 1967 U.S. Code Cong. & Admin. News 2188; 1978 U.S. Code Cong. & Admin. News 2650; 1986 U.S. Code Cong. & Admin. News 6005.
Implementing Regulations: 9 C.F.R. Parts 301-335 (1989).

Agricultural Adjustment Act of 1933, as amended, 7 U.S.C. 601-624--authorizes the President to limit agricultural imports by imposition of quotas if it is determined that imports pose a threat to the well-being of US farmers. Authorizes the Secretary of Agriculture to issue product marketing orders to regulate the orderly exchange of commodities in interstate commerce.
Highlights of Recent Legislation: New sec. 624(f) permits the President to exempt Canadian products from any import restrictions imposed under sec. 624.
Legislative History: 1948 U.S. Code Cong. Service 2320; 1950 U.S. Code Cong. Service 2596; 1951 U.S. Code Cong. Service 1465; 1988 U.S. Code Cong. & Admin. News 2395.
Implementing Regulations: 7 C.F.R. Chapt. IX & X (1990); 7 C.F.R., Part 6 (1990)[import limits].

Agricultural Trade Development and Assistance Act, as amended, 7 U.S.C. 1727--authorizes the export sale of farm commodities for overseas relief, including the Food for Peace Program.
Legislative History: 1954 U.S. Code Cong. & Admin. News 2509; 1977 U.S. Code Cong. & Admin. News 748; 1985 U.S. Code Cong. & Admin. News 1103.
Implementing Regulations: 7 C.F.R. 1495.1 (1990)[barter program].

Commodity Credit Corporation Charter Act, 15 U.S.C. 714 et seq.--authorizes the Corporation to support commodity prices via payments, loans, and purchases.
Legislative History: 1948 U.S. Code Cong. Service 2138.
Implementing Regulations: 7 C.F.R. Parts 1402-1498 (1990).

Agricultural Trade Act of 1978, as amended, 7 U.S.C. 1707a--authorizes the Commodity Credit Corporation to finance exports in order to maintain and expand foreign markets for US agricultural commodities.
Legislative History: 1966 U.S. Code Cong. & Admin. News 4410; 1978 U.S. Code Cong. & Admin. News 3664; 1981 U.S. Code Cong. & Admin. News 1965; 1985 U.S. Code Cong. & Admin. News 1103.
Implementing Regulations: 7 C.F.R. 17.1 et seq. (1990).

Forest Service Enabling Act, as amended, 16 U.S.C. 471a et seq.--established the U.S. Forest Service in the Department of Agriculture and set forth criteria for designating and managing national forests.
Legislative History: 1976 U.S. Code Cong. & Admin. News 6662; 1978 U.S. Code Cong. & Admin. News 90; 1986 U.S. Code Cong. & Admin. News 6751.
Implementing Regulations: 36 C.F.R. 223.1 et seq. (1989).

Federal Land Policy and Management Act of 1976, as amended, 43 U.S.C. 1752--permits use of national forests and grasslands for grazing and authorizes the issuance of grazing permits and rights of way.

DEPARTMENT OF AGRICULTURE

Legislative History: 1976 U.S. Code Cong. & Admin. News 6175; 1978 U.S. Code Cong. & Admin. News 4069.

Implementing Regulations: 43 C.F.R. Chapt. II, Subchapt. D (1989).

Federal Import Milk Act, 21 U.S.C. 141-149--regulates the importation of milk and cream into the U.S. for the purpose of promoting the U.S. diary industry and protecting the public health.

Legislative History: 1959 U.S. Code Cong. & Admin. News 1675; 1960 U.S. Code Cong. & Admin. News 2963.

Implementing Regulations: 9 C.F.R. Chapt. I (1989).

Wilderness Act, 16 U.S.C. 1131-1136--establishes a National Wilderness Preservation System comprised of Federally-owned areas designated by Congress as "wilderness areas," and directs that they be managed by the agency under whose jurisdiction they were when so designated.

Legislative History: 1964 U.S. Code Cong. & Admin. News 3615.

Implementing Regulations: 36 C.F.R. 251.1 et seq. (1989); 43 C.F.R. Parts 19 & 8560 et seq. (1989); 50 C.F.R. 35.1 et seq. (1989).

DEPARTMENT OF COMMERCE

14th Street and Constitution Avenue, N.W.
Washington, D.C. 20230

DESCRIPTION: The Department of Commerce promotes and serves the nation's international trade, economic growth, and technological advancement. It offers assistance and information to increase U.S. companies' competitiveness in the world economy; attempts to prevent unfair foreign trade competition; provides social and economic statistics and analyses for business and government planners; provides research and support for the increased use of scientific, engineering, and technological development; works to improve understanding and benefits of the Earth's physical environment and oceanic resources; grants patents and registers trademarks; develops policies and conducts research on telecommunications; assists domestic economic development; promotes travel to the U.S.; and promotes the growth of minority businesses.

(Area Code 202)
Secretary: Robert A. Mosbacher 377-2112
Procurement Information 377-1472
Public Affairs 377-3263
Publications 377-5394
Small and Disadvantaged Business Utilization 377-1472
Office of Business Liaison.............................377-3176
Facsimile: 377-4054
Export Administration Referral and Review Board 377-5264
Inspector General's Hotline:
Washington, D.C. Metro Area 377-2495
Outside Washington, D.C. Metro Area ....(800) 424-5197
Facsimile: 377-5264

Freedom of Information Act Office 377-3271
There is a copying charge of 7 cents per page for FOIA requests. There is also a variable per hour search fee. If the total cost for a request is less than 100 pages plus two hours of search time, the fee is waived. All Freedom of Information Act requests will receive a response within 10 working days.

(Area Code 202)
Privacy Act Office 377-3271
There is a copying charge of 7 cents per page for Privacy Act requests. Privacy Act Requests generally receive a response within 10 working days.

Main Library (Room 7043) 377-5511
The library is open to the public from 1:00 PM until 4:00 PM, Monday through Friday. Materials may be copied at a cost of 15 cents per page. They are not able to answer reference questions over the phone.

Law Library (Room 1894) 377-5517
The law library is open to the public from 8:30 AM until 5:00 PM, Monday through Friday. A picture identification is required for entry. Materials may not be removed from the library, but loans can be arranged.

OFFICE OF THE GENERAL COUNSEL (Room 5870)

The General Counsel is the chief legal adviser to the Secretary of Commerce and the Department. The General Counsel is responsible for providing legal advice and guidance on all matters involving the programs of the Department other than those relating to the issuance of patents and the registration of trademarks. The General Counsel also supervises the development of the Department's legislative and regulatory programs.

The principal responsibilities of the Office of the General Counsel (OGC) include identifying and resolving legal issues affecting American productivity, technology and innovation, and the ability of U.S. goods and services to compete in world markets. It also assists the Department in resolving legal issues that arise in connection with the collection, dissemination, and protection of important economic and technical information. In addition, OGC performs a wide range of legal services necessary for the administration of the Department's trade programs; ocean, coastal, and atmospheric programs; telecommunications and information programs; business development programs; and its various economic, scientific, and technical activities and operations. The Office also provides a wide array of services in connection with Departmental personnel law, contracts, interpretation of administrative statutes and regulations, the Freedom of Information Act, and general management issues.

The organizational structure of the Office of the General Counsel consists of nine component offices: the Immediate Office, Office of the Assistant General Counsel for Administration, Office of the Assistant General Counsel for Finance and Litigation, Office of the Assistant General Counsel for Legislation and Regulation, Office of the Chief Counsel for Economic Affairs, Office of the Chief Counsel for International Commerce, Office of the Chief Counsel for Export Administration, Office of the Chief Counsel for Import Administration, and Office of the Chief Counsel for Technology Administration.

Also under the supervision of the General Counsel, but generally autonomous, are five bureau counsel offices. Each bureau legal office head provides programmatic legal advice to their respective client. Two of the five bureau legal offices, the National Oceanic and Atmospheric Administration and the Economic Development Administration, have attorneys in regional offices as well as in the Washington, D.C. area.

(Area Code 202)
General Counsel: Wendell L. Willkie, II 377-4772
Deputy General Counsel: Dan Haendel 377-4772
Assistant General Counsel for Administration:
Barbara S. Fredericks 377-5387
Assistant General Counsel for Finance and Litigation:
James K. White 377-1328

(Area Code 202)
Assistant General Counsel for Legislation and
Regulation: Michael A. Levitt 377-3151
Chief Counsel for:
Economic Affairs: Robert Ellert 377-5394
Economic Development Administration:
Joseph M. Levine 377-4687

(Area Code 202)

Export Administration:
Thomas H. Stillman 377-5301
Import Administration: Stephen J. Powell 377-8915
International Commerce: Eleanor R. Lewis 377-0937
Minority Business Development Agency:
Otto Barry Bird (Acting) 377-5045

(Area Code 202)

National Oceanic and Atmospheric Administration:
Thomas A. Campbell 377-4080
National Telecommunications and Information
Administration: Jean Prewitt 377-1816
Patent and Trademark Office:
Solicitor: Fred E. McKelvey ....(703) 557-4035
Technology Administration: James V. Lacy 377-1984

Office of the Assistant General Counsel for Administration (Room 5883)

The Assistant General Counsel (AGC) for Administration is responsible for the coordination of all legal matters involving Departmental activities and interests in the field of administrative law. The AGC is the source of legal expertise in specific areas of Departmental authority, ethics and standards of conduct, personnel, property, management, administrative law, civil rights, labor relations, collective bargaining, merit pay, civil service reform, travel allowance, and employee benefits. The AGC also advises on special statutes such as the Freedom of Information Act, the Hatch Act, the Privacy Act, and the Federal Advisory Committee Act. The office provides legal expertise in the conduct of litigation involving adverse actions, civil rights, and cases before the Merit Systems Protection Board and the Federal Labor Relations Authority and other labor law forums. The Office consists of four divisions: the immediate office, the Personnel Law Division, the Labor Law Division, and the General Law Division.

(Area Code 202)

Assistant General Counsel for Administration:
Barbara Fredericks 377-5387

The **Personnel Law Division** provides advice and opinions on questions of personnel law and represents the Department in administrative proceedings and judicial litigation involving personnel actions and related matters. Division attorneys represent the Department in administrative proceedings before the Merit Systems Protection Board and the Equal Employment Opportunity Commission. The Division is also responsible for assisting the Department of Justice in connection with litigation arising out of personnel actions or alleged discrimination, including the preparation of litigation reports and assistance in discovery and trial preparation.

(Area Code 202)

Chief: Gordon B. Fields 377-5017

The **Labor Law Division** provide advice and opinions on questions of labor law and represents the Department in administrative proceedings and judicial litigation involving labor-management relations and related personnel actions. Division attorneys represent the Department in administrative proceedings before the Federal Labor Relations Authority, the Federal Service Impasses Panel, and the Federal Mediation and Conciliation Service. They represent the Department before third-party arbitrators under negotiated grievance procedures. The Division also assists the Department of Justice in connection with litigation arising out of labor actions, including the preparation of litigation reports and assistance in discovery and trial preparation.

(Area Code 202)

Chief: Erica F. Cooper 377-0124

The **General Law Division** provides advice and opinions concerning the administration and management of the Department, areas which in general are governed by statutes and regulations of Government-wide applicability, as distinguished from program statutes and regulations. Attorneys in this Division handle matters arising under the Freedom of Information Act, Privacy Act, and the Federal Advisory Committee Act, as well as providing advice in a number of miscellaneous areas, such as those involving the Administrative Procedure Act, appropriations and budget matters, the classification and protection of records, printing and publishing, and property and record management and disposition.

(Area Code 202)

Chief: Eric W. Moll 377-5391

Office of the Assistant General Counsel for Finance & Litigation (Room 5896)

The Assistant General Counsel for Finance and Litigation provides legal advice and services to Department officials on all financial assistance, loans, loan guarantees, and general finance legal matters. This Office represents the Department on all general and commercial litigation matters, including procurement, tort and admiralty claims, collections, bankruptcies and foreclosures. The Office consists of four divisions: the immediate office, General Litigation Division, Commercial Litigation Division, and Contract Law Division.

(Area Code 202)

Assistant General Counsel for Finance and Litigation:
James K. White 377-1328

The **General Litigation Division** provides advice and opinions on general litigation issues and questions, all matters of tort liability, claims administration, certain collection activities, interpretation of laws and regulations regarding these matters, and related problems. Division attorneys actively assist the Department of Justice in the defense of all tort litigation and certain general litigation cases wherein Department of Commerce Personnel or activities are involved. Many of these cases involve aviation or maritime accidents wherein negligence is alleged on the part of the National Weather Service (NWS) in its failure to issue a proper forecast or timely warning. Division attorneys also receive and adjudicate all tort claims filed against the Department; pursue collection claims and litigation against those owing the Department money as a result of tort claims filed against the Department; and receive and respond to subpoenas, other requests for the production of documents, or the appearance of Department employees in litigation proceedings. Division attorneys also handle a caseload of commercial litigation cases involving defaulted loans and grants regarding NOAA's fishing vessel loan guarantees and direct loan programs.

(Area Code 202)

Chief: M. Timothy Conner 377-1067

The **Commercial Litigation Division** represents the Department in loan liquidation and commercial litigation matters, claims, debt collection, and the interpretation of laws and regulations regarding these matters and related problems. Division attorneys assist the Department of Justice and U.S. Attorneys offices in all matters in which the Division is involved, and serve as Special Assistant U.S. Attorneys responsible for all aspects of Division litigation otherwise conducted by the Department of Justice. Such litigation includes bankruptcy matters, collection, liquidation and collateral protection activities, environmental matters, false claims, fraud, and Davis-Bacon and related acts. The Division represents the Department's Economic Development Administration (EDA) and presently handles 200 cases representing claims of $540,000,000. The representation includes Trade Adjustment Assistance programs, collection efforts of EDA projects incapable of continuing viable operations, as well as those which are in bankruptcy or receivership. The caseload in this Division includes an increasing number of guaranty denials involving potential losses of between two and 20 million dollars per case.

(Area Code 202)
Chief: George E. Maden 377-1362

The **Contract Law Division** represents the Department in contract litigation and provides advice and legal opinions concerning bid and proposal solicitations, the award and administration of procurement contracts, and the award and administration of grants and cooperative agreements. Attorneys in this Division represent the Department before the General Accounting Office on protests against contract award, before the General Services Administration (GSA) Board of Contract Appeals in protest of contractual solicitation matters relating to ADP procurements under the Brooks Act (41 U.S.C. section 759), and serve as trial attorneys before the GSA Board of Contract Appeals on appeals against contracting officer decisions on contract-related disputes claims. Attorneys in this Division also work with the Department of Justice and U.S. Attorneys on contract matters in the U.S. Claims Court and U.S. District Courts. These may involve direct appeal of contracting officer decisions to the Claims Court or suits in the Claims Court and District Courts by unsuccessful offerors to enjoin contract award or contract performance. Division attorneys review for legal sufficiency the Department's position in appeals made by adversely affected parties against decisions to contract out or perform in-house commercial and industrial activities pursuant to cost comparisons implementing OMB Circular A-76.

(Area Code 202)
Chief: Jerry A. Walz 377-1122

Office of the Assistant General Counsel for Legislation & Regulation (Room 5876)

The Assistant General Counsel for Legislation and Regulation evaluates proposed legislation and regulations in terms of their foreseeable impact on Department policies, procedures, methods of operation, and existing legislation. It also directs studies and analyses of legislative requirements, including the need for legislation in areas such as export and import controls, unfair trade remedies, domestic economic issues, regulatory aspects of legislative initiatives, and environmental issues. On the regulatory side, this office is responsible for the coordination and compliance by all Department offices with Executive Orders governing the regulatory process. the Regulatory Flexibility Act, the Administrative Procedure Act, and other administrative or procedural regulatory requirements.

(Area Code 202)
Assistant General Counsel for Legislation and Regulation: Michael A. Levitt 377-3151

OFFICE OF INSPECTOR GENERAL (Room 7898-C)

The Office of Inspector General (OIG) was established pursuant to the Inspector General Act of 1978 as an independent and objective office within the agency to conduct and supervise audits and investigations relating to agency programs and operations. It provides leadership and recommends policies designed to detect and prevent waste, fraud, and abuse, and to promote economy, efficiency, and effectiveness in the administration of agency programs and operations. The OIG is responsible for all audits and investigative activities, with the exception of special purpose activities, such as fishery enforcement and export licensing enforcement.

The small Legal Staff provides legal assistance to auditors, investigators, and inspectors of departmental programs and grantees, and handles all subpoenas, FOIA, and legislative review work.

(Area Code 202)
Inspector General: Frank D. DeGeorge 377-4661
Office of Investigations 377-5497

(Area Code 202)
Counsel to the Inspector General: K. Wayne Weaver 377-5992
Facsimile 789-0522

OFFICE OF THE UNDER SECRETARY FOR ECONOMIC AFFAIRS (Room 4848)

The Office of the Under Secretary for Economic Affairs analyzes economic developments, develops economic policy options, and oversees the collection and dissemination of a major share of U.S. Government economic and demographic statistics. Economic Affairs also supervises studies of major economic and business developments, promotes efforts to improve productivity, and analyzes supply and demand for strategic materials.

DEPARTMENT OF COMMERCE

The Office of Chief Counsel for Economic Affairs (Room 4610) provides programmatic legal advice and assistance to the Office of the Under Secretary for Economic Affairs and offices reporting to the Under Secretary, which are: Bureau of the Census, Bureau of Economic Analysis, Office of Business Analysis, Office of Economic Policy, Office of Strategic Resources, Office of Economic Conditions, and Office of the Chief Economist. The legal work performed in the Office of Chief Counsel for Economic Affairs reflects the nature of the client's program responsibilities in areas such as economic policy and gathering and disseminating statistical information. The office also drafts testimony, legislation, legal opinions, letters, memoranda, etc., and provides legal advice on a wide variety of issues relating to its clients' program responsibilities.

(Area Code 202)

Under Secretary for Economic Affairs:
Michael R. Darby 377-3727
Chief Counsel for Economic Affairs: Robert B. Ellert ..377-5394

(Area Code 202)

Deputy Chief Counsel: Philip C. Freije 377-5165
Deputy Chief Counsel/Census Bureau:
J. Patrick Heelen ....(301) 763-2818

OFFICE OF UNDER SECRETARY FOR TECHNOLOGY (TECHNOLOGY ADMINISTRATION) (Room 4824)

The Office of Under Secretary for Technology (Technology Administration) is the Federal Government's advocate for government policies and actions to eliminate statutory, regulatory, or other barriers to the rapid U.S. commercialization of science and technology. The Office advises the Secretary of Commerce and the President's Science Adviser regarding the needs and commercial relevance of Federally-funded research and development, fosters and promotes Federal investment in R&D, technical standards, and intellectual property protection necessary for optimal U.S. commercial development of new products and processes. The Office includes the following major divisions: National Technical Information Service (NTIS), National Institute of Standards and Technology (NIST), Office of International Technology Policy and Programs, Office of Technology Assessment and Product Development, Office of Technology Commercialization, and the Japanese Technical Literature Program.

The legal work performed in the Office of the Chief Counsel for Technology Administration (Room 4410) reflects the nature of each respective client's program responsibilities, such as the utilization, transfer and dissemination of Federally-funded technologies, including scientific, engineering, and technical information. Other prevalent issues include patent policy, intellectual property, the implementation of the Stevenson-Wydler Technology Transfer Act, related science, standards, technology, and innovation issues, and the applicability of antitrust issues thereto. This office also drafts testimony, legislation, legal opinions, memoranda, and provides legal advice on a wide variety of issues relating to its clients' responsibilities.

(Area Code 202)

Under Secretary for Technology: Dr. Robert M. White ...377-1984
Chief Counsel for Technology Administration:
James V. Lacy..377-1984
Deputy Chief Counsel/National Institute of Standards
and Technology Michael R. Rubin ....(301) 975-2803
or (202) 377-1984

(Area Code 202)

Senior Patent Attorney: Thomas Zack 377-5394
Patent Attorney: Alvin Englert 377-5394
Attorney Advisor: Philip Greene 377-5394

DATABASES AND PUBLICATIONS OF INTEREST

Publications:

For information regarding publications of the Department of Commerce, see each of the following Administrations and the U.S. Patent Office. Each Administration and the U.S. Patent Office has its own Publications Office.

The following publications can be purchased from the **U.S. Government Printing Office.** Stock numbers and prices for annual subscriptions are shown below. Submit requests for these publications to: The Superintendent of Documents, U.S. Government Printing Office, Washington, D.C. 20402. Tel: 202/783-3238.

Commerce Publications Update is a biweekly bulletin highlighting all of the latest Commerce publications. Price: $21.00 per year. GPO Stock# 703-014-00000-3.

Commerce Business Daily is a daily (Monday-Friday) synopsis of U.S. Government proposed procurement, sales, and contract awards of particular value to firms interested in bidding on U.S. Government purchases, surplus property offered for sale, or in seeking subcontract opportunities from prime contractors. It includes information received daily from military and civilian procurement offices. Price: domestic - $208.00 per year (non-priority mail); $261.00 (priority mail); foreign - $260.00 (plus additional cost based on International Postal Zone-sent airmail). A special six-month introductory rate is available at one-half the yearly price. GPO Stock# 703-013-00000-7.

ECONOMIC DEVELOPMENT ADMINISTRATION
14th Street and Constitution Avenue, N.W.
Washington, D.C. 20230

The Economic Development Administration (EDA) generates and protects jobs in economically distressed areas. Its programs encourage a combination of private and public sector economic development efforts to raise depressed areas to a level of continuing national prosperity. Such programs include millions of dollars in financial assistance grants under its Public Works and Development Facilities program, business loans, technical assistance projects, economic adjustment grants, economic development planning grants, and research grants.

(Area Code 202)

Assistant Secretary for Economic Development:
James L. Perry (Acting) 377-5081
Public Affairs 377-5113

(Area Code 202)

Freedom of Information Act/Privacy Act Office 377-4687
Facsimile 377-0995

OFFICE OF CHIEF COUNSEL (Room 7001-A)

The Chief Counsel directs and coordinates the work of a staff of attorneys in Washington, D.C. and in the EDA regional offices, providing general policy guidance and evaluating attorneys' work products for conformance with legal standards. It is the Chief Counsel's responsibility to supervise all legal activities required to implement programs authorized by the Public Works and Economic Development Act of 1965, as amended (PWEDA) and by other statutes administered by EDA. Through his staff, the Chief Counsel reviews and approves the legal aspects of each proposed EDA project, and represents the Administration on all legal matters before other Commerce operating units, other Federal agencies, and the public.

(Area Code 202)

Chief Counsel for Economic Development Administration:
Joseph M. Levine 377-4687

(Area Code 202)

Deputy Chief Counsel: James F. Marten 377-5441
Senior Counsel: Edward M. Levin 377-4687

REGIONAL OFFICES

Atlanta
Regional Counsel: Jerry Foster
Economic Development Administration, U.S. Department of Commerce, 401 W. Peachtree Street, N.W., Atlanta, GA 30308. Tel: 404/730-3006.

Austin
Regional Counsel: Margo Harvey
Economic Development Administration, U.S. Department of Commerce, Suite 201, Grant Building, 611 East Sixth Street, Austin, TX 78701. Tel: 512/482-5461.

Chicago
Regional Counsel: Charlene Degen
Economic Development Administration U.S. Department of Commerce, 175 West Jackson Boulevard, Chicago, IL 60604. Tel: 312/353-7706.

Denver
Regional Counsel: Thomas Vine
Economic Development Administration., U.S. Department of Commerce, 1244 Speer Boulevard, Room 670, Denver, CO 80204. Tel: 303/844-4714.

Philadelphia
Regional Counsel: Lisa Bremer
Economic Development Administration, U.S. Department of Commerce, Liberty Square Building, 105 South 7th Street, Philadelphia, PA 19106. Tel: 215/597-4603.

Seattle
Regional Counsel: James Sullivan
Economic Development Administration, U.S. Department of Commerce, Jackson Federal Building, 915 Second Avenue, Seattle, WA 98714. Tel: 206/442-0596.

BUREAU OF EXPORT ADMINISTRATION
14th Street and Constitution Avenue, N.W.
Washington, D.C. 20230

The Bureau of Export Administration provides high-level direction for national export control policy and administration, strong enforcement of export laws, and improved service to business. U.S. laws prevent the unauthorized transfer of high technology that would harm America's national security. These laws also control exports for reasons of foreign policy or short supply of certain domestic products. In addition, the Bureau of Export Administration administers and enforces the antiboycott provisions of the Export Administration Act.

(Area Code 202)

Under Secretary for Export Administration:
Dennis E. Kloske 377-1455
Office of Public Affairs/Publications 377-2721

(Area Code 202)

Freedom of Information Act/Privacy Act Office 377-2593
Facsimile 377-2387

OFFICE OF CHIEF COUNSEL FOR EXPORT ADMINISTRATION (Room 3329)

The Chief Counsel provides legal services relating to all programs of the Under Secretary of Commerce for Export Administration. Principal programs are the administration and enforcement of the laws that control exports for reasons of national security, nuclear nonproliferation and foreign policy, and the enforcement of the antiboycott laws.

DEPARTMENT OF COMMERCE

Attorneys in the Chief Counsel's Office provide expert legal advice on domestic and international legal issues relevant to the administration and enforcement of these laws and the complex regulations which implement them. They also provide legal support in connection with interagency and international deliberations concerned with transfers of technology. The Office frequently faces challenging issues regarding the extraterritorial reach of U.S. law.

The enforcement and litigation attorneys in the Office review investigatory records and supporting analyses from the Office of Export Enforcement and the Office of Antiboycott Compliance concerning alleged violations of the Export Administration Act. They determine whether violations of the statute and regulations are disclosed by the investigatory material, whether there is a sound legal basis for pursuing alleged violations, and represent the Department in hearings before an Administrative Law Judge.

Attorneys in the Chief Counsel's Office also participate in negotiating consent settlements and in referring cases to the Justice Department involving alleged criminal violations. They also assist in the preparation of briefs, memoranda of law, and other legal documents for the use by U.S. Attorneys.

(Area Code 202)

Chief Counsel for Export Administration:
Thomas Stillman 377-5301
Deputy Chief Counsel: Cecil Hunt 377-5301

(Area Code 202)

Deputy Chief Counsel/Enforcement & Litigation:
Pamela P. Breed 377-5311
Senior Counsel: Roman W. Sloniewsky 377-5304

PUBLICATIONS OF INTEREST

The following publication can be purchased from the **U.S. Government Printing Office.** Stock number and price for annual subscription are shown below. Submit requests for this publication to: The Superintendent of Documents, U.S. Government Printing Office, Washington, D.C. 20402. Tel: 202/783-3238.

Export Administration Regulations (1989) is a compilation of official regulations and policies governing the export licensing of commodities and technical data. The subscription service consists of a basic manual with supplementary material issued as Export Administration Bulletins for approximately one year. Price: $87.00 per year domestic; $108.75 foreign. GPO Stock# 903-014-00000-8.

INTERNATIONAL TRADE ADMINISTRATION
14th Street and Constitution Avenue, N.W.
Washington, D.C. 20230

The International Trade Administration (ITA) is responsible for most non-agricultural trade operations of the Government and works with the Office of the U.S. Trade Representative in coordinating U.S. trade policy. It operates through four principal units: Trade Development, International Economic Policy, Trade Administration, and the U.S. and Foreign Commercial Service.

(Area Code 202)

Under Secretary for International Trade:
J. Michael Farren 377-2867
Facsimile 377-5933

(Area Code 202)

Office of Public Affairs
Director 377-3808
Publications Division 377-5487

OFFICE OF CHIEF COUNSEL FOR INTERNATIONAL COMMERCE (Room 5624)

The legal responsibilities of the International Trade Administration are divided between two Offices of Chief Counsel: 1) the Office of Chief Counsel for International Commerce and, 2) the Office of Chief Counsel for Import Administration.

The Office of the Chief Counsel for International Commerce (CC/IC) provides legal advice and support to the Under Secretary for International Trade and to the elements of the International Trade Administration (ITA) headed by the Assistant Secretary for Trade Development, the Assistant Secretary for International Economic Policy, and the Director General of the U.S. and Foreign Commercial Service. The Office also advises the U.S. Travel and Tourism Administration on international services trade negotiations and trade promotion.

The Office's legal responsibilities fall into a number of major areas:

* **Trade Policy Process:** The Office advises on and participates in developing ITA, Departmental, and U.S. Government strategies and positions on trade matters, including cases under Section 301 of the Trade Act of 1974 (enforcement of U.S. rights under trade agreements and response to certain foreign practices; Section 337 of the Tariff Act of 1930 (unfair practices in import trade); Section 201 of the Trade Act of 1974 (relief from injury caused by import competition); Section 406 of the Trade Act of 1974 (relief from market disruption caused by imports from communist countries); the Generalized System of Preferences; and statutory programs to monitor and analyze foreign investment in the U.S.

* **Multilateral Agreements and Negotiations:** The Office advises in interpretation and application of the General Agreement on Tariffs and Trade (GATT) and the GATT Codes, and is actively involved in the Uruguay Round of Multilateral Trade Negotiations. The Office also advises on and participates in UN, OECD, and other multilateral negotiations on trade, intellectual property rights, and investment.

* **Bilateral Trade Negotiations and Issues:** The Office has a major role in developing Commerce and U.S. negotiating strategies and in negotiating bilateral trade agreements.

* **Industry Sectors:** The Office provides legal advice to ITA's industry sector offices on domestic regulatory proposals, legislation, and foreign trade practices affecting industries' international competitiveness, and provides legal support to the Trade Adjustment Assistance Program.

* **Export Promotion:** Attorneys in the Office serve as counsel for ITA's administration of the Export Trading Company Act, under which nearly 100 export trade arrangements have received antitrust immunity. The Office also advises on export development activities and the activities of domestic and overseas commercial officers.

* **Business Practices:** Attorneys advise on a variety of practical aspects of international business, including trade information, trade finance, international taxation, intellectual property protection, joint ventures, technology licensing, international marketing through agents and distributors, and resolution of international business disputes.

In these activities, CC/IC attorneys work closely not only with ITA officials, but also with trade policy officials in the Office of the U.S. Trade Representatives and other Government agencies, and with the private sector.

(Area Code 202)

Chief Counsel for International Commerce:
Eleanor R. Lewis 377-0937

(Area Code 202)

Senior Counsel for International Commercial Transactions: John Masteron 377-8915

OFFICE OF CHIEF COUNSEL FOR IMPORT ADMINISTRATION (Room 3099B)

The Office of Chief Counsel for Import Administration (CC/IA) provides legal support and counsel to the International Trade Administration's Office of Import Administration in connection with the administration of the following laws affecting the importation of merchandise into the United States:

(a) countervailing duty (19 U.S.C. 1671 et seq).
(b) antidumping duty (19 U.S.C. 1673 et seq).
(c) Foreign Trade Zones Act (19 U.S.C. 81a et seq).
(d) Educational, Scientific and Cultural Materials Importation Act (19 U.S.C. 1202).
(e) Insular Possessions Watch Industry Program (19 U.S.C. 1202).
(f) Steel Import Stabilization Act (19 U.S.C. 2253 note).
(g) national security import cases under section 232 of the Trade Expansion Act of 1962 (19 U.S.C 1862).
(h) Defense Production Act of 1950.
(i) quota cheese program (19 U.S.C. 1202 note).

The Office is also responsible for representing the International Trade Administration's interest in litigation arising under these laws. In this regard, attorneys in this Office help the Justice Department prepare each case for litigation in both the Court of International Trade and the Court of Appeals for the Federal Circuit; participation includes brief-writing and, from time to time, presentation of oral argument.

Legal Support includes advice on and active participation in the formulation of U.S. positions and strategies concerning bilateral and multilateral international trade activities. This Office provides advice on matters concerning implementation of the General Agreement on Tariffs and Trade (GATT) in import matters and Multilateral Agreement on the Importation of Educational, Scientific, and Cultural Materials (The Florence Agreement and Nairobi Protocol). The Office is actively involved in the Uruguay Round negotiations, primarily the Negotiating Group on Subsidies and Countervailing Measures and the MTN Codes Negotiating Group.

The CC/IA Office also provides legal support to the Import Administration in connection with the following international trade dispute mechanisms conducted by other agencies:

(a) injury from increased imports under section 201 of the Trade Act of 1974 (19 U.S.C. 2251). [International Trade Commission]

(b) unfair practices in the import trade under section 337 of the Tariff Act of 1930 (19 U.S.C. 1337). [International Trade Commission]

(c) market disruption by imports from communist countries under section 406 of the Trade Act of 1974 (19 U.S.C. 2436(a)). [International Trade Commission]

(d) general investigations of tariffs and trade matters under section 332 of the Tariff Act of 1930 (19 U.S.C. 1332). [International Trade Commission]

(e) enforcement of U.S. rights under trade agreements, under section 301 of the Trade Act of 1974 (19 U.S.C. 2411). [U.S. Trade Representative]

(f) elimination of income tax credits under section 103 of the Revenue Act of 1971 (26 U.S.C. 48(a)(7)(D). [U.S. Trade Representative]

The Office of the Chief Counsel for Import Administration also provides legal analysis and advice, as requested, on other legal matters concerning importation of merchandise into the United States, including miscellaneous tariff bills, the generalized system of preferences, classification and valuation, tariff schedule, country of origin, U.S. Customs Service practices, and certain reciprocity provisions.

DEPARTMENT OF COMMERCE

(Area Code 202)

Chief Counsel for Import Administration:
Stephen Powell 377-8915
Senior Counsel for:
Antidumping/Countervailing Duty Proceedings:
Lynn Kaymark 377-0836

(Area Code 202)

Antidumping Litigation: Bernice Browne 377-3296
Countervailing Duty Litigation: John McInerney 377-5589
Trade Agreements: Lisa Koteen 377-5340

DATABASES AND PUBLICATIONS OF INTEREST

Database:

Antidumping Central Records Information Management System (CRIMS) is an internal database index of the International Trade Administration prepared for judicial review of duty cases. Public documents in an individual case can be reviewed in the Public Reading Room (B099) of the Department of Commerce, 14th and Constitution Ave., N.W. Washington, D.C. 20230, Monday through Friday from 8:30 AM until 5:00 PM.

Publications:

The following publications can be purchased from the **U.S. Government Printing Office.** Stock numbers and prices for annual subscriptions are shown below. Submit requests for these publications to: The Superintendent of Documents, U.S. Government Printing Office, Washington, D.C. 20402. Tel: 202/783-3238.

Overseas Business Reports contains information on the economic outlook, industry trends, trade regulations, distribution and sales channels, transportation, credit and other aspects of business in various countries. It is published at irregular intervals at an annual cost of $14.00 domestic; $17.50 foreign. GPO Stock# 803-007-00000-4.

Foreign Economic Trends contains information on the implications of foreign trade for the United States and covers most countries in the world. Price: $55.00 per year domestic; $68.75 foreign. GPO Stock# 803-006-00000-8.

U.S.-Canada Free Trade Agreement summarizes the 1988 trade agreement, including details of its effect on agriculture, auto trade, cultural industries, financial services and trade remedies. It can be obtained free of charge by writing the Office of Canada, International Trade Administration, 14th and Constitution Avenue, N.W., Washington, D.C. 20230. The full text can be obtained at a cost of $32.00. GPO Stock# 052-071-00826-8.

Business America, The Magazine of International Trade. A bi-weekly publication designed to help American exporters penetrate overseas markets by providing them with timely information on opportunities for trade and methods of doing business in foreign countries. Includes news of congressional and government actions affecting trade, economic and market reports gathered by the Foreign Commercial Service, and other trade news gathered by the International Trade Administration and other agencies as well as foreign governments. Price: $49.00 per year domestic; $61.25 per year foreign. GPO Stock# 703-011-00000-4.

MINORITY BUSINESS DEVELOPMENT AGENCY
14th Street and Constitution Avenue, N.W.
Washington, D.C. 20230

The Minority Business Development Agency (MBDA) is the only Federal agency that administers programs to generate business opportunities for minority firms in Government and private markets. It provides an array of management, marketing, financial, and technical assistance to the nation's 700,000 minority-owned businesses.

(Area Code 202)

Director: Kenneth E. Bolton 377-5061
Communications: 377-1936

(Area Code 202)

FOIA/Privacy Act Office 377-2881
Facsimile 377-5117

OFFICE OF CHIEF COUNSEL (Room 5060)

The Office of Chief Counsel provides programmatic legal services and counsel to the Director, Minority Business Development Agency, and the heads of the program staff offices to implement the Federal Government's minority business development programs under the provisions of 15 U.S.C. section 1512, Executive Orders 1165 and 12432, and all other relevant statutes and regulations. The Office develops all rules and regulations for the various programs; analyzes the legal implications to MBDA of policies and procedures developed by other Federal agencies that affect the minority business enterprise program; provides advice on the programs' legal requirements; reviews or prepares all contracts, interagency agreements, grants, and cooperative agreements proposed by MBDA; and prepares or clears all legislative proposals initiated by the Agency.

(Area Code 202)

Chief Counsel: Otto Barry Bird (Acting) 377-5045
Attorney Advisors:
John C. Smith 377-5045

(Area Code 202)

Michelle O. McClelland 377-5045
Dinah I. Flynn 377-5045

NATIONAL OCEANIC AND ATMOSPHERIC ADMINISTRATION
14th and Constitution Avenue, N.W.
Washington, D.C. 20230

The National Oceanic and Atmospheric Administration (NOAA) conducts research and gathers data about the oceans, atmosphere, space, and the sun, and applies this knowledge to products and services that benefit all Americans. Some NOAA employees are located at the Washington Science Center, Building 5, 6010 Executive Blvd., Rockville, MD 20852. These offices are indicated below by the area code 301.

(Area Code 202)

Under Secretary for Oceans & Atmosphere/NOAA
Administrator: John Knauss 377-3436
Procurement Information .... (301) 443-8222
Public Information 377-8090
FOIA/Privacy Act Office 443-8967
Facsimile 377-8203

(Area Code 202)

Library 443-8330
There is a reference desk in the lobby of NOAA which also serves as a publications information office. It is open Monday through Friday from 8:00 AM to 4:30 PM and copying machines are available.

OFFICE OF GENERAL COUNSEL (Room 5814)

The Office of General Counsel provides a wide range of legal and policy advice relating to NOAA's mission and responsibilities. Of predominant importance are agency operations (including enforcement) under the Magnuson Fishery Conservation and Management Act, Marine Mammal Protection Act, Endangered Species Act, several international conventions and numerous statutes providing assistance to the U.S. fishing industry in the form of loan guarantees, Federal grants, and seafood inspection and marketing services.

Other responsibilities include the implementation of Federal laws governing the management, protection, and study of the nation's coastal regions, including the Coastal Zone Management Act, and Title III of the Marine Protection, Research, and Sanctuaries Act, and implementation of the Ocean Thermal Energy Conversion Act of 1980, and the Deep Seabed Hard Minerals Resources Act.

Attorneys in the Office also deal with habitat protection and the assessment of damages to natural resources arising from marine pollution; the protection of wildlife habitats over which NOAA exercises management jurisdiction; consultation with other Federal agencies on permitting and licensing activities; ocean and atmospheric research and services (through the National Weather Service); natural aeronautical surveying, mapping and charting, and marine research (through the National Ocean Service); satellite commercialization (through the National Environmental Satellite, Data and Information Service); and environmental, atmospheric, and climatic research and data services.

(Area Code 202)

General Counsel: Thomas A. Campbell 377-4080
Deputy General Counsel for:
Policy, Research, and Services: James W. Brennan 377-3043
Fisheries, Enforcement, and Regions:
Jay S. Johnson 377-3043
Assistant General Counsel for:
Enforcement and Litigation: Eileen M. Cooney .. (301) 427-2292
Fisheries: Margaret F. Hayes .... (301) 427-2231
Ocean Services: Margo E. Jackson 673-5200

(Area Code 202)

Senior Counselor for:
Legislation and Environmental Legal Affairs:
Lisa L. Lindeman 377-4080
Weather Services: John Milholland 377-4053
Satellite Services: John Milholland 377-4053
Special Counsel for Natural Resources:
Grayson R. Cecil 377-3043

FIELD OFFICES

NOAA has five regional offices, each of which has a Regional Counsel and staff attorneys.

Gloucester
Regional Counsel: Joel G. MacDonald
NOAA, U.S. Department of Commerce, 1 Blackburn Drive,
Gloucester, MA 01930. Tel: 508/281-9211. FAX: 508/281-9389.

Juneau
Regional Counsel: Craig R. O'Connor
NOAA, U.S. Department of Commerce, 709 West 9th Street,
P.O Box 21109, Juneau, AK 99802-1109. Tel: 907/586-7414.
FAX: 907/871-7263.

St. Petersburg
Regional Counsel: John L. Pedrick Jr.
NOAA, U.S. Department of Commerce, 9450 Koger Blvd.,
St. Petersburg, FL 33702. Tel: 813/893-3617. FAX: 813/893-3404.

Seattle
Regional Counsel: Douglas M. Ancona
NOAA, U.S. Department of Commerce, 7600 Sand Point Way, N.E.,
BIN C15700, Seattle, WA 98115. Tel: 206/526-6075.
FAX: 206/392-6542.

Terminal Island
Regional Counsel: Martin B. Hochman
NOAA, U.S. Department of Commerce, 300 S. Ferry Street,
Room 2013, Terminal Island, CA 90731. Tel: 213/514-6181.
FAX: 213/514-6053.

PUBLICATIONS OF INTEREST

Weather Records in Private Litigation is part of NOAA's Environmental Information Summaries C-1 containing information on how to obtain certified copies of weather reports. It is published irregularly with the last one dated January 1988. It can be obtained free of charge from the National Climatic Data Center, Federal Building, Asheville, NC 28801-2696. Tel: 704/259-0682.

NATIONAL TELECOMMUNICATIONS AND INFORMATION ADMINISTRATION

14th Street and Constitution Avenue, N.W.
Washington, D.C. 20230

The National Telecommunications and Information Administration (NTIA) develops domestic and international communications and information policy and presents Executive Branch views and recommendations before the Congress, the Federal Communications Commission, and international technical, economic, and regulatory organizations. NTIA serves as the President's principal adviser on telecommunications policy; manages the Federal Government's substantial use of the radio frequency spectrum; conducts radio and other communications system research; and participates in trade and telecommunications regulatory discussions with Japan, the European Economic Community, and individual European countries.

(Area Code 202)

Assistant Secretary for Communications & Information/ NTIA Administrator: Janice Obuchowski 377-1840
Procurement Operations 377-8062

(Area Code 202)

Public Information 377-1551
Publications Information 377-5802
Facsimile 377-1635

OFFICE OF CHIEF COUNSEL (Room 4717)

Attorneys in the Office of Chief Counsel concentrate primarily on various aspects of telecommunications law required to implement NTIA's domestic and international responsibilities. Attorneys in the Office: develop and prepare petitions, comments, and other filings with the Federal Communications Commission and other regulatory agencies; draft and review legislative testimony and analyze legislative proposals; provide legal counsel to the Public Telecommunications Facilities Program (PTFP) with regard to the eligibility of grant applications, legal review of applications submitted, advice on post-award problems, and the drafting of regulations; and provide legal assistance on Comsat and INTELSAT/INMARSAT oversight.

(Area Code 202)

Chief Counsel: Jean M. Prewitt 377-1816

(Area Code 202)

Deputy Chief Counsel: Phyllis Hartsock 377-1816

U.S. PATENT AND TRADEMARK OFFICE

2121 Crystal Drive, Crystal Park 2
Arlington, VA 22202

The role of the U.S. Patent and Trademark Office is to provide patent protection for inventions and to register trademarks. It serves the interest of inventors and businesses with respect to their inventions and corporate, product, and service identifications. The Office advises and assists the Department of Commerce and other Government agencies in matters involving "intellectual property" such as patents, trademarks and semiconductor mask works. In discharging its duties, the Patent and Trademark Office examines applications and grants patents on inventions when applicants are entitled to them, performing similar functions relating to trademarks.

(Area Code 703)

Assistant Secretary and Commissioner of Patents and Trademarks: Harry F. Manbeck Jr 557-3071
Procurement Information 557-0014
Public Information 557-5168

(Area Code 703)

Publications Information 557-9737
FOIA/Privacy Act 557-4035
Facsimile 557-8331

BOARD OF PATENT APPEALS AND INTERFERENCES (Room 12C12)

1225 Jefferson Davis Highway, Crystal Gateway 2, Arlington, VA 22202

The Board of Patent Appeals and Interferences has the sole power to (1) hear and adjudicate appeals from decisions of the Primary Examiners as to patentability in applications for patents, for reissue of patents, and for reexamination of patents; (2) to declare and to conduct proceedings in interferences; and (3) to determine priority of invention. Final decisions of the Board may be appealed to the U.S. Court of Appeals for the Federal Circuit or civil action may be taken.

Examiners-in-Chief participate in the appellate and administrative responsibilities of the Board and exercise independent judgment on all matters before him/her on appeal, subject to administrative and policy direction of the Commissioner, and may be responsible for conducting interlocutory proceedings in interference and for determining questions of priority of invention and patentability between interference parties. Appeals filed in accordance with 35 U.S.C. 134 and interferences declared in accordance with 35 U.S.C. 135 involve complex legal and technical questions.

There are currently around 50 Examiners-in-Chief and each is assigned to work in either the chemical, electrical, or mechanical area.

The decisions of the Board of Patent Appeals and Interferences are reported in either full text or digest in U.S. Patents Quarterly. The weekly publication can be obtained from the Bureau of National Affairs, 9435 Key West Ave., Rockville, MD 20850. Tel: 301/258-1033 or 800/372-1033. The annual cost is $1,020.00.

(Area Code 703)

Chairman: Saul I. Serota 557-4072
Chief Clerk of Board: T. Maxine Duvall 557-4101

Ex Parte Legal Clerks
- Groups 110, 150 Karen I. Sweeney 557-4109
- Group 120 Eleanor R. Green 557-4108
- Groups 130, 180 Paula Goldring 557-3100
- Groups 210, 230, 250, 260, 290 Wanda Tigner 557-4107
- Groups 240, 310, 320 Easlene Lowery 557-7189
- Groups 330, 340, 350 Mabel A. Neal 557-4106

Inter Partes Legal Clerks
- Margaret E. Branson 557-4011
- Olivia M. Duvall 557-4006
- Carrie L. Evans 557-4004

OFFICE OF THE SOLICITOR (Suite 918)

2121 Crystal Drive, Crystal Park 2, Arlington, VA. 22202

The patent attorneys in the Office of the Solicitor are responsible for preparing, arguing, and conducting selected technical and controversial court cases which require extensive research and analysis, including eliciting and evaluating expert testimony. They provide counsel in a wide range of areas, including: the interpretation of patent and trademark statutes and regulations; proposed legislation and regulatory provisions; proposed cooperative agreements to which the Patent and Trademark Office is a party; and ownership of patents and rights to inventions made by Government employees under the provisions of Executive Orders 10096 and 10930. The Solicitor's Office also examines patent attorneys and agents seeking admission and registration to practice before the U.S. Patent and Trademark Office, and initiates and prosecutes proceedings to disbar registered patent attorneys and agents.

(Area Code 703)

Solicitor: Fred E. McKelvey 557-4035
Deputy Solicitor: Albin F. Drost (Acting) 557-4035
Associate Solicitors:
- Lee Barrett 557-4035
- Muriel E. Crawford 557-4035
- John W. Dewhirst 557-4035
- Robert D. Edmonds 557-4035
- Jameson Lee 557-4035
- Harris A. Pitlick 557-4035
- John Raubitschek 557-4035
- Richard E. Schafer 557-4035
- Nancy C. Slutter 557-4035
- Linda M. Skoro 557-4035

OFFICE OF THE COMMISSIONER FOR PATENTS (Suite 919)

2121 Crystal Drive, Crystal Park 2, Arlington, VA 22202

The Patent and Trademark Office judges the patentability of engineering discoveries made by research and development engineers, inventors, and scientists throughout the world. This is accomplished by a highly competent corps of scientists and engineers called Patent Examiners. There are currently around 1,500 Patent Examiners at the U.S. Patent and Trademark Office, about one-third of whom have a law degree.

Working in an assigned area of technology, a Patent Examiner analyzes the subject matter of the application for a patent, as well as the prior art in the field, and determines whether the claimed invention is patentable. He/she applies procedural and substantive law and grants or rejects the claims of the application. Areas of technical specialization fall generally under one of the following options: Engineering Options; Chemistry Option; Physics Option; Applied Physical Science Option; Biology Option; and Electronics, Marine Technology, Textile Technology, Food Technology Options.

(Area Code 703)

Assistant Commissioner: James E. Denny (Acting) 557-4279
Patent Policy and Projects Administrator:
- Charles E. Van Horn 557-3054

Deputy Assistant Commissioner:
- Stephen G. Kunin (Acting) 557-3811

(Area Code 703)

Patent Examination
Petitions Information 557-4282
Petitions Examiner: Jeffrey V. Nase 557-4282

CHEMICAL EXAMINING GROUPS

Group 110:
General, Metallurgical, Inorganic, Petroleum, Electrical Chemistry, and Engineering
Director: Dennis E. Talbert 557-9600
General Information 557-2517

Group 120:
Organic Chemistry
Director: John Terapane 557-0661
General Information 557-3920
Biotechnology-Chemical Library: Mary C. Lee 557-3779

Group 130:
Specialized Chemical Industries and Chemical Engineering
Director: Barry Richman 557-3804
General Information 557-2475

Group 150:
High Polymer Chemistry, Plastics, Coating, Photography, Stock Materials, and Compositions
Director: James O. Thomas Jr 557-6533
General Information 557-6525

Group 180:
Biotechnology
Director: John E. Kittle 557-3637
General Information 557-6941
Biotechnology-Chemical Library: Charles F. Warren ..557-7387

ELECTRICAL EXAMINING GROUPS

Group 210:
Industrial Electronics, Physics, and Related Elements
Director: Donald G. Kelly 557-2488
General Information 557-5080

Group 220/290:
Utility and Design Applications
Director: Robert Garrett 557-2877
General Information 557-2037
Licensing and Review: Hilda H. Grimes 557-4948

(Area Code 703)

Group 230:
Information Processing;, Storage, and Retrieval
Director: Gerald Goldberg 557-5088
General Information 557-2878

Group 240:
Packages, Cleaning, Textiles, and Geometrical Instruments
Director: Trygve M. Blix 557-2906
General Information 557-2900

Group 250:
Electronic and Optical Systems and Devices
Director: Edward E. Kubasiewicz 557-2084
General Information 557-3311

Group 260:
Communications, Measuring, Testing, and Lamp Discharge
Director: Stephen G. Kunin 557-7075
General Information 557-3321

MECHANICAL EXAMINING GROUPS

Group 310:
Handling and Transporting Media
Director: Bobby R. Gray 557-3677
General Information 557-3618

Group 320:
Material Shipping, Article Manufacturing, and Tools
Director: Edward R. Kazenske 557-3547
General Information 557-3694

Group 330:
Surgery, Plant and Animal Husbandry, Amusement and Exercise Devices, and Printing
Director: John Love 557-3164
General Information 557-3125

Group 340:
Solar, Heat, Power, and Fluid Engineering Devices
Director: Nicholas Godici 557-3340
General Information 557-2122

Group 350:
General Constructions, Petroleum, and Mining Engineering
Director: Al Lawrence Smith 557-3414
General Information 557-6200

OFFICE OF THE ASSISTANT COMMISSIONER FOR TRADEMARKS (Room 1008)

1755 Jefferson Davis Highway, Crystal Square, Bldg 5, Arlington, VA 22202

The Office Assistant Commissioner for Trademarks provides administrative and policy direction for the registration of trademarks and related operations performed by authorized personnel; provides guidelines governing trademark examination; decides petitions to the Commissioner concerning procedural questions; establishes criteria for quality review of trademark applications; establishes program activity targets and continually evaluates status against programs objectives; provides training to attorney advisors (trademarks) in trademark practice and procedure; oversees contracts with private vendors relating to trademark processing; and coordinates design, development and maintenance of the trademark automated systems and databases.

(Area Code 703)

Assistant Commissioner: Jeffrey M. Samuels 557-3061
Trademark Legal Administrator: Lynne G. Beresford 557-9514

Trademark Trial and Appeal Board

The Trademark Trial and Appeal Board is the administrative tribunal for deciding appeals from examiners' refusals to register trademarks, and for determining certain inter partes proceedings. These involve actions to oppose registration of a mark or to cancel an existing registration. Decisions of the Board may be appealed to a U.S. Court of Appeals.

The Board currently consists of a Chairman, seven members (called "Attorney Examiners") and six interlocutory attorneys.

(Area Code 703)

Chairman: J. David Sams 557-3551
Clerk of the Board 557-3551
Trademark Administrator: Erma S. Brown 557-3551

Attorney Examiners:
Robert Cissel 557-3551
Tim Hanak 557-3551
Jeffrey Quinn 557-3551
Janet Rice 557-3551
Louise Rooney 557-3551
Ellen Seeherman 557-3551
Rany Sims 557-3551

(Area Code 703)

Interlocutory Attorneys:
- Marc Bergsman 557-3551
- Carla Calcagno 557-3551
- Beth Chapman 557-3551

(Area Code 703)

Paula Hairston 557-3551
Douglas Hohein 557-3551
Helen Wendel 557-3551

Trademark Examining Operation (Room 3C06)

2011 Jefferson Davis Highway, Crystal Plaza 2, Arlington, VA 22202

Federal statutes provide owners of trademarks, which have been registered with the U.S. Patent and Trademark Office, protection against infringement by others. Determination of whether a trademark is registrable is the job of the Trademark Attorney. The Trademark Attorney thus analyzes applications and determines whether or not they conform with applicable statutes, rules, and precedents; classifies goods or services; researches previously issued registrations to resolve questions of ownership, relationship between users, right to an adversary proceeding, etc; and makes a determination of registrability and renewability.

Trademark Attorneys also examine service marks (TV titles, character names associated with a service), collective marks (trade associations), membership marks (union, fraternal organizations), and certification marks (e.g., seal of Good Housekeeping).

The decisions of the Trademark Trial and Appeals Board can be found in U.S. Patents Quarterly. The weekly publication can be obtained from the Bureau of National Affairs, 9435 Key West Avenue, Rockville, MD 20850. Tel: 301/258-1033 or 800/372-1033. The annual cost is $1,020.00.

(Area Code 703)

Director David E. Bucher 557-3268
Trademark Examining Law Office Managing Attorneys:
- Law Officer I Deborah Cohn 557-3273
- Law Officer II Ronald Williams 557-3277
- Law Officer III Myra S. Kurzbard 557-9560
- Law Officer IV Thomas S. Lamone 557-9550

(Area Code 703)

- Law Officer V Paul E. Farenkopf 557-5380
- Law Officer VI Ronald E. Wolfington 557-2937
- Law Officer VII Thomas Howell 557-5237
- Law Officer VIII Sidney I. Moskowitz 557-5242

Trademark Services Division Director: Doreane I. Poteat 557-5249

DATABASES AND PUBLICATIONS OF INTEREST

Databases:

The following databases are available from the Department of Commerce. These records can be obtained from the addresses listed below.

Technology Assessment and Forecast (TAF) Program is a database containing more than 27 million documents which make up the categorized U.S. patent file. Patent information is disseminated to users through the following various methods:

1) **Publications** are prepared on topics of general interest. The **Patent Profiles** series includes surveys of U.S. patenting activity in biotechnology, solar energy, and microelectronics. The ten **Technology Assessment and Forecast Reports** include reviews of technology areas having the most new patents or the most foreign inventors, explanations of information available by studying patents; comparisons of the patenting activity of major corporations; and analyses of the inventions patented in selected technology. The TAF Program also publishes reports on design patents, industrial robots, and annual statistics of industrial patent activity. The costs vary from $6.50 to $95.00 according to report. A complete list of publications and costs can be obtained from the National Technical Information Service, 5285 Port Royal Road, Springfield, VA 22161. Tel: 703/487-4650.

2) **Custom Patent Reports** are generated from the TAF data cost base and prepared in response to specific requests. These include: Technology Profile Report which has four parts: a) patenting activity percentages and time-series distribution by general assignment category and origin of patents; b) a ranked listing of organizations, and counts of patents granted by both year of application filing and year of grant; c) lists of organizations alphabetically with patent numbers and titles; and d) names and addresses of the inventors of patents assigned to individuals or unassigned at time of issue, including patent numbers and titles. **Organizational Profile Report** profiles patent activity, usually of a specified organization, with specific patent numbers and titles. **Multi-Corporate Patent Activity Profile** profiles the activity of up to eight organizations simultaneously, facilitating comparisons between organizations but giving no patent numbers or titles. **Enterprise Patenting Report** shows the number of patents per year for a parent company and its patenting subsidiaries.

These **Custom Patent Reports** are provided on a cost reimbursable basis with costs varying from as low as $50.00 to several thousand dollars. For more information contact the Office of Documentation Information, U.S. Patent and Trademark Office, CM2-304, Washington, D.C. 20231. Tel: 703/557-0433.

3) **Statistical Reports** can be obtained which cover all patents in the data base and show yearly levels of patenting distributed by state or country of origin, category of ownership and/or technology class within the U.S. Patent Classification (USPC) System. These reports are free of charge from the Office of Documentation Information, U.S. Patent and Trademark Office, CM2-304, Washington, D.C. 20231. Tel: 703/557-5652.

The **Office of Electronic Data Conversion and Dissemination** within the Patent and Trademark Office disseminates a variety of information in electronic form. An example of the 1990 patent products are:

1) **Patent Full Text File** contains the full text of each patent issued. Some of the data included are: patent number, series code and application number, type of patent, filing date, title, abstract, assignee name and address at time of issue, attorney, agent, or firm/legal representative, related U.S. patent documents, classification information, field of search, U.S. and foreign references, priority data, and claims. Each weekly update contains approximately 2,000 patents. The annual charge for this weekly service is $8,980.00 and can be obtained from the Office of Electronic Data Conversion and Dissemination, U.S. Patent and Trademark Office, Crystal Park 2, Suite 1100B, Washington, D.C. 20231. Tel: 703/557-6154. This file is commercially available through Meade Data Central's LEXPAT. Tel: 800/543-6862.

2) **Patent Attorney Roster File** contains records for attorneys and/or agents who are registered to practice before the Patent and Trademark Office. It provides their names and addresses and contains approximately 12,500 names and is often used for mass mailings. Its costs is $300.00 and is issued on demand. It can be ordered through the Office of Electronic Data Conversion and Dissemination, U.S. Patent and Trademark Office, Crystal Park 2, Suite 1100B, Washington, D.C. 20231. Tel: 703/557-6154.

3) **Patent Master Classification File (MCF)** contains the classes and subclasses of technology that all patents are assigned by the Patent Examining Corps. It is broken into approximately 120,000 categories. The MCF is completely updated each time it is issued, relating all issued patents since 1790 to their current classification. MCF can be obtained at an annual cost of $510.00 from the Office of Electronic Data Conversion and Dissemination, U.S. Patent and Trademark Office, Crystal Park 2, Suite 1100B, Washington, D.C. 20231. Tel: 703/557-6154. Commercial availability: IFI/Plenum and DIALOG (Tel: 800/334-2564); Derwent, Inc. (Tel: 800/421-7229); and NERAC (Tel: 203/486-4533). The public, through the Patent Depository Libraries (PDL), may search the MCF by using the DC-ROM system provided to each PDL by the Patent and Trademark Office.

4) **Trademark Weekly Text File** contains the text data of pending and registered trademarks. Some of the fields include: word mark, serial number, registration number, filing date, and TTAB (Trademark Trial and Appeal Board) data. This weekly file can be obtained at an annual cost of $4,850 from the Office of Electronic Data Conversion and Dissemination, U.S. Patent and Trademark Office, Crystal Park 2, Suite 1100B, Washington, D.C. 20231. Tel: 703/557-6154. This file is commercially available from The Trademark Register through Bell Atlantic Gateway Operator 2606 (Tel: 800/638-6363) and Maxwell Online's U.S. Trademark Watch (Tel: 800/456-7248).

5) **Trademark Image File** contains the images of pending and registered trademarks and the corresponding serial/registration number. The retrospective file is available from the present to April 1, 1987 and contains approximately 500 images per each weekly update. This weekly file costs $3,945.00 annually and can be obtained from the Office of Electronic Data Conversion and Dissemination. U.S. Patent and Trademark Office, Crystal Park 2, Suite 1100B, Washington, D.C. 20231. Tel: 703/557-6154. This file is commercially available through Thomson and Thomson or through DIALOG. Tel: 800/227-7229.

Publications:

Facts About Trademarks contains information about the advantages and procedures of filing a trademark application, including blank application forms. It can be obtained free of charge by contacting the Office of Public Information, U.S. Patent and Trademark Office, 2121 Crystal Drive, Crystal Park 2, Arlington, VA 22202. Tel: 703/557-5168.

The following publications can be purchased from the **U.S. Government Printing Office.** Stock numbers and prices for annual subscriptions are shown below. Submit requests for these publications to: The Superintendent of Documents, U.S. Government Printing Office, Washington, D.C. 20402. Tel: 202/783-3238.

General Information Concerning Patents contains information on patents including the workings of the Patent and Trademark Office, what applicants must do, and definitions of patents, copyrights, and trademarks. Price: $2.00. GPO Stock# 003-004-00641-2.

Manual of Classification (Patent Office), December 1988 lists the numbers and descriptive titles of the Patent Office classes and subclasses, as well as the Design Classes. Subscription service consists of a two-volume basic manual, the index to Classification of Patents, and semiannual replacement pages for the manual for an indeterminate period. Price: $66.00 domestic; $82.50 foreign. GPO Stock# 903-006-00000-5.

Manual of Patent Examining Procedure (1988) is a consolidated reprint providing information on practices and procedures related to the prosecution of patent applications before the U.S. Patent and Trademark Office. Subscription service consists of a basic manual and supplementary material for an indeterminate period. Price: $78.00 domestic; $97.50 foreign. GPO Stock# 903-007-00000-1.

Trademark Manual of Examining Procedure, 1987 provides trademark examiners in the Patent Office, trademark applicants, and attorneys for applicants with a reference work on the practices and procedures related to the prosecution of applications to register marks in the Patent Office. Subscription service consists of a basic manual and semiannual changes for an indeterminate period. Price: $14.00 domestic; $17.50 foreign. GPO Stock# 903-010-00000-2.

Official Gazette of the U.S. Patent and Trademark Office: Patents is published weekly and contains the Patents, Patent Office Notices, and Designs issued each week. The annual indexes are not included as part of the subscription service but are sold separately. Subscribers will be notified when the indexes are published. Price: $593.00 a year domestic (priority mail) or $449.00 a year (non-priority mail); $561.25 a year foreign. Foreign airmail distribution available upon request, plus an additional cost based upon International Postal Zone. GPO Stock# 703-033-00000-8.

Official Gazette of the U.S. Patent and Trademark Office: Trademarks is published weekly and contains Trademarks, Trademark Notices, Marks Published for Opposition, Trademark Registrations Issued, and Index of Registrants. Price: $312.00 a year domestic; $390.00 a year foreign. GPO Stock# 703-034-00000-4.

Patent and Trademark Office Notices is published weekly. Price: $82.00 a year domestic (priority mail) or $59.00 a year (non-priority mail); $73.75 a year foreign. Foreign airmail distribution available upon request, plus an additional cost based upon International Postal Zone. GPO Stock# 703-035-00000-1.

DEPARTMENT OF COMMERCE
KEY LEGAL AUTHORITIES

Major Regulations:

Acquisition Regulations--48 C.F.R. Parts 1301-1353 (1988).
General Departmental Regulations--15 C.F.R. Parts 0-26 (1990).
Census Bureau--15 C.F.R. Parts 30-100 (1990).
Economic Development Administration--13 C.F.R. Parts 301-318 (1989).
International Trade Administration--19 C.F.R. Parts 353-356 (1989).
Minority Business Development Administration--15 C.F.R. Part 1400 (1989).
National Oceanic & Atmospheric Administration--15 C.F.R. Parts 902-909 & 945 (1989); 50 C.F.R. Parts 204-299 (1989).
National Telecommunications & Information Administration--15 C.F.R. Part 2301 (1989).
Patent & Trademark Office--**37 C.F.R. Parts 1-150 (1989).**
Rules of Practice & Procedure: Patent Cases--37 C.F.R. Part 1 (1989).

Rules of Practice & Procedure: Trademark Cases--37 C.F.R. Part 2 (1989).
Rules of Practice & Procedure: Patent Office--37 C.F.R. Parts 10-15a(1989).

National Institute of Standards & Technology Act, 15 U.S.C. 271-282a--renamed the National Bureau of Standards and expanded its duties to cover technology services, a computer standards program, establishment of regional centers for the transfer of manufacturing technology, assistance to state technology programs, a new non-energy inventions program, an advanced technology program, and the assessment of emerging technologies.
Legislative History: 1988 U.S. Code Cong. & Admin. News 3269.
Implementing Regulations: 15 C.F.R. Parts 7, 9-10, 16, & 200-255 (1990).

Fair Packaging & Labeling Act, as amended, 14 U.S.C. 1451, 1454--directs the Secretary of commerce to determine whether the ability of consumers to make value comparisons among products is impaired by the undue proliferation of weights, measures, or quantities in which such products are being distributed at retail and to request manufacturers, packers, and distributors, where a determination of undue proliferation has been made, to participate in the development of a voluntary product standard.
Legislative History: 1966 U.S. Code Cong. & Admin. News 4069.
Implementing Regulations: 15 C.F.R. 12.1 et seq. (1990).

Educational, Scientific, & Cultural Materials Importation Act of 1966, as amended, 19 U.S.C. 1202--implements the multilateral Agreement on the Importation of Educational, Scientific, & Cultural Materials ("Florence Agreement"), which provides for the duty-free importation of instruments and apparatus for the use of any nonprofit institution established for educational or scientific purposes if no instrument or apparatus of equivalent scientific value for the intended purpose is manufactured in the U.S.
Legislative History: 1966 U.S. Code Cong. & Admin. News 3254.
Implementing Regulations: 15 C.F.R. Part 301 (1989).

Export Trading Company Act of 1982, 15 U.S.C. 4001-4053--designed to promote the formation of export trade associations and companies by modifying the antitrust laws for the limited purpose of allowing bank holding companies and other entities to invest in such organizations; established a regulatory review procedure in the Department of Commerce.
Legislative History: 1982 U.S. Code Cong. & Admin. News 2431.
Implementing Regulations: 15 C.F.R. Parts 325 & 400 (1989).

Foreign Trade Zones Act of 1934, as amended, 19 U.S.C. 81a--authorized the formation of foreign trade zones, defined as isolated, enclosed, and policed areas operated as public utilities in or adjacent to a port of entry and furnished with facilities for lading, unlading, handling, storing, manipulating, manufacturing, exhibiting, and reshipping goods. Goods may be brought into a zone without being subject to U.S. customs law governing entry or payment of a duty and may be reshipped to foreign ports duty-free.
Legislative History: 1950 U.S. Code Cong. Service 2533; 1984 U.S. Code Cong. & Admin. News 4910. 19 C.F.R. Part 146.0 et seq., 196, 252, & 290 (1989).

Export Administration Act of 1979, as amended, 50 U.S.C. App. 2401-2420--establishes a system of export controls over goods consistent with U.S. national security, foreign policy, and economic objectives, and also a procedure for obtaining export licenses.
Legislative History: 1979 U.S. Code Cong. & Admin. News 1147; 1985 U.S. Code Cong. & Admin. News 108; 1988 U.S. Code Cong. & Admin. News 1547.
Implementing Regulations: 15 C.F.R. Parts 768-799 (1989).

Trade Fair Act of 1959, 19 U.S.C. 1751-1756--authorizes the Secretary of Commerce to advise the Secretary of the Treasury of a "trade fair designation," which confers special customs entry and disposition privileges on articles imported for a trade fair.
Legislative History: 1959 U.S. Code Cong. & Admin. News 1436.
Implementing Regulations: 19 C.F.R. Part 147 (1989).

International Investment Survey Act of 1976, as amended, 22 U.S.C. 3101-3108--directs the Department of Commerce to carry out a continuing data collection effort with respect to international trade and internal and external investment in services and, to that end, imposes certain recordkeeping and reporting requirements on persons subject to U.S. jurisdiction.
Legislative History: 1976 U.S. Code Cong. & Admin. News 4663; 1981 U.S. Code Cong. & Admin. News 99; 1984 U.S. Code Cong. & Admin. News 4910.
Implementing Regulations: 15 C.F.R. Part 801 (1989).

Coastal Zone Management Act of 1972, as amended, 16 U.S.C. 1451 et seq.--authorizes the National Oceanic & Atmospheric Administration to approve state coastal zone management programs and to administer a development grant program.
Legislative History: 1972 U.S. Code Cong. & Admin. News 4776.
Implementing Regulations: 15 C.F.R. Part 923 et seq. (1989).

Deep Seabed Hard Mineral Resources Act, 30 U.S.C. 1401 et seq.--directs the National Oceanic & Atmospheric Administration to regulate the issuance of licenses to U.S. citizens to explore for deep seabed hard minerals, such as manganese nodules.
Legislative History: 1980 U.S. Code Cong. & Admin. News 1600.
Implementing Regulations: 15 C.F.R. Part 970 (1989).

Ocean Thermal Energy Act of 1980, as amended, 42 U.S.C. 9101 et seq.--makes the National Oceanic & Atmospheric Administration the licensing authority over ownership, construction, and operation of ocean thermal energy conversion facilities and plantships.
Legislative History: 1980 U.S. Code Cong. & Admin. News 2407.
Implementing Regulations: 15 C.F.R. Part 981 (1989).

Census Enabling Legislation, 13 U.S.C. 1 et seq.; 15 U.S.C. 192a--authorizes the Census Bureau to conduct special population censuses at the request and expense of a community, and establishes fees for Census services and statistics.
Implementing Regulations: 15 C.F.R. Part 50 (1990).

Public Works and Economic Development Act of 1965, as amended, 42 U.S.C. 3211 et seq.--establishes a program to provide assistance to economically distressed areas in order to alleviate substantial and persistent unemployment and underemployment and to stabilize and diversify the economy of such areas.
Legislative History: 1965 U.S. Code Cong. & Admin. News 2788.
Implementing Regulations: 13 C.F.R. Part 301 et seq. (1989).

Tariff Act of 1930, as amended, 19 U.S.C. 1673-1677h--imposes "antidumping" duties on imported goods sold in the U.S. at less than their fair value, and "countervailing" duties to offset any disadvantage to U.S.-manufactured goods competing against foreign goods that receive manufacturing, production, or export benefits from another country.
Legislative History: 1979 U.S. Code Cong. & Admin. News 381; 1984 U.S. Code Cong. & Admin. News 4910; 1988 U.S. Code Cong. & Admin. News 1547.
Implementing Regulations: 19 C.F.R. Part 355-355 (1989).

Marine Mammal Protection Act of 1972, as amended, 16 U.S.C. 1361-1407 (1989)--restricts the taking, possession, transportation, selling, offering for sale, and importing of marine mammals, and directs the National Oceanic & Atmospheric Administration to enforce the Act and administer the granting of limited exceptions thereto.
Legislative History: 1972 U.S. Code Cong. & Admin. News 4144; 1976 U.S. Code Cong. & Admin. News 593; 1981 U.S. Code Cong. &

Admin. News 1458; 1986 U.S. Code Cong. & Admin. News 6240; 1988 U.S. Code Cong. & Admin. News 6154.

Implementing Regulations: 50 C.F.R. Parts 17, 216-230 (1989).

Fish & Wildlife Act of 1956, as amended, 16 U.S.C. 742(c)--creates a revolving Fisheries Loan Fund to assist owners/operators of commercial fishing vessels to avoid default on primary vessel financing and to cover vessel operating losses.

Legislative History: 1956 U.S. Code Cong. & Admin. News 4590; 1986 U.S. Code Cong. & Admin. News 6240.

Implementing Regulations: 50 C.F.R. Parts 250-259 (1989).

Agricultural Marketing Act of 1946, as amended, 7 U.S.C. 1621 et seq.--directs the National Marine Fisheries Service of the Department's National Oceanic & Atmospheric Administration to develop grade standards and to inspect and certify transportation facilities and rates for fish, shellfish, and related produce.

Legislative History: 1946 U.S. Code Cong. Service 1584; 1955 U.S. Code Cong. & Admin. News 2727; 1977 U.S. Code Cong. & Admin. News 1704; 1985 U.S. Code Cong. & Admin. News 1103.

Implementing Regulations: 50 C.F.R. Parts 260-299 (1989).

Patent Act of 1952, as amended, 35 U.S.C. 1 et seq.--the basic patent statute of the U.S.

Legislative History: 1964 U.S. Code Cong. & Admin. News 2122; 1974 U.S. Code Cong. & Admin. News 7113; 1975 U.S. Code Cong. & Admin. News 1220.

Implementing Regulations: 37 C.F.R. Part 1 et seq. (1989).

Trademark Act of 1946 ("Lanham Act"), as amended, 15 U.S.C. 1051 et seq.--the basic Federal trademark law, designed to make actionable the deceptive and misleading use of trademarks, tradenames, and service marks in interstate and foreign commerce, and to protect against unfair competition.

Highlights of Recent Legislation: The Trademark Law Revision Act of 1988, Pub.L. 100-667, 102 Stat. 3935, significantly amended the Trademark Act by (1) eliminating the requirement that U.S. citizens and businesses, unlike their foreign counterparts, must use a mark in commerce before filing a registration application ("pre-application use requirement"); decreases the term of registration and renewal from 20 to ten years; and confers Federal trademark rights only if the mark is actually used in the ordinary course of trade.

Legislative History: 1946 U.S. Code Cong. Service 1274; 1962 U.S. Code Cong. & Admin. News 2844; 1974 U.S. Code Cong. & Admin. News 7113; 1982 U.S. Code Cong. & Admin. News 765; 1988 U.S. Code Cong. & Admin. News 5577.

Implementing Regulations: 37 C.F.R. Part 1 et seq. (1989).

DEPARTMENT OF DEFENSE

The Pentagon
Washington, D.C. 20301-1600

DESCRIPTION: The Department of Defense (DOD) is the parent organization of 13 Defense agencies and the three military departments (Department of the Army, Department of the Navy, and Department of the Air Force) and their subordinate armed forces (Army, Navy, and Air Force; the Marine Corps is part of the Department of the Navy). The military departments are responsible for recruiting, training and equipping their armed forces, but operational control of those forces in combat is assigned to one of the unified and specified commands, which report directly to the Secretary of Defense.

More than five million people, including active duty service members, civilian employees, and Reserve Forces, work for the Department of Defense, including more than two million active duty service personnel and 1.1 million civilians. The Department administers almost 1,300 military installations and properties, almost 900 of them in the U.S. and the rest in 21 other countries.

(Area Code 202)
Secretary: Richard Cheney 695-5261
Public Affairs/Publications Information 697-5737
General Information 545-6700
Legislative Reference Services 697-1305
Freedom of Information Act Office 697-1180
Privacy Act Office 694-3027
Small and Disadvantaged Business Utilization 694-1151
Defense Hotline for Waste, Fraud and Abuse 693-5080
Outside Washington, D.C. Metro Area ....(800) 424-9098

Uniformed Services University of the Health Sciences
General Counsel: Charles Mannix ....(301) 295-3028
Legal Advisor to the Assistant Secretary for Intelligence
Oversight: Capt George L. Michael III 695-9542
Office of the National Ombudsman, National Committee for
Employer Support of the Guard and Reserve
National Ombudsman: (vacant) ....(800) 336-4590
Or, in Virginia ....(703) 696-1400

OFFICE OF THE GENERAL COUNSEL (Room 3E999)

The Office of the General Counsel is the chief legal organization in the Department of Defense. The Office is responsible for the provision of advice to high-level policymakers in the Office of the Secretary of Defense. In addition, the Office works closely with senior attorneys and policymakers from the military departments, and with officials from the Departments of Justice, State, Treasury, and other Federal Government agencies.

The Office is divided into sub-offices: International and Intelligence; Logistics; Fiscal Matters; Legal Counsel; and Personnel and Health Policy. The issues considered by the Office involve virtually all areas of the law, with particular focus on international relations, the Uniform Code of Military Justice, procurement policy, the appropriations process, environmental concerns, property law, labor-management relations, administrative procedure, industrial security, counter-intelligence policy, and national intelligence. The Office frequently engages in special projects for the Secretary of Defense.

(Area Code 202)
General Counsel: Honorable Terrence O'Donnell 695-3341
Deputy General Counsel: Leonard Niederlehner 697-7248
Assistant General Counsel/Fiscal and Inspector
General: Manuel Briskin 695-5864
Assistant General Counsel/International and
Intelligence: John H. McNeill 695-2604

(Area Code 202)
Assistant General Counsel/Legal Counsel:
Michael A. Sterlacci 697-2714
Assistant General Counsel/Logistics: Dennis Trosch 697-5387
Assistant General Counsel/Personnel and Health Policy:
Robert L. Gilliat 697-9341

OFFICE OF THE INSPECTOR GENERAL (Room 1000)

400 Army Navy Drive, Arlington, VA 22202

The Office of Inspector General is charged with preventing fraud, waste and abuse as well as promoting economy, efficiency and effectiveness in departmental programs and operations. The Office's specific functions are to: conduct and supervise audits and criminal investigations relating to departmental programs and operations; recommend policies to prevent and detect fraud, waste and abuse and increase economy, efficiency and effectiveness in such programs and operations; and keep the Secretary of Defense and the Congress informed about programs and corrective actions needed in administering departmental operations.

(Area Code 202)
Inspector General: Susan J. Crawford 695-4249
Assistant Inspector General for Criminal Investigations
Policy and Oversight: Morris B. Silverstein 694-8957

(Area Code 202)
Assistant Inspector General for Investigations and
Director of Defense Criminal Investigative Service:
Donald Mancuso 693-0031

OFFICE OF CIVILIAN HEALTH AND MEDICAL PROGRAM OF THE UNIFORMED SERVICES (OCHAMPUS)

Bldg 618, Fitzsimons Army Medical Center, Aurora, CO 80045

The Office of Civilian Health and Medical Program of the Uniformed Services (OCHAMPUS) administers a civilian health and medical care program for spouses and dependent children of active duty, retired, and deceased service members.

The Office of General Counsel provides advice and counsel on administrative and contract law matters; maintains liaison with the General Counsel of the Department of Defense and counsel for other Federal, state, and local agencies on legal matters involving OCHAMPUS; monitors debt collection activities to recover Government funds under the Federal Medical Care Recovery Act and the Federal Claims Collection Act; reviews cases of suspected fraud, monitors case investigation and prosecution, and initiates final case disposition; provides litigation support to the Department of Justice in cases involving OCHAMPUS; and administers the hearings and appeals system to ensure due process for dissatisfied beneficiaries, participating providers, and providers denied the status of CHAMPUS-authorized providers.

There are also contract Hearing Officers who conduct hearings in geographically dispersed locations, primarily in Washington, D.C., Florida, Texas, and California. Although Hearing Officers can be based anywhere in the U.S., they must travel to the site of the hearing.

(Area Code 303)

Director: Capt. Thomas McDavid 361-8606
General Counsel: Robert Seaman 361-8506

(Area Code 303)

Office of Appeals and Hearings
Chief: Donald F. Wagner 361-8506

ARMED SERVICES BOARD OF CONTRACT APPEALS

Hoffman Building II, 200 Stovall Street, Alexandria, VA 22332

The Members of the Board (who have by charter the title Administrative Judge) perform quasi-judicial duties in adversary proceedings involving disputes relating to contracts between components of the Department of Defense and their contractors. On occasion, the Board may also handle contract appeals on behalf of some civilian agencies, such as the Department of Health and Human Services, and the Agency for International Development, which do not have their own board of contract appeals. In general, an Administrative Judge presides at formal hearings, makes decisions on the basis of the record, and prepares written opinions to explain and justify decisions.

The decisions of the Armed Services Board of Contract Appeals can be found in the Board of Contract Appeals Reporter, a bi-weekly publication which reports the decisions of the following Boards of Contract Appeals: Agriculture, Armed Services, Corps of Engineers, Department of Transportation, Energy, General Services Administration, Department of Housing and Urban Development, Interior, Labor, National Aeronautics and Space Administration, U.S. Postal Service, and Department of Veterans Affairs. Annual Price $760.00. Contact: Commerce Clearing House, Inc., 4025 West Peterson Avenue, Chicago, IL 60646. Tel: 312/583-8500. Or in Washington, D.C., call 202/626-2200.

(Area Code 703)

Chairman: Paul Williams 756-8501
Vice Chairman: V. John Riismandel 756-8501
Vice Chairman: William J. Ruberry 756-8501

(Area Code 703)

Vice Chairman: Alan M. Spector 756-8501
Recorder: Edward S. Adamkewicz 756-8502

ASSISTANT SECRETARY (FORCE MANAGEMENT AND PERSONNEL)

(Area Code 703)

General Counsel for DOD Dependent Schools:
Robert Terzian 325-0256

Military Manpower and Personnel Policy
Legislative and Legal Policy for Deputy Assistant Secretary Director: Col. Ted Borek ....(202) 697-3387

ASSISTANT SECRETARY (PUBLIC AFFAIRS)

(Area Code 703)

American Forces Information Service
General Counsel: Normand V. Lussier 274-4828

DEFENSE ADVANCED RESEARCH PROJECTS AGENCY

1400 Wilson Boulevard, Architect Building, Arlington, VA 22209

(Area Code 202)

General Counsel: Richard Dunn 694-6831

DEFENSE COMMUNICATIONS AGENCY
8th Street and South Courthouse Road
Arlington, VA 22204

The mission of the Defense Communications Agency (DCA) is to perform system engineering and technical support for the Defense Communications System, the National Military Command System, the Department of Defense, and other Government agencies. There are two attorneys in the headquarters office, the General Counsel and Deputy General Counsel. The only other attorneys (two) are located in Scott AFB, IL, who work for the agency's Defense Commercial Communications Office, handling long-line communications leases for the Department of Defense.

(Area Code 202)
Director: Lt. Gen. John T. Myers 692-0018
Inspector General: Col. Edward Henderson 692-9012
Corporate Exchange Branch/Public Affairs 692-2006
Freedom of Information Act/Privacy Act Office 692-2000
Facsimile 692-2045

(Area Code 202)
Law Library 692-0373
The Law Library is not open to the public, but the librarian will answer brief questions over the phone.

OFFICE OF GENERAL COUNSEL (Room 4210)

The Office of General Counsel provides legal advice to DCA headquarters and its field activities. Responsibilities include: providing liaison with Congress; determining appropriate action to be taken in cases involving fraud and violations of Standards of Conduct and Conflict of Interest regulations; reviewing all audit and investigation reports; and providing guidance on contract compliance and all significant labor relations matters. The office also serves as the agency focal point of contact for all international logistics negotiations with foreign governments and with the Office of the Secretary of Defense.

(Area Code 202)
General Counsel: Susan Chadick (Acting) 692-2009
Chief Regulatory Counsel (Telecoms): Carl Smith 692-6957

Illinois Office
Chief Counsel: Cliff Hasagawa
Defense Commercial Communications Office, Scott Air Force Base, IL 62225-8400. Tel: 618/256-4023.

DEFENSE CONTRACT AUDIT AGENCY
Building 4, Cameron Station
Alexandria, VA 22304-6178

The Defense Contract Audit Agency (DCAA) is an independent defense agency responsible for performing all contract audits for the Department of Defense (DOD). A worldwide organization, it is the largest audit agency in the Federal Government. In addition to performing all contract audits and providing accounting and financial advisory services on DOD contracts, DCAA also provides these services for some 83 non-DOD agencies and for some allied nations that purchase U.S.-produced defense supplies and equipment. DCAA audits about 13,000 business enterprises, including all large defense contractors, and issues approximately 60,000 audit reports annually. Results of audits are provided to procurement and contract officials for use in the negotiation, administration, and settlement of contracts and subcontracts.

The agency's headquarters is in Alexandria, VA. Six regional offices and 450 field offices are located throughout the U.S. and overseas.

The Defense Legal Service provides legal and legislative advice to the Director, members of his staff, and to Regional Directors. The Defense Legal Service staff is responsible for all legal matters relating to contract audit in DOD, and is responsible for the legal sufficiency of directives, instructions, regulations, determinations, and related correspondence. The attorneys represent the agency in administrative proceedings and provide liaison and legal support in contract dispute trials. The General Counsel also serves as the Agency Ethics Official and Standards of Conduct Counselor.

In addition, the Defense Legal Service develops and administers procedures for the comprehensive reporting of all instances of irregular conduct and assists regional management in ensuring implementation of such procedures.

(Area Code 703)
Director: William H. Reed 274-6785
Public Information 274-7319

(Area Code 703)
Freedom of Information Act/Privacy Act Office 274-4400
Facsimile 274-7567

DEPARTMENT OF DEFENSE

OFFICE OF GENERAL COUNSEL (Room 4A175)

(Area Code 703)

General Counsel: John J. Quill 274-7321
Deputy General Counsel: Kirk B. Moberley 274-7383
Deputy General Counsel: John N. Ford 274-7322
Assistant General Counsel: Paul Bley 274-7800
Assistant General Counsel: Thomas H. Alphin 274-7800

Western Regional Office
Counsel: Sandra Mason
450 Golden Gate Avenue, Box 36116, San Francisco, CA 94102-3563. Tel: 415/556-6137.

DEFENSE INTELLIGENCE AGENCY
The Pentagon
Washington, D.C. 20340-3042

The Defense Intelligence Agency (DIA) is responsible for producing and disseminating military intelligence to satisfy the intelligence requirements of the Secretary of Defense, the Joint Chiefs of Staff, major components of DOD, and other authorized requirements. It accomplishes this either by use of internal resources or through cooperation with other intelligence agencies.

(Area Code 202)

Director: Lt. Gen. Harry E. Soyster 695-7353
Inspector General: Col Joseph Breen ....(703) 284-1254
Public Affairs 695-0071

(Area Code 202)

Freedom of Information Act Office 373-3911
Privacy Act Office 373-4291
Facsimile ....(703) 284-1144

OFFICE OF GENERAL COUNSEL (Room 2E238)

The Office of General Counsel provides legal counsel on substantive and procedural questions relating to the functioning of DIA. Responsibilities include: developing the Agency's position on legislation; representing the Agency on legal and public policy matters; interpreting laws, executive orders, and Defense Department Directives; coordinating the Agency's defense with the Justice Department in all law suits; monitoring the Agency's responsiveness under the Freedom of Information Act/Privacy Acts; and coordinating acquisition efforts. Attorneys in the office also provide legal advice on disciplinary actions (military and civilian), investigations, security matters, contracts, patents and copyrights, EEO, and international law. In addition to directing all activities of the office, the General Counsel serves as the Agency Ethics Official and as a member of the Contract Review Board.

(Area Code 202)

General Counsel: William J. Allard 697-3945

(Area Code 202)

Deputy General Counsel: Robert H. Berry Jr 697-3945

DEFENSE INVESTIGATIVE SERVICE
1900 Half Street, S.W.
Washington, D.C. 20234-1700

The Defense Investigative Service (DIS) consists of a Headquarters office; two Operations Centers; eight regional offices (and their subordinate field offices and resident agencies) located in the 50 states and Puerto Rico; the Office of Industrial Security, International-Europe in Brussels, Belgium and Mannheim, Federal Republic of Germany; and the Office of Industrial Security, International-Far East in Yokohama, Japan and Seoul, Korea.

DIS conducts all personnel security investigations for Department of Defense (DOD) components and, when authorized, for other U.S. Government activities. DIS is also responsible for the four major programs involving industrial security, manages the Defense Central Index of Investigations, a centralized list of all Defense components investigative files, and security clearance information pertaining to DOD personnel.

(Area Code 202)

Director: John F. Donnelly 475-0966
Inspector General: James R. Connolly 475-1195
Public Information 475-1062

(Area Code 202)

Publications 475-1030
Freedom of Information Act/Privacy Act Office 475-1062
Facsimile 475-9240

OFFICE OF GENERAL COUNSEL (ROOM 6126)

The Office of General Counsel reviews agency policy, procedures, and directives for legality and propriety; monitors legislation, Supreme Court and other court decisions that may affect the operations and administration of DIS; drafts legislation; interprets Public Laws, Executive Orders and Department of Defense Directives; serves as liaison for legal matters with the DOD General Counsel, the General Counsels of the Military Departments, Judge Advocates General, and U.S. Attorneys; assists in the preparation of litigation against the agency and agency personnel; provides advice and assistance on legal questions which arise in the course of the conduct of DIS investigations; and handles standards of conduct and ethics matters.

(Area Code 202)
General Counsel: Thomas N. Willess 475-1465
Assistant General Counsel: Steven M. Tevlowitz 475-1465

(Area Code 202)
Assistant General Counsel: vacant 475-1465

DEFENSE LOGISTICS AGENCY
Building 3, Cameron Station
Alexandria, VA 22304-6100

The mission of the Defense Logistics Agency is to provide effective and economical support to the Department of Defense, Federal civilian agencies, foreign governments, and others as authorized, for assigned materiel commodities and supply items, including weapons systems, logistics services, contract administration services, and other support services as directed by the Secretary of Defense.

(Area Code 703)
Director: Lt. Gen. Charles McCausland 274-6111
Public Affairs 274-6135
Publications 274-6011

(Area Code 703)
Freedom of Information Act/Privacy Act Office 274-6234
Facsimile 274-7920

OFFICE OF GENERAL COUNSEL (Room 3D305)

The Office of the General Counsel provides legal advice and services on matters involving or affecting the Agency. An attorney in the Office of General Counsel may be called upon to perform the following functions:

*conduct legislative and legal research incident to the development, analysis, and implementation of DLA programs and operations;
*handle all court litigation, including appeals;
*represent DLA in bid protests filed at the General Accounting Office and in cases referred by the Special Counsel, Merit Systems Protection Board;
*represent DLA in administrative litigation;
*administer the DLA Standards of Conduct Program and serve as the DLA Ethics Counselor;
*exercise delegated authority to suspend and debar contractors;
*resolve infringement claims relating to patents, trademarks, and copyrights; and
*draft proposed legislation, comment on legislative proposals, and prepare congressional testimony for DLA witnesses.

(Area Code 703)
General Counsel: Karl W. Kabeiseman 274-6156

Counsel Europe: Bruce Krasker
Counsel Europe (Weisbaden, West Germany), APO New York 09634-5000. Tel: 49-6121-840868.

REGIONAL OFFICES

Supply Centers manage some 3.9 million items, all of the consumables in the Defense Department inventory. They also forecast demands, process requisitions, award contracts, monitor inventory levels, and schedule production.

Alexandria, VA
Counsel: Bernard Duval
Defense Fuel Supply Center, Cameron Station, Alexandria, VA 22304-6160. Tel: 703/274-7445.

Columbus, OH
Counsel: Thomas Hillin
Defense Construction Supply Center, 3990 East Broad Street, Columbus, OH 43216-5000. Tel: 614/238-3284.

Dayton
Counsel: Charles Roedersheimer
Defense Electronics Supply Center, 1507 Wilmington Pike, Dayton, OH 45444-5010. Tel: 513/296-6211.

Philadelphia
Counsel: Walter Pierce
Defense Industrial Supply Center, 700 Robbins Avenue, Philadelphia, PA 19111-5096. Tel: 215/697-2739.

Richmond
Counsel: Philip Eckert
Defense General Supply Center, Office of Counsel, Richmond, VA 23297-5000. Tel: 804/275-4811.

DEPARTMENT OF DEFENSE

Depots receive, store, and issue the full range of commodities (except bulk fuel) managed by the supply centers.

Mechanicsburg, PA
Counsel: John Fritz
Defense Depot Mechanicsburg, 5450 Carlisle Pike, P.O. Box 2030, Mechanicsburg, PA 17055-0789. Tel: 717/790-7464.

Memphis
Counsel: Ralph J. May, Jr.
Defense Depot Memphis, Office of Counsel, Memphis, TN 38114-5000. Tel: 901/775-6306.

Ogden
Counsel: Gregory T. Allen
Defense Depot Ogden, Office of Counsel, Ogden, UT 84407-5000. Tel: 801/399-7750.

Tracy, CA
Counsel: Nancy C. Rusch
Defense Depot Tracy, Office of Counsel, Tracy, CA 95376-5000. Tel: 209/832-9750.

Service Centers perform technical and logistics functions such as maintaining the Federal Supply Catalog, disposing of surplus inventory, maintaining a general reserve of machine tools and plant equipment, acting as a central repository of scientific and technical information, and managing the national reserve of strategic materials.

Alexandria, VA
Counsel: Robert Burton (acting)
DLA Administrative Support Center, Office of Counsel, Cameron Station, Room 3C346, Alexandria, VA 22304-6130. Tel: 703/274-5825.

Arlington, VA
Counsel: Rodney Ficker
Defense National Stockpile Center, 1745 Jefferson Davis Highway, Ste 100, Crystal Square, Bldg 4, Arlington, VA 22202. Tel: 202/746-7348.

Battle Creek
Counsel: Bruce W. Baird
Defense Reutilization and Marketing Service, Federal Center, 74 North Washington, Battle Creek, MI 49017-3091. Tel: 616/961-5986.

Camp H.M. Smith, HI
Counsel: Sharron Philo
Defense Reutilization and Marketing Service, ATTN: DRMS-G-P, Camp H.M. Smith, HI 96861-5010. Tel: 808/477-1223.

Columbus, OH
Counsel: David Permar
DLA Systems Automation Center, P.O. Box 1605, Columbus, OH 43216-5002. Tel: 614/238-9399.

Memphis
Counsel: Cynthia Emerson
Defense Reutilization and Marketing Service, ATTN: DRMS-G-M, 2163 Airways Blvd, Memphis, TN 38114-5247. Tel: 901/775-6342.

Ogden
Counsel: Thompson Fehr
Defense Reutilization and Marketing Service, ATTN: DRMS-G-O, 500 West 12th Street, Ogden, UT 84407-5001. Tel: 801/399-7760.

Contract Management Districts support the procurement of material by administering contracts after they have been awarded by the military services, defense agencies, some civil agencies, and some foreign governments.

Boston
Counsel: Paula Loviner
Defense Contract Management Region, Boston, 495 Summer Street, Boston, MA 02210-2184. Tel: 617/451-4269.

Chicago
Counsel: Robert Eaton
Defense Contract Management Region, Chicago, O'Hare International Airport, P.O. Box 66475, Chicago, IL 60666-0475. Tel: 312/694-6275.

Cleveland
Counsel: Frederick Condon
Defense Contract Management Region, Chicago, A.J.C. Federal Office Bldg, 1240 East 9th Street, Cleveland, OH 44199-2063. Tel: 216/522-5240.

Dallas
Counsel: Faith Biggs
Defense Contract Management Region, Dallas, 1200 Main Street, Dallas, TX 75202-4399. Tel: 214/670-1241.

El Segundo
Counsel: Anthony Carr
Defense Contract Management Region, Los Angeles, Pacific Corporate Towers, 222 North Sepulveda Blvd, Ste 1116, El Segundo, CA 90245-4320. Tel: 213/335-4480.

Marietta, GA
Counsel: Martha Henson
Defense Contract Management Region, Atlanta, 805 Walker Street, Marietta, GA 30060-2789. Tel: 404/590-6260.

New York
Counsel: David Drabkin
Defense Contract Management Region, New York, 201 Varick Street, New York, NY 10014-4811. Tel: 212/807-3008.

Philadelphia
Counsel: Alvin LaCoste
Defense Contract Management Region, Philadelphia, 2800 South 20th Street, P.O. Box 7478, Philadelphia, PA 19101-7478. Tel: 215/952-4017.

St. Louis
Counsel: Marvin Stein
Defense Contract Management Region, St. Louis, 1222 Spruce Street, St. Louis, MO 63103-2811. Tel: 314/331-5232.

Other Regional Offices

Alameda
Counsel: Richard Lavin
Defense Subsistence Region, Pacific, Defense Personnel Supply Center, 2155 Mariner Square Loop, Alameda, CA 94501-1022. Tel: 415/869-8160.

Philadelphia
Counsel: Michael Trovarelli
Defense Personnel Support Center, 2800 South 20th Street, Philadelphia, PA 19101-8419. Tel: 215/737-2630.

DEFENSE MAPPING AGENCY
8613 Lee Highway
Fairfax, VA 22031-2137

The mission of the Defense Mapping Agency (DMA) is to enhance national security and support the nation's strategy of deterrence by producing and distributing mapping, charting (nautical and aeronautical), and geodetic products and services. Agency components include: the DMA Aerospace Center in St Louis, MO; the DMA Hydrographic/Topographic Center in Brookmont, MD; the Defense Mapping School in Fort Belvoir, VA; the DMA Inter-American Geodetic Survey in Fort Sam Houston, TX; the DMA Systems Center in Reston, VA; and the DMA Office of Telecommunications Services in Reston, VA.

(Area Code 703)
Director: Maj. Gen. Robert F. Durkin 285-9302
Inspector General: Col. Raymond Abrahamson 285-9165
Public Affairs 285-9138

(Area Code 703)
Freedom of Information Act Office 285-9138
Privacy Act Office 285-9140
Facsimile 285-9374

OFFICE OF GENERAL COUNSEL (Room 2N20)

The Office of the General Counsel, located in DMA headquarters office provides legal services and represents DMA before all courts and boards, with the exception of the labor relations program, where only representational services are provided when specifically requested. The General Counsel is also the Agency Ethics Official and is responsible for the standards of conduct program.

(Area Code 703)
General Counsel: Edward J. Obloy 285-9315
Deputy General Counsel: John Perruzzi 285-9315

Contract Law Division
Associate General Counsel: Andrew H. Deranger (301) 227-4143

OFFICES OUTSIDE HEADQUARTERS:

Hydrographic/Topographic Center (Brookmont, MD)
Defense Mapping Agency, 6500 Brooks Lane, Washington, D.C. 20315-0030

Associate General Counsel: Kermit A. Sande ...(301) 227-2268

Aerospace Center
Defense Mapping Agency, 3200 South 2nd Street, St. Louis, MO 62301

Associate General Counsel: Howard Bishop ......(314) 263-4501

Systems Center
Defense Mapping Agency, 12100 Sunset Hills Road, Suite 200, Reston, VA 22090-3207

Associate General Counsel: Paul C. Kelbaugh ...(703) 285-9315

DEFENSE NUCLEAR AGENCY
6801 Telegraph Road
Alexandria, VA 22310-3398

The Defense Nuclear Agency (DNA) provides support to senior officials of the Defense Department (DOD) and other Federal agencies on matters concerning nuclear weapons, nuclear weapons system acquisition, nuclear weapons effects on weapons systems and forces, and other aspects of the DOD nuclear program. During wartime and periods of international crisis, DNA assists in analyzing nuclear weapons planning and action options.

(Area Code 703)
Director: Major General Gerald G. Watson 325-7004
Inspector General: Capt. James H. Morris 325-7096
Public Information 325-7095

(Area Code 703)
Freedom of Information Act/Privacy Act Office 325-7095
Facsimile 325-7366

OFFICE OF GENERAL COUNSEL (Room 109)

The Office of the General Counsel provides legal advice and assistance to senior officials of DNA and to the Director of the Armed Forces Radiobiology Research Institute. Responsibilities include providing legal advice on procurement and acquisition activities, on litigation, and on legislation affecting the agency. Attorneys in the office also ensure DNA's compliance with provisions of the National Environmental Policy Act, advise on policies and procedures relating to the Privacy Act and the Freedom of Information Act, and advise on all standards of conduct and conflict of interest matters.

(Area Code 703)
General Counsel: Robert L. Brittigan 325-7681

(Area Code 703)
Deputy General Counsel: David C. Rickard 325-7681

DEFENSE SECURITY ASSISTANCE AGENCY
The Pentagon
Washington, D.C. 20301-2800

The Defense Security Assistance Agency (DSAA) directs the execution of security assistance programs, such as military assistance and foreign military sales. The Agency supervises the formulation of detailed Security Assistance programs; conducts international logistics and sales negotiations with foreign countries; manages a credit financing program; maintains liaison with Congress on related legislation; and supervises Department of Defense elements in foreign countries responsible for managing Security Assistance programs.

(Area Code 202)
Director: Lt. Gen. Charles W. Brown 695-3291
Public Affairs 697-5131
Freedom of Information Act/Privacy Act Office 697-2859
Facsimile 695-0081

OFFICE OF GENERAL COUNSEL (Room 4B730)

The General Counsel handles all legal responsibilities for the Agency.

(Area Code 202)
General Counsel: Jerome H. Silber 697-8000

NATIONAL SECURITY AGENCY
Ft. George C. Meade, MD 20755-6000

The National Security Agency (NSA) is responsible for coordinating and performing highly specialized technical functions in support of U.S. Government activities to protect U.S. communications and produce foreign intelligence information. The agency has three primary missions: a communications security mission, a computer security mission, and a foreign intelligence information mission.

(Area Code 301)
Director: Vice Admiral William O. Studeman 688-7111
Inspector General: Robert K. Price 688-6666
Public Affairs 688-6524
Freedom of Information Act/Privacy Act Office 688-6527

OFFICE OF GENERAL COUNSEL (ROOM 2B8140)

The Office of General Counsel provides legal advice to senior agency officials, including interpreting law and regulations applicable to the agency's missions and activities, and representing the agency on all legal matters in dealings with other Federal departments and agencies, private organizations, and the general public. The General Counsel handles litigation involving NSA, develops and presents the agency's legislative program, and is responsible for legal oversight of certain agency activities to ensure compliance with law and regulations.

(Area Code 301)
General Counsel: Paul Brady 688-6705
Deputy General Counsel: Richard S. Surrey 688-6705

STRATEGIC DEFENSE INITIATIVE ORGANIZATION
The Pentagon
Washington, D.C. 20301-7100

The Strategic Defense Initiative Organization (SDIO) directs the conduct of a vigorous research program including advanced technologies, that will provide the basis for an informed decision regarding the feasibility of eliminating the threat posed by nuclear ballistic missiles of all ranges, and of increasing the contribution of defensive systems to U.S. and allied security. Consistent with international treaty obligations, the Secretary of Defense has invited U.S. allies to participate formally in the SDI research program.

(Area Code 202)
Director: Henry F. Cooper..............................695-7060
Public Affairs 695-8743

(Area Code 202)
Freedom of Information Act/Privacy Act Office 693-1500
Facsimile 693-1697

OFFICE OF GENERAL COUNSEL (Room 1E1080)

The General Counsel manages the agency's legal program, serves as legal advisor to the Director, and ensures that SDIO's program is conducted in compliance with U.S. treaty obligations. This position is also in the Defense Legal Services Agency and reports professionally to the General Counsel, Department of Defense, who is head of the Defense Legal Services Agency.

(Area Code 202)
General Counsel: William Carroll 693-1784

The **Assistant General Counsel (Treaty Compliance and International Law)** performs complex legal assignments relating to compliance of the SDI program with U.S. treaty obligations, customary international law, and other international aspects of the program.

(Area Code 202)
Assistant General Counsel (Treaty Compliance & International Law): Lt. Col. James Gravelle 693-1784

The **Assistant General Counsel (General and Administrative Law)** performs complex legal assignments relating to general and administrative laws affecting the SDI program, including areas of environmental law, Ethics in Government, Standards of Conduct, and similar statutes; advises on Freedom of Information and Privacy Acts; and manages the agency's legislative program.

(Area Code 202)
Assistant General Counsel (General & Administrative Law): Lt. Col. Michael Vanzandt 693-1784

The **Assistant General Counsel (Contracting, Fiscal, and Program Fraud)** handles complex legal assignments relating to Federal acquisition law, appropriations law, and implementing regulations; and manages the agency's program to combat contract fraud.

(Area Code 202)
Assistant General Counsel (Contracting, Fiscal, & Program Fraud): William Zanca 693-1784

The **Assistant General Counsel (Contracting and Government Ethics)** handles complex legal assignments relating to Federal acquisition law and Government ethics, including: advising SDIO technical and contracting personnel on procurement law; representing the agency in administrative forums involved in resolution of contract protests, claims, and disputes; and preparing delegations of authority and memoranda of understanding required for negotiation of cooperative research projects with Allies.

(Area Code 202)
Assistant General Counsel (Contracting & Government Ethics): James Tate 693-1784

DEPARTMENT OF DEFENSE

PUBLICATIONS OF INTEREST

Department of Defense Directives can be obtained from U.S. Naval Publications and Forms Center, 5801 Tabor Ave, Attn: Code 301, Philadelphia, PA. 19120.

The following publications can be purchased from the **U.S. Government Printing Office**. Stock numbers and prices for annual subscriptions are shown below. Submit requests for these publications to: The Superintendent of Documents, U.S. Government Printing Office, Washington, D.C. 20402. Tel: 202/783-3238.

How to Buy Surplus Personal Property from the United States Department of Defense. A pamphlet providing information necessary to purchase personal property from the Department of Defense, bidder's lists, and types of property sold. Price: $1.50. GPO Stock# 008-007-03288-7.

Companies Participating in the Department of Defense Subcontracting Program. Quarterly. This publication summarizes information submitted by DOD prime contractors required to submit reports on subcontracting to small and small disadvantaged businesses. Approximately 900 companies, listed alphabetically and indicating their location, date of latest Government subcontracting surveillance review, net value of subcontract awards, and amount and percent of awards. The report has a section for each military department and the Defense Logistics Agency. Annual subscription price: $15.00 domestic; $18.75 foreign. GPO Stock# 708-066-00000-1.

DOD Federal Acquisition Regulation Supplement. 1988. Contains guidelines on the provisions, clauses, and cost principles authorized for DOD contracts, as well as the procedures and actions necessary for awarding and administering the contracts. Subscription service consists of a basic manual and changes for an indeterminate period. In looseleaf form, punched for 3-ring binder. Price: $102.00 domestic; $127.50 foreign. GPO Stock# 908-011-00000-7.

Manual for Courts-Martial. 1984. This procedural and practice manual implements the Uniform Code of Military Justice (10 U.S.C. 801-940) and applies to all of the military services. It also contains the Military Rules of Evidence. Price: $13.00 domestic; $16.25 foreign. GPO Stock# 008-000-00403-0.

JOINT CHIEFS OF STAFF
The Pentagon
Washington, D.C. 20318

(Area Code 202)
Chairman: General Colin Powell 697-9121
Legal and Legislative Counsel: Col Fred Green 697-1137

(Area Code 202)
Public Affairs 697-4272
Facsimile 697-8758

DEPARTMENT OF THE AIR FORCE
The Pentagon
Washington, D.C. 20330-1000

The Department of the Air Force manages the air defenses of the U.S. It is responsible for the procurement of air weapons and the recruitment, retention, and training of members of the U.S. Air Force.

(Area Code 202)

Secretary of the Air Force: Donald B. Rice 697-8141
Public Affairs 697-6061
Publications 767-6071
Office of Small & Disadvantaged Business Utilization ..697-4126
Freedom of Information Act Office 695-4992
Privacy Act Office 697-3491
Facsimile 697-1215

(Area Code 202)

Law Library (Judge Advocate's Library) 767-1520
The law library is open to the public on a very limited basis, from 7 AM until 4 PM. The library is located in Room 102, Building #5683, Bolling Air Force Base.

OFFICE OF THE INSPECTOR GENERAL (Room 4E1076)

The Inspector General is responsible to the Secretary of the Air Force for the optimum effectiveness of the U.S. Air Force, and for inspection, safety, investigation, security, counterintelligence, complaint processing, enforcement, fraud, waste and abuse, and antiterrorist programs.

(Area Code 202)

Inspector General: Lt. Gen. Bradley C. Hosmer 697-6733
Facsimile 697-4293

(Area Code 202)

Office of Special Investigations
Assistant Inspector General and Commander:
Brig. Gen. Francis R. Dillon 767-5228
Judge Advocate: Col. Robert E. Reed 767-5312

OFFICE OF GENERAL COUNSEL (Room 4E856)

The Air Force Office of General Counsel has the following areas of responsibility:

The **General Counsel** is the final legal authority on all matters arising within or referred to the Department of the Air Force, except those relating to the administration of military justice.

(Area Code 202)

General Counsel: Ann C. Petersen 697-0941

The **Deputy General Counsel** assists in providing legal advice on all matters arising within or referred to the Department of the Air Force, except those relating to the administration of military justice.

Deputy General Counsel: vacant 697-4406

The **Assistant General Counsel for Procurement** provides advice and counsel regarding procurement law and legal policy affecting all procurement activities of the Air Force.

Assistant General Counsel for Procurement: John Janecek 697-3900

The **Assistant General Counsel for Installations and Environment** provides advice on legal matters involving the acquisition, use, and disposal of real property; military construction; land use and zoning; family housing; and environmental protection, including pollution control, environmental policy, and occupational safety and health laws.

(Area Code 202)

Assistant General Counsel for Installations and Environment: Grant C. Reynolds 697-7479

The **Assistant General Counsel for Civilian Personnel and Fiscal** provides legal advice and counsel in fields of civilian personnel law, EEO, labor-management relations, fiscal law, conflict of interest, standards of conduct, Freedom of Information, and privacy.

Assistant General Counsel for Civilian Personnel and Fiscal: Walter A. Willson 695-4975

The **Assistant General Counsel for Military Affairs** provides legal advice on matters relating to military personnel, intelligence, counterintelligence, and investigative matters.

Assistant General Counsel for Military Affairs: Florence W. Madden 695-5663

The **Assistant General Counsel for International Matters and Civil Aviation** provides legal advice and assistance to the Secretary and Air Staff on international and civil aviation matters of interest to the Air Force.

Assistant General Counsel for International Matters and Civil Aviation: Boyd W. Allen Jr 695-5067

AIR FORCE REVIEW BOARD

(Area Code 202)

Deputy: Joe G. Lineberger 692-7571

(Area Code 202)

Board for the Correction of Military Records 692-4726

CHIEF OF STAFF OF THE AIR FORCE

(Area Code 202)

Chief of Staff: Gen. Larry D. Welch 697-9225
Public Affairs 697-6061

(Area Code 202)

Freedom of Information Act/Privacy Act Office 694-3527

OFFICE OF THE JUDGE ADVOCATE GENERAL (ROOM 4E112)

The Air Force JAG Department numbers about 1,400 attorneys assigned to one of 136 Air Force facilities throughout the world. Primary areas of practice include:

Military Justice--participating in trials by courts-martial as judges, trial counsel (prosecutors), and defense counsel. Defense counsel also represent Air Force members in nonjudicial punishment proceedings and adverse administrative proceedings. New judge advocates generally do not become defense counsels until after at least one year of active duty.

Government Contract Law--formal advertising and negotiation of contracts; performance monitoring, including modification, termination, inspection and acceptance; and dispute management, including protests by unsuccessful offerors, and appeals. JAGs are also assigned as Air Force representatives at major contractors.

Labor Law--representation in arbitration hearings, grievance hearings, EEO administrative hearings, and proceedings before the Federal Services Impasse Panel; serving as members of management team for negotiating new collective bargaining agreements.

Environmental and Real Property Law--advising commanders and staff officers on the requirements of the National Environmental Policy Act; reviewing environmental impact statements for legal sufficiency; negotiating with environmental agencies at all levels; appearing before Government agencies on a variety of issues, including applications, rulemaking and variances; dealing with land use problems in the vicinity of military airports, including compliance with local zoning ordinances, applications for zoning variances, nuisances, and unconstitutional takings.

Claims--supervising portions of Air Force-wide claims programs; ensuring prompt and fair payment of household goods claims and recovering damages from the responsible common carrier; and investigating and evaluating tort-type claims ranging from auto accidents and medical malpractice to multi-jurisdictional aircraft accidents.

International Law--researching problems concerning the law of armed conflict and giving instructional presentations to ensure Air Force members are familiar with the law of armed conflict. JAG officers assigned overseas advise commanders on agreements governing the status of U.S. forces; participate in the negotiation of bilateral arrangements; monitor foreign criminal trials and prison conditions of U.S. military members to ensure they are granted applicable procedural safeguards; and solve foreign civil law problems dealing with customs, taxes, claims, and real estate.

Legal Assistance--providing assistance to active duty and retired military members and their dependents on such issues as taxes, domestic relations, wills, powers of attorney, property transactions, landlord and tenant relations, debtor-creditor rights, consumer affairs, adoption, and citizenship.

(Area Code 202)

The Judge Advocate General: MG Keithe Nelson 694-5732
Deputy Judge Advocate General/JAA: MG David Morehouse 694-5733

Executive Assistant to the Judge Advocate General/JAE:
Col. Olan Waldrop 694-5734
Professional Development Division/JAEC:
Col. William Dugan 694-3021
Special Assistant for Reserve Affairs/JAER:
Col. Maximilian Welker 694-3021
Recruiting Division/JAECR: Maj. Carol DiBattiste 694-5941
Executive Services Division/JAES:
Maj. Robert Schwartz 697-4378
Legal Information Systems Division/JAEX:
Maj. Colby Blake (Bolling AFB, DC) 767-1660

Directorate of Civil Law/JAC: Col. Frank Losey 694-4069
Preventive Law & Legal Aid Group/JACA:
LTC Tom Fiscus 697-0413
Claims & Tort Litigation Staff/JACC:
Col. Edward Hornbrook (Bolling AFB, DC) 767-1571
Environmental Law Division/JACE:
LTC Fred Kuhn (Bolling AFB) 767-4823
International Law Division/JACI:
Col. Francis Moran 695-9631
General Litigation Division/JACL:
Col. Michael Emerson 475-7635
General Litigation Division-Utilities Litigation/JACL (ULT):
LTC Bruce Barnard (Tyndall AFB, FL) ...(904) 283-6347

(Area Code 202)

General Law Division/JACM: Everett Hopson Jr 694-4075
Contract Law Division/JACN: LTC William Henabray 694-8758
Patents Division/JACP: Don Singer 475-1386
Patents Division-Patent Prosecution Office/JACPB:
Jacob Erlich (Waltham, MA) ....(617) 377-4075
Patents Division-Patent Prosecution Office/JACPD:
Thomas Kundert (Wright-Patterson AFB, OH) ....(513) 225-2838
Patents Division-Patent Infringement Investigation Office/JACPI: Edward Nypaver ....(513) 225-2872

Directorate of the U.S. Air Force Judiciary/JAJ:
Col. Thomas Hemingway (Bolling AFB, DC) 767-1535
Court of Military Review/JAR:
Col. Patrick O'Brien (Bolling AFB, DC) 767-1550
Defense Services Division/JAJD:
Col. Richard Dixon (Bolling AFB, DC) 767-1562
Government Trial & Appellate Counsel Division/JAJG:
Col. Joe Lamport (Bolling AFB, DC) 767-1546
Military Justice Division/JAJM:
(Vacant) (Bolling AFB, DC) 767-1539
Clemency, Corrections, & Official Review/JAJR:
Thomas Markiewicz (Bolling AFB, DC) 767-1535
Trial Judiciary Division/JAJT:
Col. John Howell (Bolling AFB, DC) 767-1543

Directorate of Legal Information Services/JAS:
Col. Michael Wims (Lowry AFB, CO) .....(303) 370-7531

DEPARTMENT OF DEFENSE

FIELD OFFICES

Staff/Senior Judge Advocate: Col. John Wheeler
Air Force District of Washington, AFDW/JA, Bolling Air Force Base, DC 20332. Tel: 202/767-4772.

Staff/Senior Judge Advocate: Col. Robert Reed
Headquarters, Air Force Office of Special Investigations, HQ AFOSI/JA, Bolling Air Force Base, DC 20332.
Tel: 202/767-5312.

Staff/Senior Judge Advocate: Maj. Leo Wegemer
AFOSR/JA, Bolling Air Force Base, DC 20332.
Tel: 202/767-4966.

Staff/Senior Judge Advocate: Maj. Allan Curlee
National Guard Bureau, NGB/JA, Washington, DC 20310.
Tel: 202/697-5632.

Alabama
Staff/Senior Judge Advocate: LTC Samuel Roser
HQ CDS/JA, Gunter Air Force Base, AL 36114.
Tel: 205/279-3385.

Staff/Senior Judge Advocate: Col. Henry Fowler
HQ AU/JA, Maxwell Air Force Base, AL 36112.
Tel: 205/293-7931.

Staff/Senior Judge Advocate: Col. Donald Rasher
HQ AUCPD/JA, Maxwell Air Force Base, AL 36112.
Tel: 205/293-2802.

Staff/Senior Judge Advocate: Maj. Tony Montgomery
HQ AFROTC/JA, Maxwell Air Force Base, AL 36112.
Tel: 205/293-6742.

Staff/Senior Judge Advocate: Maj. Kathleen O'Reilly
3800 ABW/JA, Maxwell Air Force Base, AL 36112.
Tel: 205/293-2786.

Staff/Senior Judge Advocate: Maj. Thomas Nied
CAP-USAF/JA, Maxwell Air Force Base, AL 36112.
Tel: 205/293-6644.

Alaska
Staff/Senior Judge Advocate: Maj. Peter Carey
343 CSG/JA, Eielson Air Force Base, AK 99702.
Tel: 907/377-4114.

Staff/Senior Judge Advocate: Col. Richard Purdon
HQ AAC/JA, Elmendorf Air Force Base, AK 99506.
Tel: 907/552-3451.

Staff/Senior Judge Advocate: LTC Robert Gibson
21 CSG/JA, Elmendorf Air Force Base, AK 99506.
Tel: 907/552-3046.

Arizona
Staff/Senior Judge Advocate: LTC James Russell
836 AD/JA, Davis-Monthan Air Force Base, AZ 85707.
Tel: 602/750-5242.

Staff/Senior Judge Advocate: LTC Charles Wilcox
832 AD/JA, Luke Air Force Base, AZ 85309.
Tel: 602/856-6901.

Staff/Senior Judge Advocate: Maj. Michael Wilson
82 ABG/JA, Williams Air Force Base, AZ 85240.
Tel: 602/988-6866.

Arkansas
Staff/Senior Judge Advocate: Maj. Deborah Suchenski
97 BMW/JA, Eaker Air Force Base, AR 72317.
Tel: 501/762-7133.

Staff/Senior Judge Advocate: Maj. Robert Kaszczuk
314 CSG/JA, Little Rock Air Force Base, AR 72099.
Tel: 501/988-6881.

California
Staff/Senior Judge Advocate: Maj. George Ledbetter
AFRCE-BMS/DES, Norton Air Force Base, CA 92409.
Tel: 714/382-2003.

Staff/Senior Judge Advocate: LTC Lloyd Leroy
9 SRW/JA, Beale Air Force Base, CA 95903.
Tel: 916/634-2815.

Staff/Senior Judge Advocate: LTC Charles Beckenhauer
93 BMW/JA, Castle Air Force Base, CA 95342.
Tel: 209/726-2421.

Staff/Senior Judge Advocate: Col. Kenneth Rengert
AFFTC/JA, Edwards Air Force Base, CA 93523.
Tel: 805/277-4310.

Staff/Senior Judge Advocate: LTC Michael Madrid
831 AD/JA, George Air Force Base, CA 92394.
Tel: 619/269-3630.

Staff/Senior Judge Advocate: Maj. Jay McFayden
AFPRO DET 36/JA, El Segundo, Los Angeles, CA 90009.
Tel: 213/414-6405.

Staff/Senior Judge Advocate: Col. Albert Lahendro
SD/JA, Los Angeles Air Force Base, CA 90009.
Tel: 213/643-1272.

Staff/Senior Judge Advocate: Col. Richard Rothenburg
HQ 15 AF/JA, March Air Force Base, CA 92518.
Tel: 714/655-4247.

Staff/Senior Judge Advocate: LTC Willard Pope
22 AREFW/JA, March Air Force Base, CA 92518.
Tel: 714/655-4454.

Staff/Senior Judge Advocate: Maj. John Suhar
323 FTW/JA, Mather Air Force Base, CA 95655.
Tel: 918/364-3277.

Staff/Senior Judge Advocate: Col. Alvin Schlechter
SM-ALC/JA, McClellan Air Force Base, CA 95652.
Tel: 916/643-3150.

Staff/Senior Judge Advocate: LTC Douglas Kohrt
63 ABG/JA, Norton Air Force Base, CA 92409.
Tel: 714/382-7783.

Staff/Senior Judge Advocate: LTC Jeff Denson
BMO/JA, Norton Air Force Base, CA 92409.
Tel: 714/382-6433.

Staff/Senior Judge Advocate: Maj. William Hill
1004 SSG/JA, Onizuka Air Force Base, CA 94088.
Tel: 408/752-3587.

Staff/Senior Judge Advocate: Col. Howard Sweeney
HQ 22 AF/JA, Travis Air Force Base, CA 94535.
Tel: 707/438-2508.

Staff/Senior Judge Advocate: LTC John Hannah
60 ABG/JA, Travis Air Force Base, CA 94535.
Tel: 707/438-3251.

Staff/Senior Judge Advocate: Capt. Brian Gavigan
USAFMEDCEN/SGJ, Travis Air Force Base, CA 94535.
Tel: 707/438-8503.

Staff/Senior Judge Advocate: LTC Conley Meredith
1 STRAD/JA, Vandenberg Air Force Base, CA 93437.
Tel: 805/866-5821.

Staff/Senior Judge Advocate: Maj. John Karns
WSMC/JA, Vandenberg Air Force Base, CA 93437.
Tel: 805/866-3052.

Colorado
Staff/Senior Judge Advocate: Col. Michael Wims
JAS, Lowry Air Force Base, CO 80279. Tel: 303/370-7531.

Staff/Senior Judge Advocate: Col. Jeffrey Graham
U.S. Air Force Academy, USAFA/JA, Colorado Springs, CO 80840.
Tel: 303/472-3642.

Staff/Senior Judge Advocate: Col. Richard Lee
U.S. Air Force Academy, USAFA/DFL, Colorado Springs, CO 80840.
Tel: 303/472-3680.

Staff/Senior Judge Advocate: Maj. Jay Lauer
2 SPACE WG/JA, Falcon Air Force Base, CO 80912.
Tel: 719/550-5050.

Staff/Senior Judge Advocate: Col. Jeffrey Cook
LTTC/JA, Lowry, CO 80230. Tel: 303/370-2470.

Staff/Senior Judge Advocate: Col. Robert Abbott
HQ AFAFC/JA, Lowry Air Force Base, CO 80279.
Tel: 303/370-7514.

Staff/Senior Judge Advocate: Col. Ronald Rakowsky
HQ ARPC/JA, Lowry Air Force Base, CO 80279.
Tel: 303/370-4915.

Staff/Senior Judge Advocate: Col. Phillip Johnson
Space Command, HQ SPACECOM/JA, Peterson Air Force Base, CO
80914. Tel: 719/554-3916.

Staff/Senior Judge Advocate: LTC John Morisonorton
3rd SSW/JA, Peterson Air Force Base, CO 80914.
Tel: 719/554-4871.

Delaware
Staff/Senior Judge Advocate: Maj. Bruce Brown
436 ABG/JA, Dover Air Force Base, DE 19902.
Tel: 302/678-6526.

Florida
Staff/Senior Judge Advocate: LTC Bruce Barnard
JACL (ULT), Tyndall Air Force Base, FL 32403.
Tel: 904/283-6347.

Staff/Senior Judge Advocate: Col. John Thornton
MSD/JA, Eglin Air Force Base, FL 32542. Tel: 904/882-4611.

Staff/Senior Judge Advocate: LTC Curtis Bentz
31 TFW/JA, Homestead Air Force Base, FL 33039.
Tel: 305/257-7207.

Staff/Senior Judge Advocate: Col. Robert Bosser
23 AF/JA, Hurlburt Field, FL 32544. Tel: 904/884-2251.

Staff/Senior Judge Advocate: LTC Howard Few
834 CSG/JA, Hurlburt Field, FL 32544. Tel: 904/884-7821.

Staff/Senior Judge Advocate: LTC Bradford Vassey
56 TTW/JA, MacDill Air Force Base, FL 33608.
Tel: 813/830-4421.

Staff/Senior Judge Advocate: LTC Gordon Edgin
USSOCOM/SOJA, MacDill Air Force Base, FL 33608.
Tel: 813/830-3252.

Staff/Senior Judge Advocate: LTC Bill Camp
USCENTCOM/CCJA, MacDill Air Force Base, FL 33608.
Tel: 813/830-6422.

Staff/Senior Judge Advocate: Col. William Mckenna
ESMC/JA, Patrick Air Force Base, FL 32925.
Tel: 305/494-7356.

Staff/Senior Judge Advocate: LTC Joel Oxley
USAFADWC/JA, Tyndall Air Force Base, FL 32403.
Tel: 904/283-4681.

Staff/Senior Judge Advocate: LTC Warren Humphreys
HQ AFESC/JA, Tyndall Air Force Base, FL 32403.
Tel: 904/283-6460.

Georgia
Staff/Senior Judge Advocate: Maj. Bryan Lawler
347 TFW/JA, Moody Air Force Base, GA 31699.
Tel: 912/333-3414.

Staff/Senior Judge Advocate: Col. Richard Bexten
WR-ALC/JA, Robins Air Force Base, GA 31098.
Tel: 912/926-3961.

Staff/Senior Judge Advocate: LTC William Waller
HQ AFRES/JA, Robins Air Force Base, GA 31098.
Tel: 912/926-5255.

Hawaii
Staff/Senior Judge Advocate: Maj. David Fahey
CINCPAC/J-73, Camp Smith, HI 96861. Tel: 808/477-1193.

Staff/Senior Judge Advocate: Col. Raul Barbara
HQ PACAF/JA, Hickam Air Force Base, HI 96853.
Tel: 808/449-2042.

Staff/Senior Judge Advocate: Col. Bryan Caldwell
15 ABW/JA, Hickam Air Force Base, HI 96853.
Tel: 808/449-1737.

Staff/Senior Judge Advocate: LTC Stephen Hedlund
Army & Air Force Exchange Service-Pacific, HQ AAFES-PAC,
919 Ala Moana Blvd, Honolulu, HI 96814. Tel: 808/533-8421.

Idaho
Staff/Senior Judge Advocate: Maj. Rebecca Weeks
366 TFW/JA, Mountain Home Air Force Base, ID 83648.
Tel: 208/828-2238.

Illinois
Staff/Senior Judge Advocate: Col. Gordon Finley
CTTC/JA, Chanute Air Force Base, IL 61868.
Tel: 217/495-2110.

Staff/Senior Judge Advocate: Col. Robert Bridge
HQ MAC/JA, Scott Air Force Base, IL 62225.
Tel: 618/256-2325.

Staff/Senior Judge Advocate: Col. Tim Anderson
HQ AFCC/JA, Scott Air Force Base, IL 62225.
Tel: 618/256-3271.

Staff/Senior Judge Advocate: LTC Francis Bergan
375 ABW/JA, Scott Air Force Base, IL 62225.
Tel: 618/256-2358.

Staff/Senior Judge Advocate: Capt. Steve Chilian
USAFMEDCEN/SGJ, Scott Air Force Base, IL 62225.
Tel: 618/256-7477.

Indiana
Staff/Senior Judge Advocate: Maj. William Love
305 AREFW/JA, Grissom Air Force Base, IN 46971.
Tel: 317/689-2231.

DEPARTMENT OF DEFENSE

Kansas
Staff/Senior Judge Advocate: Maj. David Thomas
384 BMW/JA, McConnell Air Force Base, KS 67221.
Tel: 316/652-3590.

Louisiana
Staff/Senior Judge Advocate: Col. Andrew Egeland
HQ 8 AF/JA, Barksdale Air Force Base, LA 71110.
Tel: 318/456-2461.

Staff/Senior Judge Advocate: LTC William Kirschner
23 TFW/JA, England Air Force Base, LA 71311.
Tel: 318/448-2285.

Staff/Senior Judge Advocate: LTC Jay Cohen
2 BMW/JA, Barksdale Air Force Base, LA 71110.
Tel: 318/456-2561.

Maine
Staff/Senior Judge Advocate: Maj. Scott McLauthlin
42 BMW/JA, Loring Air Force Base, ME 04751.
Tel: 207/999-7262.

Maryland
Staff/Senior Judge Advocate: BG Thomas Jeter
Headquarters, Air Force Systems Command, HQ AFSC/JA, Andrews Air Force Base, MD 20334. Tel: 301/981-2563.

Staff/Senior Judge Advocate: LTC James Potuk
1776 ABW/JA, Andrews Air Force Base, MD 20331.
Tel: 301/981-3622.

Staff/Senior Judge Advocate: Maj. Kathryn Ducharme
USAFMEDCEN/SGJ, Andrews Air Force Base, MD 20331.
Tel: 301/981-7440.

Massachusetts
Staff/Senior Judge Advocate: Col. James Roan
ESD/JA, Hanscom Air Force Base, MA 01730. Tel: 617/377-4077.

Staff/Senior Judge Advocate: Maj. Flayo Kirk
AFCAC/JA, Hanscom Air Force Base, MA 01731.
Tel: 617/377-8645.

Staff/Senior Judge Advocate: Maj. Michael McGrath
3245 ABG/JA, Hanscom Air Force Base, MA 01731.
Tel: 617/377-2361.

Michigan
Staff/Senior Judge Advocate: LTC Jack Smith
410 BMW/JA, K.I. Sawyer Air Force Base, MI 49843.
Tel: 906/346-2216.

Staff/Senior Judge Advocate: Maj. Steve Donnelly
379 BMW/JA, Wurtsmith Air Force Base, MI 48753.
Tel: 517/747-6436.

Mississippi
Staff/Senior Judge Advocate: Maj. John Thrasher
14 ABG/JA, Columbus Air Force Base, MS 39701.
Tel: 601/434-7030.

Staff/Senior Judge Advocate: Col. William Snyder
KTTC/JA, Keesler Air Force Base, MS 39534.
Tel: 601/377-3510.

Staff/Senior Judge Advocate: Maj. Paul Pirog
KTTC/SGJ, Keesler Air Force Base, MS 39534.
Tel: 601/377-6313.

Missouri
Staff/Senior Judge Advocate: Maj. Katherine Kennedy
351 SMW/JA, Whiteman Air Force Base, MO 65305.
Tel: 816/687-3422.

Montana
Staff/Senior Judge Advocate: LTC Jeffrey Grundtisch
40 AD/JA, Malmstrom Air Force Base, MT 59402.
Tel: 406/731-2878.

Nebraska
Staff/Senior Judge Advocate: BG Roger Jones
Strategic Air Command, HQ SAC/JA, Offutt Air Force Base, NE 68113. Tel: 402/294-6321.

Staff/Senior Judge Advocate: LTC Glenn Gamboa
55 SRW/JA, Offutt Air Force Base, NE 68113.
Tel: 402/294-3732.

Nevada
Staff/Senior Judge Advocate: Maj. Erich Hart
4450 TG/JA, Nellis Air Force Base, NV 89191.
Tel: 702/652-5864.

Staff/Senior Judge Advocate: Mol. Michael Lumbard
554 OSW/JA, Nellis Air Force Base, NV 89191.
Tel: 702/652-4213.

New Hampshire
Staff/Senior Judge Advocate: Maj. Cheryl Nilsson
509 BMW/JA, Pease Air Force Base, NH 03803.
Tel: 603/430-4124.

New Jersey
Staff/Senior Judge Advocate: Col. Jimmy Puett
HQ 21 AF/JA, McGuire Air Force Base, NJ 08641.
Tel: 609/724-3647.

Staff/Senior Judge Advocate: LTC Michael McDonald
438 ABG/JA, McGuire Air Force Base, NJ 08641.
Tel: 609/724-4601.

New Mexico
Staff/Senior Judge Advocate: Maj. Mark Bell
27 TFW/JA, Cannon Air Force Base, NM 88103.
Tel: 505/784-2211.

Staff/Senior Judge Advocate: LTC Howard Donaldson
833 AD/JA, Holloman Air Force Base, NM 88330.
Tel: 505/479-7216.

Staff/Senior Judge Advocate: Col. Robert Allen
HQ AFCMD/JA, Kirtland Air Force Base, NM 87117.
Tel: 505/844-0846.

Staff/Senior Judge Advocate: LTC Charles Brower
1606 ABW/JA, Kirtland Air Force Base, NM 87117.
Tel: 505/844-2943.

New York
Staff/Senior Judge Advocate: LTC David Benderson
416 BMW/JA, Griffiss Air Force Base, NY 13441.
Tel: 305/330-3071.

Staff/Senior Judge Advocate: Maj. Michael Bell
RADC/JA, Griffiss Air Force Base, NY 13441.
Tel: 315/330-2087.

Staff/Senior Judge Advocate: Maj. Larry Kudrle
380 BMW/JA, Plattsburg Air Force Base, NY 12903.
Tel: 518/565-5476.

North Carolina
Staff/Senior Judge Advocate: Maj. Richard Slipsky
317 CSG/JA, Pope Air Force Base, NC 28308.
Tel: 919/394-2341.

Staff/Senior Judge Advocate: Maj. Jarisse Sanborn
4 TFW/JA, Seymour Johnson, NC 27531. Tel: 919/736-6256.

North Dakota
Staff/Senior Judge Advocate: LTC Steven Linder
42 AD/JA, Grand Forks Air Force Base, ND 58205.
Tel: 701/747-3605.

Staff/Senior Judge Advocate: LTC Richard McDonald
57 AD/JA, Minot Air Force Base, ND 58705. Tel: 701/723-3026.

Ohio
Staff/Senior Judge Advocate: Thomas Kundert
JACPD, Wright-Patterson Air Force Base, OH 45433.
Tel: 513/225-2838.

Staff/Senior Judge Advocate: Edward Nypaver
JACPI, Wright-Patterson Air Force Base, OH 45433.
Tel: 513/225-2872.

Staff/Senior Judge Advocate: BG Nolan Sklute
HQ AFLC/JA, Wright-Patterson Air Force Base, OH 45433.
Tel: 513/257-6514.

Staff/Senior Judge Advocate: Col. Mike Petherick
2750 ABW/JA, Wright-Patterson Air Force Base, OH 45433.
Tel: 513/257-6141.

Staff/Senior Judge Advocate: Col. Robert Schaefer
HQ AFCLC/JA, Wright-Patterson Air Force Base, OH 45433.
Tel: 513/255-3203.

Staff/Senior Judge Advocate: Maj. Bill Wells
USAFMEDCEN/SGJ, Wright-patterson Air Force Base, OH 45433.
Tel: 513/257-9147.

Staff/Senior Judge Advocate: Maj. Fraser Jones
AGMC/JA, Newark Air Force Base, OH 43057. Tel: 614/522-7874.

Oklahoma
Staff/Senior Judge Advocate: Maj. Richard Tobin
443 ABG/JA, Altus Air Force Base, OK 73523.
Tel: 405/481-7294.

Staff/Senior Judge Advocate: Capt. Allen Detert
HQ EID/JA, Tinker Air Force Base, OK 73145.
Tel: 405/734-9981.

Staff/Senior Judge Advocate: Col. Harmon Massey
OC-ALC/JA, Tinker Air Force Base, OK 73145.
Tel: 405/739-2695.

Staff/Senior Judge Advocate: Capt. Kevin Corcoran
71 ABG/JA, Vance Air Force Base, OK 73705.
Tel: 405/249-7404.

South Carolina
Staff/Senior Judge Advocate: Maj. Bradley Grant
437 ABG/JA, Charleston Air Force Base, SC 29404.
Tel: 803/566-5502.

Staff/Senior Judge Advocate: Maj. Felix Stalls
354 TFW/JA, Myrtle Beach Air Force Base, SC 29579.
Tel: 803/238-7624.

Staff/Senior Judge Advocate: Col. Bryan Hawley
HQ 9 AF/JA, Shaw Air Force Base, SC 29152.
Tel: 803/668-2966.

Staff/Senior Judge Advocate: LTC Michael Hoover
363 TFW/JA, Shaw Air Force Base, SC 29152.
Tel: 803/668-2315.

South Dakota
Staff/Senior Judge Advocate: LTC Charles Williams
12 AD/JA, Ellsworth Air Force Base, SD 57706.
Tel: 605/385-2328.

Tennessee
Staff/Senior Judge Advocate: Maj. Ronald Allen
AEDC/JA, Arnold Air Force Base, TN 37289.
Tel: 615/454-7814.

Texas
Staff/Senior Judge Advocate: Col. William Moorman
HQ 12 AF/JA, Bergstrom Air Force Base, TX 78743.
Tel: 512/369-2865.

Staff/Senior Judge Advocate: LTC Robert Sutemeier
67 TRW/JA, Bergstrom Air Force Base, TX 78743.
Tel: 512/369-3781.

Staff/Senior Judge Advocate: LTC Joseph Euretig
HQ HSD/JA, Brooks Air Force Base, TX 78235.
Tel: 512/536-3301.

Staff/Senior Judge Advocate: Maj. Charles Wintermeyer
HSD/EVJ, Brooks Air Force Base, TX 78235.
Tel: 512/536-2506.

Staff/Senior Judge Advocate: LTC Michael Fox
7 BMW/JA, Carswell Air Force Base, TX 76127.
Tel: 817/735-7594.

Staff/Senior Judge Advocate: Maj. William Lyell
96 BMW/JA, Dyess Air Force Base, TX 79607.
Tel: 915/696-2232.

Staff/Senior Judge Advocate: Maj. Frank Posey
GTTC/JA, Goodfellow Air Force Base, TX 76908.
Tel: 915/657-3202.

Staff/Senior Judge Advocate: Col. Allen Hoppe
SA-ALC/JA, Kelly Air Force Base, TX 78241.
Tel: 512/925-5010.

Staff/Senior Judge Advocate: Col. Franklin Flatten
Electronics Security Command, HQ ESC/JA, Kelly Air Force Base, TX 78243. Tel: 512/925-2291.

Staff/Senior Judge Advocate: Maj. Marilyn Barton
HQ CESD/JA, Kelly Air Force Base, TX 78243.
Tel: 512/925-2291.

Staff/Senior Judge Advocate: Col. Verlin Dickman
Headquarters, Army & Air Force Exchange Service,
HQ AAFES-GC, Dallas, TX 75222. Tel: 214/780-3641.

Staff/Senior Judge Advocate: Maj. Michael Pitou
General Dynamics, AFPRO DET 27/JA, Fort Worth, TX 76101
Tel: 817/763-4452.

Staff/Senior Judge Advocate: Col. James Miller
AFMTC/JA, Lackland Air Force Base, TX 78236.
Tel: 512/671-3367.

Staff/Senior Judge Advocate: Maj. Kenneth Kramer
WHMC/SGJ, Lackland Air Force Base, TX 78236.
Tel: 512/670-7808.

Staff/Senior Judge Advocate: Maj. Noel Phetteplace
47 ABG/JA, Laughlin Air Force Base, TX 78843.
Tel: 512/298-5172.

Staff/Senior Judge Advocate: Col. Kenneth Joyce
HQ AFMPC/JA, Randolph Air Force Base, TX 78150.
Tel: 512/652-6691.

Staff/Senior Judge Advocate: Col. James McDade
HQ ATC/JA, Randolph Air Force Base, TX 78150.
Tel: 512/652-4511.

Staff/Senior Judge Advocate: LTC Charles Jones
12 ABG/JA, Randolph Air Force Base, TX 78150.
Tel: 512/652-6781.

Staff/Senior Judge Advocate: Maj. Howard Altschwager
64 ABG/JA, Reese Air Force Base, TX 79489.
Tel: 806/885-3505.

Staff/Senior Judge Advocate: Col. Dennis Kansala
HQ STTC/JA, Sheppard Air Force Base, TX 76311.
Tel: 817/851-2312.

Staff/Senior Judge Advocate: Capt. Marc Van Nuys
3790 MSTW/MSJ, Sheppard Air Force Base, TX 76311.
Tel: 817/851-2348.

Utah
Staff/Senior Judge Advocate: Col. John Brancato
OO-ALC/JA, Hill Air Force Base, UT 84056.
Tel: 801/777-6756.

Virginia
Staff/Senior Judge Advocate: Col. Phil Mills
HQ TAC/JA, Langley Air Force Base, VA 23665.
Tel: 804/764-7651.

Staff/Senior Judge Advocate: Col. Robert Cerha
1 AF/JA, Langley Air Force Base, VA 23665.
Tel: 804/764-7651.

Staff/Senior Judge Advocate: LTC Michael Ford
1 TFW/JA, Langley Air Force Base, VA 23665.
Tel: 804/764-3276.

Washington
Staff/Senior Judge Advocate: LTC Peter Held
92 BMW/JA, Fairchild Air Force Base, WA 99011.
Tel: 509/247-5231.

Staff/Senior Judge Advocate: LTC George Ash
62 ABG/JA, McChord Air Force Base, WA 98438.
Tel: 206/984-5512.

Staff/Senior Judge Advocate: Maj. Michael Benner
Boeing Corp., AFPRO DET 9/JA, Seattle, WA 98124.
Tel: 206/773-7227.

Wyoming
Staff/Senior Judge Advocate: LTC Chester Morgan, 90 SMW/JA, F.E. Warren Air Force Base, WY 82005. Tel: 307/775-2256.

OVERSEAS

Azores
Staff/Senior Judge Advocate: Maj. William Beazley
1605 MASW/JA, Lajes Field, APO New York 09406.

Germany
Staff/Senior Judge Advocate: LTC John Martinez
36 TFW/JA, Bitburg Air Force Base, APO New York 09132.
Tel: 011-49-6561-61-7665.

Staff/Senior Judge Advocate: Maj. Chris Dooley
DET 2 36 TFW/JA, Geilenkirchen, APO New York 09104.

Staff/Senior Judge Advocate: LTC Michael Schlabs
50 TFW/JA, Hahn Air Base, APO New York 09122.
Tel: 011-49-6543-51-6177.

Staff/Senior Judge Advocate: Maj. Robert Thomas
600 CSS/JA, Hessisch-Oldendorf Air Station, APO New York 09669.

Staff/Senior Judge Advocate: LTC Rich Pennington
7100 CSW/JA, Lindsey Air Base, APO New York 09634.
Tel: 011-49-6121-82-3669.

Staff/Senior Judge Advocate: Capt. Bill White
USAFMEDCEN/SGJ, Lindsey Air Base, APO New York 09220.
Tel: 011-49-6121-82-7264.

Staff/Senior Judge Advocate: LTC Harold Fievet
Army & Air Force Exchange Service, Europe (Munich), HQ AAFES-EUR-GC, APO New York 09245.

Staff/Senior Judge Advocate: Col. Thomas Hemingway
U.S. Air Force, Europe, HQ USAFE/JA, Ramstein Air Base, APO New York 09094. Tel: 011-49-6371-47-6826.

Staff/Senior Judge Advocate: Col. Ralph Summerfield
377 CSW/JA, Ramstein Air Base, APO New York 09094.
Tel: 011-49-6371-47-2013.

Staff/Senior Judge Advocate: LTC Gary Grunick
435 TAW/JA, Rhein-Main Air Base, APO New York 09097.
Tel: 011-49-69-699-7275.

Staff/Senior Judge Advocate: Col. Charles Heimburg
HQ 17 AF/JA, Sembach Air Base, APO New York 09136.
Tel: 011-49-6302-67-6103.

Staff/Senior Judge Advocate: LTC Harry Yee
66 ECW/JA, Sembach Air Base, APO New York 09136.
Tel: 011-49-6302-67-7774.

Staff/Senior Judge Advocate: LTC Chuck Matthewson
52 TFW/JA, Spangdahlem Air Base, APO New York 09126.
Tel: 011-49-6565-61-6796.

Staff/Senior Judge Advocate: Col. William Eckhardt
European Command, HQ EUCOM/ECLA, Stuttgart, APO New York 09128.

Staff/Senior Judge Advocate: Maj. Sam Rupe
7350 ABG/JA, Tempelhof Central Airport (Berlin), APO New York 09611.

Staff/Senior Judge Advocate: Maj. Dartt Demaree
26 TRW/JA, Zweibrucken Air Base, APO New York 09860.
Tel: 011-49-6332-47-2171.

Greece
Staff/Senior Judge Advocate: Maj. Chuck Ketchel
JUSMAG Greece, Athens, APO New York 09235.

Staff/Senior Judge Advocate: Col. Robert Senander
7206 ABG/JA, Hellenikon Air Base, APO New York 09223.
Tel: 011-301-989-8420.

Staff/Senior Judge Advocate: Maj. Donald Walsh
7276 ABG/JA, Iraklion Air Base, Crete, APO New York 09291
Tel: 011-30-81761-196.

Guam
Staff/Senior Judge Advocate: Maj. Robert Curione
633 ABW/JA, Anderson Air Force Base, Guam 96334.

Iceland
Staff/Senior Judge Advocate: Maj. David Northrup
AF Iceland/JA, Keflavik Naval Air Station, APO New York 09673.

Staff/Senior Judge Advocate: Capt. Thomas Kiniffen
IDF/JA, Keflavik Airport, APO New York 09571.
Tel: 011-354-257014.

Italy
Staff/Senior Judge Advocate: Maj. Victor Donovan
40 TACG/JA, Aviano Air Base, APO New York 09293.
Tel: 011-39-434-651141.

Staff/Senior Judge Advocate: Maj. Gary Rowell
487 TMW/JA, Comiso Air Base, APO New York 09694.
Tel: 011-39-932-732611.

Staff/Senior Judge Advocate: Maj. William Burd
7275 ABG/JA, San Vito Dei Normanni Air Base, APO New York 09240. Tel: 011-39-831-423401.

Japan
Staff/Senior Judge Advocate: Col. Mark Anderson
313 AD/JA, Kadena Air Base, APO San Francisco 96239.
Tel: 011-8109-893-6117-341-509.

Staff/Senior Judge Advocate: Maj. Donald Plude
432 TFW/JA, Misawa Air Base, APO San Francisco 96519.
Tel: 011-81-176-53-5181.

Staff/Senior Judge Advocate: Col. William Elliott
HQ 5 AF/JA, Yokota Air Base, APO San Francisco 96328.
Tel: 011-81-0425-2511, Ext. 7020.

Staff/Senior Judge Advocate: LTC Jeffrey Infelise
475 ABW/JA, Yokota Air Base, APO San Francisco 96328.
Tel: 011-81-0425-2511, Ext. 7020.

Korea
Staff/Senior Judge Advocate: LTC Stephen Duggan
8 TFW/JA, Kunsan Air Base, APO San Francisco 96264.
Tel: 011-82-27-910-5194.

Staff/Senior Judge Advocate: Col. Lewis Brewer
HQ 7 AF/JA, Osan Air Base, APO San Francisco 96570.
Tel: 011-82-333-414-4044.

Staff/Senior Judge Advocate: LTC Terrence Curtin
51 TFW/JA, APO San Francisco 96570.

Staff/Senior Judge Advocate: Capt. William Lavery
460 CSS/JA, Taegu Air Base, APO San Francisco 96213.

Staff/Senior Judge Advocate: Col. John Duncan
HQ USFK/JAJ, Yongsan Air Base, APO San Francisco 96301.
Tel: 011-82-2-791-3-6033.

Netherlands
Staff/Senior Judge Advocate: Maj. David Ehrhart
32 TFS/JA, Soesterberg Air Base, APO New York 09292.
Tel: 011-31-3463-8533.

Norway
Staff/Senior Judge Advocate: Capt. Harry Batey
7240 ABS/JA, Oslo, APO New York 09085.

Panama
Staff/Senior Judge Advocate: LTC Martin Jayne
24 COMPW/JA, Howard Air Force Base, APO Miami 34001.

Staff/Senior Judge Advocate: LTC Thomas Tudor
Southern Command, HQ USSOUTHCOM, Quarry Heights, APO Miami 34003.

Philippines
Staff/Senior Judge Advocate: Col. William Sherman
13 AF/JA, Clark Air Base, APO San Francisco 96274.
Tel: 011-6345-35-33995.

Staff/Senior Judge Advocate: Capt. Frank Wood
HQ, AAFES/GLC, Clark Air Base, APO San Francisco 96274.
Tel: 011-6532-25149.

Staff/Senior Judge Advocate: Maj. Tim Hickey
13 MED CEN/SGJ, Clark Air Base, APO San Francisco 96274.
Tel: 011-6345-35-33995.

Staff/Senior Judge Advocate: Maj. Dave Stephenson
U.S. Embassy, Manila, APO San Francisco 96528.

Spain
Staff/Senior Judge Advocate: LTC James Nero
JUSMG-MAAG, Madrid, APO New York 09285.

Staff/Senior Judge Advocate: Col. William Thompson
HQ 16 AF/JA, Torrejon Air Base, APO New York 09283.
Tel: 011-341-665-5095.

Staff/Senior Judge Advocate: LTC Charles Orck
401 TFW/JA, Torrejon Air Base, APO New York 09283.
Tel: 011-341-665-5305.

Staff/Senior Judge Advocate: Maj. Rodney Wolthoff
406 TFTW/JA, Zaragoza Air Base, APO New York 09286.
Tel: 011-3476-326-711.

Turkey
Staff/Senior Judge Advocate: LTC Dennis Yoder
HQ TUSLOG/JA, Ankara Air Station, APO New York 09254
Tel: 011-9041259943.

Staff/Senior Judge Advocate: Maj. Richard Price
HQ JUSMMAT/JA, Ankara Air Force Base, APO New York 09254

Staff/Senior Judge Advocate: Maj. Charles Hasskamp
39 TACG/JA, Incirlik Air Base, APO New York 09289
Tel: 011-90-711-19062/EXT 6540.

Staff/Senior Judge Advocate: Maj. Jeanne Rueth
7241 ABG/JA, Izmir Air Station, APO New York 09224.
Tel: 011-9051-138449.

United Kingdom
Staff/Senior Judge Advocate: LTC Stephen Donohue
RAF Alconbury, 10 TFW/JA, APO New York 09238.
Tel: 011-44-480-822535.

Staff/Senior Judge Advocate: Maj. Rocco Lamuro
7274 ABG/JA, RAF Chicksands Base, APO New York 09193.
Tel: 011-44-462-812571 EXT 219/261.

Staff/Senior Judge Advocate: Maj. Timothy Wilson
501 TMW/JA, RAF Greenham Common, APO New York 09150.
Tel: 011-44-635-512000.

Staff/Senior Judge Advocate: LTC Mike Bartley
48 TFW/JA, RAF Lakenheath, APO New York 09179.
Tel: 011-44-638-523553.

Staff/Senior Judge Advocate: Col. James Howey
HQ 3 AF/JA, RAF Mildenhall, APO New York 09127.
Tel: 011-44-638-512055.

Staff/Senior Judge Advocate: Maj. James Conrad
513 ACCW/JA, RAF Mildenhall, APO New York 09127.
Tel: 011-44-638-512028.

Staff/Senior Judge Advocate: LTC Daniel Hass
20 TFW/JA, RAF Upper Heyford, APO New York 09194.
Tel: 011-44-869-8234845.

DEPARTMENT OF DEFENSE

OTHER AIR FORCE LEGAL OFFICES

(Area Code 202)

National Guard Bureau
Chief Counsel: James C. Hise 695-5149

Office of Scientific Research
Judge Advocate: Maj. Leo Wegemer 767-4966

(Area Code 301)

Air Force Systems Command
Bldg 1535, Andrews Air Force Base, MD 20334

Staff Judge Advocate: Brig. Gen. James C. Roan 981-2563

PUBLICATIONS OF INTEREST

The following publications can be purchased from the **U.S. Government Printing Office.** Stock numbers and prices for annual subscriptions are shown below. Submit requests for these publications to: The Superintendent of Documents, U.S. Government Printing Office, Washington, D.C. 20402. Tel: 202/783-3238.

Air Force Federal Acquisition Regulations Supplement. October 1988. A supplement to the Federal Acquisition Regulation for use in acquiring supplies and services for the Air Force. Subscription service consists of a basic manual and supplementary material for an indeterminate period. In looseleaf form, punched for 3-ring binder. Price: $92.00 domestic; $115.00 foreign. GPO Stock# 908-013-00000-0.

The Reporter. Published quarterly. A legal journal which provides a forum for the exchange of information pertinent to the practice of law in the military as well as the civilian community. Each issue contains three to six articles on current topics of interest in the law and sections devoted to military justice, claims, and tort litigation and preventive law. Price: $9.00/year domestic; $11.25/year foreign. GPO Stock# 708-047-00000-7.

Air Force Law Review. Published semiannually by the Office of the Judge Advocate General of the Air Force, this Review provides a means for exchange of ideas and information. It contains a survey of important legislative, administrative, and judicial developments in military and related law fields. Price: $5.00/year domestic; $6.25/year foreign. GPO Stock# 708-005-00000-2.

DEPARTMENT OF THE ARMY
The Pentagon
Washington, D.C. 20310-0104

DESCRIPTION: The mission of the Department of the Army is to organize, train, and equip active duty and reserve forces for the preservation of peace, security, and the defense of our nation. The Army also administers programs aimed at protecting the environment, improving waterway navigation, flood and beach erosion control, and water resource development. It supports the National Civil Defense Program, provides military assistance to Federal, State, and local government agencies, including natural disaster relief assistance, and provides emergency medical air transportation services.

(Area Code 202)

Secretary of the Army: M.P.W. Stone 695-3211
Public Affairs 695-0363
Publications ....(703) 487-4689
Freedom of Information Act/Privacy Act Office ...(703) 325-6163
Office of Small & Disadvantaged Business Utilization ..695-9800
Facsimile 697-8036

(Area Code 202)

Inspector General's Hotline:
Washington, D.C. Metro Area 695-1578
Virginia ....(800) 572-9000
Outside Washington, D.C. Metro Area ....(800) 752-9747

Pentagon Library (Room 1A518) 697-4301
The library includes law materials, but DOD identification is required. The librarians will answer brief reference questions

OFFICE OF THE GENERAL COUNSEL (Room 2E722)

The Army Office of the General Counsel provides legal advice to the Secretary of the Army and the senior Army leadership on every conceivable legal issue which arises during the course of the Army's business, including: legislative matters affecting the Army, civil lawsuits to which the Army is a party, environmental legal issues, Freedom of Information Act (FOIA) and Privacy Act matters, every facet of Government acquisition and procurement, and intelligence and operational matters. The attorneys in this office do not perform in-court litigation.

(Area Code 202)

General Counsel: William J. Haynes II 697-9235
Special Assistant for Fiscal Law and Policy: Matt Reres 695-4296
Principal Deputy General Counsel: Vacant 697-4807
Deputy General Counsel (Acquisition): Anthony H. Gamboa 697-5120
Deputy General Counsel (Installations and Operations):
Thomas W. Taylor 695-0562
Deputy General Counsel (Military and Civil Affairs):
Darrell L. Peck 697-6493
Army Contract Adjustment Board Recorder: John Krump 697-4349

US Army Information Systems Selection and Acquisition Agency
Director: David Borland ....(703) 325-9760
Chief Counsel: Col. Richard T. Altieri ....(703) 325-9490

(Area Code 202)

Army Military Review Boards Agency
Director/Deputy Assistant Secretary:
John W. Matthews 697-9641
Army Board for Correction of Military Records
Executive Secretary: David Kinneer 697-4254

Army Clemency and Review Board
Chairman: James E. Vick 697-7775

Army Discharge Review Board
President: Col. James W. Rowe 692-4606

OFFICE OF THE INSPECTOR GENERAL (Room 1E736)

The Office of Inspector General inquires into and reports upon any matter that affects the discipline or military efficiency of the Army and makes such inspections, investigations, and reports as the Secretary of the Army or the Chief of Staff directs.

(Area Code 202)
Inspector General: Lt. Gen. Johnnie H. Corns 695-1500

(Area Code 202)
Legal Advisor: Col. Herbert D. Williams 697-9734

AUDITOR GENERAL (Room 1301)

3101 Park Center Drive, Alexandria, VA 22302-1596

(Area Code 703)
Auditor General: Harold L. Stugart 756-2809

(Area Code 703)
Counsel: William J. Guinan 756-2802

CHIEF OF STAFF OF THE ARMY (Room 3E668)

(Area Code 202)
Chief of Staff: General Carl E. Vuono 695-2077
Public Affairs 697-7589
Freedom of Information Act/Privacy Act Office 695-7922

(Area Code 202)
US Army Civilian Appellate Review Agency Administrator:
William B. Smith ....(703) 756-1423
Facsimile 695-9439

OFFICE OF THE JUDGE ADVOCATE GENERAL (Room 2E444)

The Judge Advocate General's Corps is the legal branch of the Army. Its attorneys prosecute and defend criminal cases; represent members of the armed forces in administrative hearings; advise commanders; do procurement work; advise members of the Army and their dependents on a broad range of legal matters; and determine claims against the U.S., among other duties.

The JAG Corps employs three classes of attorneys: active duty attorneys; Reserve component attorneys; and civilian attorneys.

Active Duty Attorneys: More than 1,800 judge advocates on active duty serve throughout the U.S. and in 11 foreign countries. The attorneys practice in the following areas:

Criminal Law--prosecuting or defending soldiers at courts-martial; serving as appellate counsel; examining records of trial for legal sufficiency; and reviewing petitions for new trials or other relief. Selected career officers serve as judges at both trial and appellate levels.

Legal Assistance--counseling soldiers, military retirees and family members with personal legal problems; drafting wills; answering tax questions; assisting with immigration and naturalization matters; advising on consumer affairs; drafting separation agreements; and counseling clients regarding adoptions and other family law matters. In several states, a judge advocate may represent clients in Federal and state courts in civil cases.

Administrative Law--advising Army commanders on military personnel law (validity of enlistments, legal sufficiency of involuntary discharges and characterization of service, and disability determinations); environmental law; lawfulness of expenditures of appropriated and nonappropriated funds; support to other Federal agencies, foreign governments and organizations, state and local governments, and private organizations; lawful avenues for disposal of excess or obsolete Government property; liability of military personnel and civilian employees for loss of or damage to Government property; Privacy Act and Freedom of Information Act matters; and review of administrative investigations for compliance with due process standards.

Claims and Tort Liability--investigating and settling claims filed against the Army by military personnel, other U.S. citizens and organizations, and foreign nationals under the various claims statutes and international agreements; and pursuing claims in favor of the U.S.

JAG Corps officers specialize in:

Contract Law--reviewing contracts for supplies, services, construction, and research and development; rendering legal opinions on procurement procedures, bid protests, contract terminations, and contract appeal disputes; serving as legal advisors to contracting officers and boards of award; reviewing qualifications of potential contractors; monitoring contracts with foreign sources; and litigating contract disputes before the Armed Services Board of Contract Appeals.

Labor Law--advising on the management of civilian employees under U.S. Office of Personnel Management rules; representing the Army in administrative hearings before the Merit Systems Protection Board and the Federal Labor Relations Authority; and advising on labor-management relations for both private and public sector union matters.

International Affairs--providing legal advice on a wide range of international law matters affecting Army interests abroad, including: interpreting international agreements and foreign laws; participating in negotiating and drafting international agreements such as base rights, status of forces and personnel exchange agreements; performing legal liaison functions between Army commands and host nation judicial authorities; observing and reporting on foreign trials of U.S. personnel; assisting U.S. personnel confined in foreign prisons; reviewing military operations plans and providing advice on the laws of war, rules of engagement, domestic law relating to employment of forces and support of our allies, and the legal aspects of civil affairs.

Civil Litigation--investigating and preparing cases for trial through preparation of pleadings, motions and briefs to be used by the JAG Corps or U.S. Department of Justice trial or appellate attorneys.

Teaching--Selected JAG Corps officers teach on faculties of The Judge Advocate General's School, Charlottesville, VA; the U.S. Military Academy, West Point, NY; and other military schools throughout the U.S.

Medical Law--A few judge advocates specialize in the legal problems peculiar to hospital administration, medical practice and medical research. They work in hospitals where they are involved in such matters as the credentialing of health care professionals, human-subject research, and risk management programs, or in legal offices where they handle medical malpractice claims.

(Area Code 202)

Judge Advocate General:
Maj. Gen. William Suter (Acting) 697-5151
Assistant Judge Advocate General: Vacant 697-6308
Facsimile...697-4337

Military Law
Assistant Judge Advocate General: Brig. Gen.
Donald W. Hansen 695-5947
Labor and Employment Office Chief:
Col. Calvin M. Lederer 695-9300
Legal Assistance Office Chief:
Lt. Col. Donald L. Hansen 697-3170
Administrative Law Division Chief:
Col. William Lehman..........................695-3585
Criminal Law Division Chief: Col. Francis A. Gilligan 695-6433
International Affairs Division Chief: Col.
James A. Burger 695-3170

(Area Code 202)

Civil Law
Assistant Judge Advocate General: Brig. Gen.
John L. Fugh 697-4769
Contract Law Division Chief: Col. Maurice J. O'Brien 693-4071
Environmental Law Division Chief: Lt. Col.
Scott Issacson 697-1351
Litigation Division Chief: Col. William A. Aileo 695-1721
Procurement Fraud Division Chief: Col.
James C. Gleason 504-4278

Law Library (Room 203) ....(703) 756-2608
The library is open to the public from 7:45 AM until 4:15 PM. Call before you visit.

U.S. ARMY LEGAL SERVICES AGENCY
5611 Columbia Pike, Falls Church, VA 22041

(Area Code 703)

Commander: Kenneth Gray (Acting) 756-1862
Legal Administrator: Michael Parker 756-1774
Clerk of the Court: Attorney Advisor
William S. Fulton Jr. 756-1888
Regulatory Law Office Chief: vacant 756-2015
Trial Counsel Assistance Program Office Chief:
Lt. Col. John T. Meixell 756-1804
Contract Appeals Division Chief: Col. Ronald P. Cundick 756-2023
Defense Appellate Division Chief: Robert Kirby 756-1807
Examination and New Trials Division Chief:
William S. Fulton, Jr 756-1701
Government Appellate Division Chief: Alfred Arquila ...756-1454
Patents, Copyrights and Trademarks Division Chief:
Anthony T. Lane 756-2430
Trial Judiciary Chief: Col. Howard C. Eggers 756-1719
US Army Court of Military Review Chief Judge: Vacant ..756-1862
Facsimile 756-1984

THE JUDGE ADVOCATE GENERAL'S SCHOOL
Charlottesville, VA 22903

(Area Code 804)

Commandant: Col. T.M. Strassburg 972-6301

U.S. ARMY CLAIMS SERVICE
Building 4411, Fort Meade, MD 20755

(Area Code 301)

Commander: Col. Jack F. Lane Jr 677-7622

U.S. ARMY JAG FIELD OFFICES

Washington, D.C.
Acting Judge Advocate General: MG William K. Suter
Office of the Judge Advocate General, DA, Washington, D.C. 20310. Tel: 202/697-5151.

Assistant Judge Advocate General for Civil Law: BG John L. Fugh
Office of the Judge Advocate General, DA, Washington, D.C. 20310. Tel: 202/697-4769.

Assistant Judge Advocate General for Military Law:
BG Donald W. Hansen, Office of the Judge Advocate General, DA, Washington, D.C. 20310. Tel: 202/695-5947.

Staff Judge Advocate: Col. John R. Howell
HQ, Military District of Washington, Washington, D.C. 20319. Tel: 202/475-1710.

Chief Attorney: LTC Kevin E. O'Brien
Headquarters Services-Washington, Washington, D.C. 20210. Tel: 202/695-5994.

Center Judge Advocate: Col. Wayne Johnston
Walter Reed Army Medical Center, Washington, D.C. 20307. Tel: 202/576-2531.

Alabama
Staff Judge Advocate: Col. Roger G. Darley
HQ, USA Strategic Defense Command, P.O. Box 1500, Huntsville, AL 35807. Tel: 205/895-4520.

Staff Judge Advocate: LTC David Bornhorst
HQ, USA Chemical & MP Centers, Ft. McClellan, AL 36205. Tel: 205/848-5435.

Staff Judge Advocate: LTC Everett M. Urech
HQ, USA Aviation Center & Ft. Rucker, Ft. Rucker, AL 36362. Tel: 205/255-5491.

Alaska
Staff Judge Advocate: LTC Michael J. Marchand
HQ, 6th Infantry Division, Ft. Richardson, AK 99505. Tel: 907/863-9137.

Arizona
Staff Judge Advocate: Col. Harry C. Beans III
USA Information Systems Command & US Army Garrison, Ft. Huachuca, AZ 85613. Tel: 602/533-3181.

Post Judge Advocate: MAJ(P) Jay D. McQueen
US Army Garrison, Yuma Proving Grounds, AZ 85365. Tel: 602/328-2838.

California
Staff Judge Advocate: Col. Jack P. Hug
HQ, Sixth US Army, Presidio of San Francisco, CA 94129. Tel: 415/561-3131.

Staff Judge Advocate: LTC(P) Craig Schwender
HQ, Presidio of San Francisco, Presidio of San Francisco, CA 94129. Tel: 415/561-5591.

Staff Judge Advocate: LTC Richard Wright
MTMC, Western Area, Oakland, CA 94626. Tel: 415/466-2921.

Staff Judge Advocate: LTC Edward R. Ziegler
HQ, National Training Center, Ft. Irwin, CA 92310. Tel: 619/386-3251.

Colorado
Staff Judge Advocate: Col. Robert P. Williams
HQ, 4th Infantry Division & Ft. Carson, Ft. Carson, CO 80913. Tel: 719/579-5361.

Center Judge Advocate: LTC Robert J. Short
Fitzsimons Army Medical Center, Aurora, CO 80054. Tel: 303/361-3138.

Florida
Staff Judge Advocate: Col. Raymond C. Ruppert
HQ, US Central Command, MacDill AFB, FL 33608. Tel: 813/830-6422.

Staff Judge Advocate: Col. Albert E. Vernon III
HQ, US Special Operations Command, MacDill AFB, FL 33608. Tel: 813/830-3252.

Georgia
Staff Judge Advocate: Col. John T. Holloman
HQ, USA Signal Center & Ft. Gordon, Ft. Gordon, GA 30905. Tel: 404/791-3148.

Staff Judge Advocate: Col. Jerome X. Lewis
HQ, Third US Army, Ft. McPherson, GA 30330. Tel: 404/752-4877.

Staff Judge Advocate: Col. Vahan Moushegian Jr
HQ, 24th Infantry Division & Ft. Stewart, St. Stewart, GA 31314. Tel: 912/767-7713.

Staff Judge Advocate: Col. Michael J. Nardotti Jr
HQ, USA Infantry Training Center & Ft. Benning, Ft. Benning, GA 31905. Tel: 404/545-4611.

Staff Judge Advocate: Col. Carroll J. Tichenor
HQ, FORSCOM, Ft. McPherson, GA 30030. Tel: 404/752-2435.

Staff Judge Advocate: LTC Robert T. Jackson Jr
US Army Garrison, Ft. McPherson, GA 30330. Tel: 404/752-4270.

Staff Judge Advocate: Col. Edwin P. Wasinger
HQ, Second US Army, Ft. Gillem, GA 30050. Tel: 404/362-3343.

Hawaii
Staff Judge Advocate: Col. George G. Jacunski
HQ, USA Western Command, Ft. Shafter, HI 96858. Tel: 808/438-9470.

Staff Judge Advocate: LTC Patrick W. Fligg
HQ, USA SUPCOM-Hawaii, Ft. Shafter, HI 96858. Tel: 808/438-2472.

Staff Judge Advocate: LTC William R. Hagan
HQ, 25th Infantry Division, Schofield Barracks, HI 96857. Tel: 808/655-4884.

Illinois
Staff Judge Advocate: Col. Bartlett J. Carroll Jr
HQ, Fourth US Army, Ft. Sheridan, IL 60037. Tel: 312/926-5556.

Staff Judge Advocate: Col. Brian Schempf
HQ, USA Recruiting Command, Ft. Sheridan, IL 60037. Tel: 312/926-2063.

Staff Judge Advocate: Col. Michael J. Brawley
HQ, US Army Garrison, Ft. Sheridan, IL 60037. Tel: 312/926-3967.

Indiana
Staff Judge Advocate: LTC Thomas A. Pyrz
HQ, USA Solder Spt Center & Ft. Harrison, Ft. Harrison, IN 46216. Tel: 317/549-5260.

DEPARTMENT OF DEFENSE

Kentucky
Staff Judge Advocate: Col. Malcolm H. Squires
HQ, 101st Airborne Division & Ft. Campbell, Ft. Campbell, KY 42223. Tel: 502/798-5890.

Louisiana
Staff Judge Advocate: Col. Arthur L. Hunt
HQ, 5th Infantry Division & Ft. Polk, Ft. Polk, LA 71459. Tel: 318/535-2019.

Kansas
Staff Judge Advocate: Col. Jonathan C. Gordon
HQ, 1st Infantry Division & Ft. Riley, Ft. Riley, KS 66442. Tel: 913/239-2217.

Staff Judge Advocate: LTC Michael B. Kearns
USA Correctional Activity, Ft. Riley, KS 66442. Tel: 913/239-6233.

Staff Judge Advocate: Col. Paul J. Rice
USA CAC & Ft. Leavenworth, Ft. Leavenworth, KS 66027. Tel: 913/684-4941.

Kentucky
Staff Judge Advocate: Col. Thomas P. DeBerry
HQ, USA Armor Center & Ft. Knox, Ft. Knox, KY 40121. Tel: 502/624-1255.

Maryland
Staff Judge Advocate: Col. Arthur G. Haessig
HQ, First US Army, Ft. Meade, MD 20755. Tel: 301/677-4016.

Commander: Col. Jack F. Lane
US Army Claims Service, Ft. Meade, MD 20755. Tel: 301/677-7622.

Staff Judge Advocate: LTC Demmon F. Canner
US Army Garrison, Ft. Meade, MD 20755. Tel: 301/677-2576.

Staff Judge Advocate: Col. Patrick J. Mackey
USA Test & Evaluation Command, Aberdeen Proving Ground, MD 21005. Tel: 301/278-5281.

Legal Advisor: Col. Buren R. Shields
USA Toxic & Hazardous Materials Agency, Aberdeen Proving Ground, MD 21010. Tel: 301/671-2657.

Staff Judge Advocate: LTC Gregory L. Edlefsen
HQ, 7th Signal Command & Ft. Ritchie, Ft. Richie, MD 21719. Tel: 301/878-5771.

Command Judge Advocate: LTC George H. Sisson
USA Medical Research & Development Command, Ft. Detrick, MD 21701. Tel: 301/663-2065.

Massachusetts
Staff Judge Advocate: LTC Robert F. Gonzales
US Army Garrison, Ft. Devens, MA 01433. Tel: 508/796-2255.

Missouri
Staff Judge Advocate: Col. John R. Hamilton
HQ, USA Aviation Systems Command, St. Louis, MO 63210. Tel: 314/263-3391.

Command Judge Advocate: MAJ(P) Gary M. Manuel
USA Reserve Personnel Center, 9700 Page Boulevard, St. Louis, MO 63132. Tel: 314/263-7908.

Staff Judge Advocate: Col. Richard J. Mackey
HQ, USATC Eng & Ft. Leonard Wood, Ft. Leonard Wood, MO 65473. Tel: 314/368-2116.

New Jersey
Staff Judge Advocate: Col. Daniel B. Limbaugh
HQ, USA Training Center & Ft. Dix, Ft. Dix, NJ 08640. Tel: 609/562-2455.

Staff Judge Advocate: LTC John C. Greenhaugh
HQ, CECOM & Ft. Monmouth, Ft. Monmouth, NJ 07703. Tel: 201/532-4442.

Staff Judge Advocate: LTC Joseph A. Rehyansky
Military Traffic Management Command, Eastern Area, Bayonne, NJ 07002. Tel: 201/823-7121.

New Mexico
Staff Judge Advocate: LTC Vincent J. Faggioli
USA White Sands Missile Range, White Sands, NM 88002. Tel: 505/678-1263.

New York
Staff Judge Advocate: Col. William P. Greene, Jr
US Military Academy, West Point, NY 10996. Tel: 914/938-2781.

Staff Judge Advocate: LTC Donald Morgan
HQ, 10th Infantry Division & Ft. Drum, Ft. Drum, NY 13602. Tel: 315/772-6369.

Staff Judge Advocate: LTC James J. Murphy
HQ, NY Area Command & Ft. Hamilton, Brooklyn, NY 11252. Tel: 718/630-4024.

North Carolina
Staff Judge Advocate: Col. John R. Bozeman
HQ, XVIIIth Abn Corps & Ft. Bragg, Ft. Bragg, NC 28307. Tel: 919/396-5506.

Staff Judge Advocate: LTC Fred E. Bryant
HQ, 1st SOCOM, Ft. Bragg, NC 28307. Tel: 919/396-1606.

Staff Judge Advocate: LTC James J. Smith
HQ 82d Airborne Division, Ft. Bragg, NC 28307. Tel: 919/432-0730.

Oklahoma
Staff Judge Advocate: Col. Thomas N. Tromey
HQ, USA Field Artillery Center & Ft. Sill, Ft. Sill, OK 73503. Tel: 405/351-3311.

Puerto Rico
Staff Judge Advocate: LTC Dickson Kesler
US Army Garrison, Ft. Buchanan, PR, APO Miami 34040. Tel: 809/967-4176.

South Carolina
Staff Judge Advocate: Col. Allan A. Toomey
HQ, USA Training Center & Ft. Jackson, Ft. Jackson, SC 29207. Tel: 803/751-7657.

Texas
Staff Judge Advocate: Col. Richard S. Arkow
HQ, Fifth US Army, Ft. Sam Houston, TX 78234. Tel: 512/221-2208.

Staff Judge Advocate: LTC James M. Norton
US Army Garrison, Ft. Sam Houston, TX 78234. Tel: 512/221-6484.

Staff Judge Advocate: Col. Robert D. Hamel
HQ, USA Health Services Command, Ft. Sam Houston, TX 78324. Tel: 512/221-3400.

Staff Judge Advocate: Col. Alexander M. Walczak
HQ, III Corps & Ft. Hood, Ft. Hood, TX 76544. Tel: 817/287-3421.

Staff Judge Advocate: LTC Gerald J. Leeling
HQ, 2d Armored Division, Ft. Hood, TX 76546.
Tel: 817/287-4912.

Staff Judge Advocate: LTC Philip E. Lower
HQ, 1st Cav Division, Ft. Hood, TX 76544. Tel: 817/287-9411.

Staff Judge Advocate: Col. Charles E. Bonney
HQ, US Army Air Defense Center & Ft. Bliss, Ft. Bliss, TX 79916. Tel: 915/568-5102.

Command Judge Advocate: LTC James E. Bailey III
Academy of Health Sciences, Ft. Sam Houston, TX 78234.
Tel: 512/221-5549.

Utah
Post Judge Advocate: Maj. Robert L. Horalek
US Army Dugway Proving Ground, Dugway Proving Ground, UT 84022.
Tel: 801/831-3333.

Virginia
Commander/Chief Judge: Col. Kenneth D. Gray
USA Legal Services Agency, Falls Church, VA 22041.
Tel: 703/756-1862.

Staff Judge Advocate: Col. Daniel L. Rothlisberger
HQ, Military Traffic Management Command. 5611 Columbia Pike, Room 405, Falls Church, VA 22041. Tel: 703/756-1580.

Staff Judge Advocate: LTC Brent Green
HQ, USA Criminal Investigation Command, 5611 Columbia Pike, Falls Church, VA 22041. Tel: 703/756-2281.

Staff Judge Advocate: Col. Anthony L. Wagner
USA Material Command, 5001 Eisenhower Avenue, Alexandria, VA 22333. Tel: 703/274-8003.

Chief Counsel: Col. Richard T. Altieri
USA Information Systems Selection & Acquisition Activity, 2461 Eisenhower Avenue, Room 954, Alexandria, VA 22331.
Tel: 703/325-9490.

Command Judge Advocate: LTC William S. Key III
USA Total Personnel Command, Alexandria, VA 22332.
Tel: 703/325-9490.

Command Judge Advocate: LTC John G. Thomas III
USA Community & Family Support Center, Alexandria, VA 22331.
Tel: 703/325-9633.

Command Judge Advocate: LTC Robert A. Youmans
HQ, USA Strategic Defense Command, Arlington, VA 22215.
Tel: 202/746-0300.

Staff Judge Advocate: Col. Malcolm S. Magers
HQ, TRADOC, Ft. Monroe, VA 23651. Tel: 804/727-2302.

Staff Judge Advocate: Col. Frederick E. Moss
HQ, Ft. Belvoir, Ft. Belvoir, VA 22060. Tel: 703/664-4344.

Staff Judge Advocate: Col. Francis D. O'Brien
HQ, USA INSCOM, Ft. Belvoir, VA 22060. Tel: 703/706-1245.

Staff Judge Advocate: LTC Buris C. Dale Jr
HQ, USA Transportation Center & Ft. Eustis, Ft. Eustis, VA 23604. Tel: 804/878-2205.

Staff Judge Advocate: LTC Larry R. Dean
HQ, USA Quartermaster Center & Ft. Lee, Ft Lee, VA 23801.
Tel: 804/734-4058.

Washington
Staff Judge Advocate: Col. Brooks LaGrua
HQ, I Corps & Ft. Lewis, Ft. Lewis, WA 98433.
Tel: 206/967-4540.

Staff Judge Advocate: LTC Brian X. Bush
HQ, 9th Infantry Division, Ft. Lewis, WA 98433.
Tel: 206/967-5945.

OVERSEAS

Panama
Staff Judge Advocate: Col. John K. Wallace III
HQ, US Southern Command (Panama), APO Miami 34003.
Tel: (11) 507-82-3454.

Staff Judge Advocate: LTC James S. Russell
HQ, US Army South (Panama), APO Miami 34004.
Tel: (507) 87-6205

Italy
Staff Judge Advocate: Col. James R. Baker
US Army South Eur Task Force & 5th SUPCOM (Vicenza), APO New York 09168. Tel: (39) 444-51-7818.

Legal Advisor: Col. Tony Toomepuu
Allied Forces Southern Europe/AF South, US Army Element Box 130 (Naples), FPO 09524. Tel: (39) 81721-6001.

Korea
Judge Advocate: Col. Norman G. Cooper
HQ, Eighth US Army (Korea), APO San Francisco 96301.
Tel: (011) 822-7913-6003.

Staff Judge Advocate: Col. Anthony P. DeGiulio
HQ, 19th SUPCOM (Korea), APO San Francisco 96212.
Tel: (011) 82-53-620-7692.

Staff Judge Advocate: Col. James D. Polley
HQ, Combined Field Army (Korea), APO San Francisco 96358.
Tel: (011) 315-732-6017.

Staff Judge Advocate: LTC William C. Kirk
HQ, 2d Infantry Division (Korea), APO San Francisco 96224.
Tel: (011) 82-351-60-1888.

Japan
Staff Judge Advocate: Col. Paul A. Robblee Jr
HQ, US Army Japan, APO San Francisco 96343.
Tel: (462) 51-1520-4041.

Staff Judge Advocate: LTC James A. Braga
HQ, 10th Area Support Group, Okinawa, Japan, APO San Francisco 96331. Tel: (989) 56-5617-4784.

Germany
Staff Judge Advocate: Col. Dennis M. Corrigan
HQ, 21st TAACOM (Kaiserslautern), APO New York 09325.
Tel: (49) 631-411-8491.

Office of the Judge Advocate: Col. Thomas M. Crean
HQ, USA Europe & Seventh Army (Heidelberg), APO New York 09403.
Tel: (49) 6221-57-6744.

Staff Judge Advocate: Col. Donald Deline
HQ, V Corps (Frankfurt), APO New York 09079.
Tel: (49) 69-151-6336.

Legal Advisor: Col. William G. Eckhardt
HQ, US European Command (Vaihingen), APO New York 09128.
Tel: (49) 0711-680-7354.

Staff Judge Advocate: Col. Walter B. Huffman
HQ, VII Corps (Stuttgart), APO New York 09107.
Tel: (49) 711-729-2817.

Staff Judge Advocate: Col. William H. Lantz Jr
HQ, US Army Berlin, APO New York 09742. Tel: (49) 030-819-6017.

Staff Judge Advocate: LTC John D. Altenburg
HQ, 1st Armored Division (Ansbach), APO New York 09326.
Tel: (49) 981-83-8781.

Staff Judge Advocate: LTC Waldo W. Brooks
HQ, 2d Armored Division (FWD), (Garlstedt), APO New York 09355.
Tel: (49) 4795-77-6717.

Staff Judge Advocate: LTC John T. Burton
HQ, 3d Armored Division (Frankfurt), APO New York 09039.
Tel: (49) 69-1549-8215.

Staff Judge Advocate: LTC Dayton M. Cramer
HQ, 8th Infantry Division (Bad Kreuznach), APO New York 09111.
Tel: (49) 671-609-6412.

Staff Judge Advocate: LTC James H. Rosenblatt
HQ, 32d USA Air Defense Command, APO New York 09175.
Tel: (49) 6151-69-7358.

Staff Judge Advocate: LTC Joseph E. Ross
HQ, 1st Infantry Division (Fwd)-(Goeppingen), APO New York 09137. Tel: (49) 7161-618-3724.

Staff Judge Advocate: LTC Lee Schinasi
HQ, 3d Infantry Division (Wuerzburg), APO New York 09036.
Tel: (49) 931-889-6194.

U.S. ARMY MATERIEL COMMAND

Headquarters, 5001 Eisenhower Avenue
Alexandria, VA 22333-0001

The U.S. Army Materiel Command provides materiel and related services to the Army and other U.S. and foreign agencies as directed. Principal functions include research and development; product production and maintenance engineering; testing and evaluation of materiel; production and procurement of materiel; and the maintenance, distribution, and disposal of materiel.

(Area Code 703)
Commanding General: General William G.T. Tuttle Jr 274-9625
Public Affairs 274-8010

(Area Code 703)
Freedom of Information Act/Privacy Act Office 274-8031
Facsimile 274-4723

OFFICE OF THE COMMAND COUNSEL (Room 7806)

The Office of Command Counsel serves as legal advisor to the Commanding General of the U.S. Army Materiel Command (AMC), and to subordinate commands, installations, and field activities in areas of law and patents. The Office also monitors all AMC actions concerning procurement fraud and procurement irregularities.

(Area Code 703)
Command Counsel: Edward J. Korte 274-8031
Deputy Command Counsel: Robert B. MacFarlane 274-8031
Deputy Command Counsel/Command Judge Advocate:
Col. Thomas Kullman 274-8049

The Office of Command Counsel is organized in four divisions:

The **Employment/Contract Proceedings Division** provides legal services relating to labor-management relations and civilian personnel law, litigation (except matters relating to intellectual property), bankruptcy, admiralty, contract and tort claims, appeals, contract adjustments, debarment, and suspension actions involving procurement fraud and irregularity. Attorneys in the Division also review and supervise the preparation of cases appearing before the Armed Services Board of Contract Appeals and other tribunals.

(Area Code 703)
Chief: Stephen A. Klatsky 274-8080

The **General Law Division** provides legal advice and assistance on issues involving military justice, standards of conduct and conflicts of interest, professional ethics, military personnel law, environmental law, taxation, all aspects of property law, administrative law, congressional inquiries, and proposed legislation.

(Area Code 703)
Chief: Col. Thomas Kullman 274-8049

The **Acquisition Law Division** provides legal services and advice involving the worldwide administration and execution of AMC legal procurement programs and the use of appropriated and nonappropriated funds. This Division also has two branches: a Protest Branch, which evaluates all protests against awards and represents the Army before the General Accounting Office; and the Acquisition Law Branch, which provides advice on contracting policies, contract types, procurement regulations, and special research and development problems relating to grants and contracts.

(Area Code 703)
Chief: Robert B. MacFarlane 274-8045

The **Protest Division** handles GAO and GSBCA protests.

(Area Code 703)
Chief: Richard Couch 274-8045

U.S. Army Laboratory Command
ATTN: SLCIS-CC-IP, 2800 Powder Mill Road (HDL,ISA), Adelphi, MD 20783-1145

The patent law responsibilities of the Office of Command Counsel are handled by the **U.S. Army Laboratory Command** in Adelphi, MD. The patent attorneys there provide legal advice and services on all matters involving intellectual property, including inventions, patents, copyrights, trademarks, technical data, foreign licensing, and other international programs involving proprietary rights.

Chief of Intellectual Property: Saul Elbaum ...(301) 394-3790

AMC AND ITS SUBORDINATE LEGAL OFFICES

1. **Office of the Command Counsel**
Command Counsel: Edward J, Korte
HQ, U.S. Army Materiel Command, Attn: Office of the Command Counsel, AMCCC, 5001 Eisenhower Avenue, Alexandria, VA 22333-0001. Tel: 703/274-8031.

2. **U.S. Army Armament, Munitions & Chemical Command (D)**
Chief Counsel: Benjamin Halperin
Deputy Chief Counsel: Francis A. Cassidy
Adversary Proceedings Division: Robert F. McQuillan, Chief
Patent Law Division: Edward Goldberg, Chief
U.S. Army Armament, Munitions & Chemical Command (D), AMSMC-GC(D), Picatinny Arsenal, NJ 07806-5000. Tel: 201/724-6597.

3. **U.S. Army Armament, Chemical, Research, Development and Engineering Center**
Chief Counsel: Robert W. Poor
U.S. Army Armament, Chemical, Research, Development and Engineering Center, Edgewood Area, Attn: AMSMC-GCC(A), Counsel, Aberdeen Proving Ground, MD 21010-5423. Tel: 301/671-2703.

4. **U.S. Army Armament, Munitions & Chemical Command (R)**
Chief Counsel: Marvin L. Hancks
Deputy Chief Counsel: Col. Raymond K. Costello
Adversary Proceedings Division: Robert K. Droll, Chief
General Law/Congressional Affairs Division: Don Lappin, Chief
Procurement Law Division: Mike G. Patramanis, Chief
U.S. Army Armament, Munitions & Chemical Command (R), Attn: AMSMC-GC(R), Rock Island, IL 61299-6000. Tel: 309/782-4051.

Counsel: Lynn M. Sturges
McAlester Army Ammunition Plant, SMCMC-GC, McAlester, OK 74501-5000. Tel: 918/421-2439.

Counsel: William F. Sayegh
Pine Bluff Arsenal, SMCPB-JA, Pine Bluff, AR 71602-9500. Tel: 501/543-3131.

Counsel: James G. Gilliam
Rocky Mountain Arsenal, Attn: XRMAC-GC, Counsel, Commerce City, CO 80022-2180. Tel: 303/289-0147.

Counsel: Earl T. Hilts
Watervliet Arsenal, Attn: SMCWV-GC, Counsel, Watervliet, NY 12189-4050. Tel: 518/266-5413.

5. **U.S. Army Communications-Electronics Command**
Chief Counsel: Victor Ferlise
Deputy Chief Counsel: Robert B. Saphro
Adversary Proceedings Division: Marc A. Moller
Staff Judge Advocate: LTC John C. Greenhaugh, Chief
Legal Services Branch: CPT Joseph Bestul
Civil Law Branch: CPT Rafe Foster
Criminal Law Branch: CPT Robert L.Carey
Procurement Law Division: Mark A. Sagan, Chief
ISEC Legal Counsel: William J. Kampo, Jr.
Assistant Chief Counsel for Intellectual Property Law: Sheldon Kanars
Patent/Data Procurement Branch: Michael Zelenka, Chief
Patent Prosecution Branch: vacant, Chief
U.S. Army Communications-Electronics Command, AMSEL-LG, Fort Monmouth, NJ 07703-5000. Tel: 201/532-3120.

Chief Counsel: Dominic A. Femino, Jr.
Installation Judge Advocate Division: CPT C.N. Patterson
Procurement Law Division: Christopher E. Kernan, Chief
U.S. Army Communications-Electronics Command, Vint Hill Legal Office, Vint Hill Farms Station, Attn: Counsel, SELCE-LG, Warrenton, VA 22186-5196. Tel: 703/349-5259.

Chief Counsel: Dominic J. Brognano
U.S. Army Communications-Electronics Command, Night Vision and Electro-Optics Center, Attn: Counsel, AMSEL-LG-VHFS-B, Fort Belvoir, VA 22060-5677. Tel: 703/664-1058.

6. **U.S. Army Depot Systems Command**
Chief Counsel: Patrick R. Sheldon
Acquisition/Labor Law Division: Melvin Howry, Chief
Environmental/Safety Law Division: Dennis L. Bates, Chief
U.S. Army Depot Systems Command, Attn: Chief Counsel, AMSDS-CC, Chambersburg, PA 17201-4170. Tel: 717/267-5180

Chief Deputy Counsel: Leslie K. Mason
Anniston Army Depot, Attn: Counsel, SDSAN-L, Anniston, AL 36201-5005. Tel: 205/235-6334.

Counsel: James T. Abbott
Corpus Christi Army Depot, Attn: Counsel, SDSCC-GJ, Corpus Christi, TX 78419-6080. Tel: 512/939-3432.

Chief Counsel: Patrick R. Sheldon
Letterkenny Army Depot, Attn: Counsel, SDSLE-DL, Chambersburg, PA 17201-4150. Tel: 717/267-5180.

Counsel: Leslie E. Renkey
Lexington-Blue Grass Army Depot, Attn: Counsel, SDSLB-LE, Lexington, KY 40511-5003. Tel: 606/293-3932.

Counsel: James E. Toms
New Cumberland Army Depot, Attn: Counsel, SDSNC-L, New Cumberland, PA 17070-5001. Tel: 770/782-7971.

Counsel: Joseph G. Martin
Red River Army Depot, Attn: Counsel, SDSRR-AL, Texarkana, TX 75507-5000. Tel: 214/334-3258.

Counsel: Elizabeth Buchanan
Sacramento Army Depot, Attn: Counsel, SDSSA-ALO, Sacramento, CA 95813-5020. Tel: 916/388-3274.

Counsel: CPT David K. Ettman
Seneca Army Depot, Attn: Counsel, SDSSE-PL, Romulus, NY 14541-5001. Tel: 607/869-8230.

Counsel: David S. Riley
Sharpe Army Depot, Attn: Counsel, SDSSH-CL, Lathrop, CA 95331-5120. Tel: 209/982-2021.

Counsel: CPT Daniel A. Culver
Sierra Army Depot, SDSSI-JA, Herlong, CA 96113-5007. Tel: 916/827-4548.

Counsel: Michael Futch
Tobyhanna Army Depot, Attn: Counsel, SDSTO-JD, Tobyhanna, PA 18466-5054. Tel: 717/894-7210.

Counsel: Roger Corman
Tooele Army Depot, SDSTE-LEG, Tooele, UT 84074-5027. Tel: 801/833-2536.

7. **U.S. Army Laboratory Command**
Chief Counsel: Col. William M. Whitten, III
Acquisition Law Division: Robert R. Chase, Chief
Administrative Law/Litigation Division: Timothy Connolly, Chief
Intellectual Property Law Division: Saul Elbaum, Chief
U.S. Army Laboratory Command, AMSLC-CC, 2800 Powder Mill Road (HDL,ISA), Adelphi, MD 20783-1145. Tel: 301/394-1070.

Chief Counsel: James C. Savage
U.S. Army Laboratory Command, Army Materials Technology Laboratory, SLCMT-DL, Watertown, MA 02172-0001. Tel: 617/923-5276.

Chief Counsel: Mark H. Rutter
U.S. Army Laboratory Command, Army Research Office, SLCRO-LO, P.O. Box 12211, Research Triangle Park, NC 27709-2211. Tel: 919/549-0641, ext 292.

8. U.S. Army Missile Command
Chief Counsel: William V. Black
Acquisition Law Division: Robert J. Spazzarini, Chief
Branch A: Karolyn E. Voight, Chief
Branch B: Fred W. Allen, Chief
Branch C: Carl R. Stephens, Chief
Branch D: LTC Joseph F. Cirelli, Chief
Staff Judge Advocate: Col. David B. Briggs
Legal Services Division: Donald B. Hankins, Chief
Adversary Proceedings Division: Emanuel A. Coleman, Chief
Intellectual Property Law Division: Hugh P. Nicholson, Chief
Acquisition Group: Jack M. Glandon
Patent Prosecution Group: Freddie M. Bush
U.S. Army Missile Command, AMSMI-GC, Redstone Arsenal, AL 35898-5120. Tel: 205/876-3405.

9. U.S. Army Tank-Automotive Command
Chief Counsel: Albert A. Dawes
Adversary, Administrative & Military Law Division: Frank R. Ortisi, Chief
Intellectual Property Law Division: Peter A. Taucher, Chief
Procurement Law Division: Ronald M. Goldstone, Chief
U.S. Army Tank-Automotive Command, AMSTA-L, Warren, MI 48397-5000. Tel: 313/574-6289.

10. U.S. Army Test & Evaluation Command
Chief Counsel/Staff Judge Advocate: Col. Patrick J. Mackey
Civil Law Division: Laura Rothenberg Haug, Chief
Procurement Law Division: Maj. John K. Northrop, Chief
Legal Assistance Division: CPT Andrew Ivchenko, Chief
Criminal Law Division: Maj. Wellington T. Matthews, Jr., Chief
Claims Division: CPT Reynold P. Masterton, Chief
U.S. Army Test & Evaluation Command, AMSTE-JA, Aberdeen Proving Ground, MD 21005-5055. Tel: 301/278-5293.

Office of the Judge Advocate: Maj. Robert Horalek
U.S. Army Dugway Proving Ground, STEDP-JA, Dugway, UT 84022-5000. Tel: 801/831-3333.

Staff Judge Advocate: Vincent J. Faggioli
Deputy Chief Counsel: R.G. Walker
Deputy Staff Judge Advocate: CPT Charles V.S. Platt
Chief Legal NCO: L.B. Scott, Jr.
Criminal Law/Legal Assistance: CPT Jeffrey W. Fletcher
Claims/Environmental: Robert F. Colvin
Procurement/EEO/Labor/Civilian Personnel: John M. Lenko
U.S. Army White Sands Missile Range, STEWS-JA, White Sands Missile Range, NM 88002-5075. Tel: 505/678-1263.

Command Judge Advocate: Maj. Jay D. McQueen
U.S. Army Yuma Proving Ground, STEYP-JA, Yuma, AZ 85365-9102. Tel: 602/328-2608.

11. U.S. Army Aviation Systems Command
Chief Counsel: Col. John R. Hamilton
Deputy Chief Counsel: Harvey Reznick
AH-64 Developmental Systems and CH-47 Branch: M. Bruce Jones, Chief
UH-60 and Bell Systems Branch: Robert L. Norris, Chief
Special Requirements Branch: LTC Michael J. Dicharry, Chief
General Law Division: Robert H. Garfield, Chief
Intellectual Property Law Division: Arthur H. Tischer, Chief
U.S. Army Aviation Systems Command, AMSAV-J, 4300 Goodfellow Blvd, St. Louis, MO 63120-1798. Tel: 314/263-3391.

Chief Counsel: Laurence M. Smail
U.S. Army Aviation Systems Command, U.S. Army Aviation Research & Technology Activity, SAVRT-TY-OC, Fort Eustis, VA 23604-5577. Tel: 804/878-4205.

12. U.S. Army Troop Support Command
Chief Counsel: Leonard E. Glaser, Chief
U.S. Army Troop Support Command, AMSTR-J, 4300 Goodfellow Blvd, St. Louis, MO 63120-1798. Tel: 314/263-1280.

Chief Counsel: John E. Metcalf
Procurement Law: Lloyd E. Webber
General Law: Paul M. Curran
Patent Attorney: Charles D. Miller
U.S. Army Belvoir Research, Development & Engineering Center, STRBE-L, Fort Belvoir, VA 22060-5606. Tel: 703/664-5839.

Chief Counsel: Jerome C. Brennan
Procurement/General Law: Melinda J. Loftin
Intellectual Property Law: Richard J. Donahue
U.S. Army Natick Research, Development & Engineering Center, STRNC-ZSL, Natick, MA 01760-5000. Tel: 617/651-4322.

13. U.S. Army Materiel Command, Europe
Chief Counsel: LTC Thomas P. Burns, III
U.S. Army Materiel Command, Europe, AMXEU-CJ, APO New York 09333-4747. Tel: 011-49-6221-57-7058.

14. SANG (Saudia Arabian National Guard)
Chief Counsel: Ted M. Williamson
Project Manager, SANG (Saudia Arabian National Guard) Modernization Program, AMCPM-NGZ, APO New York 09038-5005. Tel: Riyadh, Saudi Arabia Through Oversees Operator, ask for Country Code 966, City Code 1, ask for 464-6156, Ext. 207. Messages can also be forwarded by contacting PM SANG's Washington's office in the AMC HG building. Commercial telephone is 703/274-9126.

U.S. ARMY CORPS OF ENGINEERS

Headquarters, 20 Massachusetts Avenue, N.W.
Washington, D.C. 20314-1000

DESCRIPTION: The U.S. Army Corps of Engineers is the world's largest construction agency and the nation's principal developer of water resources. Under its Civil Works Programs, the Corps builds dams, reservoirs, and levees, deepens harbors, and widens waterways to help provide flood protection, increase water and power supplies, lower transportation costs, and develop recreational areas. It also regulates dredging and filling of the nation's navigable waterways under the Water Pollution Control Act of 1972 and has other responsibilities for water resource management and pollution control.

(Area Code 202)

Commander: Lt. Gen. Henry J. Hatch 272-0001
General Information 272-0660
Office of Small & Disadvantaged Business Utilization ..272-0725

(Area Code 202)

Freedom of Information Act/Privacy Act Office 272-0018
Facsimile 504-4609

OFFICE OF THE CHIEF COUNSEL (Room 8220)

Corps attorneys handle procurement matters ranging from drafting and negotiation of contracts to disputes over contract awards and terminations. Corps lawyers are also actively involved in the administrative processing of tort claims and in contractual and non-contractual claims arising from real estate management for and against the Government through prescribed administrative channels. When the Corps of Engineers is a party in litigation enforcement and adversary proceedings in the U.S. District Courts, the U.S. Court of Claims, or Federal appellate courts, Corps attorneys work on a variety of suits which emanate from military and civil works functions.

For example, Corps attorneys work on enforcement actions under its regulatory authorities, viz. Section 10 of the Rivers and Harbors Act, Section 404 of the Clean Water Act, environmental lawsuits, admiralty cases, tort actions, prosecutions of fraud and other crimes against the Government, real estate suits in condemnation, inverse condemnation and quiet title. They also deal with copyright, patent, civil rights, personnel, and the Freedom of Information Act cases.

(Area Code 202)

Chief Counsel: Lester Edelman 272-0018
Deputy Chief Counsel: Craig R. Schmauder (Acting) 272-0018
Chief Trial Attorney: Frank Carr 272-0033
Assistant Chief Counsel for:
American Indian Affairs: Rebecca Ramson ....(503) 326-3891
Environmental Law and Regulatory Programs:
Lance Wood 272-0035
Legislation and General Law: Ronald C. Allen 272-0030
Litigation: Martin R. Cohen 272-0027
Procurement: Michael J. Adams 272-0021

Senior Counsel for: (Area Code 202)
Military Programs and International Law:
Rupert Jennings 272-0030
Civil Litigation: Carolyn J. Lynch 272-0027
Environmental Restoration: John J. Mahon 272-0021
Assistant Counsel for:
General Law: Charles T. Flachbarth 272-0030
Legal Services, Policy and Programs: Ramon Powell ...272-0035
Legislation: Susan Bond 272-0030
Litigation/Water Rights: Russell W. Petit 272-0027
Procurement/Policy & Regulations: Kenneth R. Powers ..272-0021
Facsimile 504-4123

U.S. ARMY CORPS OF ENGINEERS: DIVISION AND DISTRICT COUNSEL

DIVISION COUNSEL: EUROPE

U.S. Army Engineer Division-Europe, CEEUD-OC, (Frankfurt), APO New York 09757. Tel: 011-45-69-1516154

DIVISION COUNSEL: HUNTSVILLE

U.S. Army Engineer Division-Huntsville, CEHND-OC, P.O. Box 1600, Huntsville, AL 35807. Tel: 205/895-5460

DIVISION COUNSEL: LOWER MISSISSIPPI VALLEY

U.S. Army Engineer Division-Lower Mississippi Valley, CELMV-OC, P.O. Box 80, Vicksburg, MS 39181. Tel: 601/634-5750.

District Counsel: Memphis
U.S. Army Engineer District-Memphis, CELMM-OC, B-202, 167 N. Mid-America Mall, Clifford Davis Federal Building, Memphis, TN 38103. Tel: 901/521-3221.

District Counsel: New Orleans
U.S. Army Engineer District-New Orleans, CELMN-OC, P.O. Box 60267, New Orleans, LA 70160. Tel: 504/862-2204.

District Counsel: St. Louis
U.S. Army Engineer District-St. Louis, CELMS-OC, 210 Tucker Boulevard, N., St. Louis, MO 63101. Tel: 314/263-5660.

District Counsel: Vicksburg
U.S. Army Engineer District-Vicksburg, CELMK-OC, P.O. Box 60, Vicksburg, MS 39181. Tel: 601/631-5010.

DIVISION COUNSEL: MISSOURI RIVER

U.S. Army Engineer Division-Missouri River, CEMRD-OC, P.O. Box 103 Downtown Station, Omaha, NE 68101. Tel: 402/221-7201.

District Counsel: Kansas City
U.S. Army Engineer District-Kansas City, CEMRK-OC, 700 Federal Building, Kansas City, MO 64106. Tel: 816/426-3201.

District Counsel: Omaha
U.S. Army Engineer District-Omaha, CEMRO-OC, 215 North 17th Street, Omaha, NE 68102. Tel: 402/221-3900.

DIVISION COUNSEL: NEW ENGLAND

U.S. Army Engineer Division-New England, CENED-OC, 424 Trapelo Road, Waltham, MA 02254. Tel: 617/647-8220.

DIVISION COUNSEL: NORTH ATLANTIC

U.S. Army Engineer Division-North Atlantic, CENAD-OC, 90 Church Street, New York, NY 10007. Tel: 212/264-7101.

District Counsel: Baltimore
U.S. Army Engineer District-Baltimore, CENAB-OC, P.O. Box 1715, Baltimore, MD 21203. Tel: (301) 962-4545.

Engineer Activity: Capital Area
U.S. Army Engineer Activity-National Capital Area, CENAC-OC, Ft. Myer, VA 22211. Attn: NAC. Tel: 703/696-6400.

District Counsel: New York
U.S. Army Engineer District-New York, CENAN-OC, 26 Federal Plaza, New York, NY 10278. Tel: 212/264-0100.

DEPARTMENT OF DEFENSE

District Counsel: Norfolk
U.S. Army Engineer District-Norfolk, CENAO-OC,
803 Front Street, Norfolk, VA 23510. Tel: 804/441-7601.

District Counsel: Philadelphia
U.S. Army Engineer District-Philadelphia, CANAP-OC,
U.S. Customs House, 2nd & Chestnut Streets, Philadelphia,
PA 19106. Tel: 215/597-4848.

DIVISION COUNSEL: NORTH CENTRAL
U.S. Army Engineer Division-North Central, CENCD-OC,
536 S. Clark Street, Chicago, IL 60605. Tel: 312/353-6310.

District Counsel: Buffalo
U.S. Army Engineer District-Buffalo, CENCB-OC,
1776 Niagara Street, Buffalo, NY 14207. Tel: 716/879-4200.

District Counsel: Chicago
U.S. Army Engineer District-Chicago, CENCC-OC,
219 S. Dearborn Street, Chicago, IL 60604. Tel: 312/353-6400.

District Counsel: Detroit
U.S. Army Engineer District-Detroit, CENCE-OC,
P.O. Box 1027, Detroit, MI 48231. Tel: (313) 226-6762.

District Counsel: Rock Island
U.S. Army Engineer District-Rock Island, CENCR-OC,
Clock Tower Building, Rock Island, IL 61204.
Tel: 309/788-6361.

District Counsel: St. Paul
U.S. Army Engineer District-St. Paul, CENCS-OC,
1421 U.S. Post Office & Custom House, 180 East Kellogg
Boulevard, St. Paul, MN 55101. Tel: 612/220-0200.

DIVISION COUNSEL: NORTH PACIFIC
U.S. Army Engineer Division-North Pacific, CENPD-OC,
P.O. Box 2870, Portland, OR 97208. Tel: 503/326-3700.

District Counsel: Alaska
U.S. Army Engineer District-Alaska, CENPA-OC,
P.O. Box 898, Anchorage, AK 99506. Tel: 907/753-2504.

District Counsel: Portland
U.S. Army Engineer District-Portland, CENPP-OC,
319 S.W. Pine Street, Room 401, Portland, OR 97204.
Tel: 503/326-6000.

District Counsel: Seattle
U.S. Army Engineer District-Seattle, CENPS-OC,
P.O. Box C-3755, Seattle, WA 98124. Tel: 206/764-3692.

District Counsel: Walla Walla
U.S. Army Engineer District-Walla Walla, CENPW-OC,
Building 602, City-County Airport, Walla Walla, WA 99362.
Tel: 509/522-6506.

DIVISION COUNSEL: OHIO RIVER
U.S. Army Engineer Division-Ohio River, CEORD-OC,
P.O. Box 1159, Cincinnati, OH 45201. Tel: 513/684-3002.

District Counsel: Huntington
U.S. Army Engineer District-Huntington, CEORH-OC,
502-8th Street, Huntington, WV 25701. Tel: 304/529-5395.

District Counsel: Louisville
U.S. Army Engineer District-Louisville, CEORL-OC,
P.O. Box 59, Louisville, KY 40201. Tel: 502/582-5601.

District Counsel: Nashville
U.S. Army Engineer District-Nashville, CEORN-OC,
P.O. Box 1070, Nashville, TN 37202. Tel: 615/736-5626.

District Counsel: Pittsburgh
U.S. Army Engineer District-Pittsburgh, CEORP-OC,
William S. Moorehead Federal Building, 1000 Liberty Avenue,
Pittsburgh, PA 15222. Tel: 412/644-6800.

DIVISION COUNSEL: PACIFIC OCEAN
U.S. Army Engineer Division-Pacific Ocean, CEPOD-OC,
Ft. Shafter, HI 96858. Tel: 808/438-1500.

District Counsel: Far East
U.S. Army Engineer District-Far East, CEPOF-OC,
(Seoul, Korea) APO San Francisco 96301.
Tel: (011) 82-2-274-4241

District Counsel: Honolulu
U.S. Army Engineer District-Honolulu, CEPO-OC,
Ft. Shafter, HI 96858. Tel: 808/438-1500.

District Counsel: Japan
U.S. Army Engineer District-Japan, CEPOJ-OC,
APO San Francisco 96343. Tel: 0462-51-1520.

DIVISION COUNSEL: SOUTH ATLANTIC
U.S. Army Engineer Division-South Atlantic, CESAD-OC,
77 Forsyth Street, S.W., Room 313, Atlanta, GA 30335.
Tel: 404/331-6711.

District Counsel: Charleston
U.S. Army Engineer District-Charleston, CESAC-OC,
Federal Building, 334 Meeting Street, Room 633,
Charleston, SC 29403. Tel: 803/724-4229.

District Counsel: Jacksonville
U.S. Army Engineer District-Jacksonville, CESAJ-OC,
P.O. Box 4970, Jacksonville, FL 32232. Tel: 904/791-2241.

District Counsel: US Army Middle East Africa
U.S. Army Middle East Africa, CESAI-OC,
P.O. Box 2250, Winchester, VA 22601. Tel: 703/665-3600.

District Counsel: Mobile
U.S. Army Engineer District-Mobile, CESAM-OC,
P.O. Box 2288, Mobile, AL 36628. Tel: 205/690-2511.

District Counsel: Savannah
U.S. Army Engineer District-Savannah, CESAS-OC,
P.O. Box 889, Savannah, GA 31402. Tel: 912/944-5436.

District Counsel: Wilmington
U.S. Army Engineer District-Wilmington, CESAW-OC,
P.O. Box 1890, Wilmington, NC 28402. Tel: 919/251-4501.

DIVISION COUNSEL: SOUTH PACIFIC
U.S. Army Engineer Division-South Pacific, CESPD-OC,
630 Sansome Street, Room 720, San Francisco, CA 94111.
Tel: 415/556-0914.

District Counsel: Los Angeles
U.S. Army Engineer District-Los Angeles, CESPL-OC,
P.O. Box 2711, Los Angeles, CA 90053. Tel: 213/894-5300.

District Counsel: Sacramento
U.S. Army Engineer District-Sacramento, CESPK-OC,
650 Capitol Mall, Sacramento, CA 95814. Tel: 916/551-2005.

District Counsel: San Francisco
U.S. Army Engineer District-San Francisco, CESPN-OC,
211 Main St, San Francisco, CA 94105. Tel: 415/974-0358.

DIVISION COUNSEL: SOUTHWESTERN

U.S. Army Engineer Division-Southwestern, CESWD-OC,
1114 Commerce Street, Dallas, TX 75242. Tel: 214/767-2502.

District Counsel: Albuquerque
U.S. Army Engineer District-Albuquerque, CESWA-OC,
P.O. Box 1580, Albuquerque, NM 87103. Tel: 505/766-2732.

District Counsel: Fort Worth
U.S. Army Engineer District-Fort Worth, CESWF,
P.O. Box 17300, Ft. Worth, TX 76102. Tel: 817/334-2300.

District Counsel: Galveston
U.S. Army Engineer District-Galveston, CESWG-OC,
444 Barracuda Ave, Galveston, TX 77553. Tel: 409/766-3001.

District Counsel: Little Rock
U.S. Army Engineer District-Little Rock, CESWL-OC,
700 W. Capitol, Room B-304, Little Rock, AR 72201.
Tel: 501/378-5531.

District Counsel: Tulsa
U.S. Army Engineer District-Tulsa, CESWT-OC,
224 South Boulder, Tulsa, OK 74103. Tel: 918/581-7311.

BOARDS AND COMMISSIONS

Counsel: William N. Lovelady
Coastal Engineering Research Board, CEERB-OC,
P.O. Box 631, Vicksburg, MS 39181. Tel: (601) 634-2513.

Counsel: Claude Bagley
Mississippi River Commission, CEMRC-OC
P.O. Box 80, Vicksburg, MS 39181. Tel: (601) 634-5750.

SEPARATE FIELD OPERATING ACTIVITIES

Counsel: Howard Goldman
U.S. Army Engineering and Housing Support Center, CEHSC-OC,
Building 2593, Ft. Belvoir, VA 22060. Tel: (703) 355-2160.

Chief Counsel and Staff Judge Advocate: Patrick J. Mackey
US Army Toxic and Hazardous Materials Agency, CETHA-OC,
Aberdeen Proving Ground, MD 21010. Tel: 301/278-4285.

Counsel: Cathy Kurke
U.S. Army Engineer Studies Center, CEESC-OC,
Casey Building #2594, Ft. Belvoir, VA 22060.
Tel: (703) 355-2373.

Counsel: Cathy Kurke
U.S. Army Corps of Engineers Water Resources Support Center,
CEWRC-OC, Casey Building #2594, Ft. Belvoir, VA 22060.
Tel: (703) 355-2250.

Counsel: Cathy Kurke
U.S. Army Humphreys Engineer, CEHEC-OC,
Center Support Activity, Kingman Building, #1A01,
Ft. Belvoir, VA 22060. Tel: (703) 355-2214.

BOARD OF CONTRACT APPEALS

20 Massachusetts Avenue, N.W., Washington, D.C. 20314

The U.S. Army Corps of Engineers Board of Contract Appeals is an independent, quasi-judicial tribunal that hears and decides appeals from final decisions rendered by contracting officers in the administration of civil works contracts let by the U.S. Army Corps of Engineers and several other Federal agencies, as well as contracts awarded by the Washington Area Metropolitan Transit Authority (WMATA). The Board's professional staff consists of seven Administrative Judges and two Hearing Examiners, all of whom are practicing attorneys, and a few law clerks who are law students.

Each Administrative Judge has a docket of appeals which is assigned by the Chairman, generally at random. Proceedings are adversarial in nature and Judges manage their dockets, conduct full evidentiary hearings, and render decisions based on findings of fact and opinions of law. The decision then proceeds through the concurrence process to two other Administrative Judges (one of whom normally is the Chairman) who review the record and proposed decision and then register concurrence or dissent.

Appeals of decisions are to the Court of Appeals for the Federal Circuit (in the case of appeals arising from Federal contracts subject to the Contract Disputes Act) or to the appropriate Federal District Court (in the case of appeals from WMATA contracts). Review at the judicial appellate level is in accordance with the standards for review of administrative action, that is, the Board's findings of facts are conclusive upon the court unless they are arbitrary, capricious, grossly erroneous, or not supported by substantial evidence. The Board's conclusions of law have no finality, but are accorded substantial deference based on the Board's subject matter expertise.

Decisions of the Board of Contract Appeals can be found in the Board of Contract Appeals Reporter, a bi-weekly publication which reports the decisions of the following Boards of Contract Appeals: Agriculture, Armed Services, Corps of Engineers, Department of Transportation, Energy, General Services Administration, Department of Housing and Urban Development, Interior, Labor, National Aeronautics and Space Administration, U.S. Postal Service, and Department of Veterans Affairs. Annual Price $760.00. Contact: Commerce Clearing House, Inc., 4025 West Peterson Avenue, Chicago, IL 60646. Tel: 312/583-8500. Or in Washington, D.C., call 202/626-2200.

	(Area Code 202)
Chairman: Richard C. Solibakke	272-0369
Vice Chairman: Charles Sheridan	272-0369
Administrative Judges:	
Robert Peacock	272-0369
Wesley Jockisch	272-0369
Edward Ketchen	272-0369
Administrative Judge/WMATA: Donald Frenzen	272-0369
Recorder: Ruth Price	272-0369

DEPARTMENT OF DEFENSE

OTHER ARMY LEGAL OFFICES

(Area Code 202)

National Guard Bureau
Chief Counsel: James C. Hise 695-5149
Inspector General: Col. John L. Patrick 693-3837

U.S. Army Community and Family Support Center
Command Judge Advocate: Lt. Col. John L. Thomas (703) 325-9633

U.S. Total Army Personnel Command
Command Judge Advocate: Lt. Col. William S. Key (703) 325-8855

Criminal Investigation Command
Staff Judge Advocate: Lt. Col Brent P. Green ..(703) 756-2281

Intelligence and Security Command
Staff Judge Advocate: Col. Francis D. O'Brien .(703) 706-1245

DATABASES AND PUBLICATIONS OF INTEREST

DATABASE:

CELDS (Computer-aided Environmental Legislative Data System) is part of the Environmental Technical Information System (ETIS) database maintained by the U.S. Army Corps of Engineers. **CELDS** is a collection of abstracted Federal and state environmental regulations covering seventeen subject areas such as air quality, pesticides, radiation, toxic substances and hazardous waste. Database information is continuously updated. Subscription service is available to those users desiring online access to ETIS programs. The fees are $200.00 (one-time subscription fee); $20.00/hour (telecommunications charge, if applicable); $20.00 (annual maintenance fee); $90.00/hour (connect time, billed monthly); and $15.00 (one time charge per additional login). The ETIS office offers individual assistance for **CELDS** information retrieval. ETIS staff searches cost $90.00/hour (computer connect time, prorated per minute); $25.00/hour (staff time, prorated per quarter hour); $1.00/page (FAX); and 10 cents/page (Xeroxing). For information, contact Environmental Technical Information System, University of Illinois at Urbana-Champaign, 1003 W. Nevada St., Urbana, IL 61801. Tel: 217/333-1369.

PUBLICATIONS:

The following publications can be purchased from the **U.S. Government Printing Office.** Stock numbers and prices for annual subscriptions are shown below. Submit requests for these publications to: The Superintendent of Documents, U.S. Government Printing Office, Washington, D.C. 20402. Tel: 202/783-3238.

Army Federal Acquisition Regulations Supplement. April 1988. This Army supplement to the Federal Acquisition Regulation is a subscription service consisting of a basic manual and changes for an indeterminate period. Price: $100.00 domestic; $125.00 foreign. GPO Stock# 908-020-00000-6.

The Army Lawyer. Published monthly by the Judge Advocate General's School for the official use of Army lawyers in the performance of their legal responsibilities. The publication covers current issues in criminal law, government procurement law, tort law, labor and employment law, and international law. Price: $13.00 domestic; $16.25 foreign. GPO Stock# 708-011-00000-2.

Military Law Review. Quarterly. Designed as a medium for the military lawyer, active and reserve, to share the product of his/her experience and research with fellow lawyers. Price: $12.00 a year domestic; $15.00/year foreign. GPO Stock# 708-038-0000 8.

DEPARTMENT OF THE NAVY
The Pentagon
Washington, D.C. 20360-5110

DESCRIPTION: The U.S. Navy is responsible for the maritime aspects of the defense of the U.S., including the planning, implementation and execution of global maritime strategy, which has as its objectives--

*prevention of the seas becoming a hostile medium of attack against the U.S. and its allies;

*ensuring unimpeded U.S. use of its ocean lifelines to its allies, its forward-deployed forces, its energy and mineral resources, and its trading partners; and

*the ability to project force in support of national security objectives and to support combat ashore, should deterrence fail.

(Area Code 202)

Secretary of the Navy:
Honorable H. Lawrence Garrett, III 695-3131
Special Assistant for Legal and Legislative Affairs:
Cdr. Peter L. Fagan 697-6935
Small and Disadvantaged Business Utilization Office ...692-7122

(Area Code 202)

Public Affairs 697-7491
Publications 695-0965
Freedom of Information Act/Privacy Act Office 694-5032
Facsimile 694-3477

OFFICE OF THE NAVAL INSPECTOR GENERAL

The Naval Inspector General is detailed from officers on active duty in the line, for the purpose of inquiring into and reporting upon any matter that affects the discipline or military efficiency of the Navy and makes such inspections, investigations, and reports as the Secretary of the Navy or the Chief of Naval Operations directs.

(Area Code 202)

Inspector General: Rear Adm. Ming E. Chang 433-2000
Special Assistant/Contract Law: Mark O'Brien 433-2222

(Area Code 202)

Special Assistant/Legal and Legislative Matters:
Capt. Patricia Gormley 433-2222
Facsimile 433-3277

OFFICE OF THE GENERAL COUNSEL (Room 4E724)

The Office of the General Counsel (OGC) functions as a large law firm and is a vital part of the U.S. Government. It is separate in both organization and practice from the Navy's Judge Advocate General's Corp. The General Counsel is the personal legal advisor to the Secretary of the Navy, and OGC attorneys assist in providing legal services to the Secretary, his staff, and personnel throughout the Navy.

The legal work of OGC is extremely sophisticated as well as varied. The bulk of the work centers around the U.S. Navy's primary activity of building and supplying its fleet of ships and aircraft. As a result, the principal area of OGC's practice is Government contract law, which is similar in nature to a business and commercial law practice. Many of the cases involve several hundred million dollars in purchases or claims. Additionally, OGC attorneys work in areas such as real estate law, utilities law, environmental law, admiralty law, and increasingly in civilian personnel law. OGC also includes approximately 64 patent attorneys.

In addition to varied legal work, the OGC includes many offices/commands with varied missions. The Washington, D.C. area alone includes the Naval Facilities Engineering Command, the Naval Research Laboratory, the Naval Data Automation Center, the Automatic Data Processing Selection Office, the Naval Regional Contracting Center, the Office of the Navy Inspector General, the Naval Telecommunications Command, and the Strategic Systems Project Office of the Naval Sea Systems Command.

(Area Code 202)

General Counsel: Craig S. King 694-1994
Principal Deputy General Counsel:
Chester Paul Beach Jr 694-5066
Deputy General Counsel/Logistics: Harvey J. Wilcox ...692-7136
Assistant General Counsel/Acquisition: Edward L. Saul .692-7155
Assistant General Counsel/Civilian Personnel Law:
Joseph G. Lynch 692-7186

(Area Code 202)

Assistant General Counsel/Ethics: Roger T. McNamara ...692-7172
Associate General Counsel/Litigation:
C. John Turnquist 746-1000
Associate General Counsel/Management: Fred A. Phelps ...692-7328
Facsimile 746-1032

FIELD OFFICES

California

Counsel: Ann Wansley
Naval Aviation Depot, Bldg 5A, Code 011, Alameda, CA 94501-5021. Tel: 415/263-6644.

Counsel: Randall B. Pyles
U.S. Marine Corps, Western Area Counsel Office, Bldg 1160, Room 246, Camp Pendleton, CA 92055-5001. Tel: 619/725-5610.

Counsel: Johnny S. Unpingo
Naval Weapons Center, Code 012, China Lake, CA 93555-6001. Tel: 619/437-3481.

Counsel: Virginia K. Stewart
Naval Weapons Station, Code L, Concord, CA 94520-5000. Tel: 415/671-5576/5575.

Counsel: Ronald G. Ress
COMCABWEST Code AQ, Marine Corps Air Station, El Toro, CA, 92709-5000. Tel: 714/651-3805.

Counsel: vacant
Naval Regional Contracting Center Detachment, Long Beach, CA, 90822-5095. Tel: 213/547-6676.

Counsel: Samuel Pinn, Jr.
Long Beach Naval Shipyard, Bldg 300. Rm 155, Naval Sea Systems Command, Long Beach, CA 90822. Tel: 213/547-8124/8130.

Counsel: Vacant
Naval Supply Center, Code 01, Bldg 311-2E, Oakland, CA 94625-5000, Tel: 415/466-4260.

Counsel: Allan Freidson
Military Sealift Command, Pacific Naval Supply Center, Bldg 310, Oakland, CA 94625-5010. Tel: 415/466-4923.

Counsel: Richard L. Spector
Public Works Center, San Francisco Bay, P.O. Box 24003, Oakland, CA. 94623-5000. Tel: 415/466-3348.

Counsel: Donald S. Safford
Pacific Missile Test Center, Code 009C, Point Mugu, CA 93042-5000. Tel: 805/989-7735/1696.

Counsel: Scott E. Miller
Naval Ship Weapon Systems Engineering Station, Code 00C, Port Hueneme, CA 93043-5007. Tel: 805/982-8246.

Counsel: Arthur F. Thibodeau
NAVFAC Contracts Office, Naval Construction Battalion Center, Code 27C, Bldg 90, Port Hueneme, CA 93043-5000. Tel: 805/985-3997.

Douglas P. Hinds
Western Division,Litigation Office, Legal Services Support Group, Office of the General Counsel, P.O. Box 727, San Bruno, CA 94066-0720. Tel: 415/877-7109.

Counsel: Vacant
Western Division, Naval Facilities Engineering Command, P.O. Box 727, San Bruno, CA 94066-0720. Tel: 415/877-7113.

Counsel: Linda B. Oliver
Naval Electronic Systems Engineering Center, P.O. Box 80337, San Diego, CA 92138-3288. Tel: 619/524-3141.

DEPARTMENT OF DEFENSE

Counsel: Stephen E. Katz
Naval Regional Contracting Center, Code 02, 937 North Harbor Drive, San Diego, CA 92132. Tel: 619/532-2198/96.

Counselor for the Supervisor of Ship Building, Conversion and Repair: Michael A. Reilly
USN, Code 130, Naval Station, Box 119, San Diego, CA 02136. Tel: 619/556-1068.

Counsel: John W. Higley
Naval Aviation Depot, North Island NAS, San Diego, CA 92135-5112. Tel: 619/545-2929.

Counsel: Timothy K. Dowd
Naval Ocean Systems Center, Code 0012, San Diego, CA 92152-5000. Tel: 619/553-3001.

Counsel: Jan M. Whitacre
Code 09C, Navy Public Works Center, Box 113, Naval Station, San Diego, CA 92136-5113. Tel: 619/556-1549.

Counsel: Jack L. Wells
NAVFAC Detachment, Broadway Complex Project Office, 555 West Beech Street, Suite 101, San Diego, CA 92101-2937. Tel: 619/532-3290.

Counsel: Daryl C. Dawson
Southwest Division, Naval Facilities Engineering Command, San Diego, CA 92132-5190. Tel: 619/532-2316.

Counsel to Supervisor of Shipbuilding, Conversion and Repair: Collin Lau
USN, Code 130, San Francisco, CA 94124-2996. Tel: 415/641-2546.

Counsel: Dennis O. Sanders
Naval Weapons Station, Code L, Bldg 206, Seal Beach, CA 90740-5000. Tel: 213/594-7603.

Counsel: Harold M. Dixon
Strategic Systems Program Office, Code SPLE-5, 1111 Lockheed Way, Bldg 181-B, Sunnyvale, CA 04089-3509. Tel: 408/756-3662.

Counsel: Joseph F. Smith
Mare Island Naval Shipyard, Code 107, Vallejo, CA 94592-5100. Tel: 707/646-4157.

Counsel: Robert E. Moyer
Counsel: Naval Regional Contracting Center, Code 1020, Mail Stop P28, Mare Island Naval Shipyard, Vallejo, CA 94592-5100. Tel: 707/648-2601.

Counsel: Kay F. Teeters
Office of Civilian Personnel Management, Northwest Region, 2890 North Main Street, Suite 301, Walnut Creek, CA 94596-2739. Tel: 415/246-5994.

Connecticut
Counsel for the Supervisor of Shipbuilding, Conversion and Repair: Patricia A. Kilcoyne
USN, Groton, CT 06340. Tel: 203/446-5068/7486.

District of Columbia
Counsel: Lynn L. Bush
Chesapeake Division, Code 09C, Naval Facilities Engineering Command, Washington Navy Yard, Bldg 212, Washington, D.C. 20374-2121. Tel: 202/433-3636.

Counsel: Robert H. Swennes, II
Naval Research Laboratory, 4555 Overlook Avenue, SW, Washington, D.C. 20375-5000. Tel: 202/767-2244.

Counsel: David P. Andross
Naval Data Automation Command, Washington Navy Yard, Bldg 166, Washington, D.C. 20374-1662. Tel: 202/433-4025.

Counsel: Mark R. Wiener
Automatic Data Processing Selection Office, Washington Navy Yard, Bldg 218, Washington, D.C. 20374-2181. Tel: 202/433-2636.

Counsel: Peter D. Butt
Naval Regional Contracting Center, Washington Navy Yard, Bldg 200, Code 04S, Washington, D.C. 20374-2004. Tel: 202/433-7167.

Counsel: Karen McCoy
Navy Regional Data Automation Center, Washington Navy Yard, Bldg 196, Washington, D.C. 20374-2004. Tel: 202/433-3524.

Counsel: Michael F. Bowman
Navy Inspector General, Washington Navy Yard, Bldg 200, Rm 100, Washington, D.C. 20374-2001. Tel: 202/433-2222.

Counsel: Eric A. Lile
Naval Telecommunications Command, 4401 Massachusetts Avenue, Washington, D.C. 20390-5290. Tel: 202/282-2522.

Counsel: Cornelius J. Collins, Jr.
Marine Corps Research Development & Acquisition Command, Washington, D.C. 20380-0001. Tel: 202/694-2490.

Florida
Counsel: Kenneth J. Emmanuel
Naval Aviation Depot, Code 007-NAS, Jacksonville, FL 32212-0016. Tel: 904/772-3791.

Counsel: James L. Gardner
Naval Supply Center, Code 03, P.O. Box 97, Jacksonville, FL 32212-0097. Tel: 904/772-5252.

Counsel for the Supervisor of Shipbuilding, Conversion and Repair: Mary P. Argenzio-West
USN, Code 130, Drawer T, Mayport Naval Station, Jacksonville, FL 32228-0020. Tel: 904/246-5008.

Counsel: Bernard T. Decker
Naval Training Systems Center, Code 004, 12350 Research Parkway, Orlando, FL 32826-3224. Tel: 407/380-8107.

Counsel: Starr J. Sinton
Naval Coastal Systems Center, Code 051, Panama City, FL 32407-5000. Tel: 904/234-4646.

Counsel: James R, Russell
Naval Aviation Depot, Code 007, Naval Air Station, Pensacola, FL 32508-5300. Tel: 904/452-3745.

Counsel: Kenneth J. Densmore
Chief of Naval Education & Training, Code 00D, Bldg 268, Pensacola, FL 32508-5110. Tel: 904/452-4828.

Counsel: Mark S. Lewis
Public Works Center, Naval Air Station, Bldg 458, Pensacola, FL 32508-6400. Tel: 904/452-3502

Georgia
Counsel: Michael G. Winchell
Southeastern Bases, Marine Corps Logistics Base, Albany, Georgia 31704-5000. Tel: 912/439-5449.

Counsel for Officer in Charge of Construction: David J. Rowland
Trident, Naval Facilities Engineering Command, 293 Point Peter Road, St. Mary's, GA 31558-0768. Tel: 912/673-2402.

Hawaii
Counsel: Paul M. Sullivan
Naval Facilities Engineering Command, Pacific Division, Pearl Harbor, HI 96860-7300. Tel: 808/471-8460.

Counsel: Jeffrey A. Wayne
Officer in Charge of Construction, Contracts, Mid-Pacific, Pearl Harbor, HI 96860-5420. Tel: 808/474-5147.

Counsel: Elizabeth Rivera
Naval Supply Center, P.O. Box 300Pearl Harbor, HI 96860-5300. Tel: 808/474-0611.

Counsel: Abigail D. Ogawa
Navy Public Works Center, Pearl Harbor, HI 96860-5350. Tel: 808/471-4535.

Counsel: Thomas H. Peters
Pearl Harbor Naval Shipyard, Code 107, P.O.Box 400, Pearl Harbor, HI 96860-5350. Tel: 808/474-0270.

Illinois
Counsel: James A. Sparks
Navy Public Works Center, Code 09C, Bldg 1A, Great Lakes, IL 60088-5600. Tel: 312/688-3780.

Indiana
Counsel: Pedro DeJesus
Naval Weapons Support Center, Crane, IN 47522-5000. Tel: 812/ 854-1130.

Counsel: Donald J. Sherfick
Naval Avionics Center (Code 007), 6000 East 21st Street, Indianapolis, IN 46219-2189. Tel: 317/353-7007.

Kentucky
Counsel: Dorothy E. O'Brien
Code 00L, Naval Ordnance Station, 5400 Southside Drive, Louisville, KY 40214-5001. Tel: 502/364-5331.

Maine
Counsel: David Agazarian
Supervisor of Shipbuilding, Conversion, and Repair, USN, Code 130, 574 Washington Street, Bath, ME 04530-0998. Tel: 207/443-6611, Ext. 349.

Maryland
Counsel: John E. Bjerke
David Taylor Research Center, Code 005L, Bethesda, MD 20084-5000. Tel: 301/227-1890.

Counsel: David A. Spevak
Intellectual Property, Naval Medical Research and Development Command, Bethesda, MD 20814-5000. Tel: 301/295-1453.

Counsel: John R. Osing
Naval Medical Materiel Support Command Health Services Contracting Support Detachment Fort Detrick, Frederick, MD 21701-5015. Tel: 301/663-2157/8.

Counsel: Susan K. Luther
Naval Ordnance Station, Indian Head Supply Department, Code LC, Indian Head, MD 20640-5000. Tel: 301/283-7688.

Counsel: Anthony J. Sweeney
Naval Aviation Depot Operations Center Building 449, Patuxent River, MD 20670-5449. Tel: 301/863-3284.

Counsel: Vacant
Procurement Office, Supply Department, Bldg 588, Naval Air Station, Patuxent River, MD 20670-5409. Tel: 301/863-1826.

Counsels:Kenneth E. Walden / Benjamin M. Plotkin
Office of Counsel, Naval Surface Warfare Center, White Oak Laboratory, Silver Spring, MD 20903-500. Tel: 301/394-2174.

Massachusetts
Counsel for the Supervisor of Shipbuilding, Conversion and Repair: Brian M. Kingston
USN, Code 130, 495 Summer Street, Boston, MA 02210. Tel: 617/451-4606.

Mississippi
Counsel for the Supervisor of Shipbuilding, Conversion and Repair: William E. Pressly
USN, Code 130, Pascagoula, MS 39568-2210. Tel: 601/769-4200.

Counsel: Vacant
Naval Ocean Research and Development Activity, Code 150, Stennis Space Center, MS 39529-5004. Tel: 601/688-4825.

Counsel: Robert E. Young
c/o Commander, Naval Oceanography Command, Code N12, Stennis Space Center, MS 39529-5004. Tel: 601/688-5867.

Missouri
Charles M. Stringer
Marine Corps Finance Center, Kansas City, MO 64197-0001. Tel: 816/926-7123.

Counsel: Michael A. Guerra
Naval Plant Representative Office, McDonnell-Douglas Corporation, P.O. Box 516, St. Louis, MO 63166-0516. Tel: 314/232-5176.

New Hampshire
Counsel: James L. Fender
Portsmouth Naval Shipyard, Code 100L, Portsmouth, NH 03801-2590. Tel: 207/438-2880.

New Jersey
Counsel: John P. McCambridge
Military Sealift Command, Atlantic, Military Ocean Terminal, Bldg 42, Code L7, Bayonne, NJ 07002-5399. Tel: 201/823-7510.

Counsel: Lenore K. Strakowsky
Naval Air Engineering Center, Code 00G, Bldg 129, Lakehurst, NJ 08733-5028. Tel: 201/323-2738.

New York
Counsel: Anne D. Davenport
Naval Plant Representative Office, Grumman Aerospace Corporation, Code 09A, Bethpage, NY 11714-3593. Tel: 516/575-2127.

Counsel for the Supervisor of Shipbuilding, Conversion and Repair: Anthony J. Molligo
USN, Code 130, Flushing and Washington Avenue, Brooklyn, NY 11251-9000. Tel: 718/834-2388.

Naval Supply Systems Command Field Counsel: Demetria T. Carter, New York Navy Resale & Services Support Office, Fort Wadsworth, Staten Island, NY 10305-5097. Tel: 718/390-3921.

North Carolina
Counsel: F.M. Lorenz, Col, USMC,
Eastern Area Counsel Office, Marine Corps Base, Camp Lejeune, NC 28542. Tel: 919/451-5860

Ohio
Counsel: Gary R. Bryant-Wolf
Navy Finance Center, 1240 East 9th Street, Room 2757, Cleveland, OH 44199-2055. Tel: 216/522-5396.

Pennsylvania
Counsel: Carl S. Chronister
Navy Ships Parts Control Center, P.O. Box 2020, Mechanicsburg, PA 17055-0788. Tel: 717/790-2424.

DEPARTMENT OF DEFENSE

Counsel: Michael J. Cunningham
Naval Regional Contracting Center, Bldg 600, U.S. Naval Base, Philadelphia, PA 19112-5082. Tel: 215/897-5408.

Counsel: Frank H. Lewis
Northern Division, Naval Facilities Engineering Command, Bldg 77, U.S. Naval Base, Philadelphia, PA 19112-5094. Tel: 215/897-6105/6.

Counsel: Harry D. Boonin
Aviation Supply Office, 700 Robbins Avenue, Philadelphia, PA 19111-5098. Tel: 215/697-2142.

Counsel: Jerome A. Snyder
Philadelphia Naval Shipyard, Code 107, Bldg 4, Room 1497, Department of the Navy, Philadelphia, PA 19112-5083. Tel: 215/897-4310/3669.

Counsel: Carl N. German
Naval Ship Systems Engineering Station, Code 00L, Philadelphia, PA 19112-5083. Tel: 215/897-7445.

Counsel: Robert G. Janes
Naval Air Development Center, Code 095, Warminster, PA 18974-5000. Tel: 215/441-3000.

Rhode Island
Counsel: Kenneth E. Nelligan
Naval Underwater Systems Center, Bldg 11, Newport, RI 02840-5047. Tel: 401/841-3653.

South Carolina
Counsel: J. William Green
Southern Division, Naval Facilities Engineering Command, P.O. Box 10068, Charleston, SC 29411. Tel: 803/743-0706.

Counsel: Robert C. Peterson
Naval Supply Center, Charleston, SC 29408-6303. Tel: 803/743-4502.

Counsel: Michael L. Geffen
Charleston Naval Shipyard, U.S. Naval Base, Bldg 234, Code 107, Charleston, SC 29408-6100. Tel: 803/743-3178.

Counsel: Gail R. Heriot
Naval Weapons Station, Code C8, Charleston, SC 29408-7000. Tel: 803/764-7888.

Virginia
Counsel: Pamela H. Page
Office of Civilian Personnel Management, Capitol Region, Code CAPR-09L, 801 North Randolph Street, Arlington, VA 22203-1927. Tel: 703/696-4029.

Counsel: Thomas J. Greenley
Naval Surface Weapons Center, Code C7, Dahlgren, VA 22448-5000. Tel: 202/663-7578.

Counsel for the Supervisor of Shipbuilding Conversion and Repair: Lawrence M. Spigel
USN, Newport News, VA 23607-2785. Tel: 804/380-7041.

Counsel, Atlantic Division: John S. Wittman
Naval Facilities Engineering Command, U.S. Naval Base, Norfolk, VA 23511-6287. Tel: 804/444-9507.

Counsel: Theodore H. Hoffman
Naval Supply Center, Code 08, Norfolk, VA 23512-5000. Tel: 804/444-4331.

Counsel: Cara C. Bellassai
Navy Acquisition Management Training Office, Code 04, Naval Supply Center, Bldg WI43-6, Norfolk, VA 23512-5000. Tel: 804/445-4998.

Counsel: David E. Kirkpatrick
Naval Aviation Depot, Code 005, Norfolk, VA 23511-5899. Tel: 804/444-5858.

Counsel: Alex H. Adkins
Office of Civilian Personnel Management, Southeast Region, Bldg A-67, Naval Station, Norfolk, VA 23511-6098. Tel: 804/444-7470.

Counsel: David R. Forbes
Norfolk Naval Shipyard, Code 107, Portsmouth, VA 23709-5000. Tel: 804/396-8625.

Counsel: Stephen P. Anderson
Supervisor of Shipbuilding, Conversion and Repair, USN, Code 130A, P.O. Box 215, Portsmouth, VA 23705-0215. Tel: 804/396-7779.

Counsel: Richard D. Hine
Marine Corps Combat Development Command, Lejeune Hall, Quantico, VA 22134. Tel: 703/640-3009.

Washington
Counsel: Lawrence E. Little
Naval Supply Center, Puget Sound, Code 03, Bremerton, WA 98314-5100. Tel: 206/476-2939.

Counsel for the Supervisor of Shipbuilding, Conversion and Repair: Jesse W. Bendahan
USN, Seattle, WA 98115. Tel: 206/526-3408.

Counsel: John H. Wright
Engineering Field Activity, Northwest, Western Division, Naval Facilities Engineering Command, 3505 N.W. Anderson Hill Road, P.O. Box 2366, Silverdale, WA 98383-2366. Tel: 206/476-5779.

England
Counsel: Counsel for the Commander in Chief: Charles H.T. Springer (London, England)
U.S. Naval Forces, Europe, Department of the Navy, Box 4, FPO New York 09553-2000. Tel: 011-409-4183-14283 Ext 4030.

Counsel: John L. DeGurse, Jr.
Military Sealift Command, Europe, FPO New York 09553-2000. Tel: 011-441-868-2366 Ext 351.

Italy
Counsel: Charles P. Mead
Naval Regional Contracting Center, U.S. Naval Support Activity, Naples, Italy, Box 50, FPO New York 09521 Tel: NSA 760-4125. Direct Dial: 9-011-39-81-724-4125/6.

Counsel, Atlantic Division: Deborah G. Sciascia
Naval Facilities Engineering Command, NSA, Box 51, FPO New York 09521, Naples, Italy. Tel: NSA 724-4133. Direct Dial: 011-39-81-570-6065/6028.

Japan
Counsel, Far East Asia: William B. Garvais
Military Sealift Command, FPO Seattle 98760-2600. Yokohama, Japan. Tel: 9-011-81-045-641-0794.

Counsel: Otto A. Thompson, Jr.
Naval Supply Depot, FPO Seattle 98762-1500. Yokosuka, Japan. Tel: 9-011-81-46-826-1911/7734.

Guam Mariana Islands
Counsel for the Officer in Charge of Construction: Gary W. Lunter
Naval Facilities Engineering Command Contracts, Guam Mariana Islands, FPO San Francisco, CA 96630. Tel: (011) 671-339-2117.

Philippines
Counsel: Vacant
Naval Supply Depot, Philippines, Box 33, FPO San Francisco, CA 96651. Tel: 9-011-63-898-843-583. (Republic of the Philippines, Subic Bay)

Counsel: David C. Coker
Office in Charge of Construction, Naval Facilities Engineering Command Contracts, Southwest Pacific, APO San Francisco, CA 96528. Tel: 011-63-288-9611.
(Republic of the Philippines, Manila)

Spain
Counsel, Officer in Charge of Construction: Lawrence J. Lippolis
Naval Facilities Engineering Command Contracts, Mediterranean, APO New York 09285.(Madrid, Spain) Tel: Madrid 341-266-7585. International Area: Code 341 then 541-6852-7129.

OFFICE OF THE CHIEF OF NAVAL OPERATIONS

(Area Code 202)

Chief of Naval Operations: Adm. Carlisle A.H. Trost 695-6007
Special Assistant for Legal Matters:
Rear Adm. Everette D. Stumbaugh 694-7420
Special Assistant for Naval Investigative Matters:
Rear Adm. William L. Schachte .... (703) 325-9820
Special Counsel: Cdr. Paul Thompson 695-9791
Facsimile 697-6290

Office of the Vice Chief of Naval Operations
Assistant for Legal and Legislative Matters:
Cdr. R.B. Swanson 695-3480
Freedom of Information Act Office 694-2817
Facsimile 694-8151

Office of the Deputy Chief of Naval Operations (Manpower, Personnel and Training)
Special Assistant for Legal Support:
Capt. Biff Le Grand 694-2225
Facsimile 693-1746

Bureau of Medicine and Surgery
Special Assistant for Medico-Legal Matters:
Cdr. John K. Heneberry 653-1363
Facsimile 653-1280

Office of Naval Intelligence
Assistant Director for Legal Matters:
Lt. Cdr. Joseph Callahan 697-0045
Facsimile 694-0230

Strategic Systems Programs
Counsel: Norman Shaw 695-2047
Facsimile 695-0453

Military Sealift Command
Counsel: Richard S. Haynes 433-0140
Inspector General: Com. Annette Brown 433-5099
Facsimile 433-0602

Naval Air Systems Command
Counsel: Margaret A. Olsen 692-7021
Associate General Counsel for Intellectual Property:
John L. Forrest 692-3456
Inspector General: Capt. Dennis H. Christian 692-8582
Assistant Commander for Contracts: Rear Adm.
W.R. Morris 692-0916
Small Business Office 692-0935
Facsimile 746-1597

Naval Data Automation Command
Counsel: David Andross 433-4025
Inspector General: Cdr. Charles Whittaker 433-4309
Facsimile 433-6442

Naval Facilities Engineering Command
Counsel: Matthew K. McElhaney .... (703) 325-9067
Deputy Commander for Contracts: Paul Buonaccorsi (703) 325-9121
Small Business Economic Utilization and Contractor
Liaison Office .... (703) 325-8549
Contract Award and Review Board .... (703) 325-8548

(Area Code 202)

Inspector General: Capt. Warren Garbe .... (703) 325-8548
Facsimile .... (703) 325-0979

Naval Intelligence Command
Inspector General: Jim C. Runyon .... (301) 763-3557
Facsimile .... (301) 763-1469

Naval Investigative Service Command
Director: Rear Adm. William L. Schachte 433-8800
Staff Judge Advocate: Major Ron McNeil 433-9617

Counsel: John M. Shea 433-9617
Director for Criminal Investigations: Robert Powers .. 433-9249
Director for Information/Personnel Security:
Charles Van Page 433-8841
Director for Law Enforcement/Physical Security:
James O'Hara 433-9077
Inspector General: Peter Reilly 433-8826
Facsimile 433-9322

Naval Sea Systems Command
Counsel: Eugene P. Angrist .... (703) 602-8170
Staff Judge Advocate: Cdr. John M. Tapajcik ... (703) 602-4369
Deputy Commander for Contracts:
Capt. Eugene B. Harshbarger .... (703) 602-7977
Facsimile .... (703) 602-2631

Naval Security Group Command
Staff Judge Advocate Officer: vacant 282-2620
Inspector General: Capt. Charles Authement 282-0306
Facsimile 282-0329

Naval Supply Systems Command
Counsel: Charles J. McManus 695-5519
Deputy Commander for Contracting Management:
Capt. Phillip H. Harrington 695-4377
Inspector General: Capt. J.F. Anderson 695-5391
Public Affairs 697-3795
Small & Disadvantaged Business Utilization Office ... 697-5952
Facsimile 695-5829

Naval Telecommunications Command
Counsel: Eric Lile 282-2522
Inspector General: Capt. Eugene Davis 282-0495
Facsimile 282-0366

Naval Legal Service Command
Commander: Rear Adm. John E. Gordon .... (703) 325-9820
Deputy Assistant/Inspector General:
Capt. James E. Riley .... (703) 325-6117
Facsimile .... (703) 325-2159

Naval Military Personnel Command
Legal Counsel: Capt. Biff LeGrand 694-2225
Facsimile 693-1746

Space and Naval Warfare Systems Command
Counsel: Harvey J. Nathan .... (703) 602-8458
Inspector General: Capt. Henry Chakley .... (703) 602-7534
Contracts Office .... (703) 602-7777
Facsimile .... (703) 602-1717

DEPARTMENT OF DEFENSE

OFFICE OF THE JUDGE ADVOCATE GENERAL

200 Stovall Street, Alexandria, VA 22332-2400

There are currently about 1,000 attorneys who are Naval officers within the Office of The Judge Advocate General. The duties of Judge Advocates and the personnel policies and programs governing them vary from base to base and ship to ship. One of the primary clients at any base or ship is the base or ship commander, whose job is similar to that of a city manager; as a result, the variety of legal problems is limitless. Judge Advocates are involved with problems concerning military justice; claims for and against the Government; legal assistance; and such other areas as labor, environmental, international, real property, government contracts, and administrative law.

(Area Code 202)

Judge Advocate General: Rear Admiral Everette D. Stumbaugh 694-7420
Deputy Judge Advocate General:
Rear Admiral John E. Gordon ....(703) 325-9820
Special Assistant for Fleet Affairs:
Capt. Robert C. Berley ....(703) 325-6117
Inspector General: Capt. James E. Riley ....(703) 325-6118
Navy-Marine Corps Appellate Review Activity
Officer in Charge: Col. Charles H. Mitchell Jr (703) 325-9820
Appellate Defense Division Director:
Capt. Arthur R. Philpott 433-4161
Appellate Government Division Director:
Cdr. Thomas W. Osborne 433-2998
Navy-Marine Corps Court of Military Review Chief Judge:
Capt. Edward M. Byrne 433-2272
Navy-Marine Corps Trial Judiciary Chief Judge:
Capt. Ron E. Garvin 433-4682
Facsimile ....(703) 325-9152

Operations and Management
Assistant Judge Advocate General:
Rear Admiral William L. Schachte 433-8800
Principal Deputy Assistant Judge Advocate General:
Capt. H.E. Grant ....(703) 325-9850
Deputy Assistant Judge Advocate General for:
Fiscal and Administrative Support:
Dennis J. Oppman ....(703) 325-0786
Management and Plans:
Cdr. John E. Dombroski ....(703) 325-8312
Military Personnel/JAG Corps Assignment/
Placement: Capt. Peter Wilie .(703) 325-9830
Reserve and Retired Personnel Programs:
Cdr. Richard Ozmun ....(703) 325-9736

Civil Law
Assistant Judge Advocate General:
Capt. Timothy D. Keating ....(703) 325-9850
Deputy Assistant Judge Advocate General for:
Administrative Law: Capt. David A. Guy .(703) 325-9860
Environmental Law:
Capt. Richard M. Mollison 692-2247
International Law: Capt. John Henriksen 697-9161
Special Programs: Cdr. Robert Monahan (703) 325-9536

General Law
Assistant Judge Advocate General:
Capt. John J. Geer Jr ....(703) 325-9850
Deputy Assistant Judge Advocate General for:
Admiralty: Capt. Patrick C. Turner ....(703) 325-9744
Civil Affairs: Col. R.M. McBride ....(703) 325-9752
Claims and Tort Litigation: Mike Hannas (703) 325-9880
General Litigation:
Capt. Dennis L. Mandsager ....(703) 325-9870
Investigations: Col. R. McBride (Acting)(703) 325-9530
Legal Assistance: Cdr. Joseph Scranton (703) 325-7920

Military Justice
Assistant Judge Advocate General:
Col. Charles H. Mitchell Jr ....(703) 325-9820
Deputy Assistant Judge Advocate General for Military Justice: Capt. Thomas K. Kahn ....(703) 325-9890

NAVAL LEGAL SERVICE OFFICES

Washington, DC
Commanding Officer: Capt. Craig Vanderhoef
U.S. Naval Legal Service Office, Washington Navy Yard, 9th and M Streets SE, Bldg 200-3, Washington, DC 20374-2003.
Tel: 202/433-3374.

California
Commanding Officer: Capt. Howard D. Bohaboy
U.S. Naval Legal Service Office, Naval Station, Treasure Island, Bldg #450, Room 205, San Francisco CA 94130-5029.
Tel: 415/986-6166.

Commanding Officer: Capt. Thomas A. Morrison
U.S. Naval Legal Service Office, Naval Station (Building #2) Long Beach, CA 90822-5075. Tel: 213/547-8336.

Commanding Officer: Capt. Allen C. Rudy, Jr.
U.S. Naval Legal Service Office, Naval Station, Box 138, Building #73, Room 206, San Diego, CA 92136-5138.
Tel: 619/556-1697/1699.

Connecticut
Commanding Officer: Cdr. Patrick W. Kelley
U.S. Naval Legal Service Office, Box 10, NAVSUBASE, New London, Building #137, 2nd Floor, Groton, CT 06349-5010.
Tel: 203/449-3741.

Florida
Commanding Officer: Capt. Richard Zimmerman
U.S. Naval Legal Service Office, Box 217, Naval Station, Building #T-31, 1st Floor, Mayport, FL 32228-0217.
Tel: 904/246-5708.

Commanding Officer: Capt. Frederic G. Derocher
U.S. Naval Legal Service Office, Box 107, NAS, Building #8, Room 224, Ranger Street, Jacksonville, FL 32212-0107. Tel: 904/772-2565.

Commanding Officer: Capt. Russell A. Johnson
U.S. Naval Legal Service Office, NAS, Building #45, 3rd Floor, Room 313, Pensacola, FL 32508-6000. Tel: 904/452-4576.

Hawaii
Commanding Officer: Capt. Arthur R. Thomas
U.S. Naval Legal Service Office, Box 124, Naval Base, Building #1E, 4th Floor, Pearl Harbor, HI 96860-5110. Tel: 808/471-0291.

Illinois
Commanding Officer: Capt. Geoffrey Greiveldinger
U.S. Naval Legal Service Office, Naval Training Center, Building #1, Room 230, Great Lakes, IL 60088-5029. Tel: 312/688-4753.

Pennsylvania
Commanding Officer: Capt. Charles W. Tucker
U.S. Naval Legal Service Office, Naval Base, Building 6, Philadelphia, PA 19112-5096. Tel: 215/897-6600.

Rhode Island
Commanding Officer: Capt. Thomas Watson
U.S. Naval Legal Service Office, Naval Education & Training Center, Building #360, Newport, RI 02841-5030. Tel: 401/841-2176.

Commanding Officer: Capt. Peter A. Hewit
U.S. Naval Legal Service Office, Naval Education and Training Center, Bldg #360-N, Newport, RI 02841-5018. Tel: 401/841-3491.

South Carolina
Commanding Officer: Capt. Ronald W. Scholz
U.S. Naval Legal Service Office, Naval Base, Building #NH-55, Room 122, Charleston, SC 29408-5400. Tel: 803/743-3138.

Tennessee
Commanding Officer: Capt. James G. Orr
U.S. Naval Legal Service Office, NAS, Memphis, Building #5-794, 2nd Floor, East Wing, Millington, TN 38054-5030. Tel: 901/873-5201.

Texas
Commanding Officer: CDR Richard G. Stewart, Jr.
U.S. Naval Legal Service Office, NAS, Building #3, Corpus Christi, TX 78419-5214. Tel: 512/939-3765.

Virginia
Deputy Judge Advocate General and Commander of Naval Legal Service Command: Rear Admiral John E. Gordon
200 Stovall Street, Alexandria, VA 22332-2400. Tel: 703/325-9820.

Commanding Officer: Duvall M. Williams, Jr.
U.S. Naval Legal Service Office, Naval Base, Building A50, Room 125, Norfolk, VA 23511-6198. Tel: 804/444-7561.

Washington
Commanding Officer: Capt. Ronald J. Beachy
U.S. Naval Legal Service Office, Building #9, Room 215, 7500 Sand Point Way, NE, Seattle, WA 98115-5002. Tel: 206/526-3083.

Guam
Commanding Officer: CDR Glenn N. Gonzalez
U.S. Naval Legal Service Office, U.S. Naval Legal Service Office Guam, Box 3169, Sect. 4, Code 30.84, U.S. Naval Station Guam. FPO San Francisco, CA 96630-2400. Tel: 011-671-333-2061/2/3/4/5.

Italy
Commanding Officer: Capt. Richard B. Schiff
U.S. Naval Legal Service Office, Edilizia Building II, VIA Scarfoglia, Agnano, Italy, Box 8, U.S. Naval Support Activity, FPO New York 09521. Tel: 39-81-724-4482.

Japan
Commanding Officer: Capt. Winston Hughes
U.S. Naval Legal Service Office, Box 14, Building #1555, 2nd Deck, FPO Seattle, 98762-2400. Yokosuka, Japan. Tel: 011-81-468-26-1911.

Philippines
Commanding Officer: Capt. Robert R. Rossi
U.S. Naval Legal Service Office, U.S. Naval Base, Box 35, Building 156, FPO San Francisco, CA 96651-2400. (Subic Bay) Tel: 011-63-47-384-6332/3/4.

OTHER NAVAL LEGAL OFFICES/LEGAL PERSONNEL

(Area Code 202)

Board for Correction of Naval Records
Executive Director: W. Dean Pfeiffer 694-1402

Naval Council of Personnel Boards
Counsel: Capt. Kenneth Drew 696-4366
Employee Appeals Review Board Chairman:
Kenneth Friedman (Acting) 696-4660
Naval Clemency and Parole Board: vacant 696-4592
Naval Discharge Review Board: Capt. A.W. Rehfield ...696-4881

(Area Code 202)

Office of Civilian Personnel Management
Counsel: Jan Gnerlich 696-4717

Office of the Chief of Naval Research
Corporate Counsel: Sophie Krasik 696-4271
Inspector General: M. Ed Hite 696-6692

U.S. MARINE CORPS HEADQUARTERS
Columbia Pike and Southgate Road, Arlington Annex
Arlington, VA 20380

DESCRIPTION: The primary mission of the United States Marine Corps is to provide Fleet Marine Forces of combined arms, together with supporting air components, for service with the Fleet in the seizure or defense of advanced naval bases and for the conduct of such land operations as may be essential to the prosecution of a naval campaign.

The Marine Corps provides detachments and organizations for service on armed vessels of the Navy and security detachments aboard naval stations/bases and other governmental installations and is also responsible for developing, in coordination with the other military services, the tactics, doctrine, techniques, and equipment employed by landing forces in amphibious operations.

(Area Code 202)

Commandant: Gen. Alfred M. Gray 694-2500
Public Affairs 694-8010
Inspector General: Major Gen. O.K. Steele 694-1533

(Area Code 202)

Freedom of Information Act/Privacy Officer 694-4008
Facsimile 695-5034

OFFICE OF THE COUNSEL FOR THE COMMANDANT (Room 2133)

(Area Code 202)

Counsel for the Commandant: Peter M. Murphy 694-2150
Deputy Counsel: Robert P. Cali 694-2490
Associate Counsel/Procurement: George Brezna 694-2150
Associate Counsel/Marine Corps Research and Development Acquisition Command: Neil Collins 696-0679

(Area Code 202)

Associate Counsel/Environmental Law: Lt. Col. Paul Wilbor 696-2150
Associate Counsel/Civilian Personnel Law: Major Richard H. Zales 694-4067
Associate Counsel/Land Use: Lt. Col. John P. Hertell 694-4067

U.S. MARINE CORPS JUDGE ADVOCATE DIVISION

Marine Judge Advocates draft wills and leases, advise military personnel on domestic relations and consumer protection matters, and advise commanders in the field. They also work in international, labor, torts, environmental, family, and aviation law. Judge advocates have appeared before Federal district courts, courts of appeal, the Merit Systems Protection Board, the Equal Employment Opportunity Commission, and the Nuclear Regulatory Commission.

(Area Code 202)

Staff Judge Advocate to the Commandant/Director: Brig. General Michael E. Rich 694-2737
Chief Defense Counsel: Col. George Lange III 694-2543
Military Law Branch Head: Lt. Col. Michael J. Cummings 694-1740

(Area Code 202)

Operational Law Branch Head: Lt. Col. Terry R. Kane 694-6799
Facsimile.. 695-5111

OFFICE OF STAFF JUDGE ADVOCATE TO THE COMMANDANT

Headquarters

Staff Judge Advocate to the Commandant/Director, Judge Advocate Division: Brigadier General M.E. Rich
Headquarters, U.S. Marine Corps, Washington, D.C. 20380.
Tel: 202/694-2737.

Deputy Staff Judge Advocate to the Commandant/Deputy Director, Judge Advocate Division: Col. G.W. Bond
Headquarters, U.S. Marine Corps, Washington, D.C. 20380.
Tel: 202/694-2737.

Arizona

Director, Joint Law Center: Lt. Colonel R.W. Grove
Marine Corps Air Station, Yuma, AZ 85364. Tel: 602/726-2890.

California

Staff Judge Advocate: Colonel J.P. McHenry
Marine Corps Recruit Depot, San Diego, CA 92140.
Tel: 619/524-4088.

Staff Judge Advocate: Lt. Colonel D.R. Jillisky
Marine Corps Air Ground Command, Twentynine Palms, CA 92278.
Tel: 619/368-6784.

Staff Judge Advocate: Major G.E. Lattin
7th Marine Expeditionary Brigade, Twentynine Palms, CA 92278. Tel: 619/368-6882.

Staff Judge Advocate: Colonel (Sel) W.J. Lucas
Marine Corps Air Station/COMCABWEST, El Toro, CA 92709.
Tel: 714/726-3727.

Staff Judge Advocate: Major E.J. McKay Jr
Marine Corps Logistics Base, Barstow, CA 92311.
Tel: 619/577-6879.

Staff Judge Advocate: Colonel G.L. Miller
Marine Corps Base, Camp Pendleton, CA 92055.
Tel: 619/725-5943.

Staff Judge Advocate: Colonel M.L. Haiman
I MEF/1st Marine Division, Camp Pendleton, CA 92055.
Tel: 619/725-8796.

Staff Judge Advocate: Lt. Colonel Ross Rayburn
1st Force Service Support Group, Camp Pendleton, CA 92055.
Tel: 619/725-8771.

Officer in Charge, Legal Service Support Section: Lt. Colonel R.E. Pearcy II
1st Force Service Support Group, Camp Pendleton, CA 92055.
Tel: 619/725-8772.

Staff Judge Advocate: Major S.M. Womack
5th Marine Expeditionary Brigade, Camp Pendleton, CA 92055.
Tel: 619/725-5148.

Regional Defense Counsel-Western Region: Lt. Colonel J.L. Siegel
Marine Corps Base, Camp Pendleton, CA 92055.
Tel: 619/725-4820.

Staff Judge Advocate, 3d MAW/Director, Legal Services, Marine Air Bases: Colonel E.J. Kline
Marine Corps Air Station, El Toro, CA 92709.
Tel: 714/726-3727.

Georgia

Staff Judge Advocate: Major E.B. Healey
Marine Corps Logistics Base, Albany, GA 31704.
Tel: 912/439-5213.

Hawaii
Staff Judge Advocate: Colonel E.W. Welch
Headquarters, Fleet Marine Force-Pacific, Camp Smith, HI 96861. Tel: 808/477-1638.

Staff Judge Advocate: Lt. Colonel D.L. Davis
1st Marine Expeditionary Brigade, Kaneohe Bay, HI 96863. Tel: 808/257-2160.

Louisiana
Staff Judge Advocate: Lt. Colonel R.D. Marlow
4th Marine Division, 4400 Dauphine Street, New Orleans, LA 70146. Tel: 504/948-5506.

Staff Judge Advocate: Lt. Colonel W.E. Bubsey
4th Marine Aircraft Wing, 4400 Dauphine Street, New Orleans, LA 70146. Tel: 504/948-1235.

North Carolina
Staff Judge Advocate: Colonel J.A. Cathcart
Marine Corps Base, Camp Lejeune, NC 28542. Tel: 919/451-5675.

Staff Judge Advocate: Colonel J.E. Goodrich
II MEF/2d Marine Division, Camp Lejeune, NC 28542. Tel: 919/451-8544.

Staff Judge Advocate: Lt. Colonel R.W. Leas
2d Force Service Support Group, Camp Lejeune, NC 28542. Tel: 919/451-5806.

Officer in Charge, Legal Service Support Group: Lt. Colonel W. Hellmer
2d Force Service Support Group, Camp Lejeune, NC 28542. Tel: 919/451-8308.

Staff Judge Advocate: Major C.H. Beale III
6th Marine Expeditionary Brigade, Camp Lejeune, NC 28542. Tel: 919/451-1389.

Regional Defense Counsel-Eastern Region: Lt. Colonel K. Naugle
Marine Corps Base, Camp LeJeune, NC 28542. Tel: 919/451-2286.

Director, Joint Law Center: Major S.L. Murray
Marine Corps Air Station, New River, NC 28545. Tel: 919/451-6386.

Staff Judge Advocate: Lt. Colonel A.W. Keller
Marine Corps Air Station/COMCABEAST, Cherry Point, NC 28533. Tel: 919/466-3559.

Staff Judge Advocate, 2d MAW/Director, Legal Services, Marine Air Bases Eastern Area: Colonel R.L. Vogel
Marine Corps Air Station, Cherry Point, NC 28533. Tel: 919/466-3559.

South Carolina
Staff Judge Advocate: Colonel G.W. Jones
Marine Corps Recruit Depot, Parris Island, SC 29905. Tel: 803/525-2292.

Director, Joint Law Center: Major C.F. Meyers
Marine Corps Air Station, Beaufort, SC 29904. Tel: 803/522-7382.

Virginia
Staff Judge Advocate: Col. M. C. Wholley
Marine Corps Base, Marine Corps Combat Development Command, Quantico, VA 22134. Tel: 703/640-2776.

Staff Judge Advocate: Colonel (Sel) D.E. Clancey
Headquarters, Fleet Marine Force-Atlantic, Norfolk, VA 23515. Tel: 804/444-6455.

Staff Judge Advocate: Lt. Colonel G.E. Holmes
4th Marine Expeditionary Brigade, NAB Little Creek, Norfolk, VA 23521. Tel: 804/363-8661.

OVERSEAS

Staff Judge Advocate: Lt. Colonel L.F. Henley Jr
Marine Corps Base, Camp Butler, Japan, FPO Seattle 98773.

Staff Judge Advocate: Lt. Colonel J.P. Fladeboe
Marine Corps Air Station-Iwakuni, FPO Seattle 98764. Tel: 011-81-827-21-4171 ext. 5591.

Staff Judge Advocate: Colonel W.L. Campbell
III MEF/3d Marine Division-Okinawa, FPO San Francisco 96602.

Officer in Charge, Legal Service Support Section: Colonel W.L. Campbell
3d Force Service Support Group-Okinawa, FPO San Francisco 96604.

Staff Judge Advocate: Lt. Colonel C.L. Carver
1st Marine Aircraft Wing-Okinawa, FPO San Francisco 96603.

Staff Judge Advocate: Lt. Colonel J. Composto
3d Force Service Support Group (Okinawa), FPO San Francisco 96604.

Staff Judge Advocate: Lt. Colonel M.J. Reardon
9th Marine Expeditionary Brigade (Okinawa), FPO San Francisco 96602.

Regional Defense Counsel-Pacific Region: Lt. Colonel H.A. Hopson
Marine Corps Base, Camp Butler, Japan, FPO Seattle 98773.

DEPARTMENT OF DEFENSE
KEY LEGAL AUTHORITIES

Major Regulations:

General Departmental Regulations: 32 C.F.R. Parts 1-399 (1989).
Defense Logistics Agency: 32 C.F.R. Parts 1280-1293 (1989).
Defense Acquisition Regulations (DAR): 32 C.F.R. Parts 1-39-(1984)[applicable only to contracts which preceded the effective date of the Federal Acquisition Regulation (FAR), Title 48 C.F.R., effective April 1, 1984].
Rules of Practice & Procedure-Courts of Military Review: 32 C.F.R. Part 150 (1989).
Personnel & Industrial Security Regulations: 32 C.F.R. Parts 154-159a (1989).
Department of the Army: 32 C.F.R. Parts 400-656 (1989).
Department of the Navy: 32 C.F.R. Parts 700-775 (1989).
Department of the Air Force: 32 C.F.R. Parts 800-989(1989).
U.S. Army Corps of Engineers: 33 C.F.R. Parts 203-384 (1989).
Department of the Navy Acquisition Regulation Supplement: 48 C.F.R. Parts 5215-5252 (1988).
Department of the Air Force Acquisition Regulation Supplement: 48 C.F.R. Parts 5315-5350 (1988).

DEPARTMENT OF DEFENSE

10 U.S.C. 2397-2397c--established standards of conduct, limitations on employment, and reporting requirements for potential conflicts of interest for current and former employees of defense contractors, former Department of Defense officials, and contacts between Department of Defense procurement officials and defense contractors.
Legislative History: 1982 U.S. Code Cong. & Admin. News 2598; 1985 U.S. Code Cong. & Admin. News 472; 1986 U.S. Code Cong. & Admin. News 5627.
Implementing Regulations: 32 C.F.R. Parts 40-40a (1989).

Military Selective Service Act of 1967, as amended, 50 U.S.C. App. 451 et seq.--established the selective service system and defined the parameters of the military service obligation.
Legislative History: 1967 U.S. Code Cong. & Admin. News 1308.
Implementing Regulations: 32 C.F.R. Part 50 (1989).

Armed Forces Reserve Act of 1952, as amended, 10 U.S.C. 261 et seq.--the basic statute governing the military Reserve Components.
Legislative History: 1952 U.S. Code Cong. & Admin. News 2005.

42 U.S.C. 665--obligates the Department of Defense to require child, or child and spousal support allotments from the pay and allowances of armed forces members who have failed to make periodic payments under a support order for two months or longer.
Legislative History: 1982 U.S. Code Cong. & Admin. News 781.
Implementing Regulations: 32 C.F.R. Part 54 (1989).

10 U.S.C. 1408--requires Department of Defense components to pay retired or retainer pay to the spouse or former spouse of a member or former member of the armed forces when required to do so by a court order.
Legislative History: 1984 U.S. Code Cong. & Admin. News 4174.
Implementing Regulations: 32 C.F.R. Part 63 (1989).

10 U.S.C. 1553--directs each military department to establish a Discharge Review Board to review the discharge or dismissal of former members of the armed forces on the Board's own motion or upon the request of the former member, his/her surviving spouse, next of kin, or legal representative after his/her death.
Legislative History: 1958 U.S. Code Cong. & Admin. News 4352.
Implementing Regulations: 32 C.F.R. Part 70 (1989).

10 U.S.C. 1076 et seq.--establishes and sets policy for the Civilian Health and Medical Program of the Uniformed Services (CHAMPUS), the comprehensive health care program for military dependents.
Legislative History: 1958 U.S. Code Cong. & Admin. News 4615.
Implementing Regulations: 32 C.F.R. Part 199 (1989).

Vietnam Era Veterans' Readjustment Assistance Act of 1974, as amended, 38 U.S.C. 2021-2026--protects the rights to reemployment with the same employer of persons inducted into the armed forces and reservists who volunteer for active duty.
Legislative History: 1974 U.S. Code Cong. & Admin. News 6313.
Implementing Regulations: 5 C.F.R. 353.101 et seq. (1989).

Uniform Code of Military Justice, as amended, 10 U.S.C. 801-940--sets forth the judicial and criminal provisions governing armed forces personnel and proceedings.
Legislative History: 1966 U.S. Code Cong. & Admin. News 3362.

Soldiers' and Sailors' Civil Relief Act of 1940, as amended, 50 U.S.C. App. 501-591--suspends enforcement of certain civil liabilities of persons in U.S. military service, including temporary suspension of legal proceedings during the period of such service.

Defense Production Act of 1950, as amended, 50 U.S.C. App. 2061-2166--authorizes the diversion of resources to military use and facilitates the expansion of productive facilities when necessary for national defense.
Legislative History: 1950 U.S. Code Cong. Service 3620.

Contract Disputes Act of 1978, as amended, 41 U.S.C. 601-613--generic statute authorizing Federal agencies to establish Boards of Contract Appeals to adjudicate contract disputes between the Government and Federal contractors.
Legislative History: 1978 U.S. Code Cong. & Admin. News 5235.

Export Administration Act of 1979, as amended, 50 U.S.C. App. 2401-2420--established U.S. export control policy and delegated certain authorities under the Act to the Department of Defense.
Legislative History: 1979 U.S. Code Cong. & Admin. News 1147; 1985 U.S. Code Cong. & Admin. News 108; 1988 U.S. Code Cong. & Admin. News 1547.

River and Harbor Act, 33 U.S.C. 1 et seq.--authorizes the Secretary of the Army to regulate the use, administration, and navigation of the navigable waters of the U.S. as public necessity may require for the protection of life and property, or for operations of the U.S in channel improvement, covering all matters not specifically delegated by law to other executive departments.

DEPARTMENT OF EDUCATION

400 Maryland Avenue, S.W.
Washington, D.C. 20202

DESCRIPTION: The Department of Education, which was established in 1980, coordinates and improves the administration of Federal education programs. The Department develops and implements programs and policies aimed at promoting equal access to education and improving the quality of education at all levels.

(Area Code 202)

Secretary: Lauro F. Cavazos 401-3000
Procurement Information 708-6821
Small and Disadvantaged Business Utilization 401-1500
Hot Line for Fraud, Waste, and Abuse
  Washington, D.C. Metro Area 755-2770
  Outside Washington, D.C. Metro Area .... (800) 647-8733
Public Affairs 401-1576
Facsimile 401-3130

Freedom of Information Act Office 401-0768
The FOIA office accepts written requests only. Requestors are divided into three groups: commercial, news media and research groups, and other. The first two groups are charged a copying fee of 10 cents per page. The cost for search and review is based on the salary of the person doing the search. The third group ("other") is also charged a copying fee of 10 cents per page, but the first 100 pages are free. They are also given two free hours of search time, but not review time. Call for more fee schedule information.

(Area Code 202)

Privacy Act Office 401-0768
The Privacy Act office accepts written requests only. A fee schedule does exist, but there is usually no charge for requests.

Library (Room 101) 357-6884
The library is open to the public Monday through Thursday from 9:00 AM until 4:00 PM. Books may be borrowed only if the person's company or school participates in interlibrary loan with the Department of Education Library.

OFFICE OF THE GENERAL COUNSEL (Room 4091)

The Office of the General Counsel (OGC) plays a critical role in many of the most challenging and controversial issues facing the Department, including constitutional issues related to the separation of church and state, equal protection, and due process; educational policy issues; the Federal role in education; and issues arising in the administrative operation of the Department.

Generally, the Office of General Counsel provides legal services to the Secretary of Education and other departmental officials, including: representing the Department in administrative litigation; assisting the Department of Justice in court litigation; drafting legislation and regulations; providing legal services with respect to administrative matters, such as those related to personnel, contracts, ethics, privacy and the Freedom of Information Act; and providing legal advice related to the administration of Federal aid to education programs and civil rights enforcement laws, such as Title VI of the 1964 Civil Rights Act, sex equity laws, and Section 504 of the Rehabilitation Act. The Office of General Counsel has no regional offices.

(Area Code 202)

General Counsel: Edward C. Stringer 401-2600
Senior Counsel: Theodore Sky 401-2603
Counsel to the Inspector General:
  Sarah Kemble 401-1730
  Ellen Bass 453-5816

The Office of General Counsel has two Deputy General Counsels: a Deputy General Counsel for Departmental Services and a Deputy General Counsel for Program Service.

The **Deputy General Counsel for Departmental Service** supervises the work of the following divisions:

*** Division of Business and Administrative Law,** which provides legal services required for the administration of the Department. The division handles legal issues arising with respect to contracts, grants, ethics, standards of conduct, EEO litigation and adverse actions, grievances, labor relations, personnel issues, budget/appropriations, the Freedom of Information Act, Privacy Act, Hatch Act, Government in Sunshine Act, the Family Educational Rights and Privacy Act, Equal Access to Justice Act, and claims by and against the Department in any of these areas.

*** Division of Legislative Counsel,** which drafts legislation and provides legal advice required in the development of legislative policies by the Department. The Division also reviews proposed congressional testimony and acts as liaison with the Office of Management and Budget (OMB) on legislative matters.

*** Division of Regulations Management,** which develops and monitors procedures for the preparation and clearance of regulations by the Department. The Division also advises on laws governing the need for regulations and procedures for their issuance.

(Area Code 202)

Deputy General Counsel: Mark A. Shiffrin 401-2603
Assistant General Counsel for Business and Administrative
  Law Division: William Haubert (Acting) 401-3690
Agency Ethics Official: Steven Y. Winnick 401-3124
Assistant General Counsel for Legislative Counsel
  Division: Jack Kristy 401-2670
Assistant General Counsel for Regulations Management
  Division: Steven N. Schatken 401-2670

The **Deputy General Counsel for Program Service** supervises and coordinates the work of these divisions:

*** Division of Educational Equity,** which provides legal advice in support of civil rights enforcement activities of the Department pertaining to race, national origin, sex, hardship, and age discrimination, in connection with provisions of Title VI of the 1964 Civil Rights Act, Title IX of the Education Amendments of 1972, the Education of the Handicapped Act, the Rehabilitation Act of 1973, the Bilingual Education Act, and the Women's Educational Equity Act. The Division also provides legal services relating to Federal aid-to-education and civil rights statutes, regulations, and policies, and works with Justice Department attorneys to represent the Department in court litigation.

* **Division of Elementary, Secondary, Adult, and Vocational Education,** which provides legal services for elementary and secondary school programs as well as to the Office of Vocational and Adult Education and other units within the Department. The Division is also involved in enforcement of grant conditions through audits, and aid to children attending private schools.

* **Division of Postsecondary Education and Education Research,** which provides legal services for postsecondary education programs and for research and library programs. The Division is heavily involved in enforcement efforts to eliminate fraud and abuse by some schools and financial institutions participating in the student financial aid programs, and to reduce the number of student loan default cases.

(Area Code 202)

Deputy General Counsel: Steven Y. Winnick 401-3124
Assistant General Counsel for Educational Equity Division: Susan Craig 401-2666
Assistant General Counsel for Elementary, Secondary, Adult, and Vocational Educational Division: Philip Rosenfelt 401-0807
Assistant General Counsel for Postsecondary Education and Educational Research Division: Harold Jenkins 401-2732

OFFICE OF HEARINGS AND APPEALS (Room 3053)

Decisions of the Office of the Administrative Law Judges is issued every two months. Contact Frank Furey, Senior Attorney on 202/401-2754 and ask to be placed on the distribution list. At present, this publication is distributed at no charge. Note: cases pursuant to the Higher Education Act are not included, but a copy of an individual decision may be obtained by contacting Frank Furey, Senior Attorney. Multiple copies or copies of this kind of decision over a period of time would have to be requested under FOIA.

(Area Code 202)

Director: Dan DeLacy 401-2754
Senior Attorney: Frank Furey 401-2754
Administrative Law Judges:
Judge John F. Cook 401-1162
Judge Allan Lewis 401-1162
Judge Daniel Shell 401-1162

(Area Code 202)

Civil Rights Reviewing Authority Staff Director:
Richard Slippen 245-0425
Education Appeal Board Staff Chairman:
Ernest C. Canellos 401-2754
Docket Clerk: Janice Pope 401-2754

OFFICE OF INSPECTOR GENERAL (Room 4006)

The Office of Inspector General is responsible for conducting audits and investigations relating to agency programs and operations; reviewing legislation and regulations with respect to agency programs and operations; and directing activities aimed at preventing and detecting fraud and abuse, and promoting economy and efficiency of programs and operations. The office refers evidence of criminal actions to the Justice Department or U.S. Attorney Offices, as appropriate.

(Area Code 202)

Inspector General: James B. Thomas Jr 453-4039
Counsel to the Inspector General: Ellen Bass 453-4039

(Area Code 202)

Facsimile 732-1238

OFFICE OF THE ASSISTANT SECRETARY FOR CIVIL RIGHTS

330 C Street, S.W.
Washington, D.C. 20202

The Office for Civil Rights (OCR) protects the rights of students in education programs or activities that receive financial assistance from the U.S. Department of Education. Some employees of these programs are also protected under the laws OCR enforces. These laws are Title VI of the Civil Rights Act of 1964, Title IX of the Education Amendments of 1972, Section 504 of the Rehabilitation Act of 1973, and the Age Discrimination Act of 1975. In addition, OCR assists the Department in implementing civil rights provisions in other education statutes, particularly the Education of the Handicapped Act, the Carl D. Perkins Vocational Education Act, and Title VII of the Education for Economic Security Act (the Magnet Schools Assistance Program). Under these laws, programs and activities funded by the U.S. Department of Education must be operated in a manner that ensures that people who meet the programs' qualifications and eligibility requirements are given an equal opportunity to participate, regardless of their race, color, national origin, sex, handicap, or age.

The Office for Civil Rights relies primarily on its complaint investigation and compliance review process to ensure compliance with the principal statutes it enforces. The Office investigates complaints filed by individuals, or their representatives, who believe that they have been discriminated against; initiates compliance reviews of recipient institutions and agencies; and monitors the progress in eliminating discriminatory practices of institutions and agencies that are implementing plans negotiated by OCR. When efforts to achieve voluntary compliance with the civil rights laws fail, OCR initiates enforcement action against recipients.

The Office for Civil Rights also provides technical assistance to help recipients of Department of Education funds achieve voluntary compliance by understanding their legal obligations, and to help those protected by the laws understand their rights.

As part of its coordinating responsibility, the U.S. Department of Justice has designated the U.S. Department of Education as the lead Federal agency on civil rights matters with elementary and secondary schools and with institutions of higher education. The purpose of these delegations is to avoid duplication of effort and ensure consistency of approach in cases where recipients receive funds from more than one Federal agency.

(Area Code 202)

Assistant Secretary for Civil Rights:
William L. Smith (Acting) 732-1213
Facsimile 732-1462

Policy and Enforcement Service
Director: Cathy H. Lewis 736-1635

(Area Code 202)

Enforcement Division Director: Frank Krueger 732-1710
Elementary and Secondary Education Branch Chief:
Richard T. Foster 732-1649
Postsecondary Education Branch Chief: Jeanette Lim ..732-1653

REGIONAL CIVIL RIGHTS OFFICES

Region I (Boston)

Chief Regional Attorney: Brenda Wolff
U.S. Department of Education, Office for Civil Rights,
J.W. McCormack Post Office and Courthouse Building, Room 222,
Boston, MA 02109-4557. Tel: 617/223-9679. FAX: 617/223-9669.

Region II (New York)

Chief Regional Attorney: Tobian Schwartz
U.S. Department of Education, Office for Civil Rights,
26 Federal Plaza, 33rd Floor, Room 33-130,
New York, NY 10278-0082. Tel: 212/264-1320. FAX: 212/264-4427.

Region III (Philadelphia)

Chief Regional Attorney: Lee Nell
U.S. Department of Education, Office for Civil Rights,
3535 Market Street, Room 6300, Philadelphia, PA 19104-3326.
Tel: 215/596-6175. FAX: 215/596-4862.

Region IV (Atlanta)

Chief Regional Attorney: Barbara Shannon
U.S. Department of Education, Office for Civil Rights,
101 Marietta Tower, 27th Floor, Suite 2702, P.O. Box 1705,
Atlanta, GA 30301-1705. Tel: 404/331-5206. FAX: 404/841-5382.

Region V (Chicago)

Chief Regional Attorney: John Fry
U.S. Department of Education, Office for Civil Rights,
401 South State Street, Room 700-C, Chicago, IL 60605-1202.
Tel: 312/886-5092. FAX: 312/353-4888.

Region VI (Dallas)

Chief Regional Attorney: Joan Sessons Ford
U.S. Department of Education, Office for Civil Rights,
1200 Main Tower Building, Suite 2260, Dallas, TX 75202-9998.
Tel: 214/767-3017. FAX: 214/729-3634.

Region VII (Kansas City)

Chief Regional Attorney: Stephan D. Stratton
U.S. Department of Education, Office for Civil Rights,
10220 North Executive Hill Boulevard, 8th Floor, P.O. Box 901381, Kansas City, MO 64190-1381. Tel: 816/891-8192.
FAX: 816/374-6442.

Region VIII (Denver)

Chief Regional Attorney: David Dunbar
U.S. Department of Education, Office for Civil Rights,
Federal Office Building, 1961 Stout Street, Room 330,
Denver, CO 80294-3608 Tel: 303/844-5313. FAX: 303/564-2524.

Region IX (San Francisco)

Chief Regional Attorney: Paul Grossman
U.S. Department of Education, Office for Civil Rights,
Old Federal Building, 50 United Nations Plaza, Room 239, San Francisco, CA 94102-1925. Tel: 415/744-2834. FAX: 415/556-6770.

Region X (Seattle)

Chief Regional Attorney: Randall Jones
U.S. Department of Education, Office for Civil Rights,
915 Second Avenue, Room 3310, Seattle, WA 98174-1099.
Tel: 206/442-2990. FAX: 206/399-1232.

U.S. DEPARTMENT OF EDUCATION
KEY LEGAL AUTHORITIES

Major Regulations:

General Departmental Regulations: 34 C.F.R. Parts 1-790 (1989).
Department of Education Acquisition Regulations, 48 C.F.R. Part 3401 et seq. (1989).
Rules of Practice & Procedure:
Education Appeals Board, 34 C.F.R. Part 78 (1989).
Office of Administrative Law Judges, 34 C.F.R. Part 81 (1989).
Hearings, decisions, and administrative reviews under Title VI of the Civil Rights Act of 1964: 34 C.F.R. Part 101 (1989).

General Educational Provisions Act, as amended, 20 U.S.C. 1221--the general enabling legislation for the Department of Education.
Legislative History: 1967 U.S. Code Cong. & Admin. News 2730; 1978 U.S. Code Cong. & Admin. News 4971.

Title IX of the Education Amendments of 1972, 20 U.S.C. 1681 et seq.--designed to eliminate discrimination on the basis of sex in any education program or activity receiving Federal financial assistance.
Legislative History: 1972 U.S. Code Cong. & Admin. News 2462; 1974 U.S. Code Cong. & Admin. News 6779; 1976 U.S. Code Cong. & Admin. News 4713.
Implementing Regulations: 34 C.F.R. Part 106 (1989).

Elementary & Secondary Education Act of 1965, as amended, 20 U.S.C. 2701 et seq.--the basic Federal public education assistance statute.
Legislative History: 1988 U.S. Code Cong. & Admin. News 101.
Implementing Regulations: 34 C.F.R. Part 200 et seq. (1989).

Women's Educational Equity Act, as amended, 20 U.S.C. 3041-3045--provides funds for projects designed to promote educational equity for women, with special emphasis on women who suffer multiple discrimination, bias, or stereotyping based on sex and race, ethnic origin, disability, or age.
Legislative History: 1988 U.S. Code Cong. & Admin. News 101.
Implementing Regulations: 34 C.F.R. Parts 245-247 (1989).

Civil Rights Restoration Act of 1987, Pub. L. 100-259--overturned the Supreme Court's 1984 decision in Grove City College v. Bell, 465 U.S. 555, and restored the effectiveness of the four major civil rights statutes that prohibit discrimination in federally assisted programs: Title IX of the Education Amendments of 1972, Title VI of the Civil Rights Act of 1964, Section 504 of the Rehabilitation Act of 1973, and the Age Discrimination Act of 1975. The Act provides that when Federal financial assistance is extended to any part of a college, university, other postsecondary institution, or public system of higher education, all of the operations of the institution or education systems are covered. The Act does leave the religious tenet exemption in Title IX intact and clarifies that the exemption is as broad as the Title IX coverage of education programs and activities.
Legislative History: 1988 U.S. Code Cong. & Admin. News 28.

Civil Rights Act of 1964, as amended, 42 U.S.C. 2000d-1--mandates nondiscrimination on grounds of race, color, or national origin in programs and activities receiving Federal financial assistance.
Implementing Regulations: 34 C.F.R. Part 100 (1989).

Education for All Handicapped Children Act of 1975, as amended, 20 U.S.C. 1401 et seq.--assures that all handicapped children have available to them a free and appropriate public education designed to meet their unique needs and to assure that the rights of handicapped children and their parents or guardians are protected; requires that each school child have a detailed individualized education plan.
Legislative History: 1975 U.S. Code Cong. & Admin. News 1425.
Implementing Regulations: 34 C.F.R. Part 104 (1989).

Stafford Student Loan Program Act, as amended, 20 U.S.C. 1071 et seq.--provides authority for student loan insurance programs.
Legislative History: 1986 U.S. Code Cong. & Admin. News 2572; 1988 U.S. Code Cong. & Admin. News 1070.

Military Selective Service Act of 1967, as amended, 50 U.S.C. App. 462(f)--provides offenses and penalties for failure to register with the Selective Service System before receiving any grant, loan, or work assistance under Title IV of the Higher Education Act of 1965.

Internal Revenue Code, 26 U.S.C. 6402(d) & (e)--collection of debts owed to Federal agencies-upon receiving notice from any Federal agency that a named person owes a past due legally enforceable debt (e.g. a defaulted student loan) then the IRS may reduce the amount of any overpayment of taxes payable to such person by the amount of such debt.

Exec. Order No. 11034, as amended, 3 C.F.R., 1959-1963 Comp., p. 614--delegates authority to administer portions of educational and cultural exchange programs to the Secretary of Education.

DEPARTMENT OF ENERGY

Forrestal Building, 1000 Independence Avenue, S.W.
Washington, D.C. 20585

DESCRIPTION: The U.S. Department of Energy (DOE) coordinates and administers the energy functions of the Federal Government. The Department is responsible for long-term, high-risk research and development of energy technology; the marketing of Federal power; energy conservation; the nuclear weapons programs; energy regulatory programs; and a central energy data collection and analysis program.

(Area Code 202)
Secretary: James D. Watkins 586-6210
Assistant to Secretary (Counselor): Nancy Wolicki 586-5500
Procurement Operations 586-1370
Small and Disadvantaged Business Utilization 254-5602
Publications/Public Inquiries 586-5575
Inspector General's Hot Line:
Washington, D.C. Metro Area 586-4073
Outside Washington, D.C. Metro Area ....(800) 541-1625
Facsimile..586-7644

Freedom of Information Act/Privacy Act Office...........586-5955
There is a copying fee of 5 cents per page, unless the total amount of material copied is less than 300 pages, in which case there is no fee. Freedom of Information Act searches and reviews must be requested in writing. Telephone requests will not be accepted. The fee for this service varies depending on who does the search or review, since the rate is based on that person's hourly salary plus 16%.

(Area Code 202)
Library (Room GA-138)..................................586-9534
The library is open from 8:30 AM until 5:00 PM, Monday through Friday. Although the library is open to the public, escort by someone with a valid building access badge is required. A copying machine is available at no charge. Loan of materials in the circulating collection may be arranged through the Interlibrary Loan Program.

Law Library (Room 6A-156)...............................586-4848
The law Library is open from 8:30 AM until 5:30 PM, Monday through Friday. It is open to the public only by special prior arrangement and only if the needed material cannot be found in any other library. Escort by someone with a valid building access pass is required.

OFFICE OF THE GENERAL COUNSEL (Room 6A-245)

The Office of General Counsel provides comprehensive legal services to the Secretary and the Department. These services include legal counsel with respect to every program and function of the Department, with the exception of the Federal Energy Regulatory Commission; legal review of all significant Departmental proposed actions; and the defense of those matters through both judicial and administrative litigation in both Federal and state courts, at trial and appellate levels.

The Office of General Counsel also participates in the negotiation and drafting of international agreements for cooperative research and developmental activities in several energy fields.
In the area of emergency preparedness, the Office of General Counsel works with other DOE offices and other agencies to improve domestic emergency preparedness, and with other agencies and international organizations to implement international energy emergency preparedness. In addition to its Washington, D.C. headquarters office, the Office of General Counsel also has attorneys in its regional Operations and Area Counsel Offices.

The Office of General Counsel supports the Economic Regulatory Administration (ERA) in its efforts to reduce regulation of natural gas imports and exports in order to promote competition. This support includes providing counsel to ERA with respect to natural gas import cases involving novel questions of fact and law as they apply to the proper role of Government regulation in a rapidly changing energy marketplace.

A final, discrete responsibility of the Office is to administer DOE's Standards of Employee Conduct program and regulations, including the financial disclosure program and other regulations and policy requirements respecting employee conduct.

(Area Code 202)
General Counsel: Stephen A. Wakefield 586-5281
Deputy General Counsel: Eric J. Fygi 586-5284

To fulfill these responsibilities, the Office of General Counsel is divided into four sections:

The **Office of the Deputy Counsel for Energy Resources** ensures that the General Counsel's responsibilities with respect to environmental, legislative, defense and nuclear energy programs, and natural gas and mineral leasing are met.

***The Assistant General Counsel for Environment** provides legal support to DOE's environmental protection and health and safety programs.

***The Assistant General Counsel for Legislation** is responsible for preparing the Department's legislative proposals and coordinating DOE policy on pending legislation.

***The Assistant General Counsel for Nuclear Affairs** ensures that legal advice and support is provided to DOE's nuclear weapons programs. Staff attorneys also assist in the negotiation, drafting, and implementation of related treaties and international agreements.

***The Assistant General Counsel for Natural Gas and Mineral Leasing** provides legal advice and assistance in the formulation and implementation of policy and activities related to DOE's domestic and international natural gas responsibilities, including the negotiation and drafting of international agreements. The office also provides legal and policy advice concerning DOE's mineral leasing and related coastal zone management responsibilities.

DEPARTMENT OF ENERGY

(Area Code 202)

Deputy General Counsel: Mark C. Schroeder 586-6732
Assistant General Counsel for:
Environment: William J. Dennison (Acting) ... 586-6947
Legislation: Robert G. Rabben 586-6718
Nuclear Affairs: Stephen M. Sohinki 586-6975
Natural Gas and Mineral Leasing: James White 586-6667

The **Office of Deputy Counsel for Litigation** ensures that the General Counsel's responsibilities with respect to litigation functions are met.

***The Office of the Assistant General Counsel for General Litigation** primarily provides defensive litigation services in areas traditionally perceived as general law subjects, such as personnel, labor, EEO, privacy, the Freedom of Information Act, torts, contracts, procurement, etc.

***The Office of the Assistant General Counsel for Special Litigation** handles matters arising from Departmental programs that result in litigation, such as Fuel Use Act programs, etc. Certain other cases, many involving considerable interaction with state and local governments, are also assigned to Special Litigation.

(Area Code 202)

Deputy General Counsel: Marc Johnston (Acting) 586-2909
Assistant General Counsel for:
General Litigation: Marc Johnston 586-8700
Special Litigation: vacant 586-8700

The **Office of the Deputy General Counsel for Programs** ensures that the General Counsel's responsibilities with respect to the Department's domestic and international energy emergency preparedness, procurement and finance matters, power marketing activities, and the conduct of interventions in state and Federal utility regulatory proceedings are met.

***The Assistant General Counsel for Regulatory Interventions and Power Marketing** represents the Department in various state and Federal utility regulatory proceedings. The office also provides legal support to DOE program offices for the development of national energy policies regarding electric utilities and other regulated energy areas.

***The Assistant General Counsel for Procurement and Finance** provides legal support for the Department's massive contractual expenditures, which are second in magnitude only to those of the Department of Defense. Staff attorneys assist in the development of regulations pertaining to procurements, agreements, grants, and other types of financial assistance; review and comment on related legislation and regulations; assist in the preparation of contract solicitation documents and other contractual documents; and represent the Department in connection with GAO protests and contract disputes. A separate responsibility of the office is to prepare and review loan guaranty agreements, trust incentives, credit agreements, technology agreements, and related financial documents for the Department's multi-million dollar synthetic fuels, alcohol fuels, and geothermal loan guarantee programs.

***The Assistant General Counsel for International Affairs** provides legal advice concerning energy emergency preparedness and response, including the use of extraordinary legal authorities such as those contained in the Defense Production Act, the International Emergency Economic Powers Act, and the Trade Expansion Act. As part of that mission, staff attorneys provide overall legal advice in the formulation and implementation of policy related to the Strategic Petroleum Reserve and related programs and agreements.

(Area Code 202)

Deputy General Counsel: Jerry Z. Pruzan 586-6942
Assistant General Counsel for Regulatory Interventions
and Power Marketing: Lawrence A. Gollomp 586-6958
Assistant General Counsel for Procurement and Finance:
Lawrence R. Oliver 586-2440
Assistant General Counsel for International Affairs:
Craig S. Bamberger 586-2900

The **Office of the Deputy General Counsel for Legal Services** ensures that the General Counsel's responsibilities in the areas of standards of employee conduct, FOIA, intellectual property, energy conservation, and regulatory matters are met.

***The Assistant General Counsel for Patents** conducts a program to protect the Department's interests in intellectual property matters. This requires the evaluation of intellectual property arising from DOE-funded activities, and determining the need for prosecuting domestic and foreign patent applications. Attorneys in this office also review all patent applications on nuclear inventions submitted to the U.S. Patent and Trademark Office to determine whether the application should be classified or if DOE should take title to the application. Duties include: developing DOE policy and regulations for the licensing of patents and patent applications owned by the Department; administering the DOE patent licensing program; negotiating with DOE contractors regarding patent, data, and copyright matters; negotiating intellectual property provisions in all interagency and international agreements; conducting related litigation in judicial and administrative proceedings; and managing the activities of field patent counsel. There are currently around seven patent attorneys in the Washington Headquarters office and around 24 in field offices.

***The Assistant General Counsel for General Law** provides advice with respect to laws of general applicability, such as questions of constitutional, fiscal, or administrative law. The office provides continuing legal services in connection with DOE's Freedom of Information Act (FOIA) and Privacy Act regulations, as well as legal review of regulations relating to protective force and arrest standards.

***The Assistant General Counsel for Conservation and Regulations** is responsible for providing legal advice and support in connection with the development and administration of DOE's conservation and renewable energy programs and activities, including state grants programs, industrial energy conservation programs, weatherization programs, and all other energy conservation and renewable energy activities and associated loan guarantee programs.

(Area Code 202)

Deputy General Counsel: William A. Crane 586-5246
Assistant General Counsel for:
Patents: Richard E. Constant 586-2802
General Law: Ralph D. Goldenberg 586-8665
Conservation and Regulations:
Lawrence V. Robertson 586-9507

FIELD OFFICES

Albuquerque Operations Office
Chief Counsel: James A. Stout
U.S. Department of Energy, Albuquerque Operations Office
P.O. Box 5400, Albuquerque, NM 87115. Tel: 505/845-6265.

Chicago Operations Office
Chief Counsel: Martin Samber
U.S. Department of Energy, Chicago Operations Office,
9800 South Cass Avenue, Argonne, IL 60439. Tel: 708/972-2032.

Idaho Operations Office
Chief Counsel: Ignacio Resendez
U.S. Department of Energy, Idaho Operations Office, 785 DOE Place, Idaho Falls, ID 83402. Tel: 208/526-1633.

Nevada Operations Office
Chief Counsel: Richard Amick
U.S. Department of Energy, Nevada Operations Office, P.O. Box 98518, Las Vegas, NV 89114-4100. Tel: 702/295-3581.

Oak Ridge Operations Office
Chief Counsel: Bill Snyder
U.S. Department of Energy, Oak Ridge Operations Office P.O. Box X-2001, Oak Ridge, TN 37831. Tel: 615/576-1200.

Richland Operations Office
Chief Counsel: Eugene Pride
U.S. Department of Energy, Richland Operations Office, 825 Jadwin Avenue, Richland, WA 99352. Tel: 509/376-7311.

San Francisco Operations Office
Chief Counsel: Peter Bernard
U.S. Department of Energy, San Francisco Operations Office, 1333 Broadway, Oakland, CA 94612. Tel: 415/273-4357.

Savannah River Operations Office
Chief Counsel: Warren Bergholz
U.S. Department of Energy, Savannah River Operations Office, P.O. Box A, Aiken, SC 29802. Tel: 803/725-2497.

Strategic Petroleum Reserve Project Office
Project Counsel: Jocelyn Guarisco
U.S. Department of Energy, Strategic Petroleum Reserve, Project Management Office, 900 Commerce Road East, New Orleans, LA 70123. Tel: 504/734-4294.

Pittsburgh Naval Reactors Office
Chief Counsel: James S. Carey Jr.
U.S. Department of Energy, Pittsburgh Naval Reactors Office, P.O. Box 109, West Mifflin, PA 15122. Tel: 412/476-7202.

Schenectady Naval Reactors Office
Chief Counsel: Henry VanDyke
U.S. Department of Energy, Schenectady Naval Reactors Office, P.O. Box 1069, Schenectady, NY 12301. Tel: 518/395-4227.

Kansas City Area Office
Chief Counsel: Patrick G. Currier
U.S. Department of Energy, Kansas City Area Office, P.O. Box 410202, Kansas City, MO 64141. Tel: 816/997-3341.

Los Alamos Area Office
Counsel: Joyce H. Laeser
U.S. Department of Energy, Los Alamos Area Office, 528 35th Street, Los Alamos, NM 87544. Tel: 505/667-4667.

Rocky Flats Area Office
Chief Counsel: Greg Fess
U.S. Department of Energy, Rocky Flats Area Office, P.O. Box 928, Golden, CO 80402-0928. Tel: 303/966-7000.

Morgantown Energy Technology Center
Chief Counsel: Charles H. Seehorn
U.S. Department of Energy, Morgantown Energy Technology Center, 3610 Collins Ferry Road, P.O. Box 880, Morgantown, WV 26507-0880. Tel: 304/291-4527.

Pittsburgh Energy Technology Center
Chief Counsel: C.W. McBride
U.S. Department of Energy, Pittsburgh Energy Technology Center, Cochrans Mills Road, P.O. Box 10940, Pittsburgh, PA 15236-0940. Tel: 412/892-6161.

POWER ADMINISTRATIONS

Four of the Power Administration offices (the Bonneville Power Administration, Western Area Power Administration, Southeastern Power Administration, and Southwestern Power Administration) have attorneys on their staffs; the Alaska Power Administration has none.

Bonneville Power Administration
Administrator: James J. Jura
General Counsel: Harvey P. Spigal
P.O. Box 3621, Portland, OR 97208. Tel: 503/230-4201. Fax: 503/230-7405.
Washington, D.C. Liaison Office
Assistant Administrator: Stephen J. Wright. Tel: 202/586-5640.

Western Area Power Administration
Administrator: William H. Clagett
General Counsel: Michael S. Hacskaylo
P.O. Box 3402, Golden, CO 80401-3398. Tel: 303/231-1534. Fax: 303/231-1632.
Washington, D.C Liaison Office:
Assistant Administrator: Ronald Greenhalgh. Tel: 202/586-5581.

Alaska Power Administration
Administrator: Robert J. Cross
709 W. 9th Street, Room 835, Juneau, AK 99802-0050. Tel: 907/586-7405. Fax: 907/586-7270

Washington, D.C. Liaison Office
Director: Rodney L. Adelman. Tel: 202/586-2008

Southeastern Power Administration
Administrator: John A. McAllister Jr.
Attorney: D. Lee Rampey
Samuel Elbert Building, Elberton, GA 30635
Tel: 404/283-9911. FAX: 404/283-9928.
Washington, D.C. Liaison Office
Director: Rodney D. Adelman. Tel: 202/586-2008

Southwestern Power Administration
Administrator: J. M. Shafer
Attorney Advisor: Charles Borchardt
1 Williams Towers II, 16th Floor, Tulsa, OK 74101
Tel: 918/581-7426. FAX: 918/581-7530
Washington, D.C. Liaison Office
Director Rodney L. Adelman. Tel: 202/586-2008

OFFICE OF INSPECTOR GENERAL (Room 5D-039)

The responsibility of the Inspector General is to direct investigations and audits of agency activities and operations to ensure their effectiveness and efficiency, and to detect fraud, waste and abuse.

(Area Code 202)
Inspector General: John C. Layton........................586-4393
Counsel to the Inspector General: Sanford J. Parnes.....586-2414
Facsimile...586-7851

(Area Code 202)
Office of Investigations
Assistant Inspector General: Charles Croxton (Acting) 586-4143

DEPARTMENT OF ENERGY

BOARD OF CONTRACT APPEALS

Webb Building, 4040 N. Fairfax Drive, Arlington, VA 22203

The Energy Board of Contract Appeals is a quasi-judicial arm of the Department, which, under statute, or acting for the Secretary, hears and resolves appeals pertaining to contract-related and other delegated matters. There are three members of the Board, all of whom are Administrative Judges: a Chairman, a Vice Chairman, and a Member. Depending on the nature of the case, the Chairman, Vice Chairman, and Member may sit as the Contract Adjustment Board, Financial Assistance Appeals Board, Invention Licensing Appeals Board, or Patent Compensation Board.

Single copies of decisions may be obtained by contacting the Recorder, 703/235-2700.

Copies of all Board of Contract Appeals decisions are sent to the Energy Department's FOIA Reading Room, located in Room 1E-190 in the Forrestal Building. The Reading Room is open to the public from 9:00 AM to 4:00 PM, Monday through Friday. Tel: 202/586-6020.

Decisions of the Board of Contract Appeals are available from Commerce Clearing House in the publication Board of Contract Appeals Reporter, a bi-weekly publication which reports the decisions of the following Boards of Contract Appeals: Agriculture, Armed Services, Corps of Engineers, Department of Transportation, Energy, General Services Administration, Department of Housing and Urban Development, Interior, Labor, National Aeronautics and Space Administration, U.S. Postal Service, and Department of Veterans Affairs. Annual Price $760.00. Contact: Commerce Clearing House, Inc., 4025 West Peterson Avenue, Chicago, IL 60646. Tel: 312/583-8500. Or in Washington, D.C., call 202/626-2200.

	(Area Code 703)
Chairman: E. Barclay Van Doren	235-2700
Vice Chairman: Sherman P. Kimball	235-2700
Member: Beryl S. Gilmore	235-2700
Recorder: Betty A. Hudson (Acting)	235-2700

OFFICE OF HEARINGS AND APPEALS (Room 6G030)

The Office of Hearings and Appeals (OHA) is the adjudicative branch of the U.S. Department of Energy. It conducts four basic categories of administrative proceedings: exception proceedings, enforcement proceedings, refund proceedings, and proceedings arising under the Freedom of Information Act. In exception, enforcement, and refund proceedings, OHA acts as an administrative forum of first instance, or trial court. In the Freedom of Information Act proceedings, it serves as the administrative appellate body.

Exception proceedings are initiated when a party requests to be exempted (i.e., "excepted") from complying with one of DOE's programs. The Office examines the facts presented, reviews case law involving similar claims, and issues a written decision granting or denying the request.

Enforcement proceedings are initiated when a party contests a Proposed Remedial Order (PRO), a charging document similar to a civil complaint, issued by the Economic Regulatory Administration (the enforcement arm of DOE), alleging that it has violated a DOE regulation. The ERA's goal in issuing a PRO is to have a party who violated the regulations refund any improper funds it realized through those violations.

In these cases, OHA acts as a trial court and determines whether the allegations in the PRO are correct and, if they are, the extent of the cited party's liability. Enforcement proceedings may include hearings for the purpose of evidentiary presentations and/or oral arguments; however, OHA does not conduct trials in the classic "court room" sense of the term. Rather, the facts and legal arguments in the cases pending before the Office are developed primarily through an extensive pleadings practice.

Decisions reached by OHA in these cases are appealable as follows: first, to the Federal Energy Regulatory Commission which acts as the administrative appellate forum in these instances; second, to the U.S. District Court (venue lies either in the cited party's home district or in the District of Columbia); third, to the Temporary Emergency Court of Appeals, a special Federal appellate court whose jurisdiction is limited to the review of cases arising under the statutes and regulations administered by DOE. Because of the large amount of money at stake in these proceedings, appeals are common.

OHA normally assumes jurisdiction over funds paid to DOE by firms accused of regulatory violations. Refund proceedings are then conducted in order to make restitution to parties adversely affected by proven or alleged regulatory violations.

The final type of case heard by OHA concerns appeals arising under the Freedom of Information Act. These cases are normally initiated when an the Freedom of Information Act request filed with a specified DOE office or program has been denied, and the party making the request seeks a review of that determination.

OHA is an independent adjudicative body and the Director, who has independent authority for the operation of the Office, is responsible for policy development on both procedural and substantive issues. There are three Deputy Directors and an Associate Director, each of whom heads a staff of approximately ten attorneys and three economic analysts. Each staff handles the same types and numbers of cases.

Each case is assigned to an OHA staff member, who becomes responsible for all procedural aspects of the case, including the development and evaluation of facts and legal arguments. The staff attorney will then participate on any OHA hearing panel convened in the case and will draft DOE's final opinion (i.e., the "Decision and Order") disposing of the case on its merits.

Decisions of the Office of Hearings and Appeals are available in OHA's Public Reference Room (Room 1E-234, Forrestal Building) from 1:00 PM through 5:00 PM, Monday through Friday. Copying is free for the first 100 pages; five cents per page thereafter.

Decisions of the Office of Hearings and Appeals are also available from Commerce Clearing House in a weekly looseleaf service entitled **Federal Energy Guidelines.** This publication also includes regulations, interpretations, related court decisions etc. Price: $790.00 a year. Contact: Commerce Clearing House, 4025 West Peterson Avenue, Chicago, IL 60646. Tel: 312/583-8500. Or, in Washington, D.C. call 202/626-2200.

(Area Code 202)
Director: George B. Breznay 586-5510
Office of Legal Analysis Deputy Director: Thomas Mann ..586-2094

(Area Code 202)
Docket and Publications Division 586-4924

ECONOMIC REGULATORY ADMINISTRATION

The Economic Regulatory Administration (ERA) administers all of the Energy Department's regulatory programs not assigned to the Federal Energy Regulatory Commission. These consist of (1) ongoing enforcement activities generated by the oil price and allocation regulations implementing the Emergency Petroleum Allocation Act of 1973 (EPAA); (2) the natural gas import and export licensing program; (3) electricity export licensing activities; (4) the issuance of Presidential permits for construction and use of transmission facilities for international exchanges of electricity; and (5) the coal conversion program.

(Area Code 202)
Administrator: Chandler L. Van Orman 586-6781

Office of Enforcement of Litigation (Room 5B-168)

The Office of Enforcement Litigation is the result of a recent merger and reorganization of ERA legal activities. This office performs the same functions as its predecessors, the Office of the Solicitor and the Office of the Special Counsel, primarily enforcing EPAA price and allocation regulations, including the prosecution of overcharge violations through administrative and court tribunals, as well as negotiating settlements. Federal oil price and allocation controls were eliminated in 1981, but almost 200 cases remain to be resolved.

The office is headed by a chief counsel and has three directorates: the Directorate of Judicial Litigation, the Directorate of Administrative Litigation, and the Directorate of Enforcement Support.

(Area Code 202)
Chief Counsel: Milton C. Lorenz 586-8900
Deputy Chief Counsel for Analysis and Review: vacant 586-2967
Judicial Litigation Division Director: Don Crockett 586-5411
Administrative Litigation Division Director:
Diana Clark 586-4275
Enforcement Support Division Director: Ben Lemos 586-5005

Field Office:

Dallas
Director: Ben Lemos
Attorney-Advisor: Victor Hanson
U.S. Department of Energy, Economic Regulatory Administration, Frito-Lay Tower, Ste 225-B, P.O. Box 45608, Dallas, TX 75245-0608. Tel: 214/655-6912.

ENERGY INFORMATION ADMINISTRATION (Room 2H-027)

(Area Code 202)
Administrator: Helmut A. Merklein 586-4361
National Energy Information Center 586-8800

(Area Code 202)
Publications Information...............................586-8800

FEDERAL ENERGY REGULATORY COMMISSION
825 North Capitol Street, N.E.
Washington, D.C. 20426

DESCRIPTION: The Federal Energy Regulatory Commission (FERC) is an independent agency created in 1977 which regulates natural gas, electric utilities, hydroelectric power, and oil pipelines. Charged with ensuring that Americans have ample gas and electricity at just and reasonable rates, the Commission administers laws designed to improve energy self-sufficiency by providing incentives for creating new energy supplies. The two laws under the 1978 National Energy Act which are of particular interest to the Commission are the Natural Gas Policy Act of 1978 (NGPA) and the Public Utility Regulatory Policies Act of 1978 (PURPA).

The Commission carries out its assigned functions both by adjudicatory proceedings and rulemakings. Final decisions, based on the record gathered before the agency, are appealable to the U.S. Courts of Appeals and ultimately to the U.S. Supreme Court.

(Area Code 202)
Chairman: Martin Allday.................................208-0000
Executive Director: George Pratt.........................208-0300
Procurement Information.................................208-1869
Legal Reference and Records Management Branch 208-2300

(Area Code 202)
Public Reference Branch 208-0118
Docket...208-0715
Freedom of Information Act/Privacy Act Office 208-0055
Facsimile..208-2106

DEPARTMENT OF ENERGY

OFFICES OF THE COMMISSIONERS (Room 9000)

The Commission is composed of five members appointed by the President for four-year terms, one of whom is chosen by the President to serve as Chairman.

There are currently ten attorneys serving as Legal Advisors to the Chairman and Commissioners. Legal Advisors study, investigate, and provide advice on questions of law or administrative/regulatory policy involved in the operations of the Commission. The work includes providing advice on such matters as: legal aspects of cases or matters before the Commission, the effect of proposed actions on various electric power and natural gas utilities, changes in Commission rules and regulations, investigations of violations, jurisdictional issues, determinations of the interstate nature of sales of energy, and proposed legislation affecting the Commission. Legal Advisors also prepare drafts of proposed or final decisions and opinions for Commission consideration; prepare material for opinions of the Commissioner, including separate or dissenting opinions; conduct special studies on proposed policies or rules; and perform legal research requiring the interpretation and analysis of statutes, legislation, and court decisions.

(Area Code 202)

Chairman: Martin L. Allday 208-0000
Chief of Staff and Counselor: Howard H. Shafferman 208-0550
Deputy Chief of Staff and Senior Legal Advisor:
Lee A. Alexander 208-0137
Legal Advisors:
John Clements 208-0315
Michael D. Hornstein 208-0455

Commissioner: Jerry J. Langdon 208-0377
Legal Advisors:
Catherine Wakelyn 208-0377
Janice Macpherson 208-0377
Randy Parker 208-0377

(Area Code 202)

Commissioner: Elizabeth Anne Moler 208-0383
Legal Advisors:
Mary Kelly 208-0383
Robert Fallon 208-0383
John Conway 208-0383

Commissioner: Charles A. Trabandt 208-0366
Legal Advisors:
Penelope S. Ludwig 208-0366
George C. O'Connor 208-0366
Joshua Rokach 208-0366

OFFICE OF THE GENERAL COUNSEL (Room 8000)

The Office of the General Counsel provides a variety of legal services to the Commission. Lawyers in the office draft rulemaking orders, prepare analyses, draft orders and opinions, participate in Commission hearings, and defend orders of the agency in Federal courts.

The office has five major divisions: the Office of the Associate General Counsel for Hydroelectric and Electric; Office of the Associate General Counsel for Gas and Oil; Office of the Associate General Counsel for Enforcement, General Law, and Rulemaking: Office of the Associate General Counsel for Administrative Litigation; and Office of the Solicitor. Despite the office or section to which one is assigned, an attorney's work typically focuses on the following areas:

***Advisory and Rulemaking.** Attorneys perform legal research and analysis and prepare draft rulemakings, orders, and opinions for Commission action.

***Administrative Litigation.** Attorneys prepare briefs and pleadings for cases for trial and argue cases involving complex issues before Administrative Law Judges. Attorneys also conduct settlement conferences and prepare settlement agreements.

***Appellate Litigation.** Attorneys defend the Commission's regulatory decisions which have been appealed to the various U.S. Courts of Appeals. They also represent the Commission in cases filed in the Supreme Court where the Commission is a party or has a significant interest.

***Enforcement.** Attorneys initiate and execute investigations of possible violations of the statutes administered by the Commission and the rules, orders, and regulations issued by the Commission. Attorneys issue subpoenas, take evidence, obtain documentary records, and prepare and try violations before Administrative Law Judges and Federal District Courts.

***General Law.** Attorneys advise and represent the Commission before Federal Courts and administrative tribunals on general legal issues, including contracts and procurement, the Freedom of Information Act, privacy issues, and various personnel matters, such as EEO, labor-management relations, and conflicts of interest.

(Area Code 202)

General Counsel: William S. Scherman....................208-1000
Deputy General Counsel: David N. Cook....................208-0955
Solicitor: Jerome M. Feit...............................208-1191

Hydroelectric and Electric
Associate General Counsel: Cynthia A. Marlette........208-2124
Assistant General Counsel for Electric Rates and
Corporate Regulation: Daniel L. Larcamp 208-2088
Assistant General Counsel for Hydroelectric Licensing:
K. Kristina Nygaard 208-0633

Administrative Litigation
Associate General Counsel: Richard L. Miles 208-0702
Assistant General Counsel for Hydroelectric and
Electric Litigation: C. Stephen Angle 208-0361

(Area Code 202)

Enforcement, General Law and Rulemaking
Associate General Counsel: Michael Schopf.............208-0597
Assistant General Counsel for:
Enforcement: Ellen K. Schall 208-0438
General Legal Services: Kathleen McDonough ...208-2238

Gas and Oil
Associate General Counsel: Susan J. Court.............208-0448
Assistant General Counsel for:
Gas and Oil Litigation: William Froehlich ...208-0488
Pipeline Certificates: Robert F. Christin ...208-1022
Pipeline Rates and Valuation: Andrea Wolfman 208-2097
Rate Filings Regulation: Howard B. Schneider 208-0702

REGIONAL OFFICES

Although FERC has regional offices in Atlanta, Chicago, New York, Portland, and San Francisco, all attorneys are located in the headquarters office in Washington, D.C.

OFFICE OF ADMINISTRATIVE LAW JUDGES (Room 921)

810 1st Street, N.E., Washington, D.C. 20426

Within the Federal Energy Regulatory Commission (FERC) the Administrative Law Judges play a judicial role and are, in effect, the trial judiciary of the agency. In all cases set for hearing by the Commission, the Administrative Law Judges preside over the hearing and issue an initial decision at its conclusion, operating in much the same fashion as a Federal District Court Judge presiding over a civil, non-jury case. Hearings are conducted under the Interstate Commerce Act, the Natural Gas Policy Act, the Public Utility Regulatory Policies Act, and the Powerplant and Industrial Fuel Use Act.

The decisions of the FERC Administrative Law Judges (and all other FERC materials) are available at: The Reference and Information Center, 941 North Capitol Street, N.E., Room 3308, Washington, D.C. 20436. (202/208-0118). This Center is open to the public from 8:30 AM through 5:00 PM, Monday through Friday. Copying is free for the first 10 pages; subsequent pages are either 15 cents or 17 cents each, depending on the age of the material (the older items are in computer form).

(Area Code 202)

Chief Administrative Law Judge: Curtis L. Wagner, Jr ...357-0500
Legal Assistant: Martha E. Altamar 357-0500

(Area Code 202)

Administrative Officer: Susie J. Waller 357-0500

DATABASES AND PUBLICATIONS OF INTEREST

Database:

Federal Energy Regulatory Commission

CIPS (Commission Issuance Posting System). This is a database containing copies of all Commission formal issuances, including opinions, orders, initial decisions, and the Commission agenda, as well as proposed, interim, and final rulings. All available free of charge to anyone with a computer and a modem. For further information, call 202/208-2474.

Copies of specific orders and other items. To obtain a copy of a specific order, notice, filing, etc., submit a written request to: Reference and Information Center, Federal Energy Regulatory Commission, Room 3308, 941 N. Capitol Street, N.E., Washington, D.C. 20426. Tel: 202/208-1371.

Service List. To get on a mailing list ("Service List") to receive copies of all material issued concerning a particular docket number, submit a written request to: The Secretary of the Commis-sion, Federal Energy Regulatory Commission, 825 N. Capitol Street, N.E., Room 3110, Washington, D.C. 20426. Tel: 202/208-0400.

Publications:

Department of Energy

The following publication can be purchased from the **U.S. Government Printing Office.** Stock numbers and prices for annual subscriptions are shown below. Submit requests for these publications to: The Superintendent of Documents, U.S. Government Printing Office, Washington, D.C. 20402. (202/783-3238).

Department of Energy Acquisition Regulation. Supplements the Federal Acquisition Regulation for procuring supplies and services for the U.S. Department of Energy. Subscription service consists of a basic manual and supplemental material for an indeterminate period. Latest update published March 1990. In looseleaf form, punched for 3-ring binder. Price: $67.00 domestic; $83.75 foreign. GPO Stock# 961-002-00000-1.

DEPARTMENT OF ENERGY

KEY LEGAL AUTHORITIES

Major Regulations:

General Departmental Regulations: 10 C.F.R. Parts 200-1060 (1989).
Rules of the Board of Contract Appeals: 10 C.F.R. Part 703 (1989).
Federal Energy Regulatory Commission (FERC): 18 C.F.R. Parts 1-1313 (1989).
FERC Rules of Practice & Procedure: 18 C.F.R. Part 385 (1989).

Department of Energy Organization Act, 42 U.S.C. 7101 et seq.--the basic enabling and organizational statute of the Department and, within the Department, the autonomous Federal Energy Regulatory Commission.
Legislative History: 1977 U.S. Code Cong. & Admin. News 854.

Powerplant & Industrial Fuel Use Act of 1978, as amended, 42 U.S.C. 8301 et seq.--designed to reduce oil imports and encourage the development, use, and conservation of domestic energy resources.
Legislative History: 1978 U.S. Code Cong. & Admin. News 8173; 1987 U.S. Code Cong. & Admin. News 270.
Implementing Regulations: 18 C.F.R. Part 287 (1989).

Wind Energy Systems Act of 1980, as amended, 42 U.S.C. 9201 et seq.--to encourage and assist in the development of wind energy.
Legislative History: 1980 U.S. Code Cong. & Admin. News 2691; 1986 U.S. Code Cong. & Admin. News 1833.

DEPARTMENT OF ENERGY

Energy Conservation Standards for New Buildings Act of 1976, as amended, 42 U.S.C. 6831-6870--mandates energy performance standards for new commercial and residential buildings receiving Federal financial assistance and encourages the development of voluntary performance standards for other buildings.
Legislative History: 1976 U.S. Code Cong. & Admin. News 2005; 1981 U.S. Code Cong. & Admin. News 396; 1987 U.S. Code Cong. & Admin. News 3317.

National Energy Conservation Policy Act, as amended, 42 U.S.C. 8201 et seq.--this basic energy conservation statute concentrates on residential energy conservation, utility programs, and Federal energy initiatives.
Legislative History: 1978 U.S. Code Cong. & Admin. News 8114; 1986 U.S. Code Cong. & Admin. News 2028.

Energy Conservation and Production Act, as amended, 42 U.S.C. 6801 et seq.--intended to conserve energy through electric utility regulatory reform and rate design initiatives and a weatherization assistance program for low-income persons.
Legislative History: 1976 U.S. Code Cong. & Admin. News 2005; 1987 U.S. Code Cong. & Admin. News 3317.

Nuclear Waste Policy Act of 1982, as amended, 42 U.S.C. 10101 et seq.--establishes a schedule for siting, construction, and operation of civilian radioactive waste repositories; establishes a Nuclear Waste Fund consisting of payments by the generators and owners of such waste and spent fuel to pay for disposal; and sets up an interim storage program.
Legislative History: 1982 U.S. Code Cong. & Admin. News 3792; 1987 U.S. Code Cong. & Admin. News 2313-1.

Federal Nonnuclear Energy Research & Development Act of 1974, as amended, 42 U.S.C. 5901 et seq.--designed to stimulate development of all potentially beneficial energy sources and utilization technologies.
Legislative History: 1974 U.S. Code Cong. & Admin. News 6861; 1986 U.S. Code Cong. & Admin. News 1833.

National Appliance Energy Conservation Act, as amended, 42 U.S.C. 6291 et seq.--established an energy efficiency testing and labeling program for covered consumer products other than automobiles.
Legislative History: 1975 U.S. Code Cong. & Admin. News 1762; 1978 U.S. Code Cong. & Admin. News 8114; 1987 U.S. Code Cong. & Admin. News 52; 1988 U.S. Code Cong. & Admin. News 784.

Energy Policy & Conservation Act, as amended, 42 U.S.C. 6201 et seq.--one of the generic U.S. energy statutes covering a broad range of energy concerns including: (1) granting standby energy rationing authority to the President; (2) establishing a Strategic Petroleum Reserve; (3) price incentives and production requirements designed to increase domestic fossil fuel supplies; (4) energy conservation programs; (5) fuel efficiency requirements; (6) increasing coal usage; and (7) an energy data program.
Legislative History: 1975 U.S. Code Cong. & Admin. News 1762; 1985 U.S. Code Cong. & Admin. News 86.

Atomic Energy Act of 1954, as amended, 42 U.S.C. 2011 et seq.--the fundamental statutory basis for the nuclear power industry, assigning regulatory authority to the Nuclear Regulatory Commission and developmental responsibilities to the Department of Energy.
Legislative History: 1954 U.S. Code Cong. & Admin. News 3456; 1978 U.S. Code Cong. & Admin. News 7433; 1988 U.S. Code Cong. & Admin. News 1424.

Public Utilities Regulatory Policies Act of 1978, as amended, 16 U.S.C. 2601 et seq.--designed to conserve electric energy while preserving reasonable retail rates for consumers; improve wholesale distribution of electric energy; reform Federal Energy Regulatory Commission procedures; encourage hydroelectric development; conserve natural gas and insure equitable rates to consumers; and encourage the development of crude oil transportation systems.
Legislative History: 1978 U.S. Code Cong. & Admin. News 7659.
Implementing Regulations: 18 C.F.R. Parts 290-294 (1989).

Federal Power Act, as amended, 16 U.S.C. 791 a et seq.--the generic Federal utility regulatory statute.
Legislative History: 1960 U.S. Code Cong. & Admin. News 2944; 1978 U.S. Code Cong. & Admin. News 7659; 1980 U.S. Code Cong. & Admin. News 1743; 1986 U.S. Code Cong. & Admin. News 2496.
Implementing Regulations: 18 C.F.R. Parts 4-141 (1989).

Natural Gas Policy Act of 1978, 15 U.S.C. 3301 et seq.--established price controls for natural gas at the wellhead and throughout the distribution system and directed the Federal Energy Regulatory Commission to administer the statute.
Legislative History: 1978 U.S. Code Cong. & Admin. News 8800.
Implementing Regulations: 18 C.F.R. Parts 270-286 (1989).

Natural Gas Act, as amended, 15 U.S.C. 717-717z--the generic statute regulating natural gas companies.
Legislative History: 1978 U.S. Code Cong. & Admin. News 7659; 1988 U.S. Code Cong. & Admin. News 2692.
Implementing Regulations: 18 C.F.R. Parts 152-260 (1989).

Interstate Commerce Act, as amended, 49 U.S.C. 1 et seq.--authorizes the Federal Energy Regulatory Commission to regulate oil pipeline carrier rates.
Implementing Regulations: 18 C.F.R. Parts 340-362 (1989).

DEPARTMENT OF HEALTH AND HUMAN SERVICES

200 Independence Avenue, S.W.
Washington, D.C. 20201

DESCRIPTION: The Department of Health and Human Services (HHS) is among the largest and most diverse of Federal agencies. Among the Department's areas of responsibility are the world's largest social insurance program (Social Security), one of the world's largest medical insurance programs (Medicare and Medicaid), the world's largest medical research center (the National Institutes of Health), and one of the nation's primary consumer protection agencies (the Food and Drug Administration). These programs, and the many others within the Department, deal with some of the most complex and difficult social, scientific, and ethical issues of our day. Such issues result in thousands of Federal court cases filed annually against or by the Department. Hundreds of regulations touching virtually every aspect of American life are considered by the Department each year.

(Area Code 202)

Secretary: Louis W. Sullivan 245-7000
Information Operator 475-0257
Public Affairs 245-1850
Small and Disadvantaged Business Utilization 245-7300
Docket 245-6648
Inspector General's Hot Line:
Washington, D.C. Metro Area .... (301) 965-5953
Outside Washington, D.C. Metro Area .... (800) 368-5779
Facsimile 472-6297

Freedom of Information Act/Privacy Act Office 472-7453
The HHS FOIA/Privacy Act Office serves all HHS offices. To make FOIA/PA requests, write to: HHS Freedom of Information Act/PA Officer, Room 645-F, Hubert Humphrey Bldg, 200 Independence Avenue, S.W., Washington, D.C. 20201.

(Area Code 202)

Law Library (Room G-400) 619-0190
Cohen Bldg, 330 Independence Avenue, S.W., Washington, D.C. 20201
The law library is open to the public from 9:00 AM until 5:30 PM. Materials are on the topics of health, family relations, social security and public assistance. Photocopying is free up to 25 copies; bring your own paper if you plan to photocopy extensively.

National Library of Medicine .... (301) 496-6095
National Institutes of Health Campus, 8600 Rockville Pike, Bethesda, MD 20894
The library is open 8:30 AM until 9:00 PM Monday through Thursday; and 8:30 AM until 5:00 PM Friday and Saturday; (closed Sunday). There is an extensive collection of information on 40 fields of medicine. The library is open to the public, but stacks are closed, so you must allow time to have information retrieved. There is a small collection of materials in the Reading Room. Photocopying is available at 10 cents a page.

OFFICE OF THE GENERAL COUNSEL (ROOM 722-A)

The General Counsel is the chief legal officer of the Department and heads an office of attorneys in the Washington, D.C. headquarters offices as well as in regional offices. The work of the Office of General Counsel falls into three general categories: litigation, regulations, and program review. Most of the Office's work is performed by lawyers in the various Divisions, which are organized according to subject matter expertise or program for which they act as counsel. The Divisions range in size from 10 to more than 75 attorneys, but each is headed by an Associate General Counsel.

A substantial portion of attorneys' time is spent representing the Department's interests in thousands of cases which are filed annually in Federal courts. This litigation covers a broad spectrum of issues, subject matter, and procedural variations. Another important role of the Office is the regulatory process, where attorneys review and assist in revising proposed regulations at every stage. Like the Department's litigation, its regulations touch upon many significant issues of health, medical practice, and social policy.

(Area Code 202)

General Counsel: Michael J. Astrue 245-7741
Principal Deputy General Counsel:
Grover G. Hankins 245-7780
Deputy General Counsel: Beverly Dennis, III 245-7721
Deputy General Counsel/Legal Counsel: Susan Zagame 245-6318
Special Assistant to General Counsel: David V. Foster 245-6318

The **Business and Administrative Law Division** provides legal advice on matters affecting the general operation of the Department. Attorneys in this Division handle a diverse array of problems and lawsuits, including matters arising under the Freedom of Information Act, patent law, Federal Tort Claims Act (including medical malpractice), Federal contract law, labor law, environmental law, and the Ethics in Government Act.

(Area Code 202)

Associate General Counsel: Sandra H. Shapiro 619-0150
Deputy Associate General Counsel: (vacant) 619-0150
Administrative Law Branch Chief:
Timothy White (Acting) 619-2155
Business Law Branch Chief: Ronald B. Guttmann 619-3709
Litigation Branch Chief: Timothy M. White 619-2155

DEPARTMENT OF HEALTH AND HUMAN SERVICES

The **Civil Rights Division** provides legal representation to the Department's Office for Civil Rights (OCR). OCR is responsible for enforcing various civil rights laws in connection with the Department's programs. Attorneys advise OCR staff in the conduct of civil rights investigations and enforcement proceedings. Division attorneys frequently participate in compliance negotiations with OCR staff and represent the Department in formal administrative proceedings.

(Area Code 202)

Associate General Counsel: George Lyon 619-0900
Compliance and Enforcement Branch Chief:
Wendy Pailen 619-1748
Policy Branch Chief: Edwin Woo 619-0747

The **Family Support and Human Development Division** provide legal services to the Family Support Administration and Office of Human Development Services, which administer entitlement and block grant programs, including Aid to Families with Dependent Children (AFDC) and Head Start.

(Area Code 202)

Associate General Counsel: Frank Dell'Acqua 475-4505
Chief of Litigation: John B. Watson 475-4505

The **Food and Drug Division** acts as counsel to the Food and Drug Administration (FDA). The FDA, which is one of the Government's principal consumer protection agencies, is responsible for ensuring the safety, effectiveness, and proper labeling of foods, drugs, and cosmetics. Attorneys in this Division gain substantial Federal court litigation experience in matters ranging from seizure actions against adulterated and mis-branded products to complex actions involving major drug, food, or cosmetic companies.

(Area Code 301)

Associate General Counsel: Margaret Jane Porter 443-4370
Deputy Associate General Counsel:
Jeffrey B. Springer 443-4370
Deputy Chief Counsel for Administration:
Kenneth Baumgartner 443-4360
Deputy Chief Counsel for Litigation: Arthur N. Levine 443-4390
Deputy Chief Counsel for Regulations and Hearings:
Linda R. Horton 443-1345
Associate Chief Counsel for Biologics: Ann Wion 443-1345
Associate Chief Counsel for Drugs:
David G. Adams 443-4350
Margaret Pendergast 443-1345
Ann Witt 443-4360
Associate Chief Counsel for Enforcement:
Eric M. Blumberg 443-4380
Catherine L. Copp 443-1770
Mary K. Pendergast 443-1345
Robert M. Spiller Jr 443-3235
Associate Chief Counsel for Environmental Affairs:
Richard Geyer 443-4390
Associate Chief Counsel for Food:
Philip Derfler 443-4390
Catherine L. Copp 443-1770
Denise Zavagno 443-1770
Associate Chief Counsel for Medical Devices:
Mark A. Heller 443-3235
Donald Segal 443-3235
Associate Chief Counsel for Radiological Health:
Fletcher E. Campbell 443-3235
Associate Chief Counsel for Veterinary Medicine:
Richard Geyer 443-4390
Michael M. Landa 443-1770

The **Health Care Financing Division** represents the Health Care Financing Administration, the agency responsible for administering the Medicare and Medicaid programs.

Associate General Counsel: Darrel J. Grinstead (202) 619-0300
Deputy Associate General Counsel for Litigation:
Henry Goldberg ....(301) 965-8864

(Area Code 202)

Deputy Associate General Counsel for Program Review:
Robert P. Jaye 619-0300
Deputy Associate General Counsel for Regulations:
Edward Steinhouse ....(301) 965-8868

The **Inspector General Division** is responsible for investigating allegations of fraud, waste, and abuse in programs within (or funded by) the Department. Attorneys in this Division provide legal counsel to the Inspector General with respect to proposed civil and criminal proceedings and, where appropriate, institute administrative or civil actions to remedy alleged abuses.

(Area Code 202)

Associate General Counsel: D. McCarty Thornton 619-0335
Chief of Litigation: (vacant) 619-1306

The **Legislation Division.** Attorneys in this Division draft and analyze bills affecting programs within the Department's jurisdiction. In addition, the Division acts as the focal point within the Department for review of proposed reports to Congress and the Office of Management and Budget.

(Area Code 202)

Associate General Counsel: Frances White 245-7760

The **Public Health Division** represents a variety of agencies involved in medical research (e.g., the National Institutes of Health) and public health issues (e.g., Public Health Service, National Institute of Occupational Safety and Health). A substantial portion of the Division's work involves providing formal and informal legal advice on a variety of health-related issues.

(Area Code 301)

Associate General Counsel: Richard J. Riseberg 443-2644
Deputy Associate General Counsel: Joel M. Mangel 443-2644
ADAMHA Branch Chief: Chris Pascal 443-1212
Centers for Disease Control Branch Chief:
Gene Matthews ....(404) 639-3428
Health Resources and Services Administration Branch
Chief: Donald Young 443-2240
Indian Health Services Branch Chief: Duke McCloud ...443-3096
NIH Branch Chief: Robert Lanman 496-4108
Patent Branch Chief: Leroy Randall 496-7056

The **Social Security Division** provides legal advice and representation to the Department's largest agency, the Social Security Administration (SSA). Division attorneys draft and interpret regulations, and represent the agency in thousands of Federal court actions which are filed annually. Due to the agency's large volume of litigation, a number of Social Security cases, frequently involving significant constitutional issues, reach the Supreme Court each term.

(Area Code 301)

Associate General Counsel: Donald A. Gonya 965-0600
Deputy Associate General Counsel: Randolph W. Gaines 965-3135
Deputy Associate General Counsel for Disability
Litigation: A. George Lowe 965-3177
Disability Litigation Branch I:
Carlotta Wells, Chief 965-3209
Disability Litigation Branch II:
Etzion Brand, Chief 965-3181
Disability Litigation Branch III:
Catherine Tackney, Chief 965-7178
Disability Litigation Branch IV:
Marlene Heiser, Chief 965-3202
Retirement, Survivor and Supplemental Assistance
Litigation Branch Chief: John M. Sacchetti ..965-3169
Deputy Associate General Counsel for Programs:
John B. Watson 965-3137
Retirement, Survivors and Disability Programs Branch
Chief: Mary J. Gludt 965-3146
Supplemental Security Income Program Branch Chief:
Gwenda Jones Kelley 965-0495

REGIONAL OFFICES

These offices provide legal services to the Regional Director and the regional representatives of constituent agencies. Attorneys in these offices perform a wide range of administrative law functions, which include writing legal opinions, preparing and reviewing contracts and other legal documents, commenting on proposed state legislation, conducting administrative hearings, and preparing briefs for and otherwise assisting U.S. Attorneys' Offices in civil/criminal litigation.

Region I (Boston)

Chief Counsel: Samuel C. Fish
U.S. Department of Health and Human Services, John F. Kennedy Federal Building, Government Center, Room 2407, Boston, MA 02203. Tel: 617/565-2370.

Region II (New York)

Chief Counsel: Annette Blum
U.S. Department of Health and Human Services, Room 3908, 26 Federal Plaza, New York, NY 10278. Tel: 212/264-4610.

Region III (Philadelphia)

Chief Counsel: Eileen Bradley
U.S. Department of Health and Human Services, Gateway Building, Room 9100, 3535 Market Street, Philadelphia, PA 19101. Tel: 215/596-1242.

Region IV (Atlanta)

Chief Counsel: Bruce Granger
U.S. Department of Health and Human Services, Suite 521, 101 Marietta Tower, Atlanta, GA 30323. Tel: 404/331-2377.

Region V (Chicago)

Chief Counsel: Donna Weinstein
U.S. Department of Health and Human Services, 105 W. Adams Street, 19th Floor, Chicago, IL 60603. Tel: 312/353-1640.

Region VI (Dallas)

Chief Counsel: Gayla Fuller
U.S. Department of Health and Human Services, Suite 1330, 1200 Main Tower Bldg, Dallas, TX 75202. Tel: 214/767-2995.

Region VII (Kansas City)

Chief Counsel: Frank Smith
U.S. Department of Health and Human Services, 601 East 12th St, Room 535, Kansas City, MO 64106. Tel: 816/426-3593.

Region VIII (Denver)

Chief Counsel: Ronald S. Luedeman
U.S. Department of Health and Human Services, Room 1106, 1961 Stout Street, Denver, CO 80294. Tel: 303/844-5101.

Region IX (San Francisco)

Chief Counsel: Richard K. Waterman
U.S. Department of Health and Human Services, 50 United Nations Plaza, Room 420, San Francisco, CA 94102. Tel: 415/556-5642.

Region X (Seattle)

Chief Counsel: Patrick McBride
U.S. Department of Health and Human Services, Suite 702, 2201 Sixth Avenue, Seattle, WA 98121. Tel: 206/442-0470.

OFFICE OF THE INSPECTOR GENERAL (ROOM 5250)

330 Independence Avenue, S.W., Washington, D.C. 20201

The mission of the Office of Inspector General (OIG), as mandated by Public Law 94-505, is to protect the integrity of Department of Health and Human Services' (HHS) programs as well as the health and welfare of beneficiaries served by those programs. This statutory mission is carried out through a nationwide network of audits, investigations and inspections conducted by three OIG operating components: the Office of Audit, the Office of Investigations, and the Office of Analysis and Inspections. The OIG also informs the Secretary of Health and Human Services of program and management problems, and recommends courses of action to correct them.

(Area Code 202)
Inspector General: Richard P. Kusserow 619-3148
Principal Deputy Inspector General:
Bryan B. Mitchell 619-3146
General Counsel: Max Thornton (Acting) 619-0335
Office of Inspector General Hotline:
Washington, DC Metro Area ....(301) 965-5953
Outside Washington, DC Metro Area ....(800) 368-5779
Facsimile 619-1487

Office of Investigations

The OIG's Office of Investigations (OI) conducts criminal investigations of wrongdoing against the Department's programs. The OI also investigates cases which fall short of criminality, involving abuse of HHS programs or beneficiaries and unjust enrichment by service providers. The investigative efforts of OI lead to judicial convictions, sanctions or civil money penalties. The OI also oversees State Medicaid Fraud Control Units which investigate and prosecute provider fraud in the Medicaid program.

(Area Code 202)
Deputy Inspector General for Investigations and Enforcement:
Larry D. Morey 619-3208
Assistant Inspector General for Civil and Administrative
Remedies: Eileen T. Boyd 619-0070
Assistant Inspector General for Criminal
Investigations: Robert A. Simon 619-0529
Assistant Inspector General for Investigations Policy
and Oversight: Paul F. Conroy 619-3210
State Fraud Branch Chief: Jim J. Shields 619-1520

DEPARTMENT OF HEALTH AND HUMAN SERVICES

DEPARTMENTAL APPEALS BOARD (ROOM 637-D)

Created in 1974, the Departmental Appeals Board (DAB) provides impartial review of disputed decisions of HHS operating components under agency grant programs, and provides hearings required in "civil penalty" programs of the Inspector General. The Board provides both relatively formal adjudication and informal mediation services. In 1988, the Secretary also gave the Board responsibility for adjudicating disputed civil penalties imposed under a wide range of new statutory authorities. The Board has two divisions:

***The Civil Remedies Division,** which includes the Board's Administrative Law Judges, primarily provides formal hearings in cases which typically involve allegations of fraud by physicians and other providers in the Medicaid and Medicare programs. In these cases, the Inspector General may seek recovery of funds, imposition of a penalty, and suspension from the programs. ALJ's decisions are appealable to the Appellate Division of the Board.

***The Appellate Division,** which essentially was the Board before the addition of civil remedies responsibilities, includes the five Board Members (one of whom is the Chairman, all of whom are appointed by the Secretary). The Appellate Division primarily reviews "disallowances" in numerous HHS grant programs, the most prominent of which are Medicaid and AFDC. A "disallowance" is an agency decision that a grantee (typically a state, Head Start, or community services agency) has spent grant funds improperly. Also reviewed are decisions in cost allocation disputes, debarment and suspension (e.g., where a researcher falsifies data), civil remedies decisions, and many other matters. The Appellate Division's process is innovative and relatively flexible, designed to offer fast and simple dispute resolution fitted to the needs of each case.

(Area Code 202)

Chairman: Norval (John) D. Settle 475-0007
Executive Secretary: Neil H. Kaufman 475-0006
Docket 475-0001
Administrative Law Judge: Charles E. Stratton 475-6090
Administrative Law Judge: Steven T. Kassel ......(404) 331-2194
101 Marietta Towers, Room 1621, Atlanta, GA 30323

(Area Code 202)

Library (Room 642-G) 475-0340
The library is available for reference Monday through Friday from 7:00 AM until 6:00 PM. Photocopying is available. A limited number of copies can be made for no charge. For additional information, contact the Administrative Assistant, Mary Pitts at 202/475-0340.

OFFICE OF EQUAL OPPORTUNITY AND CIVIL RIGHTS (Room 338-F)

(Area Code 202)

Complaints Processing and Adjudications Officer: (vacant) 245-1787

(Area Code 202)

Small and Disadvantaged Business Utilization and Civil Rights Officer: Cynthia Haile Selassie 245-1787

FAMILY SUPPORT ADMINISTRATION (Suite 600)

370 L'Enfant Promenade, S.W., Washington D.C. 20447

(Area Code 202)

Office of Child Support Enforcement Assistant Secretary: Jo Anne B. Barnhart 252-4500

FOOD AND DRUG ADMINISTRATION

5600 Fishers Lane
Rockville, MD 208578

DESCRIPTION: The Food and Drug Administration enforces the Federal Food, Drug and Cosmetic Act and other statutes within its jurisdiction. Its activities are directed toward protecting the nation's health against impure and unsafe foods, drugs and cosmetics, and other potential hazards. It is responsible for assessing the safety of food additives, human drugs, biological drugs, animal drugs, medical devices, radiation-emitting products, color additives, and cosmetics.

The Office of Chief Counsel, also known as the Food and Drug Division, Office of the General Counsel, represents the FDA in all court proceedings and administrative hearings; provides legal advice and policy guidance for FDA-administered programs; acts as liaison to the Justice Department and other Federal departments in connection with FDA legal matters; drafts or reviews all FDA proposed and final regulations and Federal Register notices; performs legal research and gives legal opinions on regulatory issues and actions; reviews and gives legal opinions on petitions submitted to the FDA; reviews proposed legislation affecting FDA that originates in the Department of HHS or on which Congress requests the views of the Department; and provides legal advice and assistance to the Office of the Secretary on matters within the Office's expertise. The Office also handles legal matters involving the Administrative Procedure Act, Federal Advisory Committee Act, Federal Tort Claims Act, and other Federal statutes.

(Area Code 301)

Commissioner: James Benson (Acting) 443-2410
Administrative Law Judge: Daniel J. Davidson 443-5315
Dockets Management 443-1753

Office of Health Affairs
Associate Commissioner: Stuart L. Nightingale, MD ...443-6143
Special Assistant to the Associate Commissioner for Health Affairs: Carol Kimbrough 443-6143
Health Assessment Policy Staff Regulatory Counsel:
Nancy Pirt 443-1382
I. David Wolfson 443-1382
Vacant...443-1382

(Area Code 301)

Office of Regulatory Affairs
Associate Commissioner: Ronald Chesemore 443-1594
Assistant Associate Commissioner:
William L. Schwemer 443-3283

Office of Enforcement
Director: Alan L. Hoeting 443-7400
Compliance Management and Operations Division
Director: Charles H. Everline 443-1745
Compliance Policy Division Director: (vacant) 443-2390
Regulations Policy Division Director:
Robert L. Spencer 443-3480

HEALTH CARE FINANCING ADMINISTRATION
6325 Security Boulevard
Baltimore, MD 21207

Administrator: Dr. Gail Wilensky ....(202) 245-6726
Office of Attorney Advisor Director:
Anthony J. Tirone ....(301) 966-3175
Public Affairs ....(202) 245-6113
Publications Information ....(301) 966-7843
FOIA ....(301) 966-5352
Privacy Act ....(301) 966-6079

PROVIDER REIMBURSEMENT REVIEW BOARD (Room 104)
Professional Building, 6660 Security Blvd, Baltimore, MD 21207

(Area Code 301)

Chairman: Elise D. Smith 966-5591

BUREAU OF POLICY DEVELOPMENT (Room 100)
East Highrise Building, 6325 Security Boulevard, Baltimore, MD 21207

(Area Code 301)

Office of Eligibility Policy
Hearings Staff Director: Kathleen A. Buto 966-5674

SOCIAL SECURITY ADMINISTRATION
6401 Security Boulevard
Baltimore, MD 21235

DESCRIPTION: The Social Security Administration (SSA) administers a national program of contributory social insurance whereby employees, employers, and the self-employed pay contributions that are pooled in special trust funds.

(Area Code 301)

Commissioner: Gwendolyn S. King 965-3120
Associate General Counsel: Donald Gonya 965-2410
Office of Public Inquires 965-7700

(Area Code 301)

FOIA 965-3962
Privacy Act 965-3962
Public Information ....(800) 234-5772

PROGRAMS (Room 100)

(Area Code 301)

Deputy Commissioner for Programs: Louis D. Enoff 965-0100

(Area Code 301)

Litigation Staff Director: Arleen Gahan 965-1507

DEPARTMENT OF HEALTH AND HUMAN SERVICES

OFFICE OF DISABILITY (Room 560)

(Area Code 301)

Associate Commissioner: Susan Parker 965-3424
Federal Disability Determination Service Director:
Robert E. Emrich 966-4800
Disability Claims Information ....(800) 234-0035

Note: This number should be used by individuals who have filed with the Office of Disability. It should not be used for general information.

OFFICE OF HEARINGS AND APPEALS (Suite 1600)

1 Skyline Tower, 5107 Leesburg Pike, Falls Church, VA 22041

The Office of Hearings and Appeals (OHA) of the Social Security Administration (SSA) is responsible for administering the appeals process under various titles of the Social Security Act. This process enables a claimant who has received an unfavorable decision by SSA to seek redress by presenting his or her case at a hearing before an Administrative Law Judge.

The Office of Hearings and Appeals currently employs approximately 660 Administrative Law Judges and 500 Attorneys and Law Clerks in its 132 Hearing Offices located throughout the United States. There are also 19 Attorney-Examiners who serve as members of the Appeals Council in its Central Office in Arlington, VA.

Attorney-Advisers serve as legal assistants to one or more Administrative Law Judges (ALJs) in a Hearing Office. Administrative Law Judges hold hearings and render decisions on appeals from determinations made in the course of the administration of Titles II, XVI, and XVIII of the Social Security Act. The Attorney-Advisers render legal advice and assistance to the Administrative Law Judges in prehearing development and preparation of cases for hearing, preparation of the decision, and post-hearing development. Legal problems involve research and interpretation of complex provisions of the Social Security Act, implementing regulations, related Federal and state laws, the Administrative Procedure Act, and precedent Social Security rulings and court decisions. Legal issues must be determined according to the various medical, social, and economic variables in each case, taking into consideration all of the factors as they relate to Federal, state, and local laws, agency policy, regulations, and precedents. Duties include conducting independent legal research, determining the need for additional testimony, reviewing/interpreting briefs, preparing analyses, and preparing a defensible legal decision in final form for the Administrative Law Judge's approval.

Trial Attorneys participate in case processing and presentation. They review and analyze cases, prepare the administrative record, develop and present relevant evidence, and examine/cross-examine witnesses. Trial Attorneys also review initial decisions issued by Administrative Law Judges and recommend that cases should be forwarded to the Appeals Council for consideration.

The 19 Attorney-Examiners serve as members of the Appeals Council which constitutes the adjudicative head of the agency. Each one exercises independent judgment and discretion in reviewing decisions of ALJ's and rendering the final administrative disposition of cases from a defined geographical area. The Attorney-Examiner may grant, dismiss, or deny the request for review of the ALJ's decision, which will result in the issuance of a decision affirming, modifying, or reversing the hearing decision. Decisions by Appeals Council Members are final and binding on all parties unless a civil action is filed in a Federal District Court.

(Area Code 703)

Associate Commissioner: Eileen Bradley 756-9200
Special Counsel: Donald Przybylinski 756-9170
Deputy Associate Commissioner: (vacant) 756-9200
Chief Administrative Law Judge: Theodore Haynes 756-5000
Deputy Chief Administrative Law Judge: (vacant) 756-5000
Office of Docket and File Management 756-9570

(Area Code 703)

Office of Appellate Operations:
Chairman: Eileen Bradley 756-9200
Executive Director: William J. Taylor 756-9100

REGIONAL OFFICES

Each of the regional offices has an Administrative Law Judge and a Regional Management Officer. Contact the Regional Management Officer for docket and other administrative information. Officer for docket and other administrative information.

Region I (Boston)

Regional Management Officer: Al Sapienza
Office of Hearings and Appeals, John F. Kennedy Federal Building, Room E-310, Boston, MA 02203. Tel: 617/565-1370.
(Jurisdiction: CT, ME, MA, NH, RI, VT)

Region II (New York)

Regional Management Officer: Arthur DeRuve
Office of Hearings and Appeals, 26 Federal Plaza, Room 34-130, New York, NY 10278. Tel: 212/264-4036.
(Jurisdiction: NY, NJ, PR, VI)

Region III (Philadelphia)

Regional Management Officer: Mary Meiss
Office of Hearings and Appeals, The Gateway Bldg, Rm 11100, 36th and Market Streets, Philadelphia, PA 19101. Tel: 215/596-6975.
(Jurisdiction: DE, MD, PA, VA, WV, DC)

Region IV (Atlanta)

Regional Management Officer: Fred Ponder
Office of Hearings and Appeals, Marietta Tower Bldg, 17th Floor, 101 Marietta Street, N.W., Atlanta, GA 30323. Tel: 404/331-5685.
(Jurisdiction: AL, FL, GA, KY, MS, NC, SC, TN)

Region V (Chicago)

Regional Management Officer: Patricia Carey
Office of Hearings and Appeals, Bankers Bldg, 18th Floor, 105 West Adams, Chicago, IL 60603. Tel: 312/353-0567.
(Jurisdiction: IL, IN, MI, MN, OH, WI)

Region VI (Dallas)

Regional Management Officer: Andrew Hickam
Office of Hearings and Appeals,1200 Main Tower, Room 1135, Dallas, TX 75202. Tel: 214/767-9401.
(Jurisdiction: AR, LA, NM, OK, TX)

Region VII (Kansas City)

Regional Management Officer: Alan Jacobs
Office of Hearings and Appeals, Federal Office Bldg, Room 505, 911 Walnut Street, Kansas City, MO 64106. Tel: 816/426-5246.
(Jurisdiction: IA, KS, MO, NB)

Region VIII (Denver)

Regional Management Officer: Matthew Trocheck
Office of Hearings and Appeals, Colonnade Center, Suite 600, 1244 Speer Blvd, Denver, CO 80204. Tel: 303/844-6100.
(Jurisdiction: CO, MT, ND, SD, UT, WY)

Region IX (San Francisco)

Regional Management Officer: Paul Meyers
Office of Hearings and Appeals,75 Hawthorne Street, 6th Floor, San Francisco, CA 94105. Tel: 415/744-4615.
(Jurisdiction: AZ, CA, HI, NV)

Region X (Seattle)

Regional Management Officer: James Ferguson
Office of Hearings and Appeals, Room 910, Mailstop RX-60, 2201 Sixth Ave, Seattle, WA 98121. Tel: 206/442-1322.
(AK, ID, OR, WA)

DATABASES AND PUBLICATIONS OF INTEREST

Databases and Bulletin Boards:

Departmental Appeals Board, Electronic Bulletin Board. The Departmental Appeals Board Electronic Bulletin Board is a computerized database that provides summaries of Departmental Appeals Board decisions, the full text of the decisions, and related index materials. It can be accessed through any microcomputer using a 1200 baud modem. There is no fee for use of the Bulletin Board, but usage is limited to one hour per day per user. For information call 202/474-0008.

Food and Drug Administration, Electronic Bulletin Board. The FDA Electronic Bulletin Board provides the full texts of announcements the moment that they are released. The bulletin board It offers FDA news releases, recalls, FDA Federal Register summaries, the FDA Drug Bulletin, selected stories from the FDA Consumer magazine, Congressional testimony, speeches delivered by FDA officials, and a special section on AIDS. It is designed for users with little computer experience and is available 24 hours a day, 7 days a week. To obtain FDA's free packet of information about the bulletin board, contact FDA at 301/443-3285 or write: U.S. Food and Drug Administration, 5600 Fishers Lane, Rockville, MD 20857. The bulletin board can be accessed through BT TYMNET. For pricing or equipment information, contact BT TYMNET Customer Support at 301/770-4280, 6120 Executive Boulevard, Suite 500, Rockville, MD 20852. Pricing information is also available from BT TYMNET at 800/872-7654.

Food and Drug Administration, Adverse Reaction Database. The FDA Adverse Reaction Database includes all adverse reactions to prescription drugs that are reported to FDA. The database was started in 1970 and contains over 100,000 records. Search requests must be submitted in writing and should include the trade name, generic name, and manufacturer of the drug. Reports list adverse reactions that are not normally found in the product insert. They also include summaries of case reports that show each specific case, the case accession number, and the adverse reactions encountered in the case. These reports cost $50.00 per drug. A second type of report is available describing specific cases in detail. The case reports should be requested by accession number. The cost of case reports is 50 cents per page plus staff search time, which is billed at $10.00 per hour or $20.00 per hour depending on the level of staff required to complete the search. Allow at least two to three weeks per search. Search charges are billed once per month. Contact: U.S. Food and Drug Administration, Division of Epidemiology and Surveillance, 5600 Fishers Lane (HFD737), Room 15B23, Rockville, MD 20857. Tel: 301/443-6260.

Food and Drug Administration, Product Defects Database. The FDA's Product Defects Database was started in 1974 and includes product defect information that has been reported to FDA. Only drugs produced in the U.S. are covered. Search requests must be submitted in writing and should include the trade name, generic name, and manufacturer of the drug. It is helpful to include the type of defect when known. Searches are performed on a cost reimbursement basis. Typical searches cost $10.00 to $60.00. All incidents meeting the search criteria are included in the search reports. A typical incident will be described in one to five lines. Allow at least two to three weeks per search. Search charges are billed once per month. Contact: U.S. Food and Drug Administration, Division of Epidemiology and Surveillance, 5600 Fishers Lane (HFD737), Room 15B23, Rockville, MD 20857. Tel: 301/443-6260.

BIOETHICSLINE. BIOETHICSLINE is a National Library of Medicine (NLM) online bibliographic database focused on questions of ethics and public policy. Its scope spans the literature of the health sciences, law, religion, philosophy, social sciences, and the popular media. For example, the database contains citations on such topics as euthanasia, organ donation and transplantation, the allocation of health care resources, patients' rights, codes of professional ethics, in vitro fertilization and other reproductive technologies, genetic intervention, abortion, behavior control and mental health therapies, and human experimentation. Published each year since 1975, BIOETHICSLINE currently contains approximately 30,000 records and is updated bimonthly. It is growing at the rate of approximately 2,400 records per year. The database is produced by the Information Retrieval Project at the Kennedy Institute of Ethics, Georgetown University, Washington, D.C. 20057. Tel: 202/625-8709 in the Washington, D.C. metropolitan area or 800/MED-ETHX outside the Washington, D.C. metropolitan area. The National Center for Bioethics will conduct searches of BIOETHICSLINE at no charge. BIOETHICSLINE is also available through the National Library of Medicine's MEDLAR system. NLM charges about $24.00 per computer connect hour during prime time (10:00 AM to 5:00 PM, Eastern time) and about $17.00 per hour at all other times. NLM also charges 25 cents for each page printed offline. A hard copy version of the database is published annually as the Bibliography of Bioethics. Volume 16, available November 1990, is $45.00 in the U.S. and Canada; $50.00 elsewhere.

Publications:

Deciding to Forego Life-Sustaining Treatment: Ethical, Medical, and Legal Issues in Treatment Decisions. President's Commission for the Study of Ethical Problems in Medicine and Biomedical and Behavioral Research, 1983. Available from National Technical Information Service, Springfield, VA 22161. Price: $11.00 plus $3.00 for handling. Document no. PB 83226836.

DEPARTMENT OF HEALTH AND HUMAN SERVICES

Handbook of Child Support Enforcement. Contains suggestions for resolving enforcement child support problems. Lists the basic steps to follow to obtain child support enforcement services. 1985. Available from Consumer Information Center-P, P.O. Box 100, Pueblo, CO 81002. Free. If you order two or more free publications, include a check for $1.00 payable to Superintendent of Documents. Booklet number 505W.

Wage Withholding for Child Support--An Employer's Guide for Small Businesses. As of November 1990, employers have legal responsibilities for enforcing child support. This booklet provides an overview of the law. It also lists telephone numbers of State Child Support Agency Wage Withholding Offices. Available from Consumer Information Center-P, P.O. Box 100, Pueblo, CO 81002. Free. If you order two or more free publications, include a check for $1.00 payable to Superintendent of Documents. Booklet number 502W.

Food and Drug Interactions. This four-page booklet describes how some commonly used drugs affect nutritional needs. It also discusses how foods affect drug actions and how to avoid ill effects. 1988. Available from Consumer Information Center-P, P.O. Box 100, Pueblo, CO 81002. Free. If you order two or more free publications, include a check for $1.00 payable to Superintendent of Documents. Booklet number 549W.

The following publications can be purchased from the **U.S. Government Printing Office.** Stock numbers and prices for annual subscriptions are shown below. Submit requests for these publications to: The Superintendent of Documents, U.S. Government Printing Office, Washington, D.C. 20402. (202/783-3238).

Compilation of the Social Security Laws, Including the Social Security Act, as Amended, and Related Enactments, Through January 1, 1989, Volume I. Contains an index of the Social Security Act as well as selected provisions of the Act and the Internal Revenue Code. Price: $31.00 domestic, $38.75 foreign. GPO Stock# 052-070-06583-4.

Compilation of the Social Security Laws, Including the Social Security Act, as Amended, and Related Enactments, Through January 1, 1989, Volume II. Includes applicable provisions of the Internal Revenue Code as well as other relevant public laws which effect the operating procedures of the Social Security Act. Price: $30.00 domestic, $37.50 foreign. GPO Stock# 052-070-06584-2.

Social Security Handbook (1988). Rulings are published as needed and consolidated annually. A cumulative manual is published every 5 years. This handbook contains rulings as amended through December 31, 1987. Price: $13.00 domestic, $16.25 foreign. GPO Stock# 017-070-00437-7.

Social Security and Acquiescence Rulings. Published irregularly. Contains interpretations and decisions of the Social Security Administration, as well as rulings of the U.S. Courts of Appeals that are in disagreement with the Administration's decisions, changes in Title II of the Social Security Act and related regulations, and items of general interest. Service consists of approximately 25 Social Security Rulings and eight Acquiescence Rulings. Price: $35.00 a year domestic; $43.75 a year foreign. GPO Stock# 817-003-00000-1.

These irregular issues are combined annually into the Social Security Rulings Cumulative Bulletin, which is not included in the subscription service but is sold as a separate publication at various prices.

Social Security Rulings on Federal Old Age, Survivors, Disability, Supplemental Income, and Black Lung Benefits. Cumulative edition 1988. Contains Presidential decisions based on case decisions, policy statements, decisions of administrative law judges, and the Appeals Council. Price: $6.00 domestic, $7.50 foreign. GPO Stock# 017-070-00445-8.

Approved Drug Products with Therapeutic Equivalence Evaluations (1990). Lists current marketed prescription drug products that have been approved on the basis of their safety and effectiveness by the Food and Drug Administration. Subscription service consists of a basic manual and supplemental material for an indeterminate period. Price: $91.00 a year domestic; $113.75 foreign. Stock# 917-016-00000-3.

FDA Consumer. Contains information written especially for consumers about Food and Drug Administration regulatory and scientific decisions, and about the safe use of products regulated by FDA. Published ten times a year. Price: $12.00 a year domestic; $15.00 foreign. GPO Stock# 717-009-00000-2.

FDA Enforcement Report. This weekly publication of the Food and Drug Administration contains information on prosecutions, seizures, injunctions, and recalls. Price: $51.00 a year domestic; $63.75 a year foreign. GPO Stock# 717-010-00000-1.

Federal Food, Drug, and Cosmetics Act as Amended and Related Laws. Price: $7.50 domestic, $9.38 foreign. GPO Stock# 017-012-00347-8.

Requirements of Laws and Regulations Enforced by Food and Drug Administration. Price: $2.75 domestic, $3.44 foreign. GPO Stock# 017-012-00343-5.

Medicare Coverage Issues Manual. HFCA Publication #6. 1990. Consolidated reprint. Contains the appendices previously issued in Medicare Hospital Manual, HFCA #10; Medicare Intermediary Manual, Part A, Claims Process, Part 3, HFCA #13-3; and Medicare Carriers Manual, Part B, Claims Process, Part 3, HFCA #14-3. Subscription service consists of a basic manual and transmittals issued for an indeterminate period. Price: $115.00 domestic; $143.75 foreign. GPO Stock# 917-012-00000-8.

Medicare Provider Reimbursement Manual. HFCA Publication #15-1. 1990. Consolidated reprint. Provides guidelines and policies to implement Medicare regulations which set forth principles for determining the reasonable cost of provider services. Subscription service consists of a basic manual and supplementary material issued for an indeterminate period. In looseleaf form, punched for 3-ring binder. Price: $91.00 domestic; $113.75 foreign. GPO Stock# 917-007-00000-4.

DEPARTMENT OF HEALTH AND HUMAN SERVICES
KEY LEGAL AUTHORITIES

Major Regulations:

General Departmental Regulations: 45 C.F.R. Part 1-199 (1989).
HHS Acquisition Regulation: 41 C.F.R. Chapt. 3 (1989); 48 C.F.R. Part 301 et seq. (1989).
Child Support Enforcement Office: 45 C.F.R. Parts 301-307 (1989).
Community Services Office: 45 C.F.R. 1010 et seq. (1989).
Family Assistance Office: 45 C.F.R. 201 et seq. (1989).
Food & Drug Administration: 21 C.F.R. 1 et seq. (1989).
Health Care Financing Administration: 42 C.F.R. 401 et seq. (1989).

Medicaid: 42 C.F.R. 430 et seq. (1989).
Medicare: 42 C.F.R. 401 et seq. (1989).
Peer Review: 42 C.F.R. 462 et seq. (1989).
Human Development Services Office: 45 C.F.R. 1301 et seq. (1989).
Public Health Service: 42 C.F.R. 1 et seq. (1989).
Public Health Service Acquisition Regulations: 48 C.F.R. PHS 301 et seq. (1989).
Refugee Resettlement Office: 45 C.F.R. Parts 400-402 (1989).
St. Elizabeth's Hospital: 42 C.F.R. Parts 301-306 (1989).
Social Security Administration: 20 C.F.R. Part 401 et seq. (1989).
Rules of Practice & Procedure:
Grant Appeals Board: 45 C.F.R. Part 16 (1989).
Informal Grant Appeals: 45 C.F.R. Part 75 (1989).
Civil Rights Hearings: 45 C.F.R. Part 81 (1989)

Human Subject Research, 42 U.S.C. 289--requires entities that apply for Health & Human Services grants, contracts, or cooperative agreements for projects involving human subject biomedical or behavioral research take steps to protect the rights of the human subjects of such research.
Legislative History: 1985 U.S. Code Cong. & Admin. News 672.
Implementing Regulations: 45 C.F.R. Part 46 (1989).

Public Health Service Act, as amended, 42 U.S.C. 201 et seq.--omnibus statute covering the duties and functions of the Public Health Service, including the (1) Commissioned Corps; (2) National Institutes of Health; (3) Centers for Disease Control; etc.
Legislative History: 1944 U.S. Code Cong. Service 1211; 1946 U.S. Code Cong. Service 1259; 1959 U.S. Code Cong. & Admin. News 1675; 1970 U.S. Code Cong. & Admin. News 4566; 1983 U.S. Code Cong. & Admin. News 3577; 1986 U.S. Code Cong. & Admin. News 42.
Implementing Regulations: 42 C.F.R. Part 1 et seq. (1989); 45 C.F.R. Part 83 (1989)[administration and enforcement of secs. 799A & 845 of the Act, denying Federal support to certain entities that may discriminate on the basis of sex in the admission of individuals to their training programs].

Age Discrimination Act of 1975, as amended, 42 U.S.C. 6101 et seq.--prohibits discrimination on the basis of age in programs or activities receiving Federal financial assistance while allowing such recipients to continue to use certain permitted age distinctions and non-age factors; and directs the Department of Health & Human Services to issue general governmentwide regulations implementing the Act.
Legislative History: 1975 U.S. Code Cong. & Admin. News 1252; 1978 U.S. Code Cong. & Admin. News 3388; 1988 U.S. Code Cong. & Admin. News 3.
Implementing Regulations: 45 C.F.R. Part 90 (1989).

Older Americans Act of 1965, as amended, 42 U.S.C. 3001 et seq.--makes available comprehensive aging programs, including health, education, and social services.
Legislative History: 1965 U.S. Code Cong. & Admin. News 1884; 1978 U.S. Code Cong. & Admin. News 3388; 1981 U.S. Code Cong. & Admin. News 2530; 1984 U.S. Code Cong. & Admin. News 2974; 1987 U.S. Code Cong. & Admin. News 866.
Implementing Regulations: 45 C.F.R. Parts 1321-1328 (1989).

Immigration & Nationality Act, Title IV, as amended, 8 U.S.C. 1522(a)(9)--established the Office of Refugee Resettlement in the Department of Health & Human Services and directed it to provide certain resettlement services to refugees.
Legislative History: 1980 U.S. Code Cong. & Admin. News 141.
Implementing Regulations: 45 C.F.R. Part 400 et seq. (1989).

Equal Opportunity Act of 1964, Title V, as amended ("Head Start Act"), 42 U.S.C. 9831 et seq.--authorized the Head Start child development services program.
Legislative History: 1981 U.S. Code Cong. & Admin. News 396; 1984 U.S. Code Cong. & Admin. News 4847; 1986 U.S. Code Cong. & Admin. News 2092; 1988 U.S. Code Cong. & Admin. News 101.
Implementing Regulations: 45 C.F.R. Parts 1301-1305 (1989).

Native American Programs Act of 1974, as amended, 42 U.S.C. 2991 et seq.--promotes economic and social self-sufficiency for Native Americans.
Legislative History: 1974 U.S. Code Cong. & Admin. News 8043.
Implementing Regulations: 45 C.F.R. Part 1336 (1989).

Child Abuse Prevention & Treatment Act, as amended, 42 U.S.C. 5101 et seq.--established a National Center on Child Abuse and Neglect designed to assist national, state, and local organizations to improve and expand prevention and treatment activities, and established an adoption information clearinghouse in the Department of Health & Human Services.
Legislative History: 1974 U.S. Code Cong. & Admin. News 2763 & 8043; 1978 U.S. Code Cong. & Admin. News 557; 1984 U.S. Code Cong. & Admin. News 2918; 1988 U.S. Code Cong. & Admin. News 72.
Implementing Regulations: 45 C.F.R. Part 1340 (1989).

Adoption Assistance & Child Welfare Act of 1980, as amended, 42 U.S.C. 670 et seq.--authorizes Federal payments for foster care and adoption assistance for children with special needs, including abandoned infants.
Legislative History: 1980 U.S. Code Cong. & Admin. News 1448; 1986 U.S. Code Cong. & Admin. News 42 & 4075.
Implementing Regulations: 45 C.F.R. Parts 1335-1357 (1989).

Developmental Disabilities Assistance & Bill of Rights, as amended, 42 U.S.C. 6000 et seq.--the statutory authority for the developmental disabilities programs of the U.S. Government; requires grantees to meet affirmative action requirements with respect to employing handicapped individuals; and specifies the rights of persons with developmental disabilities.
Legislative History: 1984 U.S. Code Cong. & Admin. News 2662.
Implementing Regulations: 45 C.F.R. Parts 1385-1388 (1989).

Federal Food, Drug, & Cosmetic Act, as amended, 21 U.S.C. 301 et seq.--prohibits the introduction or receipt into interstate commerce of any adulterated or misbranded food, drug, device, or cosmetic and related acts, mandates the registration of drug and device producers and the pre-market approval of drugs and devices, and imposes other regulatory requirements.
Legislative History: 1954 U.S. Code Cong. & Admin. News 2626; 1958 U.S. Code Cong. & Admin. News 5300; 1960 U.S. Code Cong. & Admin. News 2887; 1962 U.S. Code Cong. & Admin. News 2884; 1965 U.S. Code Cong. & Admin. News 1895; 1968 U.S. Code Cong. & Admin. News 2607 & 4594; 1970 U.S. Code Cong. & Admin. News 4566; 1972 U.S. Code Cong. & Admin. News 3993; 1976 U.S. Code Cong. & Admin. News 709; 1980 U.S. Code Cong. & Admin. News 2858; 1988 U.S. Code Cong. & Admin. News 5659.

Fair Packaging & Labeling Act, as amended, 15 U.S.C. 1451 et seq.--designed to insure that packages and their labels permit consumers to obtain accurate information as to the quantity of their contents, and to facilitate value comparisons by making unlawful unfair and deceptive packaging and labeling.
Legislative History: 1966 U.S. Code Cong. & Admin. News 4069.

Controlled Substances Act, as amended, 21 U.S.C. 801 et seq.--authorizes the Department of Health & Human Services (HHS) to determine the qualifications and competency of practitioners wishing to conduct research with listed controlled substances and the merits of the research protocol, and directs HHS to determine the safety and effectiveness of new drugs to be used in the treatment of narcotics addicts.
Legislative History: 1970 U.S. Code Cong. & Admin. News 4566; 1984 U.S. Code Cong. & Admin. News 3182 & 3994; 1986 U.S. Code Cong. & Admin. News 5393 & 6139; 1988 U.S. Code Cong. & Admin. News 5937.

Consumer Patient Radiation Health & Safety Act, as amended, 42 U.S.C. 10007-10008--directs the Department of health & Human Services to establish and electronic product radiation control program to include development and administration of performance standards to control emissions of radiation from electronic products.
Legislative History: 1968 U.S. Code Cong. & Admin. News 4312; 1976 U.S. Code Cong. & Admin. News 4947.

DEPARTMENT OF HEALTH AND HUMAN SERVICES

Implementing Regulations: 21 C.F.R. Part 1000 et seq. (1989).

Radiation Control for Health & Safety Act of 1968, 42 U.S.C. 263b et seq.--authorizes the Department of Health & Human Services, in conjunction with the Environmental Protection Agency and the Department of Veterans Affairs, to promulgate Federal radiation guidelines.
Legislative History: 1981 U.S. Code Cong. & Admin. News 396.

Patent Term Restoration, 35 U.S.C. 155-156--authorizes the Department of Health & Human Services to review patent term restoration applications for certain human drug products, medical devices, and food or color additives.
Legislative History: 1983 U.S. Code Cong. & Admin. News 1615; 1984 U.S. Code Cong. & Admin. News 2647; 1988 U.S. Code Cong. & Admin. News 5659.
Implementing Regulations: 21 C.F.R. Part 60 (1989).

Federal Import Milk Act, 21 U.S.C. 141-149--regulates the importation of milk and cream into the U.S. for the purpose of promoting the U.S. diary industry and protecting the public health.
Legislative History: 1959 U.S. Code Cong. & Admin. News 1675; 1960 U.S. Code Cong. & Admin. News 2963.
Implementing Regulations: 21 C.F.R. Chapt. I (1989).

Tea Importation Act, 21 U.S.C. 41 et seq.--prohibits the importation of any merchandise as tea inferior in purity, quality, and fitness for consumption to the standards fixed and established by the Secretary of Health & Human Services.
Legislative History: 1962 U.S. Code Cong. & Admin. News 1641; 1988 U.S. Code Cong. & Admin. News 1547.
Implementing Regulations: 21 C.F.R. Part 1220 (1989).

Parent Locator Service, 42 U.S.C. 653--directs the Department of Health & Human Services to established a Parent Locator Service designed to obtain and transmit to any authorized person information as to the whereabouts of any absent parent when the information is to be used to enforce support obligations against such parent.
Legislative History: 1974 U.S. Code Cong. & Admin. News 8133; 1981 U.S. Code Cong. & Admin. News 396; 1984 U.S. Code Cong. & Admin. News 697 & 2397; 1988 U.S. Code Cong. & Admin. News 2776.

Social Security Act, as amended, 42 U.S.C. 301 et seq.--the generic social insurance and services statute of the U.S., establishing trust funds and eligibility criteria for old age, survivors, and disability insurance benefits, aid to needy families with children, child welfare services, child support programs, services to the aged, blind, and disabled, unemployment insurance, supplemental security income for the aged, blind, and disabled, and health insurance programs, e.g., Medicare and Medicaid.
Legislative History: 1950 U.S. Code Cong. & Admin. News 3287.
Implementing Regulations: 42 C.F.R. Part 400 et seq. (1989); 20 C.F.R. Part 401 et seq. (1989).

Federal Coal Mine Health & Safety Act of 1969, as amended, 30 U.S.C. 801 et seq.--provides a benefit program for coal miners with Black Lung disease.
Legislative History: 1969 U.S. Code Cong. & Admin. News 2503; 1977 U.S. Code Cong. & Admin. News 3401.
Implementing Regulations: 20 C.F.R. Part 410 (1989).

DEPARTMENT OF HOUSING AND URBAN DEVELOPMENT

451 Seventh Street, S.W.
Washington, D.C. 20410

DESCRIPTION: The Department of Housing and Urban Development (HUD) administers the Federal Government's major programs of assistance for housing and for the nation's communities. HUD administers mortgage insurance programs to help families become homeowners, rental subsidy assistance for lower-income families, programs to aid neighborhood rehabilitation and the preservation of our urban centers from blight and decay, and community development assistance to increase the supply of low and moderate income housing, eliminate slums, conserve existing housing, and improve public service. HUD is also responsible for the administration and enforcement of the Federal fair housing laws and has other important regulatory functions, including the administration of the Real Estate Settlement Procedures Act, the Interstate Land Sales Full Disclosure Act, and the National Manufactured Housing Construction and Safety Standards Act.

(Area Code 202)

Secretary: Jack Kemp 708-0417
Office of Procurement and Contracts 708-1290
Public Affairs 708-0980
Small and Disadvantaged Business Utilization 708-1428
Fair Housing and Equal Opportunity Hotline:
Washington, DC Metro Area 708-3500
Outside Washington, DC Metro Area .... (800) 424-8590
Hotline for Fraud, Waste and Mismanagement 708-4200
Facsimile 708-0299

Library and Information Services 708-1420
HUD has a Library and Information Services Office which provides information on programs and publications, as well as refers questions to the correct administrative office. To obtain the publications of HUD's various units, call the number listed above. Questions about programs and issues are preferred in writing: Office of Housing and Urban Development, 451 7th Street S.W., Rm 8141, Washington, D.C. 20410. Attn: Library and Information Services.

(Area Code 202)

Freedom of Information Act Office 708-2749
Questions must be in writing; no requests will be taken over the phone. There is no charge for information and no page limit within reason. Submit requests to the Freedom of Information Act Officer, Rm 10132, at the HUD address cited at the beginning of this listing.

Privacy Act Office 708-2374

Library (Room 8141)
Main library 708-2370
Law library 708-2370
The library is open to the public from 8:45 AM until 5:15 PM Monday through Friday. However, only HUD employees may remove materials from the library. The library will not do searches, but will give assistance. Free photocopying available.

OFFICE OF GENERAL COUNSEL (Room 10214)

The Office of General Counsel provides a wide range of legal services to the Department, including:

*managing HUD litigation. Although the Department of Justice normally argues HUD's cases in court, HUD attorneys are responsible for case preparation and brief writing, and participate in trial and appellate presentation of cases;
*providing legal opinions on the operation of agency programs and on the interpretation of legislation;
*managing administrative hearings. These include hearings on interstate land sales, disputed personnel actions, and suspension or debarment procedures involving mortgagees or recipients of HUD program assistance;
*reviewing and processing HUD rules and regulations;
*developing and reviewing contracts, agreements, financing documents, and other documents used in HUD programs and activities; and
*drafting new legislation, interpreting statutes relating to HUD operations, and communicating the Department's views on legislation to the Congress.

(Area Code 202)

General Counsel: Frank Keating 708-2244
Deputy General Counsel: J. Stephen Britt 708-1240

The Office of General Counsel consists of six major offices. Attorneys assigned to these offices have broad responsibilities for specific areas of law. These offices are: Office of Insured Housing and Finance; Office of Assisted Housing and Community Development; Office of General and Administrative Law; Office of Program Enforcement; Office of Litigation; and Office of Legislation and Regulations.

Office of Assisted Housing and Community Development
Associate General Counsel: Robert S. Kenison 708-0212
Assistant General Counsel for Action Grants Division:
A. Heaton Nash 708-1298

(Area Code 202)

Assistant General Counsel for Assisted Housing Division:
George Weidenfeller 708-0992
Assistant General Counsel for Block Grants Division:
Vincent R. Landau 708-2027

Office of Equal Opportunity and Administrative Law
Associate General Counsel: Carolyn Lieberman 708-2203
Assistant General Counsel for Administrative Law:
Charles M. Farbstein 708-3137
Assistant General Counsel for General Law:
Harry Carey 708-0570

Office of Insured Housing and Finance
Associate General Counsel: John J. Daly (Acting) 708-1274
Assistant General Counsel for Finance Division:
Richard F. Lasner (Acting) 708-3260

(Area Code 202)

Assistant General Counsel for Home Mortgage Division:
David N. Pinsky 708-0303
Assistant General Counsel for Multifamily Mortgage Division:
David R. Cooper 708-4090

Office of Legislation and Regulations
Associate General Counsel: Edward J. Murphy, Jr 708-1793
Assistant General Counsel for Legislation Division:
James F. Lischer 708-1793
Assistant General Counsel for Regulations Division:
Grady J. Norris 708-3055
Rules Docket Clerk: Joan Campion 708-2084

Office of Litigation
Associate General Counsel: Gershon M. Ratner 708-0300
Associate General Counsel for Assisted & Fair Housing Litigation: Howard M. Schmeltzer 708-0300
Assistant General Counsel for Insured Housing & Community Development Litigation: Angelo Aiosa 708-1042
Facsimile 708-3351

Office of Program Enforcement
Associate General Counsel: John P. Kennedy 708-2568
Assistant General Counsel for Affirmative Litigation Division: Herbert Goldblatt 708-0557
Assistant General Counsel for Inspector General & Administrative Proceedings Division:
Patricia M. Black 708-3200
Assistant General Counsel for Program Compliance Division:
Peter S. Race 708-4184

REGIONAL AND FIELD OFFICES

HUD has ten major regional offices and 36 field offices. The principal attorney in the smaller offices has the title of either Chief Counsel or Chief Attorney, depending on the size of the office.

The Regional Counsel serves as the principal advisor to the Regional Administrator-Regional Housing Commissioner on legal matters. The Regional Counsel offices: provide legal counsel and assistance on all HUD programs and activities in the region; provide advice and guidance to Chief Counsel and Chief Attorneys; review equal opportunity enforcement activities and provide legal counsel to the Director, Office of Fair Housing and Equal Opportunity; and perform functions relating to Standards of Conduct, the Freedom of Information Act, adverse actions, tort claims, foreclosure actions, and litigation which involves regional or field office programs.

Listed below are HUD's Regional Counsel Offices, the Field Offices within each region which have attorneys on their staffs, and the names of key attorney personnel:

Region I (Boston)

Regional Counsel: Marvin H. Lerman
Associate Regional Counsel: Kathy E. Machan, William Poole, Sheila Mondshein, and Ellen Perry Dole
U.S. Department of Housing and Urban Development, Thomas P. O'Neill Jr. Federal Bldg, Rm 375, 10 Causeway Street, Boston, MA 02222-1092. Tel: 617/565-5234.

Field Offices

Hartford
Chief Counsel: Alan Cohen
Attorney-Advisor: David Furie
U.S. Department of Housing and Urban Development, 330 Main Street, First Floor, Hartford, CT 06106-1860.
Tel: 203/240-4523.

Manchester
Chief Attorney: David Aborn
U.S. Department of Housing and Urban Development, Norris Cotton Federal Bldg, 275 Chestnut Street, Manchester, NH 03101-2487.
Tel: 603/666-7681.

Region II (New York)

Regional Counsel: John Dellera
Deputy Regional Counsel: Benjamin Skurnick
Associate Regional Counsel: Irwin Horowitz, Louis Smigel, and John Cahill
U.S. Department of Housing and Urban Development, 26 Federal Plaza, New York, NY 10278-0068. Tel: 212/264-8053.

Field Offices

Newark
Chief Attorney: Brigid Bohan
General Attorneys: William Donzeiser, Sam Rosenblum, and Shie-Fong Sun
U.S. Department of Housing and Urban Development, Military Park Bldg, 60 Park Place, Newark, NJ 07102-5504.
Tel: 201/877-1662.

Buffalo
Chief Counsel: James Brylinski
General Attorneys: Diane Schwach and Louis Avino
U.S. Department of Housing and Urban Development, 465 Main Street, Fifth Floor, Buffalo, NY 14203-1780. Tel: 716/846-5755.

San Juan
Chief Counsel: Roque Sierra-Cruz
General Attorneys: Jennifer Bingham and Ivonne Ramirez
U.S. Department of Housing and Urban Development, 159 Carlos Chardon Avenue, San Juan, PR 00918-1804. Tel: 809/753-4201.

Region III (Philadelphia)

Regional Counsel: Peter Campanella
Associate Regional Counsel: Ann Harrison and Robert Dinney
U.S. Department of Housing and Urban Development, Liberty Square Bldg, 105 South Seventh Street, Philadelphia, PA 19106-3392. Tel: 215/597-2560

Field Offices

Baltimore
Chief Counsel: Joseph McSweeney
Attorneys-Advisors: Michael Fraticelli and John Sullivan
U.S. Department of Housing and Urban Development, Equitable Bldg, 10 North Calvert Street, 3rd Floor, Baltimore, MD 21202-1865. Tel: 301/962-2520.

Pittsburgh
Chief Counsel: John Bates
Attorney-Advisors: Anthony DeFrank, Suzanne McLaughlin, and Maria Mayercheck
U.S. Department of Housing and Urban Development, 412 Old Post Office Courthouse, 7th and Grant Streets, Pittsburgh, PA 15219-1906. Tel: 412/644-6388.

Richmond
Chief Counsel: Irene Deneau
Attorney-Advisor: Gabriel Peaseley
U.S. Department of Housing and Urban Development, Federal Bldg, First Floor, 400 North 8th Street, Richmond, VA 23240-0170. Tel: 804/771-2721.

Chief Counsel: Michael Reardon
Attorney-Advisors: Elizabeth Hughes, Russ Conlin, and Howard Sims
U.S. Department of Housing and Urban Development, 451 Seventh Street, S.W., Rm 3158, Washington, DC 20410-5500. Tel: 202/453-4500.

Region IV (Atlanta)

Regional Counsel: Raymond Buday Jr.
Associate Regional Counsel: James Blackmon, Donnie Murray, Jessica Parks, and Kathelene Coughlin
U.S. Department of Housing and Urban Development, Richard B. Russell Federal Bldg, 75 Spring Street, S.W., Atlanta, GA 30303-3388. Tel: 404/331-5136.

Field Offices

Birmingham
Chief Counsel: Robert Moore
U.S. Department of Housing and Urban Development, Daniel Bldg, 15 South 20th Street, Birmingham, AL 35233-2096. Tel: 205/731-1617.

Columbia
Chief Counsel: Edwin Brading
Attorney-Advisor: Sharon Shuler
U.S. Department of Housing and Urban Development, Strom Thurmond Federal Bldg, 1835-45 Assembly Street, Columbia, SC 29201-2480. Tel: 803/765-5592.

Greensboro
Chief Counsel: Max Redding
Attorney-Advisor: Janice Scott
U.S. Department of Housing and Urban Development, 415 North Edgeworth Street, Greensboro, NC 27401-2107. Tel: 919/333-5363.

Jackson
Chief Counsel: Jerry Moize
U.S. Department of Housing and Urban Development, Doctor A. H. McCoy Federal Bldg, 100 West Capitol Street, Ste 910, Jackson, MS 39269-1096. Tel: 601/965-4738.

Jacksonville
Chief Counsel: Gerald Wright
Attorney-Advisors: Frank Ferlita and Jerry Harward
U.S. Department of Housing and Urban Development, 325 West Adams Street, Jacksonville, FL 32202-4303. Tel: 904/791-2626.

Knoxville
Chief Counsel: James Fisher
U.S. Department of Housing and Urban Development, John J. Duncan Federal Bldg, Third Floor, 710 Locust Street, Knoxville, TN 37902-2526. Tel: 615/549-9384.

Louisville
Chief Counsel: Robert Kuhnle
Attorney-Advisor: Michael Powers
U.S. Department of Housing and Urban Development, 601 West Broadway, Louisville, KY 40201-1044. Tel: 502/582-5251.

Nashville
Chief Attorney: David Rogers
Attorney-Advisor: Thomas Derryberry
U.S. Department of Housing and Urban Development, 251 Cumberland Bend Dr, Ste 200, Nashville, TN 37228-1803. Tel: 615/736-5213.

Region V (Chicago)

Regional Counsel: Lewis Nixon
Associate Regional Counsel: Estelle Linn, Emil Vitucci, John Jensen, John Mahoney, Joseph Paige, Robert Leong, Karen Grant Dixson, and Geoffrey Roupas
U.S. Department of Housing and Urban Development, 626 West Jackson Blvd, Chicago, IL 60606-5601. Tel: 312/353-5680.
And:
U.S. Department of Housing and Urban Development, 547 West Jackson Blvd, Chicago, IL 60606-5760. Tel: 312/353-7660.

Field Offices

Cincinnati
Chief Attorney: Earl Cox
U.S. Department of Housing and Urban Development, Federal Office Bldg, Rm 9002, 550 Main Street, Cincinnati, OH 45202-3253. Tel: 513/684-2884.

Columbus
Chief Attorney: Jerry Grier
Attorney-Advisor: William Cusack
U.S. Department of Housing and Urban Development, 200 North High Street, Columbus, OH 43215-2499. Tel: 614/469-7345.

Cleveland
Chief Attorney: Milton Aponte
Attorney-Advisor: Angel Arroyo
U.S. Department of Housing and Urban Development, One Playhouse Square, Rm 420, 1375 Euclid Avenue, Cleveland, OH 44115-1832. Tel: 216/522-4065.

Detroit
Chief Counsel: Sheila Walker
Attorney-Advisors: John McFadden, Linda Johnson, Norman Clark
U.S. Department of Housing and Urban Development, Patrick V. McNamara Federal Bldg, 477 Michigan Avenue, Detroit, MI 48226-2592. Tel: 313/226-6280.

Indianapolis
Chief Counsel: Keith Lerch
Attorney-Advisor: Thomas O'Malley
U.S. Department of Housing and Urban Development, 151 North Delaware Street, Indianapolis, IN 46204-2526. Tel: 317/269-6303.

Milwaukee
Chief Counsel: Jeremy Beitz
U.S. Department of Housing and Urban Development, Henry S. Reuss Federal Plaza, Ste 1380, 310 West Wisconsin Avenue, Milwaukee, WI 53203-2289. Tel: 414/291-3214.

Minneapolis
Chief Counsel: Stephen Gronewold
Attorney-Advisor: Seval Charles Sorenson
U.S. Department of Housing and Urban Development, 220 Second Street, South, Minneapolis, MN 55401-2195. Tel: 612/370-3000.

Region VI (Fort Worth)

Regional Counsel: Thomas Peeler
Associate Regional Counsel: Charlene Berry, George Peeler, and Jack Stark
U.S. Department of Housing and Urban Development, 1600 Throckmorton, Fort Worth, TX 76113-2905. Tel: 817/885-5401.

Field Offices

Little Rock
Chief Counsel: John Munday
Attorney-Advisor: Robert Taylor
U.S. Department of Housing and Urban Development, Lafayette Bldg, Ste 200, 523 Louisiana Street, Little Rock, AR 72201-3707. Tel: 501/378-5401.

New Orleans
Chief Counsel: Florence Quail
U.S. Department of Housing and Urban Development, Fisk Federal Bldg, 1661 Canal Street, New Orleans, LA 70112-2887. Tel: 504/589-7200.

Oklahoma City
Chief Counsel: Clarence Wilson
Attorney-Advisor: Susan Ferrell
U.S. Department of Housing and Urban Development, Murrah Federal Bldg, 200 N.W. Fifth Street, Oklahoma City, OK 73102-3202. Tel: 405/231-4891.

San Antonio
Chief Counsel: Marcia Weiner
Attorney-Advisors: Vito Spano and Mary Thomas
U.S. Department of Housing and Urban Development, Washington Square, 800 Dolorosa, San Antonio, TX 78207-4563. Tel: 512/229-6806.

Region VII (Kansas City)

Regional Counsel: Joseph James
Associate Regional Counsel: William Nichols and Eugene Lipscomb
U.S. Department of Housing and Urban Development, 1103 Grand Avenue, Kansas City, MO 64106-2496. Tel: 816/374-6432.

Field Offices

St. Louis
Chief Counsel: Donald Flint
Attorney-Advisors: Barbara Kirschten and Daniel Dugan
U.S. Department of Housing and Urban Development, 210 North Tucker Blvd, St. Louis, MO 63101-1997. Tel: 314/425-4761.

Omaha
Chief Counsel: Joyce Haile-Selassie
Attorney-Advisor: Deborah McKeone
U.S. Department of Housing and Urban Development, 210 South 16th Street, Omaha, NE 68102-1622. Tel: 402/221-3703.

Region VIII (Denver)

Regional Counsel: Michal Stover
Deputy Regional Counsel: Diane DiQuinzio
Associate Regional Counsel: Thomas Coleman
U.S. Department of Housing and Urban Development, Executive Tower Bldg, 1405 Curtis Street, Denver, CO 80202-2349. Tel: 303/844-4513.

Region IX (San Francisco)

Regional Counsel: Beverly Agee
Deputy Regional Counsel: David Sutton
Associate Regional Counsel: Alfred DeMartini, Maurice Laymon, and Randall Akers*
U.S. Department of Housing and Urban Development, Phillip Burton Federal Bldg and U.S.Courthouse, 450 Golden Gate Avenue, San Francisco, CA 94102-3448. Tel: 415/556-4752.

*Assigned to Phoenix Office of Indian Programs (see Phoenix Field Office address below)

Field Offices

Honolulu
Chief Counsel: Susan Lee
U.S. Department of Housing and Urban Development, Prince Jonah Federal Bldg, 300 Ala Moana Blvd, Honolulu, HI 96850-4991. Tel: 808/541-1343.

Los Angeles
Chief Counsel: Janine Dolezel
Attorney-Advisors: Carl Kao and Nancy Feldman
U.S. Department of Housing and Urban Development, 1615 W. Olympic Blvd, Los Angeles, CA 90015-3801. Tel: 213/251-7122.

Phoenix
Chief Attorney: Raymond Kemp
U.S. Department of Housing and Urban Development, 1 North First Street, Third Floor, Phoenix, AZ 85002-3468. Tel: 602/261-4434.

Sacramento
Chief Attorney: Dexter Bergounous
U.S. Department of Housing and Urban Development, 777-12th Street, Ste 200, Sacramento, CA 95814-1997. Tel: 916/551-1351.

Region X (Seattle)

Regional Counsel: Waller Taylor III
Associate Regional Counsel: John VanderMolen
U.S. Department of Housing and Urban Development, Arcade Plaza Bldg, 1321 Second Avenue, Seattle, WA 98101-2054. Tel: 206/442-5414.

Field Offices

Portland
Chief Attorney: Robert Chatham
Attorney-Advisor: Thomas Giere
U.S. Department of Housing and Urban Development, 520 Southwest Sixth Avenue, Portland, OR 97204-1596. Tel: 503/221-2561.

Anchorage
Chief Counsel: Susan Olsen
U.S. Department of Housing and Urban Development, Federal Building-U.S. Courthouse, 222 West 8th Avenue, #64, Anchorage, AK 99513-7537. Tel: 907/271-4170.

OFFICE OF INSPECTOR GENERAL

The Office of Inspector General's (OIG) mission is to conduct audits and investigations of HUD programs and activities to determine their efficiency and effectiveness, and to prevent and detect fraud and abuse. The Inspector General has access to all records, reports, audits, reviews, documents, papers, recommendations or other material relating to the Department's programs and operations. This information is used by the Inspector General to assure that HUD-funded activities and operations are being conducted efficiently and effectively to meet legislative requirements and other goals.

(Area Code 202)
Inspector General: Paul A. Adams 708-0430

(Area Code 202)
Facsimile..708-1354

THE BOARD OF CONTRACT APPEALS (Room 3229)

Interstate Commerce Commission Building, 12th Street & Constitution Ave, N.W., Washington, D.C. 20401
(Mailing Address: 451 Seventh St, SW, Room 2131, Washington, D.C. 20401)

The HUD Board of Contract Appeals is the Department's independent forum for deciding appeals by contractors from final written decisions of HUD contracting officers. It consists of three administrative judges, who have the titles of Chairman, Vice Chairman, and Member. The Board is empowered to hear and make determinations on administrative appeals, the debarment and suspension of contractors, and Mortgage Review Board decisions.

The Board has the flexibility to provide either a full trial with discovery, subpoenas, and formal trial procedures, or more informal, expedited hearings for appellants with small claims against the Department. Most final decisions of the Board regarding contract disputes are written; certain debarment decisions are rendered from the bench upon agreement of both parties. Over half of the Board's hearings are held in the appellant's city to accommodate small business and pro se appellants.

To obtain the rules of procedure on contract appeal cases, see 24 C.F.R. 20.10 (1989); for debarment and suspension cases (including mortgagee review cases), see 24 C.F.R. Part 24 (1989); for IRS tax offset cases, see 24 C.F.R. 17.150-17.161 (1989); and for rules governing proceedings before Departmental Hearing Officers, see 24 C.F.R. Part 26 (1989). For other procedural information, contact the Law Clerk or Docket Clerk on 275-6233.

The decisions of the HUD Board of Contract Appeals are reported in the Board of Contract Appeals Reporter, a bi-weekly publication which reports the decisions of the following Boards of Contract Appeals: Agriculture, Armed Services, Corps of Engineers, Department of Transportation, Energy, General Services Administration, Department of Housing and Urban Development, Interior, Labor, National Aeronautics and Space Administration, U.S. Postal Service, and Department of Veterans Affairs. Annual Price $760.00. Contact: Commerce Clearing House, Inc., 4025 West Peterson Avenue, Chicago, IL 60646. Tel: 312/583-8500. Or in Washington, D.C., call 202/626-2200.

(Area Code 202)
Chairman and Administrative Judge: David T. Anderson...275-6233
Vice Chair and Administrative Judge: Jean S. Cooper....275-6233

(Area Code 202)
Board Member: Timothy J. Greszko........................275-6233
Docket Clerk or Law Clerk...............................275-6233

OFFICE OF ADMINISTRATIVE LAW JUDGE (Room 2156)

The Office of Administrative Law Judge provides the administrative adjudication system for HUD where required by statute, Executive Order, or Departmental rule. The Administrative Law Judge is an independent, impartial trier of fact in on-the-record hearings similar to a trial judge conducting civil trials without a jury. The Judge conducts formal and informal hearings in various locations throughout the United States. Generally, the Judge's decision becomes the final decision of the Department.

The Administrative Law Judge determines issues under a variety of statutes and regulations, including: the Interstate Land Sales Full Disclosure Act; the Civil Rights Act of 1964, Title VI; the Housing and Urban Development Act of 1968, Section 3 (Jobs in Housing); the Housing and Community Development Act of 1974 (Community Development Block Grants); the National Manufactured Housing Construction and Safety Standards Act of 1974; the debarment, suspension, and ineligibility of contractors and grantees in Departmental programs and related proceedings; and other administrative procedures requiring the expertise of an Administrative Law Judge.

Decisions of the Administrative Law Judges are not published; however, requests for a printed copy of the decision rendered in a specific case can be obtained by calling the Docket Clerk, Tel: 202/708-2540. Excerpts of the decisions of the Administrative Law Judges in cases involving the Fair Housing Amendments Act of 1988 can be found in Fair Housing-Fair Lending, a monthly updated publication of Prentice Hall, Law and Business Division. Tel: 1-800-223-0231. The annual subscription, with monthly report bulletins, costs $390.00.

(Area Code 202)
Chief Administrative Law Judge: Alan W. Heifetz 755-2540
Administrative Law Judge: William C. Cregar 755-2540
Administrative Law Judge: Robert A. Andretta 755-2540
Administrative Law Judge: Thomas C. Heinz 755-2540

(Area Code 202)
Paralegal/Chief Docket Clerk: Janet Rouamba 755-2540
Facsimile...619-8139

To obtain information on rules and procedures, call 755-2540.

DATABASES AND PUBLICATIONS OF INTEREST

Database:

HUD USER is a research information service sponsored by HUD's Office of Policy Development and Research. This system consists of research-oriented materials on such topics as affordable housing, building technology, community development, services for the elderly and handicapped, and neighborhood rehabilitation and conservation. The following services are offered:

- **HUD USER ONLINE:** BRS has the rights to approximately 145 bibliographic and full-text databases. The basic on-line connect cost varies depending on which database is used. For more information call 1-800-289-4277 or 703/442-0900, or write BRS, 8000 West Park Drive, McLean, VA 22102.

- **Document Delivery:** Printed copies of recently published reports may be obtained for $3 if the materials are currently in stock. Those reports not in stock may be obtained at a higher cost. For information, call 1-800-245-2691 or write **HUD USER**, P.O. Box 6091, Rockville, MD 20850.

- **Recent Research Results:** This free bulletin features information on HUD's policies, programs, publications and research activities. Call 800/245-2691 to order.

- **HUD USER** Standard Searches: Reports on key topics in housing and urban development are available for $10 and custom searches are available for $20. Call 800/245-2691 for information.

- Copies of non-copyrighted documents from **HUD USER ONLINE** are available in microfiche, contact: **HUD USER**, P.O. Box 6091, Rockville, MD 20850, or call 800/245-2691.

Publication:

Fair Housing-Fair Lending is an annual subscription with monthly report bulletins covering Federal and state equal housing opportunity law as represented in statutes, regulations, guidelines and court decisions. An annual subscription costs $390.00 and can be obtained from Prentice Hall, Law and Business Division. Tel: 800/223-0231.

DEPARTMENT OF HOUSING AND URBAN DEVELOPMENT
KEY LEGAL AUTHORITIES

Major Regulations:

General Departmental Regulations: 24 C.F.R. Part 0 et seq. (1989).
Department of Housing & Urban Development Acquisition Regulations: 48 C.F.R. Part 2400 (1989).
Government National Mortgage Association ("Ginnie Mae") Regulations: 24 C.F.R. Parts 300-390 (1989).
Homeless Shelter Assistance Programs: 24 C.F.R. Parts 575-576 (1989).
Rules of Practice and Procedure:
- **In General:** 24 C.F.R. Part 2 (1989).
- **Rulemaking:** 24 C.F.R. Part 10 (1989).
- **Board of Contract Appeals:** 24 C.F.R. Part 20 (1989).
- **Mortgagee Review Board:** 24 C.F.R. Part 25 (1989).
- **Proceedings Before a Hearing Officer:** 24 C.F.R. Part 26 (1989).
- **Interstate Land Sales Registration Program:** 24 C.F.R. Part 1720 (1989).

Department of Housing and Urban Development Act, as amended, 42 U.S.C. 3531 et seq.--the enabling statute for HUD, describing the Department's mission, powers and duties, as well as its organizational structure.
Legislative History: 1965 U.S. Code Cong. & Admin. News 3011.

Fair Housing Act of 1968, as amended, 42 U.S.C. 3601 et seq.--prohibits discrimination in the sale or rental of housing on the basis of race, color, religion, sex, familial status, or handicap. The Act extends to all real estate transactions including sale, rental, financing, and access to brokerage services.
Highlights of Recent Amendments: Extended coverage to include discrimination on the basis of (1) familial status and (2) handicap.
Legislative History: 1968 U.S. Code Cong. & Admin. News 1837; 1988 U.S. Code Cong. & Admin. News 2173.
Implementing Regulations: 24 C.F.R. Parts 105-115 (1989).

Civil Rights Act of 1964, Title VI, 42 U.S.C. 2000d et seq.--provides that no person in the U.S. shall be excluded from participating in, be denied the benefits of, or otherwise be subject to discrimination, on the grounds of race, color, or national origin, under any program or activity receiving Federal financial assistance.
Legislative History: 1964 U.S. Code Cong. & Admin. News 2355.
Implementing Regulations: 24 C.F.R. Part 1 (1989).

National Housing Act, as amended, 12 U.S.C. 1701 et seq.--the generic Federal housing and homeownership assistance and financing statute.
Legislative History: 1968 U.S. Code Cong. & Admin. News 2873.

Real Estate Settlement Procedures Act (RESPA), 12 U.S.C. 2601 et seq.--requires every transaction involving Federally-related mortgage loans to be in a standard form for the statement of settlement costs. This form (HUD-1) itemizes all settlement charges imposed upon the borrower and seller and indicates whether the lender or borrower or both are covered by any title insurance premium included in such settlement charges. Each lender must provide a booklet explaining the nature and cost of real estate settlement services, prepared by the Secretary, as well as a Good Faith Estimate of closing costs to every person from whom the lender receives, or for whom it prepares, a written application.
Legislative History: 1974 U.S. Code Cong. & Admin. News 6546.
Implementing Regulations: 24 C.F.R. Part 3500 (1989).

National Manufactured Housing Construction and Safety Standards Act of 1974, as amended, 42 U.S.C. 5401 et seq.--specifies that manufacturers who build mobile homes for sale in the U.S. must comply with HUD construction and safety standards, and are subject to inspection during construction by HUD-approved, third-party inspection agencies. The Act also accords consumers with defective manufactured homes remedies ranging from the right to be notified that their home contains a defect to the right to a refund or exchange in extreme circumstances, and also prohibits dealers from selling homes in which they know there exists a failure to conform to Federal standards.
Highlights of Recent Amendments: 24 U.S.C. 5403(i): added energy conservation standards.
Legislative History: 1974 U.S. Code Cong. & Admin. News 4340; 1984 U.S. Code Cong. & Admin. News 3817.
Implementing Regulations: 24 C.F.R. Parts 3280, 3282, & 3283 (1989).

Housing and Community Development Act of 1974, 12 U.S.C. 1706(e) --authorizes "urban homesteading," which is designed to use existing housing stock to provide home ownership, encourages public and private investment in selected neighborhoods, and assists in their preservation and revitalization. The program provides for the transfer without payment of Federally-owned properties to a local urban homesteading agency (LUHA) for use in HUD-approved local urban homesteading programs.
Legislative History: 1974 U.S. Code Cong. & Admin. News 4353.
Implementing Regulations: 24 C.F.R. Part 590 (1988).

Interstate Land Sales Full Disclosure Act, as amended, 15 U.S.C. 1701 et seq.--requires developers who sell land consisting of 100 or more nonexempt lots, any one of which is less than 20 acres, who use any means of interstate commerce or the mails to promote their properties, to register with HUD. Purchasers must be provided with a Property Report which gives key facts about the development and the developer. The registration procedure requires the developer to file a statement of record, including the Property Report, disclosing all pertinent facts about the land, its ownership, control, amenities, restrictions, and the nature of the purchase or lease transaction.
Legislative History: 1968 U.S. Code Cong. & Admin. News 2873; 1974 U.S. Code Cong. & Admin. News 4357; 1979 U.S. Code Cong. & Admin News 2346.
Implementing Regulations: 24 C.F.R. Part 1700 (1989).

Uniform Relocation Assistance and Real Property Acquisition Policies Act of 1970, as amended, 42 U.S.C. 4601 et seq.--encourages and expedites the acquisition of real property by Federal entities through agreements with owners in order to avoid litigation and relieve congestion in the courts, and requires that:
* Every reasonable effort will be made to acquire real property through negotiation.
* Real property will be appraised before the initiation of negotiations, and the owner or his designated representative may accompany the appraiser during the inspection.
* Before the start of negotiations for the real property, a just compensation will be determined and an offer will be made.
* No person occupying real property will be required to leave his dwelling or move his business without 90 days written notice.

Highlights of Recent Amendments: authorizes heads of Federal agencies to prescribe a procedure to waive the appraisal requirement in cases involving the acquisition by sale or donation of property with a low fair market value, and if an acquisition of property would leave the owner with an uneconomic remnant (as determined by the Secretary), the agency must offer to buy the uneconomic remnant.
Legislative History: 1970 U.S. Code Cong. & Admin. News 5850; 1987 U.S. Code Cong. & Admin. News 66, 241.

Implementing Regulations: 24 C.F.R. Part 42 (1989); 49 C.F.R. Part 24 (1989).

Multifamily Mortgage Foreclosure Act of 1981, as amended, 12 U.S.C. 3701-3717--creates a uniform Federal remedy for the foreclosure of mortgages covering multi-unit residential and non-residential project mortgages held by the Secretary of HUD under Title II of the National Housing Act and 45 U.S.C. 1452b.
Legislative History: 1981 U.S. Code Cong. & Admin. News 396.
Implementing Regulations: 24 C.F.R. Part 27 (1989).

Lead-Based Paint Poisoning Prevention Act, as amended, 42 U.S.C. 4821-4846--directs the Secretary of HUD to establish procedures to eliminate, as far as practicable, lead-based paint poisoning hazards in Federally-assisted housing.
Legislative History: 1970 U.S. Code Cong. & Admin. News 6131; 1988 U.S. Code Cong. & Admin. News 4395.
Implementing Regulations: 24 C.F.R. Part 35 (1989).

Exec. Order No. 11063, 3 C.F.R., 1959-1963 Comp., p. 652, as amended by **Exec. Order No. 12259,** 3 C.F.R., 1980 Comp., p. 307, "Equal Opportunity in Housing."

DEPARTMENT OF INTERIOR

1849 C Street, N.W.
Washington, D.C. 20240

DESCRIPTION: The jurisdiction of the Department of the Interior includes the administration of over 500 million acres of Federal land, and trust responsibilities for approximately 50 million acres of land, mostly Indian reservations; the conservation and development of fish and wildlife resources; the coordination of Federal and state recreation programs; the preservation and administration of the nation's scenic and historic areas; the reclamation of arid lands in the West through irrigation; the operation and coordination of manpower and youth training programs; and the management of hydroelectric power systems.

(Area Code 202)

Secretary: Manuel Lujan Jr 208-7351
Procurement Information 208-3105
Public Affairs 208-3171
Publications Information 208-4841
Small and Disadvantaged Business Utilization 208-3493
Hot Line for Fraud, Waste and Abuse
  Washington, D.C. Metro Area 208-2424
  Outside Washington, D.C. Metro Area .... (800) 424-5081
Facsimile 208-5048

Main Library (Room 1140) 208-5815
The main Department of Interior library (called the Natural Resources Library) is open to the public Monday through Friday from 8:00 AM until 4:00 PM. Only Department of Interior employees may remove materials from the library. If you want to photocopy materials, please bring your own paper. The automated card catalog is accessible to the public.

Law Library (Room 7100 West) 208-4571
The library is open to the public Monday through Friday from 7:45 AM until 6:00 PM. Only Department of Interior employees may remove materials from the library. If you want to photocopy materials, please bring your own paper. The automated card catalog is accessible to the public.

(Area Code 202)

Freedom of Information Act/Privacy Act Office 208-6191
The Information Act/Privacy Act Offices are decentralized within the agency. If you have a FOIA/Privacy Act request, call the main number listed above and ask for the FOIA/Privacy Act office for a specific Bureau or Service. The following names, addresses and phone numbers are Department of Interior offices which set policy and establish procedures regarding FOIA/Privacy Act.

FOIA and Privacy Act: Ms. Alexandra Mallus
U.S Department of the Interior, (DRD-PMI), MS-2242-MIB, Washington, D.C. 20240. Tel: 202/208-5342.

FOIA Appeals Officer: William Wolff
U.S. Department of the Interior, (DRD-PMI), MS-2242-MIB, Washington, D.C. 20240. Tel: 202/208-5339.

Legal Contact: John Trezise
Office of the Solicitor, Division of General Law, U.S. Department of the Interior, MS-6531-MIB, Washington, D.C. 20240. Tel: 202/208-5216

OFFICE OF THE SOLICITOR (ROOM 5352)

The Solicitor is the principal legal advisor of the Secretary and is the chief law enforcement officer of the Department. The Solicitor's Office consists of a headquarters organization in Washington, D.C. and regional and field offices located at 19 locations throughout the U.S. The Washington, D.C. office is organized into six major legal divisions and an administrative division.

(Area Code 202)

Solicitor: Thomas L. Sansonetti 208-4423
Deputy Solicitor: Jennifer A. Salisbury 208-4813
Special Assistant: Jill Fallon 208-5301
Special Assistant: Candace Strother 208-4423
Docket 208-6503
Contact Carol Kesterson, Chief Docket and Record Control Administrator. The office receives summons, complaints, pleadings, and orders and sends them on to the appropriate department or to the Justice Department for litigation. This office keeps the docket on all lawsuits or complaints for the Department of Interior.

The **Division of Administration** provides all administrative and management support services. It has four subdivisions: the Budget and Accounting Branch; the Personnel Services Branch; the Management Information Systems Branch; and the Docket, Records, Mail and Distribution Branch.

(Area Code 202)

Director: Terence C. Wiles 208-6115
Ethics Specialist: Lori Jarmen 208-6115
Dockets and Records Control/Branch Chief:
  Carol A. Kesterson 208-6503

The **Division of Audit and Investigation** provides legal advice and services to the Office of the Inspector General with respect to: audits and investigations of the Department's programs, operations, and employee conduct; the review of legislation; investigation of employee complaints; and reports to Congress.

(Area Code 202)

Associate Solicitor: Thomas E. Robinson 208-3275

The **Division of Conservation and Wildlife** is responsible for legal matters arising in connection with the programs and activities of the National Park Service and the Fish and Wildlife Service. In addition, the Division provides legal assistance and counsel to the Assistant Secretary for Fish and Wildlife and Parks. The Division has three Branches, each of which is under the direction of an Assistant Solicitor: the Branch of Parks and Recreation, the Branch of National Capital Region, and the Branch of Fish and Wildlife.

(Area Code 202)

Associate Solicitor: Martin J. Suuberg 208-4344
Assistant Solicitor for Fish and Wildlife:
  Charles P. Raynor 208-6172

Assistant Solicitor for National Capital Parks:
Richard C. Robbins 208-4338
Assistant Solicitor for Parks and Recreation:
David A. Watts 208-7957

The **Division of Energy and Resources** is responsible for legal matters arising in connection with the programs and activities of the Bureaus of Land Management, Mines and Reclamation; the Geological Survey; and the Minerals Management Service. The Division is also responsible for legal services pertaining to programs and activities of the Department related to electric power, and the Law of the Sea and international law affecting marine minerals, pollution, and related matters. In addition, the Division provides legal assistance and counsel to the Assistant Secretaries of Water and Science and of Land and Minerals Management. The Division has four branches, each of which is under the direction of an Assistant Solicitor: the Branch of Offshore Minerals and Royalty Management; the Branch of Onshore Minerals, the Branch of Land Use, and the Branch of Water and Power.

(Area Code 202)
Associate Solicitor: Michael A. Poling 208-5757
Deputy Associate Solicitor: Paul B. Smyth 208-4506
Assistant Solicitor for:
Land Use and Realty: A. Scott Loveless 208-4444
Offshore Minerals and Royalty Management:
L. Poe Leggette 208-4325
Onshore Minerals: vacant 208-4803
Water and Power: Patricia S. Bangert 208-4379

The **Division of General Law** is responsible for procurement and tort claims, patents, EEO, territories, labor law, and administrative and other general law functions. The Division also has the initial lead responsibility for providing legal services in the environmental area pertaining to the administration of the National Environmental Policy Act. The Division has three branches, each of which is under the direction of an Assistant Solicitor: the Branch of Procurement and Patents, the Branch of Administrative Law and General Legal Services, and the Branch of Equal Opportunity Compliance.

(Area Code 202)
Associate Solicitor: Jennifer A. Salisbury 208-4722
Deputy Associate Solicitor: Timothy S. Elliott 208-4722
Assistant Solicitor for:
Administrative Law and General Legal Services:
John Trezise 208-5216
Equal Opportunity Compliance: Robert Walter 208-6346
Procurement and Patents: Justin P. Patterson 208-6201

The **Division of Indian Affairs** is responsible for all legal matters pertaining to the administration of Indian affairs. The Division has four branches, each of which is under the direction of an Assistant Solicitor: the Branch of Water and Power, the Branch of Land and Minerals, the Branch of Tribal Government and Alaska, and the Branch of General Indian Legal Activities.

(Area Code 202)
Associate Solicitor: William G. Lavell 208-3401
Deputy Associate Solicitor: Charles B. Hughes 208-3401
Assistant Solicitor for:
General Indian Legal Activities:
Duard R. Barnes 208-4388
Land and Minerals: Michael Cox 208-4361
Tribal Government and Alaska: Scott Keep 208-5134
Water and Power: Ann Crichton 208-6967

The **Division of Surface Mining** is responsible for providing legal advice to the Office of Surface Mining (OSM) and the Assistant Secretary-Energy and Minerals relating to implementation of the Surface Mining Control and Reclamation Act of 1977. The Division also represents OSM in all administrative hearings and litigation, and assists the Department of Justice in the conduct of Federal court litigation. The Division has four branches, each of which is under the direction of an Assistant Solicitor: the Branch of Litigation, the Branch of Enforcement and Collections, the Branch of Regulatory Programs, and the Branch of Governmental Relations.

(Area Code 202)
Associate Solicitor: Donald H. Vish 208-3175
Special Assistant: Christopher Warner 208-5207
Deputy Associate Solicitor: Robert S. More 208-3175
Assistant Solicitor for:
Enforcement and Collections: Frank Conforti 208-4582
Litigation: Glenda H. Owens 208-4671
Regulatory Programs: Joel M. Yudson 208-6347

Field Offices: The Division of Surface Mining has three field offices. Their addresses are listed below.

Golden
Field Solicitor: Albert Kashinski
U.S. Department of the Interior, Division of Surface Mining, 703 Sims St, Suite 472, Golden, CO 80401. Tel: 303/236-8444.

Knoxville
Field Solicitor: J.T. Begley
U.S. Department of the Interior, Division of Surface Mining, P.O. Box 15006, Knoxville, TN 37901. Tel: 615/673-4233.

Pittsburgh
Field Solicitor: Janet A. Goodwin
U.S. Department of the Interior, Division of Surface Mining, Ten Parkway Center, Pittsburgh, PA 15220. Tel: 412/937-4000.

REGIONAL AND FIELD OFFICES

With the exception of the Division of Surface Mining field offices listed above, each of the other Solicitor's field offices has responsibility for the execution of legal work in connection with programs and activities conducted by bureaus in its particular vicinity. These offices are listed below.

Alaska Regional Office (Anchorage)

Regional Solicitor: Jon Tangen
U.S. Department of the Interior, 222 West 8th Avenue, Room A25, Anchorage, AK 99513. Tel: 907/271-4131.

Intermountain Regional Office (Salt Lake City)

Regional Solicitor: Lynn Collins
Assistant Regional Solicitor: David K. Grayson
U.S. Department of the Interior, 6201 Federal Bldg, 125 South State Street, Salt Lake City, UT 84138-1180. Tel: 801/524-5677.

Field Office: Boise
Field Solicitor: William Dunlop
U.S. Department of the Interior, Federal Bldg, U.S. Courthouse, 550 W. Fort Street, Box 020, Boise, ID 83724.Tel: 208/334-1911.

Field Office: Phoenix
Field Solicitor: Fritz Goreham
U.S. Department of the Interior, 1 Renaissance Square, Suite 500, 2 North Central, Phoenix, AZ 85004.
Tel: 602/379-4756.

Northeast Regional Office (Newton Corner)

Regional Solicitor: Anthony R. Conte
Senior Attorney: James E. Epstein
U.S. Department of the Interior, One Gateway Center, Suite 612, Newton Corner, MA 02158-2868. Tel: 617/965-5100.

Pacific Northwest Regional Office (Portland)

Regional Solicitor: Lawrence E. Cox
Assistant Regional Solicitor: Donald P. Lawton
Assistant Regional Solicitor: Arthur V. Biggs
Assistant Regional Solicitor: William D. Back
U.S. Department of the Interior, Lloyd 500 Bldg, Suite 607, 500 N.E. Multnomah Street, Portland, OR 97232. Tel: 503/231-2126.

Field Office: Billings
Field Solicitor: Richard Aldrich
U.S. Department of the Interior, 316 North 26th Street, Room 3004, Billings, MT 59101. Tel: 406/657-6331.

Field Office: Twin Cities
Field Solicitor: Mariana Shulstad
U.S. Department of the Interior, 686 Federal Building, Ft. Snelling, Twin Cities, MN 55111. Tel: 612/725-3540.

Pacific Southwest Regional Office (Sacramento)

Regional Solicitor: William M. Wirtz (Acting)
U.S. Department of the Interior, 2800 Cottage Way, Room E-2753, Sacramento, CA 95825-1890. Tel: 916/978-4821.

Field Office: San Francisco
Field Solicitor: Ralph Mihan
U.S. Department of the Interior, 450 Golden Gate Avenue, Room 14126, San Francisco, CA 94102. Tel: 415/556-8807.

Rocky Mountain Regional Office (Golden)

Regional Solicitor: Gina Guy
Assistant Regional Solicitor: Albert V. Witham
Assistant Regional Solicitor: Lowell L. Madsen
U.S. Department of the Interior, 730 Simms Street, Suite 450, Golden, CO 80401. Tel: 303/236-8444.

Southeast Regional Office (Atlanta)

Regional Solicitor: Roger S. Babb
Assistant Regional Solicitor: Kahlman R. Fallon
U.S. Department of the Interior, Richard B. Russell Federal Building, 75 Spring Street, S.W., Suite 1328, Atlanta, GA 30303. Tel: 404/331-4447.

Southwest Regional Office (Tulsa)

Regional Solicitor: Timothy Vollmann
Assistant Regional Solicitor: Emmett M. Rice
Assistant Regional Solicitor: M. Sharon Blackwell
U.S. Department of the Interior, Page Belcher Federal Bldg, Room 3068, 333 West Fourth St, Tulsa, OK 74101. Tel: 918/581-7502.

Field Office: Pawhuska
Attorney: William Haney
U.S. Department of the Interior, Osage Agency, Grand View Ave., Pawhuska, OK 74056. Tel: 918/287-2495 ext 247.

Field Office: Santa Fe
Field Solicitor: Gayle Manges
U.S. Department of the Interior, Federal Building, Cathedral Pl., Room 226, Santa Fe, NM 87501. Tel: 505/988-6200.

Field Office: Window Rock
Field Solicitor: Theresa Gomez
U.S. Department of the Interior, BIA Administrative Bldg #1, Room 26, Window Rock Drive, Window Rock, AZ 86515. Tel: 602/871-5151, ext 5116.

OFFICE OF THE INSPECTOR GENERAL (Room 5359)

The Office of the Inspector General provides policy direction and conducts, supervises, and coordinates all audits, investigations, and other activities in the Department designed to promote economy and efficiency or prevent and detect fraud and abuse. The Office also reviews existing and proposed legislation and regulations and makes recommendations to the Secretary and Congress in order to prevent and detect fraud and abuse in Departmental programs.

(Area Code 202)
Inspector General: James R. Richards 208-5745
Assistant Inspector General for Investigations:
Thomas T. Sheehan 208-6752

(Area Code 202)
Facsimile 208-4998

OFFICE OF CONGRESSIONAL AND LEGISLATIVE AFFAIRS (Room 6243)

The Office of Legislative Counsel consults with the Office of the Secretary in determining policy relating to proposed or pending legislation; reviews legislative documents and monitors the preparation of coordinated reports; coordinates Interior Department representation at congressional hearings; maintains contacts on legislative matters with the Congress and other Federal agencies; and provides legislative information for use within the Department.

(Area Code 202)
Legislative Counsel: Pamela E. Sommers 208-6706

(Area Code 202)
Assistant Legislative Counsel: Ralph Hill, Jr 208-4547

OFFICE OF HEARINGS AND APPEALS (Room 1110)

4015 Wilson Blvd, Arlington, VA 22203

The Office of Hearings and Appeals (OHA) handles the quasi-judicial responsibilities of the Department of the Interior, hearing, considering, and determining matters within the jurisdiction of the Department involving hearings, appeals, and other secretarial review functions. The Office of Hearings and Appeals is headquartered in Arlington, VA, with Administrative Law Judges in field locations where indicated.

(Area Code 703)

Director: Charles B. Cates 235-3810
Deputy Director: vacant 235-3810
Special Counsel:
Frances A. Patton 235-3810
Bruce A. Johnson 235-3810
Facsimile 235-1631

There are two major functions within OHA: the **Hearings Division**, and the **Appeals Boards** which include the Board of Contract Appeals, the Board of Land Appeals, and the Board of Indian Appeals.

The **Hearings Division** consists of Administrative Law Judges who are authorized to conduct hearings in cases under the Administrative Procedure Act, hearings in Indian probate matters, and hearings in other cases arising under Departmental statutes and regulations. There is currently one Administrative Law Judge in the headquarters office, one in Knoxville, and three in Salt Lake City. There are also Administrative Law Judges handling Indian probate matters in each of the following locations: Albuquerque, Billings, Oklahoma City, Phoenix, Rapid City, Sacramento, and Twin Cities, MN.

The decisions of the Administrative Law Judges, mainly those involving surface mining cases, can be obtained by subscription from the Office of Hearings, 4015 Wilson Blvd., Arlington, VA 22203. Tel: 703/235-3799. Annual price: $45.00. If you have a request for a specific case, you can call the office at the above number for a copy of that record.

(Area Code 703)

Chief Administrative Law Judge: Parlen L. McKenna ...235-3800
Legal Staff Assistant (Docket Supervisor):
Joanne F. Summerbell 235-3800
Administrative Law Judge: vacant 235-3800

The **Board of Land Appeals**, the largest Appeals Board, decides appeals relating to the use and disposition of public lands and their resources, including land selections arising under the Alaska Native Claims Settlement Act, as well as to the use and disposition of mineral resources in certain acquired lands of the U.S. and in submerged lands of the Outer Continental Shelf. Cases appealed to this Board involve mining claims, mineral leasing, grazing, homestead, rights-of-way, and public sale laws.

The decisions of the Administrative Law Judges of the Board of Land Appeals can be obtained by subscription from the Office of Hearings, 4015 Wilson Blvd., Arlington, VA 22203. Tel: 703/235-3799. Annual price: $475.00. If you have a request for a specific case, you can call the office at the above number for a copy of that record. Online WESTLAW users can also access these decisions.

(Area Code 703)

Chief Administrative Judge: William Philip Horton ...235-3750
Deputy Chief Administrative Judge: Bruce R. Harris ..235-3750
Legal Staff Assistant: Betty Jo Brownlee 235-3750
Administrative Judges:
Franklin D. Arness 235-3750
James L. Burski 235-3750
James L. Byrnes 235-3750
Gail M. Frazier.............................235-3750
C. Randall Grant Jr 235-3750
David L. Hughes 235-3750
William A. Irwin 235-3750
John H. Kelly 235-3750
Robert W. Mullen 235-3750

The **Board of Contract Appeals** decides appeals dealing with the procurement of services; the procurement of construction, repair, or maintenance of real property; or the disposal of personal property.

The decisions of the Board of Contract Appeals can be obtained by subscription from the Office of Hearings, 4015 Wilson Blvd., Arlington, VA 22203. Tel: 703/235-3799. Annual price: $80.00. If you have a request for a specific case, you can call the office at the above number for a copy of that record. Online WESTLAW users can also access the decisions.

Board of Contract Appeals Reporter is a bi-weekly publication which reports the decisions of the Department of Interior's Board of Contract Appeals, as well as the rulings of other Boards of Contract Appeals. Annual Price $760.00. Contact: Commerce Clearing House, Inc., 4025 West Peterson Avenue, Chicago, IL 60646. Tel: 312/583-8500. Or in Washington, D.C., call 202/626-2200.

(Area Code 703)

Chairman: Russell C. Lynch 235-3813
Legal Assistant/Recorder: Edward P. Dronenburg 235-3813
Vice Chairman: G. Herbert Packwood 235-3813
Members:
William F. McGraw 235-3813
Bernard V. Parrette 235-3813
vacant......................................235-3813
Attorney Advisors:
Stephen J. McGuire..........................235-3813
Scott W. Wheeler 235-3813

Regional Offices: The Board of Contract Appeals has two regional offices. Their addresses are listed below.

Knoxville
Administrative Law Judge: David Torbett
U.S. Department of the Interior, Board of Contract Appeals,
710 Locust Street, Suite 1116, Knoxville, TN 37902.
Tel: 615/549-9329.

Salt Lake City
Administrative Law Judges: Raymond Child, John Rampton, Harvey Sweitzer
U.S. Department of the Interior, Board of Contract Appeals,
6432 Federal Bldg, Salt Lake City, UT 84138.
Tel: 801/524-5344.

The **Board of Indian Appeals** handles cases arising under hundreds of treaties, statutes, and regulations bearing on the Department's dealing with Indians. For example, the Board adjudicates appeals involving rights-of-way over Indian lands; farming, grazing, and other leases held on Indian lands; rights to receive financial assistance; contracting privileges of Indian enterprises and tribes; sale or transfer of trust or restricted Indian lands; tribal powers of self-government; tribal government and election issues; and restoration of lands to Indian tribes.

The decisions of the Board of Indian Appeals can be obtained by subscription from the Office of Hearings, 4015 Wilson Blvd., Arlington, VA 22203. Tel: 703/235-3799. Annual price: $75.00. If you have a request for a specific case you can call the office at the above number for a record of that case. Online WESTLAW users can also access the decisions of the Board.

(Area Code 703)

Chief Administrative Judge: Kathryn A. Lynn 235-3816
Legal Assistant: Vickie L. Matthews 235-3816
Administrative Judges:
Anita S. Vogt...............................235-3816
vacant......................................235-3816

DEPARTMENT OF THE INTERIOR

ENFORCEMENT AND SECURITY MANAGEMENT DIVISION (Room 5042)

(Area Code 202)
Chief: John Gannon 208-4108

(Area Code 202)
Law Enforcement Branch Chief: Harry A. DeLashmutt 208-6319

ADVISORY COUNCIL ON HISTORIC PRESERVATION (Room 809)

1100 Pennsylvania Ave, N.W., Washington, D.C. 20004

(Area Code 202)
Chairman: John F.W. Rogers 786-0503
General Counsel: John M. Fowler 786-0503

(Area Code 202)
Executive Director: Robert D.Bush 786-0503

PUBLICATIONS OF INTEREST

Index Digest is the computer printout of published and unpublished headnotes of the Board of Land Appeals, the Board of Indian Appeals, and the Board of Contract Appeals, and the published Solicitor's opinions. It is published quarterly and bound in paperback at the end of each year. After five years, it is bound in hardback. Annual price: $65.00. Contact the Office of Hearings, 4015 Wilson Blvd., Arlington, VA 22203.
Tel: 703/235-3799.

Surface Mining Law Summary is a looseleaf publication, updated periodically. It contains decisions of the Administrative Law Judges of the Board of Land Appeals and the decisions of the Administrative Law Judges of the Hearings Division in selected surface mining cases. Annual price: $375.00. Contact: Surface Mining Law Summary, Inc. P.O. Box 281, Corbin, KY 40701. Tel: 606/528-9481.

The following publications can be purchased from the U.S. Government Printing Office. Stock numbers and prices for annual subscriptions are shown below. Submit requests for these publications to: The Superintendent of Documents, **U.S. Government Printing Office,** Washington, D.C. 20402. Tel: 202/783-3238.

Decisions of the Department of the Interior contains significant decisions by the U.S. Department of the Interior on appeals, claims, and acts. It is published monthly and placed in bound volumes at the end of the year.

Volume 95 (1988). Annual price: $14.00 domestic; $17.50 foreign. GPO Stock# 724-010-00000-8.

Volume 96 (1989). Annual price: $11.00 domestic; $13.75 foreign. GPO Stock# 724-011-00000-4.

Volume 97 (1990). Annual price: $11.00 domestic; $13.75 foreign. GPO Stock #724-013-00000-7.

DEPARTMENT OF THE INTERIOR
KEY LEGAL AUTHORITIES

Major Regulations:

General Departmental Regulations: 43 C.F.R. Parts 1-9269 (1989).
Department of Interior Acquisition Regulations: 48 C.F.R. Part 1401 et seq. (1989).
Rules of Practice & Procedure: 43 C.F.R. Parts 1, 4, 14, 1810-1880 (1989).
Fish & Wildlife Service: 50 C.F.R. Part 1 et seq. (1989).
Geological Survey: 30 C.F.R. Parts 400-402 (1989).
Bureau of Indian Affairs: 25 C.F.R. Part 1 et seq. (1989).
Bureau of Land Management: 43 C.F.R. Part 1600 et seq. (1989).
Minerals Management Service: 30 C.F.R. 201 et seq. (1989).
Bureau of Mines: 30 C.f.r. 601 et seq. (1989).
National Park Service: 36 C.F.R. 1 et seq. (1989).
Bureau of Reclamation: 43 C.F.R. Parts 230-431 (1989).
Surface Mining & Reclamation Appeals Board: 30 C.F.R. 301 et seq. (1989).
Surface Mining & Reclamation Enforcement Office: 30 C.F.R. 700 et seq. (1989).

Geothermal Steam Act of 1970, as amended, 30 U.S.C. 1001 et seq.--leases may be issued for withdrawn lands, for acquired lands, and for geothermal resources in lands which have passed from Federal ownership subject to a reservation to the United States, with certain exceptions.

Highlights of Recent Amendments: 30 U.S.C. 1005 at section (g). Any geothermal lease for land which has not produced or utilized any geothermal steam in commercial quantities by the end of its primary lease term (10 years), or by the end of any extension, may be extended for successive 5 year periods not exceeding an additional 25 years for a total of 50 years.
Legislative History: 1970 U.S. Code Cong. & Admin. News 5113; 1988 U.S. Code Cong. & Admin. News 2350.
Implementing Regulations: 43 C.F.R. Part 3200 et seq. (1989).

Indian Child Welfare Act of 1978, as amended, 25 U.S.C 1901 et seq.-- establishes minimum Federal standards for the removal of Indian children from their families and the placement of such children in foster or adoptive homes, and provides assistance to Indian tribes and organizations in the operation of child and family service programs.
Legislative History: 1978 U.S. Code Cong. & Admin. News 7530.
Implementing Regulations: 25 C.F.R. Part 23 (1989).

Oil Pollution Prevention, 43 U.S.C. 1334--during the exploration, development and transportation of oil and gas, the lessee must take measures to prevent unauthorized discharge of pollutants into the offshore waters, and must not create conditions which pose an unreasonable risk to public health, property, aquatic life or wildlife.

Legislative History: 1953 U.S. Code Cong. & Admin. News 2177; 1978 U.S. Code Cong. & Admin. News 1450.
Implementing Regulations: 30 C.F.R. Part 250 (1989).

Bureau of Reclamation Act of 1902, as amended, 43 U.S.C. 371 et seq.--designed to provide viable farm opportunities on land recovery reclamation project water. The law requires reimbursement to the Federal government of the full cost of providing irrigation water to land holdings which exceed established limits, with certain exceptions.
Legislative History: 1982 U.S. Code Cong. & Admin. News 2570; 1987 U.S. Code Cong. & Admin. News 2313.
Implementing Regulations: 43 C.F.R. Part 426 (1989).

Federal Oil and Gas Management Act of 1982, as amended, 30 U.S.C. 1701 et seq.--implements and maintains the royalty management system for the collection and disbursement of oil and gas lease revenues on Federal lands, Indian lands and the Outer Continental Shelf.
Legislative History: 1982 U.S. Code Cong. & Admin. News 2268; 1987 U.S. Code Cong. & Admin. News 2313.
Implementing Regulations: 30 C.F.R. Part 218 (1989).

Federal Land Policy and Management Act of 1976, as amended, 43 U.S.C. 1701 et seq.--establishes a process for the development, approval, maintenance, amendment, and revision of resource management plans, programs and budgets.
Legislative History: 1976 U.S. Code Cong. & Admin. News 6175.
Implementing Regulations: 43 C.F.R. Parts 24, 1600-1610 (1989).

Exec. Order No. 10355, 3 C.F.R., 1949-1953 Comp., p.873--delegating to the Secretary of Interior the authority to reserve or withdraw U.S. lands for public purposes.

Earthquake Hazards Reduction Act of 1977, as amended, [CITATION?]--attempts to reduce, abate and mitigate the potential loss of life and property as the result of an earthquake, by assessing earthquake risks, planning prevention or reducing risks and organizing emergency operations.
Legislative History: 1977 U.S. Code Cong. & Admin. News 2785: 1980 U.S. Code Cong. & Admin. News 4726.
Implementing Regulations: 44 C.F.R. Part 361 (1989).

Surface Mining Control and Reclamation Act of 1977, as amended, 30 U.S.C. 1201 et seq.--sets guidelines for controlling surface coal mining operations. The Act requires review and approval or disapproval of state programs for controlling surface coal mining operations and reclaiming abandoned mined lands.
Legislative History: 1977 U.S. Code Cong. & Admin. News 593.
Implementing Regulations: 30 C.F.R. Part 700 (1989); 43 C.F.R. Part 3400 (1989).

Coal Leasing Act, as amended, 30 U.S.C. 201 et seq.--establishes policies for the development of coal deposits on Federal lands through a leasing system involving land use planning and environmental assessment/impact statement processes.
Legislative History: 1976 U.S. Code Cong. & Admin. News 1943; 1978 U.S. Code Cong. & Admin. News 4736.
Implementing Regulations: 43 C.F.R. Parts 3000 et seq. (1989).

Right of Way Leasing Act of 1930, as amended, 30 U.S.C. 301 et seq.--authorizes either the leasing of oil and gas deposits under railroad and other rights of way to the owner of the right of way or the entering of a compensatory royalty agreement with adjoining land owners.
Implementing Regulations: 43 C.F.R. Part 3100 (1989).

Marine Mammal Protection Act of 1972, as amended, 16 U.S.C. 1361 et seq.--authorizes appropriations to make grants or provide other forms of financial assistance for the purpose of undertaking research relevant to the protection and conservation of marine mammals.
Legislative History: 1972 U.S. Code Cong. & Admin. News 4144.
Implementing Regulations: 50 C.F.R. Part 82 (1989).

Act of June 8, 1906, 16 U.S.C. 432--establishes a permitting system in the Department of the Interior, Department of Agriculture, and Department of the Army whereby permits may be granted by the respective departments to properly qualified institutions for the examination of ruins, excavation of archaeological sites, and the gathering of antiquities upon lands under their respective jurisdictions, subject to any rules and regulations the respective departments may prescribe.
Implementing Regulations: 25 C.F.R. Part 261 et seq. (1989); 43 C.F.R. Part 3 (1989).

Archaeological Resources Protection Act of 1979, as amended, 16 U.S.C. 470aa-470mm--protects archaeological resources and sites on public and Indian lands and directs the Departments of the Interior, Agriculture, and Defense, and the Tennessee Valley Authority to regulate the permitting system and enforce the law; and makes unlawful the (1) unauthorized excavation, removal, damage, alteration, or defacement of archaeological resources; (2) trafficking in such resources if the excavation or removal was unlawful under Federal law; and (3) trafficking, in interstate or foreign commerce, in archaeological resources if the excavation, removal, sale, purchase, exchange, transportation, or receipt is wrongful under state or local law.
Legislative History: 1979 U.S. Code Cong. & Admin. News 1709; 1988 U.S. Code Cong. & Admin. News 3625 & 3983.
Implementing Regulations: 43 C.F.R. Part 7 (1989).

Wilderness Act, 16 U.S.C. 1131-1136--establishes a National Wilderness Preservation System comprised of Federally-owned areas designated by Congress as "wilderness areas," and directs that they be managed by the agency under whose jurisdiction they were when so designated.
Legislative History: 1964 U.S. Code Cong. & Admin. News 3615.
Implementing Regulations: 36 C.F.R. 251.1 et seq. (1989); 43 C.F.R. Parts 19 & 8560 et seq. (1989); 50 C.F.R. 35.1 et seq. (1989).

Alaska National Interest Lands Conservation Act, as amended, 16 U.S.C. 3101 et seq.--protects scenic, natural, cultural, and environmental values on public lands in Alaska, balancing the natural interest in these values against the economic and social needs of the State and its people.
Legislative History: 1980 U.S. Code Cong. & Admin. News 5070; 1988 U.S. Code Cong. & Admin. News 1356.
Implementing Regulations: 43 C.F.R. Part 3000 et seq. (1989).

National Wildlife Refuge System Administration Act of 1966, as amended, 16 U.S.C. 668dd-668ee--designates all lands, waters, and interests therein administered by the Secretary of the Interior as the national Wildlife Refuge System, prohibiting certain activities while permitting others therein, and directs the Secretary to enforce the Act.
Legislative History: 1966 U.S. Code Cong. & Admin. News 3342; 1976 U.S. Code Cong. & Admin. News 271; 1988 U.S. Code Cong. & Admin. News 5366.
Implementing Regulations: 43 C.F.R. 3100.0-3 et seq. (1989); 50 C.F.R. 25.11 et seq. (1989).

Wild Free-Roaming Horses & Burros Act, as amended, 16 U.S.C. 1331-1340--protects horses and burros roaming wild and free on U.S. public lands from capture, harassment, branding, and death, and makes unlawful any of these acts.
Legislative History: 1971 U.S. Code Cong. & Admin. News 2149; 1978 U.S. Code Cong. & Admin. News 4069.
Implementing Regulations: 36 C.F.R. 261.1 et seq. (1989); 43 C.F.R. Part 4700 et seq. (1989).

Endangered Species Act of 1973, as amended, 16 U.S.C. 1531-1544--protects various species of fish, wildlife, and plants facing extinction.

Legislative History: 1973 U.S. Code Cong. & Admin. News 2989; 1982 U.S. Code Cong. & Admin. News 2807; 1988 U.S. Code Cong. & Admin. News 2700.
Implementing Regulations: 7 C.F.R. 355.1 et seq. (1990); 50 C.F.R. 17.1 et seq. & 424.01 et seq. (1989).

Wild & Scenic Rivers Act, as amended, 16 U.S.C. 1271 et seq.--protects certain rivers by including them in a national wild and scenic rivers system and by setting forth criteria whereby additional components may be added to the system.
Legislative History: 1968 U.S. Code Cong. & Admin. News 3801; 1974 U.S. Code Cong. & Admin. News 3006; 1980 U.S. Code Cong. & Admin. News 5070; 1988 U.S. Code Cong. & Admin. News 3574.
Implementing Regulations: 36 C.F.R. 251.9 et seq. (1989); 43 C.F.R. 8300.0-1 et seq. (1989).

National Trails System Act, as amended, 16 U.S.C. 1241-1251--established a National Trails System and provides for administration by the Secretaries of the Interior and Agriculture.
Legislative History: 1968 U.S. Code Cong. & Admin. News 3855; 1983 U.S. Code Cong. & Admin. News 112; 1988 U.S. Code Cong. & Admin. News 2607.
Implementing Regulations: 36 C.F.R. 251.9 et seq. (1989); 43 C.F.R. 8000.0-1 et seq. (1989).

Mineral Lands Leasing Act of 1920, as amended, 30 U.S.C. 181-287--governs the disposition of deposits of energy and certain non-energy minerals owned by the U.S. (excluding certain specified lands and petroleum reserves).
Legislative History: 1960 U.S. Code Cong. & Admin. News 3313; 1981 U.S. Code Cong. & Admin. News 1740; 1987 U.S. Code Cong. & Admin. News 2313-1.
Implementing Regulations: 30 C.F.R. Chapt. II, Subchapt. A & Chapt. VII, Subchapt. D (1989); 43 C.F.R. Part 3000 et seq. (1989).

Mineral Leasing Act for Acquired Lands, as amended, 30 U.S.C. 351-359--governs the disposition of energy and certain non-energy mineral deposits owned or subsequently acquired by the U.S. within lands acquired by the U.S., excepting lands acquired by foreclosure or otherwise for resale.
Legislative History: 1947 U.S. Code Cong. Service 1661; 1976 U.S. Code Cong. & Admin. News 1943; 1981 U.S. Code Cong. & Admin. News 1740.
Implementing Regulations: 32 C.F.R. 235.1 et seq. (1989); 43 C.F.R. Part 3000 et seq. (1989).

Federal Oil & Gas Royalty Management Act of 1982, as amended, 30 U.S.C. 1701-1757--established a royalty management system for oil and gas leases on Federal lands, Indian lands, and the outer continental shelf.
Legislative History: 1982 U.S. Code Cong. & Admin. News 4268.
Implementing Regulations: 30 C.F.R. 229.100 et seq. (1989); 43 C.F.R. Part 3160 (1989).

Federal Water Pollution Control Act, as amended ("Clean Water Act"), 33 U.S.C. 1251-1376--provides that natural resource trustees may assess damages to natural resources resulting from a discharge of oil or release of a hazardous substance and may seek to recover those damages.
Legislative History: 1972 U.S. Code Cong. & Admin. News 3668; 1977 U.S. Code Cong. & Admin. News 4326; 1987 U.S. Code Cong. & Admin. News 5.
Implementing Regulations: 43 C.F.R. Part 11 (1989).

Comprehensive Environmental Response, Compensation, and Liability Act of 1980, as amended ("CERCLA"), 42 U.S.C. 9601 et seq.--provides that natural resource trustees may assess damages to natural resources resulting from a discharge or release of a hazardous substance and may seek to recover those damages.
Legislative History: 1980 U.S. Code Cong. & Admin. News 6119; 1986 U.S. Code Cong. & Admin. News 2835.
Implementing Regulations: 43 C.F.R. Part 11 (1989).

Trans-Alaska Pipeline Authorization Act, as amended, 43 U.S.C. 1651-1655--establishes a Liability Fund to compensate persons for damages caused by discharges of oil from vessels loaded at pipeline terminal facilities.
Legislative History: 1973 U.S. Code Cong. & Admin. News 2417.
Implementing Regulations: 43 C.F.R. Part 29 (1989).

Recreation & Public Purposes Act, as amended, 43 C.F.R. 869--authorizes the Secretary of the Interior to dispose of public lands to certain entities for any public or recreational purposes.
Legislative History: 1954 U.S. Code Cong. & Admin. News 2316; 1959 U.S. Code Cong. & Admin. News 1573; 1988 U.S. Code Cong. & Admin. News 3813.
Implementing Regulations: 43 C.F.R. Part 2400 et seq. (1989).

Public Rangelands Improvement Act of 1978, 43 U.S.C. 1901-1908--established a management system for public rangelands and a fee schedule for public grazing use.
Legislative History: 1978 U.S. Code Cong. & Admin. News 4069.
Implementing Regulations: 36 C.F.R. 222.1 et seq. (1989); 43 C.F.R. Part 4100 (1989).

Taylor Grazing Act, as amended, 43 U.S.C. 315 et seq.--authorizes the Secretary of the Interior to establish portions of U.S. public lands as grazing districts and administer them accordingly.
Implementing Regulations: 43 C.F.R. Part 4100 et seq. (1989).

Indian Mineral Development Act of 1982, 25 U.S.C. 2101-2108--authorizes any Indian tribe, subject to approval by the Secretary of the Interior and any limitation in its constitution or charter, to enter into agreements for the exploitation of any mineral resources in which it owns an interest.
Legislative History: 1982 U.S. Code Cong. & Admin. News 3465.
Implementing Regulations: 25 C.F.R. Part 211 et seq. (1989); 43 C.F.R. Part 3160 (1989).

Outer Continental Shelf Lands Act, as amended, 43 U.S.C. 1331-1356, 1801-1866--establishes U.S. jurisdiction over the outer continental shelf and governs the disposition of outer continental shelf minerals.
Legislative History: 1953 U.S. Code Cong. & Admin. News 2177; 1978 U.S. Code Cong. & Admin. News 1450.
Implementing Regulations: 30 C.F.R., Chapt. II (1989).

Exec. Order No. 11644, 3 C.F.R., 1971-1975 Comp., p. 666, "Use of Off-Road Vehicles on the Public Lands."

DEPARTMENT OF JUSTICE

10th Street and Constitution Avenue, N.W.
Washington, D.C. 20530
NOTE: The public entrance is located at 10th Street and Pennsylvania Avenue, N.W.

DESCRIPTION: The Attorney General is the Federal Government's chief legal officer. The U.S. Government is the Attorney General's client. The Department of Justice, with almost 80,000 employees worldwide, is the Attorney General's staff. The Justice Department employs approximately 6,000 attorneys nationwide.

A primary responsibility of the Department of Justice is to represent the United States in court. Attorneys in the general counsel offices of other departments and agencies perform the day-to-day legal duties of the Federal Government, such as negotiating contracts, settling complaints, and providing legal advice to other Government officials. However, when a department or agency is involved in litigation, the matter is generally turned over to the Department of Justice.

The Judiciary Act of 1789 authorized the Attorney General to render opinions on questions of law when requested by the President or the heads of executive departments. This authority is now codified at 28 U.S.C. 511-513.

(Area Code 202)
Attorney General: Richard L. Thornburgh 514-2001
Information Operator 514-2000
Public Affairs 514-2007
Office of Small and Disadvantaged Business Utilization 501-6271
Office of Justice Programs/Office of Congressional
and Public Affairs 307-0781
Immigration Related Unfair Employment Practices
Hot Line: ....(800) 255-7688
Facsimile..514-4371

(Area Code 202)
Freedom of Information Act/Privacy Act Office 514-3642
This office will answer general questions on FOIA and the Privacy Act and will refer callers to the appropriate office within the Justice Department, if necessary. You may send your request to: FOIA/PA Section, Justice Management Division, U.S. Department Of Justice, 10th and Constitution Avenue, N.W., Washington, D.C. 20530.

Library (Room 5400) 514-3695
The library is open to the public from 9:00 AM until 5:30 PM, Monday through Friday. An appointment is necessary, and a photo ID is needed for admittance. Photocopying is 10 cents a page.

OFFICE OF THE ATTORNEY GENERAL (Room 5111)

The Office of the Attorney General provides overall policy and program direction for the offices, boards, divisions, and bureaus of the Department of Justice. The Office represents the U.S. in legal matters generally, prosecutes violations of Federal law, and offers legal advice and opinions to the President, Cabinet, and heads of executive agencies. It also provides comments on pending legislation and makes recommendations to the President concerning appointments to Federal judicial positions as well as appointments of U.S. Attorneys and U.S. Marshals.

(Area Code 202)
Attorney General: Richard L. Thornburgh 514-2001

Office of the Deputy Attorney General
Deputy Attorney General: William P. Barr (Acting) 514-2101
Principal Associate Deputy Attorney General:
John A. Smietanka 514-2105
Assistant Attorneys General:
Administration: Harry H. Flickinger 514-3101
Office of Legal Counsel: J. Michael Luttig (Acting) ..514-2041

(Area Code 202)
Office of Legislative Affairs: Lee Rawls (Acting) 514-3752
Antitrust Division: James F. Rill 514-2401
Civil Division: Stuart M. Gerson 514-3301
Civil Rights Division: John R. Dunne 514-2151
Criminal Division: Edward S.G. Dennis Jr 514-2601
Environment and Natural Resources Division:
Richard B. Stewart 514-2701
Tax Division: Shirley D. Peterson 514-2901
Office of Justice Programs: Richard Bender Abell 307-5933

OFFICE OF THE SOLICITOR GENERAL (Room 5143)

The major function of the Solicitor General's Office is to supervise and conduct Government litigation in the U.S. Supreme Court. The staff participates in preparing the petitions, briefs, and other papers filed by the Government in its U.S. Supreme Court litigation. Another function of the Office is to review all cases lost by the Department of Justice in the lower courts to determine whether they should be appealed and, if so, what position should be taken. The Solicitor General also determines whether the Government will participate as amicus curiae, or intervene, in cases in any appellate court. The Office does not, however, ordinarily participate directly in the preparation of the briefs or arguments in any court other than the U.S. Supreme Court.

(Area Code 202)
Solicitor General: Kenneth W. Starr 514-2201
Principal Deputy Solicitor General:
John G. Roberts Jr 514-2206
Facsimile 514-3648

Deputy Solicitors General: (Area Code 202)
vacant 514-4218
David L. Shapiro 514-2208
Lawrence G. Wallace 514-2211
William C. Bryson 514-4037

DEPARTMENT OF JUSTICE

JUSTICE MANAGEMENT DIVISION (Room 1111)

The Justice Management Division exercises Department-level oversight and control over selected management operations.

***The Office of the General Counsel** provides legal support to the offices, boards, divisions, and bureaus of the Department in administrative law areas. The Office has operational responsibility for the Department's ethics-in-Government functions, and its Newspaper Preservation Act functions.

***The Litigation Systems Staff** provides training, research, and user assistance in the operation of the Justice Retrieval and Inquiry System (JURIS). JURIS is a computer-assisted legal research system developed and operated by the Department of Justice for use by the Federal legal community.

(Area Code 202)

Assistant Attorney General/Administration:
Harry H. Flickinger 514-3101
Deputy Assistant Attorney General/Administration:
Anthony C. Moscato 514-3101
Deputy Assistant Attorney General/Information and Administrative Services: Stephen R. Colgate 514-5501
Deputy Assistant Attorney General/Controller:
Michael J. Roper 514-1843

(Area Code 202)

Deputy Assistant Attorney General/Debt Collection Management: Robert N. Ford 514-5343
Facsimile 514-1778

Federal Law Enforcement Training Center, Glynco, GA.
Associate Assistant Attorney General:
William E. Hall ....(912) 267-2914

OFFICE OF THE INSPECTOR GENERAL (Room 6649)

The Inspector General is responsible for providing policy direction, for conducting investigations and audits relating to the economy and efficiency of the Department's programs and operations, and for detecting and preventing fraud and abuse in programs and operations administered or financed by the Department. Two special restrictions apply to the Inspector General of the Department of Justice. First, cases involving the conduct of a departmental attorney, criminal investigative or law enforcement position relating to a violation of law, regulation, order, or other applicable standard of conduct are to be referred by the Inspector General to the Counsel, Office of Professional Responsibility. Second, a specific statutory provision authorizes the Attorney General to prohibit the Inspector General from undertaking or continuing an investigation or audit that might disclose sensitive information regarding ongoing cases, undercover operations, informants, or intelligence and national security matters.

(Area Code 202)

Inspector General: Anthony C. Moscato (Acting) 514-3435
Executive Assistant: Thomas F. McLaughlin 514-3435
Deputy Inspector General: Robert Ashbaugh 514-3435
Assistant General Counsel: Deborah Westbrook (Acting) ..514-3435

Assistant Inspectors General for: (Area Code 202)
Audits: Guy Zimmerman ....(703) 756-6121
Investigations: Louis A. De Martinis 633-3510
Inspections: Robert D. Schmidt 633-3611
Management & Planning: Allen Vander-Staay 514-3435

OFFICE OF PROFESSIONAL RESPONSIBILITY (Room 4304)

The Office of Professional Responsibility oversees all investigations of allegations of criminal or ethical misconduct by all employees of the Department. At the Counsel's discretion, the Office frequently conducts its own investigations into those allegations. The Office may also participate in or direct an investigation conducted by another component of the Department, or may simply monitor an investigation conducted by an appropriate agency having jurisdiction over the matter.

(Area Code 202)

Counsel: Michael E. Shaheen Jr 514-3365
Deputy Counsel: Richard M. Rogers 514-3365

Waste, Fraud and Abuse Hot Line ....(800) 869-4499
This number is for reporting of misconduct of Justice Department employees.)

OFFICE OF LEGAL COUNSEL (Room 5214)

The principal function of this office is to assist the Attorney General in the role of legal adviser to the President and Executive Branch agencies. The Attorney General has delegated to the OLC the responsibility for preparing formal Attorney General opinions, rendering informal opinions to Federal agencies, assisting the Attorney General in the performance of his function as legal advisor to the President, and rendering opinions to the Attorney General and the heads of various Department of Justice units. OLC frequently considers legal issues of particular complexity and importance about which two or more agencies disagree, and serves as final arbiter within the Executive Branch on legal questions, both constitutional and statutory. The staff also prepares and delivers testimony to Congress on a variety of legal issues, particularly constitutional issues.

(Area Code 202)

Assistant Attorney General: J. Michael Luttig (Acting) 514-2041
Principal Deputy Assistant Attorney General:
J. Michael Luttig 514-2051

Deputy Assistant Attorneys General:
John O. McGinnis 514-3657
vacant 514-2059

OFFICE OF POLICY DEVELOPMENT (Room 4234)

This office serves as the Attorney General's principal policy development staff, providing thorough legal and policy analysis necessary to the development of new Department initiatives. Issues considered by the office have included separation of powers disputes, religious liberty conflicts, and approaches to constitutional litigation. The office has also been involved in matters of court reform, white collar crime, criminal procedure, civil rights, and social policy.

(Area Code 202)

Director: Thomas M. Boyd 514-4601
Deputy Director: Kevin R. Jones 514-4604
Special Counsel:
Diane G. Culp 514-4016
Grace Mastalli 514-4606

Office of Asylum Policy and Review Unit
Director: Henry L. Curry 514-2415
Deputy Director and Counsel: vacant 514-2415
Associate Director and Deputy Counsel:
Antonia Chambers 514-2415

OFFICE OF LEGISLATIVE AFFAIRS (Room 4119)

The office supervises the Department's legislative program and responds to requests and inquiries from congressional committees, individual members, and their staffs. Responsibilities also include appearing before congressional committees on justice-related matters and advising the President on the legal sufficiency of much of the legislation enacted by Congress and presented to him for approval.

(Area Code 202)

Assistant Attorney General: Lee Rawls (Acting) 514-3752
Deputy Assistant Attorneys General:
Bruce Navarro 514-4045
Vacant 514-4054

Senior Legislative Counsels:
Nicholas Wise 514-3951
Kevin Holsclaw 514-2138

OFFICE OF LIAISON SERVICES (Room 4213)

The Office of Liaison Services (OLS) represents the Attorney General and the Department of Justice in its dealings with external interest groups, justice and law enforcement-related constituencies, and virtually all legislatures and governmental entities, with the exception of Congress.

(Area Code 202)

Director: William C. Lucas 514-3465
Deputy Director: Cheryl C. Nolan 514-3465
Attorney Advisor: Barbara S. Bruin 514-3465

Senior Liaison Officers:
Michael Dee 514-3465
Dennis Bartlett 514-3465

ANTITRUST DIVISION (Room 3107)

The mission of the Antitrust Division is the promotion and maintenance of competition in the American economy. Private anticompetitive conduct is subject to criminal and civil action under the Sherman and Clayton Acts, which prohibit conspiracies in restraint of trade, monopolization, and anticompetitive mergers. The highest priorities of the Antitrust Division are the prosecution of criminal bid-rigging and price-fixing cases and the review of mergers and acquisitions to identify and prohibit those which will result in reduction of competition and consequent injury to consumers. In carrying out these responsibilities, Division attorneys conduct grand jury proceedings, issue and enforce merger discovery requests and civil investigative demands, and handle all litigation that arises out of such civil and criminal investigations. In addition to these top priority efforts, the Division intervenes, or participates before administrative agencies, in proceedings requiring consideration of the antitrust laws or competitive policies.

Ten of the Division's sections and more than half of the Division's attorneys are located in Washington, D.C. Seven field offices, which emphasize criminal prosecution, are located throughout the country.

*** Litigation I and II Sections.** Two of the litigating sections (Litigation I and II), located in the Washington, D.C. area, are responsible for conducting investigations and handling litigation, both criminal and civil, and negotiating, enforcing, and monitoring consent judgments, relating to a group of commodities and services for which each of the sections have responsibility and expertise. Each section is also responsible for participating in legislative and administrative activities that relate to its commodity jurisdiction.

***Field Offices.** The Division's seven field offices, located in Atlanta, Chicago, Cleveland, Dallas, New York, Philadelphia, and San Francisco, are responsible for investigating and litigating antitrust violations in specific geographical areas in a wide variety of commodities and industries. The field offices have been assigned the primary responsibility for a new initiative by the Antitrust Division to use the antitrust laws to attack mob infiltration of legitimate businesses. In addition, the field offices serve as the Division's liaison with U.S. Attorneys, state attorneys general, and other law enforcement agencies within their areas.

***The Professions and Intellectual Property Section** investigates and prosecutes all violations of the antitrust laws involving the professions, including the health care industry, intellectual property rights (e.g., copyrights, trademarks, and patents), and labor. In addition, it has jurisdiction over a variety of services and commodities, including motion pictures, books and newspapers, pharmaceuticals, and educational institutions.

***The Transportation, Energy, and Agriculture Section** enforces antitrust laws in the airline, railroad, motor carrier, and ocean carrier industries; in the energy industries, which include petroleum, natural gas, electric power, and coal; and in all matters pertaining to agriculture and related commodities. The Section is also active in legislative activities relating to the deregulation of various transportation, energy, and agricultural industries, and prepares reports to Congress and the Executive Branch on policy issues related to those commodities.

***The Communications and Finance Section** is responsible for the enforcement of the antitrust laws and competition advocacy in the banking, finance, securities, and communications industries. It also participates in proceedings before such agencies as the Federal Reserve Board and the Securities and Exchange Commission.

***The Foreign Commerce Section** fosters competition in U.S. foreign trade; develops policy on issues of trade and international antitrust enforcement; participates in regulatory agency proceedings before the International Trade Commission; and coordinates the Division's review of applications for export trading company certificates. The Section also works with the Department of State concerning investigations and cases that the Division initiates involving foreign corporations and nationals.

***The Appellate Section** represents the Division in all appeals to the U.S. Courts of Appeals and, in conjunction with the Solicitor General's Office, all appeals before the U.S. Supreme Court. In addition, the Section represents the U.S. as statutory respondent in proceedings to review orders of several Federal agencies, such as the Interstate Commerce Commission and the Federal Communications Commission.

***The Legal Policy Section** is responsible for providing analysis of complex antitrust matters; for the development and submission to Congress of the Division's legislative program; and for long-range planning projects and programs. The Section is also involved in making recommendations concerning Division enforcement policies, reviewing investigations and case recommendations for legal and policy considerations, and researching legislative matters.

(Area Code 202)

Assistant Attorney General: James F. Rill 514-2401

Deputy Assistant Attorney General/Economic Analysis:
Robert D. Willig 514-2408
Chief of Economic Litigation Section: Jon M. Joyce ...307-6665
Chief of Economic Regulatory Section:
I. Curtis Jernigan 307-6332

Deputy Assistant Attorney General/Litigation:
Judy Whalley 514-2562
FOIA Branch Chief: Leo D. Neshkes 514-2692
Litigation I Section: Anthony V. Nanni 307-6694
Litigation II Section: P. Terry Lubeck 307-0924

(Area Code 202)

Deputy Assistant Attorney General/Policy and Legislation:
Michael Boudin 514-2411
Appellate Section Chief: Catherine G. O'Sullivan 514-2413
Legal Policy Section Chief: Neil E. Roberts 514-2512

Deputy Assistant Attorney General/Regulatory Affairs:
Alison L. Smith 514-2404
Communications and Finance Section Chief:
B. Barry Grossman 514-5621
Foreign Commerce Section Chief: Charles S. Stark 514-2464
Professions and Intellectual Property Section Chief:
Robert E. Bloch 307-0467
Transportation, Energy and Agriculture Section Chief:
Mark C. Schechter 307-6349

REGIONAL OFFICES

Atlanta Region
Regional Chief: John T. Orr
U.S. Department of Justice, Antitrust Division,
75 Spring Street, S.W., Richard B. Russell Bldg, Suite 1394,
Atlanta, GA 30303. Tel: 404/331-7100.
(Jurisdiction: AL, FL, GA, MS, NC, SC, TN)

Chicago Region
Regional Chief: Kent Brown
U.S. Department of Justice, Antitrust Division,
230 South Dearborn Street, John C. Kluczynski Bldg, Room 3820
Chicago, IL 60604. Tel: 312/353-7530.
(Jurisdiction: Northeastern CO, IL, IN, IA, KS, Western MI, MN, MO, NE, ND, SD, WI)

Cleveland Region
Regional Chief: John A. Weedon
U.S. Department of Justice, Antitrust Division,
1240 East 9th Street, 995 Celebrezze Federal Bldg, Cleveland, OH 44199-2089. Tel: 216/522-4070.
(Jurisdiction: KY, Eastern MI, OH, WV)

Dallas Region
Regional Chief: Alan A. Pason
U.S. Department of Justice, Antitrust Division,
1100 Commerce Street, Earl Cabell Federal Bldg, Room 8C6,
Dallas, TX 75242. Tel: 214/767-8051.
(Jurisdiction: AR, LA, NM, OK, TX)

New York Region
Regional Chief: Ralph T. Giordano
U.S. Department of Justice, Antitrust Division,
26 Federal Plaza, Room 3630, New York, NY 10278-0096.
Tel: 212/264-0390.
(Jurisdiction: CT, ME, MA, NH, Northern NJ, NY, RI, VT)

Philadelphia Region
Regional Chief: John J. Hughes
U.S. Department of Justice, Antitrust Division,
1 Independence Square-West, 7th and Walnut Streets,
Curtis Center, Suite 650, Philadelphia, PA 19106.
Tel: 215/597-7405.
(Jurisdiction: DE, DC, MD, Southern NJ, PA, VA)

San Francisco Region
Regional Chief: Gary R. Spratling
U.S. Department of Justice, Antitrust Division,
450 Golden Gate Avenue, P.O. Box 36046, San Francisco, CA 94102. Tel: 415/556-6300.
(Jurisdiction: AK, CA, CO [except northeastern], HI, ID, MT, NV, OR, UT, WA, WY)

CIVIL DIVISION (Room 3143)

The Civil Division functions as the "Government's law firm." Its clients include more than 100 Federal agencies and commissions, individual Federal employees acting in their official capacities, in some instances members of Congress and the Federal judiciary, and the people of the United States. Because the Government engages in buying, selling, and other activities similar to those of a modern corporation, the Division also handles the complete spectrum of legal problems encountered by private enterprise. Division cases frequently have wide-reaching domestic and foreign policy implications.

The ever-increasing scope of civil litigation has greatly expanded the Division's responsibilities and caseload. This has been particularly true in the areas of debt recoveries, fraud and abuse in Federal programs, toxic tort claims, aviation litigation, and deportation and detention of aliens.

(Area Code 202)
Assistant Attorney General: Stuart M. Gerson 514-3301
Special Counsel to the Assistant Attorney General:
Col. William A. Aileo 514-3886
Lisa Farringer 514-3045

Law Library (Room 3300) 514-3523
The library is open from 9:00 AM until 5:30 PM, Monday through Friday by appointment only.

The Division's litigation is organized in six areas: commercial, Federal programs, torts, immigration, consumer, and appellate. The Division also employs a small number of attorneys in its field offices located in New York and San Francisco.

* **The Commercial Litigation Branch,** handles civil trial and appellate cases involving billions of dollars in claims both for and against the Government. The Branch prosecutes claims for the recovery of losses resulting from frauds upon Federal programs and contracts, and the bribery and corruption of public officials; initiates litigation to protect the Government's interest in bankruptcy and reorganization proceedings; and collects monies owed to the United States as a result of civil judgments and compromises. In disputes arising under contracts, grants, loans, loan guarantees, and insurance programs, the Branch represents the Government and its agencies both affirmatively and defensively. The attorneys in the Office of Foreign Litigation defend the international trade policies of the U.S. and defend and assert the Government's financial and commercial interests in foreign countries and under foreign treaties. In the area of patent and copyright claims, the Intellectual Property attorneys defend the Government against allegations of patent and copyright infringement as well as prosecuting violations of Government-owned patents.

(Area Code 202)
Deputy Assistant Attorney General/Commercial Litigation Branch: Stuart E. Schiffer 514-3306
Foreign Litigation Office Director: David Epstein ... 514-7455
Special Litigation Counsel:
JoanBernott................................ 514-7300
James G. Bruen Jr 307-0493
International Trade Field Office/New York City:
Attorney-in-Charge: Joseph I. Liebman (212) 264-9232

Field Offices (Commercial Litigation Branch)

International Trade Field Office
Attorney-In-Charge: Joseph I. Liebman
U.S. Department of Justice, 26 Federal Plaza, Suite 339, New York, NY 10278. Tel: 212/264-9232.

Commercial Field Office:
Legal Officer: Gerard F. Charig
U.S. Department of Justice
Koniginstrasse 5, 8 Munich 22, West Germany.
Tel: 9-011-49-89-285161

* **The Federal Programs Branch** handles suits challenging the propriety, legality, or constitutionality of various Government policies, programs, or actions. The Branch principally handles the defense of Government activity from domestic welfare programs to international agreements. The Branch is responsible for such diverse matters as litigation of Federal banking statutes and regulations, suits challenging auto safety laws, and litigation involving the effect of Federal budget actions on various regulatory programs.

* **The Office of Consumer Litigation** is responsible for the enforcement of Federal consumer protection laws through civil and criminal litigation. Affirmative litigation covers such areas as adulterated and misbranded foods and drugs, unsafe household products, unfair credit practices, and deceptive advertising. To address those issues which are beyond Federal jurisdiction, the Office also maintains liaison with state and local enforcement agencies.

(Area Code 202)
Deputy Assistant Attorney General/Federal Programs Branch and Office of Consumer Litigation: Leslie H. Southwick 514-5421
Federal Programs Directors:
David J. Anderson 514-3354
Brook Hedge 514-3501
Dennis G. Linder 514-3314
Special Litigation Counsel: Neil H. Koslowe 514-3418

(Area Code 202)

Office of Consumer Litigation
550-11th Street, N.W., Washington, D.C. 20004
Director: John R. Fleder 514-6786
Assistant Director: Margaret A. Cotter 307-0134
Assistant Director: Lawrence G. McDade 307-0138

* **The Torts Branch** is responsible for traditional problems in tort law, such as personal injury and medical malpractice, as well as new issues such as exposure to toxic substances (e.g. radiation and asbestos), and suits filed in the aftermath of major bank failures. In addition, the Branch represents present and former Government officials who are personally sued for monetary damages as a result of actions taken in the course of their duties. The Branch also represents the Government in its role as owner of ships and regulator of the nation's coastal waters and inland waterways. Finally, aviation litigation arises from damages involving Government-owned aircraft or resulting from the Government's role in air traffic control, aircraft and airport certification, and dissemination of weather information.

(Area Code 202)

Deputy Assistant Attorney General/Torts Branch:
Stephen C. Bransdorfer 514-3309
Special Litigation Counsel:
John C. Kruse 501-6059
Barbara B. O'Malley 501-7080
Attorney-in-Charge/New York:
Janis G. Schulmeisters ....(212) 264-0480
Attorney-in-Charge/San Francisco:
Philip A. Berns ....(415) 556-3146

Field Offices: Torts Branch

Attorney-in-Charge: Janis G. Schulmeisters
U.S. Department of Justice, 26 Federal Plaza, Suite 320, New York, NY 10278. Tel: 212/264-0480.

Attorney-In-Charge: Phillip A. Berns
U.S. Department of Justice, 450 Golden Gate Avenue, 15th Floor, Box 36028, San Francisco, CA 94102. Tel: 415/556-3146.

* **The Office of Immigration Litigation** conducts civil trial and appellate litigation under the immigration and naturalization laws. Litigation activities include district and circuit court challenges to the apprehension, detention, and deportation of aliens, the issuance of visas and passports, and the response of the Government to applications for naturalization, political asylum, and other immigration benefits. The Office also defends litigation raising constitutional challenges to the immigration laws, and for the defense and prosecution of cases arising under the amnesty and employer sanction provisions of the recent immigration reforms.

(Area Code 202)

Deputy Assistant Attorney General/Office of Immigration Litigation: Steven R. Valentine 514-1258
Immigration Litigation Director: Robert L. Bombaugh..501-7030

Office of Management Programs:
Director: Kenneth L. Zwick 514-4552

Office of Litigation Support
Directors:
Clarisse Abramadis (Acting) 307-2530
Eric B. Donovan (Acting) 307-2539

* **The Appellate Staff** briefs and argues cases before the Federal courts of appeals. The Staff's caseload generally includes only those cases that present the most important issues or have national impact.

Deputy Assistant Attorney General/Appellate Staff:
Patricia M. Bryan 514-4015
Appellate Staff Director: Robert E. Kopp 514-3311

CIVIL RIGHTS DIVISION (Room 5744)

The Civil Rights Division is responsible for enforcing the nation's laws and Executive Orders relating to civil rights. These laws now prohibit discrimination on the basis of race, national origin, color, religion, sex, age, and handicapping condition. Collectively, they guarantee individual rights in most areas of American society, including voting, education, employment, credit, housing, public accommodations and facilities, Federally funded and conducted programs, and institutions such as mental hospitals and prisons. Except for criminal enforcement work, where cases are normally tried before a jury, the suits filed by the Division are in equity--usually before a single judge seeking injunctive relief. The Civil Rights Division does not have regional offices. All Division employees are in Washington D.C. but are required to travel since litigation activities occur in all parts of the U.S.

* **The Appellate Section** handles appeals arising from the Division's litigation and develops the Division's amicus curiae participation in appellate courts.

* **The Coordination and Review Section** ensures that all Federal executive agencies effectively and consistently implement Federal statutes prohibiting discrimination on the basis of race, color, national origin, handicap, religion, or sex. The Section also issues interpretations in individual administrative cases and provides guidance to agencies on new civil rights issues.

* **The Criminal Section** enforces Federal statutes designed to preserve personal liberties. The Section reviews approximately 7,500 complaints annually for prosecutive merit and seeks indictments in 50-60 cases per year.

* **The Educational Opportunities Section** enforces Federal statutes which require nondiscrimination in public education. The Section's enforcement efforts involve elementary and secondary schools, as well as public colleges and universities.

* **The Voting Section** enforces Federal provisions which pertain to nondiscrimination in the exercise of voting rights. In enforcing the Voting Rights Act, the Section brings lawsuits against states, counties, cities, and other jurisdictions to remedy denials and abridgements of the right to vote; administratively reviews changes in voting laws and procedures; and monitors election day activities through the assignment of Federal observers.

* **The Employment Litigation Section** enforces Federal prohibitions against discrimination in employment. The Department of Justice is the sole Federal agency empowered to initiate litigation to redress employment discrimination by units of state and local government. The Section also has litigating responsibility in the employment area in the private sector on referral from the Department of Labor of cases against Federal contractors.

* **The Housing and Civil Enforcement Section** enforces the Federal prohibitions against discrimination in housing, consumer credit, public accommodations, and the provision of municipal services under Federally funded programs. The bulk of the Section's efforts is in the fair housing area, and authority in this area has been substantially expanded by the Fair Housing Amendments Act of 1988.
Under this Act, the Section was given added authority to seek damages and civil penalties, in addition to injunctive relief, in fair housing cases; to seek relief for individual victims of discrimination as well as against the "pattern and practice" of discrimination; and to seek relief where there is discrimination on the basis of handicap in addition to race, color, religion, national origin, and sex.

* **The Special Litigation Section** ensures the rights of persons confined in penal institutions or committed to facilities for the mentally ill, developmentally disabled, elderly, and juveniles. The Section also enforces Section 504 of the Rehabilitation Act of 1973 which prohibits discrimination against physically and mentally handicapped persons by recipients of Federal financial assistance.

(Area Code 202)

Assistant Attorney General: John R. Dunne 514-2151

Library (Room 7618) 514-4098
The library is open from 8:00 AM until 4:30 PM, Monday through Friday by appointment only.

Deputy Assistant Attorney General:
Gerald W. Jones (Acting) 307-2767
Coordination and Review Section Chief:
Stewart B. Oneglia 307-2222
Special Litigation Section Chief: Arthur E. Peabody 514-6255
Special Litigation Counsel:
Alexander C. Ross 514-2303
James M. Schermerhorn 514-4701
Voting Section Chief: Barry H. Weinberg 307-3266

(Area Code 202)

Deputy Assistant Attorney General: James P. Turner 514-3828
Criminal Section Chief: Linda K. Davis 514-3204
Employment Litigation Section Chief: James S. Angus 514-3831
Administration Section Chief: Robert K. Bratt 514-4224

Deputy Assistant Attorney General: Roger Clegg 514-2163
Appellate Section Chief: David Flynn 514-2195
Educational Opportunities Section Chief:
Nathaniel Douglas 514-4092
Housing and Civil Enforcement Section Chief:
Paul Hancock 514-4713

CRIMINAL DIVISION (Room 2107)

The Criminal Division formulates Federal criminal law enforcement policies, coordinates the implementation of those policies, and conducts selected prosecutions. The Division oversees the prosecution of criminal offenses under more than 900 statutes.

Although most criminal prosecutions are conducted by U.S. Attorneys, the Criminal Division asserts direct responsibility for certain general categories of offenses and, in some specific cases, when circumstances warrant, Division intervention. The Criminal Division also supervises certain civil litigation regarding Federal liquor, narcotics, counterfeiting, gambling, firearms, customs, agriculture, and litigation resulting from petitions for writs of habeas corpus by members of the Armed Forces, actions brought by or on behalf of Federal prisoners, alleged investigative misconduct, and certain legal actions related to national security issues.

* **The Organized Crime and Racketeering Section** conducts investigations and prosecutes cases to suppress the illicit activities of organized crime in major U.S. cities.

* **The Narcotics and Dangerous Drug Section** investigates and prosecutes high level drug traffickers and members of criminal organizations involved in the importation, manufacture, shipment, or distribution of illicit narcotics and dangerous drugs, with particular emphasis on litigation attacking the financial underpinnings of those criminal organizations.

* **The Public Integrity Section** investigates and prosecutes corruption cases involving public officials and the electoral system at the Federal, state, and local levels.

* **The Fraud Section** directs Federal efforts against fraud and white collar crime, focusing primarily on frauds that involve Government programs and procurement, international and multi-district fraud, the security and commodity exchanges, banking practices, and consumer victimization.

* **The Internal Security Section** investigates and prosecutes cases affecting the national security, foreign relations, and the export of military and strategic commodities and technology. It also administers and enforces the Foreign Agents Registration Act of 1938 and related statutes. The Section has exclusive prosecutorial responsibility for criminal statutes regarding espionage, sabotage, neutrality, and atomic energy. Criminal cases involving classified information, especially the application of the Classified Information Procedures Act, are coordinated by this Section.

* **The General Litigation and Legal Advice Section** investigates and prosecutes cases under Federal criminal statutes regarding crimes against the Government and the public. This Section provides legal advice to U.S. Attorneys and investigative agencies and also handles certain civil matters, including the defense of suits against actions taken by the Bureau of Prisons and the U.S. Parole Commission.

* **The Appellate Section** assists the Office of the Solicitor General in obtaining favorable constitutional and statutory interpretations in criminal cases being heard on appeal before the U.S. Supreme Court and the 12 U.S. Courts of Appeals.

* **The Office of Special Investigations** takes appropriate legal action leading to the denaturalization and/or deportation of Nazi war criminals who entered the U.S. illegally.

* **The Office of International Affairs** provides legal support on international criminal justice enforcement matters, pursuant to treaties concerning extradition, mutual legal assistance, and prisoner exchange.

* **The Office of Enforcement Operations** oversees the use of sophisticated investigative techniques such as witness protection and electronic surveillance. It also supports Government prosecutors by approving grants of immunity and responding to inquiries under the Freedom of Information Act and the Privacy Act.

* **The Asset Forfeiture Office** assists in the prosecution of both civil and criminal asset forfeiture cases, particularly regarding narcotics trafficking, organized crime, and customs violations. The Office adjudicates all judicial petitions for remission or mitigation of forfeited assets and determines equitable sharing of judicially forfeited assets with state and local law enforcement agencies.

* **The Office of Legislation** develops legislative proposals, legal memoranda, and congressional testimony on legislation affecting the Federal criminal justice system.

* **The Office of Administration** provides administrative support to each section and office of the Division.

* **The Office of Policy and Management Analysis** develops and recommends positions on policy and management issues for Department and Division officials.

* **National Obscenity Enforcement Unit** targets the major offenders of the applicable Federal criminal obscenity and child pornography statutes, and coordinates the investigation of multi-district and international cases. The Unit also assists U.S. Attorneys and state and local prosecutors, and conducts public information and educational programs for government and private-sector groups.

(Area Code 202)

Assistant Attorney General: Edward S.G. Dennis Jr 514-2601
Special Counsels:
Michael Olmstead 514-2419
Dana Biehl 514-4674

Library (Room 7100) 514-1141
The library is open from 9:00 AM until 5:30 PM, Monday through Friday by appointment only. Admittance is limited.

Deputy Assistant Attorney General: John C. Keeney 514-2621
Office of Enforcement Operations Director:
Frederick D. Hess 514-3684
Organized Crime and Racketeering Section Chief:
Michael deFeo 514-4202
Public Integrity Section Chief: Gerald E. McDowell ...514-1412

Deputy Assistant Attorney General: Paul L. Maloney 514-2636
National Obscenity Enforcement Unit Director:
Patrick A. Trueman 514-5780
Fraud Section Chief: Laurence Urgenson 514-0640
Appellate Section Chief: Sidney M. Glazer 514-3521
Office of Legislation Director: Roger A. Pauley 514-3202

(Area Code 202)

Deputy Assistant Attorney General: Mark M. Richard 514-2333
Office of International Affairs Director:
Drew Arena 514-0000
Office of Special Investigations Director: Neal Sher 514-1346
Asset Forfeiture Office Director:
Laurence W. Fann (Acting) 514-1263
Narcotics and Dangerous Drug Section Chief:
Charles Saphos 514-0917
Money Laundering Office Director:
Michael Zeldin (Acting) 514-1758

Deputy Assistant Attorney General:
David Margolis (Acting) 514-3792
Internal Security Section Chief: John L. Martin 514-1187
General Litigation and Legal Advice Section Chief:
Lawrence Lippe 514-1026
Office of Policy and Management Analysis Director:
Julie E. Samuels 514-3062
Office of Administration Director: Donald Chendorain 514-5749

ENVIRONMENT AND NATURAL RESOURCES DIVISION (Room 2603)

The Environment and Natural Resources Division (formerly known as the Land and Natural Resources Division) handles litigation involving the protection and enhancement of the American environment and wildlife resources; the acquisition, administration, and disposition of public land, water, and mineral resources; and the safeguarding of Indian rights and property. In addition, the Division is responsible for enforcing the nation's civil and criminal environmental laws as well as defending all environmental challenges to Government programs and activities.

* **The Environmental Defense Section** defends the Federal Government in suits brought both by major corporations, which interpret various environmental statutes and regulations as being far too stringent, and by environmental groups which interpret them as being far too lax. The Section is also responsible for defending a variety of Federal agencies in actions brought to clean up pollution generated from Federal facilities and installations.

* **The Environmental Crimes Section** prosecutes individuals and industries which have knowingly endangered the environment. The Section works closely with the FBI in examining violations of such statutes as the Clean Air Act, the Comprehensive Environmental Response, Compensation and Liability Act (Superfund), and the Resource Conservation and Recovery Act (RCRA), among others.

* **The Environmental Enforcement Section** brings civil enforcement cases, primarily on behalf of EPA, related to the control and abatement of pollution of air and water resources, the regulation and control of toxic substances and pesticides, and the environmental hazards posed by hazardous wastes. The statutes enforced by the Section include Superfund, RCRA, the Clean Air and Water Acts, and the Toxic Substances Control Act.

* **The Wildlife and Marine Resources Section** prosecutes and defends criminal and civil cases arising under the Federal wildlife laws, and laws concerning the conservation and management of marine fish and mammals. Prosecutions focus on smugglers and black market dealers in protected wildlife. The defensive civil litigation, particularly under the Endangered Species Act and the Migratory Bird Treaty Act, often pit the needs of protected species against the pressures for development and economic exploitation of resources.

* **The General Litigation Section** conducts trial work in the Federal district courts and the U.S. Claims Court involving all matters concerning Federal property and natural resources not subject to one of the Division's specialized sections. This includes litigation under the National Environmental Policy Act, the Federal Land Policy Management Act, and the National Historic Preservation Act. In addition, the Section represents the U.S. in all legal and equitable claims asserted by Indian tribes on the grounds that the U.S. has failed to live up to its obligations to the tribes.

* **The Indian Resources Section** represents the U.S. in its trust capacity for all legal and equitable claims asserted by individual Indians or Indian tribes. These suits include establishing water rights, establishing and protecting hunting and fishing rights, collecting damages for trespass on Indian lands, and establishing reservation boundaries and rights to land.

* **The Land Acquisition Section** is responsible for acquiring land for the Federal Government, either by direct purchase or condemnation proceedings. The purposes for acquiring land vary greatly from establishing public parks to creating missile sites.

* **The Policy, Legislation and Special Litigation Section** provides staff support for the Division's activities, including its legislative program, and handles special litigation projects. Other duties include responding to citizens' requests, serving as the Division's liaison with the media, and serving as the Division's ethics officers.

* **The Appellate Section** handles all appeals in cases initially tried in lower courts by other sections within the Division. In addition, the Section drafts the briefs for all Division cases which reach the level of the U.S. Supreme Court, and formulates recommendations to the Solicitor General that seek authority to appeal unfavorable decisions.

* **The Executive Office** handles the Division's administrative functions and oversees an active automated litigation support program.

(Area Code 202)

Assistant Attorney General: Richard B. Stewart 514-2701
Special Counsel to the Assistant Attorney General:
JonathanWiener..............................514-2744
Facsimile 514-0557

Library (Room M-2333) 514-2768
This library is open to the public by appointment only from 9:00 AM to 5:30 PM Monday through Friday.

Deputy Assistant Attorney General: Myles E. Flint 514-2718
Appellate Section Chief: Peter R. Steenland 514-2748
Indian Resources Section Chief: Joel H. Meshorer 272-4111
Wildlife & Marine Resources Section Chief:
James C. Kilbourne (Acting) 514-1811
General Litigation Section Chief: William Cohen 272-6851
Special Litigation Counsel: Frederick Disheroon 514-2672
Jean Kingrey 514-2724

(Area Code 202)

Deputy Assistant Attorney General: George W. Van Cleve 514-4760
Environmental Enforcement Section Chief: David Buente 514-5271

Deputy Assistant Attorney General: Barry M. Hartman 514-5242
Environmental Defense Section Chief: Margaret Strand 514-2219
Policy, Legislation and Special Litigation Section
Chief: Anne Shields 514-2586
Land Acquisition Chief: William Kollins 272-6776
Environmental Crimes Section Chief: Jerry G. Block ...272-9877

Deputy Assistant Attorney General:
Peter R. Steenland (Acting) 514-2748

TAX DIVISION (Room 4143)

The Tax Division represents the U.S. and its officers in all civil and criminal litigation involving Federal, state, and local taxes in all courts, except the U.S. Tax Court. The Internal Revenue Service (IRS) is the Division's principal client, and the Division's primary activities are the collection of Federal revenues through the institution of many types of civil actions; the defense of tax refund and a variety of other civil suits brought by taxpayers; the enforcement of criminal tax laws; and the handling of appellate tax cases, both civil and criminal. Attorneys in the Tax Division are stationed in Washington, D.C., except for a small staff located in the Division's Dallas field office.

* **The Appellate Section** handles appeals in civil tax cases. Appellate Section attorneys prepare briefs and present oral arguments in the courts of appeals, various state appellate courts and, on assignment from the Office of the Solicitor General, in the U.S. Supreme Court.

* **The Criminal Enforcement Sections** promote the uniform enforcement of the nation's criminal tax laws. Attorneys in the three regional trial sections review and analyze the recommendations for prosecution of tax offenses received from both the IRS and U.S. Attorneys to determine whether prosecution should be authorized. Trial attorneys from the regional sections conduct and participate directly in major grand jury investigations. They also handle the trial of these cases and provide assistance to many U.S. Attorneys' Offices in specific criminal tax litigation. Attorneys in the Criminal Appeals and Tax Enforcement Policy Section handle appeals in criminal tax cases and, working with personnel form the IRS and from U.S. Attorneys' Offices, help establish the policies which govern the litigation of criminal tax cases.

* **The Civil Trial Sections.** The Claims Court Section defends all tax refund suits filed in that Court. Five Civil Trial Sections, organized along geographic lines, represent the Government in tax refund suits in the U.S. District Courts and handle a wide variety of other litigation in Federal and state courts.

* **Offices. The Office of Review** evaluates settlement offers and furnishes advice and assistance to the trial sections on particularly complex cases. **The Office of Legislation and Policy** (Senior Legislative Counsel) conducts legal research on proposed legislation which may affect the litigation done by the Division.

(Area Code 202)

Assistant Attorney General: Shirley D. Peterson 514-2901
Counselor to the Assistant Attorney General:
Francis Allegra 514-2987
Facsimile 368-2085

Library (Room 4335) 514-2819
The library is open from 8:30 AM until 5:30 PM, Monday through Friday by appointment only.

Deputy Assistant Attorney General: Brian C. Griffin 514-2967
Senior Legislative Counsel: Stephen J. Csontos 307-6419
Appellate Section Chief: Gary Allen 514-3361
Office of Review Chief: Milan D. Karlan 307-6567

Deputy Assistant Attorney General: James A. Bruton 514-2915
Criminal Enforcement Section Director:
Stanley F. Krysa 514-2973
Criminal Enforcement Section Chiefs:
Northern Region: George T. Kelley 514-3036
Southern Region: J. Randolph Maney Jr 514-4334
Western Region: Ronald A. Cimino 514-5247

(Area Code 202)

Criminal Appeals and Tax Enforcement Policy Section
Chief: Robert Lindsay 514-3011

Deputy Assistant Attorney General: Michael L. Paup 514-5109
Office of Special Litigation Chief: Claire Fallon ...514-6502
Civil Trial Section Chiefs:
Central Region: Edward J. Snyder 307-6426
Northern Region: D. Patrick Mullarkey 307-6533
Southern Region: Steven Shapiro 514-5905
Western Region: Stephen G. Fuerth 307-6413
Claims Court Section Chief: Mildred L. Seidman 307-6440

Senior Litigation Counsel: John J. McCarthy 307-6398
Special Litigation Counsel:
Ernest J. Brown 514-3363
Jonathan S. Cohen 514-2970
Dennis M. Donohue 307-6492
Donald J. Gavin 307-6400

COMMUNITY RELATIONS SERVICE
5500 Friendship Boulevard
Chevy Chase, MD 20815

The Community Relations Service (CRS) assists communities by mediating disputes relating to allegations of race, color, or national origin discrimination, and assists in resettlement efforts for Cuban and Haitian entrants. The conciliation and mediation services provided by CRS serves as an alternative to litigation, and as a means of resolving racial conflicts without violence and economic loss. CRS also makes its services available to the judiciary. Federal District Courts refer cases to CRS dealing with housing, allegations of excessive use of force by police, multi-district school desegregation, and bilingual education programs.

CRS operates out of ten regional offices located in Boston, New York, Philadelphia, Atlanta, Chicago, Dallas, Kansas City, Denver, San Francisco, and Seattle, with headquarters in Chevy Chase, MD.

(Area Code 301)

Director: Grace Flores-Hughes 492-5929
General Counsel: Linda L. Martin 492-5939

(Area Code 301)

Facsimile 492-5984

EXECUTIVE OFFICE FOR IMMIGRATION REVIEW
5107 Leesburg Pike, Suite 2400
Falls Church, VA 22041

The Executive Office for Immigration Review, which administers and interprets the immigration laws, is completely independent of the Immigration and Naturalization Service, the organization charged with the enforcement of the immigration laws.

(Area Code 703)
Director: David L. Milhollan 756-6169

(Area Code 703)
Counsel to the Director: Gerald S. Hurwitz 756-6470

BOARD OF IMMIGRATION APPEALS

The Board of Immigration Appeals is a quasi-judicial organization which has nationwide jurisdiction to hear appeals from certain decisions entered by INS District Directors and Immigration Judges. Board decisions are binding on all Service officers and Immigration Judges, unless modified or overruled by the Attorney General, and are subject to judicial review in Federal courts. The majority of appeals reaching the Board involve orders of deportation and applications for relief from deportation. Other cases before the Board include exclusion proceedings involving aliens seeking admission to the U.S., petitions to classify the status of alien relatives for the issuance of preference immigrant visas, fines imposed on carriers for violations of immigration laws, and motions to reopen and reconsider decisions previously rendered.

(Area Code 703)
Chairman: David L. Milhollan 756-6169
Chief Attorney Examiner: David B. Holmes 756-6170

(Area Code 703)
Immigration Appeals Docket 756-6180

OFFICE OF THE CHIEF IMMIGRATION JUDGE

The Office of the Chief Immigration Judge is responsible for general supervision and direction of Immigration Judges in the performance of their duties. The Office includes a headquarters staff of management and legal personnel structured as Assistant Chief Immigration Judges, a Criminal Alien Unit, and a Central Operations Unit. The Immigration Judges, located in field offices nationwide, preside at formal, quasi-judicial deportation and exclusion proceedings. Their decisions are administratively final unless appealed or certified to the Board of Immigration Appeals.

(Area Code 703)
Chief Immigration Judge: William R. Robie 756-6247
Assistant Chief Immigration Judges:
H. Jere Armstrong 756-6569
Thomas L. Pullen 756-6569
M. Christopher Grant 756-6569

(Area Code 703)
Mary Ann Mohan 756-6617
Jill H. Dufresne 756-6569
Chief Central Operations Unit: Anthony A. Padden 756-6558
Docket Unit 756-7138

OFFICE OF THE CHIEF ADMINISTRATIVE HEARING OFFICER

The Office of the Chief Administrative Hearing Officer (OCAHO) provides overall program direction for the Administrative Law Judges (ALJs) to adjudicate cases arising under Sections 101 and 102 of the Immigration Reform and Control Act of 1986. Section 101 provides for sanctions against employers or entities who (1) hire, recruit, or refer for a fee, or continue to employ unauthorized aliens; (2) refuse to comply with the employment verification system; or (3) require the execution of an indemnity bond to protect themselves from potential liability for unlawful employment practices. Section 102 provides for the imposition of penalties against employers who discriminate against any individual (other than an unauthorized alien) in employment-related situations because of the individual's national origin or citizenship status. Such judicial proceedings will be initiated by complaints filed with OCAHO and referred to Administrative Law Judges. The Administrative Law Judges hold hearings and related administrative proceedings and render decisions on the complaints referred to them. They impose sanctions and penalties as prescribed by law in appropriate cases and may, where warranted, award attorney's fees, back pay, and issue cease and desist orders. The Chief Administrative Hearing Officer conducts administrative review and takes the final agency action with respect to cases decided by Administrative Law Judges under Section 101. The OCAHO is located in Falls Church, VA, and hearings are conducted there and in locations across the country.

(Area Code 703)
Chief Administrative Hearing Officer: Jack E. Perkins ..756-3864
Deputy Chief Administrative Hearing Officer:
Ronald Vincoli 756-3864

(Area Code 703)
Counsel: Billy Jack Rivers 756-3858
Administrative Law Judge: Marvin H. Morse 756-3861
Case Management Office 756-3872

IMMIGRATION AND NATURALIZATION SERVICE
425 I Street, N.W.
Washington, D.C. 20536

The Immigration and Naturalization Service (INS) enforces the immigration laws of the United States, and adjudicates applications for naturalization and other types of benefits available to individuals under the immigration and nationality laws. The passage of the Immigration Reform and Control Act of 1986, the most comprehensive revision of the immigration laws of the U.S. in 30 years, introduced new provisions for legalization, employer sanctions, and temporary workers. Service attorneys provide on-the-spot legal assistance to line law enforcement officers, such as investigators, adjudicators, border patrol agents, and immigration inspectors; they provide expertise and litigation assistance to U.S. Attorneys; and represent the Government before administrative and Federal district courts.

(Area Code 202)

Commissioner: D. Gene McNary 514-1900
General Counsel: William P. Cook 514-2895
Deputy General Counsel: Paul W. Virtue 514-2895
Deputy Commissioner: Richardo Inzunza 514-2961
Director of Foreign Operations: Luis Del Rio 514-4660
Director Refugee, Asylum, and Parole Division: Jan Ting 514-2361
Facsimile 514-3296

Enforcement
Associate Commissioner: Michael Williams (Acting) ... 514-3032
Assistant Commissioner for Anti-Smuggling Activities Division: Arthur Dunlap 514-3928
Assistant Commissioner for Detention and Deportation Division: Joan C. Higgins 514-2543
Assistant Commissioner for Border Patrol Division: William Bonnette (Acting) 514-3073

(Area Code 202)

Assistant Commissioner for Employer and Labor Relations Division: John R. Schroeder 514-2471
Assistant Commissioner for Intelligence Division: George Reagan 514-4402
Assistant Commissioner for Investigations Division: John F. Shaw 514-1189

Examinations
Associate Commissioner: James A. Puleo (Acting) 514-2982
Assistant Commissioner for Adjudications Division: James P. Puleo 514-3228
Assistant Commissioner for Inspections Division: Harvey A. Adler (Acting) 514-3019
Assistant Commissioner for Legalization Division: Terrance O'Reilly 514-4657
Administrative Appeals Unit Director: Thomas W. Simmons 376-2080
Outreach Program Director: Edward B. Duarte 514-4123

REGIONAL OFFICES

Eastern Region
Regional Commissioner: Stanley S. McKinley
U.S. Department of Justice, Immigration and Naturalization Service, 11 Elmwood Avenue, Federal Office Bldg, Burlington, VT 05401. Tel: 802/951-6201.
(Jurisdiction: CT, DE, DC, ME, MD, MA, NH, NJ, NY, PA, PR, RI, VT, Virgin Islands, VA, WV)

Northern Region
Regional Commissioner: Carl Houseman (Acting)
U.S. Department of Justice, Immigration and Naturalization Service, Bishop Henry Whipple Federal Building, Fort Snelling, Twin Cities, MN 55111. Tel: 612/725-3850.
(Jurisdiction: AK, CO, ID, IL, ID, IA, KS, MI, MN, MO, MT, NE, ND, OH, OR, SD, UT, WA, WI, WY)

Southern Region
Regional Commissioner: Ruth Anne Myers (Acting)
U.S. Department of Justice, Immigration and Naturalization Service, 7701 North Stemmons Freeway, Skyline Center Bldg C, Dallas, TX 75247. Tel: 214/767-7011.
(Jurisdiction: AL, AR, FL, GA, KY, LA, MS, NM, NC, OK, SC, TN, TX)

Western Region
Regional Commissioner: Benjamin G. Davidian
U.S. Department of Justice, Immigration and Naturalization Service, 24000 Avilia Road, Laguna Niguel, CA 92677.
Tel: 714/643-4236.
(Jurisdiction: AZ, CA, HI, NV)

OFFICE OF SPECIAL COUNSEL FOR IMMIGRATION-RELATED UNFAIR EMPLOYMENT PRACTICES
1100 Connecticut Avenue, N.W., Suite 800
Washington, D.C. 20036

The Office of Special Counsel for Immigration Related Unfair Employment Practices investigates and prosecutes employers charged with national origin and citizenship status discrimination. Injured parties file charges of discrimination directly with the Office of Special Counsel. Attorneys in the Office investigate the charges, negotiate settlements, and recommend to the Special Counsel whether to file a complaint. Complaints are filed with Administrative Law Judges trained to hear these cases. Appeals are filed with the U.S. Circuit Courts.

(Area Code 202)

Special Counsel: Andrew M. Strojny (Acting) 653-8121
Hot Line ....(800) 255-7688

NOTE: The Hot Line is for questions relating to citizenship status or for national origin employment discrimination charges.

OFFICE OF INTELLIGENCE POLICY AND REVIEW (Room 6325)

This office assists the Attorney General by providing legal advice and recommendations regarding national security matters, reviewing Executive Orders, directives, and procedures relating to the intelligence community, and approving certain intelligence-gathering activities. The Office also provides advice to Departmental units and other Executive Branch agencies on the interpretation and application of the Constitution, statutes, regulations, and directives relating to U.S. national security activities.

All representation of the U.S. before the Foreign Intelligence Surveillance Court is conducted by the Office of Intelligence Policy and Review. In coordination with the Criminal Division and U.S. Attorney, the Office prepares motions and briefs required in the U.S. District Court or Court of Appeals whenever surveillance authorized under the Act is challenged. The Office also monitors certain intelligence and counterintelligence investigations to ensure conformity with applicable laws and procedures. It regularly briefs the congressional intelligence committees on all of these activities.

(Area Code 202)

Counsel for Intelligence Policy: Mary C. Lawton 514-5600
Deputy Counsel for Intelligence Operations:
Allan N. Kornblum 514-2882

(Area Code 202)

Deputy Counsel for Intelligence Policy:
Americo R. Cinquegrana 514-5604

EXECUTIVE OFFICE FOR U.S. TRUSTEES
320 First Street, N.W.
Washington, D.C. 20001

The U.S. Trustees Offices handle the administration and oversight of cases filed pursuant to chapters 7, 11, and 13 of Title I of the Bankruptcy Reform Act of 1978. The law provides for 21 separate U.S. Trustee regions covering the 94 judicial districts. Each region is headed by a U.S. Trustee appointed by the Attorney General for a five-year term. The Executive Office for U.S. Trustees, located in Washington, D.C., administers the program for the Department of Justice.

The U.S. Trustees establish, supervise, and maintain panels of private trustees to serve in chapter 7 liquidation cases and supervise the standing trustees who administer chapter 12 and chapter 13 plans. In chapter 11 cases where businesses continue to operate as debtors in possession, the U.S. Trustees play an active administrative role which includes requiring debtors to file monthly financial reports, and ensuring that current tax liabilities are paid and adequate insurance coverage maintained. The U.S. Trustees' statutorily mandated duties also include monitoring the employment and compensation of professionals in a case and policing the system for criminal activity or abusive rulings.

The U.S. Trustees also do appellate work. Appeals from the bankruptcy court are normally to the district court. On occasion, the U.S. Supreme Court also hears bankruptcy issues that allow U.S. Trustee input to the Department's Civil Division and Office of the Solicitor General.

(Area Code 202)

Director and Counsel: John Logan (Acting) 307-1399
Deputy Director: vacant 307-1399
General Counsel: John Logan 301-1391

Region 1

Boston
U.S. Trustee: Virginia A. Greiman
U.S. Department of Justice, Office of the U.S. Trustee,
10 Causeway Street, Room 472, Boston, MA 02222-1043.
Tel: 617/565-6360.

Portland
Assistant U.S. Trustee: Paulette P. Parker
U.S. Department of Justice, Office of the U.S. Trustee,
66 Pearl Street, Room 322, Portland, ME 04101.
Tel: 207/780-3564.

Worcester
Paralegal Specialist: John M. Doherty
U.S. Department of Justice, Office of the U.S. Trustee,
44 Front Street, Suite 440, Worcester, MA 01608.
Tel: 508/793-0555.

Region 2

New York City
U.S. Trustee: Harold D. Jones
U.S. Department of Justice, Office of the U.S. Trustee, One Bowling Green, Room 534, New York, NY 10004. Tel: 212/668-7663.

Buffalo
Assistant U.S. Trustee: Christopher K. Reed
U.S. Department of Justice, Office of the U.S. Trustee, 42 Delaware Avenue, Suite 100, Buffalo, NY 14202. Tel: 716/846-5541

Garden City
Assistant U.S. Trustee: Neal S. Mann
U.S. Department of Justice, Office of the U.S. Trustee, 825 East Gate Blvd, Suite 304, Garden City, NY 11530. Tel: 718/917-7071.

Albany
Assistant U.S. Trustee: Kim Lefebvre
U.S. Department of Justice, Office of the U.S. Trustee, 50 Chapel Street, 1st Floor, Albany, NY 12207. Tel: 518/472-7001.

New Haven
Assistant U.S. Trustee: Eric J. Small
U.S. Department of Justice, Office of the U.S. Trustee, 105 Court Street, Room 402, New Haven, CT 06511. Tel: 203/773-2210.

Rochester
Attorney Advisor: Trudy A. Nowak
U.S. Department of Justice, Office of the U.S. Trustee, 100 State Street, Room 609, Rochester, NY 14614. Tel: 716/263-5812.

Utica
Attorney Advisor: Richard Croak
U.S. Department of Justice, Office of the U.S. Trustee, 10 Broad Street, Room 225, Utica, NY 13501. Tel: 315/793-8191.

Region 3

Newark
Assistant U.S. Trustee: Novalyn L. Winfield
U.S. Department of Justice, Office of the U.S. Trustee, 60 Park Place, Suite 210, Newark, NJ 07102. Tel: 201/645-3014.

Harrisburg
Assistant U.S. Trustee: John J. Grauer
U.S. Department of Justice, Office of the U.S. Trustee, 225 Market Street, Suite 503, Harrisburg, PA 17101. Tel: 717/782-4907.

Philadelphia
Assistant U.S. Trustee: James J. O'Connell
U.S. Department of Justice, Office of the U.S. Trustee, 200 Chestnut Street, Room 607, Philadelphia, PA 19106. Tel: 215/597-4411.

Pittsburgh
Assistant U.S. Trustee: Stephen Goldring
U.S. Department of Justice, Office of the U.S. Trustee, 1000 Liberty Avenue, Room 319, Pittsburgh, PA 15222. Tel: 412/644-4756.

Region 4

Columbia
U.S. Trustee: John E. Waites
U.S. Department of Justice, Office of the U.S. Trustee, 1835 Assembly Street, Room 1108, Columbia, SC 29201. Tel: 803/765-5599.

Alexandria
Assistant U.S. Trustee: Dennis Early
U.S. Department of Justice, Office of the U.S. Trustee, 421 King Street, Room 410, Alexandria, VA 22314. Tel: 703/557-0746.

Norfolk
Assistant U.S. Trustee: Debera F. Conlon
U.S. Department of Justice, Office of the U.S. Trustee, 200 Granby Street, Room 433, Norfolk, VA 23510. Tel: 804/441-6012.

Roanoke
Assistant U.S. Trustee: Thomas W. Kennedy
U.S. Department of Justice, Office of the U.S. Trustee, 210 Franklin Road, SW, Room 806, Roanoke, VA 24011. Tel: 704/982-4306.

Charleston, WV
Assistant U.S. Trustee: John J. Nesius
U.S. Department of Justice, Office of the U.S. Trustee, 500 Virginia Street East, Room 590, Charleston, WV 25301. Tel: 304/347-5310.

Rockville
Assistant U.S. Trustee: Jason P. Green
U.S. Department of Justice, Office of the U.S. Trustee, 51 Monroe Street, Plaza Two, Rockville, MD 20850. Tel: 301/443-1867.

Baltimore
Assistant U.S. Trustee: A. Grey Staples, Jr
U.S. Department of Justice, Office of the U.S. Trustee, 31 Hopkins Plaza, Room G-13, Baltimore, MD 21201. Tel: 301/962-3910.

Region 5

New Orleans
U.S. Trustee: William F. Baity
U.S. Department of Justice, Office of the U.S. Trustee, 400 Poydras Street, Suite 1820, New Orleans, LA 70130. Tel: 504/589-4018.

Shreveport
Assistant U.S. Trustee: Victoria E. Young
U.S. Department of Justice, Office of the U.S. Trustee, 500 Fannin Street, Room 5B07, Shreveport, LA 71101-3099. Tel: 318/226-5460.

Jackson, MS
Assistant U.S. Trustee: Ronald H. McAlpin
U.S. Department of Justice, Office of the U.S. Trustee, 100 W. Capital Street, Suite 808, Jackson, MS 39269. Tel: 601/965-5241.

Region 6

Dallas
U.S. Trustee: William T. Neary
U.S. Department of Justice, Office of the U.S. Trustee, 1100 Commerce Street, Room 9060, Dallas, TX 75242. Tel: 214/767-8967.

Tyler
Bankruptcy Analyst: Michael A. Ley
U.S. Department of Justice, Office of the U.S. Trustee, 211 West Ferguson, Room 208, Tyler, TX 75702.
Tel: 214/597-8312.

Region 7

Houston
U.S. Trustee (Acting): Ben T. Head
U.S. Department of Justice, Office of the U.S. Trustee, 440 Louisiana Street, Suite 2500, Houston, TX 77002.
Tel: 713/653-3000.

Austin
U.S. Trustee (Acting): Ben T. Head
U.S. Department of Justice, Office of the U.S. Trustee, 308 East 8th Street, Room 906, Austin, TX 78701.
Tel: 512/482-5328.

San Antonio
Assistant U.S. Trustee: Barbara Kurtz
U.S. Department of Justice, Office of the U.S. Trustee, 615 East Houston Street, Room 343, San Antonio, TX 78205.
Tel: 512/229-4640.

Region 8

Memphis
U.S. Trustee: E. Franklin Childress
U.S. Department of Justice, Office of the U.S. Trustee, 969 Madison Avenue, Suite 1411, Memphis, TN 38104.
Tel: 901/521-3251.

Louisville
Assistant U.S. Trustee: Joseph J. Golden
U.S. Department of Justice, Office of the U.S. Trustee, 510 West Broadway, Suite 904, Louisville, KY 40202.
Tel: 502/582-6000.

Chattanooga
Assistant U.S. Trustee: William R. Sonnenburg
U.S. Department of Justice, Office of the U.S. Trustee, 900 Georgia Avenue, Room 48, Chattanooga, TN 37402.
Tel: 615/752-5153.

Nashville
Assistant U.S. Trustee: Beth R. Derrick
U.S. Department of Justice, Office of the U.S. Trustee, 701 Broadway, Room 313, Nashville, TN 37203.
Tel: 615/736-2254.

Region 9

Cleveland
U.S. Trustee: Conrad J. Morgenstern
U.S. Department of Justice, Office of the U.S. Trustee, 113 St. Clair Avenue, NE, Suite 200, Cleveland, OH 44114.
Tel: 216/522-7800.

Columbus
Assistant U.S. Trustee: Charles M. Caldwell
U.S. Department of Justice, Office of the U.S. Trustee, 50 West Broad Street, Suite 325, Columbus, OH 43215.
Tel: 614/469-7411.

Grand Rapids
Assistant U.S. Trustee: Ellen G. Ritteman
U.S. Department of Justice, Office of the U.S. Trustee, 190 Monroe Ave, NW, Room 200, Grand Rapids, MI 49503.
Tel: 616/456-2002.

Detroit
Assistant U.S. Trustee: Marion J. Mack
U.S. Department of Justice, Office of the U.S. Trustee, 477 Michigan Avenue, Room 1760, Detroit, MI 48226.
Tel: 313/226-7999.

Cincinnati
Attorney: Neal J. Weill
U.S. Department of Justice, Office of the U.S. Trustee, 5th, Main & Walnut Streets, Room 245, Cincinnati, OH 45202.
Tel: 513/684-6988.

Region 10

Indianapolis
U.S. Trustee: E. Franklin Childress
U.S. Department of Justice, Office of the U.S. Trustee, 46 East Ohio Street, Room 258, Indianapolis, IN 46204.
Tel: 317/226-6101.

Peoria
Assistant U.S. Trustee: Randall W. Moon
U.S. Department of Justice, Office of the U.S. Trustee, 100 NE Monroe Street, Room 333, Peoria, IL 61602.
Tel: 309/671-7854.

South Bend
Assistant U.S. Trustee: Alexander L. Edgar
U.S. Department of Justice, Office of the U.S. Trustee, 100 East Wayne Street, Room 555, South Bend, IN 46801.
Tel: 219/236-8105.

Region 11

Chicago
U.S. Trustee: M. Scott Michel
U.S. Department of Justice, Office of the U.S. Trustee, 175 West Jackson Blvd, Room A-1335, Chicago, IL 60604.
Tel: 312/886-5785.

Milwaukee
Assistant U.S. Trustee: John R. Byrnes
U.S. Department of Justice, Office of the U.S. Trustee, 517 East Wisconsin Avenue, Room 560, Milwaukee, WI 53202.
Tel: 414/291-4499.

Madison
Assistant U.S. Trustee: Sheree L. Gowey
U.S. Department of Justice, Office of the U.S. Trustee, 14 West Mifflin Street, Room 310, Madison, WI 53703.
Tel: 608/264-5522.

Region 12

Cedar Rapids
U.S. Trustee: Wesley B. Huisinga
U.S. Department of Justice, Office of the U.S. Trustee, 425 Second Street, SE, Room 675, Cedar Rapids, IA 52401.
Tel: 319/364-2211.

Des Moines
Assistant U.S. Trustee: Terry L. Gibson
U.S. Department of Justice, Office of the U.S. Trustee, 210 Walnut Street, Room 517, Des Moines, IA 50309.
Tel: 515/284-4982.

Minneapolis
Assistant U.S. Trustee: Mark H. Weber
U.S. Department of Justice, Office of the U.S. Trustee, 331 Second Avenue, South, Suite 540, Minneapolis, MN 55401.
Tel: 612/348-1900.

Sioux Falls
Assistant U.S. Trustee: Charles L. Nail
U.S. Department of Justice, Office of the U.S. Trustee, 300 North Dakota Avenue, Suite 510, Sioux Falls, SD 57102. Tel: 605/330-4450.

Region 13

Kansas City
U.S. Trustee: John R. Stonitsch
U.S. Department of Justice, Office of the U.S. Trustee, 911 Walnut Street, Room 806, Kansas City, MO 64106 Tel: 816/426-7959.

St. Louis
Assistant U.S. Trustee: James S. Cole
U.S. Department of Justice, Office of the U.S. Trustee, 815 Olive Street, Room 324, St. Louis, MO 63101 Tel: 314/539-2976.

Omaha
Assistant U.S. Trustee: Patricia M. Dugan
U.S. Department of Justice, Office of the U.S. Trustee, 210 South 16th Street, Suite 450, Omaha, NE 68102. Tel: 402/221-4300.

Little Rock
Assistant U.S. Trustee: Charles W. Tucker, Jr.
U.S. Department of Justice, Office of the U.S. Trustee, 500 South Broadway, Suite 201, Little Rock, AR 72201. Tel: 501/378-7357.

Region 14

Phoenix
U.S. Trustee: Virginia A. Mathis
U.S. Department of Justice, Office of the U.S. Trustee, 320 North Central Avenue, Room 100, Phoenix, AZ 85004. Tel: 602/261-3092.

Region 15

San Diego
U.S. Trustee: Edward A. Infante
U.S. Department of Justice, Office of the U.S. Trustee, 101 West Broadway, Suite 440, San Diego, CA 92101. Tel: 619/557-5013.

Honolulu
Assistant U.S. Trustee: Gayle J. Lau
U.S. Department of Justice, Office of the U.S. Trustee, 300 Ala Moana Blvd, Room 6321, Honolulu, HI 96850. Tel: 808/541-3360.

Guam
Attorney Advisor: Timothy H. Bellas
U.S. Department of Justice, Office of the U.S. Trustee, 238 Archbishop Flores, Suite 805, Agana, Guam 96910. Tel: 671/472-7336.

Region 16

Los Angeles
U.S. Trustee: Davis H. Von Wittenburg
U.S. Department of Justice, Office of the U.S. Trustee, 300 N. Los Angeles Street, Room 3101, Los Angeles Street, CA 90012. Tel: 213/894-6811.

Santa Ana
Assistant U.S. Trustee: Arthur M. Marquis
U.S. Department of Justice, Office of the U.S. Trustee, 600 West Santa Ana Blvd, Room 501, Santa Ana, CA 92701. Tel: 714/836-2691.

San Bernardino
Attorney Advisor: Timothy J. Farris
U.S. Department of Justice, Office of the U.S. Trustee, 699 North Arrowhead Avenue, Room 106, San Bernardino, CA 92401. Tel: 714/383-5850.

Region 17

San Francisco
U.S. Trustee: Anthony G. Sousa
U.S. Department of Justice, Office of the U.S. Trustee, 601 Van Ness Avenue, Suite 2008, San Francisco, CA 94102. Tel: 415/556-7900.

Fresno
Assistant U.S. Trustee: Edward R. Kandler
U.S. Department of Justice, Office of the U.S. Trustee, 1130 "O" Street, Suite 1110, Fresno, CA 93721. Tel: 209/487-5400.

Oakland
Attorney: Barbara R. Serlin
U.S. Department of Justice, Office of the U.S. Trustee, 1401 Lakeside Drive, Suite 1260, Oakland, CA 94612. Tel: 415/273-7800.

Las Vegas
Assistant U.S. Trustee: Erika P. Rogers
U.S. Department of Justice, Office of the U.S. Trustee, 600 Las Vegas Blvd, South, Suite 430, Las Vegas, NV 89101. Tel: 702/388-6600.

Reno
Attorney Advisor: Elizabeth Root
U.S. Department of Justice, Office of the U.S. Trustee, 350 South Center Street, Suite 280, Reno, NV 89501. Tel: 702/784-5335.

San Jose
Assistant U.S. Trustee: Ernest M. Robles
U.S. Department of Justice, Office of the U.S. Trustee, 280 South First Street, Room 268, San Jose, CA 95113. Tel: 408/291-7450.

Sacramento
Attorney Advisor: Donna S. Tamanaha
U.S. Department of Justice, Office of the U.S. Trustee, 915 "L" Street, Suite 1150, Sacramento, CA 95814. Tel: 916/551-3300.

Region 18

Seattle
U.S. Trustee: Mary Jo Heston
U.S. Department of Justice, Office of the U.S. Trustee, 1200 6th Avenue, Room 600, Seattle, WA 98101. Tel: 206/442-2000.

Boise
Assistant U.S. Trustee: Jeffrey G. Howe
U.S. Department of Justice, Office of the U.S. Trustee, 304 North Eighth Street, Room 347, Boise, ID 83702. Tel: 208/334-1300.

Portland
Assistant U.S. Trustee: Pamela J. Griffith
U.S. Department of Justice, Office of the U.S. Trustee, 851 Southwest 6th Avenue, Suite 1300, Portland, OR 97204.
Tel: 503/326-4000.

Spokane
Assistant U.S. Trustee: Robert D. Miller
U.S. Department of Justice, Office of the U.S. Trustee, North 221 Wall Street, Suite 538, Spokane, WA 99201.
Tel: 509/353-2999.

Great Falls
Assistant U.S. Trustee: Neal Jensen
U.S. Department of Justice, Office of the U.S. Trustee, 301 Central Avenue, Suite 204, Great Falls, MT 59401
Tel: 406/761-8777.

Anchorage
Attorney Advisor: Barbara L. Franklin
U.S. Department of Justice, Office of the U.S. Trustee, 605 West Fourth Avenue, Suite 258, Anchorage, AK 99501.
Tel: 907/271-2600.

Eugene
Attorney Advisor: Paul J. Garrick
U.S. Department of Justice, Office of the U.S. Trustee, 44 West Broadway, Suite 500, Eugene, OR 97401
Tel: 503/465-6666.

Region 19

Denver
Acting U.S. Trustee: David D. Bird
U.S. Department of Justice, Office of the U.S. Trustee, 1845 Sherman Street, Suite 300, Denver, CO 80203.
Tel: 303/844-5188.

Cheyenne
Assistant U.S. Trustee: Royann Fransen
U.S. Department of Justice, Office of the U.S. Trustee, 2120 Capital Avenue, Room 8010, Cheyenne, WY 82001.
Tel: 307/772-2790.

Salt Lake City
Assistant U.S. Trustee: Michael J. Straley
U.S. Department of Justice, Office of the U.S. Trustee, 9 Exchange Place, Suite 100, Salt Lake City, UT 84111.
Tel: 801/524-5734.

Region 20

Wichita
U.S. Trustee: Carol Park Wood
U.S. Department of Justice, Office of the U.S. Trustee, 401 North Market Street, Room 180, Wichita, KS 67202.
Tel: 316/269-6637.

Oklahoma City
Attorney Advisor: Mark B. Toffoli
U.S. Department of Justice, Office of the U.S. Trustee, 201 NW Dean A. McGee Avenue, Room 516, Oklahoma City, OK 73102.
Tel: 405/231-5950.

Tulsa
Assistant U.S. Trustee: Katherine M. Vance
U.S. Department of Justice, Office of the U.S. Trustee, 333 West Fourth Street, Room 3130, Tulsa, OK 74103.
Tel: 918/581-6670.

Albuquerque
Assistant U.S. Trustee: Patricia D. Webb
U.S. Department of Justice, Office of the U.S. Trustee, 320 Central Avenue, SW, Room 34, Albuquerque, NM 87103.
Tel: 505/766-3103.

Region 21

Atlanta
U.S. Trustee: Robert L. Coley
U.S. Department of Justice, Office of the U.S. Trustee, 75 Spring Street, SW, Suite 1418, Atlanta, GA 30303.
Tel: 404/331-4437.

Miami
Assistant U.S. Trustee: David D. Bird
U.S. Department of Justice, Office of the U.S. Trustee, 51 SW First Avenue, Room 1204, Miami, FL 33130.
Tel: 305/536-7285.

Savannah
Assistant U.S. Trustee: Jack K. Berry
U.S. Department of Justice, Office of the U.S. Trustee, 222 West Oglethorpe Avenue, Suite 302, Savannah, GA 31410.
Tel: 912/944-4112.

Tampa
Assistant U.S. Trustee: Lynne L. England
U.S. Department of Justice, Office of the U.S. Trustee, 4921 Memorial Highway, Room 340, Tampa, FL 33634.
Tel: 813/225-7197.

Hato Rey
Attorney Advisor: Alejandro Oliveras
U.S. Department of Justice, Office of the U.S. Trustee, Chardon Street, Room 638, Hato Rey, PR 00918.
Tel: 809/766-5851.

Macon
Attorney Advisor: Mark W. Roadarmel
U.S. Department of Justice, Office of the U.S. Trustee, 433 Cherry Street, Suite 510, Macon, GA 31201.
Tel: 912/752-3544.

Tallahassee
Attorney: Charles S. Glidewell
U.S. Department of Justice, Office of the U.S. Trustee, 227 North Bronough Street, Room 1047, Tallahassee, FL 32301.
Tel: 904/681-7660.

FOREIGN CLAIMS SETTLEMENT COMMISSION OF THE U.S.

1111 20th Street, N.W.
Washington, D.C. 20579

The Foreign Claims Settlement Commission is a quasi-judicial agency responsible for adjudicating claims of U.S. nationals against foreign countries which have nationalized, expropriated, or otherwise taken property without paying compensation as required by international law. The Commission also advises Congress and other agencies, including the Department of State, on matters relating to international claims. In addition, the Commission has authority to determine any further claims that may be filed by U.S. military personnel and civilians, or their survivors, for mistreatment by the enemy while captured or interned during the Vietnam Conflict.

DEPARTMENT OF JUSTICE

(Area Code 202)

Chairman: Stanley J. Glod 653-6159
Chief Counsel: David Bradley 653-5883

NOTE: Decisions of the Commission are available in the Reading Room.

OFFICE OF JUSTICE PROGRAMS
633 Indiana Avenue, N.W.
Washington, D.C. 20530

The Office of Justice Programs (OJP), headed by an Assistant Attorney General, coordinates financial and technical assistance to state and local governments; provides staff support for the Bureau of Justice Statistics, the National Institute of Justice, and the Office of Juvenile Justice and Delinquency Prevention, the Office for Victims of Crime, and the Bureau of Justice Assistance.

(Area Code 202)

Assistant Attorney General: Richard Bender Abell 307-5933
Deputy Assistant Attorney General: Clifford J. White 307-5933

(Area Code 202)

Facsimile 514-6383

OFFICE OF GENERAL COUNSEL

The OJP Office of General Counsel provides legal advice to the agencies authorized by the Omnibus Crime Control and Safe Streets Act of 1968, the Victims of Crime Act of 1984, and the Juvenile Justice and Delinquency Program Prevention Act of 1974. The Office represents the five OJP program offices in administrative hearings and advises on legal questions arising under grants, contracts, and the statutes and regulations governing the expenditure of Federal grant or contract funds.

(Area Code 202)

General Counsel Walter W. Barbee (Acting) 307-0790
Associate General Counsel:
Gregory C. Brady 307-6235
John J. Wilson 307-0793

(Area Code 202)

Attorney Advisors:
Randall P.K. Davis 307-6235
Yvette D. Mouton 307-6235

Office of Civil Rights Compliance
Director: Winifred A. Dunton 307-0690

BUREAU OF JUSTICE ASSISTANCE

The Bureau of Justice Assistance (BJA) administers block grant and discretionary grant programs to assist state and local criminal justice agencies in carrying out general criminal justice system improvements and drug law enforcement programs for police, court, or correctional systems.

(Area Code 202)

Director: Gerald P. Regier (Acting) 514-6278

(Area Code 202)

Facsimile 514-5956

BUREAU OF JUSTICE STATISTICS

The Bureau of Justice Statistics (BJS) collects, analyzes, and disseminates statistical information on crime, victims of crime, criminal offenders, and the operation of justice at all levels of government.

(Area Code 202)

Director: Steven Dillingham 307-0765
Chief of Federal Statistical Programs Information
Policy: Carol Kaplan 307-0759

Bureau of Justice Clearinghouse ....(800) 732-3277
BJS distributes its reports through the National Criminal Justice Reference Service (NCJRS). There are up to 500 abstracts available in its database.

OFFICE OF JUVENILE JUSTICE AND DELINQUENCY PREVENTION

The Office of Juvenile Justice and Delinquency Prevention (OJJDP) coordinates Federal efforts relating to juvenile justice and delinquency prevention, and administers the Missing Children's Assistance Program to coordinate the Federal response to the interstate problem of missing children.

(Area Code 202)

Administrator: Robert W. Sweet Jr 307-5911

Juvenile Justice Clearinghouse .... (800) 638-8736
There is a database for information on juvenile delinquency maintained through The National Criminal Justice Reference Service. The cost of a custom search is $48 which gives you up to 400 abstracts. There is no case law or legislative information in this database. The service may also be accessed through DIALOG.

National Center for Missing & Exploited Children (800) 843-5678
This number is for reporting sightings of missing children and exploitation of children other than in a home setting. The organization will also send educational and preventative materials. The telephones are staffed from 7:30 AM until 11:30 PM EST. An answering service is on the remainder of the time.

OFFICE FOR VICTIMS OF CRIME

Office for Victims of Crime (OVC) awards grants and contracts designed to ultimately balance the system of justice by recognizing that crime victims are an integral part of the criminal justice process and must be afforded the fairness, respect, and courtesy they deserve.

(Area Code 202)

Director: Dr. Jane Burnley 307-5983
Deputy Director: vacant 724-5947

National Victims of Crime Resource Center .... (800) 627-6827
There is a National Victims Resource Center which provides information to those who assist victims of crime. Database and publications are available and they are developing a victim compensation legislative database.

NATIONAL INSTITUTE OF JUSTICE

The National Institute of Justice (NIJ) is the principal Federal agency for research, development, evaluation, and dissemination of new knowledge to improve and strengthen the criminal justice system. Priority is given to policy-relevant research that can yield approaches and information which state and local agencies can use to prevent and reduce crime and improve the administration of justice.

(Area Code 202)

Director: vacant 307-2942

NIJ DATABASES AND PUBLICATIONS OF INTEREST

The National Criminal Justice Reference Service (NCJRS) is an international clearinghouse of the latest criminal justice research. Its services include the following:

Databases:

*** Database of Criminal Justice Information:** A computerized clearinghouse of 90,000 criminal justice related information sources. It features summaries of books, reports, and articles - government and non-government, published and non-published - as well as audiovisual materials.

*** Reference and Referral Services.** Highly trained criminal justice information specialists have direct online access to the NCJRS database on such topics as law enforcement, drugs and crime, courts, juvenile justice, statistics, and victims of crime. Topical searches cost $17.50. A topical bibliography on a specific subject costs $5.00. Information specialists will also do a custom search tailored to a need for $48.00. If the service does not have the information you need, specialized librarians will refer you to another source. Documents in the data base are accessible by interlibrary loan or by visiting the NCJRS Reading Library at 1600 Research Blvd, Rockville, MD. Hours are Monday through Friday, 8:30 AM to 5:00 PM. You may also access this database by using the DIALOG service.

*** Specialized Data Bases.** These data bases are also available by calling the toll-free 800 number below: **Federal Criminal Justice Research Data Base, Criminal Justice Calendar Data Base, Juvenile Justice Automated Conference Calendar.**

Publications:

*** Publications:** By registering with NCJRS you will receive a bi-monthly publication, NIJ REPORTS. There are other publications regularly sent to registered users such as: a Research in Brief series, AIDS Bulletin and Research in Action series.

For more information or to order any of the above NCJRS products or services call (800) 851-3420 or (301) 251-5500 in Maryland and the Metropolitan Washington D.C. Area. Or, write: National Institute of Justice/-NCJRS, Box 6000, Dept. AFA, Rockville, MD 20850. Registration with NCJRS is free. If you call the above number for a registration form, you will be put on their mailing list.

EXECUTIVE OFFICE FOR U.S. ATTORNEYS (Room 1619)

The Executive Office for the U.S. Attorneys has supervisory responsibilities with regard to U.S. Attorneys' non-litigative functions, including general executive assistance, certain administrative and legal services, personnel, training, and oversight. The Legal Services Section provides counsel to the Executive Office for U.S. Attorneys and to the U.S. Attorneys Offices. Responsibilities include making conflict of interest and ethical conduct determinations; handling recusals and cross-designation requests; advising U.S. Attorneys on personnel issues; handling Freedom of Information Act/Privacy Act requests; and monitoring and drafting legislation.

U.S. Attorneys' Offices. The U.S. Attorneys are responsible for the vast bulk of the criminal and civil litigation for the United States. Federal law places upon the Attorney General responsibility for the conduct of all litigation affecting the interests of the U.S. This responsibility is discharged by delegating authority to offices throughout the country to handle such litigation and appear in the various Federal courts as the Government's advocates. These field officers are the U.S. Attorneys.

There are 93 U.S. Attorneys stationed throughout the U.S., Puerto Rico, the Virgin Islands, Guam, and the Northern Marianas. One U.S. Attorney is assigned to each judicial district with the exception of Guam and the Northern Marianas, where a single U.S. Attorney serves in both districts.

The U.S. Attorneys perform their responsibilities with the support of approximately 3,000 Assistant U.S. Attorneys and 3,500 non-attorney personnel. U.S. Attorneys are appointed by the President and confirmed by the Senate for terms of four years.

Note: As of January 1990, U.S. Strike Forces were merged into the U.S. Attorneys offices.

(Area Code 202)

Director: Laurence S. McWhorter 514-2121
Legal Counsel: Manuel Rodriguez 514-4024
Freedom of Information Act/Privacy Act Attorney Advisor:
Bonnie Gay 501-7826
Organized Crime Drug Enforcement Task Force
Administration Staff Director: Frederick W. Kramer ..514-1860
Law Enforcement Coordinating Committee/Victim Witness
Assistant Director: Nancy Allen 514-3982
Facsimile 514-0323

(Area Code 202)

Office of Legal Education
Director: Thomas Schrup 514-4104
Attorney General's Advocacy Institute
Director: Vacant 514-4104

Legal Education Institute Associate Director:
Susan Moss 501-7467

U.S. ATTORNEYS

MIDDLE DISTRICT OF ALABAMA
P.O. Box 197, Montgomery, AL 36101 ....(205) 223-7280

U.S. Attorney: James Eldon Wilson
First Assistant U.S. Attorney: D. Broward Segrest
Civil Chief: Kenneth E. Vines
Criminal Chief: Charles R. Niven
Financial Litigation Chief: Calvin C. Pryor
Lead Drug Task Force Attorney: Steven M. Reynolds

NORTHERN DISTRICT OF ALABAMA
200 Federal Building, 1800 Fifth Avenue,
Birmingham, AL 35203 ....(205) 731-1785

U.S. Attorney: Frank Donaldson
First Assistant U.S. Attorney: Leon Fred Kelly Jr.
Civil Chief: George Batcheler
Criminal Chief: Bud Henry
Lead Drug Task Force Attorney: Joe McLean

SOUTHERN DISTRICT OF ALABAMA
Room 305, U.S. Courthouse, 113 St. Joseph Street,
Mobile, AL 36602 ....(205) 690-2845

U.S. Attorney: J.B. Sessions III
First Assistant U.S. Attorney: Edward J. Vulevich Jr.
Civil Chief: Edward J. Vulevich Jr.
Criminal Chief: Ginny S. Granade
Lead Drug Task Force Attorney: Gloria Bedwell

DISTRICT OF ALASKA
Room C-252, Federal Building and U.S. Courthouse,
701 C Street, Mail Box 9
Anchorage, AK 99513 ....(907) 271-5071

Fairbanks Branch Office: Room 310 New Federal Building and U.S. Courthouse, 101 12th Avenue, Box 2, Fairbanks, AK 99701 ....(907) 456-0245

U.S. Attorney: Mark R. Davis
First Assistant U.S. Attorney: vacant
Civil Chief: vacant
Criminal Chief: vacant
Lead Drug Task Force Attorney: Crandon Randell

DISTRICT OF ARIZONA
4000 U.S. Courthouse, 230 First Avenue,
Phoenix, AZ 85025 ....(602) 379-3011

Tucson Branch Office: 110 South Church Street, Suite 8310,
Tucson, AZ 85701 ....(602) 670-6511

U.S. Attorney: Stephen N. McNamee
First Assistant U.S. Attorney: Roger W. Dokken
Chief U.S. Attorney: Daniel G. Knauss (Tucson)
Civil Chiefs: Don B. Overall (Tucson)
James P. Loss (Phoenix)
Criminal Chief: Jon R. Cooper (Tucson)
Appellate Chief: vacant
Lead Drug Task Force Attorneys: James Lacey (Phoenix)

EASTERN DISTRICT OF ARKANSAS
P.O. Box 1229, Little Rock, AR 72203 ....(501) 378-5342

U.S. Attorney: Charles A. Banks
First Assistant U.S. Attorney and Criminal Chief:
Kenneth Stoll
Civil Chief: Richard Pence

WESTERN DISTRICT OF ARKANSAS
P.O. Box 1524, Fort Smith, AR 72901 ....(501) 783-5125

U.S. Attorney: J. Michael FitzHugh
Supervisory Assistant U.S. Attorneys:
Debra J. Groom
Steven Snyder
Larry McCord

CENTRAL DISTRICT OF CALIFORNIA
312 North Spring Street,
Los Angeles, CA 90012 ....(213) 894-2434

Santa Ana Branch Office: 751 West Santa Ana Boulevard,
Santa Ana, CA 92701 ....(714) 836-2098

U.S. Attorney: Robert L. Brosio
Civil Chief: Frederick M. Brosio
Criminal Chief: Robert L. Brosio
Regional Lead Drug Task Force Coordinator:
James P. Walsh Jr.
Strike Force Chief: Julie Warner-Simon

EASTERN DISTRICT OF CALIFORNIA
3305 Federal Building, 650 Capitol Mall,
Sacramento, CA 95814 ....(916) 551-2700

Fresno Branch Office: 4304 Federal Building,
1130 O Street, Fresno, CA 93721 ....(209) 487-5172

U.S. Attorney: David F. Levi
First Assistant U.S. Attorney: Richard F. Jenkins
Civil Chief: Greg Hollows
Criminal Chief: Doug Hendricks
Lead Drug Task Force Attorney: Thomas Couris

NORTHERN DISTRICT OF CALIFORNIA
450 Golden Gate Avenue, Box 36055,
San Francisco, CA 94102 ....(415) 556-1126

San Jose Branch Office: 280 South First Street, Room 371,
San Jose, CA 95113 ....(408) 291-7221

U.S. Attorney: Joseph P. Russoniello
First Assistant U.S. Attorney: William McGivern
Civil Chief: Stephen L. Schirle
Criminal Chief: Floy E. Dawson
Lands Chief: Paul Locke
Tax Chief: Jay R. Weill
Regional Drug Task Force Coordinator: Matthew B. Pavone
Strike Force Chief: Jeff Anderson

SOUTHERN DISTRICT OF CALIFORNIA
940 Front Street, Room 5-N-19, U.S. Courthouse,
San Diego, CA 92189 ....(619) 557-5610

U.S. Attorney: William Branniff
Chief Assistant U.S. Attorney: James W. Brannigan Jr
Civil Chief: John Neece
Criminal Chief: Maria T. Arroyo-Tabin
Regional Drug Task Force Coordinator: Stephen G. Nelson

DISTRICT OF COLORADO
1961 Stout Street, Suite 1200, Federal Office Building,
Drawer 3615, Denver, CO 80294 ....(303) 844-2081

U.S. Attorney: Michael J. Norton
First Assistant U.S. Attorney: Robert Gay Guthrie
Civil Chief: William Pharo
Criminal Chief: James R. Allison
Regional Drug Task Force Coordinator: William D. Welch

DISTRICT OF CONNECTICUT
P.O. Box 1824, New Haven, CT 06508 ....(203) 773-2108

Hartford Branch Office: Federal Building, Room 250,
450 Main Street, Hartford, CT 06103 ....(203) 722-2507

Bridgeport Branch Office: Room 309, Federal Building
and Courthouse, 915 Lafayette Boulevard,
Bridgeport, CT 06603 ....(203) 579-5596

U.S. Attorney: Stanley A. Twardy
Deputy Assistant U.S. Attorney: Richard N. Palmer
Assistant U.S. Attorney in Charge of Bridgeport Office:
Linda K. Lager
Civil Chief: John B. Hughes
Criminal Chief: John H. Durham
Lead Assistant U.S. Attorney/Drug Task Force:
Donna L. Fatsi
Strike Force Chief: Robert Devlin

DISTRICT OF DELAWARE
J. Caleb Boggs Federal Building, 844 King Street, Room 5110,
Wilmington, DE 19801 ....(302) 573-6277

U.S. Attorney: William C. Carpenter Jr
Supervisory Assistant U.S. Attorney: Richard Andrews

DISTRICT OF COLUMBIA
Judiciary Center Building, 555 Fourth Street, N.W.,
Washington, D.C. 20001 ....(202) 272-9600

U.S. Attorney: Jay B. Stephens
Principal Assistant U.S. Attorney: William J. Birney
Civil Chief: John Bates
Criminal Chief: H. Marshall Jarrett

MIDDLE DISTRICT OF FLORIDA
Robert Timberlake Building, Room 410, 500 Zack Street,
Tampa, FL 33602 ....(813) 225-7300

Jacksonville Branch Office: P.O. Box 600,
Jacksonville, FL 32201 ....(904) 791-2682

Orlando Branch Office: 501 Federal Building,
80 North Hughey Avenue, Orlando, FL 32801 ....(407) 648-6700

Fort Myers Branch Office: First, Lee, Jackson, and Bay
Streets, Suite 312, Fort Myers, FL 33901 ....(813) 337-7700

U.S. Attorney: Robert W. Genzman
First Assistant U.S. Attorney: Greg Kehoe
Civil Chief: Gary Takacs
Criminal Chief: Terry Zitek
Chief Assistant U.S. Attorney/Jacksonville:
Curtis Fallgatter
Chief Assistant U.S. Attorney/Orlando:
Robert Moreno-Carreras
Lead Drug Task Force Attorney: Karla L. Spaulding
Strike Force Chief: Kevin March

NORTHERN DISTRICT OF FLORIDA
227 North Bronough Street, Suite 4014,
Tallahassee, FL 32301 ....(904) 681-7360

Pensacola Branch Office: 114 East Gregory Street,
Pensacola, FL 32501 ....(904) 434-3251

U.S. Attorney: Lyndia Barrett
Civil Chief: Ken Sukhia
Criminal Chief: Lyndia Barrett
Attorney in Charge/Pensacola: Samuel A. Alter
Lead Drug Task Force Attorney: David McGee

SOUTHERN DISTRICT OF FLORIDA
155 South Miami Avenue, Miami, FL 33130 ....(305) 536-4471

Fort Lauderdale Branch Office: 299 East Broward Boulevard,
Room 202-B, Fort Lauderdale, FL 33301 ....(305) 527-7254

West Palm Beach Branch Office: 701 Clematis Street,
West Palm Beach, FL 33401 ....(305) 655-1029

U.S. Attorney: Dexter W. Lehtinen
Civil Chief: Robyn Hermann
Appellate Chief: Linda Hertz
Economic Crimes Chief: Caroline Heck
General Crimes Chief: Myles Malman
Narcotics Chief: James McAdams
Regional Drug Task Force Coordinator: Lee S. Massey
Strike Force Chief: Bob Lehner

MIDDLE DISTRICT OF GEORGIA
P.O. Box U, Macon, GA 31202 ....(912) 752-3511

U.S. Attorney: Edgar W. Ennis Jr
First Assistant U.S. Attorney: Sam Wilson
Civil Chief: Frank L. Butler
Criminal Chief: Miriam W. Duke
Lead Drug Task Force Attorney: Deborah A. Griffin

NORTHERN DISTRICT OF GEORGIA
Richard Russell Building, 75 Spring Street, Room 1800,
Atlanta, GA 30335 ....(404) 331-6954

U.S. Attorney: Robert L. Barr
First Assistant U.S. Attorney/Criminal Chief:
Ray Rukstele
Civil Chief: Curtis Anderson
Regional Drug Task Force Coordinator: Gordon H. Miller
Strike Force Chief: Jim Deichert

SOUTHERN DISTRICT OF GEORGIA
P.O. Box 8999, Savannah, GA 31412 ....(912) 232-3145

Augusta Branch Office: P.O. Box 2017,
Augusta, GA 30903 ....(404) 724-0517

U.S. Attorney: Hinton R. Pierce
First Assistant U.S. Attorney: Edmund A. Booth Jr
Criminal Chief: William McAbee II
Lead Drug Task Force Attorney: Joe Newman

DISTRICT OF GUAM
Pacific News Building, 238 O'Hara Street, Suite 502-A,
Agana, Guam 96910 9-011-671-471-7332

Northern Mariana Islands Branch Office:
Origuchi Building, Third Floor, P.O. Box 377,
Saipan, CM 96950 9-011-670-234-9133

U.S. Attorney: D. Paul Vernier
Assistant U.S. Attorney: D. Paul Vernier
Assistant U.S. Attorney/Northern Mariana Islands:
Richard W. Pierce
Lead Drug Task Force Attorney: Frederick Black

DISTRICT OF HAWAII
PJKK Federal Building, Room C-242, Box 50183,
300 Ala Moana Blvd, Honolulu, HI 96850 ....(808) 541-2850

U.S. Attorney: Daniel A. Bent
First Assistant U.S. Attorney/Criminal Chief:
Elliot Enoki
Civil Chief: Michael Chun
Assistant U.S. Attorneys: John Peyton, Les Osborne,
and Mark Bennett
Lead Drug Task Force Attorney: John Peyton Jr

DISTRICT OF IDAHO
Room 328 Federal Building, Box 037, 550 West Fort Street,
Boise, ID 83724 ....(208) 334-1211

U.S. Attorney: Maurice O. Ellsworth
Assistant U.S. Attorneys: Joanne Rodriguez and
Warren Derbidge

CENTRAL DISTRICT OF ILLINOIS
P.O. Box 375, Springfield, IL 62705 ....(217) 492-4450

Peoria Branch Office: 252 Federal Building,
100 Northeast Monroe St, Peoria, IL 61602 ....(309) 671-7050
Danville Branch Office: 14 Towne Centre, 2 East Main St,
Danville, IL 61832 ....(217) 446-8546

U.S. Attorney: J. William Roberts
First Assistant U.S. Attorney/Criminal Chief:
Byron G. Cudmore
Civil Chief: James A. Lewis

NORTHERN DISTRICT OF ILLINOIS
Everett McKinley Dirksen Building, Room 1500-S,
219 South Dearborn St, Chicago, IL 60604 ....(312) 353-5300

Rockford Branch Office: 211 South Court Street,
Rockford, IL 61101 ....(815) 987-4277

U.S. Attorney: Ira H. Raphaelson
First Assistant U.S. Attorneys: Joan Safford and
Ira Raphaelson
Civil Chief: Nancy Needles
Criminal Chief: Vicki Peters
Regional Drug Task Force Coordinators:
Thomas J. Scorza and John Farrell
Strike Force Chief: Gary Shapiro

SOUTHERN DISTRICT OF ILLINOIS
750 Missouri Avenue, Room 330, East St. Louis,
IL 62201 ....(618) 482-9361

Benton Branch Office: PO Box D, Benton, IL 62812 (618) 439-3808
Alton Branch Office: 501 Belle, Room 230, Alton,
IL 62002 ....(618)463-6409

U.S. Attorney: Frederick J. Hess
First Assistant U.S. Attorney: Clifford J. Proud
Civil Chief: Robert L. Simpkins

NORTHERN DISTRICT OF INDIANA
4th Floor, Federal Building, 507 State Street,
Hammond, IN 46320 ....(219) 937-5215

Fort Wayne Branch Office: 220 Federal
Building, 1300 South Harrison Street,
Fort Wayne, IN 46802 ....(219) 422-2595

South Bend Branch Office: 302 Federal Building,
204 South Main St, South Bend, IN 46601 ....(219) 236-8287

U.S. Attorney: James G. Richmond
First Assistant U.S. Attorney: John F. Hoehner
Civil Chief: John P. Klingeberger

Criminal Chief: David A. Capp
Assistant U.S. Attorney in Charge/Southbend:
William T. Grimmer

SOUTHERN DISTRICT OF INDIANA
U.S. Courthouse, Fifth Floor, 46 East Ohio Street,
Indianapolis, IN 46204 ....(317) 226-6333

U.S. Attorney: Deborah J. Daniels
First Assistant U.S. Attorney: Timothy Morrison
Civil Chief: Harold Bickham
Criminal Chief: Larry Mackey
Organized Crime and Drug Enforcement Task Force Chief: John Thar

NORTHERN DISTRICT OF IOWA
425 Second Street, S.E., Suite 950, The Center,
Cedar Rapids, IA 52401 ....(319) 363-6333

Sioux City Branch Office: P.O. Box 3629,
Sioux City, IA 51102 ....(712) 233-3227

U.S. Attorney: Charles W. Larson
First Assistant U.S. Attorney: Robert L. Tieg
Supervisory Assistant U.S. Attorney: Willis A. Buell

SOUTHERN DISTRICT OF IOWA
115 U.S. Courthouse, East First and Walnut Streets,
Des Moines, IA 50309 ....(515) 284-6257

U.S. Attorney: Gene W. Sheppard
Civil Chief: Robert Dopf
Criminal Chief: Joseph S. Beck

DISTRICT OF KANSAS
444 Quincy Street, Topeka, KS 66683 ....(913) 295-2850

Wichita Branch Office: 306 U.S.Courthouse, 401 North
Market Street, Wichita, KS 67202 ....(316) 269-6481

Kansas City Branch Office: 412 Federal Building, 812 North
Seventh Street, Kansas City, KS 66101 ....(913) 236-3730

U.S. Attorney: Benjamin L. Burgess Jr
Supervisory Assistant U.S. Attorney/Wichita:
Jackie N. Williams
Supervisory Assistant U.S. Attorney/Topeka:
Richard L. Hathaway
Supervisory Assistant U.S. Attorney/Kansas City:
Janice M. Karlin

EASTERN DISTRICT OF KENTUCKY
P.O. Box 1490, Lexington, KY 40591 ....(606) 233-2661

Covington Branch Office: P.O. Box 72,
Covington, KY 41012 ....(606) 292-3184

U.S. Attorney: Louis G. Defalaise
First Assistant U.S. Attorney/Criminal Chief:
Robert F. Trevey
Civil Chief: Marianna J. Read
Assistant U.S. Attorney in Charge/Covington:
James A. Zerhusen
Lead Drug Task Force Attorney: Jane Graham

WESTERN DISTRICT OF KENTUCKY
Bank of Louisville Building, 510 West Broadway,
Tenth Floor, Louisville, KY 40202 ....(502) 582-5911

U.S. Attorney: Joseph M. Whittle
First Assistant U.S. Attorney: C. Cleveland Gambill
Civil Chief: Michael Spalding
Criminal Chief: Dwayne Schwartz
Financial Chief: Jane Bondurant
Lead Drug Task Force Attorney: David Grise

EASTERN DISTRICT OF LOUISIANA
Hale Boggs Federal Building, Rm 210, 501 Magazine Street,
New Orleans, LA 70130 ....(504) 589-2921

U.S. Attorney: John Volz
First Assistant U.S. Attorney: Albert Winters
Civil Chief: Nancy Nungesser
Criminal Chief: Lance Africk
Lead Drug Task Force Attorney: Lawrence Benson
Strike Force Chief: Jim Letten

MIDDLE DISTRICT OF LOUISIANA
352 Florida Street, Baton Rouge, LA 70801 ....(504) 389-0443

U.S. Attorney: Raymond P. Lamonica
First Assistant U.S. Attorney: James Stanley Lemelle
Lead Drug Task Force Attorney: Edward Gonzales

WESTERN DISTRICT OF LOUISIANA
Room 3-B12 Federal Building, Shreveport, LA 71101 (318) 226-5277

Lafayette Branch Office: Room 305 Federal Building and
U.S. Courthouse, 705 Jefferson Street, Lafayette,
LA 70501 ....(318) 264-6618

U.S. Attorney: Joseph S. Cage Jr
First Assistant U.S. Attorney/Shreveport: John P. Lydick
Attorney in Charge/Lafayette: Gerald J. Bertinot
Lead Drug Task Force Attorney: Judith Lombardino

DISTRICT OF MAINE
P.O. Box 1588, Portland, ME 04104 ....(207) 780-3257

Bangor Branch Office: P.O. Box 1196, Bangor, ME
04401 ....(207) 945-0374

U.S. Attorney: Richard S. Cohen
First Assistant U.S. Attorney: John S. Gleason III
Chief, Organized Crime and Drug Enforcement Task Force: William
Browder Jr
Attorney in Charge/Bangor: Jay P. McCloskey

DISTRICT OF MARYLAND
8th Floor, U.S. Courthouse, 101 West Lombard Street,
Baltimore, MD 21201 ....(301) 539-2940

U.S. Attorney: Breckinridge L. Willcox
First Assistant U.S. Attorney: Gary P. Jordan
Civil Chief: David P. King
Criminal Chief: Donna H. Triptow
Regional Drug Task Force Coordinator: Harvey Ellis Eisenberg

DISTRICT OF MASSACHUSETTS
1107 John W. McCormack Federal Building, U.S. Post Office
and Courthouse, Boston, MA 02109 ....(617) 223-9400

Springfield Branch Office: 1550 Main Street, Room 533,
U.S. Courthouse, Springfield, MA 01103 ....(413) 785-0235

U.S. Attorney: Wayne A. Budd
Executive Assistant U.S. Attorney: Susan H. Spurlock
First Assistant U.S. Attorney: Kevin Sharkey
Civil Chief: Judith S. Yogman
Criminal Chief: A. John Pappalardo
Regional Drug Task Force Coordinator: Jonathan Chiel
Strike Force Chief: Diane Kottmeyer

EASTERN DISTRICT OF MICHIGAN
817 Federal Building, 231 West Lafayette, Detroit,
MI 48226 ....(313) 237-0400

Bay City Branch Office: P.O. Box 26, 204 Federal Building,
1000 Washington St, Bay City, MI 48707 ....(517) 895-5712

Flint Branch Office: 204 Federal Building, 600 Church Street, Flint, MI 48502 ....(313) 766-5177

U.S. Attorney: Stephen J. Markman
First Assistant U.S. Attorney: Ross Parker
Civil Chief: Michael Wicks
Criminal Chief: Alan Gershel
Appellate Chief: Patricia Blake
Regional Drug Task Force Coordinator: Michael Leibson
Strike Force Chief: Keith Corbett

WESTERN DISTRICT OF MICHIGAN
399 Federal Bldg, Grand Rapids, MI 49503 ....(616) 456-2404

U.S. Attorney: John A. Smietanka
Chief Assistant U.S. Attorney: Thomas Gezon
Civil Chief: Dan Laville
Criminal Chief: Donald Davis
Lead Drug Task Force Attorney: John Bruha

DISTRICT OF MINNESOTA
234 U.S. Courthouse, 110 South Fourth Street, Minneapolis, MN 55401 ....(612) 348-1500

St. Paul Branch Office: 678 U.S. Courthouse, 316 North Robert Street, St. Paul, MN 55101 ....(612) 725-7171

U.S. Attorney: Jerome G. Arnold
First Assistant U.S. Attorney: Francis X. Hermann
Civil Chief: Mary Carlson
Criminal Chief: Thorwald H. Anderson

NORTHERN DISTRICT OF MISSISSIPPI
P.O. Drawer 886, Oxford, MS 38655 ....(601) 234-3351

U.S. Attorney: Robert Q. Whitwell
First Assistant U.S. Attorney/Criminal Chief: Alfred Morton III
Civil Chief: William Dye
Lead Drug Task Force Attorney: Thomas Dawson

SOUTHERN DISTRICT OF MISSISSIPPI
245 East Capitol Street, Room 324, Jackson, MS 39201 ....(601) 965-4480

Biloxi Branch Office: P.O. Box 1417, Biloxi, MS 39533 ....(601) 432-5521

U.S. Attorney: George L. Phillips
First Assistant U.S. Attorney: Kent McDaniel
Civil Chief: Dan Lynn
Criminal Chief: James Tucker
Assistant U.S. Attorney in Charge/Biloxi: Don Waits
Lead Drug Task Force Attorney: Richard Starrett

EASTERN DISTRICT OF MISSOURI
Room 414, U.S. Court & Custom House, 1114 Market Street, St. Louis, MO 63101 ....(314) 539-2200

U.S. Attorney: Thomas E. Dittmeier
First Assistant U.S. Attorney/Criminal Chief: Terry I. Adelman
Civil Chief: Joseph Moore
Regional Drug Task Force Coordinator: Debra E. Herzog

WESTERN DISTRICT OF MISSOURI
549 U.S. Courthouse, 811 Grand Avenue, Kansas City, MO 64106 ....(816) 426-3122

Springfield Branch Office: 222 N. John Q. Hammons, Suite 1200, Springfield, MO 65806 ....(417) 831-1892

U.S. Attorney: Jean Paul Bradshaw II
First Assistant U.S. Attorney: Robert E. Larsen
Civil Chief: Alleen S. Castellani
Criminal Chief: Linda Sybrant
Assistant U.S. Attorney in Charge/Springfield: Michael A. Jones
Strike Force Chief: Richard Marien

DISTRICT OF MONTANA
P.O. Box 1478, Billings, MT 59103 ....(406) 657-6101

Butte Branch Office: 167 Federal Building, 400 North Main, Butte, MT 59701 ....(406) 723-6611

Great Falls Branch Office: P.O. Box 3446, Room 212, Federal Building, 215 First Avenue, Great Falls, MT 59401 ....(406) 761-7715

Helena Branch Office: Drawer 10031, Federal Building, 301 South Park Avenue, Helena, MT 59626 ....(406) 449-5370

U.S. Attorney: Lorraine I. Gallinger
Civil Chief: Lorraine I. Gallinger
Criminal Chief: Robert Zimmerman
Lead Drug Task Force Attorney: James E. Seykora

DISTRICT OF NEBRASKA
P.O. Box 1228, DTS, Omaha, NE 68101 ....(402) 221-4774

Lincoln Branch Office: 520 Federal Building, 100 Centennial Mall North, Lincoln, NE 68508 ....(402) 437-5241

U.S. Attorney: Ronald D. Lahners
First Assistant U.S. Attorney: Thomas D. Thalken
Attorney in Charge/Lincoln: Sally R. Johnson

DISTRICT OF NEVADA
Box 16030, Las Vegas, NV 89101 ....(702) 388-6336

Reno Branch Office: 300 Booth Street, Room 2-032, Reno, NV 89509 ....(702) 784-5439

U.S. Attorney: Richard J. Pocker
Chief Assistant U.S. Attorney: Richard J. Pocker
Civil Chief: Shirley Smith (Reno)
Assistant U.S. Attorney in Charge/Reno: Brian L. Sullivan
Lead Drug Task Force Attorney: Thomas Green
Strike Force Chief: Terry Lord

DISTRICT OF NEW HAMPSHIRE
55 Pleasant Street, Room 439, P.O. Box 480, Concord, NH 03302 ....(603) 225-1552

U.S. Attorney: Jeffrey R. Howard
Assistant U.S. Attorney: Susan L. Howard

DISTRICT OF NEW JERSEY
Federal Building, 970 Broad Street, Room 502, Newark, NJ 07102 ....(201) 621-2700

Trenton Branch Office: 402 East State Street, Room 502, Trenton, NJ 08608 ....(609) 989-2190

Camden Branch Office: Post Office Building, 401 Market Street, Fifth Floor, Camden, NJ 08101 ....(609) 757-5026

U.S. Attorney: Samuel A. Alito Jr
First Assistant U.S. Attorney: Michael Chertoff
Civil Chief: Jerome Merin
Criminal Chief: Paul J. Fishman
Lead Drug Task Force Attorney: Joseph Greenaway
Strike Force Chief: Bob Stewart

DISTRICT OF NEW MEXICO
P.O. Box 607, Albuquerque, NM 87103 ....(505) 766-3341

Las Cruces Branch Office: U.S. Courthouse, 200 East Griggs Street, Room E-108, Las Cruces, NM 88001 ....(505) 523-5614

U.S. Attorney: William L. Lutz
Civil Chief: Lowell Harris
Criminal Chief: Don Svet
Lead Drug Task Force Attorney: Larry Gomez

EASTERN DISTRICT OF NEW YORK
U.S. Courthouse, 225 Cadman Plaza East,
Brooklyn, NY 11201 ....(718) 330-7060

Garden City Branch Office: 825 East Gate Boulevard,
Garden City, NY 11530 ....(516) 228-8630

Hauppauge Branch Office: 300 Rabro Drive,
Hauppauge, NY 11788 ....(516) 234-1250

U.S. Attorney: Andrew J. Maloney
First Assistant U.S. Attorney: Lawrence A. Urgenson
Civil Chief: Robert L. Begleiter
Criminal Chief: William J. Muller
Lead Drug Task Force Attorney: David W. Shapiro
Strike Force Chief: Leonard Michaels

NORTHERN DISTRICT OF NEW YORK
369 Federal Building, 100 South Clinton Street,
Syracuse, NY 13260 ....(315) 423-5165

Albany Branch Office: U.S. Courthouse and Post Office,
2nd Floor, 445 Broadway, Albany, NY 12207 ....(518) 472-5522

Binghamton Branch Office: 319 Federal Building,
Binghamton, NY 13901 ....(607) 772-2888

U.S. Attorney: Frederick J. Scullin Jr
Chief Assistant U.S. Attorney: Joseph Pavone
Civil Chief: William H. Pease
Assistant U.S. Attorney in Charge/Albany: David R. Homer
Assistant U.S. Attorney in Charge/Binghamton:
Gary L. Sharpe
Lead Drug Task Force Attorneys:
John McCann (Albany)
Thomas Walsh (Binghamton)
John Duncan (Syracuse)
Strike Force Chief: Kevin McCormack

SOUTHERN DISTRICT OF NEW YORK
One St. Andrews Plaza, New York, NY 10007 ....(212) 791-0055

White Plains Branch Office: 101 East Post Road,
White Plains, NY 10601 ....(914) 683-9577

U.S. Attorney: Otto Obermaier
Deputy Assistant U.S. Attorney: Louis Freeh
Civil Chief: Steven Obus
Criminal Chief: David Denton
Regional Drug Task Force Coordinator: Anne T. Vitale

WESTERN DISTRICT OF NEW YORK
502 U.S. Courthouse, 68 Court Street,
Buffalo, NY 14202 ....(716) 846-4811

Rochester Branch Office: 233 U.S. Courthouse, 100 State
Street, Rochester, NY 14614 ....(716) 263-6760

U.S. Attorney: Dennis C. Vacco
First Assistant U.S. Attorney: Roger P. Williams
Civil Chief: Louis J. Gicale Jr
Criminal Chief: Kathleen M. Mehltretter
Lead Drug Task Force Attorneys:
Joseph M. Guerra (Buffalo)
Bradley E. Tyler (Rochester)
Strike Force Chief: Richard Endler

EASTERN DISTRICT OF NORTH CAROLINA
P.O. Box 26897, Raleigh, NC 27611 ....(919) 856-4530

U.S. Attorney: Margaret P. Currin
Chief Assistant and Civil Chief: Rudolph A. Renfer Jr
Criminal Chief: John S. Bruce
Lead Drug Task Force Attorney: Doug McCullugh

MIDDLE DISTRICT OF NORTH CAROLINA
P.O. Box 1858, Greensboro, NC 27402 ....(919) 333-5351

U.S. Attorney: Robert H. Edmunds Jr
Chief Assistant U.S. Attorney: Benjamin White Jr
Lead Drug Task Force Attorney: David Smith

WESTERN DISTRICT OF NORTH CAROLINA
Room 306, U.S. Courthouse, 100 Otis Street,
Asheville, NC 28801 ....(704) 259-0661

Charlotte Branch Office: Room 260 U.S.Courthouse,
401 West Trade St, Charlotte, NC 28202 ....(704) 371-6222

U.S. Attorney: Thomas J. Ashcraft
Chief Assistant U.S. Attorney/Charlotte: Carl Horn III
Lead Drug Task Force Attorney: Max Cogburn Jr

DISTRICT OF NORTH DAKOTA
P.O. Box 2505, Fargo, ND 58108 ....(701) 239-5671

Bismarck Branch Office: P.O. Box 699,
Bismarck, ND 58502 ....(701) 250-4396

U.S. Attorney: H. Gary Annear
First Assistant U.S. Attorney: Mr. Lynn Crooks
Assistant U.S. Attorney/Bismarck: Mr. Lynn C. Jordheim
Financial Litigation Unit: Linda L. Webb

NORTHERN DISTRICT OF OHIO
Suite 500, 1404 East Ninth Street,
Cleveland, OH 44114 ....(216) 363-3900

Toledo Branch Office: 307 U.S. Courthouse, 1716 Spielbusch
Avenue, Toledo, OH 43624 ....(419) 259-6376

Akron Branch Office: 208 Federal Building, 2 South Main St,
Akron, OH 43624 ....(216) 375-5716

U.S. Attorney: Joyce J. George
First Assistant U.S. Attorney: William J. Edwards
Civil Chief: Marcia Walker Johnson
Criminal Chief: J. Matthew Cain
Attorney in Charge/Toledo: Patrick Foley
Appellate Chief: Emily M. Sweeny
Lead Drug Task Force Attorney: Kenneth S. McHargh
Strike Force Chief: Steve Jigger

SOUTHERN DISTRICT OF OHIO
85 Marconi Boulevard, Room 200, Columbus, OH
43215 ....(614) 469-5715

Cincinnati Branch Office: 220 U.S. Post Office and
Courthouse, Fifth & Walnut Streets, Cincinnati, OH
45202 ....(513) 684-3711

Dayton Branch Office: P.O. Box 280, Mid-City Station,
Dayton, OH 45402 ....(513) 225-2910

U.S. Attorney: D. Michael Crites
First Assistant U.S. Attorney: Barbara Beran
Senior Assistant U.S. Attorney/Columbus: James Rattan
Senior Assistant U.S. Attorney/Cincinnati: Anthony Nyktas
Senior Assistant U.S. Attorney/Dayton: James Wilson
Lead Drug Task Force Attorney: William Hunt

EASTERN DISTRICT OF OKLAHOMA
333 Federal Courthouse and Office Building, Fifth and Okmulgee, Muskogee, OK 74401 ....(918) 687-2543

U.S. Attorney: Roger Hilfiger
Criminal Chief: Sheldon Sperling

NORTHERN DISTRICT OF OKLAHOMA
3600 U.S. Courthouse, 333 West Fourth Street, Tulsa, OK 74103 ....(918) 581-7463

U.S. Attorney: Tony M. Graham
First Assistant U.S. Attorney: Ben Baker
Civil Chief: Peter Bernhardt
Criminal Chief: Kenneth P. Snoke

WESTERN DISTRICT OF OKLAHOMA
Room 4434, U.S. Courthouse and Federal Office Building, Oklahoma City, OK 73102 ....(405) 231-5281

U.S. Attorney: Timothy D. Leonard
First Assistant U.S. Attorney: John E. Green
Civil Chief: Roger Griffith

DISTRICT OF OREGON
312 U.S. Courthouse, 620 SW Main Street, Portland, OR 97205 ....(503) 221-2101

Eugene Branch Office: Room 438, Federal Courthouse, 211 East Seventh Ave, Eugene, OR 97401 ....(503) 687-6771

U.S. Attorney: Charles H. Turner
First Assistant U.S. Attorney/Civil: Jack C. Wong
Civil Chief: Jack G. Collin
Criminal Chief: Baron C. Sheldahl
Supervisory Assistant U.S. Attorney/Eugene: Thomas Coffin
Lead Drug Task Force Attorney: Kenneth C. Bauman

EASTERN DISTRICT OF PENNSYLVANIA
3310 U.S. Courthouse, 601 Market Street, Independence Mall West, Philadelphia, PA 19106 ....(215) 597-2556

U.S. Attorney: Michael Baylson
First Assistant U.S. Attorney: Thomas H. Lee
Civil Chief: James G. Sheehan
Criminal Chief: Terri Marinari
Appeals Chief: Walter S. Batty Jr
Financial Litigation Chief: Serena H. Dobson
Strike Force Chief: Joel Friedman

MIDDLE DISTRICT OF PENNSYLVANIA
P.O. Box 309, Scranton, PA 18501 ....(717) 348-2800

Harrisburg Branch Office: P.O. Box 11754, Harrisburg, PA 17108 ....(717) 782-4882

Lewisburg Branch Office: Room 307, Federal Building, Lewisburg, PA 17837 ....(717) 524-4415

U.S. Attorney: James J. West
Assistant U.S. Attorneys/Scranton: Malachy E. Mannion and Barbara K. Whitaker
Assistant U.S. Attorneys/Harrisburg: David C. Shipman and Sally Lied
Assistant U.S. Attorney/Lewisburg: Frederick E. Martin

WESTERN DISTRICT OF PENNSYLVANIA
633 U.S. Post Office and Courthouse, 7th Avenue and Grant Street, Pittsburgh, PA 15219 ....(412) 644-3500

Erie Branch Office: Room 137, Federal Building and Courthouse, 617 State St, Erie, PA 16501 ....(814) 452-2906

U.S. Attorney: Thomas W. Corbett Jr
First Assistant U.S. Attorney: Charles D. Sheehy
Civil Chief: Amy Reynolds Hay
Criminal Chief: Craig R. McKay
Lead Drug Task Force Attorney: Bruce Teitelbaum

DISTRICT OF PUERTO RICO
Room 101, Federal Office Building, Carlos E. Chardon Ave, Hato Rey, PR 00918 ....(809) 766-5656

Old San Juan Branch Office: Criminal Division/San Juan, Old Post Office Building, Old San Juan, PR 00902 (809) 729-6766

U.S. Attorney: Daniel F. Lopez-Romo
Executive Assistant U.S. Attorney: Charles E. Fitzwilliam
Civil Chief: Osvaldo Carlo-Linares
Criminal Chief: Juan A. Pedrosa
Lead Drug Task Force Attorney: Salixto Medina-Malave

DISTRICT OF RHODE ISLAND
Westminster Square Building, 10 Dorrance Street, 10th Fl, Providence, RI 02903 ....(401) 528-5477

U.S. Attorney: Lincoln C. Almond
Criminal Chief: Edwin Gale
Strike Force Chief: Mike Davitt

DISTRICT OF SOUTH CAROLINA
P.O. Box 2266, Columbia, SC 29202 ....(803) 765-5483

Charleston Branch Office: P.O. Box 978, Charleston, SC 29402 ....(803) 724-4381

Greenville Branch Office: P.O. Box 10067, Greenville, SC 29603 ....(803) 232-5646

U.S. Attorney: E. Bart Daniel
First Assistant U.S. Attorney: John W. McIntosh
Civil Chief: John B. Grimball
Criminal Chief: John M. Barton
Assistant U.S. Attorney in Charge/Charleston: Robert H. Bickerton
Assistant U.S. Attorney in Charge/Greenville: James D. McCoy III
Lead Drug Task Force Attorney: Robert C. Jendron Jr

DISTRICT OF SOUTH DAKOTA
P.O. Box 1073, Sioux Falls, SD 57101 ....(605) 330-4400

Rapid City Branch Office: P.O. Box 2893, Rapid City, SD 57709 ....(605) 342-7822

Pierre Branch Office: 326 Federal Building and U.S. Courthouse, 225 South Pierre Street, Pierre, SD 57501 ....(605) 225-0250

Aberdeen Branch Office: 336 Post Office and Courthouse, 102 SE Fourth Ave, Aberdeen, SD 57401 ....(605) 225-0250 ext 264

U.S. Attorney: Philip N. Hogen
First Assistant U.S. Attorney/Sioux Falls: Ted L. McBride
Assistant U.S. Attorney/Pierre: David L. Zuercher
Assistant U.S. Attorney/Rapid City: Robert A. Mandel

EASTERN DISTRICT OF TENNESSEE
P.O. Box 872, Knoxville, TN 37901 ....(615) 673-4561

Chattanooga Branch Office: 359 U.S. Post Office and Courthouse, Chattanooga, TN 37402 ....(615) 752-5140

Greeneville Branch Office: 101 U.S. Courthouse, 101 West Summer Street, Greeneville, TN 37743 ....(615) 639-6759

Johnson City Branch Office: 208 Sunset Drive, Suite 509, Johnson City, TN 37604 ....(615) 282-1889

U.S. Attorney: John W. Gill Jr
Chief Assistant U.S. Attorney: Russ Dedrick
Assistant U.S. Attorney in Charge/Chattanooga:
Curtis L. Collier
Lead Drug Task Force Attorney: James R. Dedrick

MIDDLE DISTRICT OF TENNESSEE
Room 879, U.S. Courthouse, 801 Broadway,
Nashville, TN 37203 ....(615) 736-5151

U.S. Attorney: Joe B. Brown
First Assistant U.S. Attorney: William M. Cohen
Civil Chief: C. Douglas Thoresen
Lead Drug Task Force Attorney: Peter Strianse

WESTERN DISTRICT OF TENNESSEE
1026 Federal Office Building, 167 North Main Street,
Memphis, TN 38103 ....(901) 521-4231

Jackson Branch Office: U.S. Post Office and Courthouse Building, Room 308, 109 South Highland, Jackson, TN 38302 ....(901) 424-5566

U.S. Attorney: W. Hickman Ewing Jr
Executive/Civil Chief: Bob Williams
Criminal Chief: Devon Gosnell
First Assistant U.S. Attorney/Jackson: Daniel Clancy
Lead Drug Task Force Attorney: Tim DiScenza

EASTERN DISTRICT OF TEXAS
700 North St, Ste 102, Beaumont, TX 77701 ....(409) 839-2538

Tyler Branch Office: 110 North College, Suite 600, Tyler, TX 75702 ....(214) 597-8146

Sherman Branch Office: One Grand Centre, Suite 504, 1 Grand Avenue, Sherman, TX 75090 ....(214) 868-9454

U.S. Attorney: Robert J. Wortham
First Assistant U.S. Attorney: Ruth Yeager
Chief Assistant U.S. Attorney/Beaumont: L. Stuart Platt

NORTHERN DISTRICT OF TEXAS
310 U.S. Courthouse, Tenth and Lamar Streets,
Fort Worth, TX 76102 ....(817) 334-3291

Dallas Branch Office: US Federal Building and Courthouse, Room 16G28, 1100 Commerce Street, Dallas, TX 75242(214) 767-0951

Lubbock Branch Office: U.S. Federal Building and Courthouse, Room C-201, 1205 Texas Avenue, Lubbock, TX 79401 (806) 743-7351

Amarillo Branch Office: P.O. Box 13236, Amarillo, TX 79101 ....(806) 376-2356

U.S. Attorney: Marvin Collins
First Assistant U.S. Attorney: Richard Stephens (Dallas)
Civil Chief: Charles D. Cabannis (Dallas)
Criminal Chief: Jack Williamson (Dallas)
Assistant U.S. Attorneys in Charge:
Amarillo: James P. Laurence
Lubbock: Roger McRoberts
Lead Drug Task Force Attorney: James Jacks (Dallas)

SOUTHERN DISTRICT OF TEXAS
P.O. Box 61129, Houston, TX 77208 ....(713) 229-2600

Laredo Branch Office: P.O. Box 886, Laredo, TX 78040 ....(512) 723-6523

Brownsville Branch Office: P.O. Box 1671, Brownsville, TX 78521 ....(512) 548-2544

Corpus Christi Branch Office: Wilson Plaza, Suite 1200, 606 N. Carancahua Street, Corpus Christi, TX 78476(512) 888-3111

McAllen Branch Office: Texas Commerce Bank Building, 1701 West Highway 83, Suite 858, McAllen, TX 78501(512) 630-3173

U.S. Attorney: Henry K. Oncken
First Assistant U.S. Attorney: Stephen Morris
Civil Chief: Jack Shepherd
Criminal Chief: Thomas Woodward
Regional Drug Task Force Coordinator: Kenneth Magidson
Strike Force Chief: Philip Hilder

WESTERN DISTRICT OF TEXAS
727 East Durango Boulevard, Suite A-601,
San Antonio, TX 78206 ....(512) 229-6500

El Paso Branch Office: 353 U.S. Courthouse, 511 East San Antonio Avenue, El Paso, TX 79901 ....(915) 534-6884

Austin Branch Office: 816 Congress Avenue, Suite 650, First City Centre, Austin, TX 78701 ....(512) 482-5858

Midland Branch Office: U.S. Courthouse, 200 East Wall Street, Midland, TX 79701 ....(915) 684-4120

Waco Branch Office: P.O. Box 828, Waco, TX 76703 (817) 753-3833

U.S. Attorney: Ronald F. Ederer
Civil Chief: Raymond Nowak
Criminal Chief: John Murphy
Lead Drug Task Force Attorney: Bill Johnson

DISTRICT OF UTAH
Room 476, U.S. Courthouse, 350 South Main Street,
Salt Lake City, UT 84101 ....(801) 524-5682

U.S. Attorney: Dee V. Benson
First Assistant U.S. Attorney: Paul M. Warner
Civil Chief: Joseph W. Anderson
Criminal Chief: Stewart C. Walz

DISTRICT OF VERMONT
P.O. Box 570, Burlington, VT 05402 ....(802) 951-6725

Rutland Branch Office: P.O. Box 10, Rutland, VT 05701 ....(802) 773-0231

U.S. Attorney: George J. Terwilliger III
Civil Chief: Helen Toor
Criminal Chief: David Kirby
Assistant U.S. Attorney in Charge/Rutland: Charles A. Caruso

DISTRICT OF VIRGIN ISLANDS
P.O. Box 1440, Charlotte Amalie, St. Thomas, VI
00801 ....(809) 774-5757

St. Croix Branch Office: P.O. Box 3239, Christiansted, St. Croix, VI 00820 ....(809) 773-3920

U.S. Attorney: Terry Halpern
Chief Assistant U.S. Attorney: Hugh P. Mabe
Lead Drug Task Force Attorneys: Richard K. Harris and
Salixto Medina-Malave

EASTERN DISTRICT OF VIRGINIA
1101 King Street, Suite 502, Alexandria, VA 22314 (703) 557-9100

Richmond Branch Office: P.O. Box 1257, Richmond, VA 23210 ....(804) 771-2186

Norfolk Branch Office: U.S. Courthouse, 600 Granby Street, Norfolk, VA 23510 ....(804) 441-6331

U.S. Attorney: Henry E. Hudson
First Assistant U.S. Attorney: Kenneth Melson
Civil Chief: Robert W. Jaspen
Criminal Chief: Justin W. Williams

WESTERN DISTRICT OF VIRGINIA
P.O. Box 1709, Roanoke, VA 24008 ....(703) 982-6250

Abingdon Branch Office: P.O. Box 1098, Abingdon, VA 24210 ....(703) 628-4161

U.S. Attorney: John Perry Alderman
First Assistant U.S. Attorney: E. Montgomery Tucker

EASTERN DISTRICT OF WASHINGTON
P.O. Box 1494, Spokane, WA 99210 ....(509) 353-2767

Yakima Branch Office: P.O. Box 1363, Yakima, WA 98901 ....(509) 575-5836

U.S. Attorney: John E. Lamp
First Assistant U.S. Attorney: Carroll D. Gray
Lead Drug Task Force Attorney: Frank A. Wilson

WESTERN DISTRICT OF WASHINGTON
3600 Seafirst Fifth Avenue Plaza, 800 Fifth Avenue, Seattle, WA 98104 ....(206) 442-7970

Tacoma Branch Office: Suite 350, 1145 Broadway Plaza, Tacoma, WA 98402 ....(206) 593-6316

U.S. Attorney: Mike McKay
Civil Chief: Susan E. Barnes
Criminal Complaints: Kenneth R. Parker
Criminal Trial Chief: David E. Wilson
Lead Drug Task Force Attorney: Francis Diskin

NORTHERN DISTRICT OF WEST VIRGINIA
P.O. Box 591, Wheeling, WV 26003 ....(304) 232-4026

Elkins Branch Office: P.O. Box 190, Elkins, WV 26241 ....(304) 636-1739

Clarksburg Branch Office: P.O. Box 750, Clarksburg, WV 26302 ....(304) 623-5390

Martinsburg Branch Office: U.S. Courthouse and Post Office Building, Rm 236, Martinsburg, WV 25401 ....(304) 267-8040

U.S. Attorney: William A. Kolibash
First Assistant U.S. Attorney: Betsy Steinfield
Assistant U.S. Attorney in Charge/Clarksburg: David E. Godwin
Lead Drug Task Force Attorney: John Reed

SOUTHERN DISTRICT OF WEST VIRGINIA
P.O. Box 3234, Charleston, WV 25332 ....(304) 345-2200

Huntington Branch Office: P.O. Box 1239, Huntington, WV 25714 ....(304) 529-3258

U.S. Attorney: Michael W. Carey
First Assistant U.S. Attorney: Charles T. Miller
Civil Chief: Kurt E. Entsminger
Criminal Chief: Nancy C. Hill
Lead Drug Task Force Attorney: Hunter P. Smith

EASTERN DISTRICT OF WISCONSIN
330 Federal Building, 517 East Wisconsin Avenue, Milwaukee, WI 53202 ....(414) 297-1700

U.S. Attorney: John E. Fryatt
First Assistant U.S. Attorney: Patricia J. Gorence
Civil Chief: Nathan A. Fishbach
Criminal Chief: Eric J. Klumb
Narcotics Chief: R. Jeffrey Wagner

WESTERN DISTRICT OF WISCONSIN
120 North Henry Street, Room 420, Madison, WI 53703 ....(608) 264-5158

U.S. Attorney: Patrick J. Fiedler
First Assistant U.S. Attorney: Grant C. Johnson
Civil Chief: Richard D. Humphrey

DISTRICT OF WYOMING
P.O. Box 668, Cheyenne, WY 82003 ....(307) 772-2124

Casper Branch Office: 111 South Wolcott, Room 138, Casper, WY 82601 ....(307) 261-5434

U.S. Attorney: Richard A. Stacy
Senior Assistant U.S. Attorney: Francis Leland Pico

DRUG ENFORCEMENT ADMINISTRATION

600 Army-Navy Drive, Arlington, VA 22202
(Mailing Address: Washington, D.C. 20537)

The Drug Enforcement Administration is the primary narcotics enforcement agency for the U.S., as well as one of the largest regulatory bodies in the Federal Government, regulating the entire controlled substances industry.

The Office of Chief Counsel, located in Washington, D.C., has the overall responsibility for providing legal advice within DEA, and representing DEA in various administrative proceedings, reviewing proposed legislation and performing legal liaison with other Government agencies. The Office reviews bilateral and multilateral agreements involving foreign nations; maintains liaison with the State Department and the Department of Justice's Criminal Division regarding extradition treaties and letters rogatory; assists foreign governments in the preparation of drug related laws; and drafts laws, regulations, and guidelines necessary to implement U.S. obligations. The activities of the Office are performed by four sections:

* **Civil-Administrative Section:** which processes all tort claims up to $5,000 against DEA; assists in defense of civil actions against the agency and/or its employees; represents management in Merit Systems Protection Board proceedings involving DEA employees; reviews all contracts; and provides other legal counsel on administrative and management matters.

* **Criminal Law Section:** which serves as the principal legal adviser to DEA's Administrator on all criminal law issues raised by DEA's worldwide drug enforcement and intelligence efforts. It plays a major role in developing policies and procedures governing the conduct of all criminal investigations by DEA and is frequently called upon by U.S. Attorneys and other elements of the Executive Branch for advice and assistance on criminal issues relating to drug enforcement.

* **Diversion-Regulatory Section:** which represents DEA in all administrative hearings relating to drug control, quotas, and the denial or revocation of registrants. The Section is responsible for the legal training of state and Federal personnel with respect to the investigation of drug diversion cases, drafts amendments to the Code of Federal Regulations, and furnishes legal counsel necessary for the effective administration and enforcement of the regulatory features of the Controlled Substances Act.

* **Asset Forfeiture Section:** which is responsible for all administrative activities related to the seizure and forfeiture of property used in violation of the Controlled Substances Act. This Section advises on case decisions and statutes involving the forfeiture of property, assists U.S. Attorneys in the interpretation of forfeiture laws and regulations, and conducts training in the laws of asset forfeiture for prosecutors and investigators.

Office of Administrative Law Judge: The Office of Administrative Law Judge, which conducts the agency's administrative hearings under the Administrative Procedure Act, is separate and apart from the Office of Chief Counsel.

(Area Code 202)

Administrator: Terrence M. Burke (Acting) 307-8000
Office of Congressional and Public Affairs 307-7363

Office of Chief Counsel
Chief Counsel: Dennis F. Hoffman 307-7322
Deputy Chief Counsel: Robert T. Richardson 307-8020
Civil-Administrative Section Chief: Craig Richardson ...307-8040
Criminal Law Section Chief: Harry Myers 307-8030
Diversion-Regulatory Section Chief: Steven Stone 307-8010
Asset Forfeiture Section Chief: John Mahoney 307-8555

Office of the Administrative Law Judge
Chief Administrative Law Judge:
Mary Ellen Bittner (Acting) 307-8188
Hearing Clerk/Docket Information): Helen Farmer 307-8188

Operations Division (Area Code 202)
Assistant Administrator: Stephen Greene 307-7340
Cannabis Investigations Section Chief:
John Peoples 307-8333
Cocaine Investigations Section Chief:
Charles Gutensohn 307-8448
Dangerous Drugs Investigations Section Chief:
Frank Tarallo 307-8352
Heroin Investigations Section Chief: Felix Jiminez 307-7499

Office of Diversion Control
Deputy Assistant Administrator: Gene R. Haislip 307-7165

Office of Intelligence
Deputy Assistant Administrator: Richard Bly 307-8050

Office of International Programs
Deputy Assistant Administrator: Paul Higdon 307-4233

Office of Investigative Support
Deputy Assistant Administrator: Harold D. Wankel 307-8926

DRUG ENFORCEMENT ADMINISTRATION FIELD OFFICES

Atlanta Division
Division Chief: Ronald J. Caffrey
Drug Enforcement Administration, 75 Spring Street, S.W., Room 740, Atlanta, GA 30303. Tel: 404/331-4401.
(Jurisdiction: NC, SC, TN, GA)

Boston Division
Division Chief: John Coleman
Drug Enforcement Administration, 50 Staniford Street, Suite 200, Boston, MA 02114. Tel: 617/565-2800.
(Jurisdiction: CT, VT, NH, ME, RI, MA)

Chicago Division
Division Chief: Raymond Vinsik
Drug Enforcement Administration, 500 Dirksen Federal Bldg, 219 South Dearborn Street, Chicago, IL 60604. Tel: 312/353-7875.
(Jurisdiction: IL, ND, IN, WI, MN)

Dallas Division
Division Chief: Phillip Jordan
Drug Enforcement Administration, 1880 Regal Row, Dallas, TX 75235. Tel: 214/767-7151.
(Jurisdiction: TX, OK)

Denver Division
Division Chief: Phillip W. Perry
Drug Enforcement Administration, 316 U.S. Customs House, P.O. Box 1860, Denver, CO 80201. Tel: 303/844-3951.
(Jurisdiction: WY, UT, NM, CO)

Detroit Division
Division Chief: William Coonce
Drug Enforcement Administration, 357 Federal Bldg, 231 West Lafayette, Detroit, MI 48226. Tel: 313/226-7290.
(Jurisdiction: OH, MI, KY)

Houston Division
Division Chief: Mr. Marion Hamprick
Drug Enforcement Administration, 333 West Loop North, Suite 300, Houston, TX 77024. Tel: 713/681-1771.
(Jurisdiction: TX)

Los Angeles Division
Division Chief: John Zienter
Drug Enforcement Administration, 350 South Figueroa Street, Suite 800, Los Angeles, CA 90071. Tel: 213/894-2650.
(Jurisdiction: HI, NV, Guam, part of CA)

Miami Division
Division Chief: Thomas Cash
Drug Enforcement Administration, 8400 N.W. 53rd Street, Miami, FL 33166. Tel: 305/591-4870.
(Jurisdiction: FL, PR)

Newark Division
Division Chief: Michael Tobin
Drug Enforcement Administration, Federal Office Bldg, 970 Broad Street, Room 806, Newark, NJ 07102. Tel: 201/645-6060.
(Jurisdiction: NJ)

New Orleans Division
Division Chief: Ruben Monzon
Drug Enforcement Administration, 1661 Canal Street, Suite 2200, New Orleans, LA 70112. Tel: 504/589-3894.
(Jurisdiction: LA, AL, MS, AR)

New York Division
Division Chief: Robert Stutman
Drug Enforcement Administration, 555 West 57th Street, Suite 1900, New York, NY 10019. Tel: 212/399-5151.
(Jurisdiction: NY)

Philadelphia Division
Division Chief: Samuel Billbrough
Drug Enforcement Administration, William J. Green Federal Office Bldg, 600 Arch Street, Room 10224, Philadelphia, PA 19106. Tel: 215/597-9530.
(Jurisdiction: PA, DE)

Phoenix Division
Division Chief: David Wood
Drug Enforcement Administration, One North First Street, Suite 201, Phoenix, AZ 85004. Tel: 602/261-4866.
(Jurisdiction: AZ)

San Diego Division
Division Chief: Charles Hill
Drug Enforcement Administration, 402 West 35th Street, National City, CA 92050. Tel: 619/585-4200.
(Jurisdiction: San Diego, part of CA)

San Francisco Division
Division Chief: Joseph Krueger
Drug Enforcement Administration, 450 Golden Gate Ave., #12215, P.O. Box 36035, San Francisco, CA 94102. Tel: 415/556-6771.
(Jurisdiction: Just San Francisco)

Seattle Division
Division Chief: Raymond McKinnon
Drug Enforcement Administration, 220 West Mercer, Suite 301, Seattle, WA 98119. Tel: 206/442-5443.
(Jurisdiction: AK, WA, ID, OR, MT)

St. Louis Division
Division Chief: Kenneth G. Cloud
Drug Enforcement Administration, 7911 Forsythe Boulevard, Suite 500, United Missouri Bank Building, St. Louis, MO 63105.
Tel: 314/425-3241.
(Jurisdiction: MO, NE, KS, IA, SD)

Washington, D.C. Division
Division Chief: John Wilder
Drug Enforcement Administration, 400 Sixth Street, S.W., Room 2558, Washington, D.C. 20024. Tel: 202/724-7834.
(Jurisdiction: WV, MD, VA)

El Paso Intelligence Division
Division Chief: Larry Orton
Drug Enforcement Administration, 2211 East Missouri, Suite 200, El Paso, TX 79903. Tel: 915/534-6055.

FEDERAL BUREAU OF INVESTIGATION
J. Edgar Hoover Building
9th Street and Pennsylvania Avenue, N.W.
Washington, D.C. 20535

The Federal Bureau of Investigation (FBI) investigates violations of certain Federal statutes, collects evidence in cases in which the U.S. is or may be an interested party, and performs other duties imposed by law or Presidential directive. Top priority investigative emphasis has been on organized crime, foreign counterintelligence, white-collar crime, terrorism, and crime related to narcotics and other controlled substance. A high percentage of those and other investigations are conducted by legally trained special agents.

The Legal Counsel, and staff, furnish legal advice to the Director and other FBI officials, research legal questions concerning law enforcement matters, and supervise civil litigation and administrative claims involving the FBI, its personnel, and records.

All attorneys in the Legal Counsel Division are special agents of the FBI.

(Area Code 202)
Director: William S. Sessions 324-3444
Public Information 324-3000
Public Affairs 324-3000
Facsimile 324-4705

Freedom of Information Act/Privacy Act Office 324-5520

Privacy Act: Send a notarized signature from the subject of the request. The request must include complete name, date and place of birth, day time telephone number and current mailing address. Include alias name if ever used. If the search is to be sent to an attorney, clearly note address in the letter. Requests under the Privacy Act will be processed also under FOIA to give maximum disclosure and information.

Freedom of Information Act: Send letter clearly stating request. If the search is about an episode, include date and place of episode. If it is about an individual, include date and place of birth and what you are interested in identifying about the individual. If the individual is deceased, proof of death such as an obituary, copy of death certificate, or newspaper article must be included in the letter.

The cost for a search under either act is 10 cents a page. Send requests to the following address and mark on the outside of the envelope FOIA/PA. Address to: FBI, 9th and Pennsylvania Avenue, N.W., Washington, D.C. 20535

To Receive an Identification Record or Rap Sheet:
To receive a record of arrests and dispositions from the FBI, send a letter of request which includes a satisfactory proof of identity in the form of rolled ink finger print impressions on finger print cards commonly used by law enforcement agencies. Include name, date and place of birth and $14 certified check or money order payable to the Treasury of the United States. Send to: FBI, Identification Division, Washington, D.C. 20537-9700.

(Area Code 202)
Legal Counsel Division
Assistant Director: Joseph R. Davis 324-5018

National Crime Information Center Chief:
David F. Nemecek 324-2606

Congressional Affairs Office
Legislative Counsel: John S. Hooks Jr 324-4510

Investigations
Associate Deputy Director: Oliver B. Revell 324-3333

Criminal Investigative Division
Assistant Director: William M. Baker 324-4260

Inspector/Deputy Assistant Director: Robert M. Bryant 324-5740
Drug Section Chief: David W. Johnson Jr 324-5742
Organized Crime Section Chief: James E. Moody 324-5625

(Area Code 202)

Inspector/Deputy Assistant Director: Nicholas O'Hara ..324-4262
Counterterrorism Section Chief: Neil J. Gallagher ..324-4664
Violent Crimes and Major Offenders Section Chief:
Robin L. Montgomery 324-4188

Inspector/Deputy Assistant Director: Thomas F. Jones ..342-4805
Civil Rights and Special Inquiry Section Chief:
Joseph J. Jackson 324-2801
Investigative Support Section Chief: John J. Covert 324-5805
White Collar Crimes Section Chief: William Esposito 324-5590

(Area Code 202)

Intelligence Division
Assistant Director: Douglas Gow 324-4880
Deputy Assistant Directors:
Harry B. Brandon III 324-4885
Roger P. Watson 324-4883

FBI Academy, Quantico, VA
Assistant Director: Anthony E. Daniels 324-2726

FIELD DIVISIONS OF THE FBI

The name listed with each address is the **Special Agent in Charge** of that office.

Albany
Wayne R. Alford
Federal Bureau of Investigation, 445 Broadway, 5th Floor, U.S. Post Office and Courthouse, Albany, NY 12201-1219. Tel: 518/465-7551.

Albuquerque
James W. Nelson
Federal Bureau of Investigation, 301 Grand Avenue, NE, Albuquerque, NM 87102. Tel: 505/247-1555.

Anchorage
Charles Lontor
Federal Bureau of Investigation, 222 West 7th Avenue #6, Anchorage, AK 99513-7598. Tel: 907/276-4441.

Atlanta
Weldon L. Kennedy
Federal Bureau of Investigation, 77 Forsyth Street, S.W., Atlanta, GA 30303. Tel: 404/521-3900.

Baltimore
Joseph V. Corless
Federal Bureau of Investigation, 7142 Ambassador Road, Baltimore, MD 21207. Tel: 301/265-8080.

Birmingham
Allen P. Whitaker
Federal Bureau of Investigation, 2121 Building, Room 1400, Birmingham, AL 35203. Tel: 205/252-7705.

Boston
James F. Ahearn
Federal Bureau of Investigation, JFK Federal Office Building, Boston, MA 02203. Tel: 617/742-5533.

Buffalo
G. Robert Langford
Federal Bureau of Investigation, Federal Office Bldg., #1400, 111 West Huron Street, Buffalo, NY 14202. Tel: 716/856-7800.

Butte
Vacant
Federal Bureau of Investigation, U.S. Courthouse and Federal Office Building, Room 115, Butte, MT 59702. Tel: 406/782-2304.

Charlotte
Paul V. Daly
Federal Bureau of Investigation, 6010 Kenley Lane, Charlotte, NC 28217. Tel: 704/529-1030.

Chicago
James D. McKenzie
Federal Bureau of Investigation, E.M. Dirksen Federal Office Bldg., Room 905, 219 South Dearborn Street, Chicago, IL 60604. Tel: 312/431-1333.

Cincinnati
Terence D. Dinan
Federal Bureau of Investigation,Federal Office Bldg, Room 9023, 550 Main Street, Cincinnati, OH 45202. Tel: 513/421-4310.

Cleveland
William D. Branon
Federal Bureau of Investigation, Federal Office Bldg, #3005, 1240 East 9th Street, Cleveland, OH 44199. Tel: 216/522-1400.

Columbia
Frederick B. Verinder
Federal Bureau of Investigation, Strom Thurmond Federal Office Building, Suite 1357, 1835 Assembly Street, Columbia, SC 29201. Tel: 803/254-3011.

Dallas
Bobby R. Gillham
Federal Bureau of Investigation, 1801 West Lamar, Suite 300, Dallas, TX 75202. Tel: 214/720-2200.

Denver
Robert L. Pence
Federal Bureau of Investigation, Federal Office Bldg, Room 1823, Denver, CO 80202. Tel: 303/629-7171.

Detroit
Hal N. Helterhoff
Federal Bureau of Investigation, P.V. McNamara Federal Office Bldg., 477 Michigan Ave., Detroit, MI 48226. Tel: 313/965-2323.

El Paso
Richard D. Schwein
Federal Bureau of Investigation, 700 East San Antonio Avenue, Suite C-600, El Paso, TX 79901. Tel: 915/533-7451.
John Walser
Federal Bureau of Investigation, El Paso Intelligence Center, SSG Sims Street, Building 11339, El Paso, TX 79918-5100. Tel: 915/564-2000.

Honolulu
Eugene F. Glenn
Federal Bureau of Investigation, Kalanianaole Federal Office Bldg., Room 4307, 300 Ala Moana Boulevard, Honolulu, HI 96850. Tel: 808/521-1411.

Houston
Andrew J. Duffin
Federal Bureau of Investigation, 2500 East T.C. Jester Boulevard, Suite 200, Houston, TX 77008. Tel: 713/868-2266.

Indianapolis
William C. Ervin
Federal Bureau of Investigation, Federal Office Building, Room 679, 575 North Pennsylvania Street, Indianapolis, IN 46204. Tel: 317/639-3301.

Jackson, MS
Wayne R. Taylor
Federal Bureau of Investigation, Federal Office Bldg., #1553, 100 West Capitol Street, Jackson, MS 39269. Tel: 601/948-5000.

Jacksonville
James Cagnassola, Jr.
Federal Bureau of Investigation, 4th Floor, Oaks V, 7820 Arlington Expwy, Jacksonville, FL 32211. Tel: 904/721-1211.

Kansas City
Francis J. Storey, Jr.
Federal Bureau of Investigation, Room 300, U.S. Courthouse, Kansas City, MO 64106. Tel: 816/221-6100.

Knoxville
William E. Baugh, Jr.
Federal Bureau of Investigation, 6th Floor, 710 Locust Street, Knoxville, TN 37901. Tel: 615/544-0751.

Las Vegas
James P. Weller
Federal Bureau of Investigation, 700 E. Charleston Boulevard, Las Vegas, NV 89104. Tel: 702/385-1281.

Little Rock
Don K. Pettus
Federal Bureau of Investigation, Two Financial Centre, Suite 200, 10825 Financial Centre Pkwy, Little Rock, AR 72211. Tel: 501/221-9100.

Los Angeles
Lawrence G. Lawler
Federal Bureau of Investigation, Federal Office Bldg, 11000 Wilshire Boulevard, Los Angeles, CA 90024. Tel: 213/477-6565.

Louisville
Lloyd E. Dean
Federal Bureau of Investigation, Federal Office Building, Room 500, 600 Martin Luther King Place, Louisville, KY 40202. Tel: 502/583-3941.

Memphis
William D. Fallin
Federal Bureau of Investigation, C. Davis Federal Office Building, Room 841, 167 North Main Street, Memphis, TN 38103. Tel: 901/525-7373.

Miami
William A. Gavin
Federal Bureau of Investigation, 16320 N.W. Second Avenue, North Miami Beach, FL 33169. Tel: 305/944-9101.

Milwaukee
Lawrence J. Nelson
Federal Bureau of Investigation, Federal Office Building & Courthouse, Room 700, 517 East Wisconsin Avenue, Milwaukee, WI 53202. Tel: 414/276-4684.

Minneapolis
Jeffrey J. Jamar
Federal Bureau of Investigation, Federal Office Building, Room 392, Minneapolis, MN 55401. Tel: 612/339-7861.

Mobile
William L. Hinshaw
Federal Bureau of Investigation, One St. Louis Centre, 1 St. Louis Street, Mobile, AL 36602. Tel: 205/438-3674.

Newark
John C. McGinley
Federal Bureau of Investigation, Gateway 1, Market Street, Newark, NJ 07102. Tel: 201/622-5613.

New Haven
Stanley Klein
Federal Bureau of Investigation, Federal Office Building, 150 Court Street, New Haven, CT 06510. Tel: 203/777-6311.

New Orleans
John J. O'Connor
Federal Bureau of Investigation, 1250 Poydras Street, Suite 2200, New Orleans, LA 70112. Tel: 504/522-4671.

New York
Joseph W. Koletar (Admin)
William Y. Doran (Crim)
James E. Tomlinson (FCI/Soviet)
Federal Bureau of Investigation, 26 Federal Plaza, New York, NY 10278. Tel: 212/553-2700.

Norfolk
Irvin B. Wells III
Federal Bureau of Investigation, 200 Granby Street, Room 839, Norfolk, VA 23510. Tel: 804/623-3111.

Oklahoma City
Ronald A. Hoverson
Federal Bureau of Investigation, 50 Penn Pl, Suite 1600, Oklahoma City, OK 73118. Tel: 405/842-7471.

Omaha
Nicholas V. O'Hara
Federal Bureau of Investigation, Federal Office Bldg & U.S. Post Office & Courthouse, 215 North 17th Street, Omaha, NE 68102. Tel: 402/348-1210.

Philadelphia
Wayne R. Gilbert
Federal Bureau of Investigation, Wm J. Green Jr. Federal Office Building, 600 Arch Street, Philadelphia, PA 19106. Tel: 215/629-0800.

Phoenix
Herbert H. Hawkins, Jr.
Federal Bureau of Investigation, Suite 400, 201 East Indianola, Phoenix, AZ 85012. Tel: 602/279-5511.

Pittsburgh
Bob C. Reutter
Federal Bureau of Investigation, Federal Office Bldg, #1300, 1000 Liberty Avenue, Pittsburgh, PA 15222. Tel: 412/471-2000.

Pocatello
Jon D. Arbogast
Federal Bureau of Investigation, FBI-WRCSC Bldg, Pole Line & Quinn Roads, Pocatello, ID 83206. Tel: 208/238-0771.

Portland
Danny O. Coulson
Federal Bureau of Investigation, Crown Plaza Building, 1500 SW 1st Avenue, Portland, OR 97201. Tel: 503/224-4181.

Quantico
Anthony E. Daniels, Assistant Director, FBI Academy, Quantico, VA 22135. Tel: 703/640-6131.

Richmond
Terry T. O'Connor
Federal Bureau of Investigation, 200 West Grace Street, Richmond, VA 23220. Tel: 804/644-2631.

Sacramento
Terry Lee Knowles
Federal Bureau of Investigation, Federal Office Building, 2800 Cottage Way, Sacramento, CA 95825. Tel: 916/481-9110.

St. Louis
Julian W. Delarosa
Federal Bureau of Investigation, Federal Office Bldg., #2704, 1520 Market Street, St. Louis, MO 63103. Tel: 314/241-5357.

Salt Lake City
Robert M. Bryant
Federal Bureau of Investigation, Federal Office Building, Room 3203, 125 South State Street, Salt Lake City, UT 84138. Tel: 801/355-7521.

San Antonio
Charlie J. Parsons
Federal Bureau of Investigation, Old Post Office Bldg., #433, 615 East Houston, San Antonio, TX 78205. Tel: 512/225-6741.

San Diego
Thomas A. Hughes
Federal Bureau of Investigation, Federal Office Bldg, Room 6S-31, 880 Front Street, San Diego, CA 92188. Tel: 619/231-1122.

San Francisco
Richard W. Held
Federal Bureau of Investigation, 450 Golden Gate Avenue, San Francisco, CA 94102. Tel: 415/553-7400.

San Juan/Hato Rey
Harry B. Brandon III
Federal Bureau of Investigation, US Courthouse & Federal Office Building, Room 526, Hato Rey, PR 00918. Tel: 809/754-6000.

Savannah
Vacant
Federal Bureau of Investigation, 5401 Paulsen Street, Savannah, GA 31405. Tel: 912/354-9911.

Seattle
Steven L. Pomerantz
Federal Bureau of Investigation, Federal Office Bldg, Room 710, 915 2nd Avenue, Seattle, WA 98174. Tel: 206/622-0460

Springfield
Robert P. Wright
Federal Bureau of Investigation, 400 West Monroe Street, 4th Floor, Springfield, IL 62704. Tel: 217/522-9675.

Tampa
Robert W. Butler
Federal Bureau of Investigation, Federal Office Bldg, Room 610, 500 Zack Street, Tampa, FL 33602. Tel: 813/228-7661.

Washington, D.C.
W. Douglas Gow
Federal Bureau of Investigation, Washington Metropolitan Field Office, 9th & Pennsylvania Avenue, N.W., Washington, D.C. 20535. Tel: 202/324-3000.

INTERNATIONAL CRIMINAL POLICE ORGANIZATION (INTERPOL-USNCB)

600 E Street, N.W.
Washington, D.C. 20530

International Criminal Police Organization-U.S. National Central Bureau (INTERPOL-USNCB) facilitates international law enforcement cooperation as the U.S. representative to INTERPOL, an intergovernmental organization of 147 member countries. This organization addresses the problems of international criminal activity and the movement of international criminals, both individuals and members of organized groups, who have committed criminal acts that transcend international borders, affecting law enforcement capabilities within the U.S. and in other member countries. Use of the facilities of the INTERPOL-USNCB by the approximately 20,000 eligible stat and local law enforcement agencies is essentially the only medium that state and local police have for securing the assistance of a foreign police force.

(Area Code 202)

United States National Central Bureau Chief:
Janice Stromsem (Acting) 272-8383
General Counsel: vacant 272-8383
Financial/Fraud Investigations Division Assistant Chief: Edgar A. Adamson 272-8383

(Area Code 202)

Criminal Investigations Division Assistant Chief: (vacant) 272-8383
Alien/Fugitive Enforcement Division Assistant Chief: Russell G. Parry 272-8383
Drug Investigations Division Assistant Chief: Lawrence McElynn 272-8383

U.S. MARSHALS SERVICE

600 Army-Navy Drive
Arlington, VA 22202

The U.S. Marshals Service's principal areas of jurisdiction, which affect virtually every Federal law enforcement initiative, include court security, Federal fugitive apprehension, witness protection, prisoner transportation, maintenance of drug-related seized assets, and service and execution of Federal court orders, both criminal and civil. U.S. Marshals and their staffs are located in each of the 94 Federal judicial districts in the 50 states, District of Columbia, Guam, Puerto Rico, the Virgin Islands, and the Northern Mariana Islands.

The Office of Legal Counsel, located in the Service's national office in Arlington, VA, provides legal counsel and legal services to the U.S. Marshals nationwide, and serves as in-house counsel for the agency. The Office's work includes a variety of areas, including personnel and labor relations, civil tort and contract liability, criminal law, prisoner rights, ethics, FOIA/Privacy Act, legislation, Government forfeitures, admiralty, procurement, and training.

DEPARTMENT OF JUSTICE

	(Area Code 703)		(Area Code 703)
Director: Kevin M. Moore	307-9001	Facsimile	307-9177
Legal Counsel: Gerald Auerbach	307-9054		

FEDERAL BUREAU OF PRISONS
320 First Street, N.W.
Washington, D.C. 20001

The Federal Bureau of Prisons oversees the operation of the Federal Prison System, consisting of 54 correctional institutions, as well as Federal Prisons Industries, a self-sustaining Government corporation which provides work experience and industrial learning opportunities for the Federal inmate population. **The National Institute of Corrections**, which carries out a program of technical assistance and training for state and local correctional personnel, also operates under the auspices of the Bureau of Prisons.

The Bureau of Prisons has attorneys in its Office of the General Counsel and in the Bureau's regional field offices in Dallas, Atlanta, Kansas City, Philadelphia, and Belmont, CA.

The Office of General Counsel provides legal advice and assistance to management staff; provides in-house appellate review for inmate complaints filed under the Bureau's administrative remedy procedures; processes tort and other administrative claims; provides litigation assistance to U.S. Attorneys; advises on Federal sentence computation and interpretation; and provides legislative assistance on Federal prison matters.

	(Area Code 202)		(Area Code 202)
Director: J. Michael Quinlan	307-3250	Facsimile	514-6878
General Counsel: Wallace Cheney	307-3062		

REGIONAL OFFICES

South Central Region
Regional Director: Charles Turnbo
Federal Bureau of Prisons, 4211 Cedar Springs Road, Suite 300, Dallas, TX 75219. Tel: 214/767-9700.
(Jurisdiction: AR, LA, NM, OK, TX)

Southeast Region
Regional Director: Jerry T. Williford
Federal Bureau of Prisons, 523 McDonough Blvd, S.E., Atlanta, GA 30315. Tel: 404/624-5202.
(Jurisdiction: AL, FL, GA, KY, MS, NC, PR, SC, TN, VI)

North Central Region
Regional Director: Larry DuBois
Federal Bureau of Prisons, Airworld Center, 10920 Ambassador Drive, Suite 200, Kansas City, MO 64153. Tel: 816/891-1360.
(Jurisdiction: IL, IN, KS, MI, MN, MO, NE, OH, WI)

Northeast Region
Regional Director: George Wilkinson
Federal Bureau of Prisons, U.S. Customs House, 7th Floor, 2nd & Chestnut Streets, Philadelphia, PA 19106. Tel: 215/597-6317.
(Jurisdiction: CT, DE, ME, DC, MD, MA, NH, NJ, NY, PA, RI, VT, VA, WV)

Western Region
Regional Director: Cal Edwards
Federal Bureau of Prisons, 1301 Shoreway Road, 4th Floor, Belmont, CA 94002. Tel: 415/598-4700.
(Jurisdiction: AK, AZ, CA, CO, HI, ID, MT, NV, ND, OR, SD, UT, WA, WY)

U.S. PAROLE COMMISSION
5550 Friendship Boulevard
Chevy Chase, MD 20815

The U.S. Parole Commission (which will be expiring as of Oct 31, 1992) is an independent agency in the Department of Justice created to carry out a national parole policy. The Commission is directed by nine commissioners appointed for six-year terms by the President and confirmed by the Senate. The Chairman designates three commissioners to serve on the **National Appeals Board** in Chevy Chase, MD, and designates five commissioners to serve as the regional commissioners in the regional offices located in Philadelphia, Atlanta, Dallas, San Francisco, and Kansas City.

The Office of General Counsel, located in Chevy Chase, MD, provides legal assistance and advice to the Commission and prepares litigation reports for U.S. Attorneys throughout the nation.

	(Area Code 301)		(Area Code 301)
Chairman: Benjamin F. Baer	492-5990	Facsimile	492-6694
General Counsel: Michael Stover	492-5959		

REGIONAL OFFICES

North Central Region
Commissioner: Carol Pavilack-Getty
U.S. Parole Commission, 10920 Ambassador Drive, Suite 220, Kansas City, MO 64153. Tel: 816/891-1395.
(Jurisdiction: IL, IN, KS, MI, MN, MO, NE, OH, SD, WI)

Northeast Region
Commissioner: Daniel Lopez
U.S. Parole Commission, 2nd & Chestnut Streets, Customs House, 7th Floor, Philadelphia, PA 19106. Tel: 215/597-6365.
(Jurisdiction: CT, DE, DC, ME, MD, MA, NH, NJ, NY, PA, PR, RI, VT, Virgin Islands, VA, WV)

Southeast Region
Commissioner: G. MacKenzie Rast
U.S. Parole Commission, 1718 Peachtree Street, NW, Suite 250, Atlanta, GA 30309. Tel: 404/347-4126.
(Jurisdiction: AL, Canal Zone, FL, GA, KY, MS, NC, SC, TN)

South Central Region
Commissioner: Victor M.F. Reyes
U.S. Parole Commission, 525 Griffin Street, #820, Dallas TX 75202. Tel: 214/767-0024.
(Jurisdiction: AR, LA, OK, TX)

Western Region
Commissioner: Vacant
U.S. Parole Commission, 1301 Shoreway Road, 4th Floor, Belmont, CA 94002. Tel: 415/598-4800
(Jurisdiction: AK, American Samoa, AZ, CA, CO, Guam, HI, ID, MT, NV, ND, OR, UT, WA, WY)

DATABASES OF INTEREST

DRAM (Decision Recording and Monitoring System) is an in house database not available to the public but a hard copy of specifically requested information is available; e.g. parole risk statistics, lengths of sentence vis-a-vis an offense committed. Call or write the U.S. Parole Commission, 5550 Friendship Blvd., Chevy Chase, MD 20815. Tel: 301/492-5980.

OFFICE OF THE PARDON ATTORNEY

5550 Friendship Boulevard
Chevy Chase, MD 20815

The Pardon Attorney receives and reviews all petitions for Executive clemency, initiates the necessary investigations, and prepares the recommendations to the President in connection with the consideration of all forms of Executive clemency, including pardon, commutation of sentence, remission of fine, and reprieve.

(Area Code 301)
Pardon Attorney: David C. Stephenson 492-5910
Deputy Pardon Attorney: Raymond P. Theim 492-5910

(Area Code 301)
Facsimile 492-5942

DEPARTMENT OF JUSTICE

PUBLICATIONS OF INTEREST

The following publications may be ordered from the **Superintendent of Documents, U.S. Government Printing Office,** Washington, D.C. 20402. Tel: 202/783-3238:

Antitrust Division Manual is a guide to the operating policies and procedures of the Antitrust Division of the Department of Justice with a discussion of conducting investigations and litigation that the Division has employed in the past. Price for basic manual with supplements: $40.00 domestic; $50.00 foreign. Issued irregularly for an indeterminate period. GPO Stock# 927-001-00000-4.

U.S. Attorney's Manual. Subscription service for each volume consists of a basic manual and supplementary material for an indeterminate period. In looseleaf form, punched for 3-ring binder.

Volumes I and II, Titles I Through 8. October 1988. Subscription service consists of a two-volume basic manual (Volume I, Titles 1 through 3 and Volume II, Titles 4 through 8), cumulative semiannual updates, and blue sheets for an indeterminate period. Price: $485.00 domestic; $606.25 foreign. GPO Stock# 927-004-00000-3.

Volume III, Title 9, Criminal Division. Price: $434.00 domestic; $542.50 foreign. GPO Stock# 927 005 00000-0.

Volume IV, Indices. This volume is a general index which covers Titles 1 through 9. It has a comprehensive USC and CFR reference table, and also includes a prior approval listing for the Department of Justice. Price: $18.00 domestic; $22.50 foreign. GPO Stock# 927-007-00000-2.

Federal Probation: A Journal of Correctional Philosophy and Practice contains articles relating to preventive and correctional activities in delinquency and crime. Published quarterly. Price: $5.00 per year domestic; $6.25 foreign. GPO Stock# 727-001-00000-0.

FOIA (Freedom of Information Act) Update contains updated news articles pertaining to the Freedom of Information Act. Published quarterly. Price: $5.00 per year domestic; $6.25 foreign. GPO Stock# 727-002-00000-6.

FBI Law Enforcement Bulletin. Published monthly. Price: $14.00 a year domestic; $17.50 a year foreign. GPO Stock# 727-006-00000-1.

Immigration and Naturalization Service Operating Instructions, Regulations, and Interpretations contains definitions, regulations and interpretation of the INS. Updated irregularly. Price: $196.00 per year domestic; $245.00 foreign. GPO Stock# 927-002-00000-1.

Interim Decisions of the Department of Justice contains selected precedential Board of Immigration Appeals decisions which are binding on all Immigration and Naturalization Offices. Published at irregular intervals. Price: $65.00 per year domestic; $81.25 foreign. GPO Stock# 827-002-00000-3.

United States Immigration Laws: General Information is a pamphlet containing information on emigration and immigration law. Price: $1.00 domestic; $1.25 foreign. GPO Stock# 027-002-00377-2.

Sentencing Guidelines Manual, Amendments is a Department of Justice sentencing guidelines manual including amendments which took effect June 15, 1988. Price: $26.00 domestic; $32.50 foreign. GPO Stock# 052-070-00600-8.

A Citizen's Guide on Using the Freedom of Information Act and the Privacy Act of 1974 to Request Government Records gives instructions on how to make a FOIA request and a Privacy Act request for access to information. Price: $1.75 domestic; $2.19 foreign. GPO Stock# 052-071-00865-9.

Although the following publications are out of print, they are available in many law libraries as well as in all Federal Depository Libraries.

Freedom of Information Case List, 1989 Edition is a compilation of published and nonpublished judicial decisions addressing access issues under the Freedom of Information Act, 5 U.S.C. 552, as amended. This publication also contains full texts of these statutes, a revised list of related law review articles, and a "Short Guide to the Freedom of Information Act."

The Opinions of the Attorneys General. 1789-1974. 42 volumes. Only selected opinions are included. These are merely advisory statements addressing statutory interpretations or general legal problems faced by executive departments and agencies. They are not mandatory orders, although Attorneys General have asserted their binding effect. Thus, although executive department officials are not bound to follow them, they are in fact generally followed. Attorney General opinions have also had a significant influence on judicial decisionmaking. Consequently, they have great value as guides to executive and administrative rulings and requirements and serve as valuable precedents. The bound volumes include headnotes, indexes, and tables. Over time, fewer and fewer opinions have been published. In the last volume, for example, fewer than ten percent of the opinions issued by the Attorney General in the period from 1961 to 1974 have been included. Opinions for the period from 1974 to 1986 have been compiled by the Department of Justice, but have not yet been published.

Opinions of the Office of Legal Counsel of the U.S. Department of Justice. 6 volumes, covering 1977-1982. Selected memorandum opinions advising the President, the Attorney General, and other executive officers of the Federal Government with respect to their official duties. Volumes 4-6 also include selected formal opinions of the Attorney General.

DEPARTMENT OF JUSTICE

KEY LEGAL AUTHORITIES

As the chief lawyer for the U.S. Government, the Attorney General prosecutes, defends, and is otherwise involved in cases arising under hundreds of Federal laws and regulations administered by other departments and agencies of the Executive Branch. Space limitations do not permit the enumeration of all of these legal authorities, the vast majority of which are addressed in other sections of this Directory. For a discussion of Justice Department enforcement responsibilities with respect to the most significant of these many authorities, see 28 C.F.R. Part 0 (1989).

The selected legal authorities discussed below are those of importance for which the Department of Justice bears administrative or advisory responsibility beyond its customary enforcement functions.

Regulations:

General Departmental Regulations: 28 C.F.R. Part 0 et seq. (1989).

Department of Justice Acquisition Regulations: 48 C.F.R. Part 2801 et seq. (1989).

Drug Enforcement Administration: 21 C.F.R. Part 1301 et seq. (1989).

Foreign Claims Settlement Commission: 45 C.F.R. Part 500 et seq. (1989).

Immigration & Naturalization Service: 8 C.F.R. Part 1 et seq. (1989).

Prisons Bureau: 28 C.F.R. Parts 500-572 (1989).

Justice Property Management Regulations: 41 C.F.R. Part 128 (1989).

Federal Claims Collection Standards: 4 C.F.R. Part 101 et seq. (1989)[issued jointly with the U.S. General Accounting Office].

Uniform Guidelines on Employee Selection Procedures, 28 C.F.R. 50.14 (1989)--principles issued jointly by the Departments of Justice and Labor, the Equal Employment Opportunity Commission, and the Office of Personnel Management and designed to assist employers, labor organizations, employment agencies, and licensing and certification boards to comply with Federal equal employment opportunity laws.

Guidelines on Representation of Federal Officials and Employees by Department of Justice Attorneys or Private Counsel Furnished by the Department in Civil Proceedings, Congressional Proceedings, and State Criminal Proceedings in which Federal Employees are Sued or Subpoenaed in their Individual Capacities, 28 C.F.R. 50.15 et seq. (1989).

U.S. Constitution, Art. II, Sec. 2 & the authority of the President as Chief Executive--authorizes the President to grant Executive Clemency by pardon, reprieve, commutation of sentence, or remission of fine; administered by the Department of Justice's Pardon Attorney.

Implementing Regulations: 28 C.F.R. Part 1 (1989).

Clayton Anti-Trust Act, as amended, 15 U.S.C. 12-27--prohibits mergers and acquisitions that may substantially lessen competition or lead to monopolies; authorizes the Government to challenge those mergers that economic analysis demonstrates are likely to increase prices to consumers; and authorizes the Department of Justice to conduct all proceedings arising out of violations of orders issued by the Federal Trade Commission.

Sherman Antitrust Act, as amended, 15 U.S.C. 1-7--makes illegal restraints of trade and the monopolization of trade or commerce, including agreements among competitors to fix prices, regulate bids, and allocate consumers; also prohibits the monopolization of any part of interstate commerce.

Hart-Scott-Rodino Antitrust Improvements Act of 1976, as amended, 15 U.S.C. 1311 note--provides the Department and the Federal Trade Commission with procedural devices to enforce the antitrust laws with respect to anticompetitive mergers and acquisitions.

Legislative History: 1976 U.S. Code Cong. & Admin. News 2572.

Export Trading Company Act of 1982, as amended, 15 U.S.C. 4001 et seq.-- designed to increase U.S. exports of goods and services by encouraging more efficient provisions of export trade services to U.S. producers and suppliers, by reducing restrictions on trade financing provided by financial institutions, and by reducing uncertainty concerning the application of the U.S. antitrust laws to export trade.

Legislative History: 1982 U.S. Code Cong. & Admin. News 2431.

Antitrust Division Business Review Procedure, 28 C.F.R. 50.6 (1989). Although the Department is not authorized to give advisory opinions to private parties, the Antitrust Division is willing, in certain circumstances, to review proposed business conduct and state its enforcement intentions. The requesting party may rely only upon a written business review letter signed by the Assistant Attorney General, Antitrust Division or his delegate.

Merger Guidelines. Provide a framework for defining markets within which to analyze mergers, translating principles of market power into a market definition standard.

Antitrust Civil Process Act, as amended, 15 U.S.C. 1311 et seq.--authorizes the Department of Justice to serve a "civil investigative demand" requiring the pre-proceeding production of documents from a person in order to enable the Department to determine whether there has been a violation of the antitrust laws.

Legislative History: 1962 U.S. Code Cong. & Admin. News 2567; 1976 U.S. Code Cong. & Admin. News 2572; 1980 U.S. Code Cong. & Admin. News 2716.

Implementing Regulations: 28 C.F.R. Part 49 (1989).

Federal Deposit Insurance Act, as amended, 12 U.S.C. 1828(c)--directs the Department of Justice to review proposed mergers or consolidations of insured institutions requested by the responsible financial regulatory agency.

Legislative History: 1950 U.S. Code Cong. Service 3765; 1989 U.S. Code Cong. & Admin. News 86.

Outer Continental Shelf Lands Act, as amended, 43 U.S.C. 1334(a), 1334(f)(3), & 1337--authorizes the Department of Justice to advise the Departments of Energy and Interior concerning the competitive impact of proposed regulations governing the award of mineral leases on the outer continental shelf, and the Secretary of Energy regarding pipeline permits and licenses; and also authorizes antitrust reviews of actual outer continental shelf lease sales.

Legislative History: 1978 U.S. Code Cong. & Admin. News 1450.

Atomic Energy Act of 1954, as amended, 42 U.S.C. 2135--authorizes Department of Justice reviews of proposed issuances of nuclear licenses for their competitive impact.

Legislative History: 1954 U.S. Code Cong. & Admin. News 3456; 1970 U.S. Code Cong. & Admin. News 4981.

Civil Rights Act of 1964, Title VI, 42 U.S.C. 2000d et seq.--prohibits discrimination under any program or activity receiving Federal financial assistance.

Legislative History: 1964 U.S. Code Cong. & Admin. News 2355.

Implementing Regulations: 28 C.F.R. 50.3 (1989)[Enforcement Guidelines].

Civil Liberties Act of 1988, 50 U.S.C. App. 1989 et seq.--creates a trust fund to provide restitution for the World War II internment of Japanese-Americans and Aleuts, and directs the Department of Justice to identify and locate each individual eligible for such restitution.

Legislative History: 1988 U.S. Code Cong. & Admin. News 1135.

Voting Rights Act of 1965, as amended, 42 U.S.C. 1973(c) et seq.-- prohibits the enforcement in any jurisdiction covered by section 4(b) of the Act, of any voting qualification or prerequisite to voting, or standard, practice or procedure with respect to voting, different from that in force or effect.

Legislative History: 1965 U.S. Code Cong. & Admin. News 2437; 1982 U.S. Code Cong. & Admin. News 177.

Implementing Regulations: 28 C.F.R. Parts 51 & 55 (1989).

Civil Rights Of Institutionalized Persons Act of 1980, as amended, 42 U.S.C. 1977 et seq.--provides that whenever there is reasonable cause to believe that any state or political subdivision of a state is subjecting persons residing in or confined to an institution to egregious or flagrant conditions which deprive those persons of any rights, privileges, or immunities, a civil action may be brought in any appropriate U.S. district court.

Legislative History: 1980 U.S. Code Cong. & Admin. News 787; 1982 U.S. Code Cong. & Admin. News 1893.

Implementing Regulations: 28 C.F.R. Part 40 (1989).

Exec. Order No. 12250, "Leadership and Coordination of Nondiscrimination Laws"--authorizes the Attorney General to approve rules, regulations, and orders of general application under Title VI of the Civil Rights Act of 1964 and sec. 902 of the Education Amendments of 1972 et al., and directs the Department of Justice to coordinate the implementation and enforcement by Executive Branch agencies of the following laws: Title VI of the Civil Rights Act of 1964, 42 U.S.C. 2000d et seq.; Title IX of the Education Amendments of 1972, 20 U.S.C. 1681 et seq.; Sec. 504 of the Rehabilitation Act of 1973, as amended, 29 U.S.C. 794; and any other Federal statute that prohibits discrimination by, participation in, or denial of benefits under any program or activity receiving Federal financial assistance on the grounds of race, color, national origin, handicap, religion, or sex.

Narcotic Addict Treatment Act of 1974, as amended, 21 U.S.C. 802 et seq.-- outlines the procedures to determine security standards for practitioners providing either maintenance or detoxification treatment to individuals dependent upon narcotic drugs. Practitioners giving such treatment will be required to obtain special registration and comply with established standards.

Legislative History: 1974 U.S. Code Cong. & Admin. News 3029.

Implementing Regulations: 21 C.F.R. Part 1301 (1989).

Controlled Substances Act, as amended, 21 U.S.C. 801 et seq.--directs the Attorney General to control and classify listed substances; requires manufacturers, distributors, and dispensers of controlled substances to register with the Department of Justice; prescribes offenses and penalties under the Act; and establishes forfeiture procedures.

Legislative History: 1970 U.S. Code Cong. & Admin. News 4566; 1978 U.S. Code Cong. & Admin. News 9496; 1984 U.S. Code Cong. & Admin. News 3182; 1986 U.S. Code Cong. & Admin. News 5393; 1988 U.S. Code Cong. & Admin. News 5937.

Implementing Regulations: 21 C.F.R. Part 1301 et seq. (1989).

Controlled Substances Import-Export Act, as amended, 21 U.S.C. 821 et seq.-- requires every person who manufactures, distributes, or dispenses any controlled substance or who proposes to engage in manufacturing to register annually.

Legislative History: 1970 U.S. Code Cong. & Admin. News 4566; 1984 U.S. Code Cong. & Admin. News 3182.

Implementing Regulations: 21 C.F.R. Parts 1301 & 1312 (1989).

Immigration & Nationality Act of 1952, as amended, 8 U.S.C. 1101 et seq.-- outlines the procedures for importation and exportation of persons into the United States. The Executive Office for Immigration Review and the Board of Immigration Appeals were created under this Act to aid in the day to day implementation of the immigration and emigration processes.

Legislative History: 1986 U.S. Code Cong. & Admin. News 6182.

Implementing Regulations: 8 C.F.R. Part 1 et seq. (1989).

Immigration Reform & Control Act of 1986, as amended, 8 U.S.C. 1103(a), 1324b--prohibits anyone from knowingly and intentionally discriminating or engaging in a pattern or practice of discrimination against any individual with respect to hiring, recruitment, or referral for a fee of the individual for employment; and established an Office of Special Counsel for Immigration-Related Unfair Employment Practices in the Department of Justice to enforce the antidiscrimination provisions of the Act.

Legislative History: 1986 U.S. Code Cong. & Admin. News 5649.

Implementing Regulations: 28 C.F.R. Part 44 (1989).

DEPARTMENT OF JUSTICE

Victims of Crime Act of 1984, as amended, 42 U.S.C 10601 et seq.-- establishes a separate account, to be known as the Crime Victims Fund. This fund is generated through Federal criminal fines, penalty assessments, forfeited appearance bonds, and bail bonds to be distributed among the states to support crime victim compensation and assistance.
Legislative History: 1984 U.S. Code Cong. & Admin. News 3182; 1986 U.S. Code Cong. & Admin. News 1967.
Implementing Regulations: 28 C.F.R. Part 18 (1989).

Juvenile Justice and Delinquency Prevention Act of 1974, as amended, 42 U.S.C. 5601 et seq.--authorizes grants for juvenile justice and delinquency prevention programs. The Act assists States, local communities, public and private agencies, institutions, and individuals by issuing formula grants to develop and implement programs to keep juveniles in school.
Highlights of Recent Amendments: 42 U.S.C. 5771-5773--missing children provisions.
Legislative History: 1974 U.S. Code Cong. & Admin. News 5283; 1980 U.S. Code Cong. & Admin. News 6098; 1984 U.S. Code Cong. & Admin. News 3182.
Implementing Regulations: 28 C.F.R. 31.1 et seq. (1989).

U.S. Parole Commission Act of 1976, as amended, 18 U.S.C. 4201 et seq.--authorizes the granting, modification, or revocation of the paroles of eligible U.S. prisoners serving sentences of more than one year, and is responsible for the supervision of parolees and prisoners mandatorily released prior to the expiration of their sentences.
NOTE: Although this act has been repealed, its provisions remain applicable until October 31, 1992, to (1) individuals who committed acts of juvenile delinquency before November 1, 1987 and (2) certain terms of imprisonment.

National Institute of Justice Act, as amended, 42 U.S.C. 3721 et seq.-- authorized the Institute to make grants, or enter into cooperative agreements or contracts with public agencies, institutions of higher education, private organizations or individuals to conduct research to develop law enforcement and criminal justice plans. The Institute is authorized to initiate multiyear and short term research and development concerning the criminal and civil justice systems.
Legislative History: 1979 U.S. Code Cong. & Admin. News 2471; 1984 U.S. Code Cong. & Admin. News 3182.
Implementing Regulations: 28 C.F.R. Part 18 (1989).

Bankruptcy Reform Act of 1978. as amended, 28 U.S.C. 586(e) et seq.--establishes the U.S. Trustee system to assist in the administration of the bankruptcy system.
Legislative History: 1978 U.S. Code Cong. & Admin. News 5787.
Implementing Regulations: 28 C.F.R. Part 58 (1989).

Federal Sentencing Guidelines, 18 U.S.C. App., Chapts. 1-7-- the U.S. Sentencing Commission was created by Congress to establish sentencing policies for the federal criminal justice system to ensure that the purposes of sentencing are met and to provide certainty and fairness in sentencing by avoiding unwarranted disparities among similarly situated offenders. The Commission permits individualized sentences when justified by mitigating or aggravating circumstances.

Gambling Devices Act of 1962, as amended, 15 U.S.C. 1171 et seq.--makes unlawful the interstate transportation of gambling devices unless a specific state law creates an exemption from this provision and requires gambling device manufacturers and dealers to register with the Justice Department.
Legislative History: 1950 U.S. Code Cong. Service 4240; 1962 U.S. Code Cong. & Admin. News 3809.
Implementing Regulations: 28 C.F.R. Part 3 (1989).

Labor-Management Reporting & Disclosure Act of 1959, as amended, 29 U.S.C. 401 et seq.--prohibits any person who is or has been a member of the Communist party or who has been convicted of a crime enumerated in 29 U.S.C. 504(a) to serve in any labor organization capacity for 13 years after such conviction or after the end of imprisonment therefor, whichever is later; and authorizes the Department of Justice to issue Certificates of Exemption from such prohibition.
Legislative History: 1959 U.S. Code Cong. & Admin. News 2318; 1984 U.S. Code Cong. & Admin. News 3182.
Implementing Regulations: 28 C.F.R. Part 4 (1989).

Employee Retirement Income Security Act of 1974 ("ERISA"), as amended, 29 U.S.C. 1111, 1137--prohibits any person convicted of, or imprisoned as a result of such conviction of, certain specified crimes from serving in any capacity with an employee benefit plan for 13 years after conviction or the end of imprisonment, whichever is later, unless a Certificate of Exemption from this prohibition is forthcoming.
Legislative History: 1974 U.S. Code Cong. & Admin. News 4639; 1984 U.S. Code Cong. & Admin. News 3182.
Implementing Regulations: 28 C.F.R. Part 4 (1989).

Foreign Agents Registration Act of 1938, as amended, 22 U.S.C. 611-621--requires agents of foreign principals to register with the Department of Justice.
Legislative History: 1966 U.S. Code Cong. & Admin. News 2397; 1970 U.S. Code Cong. & Admin. News 3649.
Implementing Regulations: 28 C.F.R. Part 5 (1989).

18 U.S.C. 2386--requires foreign-controlled organizations engaging in political or civilian military activity, organizations engaging in both political and civilian military activity, and every organization whose purpose is the overthrow of a government, to register with the Attorney General.
Implementing Regulations: 28 C.F.R. Part 10 (1989).

31 U.S.C. 3718--authorizes the Department of Justice to contract with private counsel to pursue debts owed to the U.S.
Legislative History: 1983 U.S. Code Cong. & Admin. News 1615; 1986 U.S. Code Cong. & Admin. News 5606.
Implementing Regulations: 28 C.F.R. Part 11 (1989).

Atomic Weapons & Special Nuclear Materials Rewards Act, 50 U.S.C. 47a-47f--authorizes a reward for original information about illegal diversions, attempted illegal diversions, or conspiracies to divert special nuclear materials or atomic weapons.
Legislative History: 1974 U.S. Code Cong. & Admin. News 4050.
Implementing Regulations: 28 C.F.R. Part 13 (1989).

Federal Tort Claims Act, as amended, 28 U.S.C. 2672--authorizes Federal agencies, in accordance with regulations prescribed by the Attorney General, to settle claims against the U.S. administratively, and requires that any award, compromise, or settlement in excess of $25,000 be approved by the Department of Justice.
NOTE: Many Federal agencies have promulgated agency-specific regulations supplementing these general, Government-wide regulations.
Legislative History: 1966 U.S. Code Cong. & Admin. News 2515.
Implementing Regulations: 28 C.F.R. Part 14 (1989).

Certification & Defense of Certain Suits Against U.S. Government Employees Acting Within the Scope of Their Duties or Employment at the Time of the Incident out of which the Suit Arose:
*Medical malpractice actions against armed forces and other health care or support personnel, 10 U.S.C. 1089.
Legislative History: 1976 U.S. Code Cong. & Admin. News 4443; 1981 U.S. Code Cong. & Admin. News 1666; 1983 U.S. Code Cong. & Admin. News 1081.
*Medical malpractice actions against Department of Veterans' Affairs health care or support personnel, 38 U.S.C. 4116.
Legislative History: 1965 U.S. Code Cong. & Admin. News 3925; 1973 U.S. Code Cong. & Admin. News 1688; 1976 U.S. Code Cong. & Admin. News 6355; 1988 U.S. Code Cong. & Admin. News 432.
*Medical malpractice actions against commissioned officers or employees of the Public Health Service, 42 U.S.C. 233.

Legislative History: 1970 U.S. Code Cong. & Admin. News 1975.
*Swine flu personal injury or wrongful death cases, 42 U.S.C. 247b.

Legislative History: 1975 U.S. Code Cong. & Admin. News 469.
*Medical malpractice actions against National Aeronautics & Space Administration health care and support personnel, 42 U.S.C. 2458a.

Legislative History: 1976 U.S. Code Cong. & Admin. News 4443.
*Negligent exposure to radiation actions against Federal contractors, Department of Defense Authorization Act of 1985, sec. 1631(d), Pub.L. 98-525, 98 Stat. 2492, 2646 (1984).

Legislative History: 1984 U.S. Code Cong. & Admin. News 4174.
*Vehicular negligence actions against Federal employees, 28 U.S.C. 2679.

Legislative History: 1961 U.S. Code Cong. & Admin. News 2784; 1966 U.S. Code Cong. & Admin. News 2515.
*Medical malpractice actions against Department of State health care or support personnel, 22 U.S.C. 2702.

Legislative History: 1980 U.S. Code Cong. & Admin. News 4419.

Implementing Regulations for all of the above provisions: 28 C.F.R. Part 15 (1989).

Public Safety Officers' Benefits Act of 1976, as amended, 42 U.S.C. 3796--authorizes the Office of Justice Programs to pay a benefit of $100,000 to specified survivors of public safety officers, rescue squad and ambulance crew members found to have died as a direct and proximate result of a personal injury sustained in the line of duty.

Legislative History: 1976 U.S. Code Cong. & Admin. News 2504; 1984 U.S. Code Cong. & Admin. News 3182; 1988 U.S. Code Cong. & Admin. News 5937.

Implementing Regulations: 28 C.F.R. Part 32 (1989).

Medical Care Recovery Act, 42 U.S.C. 2651-2653--authorizes the Government to recover the costs of hospital, medical, surgical, or dental care and treatment from tortiously liable third persons.

Legislative History: 1962 U.S. Code Cong. & Admin. News 2637.

Implementing Regulations: 28 C.F.R. Part 43 (1989).

Right to Financial Privacy Act of 1978, as amended, 12 U.S.C. 3401, 3408--authorizes a Government authority to request financial records from a financial institution.

Legislative History: 1978 U.S. Code Cong. & Admin. News 9273.

Implementing Regulations: 28 C.F.R. Part 47 (1989).

Foreign Corrupt Practices Act of 1977, as amended, 15 U.S.C. 78dd-1 et seq.--makes unlawful the payment of money or gifts to foreign officials or politicians for the purpose of influencing a favorable act or decision.

Legislative History: 1977 U.S. Code Cong. & Admin. News 4098; 1988 U.S. Code Cong. & Admin. News 1547.

Implementing Regulations: 28 C.F.R. 50.18 (1989)[Foreign Corrupt Practices Act Review Letter Procedure--whereunder the Department of Justice's Criminal Division is willing, in certain circumstances, to review proposed conduct and state its present enforcement intentions.]

Inmate Accident Compensation, 18 U.S.C. 4126--authorizes payment of accident compensation to former Federal prison inmates or their dependents for impairments from injuries sustained while working in Federal Prison Industries, Inc. or in institutional work assignments involving the operation or maintenance of a Federal correctional institution.

Legislative History: 1988 U.S. Code Cong. & Admin. News 5937.

Implementing Regulations: 28 C.F.R. Part 301 (1989).

International Claims Settlement Act of 1949, as amended, 22 U.S.C. 1621-1645o--established the Foreign Claims Settlement Commission with jurisdiction to receive, examine, adjudicate, and render final decisions on U.S. Government and nationals' claims against foreign governments arising out of the nationalization or other taking of property.

Legislative History: 1950 U.S. Code Cong. Service 1949; 1955 U.S. Code Cong. & Admin. News 2745; 1968 U.S. Code Cong. & Admin. News 2710; 1986 U.S. Code Cong. & Admin. News 2398.

Implementing Regulations: 45 C.F.R. Part 500 et seq. (1989).

War Claims Act of 1948, as amended, 50 U.S.C. App. 2001 et seq.--establishes a procedure for the adjudication and settlement of U.S. government and nationals' war claims.

Legislative History: 1954 U.S. Code Cong. & Admin. News 3101; 1962 U.S. Code Cong. & Admin. News 3826; 1980 U.S. Code Cong. & Admin. News 137.

Implementing Regulations: 45 C.F.R. Part 500 et seq. (1989).

Program Fraud Civil Remedies Act of 1986, 31 U.S.C. 3801 et seq.--provides Federal agencies victimized by false, fictitious, and fraudulent claims and statements with an administrative remedy to compensate them for losses resulting therefrom.

Legislative History: 1986 U.S. Code Cong. & Admin. News 3607.

Convention on the Service Abroad of Judicial and Extrajudicial Documents in Civil or Commercial Matters, TIAS 6638, 20 UST 361 (1969)--designates the Department of Justice the Central Authority in the U.S. to receive requests for service from other contracting states and to arrange to have documents served within the U.S.

Convention on the Taking of Evidence Abroad in Civil or Commercial Matters, TIAS 7444, 23 UST 2555 (1972)--designates the Department of Justice the Central Authority in the U.S. to receive Letters of Request to take evidence from a judicial authority of another contracting state and to transmit them to the U.S. authority competent to execute them.

DEPARTMENT OF LABOR

200 Constitution Avenue, N.W.
Washington, D.C. 20210

DESCRIPTION: The mission of the Department of Labor is to promote the welfare of wage earners, improve their working conditions, and advance their employment opportunities. The Department administers a variety of Federal labor laws guaranteeing workers' rights to safe and healthful working conditions, a minimum hourly wage and overtime pay, freedom from employment discrimination, unemployment insurance, and workers' compensation. The Department also is responsible for protecting pension rights, providing job training programs, assisting jobhunters, strengthening free collective bargaining, and tracking changes in employment, prices, and other national economic measurements. Special efforts are made to assist older workers, youths, minority group members, women, disabled persons, and other groups with special needs.

(Area Code 202)

Secretary: Elizabeth Hanford Dole 523-8271
Public Affairs/Publications Information 523-7316
Publications Information (BLS) 523-1221
Small and Disadvantaged Business Utilization 523-9148
Docket 653-5052
Hot Line for Fraud, Waste and Abuse:
Washington, D.C. Metro Area 357-0227
Outside Washington, D.C. Metro Area .... (800) 424-5409
Facsimile 523-7312

(Area Code 202)

Freedom of Information Act/Privacy Act Office 523-8188
Written requests can be sent to FOIA/PA, 200 Constitution Ave., N.W., Room N2428, Washington, D.C. 20210. Specific information regarding fees can also be found in 29 CFR 70.40.

Main Library/Law Library (Room 2439) 523-6992
The law library is part of the main library and is open to the public Monday through Friday from 8:15 AM until 4:45 PM. It includes all administrative decisions by the Labor Department and congressional hearings on microfiche. The Library also has a commercial database called **Washington Alert**, which includes the latest legislation and the status of bills.

OFFICE OF THE SOLICITOR (Room S2002)

The Office of the Solicitor provides legal services to the Secretary of Labor and departmental program officials. The Office:

* litigates cases arising under various enforcement programs in administrative proceedings in U.S. District Courts and in U.S. Courts of Appeals;

* defends and protects the financial interest of the Federal Government under various workers' compensation claims and damage claims;

* ensures the legal sufficiency of all orders, regulations, written interpretations, and opinions issued to by the Department of Labor;

* conducts independent reviews of certain legal decisions issued to assist the Secretary and Under Secretary in carrying out their reviews of appeals; and

* advises officials on the legal requirements involved in the rulemaking process, including Federal Register clearance.

(Area Code 202)

Solicitor: Robert P. Davis 523-7675
Deputy Solicitor for:
National Operations: Jerry G. Thorn 523-7684
Planning and Coordination: Judith E.Kramer 523-7705
Regional Operations: Ronald G. Whiting 523-9521
Facsimile 523-9255

The Office of Solicitor is divided into eleven divisions:

The **Black Lung Benefits Division** provides litigation services necessary to protect the interests of the Government in connection with the determination of claims under Title IV of the Federal Coal Mine Safety Act (as amended by the Black Lung Benefits Reform Act of 1977 and the Black Lung Benefits Amendments of 1981); reviews all decisions made under the Act by the Department's Administrative Law Judges to determine if an appeal should be filed with the Benefits Review Board on behalf of the Department; provides advisory legal services to the Department relating to issues arising under the Black Lung Benefits Act; and develops litigation programs to further the evolution of case law and to develop the law in various unsettled areas of the Act.

(Area Code 202)

Associate Solicitor: Donald S. Shire 357-0435
Deputy Associate Solicitor: Rae Ellen James 357-0422
Counsel for Administrative Litigation & Legal Advice:
Jeffrey J. Bernstein 357-0415
Richard A. Seid 357-0419
Counsel for Black Lung Appellate Litigation:
Michael J. Denney 357-0418
Barbara J. Johnson 357-0424
Sylvia T. Kaser 357-0417

The **Civil Rights Division** provides legal services in the field of civil rights enforcement, including responsibility for litigation, interpretations, opinions, and preparation of rules, regulations and orders, such as Executive Order 11246; Sections 503 and 504 of the Rehabilitation Act of 1973; affirmative action provisions of the Vietnam Era Veterans' Readjustment Assistance Act; Title VI of the Civil Rights Act of 1964; the Freedom of Information Act; and related matters.

(Area Code 202)

Associate Solicitor: James D. Henry 523-8286
Deputy Associate Solicitor: Joseph M. Woodward 523-8293

Counsel for: (Area Code 202)
Interpretations and Advice: Gary M. Buff 523-8000
Interpretations and Advice: Jean Davis 523-8000
Litigation: Richard Gilman 523-8000
Litigation: Diane Heim 523-8000
Senior Trial Attorney: Debra Millenson 523-8262

The **Employee Benefits Division** provides necessary legal services to the Department of Labor and the Employment Standards Administration (ESA) in connection with benefit claims and workers' compensation claims. The Division provides litigation services necessary to protect the interests of the Government in connection with the determination of claims under the Longshore and Harbor Worker's Compensation Act, Title IV of the Federal Coal Mine Safety and Health Act (as amended by the Blank Lung Benefits Reform Act of 1977 and the Black Lung Benefits Amendments of 1981), including representation of the Secretary of Labor and adjudication officers of the Department before the Benefits Review Board and in court, except the Supreme Court of the U.S. Additional responsibilities include providing legal services in connection with the Federal Employees' Compensation Act, Federal Tort Claims Act, Federal Military Personnel and Civilian Employees' Claims Act, and the Comprehensive Employment and Training Act (CETA).

(Area Code 202)
Associate Solicitor: Carol A. DeDeo 357-0460
Deputy Associate Solicitor:
Cornelius S. Donoghue, Jr 357-0405
Counsel for:
Claims: Jeffrey L. Nesvet 357-0405
Federal Employees Compensation Act:
Daniel T. Franklin 357-0405
Longshore: J. Michael O'Neill 357-0405

The **Employment and Training Legal Services Division** provides all legal services required by the Assistant Secretary for Employment and Training; provides certain specified legal services required by the Assistant Secretaries or Veterans' Employment and Training, and Administration and Management, including services under the Job Training Partnership Act, CETA, and other similar acts encompassing a variety of provisions furnishing employment and training, and economic stimulus programs for the unemployed, underemployed, and economically disadvantaged.

(Area Code 202)
Associate Solicitor: Charles D. Raymond 523-7754
Deputy Associate Solicitor: Jonathan H. Waxman 523-7758
Counsel for:
Litigation: Harry L. Scheinfeld 523-7836
Program Assistance: Bruce W. Alter 523-7857
Program Assistance: A. Robert Pfeffer 523-7857
Unemployment Compensation:
Herbert A. Kelley 523-7874

The **Fair Labor Standards Division** performs all legal services in connection with the responsibilities of the Wage and Hour Division of the Employment Standards Administration in matters concerning minimum and prevailing wage compensation, overtime compensation, child and farm labor, and wage garnishment, which are administered under the following statutes: Fair Labor Standards Act of 1938; Migrant and Seasonal Agricultural Workers Protection Act; Walsh-Healey Public Contracts Act; Service Contract Act of 1965; Davis-Bacon and related acts; Energy Reorganization Authority Act; Copeland Act; Contract Work Hours and Safety Standards Act; National Foundation on the Arts and Humanities Act of 1965; Title III of the Consumer Credit Protection Act; Social Services Amendments of 1974; and the Tax Reduction and Simplification Act of 1977.

(Area Code 202)
Associate Solicitor: Monica Gallagher 523-7570
Deputy Associate Solicitor: Gail V. Coleman 523-7577
Counsel for: (Area Code 202)
Appellate Litigation: William Stone 523-7584
Employment Standards: Linda Jan S. Pack 523-7579
Legal Advice: Gregory B. Taylor 523-7626
Trial Litigation: Douglas J. Davidson 523-7620
Trial Litigation: Edwin W. Tayler 523-7650

The **Labor-Management Laws Division** provides legal services for the Assistant Secretary for Labor-Management Standards (OLMS) under the Labor-Management Reporting and Disclosure Act of 1959, as amended, and Section 7120 of the Civil Service Reform Act (CSRA). The Division also provides legal services for the Deputy Under Secretary for Labor-Management Relations and Cooperative Programs under the employee protection provisions of the Urban Mass Transportation Act; the employee protection provisions of the Redwood National Park Expansion Act and Airline Deregulation Act; and other statutes. Attorneys in the Division also provide legal services for the Assistant Secretary for Veterans Employment and Training with respect to the protection of reemployment rights of veterans under the Military Selective Service Act and related statutes; and provide legal services with respect to international labor affairs.

(Area Code 202)
Associate Solicitor: John F. Depenbrock 523-8607
Deputy Associate Solicitor: Barton S. Widom 523-8609
Counsel for:
International Affairs/Opinions:
Dennis Paquette 523-8633
Susan Webman 523-8627
Litigation: Helene Boetticher 523-8534

The **Legislation and Legal Counsel Division** provides a wide range of legal services in direct support of legislative and litigation matters concerning the Department, and provides legal counsel as required on questions arising under the Freedom of Information Act, the Privacy Act, the Federal Advisory Committee Act, the Federal Reports Act, Administrative Procedure Act, and the Equal Access to Justice Act.

(Area Code 202)
Associate Solicitor: Seth D. Zinman 523-8201
Deputy Associate Solicitor: Robert A. Shapiro 523-8101
Counsel for:
Administrative Law: Peter Galvin 523-8088
Administrative Law: Miriam Miller 523-8188
Labor Relations: Sheila Cronan 523-8088
Legislative Reports: Richard H. Crone 523-8106
Special Legal Services: Charles S. Brown 523-8065

The **Mine Safety and Health Division** provides legal advisory and litigation services to the Mine Safety and Health Administration in connection with the development of mandatory occupational health and safety standards applicable to mining and mine construction activity, and in connection with enforcement and standards of the Federal Mine Safety and Health Act of 1977 (MSHA), and provides related legal support.

(Area Code 202)
Associate Solicitor: Edward P. Clair 235-1151
Deputy Associate Solicitor: Thomas A. Mascolino 235-1155
Counsel for:
Appellate Litigation: Dennis Clark 235-1165
Coal Standards and Legal Advice:
M. Catherine Spencer 235-1157
Metal/Nonmetallic Standards and Legal Advice:
Deborah K. Green 235-1161
Trial Litigation: Douglas White 235-1153

The **Occupational Safety and Health Division** provides legal services required by the Assistant Secretary for Occupational Safety and Health in connection with the development and enforcement of occupational safety and health standards and related legal activities.

DEPARTMENT OF LABOR

(Area Code 202)

Associate Solicitor: Cynthia L. Attwood 523-7723
Deputy Associate Solicitor: Donald Shalhoub 523-7727
Counsel for:
Appellate Litigation: Ann Rosenthal 523-7718
Appellate Litigation: Barbara Werthmann 523-6824
General Legal Advice: Robert Swain (Acting) .523-6811
Health Standards: Daniel H. Jacoby 523-7711
Safety Standards: George Henschel 523-6700
Trial & Regional Litigation: Daniel Mick ...523-6822

The **Plan Benefits Security Division** provides necessary legal services to the Secretary of Labor and the Assistant Secretary, Pension and Welfare Benefits Administration, in connection with the implementation and enforcement of the Employee Retirement Income Security Act of 1974 (ERISA).

(Area Code 202)

Associate Solicitor: Marc Machiz 523-8634
Deputy Associate Solicitor: Sherwin Kaplan 523-8634

(Area Code 202)

Counsel for:
Fiduciary Litigation: Sherwin Kaplan 523-8637
General Litigation: Risa Sandler 523-8624
Regulation: Shelby Hoover 523-9590
Senior Trial Attorney: Bruce Rinaldi 523-9127

The **Special Appellate and Supreme Court Litigation Division** plans, coordinates, and directs unusually complex or sensitive litigation on behalf of the Secretary of Labor that requires, in addition to normal professional resources, high-level, close supervision as well as sophisticated litigation support, including audit capabilities and computer assisted information management.

(Area Code 202)

Associate Solicitor: Allen H. Feldman 523-8237
Deputy Associate Solicitor: Steven J. Mandel 523-8235
Senior Appellate Attorney: Nathanial I. Spiller 523-8247

FIELD OFFICES

Region I (Boston)

Regional Solicitor: Albert H. Ross
Deputy Regional Solicitor: Paul McTague
Counsel (ESA)(LHCA): Frank McDermott
Counsel (OSHA/MSHA/ETA): Jerrold Solomon
U.S. Department of Labor, John F. Kennedy Federal Building, Government Center, Room 1803, Boston, MA 02203. Tel: 617/565-2500.

The Boston Office handles litigation arising in the New England states (CT, ME, MA, NH, RI, and VT). The major program areas litigated are Wage-Hour, ETA, and OSHA.

Region II (New York)

Regional Solicitor: Patricia Rodenhausen
Deputy Regional Solicitor: Dennis Kade
Counsel (OSHA): Stephen Dubnoff
Counsel (ESA): Theodore Gotsch
U.S. Department of Labor, 201 Varick Street, Room 707, New York, NY 10014. Tel: 212/337-2078.

The New York Office encompasses NY, NJ, PR, and the Virgin Islands. The major litigation areas include OSHA and Wage-Hour.

Region III (Philadelphia)

Regional Solicitor: Marshall Harris
Deputy Regional Solicitor: Kenneth Stein
Counsel (ESA): vacant
Counsel (OSHA): Matthew Rieder
Counsel (Black Lung/MSHA): Catherine Murphy

U.S. Department of Labor, 14480 Gateway Building, 3535 Market Street, Philadelphia, PA 19104. Tel: 215/596-5157.

The Philadelphia Office is the main office in Region III and has under its jurisdiction the Arlington Branch Office. Most litigation referred to the Philadelphia Office comes from MSHA, ETA, OSHA, and Black Lung. Cases originate in all five states in the region (PA, MD, DE, VA, WV, and the District of Columbia). However, Black Lung and MSHA cases originating in VA, WV and the District of Columbia are generally handled by the Arlington (VA) Branch Office.

Arlington Branch Office
Associate Regional Solicitor: James B. Leonard
U.S. Department of Labor, Ballston Tower #3, 4015 Wilson Boulevard, Room 516, Arlington, VA 22203. Tel: 703/235-3610.

Region IV (Atlanta)

Regional Solicitor: Bobbye Spears
Deputy Regional Solicitor: James Woodson
Counsel (ESA): Anthony Cuviello
Counsel (Black Lung/OSHA/MSHA): James L. Stine
U.S. Department of Labor, 1371 Peachtree Street, N.E., Room 339, Atlanta, GA 30367. Tel: 404/347-4811.

The Atlanta Office is the main office in Region IV and is responsible for litigation arising in Alabama, Florida, Georgia, Kentucky, Mississippi, North Carolina, South Carolina and Tennessee. This region also has three Branch Offices, in Birmingham, Nashville, and Ft. Lauderdale.

Birmingham Branch Office
Associate Regional Solicitor: George D. Palmer
U.S. Department of Labor, 2015 Second Avenue, North, Suite 201, Birmingham, AL 35203. Tel: 205/731-0280.

Nashville Branch Office
Associate Regional Solicitor: Carl W. Gerig
U.S. Department of Labor, 2002 Richard Jones Road, Suite B-201, Nashville, TN 37215. Tel: 615/736-5761.

Ft. Lauderdale Branch Office
Associate Regional Solicitor: Donald R. McCoy
U.S. Department of Labor, Federal Building, 299 East Broward Boulevard, Room 407-B, Ft. Lauderdale, FL 33301. Tel: 305/527-7363.

Region V (Chicago)

Regional Solicitor: John Secaras
Deputy Regional Solicitor: Richard Fiore
Counsel (OSHA/MSHA): Alan Bean
Counsel (ESA): William Posternack
U.S. Department of Labor, 230 South Dearborn Street, Eighth Floor, Chicago, IL 60604. Tel: 312/353-8885.

This office handles legal matters arising in Illinois, Indiana, Michigan, Minnesota, Ohio and Wisconsin. There is one Branch Office, in Cleveland.

Cleveland Branch Office
Associate Regional Solicitor: William S. Kloepfer
U.S. Department of Labor, Federal Office Building, Room 881 1240 East Ninth Street, Cleveland, OH 44199. Tel: 216/522-3881.

The Cleveland Branch Office handles OSHA, MSHA, Wage-Hour and Black Lung litigation coming from Ohio and eastern Michigan.

Region VI (Dallas)

Regional Solicitor: James E. White
Deputy Regional Solicitor: William E. Everheart
Counsel (ESA): Bobbie J. Gannaway
Counsel (OSHA/MSHA): Jack Ostrander
U.S. Department of Labor, 525 South Griffin Street, Suite 501, Dallas, TX 75202. Tel: 214/767-4902.

The Dallas Regional Office handles legal matters arising from investigations and/or complaints from Texas, Arkansas, Oklahoma, Louisiana, and New Mexico. The major program areas handled include OSHA, MSHA, Wage-Hour, and ETA.

Region VII (Kansas City)

Regional Solicitor: Tedrick Housh
Deputy Regional Solicitor and Counsel (ESA): Jaylynn Fortney
Counsel (OSHA/MSHA): Stephen Reynolds
U.S. Department of Labor, 911 Walnut Street, Room 2106, Kansas City, MO 64106. Tel: 816/426-6441.

The Kansas City Regional Office, which has jurisdiction over the Denver Branch Office, provides litigation support to Wage-Hour, MSHA, OSHA, and Black Lung programs in the states of MO, IA, NE, and KS.

Denver Branch Office
Associate Regional Solicitor: Henry Mahlman
U.S. Department of Labor, Federal Office Building, 1961 Stout Street, Room 1585, Denver, CO 80294. Tel: 303/844-5521.

The Denver Branch Office handles Wage-Hour, ETA, MSHA, and OSHA legal actions which arise in the states of CO, MT, WY, UT, SD and ND.

Region IX (San Francisco)

Regional Solicitor: Daniel Teehan
Deputy Regional Solicitor: Carol Fickenscher
Counsel (OSHA): Marshall Salzman
Counsel (FLSA): Norman Nayfach
U.S. Department of Labor, 71 Stevenson Street, 10th Floor, P.O. Box 3495, San Francisco, CA 94119-3495. Tel: 415/744-6675.

The San Francisco Regional Office has operational authority over both the Seattle and Los Angeles Branch Offices. This office handles Wage-Hour and MSHA cases for northern California, Hawaii, parts of Nevada and Arizona, Guam, and the Pacific Trust Territories. It also handles almost all CETA cases and most complex cases that occur in the Region. The San Francisco Regional Office serves as a pilot site for the ERISA decentralization project.

Los Angeles Branch Office
Associate Regional Solicitor: John C. Nangle
U.S. Department of Labor, Federal Bldg, Room 3247, 300 North Los Angeles Street, Los Angeles, CA 90012. Tel: 213/894-2681.

Seattle Branch Office
Associate Regional Solicitor: Robert A. Friel
U.S. Department of Labor, 8003 Federal Office Building, 909 First Avenue, Seattle, WA 98174. Tel: 206/442-0940.

OFFICE OF INSPECTOR GENERAL (Room S1303)

The Office of Inspector General conducts and supervises audits and criminal investigations relating to Labor Department operations; investigates areas vulnerable to labor racketeering, such as employee benefit funds, labor-management relations and internal union affairs; recommends policies to prevent and detect fraud, waste and abuse and increase economy, efficiency and effectiveness in Department programs and operations; and keeps the Secretary of Labor and Congress informed about programs and corrective actions needed in administering departmental operations. In addition, the Labor Department has the only Federal OIG engaged in a cooperative effort with the U.S. Department of Justice to control the influence of organized crime in labor-management relations.

(Area Code 202)
Inspector General: Raymond Maria (Acting) 523-7296
Deputy Inspector General: Raymond Maria 523-8545
Counsel for the Inspector General: Sylvia T. Horowitz ..523-4930

(Area Code 202)
Assistant Inspector General/ Labor Racketeering:
Gustave Schick 523-9909

OFFICE OF ADMINISTRATIVE LAW JUDGES (Suite 700)
1111 20th Street, N.W., Washington, D.C. 20036

Administrative Law Judges hear cases under more than 65 Federal statutes in labor-related fields encompassing civil rights, Government contracts and grants, employee protection, immigration, workers' compensation, welfare programs, wage and hour guarantees, disbarment, and debt collection. The Administrative Law Judges also organize into rotating panels to handle certain kinds of cases, at which time they may act as the Board of Contract Appeals or the Board of Alien Labor Certification Appeals. Judges conduct hearings across the country, in addition to the cities to which they are permanently assigned.

The Office of Administrative Law Judges has its own library which is open to the public Monday through Friday from 8:00 AM until 4:00 PM. The library primarily includes cases on the Black Lung disease, INA and WPCA. Free photocopying is available.

The decisions of the Administrative Law Judges can be found in the library mentioned above. They can also be obtained by subscription from the U.S. Government Printing Office. Stock number and price for annual subscription are shown below. Submit request to: The Superintendent of Documents, U.S. Government Printing Office, Washington, D.C. 20402. Tel: 202/783-3238.

Decisions of the Office of Administrative Law Judges and Office of Administrative Appeals. Published bimonthly. Price $28.00 a year domestic; $35.00 a year foreign. GPO Stock# 729-011-00000-2.

DEPARTMENT OF LABOR

(Area Code 202)

Chief Administrative Law Judge: Nahum Litt 653-5052
Deputy Chief Judge: John M. Vittone 653-5057
Associate Chief Administrative Law Judges:
G. Marvin Bober 653-5085
James L. Guill 653-5052

(Area Code 202)

Chief Clerk: Beverly Queen 653-5052
Docket Supervisor: Yvonne Washington 653-5052
Law Librarian: Rose Martin 653-8563

DISTRICT OFFICES

The Office of Administrative Law Judges has District Offices in eight cities. Their addresses are listed below.

Boston
District Chief Judge: Chester Shatz
Office of Administrative Law Judges, U.S. Department of Labor, John W. McCormack Post Office & Courthouse, Room 409 Post Office Square, Boston, MA 02109. Tel: 617/223-9355.

Camden
District Chief Judge: vacant
Office of Administrative Law Judges, U.S. Department of Labor, 2600 Mt. Ephraim Ave., Camden, NJ 08104. Tel: 609/757-5312.

Cincinnati
District Chief Judge: Charles Campbell
Office of Administrative Law Judges, U.S. Department of Labor, 525 Vine Street, Suite 900, Cincinnati, OH 45202. Tel: 513/684-3252.

Fort Lauderdale
District Chief Judge: Everette Thomas
Office of Administrative Law Judges, U.S. Department of Labor, Mercedes City Center, Suite 605, 200 South Andrews Ave., Fort Lauderdale, FL 33301. Tel: 305/524-5880.

Hampton
District Chief Judge: Theodor Von Brand
Office of Administrative Law Judges, U.S. Department of Labor, 55 West Queens Way, Suite 201, Hampton, VA 23669. Tel: 804/722-0571.

Metairie
District Chief Judge: Augustus Simpson
Office of Administrative Law Judges, U.S. Department of Labor, Heritage Plaza Bldg, 5th Floor, 111 Veteran's Memorial Blvd, Metairie, LA 70005. Tel: 504/598-4586.

Pittsburgh
District Chief Judge: Thomas Burke
Office of Administrative Law Judges, U.S. Department of Labor, 7 Parkway Center, 875 Greentree Rd., Room 290, Pittsburgh, PA 15220. Tel: 412/644-5754.

San Francisco
District Chief Judge: Edward Burch
Office of Administrative Law Judges, U.S. Department of Labor, 211 Main Street, Suite 600, San Francisco, CA 94105. Tel: 617/233-9355.

OFFICE OF ADMINISTRATIVE APPEALS (Room S4309)

200 Constitution Avenue, N.W., Washington, D.C. 20210

The Office of Administrative Appeals assists the Secretary, Deputy Secretary, and Assistant Secretary for Employment Standards in reviewing appeals from decisions of Administrative Law Judges under certain laws and programs. These appeals arise under the Service Contract Act, Job Training Partnership Act, Trade Act, Energy Reorganization Act, and several environmental laws, unemployment insurance conformity proceedings, and cases brought by the Office of Federal Contract Compliance Programs.
In addition to the Director and Deputy Director, there are some staff attorneys working in this office.

The decisions of the Office of Administrative Appeals can be found in the office at the address listed above. The office is open Monday through Friday from 9:00 AM until 5:30 PM, but you must call first for an appointment. The decisions are also published along with the decisions of the Administrative Law Judges by the U.S. Government Printing Office in Decisions of the Office of Administrative Law Judges and Office of Administrative Appeals. This publication is cited above in the section on the Administrative Law Judges.

(Area Code 202)

Director: M. Elizabeth Culbreth 523-9728

(Area Code 202)

Deputy Director: Gresham C. Smith 523-9728

BENEFITS REVIEW BOARD (Room 757)

1111 20th Street, N.W., Washington, D.C. 20036

The Benefits Review Board is a nine-member quasi-judicial body with exclusive jurisdiction to consider and decide appeals raising substantial questions of law or fact from decisions of Administrative Law Judges with respect to cases arising under the Longshoremen's and Harbor Workers' Compensation Act and its extensions, and the Black Lung Benefits Act of 1972.

The decisions of the Benefits Review Board are kept in a library on the fifth floor at the address above. The library is open Monday through Friday from 8:45 AM until 5:00 PM.

(Area Code 202)

Chief Administrative Appeals Judge: Roy P. Smith 653-5060
Administrative Appeals Judges:
James F. Brown 653-5060
Nancy S. Dolder 653-5060
Regina S. McGranery 653-5060
Betty R. Stage 653-5060
Chief Counsel: Robert Habermann 653-5060
Assistant Chief Counsel: Lisa Lahrman 653-5600
Clerk of the Board: Linda Meekins 653-5106

EMPLOYEES' COMPENSATION APPEALS BOARD (Suite 300)

300 Seventh Street, S.W., Washington, D.C. 20210

The Employees' Compensation Appeals Board is a quasi-judicial appellate body with exclusive jurisdiction to consider and decide appeals of Federal employees from final decisions of the Office of Workers' Compensation Programs (OWCP). The jurisdiction of the Board extends to questions of fact, as well as law, and to questions involving the exercise of discretion. Board review is limited to evidence in the case record upon which the OWCP rendered its decision; new or additional evidence may not be submitted to the Board. A decision of the Board is final as to the subject matter appealed, and is not subject to court review.

Hearings are held only in Washington, D.C. The hearing procedure is informal. As new or additional evidence may not be introduced, argument must be confined to the evidence in the case record or to the legal issues raised. There is no provision for introduction of testimony or interrogation of witnesses.

In each appeal reviewing the merits of a claim, the Board's decision includes a written opinion setting forth the salient facts, the conclusions, the law, and the reasoning upon which the Board based its action.

Decisions of the Board are comprehensive and constitute a valuable fund of precedent which serves to guide the OWCP in the adjudication of claims and is an important source of reference for injured employees, attorneys, and others concerned with problems of workmens' compensation.

The decisions of the Employees' Compensation Appeals Board (ECAB) can be seen in office cited above. The office is open Monday through Friday from 8:30 AM until 5:00 PM. You must call for an appointment. The decisions of the ECAB from October 1, 1986 through September 30, 1987 have been published and can be obtained from the U.S. Government Printing Office. Stock number and price are shown below. Submit request for this publication to: The Superintendent of Documents, U.S. Government Printing Office, Washington, D.C. 20402. Tel: 202/783-3238.

Digest and Decisions of ECAB, Vol. 38 covers October 1, 1986 through September 30, 1987 with index digest supplement. Price $37.00 domestic; $46.25 foreign. GPO Stock # 029-009-00033-3.

(Area Code 202)

Chairman: Michael J. Walsh 401-8600
Members:
David S. Gerson 401-8600
George E. Rivers 401-8600
Supervisory Attorney: vacant 401-8600
Clerk of the Board: Delores G. Anderson 401-8782

WAGE APPEALS BOARD (Room N6507)

200 Constitution Avenue, N.W., Washington, D.C. 20210

The Wage Appeals Board provides independent administrative review to parties adversely affected by final decisions of the Department of Labor's Administrative Law Judges rendered under the Davis-Bacon Act and related prevailing wage statutes, and subsequently by the Administrator of the Wage and Hour Division.

The decisions of the Wage Appeals Board can be found in the Department of Labor Law Library which is open to the public Monday through Friday from 8:15 AM until 4:45 PM. Tel: 202/523-6992. If you have difficulty in finding a decision, you can contact the Executive Secretary at the number listed below.

(Area Code 202)

Chairman: Jackson M. Andrews 523-9039
Members:
Stuart Rotherman 523-9039
vacant 523-9039
Executive Secretary/Senior Attorney:
Gerald F. Krizan 523-9039

PENSION AND WELFARE BENEFITS ADMINISTRATION (Room S2524)

200 Constitution Avenue, N.W., Washington, D.C. 20210

The Pension and Welfare Benefits Administration is responsible for formulating all current and future pension and welfare policy. conducting research and providing statistical information to the pension benefits community; issuing regulations and technical guidance regarding the Employee Requirement Income Security Act (ERISA) requirement; enforcing ERISA requirements; and assisting and educating the employee benefits community. The Office provides valuable assistance to plan administrators, corporations, and individuals who have problems or questions regarding the establishment and continued operation of pension programs.

DEPARTMENT OF LABOR

(Area Code 202)

Assistant Secretary: George Ball 523-8233
Public Affairs 523-8921

Office of Regulations and Interpretations
Director: Robert J. Doyle 523-7461
Coverage Division Chief: Helene A. Benson 523-8521
Fiduciary Interpretations and Regulations Division Chief: Bette Briggs 523-6958
Regulatory Coordination Division Chief: Rudolph F. Nuissel 523-7901

(Area Code 202)

Reporting and Disclosure Division Chief: Howard D. Hensley 523-8515

Office of Exemption Determinations
Director: Ivan L. Strasfeld 523-8671

Office of Enforcement
Director: Charles Lerner 523-8840

DATABASES AND PUBLICATIONS OF INTEREST

Databases:

Labor News is a 24 hour electronic bulletin board maintained by the Department of Labor containing the full text of each day's press releases. Speeches given by the Secretary of Labor are also included. A 30 day index of the preceding 30 days is available. Potential users can obtain further information on the bulletin board by contacting the Department of Labor, Office of Public Affairs, Tel: 202/523-7343.

Publications:

OFCCP Federal Contract Compliance Manual is in the process of being updated. It is an eight volume manual. Updated chapters 2-7 can be obtained free of charge by contacting the Office of Policy, Planning and Review Division, Office of Federal Contract Compliance Programs, U.S. Department of Labor, 200 Constitution Ave., N.W., Washington, D.C. 20210. Tel: 202/523-9434. Chapter 8 will be published shortly.

U.S. Department of Labor Highlights summarizes the major programs within each agency of the Department. Each agency is covered separately in a two page summary. A single copy is free and can be obtained by contacting the U.S. Department of Labor, Office of Public Affairs, Room S1032, 200 Constitution Ave., N.W., Washington, D.C. 20210. Tel: 202/523-7343.

Handy Reference Guide to the Fair Labor Standards Act 1987 is a publication for employees and employers covering Federal laws on minimum wage, overtime pay, child labor, and more. It is available from Consumer Information Center-P, P.O. Box 100, Pueblo, CO 81002. Price: 50 cents. Booklet number 401W.

A Working Woman's Guide to Her Job Rights 1988 is a comprehensive booklet covering freedom from discrimination and harassment, maternity leave, minimum wage, pension and retirement benefits, and more. Available from Consumer Information Center-P, P.O. Box 100, Pueblo, CO 81002. Price: $2.00. Booklet number 109W.

The following publications can be purchased from the **U.S. Government Printing Office.** Stock numbers and prices for annual subscriptions are shown below. Submit requests for these publications to: The Superintendent of Documents, U.S. Government Printing Office, Washington, D.C. 20402. Tel: 202/783-3238.

OSHA Standards and Regulations. Published in six volumes, each covering a different subject. Subscription service of each volume includes changes for an indeterminate period. Looseleaf for updating.

Volume I-General Industry Standards and Interpretations. Price: $98.00 domestic; $122.50 foreign. GPO Stock# 929-005-00000-7.

Volume II-Maritime Standards and Interpretations. Price: $29.00 domestic; $36.25 foreign. GPO Stock# 929-006-00000-3.

Volume III-Construction Industry Standards and Interpretations. Price: $29.00 domestic; $36.25 foreign. GPO Stock# 929-007-00000-0.

Volume IV-Other Regulations and Procedures. Price: $55.00 domestic; $68.75 foreign. GPO Stock# 929-008-00000-6.

Volume V-Field Operations Manual. Price: $54.00 domestic; $67.50 foreign. GPO Stock# 929-004-00000-1.

Volume VI-Industrial Hygiene Technical Manual. Price: $51.00 domestic; $63.75 foreign. GPO Stock# 929-009-00000-2.

Instructions for Filing Applications for Alien Employment Certification for Permanent Employment in the United States. Published in one volume. Price $2.25. GPO Stock# 029-014-01796-5.

DEPARTMENT OF LABOR
KEY LEGAL AUTHORITIES

Regulations:

General Departmental Regulations: 29 C.F.R. Part 0 et seq. (1989).
Rules of Practice & Procedure: 29 C.F.R. Parts 6-8, 18 (1989).
Wage Rate Determinations Under Various Statutes: 29 C.F.R. Part 1 (1989).
Department of Labor Acquisition Regulations: 48 C.F.R. Part 2901 et seq. (1989).

Uniform Guidelines on Employee Selection Procedures, 28 C.F.R. 50.14 (1989)--principles issued jointly by the Departments of Justice and Labor, the Equal Employment Opportunity Commission, and the Office of Personnel Management and designed to assist employers, labor organizations, employment agencies, and licensing and certification boards to comply with Federal equal employment opportunity laws.

Rehabilitation Act of 1973, as amended, 29 U.S.C. 793 et seq.--requires, in pertinent part, Government contractors to take affirmative action to employ and advance in employment qualified handicapped individuals. This applies to all Government contracts, including Federal deposit or share insurance, the furnishing of supplies or services, or for the use of personal property in excess of $2,500.

Legislative History: 1973 U.S. Code Cong. & Admin. News 2076; 1978 U.S. Code Cong. & Admin. News 7312; 1986 U.S. Code Cong. & Admin. News 3471.

Implementing Regulations: 41 C.F.R. Part 60 (1989).

Federal Employee's Compensation Act, as amended, 5 U.S.C. 8101 et seq.-- provides for the payment of worker's compensation benefits to civilian officers and employees of all branches of the U.S. Government. The Act provides for the payment of compensation for wage loss and for permanent impairment as a result of duties in service of the U.S. In addition, eligible employees are entitled to receive medical services at Government expense. The Act also provides monetary compensation to specified survivors of an employee.

Legislative History: 1967 U.S. Code Cong. & Admin. News 1538; 1974 U.S. Code Cong. & Admin. News 5341.

Implementing Regulations: 20 C.F.R. Part 10 (1989).

Black Lung Benefits and Reform Act of 1971, as amended, 30 U.S.C. 901 et seq.--provides for the review of pending and denied claims of benefits provided to coal miners on account of total disability or death due to pneumoconiosis (black lung); establishes the black lung disability trust fund for the payment of all claims predicated upon coal mine employment which terminated prior to January 1, 1970, and for other claims for which no operator liability can be established. The fund is financed by individual coal mine operators.

Legislative History: 1969 U.S. Code Cong. & Admin. News 2503; 1972 U.S. Code Cong. & Admin. News 2305; 1978 U.S. Code Cong. & Admin. News 237; 1981 U.S. Code Cong. & Admin. News 2671.

Implementing Regulations: 20 C.F.R. Part 727 (1989).

Longshoreman's and Harbor Worker's Compensation Act, as amended, 33 U.S.C. 901 et seq.--provides compensation for disability or death of an employee if the disability or death results from an injury occurring on the navigable waters of the United States. This includes any adjoining pier, wharf, dry dock, terminal, building way, or any other adjoining area used by an employee in loading, unloading, repairing, building, or dismantling a vessel.

Legislative History: 1984 U.S. Code Cong. & Admin. News 2734.

Implementing Regulations: 20 C.F.R. Part 702 (1989).

Fair Labor Standards Act of 1938, as amended, 29 U.S.C. 201 et seq.--establishes minimum wages and maximum hours for employees and directs the Department of Labor to administer and enforce these provisions; prohibits industries engaged in commerce or in the production of goods for commerce, from providing labor conditions detrimental to the maintenance of the minimum standard of living necessary for health, efficiency, and general well-being of workers.

Legislative History: 1974 U.S. Code Cong. & Admin. News 2811; 1985 U.S. Code Cong. & Admin. News 651.

Implementing Regulations: 29 C.F.R. Part 511 et seq. (1989).

Walsh-Healy Public Contracts Act of 1936, as amended, 41 U.S.C. 35 et seq.-- provides conditions for the purchase of supplies and the making of contracts by the United States. The Act fixes terms and conditions under which the government will permit goods to be sold to it.

Legislative History: 1979 U.S. Code Cong. & Admin. News 2471; 1985 U.S. Code Cong. & Admin. News 472.

Implementing Regulations: 41 C.F.R. Parts 50-206 (1989).

Migrant and Seasonal Agricultural Work Protection Act, as amended, 29 U.S.C. 1801 et seq.--requires farm labor contractors to register in an effort to remove the restraints on commerce caused by activities detrimental to migrant and seasonal agricultural workers, agricultural associations and agricultural employers.

Legislative History: 1982 U.S. Code Cong. & Admin. News 4547; 1986 U.S. Code Cong. & Admin. News 5649.

Implementing Regulations: 29 C.F.R. Part 500 (1989).

Labor-Management Reporting & Disclosure Act of 1959, as amended, 29 U.S.C. 401 et seq.--the generic union anti-corruption statute, including a bill of rights for union members; creates a cause of action on behalf of any person whose rights hereunder are infringed; establishes charter, administrative, financial, and reporting requirements for labor organizations, their officers and employees; sets forth union election procedures; and contains various prohibitions and penalties.

Legislative History: 1959 U.S. Code Cong. & Admin. News 2318.

Implementing Regulations: 29 C.F.R. Part 401 et seq. (1989).

Consumer Credit Protection Act of 1968, as amended, 15 U.S.C. 1671 et seq.--sets guidelines in regulating commerce and in the establishment of uniform bankruptcy laws. The Act prevents the unrestricted garnishment of compensation due for personal services as well as reducing the application of garnishment as a creditor's remedy when it hinders the production and flow of goods in interstate commerce.

Legislative History: 1968 U.S. Code Cong. & Admin. News 1962; 1977 U.S. Code Cong. & Admin. News 185.

Implementing Regulations: 29 C.F.R. Part 870 (1989)[restriction on garnishment].

Service Contract Act of 1965, as amended, 41 U.S.C. 351 et seq.--provides labor standards for the protection of employees of contractors and subcontractors furnishing services to or performing maintenance services for Federal agencies.

Legislative History: 1965 U.S. Code Cong. & Admin. News 3737; 1972 U.S. Code Cong. & Admin. News 3534.

Implementing Regulations: 29 C.F.R. Part 4 (1989).

Davis-Bacon Act of 1931, as amended, 40 U.S.C. 296(a) et seq., requires that every contract in excess of 2,000 dollars to which the U.S. is a party, for construction, alteration and/or the repair of public buildings or public works which requires or involves the employment of mechanics or laborers shall contain a provision stating the minimum wages.

Legislative History: 1960 U.S. Code Cong. & Admin. News 2693; 1964 U.S. Code Cong. & Admin. News 2335.

Implementing Regulations: 29 C.F.R. Part 5 (1989).

Wagner-Peyser Act of 1933, as amended, 29 U.S.C. 49 et seq.--established the United States Employment Service to promote and develop a national system of public job service offices.

Legislative History: 1976 U.S. Code Cong. & Admin. News 5997; 1981 U.S. Code Cong. & Admin. News 396.

Implementing Regulations: 20 C.F.R. Part 652 (1989).

Job Training Partnership Act of 1982, as amended, 29 U.S.C. 1501 et seq.--establishes programs to prepare youth and unskilled adults for entry into the labor force and to afford job training to those economically disadvantaged individuals who are in need of training to obtain productive employment.

Legislative History: 1982 U.S. Code Cong. & Admin. News 2636; 1988 U.S. Code Cong. & Admin. News 1547 & 4395.

Implementing Regulations: 20 C.F.R. Part 636 (1989).

Job Corps Program, 15 U.S.C. 1691 et seq.--established for economically disadvantaged young men and women; operates exclusively as a distinct national program; sets standards and procedures for selecting individuals as enrollees; and authorizes establishment of residential and nonresidential centers for programs of education, vocational education and work experience.

Legislative History: 1982 U.S. Code Cong. & Admin. News 2636.

Implementing Regulations: 20 C.F.R. Part 684 (1989).

Dislocated Workers Program, 29 U.S.C. 1651 et seq.--provides funds for training, retraining, job search, placement, and relocation assistance to individuals affected by mass layoffs, natural disasters, Federal Government actions, or who reside in areas of high unemployment.

Legislative History: 1982 U.S. Code Cong. & Admin. News 2636; 1988 U.S. Code Cong. & Admin. News 1547.

Implementing Regulations: 20 C.F.R. Part 631 (1989).

Trade Act of 1974, as amended, 19 U.S.C. 2271 et seq.--created the Trade Adjustment Assistance program (TAA) to assist individuals who became unemployed as a result of increased imports; and also provide reemployment services and allowances for eligible individuals.

Legislative History: 1974 U.S. Code Cong. & Admin. News 7186; 1981 U.S. Code Cong. & Admin. News 396; 1986 U.S. Code Cong. & Admin. News 42.

Implementing Regulations: 20 C.F.R. Part 617 (1989).

Mine Safety and Health Act of 1977, as amended, 30 U.S.C. 801 et seq.--authorizes the Mine Safety & Health Administration to investigate, obtain and utilize information relating to accidents, injuries and illnesses occurring in mines.

Legislative History: 1969 U.S. Code Cong. & Admin. News 2503; 1977 U.S. Code Cong. & Admin. News 3401.

Implementing Regulations: 30 C.F.R. Parts 50 & 100 (1989).

Title I, Employee Retirement Income Security Act of 1974, as amended, 29 U.S.C. 1001 et seq.--protects the interests of participants in employee benefit plans and their beneficiaries by requiring the disclosure and reporting to participants and their beneficiaries of financial and other information.

Legislative History: 1974 U.S. Code Cong. & Admin. News 4639.

Implementing Regulations: 29 C.F.R. Part 2509 et seq. (1989).

Vietnam Era Readjustment Assistance Act of 1974, as amended, 38 U.S.C. 2012 et seq.--requires Government contractors to take affirmative action to employ and advance in employment qualified disabled veterans and Vietnam-era veterans. This applies to all Government contracts, including Federal deposit or share insurance, for the furnishing of supplies, services or for the use of personal property in the amount of $10,000 or more.

Legislative History: 1974 U.S. Code Cong. & Admin. News 6313; 1980 U.S. Code Cong. & Admin. News 4555; 1982 U.S. Code Cong. & Admin. News 2877.

Implementing Regulations: 41 C.F.R. 60-250 et seq. (1989).

Occupational Safety and Health Act of 1970, as amended, 29 U.S.C. 651 et seq.--outlines provisions to assure safe and healthful working conditions for employees.

Legislative History: 1970 U.S. Code Cong. & Admin. News 5177.

Implementing Regulations: 29 C.F.R. Part 1960 (1989).

Construction Safety Act of 1969, as amended, 40 U.S.C. 333 et seq.--requires that every contract which is entered into for construction, alteration and\or repair by a contractor or subcontractor will not require any laborer or mechanic employed in the performance of the contract to work in surroundings or under working conditions which are unsanitary, hazardous,or dangerous to his health or safety.

Implementing Regulations: 29 C.F.R. Part 1926 (1989).

Legislative History: 1969 U.S. Code Cong. & Admin. News 1071.

Exec. Order 11246, 3 C.F.R., 1954-1958 Comp., p. 202, "Federal Contract Compliance Program"--sets forth guidelines for the promotion and ensuring of equal opportunities for all persons employed or seeking employment with Government contractors or with contractors performing under Federally assisted construction contracts, without regard to race, color, religion, national origin or on the basis of sex.

Implementing Regulations: 41 C.F.R. Part 60-20 et seq. (1989).

DEPARTMENT OF STATE

2201 C Street, N.W.
Washington, D.C. 20520

DESCRIPTION: The Department of State assists the President in conducting the foreign relations of the United States. The Secretary of State advises the President on general foreign relations matters and the conduct of relations with foreign countries; politico-military affairs, including mutual defense, strategic policy, and arms control; international commercial and economic affairs, encompassing trade, investment, monetary affairs, and foreign aid; and intelligence matters involving the collection and analysis of information bearing on the conduct of foreign relations. The Department is the agency primarily responsible for planning and implementing foreign policy, is chiefly responsible for U.S. representation abroad, and is also involved in the promotion and administration of informational, educational, and cultural exchange programs.

The State Department carries out its responsibilities through five geographic bureaus (African Affairs; European and Canadian Affairs; East Asian and Pacific Affairs; Inter-American Affairs; and Near Eastern and South Asian Affairs) and 14 functional area bureaus (Economic and Business Affairs, Consular Affairs, Public Affairs, International Narcotic Matters, International Organization Affairs, Human Rights and Humanitarian Affairs, Intelligence and Research, International Communications and Information Policy, Politico-Military Affairs, Oceans and International Environmental and Scientific Affairs, Refugee Programs, Diplomatic Security, Administration and Information Resources Management, Personnel).

(Area Code 202)

Secretary: James A. Baker 647-4910
Procurement Information ....(703) 875-6000
Small and Disadvantaged Business Utilization ....(703) 875-6823
Public Affairs/Public Liaison/Public Information 647-6575
Publishing Services 647-1632
Inspector General's Hot Line 647-3320
Passport Information 647-0518
U.S. Visa Information 647-0510
Overseas Citizens Emergency Center
General Information...................................647-5225
Facsimile 647-7120

Freedom of Information Act/Privacy Act Office 647-8484
Only written requests are accepted. Requestors are divided into four groups: Commercial, Educational, News Media, and All Other. Commercial requestors are charged a search fee based on the salary of the person doing the search, and a copying fee of 25 cents per page. Educational requestors and news media are not charged a copying fee for the first 100 pages, and if the total search fee is under $10.00, all charges are waived. This is also the case for commercial requestors. The fourth group ("all other") are not charged for the first 100 pages of material copied and the first two hours of search time. There is no charge for Privacy Act requests.

(Area Code 202)

Library (Room 3239)....................................647-2458
The library is not open to the public, except by special permission when the information is not available in any other library. Materials will be loaned to government and non-profit agencies through the Interlibrary Loan Program. A small amount of material may be photocopied for other groups if time permits. The library will respond to telephone inquiries.

Law Library (Room 6422) 647-4130
The law library is not open to the public except by special permission. They will loan out materials through the Interlibrary Loan Program, and will also respond to telephone inquiries.

OFFICE OF THE LEGAL ADVISER (Room 6423)

The Office of the Legal Adviser furnishes legal advice on all legal problems, domestic and international, arising in the course of the Department's work. The Office is involved in the many phases of formulating and implementing the foreign policy of the U.S., and in promoting the development of international law and institutions as a fundamental element of that policy.

Attorneys in the Office handle a wide range of responsibilities. While some of these functions are similar to those performed by legal offices of other Government agencies, a large part of the Office's practice consists of unique questions of public and private international law arising only in the conduct of foreign affairs.

The principal function of an attorney in the Office is to provide legal advice and services to policy officers of the Department. Specific responsibilities include the drafting, negotiation, and interpretation of international agreements, domestic statutes, Departmental regulations, Executive Orders, and other legal documents, and the provision of advice on questions of international and domestic law.

Members of the Office represent or assist in representing the U.S. in meetings of numerous international organizations, such as the U.N. General Assembly, the Organization of American States, the Organization for Economic Cooperation and Development, the Law of the Sea Conferences, the U.N. Conference on Trade and Development, the U.N. Environmental Program, and the International Civil Aviation Organization.

The Office also participates in international negotiations involving a wide range of matters, such as Middle East peace initiatives, arms control discussions, development of multilateral codes of conduct for multinational enterprises, transfer of technology, continental shelf boundary demarcations, international commodity agreements, bilateral air transportation and shipping agreements, economic cooperation agreements, consular conventions, and private law conventions on subjects like judicial cooperation and recognition of foreign judgments.

The Office assists the Department of Justice in preparing for litigation involving the Department's interest in both Federal and state courts. Recent cases have involved the act of state doctrine, implementation of the Iran hostages and claims settlement agreements, publication of CIA information, alleged improper business payments abroad, and the executive treaty power. The Office also works with state prosecutors and the Department of Justice in extraditing fugitives from foreign countries.

An additional responsibility of the Office is to represent the U.S. before international tribunals (such as the International Court of Justice) and in international arbitrations. Further, the Office is constantly engaged in efforts aimed at contributing to the development of international law and institutions, such as research efforts aimed at exploring international legal approaches to problems like international terrorism.

Finally, the Office participates in EEO cases and grievance procedures under the Department's labor management relations programs, and is involved in the processing and litigation of the Freedom of Information Act and Privacy Act cases.

The Office currently has approximately 100 attorneys and is headed by the Legal Adviser, who reports directly to the Secretary of State. The organization of the Office corresponds closely to the Department's overall bureau structure, with regional or geographic offices (i.e., those which focus on defined areas of the world) and various functional offices which deal with specific subject matters such as economics and business, international environmental and scientific issues, or internal management.

There are four Deputy Legal Advisers immediately below the Legal Adviser. They collectively supervise the Office's nineteen Assistant Legal Advisers who manage the individual regional and functional offices.

(Area Code 202)

Legal Adviser: Edwin Williamson (Designate) 647-9598
Principal Deputy Legal Adviser:
Michael J. Matheson (Acting) 647-8460
Digest of U.S. Practice in International Law Editor:
Marian L. Nash 653-9850
Board of Appellate Review Chairman: Alan G. James 653-5089
Counselor on International Law: Robert E. Dalton 647-8460
Facsimile 647-1037

Deputy Legal Advisers:
Michael J. Matheson 647-8460
Alan J. Kreczko 647-5036
Michael K. Young 647-7990
(vacant) 647-7942

Regional Offices:

- *Office of African Affairs
- *Office of East Asian and Pacific Affairs
- *Office of European and Canadian Affairs
- *Office of Inter-American Affairs
- *Office of Near Eastern and South Asian Affairs

There are five Assistant Legal Advisers who provide legal advice and services to the corresponding regional bureaus of the Department. Each regional bureau oversees the U.S. embassies and posts and coordinates U.S. foreign relations in its particular area. Typically, attorneys assigned to support those bureaus are involved with such matters as protection of U.S. citizens and investments, problems in diplomatic and consular relations, interpretation and negotiation of treaties, military base rights and status of force issues, peaceful settlement of disputes, and trade matters. The following highlight some of the issues dealt with by attorneys in these Regional Offices:

The **Office of African Affairs:** South Africa arms embargo, apartheid, repressive laws and measures; decolonization and armed conflict; border questions; military facility and space tracking agreements; U.S. cooperation in developing African legal institutions; and recognition of new states and governments.

(Area Code 202)

Assistant Legal Adviser: John R. Byerly 647-4110

The **Office of East Asian and Pacific Affairs:** U.S. commitments in East Asia and the Pacific; U.S. military presence in Australia, Japan, Korea, and the Philippines; relations with the People's Republic of China and commercial, cultural, and other non-governmental relations with Taiwan; and U.S. policy toward Cambodia and Vietnam.

(Area Code 202)

Assistant Legal Adviser: Mary McLeod 647-8900

The **Office of European and Canadian Affairs:** The NATO Alliance; defense cooperation and military base agreements with Greece, Iceland, Portugal, Spain, and Turkey; the European Economic Community; East-West trade and economic cooperation; U.S. rights and responsibilities regarding Berlin; the development and interpretation of agreements with the Soviet Union; U.S./Canada boundary issues; and human rights issues in Eastern Europe.

(Area Code 202)

Assistant Legal Adviser: T. Michael Peay 647-3044

The **Office of Inter-American Affairs:** Relations with governments of South America, Central America, and the Caribbean; the Organization of American States; implementation of the Panama Canal treaties; Cuba, including assets control, U.S. rights at Guantanamo, radio broadcasting issues, illegal migration, and refugee issues; Central American peace efforts; and Mexico, in particular water apportionment, boundary issues, and the practice of the International Boundary and Water Commission.

(Area Code 202)

Assistant Legal Adviser: David A. Colson 647-6328

The **Office of Near Eastern and South Asian Affairs:** Problems relating to peace in the Middle East and Afghanistan; relations with and between Iraq and Iran; peacekeeping forces; international terrorism; special legal problems frequently encountered by U.S. firms seeking to do business in or with countries of the region, including investment, boycott, and illicit payment problems; and restrictions on assistance to or conducting business with certain countries in the region.

(Area Code 202)

Assistant Legal Adviser: Jonathan B. Schwartz 647-9500

Functional Offices:

- *Office of Buildings and Acquisitions
- *Office of Consular Affairs
- *Office of Economics, Business and Communications Affairs
- *Office of Education, Cultural, and Public Affairs
- *Office of Ethics and Personnel
- *Office of Human Rights and Refugees
- *Office of International Claims and Investment Disputes
- *Office of Law Enforcement and Intelligence
- *Office of Management
- *Office of Oceans, International Environmental and Scientific Affairs
- *Office of Nuclear Affairs
- *Office of Politico-Military Affairs
- *Office of Private International Law
- *Office of Treaty Affairs
- *Office of United Nations Affairs

The Office of the Legal Adviser also supports the various functional bureaus of the Department which have crosscutting worldwide responsibilities for specific program areas:

The **Office of Buildings and Acquisitions:** Provides legal advice and assistance to the Office of Foreign Buildings and to the Department's Acquisition Division regarding legal issues associated with foreign buildings and issues associated with the acquisitions process.

(Area Code 202)
Assistant Legal Adviser: Dennis Gallagher (Acting) ...875-7020

The **Office of Consular Affairs:** Deals with issues relating to the performance of consular functions; the protection of U.S. nationals and their property abroad; rights of consular officers when acting in performance of their duties; entitlement to visas and passports; loss or acquisition of U.S. nationality; prisoner transfer agreements; privileges and immunities of diplomatic and consular officers; laws and international conventions; and the enforcement and administration of immigration law.

(Area Code 202)
Assistant Legal Adviser: James G. Hergen 647-4415

The **Office of Economics, Business, and Communications Affairs:** Assists in formulating Administration positions on international trade, energy, aviation, telecommunications, monetary affairs, shipping, and investment. This includes such matters as debt rescheduling; foreign assets and export control matters; international taxation; analysis and drafting of shipping legislation; land transport issues; codes of conduct relating to international corporations; and expropriation policy and investment disputes.

(Area Code 202)
Assistant Legal Adviser: Ted A. Borek 647-5242

The Office of Education, Cultural and Public Affairs: Deals with international cultural exchange agreements; protection of cultural property; anti-lobbying and anti-propaganda standards; copyright problems; and certain residual cultural problems resulting from World War II. It also provides legal advice and services to the Bureau of Public Affairs.

(Area Code 202)
Assistant Legal Adviser: Ely Maurer 653-9848

The **Office of Ethics and Personnel:** Provides advice on the Ethics in Government Act of 1978, the Hatch Act, and other applicable laws, Executive Orders, and regulations; provides legal advice and services to the Director General of the Foreign Service, the Director of Personnel, and others involved in human resources and labor relations matters; and directs the financial disclosure reporting program.

(Area Code 202)
Assistant Legal Adviser: Dennis Foreman 647-4446

The **Office of Human Rights and Refugees:** Provides legal support to the Bureau of Refugee Programs and the Bureau of Human Rights and Humanitarian Affairs. It deals with international implementation of human rights principles and guarantees, such as those in the U.N.Charter, the Universal Declaration of Human Rights, customary international law, and other relevant treaties; problems concerning legislation on military and economic assistance; assistance from international financial institutions for states consistently violating human rights; cases and proposals involving torture, genocide, apartheid, arbitrary detention, freedom of movement, assembly, speech, and other human rights problems.

(Area Code 202)
Assistant Legal Adviser: David P. Stewart 647-9328

The **Office of International Claims and Investment Disputes:** Deals with the legal aspects of international claims and investment disputes brought by foreign nationals and governments against the U.S. Government. This primarily involves claims, both governmental and nongovernmental, before the Iran/U.S. Claims Tribunal in The Hague which include some 5,000 claims worth billions of dollars. In addition, this office resolves various tort claims and other special claims such as those brought under the Fishermen's Protective Act.

(Area Code 202)
Assistant Legal Adviser: Ronald J. Bettauer 632-7810

The **Office of Law Enforcement and Intelligence:** Coordinates international extradition and promotes mutual legal assistance in criminal and other law enforcement matters; negotiates treaties; manages the international extradition caseload; coordinates U.S. and foreign criminal proceedings with foreign policy implications; assists U.S. Federal and state law enforcement agencies with investigations in foreign countries; advises on proposed legislative initiatives and international agreements on anti-terrorism, narcotics matters, and other law enforcement issues; coordinates the legal/foreign aspects of illicit payments by U.S. firms; and advises on U.S. intelligence activities.

(Area Code 202)
Assistant Legal Adviser: Andre Surena 647-5111

The **Office of Management:** Deals with a wide variety of internal management issues relating to the operation of the Department and its posts abroad, including Government contracts; real property management; foreign building construction, sale, and leasing; legislation affecting the management and operations of the Department; taxation and zoning involving real property of foreign governments in the U.S. and U.S. overseas school programs; foreign litigation; administrative law and Department rulemaking; diplomatic law; domestic litigation; the Privacy Act; and the Public Affairs Appeals Panel on Freedom of Information Act.

(Area Code 202)
Assistant Legal Adviser: Dennis Gallagher 647-2350

The **Office of Oceans, International Environmental and Scientific Affairs:** Deals with matters relating to the Law of the Sea; the continental shelf; the exclusive economic zone; the territorial sea; high seas; international straits; marine and transfrontier pollution; fisheries; marine scientific research; ocean dumping; international navigation rights and freedoms; negotiation of fisheries agreements; law enforcement at sea, which encompasses drug interdiction, refugee matters, piracy, and mutinies; environmental problems; wildlife; marine mammals; maritime boundaries; matters dealing with scientific cooperation in Antarctica and the Arctic; and the peaceful use of science and technology.

(Area Code 202)
Assistant Legal Adviser: Joan E. Donoghue 647-1370

The **Office of Nuclear Affairs:** Deals with non-proliferation and peaceful nuclear cooperation, including interpretation and implementation of the Atomic Energy Act, other relevant U.S. legislation, the International Atomic Energy Agency statute, the Nuclear Non-Proliferation Treaty, peaceful nuclear cooperation agreements, safeguard agreements and other international instruments; nuclear export issues; and participation in international conferences.

(Area Code 202)
Assistant Legal Adviser: (vacant) 647-1043

The Office of Politico-Military Affairs: Handles matters relating to security assistance/arms export control legislation; questions on global military policy and operations; negotiation and implementation of bases and status of forces agreements; military use of nuclear energy; military aerospace matters; state aircraft and public vessels; defense policy planning; arms control and disarmament problems; war powers legislation; and law of war and conventional weapons restrictions agreements and negotiations.

(Area Code 202)

Assistant Legal Adviser: Edward R. Cummings 647-7838

The **Office of Private International Law:** Deals with the development and implementation of treaties and other international efforts to unify and harmonize private law, including U.S. participation in multilateral organizations and bilateral negotiations; and coordinates the Secretary of State's Advisory Committee on Private International Law and its specialized study groups which focus on such matters as international business transactions, arbitration, trusts, international child abduction, international negotiable instruments, and the liability of operators of transport terminals.

(Area Code 202)

Assistant Legal Adviser: Peter H. Pfund 653-9851

The **Office of Treaty Affairs:** Handles treaty law and procedures, including drafting, negotiating, applying, interpreting, and publishing treaties and other international agreements of the U.S.; and constitutional questions including the relative powers of the President and the Congress regarding treaties and Executive Agreements.

(Area Code 202)

Assistant Legal Adviser: John R. Crook 647-2044

The **Office of United Nations Affairs:** Deals with U.S. participation in the United Nations, its specialized agencies, and other international organizations; space law; relationships between governments and the mass media; human rights; draft conventions concerning terrorism; the taking of hostages; U.N. consideration of specific situations; international peacekeeping; the rights of women; peaceful settlement of international disputes; matters concerning the International Court of Justice; and problems arising out of the presence of the U.N. and other international organizations in the U.S.

(Area Code 202)

Assistant Legal Adviser: Bruce C. Rashkow 647-6771

OFFICE OF THE INSPECTOR GENERAL (Room 6817)

The State Department Office of Inspector General (OIG) is dedicated to improving operations, stimulating positive change, and detecting an preventing waste, fraud, abuse, and mismanagement. The OIG's independent role and general responsibilities are established by the 1978 Inspector General Act, as amended, and in the Foreign Service Act of 1980. The Inspector General has reporting responsibilities to both the Secretary of State and the Congress.

The OIG evaluates State Department performance, makes recommendations for improvements, and follows up to ensure compliance with law, regulations, and effective, efficient operations. In particular the OIG:

* Reviews State Department programs and operations to assess their effectiveness and use of resources;
* Recommends policy, operational, or procedural changes to correct deficiencies;
* Identifies savings through greater efficiency, alternative use of resources, and recommended collection actions; and
* Investigates and recommends judicial and management action to correct waste, fraud, abuse, or mismanagement.

(Area Code 202)

Inspector General: Sherman M. Funk 647-9450
Counsel to the Inspector General: John D. Duncan 647-5059

Attorney Advisors: (Area Code 202)
Mark Bialek 647-5059
Linda Topping 647-5059

BUREAU OF CONSULAR AFFAIRS (ROOM 300)

(Area Code 202)

Office of Citizenship Appeals and Legal Assistance
Director: William B. Wharton 326-6172

(Area Code 202)

Deputy Director: Sharon Palmer-Royston 326-6175

BUREAU FOR REFUGEE PROGRAMS (ROOM 5824)

(Area Code 202)

Director: Princeton N. Lyman 647-7360
Deputy Assistant Secretary for International Refugee Assistance: Sarah E. Moten 663-1034

(Area Code 202)

Deputy Assistant Secretary for Refugee Admissions:
Priscilla A. Clapp 647-5767
Facsimile 647-8162

COMMISSIONS

International Boundary and Water Commission, U.S. and Mexico (The Commons, 4171 N. Mesa Street, Bldg C, Ste 310, El Paso, TX 79902)

U.S. Commissioner: Narendra N. Gunaji ....(915) 534-6677
D.C. Liaison: Paul E. Storing ....(202) 647-8162

International Boundary Commission, U.S. and Canada (425 Eye Street, N.W., Ste 150, Washington, D.C. 20001-2599)

U.S. Commissioner: David Fischer ....(202) 632-8058

International Joint Commission, U.S. and Canada (2001 S Street, N.W., Room 208, Washington, D.C. 20440)

Chairman: Gordon K. Durnil ....(202) 673-6222

PUBLICATIONS OF INTEREST

International Parental Child Abduction. Available free from U.S. Department of State, ATTN: Consuelo Pachon, Office of Citizen's Consular Services, Room 4817, Washington, D.C. 20520-4818. Tel: 202/647-3666. Publication #9794.

The following gists are available for free from the **Bureau of Public Affairs**, Room 6805, U.S. Department of State, Washington, D.C. 20520-6810. Gists are two-page summaries of foreign policy issues, including a concise background review on current facts and history and a brief summary of U.S. policy.

GATT and Multilateral Trade Negotiations. June 1989.
Generalized System of Preferences. June 1989.
Trade Protection. June 1989.
US Trade Policy. June 1989.
US Export Controls and China. November 1989.
US Exports: Foreign Policy Controls. April 1989.

The following publications are available for free from the **Bureau of Public Affairs**, Room 6805, U.S. Department of State, Washington, D.C. 20520-6810.

US - Canada Free Trade Agreement. July 1989, Public Information Series, 23 pages.

Twenty-seventh Semiannual Report--Implementation of Helsinki Final Act, April 1, 1989 - September 30, 1989. February 1989. Special Report No. 183, 58 pages.

The following publications can be purchased from the **U.S. Government Printing Office.** Stock numbers and prices for annual subscriptions are shown below. Submit requests for these publications to: The Superintendent of Documents, U.S. Government Printing Office, Washington, D.C. 20402. Tel: 202/783-3238.

Digest of U.S. Practice in International Law and Digest of International Law. 1990. This document contains a bibliography of Government publications on international law. Free. GPO Stock# 021-185-00006-0.

Treaties and Other International Acts Series. Published irregularly. Contains the texts of agreements entered into by the U.S. with other nations. Price: $89.00 domestic; $111.25 foreign. GPO Stock# 844-001-00000-2.

United States Treaties and Other International Agreements. Contains the full text of U.S. treaties and agreements. Through Volume 35, the treaties and agreements have been prepared for publication in chronological order. Beginning with Volume 36, the most frequently requested treaties and agreements will be given priority for publication. The volumes are priced individually. The most recently published volumes are:

Volume 34, Part 3, 1982. Price: $48.00 domestic; $60.00 foreign. GPO Stock# 044-000-02214-1.

Volume 34, Part 4. 1982. No price available. GPO Stock# 044-000-02215-0.

Foreign Relations Series. The Foreign Relations Series presents the documentary record of U.S. foreign policy. The series is prepared by a staff of professional historians in the Office of the Historian, Department of State. The principles that guide the selection of documents and the editing of the series are set forth in the prefaces of the volumes. Although based largely upon Department of State records, volumes also include significant Presidential and White House documents, as well as important records of other agencies and foreign governments.. Nearly all the material printed was originally classified. The volumes are priced individually.

For example, the most recent volume is Foreign Relations of the United States, 1955-1957, Volume XVI, Suez Crisis, July 26-December 31, 1956. This volume represents the comprehensive official historical documentary record of U.S. diplomacy in the events surrounding the Suez crisis. Its 1,344 pages were gathered from the White House, the Department of State, the Dwight D. Eisenhower Presidential Library, and other government agencies. Nearly all the documents selected were declassified for this publication. Price: $41.00 domestic; $51.25 foreign. GPO Stock# 044-000-02251-6.

American Foreign Policy Series. The annual volume of the American Foreign Policy Series contains official statements that set forth the goals and objectives of U.S. foreign policy. The series includes texts of major official messages, addresses, statements, interviews, press conferences and briefings, reports, congressional testimony and communications by the White House, the Department of State, and other Federal agencies or officials involved in the foreign policy process. Each volume is divided into geographic and topical chapters, and then chronologically within chapters. Editorial annotations, maps, lists of names and abbreviations, and a comprehensive index by document numbers are also included.

Each volume is compiled by the professional staff in the Office of the Historian and is intended to make available in the year following the events "the best contemporary collection of public expressions of U.S. foreign policy by U.S. Government officials." Each volume is individually priced. A typical volume is American Foreign Policy: Current Documents, 1988. Price $31.00 domestic; $38.75 foreign. GPO Stock# 044-000-02256-7.

Key Officers of Foreign Service Posts: Guide for Business Representatives. Published three times a year. Lists key officers at Foreign Service posts: the Chiefs and Deputy Chiefs of Missions; the senior officers of the political, economic, commercial, and consular sections of the post; and the agricultural attache. It also lists all embassies, legations, and consulates general. Annual subscription price: $5.00 domestic; $6.25 foreign. Single copy price: $1.75 domestic; $2.19 foreign. GPO Stock# 744-006-00000-7.

Foreign Consular Offices in the United States. Contains a complete and official listing of the foreign consular offices in the United States, together with their jurisdictions and recognized consular officers. Price: $4.00 domestic; $5.00 foreign. GPO Stock# 044-000-02283-4.

Diplomatic List. This is a quarterly list of foreign diplomatic representatives in Washington, D.C., and their addresses. Annual subscription price: $7.50 domestic; $9.38 foreign. GPO Stock# 744-004-00000-4.

Standardized Regulations (Government Civilians, Foreign Areas). Published 13 times a year. Presents information on standardized regulations pertaining to civilian employees working in foreign areas. Also announces changes and updates to current regulations as well as new regulations. Price: $36.00 a year domestic; $45.00 a year foreign. GPO Stock# 744-009-00000-6.

Guide to Doing Business with the Department of State. May 1990. Price: $1.75 domestic; $2.19 foreign. GPO Stock# 044-000-02287-7.

DEPARTMENT OF STATE
KEY LEGAL AUTHORITIES

General Regulations:

General Departmental Regulations: 22 C.F.R. Part 1 et seq. (1989).
Department of State Acquisition Regulations: 48 C.F.R. Part 601 et seq. (1989).
Rules of Practice & Procedure: 22 C.F.R. Part 7 (1989).
Fee Schedule for Consular Services: 22 C.F.R. Part 22 (1989).

Immigration and Nationality Act of 1952, as amended, 8 U.S.C. 1104 et seq.--outlines the powers, duties, and functions of diplomatic and consular officers relating to the granting or refusal of visas to classified nonimmigrants and classified immigrants and of passports to U.S. nationals.
Legislative History: 1977 U.S. Code Cong. & Admin. News 1625.
Implementing Regulations: 22 C.F.R. Parts 40 et seq. (1989).

Foreign Relations Authorization Act of 1978, as amended, 22 U.S.C. 211a et seq.--outlines the procedures for the granting and issuing of passports by diplomatic representatives and consular officers.
Legislative History: 1978 U.S. Code Cong. & Admin. News 2424; 1982 U.S. Code Cong. & Admin. News 651.
Implementing Regulations: 22 C.F.R. Part 51 (1989).

Diplomatic Relations Act of 1978, as amended, 22 U.S.C. 254a et seq.--requires all missions, members of missions and their families, and those officials of the United Nations who are entitled to diplomatic immunity, to have and maintain liability insurance if they own, maintain, or use any motor vehicle, vessel or aircraft in the United States.
Legislative History: 1978 U.S. Code Cong. & Admin. News 1935; 1983 U.S. Code Cong. & Admin. News 1484.
Implementing Regulations: 22 C.F.R. Part 151 (1989).

Arms Export and Control Act of 1968, as amended, 22 U.S.C. 2778 et seq.-- applies to, and establishes strict review and control (through licensing authority) over the export of technical data and classified defense articles.
Legislative History: 1968 U.S. Code Cong. & Admin. News ????. 1976 U.S. Code Cong. & Admin. News 1378; 1987 U.S. Code Cong. & Admin. News 2314.
Implementing Regulations 22 C.F.R. Part 120-130 (1989).

Foreign Service Act of 1946, as amended, 22 U.S.C. 1171 et seq. (current version at 22 U.S.C. 4191 et seq.)--outlines the powers and duties of consular officers regarding deaths of United States citizens or nationals abroad and the handling of their estates, and established the Foreign Service Grievance System.
Implementing Regulations: 22 C.F.R. Parts 16 & 72 (1989).

Foreign Service Act of 1980, 22 U.S.C. 3901 et seq.--the basic statute governing administration of appointments to, and personnel in, the U.S. Foreign Service, including benefit programs.
Legislative History: 1980 U.S. Code Cong. & Admin. News 4419; 1983 U.S. Code Cong. & Admin. News 1414; 1987 U.S. Code Cong. & Admin. News 2314.
Implementing Regulations: 22 C.F.R. Parts 11, 16, 19 & 20 (1989).

Foreign Missions Act of 1982, as amended, 22 U.S.C. 4301 et seq.--authorized the Secretary of State to administer the treatment of foreign missions and public international organizations in the U.S., including the provision of benefits, property, location, privileges and immunities, protective services, and travel restrictions.
Legislative History: 1982 U.S. Code Cong. & Admin. News 651; 1985 U.S. Code Cong. & Admin. News 329; 1986 U.S. Code Cong. & Admin. News 5227; 1987 U.S. Code Cong. & Admin. News 2314.
Protection Guidelines: 22 C.F.R. Part 2a (1989).

International Organizations Immunities Act, 22 U.S.C. 288-288i--the basic diplomatic immunity statute, it specifies the privileges, exemptions, and immunities enjoyed by international organizations in the U.S.
Legislative History: 1945 U.S. Code Cong. Service 946.

Alien Registration Act of 1940, 8 U.S.C. 1101 et seq.--establishes the Passport Office and Visa Office in the Department of State and specifies their duties.
Legislative History: 1952 U.S. Code Cong. & Admin. News 1653; 1961 U.S. Code Cong. & Admin. News 2950; 1965 U.S. Code Cong. & Admin. News 3328; 1977 U.S. Code Cong. & Admin. News 1625; 1981 U.S. Code Cong. & Admin. News 2577; 1986 U.S. Code Cong. & Admin. News 6182.
Implementing Regulations: 22 C.F.R. Part 4 (1989).

Fishermen's Protective Act of 1967, as amended, 22 U.S.C. 1977 et seq.--established a Fishermen's Guaranty Fund administered by the Department of State and designed to reimburse owners and charterers of U.S. fishing vessels for certain losses and costs due to seizure and detention of their vessels by foreign countries under certain rights or claims not recognized by the U.S.
Implementing Regulations: 22 C.F.R. Part 33 (1989).

Comprehensive Anti-Apartheid Act of 1986, 22 U.S.C. 5001 et seq.--states U.S. policy with respect to ending apartheid and imposes sanctions on South Africa.
Legislative History: 1986 U.S. Code Cong. & Admin. News 2334.
Implementing Regulations: 22 C.F.R. Part 60 et seq. (1989).

Foreign Sovereign Immunities Act of 1976, as amended, 28 U.S.C. 1601 et seq.--authorizes foreign states to claim jurisdictional immunity from U.S. courts and leaves commercial activities immunity determinations to U.S. courts.
Legislative History: 1976 U.S. Code Cong. & Admin. News 6604.
Implementing Regulations: 22 C.F.R. Part 93 (1989).

International Child Abduction Remedies Act, 42 U.S.C. 11601 et seq.--implements the Convention on Civil Aspects of International Child Abduction, and establishes legal rights and procedures for the prompt return of children wrongfully removed or retained.
Legislative History: 1988 U.S. Code Cong. & Admin. News 386.
Implementing Regulations: 22 C.F.R. Part 94 (1989).

Executive Order No. 11295, 3 C.F.R., 1966-1970 Comp., p. 570--Rules governing the granting, issuing, and verifying of U.S. passports.

Vienna Convention on Diplomatic Relations, 23 U.S.T. 3227.

Vienna Convention on Consular Relations, 21 U.S.T. 77.

Terrorism Convention, 27 U.S.T. 3949.

DEPARTMENT OF TRANSPORTATION

400 7th Street S.W.
Washington, D.C. 20590

DESCRIPTION: The U.S. Department of Transportation (DOT) establishes the nation's overall transportation policy. It consists of the Office of the Secretary and the following operating administrations which have decentralized authority:

- Federal Aviation Administration
- Federal Highway Administration
- Federal Railroad Administration
- Maritime Administration
- National Highway Traffic Safety Administration
- Research and Special Programs Administration
- Saint Lawrence Seaway Development Corporation
- Urban Mass Transportation Administration
- U.S. Coast Guard

(Area Code 202)

Secretary: Samuel K. Skinner 366-1111
Procurement Office 366-4952
Public Affairs 366-5580
Publications Information 366-0039
Air Travel Consumer Complaints 366-2220
Office of Small and Disadvantaged Business Utilization
  Facsimile 472-3654
  Director: Alicia Casanova 366-1930
  Minority Business Resource Center 366-2852
Inspector General's Hot Line:
  Washington, D.C. Metro Area 366-1461
  Outside Washington, D.C. Metro Area .... (800) 424-9071
Facsimile 426-4508

Freedom of Information Act Office 366-4542
All requests must be in writing and there is a copying charge of 10 cents per page. The charge for search and review is based on the hourly salary of the person doing the search plus 16%. Non-commercial requestors receive 100 free pages and two free hours of search time. Waivers are determined on a case by case basis.

(Area Code 202)

Privacy Act Office 366-1887
There is no charge for Privacy Act information.

Note: All of the operating Administrations under the Department of Transportation follow the same rules and procedures of the Freedom of Information/Privacy Act offices as listed here.

Library (Room 2200) 366-2565
The law section of the library is open Monday through Friday from 7:00 AM until 5:30 PM. The reference section is open from 9:00 AM until 4:00 PM. The library is open to the public, but a photo ID is required. There are copying machines available but no check-out privileges.

Law Library (Room 2215) 366-0749
The law library is open Monday through Friday from 9:00 AM until 5:30 PM. The library is open to the public, but a photo ID is required. There are copying machines available but no check-out privileges.

OFFICE OF THE GENERAL COUNSEL (Room 10428)

The Office of General Counsel, located organizationally in the Office of the Secretary of Transportation, serves as the Department's chief legal counselor and supervises the work of the Chief Counsels' offices in each of the operating administrations. Attorneys in the Office of General Counsel represent the Department in appearances before the transportation regulatory agencies, prepare regulations, coordinate the annual legislative program, and work with the Justice Department on matters involving Federal court litigation.

(Area Code 202)

General Counsel: Philip D. Brady 366-4702
Deputy General Counsel: Rosalind A. Knapp 366-4713
Associate General Counsel: Charles D. McGrath, Jr 366-0140
Facsimile 366-7153

The Office of the General Counsel is divided into the following seven offices:

The Office of Environmental, Civil Rights, and General Law is responsible for all in-house legal duties such as preparation of departmental regulations, processing of the Freedom of Information Act requests, handling personnel grievances and contract and conflict of interest problems, and enforcing EEO stipulations in the Department's grants and contracts.

(Area Code 202)

Assistant General Counsel: Barclay W. Webber 366-4710
Deputy Assistant General Counsel:
  James Dann 366-9154
  Roberta Gabel 366-9161
Patent Counsel: Otto Wildensteiner 366-9161

The **Office of Legislation** drafts legislation, prepares congressional testimony for departmental officials, evaluates all pending transportation legislation, and works with House and Senate committees to reconcile different versions of a bill.

(Area Code 202)

Assistant General Counsel: Thomas W. Herlihy 366-4687
Deputy Assistant General Counsel: Claire Donelan 366-4687

The **Office of Regulations and Enforcement** provides legal services in support of the Department's regulatory programs.

(Area Code 202)

Assistant General Counsel: Neil Eisner 366-9306
Deputy Assistant General Counsel: Robert C. Ashby ... 366-9306
Attorney Advisors:
  Robert Klothe 366-9306
  Elaine David 366-9306
  Joanne Petrie 366-9306
  Gwyneth Radloff 366-9306

DEPARTMENT OF TRANSPORTATION

The **Office of Aviation Enforcement** and Proceedings is responsible for enforcement of all economic aviation regulations and for public counsel representation in administrative hearings involving airline acquisitions, international route awards, and domestic licensing cases. They are also responsible for legal review of all domestic airline license applications.

(Area Code 202)

Assistant General Counsel: Samuel Podberesky 366-9342
Deputy Assistant General Counsel: Kenneth Caplan 366-9349
Attorney Advisor: Dayton Lehman: 366-9349

The **Office of International Law** deals with international transportation policies/programs, and cooperates with the State Department in international negotiations affecting U.S. transportation interests.

(Area Code 202)

Assistant General Counsel: Donald Horn 366-2972
Deputy Assistant General Counsel:
Joseph A. Brooks 366-2972
Michael Jennison 366-2972
Attorney Advisors:
Lawrence Myers 366-5621
Patricia Snyder 366-5621
Pete Schwarzkopf 366-5621
Christopher Tourtellot 366-5621
Peter Block 366-5621
Kathleen McGuigan 366-5621
Gina Thomas 366-9183

The **Board for Correction of Military Records** reviews appeals from Coast Guard personnel who have been denied correction of error in their military records.

(Area Code 202)

Chairman: Robert H. Joost 366-9335
Attorney Advisor: Nancy Battaglia 366-9335

The **Office of Litigation** represents the Department before the Interstate Commerce Commission, and occasionally the Federal Maritime Commission. Adversary proceedings often involve defense of regulations under attack from carriers, airport authorities, etc. The office also participates in some Federal court appellate litigation but most Federal court work is turned over to the Justice Department, which tries cases with the advisory assistance of the office.

(Area Code 202)

Assistant General Counsel: Mary Reed (Acting) 366-4731
Deputy Assistant General Counsel: Mary Reed 366-4731
Attorney Advisors:
Alexander Millard 366-4731
Rosalind Lazarus 366-4731
Thomas Ray 366-4731
Miguel Rovira 366-4731
Paul Smith 366-4731

OFFICE OF INSPECTOR GENERAL (ROOM 9210)

The Inspector General directs an independent and objective organization whose purpose is: 1) to formulate and recommend Departmental policy, plans, and programs for audits and investigations; 2) to conduct and supervise audits and investigations relating to programs and operations of the Department; 3) to provide leadership and recommend policies for activities designed to a) promote economy, efficiency, and effectiveness in the administration of and b) to prevent and detect fraud and abuse in such programs and operations; and 4) to provide a means for keeping the Secretary and the Congress fully and currently informed about problems and deficiencies relating to the administration of such programs and operations and the necessity for and the progress of corrective actions.

(Area Code 202)

Inspector General: (vacant) 366-1959

(Area Code 202)

Acting Deputy Inspector General: Raymond J. DeCarli 366-1959

BOARD OF CONTRACT APPEALS (Room 5101)

The Board of Contract Appeals hears and decides appeals from decisions made by contracting officers relating to contracts awarded by the Department of Transportation and its constituent administrations, as well as appeals from decisions of contracting officers relating to contracts awarded by any other executive agency when such agency or the Administrator for Federal Procurement Policy has designated the Board to decide the appeal.

Board of Contract Appeals Reporter is a bi-weekly publication which reports the decisions of the following Boards of Contract Appeals: Agriculture, Armed Services, Corps of Engineers, Department of Transportation, Energy, General Services Administration, Department of Housing and Urban Development, Interior, Labor, National Aeronautics and Space Administration, U.S. Postal Service, and Department of Veterans Affairs. Annual Price $760.00. Contact: Commerce Clearing House, Inc., 4025 West Peterson Avenue, Chicago, IL 60646. Tel: 312/583-8500. Or in Washington, D.C., call 202/626-2200.

(Area Code 202)

Chairman/Chief Administrative Judge: Thaddeus V. Ware ..366-4305
Vice Chairman/Deputy Chief Administrative Judge:
Robert J. Robertory 366-4305
Recorder: Shirley Higgs 366-4305

(Area Code 202)

Administrative Judges:
Eileen P. Fennessy 366-4305
James L. Stern 366-4305

OFFICE OF HEARINGS (Room 9228)

Petitions to bring cases before the Administrative Law Judges may come from the general public or from within the Department of Transportation; however, cases which are presented to the Administrative Law Judges must originate in the Office of Aviation Enforcement and Proceedings of the Office of General Counsel. If a case is deemed meritorious by this Office, it is assigned to an Administrative Law Judge and given a docket number.

Decisions of the Administrative Law Judges can be seen in the Docket Room where copying machines are available.

(Area Code 202)

Chief Administrative Law Judge: John J. Mathias 366-2142
Administrative Law Judges:
Daniel M. Head 366-2142
Burton S. Kolko 366-2142
Ronnie A. Yoder 366-2142
Dockets (Room 4107) 366-9323

FEDERAL AVIATION ADMINISTRATION

800 Independence Avenue, S.W.
Washington, D.C. 20591

The Federal Aviation Administration (FAA) is charged with: regulating air commerce in a manner that promotes its development and safety and fulfills the requirements of national defense; controlling the use of navigable airspace of the U.S. and regulating both civil and military operations in such airspace; encouraging and developing civil aeronautics; installing and operating air navigation facilities; and developing and operating a common system of air traffic control and navigation for both military and civilian aircraft.

(Area Code 202)

Administrator: James B. Busey 267-3111
Public Information/Publications Information 267-3484
Consumer Hotline:
Washington, DC Metro Area 267-8592
Outside Washington, DC Metro Area ....(800) 322-7873
Safety Hotline:
Washington, DC Metro Area 267-9532
Outside Washington, DC Metro Area ....(800) 255-1111
Facsimile 267-3505

Freedom of Information Act Office 267-3490

Privacy Act Office 267-9895

Library (Room 930) 267-3161
The library is open to the public from 9:00 AM to 4:00 PM Monday through Friday. Copying machines are available. The law library is contained within this library.

OFFICE OF THE CHIEF COUNSEL (Room 900-E)

The Office of the Chief Counsel includes attorneys in Washington, D.C. and regional offices. The Chief Counsel serves as FAA's chief legal officer and as counsel to the Administrator. The Office consists of the following:

(Area Code 202)

Chief Counsel: Gregory S. Walden 267-3222
Deputy Chief Counsel: John H. Cassady 267-3773
Special Counsel for Airport Access: James Whitlow 267-3473
Program Management Staff Manager: Denise Hall 267-3216
Regulations Assistant: Clara Thieling 267-3123
Rules Dockets: Michael D. Triplett 267-3123
Statistics and Dockets: Gwenda Clairborne 267-3129

The **International Affairs and Legal Policy Staff,** which provides legal counsel and assistance in international matters. It formulates the U.S. position on international aviation law questions and on legal aspects on related treaty-making activities.

(Area Code 202)

Assistant Chief Counsel for International Affairs and Legal Policy Staff: Irene E. Howie 267-3515

The **Legislative Staff,** which prepares and conducts FAA's Legislative Program. It represents the agency on all legislative matters affecting the agency, including bills, resolutions, legislative proposals, executive orders, and related matters.

(Area Code 202)

Assistant Chief Counsel for Legislative Staff: Albert B. Randall 267-3217

The **Litigation Division,** which is the principal element of the office with respect to litigation. It conducts litigation in which the agency may be involved, or in which it may have an interest; provides legal services in aircraft accident investigations and hearings; processes tort claims; and monitors/reviews judicial decisions and legal proceedings before the National Transportation Safety Board.

(Area Code 202)

Assistant Chief Counsel: James S. Dillman 267-3661
Branch Manager for:
Accident Counsel: Andrew J. Dilk 267-3167
General and Administrative Litigation:
David Wiegand 267-3671

The **Regulations and Enforcement Division,** which serves as the principal element of the office for legal counsel and assistance on matters concerning the agency regulatory and enforcement program. It provides legal counsel with respect to the drafting, form, and legality of all substantive, procedural, and interpretative rules, regulations, orders, exemptions, airspace actions, and obstruction evaluation determinations which FAA adopts or issues.

(Area Code 202)

Deputy Chief Counsel: John H. Cassady 267-3773
Assistant Chief Counsel: Donald P. Byrne (Acting) ...267-3073
Slot Administration: Joanne Brown 267-8823
Branch Manager for:
Airspace and Air Traffic Law: David Bennett 267-7158
Airworthiness Law: Gary A. Michel 267-8756
Certification Law: Michael Chase 267-3491
Enforcement Policy: Allan H. Horowitz 267-3137
Enforcement Proceedings: Peter Lynch 267-9956
Operations Law: Richard C. Beitel 267-8756

DEPARTMENT OF TRANSPORTATION

The **Procurement Legal Division**, which handles proceedings involving Government contracts. Attorneys negotiate draft contracts and appear before the Department's Contract Appeals Board, a quasi-judicial body which hears appeals by contractors from decisions made by contracting officers. This office works in conjunction with the Department of Justice in litigation involving procurement cases.

(Area Code 202)

Assistant Chief Counsel: John R. McCaw 267-3480
Branch Manager for:
Acquisition Policy and Commercial Law:
Danvers Long 267-7566
Contracts and Litigation: Nancy LoBue 267-3480

The **General Legal Services Division**, which handles a variety of legal functions. Attorneys interpret statutes and internal orders that govern and affect the agency's mission, represent the agency at labor grievance hearings, and advise on Privacy Act requirements and the Freedom of Information Act requests.

(Area Code 202)

Assistant Chief Counsel: James W. Whitlow 267-3473
Branch Manager for:
Airports/Environmental Law: Richard Danforth 267-3199
General Law: John M. Walsh 267-3362
Personnel and Labor Law: Mary Whigham Jones 267-3473

FEDERAL AVIATION ADMINISTRATION TECHNICAL CENTER

Act-1, Atlantic City Airport, NJ 08405

Director: Edward T. Harris ....(609) 484-6641
Assistant Chief Counsel: Thomas E. Flatley Jr ..(609) 484-6605
Facsimile ....(609) 484-5126

REGIONAL OFFICES

The Federal Aviation Administration (FAA) has eleven regional offices staffed by attorneys. Their addresses are as follows:

Anchorage
Regional Counsel: John Curry
FAA Alaskan Region, AAL-7, 701 C Street, Box 14, Anchorage, AK 99513. Tel: 907/271-5269.

Atlanta
Regional Counsel: Ronald Hagadone
FAA Southern Region, ASO-7, P.O. Box 20636, Atlanta, GA 30320. Tel: 404/763-7204.

Atlantic City
Regional Counsel: Thomas Flatley
FAA Technical Center, ACT-7, Atlantic City Airport, Atlantic City, NJ 08405. Tel: 609/484-6605.

Burlington, MA
Regional Counsel: Amy Corbett
FAA New England Region, ANE-7, 12 New England Executive Park, Burlington, MA 01802. Tel: 617/273-7305.

Des Plaines, IL
Regional Counsel: Eileen Johnson
FAA Great Lakes Region, AGL-7, 2300 East Devon Ave, Des Plaines, IL 60018. Tel: 312/694-7313.

Fort Worth
Regional Counsel: Hayes Hettinger
FAA Southwest Region, ASW-7, 4400 Blue Mound Road, P.O. Box 1689, Fort Worth, TX 76101. Tel: 817/624-5707.

Jamaica, NY
Regional Counsel: Loretta Alkalay
FAA Eastern Region, AEA-7, Federal Building, JFK International Airport, Jamaica, NY 11430. Tel: 718/917-1035.

Kansas City, MO
Regional Counsel: Tim Titus
FAA Central Region, ACE-7, 1558 Federal Bldg, 601 E. 12th St, Kansas City, MO 64106. Tel: 816/426-5446.

Los Angeles
Regional Counsel: DeWitte Lawson
FAA Western-Pacific Region, AWP-7, P.O. Box 920007, Worldway Postal Center, Los Angeles, CA 90009. Tel: 213/297-6270.

Oklahoma City
Regional Counsel: Joe Standell
FAA Mike Monroney Aeronautical Center, 6500 South MacArthur, P.O. Box 25082, Oklahoma City, OK 73125. Tel: 405/680-3296.

Seattle
Regional Counsel: George Thompson
FAA Northwest Mountain Region, ANM-7, 17900 Pacific Highway South, C-68966, Seattle, WA 98168. Tel: 206/431-2807.

PUBLICATIONS OF INTEREST

Aviation Law Reports covers Federal aviation laws, regulations, decisions, plus air liabilities. This four-volume publication is updated semi-annually. Price: $1,375.00 per year. The publication can be ordered from Commerce Clearing House, Inc., 4025 West Peterson Avenue, Chicago, IL 60646. Tel: 312/583-8500. Or, in Washington, D.C., call 202/626-2200.

Federal Aviation Regulations. This is a subscription service in which there are several parts, all priced individually. For example, Part 1 consists of Definitions and Abbreviations. Price: $30.00 domestic; $37.50 foreign. GPO Stock# 950-006-00000-5. Part 11 deals with General Rule-Making Procedures. Price: $27.00 domestic; $33.75 foreign. GPO Stock# 950-007-00000-1. Part 13 deals with Investigation and Enforcement Procedures. Price: $34.00 domestic; $42.50 foreign. GPO Stock# 950-008-00000-8. Subscription service for each part consists of a basic manual and supplementary changes for an indeterminate period. Contact: Superintendent of Documents, U.S. Government Printing Office, Washington, D.C. 20402. Tel: 202/783-3238.

FEDERAL HIGHWAY ADMINISTRATION
400 Seventh Street, S.W.
Washington, D.C. 20590

The Federal Highway Administration (FHwA), charged with carrying out those Department of Transportation responsibilities concerned with the highway mode of land transportation, has the primary missions of assuring that the nation's highway transportation system is safe, economical, and efficient with respect to the movement of people and goods while giving full consideration to the highway's impact on the environment and social and economic conditions.

(Area Code 202)
Administrator: Thomas D. Larson 366-0650
Public Affairs/Publications Information 366-0660
FOIA/Privacy Act 366-0534

(Area Code 202)
Contracts and Procurement Office 366-4242
Small Business and Small Disadvantaged Business Office 366-4205
Facsimile 366-7239

OFFICE OF CHIEF COUNSEL (Room 4213)

The Chief Counsel serves as the principal legal officer of the Federal Highway Administration (FHwA), which carries out the highway transportation programs of the Department of Transportation. The Office of the Chief Counsel presently has attorneys in Washington, D.C., as well as in in Regional Offices.

(Area Code 202)
Chief Counsel: Larry L. Thompson 366-0740
Deputy Chief Counsel: Edward V.A. Kussy 366-0764

The **Legislation and Regulations Division** coordinates all legislative/legal activities of the agency; initiates FHwA's legislative reference service and furnishes all congressional materials and information to FHwA officials; and drafts legislative proposals, reports on legislation, and congressional testimony. The office also provides drafting assistance as requested to congressional committee staff and Members of Congress; drafts regulations, FHwA directives, and related issuances to ensure compliance with legal requirements.

(Area Code 202)
Assistant Chief Counsel: Frank L. Calhoun 366-0761
Deputy Assistant Chief Counsel: Michael Laska 366-1383

The **Right-of-Way and Environmental Law Division** provides advice on the application of environmental laws to the highway program; reviews environmental impact statements; advises on the acquisition and disposal of Federal-aid highway rights-of-way; advises on the development of related regulations and legislation; and provides legal services relating to the Uniform Relocation Assistance and Real Property Acquisition Policies Act. The office also provides litigation support on all right-of-way and environmental litigation affecting FHwA.

(Area Code 202)
Assistant Chief Counsel: L. Harold Aikens, Jr 366-0791
Deputy Assistant Chief Counsel: Virginia Cherwek 366-1372

The **Motor Carrier and Highway Safety Law Division** provides legal services regarding motor carrier safety, hazardous materials, minimum financial responsibility, highway safety, and foreign projects; provides legal advice on state laws, proposed legislation, enforcement and certification relating to truck size and weight, speed limit issues, and the 21-year old drinking age statute; and handles administrative cases in the areas of hazardous materials, driver qualification, minimum financial responsibility, and motor carrier safety cases, as well as Interstate Commerce Commission safety fitness proceedings. The office also works with the Department of Justice in all matters affecting motor carrier and highway safety issues involving FHwA.

(Area Code 202)
Assistant Chief Counsel: Paul Brennan 366-0834
Deputy Assistant Chief Counsel: David Oliver 366-0834

The **General Law Division** provides advice in the areas of Federal-aid and direct Federal highway law, contractor sanctions, contract and tort claims, administrative procedures, the Freedom of Information Act and Privacy Act, personnel issues, ethics, civil rights, labor, and procurement. It conducts and/or monitors litigation in any of these areas which involve the FHwA.

(Area Code 202)
Assistant Chief Counsel: Kathleen S. Markman 366-0780
Deputy Assistant Chief Counsel: Wilbert Baccus 366-1396

REGIONAL OFFICES

The Federal Highway Administration (FHwA) has ten regional offices staffed by attorneys. Their addresses are as follows:

Region I (Albany)

Regional Counsel: Irwin Schroeder
Federal Highway Administration, Leo W. O'Brien Federal Bldg, Room 729, Clinton Ave and North Pearl Street, Albany, NY 12207. Tel: 518/472-7909. FAX: 518/472-4242

Region III (Baltimore)

Regional Counsel: Francis J. Locke
Federal Highway Administration, George H. Fallon Federal Office Bldg, 31 Hopkins Plaza, Room 1633, Baltimore, MD 21201. Tel: 301/962-2482. FAX: 301/962-3419

Region IV (Atlanta)

Regional Counsel: James E. Scapellato
Federal Highway Administration, 1720 Peachtree Road, N.W., Ste 200, Atlanta, GA 30367. Tel: 404/347-4040. FAX: 404/347-2125.

Region V (Homewood, IL)

Regional Counsel: John K. Kraybill
Federal Highway Administration, 18209 Dixie Highway, Homewood, IL 60430-2294. Tel: 708/799-9155. FAX: 708/799-9202.

Region VI (Ft. Worth)

Regional Counsel: Jean G. Rogers
Federal Highway Administration, 819 Taylor Street, Ft. Worth, TX 76102. Tel: 817/334-2895. FAX: 817/334-4144.

Region VII (Kansas City, MO)

Regional Counsel: Helen Mountford
Federal Highway Administration, 6301 Rockhill Road, Kansas City, MO 64131. Tel: 816/926-7769. FAX: 816/926-7879.

Region VIII (Lakewood, CO)

Regional Counsel: Richard O. Jones
Federal Highway Administration, 55 Zang Street, Room 400, Lakewood, CO 80228. Tel: 303/969-6709. FAX: 303/969-6727.

Region IX (San Francisco)

Regional Counsel: David G. Ortez
Federal Highway Administration, 211 Main St, Room 1100, San Francisco, CA 94105. Tel: 415/744-2643. FAX: 415/744-2620.

Region X (Portland, OR)

Regional Counsel: Robert B. Rutledge
Federal Highway Administration, Mohawk Building, Room 312, 708 S.W. Third Avenue, Portland, OR 97204. Tel: 503/326-2076. FAX: 503/326-3928.

Region XV (Arlington, VA)

Regional Counsel: Julia Perry
Federal Highway Administration, Eastern District Federal Division Office, 1000 North Glebe Road, Arlington, VA 22201. Tel: 703/285-0100. FAX: 703/285-0011.

FEDERAL RAILROAD ADMINISTRATION
400 Seventh Street, S.W.
Washington, D.C. 20590

The purpose of the Federal Railroad Administration (FRA) is to promulgate and enforce rail safety regulations, administer railroad financial assistance programs, conduct research and development in support of improved railroad safety and national rail transportation policy, provide for the rehabilitation of Northeast Corridor rail passenger service, and operate the Alaska Railroad.

(Area Code 202)
Administrator: Gilbert E. Carmichael 366-0710
Public Affairs 366-0881
Procurement Services 366-0563

(Area Code 202)
FOIA/Privacy Act 366-0616
Facsimile 366-7009

OFFICE OF THE CHIEF COUNSEL (Room 8201)

(Area Code 202)
Chief Counsel: S. Mark Lindsey 366-0767
Deputy Chief Counsel: Michael T. Haley 366-0767

The Office of Chief Counsel contains the following divisions:

The **Commerce and Legal Services Division** provides legal advice and support in the following areas: The Alaska Railroad, intercity rail passenger programs, procurement, EEO and civil rights, conflict of interest, personnel, the Privacy Act, and environmental law. Attorneys in the Division also provide legal advice on legislative activities; assist in developing the Department's legal position in administrative proceedings and court suits that involve matters handled by the Division; and develop all public notices and regulations issued by FRA concerning matters handled by the Division.

(Area Code 202)
Assistant Chief Counsel: Robert S. Vermut (Acting) ..366-0616

The **Freight Economics and Finance Division** renders legal advice and support in matters affecting railroad economics and financial assistance programs to the states and railroad industry. Attorneys in the Division also provide legal advice on legislative activities; assist in developing the Department's legal position inadministrative proceedings and court suits that involve matters handled by the Division; develop all public notices and regulations issued by FRA concerning matters handled by the Division; and prepare drafts of DOT submissions to the Interstate Commerce Commission on rail matters.

(Area Code 202)
Assistant Chief Counsel: Robert S. Vermut 366-0616

The **Safety Division** renders legal advice and support in the following areas: preparation of railroad safety notices and regulations, enforcement of railroad safety laws and regulations, tort claims, and the Freedom of Information Act requests. Attorneys in the Division also direct the FRA program for collecting or compromising claims arising under the railroad safety laws and regulations; provide legal advice on legislative activities; develop railroad safety notices and regulations; maintain the FRA public dockets for all railroad safety regulations; provide legal assistance at public hearings held by the FRA in connection with railroad safety rulemaking proceedings and petitions for exemption from railroad safety regulations; represent FRA at public hearings held by the National Transportation Safety Board; and assist in developing the Department's legal position in administrative and court suits involving the enforcement of railroad safety laws and regulations.

(Area Code 202)
Assistant Chief Counsel: Gregory B. McBride 366-0635

FIELD OFFICES

FRA has no regional or field legal offices.

PUBLICATIONS OF INTEREST

Accident, Incident Bulletin is an annual statistical overview summarizing reportable railroad accidents/incidents. It can be obtained free of charge from FRA, Office of Public Affairs. Tel: 202/366-0881.

MARITIME ADMINISTRATION
400 Seventh Street, S.W.
Washington, D.C. 20590

The Maritime Administration (MARAD) administers programs to aid in the development, promotion, and operation of the U.S. merchant marine. It is also charged with organizing and directing emergency merchant ship operations.

The Maritime Administration administers subsidy programs, through the Maritime Subsidy Board, under which the Federal Government pays the difference between certain costs of operating ships under the U.S. flag and foreign competitive flags on essential services, and the difference between the costs of constructing ships in U.S. and foreign shipyards.

MARAD constructs or supervises the construction of merchant type ships for the Federal Government; conducts programs to develop ports and facilities to promote domestic shipping; administers a War Risk Insurance Program; conducts research and development activities to improve the merchant marine; and regulates the sales to aliens and transfers to foreign registry of ships that are fully or partially owned by U.S. citizens.

The Maritime Administration operates the U.S. Merchant Marine Academy at Kings Point, NY, and administers a Federal assistance program for the maritime academies operated by California, Maine, Massachusetts, Michigan, New York, and Texas.

(Area Code 202)
Administrator: Captain Warren G. Leback 366-5823
Office of External Affairs/Public Affairs/
Publications Information 366-5807

(Area Code 202)
FOIA/Privacy Act 366-5746
Acquisition Office 366-5757
Facsimile 366-3890

OFFICE OF THE CHIEF COUNSEL (Room 9329B)

The Office of Chief Counsel is divided into six divisions: Division of Administration, Division of Maritime Aids, Division of Ship Financing Contracts, Division of Regulations, Division of Legislation, and Division of Litigation.

The Office of Chief Counsel provides legal counsel and advice to officials at headquarters and the regions on a broad range of issues. Attorneys in the office provide advice in the interpretation and application of statutes, treaties, regulations, contracts, etc.; negotiate and settle claims in admiralty, tort, employee, and claims referred for litigation; provide legal services on procurement and acquisition matters; review and approve citizenship status of applicants under various provisions of the Merchant Marine Act of 1936 and the Merchant Ship Sales Act of 1946; review applications for Federal subsidies and other Government aids to shipping, sales, charters, and transfers of ships; prepare contracts, agreements, deeds, leases, regulations, and related documents; and draft proposed legislation and Executive Orders. MARAD attorneys also assist the Justice Department in the trial, appeal, and settlement of litigation; represent the Administration before state and Federal courts with the permission of the Justice Department; and represent the Administration in public proceedings involving all shipping matters before Federal administrative agencies and before state and local courts with the concurrence of the Department of Justice.

(Area Code 202)

Chief Counsel: Robert J. Patton, Jr (Acting) 366-5711
Deputy Chief Counsel: Robert J. Patton Jr 366-5712
Administration Division Chief: Juan Hernandez 366-5715
Legislation Division Chief: Leonard L. Sutter 366-5724
Litigation Division Chief: Sandra L. Jenkins 366-5191

(Area Code 202)

Maritime Aids Division Chief: Murray A. Bloom 366-5320
Regulations Division Chief: Edmond T. Sommer 366-5181
Ship Financing Contracts Division Chief:
Richard M. Lorr 366-5882

REGIONAL OFFICES

Even though the Maritime Administration has regional offices in New York City (Eastern Region), New Orleans (Central Region), Des Plaines, IL (Great Lakes Region), and San Francisco (Western Region), and operates the U.S. Merchant Marine Academy in Kings Point, NY, all MARAD attorneys are located in Washington, D.C. All legal matters relating to or generated by the regions are handled in the Washington, D.C. headquarters--including legal questions arising from the operation of the Merchant Marine Academy in Kings Point, NY.

NATIONAL HIGHWAY TRAFFIC SAFETY ADMINISTRATION

400 Seventh Street, S.W., Washington, D.C. 20590

The National Highway Traffic Safety Administration (NHTSA) was established in 1970 in response to a congressional mandate to reduce the mounting number of deaths, injuries, and economic losses resulting from traffic accidents on the nation's highways and to provide motor vehicle damage susceptibility and ease of repair information, motor vehicle inspection demonstrations, and protection of purchasers of motor vehicles having altered odometers, and to provide average standards for greater vehicle mileage per gallon of fuel for vehicles under 10,000 (gross vehicle weight). NHTSA carries out programs relating to the safety performance of motor vehicles and related equipment, motor vehicle drivers and pedestrians, and a uniform nationwide speed limit. The agency administers the Federal odometer law, issues theft prevention standards, and promulgates average fuel economy standards for motor vehicles.

(Area Code 202)

Administrator: Jerry R. Curry 366-1836
Public Information 366-5580
Publications Information 366-2588
FOIA/Privacy Act 366-1834

(Area Code 202)

Auto Safety Hot Line:
Washington, DC Metro Area 366-0123
Outside Washington, DC Metro Area .... (800) 424-9393
Facsimile 366-2106

OFFICE OF THE CHIEF COUNSEL (Room 5219)

As principal legal officer, the Chief Counsel provides all legal services and representation relating to all aspects of NHTSA program activities, including: providing legal advice on legislative activities; executing formal legal instruments and documents; preparing all rulemaking documents relating to the issuance of rules, regulations, and standards under the National Traffic and Motor Vehicle Safety Act, the Highway Safety Act, and the Motor Vehicle Information and Cost Savings Act; recommending enforcement actions; and preparing briefs, memoranda, and pleadings in court cases in which NHTSA's regulatory activities are challenged or involve NHTSA enforcement efforts.

(Area Code 202)

Chief Counsel: Paul J. Rice 366-9511

The Office of Chief Counsel is composed of four divisions:

The **Litigation Division** provides legal services pertaining to the defense of agency rulemaking in judicial review and to the enforcement aspects of the agency's mission; and defends the agency in other administrative and judicial litigation, such as in the Freedom of Information Act cases, contract and personnel cases.

(Area Code 202)

Assistant Chief Counsel: Kenneth Weinstein 366-5261

The **Rulemaking Division** provides legal services pertaining to regulations and the rulemaking aspects of the agency's mission; and provides advice and legal interpretation for agency officials and the public on the rules and regulations of the administration.

(Area Code 202)

Assistant Chief Counsel: Stephen P. Wood 366-2992

The **General Law Division** provides legal services pertaining to general law and administrative law issues affecting the agency and its employees. Areas of concern include contracts and procurement matters, personnel, conflict of interest situations, delegations of authority, the Freedom of Information Act, and the Privacy Act.

(Area Code 202)

Assistant Chief Counsel: Kathleen DeMeter 366-1834

The **Legislation Division** provides legal services pertaining to the agency's legislative programs. Functions include drafting legislative proposals for submission to Congress, supervising the preparation of congressional testimony, and drafting model legislation for adoption by the states.

(Area Code 202)

Assistant Chief Counsel: John G. Womack 366-5265

REGIONAL OFFICES

The National Highway Traffic Safety Administration (NHTSA) has ten regional offices staffed by regional directors or administrators who are attorneys:

Region I (Cambridge, MA)

NHTSA Regional Director: George A. Luciano
Transportation System Center, Kendall Square Code 903, Cambridge, MA 02142. Tel: 617/494-3427.
(Jurisdiction: CT, ME, MA, NH, RI, and VT)

Region II (White Plains, NY)

NHTSA Regional Director: Thomas M. Louizou
222 Mamaroneck Avenue, Room 204, White Plains, NY 10605. Tel: 914/683-9690.
(Jurisdiction: NJ, NY, PR and VI)

Region III (Hanover, MD)

NHTSA Regional Director: Frank D. Altobelli
BWI Commerce Park, 7526 Connelley Drive, Suite L, Hanover, MD 21076-1699. Tel: 301/768-7111.
(Jurisdiction: DE, DC, MD, PA, VA, and WV)

Region IV (Atlanta)

NHTSA Regional Director: Thomas J. Enright
1720 Peachtree Road, N.W., Suite 501, Atlanta, GA 30309. Tel: 404/347-4537.
(Jurisdiction: AL, FL, GA, KY, MS, NC, SC, and TN)

Region V (Homewood, IL)

NHTSA Regional Administrator: Richard M. Cook
18209 Dixie Highway, Suite A, Homewood, IL 60430. Tel: 312/799-6067.
(Jurisdiction: IL, IN, MI, MN, OH, and WI)

Region VI (Fort Worth)

NHTSA Regional Administrator: Georgia S. Jupiko
819 Taylor Street, Room 8A38, Fort Worth, TX 76102. Tel: 817/334-4300.
(Jurisdiction: AR, LA, NM, OK, and TX)

Region VII (Kansas City, MO)

NHTSA Regional Administrator: Norman B. McPherson
P.O. Box 412515, Kansas City, MO 64141. Tel: 816/926-7887.
(Jurisdiction: IA, KS, MO, and NE)

Region VIII (Denver)

NHTSA Regional Administrator: Louis R. DeCarolis
555 Zang Street, 4th Floor, Denver, CO 80228. Tel: 303/236-3444.
(Jurisdiction: CO, MT, ND, SD, UT, and WY)

Region IX (San Francisco)

NHTSA Regional Administrator: Joseph Cindrich
211 Main Street, Suite 1000, San Francisco, CA 94105. Tel: 415/974-9840.
(Jurisdiction: American Samoa, AZ, CA, Guam, HA, and NV)

Region X (Seattle)

NHTSA Regional Administrator: Curtis A. Winston
3140 Jackson Federal Building, Seattle, WA 98174. Tel: 206/442-5934.
(Jurisdiction: AK, ID, OR, and WA)

OFFICE OF ASSOCIATE ADMINISTRATOR FOR ENFORCEMENT (Room 5321)

(Area Code 202)

Associate Administrator: George L. Reagle 366-9700
Odometer Fraud Staff Chief: Richard C. Morse 366-4761

Office of Defects Investigation
Director: Michael Brownlee 366-2850

(Area Code 202)

Office of Vehicle Safety Compliance
Director: Robert F. Hellmuth 366-2832

DATABASES OF INTEREST

The **Auto Safety Hotline** is a toll-free telephone service operated by the National Highway Traffic Safety Administration (NHTSA) which provides callers with information on motor vehicle safety recalls and safety defect investigations. New car crash test results, and other safety topics are sent by mail. Consumer complaints about possible safety defects are also accepted. The number outside the Washington, D.C. metro area is 800/424-9393. Callers inside the Washington, D.C. metro area should use 202/366-0123. Hotline operators are on duty Monday through Friday from 8:00 AM to 4:00 PM.

The Office of Defects Investigation (ODI) conducts investigations of alleged safety related defect trends in motor vehicles. Currently, there are nearly 2200 ODI investigation files available for public viewing in the Technical Reference Division (TRD), including 137 active files. Current files are maintained in a paper format. TRD maintains a complete collection of manual indexes to active investigations. This collection is found in the **Monthly Defect Investigation Report** which can be obtained by sending a written request to: National Traffic Safety Administration, General Services Division (NAD-51), 400 Seventh Street, S.W., Room 6123, Washington, D.C. 20590.

The **Office of Defect Investigation (ODI)** maintains the following computer files: The **Recall File** contains records of all vehicle and vehicle equipment, including tires, safety defect and noncompliance recalls since 1966. The **Letter File** contains records of complaints submitted by vehicle owners from 1981 to present. The **Service Bulletin File** contains records of service bulletins submitted by manufacturers. The **Active Investigation File** contains records of investigations initiated by the Office of Defect Investigations since mid-1985. The **New Car Assessment Program (NCAP) File** contains records of vehicles that have been crash tested in the NCAP. To access the files of the Office of Defect

Investigation, contact the Technical Reference Service, National Highway Traffic Safety Administration, 400 7th Street, S.W., Washington, D.C. 20590. Tel: 202/366-2768. There is a search fee.

Federal Motor Vehicle Safety Standards and Regulations with Amendments and Interpretations Consolidated, 1990 contains vehicle safety procedural rules and regulations. Its annual cost is $134.00 with updates and supplements for an indeterminate period. It can be obtained from the Superintendent of Documents, U.S. Government Printing Office, Washington, D.C. 20402. Tel: 202/783-3238.

Technical Service Bulletins are maintained by the **Technical Reference Division (TRD)** dating from 1968 to present. These bulletins describe the instructions motor vehicle manufacturers provide their dealer repair services. The Office of Defect Investigation (ODI) has selected certain bulletins for their automated data files.(Information on the automated data files is listed below.) The bulletins are designated in the following categories: technical, informational, warranty, product improvement, part and recall. TRD maintains the selected safety related bulletins in a microfiche format, with the addition of an optical disk system for retrieving bulletins from 1986 to present. For information, contact National Highway Traffic Safety Administration, Technical Reference Division, 400 7th Street, S.W., Washington, D.C. 20590. Tel: 202/366-2768.

Compliance Test Reports are the results of the testing, inspection and investigation of foreign and domestic vehicles and equipment manufacturers. A **monthly compliance report news release** is issued which lists investigations opened, closed and pending during the month, identifies compliance test reports accepted and indicates how individual reports may be obtained. These releases may be requested from the Office of Public and Consumer Affairs (NOA-40), National Highway Traffic Safety Administration, 400 7th Street, S.W., Washington, D.C. 20590.

Automated Search Files, maintained by the Technical Reference Division, include Defect Investigation files, Compliance Test Reports, Technical Service Bulletins, and consumer complaints and recall campaigns as taken from the Hotline. A search of these files, with the exception of the Compliance Test Reports, will result in a computer printout, if information is available. A statement is sent with the search results which indicates the total cost and how the payment is to be paid. The cost of an average search of the above files is between $20 to $30. Information on the automated search files can be obtained by writing or calling the National Highway Traffic Safety Administration, Technical Reference Division, 400 7th Street, S.W., Washington, D.C. 20590. Tel: 202/366-2768.

Docket Files contain information and data relating to rulemaking actions, including notices of proposed rulemaking, comments received in response to notices, petitions for rulemaking or reconsideration, denials of petitions for rulemaking or reconsideration, the final rules and the technical materials used by the standards writer. This is the public record of rulemaking activities for motor vehicle and highway safety standards. Details of these rulemaking procedures may be found in 49 C.F.R. Parts 551-557 (1989). For more information, contact the Technical Reference Division, National Highway Traffic Safety Administration, 400 7th Street, S.W., Washington, D.C. 20590. Tel: 202/366-4949. There is a search fee.

TRIS, a computerized information file maintained and operated by the Transportation Research Board of the National Research Council (a private organization), contains information on various aspects of highway and automobile safety, accidents and litigation. Online Dialogue users can access TRIS or Online Search Specialists at the Transportation Research Board will conduct searches for a fee. For more information, call or write the Transportation Research Board, National Research Council, 2101 Constitution Avenue, N.W., Washington, D.C. 20418. Tel: 202/334-3251.

RESEARCH AND SPECIAL PROGRAMS ADMINISTRATION

400 Seventh Street, S.W., Washington, D.C. 20590

The Research and Special Programs Administration (RSPA) is responsible for a number of programs involving safety regulation, emergency preparedness, and research and development. It consists of the Office of Hazardous Material Transportation, the Office of Pipeline Safety, the Office of Emergency Transportation, the Office of Aviation Information Management, the Office of Program Management and Administration, and the Transportation Systems Center in Cambridge, MA.

	(Area Code 202)
Administrator: Travis P. Dungan	366-4433
Public Information	366-4433
Publications Information	366-2301
FOIA/Privacy Act	366-9638
Facsimile	366-7431

OFFICE OF CHIEF COUNSEL (Room 8405)

The Office of Chief Counsel provides legal services and representation relating to all aspects of RSPA program activities. The office participates in regulatory analysis and planning; prepares all rulemaking documents relating to the issuance of standards, rules, regulations, exemptions, certificates, and criteria; provides legal assistance to officials investigating possible violations of laws relating to RSPA programs and recommends appropriate enforcement actions; and prepares briefs, memoranda, and pleadings for court cases involving RSPA's regulatory or enforcement activities.

In addition, the Office of Chief Counsel also prepares legal opinions concerning pipeline safety and hazardous materials transportation activities, and provides legal support for RSPA administrative activities, such as procurement and personnel, research and development, emergency transportation, and transportation safety training.

(Area Code 202)

Chief Counsel: Judy Kaleta 366-4400

Deputy Chief Counsel: Barbara Betsock 366-4400

OFFICE OF PROGRAM MANAGEMENT AND ADMINISTRATION

Transportation Safety Institute, 6500 S. MacArthur Blvd, Oklahoma City, OK 73125
Director: H. Aldridge Gillespie ....(405) 680-3153
Facsimile ....(405) 680-3521

Transportation Systems Center, Kendall Square, 55 Broadway, Cambridge, MA 02142
Director: Dr. Richard R. John ....(617) 494-2222
Chief Counsel: David S. Glater ....(617) 494-2727
Facsimile ....(617) 837-2497

SAINT LAWRENCE SEAWAY DEVELOPMENT CORPORATION

400 Seventh Street, S.W., Washington, D.C. 20590

The Saint Lawrence Seaway Development Corporation is responsible for the development, operation, and maintenance of that part of the Seaway between Montreal and Lake Erie that is within the territorial limits of the U.S. Its function is to provide a safe, efficient, and effective water artery for maritime commerce, both in peacetime and in time of national emergency. The Corporation is self-sustaining, being financed from revenues received from tolls charged for the use of its facilities.

(Area Code 202)

Administrator: James L. Emery 366-0118

Chief: Procurement and Supply:
Linda Harding (Massena, NY) ....(315) 764-3244

OFFICE OF CHIEF COUNSEL (Room 5424)

The Office of Chief Counsel serves as principal legal advisor to the Administrator, furnishing advice and opinions to officials at the Washington, D.C. and Massena, N.Y. offices of the Corporation. Responsibilities include providing advice on such issues as: the interpretation and application of statutes, treaties, regulations, contracts, and executive orders; the trade and traffic program; procurement and acquisition matters; the negotiation and settlement of claims in admiralty, tort and contract, and other administrative claims; and the preparation of contracts, deeds, leases, regulations, and related documents. The Chief Counsel also directs the Corporation's Preventive Law Program and supervises litigation activities.

(Area Code 202)

Chief Counsel: Marc C. Owen 366-0108

URBAN MASS TRANSPORTATION ADMINISTRATION

400 Seventh Street, S.W., Washington, D.C. 20590

The Urban Mass Transportation Administration (UMTA) is the principal conduit of Federal financial assistance to both urban and non-urban areas for planning, developing, maintaining, and improving the nation's publicly owned and operated mass transportation systems, e.g., subways, light rail transit, commuter rail, automated guideways, and ferries. In this main role of a grant maker and lender, UMTA is responsible for ensuring that these Federal funds are spent wisely, and that the states and their local communities obtain the best possible benefits from these funds. Additionally, over the past several years UMTA has placed a new emphasis on its planning functions: the evaluation of urban transportation systems and the impact of such systems on city growth and structure.

(Area Code 202)

Administrator: Brian W. Clymer 366-4040
Public Affairs 366-4043
Publications Information 366-0201
FOIA/Privacy Act 366-4043
Facsimile 366-3472

DEPARTMENT OF TRANSPORTATION

OFFICE OF THE CHIEF COUNSEL (Room 9316)

The Office of Chief Counsel, which has attorneys in the Washington, D.C. Headquarters Office, as well as in ten regional offices provides legal advice and assistance to agency management and staff. In addition to traditional areas of legal assistance, the UMTA Chief Counsel's Office has lead responsibility for congressional oversight and authorization hearings; participates in agency policy determinations; ensures that adequate bases exist for all legal and administrative findings and determinations prerequisite to agency grants and loans; and monitors grantees to ensure their compliance with all applicable legal requirements.

The Office of the Chief Counsel has three divisions:

(Area Code 202)

Chief Counsel: Steven A. Diaz 366-4063
Deputy Chief Counsel: Theodore A. Munter 366-4063

The **Legislation and Regulations Division** drafts and reviews legislation and regulations to implement the Administration's programs.

(Area Code 202)

Assistant Chief Counsel: Daniel Duff 366-4011
Attorney Advisors:
Richard Cantor 366-4011
Susan Schruth 366-4011

The **Litigation and Opinions Division** represents UMTA before civil courts and administrative agencies, and prepares legal opinions on issues involving UMTA programs.

(Area Code 202)

Assistant Chief Counsel: Trudy B. Levy 366-0952
Attorney Advisor: Lenese Herbert 366-0952

The **Programs Division** oversees the development and management of UMTA grants and UMTA-sponsored projects, with primary responsibility in areas of contract administration, property acquisition and relocation, grantee procurement, civil rights, and other program requirements.

(Area Code 202)

Assistant Chief Counsel: Douglas Gold 366-1936
Attorney Advisors:
Linda L. Watkins 366-1936
Rita Daguillard 366-1936
Elizabeth Snyder 366-1936

REGIONAL OFFICES

The Office of the Chief Counsel also includes a single Regional Counsel in each of UMTA's ten Regional Offices, located in Boston, New York City, Philadelphia, Atlanta, Chicago, Ft. Worth, Kansas City, Denver, San Francisco, and Seattle. These Regional Counsels are day-to-day legal advisors to UMTA management and staff, with primary responsibilities in grant-making, program and policy administration, and dealings with UMTA's grantees, state/local governments, transit industries, labor, citizen action groups, and the general public.

Region I (Cambridge, MA)

Regional Counsel: vacant
Urban Mass Transportation Administration, 55 Broadway, Suite 920, Cambridge, MA 02142. Tel: 617/494-2055. FAX: 617/494-2865.

Region II (New York)

Regional Counsel: Leslie T. Rogers
Urban Mass Transportation Administration, 26 Federal Plaza, Suite 2940, New York, NY 10278. Tel: 212/264-8162.
FAX: 212/264-8973.

Region III (Philadelphia)

Regional Counsel: Nancy A. Greene
Urban Mass Transportation Administration, 841 Chestnut Street, Suite 714, Philadelphia, PA 19107. Tel: 215/597-4179.
FAX: 215/597-2767.

Region IV (Atlanta)

Regional Counsel: Paul T. Jensen
Urban Mass Transportation Administration, 1720 Peachtree Rd, NW, Suite 400, Atlanta, GA 30309. Tel: 404/347-3948.
FAX: 404/347-7849.

Region V (Chicago)

Regional Counsel: Linda C. Hart
Urban Mass Transportation Administration, 55 East Monroe Street, Rm 1415, Chicago, IL 60603. Tel: 312/353-2789.
FAX: 312/886-0351.

Region VI (Fort Worth)

Regional Counsel: (vacant)
Urban Mass Transportation Administration, 819 Taylor Street, Suite 9A32, Fort Worth, TX 76102. Tel: 817/334-3787.
FAX: 817/334-3129.

Region VII (Kansas City, MO)

Regional Counsel: Jeanmarie Homan
Urban Mass Transportation Administration, 6301 Rockhill Road, Suite 200, Kansas City, MO 64131. Tel: 816/926-5053.
FAX: 816/926-7388.

Region VIII (Denver)

Regional Counsel: Helen M. Knoll
Urban Mass Transportation Administration, 1961 Stout Street, 5th Floor, Denver, CO 80294. Tel: 303/844-3242.
FAX: 303/844-4217.

Region IX (San Francisco)

Regional Counsel: Renee M. Marler
Urban Mass Transportation Administration, 211 Main Street, Rm 1160, San Francisco, CA 94105. Tel: 415/774-3133.
FAX: 415/774-2726.

Region X (Seattle)

Regional Counsel: Shelly R. Brown
Urban Mass Transportation Administration, 3142 Federal Bldg, 915 2nd Avenue, Seattle, WA 98174. Tel: 206/442-4210.
FAX: 206/442-4999.

DATABASES AND PUBLICATIONS OF INTEREST

All of UMTA's reports are kept by the Department of Commerce's National Technical Information Service (NTIS) and entered on **DIALOG.** Information regarding these documents can be obtained from NTIS, 5285 Port Royal Road, Springfield, VA 22161. Rush sales: Tel: 1-800/336-4700. Regular sales: Tel: 703/487-4650. To identify a document: Tel: 703/487-4783.

Online **DIALOG** users can access UMTA documents on **TRIS (Transportation Research Information Services)** which is maintained by the Transportation Research Board (TRB) of the National Research Council, which is a private organization. TRB will conduct searches for a fee. Contact the Transportation Research Board, National Research Council, 2101 Constitution Ave., N.W., Washington, D.C. 20418. Tel: 202/334-3251.

U.S. COAST GUARD
2100 Second Street, S.W.
Washington, D.C. 20593-0001

The U.S. Coast Guard, which is a service within the U.S. Department of Transportation, is also a branch of the Armed Forces of the United States and operates as part of the Navy in time of war. Its responsibilities include maritime law enforcement, search and rescue missions on the high seas and on the navigable waters of the U.S., commercial vessel safety, marine environmental response operations, port and environmental safety, boating safety, and waterways management.

The U.S. Coast Guard employs civilian attorneys in the Office of Chief Counsel's Washington, D.C. headquarters office and in District Offices located throughout the U.S. The U.S. Coast Guard also employs military attorneys in these offices.

The Coast Guard "Law Firm" employs attorneys as civilian Government employees. Civilian attorneys who work for the Coast Guard are most likely to be found practicing Government contracting or involved in Government real estate transactions. However, they are not limited to that area and can practice in other areas of law except for matters concerning military justice and legal assistance.

(Area Code 202)
Commandant: Admiral J. William Kime 267-2390
Public Information 267-2229
Publications Information 267-2303
FOIA/Privacy Act 267-2324
Small and Disadvantaged Business Utilization Office ...267-2499

(Area Code 202)
National Response Center: Oil and Chemical Spills:
Washington, DC Metro area 267-2675
Outside Washington, DC Metro area ....(800) 424-8802
Facsimile 267-4158

OFFICE OF CHIEF COUNSEL (Room 3311)

(Area Code 202)
Chief Counsel: Rear Admiral Joseph E. Vorbach 267-1616
Deputy Chief Counsel: Rue B. Helsel 267-1616
Court of Military Review Chief Judge: Joseph H. Baum ...267-0045
Chief Trial Judge: Capt Douglas A. Smith 267-0071
Claims and Litigation Division Chief:
Commander William B. Thomas 267-2245
General Law Division Chief: Walter A. Nicewicz 267-1553
Legal Administration Division Chief and Legal
Assistance Director: Commander Thomas J. Barrett 267-2256

(Area Code 202)
Legislation Division Chief: Captain Kevin J. Barry 267-1467
Maritime and International Law Division Chief:
Captain Jonathan Collom 267-1527
Procurement Law Division Chief: Thomas A. Mason Jr 267-1544
Military Justice Division Chief:
Captain Ronald S. Matthew 267-0272
Regulations and Administrative Law Division Chief:
Alfred F. Bridgman Jr 267-1534

DISTRICT FIELD OFFICES

The Coast Guard has the following district and field offices staffed by attorneys:

Anchorage
Commander Ronald L. Nelson
U.S. Coast Guard Marine Safety Office, Federal Bldg & U.S. Courthouse, 701 C Street, Box 17, Anchorage, AK 99513-0065.
Tel: 907/271-3511.

Alameda
Captain Thomas F. McGrath
12th Coast Guard District, Coast Guard Island, Alameda, CA 94501-5100. Tel: 415/437-3330.

Baltimore
Commander Arthur R. Butler
U.S. Coast Guard Yard, Curtis Bay, Bldg #70, Baltimore, MD 21226-1797.

Boston
Captain Roger A. Brunell
1st Coast Guard District, Coast Guard Bldg, 408 Atlantic Ave, Boston, MA 02210-2209. Tel: 617/223-8500.

Cape May
Commander Carl V. Mosebach
U.S. Coast Guard Training Center, Cape May, NJ 08204
Tel: 609/884-6902.

Cleveland
Commander Mark A. O'Hara
9th Coast Guard District, 1240 East 9th Street, Cleveland, OH 44199-2060. Tel: 216/522-3902.

Honolulu
Commander Malcolm J. Williams
14th Coast Guard District, Prince Kalanianaole Federal Bldg, 9th Fl, 300 Ala Moana Blvd, Honolulu, HI 96850-4982.
Tel: 808/541-2108.

Juneau
Commander Michael L. Dorsey
17th Coast Guard District, P.O. Box 3-5000, Juneau, AK 99802-1217. Tel: 907/586-7398.

Kodiak
Lieutenant Arne O. Denny
U.S. Coast Guard Support Center, P.O. Box 5, Kodiak, AK 99619-5000. Tel: 907/487-5474.

Long Beach
Commander Samuel E. Burton
11th Coast Guard District, Union Bank Bldg, 400 Oceangate, Long Beach, CA 90822-5399. Tel: 213/499-5210.

Miami
Commander Paul J. Prokop
7th Coast Guard District, Federal Bldg, 51 S.W. 1st Avenue, Miami, FL 33130-1608. Tel: 305/536-5610.

New London
Commander D. Gary Beck
U.S. Coast Guard Academy, New London, CT 06320.
Tel: 203/444-8253.

New Orleans
Captain David J. Kantor
8th Coast Guard District, Hale Boggs Federal Bldg, 500 Camp Street, New Orleans, LA 70130-3396. Tel: 504/589-6188.

New York
Captain Robert C. Reining
3rd Coast Guard District, Governors Island, New York, NY 10004-5098. Tel: 212/664-7140/41.

Portsmouth, VA
Captain Michael K. Cain
5th Coast Guard District, Federal Bldg, 431 Crawford Street, Portsmouth, VA 23705-5004. Tel: 804/398-6291.

St Louis
Commander John T. Orchard
2nd Coast Guard District, 1430 Olive Street, St. Louis, MO 63103-2398. Tel: 314/425-4624.

Seattle
Captain Richard E. Peyser
13th Coast Guard District, Federal Bldg, 915 Second Avenue, Seattle, WA 98174. Tel: 206/442-7953.

Yorktown
Lt. Commander Walter J. Brudzinski
U.S. Coast Guard Training Center, Yorktown, VA 23690-5000.

OFFICE OF ADMINISTRATIVE LAW JUDGE (Room 2216)

The Chief Administrative Law Judge is assigned to the Commandant to: act as adviser and special assistant to the Commandant on matters concerning the administration of hearings; conduct hearings; train new Administrative Law Judges; review the written decisions and orders of each Administratgive Law Judge assigned to conduct a hearing; and act as advisor to the Chief Counsel in preparation of any final action of proceeding.

The decisions of the Administrative Law Judge and any appeals of decisions can be obtained by contacting the Office of the Commandant (G-LMI), Maritime and International Law Division, U.S. Coast Guard, 2100 Second Street, S.W., Washington, D.C. 20593.

(Area Code 202)
Chief Administrative Law Judge: Alfred F. Chatterton ..267-2940
Attorney Advisor: George J. Jordan 267-2940

OFFICE OF LAW ENFORCEMENT AND DEFENSE OPERATIONS (Room 3112)

(Area Code 202)
Chief: Rear Admiral Walter T. Leland 267-0977
Deputy Chief: Captain G.F. Crosby 267-1436

Operational Law Enforcement Division
Chief: Captain Samuel J. Dennis 267-1890
Assistant Chief: Commander Robert Gravino 267-1890

(Area Code 202)
Legal Advisor: Lt. Commander Joseph E. Donovan 267-1890
Aviation Law Enforcement Branch Chief: vacant 267-1776
General Law Enforcement Branch Chief:
Commander William H. Anderson 267-1155
Maritime Drug Interdiction Branch Chief:
Commander Allen K. Boetig 267-1776

DEPARTMENT OF TRANSPORTATION
KEY LEGAL AUTHORITIES

General Regulations:

General Departmental Regulations: 49 C.F.R. Part 1 et seq. (1989).
Department of Transportation Acquisition Regulations: 48 C.F.R. Part 1201 et seq. (1989).
Board of Contract Appeals Rules of Practice & Procedure: 48 C.F.R. Part 6302 (1989).
Rulemaking Procedures: 49 C.F.R. Part 5 (1989).
Research & Special Programs Administration: 49 C.F.R. Parts 100-195 (1989).
Federal Railway Administration: 49 C.F.R. Parts 200-268 (1989).
Federal Railway Administration Rules of Practice & Procedure: 49 C.F.R. Part 211 (1989).
Federal Highway Administration: 49 C.F.R. Parts 301-399 (1989).
Federal Highway Administration Rules of Practice & Procedure: 49 C.F.R. Part 386 (1989).
U.S. Coast Guard: 33 C.F.R. Part 1 et seq. (1989); 49 C.F.R. Parts 450-453 (1989).
National Highway Traffic Safety Administration: 49 C.F.R. Parts 501-594 (1989).
National Highway Traffic Safety Administration Rules of Practice & Procedure: 49 C.F.R. Parts 511, 551, 553 (1989).
Urban Mass Transportation Administration: 49 C.F.R. Parts 601-670 (1989).
Commercial Space Transportation Office: 14 C.F.R. Parts 400-415 (1989).
Federal Aviation Administration: 14 C.F.R. Part 1 et seq. (1989).
Federal Aviation Administration Rules of Practice & Procedure: 14 C.F.R. Part 11 (1989).
Federal Highway Administration: 23 C.F.R. Part 1 et seq. (1989).
Maritime Administration: 46 C.F.R. Part 201 et seq. (1989).
Maritime Administration Rules of Practice & Procedure: 46 C.F.R. Part 201 (1989).

Key Statutes:

Department of Transportation Act of 1966, as amended, 49 U.S.C. 1651 et seq.--the Department of Transportation enabling statute.
Legislative History: 1966 U.S. Code Cong. & Admin. News 3362; 1982 U.S. Code Cong. & Admin. News 4220.

Independent Safety Board Act of 1974, as amended, 49 U.S.C. 1903(a)(1)(E)--directs the National Transportation Safety Board to investigate major private vessel marine casualties in accordance with regulations prescribed jointly by the Board and the Secretary of Transportation.
Legislative History: 1974 U.S. Code Cong. & Admin. News 7669.

Hazardous Materials Transportation Act of 1974, as amended, 49 U.S.C. 1801 et seq.--regulates the transportation and handling of hazardous materials, including radioactive materials.
Legislative History: 1974 U.S. Code Cong. & Admin. News 7669.

Hazardous Liquids Pipeline Safety Act of 1979, as amended, 49 U.S.C. App. 2001 et seq.--established Federal safety standards for liquid pipelines.
Legislative History: 1979 U.S. Code Cong. & Admin. News 1971.

Natural Gas Pipeline Safety Act of 1968, as amended, 49 U.S.C. 1671 et seq.--established Federal safety standards and an inspection and compliance regulatory scheme for natural gas pipelines.
Legislative History: 1968 U.S. Code Cong. & Admin. News 3223; 1979 U.S. Code Cong. & Admin. News 1971.

Federal Aviation Act of 1958, as amended, 49 U.S.C. 1301 et seq.--established a comprehensive Federal aviation program, including aircraft safety and control, oversight of aircraft construction, and other aspects of aviation, and invested administrative responsibility in the Federal Aviation Administration.
Legislative History: 1958 U.S. Code Cong. & Admin. News 3741.

Urban Mass Transportation Act of 1964, as amended, 49 U.S.C. 1601 et seq.--designed to develop and improve mass transportation facilities, equipment, techniques, and methods; encourage the planning and establishment of areawide urban mass transportation systems; and assist state and local governments in financing such systems.
Legislative History: 1964 U.S. Code Cong. & Admin. News 2569.

Deepwater Port Act of 1974, as amended, 33 U.S.C. 1501 et seq.--authorizes and regulates the location, ownership, construction, and operation of deepwater ports in waters beyond US territorial waters, and protects marine and coastal environments from the adverse impacts of deepwater port development.
Legislative History: 1974 U.S. Code Cong. & Admin. News 7529.
Implementing Regulations: 33 C.F.R. 148.1 et seq. (1989).

Bridge Act of 1906, as amended, 33 U.S.C. 491 et seq.--governs the construction, operation, and maintenance of bridges over the navigable waters of the U.S.
Implementing Regulations: 33 C.F.R. Parts 114-116 (1989).

Shore Protection Act of 1988, 33 U.S.C. 2601-2623--designed to protect US shorelines and beaches from pollution by municipal or commercial wastes, and regulates waste handling practices.
Legislative History: 1988 U.S. Code Cong. & Admin. News 5767.

U.S. Public Vessel Medical Waste Anti-Dumping Act of 1988, 33 U.S.C. 2501-2504--prohibits the disposal of potentially infectious medical waste into ocean waters by U.S. Government-owned, chartered, or operated vessels.
Legislative History: 1988 U.S. Code Cong. & Admin. News 5767.

Inland Navigational Rules Act of 1980, 33 U.S.C. 2001 et seq.--vessel navigation safety rules administered by the U.S. Coast Guard.
Legislative History: 1980 U.S. Code Cong. & Admin. News 7068.

Act to Prevent Pollution from Ships, as amended, 33 U.S.C. 1901-1912--implements an international convention on ship pollution prevention, and establishes penalties and a private cause of action.
Legislative History: 1980 U.S. Code Cong. & Admin. News 4849; 1987 U.S. Code Cong. & Admin. News 2511.
Implementing Regulations: 33 C.F.R. Parts 151, 155, & 157 (1989).

International Navigational Rules Act of 1977, 33 U.S.C. 1601 et seq.--establishes rules for preventing ship collisions at sea.
Legislative History: 1977 U.S. Code Cong. & Admin. News 509.

Marine Protection Research & Sanctuaries Act of 1972, as amended, 33 U.S.C. 1401-1445--regulates ocean dumping and transportation

of material for the purpose of ocean dumping.
Legislative History: 1972 U.S. Code Cong. & Admin. News 4234; 1988 U.S. Code Cong. & Admin. News 5767.
Implementing Regulations: 40 C.F.R., Chapt I, Subchapt. H (1989).

Outer Continental Shelf Lands Act, as amended, 43 U.S.C. 1331 et seq.--directs the U.S. Coast Guard to enforce safety and environmental regulations promulgated under the Act.
Legislative History: 1978 U.S. Code Cong. & Admin. News 1450.
Implementing Regulations: 33 C.F.R., Chapt. I, Subchapt. N (1989).

Ports & Waterways Safety Act of 1982, as amended, 33 U.S.C. 1221 et seq., 46 U.S.C. 3701 et seq.--provides for increased supervision of vessel and port operations by the U.S. Coast Guard.
Legislative History: 1972 U.S. Code Cong. & Admin. News 2766; 1978 U.S. Code Cong. & Admin. News 3270; 1986 U.S. Code Cong. & Admin. News 1865 & 3607; 1988 U.S. Code Cong. & Admin. News 2149.
Implementing Regulations: 33 C.F.R. 160.1 et seq.; 46 C.F.R., Chapt. I, Subchapt. O (1989).

International Safe Container Act, as amended, 46 U.S.C. App. 1501-1508--regulates international maritime shipping containers.
Legislative History: 1977 U.S. Code Cong. & Admin. News 4017.
Implementing Regulations: 49 C.F.R., Chapt. IV, Subchapt. B (1989).

Coast Guard Vessel Safety & Inspection Programs, 46 U.S.C. 2101-6307.

Coast Guard Merchant Marine Licensing & Oversight, 46 U.S.C. 7101-11507.

Ocean Thermal Energy Conversion Act of 1980, as amended, 42 U.S.C. 9101 et seq.--authorizes and regulates all aspects of the ocean thermal energy conversion industry, and directs the U.S. Coast Guard to regulate the industry and establish safety and environmental requirements.
Legislative History: 1980 U.S. Code Cong. & Admin. News 2407.
Implementing Regulations: 33 C.F.R. Part 64 et seq. (1989); 46 C.F.R. Part 50 et seq. (1989).

Comprehensive Environmental Response, Compensation, & Liability Act of 1980, as amended, 42 U.S.C. 9601, 9608(a)(3)--requires certain vessels carrying hazardous cargo to establish and maintain evidence of financial responsibility and directs the Secretary of Transportation to deny entry to the U.S., and to detain departing vessels that, upon request, cannot certify compliance with the financial responsibility of the Act.
Legislative History: 1980 U.S. Code Cong. & Admin. News 6119.

Deep Seabed Hard Mineral Resources Act, as amended, 30 U.S.C. 1401 et seq.--encourages the commercial development of hard mineral resources of the deep seabed and directs the U.S. Coast Guard to enforce the provisions of the Act addressing the safety of life and property at sea.
Legislative History: 1980 U.S. Code Cong. & Admin. News 1600.

Federal Aid-Highway Act of 1956, as amended, 23 U.S.C. 101 et seq.--designed to stimulate the construction and improvement of the U.S. highway system through Federal financial assistance for state projects.
Legislative History: 1958 U.S. Code Cong. & Admin. News 3942.

Highway Beautification Act of 1965, as amended, 23 U.S.C. 131--restricts outdoor advertising in areas adjacent to the interstate highway system.
Legislative History: 1959 U.S. Code Cong. & Admin. News 2733.
Implementing Regulations: 23 C.F.R. Part 750 et seq. (1989).

Highway Safety Act of 1966, as amended, 23 U.S.C. 401 et seq.--designed to increase highway safety, primarily through Department of Transportation programs aimed at improving highway design, school bus driver training, and preventing drunk driving.
Legislative History: 1966 U.S. Code Cong. & Admin. News 2741; 1982 U.S. Code Cong. & Admin. News 3639.
Implementing Regulations: 23 C.F.R. 625.1, 1204.4 (1989).

Commercial Space Launch Act, 49 U.S.C. App. 2601 et seq.--designed to encourage the U.S. private sector to provide space launch vehicles and services by streamlining the licensing process and stimulating the use of Government-developed space technology.
Legislative History: 1984 U.S. Code Cong. & Admin. News 5328.
Implementing Regulations: 14 C.F.R. Part 1400 et seq. (1989).

Commercial Motor Vehicle Safety Act of 1986, 49 U.S.C. App. 2701 et seq.--superimposes Federal limitations on the issuance of commercial drivers' licenses and establishes safety regulations for commercial drivers and trucks.
Legislative History: 1986 U.S. Code Cong. & Admin. News 5393.

Tandem Truck Safety Act of 1984, 49 U.S.C. App. 2301 et seq.--establishes truck length and width limitations on Federally-assisted highways.
Legislative History: 1982 U.S. Code Cong. & Admin. News 3639.

Federal Railroad Safety Act of 1970, as amended, 45 U.S.C. 421 et seq.--designed to promote safety in railroad operations, reduce railroad-related accidents, and to reduce deaths and injuries to persons and damage to property caused by accidents involving any carrier of hazardous materials.
Legislative History: 1970 U.S. Code Cong. & Admin. News 4104; 1976 U.S. Code Cong. & Admin. News 1534; 1988 U.S. Code Cong. & Admin. News 695.
Implementing Regulations: 49 C.F.R. Part 211 et seq. (1989).

Regional Rail Reorganization Act of 1973, as amended, 45 U.S.C. 701 et seq.--authorizes the Government to assume control of bankrupt railroads in the Northeast and Midwest in order to provide essential rail services; and established Conrail.
Legislative History: 1973 U.S. Code Cong. & Admin. News 3242.
Implementing Regulations: 49 C.F.R. 255.1 et seq. (1989).

Rail Passenger Service Act, as amended, 45 U.S.C. 501 et seq., 851 et seq.--established the National Railroad Passenger Corporation (AMTRAK) to provide intercity railroad and commuter passenger service throughout the U.S.
Legislative History: 1970 U.S. Code Cong. & Admin. News 4735.
Implementing Regulations: 49 C.F.R. 251.1 et seq. (1989).

Boiler Inspection Acts, 45 U.S.C. 1 et seq.--the original railroad safety laws, covering primarily railroad equipment and appliances.
Legislative History: 1988 U.S. Code Cong. & Admin. News 695.
Implementing Regulations: 49 C.F.R. 231.1 et seq. (1989).

National Driver Register Act of 1982, 23 U.S.C. 401note--directed the Secretary of Transportation to establish and maintain a National Drivers Register to assist state motor vehicle departments to exchange information on individual driving records.
Legislative History: 1982 U.S. Code Cong. & Admin. News 3367.

National Traffic & Motor Vehicle Safety Act of 1966, as amended, 15 U.S.C. 1381 et seq.--establishes motor vehicle safety standards for motor vehicles and equipment in interstate commerce and support safety research and development.
Legislative History: 1966 U.S. Code Cong. & Admin. News 2709; 1982 U.S. Code Cong. & Admin. News 3169.
Implementing Regulations: 49 C.F.R. Part 501 et seq. (1989).

Motor Vehicle Information & Cost Savings Act, as amended, 15 U.S.C. 1901 et seq.--mandated fuel efficiency standards, odometer requirements, bumper standards, and other consumer protection requirements on the U.S. automobile fleet.
Legislative History: 1972 U.S. Code Cong. & Admin. News 3960; 1988 U.S. Code Cong. & Admin. News 3643.
Implementing Regulations: 49 C.F.R. Part 501 et seq. (1989).

DEPARTMENT OF THE TREASURY

15th Street and Pennsylvania Avenue, N.W.
Washington, D.C. 20220

DESCRIPTION: The Treasury Department has a wide range of critical responsibilities. These include: 1) formulating domestic and international financial, economic, and tax policy; 2) serving as the financial agent of the Government; 3) manufacturing coins and currency; 4) managing the public debt; 5) collecting Federal revenues; 6) enforcing laws related to such matters as firearms and explosives, imports and exports, counterfeiting, protection, and tax evasion; and 7) exercising general supervision over the operations of national banks and thrift institutions.

(Area Code 202)
Secretary: Nicholas F. Brady 566-2533
Public Affairs 566-2041
Hot Line for Fraud, Waste and Abuse:
Washington, D.C. Metro Area 566-7901
Outside Washington, D.C. Metro Area .... (800) 826-0407
Facsimile 566-8066
Small and Disadvantaged Business Utilization 566-9616

Freedom of Information/Privacy Act Office 566-5231
All FOIA and Privacy Act requests must be in writing and sent to the following address: FOIA/Privacy Act Requests, Disclosure Services, DO Room 1054-MT, U.S. Department of the Treasury, 1500 Pennsylvania Avenue, N.W., Washington, D.C. 20220. The fee for reproduction is 15 cents per page; checks are accepted.

(Area Code 202)
Main Library/Law Library (Room 5030) 566-2777
Interlibrary Loan 566-5212
The law library is open to the public Monday through Friday from 10:00 AM until 5:00 PM, by appointment only. The appointment must be made at least one day in advance by calling the above number. There is no reference or research assistance. Photocopying is 15 cents per page; checks are accepted. The library will loan books to anyone willing to pick up and deliver via a messenger.

OFFICE OF THE GENERAL COUNSEL (Room 3000)

The Office of the General Counsel consists of over 1900 attorneys. Headed by the General Counsel, who is the chief legal officer of the Treasury Department, the Legal Division has responsibility for all legal work in the Department. Activities of the General Counsel include consideration of legal problems relating to broad policy aspects of management of the public debt, administration of internal revenue and tariff laws, a broad range of domestic and international monetary financial issues, law enforcement operations, and related activities.

(Area Code 202)
General Counsel: Edith E. Holiday 566-2093
Deputy General Counsel: Jeanne S. Archibald 566-2977
Associate General Counsel (Legislation, Litigation, and Regulation): Richard S. Carro 566-2558
Chief Counsel for Comptroller of the Currency: Paul Allan Schott 447-1896
Chief Counsel for the Office of Thrift Supervision: Harris Weinstein 906-6268
International Tax Counsel: Philip Morrison 566-5046
Tax Legislative Counsel: Robert Wooton 566-2316
Counsel to the Inspector General: Alexandra B. Keith 566-5668

The Legal Division has five Assistant General Counsels reporting to the General Counsel:

The **Assistant General Counsel serving as Chief Counsel for the Internal Revenue Service.**

(Area Code 202)
Assistant General Counsel (IRS Chief Counsel): Abraham Shashy, Jr 566-6364

The **Assistant General Counsel for Administrative and General Law** provides legal advice concerning administrative matters. This Assistant General Counsel also supervises the Chief Counsel for the U.S. Mint and the Chief Counsel for the Bureau of Engraving and Printing.

The Office of Administrative and General Law handles legal issues that arise concerning ethics, labor relations, equal employment opportunity, and personnel law. Attorneys represent the Department in administrative proceedings and assist in representing its interests in matters before Federal courts. In addition, the Office reviews major procurements for the Department and represents it in Government contract disputes. In the burgeoning area of disclosure law, attorneys in the Office also provide legal guidance to Departmental offices in all stages of response to the Freedom of Information Act and Privacy Act requests.

(Area Code 202)
Assistant General Counsel: Kenneth R. Schmalzbach ... 566-8464
Deputy Assistant General Counsel: Barbara Fredericks 566-8464
Chief Counsel for the Bureau of Engraving and Printing: Michael B. Frosch 447-1425
Chief Counsel for the U.S. Mint: Kenneth B. Gubin ... 376-0564
Senior Counsel for Ethics: Miklos Lonkay 566-2327
Senior Counsel for Technology: William L. Murphy 566-2327

The **Assistant General Counsel for Banking and Finance** provides legal advice in connection with Government financing transactions and issues affecting the financial services industry. In its role as the Treasury Department's principal legal advisor on matters involving banks, thrifts, and other financial institutions, the Office has been involved in litigation affecting nonbank banks, bank and bank holding company activities (including IRA commingled accounts and commercial paper), and rights to payment after foreign assets have been frozen.

This Assistant General Counsel also supervises the Chief Counsel for the Bureau of the Public Debt, the Financial Management Service, and the Office of Revenue Sharing.

(Area Code 202)
Assistant General Counsel: Mary Ann Gadziala 566-8625
Deputy Assistant General Counsel: John E. Bowman 566-8737
Chief Counsel for the Bureau of the Public Debt: Calvin Ninomiya 376-4320
Chief Counsel for Financial Management Service: David Ingold 287-0673

DEPARTMENT OF THE TREASURY

The **Assistant General Counsel for Enforcement** provides legal advice in connection with the development of Treasury law enforcement policy and the enforcement of laws over which the Office has jurisdiction, including the currency reporting laws; tariff, trade, and export control laws; alcohol, tobacco, and firearms laws; and the counterfeiting and forging of currency and Federal securities. Attorneys in the office also provide legal support to the Special Assistant to the Secretary (National Security) concerning national security and intelligence issues.

The Office of the Assistant General Counsel for Enforcement includes over 100 attorneys, of whom seven are on the immediate office staff. The remaining attorneys are employed in bureaus supervised by this Assistant General Counsel, which are: the U.S. Secret Service, the Legal Counsel of the Federal Law Enforcement Training Center, the U.S. Customs Service, and the Bureau of Alcohol, Tobacco and Firearms.

(Area Code 202)

Assistant General Counsel: Robert M. McNamara, Jr ...566-5404
Deputy Assistant General Counsel: James R. Alliston 566-8261
Chief Counsel for the Bureau of Alcohol, Tobacco and Firearms: Marvin J. Dessler 566-7772
Chief Counsel for Foreign Assets Control: William B. Hoffman 376-0408
Chief Counsel for the U.S. Customs Service: Michael T. Schmitz 566-5476
Chief Counsel for the U.S. Secret Service: John J. Kelleher....................535-5771
Legal Counsel/Director, Federal Law Enforcement Training Center, Glynco, GA: Stephan Bodolay ...(912) 267-2441

The **Assistant General Counsel for International Affairs** provides advice on legal issues involving a wide variety of international trade and financial matters. This Assistant General Counsel also supervises the Chief Counsel of the Office of Foreign Assets Control.

The Office of the Assistant General Counsel for International Affairs provides legal advice in connection with a broad range of international economic and financial matters, including third world debt problems; issues involving the International Monetary Fund, the World Bank, and other multilateral development banks; international trade; currency swap arrangements; international investment, international banking and securities issues; and the application of foreign assets controls. Attorneys in the Office also draft legislation, participate in international negotiations, and work on the application of economic sanctions under the International Emergency Economic Powers Act.

(Area Code 202)

Assistant General Counsel: Russell L. Munk 566-8101
Deputy Assistant General Counsel: Marilyn L. Muench 566-8401
Senior Counsel for International Trade: John G. Murphy Jr 566-2352
Senior Counsel for Investments: Richard M. Goodman ..566-8427

The **Office of Foreign Assets Control** advises on the exercise of the President's special wartime and peacetime emergency powers under the Trading with the Enemy Act and the International Emergency Economic Powers Act. The Office assists U.S. foreign policy aims by controlling assets in the United States of "blocked" countries and the flow of funds and trade to them.

Also reporting to the General Counsel are: the Chief Counsel for the Office of the Comptroller of the Currency, the Chief Counsel of the Office of Thrift Supervision, the International Tax Counsel, the Tax Legislative Counsel, and the Counsel to the Inspector General.

Attorneys in the **Office of the International Tax Counsel** handle international tax treaties and foreign tax affairs. Attorneys in the **Office of Tax Legislative Counsel** provide advice on tax policy matters, make recommendations for Departmental tax legislation, and review some IRS rulings and regulations. The **Counsel to the Inspector General** provides legal advice on audits and inspections conducted throughout the Department to combat fraud, waste, and abuse.

OFFICE OF THE ASSISTANT SECRETARY (ENFORCEMENT)

(Area Code 202)

Assistant Secretary: Salvatore R. Martoche 566-2568

Regulatory, Tariff and Trade Enforcement
Deputy Assistant Secretary: John P. Simpson 566-9083
Office of Foreign Assets Control Director: R. Richard Newcomb 376-0395
Chief Counsel: William B. Hoffman 376-0408

(Area Code 202)

Law Enforcement
BATF Liaison: Michael Dodd 566-2127
Customs Liaison: Allen Wilk 566-2872
IRS Liaison: William McGuire 566-3047
Secret Service Liaison: Stephan Ramsey 566-8561
Office of Financial Enforcement Director: Amy Rudnick 566-8022
Office of Law Enforcement Director: Charles Brisbin ..566-8705

OFFICE OF THE ASSISTANT SECRETARY (TAX POLICY)

(Area Code 202)

Assistant Secretary: Kenneth W. Gideon 566-5561
Tax Legislative Counsel: Robert R. Wooten 566-2316
Deputy Tax Legislative Counsel: Eric Zolt 566-5455
Deputy Tax Legislative Counsel (Regulatory Affairs): Ms. Terrill Hyde 566-8277
Associate Tax Legislative Counsel:
Paul Strella 566-8277
Thomas Wessel 566-8277

(Area Code 202)

James Miller 566-8277
Gregory Marich 566-2175
International Tax Counsel: Philip D. Morrison 566-5046
Deputy International Tax Counsel: vacant 566-5992
Associate International Tax Counsel:
Marlin Risinger 566-5791
Peter Barns 566-5815

OFFICE OF INSPECTOR GENERAL (ROOM 2412)

The Inspector General initiates, conducts, and supervises internal audits and internal investigations within the Department. The Inspector General Act Amendments of 1988 further consolidated these responsibilities and provided that the Inspector General would oversee internal investigations made by the Offices of Internal Affairs and Inspection in the Bureau of Alcohol, Tobacco and Firearms, Customs, and Secret Service, and internal audits and internal investigations of the Office of the Assistant Commissioner (Inspection) in IRS.

(Area Code 202)

Inspector General: Donald E. Kirkendall 566-6900
Deputy Inspector General: Robert Cesca 566-6900

(Area Code 202)

FOIA/Privacy Act Coordinator: Ann Marie Gould 377-7482
Counsel to the Inspector General: Alexandra B. Keith ..566-5668

BUREAU OF ALCOHOL, TOBACCO AND FIREARMS
Federal Building, 1200 Pennsylvania Avenue, N.W.
Washington, D.C. 20226

DESCRIPTION: The Bureau of Alcohol, Tobacco and Firearms is responsible for law enforcement, for regulating the alcohol, tobacco and firearms industries, and for the collection of the Federal taxes imposed on distilled spirits and tobacco products. Its mission includes: curbing the illegal traffic in and criminal use of firearms; assisting law enforcement agencies in reducing crime and violence; investigating Federal explosives law violations, including arson-for-profit schemes; issuing licenses and permits; suppressing commercial bribery, consumer deception and other prohibited trade practices in the alcoholic beverage industry; suppressing the illicit manufacture and sale of alcoholic beverages for which Federal tax has not been paid; and assisting the states to eliminate interstate trafficking in, and the sale and distribution of, cigarettes in avoidance of state taxes.

(Area Code 202)

Director: Stephen E. Higgins 566-7511
Public Affairs 566-7286
Facsimile 566-7422

(Area Code 202)

Law Library 566-7477
The library is not open to the public, but the librarian will answer questions over the telephone

THE OFFICE OF THE CHIEF COUNSEL (Room 5226)

The Office of the Chief Counsel performs legal work arising in connection with the administration of laws pertaining to alcohol and tobacco taxes, and various regulatory laws pertaining to alcohol, tobacco, firearms and explosives, enforcement of which is vested in the Bureau of Alcohol, Tobacco and Firearms (ATF). It handles the legal work arising from claims against the U.S. and Bureau employees.

The work of attorneys in the Chief Counsel's Office includes litigation, legislation and regulations, interpretation of statutes and regulations, and providing advice and direction to criminal enforcement and regulatory enforcement personnel. Legal services of the office cover a broad spectrum of law, including criminal law, civil law in general, tort law, tax law, labor law, and administrative law.

(Area Code 202)

Chief Counsel: Marvin J. Dessler 566-7772
Deputy Chief Counsel: Bradley A. Buckles 566-7774
Assistant Chief Counsel for Administration:
Michelle Davis 566-7861
Assistant Chief Counsel for Alcohol and Tobacco:
John J. Manfreda 566-7803
Assistant Chief Counsel for Firearms and Explosives:
Jack B. Patterson 566-7803
Assistant Chief Counsel for Litigation: Imelda Koett ...566-7786

(Area Code 202)

Office of Law Enforcement
Associate Director: Daniel M. Hartnett 566-7585
Explosives Division Chief: James L. Brown 566-7159
Firearms Division Chief: Richard Cook 566-7158
Special Operations Division Chief: Richard Garner ...566-7488

REGIONAL OFFICES

Midwest Region

Regional Counsel: Lenore B. Mintz
Bureau of Alcohol, Tobacco and Firearms, 230 South Dearborn Street, Room 1522, Chicago, IL 60604-1505. Tel: 312/353-3862.

District Counsel: Dale L. Cayot
Bureau of Alcohol, Tobacco and Firearms, 6510A Federal Office Building, 550 Main Street, Cincinnati, OH 45202-3222. Tel: 513/684-3225.

North-Atlantic Region

Regional Counsel: Charles B. Lewis
Bureau of Alcohol, Tobacco and Firearms, 6 World Trade Center, Room 618, New York, NY 10048-0206. Tel: 212/264-8060.

Senior Attorney in Charge: Melanie S. Stinnett
Bureau of Alcohol, Tobacco and Firearms, 841 Chestnut Street, Suite 380, Philadelphia, PA 19107-4226. Tel: 215/597-2051.

Southest Region

Regional Counsel: Michael Martin
Bureau of Alcohol, Tobacco and Firearms, 3835 Presidential Parkway, Atlanta, GA 30340. Tel: 404/986-6020.

Southwest Region

Regional Counsel: Bobby S. Tyler
Bureau of Alcohol, Tobacco and Firearms, 1114 Commerce Street, Room 701, Dallas, TX 75242-1004. Tel: 214/767-2288.

Western Region

Regional Counsel: David E. Brule
Bureau of Alcohol, Tobacco and Firearms, 221 Main Street, Suite 1120, San Francisco, CA 94105-1992. Tel: 415/744-9437.

DEPARTMENT OF THE TREASURY

PUBLICATIONS OF INTEREST

Bureau of Alcohol, Tobacco and Firearms Quarterly Bulletin. Announces all new laws, regulations, codes, and rulings or changes relating to alcohol, tobacco, and firearms. Order from: The Superintendent of Documents, U.S. Government Printing Office, Washington, D.C. 20402. (202/783-3238). Price: $13.00 a year domestic; $16.25 a year foreign. GPO Stock# 748-001-00000-0.

The following publications can be ordered from the U.S. Treasury Department, **Bureau of Alcohol, Tobacco and Firearms**, Distribution Center, 7943 Angus Court, Springfield, VA 22153. (703/455-7801). All of these publications are free of charge when ordered in small quantities.

Laws and Regulations Under the Federal Alcohol Administration Act, Title 27, U.S. Code of Federal Regulations. Publication# 5100.8.

Liquor Laws and Regulations for Retail Dealers. Publication# 5170.2.

Your Guide to Federal Firearms Regulations. Publication# 5300.4.

ATF: Explosives Laws and Regulations. Publication # 5400.7.

Rulings and Procedures Relating to Alcohol, Tobacco and Wagering Matters. Publication # 5600.1.

International Traffic in Arms Regulations (ITAR): Title 22, Code of Federal Regulations, Parts 121-130. Publication# SD-P-3310.1

Selling to the Department of the Treasury. Publication# TD-P-70-06C.

COMPTROLLER OF THE CURRENCY

490 L'Enfant Plaza, S.W.
Washington, D.C. 20219

DESCRIPTION: Created in 1863, the Office of the Comptroller of the Currency (OCC) is the oldest Federal financial regulatory agency. OCC regulates and supervises the national banking system, which consists of Federally-chartered banks representing about one-third of all the banks in the country. Together, these banks hold 60 percent of all the assets and 80 percent of all the international assets of U.S. banks. OCC's primary purpose is to ensure a safe and sound financial system that preserves public confidence and makes available the widest possible variety of financial services. The major tools OCC uses to accomplish these functions are its control over the corporate form and existence of national banks, its rulemaking authority, and its power to examine the operations and management of national banks.

(Area Code 202)

Comptroller of the Currency: Robert L. Clarke 447-1750
Communications Division 447-1800
Facsimile 447-1957

Law/Banking Library 447-1843
The library is open by appointment from 8:00 AM until 5:30 PM. Photocopying is 6 cents per copy. The library has materials specific to law, banking, finance, and economics; it has all the regional reporters and state codes and their supplements. Report to the 6th Floor receptionist upon arrival.

OFFICE OF BANK SUPERVISION-POLICY

(Area Code 202)

Chief National Bank Examiner: Donald G. Coonley 447-1684

OFFICE OF CHIEF COUNSEL (5th FLOOR)

(Area Code 202)

Chief Counsel: Paul Allan Schott 447-1896
Deputy Associate Director: Edward D. Conroy 566-7585
Assistant Chief Counsel: Emily Marwell 447-1896
Assistant Chief Counsel for Policy: Kristina Whittaker 447-1896
Deputy Chief Counsel (Operations): Roberta W. Boylan ..447-1896
Deputy Chief Counsel (Policy: Robert B. Serino 447-1847

The Washington Office of the Law Department is organized into five principal divisions:

The **Legislative and Regulatory Analysis Division**, which advises the Comptroller on legislative and regulatory developments and participates in the drafting of legislation. Attorneys in this Division also serve as counsel to the Comptroller in agency administrative proceedings (seeking cease-and-desist, removal, and civil money penalty relief) by preparing final decisions for the Comptroller's signature.

(Area Code 202)

Legislative and Regulatory Analysis Division Director:
Ms. Raija Bettauer 447-1632
Assistant Directors:
Ford Barrett 447-1177
Brenda Curry 447-1632

The **Legal Advisory Services Division**, which drafts regulations and provides advice on a variety of questions arising under the banking laws and the Glass-Steagall Act, administrative procedures, and disclosure of information. Issues handled include mergers, trust activities, operating subsidiaries, insider transactions, management interlocks, national bank lending limits, and capital requirements, as well as international banking activities. This Division has three sections with separate responsibilities: Bank Powers, Bank Assets and Compliance, and Bank Structure and General Banking.

(Area Code 202)

Legal Advisory Services Division Director:
Eric Thompson 447-1880
Assistant Directors:
William Glidden 447-1881
Harold Hansen 447-1882
Peter Liebesman 447-1883

The **Enforcement and Compliance Division**, which conducts formal administrative proceedings to seek statutory remedies such as cease and desist orders, civil money penalties, and removal of bank officers and directors to ensure compliance with Federal banking laws by national banks and bank management. This Division also makes referrals to the Department of Justice concerning criminal acts involving bank officials.

(Area Code 202)

Enforcement and Compliance Division Director:
Ralph E. Sharpe 447-1818
Assistant Directors:
Robert Paisley 447-1818
Daniel Stipano 447-1818

The **Securities and Corporate Practices Division**, which provides advice, issues interpretations, drafts regulations, and handles other matters concerning a range of securities and related banking law issues and certain corporate matters. The Division also prosecutes administrative and judicial enforcement matters involving violations of Federal securities and related banking laws. Areas of responsibility include securities offerings, shareholder meetings, proxy solicitations, broker/dealer activity, Glass-Steagall Act, changes in control, trusts, mergers and consolidations, and corporate governance.

(Area Code 202)

Securities and Corporate Practices Division Director:
Ellen Broadman 447-1954
Assistant Directors:
William Dehnke 447-1954
Donald Lamson 447-1954

The **Litigation Division**, which represents the Comptroller and OCC employees in litigation and related judicial proceedings. Attorneys in this Division prepare litigation risk analyses, litigation strategy, pleadings, and legal memoranda; and conduct discovery, oral argument, and try cases on behalf of OCC.

(Area Code 202)

Litigation Division Director: L. Robert Griffin 447-1893
Assistant Director: James Gillespie 447-1893

DISTRICT COUNSELS

The Law Department also has six District Counsel offices, one in each of the national bank districts. Attorneys in these district offices assist in resolving legal questions arising in the course of examinations of national banks. Attorneys also participate in administrative hearings and provide advice on a wide range of questions raised by bank officials, bank counsel, and others. The regional offices are as follows:

Atlanta
District Counsel: H. Gary Pannell
Comptroller of the Currency, Southeastern District, Marquis One Tower, Suite 600, 245 Peachtree Center Ave, NE, Atlanta, GA 30303. Tel: 404/588-4520.

Chicago
District Counsel: James M. King
Comptroller of the Currency, Central District, 1 Financial Place, Suite 2700, 440 South LaSalle Street, Chicago, IL 60605. Tel: 312/663-8000.

Dallas
District Counsel: R. Patrick Parise
Comptroller of the Currency, Southwestern District, 1600 Lincoln Plaza, 500 North Akard, Dallas, TX 75201-3394. Tel: 214/720-7011.

Kansas City
District Counsel: Michael J. O'Keefe
Comptroller of the Currency, Mid-Western District, 2345 Grand Avenue, Suite 700, Kansas City, MO 64108. Tel: 816/556-1870.

New York
District Counsel: Wallace S. Nathan
Comptroller of the Currency, Northeastern District, 1114 Avenue of the Americas, Suite 3900, New York, NY 10036. Tel: 212/790-4010.

San Francisco
District Counsel: Joseph Pogar, Jr.
Comptroller of the Currency, Western District, 50 Fremont Street, Suite 3900, San Francisco, CA 94105. Tel: 415/545-5900.

PUBLICATIONS OF INTEREST

The following publications are issued by the **Comptroller of the Currency**. To order, cite the title(s) of the publication(s) which you want, include a check payable to Comptroller of the Currency for the total cost, and submit to: Comptroller of the Currency, P.O. Box 70004, Chicago, IL 60673-0004.

The Director's Book. Provides general guidance to directors of national banks. It outlines the responsibilities of the board and addresses in broad terms the duties and liabilities of the individual director. Price: $2.00.

Banking Bulletins and Circulars. Contains issuances sent to all national banks. Circulars provide information of continuing concern regarding OCC policies and guidelines. Bulletins inform readers of pending regulatory changes and other general information. Annual subscription price: $100.00.

Examining Bulletins and Circulars. Contains advice and instructions to OCC's staff of national bank examiners. They provide insight into how examiners are being told to evaluate the banks they supervise. Annual subscription price: $100.00.

Interpretations. Monthly. Provides legal staff interpretations, trust interpretative letters, and investment securities letters. This monthly package represents the informal views of the Comptroller's staff concerning the applications of banking law to contemplated activities or transactions. Annual subscription price: $125.00.

Weekly Bulletin. Reports on all corporate decisions by the Office nationwide each week. Applications, approvals or denials, and consummations are noted for new banks, mergers, consolidations, and purchases and assumptions that result in national banks. Annual subscription price: $250.00.

Quarterly Journal. The journal of record for the most significant actions and policies of the Office of the Comptroller of the Currency. Published in March, June, September, and December. Annual subscription price: $60.00.

Comptroller's Manual for Corporate Activities. Makes available in one place OCC policies and procedures for processing applications for forming a new national bank. It includes sample documents required from applicants as well as pertinent laws, rulings, and regulations. Price: $90.00.

Comptroller's Manual for National Banks. A looseleaf legal reference containing laws applicable to national banks with sections dealing with regulations and interpretative rulings issued by the OCC. Price: $90.00.

Comptroller's Handbook for Consumer Examinations. A looseleaf publication intended to assist the examiner in understanding those selected portions of consumer laws and regulations pertinent to an examination of a national bank. Examination procedures are also included in this volume. Price: $90.00.

Comptroller's Handbook for National Bank Examiners. A looseleaf publication containing policies and procedures for the commercial examination of national banks. Price: $90.00.

Comptroller's Handbook for National Trust Examiners. A looseleaf publication presenting policies and procedures for the examination of the fiduciary activities of national banks. Price: $90.00.

Comptroller's Handbook for Compliance. Contains all the procedures used in compliance examinations. A handbook intended for use by examiners as a supervisory tool in performing compliance examinations and by bankers as a self-assessment tool for analyzing bank compliance systems. Price: $25.00.

Fair Housing Home Loan Data System. Published for lending departments and officials of national banks, this booklet contains the final regulation for the Fair Housing Home Loan Data System, instruction forms, and examples. Price: $1.50.

Money Laundering: A Banker's Guide to Avoiding Problems. No charge.

U.S. CUSTOMS SERVICE

1301 Constitution Avenue, N.W.
Washington, D.C. 20229

DESCRIPTION: The U.S. Customs Service collects the revenue from imports and enforces customs and related laws. Responsibilities include: collecting customs duties, excise taxes, and penalties due on imported merchandise; interdicting and seizing contraband, including narcotics and illegal drugs; processing persons, carriers, cargo, and mail into and out of the United States; administering certain navigation laws; and detecting and apprehending persons engaged in fraudulent practices designed to circumvent customs and related laws; copyright, patent, and trademark provisions; and quotas. The U.S. Customs Service also administers and enforces over 400 statutory or regulatory requirements relating to international trade. Such activities include enforcing export control laws, intercepting illegal high-technology exports, and cooperating with the Drug Enforcement Administration to suppress traffic in illegal narcotics. Although headquartered in Washington, D.C., the Service is highly decentralized and most of its personnel are stationed throughout the country and overseas, where its operational functions are performed.

(Area Code 202)

Commissioner: Carol Hallett 566-2101
Facsimile 633-7645

Customs Service Library (Room 3340) 566-5406
The library is open to the public Monday through Friday from 8:30 AM until 5:00 PM. It is open by appointment, on a very limited basis.

OFFICE OF THE CHIEF COUNSEL (ROOM 3305)

The Office of Chief Counsel. As the chief legal officer of the U.S. Customs Service, the Chief Counsel reviews proposed actions to ensure compliance with legal requirements; prepares formal legal opinions; and prepares responses in all court actions, civil or criminal, involving the Service. The Chief Counsel also makes recommendations to the Department of Justice on matters involving the settlement, compromise, or dismissal of certain types of fine, penalty, and forfeiture litigation; certain tort claims litigation; and the settlement or termination of litigation in cases which do not involve a monetary amount.

Attorneys in all sections assist and coordinate with attorneys from the Department of Justice in cases involving the Customs Service pending before the U.S. Claims Court, U.S. District Courts, U.S. Courts of Appeal, the U.S. Supreme Court, and other courts. An attorney may also serve as trial counsel when requested to do so by the Department of Justice.

(Area Code 202)

Chief Counsel: Michael T. Schmitz 566-5476
Deputy Chief Counsel: Elizabeth Anderson 566-5476
Assistant Chief Counsel for the National Financial and Logistics Centers: James M. Moster .... (317) 298-1233
Facsimile 377-9282

The **Assistant Chief Counsel for Customs Court Litigation** (located in New York City) directs Customs Service national programs related to the preparation and presentation of cases in the U.S. Court of International Trade and appeals from that court to the U.S. Court of Appeals for the Federal Circuit.

Assistant Chief Counsel for the Court of International Trade Litigation: Daniel A. Pinkus .... (212) 264-9271

The Office of Chief Counsel has three divisions:

Trade, Tariff and Legislation: which handles all matters pertaining to the licensing of customshouse brokers and others permitted to conduct business granted by Customs; makes legal determinations concerning claims against the Service; provides legal advice on contracts, leases, and acquisitions; coordinates the legal review of international agreements affecting tariffs; and develops the Customs Service's legislative program.

(Area Code 202)

Assistant Chief Counsel for Trade, Tariffs and Legislation: Allan L. Martin 566-2482

Enforcement: which reviews all civil penalty and forfeiture decisions; prepares manuals and training materials on subjects of criminal and civil laws enforced by Customs; recommends regulatory or policy changes; reviews classified matters involving intelligence or national security; and assists in drafting international agreements involving enforcement issues.

(Area Code 202)

Assistant Chief Counsel for Enforcement: Steven L. Basha 566-2482

Administration: which is responsible for personnel and labor management relations, including providing legal representation in unfair labor practice hearings; assisting in the filing of petitions for review, adverse action appeals, appeals on negotiability issues, and related actions; and drafting regulations and policy issuances concerning personnel and labor relations.

(Area Code 202)

Assistant Chief Counsel for Administration: John P. Helm 566-6245

FIELD OFFICES

Attorneys in the seven **Regional Counsel Offices** (located in Boston, New York City, Miami, New Orleans, Houston, Long Beach, and Chicago) provide legal advice and support on issues arising in the course of Customs Service activities. Duties include preparing legal opinions, preparing responses in court actions, and developing and implementing regionwide programs and procedures. Three Customs Regions also have **District Counsel Offices** (located in Charleston, SC; El Paso; San Diego; San Francisco; and Seattle), which provide similar advice and services in narrower geographic areas.

Boston
Regional Counsel: John R. de Romoet
U.S. Customs Service, Room 879, 10 Causeway Street, Boston, MA 02222-1056. Tel: 617/565-6350.

Chicago
Regional Counsel: Saul N. Perla
U.S. Customs Service, Room 1520, 55 East Monroe Street, Chicago, IL 60603-5790. Tel: 312/353-7860.

Houston
Regional Counsel: James deStefano
U.S. Customs Service, 5850 Felipe Street, Houston, TX 77057-3012. Tel: 713/953-6827.

El Paso
District Counsel: David Lindsey
U.S. Customs Service, 6585 Montana Street, Suite 100, El Paso, TX 79925. Tel: 915/764-2359.

Long Beach
Regional Counsel: Paul Wilson
U.S. Customs Service, Suite 741, One World Trade Center, Long Beach, CA 90831. Tel: 213/491-7241.

San Diego
District Counsel: Alfred A. Suarez
U.S. Customs Service, 880 Front Street, Room 5-S-9, San Diego, CA 92188. Tel: 619/557-6633.

San Francisco
District Counsel: Gary L. Graff
U.S. Customs Service, 555 Battery Street, P.O. Box 2450, San Francisco, CA 94126. Tel: 415/556-9739.

Seattle
District Counsel: Patricia Olson
U.S. Customs Service, 909 First Avenue, Seattle, WA 98174. Tel: 206/442-1299.

Miami
Regional Counsel: K. Brooks Thomas
U.S. Customs Service, Suite 6320, 909 S.E. First Avenue, Miami, FL 33131-2595. Tel: 305/536-4321.

Charleston, SC
District Counsel: John Flynn
U.S. Customs Service, 200 East Bay Street, Charleston, SC 29401-2611. Tel: 803/724-4465.

New Orleans
Regional Counsel: Hattie Broussard
U.S.Customs Service, 423 Canal Street, New Orleans, LA 70130-2341. Tel: 504/589-6358.

New York
Regional Counsel: Melvyn N. Minsky
U.S. Customs Service, Room 732, 6 World Trade Center, New York, NY 10048-0945. Tel: 212/466-4562.

OFFICE OF COMMERCIAL OPERATIONS (Room 3117)

(Area Code 202)

Assistant Commissioner: D. Lynn Gordon 566-5497
Office of Regulations and Rulings Director:
Harvey B. Fox 566-2507
International Nomenclature Staff Director: Miles Harmen 566-8530
Legal Reference Staff Branch Chief: Thomas J. Budnik ..566-6955

Commercial Rulings Division
Director: John Durant 566-5868
Entry Rulings Branch Chief: William G. Rosoff 566-5856
General Classification Branch Chief: John Elkins 566-8181
Value, Special Programs, and Admissibility Branch Chief:
Marvin M. Amornick 566-2938

(Area Code 202)

Regulatory Procedures and Penalties Division
Director: Stuart P. Seidel 566-7005
Carrier Rulings Branch Chief: James B. Fritz 566-5706
Penalties Branch Chief: Edward T. Rosse 566-8317
Regulations Control and Disclosure Law Branch Chief:
Kathryn C. Peterson 566-8237

Office of Regulatory Audit
Compliance Division Director: Matthew W. Krimski 566-2812
Revenue/Enforcement Division Director: Janet Labuda .566-5739

(Area Code 202)

Office of Trade Operations
Director: Victor G. Weeren 566-8047
Field Operations Division Director: Gerald Laderberg 566-5307

(Area Code 202)

Regulatory Trade Programs Division Director:
William D. Slyne 566-2957

OFFICE OF ENFORCEMENT (Room 3104)

(Area Code 202)

Assistant Commissioner: John E. Hensley 566-2416

Office of Aviation Operations
Deputy Assistant Commissioner: R.L. Asack 535-6368

Office of Commercial Fraud Enforcement
Director: Stephen Devaughn 566-5871
Customs Fraud Enforcement Center Division
Director: John Esau 566-9269
Fraud Enforcement Field Unit
Team Leader: Jerry Cole 566-9269
Import Specialist Enforcement Team Field Unit
Team Leader: Rick Grossman 566-2535
Foreign Assets Control & Foreign Trade Zone
Team Leader: John Mallamo 535-4399
Steel and Special Interest Commodity Team
Team Leader: vacant 566-2270
Textiles Team Leader: Robert Dorsett 535-4898
Trademark and Drawback Team Leader: Robert Marcus ... 566-2816

(Area Code 202)

Office of Enforcement Operations
Director: vacant 566-2416
Fraud Investigations Division:
Director: Shelley Altenstadter 566-5871
Smuggling Investigations Division:
Director: Clark W. Settles 566-8005
Special Investigations Division:
Director: vacant 566-5401
FOIA/Privacy Act Branch Chief: Gloria Marshall 566-9201
Strategic Investigations Division:
Director: John C. Kelly Jr 566-5104

Office of Intelligence
Director: Janet Gunther 535-6600

El Paso Intelligence Center, Texas
Senior Special Agent: David Porter ....(915) 564-2000

OFFICE OF INSPECTION AND CONTROL (Room 3112)

(Area Code 202)

Assistant Commissioner: Charles Winwood 566-2366

Office of Cargo Enforcement and Facilitation
Director: Albert Tennant 566-5354

(Area Code 202)

Office of Inspectional Enforcement Liaison
Director: John B. McGowan 566-2140

Office of Passenger Enforcement and Facilitation
Director: Robert A. Bartol 566-5607

OFFICE OF INTERNATIONAL AFFAIRS (Room 3137)

(Area Code 202)

Assistant Commissioner: James W. Shaver 566-5303

PUBLICATIONS OF INTEREST

The following publications can be purchased from the **U.S. Government Printing Office.** Stock numbers and prices for annual subscriptions are shown below. Submit requests for these publications to: The Superintendent of Documents, U.S. Government Printing Office, Washington, D.C. 20402. (202/783-3238).

<u>Customs Bulletin and Decisions</u>. A weekly publication containing regulations, rulings, decisions, and notices concerning Customs and related matters in the U.S. Court of Appeals for the Federal Circuit and the U.S. Court of International Trade. Price: $114.00 per year domestic; $142.50 per year foreign. GPO Stock# 748-002-00000-6.

<u>Customs Regulations of the United States</u>. 1989. Contains regulations made and published for the purpose of carrying out customs laws administered by the U.S. Customs Service. A subscription service consisting of a basic manual and supplementary material for an indeterminate period. In looseleaf form, punched for 3-ring binder. Price: $40.00 domestic; $50.00 foreign. GPO Stock# 948-006-00000-6.

Single copies of the following publications can be obtained free of charge from: **U.S. Customs Service**, P.O. Box 7407, Washington, D.C. 20044.

<u>Importing into the United States</u>. March 1990. 88 pages. Topics addressed include entry of goods, assessment of duty, classification and value, marking, fraud, and foreign trade zones. Appendix contains copies of a pro forma invoice, carrier's certificate, corporate surety power of attorney, Customs bond, and entry summary.

<u>U.S. Import Requirements</u>. Pamphlet.
<u>U.S. Customs: International Mail Imports</u>. Pamphlet.
<u>Tariff Classification of Prospective Imports</u>. Pamphlet.
<u>Foreign Trade Zones: U.S. Customs Procedures and Requirements</u>. Pamphlet.

BUREAU OF ENGRAVING AND PRINTING
14th and C Streets, S.W.
Washington, D.C. 20228

DESCRIPTION: The Bureau of Engraving and Printing designs, engraves, and prints U.S. currency, postage stamps, Treasury obligations (bills, bonds, certificates, notes, etc.), and other U.S. securities. Attorneys in the Office of Chief Counsel handle a broad range of labor-relations and procurement activities, fiscal matters, questions relating to patent and technical data rights, and personnel, EEO, environmental, product security and tort law issues.

(Area Code 202)
Director: Peter H. Daly 447-1364
Chief Counsel: Michael B. Frosch 447-1425
Office of Advanced Counterfeit Deterrence 447-0111

(Area Code 202)
Public Information 447-0193
Facsimile 447-0915

FEDERAL LAW ENFORCEMENT TRAINING CENTER
Building 94
Glynco, GA 31524

DESCRIPTION: The Federal Law Enforcement Training Center trains all criminal law enforcement officers of the Federal Government except the FBI. Headquartered in Glynco, GA, the Center provides instruction on basic law enforcement skills and conducts advanced programs in such areas as white collar crime, procurement/contract fraud, and marine law enforcement. Highly specialized training programs are also offered to state and local law enforcement officials.

(Area Code 912)
Director: Charles F. Rinkevich 267-2224
Legal Counsel: Stephen M. Bodolay 267-2441
Facsimile 267-2217

(Area Code 912)
Office of General Training Legal Division Chief:
James King 267-2689

FINANCIAL MANAGEMENT SERVICE
401 14th Street, S.W.
Washington, D.C. 20227

DESCRIPTION: The Financial Management Service (FMS) is responsible for the Government's cash management, credit management, and debt collection programs, payments, and collections, the investment of social security and other trust funds, and the Government's central accounting and reporting system.

(Area Code 202)
Commissioner: William E. Douglas 287-0700

(Area Code 202)
Facsimile 287-0715

THE OFFICE OF CHIEF COUNSEL (Room 531)

The Office of Chief Counsel consists of attorneys and related support staff who report to the General Counsel through the Assistant General Counsel, Banking and Finance. The function of the Chief Counsel is to provide legal advice and other services, as requested, to the Commissioner and the staff of the Financial Management Service, and to assist the Department of Justice in representing the interests of the U.S. in litigation in which FMS is interested. In addition, the Office reviews for legal sufficiency major solicitations and contract awards, proposed legislation that may affect FMS, and other administrative actions and initiatives. The Office also represents the Service's interests in third party administrative proceedings before the Merit Systems Protection Board and the General Services Administration Board of Contract Appeals.

(Area Code 202)
Chief Counsel: David Ingold 287-0673

ASSISTANT COMMISSIONER (HEADQUARTERS OPERATIONS)

(Area Code 301)

Assistant Commissioner: Bland T. Brockenborough 436-6349

Adjudication Division
Director: Harvey D. Cable 436-6390

(Area Code 301)

Claims Liaison Branch Manager: Ella Redfield 436-6358
Questioned Documents Branch Manager:
Thomas Hundley 436-6368

INTERNAL REVENUE SERVICE
1111 Constitution Avenue, N.W.
Washington, D.C. 20224

DESCRIPTION: The Internal Revenue Service (IRS) administers Federal tax laws and regulations and collects tax revenues. The country is divided into seven broad multi-state regions (the North Atlantic Region, Mid-Atlantic Region, Southeast Region, Central Region, Midwest Region, Southwest Region, and Western Region), in which the chief IRS legal official is the Regional Counsel. Within these Regions, there are then 54 Internal Revenue Service Districts, each administered by a District Director whose legal advisor is the District Counsel. Districts may encompass an entire state, or a certain number of counties within a state, depending on population.

(Area Code 202)

Commissioner: Frederick T. Goldberg, Jr 566-4115
IRS Integrity Hotline (Fraud, Waste, and Abuse) (800) 366-4484
Public Information 566-4743
Freedom of Information Act/Privacy Act Reading Room ...566-3770
Tax Forms and Publications Division
To order forms call: ....(800) 424-3676
Facsimile..566-6105

Taxpayers Assistance (Room 1569) ....(800) 424-1040
This is a reading room which has the Chief Counsel's Memos, private letter rulings and issues that deal with topics on taxation. It is open to the public Monday through Friday from 9:00 AM until 4:00 PM.

(Area Code 202)

Legislative Research Group 566-3211
Although this Group's reading room (which is part of the Chief Counsel's Library) is not open to the public, they will answer questions over the phone.

Office of the Taxpayer Ombudsman
Taxpayer Ombudsman: Damon O. Holmes 566-6475
Problem Resolution Program Staff Director: Linda Martin 566-4948

Law Library 566-6342
The library is not open to the public. However, library personnel will take questions over the phone and will direct callers to where the needed information may be obtained.

OFFICE OF THE CHIEF INSPECTOR (INSPECTION)

(Area Code 202)

Chief Inspector: Teddy R. Kern 566-4656

OFFICE OF THE DEPUTY COMMISSIONER (OPERATIONS)

(Area Code 202)

Deputy Commissioner: Charles H. Brennan 566-4386

Office of Assistant Commissioner (Collection)
Assistant Commissioner: Raymond Keenan 566-4033

Office of Assistant Commissioner (Criminal Investigation)
Assistant Commissioner: Inar Morics 566-6723

Office of Assistant Commissioner (Employee Plans and Exempt Organizations)
Assistant Commissioner: Robert I. Brauer 566-3171

Office of Assistant Commissioner (Examination)
Assistant Commissioner: David G. Blattner 566-4046

(Area Code 202)

Office of International Programs
Director: Stanley Novack 447-1108
Tax Treaty Division Chief: Elvin Hedgepeth 287-4739
International Enforcement Division Chief:
Graham Clark 447-1115
Office of Taxpayer Service and Compliance:
Director: Stanley Beesley 447-1435

Office of Assistant Commissioner (Returns Processing)
Assistant Commissioner: Charles J. Peoples 566-6335

Office of Assistant Commissioner (Taxpayer Services)
Assistant Commissioner: Robert LeBaube 377-6058

OFFICE OF THE CHIEF COUNSEL (Room 3026)

The **Office of Chief Counsel** performs a variety of important legal services, such as the trial of Tax Court cases, the drafting of Treasury regulations, the review and referral of criminal prosecution recommendations, the drafting of revenue rulings, and the issuance of private tax rulings. The office also performs non-tax legal work for the IRS, including labor relations, contracts, torts, Freedom of Information Act (FOIA), and Privacy Act matters. The Chief Counsel is responsible for representing and advising IRS officials, both in the National Office (in Washington, D.C.) and in field offices, in all litigation and other legal matters, both tax and non-tax.

(Area Code 202)

Chief Counsel: Abraham N.M. Shashy Jr 566-6364
Deputy Chief Counsel: David Jordan 566-4735

Office of the National Director of Appeals
National Director: James J. Casimir 252-8221
Deputy National Director: John J. Monaco 252-8221
Technical Assistants:
Bonnie S. Franklin 252-8221
Tom Louthan (International) 252-8221
Office of TEFRA (Tax Equity and Fiscal Responsibility Act) and Tax Shelter Programs:
Director: Kathleen Novack 252-8159

National Office Organization and Responsibilities

The National Office consists of Technical, Litigation, International Tax, and Finance and Management components.

NATIONAL OFFICE TECHNICAL. The five offices reporting to the Associate Chief Counsel (Technical) are primarily responsible for developing and applying basic principles and rules for the uniform interpretation and application of Federal tax laws. Each office is responsible for administering the sections of the tax law under its jurisdiction.

The primary activities performed by attorneys in these offices include issuing private letter rulings and technical advice, initiating and drafting revenue rulings and procedures, developing and drafting regulations, participating in the development of new tax legislation, and assisting in the development of litigating positions.

The issuance of private letter rulings and technical advice involves extensive analysis of complex tax issues, and deals with both proposed and completed transactions.

The initiation and drafting of revenue rulings and revenue procedures for publication in the Internal Revenue Bulletin involves the application of the Code to various factual situations. Revenue rulings and procedures are the official published positions of the IRS and provide guidance to taxpayers and IRS personnel with respect to the most significant tax issues.

The development and drafting of regulations involve the interpretation of the intent of Congress in enacting tax legislation.

Participation in the development of new tax legislation includes developing proposals, assisting congressional staff in drafting new or amended Code provisions, and reviewing draft committee report language. Attorneys involved in the development of legislation work closely with the staff of the Joint Committee on Taxation, the Senate Finance Committee, the House Ways and Means Committee, and officials at the Office of the Tax Legislative Counsel at the Treasury Department.

The five Technical organizations are:

* **Income Tax and Accounting**, which has primary responsibility for the Federal tax laws applicable to the income, deductions, and exclusions of individuals and corporations, and the Federal tax laws applicable to tax accounting. Subjects handled include: like-kind exchanges, charitable contributions, business expenses, alternative minimum tax, alimony payments, tax penalties, tax procedure, uniform capitalization, long-term contracts, installment sales, and greenmail.

* **Corporate**, which has primary responsibility over the law applicable to reorganizations involving domestic and foreign corporations and consolidated returns. Subjects handled include general reorganizations, redemptions, liquidations, spinoffs, transfers to controlled corporations, debt v. equity determinations, bankruptcy, and transactions involving affiliated groups of corporations.

* **Passthroughs and Special Industries**, which has primary responsibility over the Federal tax laws involving entities that passthrough tax attributes to their owners, such as partnerships, trusts and estates, and S corporations. This organization is also responsible for tax issues involved with certain specialized industries such as public utilities, natural resources, and cooperatives. Subjects handled include partnerships, S corporations, classification of foreign and domestic entities, estates and trusts, passive activity losses, personal holding companies, excise taxes, estate and gift taxes, oil and gas, natural resources, tax credits, depreciation, at-risk rules, public utilities, and cooperatives.

* **Financial Institutions and Products**, which has primary responsibility over issues involving financial institutions and products, insurance companies and products, and tax exempt bonds. Subjects handled include banks, savings and loan associations, regulated investment companies, real estate investment trusts, real estate mortgage investment companies, insurance companies and products, annuities, original issue discount obligations, arbitrage bonds, new types of financial instruments, and all types of tax exempt financing.

* **Employee Benefits/Exempt Organizations**, which has primary responsibility over issues involving employee benefits, employee plans, and exempt organizations. Subjects handled include qualified employee plans, other non-qualified plans, employee stock options and other employee benefits, classification and qualification of various types of tax exempt entities, private foundations, and employment tax issues.

(Area Code 202)

Associate Chief Counsel: Kenneth Klein 566-4433
Deputy Associate Chief Counsel: Kenneth E. Kempson ..566-3785

Corporate
Assistant Chief Counsel: Mario E. Lombardo 566-3223
Deputy Chief Counsel: Donald E. Osteen 566-3224

Employee Benefits and Exempt Organizations
Assistant Chief Counsel: James J. McGovern 566-3540
Deputy Assistant Chief Counsel: Mary Oppenheimer 566-6628
Deputy Assistant Chief Counsel: Michael A. Thrasher ..566-3576

Financial Institutions and Products
Assistant Chief Counsel: James F. Malloy 566-3373
Deputy Assistant Chief Counsel: Paul A. Francis 566-3218

Income Tax and Accounting
Assistant Chief Counsel: E. Leon Kennedy (Acting) 566-4504
Deputy Assistant Chief Counsel:
David E. Dickinson (Acting) 566-3274
Irwin A. Leib 566-3805
James B. Webb 566-3183

Passthroughs and Special Industries
Assistant Chief Counsel: Paul F. Kugler 566-3767
Deputy Assistant Chief Counsel:
Richard H. Manfreda 566-3788
Geoffrey J. Taylor 566-3788

NATIONAL OFFICE LITIGATION. The Litigation function under the supervision of the Associate Chief Counsel (Litigation) in the National Office has four offices and three program responsibilities. The four offices are:

* Tax Litigation
* General Litigation
* Criminal Tax
* Disclosure Litigation

The three program areas include:

* The Industry Specialization Program
* The Special Trial Attorney Program
* The Appellate Litigation Program

The responsibilities of the four National Office Litigation offices are as follows:

* **Criminal Tax.** Attorneys in the National Office perform a variety of legal duties in connection with the operation of the criminal tax program nationwide. For example, they handle centralized criminal tax cases, search warrant and immunity applications, appeals, legislative matters, and opinions and guidelines which impact the criminal tax function nationally. These attorneys also coordinate criminal tax matters between the Criminal Tax function and the Regional and District Counsel offices.

* **Disclosure Litigation.** Attorneys assigned to the Disclosure Litigation Office handle all matters relating to the disclosure of any records or information of the IRS. Attorneys advise other Service functions as to the availability of records under the Freedom of Information Act, the Privacy Act of 1974, and the disclosure provisions of the Internal Revenue Code. In related litigation, or in cases where an employee's refusal to testify or produce Service records or information results in the employee being held in contempt of court, the Office recommends the defense and assists the Department of Justice with the pleadings, discovery, and any questions of law or fact which arise during litigation. The Office is also responsible for reviewing reports regarding possible criminal violations of section 7213 of the Code (the criminal sanctions for unlawful disclosures of tax return information) and for making prosecution recommendations to the Department of Justice with respect to such violations.

* **General Litigation.** In the National Office, General Litigation Office attorneys make recommendations to the Tax Division of the Department of Justice as to appeal and certiorari where adverse decisions are entered. Their area of responsibility is primarily collection issues, including constitutional and administrative law, property law, creditors' rights, bankruptcy, and insolvency, as well as summons enforcement. They also handle centralized court cases which generally seek injunctions against senior IRS or Treasury officials in Washington, D.C. Additional responsibilities include the preparation of legal advice memoranda and handling legislation and regulations for the General Litigation functional area.

***Tax Litigation.** Attorneys assigned to the National Office are engaged in three principal types of activities: (1) the consideration of substantive tax issues, including the review of U.S. Tax Court briefs and defense letters in U.S. District Court refund cases prepared in the field, the preparation of defense letters in all U.S. Claims Court refund cases, the preparation of Tax Litigation advice memoranda in response to field requests, and the formulation of positions to be taken in litigation; (2) appellate court work such as recommendations concerning appeal and certiorari, and the preparation of actions on decisions (acquiescence or nonacquiescence); and (3) procedural matters, such as the handling of cases at the U.S. Tax Court's weekly motions calendar and advising field offices on procedural issues.

National Office attorneys are also responsible for litigating most insurance cases and many declaratory judgment cases in the Tax Court, including those involving qualification of retirement plans, tax exempt organizations, and tax exempt bonds. They also formulate tax shelter technical positions and litigation strategy, and directly litigate major tax shelter cases; work with other National Office and field attorneys in the Industry Specialization Program and Coordinated Examination Program developing legal positions and strategies regarding issues with large revenue impact or industry-wide significance; and review proposed regulations, revenue rulings, and private letter rulings with a view to their impact on litigation.

The responsibilities of the three National Office Litigation programs are as follows:

The **Industry Specialization Program Coordinator** assures identification of key issues in specific industries and the development of technical and litigating positions in support of the examination function. This cross-functional program involves both the technical and litigating functions and ensures that any necessary expertise is devoted to the development or resolution of the substantive position.

The **Special Litigation Counsel** oversees the **Special Trial Attorney Program** throughout the country. These litigators are the Office's most senior and experienced individuals who are charged with litigating the largest and most significant cases developed by the IRS. Within this program the Associate Chief Counsel (Litigation) has a staff of special trial attorneys who try cases of national significance in the U.S. Tax Court.

The **Special Appellate Counsel** oversees the appellate recommendations made on behalf of the IRS both at the trial level as well as at the Court of Appeals and Supreme Court levels.

(Area Code 202)

Associate Chief Counsel: James J. Keightley 566-4138
Deputy Associate Chief Counsel: Patrick Dowling 566-2138
Special Appellate Counsel: Daniel F. Folzenlogen 566-3228
Special Litigation Counsel: Stephen M. Miller 252-8888

Criminal Tax Division
Assistant Chief Counsel: Barry J. Finkelstein 566-4138
Deputy Assistant Chief Counsel: Martin Klotz 566-4138

Disclosure Litigation Division
Assistant Chief Counsel: Peter V. Filpi 566-4109
Deputy Assistant Chief Counsel: John B. Cummings 566-3420

General Litigation Division
Assistant Chief Counsel: Arnold E. Kaufman 566-6481
Deputy Assistant Chief Counsel: Eliot D. Fielding ...566-6482
Docket Section 566-4458

Tax Litigation Division
Assistant Chief Counsel: Marlene Gross 566-3300
Deputy Assistant Chief Counsel: Daniel J. Wiles 566-3108
Docket 566-3333
Procedural Litigation Branch Chief: Christopher Ray 343-0033
Tax Shelter Branch Chief: Curtis Wilson (Acting) 566-4174

INTERNATIONAL TAX. The Office of the Associate Chief Counsel (International) is responsible for all international tax matters in the Office. It is structured without functional or subject matter divisions of responsibility, so attorneys handle a variety of matters. For example, attorneys may develop revenue rulings and private letter rulings, draft regulations, provide technical advice to field offices, write legal opinions, and participate in the development of legislation. They may also participate in litigation involving international issues (in conjunction with IRS field offices and the Department of Justice), in tax treaty negotiations, exchange of information matters, and treaty administration cases.

(Area Code 202)

Associate Chief Counsel: Steven Lainoff 566-9050
Deputy Associate Chief Counsel: Charles S. Triplett 566-9050
Assistant Chief Counsel:
Robert E. Culbertson Jr 377-9493
John T. Lyons 377-9493

FINANCE AND MANAGEMENT. This function, which consists of the Offices of Human Resources, Planning and Finance, and Information Systems, provides the administrative support for the Office of Chief Counsel.

General Legal Services. Attorneys assigned General Legal Services work in the National Office handle the various non-tax legal problems arising in the IRS. They represent management in all labor law litigation under the Civil Service Reform Act of 1978, including representation, unfair labor practice and arbitration cases; they handle personnel litigation arising from the Merit Systems Protection Board and discrimination litigation before the Equal Employment Opportunity Commission; they render legal advice and assistance in government contract negotiations or disputes and represent the IRS in government contract litigation before the General Services Administration Board of Contract Appeals and the U.S. General Accounting Office. They are responsible for legal advice in forfeiture matters, in disbarment actions against taxpayer representatives, and in ethical matters involving IRS employees or tax practitioners, and other administrative matters. They also assist the Department of Justice in defending the IRS or its personnel in a variety of non-tax Federal court cases, including constitutional and common law tort actions, equal employment opportunity, and personnel-related civil actions. In addition, they provide legal advice with respect to administrative claims and suits against the U.S. arising under the Federal Tort Claims Act and in ethical matters involving IRS or Chief Counsel employees or tax practitioners.

(Area Code 202)

Associate Chief Counsel: Richard J. Mihelcic 566-4148

General Legal Services Division

Assistant Chief Counsel: William F. Long Jr 252-8000
Deputy Assistant Chief Counsel: Kenneth N. Holland ..252-8000
Branch Chiefs:
Branch #1 (Labor Law): Mark S. Kaizen 252-8013
Branch #2 (Torts): Beverly Dale 252-8029
Branch #3 (Ethics): Stuart Endick 252-8044
Branch #4 (Government Contract Law):
Donald Suica 252-8062
Docket Section 252-8078

Field Office Responsibilities

Of the 11 Functions in the National Office, four have coordination and oversight responsibilities for the work performed in the **field offices.** These are the Criminal Tax, General Legal Services, General Litigation, and Tax Litigation offices. Field office responsibilities in these areas are as follows:

Criminal Tax. The Chief Counsel is the legal advisor to the Commissioner and is responsible for referring for prosecution criminal tax cases investigated by special agents of the Commissioner. Attorneys in a field office handling criminal tax work render a range of legal services. They are responsible for referring for prosecution criminal tax cases investigated by special agents of the Commissioner. They identify legal problems, offer alternative investigative approaches, and assist in the drafting of search warrants and affidavits, requests for administrative immunity, and summonses. After investigations are completed, field attorneys review reports and evidence, hold conferences with representatives of proposed defendants, and determine whether to recommend criminal prosecution. They then either forward such cases for prosecution or write declination memoranda returning the case to the District Director for civil disposition. IRS attorneys may furnish pretrial or trial assistance in criminal tax prosecutions. Selected criminal tax attorneys may be designated by the Department of Justice to try criminal tax cases in U.S. District Court.

General Legal Services. Attorneys assigned to this function in a Regional Counsel office, like their counterparts in the National Office, handle the various non-tax legal problems arising in the IRS. They represent management in all labor law litigation under the Civil Service Reform Act of 1978, including representation, unfair labor practice and arbitration cases; they handle personnel litigation arising from the Merit Systems Protection Board and discrimination litigation before the Equal Employment Opportunity Commission; they render legal advice and assistance in government contract negotiations or disputes and represent the IRS in government contract litigation before the General Services Administration Board of Contract Appeals and the U.S. General Accounting Office. They are responsible for legal advice in forfeiture matters, in disbarment actions against taxpayer representatives, and in ethical matters involving IRS employees or tax practitioners, and other administrative matters. They also assist the Department of Justice in defending the IRS or its personnel in a variety of non-tax Federal court cases, including constitutional and common law tort actions, equal employment opportunity, and personnel-related civil actions.

General Litigation. Attorneys in a District Counsel office assigned general litigation work provide legal advice and services necessary to collect and protect tax claims of the U.S. Issues handled include constitutional law, administrative law, lien law, UCC, real and personal property, bankruptcy, and decedent's estate issues. They work with attorneys from the Department of Justice in the commencement or defense of litigation brought in U.S. District Courts or state courts with respect to IRS activities. They also advise and prepare correspondence authorizing suits in connection with civil enforcement of summonses and tax return preparer matters. In many offices, the attorneys have been appointed Special Assistant U.S. Attorneys handling primarily bankruptcy cases for the IRS.

Tax Litigation. Attorneys assigned tax litigation work in a District Office are responsible for a docket of cases pending before the U.S. Tax Court. They prepare all pleadings and briefs, participate in discovery and settlement conferences, and try cases. With respect to adverse decisions, they make initial recommendations as to whether the cases should be appealed. Attorneys analyze the facts in such cases, research applicable law, and determine the position of the Service. These determinations are incorporated in letters to the Department of Justice recommending a course of action. In addition, Tax Litigation attorneys participate in settlement conferences with taxpayers' attorneys and make recommendations as to the merits of the proposed settlement.

IRS REGIONAL AND DISTRICT COUNSELS

Regional Counsel (Central Region)

(Area Code 513)

Internal Revenue Service, 7510 John Weld Peck Federal Building, CC:C, 550 Main Street, Cincinnati, OH 45202.
Regional Counsel: Clarence E. Barnes, Jr.............684-3201
Assistant Regional Counsel: James E. Rogers Jr........684-3204
Central Region Problem Resolution Office: 684-2587

District Counsel: Cincinnati (Area Code 513)
Internal Revenue Service, 7525 John Weld Peck Federal Building, C:CIN, 550 Main Street, Cincinnati, OH 45202.
District Counsel: Richard E. Trogolo..................684-3211

District Counsel: Cleveland (Area Code 216)
Internal Revenue Service, One Cleveland Center, Suite 810, C:CLE, 1375 E. Ninth Street, Cleveland, OH 44114.
District Counsel: Buckley D. Sowards..................522-3380

District Counsel: Detroit (Area Code 313)
Internal Revenue Service, 1870 McNamara Building,
C:DET, 477 Michigan Avenue, Detroit, MI 48226.
District Counsel: Oksana O. Xenos....................226-4790

District Counsel: Indianapolis (Area Code 317)
Internal Revenue Service, 513 Minton-Capehart Federal Building,
C:IND, 575 N. Pennsylvania Street, Indianapolis, IN 46204.
District Counsel: Ross E. Springer....................226-6601

District Counsel: Louisville (Area Code 502)
Internal Revenue Service, 579 Federal Office Building, C:LOU,
600 Martin Luther King Jr Place, Louisville, KY 40202.
District Counsel: Ferdinand J. Lotz III..............582-5471

Tax Shelter Office: Louisville (Area Code 502)
Internal Revenue Service, Gene Snyder Custom House &
Courthouse, Room 636-A, 601 W. Broadway, Louisville, KY 40202.
Special Litigation Assistant: Jilena A. Warner.......582-6089

Regional Director of Appeals (Area Code 513)
Internal Revenue Service, 5405 John Weld Peck Federal Building,
C:RDA, 550 Main Street, Cincinnati, OH 45202.
Regional Director: Thomas J. Yates..................684-2241

Appeals Office: Cincinnati (Area Code 513)
Internal Revenue Service, 10507 John Weld Peck Federal
Building, C:CIN:AP, 550 Main Street, Cincinnati, OH 45202.
Chief: Benny R. McCandless..........................684-3372

Appeals Office: Cleveland (Area Code 216)
Internal Revenue Service, Suite 815, One Cleveland Center,
C:CLE:AP, 1375 E. Ninth Street, Cleveland, OH 44114.
Chief: Joseph R. Brimacombe 522-7240

Appeals Office: Detroit (Area Code 313)
Internal Revenue Service, 470 McNamara Building,
C:DET:AP, 477 Michigan Avenue, Detroit, MI 48226.
Chief: Zora S. Hargrave..............................226-7720

Appeals Office: Indianapolis (Area Code 317)
Internal Revenue Service, 429 N. Pennsylvania Street,
Room 203, C:IND:AP, Indianapolis, IN 46204.
Chief: Gerald W. Wendel..............................226-7955

Appeals Office: Louisville (Area Code 502)
Internal Revenue Service, 272 Federal Office Building, C:LOU:AP,
600 Martin Luther King Jr Place, Louisville, KY 40202.
Chief: Walter Jernigan...............................582-5445

Regional Counsel (Mid-Atlantic Region)

(Area Code 215)
Internal Revenue Service, 841 Chestnut Street, Room 360,
CC:MA, Philadelphia, PA 19107.
Regional Counsel: David E. Gaston....................597-2153
Mid-Atlantic Region Problem Resolution Office: 597-3991

District Counsel: Baltimore (Area Code 301)
Internal Revenue Service, 101 W. Lombard Street,
Room 4100, MA:BAL, Baltimore, MD 21201.
District Counsel: Herbert A. Seidman.................962-3108

District Counsel: Newark (Area Code 201)
Internal Revenue Service, 970 Broad Street, Room 904,
MA:NEW, Newark, NJ 07102.
District Counsel: Matthew Magnone....................645-6510

District Counsel: Philadelphia (Area Code 215)
Internal Revenue Service, 600 Arch Street,
Room 10424, MA:PHI, Philadelphia, PA 19106.
District Counsel: H. Stephen Kesselman...............597-3442

District Counsel: Pittsburgh (Area Code 412)
Internal Revenue Service, 726 Federal Building, MA:PIT,
1000 Liberty Avenue, Pittsburgh, PA 15222.
District Counsel: Edward F. Peduzzi Jr...............644-3435

District Counsel: Richmond (Area Code 804)
Internal Revenue Service, 5215 Federal Bldg, MA:RCH,
400 N. Eighth St., Richmond VA 23240.
District Counsel: Marion B. Morton...................771-2332

District Counsel: Washington, D.C. (Area Code 202)
Internal Revenue Service, 4620 Wisconsin Avenue, N.W.,
4th Floor, MA:WAS, Washington, D.C. 20016.
District Counsel: Melvine E. Lefkowitz........634-5403 ext 262

Regional Director of Appeals (Area Code 215)
Internal Revenue Service, Philadelphia Life Building,
Room 950, MA:RDA, 615 Chestnut Street, Philadelphia, PA 19106.
Regional Director of Appeals: James A. Dougherty......597-2168

Appeals Office: Baltimore (Area Code 301)
Internal Revenue Service, 101 W. Lombard Street,
Rm 4200, MA:BAL:AP, Baltimore, MD 21201.
Chief: Susan H. Piper................................922-2504

Appeals Office: Newark (Area Code 201)
Internal Revenue Service, 970 Broad Street,
Room 702, MA:NEW:AP, Newark, NJ 07102.
Chief: Patrick J. Glynn..............................645-3670

Appeals Office: Philadelphia (Area Code 215)
Internal Revenue Service, 600 Arch Street,
Room 4454, MA:PHI:AP, Philadelphia, PA 19106.
Chief: Thomas Spaccarelli............................597-2177

Appeals Office: Pittsburgh (Area Code 412)
Internal Revenue Service, 1428 Federal Bldg,
MA:PIT:AP, 1000 Liberty Avenue, Pittsburgh, PA 15222.
Chief: Malvern P. Powell.............................644-4760

Appeals Office: Richmond (Area Code 804)
Internal Revenue Service, 11th Floor, Federal Building,
MA:RCH:AP, 400 N. Eighth Street, Richmond, VA 23240.
Chief: John D. Piper.................................771-2881

Appeals Office: Washington, D.C. (Area Code 202)
Internal Revenue Service, 4620 Wisconsin Avenue, N.W.,
Third Floor, MA:WAS:AP, Washington, D.C. 20016.
Chief: Thomas L. Kruse.......................634-5414 ext 366

Regional Counsel (Midwest Region)

(Area Code 312)
Internal Revenue Service, 230 S. Dearborn Street,
Suite 3410, CC:MW, Chicago, IL 60604.
Regional Counsel: Denis J. Conlon....................886-8290
Midwest Region Problem Resolution Office: 886-4291

District Counsel: Chicago (Area Code 312)
Internal Revenue Service, 1342 Dirksen Federal Building,
MW:CHI, 219 S. Dearborn Street, Chicago, IL 60604.
District Counsel: James F. Kidd......................886-9225

District Counsel: Des Moines (Area Code 515)
Internal Revenue Service, 439 Federal Building, MW:DM,
210 Walnut Street, Des Moines, IA 50309.
District Counsel: Mark E. O'Leary....................284-4783

District Counsel: Helena (Area Code 406)
Internal Revenue Service, Room 242, Federal Building,
MW:HEL, 301 South Park Avenue, Helena, MT 59626.
District Counsel: Virginia Schmid 449-5328

District Counsel: Kansas City (Area Code 816)
Internal Revenue Service, 2700 Federal Office Building, MW:KCY, 911 Walnut Street, Kansas City, MO 64106.
District Counsel: James E. Cannon....................426-3556

District Counsel: Milwaukee (Area Code 414)
Internal Revenue Service, 310 W. Wisconsin Avenue, Suite 760, MW:MIL, Milwaukee, WI 53203.
District Counsel: Nelson E. Shafer....................297-1106

District Counsel: Omaha (Area Code 402)
Internal Revenue Service, 3101 Federal Bldg, MW:OMA, 215 N. 17th Street, Omaha, NE 68101.
District Counsel: Ronald M. Frykberg..................221-3733

District Counsel: Springfield (Area Code 217)
Internal Revenue Service, 320 W. Washington Street, Rm 720, MW:SPR, Springfield, IL 62701.
District Counsel: Jeff P. Ehrlich.....................492-4540

District Counsel: St. Louis (Area Code 314)
Internal Revenue Service, Third Floor, Chouteau Center, MW:STL, 133 S. 11th Street, St. Louis, MO 63102.
District Counsel: Richard A. Witkowski................425-4747

District Counsel: St. Paul (Area Code 612)
Internal Revenue Service, Galtier Plaza, Suite 650, MW:STP, 175 East Fifth Street, St. Paul, MN 55101.
District Counsel: Robert F. Cunningham................290-3473

Regional Director of Appeals (Area Code 312)
Internal Revenue Service, 32nd Floor, Room 3280, MW:RDA, 230 S. Dearborn Street, Chicago, IL 60604.
Regional Director of Appeals: Paul H. Thornton 886-5730

Appeals Office: Chicago (Area Code 312)
Internal Revenue Service, 200 W. Adams Street, Suite 600, CHI:AP, Chicago, IL 60606.
Chief: John Vest......................................886-5736

Appeals Office: Kansas City (Area Code 816)
Internal Revenue Service, 1700 Federal Office Building, MW:KCY:AP, 911 Walnut Street, Kansas City, MO 64106.
Chief: James R. Wells.................................426-5572

Appeals Office: Milwaukee (Area Code 414)
Internal Revenue Service, 780 Henry S. Reuss Federal Plaza, MW:MIL:AP, 310 W. Wisconsin Avenue, Milwaukee, WI 53203.
Chief: Robert J. Collins..............................297-3406

Appeals Office: Omaha (Area Code 402)
Internal Revenue Service, 3132 Federal Building, MW:OMA:AP, 215 N. 17th Street, Omaha, NE 68102.
Chief: Edwin L. Brooke................................221-3683

Appeals Office: St. Louis (Area Code 314)
Internal Revenue Service, 133 S. 11th Street, MW:STL:AP, St. Louis, MO 63102.
Chief: Douglas E. Kelly...............................425-6070

Appeals Office: St. Paul (Area Code 612)
Internal Revenue Service, 500 Federal Building & U.S. Courthouse, MW:STP:AP, 316 N. Robert Street, St. Paul, MN 55101.
Chief: Kenneth J. Wielinski...........................290-3860

Regional Counsel (North Atlantic Region)

(Area Code 212)
Internal Revenue Service, 25th Floor, 7 World Trade Center, CC:NA, New York, NY 10048.
Regional Counsel: Agatha L. Vorsanger. 264-0290
North Atlantic Region Problem Resolution Office: 264-0839

District Counsel: Albany (Area Code 518)
Internal Revenue Service, Leo W. O'Brien Federal Building, NA:ALB, Clinton Avenue & North Pearl Street, Albany, NY 12207.
District Counsel: Gerald A. Thorpe....................472-3681

District Counsel: Boston (Area Code 617)
Internal Revenue Service, 10 Causeway Street, Room 401, NA:BOS, Boston, MA 02222.
District Counsel: Gerald J. O'Toole...................565-7838

District Counsel: Brooklyn (Area Code 516)
Internal Revenue Service, 1600 Stewart Avenue, Suite 601, NA:BRK, Westbury, NY 11590.
District Counsel: Martha Sullivan.....................832-2408

District Counsel: Buffalo (Area Code 716)
Internal Revenue Service, Suite 500, Guaranty Building, NA:BUF, 28 Church Street, Buffalo, NY 14202.
District Counsel: John E. White.......................846-5610

District Counsel: Hartford (Area Code 203)
Internal Revenue Service, 135 High Street, Room 259, NA:HAR, Hartford, CT 06103.
District Counsel: Powell W. Holly Jr..................240-4253

District Counsel: Manhattan (Area Code 212)
Internal Revenue Service, 24th Floor, 7 World Trade Center, NA:MAN, New York, NY 10048.
District Counsel: Joseph F. Maselli...................264-0277

Regional Director of Appeals (Area Code 212)
Internal Revenue Service, 90 Church Street, NA:RDA, New York, NY 10007.
Regional Director of Appeals: Kevin P. Morgan.........264-7845

Appeals Office: Boston (Area Code 617)
Internal Revenue Service, 10 Causeway Street, Room 493, NA:BOS:AP, Boston, MA 02222.
Chief: Linda M. Garrard...............................565-7900

Appeals Office: Buffalo (Area Code 716)
Internal Revenue Service, Suite 400, Guaranty Building, NA:BUF:AP, 28 Church Street, Buffalo, NY 14202.
Chief: Joseph H. Walz.................................846-5330

Appeals Office: Hartford (Area Code 203)
Internal Revenue Service, 450 Main Street, Room 335, NA:HAR:AP, Hartford, CT 06103.
Chief: Joseph F. Scherzinger..........................240-3070

Appeals Office: Long Island (Area Code 516)
Internal Revenue Service, 50 Clinton Street, NA:LI:AP, Hempstead, NY 11550.
Chief: Murray Navarro.................................565-9301

Appeals Office: New York City (Area Code 212)
Internal Revenue Service, 90 Church Street, NA:NY:AP, New York, NY 10007.
Chief: Edward M. Schaeffer............................264-7842

Regional Counsel (Southeast Region)

(Area Code 404)
Internal Revenue Service, 401 W. Peachtree Street, N.W., CC:SE, Suite 2110, Stop 180-R, Atlanta, GA 30365.
Regional Counsel: William A. Goss.....................331-6098
Southeast Region Problem Resolution Office: 331-4506

District Counsel: Atlanta (Area Code 404)
Internal Revenue Service, 401 W. Peachtree Street, N.W., SE:ATL, Suite 1400, Stop 1000-D, Atlanta, GA 30365.
District Counsel: Dean R. Morley III..................331-6120

District Counsel: Birmingham (Area Code 205)
Internal Revenue Service, 500-22nd Street, S., Room 340, SE:BIR, Birmingham, AL 35233.
District Counsel: John B. Harper......................731-1281

District Counsel: Greensboro (Area Code 919)
Internal Revenue Service, 320 Federal Place, Room 509, SE:GBO, Greensboro, NC 27401.
District Counsel: Alan I. Weinberg....................333-5285

District Counsel: Jacksonville (Area Code 904)
Internal Revenue Service, Box 35027, Federal Office Building, Room 564, SE:JAX, 400 W. Bay Street, Jacksonville, FL 32202.
District Counsel: Benjamin A. deLuna 791-2788

District Counsel: Miami (Area Code 305)
Internal Revenue Service, 1114 Federal Office Building, SE:MIA, 51 S.W. First Avenue, Stop 8000, Miami, FL 33130.
District Counsel: David R. Smith......................536-5571

District Counsel: Nashville (Area Code 615)
Internal Revenue Service, 703 U.S. Courthouse, SE:NAS, 801 Broadway, Nashville, TN 37203.
District Counsel: James E. Keeton 736-5441

District Counsel: New Orleans (Area Code 504)
Internal Revenue Service, 917 Hale Boggs Building, SE:NO, 501 Magazine Street, New Orleans, LA 70130.
District Counsel: Louis John Zeller, Jr 589-2863

Regional Director of Appeals (Area Code 404)
Internal Revenue Service, 401 W. Peachtree Street, N.W., Suite 2118, SE:RDA, Atlanta, GA 30365.
Regional Director of Appeals: Richard E. Foley........331-6848

Appeals Office: Atlanta (Area Code 404)
Internal Revenue Service, 401 W. Peachtree Street, N.W., Suite 1455, SE:ATL:AP, Atlanta, GA 30365.
Chief: Charles R. Barnes.............................331-6451

Appeals Office: Birmingham (Area Code 205)
Internal Revenue Service, 500-22nd Street, S., Room 330, SE:BIR:AP, Birmingham, AL 35233.
Chief: Bob D. Holt...................................731-1134

Appeals Office: Greensboro (Area Code 919)
Internal Revenue Service, 320 Federal Place, Room 527, SE:GBO:AP, Greensboro, NA 27401.
Chief: Larry L. Davis.................................333-5019

Appeals Office: Jacksonville (Area Code 904)
Internal Revenue Service, Box 35083, Federal Office Bldg, SE:JAX:AP, 400 W. Bay Street, Room 364, Jacksonville, FL 32202.
Chief: Christine Haveles.............................791-2492

Appeals Office: Miami (Area Code 305)
Internal Revenue Service, 316 Federal Office Building, SE:MIA:AP, 51 S.W. First Avenue, Miami, FL 33130.
Chief: Steven D. Herscovitz..........................536-5191

Appeals Office: Nashville (Area Code 615)
Internal Revenue Service, MDP 20, 801 Broadway, SE:NAS:AP, Nashville, TN 37203.
Chief: Louie C. Mays.................................736-7380

Appeals Office: New Orleans (Area Code 504)
Internal Revenue Service, 501 Magazine Street, SE:NO:AP, New Orleans, LA 70130.
Chief: Sandra T. Freeland............................589-2004

Appeals Office: Tampa (Area Code 813)
Internal Revenue Service, 2001 Pan Am Circle, Suite 203, SE:T:AP, Tampa, FL 33607.
Chief: William E. Oppenheim Jr.......................228-2540

Regional Counsel (Southwest Region)

(Area Code 214)
Internal Revenue Service, 2000SWRO, 4050 Alpha Road, 14th Floor, CC:SW, Dallas, TX 75244.
Regional Counsel: William F. Hammack (Acting) 308-7350
Southwest Region Problem Resolution Office: 308-7019

District Counsel: Albuquerque (Area Code 505)
Internal Revenue Service, 123 Fourth Street, S.W., Rm 326, SW:ABQ, Albuquerque, NM 87102.
District Counsel: Harry Beckhoff......................766-8736

District Counsel: Austin (Area Code 512)
Internal Revenue Service, 300 E. 8th Street, Suite 601, SW:AUS, Austin, TX 78701.
District Counsel: Lewis J. Hubbard Jr.................499-5662

District Counsel: Dallas (Area Code 214)
Internal Revenue Service, 12A24 Earle Cabell Federal Bldg, SW:DAL, 1100 Commerce Street, Dallas, TX 75242.
District Counsel: William F. Hammack Jr...............708-7350

District Counsel: Denver (Area Code 303)
Internal Revenue Service, 1244 Speer Boulevard, Suite 500, SW:DEN, Denver, CO 80204.
District Counsel: Martin B. Kaye......................844-3258

District Counsel: Houston (Area Code 713)
Internal Revenue Service, 10850 Richmond Avenue, Suite 350, SW:HOU, Houston, TX 77042.
District Counsel: Harold Friedman.....................954-1200

District Counsel: Oklahoma City (Area Code 405)
Internal Revenue Service, 500 W. Main, Suite 320, SW:OKL, Oklahoma City, OK 73102.
District Counsel: Michael J. O'Brien..................231-4921

District Counsel: Phoenix (Area Code 602)
Internal Revenue Service, 3225 N. Central Avenue, Suite 1500, SW:PNX, Phoenix, AZ 85012.
District Counsel: Roger Rhodes........................640-5350

District Counsel: Salt Lake City (Area Code 801)
Internal Revenue Service, Room 1311, Wallace F. Bennett Federal Bldg, SW:SLC, 125 S. State Street, Salt Lake City, UT 84138.
District Counsel: Marion K. Mortensen.................524-5815

Regional Director of Appeals (Area Code 214)
Internal Revenue Service, 8000SWRO, 4050 Alpha Road, 14th Floor, SW:RDA, Dallas, TX 75244.
Regional Director of Appeals: Claude C. Rogers Jr.....308-7450

Appeals Office: Austin (Area Code 512)
Internal Revenue Service, 300 E. 8th Street, Suite 602, SW:AUS:AP, Austin, TX 78701.
Chief: Fred R. Box...................................499-5662

Appeals Office: Dallas (Area Code 214)
Internal Revenue Service, Earle Cabell Federal Building 12A12, SW:DAL:AP, 1100 Commerce Street, Dallas, TX 75242.
Chief: Elaine C. Wedgeworth..........................767-1418

Appeals Office: Denver (Area Code 303)
Internal Revenue Service, Colonnade Center, Suite 400, SW:DEN:AP, 1244 Speer Boulevard, Denver, CO 80204.
Chief: Dwight M. Sumner..............................844-2893

Appeals Office: Houston (Area Code 713)
Internal Revenue Service, 10850 Richmond Avenue, Suite 300, SW:HOU:AP, Houston, TX 77042.
Chief: William C. Reitan.............................954-1251

Appeals Office: Oklahoma City (Area Code 405)
Internal Revenue Service, 500 W. Main, Suite 310, SW:OKL:AP, Oklahoma City, OK 73102.
Chief: Brian W. Haley....231-4226

Appeals Office: Phoenix (Area Code 602)
Internal Revenue Service, 3225 N. Central Ave, Suite 1501, SW:PNX:AP, Phoenix, AZ 85012.
Chief: Darrell P. Ladmirault....640-5301

Appeals Office: Salt Lake City (Area Code 801)
Internal Revenue Service, 125 S. State Street, Room 4311, SW:SLC:AP, Salt Lake City, UT 84138.
Chief: Robert B. Stipek....524-5925

Regional Counsel (Western Region)

(Area Code 415)
Internal Revenue Service, 1650 Mission Street, Room 514, CC:W, San Francisco, CA 94103.
Regional Counsel: Benjamin C. Sanchez....556-0932
Western Region Problem Resolution Office: 556-3035

District Counsel: Anchorage (Area Code 907)
Internal Revenue Service, 949 E. 36th Avenue, Room 607, W:ANC, Anchorage, AK 99508.
District Counsel: Jerry L. Leonard....261-4470

District Counsel: Boise (Area Code 208)
Internal Revenue Service, 550 W. Fort Street, Box 024, W:BOI, Boise, ID 83724.
District Counsel: Randall G. Durfee....334-9609

District Counsel: Honolulu (Area Code 808)
Internal Revenue Service, 7119 PJKK Federal Building, W:HON, 300 Ala Moana Boulevard, Honolulu, HI 96850.
District Counsel: William A. Sims....541-3350

District Counsel: Laguna Niguel (Area Code 714)
Internal Revenue Service, 2nd Floor, Chet Holifield Building, W:LN, 24000 Avila Road, Laguna Niguel, CA 92656.
District Counsel: Harry M. Asch....643-4325

District Counsel: Las Vegas (Area Code 702)
Internal Revenue Service, 4750 W. Oakey, Suite 403, W:LV, Las Vegas, NV 89102.
District Counsel: James W. Clark 455-1127

District Counsel: Los Angeles (Area Code 213)
Internal Revenue Service, 3018 Federal Building, W:LA, 300 N. Los Angeles Street, Los Angeles, CA 90012.
District Counsel: Joseph O. Greaves....894-3027

District Counsel: Portland (Area Code 503)
Internal Revenue Service, 222 S.W. Columbia, Suite 450, W:POR, Portland, OR 97201.
District Counsel: Wayne R. Appleman....326-3185

District Counsel: Sacramento (Area Code 916)
Internal Revenue Service, Suite 470, 4330 Watt Avenue, W:SAC, Sacramento, CA 95812.
District Counsel: Steven J. Mopsick....978-6332

District Counsel: San Diego (Area Code 619)
Internal Revenue Service, 701 B Street, Suite 901, W:SD, San Diego, CA 92101.
District Counsel: Donald W. Wolf....557-6014

District Counsel: San Francisco (Area Code 415)
Internal Revenue Service, 160 Spear Street, Room 504, W:SF, San Francisco, CA 94105.
District Counsel: J. Richard Murphy Jr....974-9104

District Counsel: San Jose (Area Code 408)
Internal Revenue Service, 55 South Market Street, Suite 505, W:SJ, San Jose, CA 95113.
District Counsel: Lawrence G. Lilly....291-4262

District Counsel: Seattle (Area Code 206)
Internal Revenue Service, 2710 Federal Bldg, W:SEA, 915 Second Avenue, Seattle, WA 98174.
District Counsel: Richard J. Shipley....442-5267

District Counsel: Thousand Oaks (Area Code 805)
Internal Revenue Service, 950 Hampshire Rd, East Pavilion, W:TO, Thousand Oaks, CA 91361.
District Counsel: James A. Nelson....371-6700

Regional Director of Appeals (Area Code 415)
Internal Revenue Service, 1650 Mission Street, Room 515, W:RDA, San Francisco, CA 94103.
Regional Director of Appeals: Donato Cantalupo....556-0790

Appeals Office: Laguna Niguel (Area Code 714)
Internal Revenue Service, 2nd Floor, Chet Holifield Building, W:LN:AP, 24000 Avila Road, Laguna Niguel, CA 92656.
Chief: Raymond E. Gump....643-4339

Appeals Office: Las Vegas (Area Code 702)
Internal Revenue Service, 4750 West Oakey Blvd, 4th Floor, W:LV:AP, Las Vegas, NV 89102.
Chief:vacant....455-1130

Appeals Office: Los Angeles (Area Code 213)
Internal Revenue Service, 300 N. Los Angeles Street, Room 3054, W:LA:AP, Los Angeles, CA 90012.
Acting Chief: Christian G. Beck....894-4710

Appeals Office: Portland (Area Code 503)
Internal Revenue Service, 222 S.W. Columbia, Suite 400, W:POR:AP, Portland, OR 97201.
Chief: George F. Kaufer....326-3281

Appeals Office: Sacramento (Area Code 916)
Internal Revenue Service, 801 I Street, Room 456, W:SAC:AP, Sacramento, CA 95812.
Chief: Oris McMillian....551-1237

Appeals Office: San Diego (Area Code 619)
Internal Revenue Service, 701 B Street, Suite 900, W:SD:AP, San Diego, CA 92101.
Chief: Charles Mason....557-6926

Appeals Office: San Francisco (Area Code 415)
Internal Revenue Service, 160 Spear Street, Suite 400, W:SF:AP, San Francisco, CA 94105.
Chief: James M. Elliott....744-9308

Appeals Office: San Jose (Area Code 408)
Internal Revenue Service, Mail Stop 77-01-0200, 55 South Market Street, Suite 516, W:SJ:AP, San Jose, CA 95113.
Chief: Jackson Kohagura....291-4030

Appeals Office: Seattle (Area Code 206)
Internal Revenue Service, 2790 Federal Building, W:SEA:AP, 915 Second Avenue, Seattle, WA 98174.
Chief: Jerald M. Peterson....442-5344

DEPARTMENT OF THE TREASURY

PUBLICATIONS OF INTEREST

The following publication can be purchased from the **U.S. Government Printing Office.** Stock numbers and prices for annual subscriptions are shown below. Submit requests for these publications to: The Superintendent of Documents, U.S. Government Printing Office, Washington, D.C. 20402. Tel: 202/783-3238.

Internal Revenue Bulletin. A weekly publication containing official IRS rulings, Treasury Decisions, Executive Orders, legislation, and court decisions pertaining to internal revenue matters. Price: $104.00 a year domestic; $130.00 a year foreign. GPO Stock# 748-004-00000-9.

Twice a year the weekly issues of the Internal Revenue Bulletin are consolidated into Cumulative Bulletins. These cumulative bulletins are not included as part of the subscription, but are sold as separate publications. Price: 1989-2: $40.00. GPO Stock# 048-004-02292-3; 1989-1: $44.00. GPO Stock# 048-004-02286-9.

Bulletin Index-Digest System. Contains the Finding List and Digests for all permanent tax matters published in the Internal Revenue Bulletin. Each subscription service consists of a basic manual and cumulative supplements for an indeterminate period.

Service #1. Income Taxes 1953-1988. Publication No. 641. Price: $42.00 domestic; $52.50 foreign. GPO Stock# 948-001-00000-4.

Service #2. Estate and Gift Taxes, 1953-1988. Publication No. 642. Price: $19.00 domestic; $23.75 foreign. GPO Stock# 948-002-00000-1.

Service No. 3. Employment Taxes, 1953-1988. Publication No. 643. Price: $19.00 domestic; $23.75 foreign. GPO Stock# 948-003-00000-7.

Service No. 4. Excise Taxes, 1953-1988. Publication No. 644. Price: $19.00 domestic; $23.75 foreign. GPO Stock #948-004-00000-3.

Cumulative List of Organizations Described in Section 170(c) of the Internal Revenue Code of 1986. Revised to September 1989. Publication No. 78. Lists contributions of organizations which are deductible under Section 170(c) of the Internal Revenue Code of 1986. Subscription service includes the revised edition containing the names of exempt organizations, through September 1989, and three cumulative quarterly supplements. Price: $41.00 domestic; $51.25 foreign. GPO Stock# 948-009-00000-5.

* * * * * * * *

Catalog of Federal Tax Forms, Form Letters, Notices, and Taxpayer Information Publications. To request a free copy contact: Internal Revenue Service, Forms Distribution Center, P.O. Box 25866, Richmond, VA 23289. Tel: 800/829-FORM.

* * * * * * * *

CCH Standard Federal Tax Reporter. Looseleaf. This multi-volume set consists of:

*Code Volumes, which print, in Internal Revenue Code section order, all provisions of the Code, and include tables and annotations cross-referencing and explaining Code sections;

*Index Volume, with a topical index, tax calendar, and rate tables, checklists, tax planning materials, the IRS Tax Shelter Examination Handbook, a glossary of tax terms, and sections covering tax treaties, tax return preparers, and bond and annuity tables;

*Compilation Volumes, in Code section order, containing the full text of the Code, final and temporary regulations, digest-annotations to letter rulings, revenue rulings, revenue procedures, and court decisions, as well as some legislative histories, plus editorial explanation;

*New Matters Volume, which has a topical index of recent developments and a legal periodicals section containing an order list of IRS publications and digests of current tax articles, information on pending tax bills before Congress, and an Illustrative Cases section;

*U.S. Tax Cases Advance Sheets Volume, which contains Treasury Department proposed regulations, tax decisions of the U.S. District Courts, U.S. Claims Court, U.S. Courts of Appeals, and the U.S. Supreme Court; and

*Citator Volumes, which list all decisions alphabetically and can be used to determine if subsequent decisions have affected earlier volumes.

Price: $1,435 for a one-year subscription; $1,305 per year for a two-year subscription. Order from Commerce Clearing House, Inc., 4025 West Peterson Avenue, Chicago, IL 60646. Tel: 800/621-6429. Or, in Washington, D.C., call 202/626-2200.

* * * * * * * *

Prentice-Hall Federal Taxes 2d. Looseleaf. This multivolume set consists of:

*Code Volumes, which reproduce, in Code section order, all Internal Revenue Code provisions, with a brief history of each provision, Code and cross-reference tables, annotations, an effective-date table, proposed regulations, a Code section index for these regulations, and a topical index;

*Index Volume, which has topical and transactions indexes to all of the materials in the Compilation Volumes (below), a Federal Tax Calendar, checklists, lists of tax forms, tax and bond tables, a Tax Elections Checklist, Tables of Rulings and of Cases, and an Index to Tax Articles;

*Compilation Volumes, which contain, in Code section order, the full text of the Code, final, temporary and proposed regulations, digest-annotations to revenue rulings and procedures and to letter rulings and court decisions, plus extensive editorial material explaining tax issues and questions, as well as information about U.S. income tax treaties;

*Current Matters Volume, which cross-references new items to Compilation Volumes items and contains a List of Current Decisions, gives information about appeals and selected pending tax legislation, and also includes several useful indexes;

*American Federal Tax Reports 2d (AFTR2d) Decisions Advance Sheets Volume, which includes decisions by the U.S. District Courts, U.S. Claims Court, U.S. Courts of Appeals, and the U.S. Supreme Court; and

*Citator Volumes, which list all decisions alphabetically and can be used to determine the effect of later decisions upon earlier ones.

Prices: 1) Income Tax Set (16 volumes, two semi-annual AFTR2d bound volumes, a Topical Index, and weekly reports): $1,150 per year; 2) Income and Excise Tax Set (17 volumes, two semi-annual AFTR2d bound volumes, a Topical Index, and weekly reports): $1,271 per year; 3) Income and Estate and Gift Tax Set (18 volumes, two semi-annual AFTR2d bound volumes, a Topical Index, and weekly reports): $1,456 per year; 4) Income, Excise and Estate and Gift Tax Set (19 volumes, two semi-annual AFTR2d bound volumes, a Topical Index, and weekly reports): $1,562 per year. Order from: Prentice-Hall, Inc., Englewood Cliffs, NJ 07632. Tel: 800/562-0245. Or, in Washington, D.C., call 202/293-0707.

* * * * * * * *

Tax Notes. Weekly report of tax developments, including Congressional action, court opinions, IRS and Treasury Department actions, General Accounting Office reports, international tax news, a calendar, digests of tax articles, and special reports. Price: $995 per year from Tax Analysts, 6830 North Fairfax Drive, Arlington, VA 22213. Tel: 800/336-0439 (703/532-1850 in Virginia).

* * * * * * * *

Federal Tax Coordinator 2d. Looseleaf. Weekly. Discusses all areas of taxation, using a subject-matter approach, with numerous citations and cross-references to related topics in other chapters; also includes analyses of matters not yet resolved, planning checklists, tax tables, and tax calendars, and also contains a Weekly Alert as part of the subscription. The text of U.S. tax treaties and annotations and proposed regulations and their preambles are also included. Price: $1,476 per year. Order from Research Institute of America, Inc., 90 Fifth Avenue, New York, NY 10011. Tel: 800/431-9025 or 202/628-6050.

Internal Memorandums of the IRS. Weekly. Contains the strategic thinking behind IRS' decisions. Price: $378 per year from Prentice-Hall, Inc., Englewood Cliffs, NJ 07632. Tel: 800/562-0245. Or, in Washington, D.C., call 202/293-0707.

UNITED STATES MINT
633 3rd Street, N.W.
Washington, D.C. 20220

DESCRIPTION: The U.S. Mint manufactures coins for the nation's commerce and circulates them through the Federal Reserve Banks. Other responsibilities include the custody, processing, and movement of Treasury gold and silver bullion; the production of foreign coins; and the manufacture of national medals, proof coin sets, and other numismatic items for sale to the public.

(Area Code 202)
Director: Donna Pope 376-0560

OFFICE OF THE CHIEF COUNSEL

The Office of the Chief Counsel provides advice and counsel to Mint officials concerning the entire range of Mint functions and activities; interprets coinage laws and other statutes and regulations which may affect Mint operations; drafts legislation and administrative regulations; prepares Departmental reports on legislative proposals having potential impact on the Mint; prepares litigation reports and assists the U.S. Attorney on all civil actions instituted against the Government which may arise from the activities of the Mint; reviews procurement and construction contract proposals and prepares reports to the Comptroller General in protests resulting from Mint activities; represents the Mint in proceedings involving labor-management relations, discrimination complaints, and other personnel actions; evaluates claims against the Mint under the Federal Tort Claims Act and the Military Personnel and Civilian Employees' Claims Act; and interprets matters relating to the Freedom of Information Act and Privacy Act.

(Area Code 202)
Chief Counsel: Kenneth B. Gubin 376-0564

BUREAU OF THE PUBLIC DEBT
999 E Street, N.W.
Washington, D.C. 20239-0001

DESCRIPTION: The Bureau of the Public Debt supports management pertaining to security issues, directs the conduct of transactions in outstanding securities, and adjudicates claims on lost, stolen, destroyed, or mutilated securities. Attorneys in the Office of Chief Counsel also provide advice on litigation in Federal and state courts involving the construction or validity of laws and regulations affecting the public debt, consulting and assisting attorneys from the Department of Justice.

(Area Code 202)
Commissioner: Richard L. Gregg 376-4300
Chief Counsel: Calvin Ninomiya 376-4320

(Area Code 202)
Facsimile 376-4391

U.S. SAVINGS BONDS DIVISION
1111 20th Street, N.W., Washington, D.C. 20226

(Area Code 202)
National Director: Catalina V. Villalpando 566-2843

(Area Code 202)
Public Affairs 634-5377

SAVINGS BONDS OPERATIONS OFFICE
200 Third Street, Parkersburg, WV 26106-1328

(Area Code 304)
Assistant Commissioner: Martin French 420-6516

(Area Code 202)
Assistant Chief Counsel: Dean Adams 420-6505

PUBLICATIONS OF INTEREST

Legal Aspects. Contains a discussion of U.S. Savings Bonds and tax liability; of particular interest to executors in estate administration. Available free of charge from the Public Affairs Office, U.S. Savings Bonds Division. (202/634-5377).

UNITED STATES SECRET SERVICE
1800 G Street, N.W.
Washington, D.C. 20223

DESCRIPTION: The U.S. Secret Service protects the President, the Vice President, their immediate families, former Presidents, distinguished foreign visitors, and U.S. officials performing special missions abroad; detects and arrests offenders for counterfeiting coins, currency, stamps, and other obligations or securities of the U.S.; detects and arrests offenders of law pertaining to electronic funds transfer frauds, credit and debit card frauds, and false identification documents; and provides security at the White House complex and various foreign diplomatic missions in the Washington, D.C. metropolitan area.

(Area Code 202)
Director: John R. Simpson 535-5700

(Area Code 202)
Public Affairs 535-5708

OFFICE OF CHIEF COUNSEL

Attorneys in the Office of Chief Counsel provide advice and assistance on complex legal questions pertaining to the Service's criminal and protective operations.

(Area Code 202)
Chief Counsel: John J. Kelleher 535-5771
Deputy Chief Counsel: Don Personett 535-5771
Facsimile 535-5665

(Area Code 202)
Office of Investigations Assistant Director:
Garry M. Jenkins 535-5716

PUBLICATIONS OF INTEREST

Know Your Money: U.S. Department of the Treasury, United States Secret Service. 20-page booklet designed to help individuals detect counterfeit currency and guard against forgery loss. Order from: U.S. Department of the Treasury, United States Secret Service, 1800 G Street, N.W., Room 805, Washington, D.C. 20225. Free of charge.

OFFICE OF THRIFT SUPERVISION
1700 G Street, N.W., 5th Floor
Washington, D.C. 20552

DESCRIPTION: The Office of Thrift Supervision (OTS) became operational in October 1989 and is part of a major reorganization of the thrift regulatory structure mandated by the Financial Institutions Reform, Recovery and Enforcement Act. In that Act, Congress gave OTS authority to charter federal thrift institutions and serve as the primary regulator of the Federal and state- chartered thrifts belonging to the Savings Association Insurance Fund. In addition to overseeing thrift institutions themselves, OTS also regulates, examines and supervises companies that own thrifts, and controls the acquisition of thrifts by these holding companies.

OTS is organized into six main divisions.

* **Supervision-Operations** oversees the examination and supervision of savings institutions by regulatory staff in 12 District Offices.

* **Supervision-Policy** is responsible for developing regulations, directives and policies to ensure the safe and sound operation of savings institutions as well as their compliance with Federal law and regulations.

* **Chief Counsel** provides a full range of legal services to the agency, including writing regulations, representing the agency in court, and taking enforcement actions against savings institutions that violate laws or regulations. This office also processes corporate filings required by the Securities and Exchange Act of 1934.

* **Congressional Relations and Communications** is responsible for publishing and communicating information about OTS and its actions and policies.

* **Management** includes all administrative functions including human resources and the agency's nationwide computer system.

* **Chief Economist** encompasses the collection and analysis of thrift industry and general economic data.

(Area Code 202)
Director: Timothy Ryan 906-6280
Facsimile 898-0230

(Area Code 202)
Information Services Division..........................416-2751

THE OFFICE OF CHIEF COUNSEL

The Chief Counsel's Office is comprised of two significant branches, Legal and Enforcement. Five divisions make up the Legal function of the Chief Counsel's office. They are 1) Regulations and Legislation; 2) Litigation; 3) Conservators and Receivers; 4) Corporate and Securities; and 5) General law.

(Area Code 202)
Chief Counsel: Harris Weinstein 906-6268
Counselor to the Chief Counsel: Dwight Smith 906-6990
Senior Counsel: Carolyn Lieberman 906-6404
Principal Deputy Chief Counsel (Legal): Eugene M. Katz 906-6856
Principal Deputy Chief Counsel (Enforcement):
Rosemary Stewart 906-7622
Senior Deputy Director: Robert DeCuir 906-7152

The **Regulations and Legislation Division** provides legal support for OTS' regulatory and legislative initiatives. In its regulatory capacity, the Division works closely with Supervision-Policy in researching and drafting regulatory initiatives. Attorneys in the Division assist in reviewing and clearing all regulations and policy statements prior to publication in the **Federal Register;** drafting opinions interpreting the regulations that govern the activities in which savings associations can engage; and providing drafting and other technical support for all of OTS' legislative initiatives.

(Area Code 202)
Associate Chief Counsel for Regulations and Legislation:
Karen Solomon 906-7240

The **Litigation Division** represents OTS in all matters before state or Federal courts, including any case where the authority of the agency to take a particular action is challenged. OTS possesses the relatively unique authority to represent itself in Federal court. Either directly or through retention of outside counsel, attorneys from the Division prepare briefs and other filings and make oral arguments to defend OTS in matters ranging from challenges to regulations or final determination to personnel matters.

(Area Code 202)
Associate Chief Counsel for Litigation: Thomas Segal 906-7230

The **Conservators and Receivers Division** is responsible for preparing the legal documentation necessary for appointing conservators or receivers for troubled institutions. Attorneys in this Division work closely with Supervision-Operations and the supervisory personnel in the 12 district offices to ensure that sufficient grounds exist for the appointment of a conservator or receiver and that the documentation properly reflects the existence of those grounds. In addition to drafting legal opinions and reviewing supervisory memoranda, this Division also drafts the Director's orders to effectuate the appointments.

(Area Code 202)
Associate Chief Counsel for Conservators and Receivers:
Ronald Brown 906-7044

The **Corporate and Securities Division** provides legal support on the statutes and regulations that govern 1) the ownership and organization of savings associations and savings association holding companies; and 2) the transactions that may be engaged in by savings associations and their affiliates. In this regard, the Division assists in drafting regulations and provides legal opinions on activities proposed in applications submitted by institutions and holding companies. The Division is also responsible for implementing and supervising compliance with the securities statutes that apply to publicly traded savings associations.

(Area Code 202)
Deputy Chief Counsel for Corporate and Securities:
Julie L. Williams 906-6459

The **General Law Division** handles most internal administrative matters, including personnel and contract actions. The Division is also responsible for drafting and interpreting the ethics statutes and regulations that govern the actions of all OTS employees.

(Area Code 202)
Deputy Chief Counsel for General Law:
Harry W. Quillian 906-6462

The **Enforcement Branch** is comprised of four primary divisions. The smallest of these divisions is devoted to policy and administrative matters and special projects, including representation of OTS on various multi-agency task forces formed for such purposes as enhancement of relationships with the Department of Justice and developing more improved and uniform enforcement policies for all Federal financial institution regulatory agencies.

Attorneys in the three larger divisions are involved in bringing enforcement actions throughout the country on behalf of OTS. These three divisions of Enforcement staff are primarily engaged in providing specialized legal support to supervisory personnel, including attorneys, in the 12 OTS District offices. Enforcement attorneys assist in determining the appropriate enforcement action to be taken and providing the legal support necessary to complete the action. The types of enforcement actions coordinated and provided by Enforcement include cease and desist orders against individuals, civil money penalties, and formal investigations conducted to determine whether enforcement action would be appropriate or to provide evidence to support an action.

(Area Code 202)
Assistant Director for Policy and Special Projects
Division: John Downing 906-7154
Director "X" Division: Stanley Hecht 906-7954
Director "Y" Division: Steve Hershkowitz 906-7160
Director "Z" Division: Steve Hom 906-7966

DISTRICT OFFICES

District 1 (Boston)

District Counsel: Gary Gegenheimer
Office of Thrift Supervision, U.S. Department of the Treasury, One Financial Center, Fl 20, Boston, MA 02111.
Tel: 617/542-3979

District 2 (New York)

District Counsel: James Porreca
Office of Thrift Supervision, U.S. Department of the Treasury, 10 Exchange Place, 18th Floor, Jersey City, NJ 07302.
Tel: 201/413-7304.

District 3 (Pittsburgh)

District Counsel: James Orie
Office of Thrift Supervision, U.S. Department of the Treasury, One Riverfront Center, 20 Stanwix Street, Pittsburgh, PA 15222-4893. Tel: 412/288-3400.

District 4 (Atlanta)

District Counsel: Thomas King
Office of Thrift Supervision, U.S. Department of the Treasury, 1475 Peachtree Street, N.E., Atlanta, GA 30309.
Tel: 404/888-8000.

District 5 (Cincinnati)

District Counsel: Gerald P. Summers
Office of Thrift Supervision, U.S. Department of the Treasury, 2000 Atrium Two, 221 East Fourth Street, Cincinnati, OH 45201-0598. Tel: 513/852-7100.

District 6 (Indianapolis)

District Counsel: F. Keith Brown
Office of Thrift Supervision, U.S. Department of the Treasury, 8250 Woodfield Crossing Blvd, Suite 305, Indianapolis, IN 46204. Tel: 317/465-0200.

District 7 (Chicago)

District Counsel: Stacey Powers
Office of Thrift Supervision, U.S. Department of the Treasury, 111 East Wacker Drive, Suite 800, Chicago, IL 60601-4360. Tel: 312/565-5712.

District 8 (Des Moines)

District Counsel: William Nassis
Office of Thrift Supervision, U.S. Department of the Treasury, 907 Walnut Street, Des Moines, IA 50309. Tel: 515/243-4211.

District 9 (Irving)

District Counsel: Deborah Jenkins
Office of Thrift Supervision, U.S. Department of the Treasury, 500 East John Carpenter Freeway, Irving, TX 75062. Tel: 214/541-8900.

District 10 (Topeka)

District Counsel: Brian McCormally
Office of Thrift Supervision, U.S. Department of the Treasury, 200 East Sixth Street, P.O. Box 828, Topeka, KS 66601-0828. Tel: 913/233-5300.

District 11 (San Francisco)

District Counsel: William Black
Office of Thrift Supervision, U.S. Department of the Treasury, 580 California Street, Fl 10, San Francisco, CA 94104. Tel: 415/393-1000.

District 12 (Seattle)

District Counsel: Gregg Golden
Office of Thrift Supervision, U.S. Department of the Treasury, 1501 Fourth Avenue, Floor 19, Seattle, WA 98101-1693. Tel: 206/340-2300.

PUBLICATIONS OF INTEREST

To order any of the following publications, submit a check (made payable to the Office of Thrift Supervision), to: Controller, Office of Thrift Supervision, 1700 G Street, N.W., Washington, D.C. 20552. Tel: 202/906-6155.

Compliance Activities Handbook. Addresses compliance examination matters related to consumer protection laws and regulations, such as the Truth in Lending Act, and those related to the public interest, such as the Community Reinvestment Act and Bank Secrecy Act. Also contains examination objectives, procedures, and checklists for performing compliance reviews. Price: $50.00 for regulated institutions; $75.00 for others.

Holding Companies Handbook. Addresses areas of particular interest when reviewing holding company operations. It focuses on methods to identify risks to thrift institutions of holding company activities. Price: $50.00 for regulated institutions; $75.00 for others.

Application Processing Handbook. Contains guidance on how to process and analyze thrift and holding company applications. Price: $50.00 for regulated institutions; $75.00 for others.

Trust Activities Handbook. Assists in the examination of thrift institutions and their subsidiaries that engage in trust activities. It summarizes requirements and other laws and regulations applicable to trust activities of regulated institutions. Price: $50.00 for regulated institutions; $75.00 for others.

Compliance: A Self-Assessment Guide. Assists thrift institutions develop or improve internal policies and programs to ensure compliance with consumer and public interest laws. It covers consumer protection laws and regulations and several other statutes, including the Bank Secrecy Act and Bank Protection Act. Price: $20.00.

Bank Secrecy Act. Preventive and corrective actions for violations of Treasury Department and Office of Thrift Supervision regulations. Price: $3.00.

Director Information Guidelines. This pamphlet helps thrift directors meet their responsibilities in overseeing the management of their institutions by providing guidelines for evaluating information received in monthly board meetings. Price: $3.00.

Legal Alert Memo Subscription Series. Issued periodically by the Chief Counsel of the Office of Thrift Supervision, this series provides national guidance on significant legal issues such as securities disclosure requirements, mergers and acquisitions, transactions with affiliates, and management interlocks. Basic subscription price: $200.00. Copies of all back issues can be purchased for $35.00.

DEPARTMENT OF THE TREASURY
KEY LEGAL AUTHORITIES

General Departmental Regulations:

General: 31 C.F.R. Part 0 et seq. (1989).
Department of Treasury Acquisition Regulations: 48 C.F.R. Part 1033 (1989).
Office of Thrift Supervision: 12 C.F.R. Chapt. V (1989).
Comptroller of the Currency: 12 C.F.R. Parts 1-35 (1990).
Comptroller of the Currency-Rules of Practice & Procedure: 12 C.F.R. Part 19 (1990).
Bureau of Alcohol, Tobacco & Firearms: 27 C.F.R. Part 1 et seq. (1989).
Bureau of Alcohol, Tobacco & Firearms-Rules of Practice & Procedure: 31 C.F.R. Part 8 (1989); 27 C.F.R. Parts 70-72 & 200 (1989).
Customs Service: 19 C.F.R. Parts 1-191 (1989).

Customs Service-Special Classes of Merchandise: 19 C.F.R. Part 12 (1989).
Internal Revenue Service: 26 C.F.R. Part 1 et seq. (1989).
Internal Revenue Service-Rules of Practice & Procedure: 31 C.F.R. Part 10 (1989).
Financial Management Service: 31 C.F.R. Parts 202-290 (1989).
Bureau of the Public Debt: 31 C.F.R. Parts 306-391 (1989).

Financial Institutions Reform, Recovery, & Enforcement Act of 1989 (FIRREA), Pub. L. 101-73, 103 Stat. 183 (8/9/89)--transferred authority to regulate the organization, incorporation, examination, and operation of savings associations and savings and loan holding companies from the former Federal Home Loan Bank Board and Federal Savings and Loan Insurance Corporation to the new Office of Thrift Supervision in the Department of the Treasury.
Legislative History: 1989 U.S. Code Cong. & Admin. News 86.

Budget & Accounting Procedures Act of 1950, as amended, 31 U.S.C. 1101 et seq.--outlines the annual Federal budget and appropriations process.
Legislative History: 1983 U.S. Code Cong. & Admin. News 4301; 1985 U.S. Code Cong. & Admin. News 979; 1987 U.S. Code Cong. & Admin. News 739; 1988 U.S. Code Cong. & Admin. News 1547 & 5937.

Second Liberty Bond Act, as amended, 31 U.S.C. 3101 et seq.--authorizes the Secretary of the Treasury to borrow on the credit of the U.S. Government the amounts necessary for expenditures authorized by law through the issuance of bills, bonds, notes, and other instruments, including Savings Bonds.
Legislative History: 1986 U.S. Code Cong. & Admin. News 5395.
Implementing Regulations: 31 C.F.R. Part 309 et seq. (1989).

National Bank Act of 1864, as amended, 12 U.S.C. 21 et seq.--the basic statute governing the organization, capitalization, regulation, and examination of national banks.
Legislative History: 1959 U.S. Code Cong. & Admin. News 2232.

Federal Deposit Insurance Act, as amended, 12 U.S.C. 1811 et seq.--requires national banking associations to make reports of condition to the Comptroller of the Currency.
Legislative History: 1950 U.S. Code Cong. & Admin. News 3765; 1989 U.S. Code Cong. & Admin. News 86.
Implementing Regulations: 12 C.F.R. 5.20 (1990).

Change in Bank Control Act of 1978, 12 U.S.C. 1817(j)--requires 60 days' notice to the appropriate Federal banking agency, and agency approval of any acquisition of control over an insured depository institution.
Legislative History: 1978 U.S. Code Cong. & Admin. News 1421 & 9273.
Implementing Regulations: 12 C.F.R. 5.50 (1990).

Edge Act, as amended, 12 U.S.C. 611-632--governs the formation by national banks of subsidiaries to engage in international banking.
Legislative History: 1978 U.S. Code Cong. & Admin. News 1421.
Implementing Regulations: 12 C.F.R. Part 20 (1990).

Depository Institution Management Interlocks Act, as amended, 12 U.S.C. 3201 et seq.--designed to foster competition by prohibiting a management official of a depository institution or holding company from also serving as a management official of another such entity if the two organizations are: (1) not affiliated, and (2) very large or located in the same area.
Legislative History: 1978 U.S. Code Cong. & Admin. News 9273; 1983 U.S. Code Cong. & Admin. News 1768; 1988 U.S. Code Cong. & Admin. News 3054; 1989 U.S. Code Cong. & Admin. News 86.
Implementing Regulations: 12 C.F.R. Part 26 (1990).

Securities Exchange Act of 1934, as amended, 15 U.S.C. 78a et seq.--governs national banks or their subsidiaries acting as municipal securities dealers and all securities subject to registration by national banks.
Implementing Regulations: 12 U.S.C. Parts 10-11 (1990).

Fair Housing Act of 1968, as amended, 42 U.S.C. 3601 et seq.--requires that national banks and their subsidiaries, which make home loans for the purpose of purchasing, construction-permanent financing,or refinancing of residential real property, maintain records and a log of the various applications and inquiries.
Legislative History: 1968 U.S. Code Cong. & Admin. News 1837.
Implementing Regulations: 12 C.F.R. Part 27 (1990).

Bank Protection Act of 1968, as amended, 12 U.S.C. 1881 et seq.--establishes minimum standards which each national or district bank must comply with regarding the installation, maintenance, and operation of security devices to deter crime; requires submission of reports with respect to the installation, maintenance, and operations of such devices.
Legislative History: 1968 U.S. Code Cong. & Admin. News 2530.
Implementing Regulations: 12 C.F.R. Part 21 (1990).

Community Reinvestment Act of 1977, as amended, 12 U.S.C. 2901 et seq.--outlines procedures to encourage national banks to help meet the credit needs of their local communities; provides banks with guidance as to how the Comptroller of the Currency will assess their records of fulfilling this obligation, including with respect to communities with low and moderate income neighborhoods.
Legislative History: 1977 U.S. Code Cong. & Admin. News 2884.
Implementing Regulations: 12 C.F.R. Part 25 (1990).

Home Mortgage Disclosure Act of 1975, as amended, 12 U.S.C. 2801 et seq.--provides the public with loan data to determine whether depository institutions are serving the housing needs of the communities in which they are located.
Legislative History: 1975 U.S. Code Cong. & Admin. News 2303.
Implementing Regulations: 12 C.F.R. Part 203 (1990).

Truth in Lending Act of 1968, as amended, 15 U.S.C. 1601 et seq.--promotes the informed use of consumer credit by requiring disclosures about its terms and costs; gives consumers the right to cancel certain credit transactions that involve a lien on a consumer's principal dwelling.
Legislative History: 1968 U.S. Code Cong. & Admin. News 1962; 1981 U.S. Code Cong. & Admin. News 74; 1982 U.S. Code Cong. & Admin. News 3054.
Implementing Regulations: 12 C.F.R. Part 226 (1990).

Equal Credit Opportunity Act of 1974, as amended, 15 U.S.C. 1691 et seq.--promotes the availability of credit to all creditworthy applicants without regard to race, color, religion, national origin, sex, marital status, or age.
Legislative History: 1974 U.S. Code Cong. & Admin. News 6119. 1976 U.S. Code Cong. & Admin. News 403.
Implementing Regulations: 12 C.F.R. Part 202 (1990).

International Lending Supervision Act of 1983, as amended, 12 U.S.C. 3901 et seq.--strengthens the bank regulatory process to insure closer supervision of international loans and authorizes Federal bank regulatory agencies to require banking institutions to maintain special reserves whenever the quality of their foreign loans deteriorates.
Legislative History: 1983 U.S. Code Cong. & Admin. News 1768.
Implementing Regulations: 13 C.F.R. Parts 3 & 20 (1990).

International Banking Act of 1978, as amended, 12 U.S.C. 3101 et seq.--sets out rules governing the international and foreign activities of U.S. banking organizations.
Legislative History: 1978 U.S. Code Cong. & Admin. News 1421.
Implementation Regulations: 12 C.F.R. Part 211 (1990).

Currency & Foreign Transactions Reporting Act, as amended, 31 U.S.C. 5311-5326--designed to combat money laundering by requiring U.S. financial agencies to report certain transactions to the Government.
Legislative History: 1984 U.S. Code Cong. & Admin. News 3182; 1988 U.S. Code Cong. & Admin. News 5937.
Implementing Regulations: 31 C.F.R. Part 103 (1989).

DEPARTMENT OF THE TREASURY

International Investment Survey Act of 1976, as amended, 22 U.S.C. 3101-3108--directs the Department of Commerce to carry out a continuing data collection effort with respect to international trade and internal and external investment in services and, to that end, imposes certain recordkeeping and reporting requirements on persons subject to U.S. jurisdiction.
Legislative History: 1976 U.S. Code Cong. & Admin. News 4663; 1981 U.S. Code Cong. & Admin. News 99; 1984 U.S. Code Cong. & Admin. News 4910.
Implementing Regulations: 31 C.F.R. Part 128-129 (1989)[Treasury Department]; 15 C.F.R. Part 801 (1989)[Commerce Department].

Fair Debt Collection Practices Act of 1977, as amended, 15 U.S.C. 1692 et seq.--outlines procedures to eliminate abusive debt collection practices by debt collectors, to insure that those who are not engaged in abusive practices are not competitively disadvantaged and to promote consistent state action to protect consumers.
Legislative History: 1977 U.S. Code Cong. & Admin. News 1695.
Implementing Regulations: 12 C.F.R. Part 202 (1990).

Garn-St. Germain Depository Institutions Act of 1982, as amended, 12 U.S.C. 216 et seq.--provides guidelines for the Federal financial supervisory agencies, including the Department of the Treasury's Office of the Comptroller of the Currency and Office of Thrift Supervision to deal with financially distressed depository institutions.
Legislative History: 1982 U.S. Code Cong. & Admin. News 3054.
Implementing Regulations: 12 C.F.R. Part 33 (1990).

Financial Institutions Regulatory and Interest Rate Control Act of 1978, as amended, 12 U.S.C. 375 et seq.--governs any extension of credit by a member bank, a bank holding company of which the member bank is a subsidiary and any other subsidiary of that bank holding company; implements the reporting requirements concerning extension of credit by a member bank to its executive officers.
Legislative History: 1978 U.S. Code Cong. & Admin. News 9273; 1982 U.S. Code Cong. & Admin. News 3054.
Implementing Regulations: 12 C.F.R. Part 215 (1990).

Depository Institutions Deregulation and Monetary Control Act of 1980, as amended, 12 U.S.C. various sections--authorizes the automatic transfer of funds and negotiable order of withdrawal (NOW) accounts at depository institutions; also authorizes Federally-chartered savings and loan associations to establish remote service units.
Legislative History: 1980 U.S. Code Cong. & Admin. News 236.
Implementing Regulations: 12 C.F.R. Part 204 (1990).

Internal Revenue Code, Title 26 U.S.C.--the fundamental tax statute of the U.S.
Implementing Regulations: 26 C.F.R. Part 0 et seq. (1989).

Anti-Smuggling Act of 1935, as amended, 19 U.S.C. 1701 et seq.--outlines the standards for the inspection, examination and search of persons, vessels, aircraft, vehicles and merchandise involved in importation, for the seizure of property; for the forfeiture and sale of seized property; and for Customs Service enforcement of controlled substances, narcotics and marihuana laws.
Implementing Regulations: 19 C.F.R. Part 162 (1989).

Bank Secrecy Act of 1970, as amended, 12 U.S.C. 1951 et seq.--requires financial recordkeeping and reporting of currency and foreign transactions by banks and businesses where such records would have a high degree of usefulness in criminal, tax or regulatory investigations or proceedings.
Legislative History: 1970 U.S. Code Cong. & Admin. News 4394.
Implementing Regulations: 12 C.F.R. Part 21 (1989)[customs enforcement]; 31 C.F.R. Part 103 (1989)[Comptroller of the Currency].

Unfair Competition Act of 1916, as amended, 15 U.S.C. 71 et seq.-prohibits any person from importing or assisting in importing any articles from a foreign country into the United States if the articles are to be sold at a price substantially less than the actual market value or wholesale price in the principal markets of the country of their production.
Implementing Regulations: 19 C.F.R. Part 207 (1989).

Tariff Act of 1930, as amended, 19 U.S.C. 1201 et seq.--contains the tariff schedules governing all imports into the U.S. and is the generic statute governing U.S. customs procedures.
Implementing Regulations: Title 19, C.F.R. (1989).

Customs Procedural Reform and Simplification Act of 1978, as amended, 19 U.S.C. 1481 et seq.--establishes a modified procedure for handling the documentary and financial aspects of import transactions; relates the amount of the customs penalty for false and material statements to Customs to the culpability of the offender.
Legislative History: 1978 U.S. Code Cong. & Admin. News 2211.
Implementing Regulations: 19 C.F.R. Parts 24 & 141 (1989).

Trade Act of 1974, as amended, 19 U.S.C. 2101 et seq.--provides procedures to safeguard American industry and labor against unfair or injurious import competition; also assists industries, workers and communities with respect to international trade issues.
Legislative History: 1974 U.S. Code Cong. & Admin. News 7186.
Implementing Regulations: 19 C.F.R. Parts 205-207 (1989).

Trade Expansion Act of 1962, as amended, 19 U.S.C. 1862--authorizes the President to retain import restrictions or duties if their decrease or elimination would threaten to impair national security.
Legislative History: 1962 U.S. Code Cong. & Admin. News 3110; 1988 U.S. Code Cong. & Admin. News 1547.
Implementing Regulations: 31 C.F.R. Part 13 (1989).

Plant Quarantine Act of 1912, as amended, 7 U.S.C. 149 et seq.--requires the Customs Service to quarantine plants entering the U.S.
Legislative History: 1957 U.S. Code Cong. & Admin. News 1184; 1982 U.S. Code Cong. & Admin. News 4426.
Implementing Regulations: 7 C.F.R. Part 352 (1990).

Foreign Trade Zones Act of 1934, as amended, 19 U.S.C. 81a--authorized the formation of foreign trade zones, defined as isolated, enclosed, and policed areas operated as public utilities in or adjacent to a port of entry and furnished with facilities for lading, unlading, handling, storing, manipulating, manufacturing, exhibiting, and reshipping goods. Goods may be brought into a zone without being subject to U.S. customs law governing entry or payment of a duty and may be reshipped to foreign ports duty-free.
Legislative History: 1950 U.S. Code Cong. Service 2533; 1984 U.S. Code Cong. & Admin. News 4910. 19 C.F.R. Part 146.0 et seq., 196, 252, & 290 (1989).
Implementing Regulations: 19 C.F.R. Part 146 (1989).

Trade Fair Act of 1959, 19 U.S.C. 1751-1756--authorizes the Secretary of Commerce to advise the Secretary of the Treasury of a "trade fair designation," which confers special customs entry and disposition privileges on articles imported for a trade fair.
Legislative History: 1959 U.S. Code Cong. & Admin. News 1436.
Implementing Regulations: 19 C.F.R. Part 147 (1989).

Trading with the Enemy Act of 1917, as amended, 50 U.S.C. App. 5(b) et seq.--outlines licensing and prohibited procedures in regard to foreign assets.

Legislative History: 1977 U.S. Code Cong. & Admin. News 4540; 1978 U.S. Code Cong. & Admin. News 1833; 1988 U.S. Code Cong. & Admin. News 547.
Implementing Regulations: 31 C.F.R. Part 500 (1989).

U.S. Secret Service Uniformed Division, 3 U.S.C. 202 et seq.--governs the Secret Service's Uniformed Division.
Legislative History: 1962 U.S. Code Cong. & Admin. News 1672; 1986 U.S. Code Cong. & Admin. News 5627.
Implementing Regulations: 31 C.F.R. Part 13 (1989).

Secret Service Act, as amended, 49 U.S.C. 781 et seq.--designates the Secret Service to seize vessels, vehicles, and aircraft that are transporting, carrying or conveying any contraband articles.
Legislative History: 1970 U.S. Code Cong. & Admin. News 4566; 1978 U.S. Code Cong. & Admin. News 5518.
Implementing Regulations: 31 C.F.R. Part 401 (1989).

Public Debt, as amended, 31 U.S.C. 306 et seq.--outlines procedures for the management of the public debt, including settlement procedures for lost, stolen or destroyed bonds as well as the selling of Treasury securities and savings bonds.
Implementing Regulations: 31 C.F.R. Parts 315 & 340 (1989).

Federal Alcohol Administration Act, as amended, 27 U.S.C. 203 et seq.--outlines the requirements governing the issuance, amendment, denial, automatic termination and annulment of basic permits and the duration of permits for manufacturers et al.
Legislative History: 1958 U.S. Code Cong. & Admin. News 3996.
Implementing Regulations: 27 C.F.R. Part 1 (1989).

Gun Control Act of 1968, as amended, 18 U.S.C. 921 et seq.--outlines the procedural and substantive requirements relative to the licensing of manufacturers and importers of firearms and ammunition, collectors of firearms and dealers in firearms.
Legislative History: 1968 U.S. Code Cong. & Admin. News 4410; 1974 U.S. Code Cong. & Admin. News 1974; 1986 U.S. Code Cong. & Admin. News 1327.
Implementing Regulations: 27 C.F.R. Part 178 (1989).

Trafficking in Contraband Cigarettes Act of 1978, as amended, 18 U.S.C. 2341 et seq.--makes it unlawful for any person knowingly to ship, transport, receive, possess, sell distribute or purchase contraband cigarettes; prohibits a person knowingly to make any false statement or representation with respect to the information to be kept in the records of any person who ships, sells, or distributes any quantity of cigarettes in excess of 60,000 in a single transaction.
Legislative History: 1978 U.S. Code Cong. & Admin. News 5518.
Implementing Regulations: 27 C.F.R. Part 270 (1989).

Organized Crime Control Act of 1970, as amended, 18 U.S.C. 841 et seq.--outlines procedural and substantive requirements in the issuing of permits and the licensing of manufacturers, importers and dealers in explosive materials.
Legislative History: 1970 U.S. Code Cong. & Admin. News 4007; 1982 U.S. Code Cong. & Admin. News 2631; 1984 U.S. Code Cong. & Admin. News 182.
Implementing Regulations: 27 C.F.R. Part 55 (1989).

Arms Export Control Act of 1976, as amended, 22 U.S.C. 2778 et seq.--concerned with the importation of arms, ammunition, and implements of war; contains procedural and administrative requirements and provisions including the registration of importers, permits and articles in transit.
Legislative History: 1976 U.S. Code Cong. & Admin. News 1378; 1977 U.S. Code Cong. & Admin. News 978.
Implementing Regulations: 27 C.F.R. Part 47 (1989).

DEPARTMENT OF VETERANS AFFAIRS

810 Vermont Avenue, N.W.
Washington, D.C. 20420

DESCRIPTION: The Department of Veterans Affairs administers broad programs of care and assistance to over 29 million veterans and their dependents and is one of the largest employers of attorneys in the U.S. Government. Its mission is to: provide quality medical care on a timely basis to all authorized veterans; provide an appropriate levels of benefits to eligible veterans and other beneficiaries; ensure that memorial affairs are handled with honor and dignity; and represent the concerns and needs of veterans within the Federal Government. The Department operates more than 500 health care facilities and over 100 cemeteries throughout the U.S.

(Area Code 202)

Secretary: Edward J. Derwinski 233-3775
Procurement Information 233-2411
Small and Disadvantaged Business Utilization 376-6996
Public Information 233-2741
Publications Information 233-2741
Docket 233-4294
Legislative Reference and Research 233-3940
Fraud, Waste and Abuse Hot Line:
Washington, D.C. Metro Area 233-5394
Outside Washington, D.C. Metro Area ....(800) 368-5899
Facsimile 233-2807

Freedom of Information Act Office 233-3616
All requests must be in writing. Requestors are divided into four groups: Commercial, Educational, News Media, and all other. Copying charge for those in the first group is 15 cents per page. The charge for search and review is based on the salary of the person doing the search. The second two groups are not charged for the first 100 pages and pay no search fee. The last group ("all other") gets 100 pages of free copying and two free hours of search time.

(Area Code 202)

Privacy Act Office 233-3616
There is no fee for Privacy Act searches, but there is a copying fee of 15 cents per page. Veterans are allowed one free copy of their benefits records.

(Area Code 202)

Law Library (Room 1039) 233-6442
The law library is open to the public Monday through Friday from 8:00 AM until 5:00 PM. Appointments are required. Materials may be copied at no charge.

OFFICE OF THE GENERAL COUNSEL (ROOM 1024)

The Office of General Counsel provides legal advice to the Secretary of Veterans Affairs, and the General Counsel is the chief legal officer of the Department. The office renders legal advice and other legal services to all department heads and top staff officials and is responsible for the Department's legislative program. Attorneys at the central office in Washington, D.C. represent the Department at congressional hearings and try cases before administrative tribunals, particularly in the contract and personnel fields. The attorneys in the 54 District Counsel offices nationwide (see list below) provide a full range of legal services involving advice and assistance on questions presented by Directors of VA Medical Centers and Regional Offices and officials of these offices. They also represent the Secretary in state courts and assist U.S. Attorneys in Federal courts in matters involving the Department.

(Area Code 202)

General Counsel: Raoul L. Carroll 233-3831
Deputy General Counsel: Robert E. Coy 233-3082
Facsimile 233-5420

The Office of General Counsel is divided into the following seven Professional Staff Groups (PSG) each of which is headed by an Assistant General Counsel:

Assistant General Counsel for:

(Area Code 202)

PSG I (Education, Loan Guaranty, Medical Care Recovery, Tort Claims, and Vocational Rehabilitation): James P. Kane 233-2189

PSG II (Automobile Allowances, Burial Benefits, Compensation and Pension, Insurance, Judicial Review of Denied Benefits):
John H. Thompson 233-3004

PSG III (Crimes and Police Matters, Ethics, Labor Relations, Medical Care Benefits and Hospital Administration, Personnel):
Audley Hendricks 233-3671

(Area Code 202)

PSG IV (Administrative Procedures, Appropriations, Architectural and Transportation Barriers, Discrimination, Information Disclosure, Patents and Copyrights): Neal C. Lawson 233-3294

PSG V (Board of Contract Appeals, Environmental/Historic Preservation, Procurement, Real Estate): William E. Thomas Jr 233-2217

PSG VI (Management and Operations):
Nicholas C. Chybinski 233-2479
Deputy General Counsel: Douglas W. Bartow ..223-4280
Deputy General Counsel (Agent Orange):
Frederick L. Conway 223-8018

PSG VII (Court of Veterans Appeals Litigation):
Barry M. Tapp 254-4938
Deputy Assistant General Counsel:
Andrew J. Mullen 254-5195
Deputy Assistant General Counsel:
Pamela L. Wood 254-5047
Docket: 254-5200

DISTRICT COUNSEL OFFICES

Washington, D.C.
District Counsel: Howard C. Lem
U.S. Department of Veterans Affairs, 941 N. Capitol Street, NE, Ste 9100, Washington, D.C. 20421. Tel: 202/275-1417.

Albuquerque
District Counsel: Donald A. Adams
U.S. Department of Veterans Affairs, VA Medical Center, Bldg 18, 2100 Ridgecrest Drive, SE, Albuquerque, NM 87108. Tel: 505/256-2780.

Atlanta
District Counsel: William M. Thigpen, III
U.S. Department of Veterans Affairs, 730 Peachtree Street, NE, Atlanta, GA 30365. Tel: 404/347-3391.

Baltimore
District Counsel: Edward J. McGarrity
U.S. Department of Veterans Affairs, Federal Bldg, 31 Hopkins Plaza, Baltimore, MD 21201. Tel: 301/962-4160.

Bay Pines, FL
District Counsel: Karen Sue Meyer
U.S. Department of Veterans Affairs, 10000 Bay Pines Blvd, Bldg 22, Rm 333, Bay Pines, FL 33504. Tel: 813/398-9390.

Boston
District Counsel: Edward J. Lukey
U.S. Department of Veterans Affairs, JFK Federal Bldg, Boston, MA 02203. Tel: 617/565-2644-49.

Boise
District Counsel: William F. Helfrick
U.S. Department of Veterans Affairs, 550 West Fort Street, P.O. Box 044, Boise, ID 83724. Tel: 208/338-7204.

Buffalo
District Counsel: John C. Dinoto
U.S. Department of Veterans Affairs, 120 LeBrun, Buffalo, NY 14215. Tel: 716/862-3719.

Cheyenne
District Counsel: Jerry L. Jones
U.S. Department of Veterans Affairs, 2360 E. Pershing Blvd, Cheyenne, WY 82001. Tel: 307/778-7332.

Cleveland
District Counsel: Harvey Wax
U.S. Department of Veterans Affairs, Federal Office Bldg, 1240 E. 9th Street, Cleveland, OH 44199. Tel: 216/522-3592.

Columbia, SC
District Counsel: John L. Pressly, Jr.
U.S. Department of Veterans Affairs, 1801 Assembly Street, Columbia, SC 29201. Tel: 803/765-5217.

Denver
District Counsel: George W. Beasley
U.S. Department of Veterans Affairs, Box 25126, 44 Union Blvd, Denver, CO 80225. Tel: 303/980-2705.

Des Moines
District Counsel: Earl E. Parson
U.S. Department of Veterans Affairs, 210 Walnut Street, Des Moines, IA 50309. Tel: 515/284-4090.

Detroit
District Counsel: John M. Mac Millan
U.S. Department of Veterans Affairs, Patrick V. McNamara Federal Bldg, Ste 1460, 477 Michigan Avenue, Detroit, MI 48226. Tel: 313/226-4242-43.

Fargo
District Counsel: Branson H. Moore
U.S. Department of Veterans Affairs, 2101 Elm Street, Fargo, ND 58102. Tel: 701/239-3781.

Harrison, MT
District Counsel: Michael D. Thompson
U.S. Department of Veterans Affairs, Ste 137, VA Center, Fort Harrison, MT 59636. Tel: 406/442-6410.

Hartford
District Counsel: Joan M. Lebovitz
U.S. Department of Veterans Affairs, 450 Main Street, Hartford, CT 06103. Tel: 203/240-3150.

Hines, IL
District Counsel: Dennis Kokinda
U.S. Department of Veterans Affairs, VAMC, Bldg 50, P.O. Box 127, Hines, IL 60141. Tel: 312/216-2216.

Honolulu
District Counsel: Frederick L. Hall, III
U.S. Department of Veterans Affairs, 300 Ala Moana Blvd, Rm 2302, P.O. Box 50188, Honolulu, HI 96850. Tel: 808/541-1605.

Houston
District Counsel: Logan A. Slaughter
U.S. Department of Veterans Affairs, 2515 Murworth Drive, Houston, TX 77054. Tel: 713/660-4352.

Huntington, WV
District Counsel: Charles C. Moore, Jr.
U.S. Department of Veterans Affairs, 640 4th Avenue, Huntington, WV 26701. Tel: 304/529-5022.

Indianapolis
District Counsel: Wilson L. Tow
U.S. Department of Veterans Affairs, 575 N. Pennsylvania Street, Rm 309, Indianapolis, IN 46204. Tel: 317/226-7876.

Jackson, MS
District Counsel: Mary E. Barrett
U.S. Department of Veterans Affairs, 1500 E. Woodrow Wilson Dr, Jackson, MS 39216. Tel: 601/364-1261.

Lincoln
District Counsel: James C. Klein
U.S. Department of Veterans Affairs, 100 Centennial Mall N., Lincoln, NE 68508. Tel: 402/437-5061.

Little Rock
District Counsel: Charles J. Pugh
U.S. Department of Veterans Affairs, VAMC, 2200 Fort Roots Dr, N. Little Rock, AR 72114. Tel: 501/370-6602.

Los Angeles
District Counsel: Lazar Benrubi
U.S. Department of Veterans Affairs, 11000 Wilshire Blvd, Los Angeles, CA 90024. Tel: 818/209-7379.

Louisville
District Counsel: Anthony G. Belak
U.S. Department of Veterans Affairs, 600 Martin Luther King Jr Place, Louisville, KY 40202. Tel: 502/582-5871.

Manchester
District Counsel: Barry J. Walker
U.S. Department of Veterans Affairs, Norris Cotton Federal Bldg, 275 Chestnut Street, Manchester, NH 03101-2487. Tel: 603/666-7573.

DEPARTMENT OF VETERANS AFFAIRS

Milwaukee
District Counsel: Ralph E. Anfang
U.S. Department of Veterans Affairs, VA Regional Office, Bldg 6, Milwaukee, WI 53295. Tel: 414/382-5010.

Montgomery
District Counsel: Lawrence Kloess, Jr.
U.S. Department of Veterans Affairs, Aronov Bldg, 474 S. Court St, Montgomery, AL 36104. Tel: 205/223-7046.

Muskogee
District Counsel: Herbert N. Standeven
U.S. Department of Veterans Affairs, VA Regional Office, 125 South Main Street, Muskogee, OK 74401. Tel: 918/687-2191.

Nashville
District Counsel: Jerry D. Stringer
U.S. Department of Veterans Affairs, Federal Courthouse Annex, 110 9th Avenue, S., Nashville, TN 37203. Tel: 615/736-5326.

Newark
District Counsel: Emil N. Addesa
U.S. Department of Veterans Affairs, 20 Washington Pl, Newark, NJ 07102. Tel: 201/645-3260.

New Orleans
District Counsel: Walter A. Hall
U.S. Department of Veterans Affairs, 701 Loyola Avenue, New Orleans, LA 70113. Tel: 504/589-6441.

New York
District Counsel: Max D. Shemtob
U.S. Department of Veterans Affairs, 252 Seventh Avenue, New York, NY 10001. Tel: 212/620-6276.

Philadelphia
District Counsel: David Adelman
U.S. Department of Veterans Affairs, 5000 Wissahickon Avenue, P.O. Box 8079, Philadelphia, PA 19101. Tel: 215/951-5487.

Phoenix
District Counsel: Gregory G. Ferris
U.S. Department of Veterans Affairs, 3225 N. Central Avenue, Rm 305, Phoenix, AZ 85012. Tel: 602/241-2742.

Pittsburgh
District Counsel: Homer D. Byrd
U.S. Department of Veterans Affairs, 1000 Liberty Avenue, Pittsburgh, PA 15222. Tel: 412/644-6670.

Portland
District Counsel: Roland V. Brown
U.S. Department of Veterans Affairs, 1220 S. West Third Avenue, Portland, OR 97204. Tel: 503/326-2441.

Providence
District Counsel: Murray Zaretsky
U.S. Department of Veterans Affairs, 380 Westminster Mall, Providence, RI 02903. Tel: 401/528-4420.

Reno
District Counsel: Susan K. Savela
U.S. Department of Veterans Affairs, VA Medical Center, 1000 Locust Street, Reno, NV 89520. Tel: 702/786-7200, ext. 526.

Roanoke
District Counsel: Robert E. Hadley
U.S. Department of Veterans Affairs, 210 Franklin Road, SW, Roanoke, VA 24011. Tel: 703/982-6162.

St. Louis
District Counsel: David E. Davenport, Jr.
U.S. Department of Veterans Affairs, 1010 Market Street, Ste 1520, St. Louis, MO 63101. Tel: 314/425-5161.

St. Paul
District Counsel: Dale E. Parker
U.S. Department of Veterans Affairs, VARO & IC, Fort Snelling, Rm 112, Bishop Henry Whipple Federal Bldg, St. Paul, MN 55111. Tel: 612/725-3122.

Salt Lake City
District Counsel: Glade S. Bigler
U.S. Department of Veterans Affairs, 125 S. State Street, P.O. Box 11500, Salt Lake City, UT 84147. Tel: 801/524-5950.

San Diego
District Counsel: Lazar Benrubi
U.S. Department of Veterans Affairs, Ste 326, 2022 Camino Del Rio N., San Diego, CA 92108. Tel: 619/557-6710. Note: The Los Angeles office has jurisdiction over this office.

San Francisco
District Counsel: Jack Nagan
U.S. Department of Veterans Affairs, 211 Main Street, San Francisco, CA 94105. Tel: 415/974-0228.

San Juan
District Counsel: Otto J. Riefkohl, II
U.S. Department of Veterans Affairs, VA Medical Center, One Veterans Plaza, San Juan, PR 00927. Tel: 809/758-7575, ext. 3227-28.

Seattle
District Counsel: Stephen M. Gold
U.S. Department of Veterans Affairs, 915 Second Avenue, Seattle, WA 98174. Tel: 206/442-5010.

Sioux Falls
District Counsel: William H. Ranney, Jr.
U.S. Department of Veterans Affairs, 2501 W. 22nd Street, P.O. Box 5046, Sioux Falls, SD 57117. Tel: 605/333-6853.

Togus, ME
District Counsel: Denise Ridge
U.S. Department of Veterans Affairs, Veterans Administration Center, VAMROC, Togus, ME 04330. Tel: 207/623-8411.

Waco
District Counsel: Richard J. Jones
U.S. Department of Veterans Affairs, 1400 North Valley Mills Dr, Waco, TX 76799. Tel: 817/757-6414.

White River Junction, VT
District Counsel: Gregory R. Valentine
U.S. Department of Veterans Affairs, 02, VAMROC, White River Junction, VT 05001. Tel: 802/296-5116.

Wichita
District Counsel: John A. Bell
U.S. Department of Veterans Affairs, 5500 East Kellogg, Wichita, KS 67218. Tel: 316/269-6704.

Winston-Salem
District Counsel: Duncan E. Sessions
U.S. Department of Veterans Affairs, 251 North Main Street, Winston-Salem, NC 27155. Tel: 919/761-3488.

OFFICE OF INSPECTOR GENERAL (Room 1100)

The Office of Inspector General is responsible for audits and investigations; review of legislation; and recommendation of policies designed to promote economy and efficiency in the administration of, or prevent and detect fraud and abuse in, the programs and operations of the Department. In this regard, the Inspector General is responsible for keeping the Secretary and the Congress fully informed about problems and deficiencies in VA programs and operations and the need for corrective action. The Inspector General has authority to inquire into all VA programs and activities of persons or parties preforming under grants, contracts or other agreement. These inquiries may be in the form of audits, surveys, criminal and other investigations, personnel security checks, or other appropriate actions.

(Area Code 202)
Inspector General: Renald P. Morani 233-2636

(Area Code 202)
Assistant Inspector General for Investigations: (vacant) 233-3093

BOARD OF VETERANS APPEALS (Room 845)

The Board of Veterans Appeals makes final determinations in appeals on all questions involving claims for veterans' benefits in over 32,000 cases per year. The Board is organized around the Office of the Chairman and 23 sections composed of usually two attorneys and one medical member. Several attorney-advisors assist in legal research.

(Area Code 202)
Chairman: Kenneth E. Eaton 233-3001
Executive Assistant to Chairman: Stephen A. Jones ...233-3275
Special Legal Assistant: Jan Donsbach 233-2978
Vice Chairman: Roger K. Bauer 233-2222

(Area Code 202)
Deputy Vice Chairmen:
David Landers 233-3163
Richard Standefer 233-3163
Appellate Index and Retrieval Staff.....................233-3365

BOARD OF CONTRACT APPEALS (Room 632)
1425 K Street, N.W., Washington, D.C. 20420

The Board of Contract Appeals is a quasi-judicial tribunal composed of Administrative Judges who conduct on-the-record, adversarial hearings and render formal decisions on contractor appeals from final decisions of Department of Veterans Affairs Contracting Officers. The Board is, in effect, a trial court which hears and decides Government contract disputes. The Board also has jurisdiction, under the Equal Access to Justice Act, to decide applications for attorney fees and expenses incurred in connection with Contract Disputes Act appeals.

The Administrative Judges are selected and appointed to serve in the same manner as Federal Administrative Law Judges. They preside over the processing of appeals, which may include significant prehearing activity, such as discovery and motions practice. Oral hearings are provided if elected by either party. Generally, a single Administrative Judge conducts the hearing although Board opinions are, in most cases the result of consideration by a panel of three Judges. Except in certain limited circumstances, decisions are issued in the form of formal, written opinions containing findings of fact and conclusions of law. Board decisions are final within the Agency, but may be appealed by either party to the U.S. Court of Appeals for the Federal Circuit.

Board of Contract Appeals Reporter is a bi-weekly publication which reports the decisions of the following Boards of Contract Appeals: Agriculture, Armed Services, Corps of Engineers, Department of Transportation, Energy, General Services Administration, Department of Housing and Urban Development, Interior, Labor, National Aeronautics and Space Administration, U.S. Postal Service, and Department of Veterans Affairs. Annual Price $760.00. Contact: Commerce Clearing House, Inc., 4025 West Peterson Avenue, Chicago, IL 60646. Tel: 312/583-8500. Or in Washington, D.C., call 202/626-2200.

(Area Code 202)
Chairman: Guy H. McMichael III 275-0430
Vice Chairman: Dan R. Anders 275-0430
Administrative Judges:
Richard W. Krepasky 275-0430
Morris Pullara Jr 275-0430
James K. Robinson 275-0430

The Hearing Examiner's functions are, in many respects, similar to those of an Administrative Judge. However, the Hearing Examiner is without authority to take any action which is potentially dispositive of an appeal or a portion thereof. On such matters, the Hearing Examiner may make recommendations to Administrative Judges. Further, the Hearing Examiner lacks authority to perform certain other functions, such as issuance of subpoenas, which are within the authority of the Administrative Judges.

The Attorney Examiner conducts extensive research of laws, legal authority and specific problems in precedent cases and prepares legal analysis and digests of evidence generated by hearings held by the Board.

The Law Clerk assists the Judges in a variety of ways, including docket management tasks, and providing advice and assistance to the Judges in their consideration of both factual and legal issues of appeals.

(Area Code 202)
Hearing Examiner: vacant 275-0430
Attorney Examiner: Shari Bell 275-9858
Law Clerk: James R. Ashburn 275-7065

NOTE: Although the Board's offices are located at 1425 K Street, N.W., the Board's mailing address is the Vermont Avenue address listed at the beginning of this listing. The Board frequently holds hearings in the field to accommodate contractors and Department of Veterans Affairs elements located outside the Washington, D.C. area.

DEPARTMENT OF VETERANS AFFAIRS

PUBLICATIONS OF INTEREST

Federal Benefits for Veterans and Dependents 1989 discusses medical, educational, loan, insurance, compensation, pension, and other programs and benefits administered by the Veterans Administration and other agencies. It lists VA facilities nationwide. It is available from Consumer Information Center-P, P.O. Box 100, Pueblo, CO 81002. Price: $2.75. Booklet number 116W.

United States Code, Title 38, Veteran's Benefits contains the exact text of laws in the field of veterans' affairs which come within the jurisdiction of the House Committee on Veterans' Affairs. Subscription service consists of a basic manual and one change per Congress (two-year period). In looseleaf form, punched for 3-ring binder. Price: $25.00 domestic; $31.25 foreign. GPO Stock# 952-002-00000-7. This publication can be purchased from the U.S. Government Printing Office. Submit request to: The Superintendent of Documents, U.S. Government Printing Office, Washington, D.C. 20402. (202/783-3238).

DEPARTMENT OF VETERANS AFFAIRS
KEY LEGAL AUTHORITIES

General Regulations:

General Departmental Regulations: 38 C.F.R. Part 0 et seq. (1989).
Department of Veterans Affairs Acquisition Regulations: 48 C.F.R. Part 801 et seq. (1989).
Board of Veterans Appeals' Rules of Practice & Procedure: 38 C.F.R. Part 19 (1989).

Department of Veterans Affairs Act, 38 U.S.C. 201 note-elevated the Veterans Administration to a Cabinet Department in order to strengthen the agency's management effectiveness and internal controls. The Act became effective March 15, 1989.
Legislative History: 1988 U.S. Code Cong. & Admin. News 3407.

Veteran's Judicial Review Act, 38 U.S.C. 4051 et seq.--established the United States Court of Veterans Appeals, under the authority vested in Congress under section 8 of Article I of the Constitution. The court provides for judicial review of certain final decisions of the Department of Veterans Affairs' Board of Veterans' Appeals. Judicial review by the Court is available only to persons who file a notice of disagreement on or after the date of enactment of the Act (November 18, 1989). The Act also provides for the payment of reasonable fees to attorneys for rendering legal representation to individuals claiming benefits under laws administered by the Department of Veterans Affairs.
Legislative History: 1988 U.S. Code Cong. & Admin. News 5782.

Veterans' Dioxin and Radiation Exposure Compensation Standards Act, 38 U.S.C. 354 note- ensures that Department of Veterans' Affairs disability compensation is provided to veterans who were exposed during service in Vietnam to a herbicide containing dioxin as well as to those exposed to ionizing radiation during the American occupation of Japan after the nuclear blasts at Nagasaki and Hiroshima.
Legislative History: 1984 U.S. Code Cong. & Admin. News 58.

Radiation Control for Health & Safety Act of 1968, 42 U.S.C. 263b et seq.--authorizes the Department of Health & Human Services, in conjunction with the Environmental Protection Agency and the Department of Veterans Affairs, to promulgate Federal radiation guidelines.
Legislative History: 1981 U.S. Code Cong. & Admin. News 396.

Federal Medical Care Recovery Act, 42 U.S.C. 2651 et seq.--authorizes the Department of Veterans Affairs to collect in full, compromise, settle, or waive any claim up to $40,000 from a tortiously liable third party for health care or treatment provided by Department of Veterans Affairs facilities or personnel.
Implementing Regulations: 28 C.F.R. Part 43 (1989).

Soldiers' and Sailors' Civil Relief Act of 1940, as amended, 50 U.S.C. App. 501-591--suspends enforcement of certain civil liabilities of persons in U.S. military service, including temporary suspension of legal proceedings during the period of such service.
Legislative History: 1960 U.S. Code Cong. & Admin. News 3404.
Implementing Regulations: 38 C.F.R. Part 7 (1989).

Veterans Benefits Act of 1958, as amended, Title 38 U.S.C.--consolidated into one Act all the benefits laws administered by the Department of Veterans Affairs, including the following key statutes:

Service-Connected Death/Disability Benefits, 38 U.S.C. 301 et seq.
Legislative History: 1959 U.S. Code Cong. & Admin. News 2159; 1960 U.S. Code Cong. & Admin. News 2234; 1976 U.S. Code Cong. & Admin. News 2537.
Implementing Regulations: 38 C.F.R. Part 4 (1989).

Dependency & Indemnity Compensation for Service-Connected Deaths, 38 U.S.C. 401 et seq.
Legislative History: 1960 U.S. Code Cong. & Admin. News 2235; 1967 U.S. Code Cong. & Admin. News 1493; 1969 U.S. Code Cong. & Admin. News 1022 & 1192; 1980 U.S. Code Cong. & Admin. News 4555; 1982 U.S. Code Cong. & Admin. News 2877; 1984 U.S. Code Cong. & Admin. News 58; 1988 U.S. Code Cong. & Admin. News 5782.

Pensions for Non-Service Connected Disability or Death or for Service, 38 U.S.C. 501 et seq.
Legislative History: 1959 U.S. Code Cong. & Admin. News 2190; 1964 U.S. Code Cong. & Admin. News 4010; 1967 U.S. Code Cong. & Admin. News 1493; 1976 U.S. Code Cong. & Admin. News 2513; 1978 U.S. Code Cong. & Admin. News 5583; 1982 U.S. Code Cong. & Admin. News 2598; 1988 U.S. Code Cong. & Admin. News 5782.

Hospital, Nursing Home, Domiciliary, & Medical Care, 38 U.S.C. 601 et seq.
Legislative History: 1960 U.S. Code Cong. & Admin. News 2758 & 3111; 1962 U.S. Code Cong. & Admin. News 2134; 1967 U.S. Code Cong. & Admin. News 1493; 1968 U.S. Code Cong. & Admin. News 4381; 1973 U.S. Code Cong. & Admin. News 1688; 1976 U.S. Code Cong. & Admin. News 6355; 1979 U.S. Code Cong. & Admin. News 169.
Implementing Regulations: 38 C.F.R. Part 17 (1989).

Life Insurance Programs, 38 U.S.C. 701 et seq.
Legislative History: 1964 U.S. Code Cong. & Admin. News 4010; 1970 U.S. Code Cong. & Admin. News 3317; 1971 U.S. Code Cong. & Admin. News 2132; 1982 U.S. Code Cong. & Admin. News 2598; 1986 U.S. Code Cong. & Admin. News 5468.
Implementing Regulations: 38 C.F.R. Part 6, 8-9 (1989).

Specially Adapted Housing for Disabled Veterans, 38 U.S.C. 801-806.
Legislative History: 1959 U.S. Code Cong. & Admin. News 2275; 1980 U.S. Code Cong. & Admin. News 3307; 1986 U.S. Code Cong. & Admin. News 5468; 1988 U.S. Code Cong. & Admin. News 432.
Implementing Regulations: 38 C.F.R. 36.4400 et seq. (1989).

Burial Benefits, 38 U.S.C. 901 et seq.
Legislative History: 1959 U.S. Code Cong. & Admin. News 1675; 1961 U.S. Code Cong. & Admin. News 2678; 1964 U.S. Code Cong. & Admin. News 2536; 1982 U.S. Code Cong. & Admin. News 2877.

Eligibility for Internment in National Cemeteries, 38 U.S.C. 1002.
Legislative History: 1973 U.S. Code Cong. & Admin. News 1401; 1986 U.S. Code Cong. & Admin. News 5468.

Vocational Rehabilitation Benefits, 38 U.S.C. 1501 et seq.
Legislative History: 1980 U.S. Code Cong. & Admin. News 4555; 1982 U.S. Code Cong. & Admin. News 2877; 1986 U.S. Code Cong. & Admin. News 5468; 1988 U.S. Code Cong. & Admin. News 539.
Implementing Regulations: 38 C.F.R. Part 21 (1989).

Education & Training Benefits, 38 U.S.C. 1401 et seq., 1601 et seq., 1700 et seq., 1770 et seq., 2000 et seq., & 2011 et seq.
Legislative History: 1962 U.S. Code Cong. & Admin. News 2594; 1968 U.S. Code Cong. & Admin. News 4484; 1972 U.S. Code Cong. & Admin. News 4331; 1976 U.S. Code Cong. & Admin. News 5241; 1980 U.S. Code Cong. & Admin. News 4555; 1982 U.S. Code Cong. & Admin. News 2598 & 2877; 1983 U.S. Code Cong. & Admin. News 1344; 1986 U.S. Code Cong. & Admin. News 5468; 1987 U.S. Code Cong. & Admin. News 314; 1988 U.S. Code Cong. & Admin. News 539.
Implementing Regulations: 38 C.F.R. Part 21 (1989).

Housing & Small Business Loans, 38 U.S.C. 1801 et seq.
Legislative History: 1970 U.S. Code Cong. & Admin. News 5134; 1976 U.S. Code Cong. & Admin. News 1344; 1981 U.S. Code Cong. & Admin. News 1685.
Implementing Regulations: 38 C.F.R. Part 36 (1989).

Veterans Reemployment Rights, 38 U.S.C. 2021-2026.
Legislative History: 1974 U.S. Code Cong. & Admin. News 6313; 1986 U.S. Code Cong. & Admin. News 5468; 1984 U.S. Code Cong. & Admin. News 5708.

Automobile & Adaptive Equipment, 38 U.S.C. 1901 et seq.
Legislative History: 1970 U.S. Code Cong. & Admin. News 5999; 1974 U.S. Code Cong. & Admin. News 6592; 1988 U.S. Code Cong. & Admin. News 432.
Implementing Regulations: 38 C.F.R. 117.119-117.119d (1989).

Board of Veterans Appeals, 38 U.S.C. 4001 et seq.
Legislative History: 1962 U.S. Code Cong. & Admin. News 2576; 1984 U.S. Code Cong. & Admin. News 58; 1988 U.S. Code Cong. & Admin. News 5782.
Implementing Regulations: 38 C.F.R. Part 19 (1989).

Protection of Patient Rights, 38 U.S.C. 4131-4134.
Legislative History: 1976 U.S. Code Cong. & Admin. News 6355; 1988 U.S. Code Cong. & Admin. News 432.
Implementing Regulations: 38 C.F.R. 17.34-17.34a (1989).

Health Professionals Educational Assistance Program, 38 U.S.C. 4301-4336.
Legislative History: 1988 U.S. Code Cong. & Admin. News 432.
Implementing Regulations: 38 C.F.R. 17.600 et seq. (1989).

ACTION

1100 Vermont Avenue, N.W.
Washington, D.C. 20525

DESCRIPTION: ACTION is the principal agency in the Federal Government for administering volunteer service programs such as: Older American Volunteer Programs; Retired Senior Volunteer Programs; the Foster Grandparents Program; the Senior Companion Program; Volunteers in Service to America (VISTA); Service Learning Programs; Young Volunteers in Action; and its Office of Volunteer Initiatives. The agency actively encourages private sector involvement by helping individuals launch local volunteer projects.

(Area Code 202)

Director: Jane A. Kenny 634-9380
Procurement Information 634-9148
Public Information 634-9108
Freedom of Information/Act Privacy Act Office 634-9242
Facsimile 634-9126

OFFICE OF GENERAL COUNSEL (Room 9200)

The General Counsel provides legal advice and representation on all matters arising under the Domestic Volunteer Service Act of 1973, as well as other legal and regulatory provisions affecting the authorities and functions of the Agency. The Office of General Counsel is divided into two Divisions:

* The **Litigation, Administration, Contracts and Ethics Division** which represents the Agency in litigation, administrative hearings, and settlement negotiations; and provides legal advice on contracts, the Freedom of Information Act and Privacy Act issues, on personnel matters (including EEO), on negotiations to settle claims under the Federal Tort Claims and Contract Disputes Acts, and on matters relating to the Ethics in Government Act, standards of conduct, and conflicts of interest.

* The **Programs, Legislation and Regulations Division** provides legal services relating to Agency program grants, cooperative agreements, and interagency agreements; provides legal advice on issues relating to recruitment, training, support, health care, and benefits of volunteers; handles liaison with regional and state offices; and provides legal advice relating to legislation affecting the agency.

(Area Code 202)

General Counsel: Frank B. Sillwell III 634-9333
Deputy General Counsel: Stewart A. Davis 634-9333
Associate General Counsel: vacant 634-9333

OFFICE OF THE INSPECTOR GENERAL (12th Floor)

The Inspector General is responsible for directing programs aimed at ensuring economy and efficiency in agency operations, and detecting fraud, waste, and abuse.

(Area Code 202)

Inspector General: Judith Denny 634-9304
Deputy Inspector General: Joseph Suszko 634-9304

ACTION
KEY LEGAL AUTHORITIES

Regulations: 45 C.F.R. Part 1206 et seq. (1989).

Domestic Volunteer Service Act of 1973, as amended, 42 USC 4951--Provides the legislative basis for the Federal Government's domestic volunteer initiatives.

Legislative History: 1973 U.S. Cong. Code & Admin. News 2155; 1979 U.S. Cong. Code & Admin. News 2183; 1984 U.S. Cong. Code & Admin. News 454.

ADMINISTRATIVE CONFERENCE OF THE UNITED STATES

2120 L Street, N.W., Suite 500
Washington, D.C. 20037

DESCRIPTION: The purpose of this small, independent Federal agency is to improve the procedures of Federal agencies so that the agencies may fairly and expeditiously carry out their responsibilities to protect private rights and public interest while administering regulatory, benefit, and other Government programs. The Conference provides a forum in which agency officials, private attorneys, university professors, and other experts in administrative law and government can combine their experience and judgment in cooperative efforts to study procedural problems and explore solutions. Although the Conference has the authority only to recommend changes in administrative procedures, the Chairman is authorized to encourage the departments and agencies to adopt the Conference's recommendations.

The staff attorneys serve as liaison to the various committees of the Conference. There are six standing committees which are each assigned a broad area of interest: Adjudication, Administration, Governmental Processes, Judicial Review, Regulation, and Rulemaking. Special purpose committees are formed on an ad hoc basis to examine particular topics.

(Area Code 202)

Chairman: Marshall J. Breger 254-7020
Facsimile 254-3077

Freedom of Information Act/Privacy Act Office 254-7020
There is generally no charge for FOIA requests, although this office does reserve the right to charge a fee if costs exceed a certain limit.

(Area Code 202)

Library (Suite 500) 254-7065
The library is open Monday through Friday from 9:00 AM until 5:30 PM. The law library is contained within this library. The library is open to the public unless meetings are scheduled.

OFFICE OF THE GENERAL COUNSEL

(Area Code 202)

General Counsel: Gary J. Edles 254-7020
Senior Staff Attorney: Charles E. Pou, Jr 254-7020

Staff Liaison for Standing Committee on Adjudication:
Nancy G. Miller 254-7020
Staff Liaison for Standing Committee on Administration:
Charles E. Pou, Jr. 254-7020
Staff Liaison for Standing Committee on Governmental Processes: David M. Pritzker 254-7020

(Area Code 202)

Staff Liaison for Standing Committee on Judicial Review:
Mary Candace Fowler 254-7020
Staff Liaison for Standing Committee on Regulation:
David M. Pritzker 254-7020
Staff Liaison for Standing Committee on Rulemaking:
Kevin Jessar 254-7020
Staff Liaison for Special Committee on Government Ethics Regulation: Michael W. Bowers 254-7020
Staff Liaison for Special Committee on Financial Services Regulation: Brian C. Murphy 254-7020

PUBLICATIONS OF INTEREST

Administrative Conference News is a newsletter published quarterly highlighting Conference activities. To obtain a free copy of this publication, write the Administrative Conference or call the Chairman's office on 202/254-7020.

1989 Annual Report. The Annual Report reviews research and implementation activities of the Conference. Conference initiatives in 1989 include: alternative means of dispute resolution, Government ethics, Banking regulation, agency actions, medical benefit programs, immigration issues, biotechnology regulation, and research activities. At the end of 1989 approximately 30 research projects were underway. These included studies on the choice of forum in Government contract litigation, FAA sanctions and enforcement procedures, the role of Inspectors General in carrying out their responsibilities of internal oversight, judicial remands of cases to administrative agencies, oversight and regulation of Government-Sponsored Enterprises and pro bono practice by Government attorneys. To obtain a free copy of this publication, write the Administrative Conference or call the Chairman's office on 202/254-7020.

ADMINISTRATIVE CONFERENCE OF THE UNITED STATES
KEY LEGAL AUTHORITIES

General Agency Regulations: 1 C.F.R. Part 301 et seq. (1989).

Administrative Conference Act, as amended, 5 U.S.C. 571-576--provides arrangements through which Federal agencies, assisted by outside experts, may cooperatively study mutual problems, exchange information, and develop recommendations for action so that private rights may be fully protected and regulatory activities and other Federal responsibilities may be carried out expeditiously in the public interest.

APPALACHIAN REGIONAL COMMISSION

1666 Connecticut Avenue, N.W.
Washington, D.C. 20235

DESCRIPTION: The Appalachian Regional Commission is a Federal-state governmental agency concerned with the economic, physical, and social development of the 13-state Appalachian region. Because of the Federal-state nature of the Commission, its staff members are not Federal employees. Commission expenses are shared equally by the Federal Government and the Appalachian states.

(Area Code 202)
Executive Director: Francis E. Moravitz 673-7874
News and Public Affairs: Ann Anderson 673-7968
Facsimile 673-7930

(Area Code 202)
Freedom of Information/Privacy Act Office 673-7871
Commission is legally not covered under the FOIA statues but has a policy of attempting to supply information voluntarily consistent with FOIA.

OFFICE OF CHIEF COUNSEL (Room 638)

The Office of the Chief Counsel represents the Commission in all legal proceedings and matters. Responsibilities include: rendering formal opinions upon request of the Commission or the Executive Director; drafting legislation, regulations, and orders; reviewing and approving contracts, leases, and other legal obligations; supervising administrative hearings; and conducting litigation and other judicial proceedings to which the Commission may be a party.

(Area Code 202)
Chief Counsel: Rita Geier 673-7871
Assistant Chief Counsel: Evangeline E. Wells 673-7871

(Area Code 202)
Assistant Chief Counsel: Charles S. Howard 673-7871

PUBLICATIONS OF INTEREST

Appalachia is a quarterly magazine highlighting the activities and projects of the Commission with special emphasis on the activities of the people in the region. To obtain a free copy, call or write the Commission.

APPALACHIAN REGIONAL COMMISSION
KEY LEGAL AUTHORITIES

Regulations: 7 C.F.R. 755.1 et seq. (1989).

Appalachian Regional Development Act of 1965, as amended, 40 U.S.C. App. 1 et seq.--provides public works and economic development programs for the Appalachian region.
Legislative History: 1975 U.S. Cong. Code & Admin. News 2157.

ARCHITECTURAL AND TRANSPORTATION BARRIERS COMPLIANCE BOARD

1111 18th Street, N.W.
Washington, D.C. 20036

DESCRIPTION: The Architectural and Transportation Barriers Compliance Board is an independent regulatory agency established under Section 502 of the Rehabilitation Act of 1973. It is responsible for ensuring compliance with the standards issued under the Architectural Barriers Act (ABA) of 1968. These standards govern accessibility by physically handicapped persons to buildings and facilities designed, constructed, altered, or leased with Federal funds since September 1969.

(Area Code 202)

Chairman: William H. McCabe 653-7834
Executive Director: Lawrence W. Roffee 653-7834
Office of Compliance & Enforcement Director:
Judy Newton 653-7951
Office of Technical & Information Services
Ruth Lusher 653-7848
Office of Publications 653-7834
Facsimile 653-7863

(Area Code 202)

Freedom of Information/Privacy Act Office 653-7834
Requests must be in writing. There are four categories of requestors: Commercial, News Media, Educational and Scientific, and Others. Search fees are $14.00 per hour and review fees are $20.00 per hour when done by a Board employee. The copying fee is 20 cents per page, with generally no charge for the first 100 pages. News media and educational requestors are not charged search and review fees. Privacy Act copying charges are 10 cents per page.

OFFICE OF GENERAL COUNSEL (Suite 501)

The Office of General Counsel concentrates on administrative law, contracts and civil rights law. Responsibilities include presenting litigation in connection with Board administrative enforcement procedures; enforcing and processing complaints filed pursuant to the ABA; providing advice and assistance in connection with the preparation and implementation of Board regulations and procedures; and preparing legislative and administrative recommendations. FOIA and Privacy Act requests are handled by the General Counsel.

(Area Code 202)

General Counsel: James Raggio 653-7834

(Area Code 202)

Deputy General Counsel: Elizabeth Stewart 653-7834

PUBLICATIONS OF INTEREST

The following publications are available free of charge. Requests must be in writing addressed to: **U.S. Architectural and Transportation Barriers Compliance Board**, Suite 501, 1111 18th Street, N.W., Washington, D.C. 20036.

Access America is a quarterly journal containing news of pending legislation and regulatory actions, staff changes, Board meetings, court decisions, related actions by other agencies, new publications, and a research and technical assistance section. Also available in cassette and large type.

Access America: The Architectural Barriers Act and You describes the Access Board and how to file complaints about inaccessible federally funded buildings and facilities. Also available in braille, large type, cassette and floppy disc.

Laws Concerning the ATBCB contains the Architectural Barriers Act of 1968 (Public Law 90-480) and sections 502 (which established the ATBCB), 506, and 507 of the Rehabilitation Act of 1973. Also available in braille and large type.

Uniform Federal Accessibility Standards) (UFAS) discusses design, construction and alteration standards for access to federally funded facilities (based on the ATBCB Minimum Guidelines and Requirements for Accessible Design). Also available in cassette.

ARCHITECTURAL AND TRANSPORTATION BARRIERS COMPLIANCE BOARD
KEY LEGAL AUTHORITIES

Regulations: 36 C.F.R. Parts 1120 et seq. (1988).

Architectural Barriers Act of 1968, as amended, 42 U.S.C. 4151 et seq.--directs the development of mandatory standards for the design, construction, and alteration of buildings to insure, whenever possible, access and use to physically handicapped persons.

Legislative History: 1968 U.S. Code Cong. & Admin. News 3214; 1970 U.S. Code Cong. & Admin. News 2477; 1976 U.S. Code Cong. & Admin. News 5558.

ARCHITECTURAL AND TRANSPORTATION BARRIERS COMPLIANCE BOARD

Rehabilitation Act of 1973, as amended, 29 U.S.C. 792--establishes the Board to ensure compliance with the Architectural Barriers Act of 1968, including enforcement of standards under the Act, investigation of alternative approaches to barriers confronting the handicapped, and to ensure that public conveyances are accessible to physically handicapped persons.

Legislative History: 1973 U.S. Code Cong. & Admin. News 2076; 1974 U.S. Code Cong. & Admin. News 6373; 1978 U.S. Code Cong. & Admin. News 496 & 7312; 1980 U.S. Code Cong. & Admin. News 3141; 1984 U.S. Code Cong. & Admin. News 15; 1986 U.S. Code Cong. & Admin. News 3471.

ARMS CONTROL AND DISARMAMENT AGENCY

320 21st Street, N.W.
Washington, D.C. 20451

DESCRIPTION: The Arms Control and Disarmament Agency (ACDA) conducts studies and provides advice relating to arms control and disarmament policy formulation; prepares for and manages U.S. participation in international negotiations; disseminates and coordinates related public information; and directs U.S. participation in international control systems.

(Area Code 202)

Director: Ronald F. Lehman II 647-9610
Deputy Director: Stephen R. Hanmer, Jr 647-8463
Publications Information 523-2801
Public Affairs/Public Information 647-8677
Facsimile 647-6721

Freedom of Information Act Office 647-0932
There is a copying fee of 20 cents per page for FOIA requests and a per hour search charge ranging from $20.00 to $35.00 depending on the grade level of the person conducting the search.

(Area Code 202)

Privacy Act Office 647-0932
There is a copying charge of 20 cents per page for Privacy Act requests.

Library (Room 5840) 647-5969
The library is open the public by appointment only from 8:00 AM until 4:30 PM, Monday through Friday. A copying machine is available at a cost of 20 cents per page. Loans may be arranged through the Interlibrary Loan Program.

OFFICE OF THE GENERAL COUNSEL (Room 5534A)

The Office of the General Counsel is responsible for all matters of domestic and international law relevant to the work of the Agency. It provides advice and assistance in drafting and negotiating arms control treaties and agreements, and on questions regarding their approval by Congress, implementation, interpretation, ratification, and revision. The office is also involved in the legal aspects of the nuclear weapons non-proliferation responsibilities of the Agency and handles legal matters relating to arms control policy formulation and related Agency legislation. It also handles the legal aspects of Agency policies and operations in areas of personnel, security, patents, contracts, procurement, fiscal, and administrative law matters.

(Area Code 202)

General Counsel: Thomas Graham, Jr 647-3582
Deputy General Counsel: Mary E. Hoinkes 647-4621

(Area Code 202)

Assistant General Counsel: Paul Lembesis 647-3596
Assistant General Counsel: David Webster 647-3596

ARMS CONTROL AND DISARMAMENT AGENCY
KEY LEGAL AUTHORITIES

Regulations: 22 C.F.R. Parts 601-607 (1989).

Arms Control and Disarmament Act, as amended, 22 U.S.C. 2251 et seq--provides a central organization with primary responsibility for U.S. arms control and disarmament policy and assessment of the effect of recommendations on foreign policies, national security policies, and the economy; management of U.S. participation in international arms control negotiations; and coordination of U.S. participation in control systems.

Legislative History: 1961 U.S. Code Cong. & Admin. News 2903; 1963 U.S. Code Cong. & Admin. News 1110; 1964 U.S. Code Cong. & Admin. News 2834; 1975 U.S. Code Cong. & Admin. News 1382; 1977 U.S. Code Cong. & Admin. News 1684; 1978 U.S. Code Cong. & Admin. News 1209; 1979 U.S. Code Cong. & Admin. News 1028; 1980 U.S. Code Cong. & Admin. News 4419; 1982 U.S. Code Cong. & Admin. News 3203; 1985 U.S. Code Cong. & Admin. News 329; 1986 U.S. Code Cong. & Admin. News 5171; 1987 U.S. Code Cong. & Admin. News 2454; 1988 U.S. Code Cong. & Admin. News 2503.

Exec. Order No. 11044, as amended, "Interagency Coordination of Arms Control Matters," 3 C.F.R., 1959-1963 Comp., p. 627--authorizes the Director of the Arms Control and Disarmament Agency to coordinate arms control policy.

CENTRAL INTELLIGENCE AGENCY

Washington, D.C. 20505

DESCRIPTION: The Central Intelligence Agency (CIA) is the primary organization advising the President and the National Security Council on foreign intelligence matters, and is responsible for: the correlation, evaluation, and dissemination of intelligence which affects national security; making recommendations to the National Security Council concerning coordination of the intelligence activities of the executive departments (including the military services) and other agencies' clandestine collection of foreign intelligence; conducting counterintelligence abroad; coordinating foreign counterintelligence activities of other agencies within the Intelligence Community outside the U.S.; subject to the Attorney General's approval, conducting counterintelligence activities within the U.S. in coordination with the FBI; and research and development of technical intelligence collection systems. The CIA collects, produces and disseminates foreign political, economic, military, geographic, sociological, and scientific and technical intelligence, and intelligence on foreign aspects of narcotics production and trafficking and international terrorism.

(Area Code 703)

Director: William H. Webster 482-6363
Public Affairs 482-7676
Facsimile 482-6790

Freedom of Information Act/Privacy Act Office
Requests for information must be in writing and give specific details. Address requests to: Central Intelligence Agency, Information and Privacy Coordinator, Washington, D.C. 20505.

OFFICE OF GENERAL COUNSEL (Room 6Y01)

The Office of General Counsel serves the Director of Central Intelligence (DCI) in both of his capacities--as head of the CIA and as head of the Intelligence Community, which includes the CIA, National Security Agency, Defense Intelligence Agency, the offices within the Department of Defense responsible for collecting specialized national foreign intelligence, the Bureau of Intelligence and Research of the Department of State, the intelligence elements of the military services, the Federal Bureau of Investigation, and the Departments of Treasury and Energy. General Counsel office attorneys ensure that the Agency operates within applicable law. Much of the practice is aimed at preventing disclosure of information that will damage national security. In addition to performing legal research, writing opinions, and drafting and reviewing proposed regulations and legislation, attorneys serve as advisors to CIA boards and panels; represent the CIA in negotiations with Federal, state and private organizations; participate in the defense of the CIA against attempts to obtain sensitive information; provide counseling on the legality of activities which other CIA components wish to undertake; and participate extensively with Department of Justice attorneys in litigation involving the CIA.

(Area Code 703)

General Counsel: Elizabeth Rindskopf 874-3200
Deputy General Counsel: J. Edwin Dietel 874-3202

The Office is divided into the divisions listed below:

The **Intelligence Community Affairs Division** provides legal counsel and assistance on matters relating to the DCI's intelligence community responsibilities, including: representing the DCI in interagency discussions and committees on a variety of intelligence policy issues involving such matters as technology transfer, international terrorism, and narcotics intelligence; and advising operational components on the international legal implications of proposed intelligence activities and on constitutional and other legal issues relating to the DCI's tasking or the collection of national foreign intelligence by elements within the intelligence community. Legal assistance on budgetary, security, and legislative oversight issues is also provided.

The **Intelligence Law Division** counsels CIA components, especially operations elements, to ensure that current and proposed intelligence activities are consistent with applicable law, Executive Orders, and internal CIA regulations; deals with ongoing or proposed sensitive, clandestine intelligence operations (often involving counterintelligence, international terrorism, and international narcotics trafficking) to ensure the legality of activities undertaken; reviews the Agency's conduct of technical collection; obtains Attorney General approval for specific operations; negotiates formal legal guidance, including legislation, concerning intelligence activities; conducts training sessions for CIA personnel in the U.S. and abroad on the laws and regulations governing their activities; handles questions of legality and propriety with the President's Intelligence Oversight Board; and assists in responding to questions on these subjects from the congressional intelligence committees.

The **Foreign Law Division** performs in-depth analyses of specialized areas of foreign and international law on a variety of high priority topics such as the regulation and control of international narcotics trafficking and foreign laws regulating munitions exports.

The **Litigation Division** is responsible for all Freedom of Information Act and Privacy Act matters, tort claims arising out of Agency activities, civil litigations involving claims for violations of constitutional or statutory rights, and litigation in which the CIA is involved as a third party. Attorneys work frequently with the Department of Justice, U.S. Attorney Offices throughout the country, and other agencies within the Intelligence Community. They also review and comment on all proposed legislation that could affect the Agency's interests or position in litigation.

The **Operations Support Division** provides legal assistance to CIA components directly involved in conducting or supporting clandestine operations; handles matters involving corporate law, U.S. and foreign tax, immigration and naturalization law, and export controls; deals with the administration of certain specially situated personnel and contractual agreements in support of operations; and acts as liaison with other Government agencies and the courts in dealing with problems arising from the requirement to maintain clandestinity in certain CIA operations.

The **Administrative Law Division** supports the Agency's Directorate of Administration, particularly the Offices of Personnel and Finance, and deals with issues related to the special personnel, fiscal, and other administrative authorities employed in pursuit of the Agency's unique mission. Division attorneys are also responsible for Ethics in Government Act compliance issues and for liaison with the Justice Department in cases of unauthorized disclosures of classified information or other misconduct by Agency employees. Legal specialty areas relevant to the Division's work include criminal, administrative, regulatory, insurance, and legislative law.

The **Management Law Division** focuses on legal issues related to the responsibilities of the Agency's Inspector General and Offices of Security, Communications, Medical Services, and Equal Employment Opportunity. The Division is also responsible for liaison with the Department of Justice in cases where law enforcement activities affect operational concerns, and in connection with unauthorized disclosures or other non-employee misconduct involving intelligence information or activities. Legal specialty areas relevant to the Division's work include criminal, telecommunications, copyright, equal employment opportunity, regulatory, and legislative law.

The **Logistics and Procurement Law Division** deals primarily with Government contracts, but also with environmental protection, real estate, patents, leases, and the movement of material and supplies. It is responsible for matters concerning firearms, munitions control and Federal/state jurisdiction, and claims arising from the operation of vehicles and the loss of employee property.

OFFICE OF INSPECTOR GENERAL (Room 2X30)

The Office of Inspector General acts on behalf of the Director of the Central Intelligence, directing and coordinating the activities of the Inspection Staff, Special Investigations Group, and the Audit Staff in conducting inspections, special investigations and audits of CIA components and the staff elements of the Defense Intelligence Agency (DIA).

(Area Code 703)

Inspector General: William F. Donnelly (Acting) 874-2553

CENTRAL INTELLIGENCE AGENCY
KEY LEGAL AUTHORITIES

General Agency Regulations: 32 C.F.R. Parts 1900-1902 (1989).

National Security Act of 1947, as amended, 50 U.S.C. 403--established the CIA for the purpose of coordinating Federal Government intelligence activities in the interest of national security, advise the National Security Council, and correlate and evaluate intelligence, and expressly denies the CIA police, subpena, and law enforcement powers and internal security functions.

Legislative History: 1947 U.S. Code Cong. Service 1483; 1949 U.S. Code Cong. Service 1395; 1953 U.S. Code Cong. & Admin. News 1339; 1960 U.S. Code Cong. & Admin. News 3338; 1964 U.S. Code Cong. & Admin. News 2834.

CIA Information Act of 1984, 50 U.S.C. 431--exempts the operational files of the CIA from the Freedom of Information Act, at the discretion of the Director of Central Intelligence.

Legislative History: 1984 U.S. Code Cong. & Admin. News 3741.

Exec. Order 12333, 3 C.F.R., 1981 Comp., p. 200, "United States Intelligence Activities."

Exec. Order 12356, 3 C.F.R., 1983 Comp., p. 166, "National Security Information."

COMMISSION ON CIVIL RIGHTS

1121 Vermont Avenue, N.W.
Washington, D.C. 20425

DESCRIPTION: The U.S. Commission on Civil Rights is an independent, bipartisan, fact-finding agency whose duties are:

* to investigate allegations that certain U.S. citizens are being deprived of their right to vote and have that vote counted by reason of color, race, religion, sex, age, handicap, or national origin;

* to study and collect information concerning legal developments constituting discrimination or a denial of equal protection of the laws under the Constitution because of color, race, religion, sex, age, handicap or national origin;

* to appraise Federal laws with respect to discrimination or equal protection of the laws under the Constitution; and

* to investigate allegations that citizens are being accorded or denied the right to vote in Federal elections as a result of fraud or discrimination.

While the Commission may hold hearings and issue subpoenas in furtherance of its fact-finding duties, it lacks enforcement powers and must refer the complaints it receives to the appropriate Federal agency for action.

Although the Commission has three field offices (the Eastern Regional Division in Washington, D.C.; the Central States Regional Division in Kansas City, MO; and the Western Regional Division in Los Angeles, CA), all of the Commission's attorneys are currently located in the headquarters office in Washington, D.C. whose address is cited at the beginning of this listing.

(Area Code 202)

Chairman: Arthur A. Fletcher 523-5571
Staff Director: Wilfredo J. Gonzalez 523-5571
Solicitor: Emma Joy Monroig 376-8514
Civil Rights Complaints .... (800) 552-6843
Publications Information 376-8110
Facsimile 376-1163

The Commission:

Chairman: Arthur A. Fletcher 523-5571
Vice Chairman: Charles Pei Wang 523-5571
Commissioner: Russell G. Redenbaugh 523-5571
Commissioner: Carl A. Anderson 523-5571
Commissioner: William B. Allen 523-5571
Commissioner: Mary Frances Berry 523-5571
Commissioner: Ester G. Buckley 523-5571
Commissioner: Glendina C. Ramirez 523-5571

(Area Code 202)

Freedom of Information Act/Privacy Act Office 376-8351
There is no standard charge for FOIA/Privacy Act requests. Address requests to: FOIA/Privacy Act, 1121 Vermont Avenue, N.W., Room 600, Washington, D.C. 20425, ATTN: Solicitor's Unit.

Library (Room 709) 376-8110
The library is open to the public from 10:00 AM until 4:00 PM, Monday through Friday. This library is the National Clearinghouse Library for Civil Rights materials. A legal collection is part of the main library. There is a photocopying charge of 10 cents per page.

OFFICE OF GENERAL COUNSEL (Room 604)

(Area Code 202)

General Counsel: Carol McCabe Booker 376-8351
Deputy General Counsel: vacant 376-8351

(Area Code 202)

Assistant General Counsel: Jeffrey P. O'Connell 376-8353

REGIONAL DIVISIONS

The Commission's three Regional Divisions are as follows. Note: There are no attorneys assigned to these offices.

Eastern Regional Division
Director: John I. Binkley
U.S. Commission on Civil Rights, 1121 Vermont Avenue, N.W., Room 710, Washington, D.C. 20425. Tel: 202/523-5264.

Central Regional Division
Director: Melvin L. Jenkins
U.S. Commission on Civil Rights, 911 Walnut Street, Room 3109, Kansas City, MO 64106. Tel: 816/426-5253.

Western Regional Division
Director: Philip Montez
U.S. Commission on Civil Rights, 3660 Wilshire Blvd, Room 810, Los Angeles, CA 90010. Tel: 213/894-3437.

PUBLICATIONS OF INTEREST

Catalogue of Publications is an annotated list of the publications available from the Commission. These include: clearinghouse publications, statutory and interim reports, staff reports, hearings, consultations, conferences and state advisory committee reports.

The publications listed below are a selection from the catalogue. The Catalogue of Publications and the following publications are free of charge and may be obtained from the **Clearinghouse Division, U.S. Commission on Civil Rights,** 1121 Vermont Ave., N.W., Washington, D.C. 20425. Tel: 202/376-8110. If available, stock numbers are listed after each publication.

Medical Discrimination Against Children with Disabilities (1989) looks at the nature and extent of the practice of withholding medical treatment and nourishment from children born with disabilities. Among areas discussed are the role of quality of life judgments, economic considerations, infant care review committees, the relationship between parents and physicians, and enforcement of the Child Abuse Amendments of 1984. Concludes that denials of treatment continue and makes recommendations to alleviate the situation. 513 pp. No. 005-901-00058-8.

The Immigration Reform and Control Act: Assessing the Evaluation Process (1989) examines the reports by the General Accounting Office on the extent of discrimination and the burden on employers under the employer sanctions provisions of the Immigration Reform and Control Act of 1986. Concludes that the law has caused at least a pattern of discrimination. Recommends that Congress extend the evaluation period and clarify certain provisions in the law. Contains other findings and recommendations. 46 pp.

Federal Enforcement of Equal Employment Requirements (1987) describes the responsibilities and policies of the Equal Employment Opportunity Commission, the Employment Litigation Section of the Justice Department's Civil Rights Division, and the Labor Department's Office of Federal Contract Compliance Programs during the Reagan Administration. CHP 93. 40 pp. No. 005-902-00041-0.

A Citizen's Guide to Understanding the Voting Rights Act (1984) explains the provisions of the 1965 Voting Rights Act as amended, including preclearance, minority language protections, and Federal observers, and how individuals and groups may make complaints and comments. Appendices include the text of the act, lists of jurisdictions covered, various sample letters, and source materials. CHP 84. 91 pp. No. 005-902-00038-0.

COMMISSION ON CIVIL RIGHTS
KEY LEGAL AUTHORITIES

Regulations: 45 C.F.R. Parts 701-706 (1989).

Civil Rights Act of 1957, as amended, 42 U.S.C. 1975-1975f--establishes and prescribes the duties of the Commission and confers subpena power on the agency.

Legislative History: 1957 U.S. Code Cong. & Admin. News 1966; 1983 U.S. Code Cong. & Admin. News 1989.

COMMODITY FUTURES TRADING COMMISSION

2033 K Street, N.W.
Washington, D.C. 20581

DESCRIPTION: The Commodity Futures Trading Commission (CFTC) oversees the regulation of commodity futures markets. It ensures the economic utility of futures markets by encouraging their competitiveness and efficiency, by ensuring their integrity, and by protecting market participants against manipulation, abusive trade practices, and fraud. In recent years, futures trading has expanded into many new markets, including foreign currencies, petroleum products, and U.S. Government securities, as well as various stock and macroeconomic indexes.

The attorneys at the Commission work either in the headquarters office in Washington, D.C. or in the regional offices. At Headquarters, most attorneys are in the Division of Enforcement, the Division of Trading and Markets, and the Office of the General Counsel, with only a few assigned to the Office of Proceedings in the Office of the Executive Director.

(Area Code 202)

Chairman: Wendy Gramm (April 1995) 254-6970
Counsel to the Chairman: Thomas M. McGivern 245-3343

Commissioner: William P. Albrecht (April, 1993) 254-6288
Counsel/Legal Assistant: Nancy E. Yanofsky 254-6288

Commissioner: Kalo A. Hineman (June 19, 1991) 254-6318
Counsel/Legal Assistant: Donald H. Heitman 254-5945

Commissioner: vacant (Nomination is pending) 254-6354
Counsel/Legal Assistant: Jay Gelderman 254-6354

Commissioner: Fowler West (April, 1992) 254-8541
Counsel/Legal Assistant: J. Douglas Leslie 254-8541

The Commissioner's term expires on date shown in parentheses. If specified term has expired, a Commissioner may continue to serve through the next session of Congress or until reappointed or replaced.

Executive Director: Dr. Ewen M. Wilson 254-3350
Office of Communication and Education Services 254-8630
Facsimile 254-6265

Office of Secretariat 254-6314
Notice of upcoming public meetings of the Commissioners can be obtained from this office.

(Area Code 202)

Freedom of Information/Privacy Act Office 254-3382
There is a 15 cents per page copying charge for FOIA requests. If a professional staff member is required to conduct the search then there is an additional $18.00 per hour search fee; if a clerical staff member can conduct the search then the hourly rate is $12.00. The costs for Privacy Act requests are identical to the FOIA request costs.

Library (Room 540) 254-5901
The library is open Monday through Friday from 8:15 AM until 4:45 PM. The public only has access to this library from 8:15 AM until 10:00 AM by appointment, although you can usually stay as long as necessary. The library has legislative reports, commodities publications, trade law, economics and agriculture related materials. The library has a law collection, primarily for lawyers at CFTC.

Reading Room (Room 211) 254-3236
The reading room is open to the public Monday through Friday from 8:00 AM until 5:30 PM. The reading room is responsible for the Commission's records. These records include: filings, rule changes that are submitted and are not confidential, disciplinary notices, comment letters responding to Federal Register announcements, and files of minutes and documents of the open commission meetings. They also keep the case log, opinions and orders. There are photocopying facilities for both paper and microfiche. Photocopying costs 15 cents per page. Information requested from the public file will be sent for only the cost of photocopying.

OFFICE OF GENERAL COUNSEL (7th Floor)

The Office of the General Counsel (OGC) represents the Commission before the U.S. Courts of Appeals and, in cooperation with the Solicitor General, before the U.S. Supreme Court. OGC also defends actions brought against the Commission or its employees in the U.S. District Courts, and in private litigation involving legal issues of interest to the Commission. The office also handles certain disciplinary and other administrative litigation, represents the Commission in matters affecting other Federal agencies, and acts as liaison to state and certain foreign governments. OGC monitors bankruptcy proceedings involving commodity professionals and represents the Commission as intervenor or amicus curiae in such proceedings. The Office reviews all substantive regulatory, legislative, and administrative matters presented to the Commission and provides advice on the application and interpretation of the Commodity Exchange Act and pertinent administrative statutes.

(Area Code 202)

General Counsel: Joanne T. Medero 254-9880
Deputy General Counsel/Legislation, Ethics and Opinions:
Pat G. Nicolette 254-9880
Deputy General Counsel/Litigation: Jay L. Whitkin 254-9880

(Area Code 202)

Deputy General Counsel/Regulatory and Enforcement Review: David R. Merrill 254-9880
Opinions Section Director: Edson G. Case Jr 254-7110

OFFICE OF THE INSPECTOR GENERAL (Room 3051)

The primary objectives of the Office of Inspector General are to promote the long term efficiency and effectiveness in the administration and operation of the Commission and to protect against fraud and abuse.

(Area Code 202)

Inspector General: Nancy Wentzler 254-9560

OFFICE OF PROCEEDINGS

2000 L Street, Washington, D.C. (Mailing address is 2033 K Street, N.W., Washington, D.C. 20581)

The Office of Proceedings, which operates under the administrative direction of the Office of the Executive Director, processes and decides customer claims against persons or firms registered under the Commodity Exchange Act. Cases forwarded by the complaints section are decided in the hearings section by either a judgment officer or an administrative law judge. Administrative law judges also decide enforcement cases brought by the CFTC against persons or firms who have violated the Commission's Act or regulations.

(Area Code 202)

Director: R. Britt Lenz 254-6790
Clerk of the Court: John Nolan 254-5008
Docket Clerk: Shiela Smith 254-5008

Administrative Law Judges:
William G. Spruill 254-6792
George H. Painter 254-6792
Robert E. Duncan 254-6793
Arthur L. Shipe 254-6791

Judgment Officers:
John C. Phillips 254-3570
Joel R. Maillie 254-3570
Philip V. McGuire 254-3570

DIVISION OF ECONOMIC ANALYSIS

(Area Code 202)

Director: Steven Manaster 254-3201
Chief Counsel: Paul M. Architzel 254-6990

DIVISION OF ENFORCEMENT

The Division of Enforcement investigates and prosecutes alleged violations of the Commodity Exchange Act and Commission regulations. Violations may involve trading commodity futures and options contracts on domestic commodity exchanges, or improper marketing of commodity futures and option contracts and similar investment vehicles under the Commission's jurisdiction.

At the conclusion of an investigation, the Division of Enforcement may recommend administrative proceedings or may seek injunctive and related ancillary relief in Federal court to halt alleged violations. Administrative sanctions may include suspension, denial, or revocation of a respondent's registration with the Commission, denial of exchange privileges, cease and desist orders, and the assessment of civil monetary penalties. Evidence gathered during an investigation which indicates criminal violations of the Act have occurred is referred to the Justice Department for prosecution.

The Division of Enforcement provides expert assistance to U.S. Attorneys and other Federal and state law enforcement agencies on case development and trials. Further, the Commission and states may join as co-plaintiffs in civil injunctive actions.

(Area Code 202)

Director: Dennis A. Klejna 254-9501
Chief Counsel: Robert F. Klein 254-8517

DIVISION OF TRADING AND MARKETS

The Division of Trading and Markets oversees the trade practice surveillance and rule enforcement activities of the self-regulatory organizations (SRO's), the 14 exchanges, and the National Futures Association. Attorneys in this Division draft regulations governing the operations of exchanges and registered futures associations, as well as regulations governing the registration, operation, surveillance, and audit of other regulated entities. The Division also supports other CFTC divisions in enforcing the provisions of the Commodity Exchange Act and the Commission's regulations.

(Area Code 202)

Director: Andrea Corchoran 254-8955
Chief Counsel: Susan C. Ervin 254-8955
Associate Chief Counsel: Lawrence B. Patent 254-8955
Assistant Chief Counsel: Barbara S.Gold 254-8955
Assistant Director for Registration Unit:
Robert P. Shiner 254-6112
Special Counsel/Contract Markets Section:
Linda Kurjan 254-8955

COMMODITY FUTURES TRADING COMMISSION

REGIONAL OFFICES

The CFTC has major regional offices in New York, Chicago, and Los Angeles, with smaller offices in Minneapolis and Kansas City.

CENTRAL REGION (Chicago)

Regional Counsel (Enforcement): Dennis M. Robb
U.S. Commodity Futures Trading Commission, 233 South Wacker Drive, Suite 4600, Chicago, IL 60606. Tel: 312/353-9004.

EASTERN REGION (New York)

Regional Counsel (Enforcement): Stephen F. Mihans
U.S. Commodity Futures Trading Commission, One World Trade Center, Suite 4747, New York, NY 10048. Tel: 212/668-2001.

WESTERN REGION (Los Angeles)

Regional Counsel (Enforcement): Kenneth Guido
U.S. Commodity Futures Trading Commission, 10880 Wilshire Blvd, Suite 1005, Los Angeles, CA 90024. Tel: 213/793-6783.

PUBLICATIONS OF INTEREST

Decisions rendered by the Commission, the Administrative Law Judges, and the Judgment Officers can be obtained by contacting the Office of Proceedings, 2033 K Street, N.W., Washington, D.C. 20581. Tel: 202/254-5008. There is a $12.00 reproduction service charge and 15 cents per page copying fee.

Commodities Futures Law Report contains semi-monthly reports on the latest court decisions and regulatory activity of the Commodity Futures Trading Commission. New regulations and interpretations covering controls and standards as issued by CFTC are reported promptly upon release. Reparation procedures for resolving complaints against registrants, as well as significant decisions from the CFTC are included. Price: $600.00 a year includes 2 vols. and semi-monthly reports from Commerce Clearing House, Inc., 4025 West Peterson Avenue, Chicago, IL 60646. Tel: 312/452-4323. Or, in Washington, D.C., call 202/626-2200.

COMMODITY FUTURES TRADING COMMISSION
KEY LEGAL AUTHORITIES

Regulations: 17 C.F.R., Chapt. I (1989).

Commodity Exchange Act, as amended, 7 U.S.C. 1 et seq.--established the CFTC to regulate trading in futures contracts for commodities and to supervise the operations of commodity exchanges.

Legislative History: 1955 U.S. Code Cong. & Admin. News 2513; 1968 U.S. Code Cong. & Admin. News 1673 & 2704; 1974 U.S. Code Cong. & Admin. News 5843; 1978 U.S. Code Cong. & Admin. News 2087; 1982 U.S. Code Cong. & Admin. News 3871; 1986 U.S. Code Cong. & Admin. News 6005.

CONSUMER PRODUCT SAFETY COMMISSION

5401 Westbard Avenue
Bethesda, MD 20207

DESCRIPTION: The Consumer Product Safety Commission (CPSC) is an independent regulatory agency that establishes mandatory and voluntary safety standards for consumer products and their packaging; bans the sale of unsafe products; establishes flammability standards for fabrics and packaging requirements for poisons; and establishes other related safety standards.

Although the Commission has three Regional Centers (located in Chicago, New York, and San Francisco), and 34 resident offices, all CPSC attorneys are located in the headquarters office in Bethesda, MD.

(Area Code 301)

Chairman: Jacqueline Jones-Smith 492-5500
Information and Public Affairs 492-6580
Facsimile .... (301) 492-6924

Product Safety and Recall Hotline .... (800) 638-2772
This number provides general information on the Commission as well as information on current product safety problems and recalls.

National Injury Information Clearinghouse 492-6424
This Clearinghouse provides incident/accident data and statistical information on product-related accidents occurring in home, school, farm, and recreational sports, including vehicles which do not have to be licensed (e.g., all-terrain vehicles). It does not deal with data on automobiles, cosmetics, food, or drugs.

Freedom of Information Act/Privacy Act 492-5785
Send request to: Consumer Product Safety Commission, FOIA Office, Washington, D.C. 20207. Attn: Todd Stevenson. There is a copying charge of 10 cents per page. If you represent a plaintiff the charge is waived for the first 100 pages, or you are refunded $10.00. There are also charges for search and review time.

(Area Code 301)

Library (Room 456). 492-6544
The library is open Monday through Friday from 8:30 AM until 5:00 PM. The law library is located in Room 225. There are standard reference books in the law library, used primarily by CPSC attorneys.

Reading Room (Room 528) 492-6800
The reading room is open to the public Monday through Friday from 7:30 AM until 5:00 PM. The reading room staff takes requests for information over the telephone and will send the information free of charge. The reading room has the following information: agenda for the Commission meetings, meeting logs and minutes, closed meeting notices, annual report, technical reports, Federal regulation notices, the Code of Federal Regulations, a compilation of laws on product safety, consent agreements, contracts, advisory opinions, decision index, legislative history, petition index, policy guidance letters, and record of Commission actions.

OFFICES OF THE COMMISSION

(Area Code 301)

Chairman: Jacqueline Jones-Smith 492-5500
Counsel and Executive Assistant: Clarence T. Bishop .. 492-5500
Special Assistant and Legal Counsel: Michele Brown ... 492-5500

Commissioner: Carol Gene Dawson 492-5520
Special Assistant and Legal Counsel: Timothy Baker ... 492-5520

(Area Code 301)

Commissioner: Anne Graham 492-5530
Counsel: vacant 492-5530

Commissioner: vacant 492-5500
Counsel: vacant 492-5500

Commissioner: vacant 492-5500
Counsel: vacant 492-5500

OFFICE OF THE GENERAL COUNSEL (Room 200)

The Office of the General Counsel provides advice and counsel to the Commissioners and organizational components on matters of law arising from operations of the Commission. It prepares the Commission's legislative program; advises on administrative litigation matters; provides final legal review of and makes recommendations to the Commission on proposed product safety standards, rules, regulations, petition actions, and substantial hazard actions; provides legal review of certain procurement, personnel, and administrative actions; and, in conjunction with the Department of Justice, is responsible for conducting all Federal court litigation to which the Commission is a party.

(Area Code 301)

General Counsel: Susan Birenbaum (Acting) 492-6980
Assistant General Counsel for Enforcement and Information Division: Alan C. Shakin 492-6980

(Area Code 301)

Assistant General Counsel for General Law Division: Richard W. Allen 492-6980
Assistant General Counsel for Regulatory Affairs Division: D. Stephen Lemberg 492-6980

CONSUMER PRODUCT SAFETY COMMISSION

OFFICE OF INSPECTOR GENERAL (Room 302)

The Inspector General directs efforts to promote the overall efficiency, effectiveness, and economy of agency programs and operations, as well as efforts to prevent and detect fraud, waste, and abuse.

(Area Code 301)
Inspector General: Thomas F. Stein 492-6573

DIRECTORATE FOR COMPLIANCE AND ADMINISTRATIVE LITIGATION
(Mailing address: Washington, D.C. 20207)

Reporting directly to the Executive Director of the Commission, the Directorate for Compliance and Administrative Litigation (whose offices are located in Bethesda, MD) conducts or supervises the conduct of compliance and administrative enforcement activity; provides advice to regulated industries on complying with all administered acts; and reviews proposed standards and rules with respect to their enforceability. The Directorate's responsibility also includes identifying and acting on safety hazards in consumer products already in distribution, promoting industry compliance with existing safety rules, and conducting litigation before an administrative law judge on administrative complaints. It also provides advice and case guidance to field offices and participates in the development of standards before their promulgation to ensure enforceability.

(Area Code 301)
Associate Executive Director: David Schmeltzer 492-6621
Administrative Litigation Division:
Director: Alan H. Schoem 492-6626

(Area Code 301)
Corrective Actions Division: Director: Marc Schoem 492-6608
Regulatory Management Division:
Director: Robert G. Poth 492-6400

CPSC REGIONAL CENTERS

Eastern Regional Center
Director: Richard D. Swackhamer
U.S. Consumer Product Safety Commission, 6 World Trade Center, Vesey Street, Room 301, New York, NY 10048. Tel: 212/264-1134.

Central Regional Center
Director: Eric B. Ault
U.S. Consumer Product Safety Commission, 230 South Dearborn Street, Room 2944, Chicago, IL 60604. Tel: 312/353-8260.

Western Regional Center
Director: Lee D. Baxter
U.S. Consumer Product Safety Commission, 555 Battery Street, Room 415, San Francisco, CA 94111. Tel: 415/556-1816.

PUBLICATIONS OF INTEREST

Compilation of Laws. Published September 1989; 122 pages. Single copies can be requested by writing: Office of Information and Public Affairs, U.S. Consumer Product Safety Commission, Washington, D.C. 20207.

CONSUMER PRODUCT SAFETY COMMISSION
KEY LEGAL AUTHORITIES

General Agency Regulations: 16 C.F.R. Parts 1000-1750 (1990).
Rules of Practice and Procedure: 16 C.F.R. Parts 1025, 1051, & 1052 (1990).

Consumer Product Safety Act, as amended, 15 U.S.C. 2051 et seq.--established the Commission to protect consumers from unreasonable risk of injury from hazardous products; authorized the ordering of an immediate recall from the market when a substantial hazard is discovered; obligates manufacturers, distributors, and retailers of consumer products to report instances of failure of a product to comply with a safety standard or of a defect which could create a substantial product hazard, including problems in design, labeling, instructions, and warnings, unintended faults, flaws, irregularities, or manufacturing or production problems; authorizes the Commission to bring civil or criminal action for failure to report a defect; directs Commission to assist industry in developing voluntary safety standards; authorizes issuance of mandatory safety standards; authorizes product testing and inspection and investigation of factory facilities; and directs Commission to monitor enforcement of existing mandatory safety standards, product bans, and labeling requirements.

Legislative History: 1972 U.S. Code Cong. & Admin. News 4573; 1976 U.S. Code Cong. & Admin. News 993; 1981 U.S. Code Cong. & Admin. News 396; 1982 U.S. Code Cong. & Admin. News 3577; 1988 U.S. Code Cong. & Admin. News 1547.

Federal Hazardous Substances Act of 1960, as amended, 15 U.S.C. 1261 et seq.--requires warning labels and regulates distribution and sale of hazardous substances suitable for household use.
Legislative History: 1960 U.S. Code Cong. & Admin. News 2833; 1966 U.S. Code Cong. & Admin. News 4095; 1969 U.S. Code Cong. & Admin. News 1231; 1986 U.S. Code Cong. & Admin. News 1566.

Poison Prevention Packaging Act of 1970, as amended, 15 U.S.C. 1471 et seq.--requires child-proof packaging to protect children from serious injury or illness resulting from household substances.
Legislative History: 1970 U.S. Code Cong. & Admin. News 5326; 1982 U.S. Code Cong. & Admin. News 3577.

Flammable Fabrics Act of 1953, as amended, 15 U.S.C. 1191 et seq.--prohibits the introduction into, or transportation in, interstate commerce of highly flammable clothing and material.
Legislative History: 1953 U.S. Code Cong. & Admin. News 1722; 1967 U.S. Code Cong. & Admin. News 2132.

Refrigerator Safety Act of 1956, 15 U.S.C. 1211 et seq.--mandates that all refrigerators sold in interstate commerce have a safety device enabling them to be easily opened from the inside.
Legislative History: 1956 U.S. Code Cong. & Admin. News 4195.

ENVIRONMENTAL PROTECTION AGENCY

401 M Street, S.W.
Washington, D.C. 20460

DESCRIPTION. The Environmental Protection Agency (EPA) is the largest Federal regulatory agency, responsible for implementing the following Federal environmental statutes:

*Under the Clean Air Act, EPA sets standards for air quality and approves state plans to achieve them.

*Under the Comprehensive Environmental Response, Compensation, and Liability Act, EPA administers the Superfund program to clean up hazardous waste sites and collect costs and damages from responsible parties.

*Under the Clean Water Act, EPA has authority to remedy and prevent pollution of lakes, streams, rivers, and bays. Under the Marine Protection Research and Sanctuaries Act, it controls ocean disposal of wastes.

*Under the Safe Drinking Water Act, EPA helps ensure safe drinking water and protects underground aquifers.

*Under the Resource Conservation and Recovery Act, EPA sets standards for the management, transportation, and disposal of solid and hazardous wastes.

*Under the Toxic Substances Control Act, EPA has authority over the manufacture, distribution, use, and disposal of chemical products that present hazards to health and the environment.

*Under the Federal Insecticides, Fungicides and Rodenticides Act, EPA regulates pesticides, fungicides, and rodent poisons that have adverse effects on human health and the environment.

*Under the Clean Air and Atomic Energy Acts, EPA has radiation control responsibilities.

Each year EPA promulgates hundreds of nationally significant regulations and is the defendant in hundreds of major lawsuits, primarily in U.S. Courts of Appeals, in which these and other regulatory actions are challenged. EPA is also engaged in hundreds of enforcement actions in Federal District Courts throughout the country.

(Area Code 202)

Administrator: William K. Reilly 382-4700
Procurement and Contracts Information 382-5024
Grants Information 382-5266
Public Information 382-2080
Public Affairs 382-4361
Communications/Publications 382-4359
Central Docket (Clean Air Act) 382-7548
Asbestos Action Program 382-3949
National Pesticides Telecommunications Network (NPTN):
In Texas ....(806) 743-3091
Toll free outside Texas ....(800) 858-PEST
Risk Communication Hotline 382-5606
Safe Drinking Water Hotline:
Washington, D.C. Metro Area 382-5533
Outside Washington, D.C. Metro Area ....(800) 428-4791
Resource Conservation and Recovery Act (RCRA)/Superfund Hotline:
Washington, D.C. Metro Area 382-3000
Outside Washington, D.C. Metro Area ...(800) 424-9346
Title III-Community Right-to-Know Hotline:
Washington, D.C. Metro Area 479-2449
Outside Washington, D.C. Metro Area ....(800) 535-0202
Inspector General's Hot Line
Washington, D.C. Metro Area 382-4977
Outside Washington, D.C. Metro Area ....(800) 424-4000
Facsimile 382-7883

Toxic Substances Control Act Information Hotline 554-1404
The hotline serves as a clearinghouse for questions on The Toxic Substance Control Act; specifically asbestos, PCB's and chemicals (including exports and imports). If contacted by telephone, they will send publications, brochures and documents on the subject.

(Area Code 202)

Freedom of Information/Privacy Act Office 382-4048
There is a 15 cents per page copying charge for FOIA requests. There is also an hourly search charge ranging from $4.00 to $20.00 (depending on the type of staff person who is required to perform the search). If the total cost of the FOIA request is less than $20.00 then the fee is waived.

Library (Room 2904) 382-5922
The main library is open to the public Monday through Friday from 8:00 AM until 5:30 PM.

Law Library (Room 2902) 382-5920
The law library is open to the public Monday through Friday from 8:15 AM until 5:30 PM. Due to the small staff of the law library, call in advance to make an appointment.

Legislative Library (Room 832) 382-5425
The library is open to the public Monday through Friday from 9:00 AM until 5:30 PM. It has copies of all bills which are related to environmental policy, as well as copies of committee reports, Senate and House reports, and current laws. Copies of bills will be sent in response to a telephone request.

NOTE: An informational Guide to EPA Libraries and Information Services is available from National Technical Information Service (NTIS), 5285 Port Royal Road, Springfield, VA 22161. Tel: 703/487-4650 or 800/336-4700. Price: $23.00. NTIS Order Number PB89144786/HDM. NTIS charges $3.00 per total order for shipping and handling.

OFFICE OF GENERAL COUNSEL (Room 537 West Tower)

The Office of General Counsel (OGC) serves as EPA legal advisor to program offices charged with developing national regulations and policies. Attorneys may be called upon to provide written legal opinions, to identify and help resolve legal and technical issues, and to draft, review, and revise regulations and associated support documents.

With the exception of pesticide cancellation proceedings, in which OGC attorneys serve as EPA's trial staff before an Administrative Law Judge, OGC litigation is largely conducted in U.S. Courts of Appeals and District Courts in conjunction with the Department of Justice. EPA cases involve difficult and complex scientific, technical, and administrative law issues. Because of the intricacy of many EPA-administered statutes, litigation frequently involves complex issues of first impression.

(Area Code 202)

General Counsel and Assistant Administrator:
E. Donald Elliot 475-8040
Deputy General Counsel: Gerald H. Yamada 475-8064
Deputy General Counsel for Litigation, Regulatory Operations and Legislation:
Raymond B. Ludwiszewski (Acting) 475-8067

The Office of General Counsel is divided into six divisions:

The **Air and Radiation Division** provides legal counsel and litigation support to the Agency's air and radiation programs and activities.

(Area Code 202)
Associate General Counsel: Alan W. Eckert 382-7606

The **Grants, Contracts, and General Law Division** provides legal counsel and litigation support with respect to financial assistance awards, information law matters, contracts for procurement and construction, and general law matters, including personnel, labor relations, appropriations, claims, patents, government ethics, and civil rights.

(Area Code 202)
Associate General Counsel: Craig B. Annear 382-5320

The **Inspector General Division** deals with issues of fraud, waste, and mismanagement within EPA.

(Area Code 202)
Associate General Counsel: Marla Diamond 475-6660

The **International Division** provides legal advice on EPA's international activities.

(Area Code 202)
Associate General Counsel: Edith Brown-Weiss 382-4550

The **Solid Waste and Emergency Response Division** provides legal counsel and litigation support on the Agency's solid waste and emergency response programs and activities.

(Area Code 202)
Associate General Counsel: Lisa K. Friedman 382-7706

The **Pesticides and Toxic Substances Division** provides legal counsel and litigation support on the Agency's pesticides and toxic substances program and activities.

(Area Code 202)
Associate General Counsel: Mark A. Greenwood 382-7505

The **Water Division** provides legal counsel and litigation support on the Agency's water, drinking water, and ocean dumping programs and activities.

(Area Code 202)
Associate General Counsel: Susan G. Lepow 382-7700

REGIONAL OFFICES

The ten Regional Offices provide counsel to the Regional Administrators and to regional program staffs on the application of national regulations to particular sources of pollution within their regions. Regional Attorneys also provide counsel on enforcement matters and work with the Department of Justice and U.S. Attorneys in preparing enforcement cases for litigation.

The Regional Offices also house libraries with valuable information and databases available to the public. Each region has an Office of Ombudsman and in some regions, hotlines are available.

Region 1 (Boston)

U.S. Environmental Protection Agency, John F. Kennedy Federal Building, Boston, MA 02203.
Regional Counsel: Harley Laing ....(617) 565-3424
Library ....(617) 565-3300
Office of Ombudsman ....(617) 573-5758
Unleaded Fuel Hotline ....(800) 821-1237
Unleaded Fuel Hotline (MA) ....(800) 631-2700
(Jurisdiction: CT, MA, ME, NH, RI, VT)

Region 2 (New York)

U.S. Environmental Protection Agency, 26 Federal Plaza, New York, NY 10278.
Regional Director: Douglas Blazey ....(212) 264-2515
Library ....(212) 264-2881
Office of Ombudsman ....(212) 264-2980
(Jurisdiction: NY, NJ, PR, Virgin Islands)

Region 3 (Philadelphia)

U.S. Environmental Protection Agency, 841 Chestnut Street, Philadelphia, PA 19107.
Regional Counsel: Marsha Malkey ....(215) 597-9370
Library ....(215) 597-0500
Office of Ombudsman ....(215) 597-9636
EPA Hotline ....(800) 438-2474
Waste Minimization Hotline ....(800) 826-5320
Waste Minimization Hotline (PA) ....(800) 334-2467
(Jurisdiction: Washington, D.C., DE, MD, PA, VA, WV)

Region 4 (Atlanta)

U.S. Environmental Protection Agency, 345 Courtland St, NE, Atlanta, GA 30365.
Regional Director: James Sargent ....(404) 347-3004
Library ....(404) 347-4216
Office of Ombudsman ....(404) 347-3004
EPA Hotline ....(800) 241-1754
(Jurisdiction: AL, FL, GA, KY, MS, NC, SC, TE)

Region 5 (Chicago)

U.S. Environmental Protection Agency, 230 South Dearborn Street, Chicago, IL 60604.
Regional Counsel: Betran Frey (Acting) ....(312) 353-2072
Library ....(312) 353-2022
Office of Ombudsman ....(312) 886-0981
EPA Hotline ....(800) 621-8431
EPA Hotline (IL) ....(800) 572-2515
(Jurisdiction: IL, IN, MI, MN, OH, WI)

Region 6 (Dallas)

U.S. Environmental Protection Agency, 1445 Ross Avenue, Dallas, TX 75202.

Regional Director: George Alexander ....(214) 655-2200
Library ....(214) 255-6444
Office of Ombudsman ....(214) 655-6760
(Jurisdiction: AK, LA, NM, OK, TX)

Region 7 (Kansas City)

U.S. Environmental Protection Agency, 726 Minnesota Avenue, Kansas City, KS 66101.

Regional Director: Martha Steincamp ....(913) 236-2803
Library ....(913) 236-2828
Office of Ombudsman ....(913) 757-2856
EPA Hotline ....(800) 223-0425
EPA Hotline (KS) ....(800) 221-7749
RCRA Hotline (IO) ....(800) 223-0424
Superfund/Dioxin Hotline (MO) ....(800) 892-5009
(Jurisdiction: IA, KS, MO, NE)

Region 8 (Denver)

U.S. Environmental Protection Agency, 999 18th St, Denver, CO 80202.

Regional Director: Thomas Speicher ....(303) 293-1692
Library ....(303) 293-1414
Office of Ombudsman ....(303) 330-1111
EPA Hotline ....(800) 525-3022
(Jurisdiction: CO, MT, ND, SD, UT, WY)

Region 9 (San Francisco)

U.S. Environmental Protection Agency, 215 Fremont Street, San Francisco, CA 94105.

Regional Director: Nancy Marve ....(415) 744-1171
Library ....(415) 974-8082
Office of Ombudsman ....(415) 974-8916
(Jurisdiction: AZ, CA, NV, HI, American Samoa, Guam)

Region 10 (Seattle)

U.S. Environmental Protection Agency, 1200 6th Avenue, Seattle, WA 98101. Tel: 206/442-1465.

Regional Director: Jackson Fox ....(206) 442-1465
Library ....(206) 399-1289
Office of Ombudsman ....(206) 442-2871
(Jurisdiction: AK, ID, OR, WA)

OFFICE OF THE INSPECTOR GENERAL (Room 301 NORTHEAST MALL)

The Office of the Inspector General in EPA is responsible for conducting and supervising objective and independent audits, evaluations, and investigations of internal programs, financial transactions, and administrative activities. The Inspector General's responsibility is to detect, report and prevent any indications of fraud, waste and abuse in EPA's programs and operations.

(Area Code 202)

Inspector General: John C. Martin 382-3137
Deputy Inspector General: Anna Hopkins Birbick 382-4112

(Area Code 202)

Office of Investigations
Assistant Inspector General: John E. Barden 382-4109

OFFICE OF ADMINISTRATIVE LAW JUDGES (Room 3706)

Mail Code A-110, 401 M Street, S.W., Washington, D.C. 20460

The Administrative Law Judges hear a broad range of cases involving EPA's responsibilities, including administrative cases in which the agency is seeking civil penalties and cases involving permits. There are six Administrative Law Judges in Washington, D.C., and one in the Atlanta field office.

The decisions of the Administrative Law Judges can be obtained by contacting the Office of Administrative Law Judges as listed above. Tel: 202/382-4865. On-line users can access these decisions through LEXIS.

(Area Code 202)

Chief Judge Henry B. Frazier 382-4860
Judge Spencer T. Nissen 382-4856
Judge Jean F. Greene 382-4856
Judge Frank W. Vanderheyden 382-3325
Judge Daniel M. Head 382-4867
Hearing Clerk: Bessie L. Hammiel 382-4865

The Office of Administrative Law Judge has one field office in Region 4. The address is listed below.

Region 4 (Atlanta)
345 Cortland Street, NE, Atlanta, GA 30365.
Administrative Law Judge: Thomas B. Yost .....(404) 347-2681
Hearing Clerk: Julia P. Mooney ....(404) 347-2681

OFFICE OF SMALL AND DISADVANTAGED BUSINESS UTILIZATION (Room 1108)

(Area Code 202)

Director: John M. Ropes 557-7777
Small Business Ombudsman: Karen Brown 557-1938
Direct Procurement Advisor: Margie A. Wilson 557-7305

Hot Line:
Washington, DC Metro Area ....(703) 557-7015
Outside Washington, DC Metro Area ....(800) 368-5888

OFFICE OF CHIEF JUDICIAL OFFICER (Room 1145 - West Tower)

The Chief Judicial Officer is the Administrator's primary advisor in administrative appeals and makes final recommendations for administrative signature.

Online LEXIS users can access decisions of the Chief Judicial Officer.

(Area Code 202)

Chief Judicial Officer: Ronald L. McCallum 382-4076
Staff Attorneys:
Timothy Dowling 382-4076
James Black 382-4076
Alice Wegman 382-4076
Katie Calder 382-4076

OFFICE OF EMERGENCY AND REMEDIAL RESPONSE (SUPERFUND)

Emergency Response Division .... (202) 475-8720
Facsimile .... (202) 755-2155
Environmental Response Branch .... (201) 340-6740
Facsimile .... (201) 321-6724

OFFICE OF THE ASSISTANT ADMINISTRATOR FOR ENFORCEMENT AND COMPLIANCE MONITORING (Room 1037 West Tower)

The Office of Enforcement and Compliance Monitoring in Washington, D.C. has attorneys who counsel national program managers on enforcement matters and represent the Agency in nationally significant enforcement cases. The Office also provides the principal direction and review in matters concerning enforcement and compliance monitoring activities for air, water, waste, pesticides, toxic substances, and radiation. The Office manages a national criminal enforcement program, ensures coordination of compliance programs, and provides technical expertise for enforcement activities.

(Area Code 202)

Assistant Administrator: James M. Strock 382-4134
Deputy Assistant Administrator: Edward E. Reich 382-4137

Air Enforcement Division
Associate Enforcement Counsel: Michael S. Alushin ... 382-2820

Hazardous Waste Enforcement Division
Associate Enforcement Counsel:
David Van Slyke (Acting) 382-3050

Pesticides and Toxic Substances Enforcement Division
Associate Enforcement Counsel:
Michael Walker (Acting) 382-4544

Water Enforcement Division
Associate Enforcement Counsel: Frederick K. Steihl .. 475-8180

National Enforcement Investigations Center (Bldg 53, Box 25227, Denver, CO 80225)
Director: Frank Covington .... (303) 236-5100
Facsimile .... (303) 236-5116
Library: .... (303) 236-5122

Office of Compliance Analysis and Program Operations
Legal Enforcement Policy Branch Chief: Robert Heiss .. 475-8777
Director: Gerald Bryan 382-4140

DATABASES AND PUBLICATIONS OF INTEREST

Databases:

The **Integrated Risk Information System (IRIS)**, developed by EPA, contains summary information related to human health risk assessment. Updated monthly, **IRIS** is the Agency's primary vehicle for communication of chronic health hazard information that represents EPA consensus positions following comprehensive review by intra-Agency work groups. **IRIS** contains chemical-specific information in summary format for over 400 chemicals and provides a description of the basis for the hazard assessment and a discussion of the uncertainties in that assessment. **IRIS** can be accessed via several methods: telecommunications link with a commercial carrier (BT Tymnet); through the National Library of Medicine's TOXNET system; and, on diskettes from the National Technical Information Service (NTIS), Tel: 703/487-4650 or 800/336-4700. For further information, contact IRIS User Support, ECAO/EPA (MS-114), 26 West Martin Luther King Dr., Cincinnati, OH 45268.

Road Maps to Information Sources on Section 313 Chemicals provides support data on EPA's preliminary exposure and risk assessment activities of the TRI (Toxic Release Inventory) Section 313 chemicals. The database contains references to EPA hazard and risk assessment review documents and online databases concerning toxicity and risk assessment; covers major Federal regulations and regulatory levels on the chemicals; provides State information on air and drinking water levels and standards; and summarizes toxicity information available on the Section 313 chemicals. The present information is from the summer of 1989. EPA hopes to update this annually. This database is available from NTIS, 5285 Port Royal Road, Springfield, VA 22161. Tel: 703/487-4650 or 800/336-4700. Price for database: $180.00. NTIS Order Number PB90-501487. Price for user's manual: $17.00 (paperback), $8.00 (microfiche). NTIS Order Number PB90-174855. NTIS charges $3.00 per total order for shipping and handling.

Publications:

EPA Regulatory Agenda provides scientific information on the status of regulations that are under development, revision, and review at EPA. It can be obtained free of charge by contacting EPA, Regulation Development Branch, 401 M Street, S.W., 415 W. Tower, Washington, D.C. 20460. Tel: 202/382-5475.

ENVIRONMENTAL PROTECTION AGENCY
KEY LEGAL AUTHORITIES

Regulations:

General Agency Regulations: 40 C.F.R. Part 1 et seq. (1989).
Rules of Practice & Procedure: 40 C.F.R. Parts 22, 24, 54, 154 (FIFRA), 164, 209 (Noise), 304 (Superfund Cost Recovery Claims Arbitration Procedures), 702 & 750 (Toxic Substances Control Act).
EPA Acquisition Regulations: 48 C.F.R. Part 1500 et seq. (1989).

Comprehensive Environmental Response, Compensation and Liability Act (CERCLA) as amended, 42 U.S.C. 9601-9657--also known as the "Superfund" Act, this statute provides for a national inventory of inactive hazardous waste sites and establishes a program for appropriate environmental response action to protect public health and the environment from the dangers posed by such sites. The Act authorizes the EPA Administrator to take emergency assistance and containment actions with respect to such sites and establishes a fund to be drawn from industry-based fees and Federal appropriations to finance such clean-up actions. CERCLA also provides for liability of persons responsible for releases of hazardous waste at such sites.
Legislative History: 1980 U.S. Code Cong. & Admin. News 6119; 1986 U.S. Code Cong. & Admin. News 2835.
Implementing Regulations: 40 C.F.R. Part 300 et seq. (1989).

Resource Conservation and Recovery Act, as amended, 42 U.S.C. 6901 et seq.--the basic environmental statute governing solid waste/hazardous waste disposal.
Legislative History: 1976 U.S. Code Cong. & Admin. News 6238; 1984 U.S. Code Cong. & Admin. News 5576; 1988 U.S. Code Cong. & Admin. News 3632.
Implementing Regulations: 40 C.F.R. Parts 255 & 260-271 (1989).

Clean Air Act, 42 U.S.C. 7401 et seq.--the fundamental Federal anti-air pollution statute, it establishes an extensive regulatory scheme designed to control the volume and level of pollutants emitted by stationary and mobile sources.
Legislative History: 1963 U.S. Code Cong. & Admin. News 1260; 1965 U.S. Code Cong. & Admin. News 3605; 1967 U.S. Code Cong. & Admin. News 1938.
Implementing Regulations: 40 C.F.R. Parts 15 & 50-99 (1989).

Federal Water Pollution Control Act, as amended ("Clean Water Act"), 33 U.S.C. 1251 et seq.--the basic Federal anti-water pollution statute, it establishes Federal regulatory authority over emitting facilities and authorizes EPA to promulgate effluent guidelines and standards.
Legislative History: 1952 U.S. Code Cong. & Admin. News 2312.
Implementing Regulations: 40 C.F.R. Parts 15, 100 et seq., 401, & 500-501 (1989).

Safe Drinking Water Act, as amended, 42 U.S.C. 300 et seq.--directs EPA to regulate national primary drinking water systems.
Legislative History: 1974 U.S. Code Cong. & Admin. News 6454; 1977 U.S. Code Cong. & Admin. News 3648; 1986 U.S. Code Cong. & Admin. News 1566.
Implementing Regulations: 40 C.F.R. Part 141 et seq. (1989).

Federal Insecticide, Fungicide and Rodenticide Act (FIFRA), as amended, 7 U.S.C. 136-136y--establishes Federal regulatory authority over pesticide usage and disposal.
Legislative History: 1972 U.S. Code Cong. & Admin. News 3993.
Implementing Regulations: 40 C.F.R. Part 152 et seq. (1989).

Toxic Substances Control Act, as amended, 15 U.S.C. 2601 et seq.--establishes a regulatory scheme for chemicals which may impact adversely on health or the environment and confers emergency authority on EPA to take action with respect to imminent chemical hazards, including asbestos.
Legislative History: 1976 U.S. Code Cong. & Admin. News 4491; 1986 U.S. Code Cong. & Admin. News 5004.
Implementing Regulations: 40 C.F.R. Part 700 et seq. (1989).

Nuclear Waste Policy Act of 1982, as amended, 42 U.S.C. 10101 et seq.--regulates the disposal and storage of radioactive waste and spent nuclear fuel, and directs EPA to develop and administer radiation protection standards for nuclear power operations and the management and disposal of spent nuclear fuel.
Legislative History: 1982 U.S. Code Cong. & Admin. News 3792; 1987 U.S. Code Cong. & Admin. News 2313-1.
Implementing Regulations: 40 C.F.R. Part 191 (1989).

Federal Food, Drug, and Cosmetic Act, as amended, 21 U.S.C. 346a--authorizes EPA to establish tolerances for pesticide chemicals in or on raw agricultural commodities.
Legislative History: 1954 U.S. Code Cong. & Admin. News 2626; 1972 U.S. Code Cong. & Admin. News 3993.
Implementing Regulations: 40 C.F.R. 163.1 et seq., 180.1 et seq. (1989).

Marine Protection, Research and Sanctuaries Act of 1972, as amended, 33 U.S.C. 1401 et seq.--regulates ocean dumping.
Legislative History: 1972 U.S. Code Cong. & Admin. News 4234; 1974 U.S. Code Cong. & Admin. News 2796; 1988 U.S. Code Cong. & Admin. News 5767.
Implementing Regulations: 40 C.F.R. Parts 220-233 (1989).

Noise Control Act of 1972, as amended, 42 U.S.C. 4901-4918--designed to control the emission of noise detrimental to the human environment.
Legislative History: 1972 U.S. Code Cong. & Admin. News 4655.
Implementing Regulations: 40 C.F.R. Parts 201-211 (1989).

Radiation Control for Health & Safety Act of 1968, as amended, 42 U.S.C. 263b et seq.--authorizes the Department of Health & Human Services, in conjunction with the Environmental Protection Agency and the Department of Veterans Affairs, to promulgate Federal radiation guidelines.
Legislative History: 1968 U.S. Code Cong. & Admin. News 4312; 1981 U.S. Code Cong. & Admin. News 396.

Uranium Mill Tailings Radiation Control Act of 1978, as amended, 42 U.S.C. 2022--authorizes EPA to regulate control of residual radioactive material at designated uranium processing or depository sites and to administer restoration of such sites following any use of subsurface minerals.
Legislative History: 1978 U.S. Code Cong. & Admin. News 7433; 1982 U.S. Code Cong. & Admin. News 3592.
Implementing Regulations: 40 C.F.R. Part 192 (1989).

Emergency Planning & Community Right-to-Know Act of 1986, as amended, 42 U.S.C. 11001-11050--established a nationwide emergency notification and response system for dealing with releases of extremely hazardous substances into the environment.
Legislative History: 1986 U.S. Code Cong. & Admin. News 2835.
Implementing Regulations: 40 C.F.R. Part 350 et seq. (1989).

Motor Vehicle Information & Cost Savings Act, 15 U.S.C. 1901, 2001 et seq.--authorizes EPA to test the U.S. automobile fleet for fuel economy and to issue regulations to enforce the fuel economy requirements of the law.

Legislative History: 1975 U.S. Code Cong. & Admin. News 1762; 1977 U.S. Code Cong. & Admin. News 854; 1980 U.S. Code Cong. & Admin. News 3845; 1988 U.S. Code Cong. & Admin. News 3016.

Implementing Regulations: 40 C.F.R. Parts 600-610 (1989).

National Environmental Policy Act of 1969, 42 U.S.C. 4321 et seq.--requires EPA (and all other Federal agencies) to consider the environmental effects of all proposed agency actions.

Legislative History: 1969 U.S. Code Cong. & Admin. News 2751.

Implementing Regulations: 40 C.F.R. Part 6 (1989).

EQUAL EMPLOYMENT OPPORTUNITY COMMISSION

1801 L Street, N.W.
Washington, D.C. 20507

DESCRIPTION: The Equal Employment Opportunity Commission's (EEOC) mission is to ensure equality of opportunity by enforcing Federal legislation prohibiting discrimination in employment through investigation, conciliation, litigation, coordination, and regulation in the Federal sector, and through education, policy research and the provision of technical assistance. The EEOC receives and investigates employment discrimination charges and complaints. If the Commission finds reasonable cause to believe that unlawful discrimination occurred, it attempts to conciliate the charge or complaint. When conciliation is not achieved, the EEOC may file lawsuits in Federal District Court against employers, labor organizations and employment agencies. The staff also conducts Commission-initiated investigations under several of its authorizing statutes, which include: Title VII of the Civil Rights Act of 1964, which prohibits employment discrimination on the basis of race, color, sex, religion, or national origin; the Age Discrimination in Employment Act, which protects workers over 40; the Equal Pay Act of 1963, which protects women and men performing substantially equal work against pay discrimination based on sex; and in the Federal sector, Section 501 of the Rehabilitation Act of 1973, which prohibits discrimination against handicapped persons. By Executive Order, the EEOC also oversees and coordinates all Federal equal employment opportunity regulations, practices, and policies.

(Area Code 202)
Chairman: Evan J. Kemp Jr 663-4001
Executive Officer: Frances M. Hart 633-4070
Attorney Advisor to the Executive Officer:
Stephen Llewellyn 633-4073
Procurement Information 634-7048
Communications and Legislative Affairs 663-4900
Freedom of Information Act/Privacy Act Office 663-4637

EEOC Hotline ....(800) USA-EEOC
This Hotline can be used to file a charge or complaint of discrimination, or for further information on EEO laws

(Area Code 202)
Law Library (Room 6502) 663-4630
This law library is open to the public (by appointment) Monday through Friday from 8:30 AM until 5:30 PM. Photocopying is available: the first ten pages are free; subsequent pages are 15 cents each.

OFFICES OF THE COMMISSIONERS

(Area Code 202)
Chairman Evan J. Kemp Jr 663-4001
Chief of Staff: Robert Funk 663-4001
Attorney Advisors: Sherry Powers 663-4001
Christopher Bell 663-4001
Isiah Smith 663-4001

Vice Chairman: R. Gaull Silberman 663-4026
Special Assistant: Susan Murphy 663-4026

(Area Code 202)
Commissioner: Joy Cherian 663-4027
Executive Assistant: Raj Gupta 663-4027
Special Assistant: Byron Spears 663-4027

Commissioner: Tony E. Gallegos 663-4036
Executive Assistant: Michael Baldonado 663-4036
Special Assistant: Gladys O. Collazo-Valencia 663-4036

OFFICE OF GENERAL COUNSEL (Room 7000)

The Office of General Counsel conducts litigation under Title VII of the Civil Rights Act, the Age Discrimination in Employment Act, and the Equal Pay Act, including class, systemic and individual cases of discrimination in direct suits, and intervention and amicus curiae participation in litigation brought by third parties, and also enforces Commission subpoenas.

(Area Code 202)
General Counsel: Donna R. Livingston (Acting) 663-4702
Deputy General Counsel: William H. Ng 663-4705

Appellate Services
Association General Counsel: Gwendolyn Young Reams ..663-4736
Assistant General Counsel for Division I:
Vella M. Fink 663-4736
Assistant General Counsel for Division II:
Vince Blackwood 663-4736
Assistant General Counsel for Division III:
Lorraine Davis 663-4736

(Area Code 202)
Systemic Litigation Services
Associate General Counsel: James N. Finney 663-4758
Assistant General Counsel for Division I:
Gerald Letwin 663-4760
Assistant General Counsel for Division II:
Karen H. Baker 663-4780

Trial Services
Associate General Counsel: Philip B. Sklover 663-4786
Assistant General Counsel: Ethel Mixon 663-4794
Trial Attorney: Paul Brenner 633-4788

(Area Code 202)
Liaison Attorney: Charles Thomas 663-4789
(Cleveland, Denver, Detroit, Indianapolis, New Orleans, Philadelphia, Seattle)

Liaison Attorney: James Scanlan 663-4795
(Atlanta, Chicago, Memphis, Milwaukee)

(Area Code 202)
Liaison Attorney: Justine Lisser 663-4773
(Houston, Miami, New York, San Francisco)
Liaison Attorney: Jerome Scanlan 663-4793
(Baltimore, Birmingham, Charlotte, Dallas, Los Angeles, San Antonio, St. Louis)

DISTRICT AND AREA OFFICES

Albuquerque
Director: Tom E. Robles
U.S. Equal Employment Opportunity Commission, Albuquerque Area Office, 505 Marquette, N.W., Suite 1105, Albuquerque, NM 87102-2189. Tel: 505/766-2061.

Atlanta
Director: Harris A. Williams
Regional Attorney: George Darden
U.S. Equal Employment Opportunity Commission, Atlanta District Office, 75 Piedmont Avenue, N.E., Suite 1100, Atlanta, GA 30335. Tel: 404/331-6093.

Baltimore
Director: Chris Roggerson
Regional Attorney: Gerald Kiel
U.S. Equal Employment Opportunity Commission, Baltimore District Office, 111 Market Place, Suite 4000, Baltimore, MD 21202. Tel: 301/962-3932.

Birmingham
Director: Warren Bullock
Regional Attorney: Jerome C. Rose
U.S. Equal Employment Opportunity Commission, Birmingham District Office, 2121 Eighth Avenue, North, Suite 824, Birmingham, AL 35203. Tel: 205/731-0082.

Boston
Director: Charles L. Looney
U.S. Equal Employment Opportunity Commission, Boston Area Office, JFK Federal Building, Room 409-B, Boston, MA 02203. Tel: 617/565-3200.

Buffalo
Director: Jon Patterson
U.S. Equal Employment Opportunity Commission, Buffalo Local Office, 28 Church Street, Room 301, Buffalo, NY 14202. Tel: 716/846-4441.

Charlotte
Director: R. Edison Elkins
Regional Attorney: Ronald Arrington
U.S. Equal Employment Opportunity Commission, Charlotte District Office, 5500 Central Avenue, Charlotte, NC 28212. Tel: 704/567-7100.

Chicago
Director: Marsha Drane
Regional Attorney: Jack Rowe
U.S. Equal Employment Opportunity Commission, Chicago District Office, 536 South Clark Street, Room 930-A, Chicago, IL 60605. Tel: 312/353-2713.

Cincinnati
Director: Earl Haley
U.S. Equal Employment Opportunity Commission, Cincinnati Area Office, 550 Main Street, Room 7015, Cincinnati, OH 45202. Tel: 513/684-2851.

Cleveland
Director: Harold Ferguson
Regional Attorney: Robert Bauders
U.S. Equal Employment Opportunity Commission, Cleveland District Office, 1375 Euclid Avenue, Room 600, Cleveland, OH 44115. Tel: 216/522-2001.

Dallas
Director: Jacqueline Bradley
Regional Attorney: vacant
U.S. Equal Employment Opportunity Commission, Dallas District Office, 8303 Elmbrook Drive, Dallas, TX 75247. Tel: 214/767-7015.

Denver
Director: Francisco J. Flores
Regional Attorney: Nelson Alston
U.S. Equal Employment Opportunity Commission, Denver District Office, 1845 Sherman Street, 2nd Floor, Denver, CO 80203. Tel: 303/866-1300.

Detroit
Director: A. William Schukar
Regional Attorney: John H. Edmonds
U.S. Equal Employment Opportunity Commission, Detroit District Office, 477 Michigan Avenue, Room 1540, Detroit, MI 48226. Tel: 313/226-7636.

El Paso
Director: Eliazar Salinas
U.S. Equal Employment Opportunity Commission, El Paso Area Office, 700 East San Antonio Street, Room B-406, El Paso, TX 79901. Tel: 915/534-6550.

Fresno
Director: David Rodriguez
U.S. Equal Employment Opportunity Commission, Fresno Local Office, 1313 P Street, Suite 103, Fresno, CA 93721. Tel: 209/487-5793.

Greensboro
Director: Daisy Crenshaw
U.S. Equal Employment Opportunity Commission, Greensboro Local Office, 324 West Market Street, Room B-27, P.O. Box 3363, Greensboro, NC 27402. Tel: 919/333-5174.

Greenville
Director: Walt Champe
U.S. Equal Employment Opportunity Commission, Greenville Local Office, 300 East Washington Street, Suite B-41, Greenville, SC 29601. Tel: 803/233-1791.

Honolulu
Director: Deborah Wong Randall
U.S. Equal Employment Opportunity Commission, Honolulu Local Office, 677 Ala Moana Boulevard, Suite 404, P.O. Box 50082, Honolulu, HI 96813. Tel: 808/541-3120.

Houston
Director: Harriet J. Ehrlich
Regional Attorney: Jim Sacher
U.S. Equal Employment Opportunity Commission, Houston District Office, 1919 Smith Street, 7th Floor, Houston, TX 77002. Tel: 713/653-3320.

Indianapolis
Director: Thomas P. Hadfield
Regional Attorney: Laurie Young
U.S. Equal Employment Opportunity Commission, Indianapolis District Office, 46 East Ohio Street, Room 456, Indianapolis, IN 46204. Tel: 317/226-7212.

EQUAL EMPLOYMENT OPPORTUNITY COMMISSION

Jackson
Director: Henrene P. Matthews
U.S. Equal Employment Opportunity Commission, Jackson Area Office, 100 West Capitol Street, Suite 721, Jackson, MS 39269. Tel: 601/965-4537.

Kansas City
Director: Joseph P. Doherty
U.S. Equal Employment Opportunity Commission, Kansas City Area Office, 911 Walnut, 10th Floor, Kansas City, MO 64106. Tel: 816/426-5773.

Little Rock
Director: W.P. Brown
U.S. Equal Employment Opportunity Commission, Little Rock Area Office, 320 West Capitol Avenue, Suite 621, Little Rock, AR 72201. Tel: 501/378-5060.

Los Angeles
Director: Dorothy Porter
Regional Attorney: Tomas Olmos
U.S. Equal Employment Opportunity Commission, Los Angeles District Office, 3660 Wilshire Boulevard, 5th Floor, Los Angeles, CA 90010. Tel: 213/251-7278.

Louisville
Director: Roosevelt Gholston Jr.
U.S. Equal Employment Opportunity Commission, Louisville Area Office, 601 West Broadway, Room 613, Louisville, KY 40202. Tel: 502/582-6082.

Memphis
Director: Walter Grabon
Regional Attorney: Joseph R. Terry Jr.
U.S. Equal Employment Opportunity Commission, Memphis District Office, 1407 Union Avenue, Suite 621, Memphis, TN 38104. Tel: 901/521-2617.

Miami
Director: Federico Costales
Regional Attorney: Segismundo Pares
U.S. Equal Employment Opportunity Commission, Miami District Office, 1 Northeast First Street, 6th Floor, Miami, FL 33132. Tel: 305/536-4491.

Milwaukee
Director: Chester V. Bailey
Regional Attorney: Sandy Neese
U.S. Equal Employment Opportunity Commission, Milwaukee District Office, 310 West Wisconsin Avenue, Suite 800, Milwaukee, WI 53203. Tel: 414/291-1111.

Minneapolis
Director: Michael Bloyer
U.S. Equal Employment Opportunity Commission, Minneapolis Local Office, 220 Second Street South, Room 108, Minneapolis, MN 55401. Tel: 612/370-3330.

Nashville
Director: Rosetta Miller Perry
U.S. Equal Employment Opportunity Commission, Nashville Area Office, 404 James Robertson Parkway, Suite 1100, Nashville, TN 37219. Tel: 615/736-5820.

Newark
Director: Corrado Gigante
U.S. Equal Employment Opportunity Commission, Newark Area Office, 60 Park Place, Room 301, Newark, NJ 07102. Tel: 201/645-6383.

New Orleans
Director: Patricia Fields Bivins
Regional Attorney: Keith Hill
U.S. Equal Employment Opportunity Commission, New Orleans District Office, 701 Loyola Avenue, Suite 600, New Orleans, LA 70113. Tel: 504/589-2329.

New York
Director: Spencer H. Lewis Jr.
Regional Attorney: James Lee (Acting)
U.S. Equal Employment Opportunity Commission, New York District Office, 90 Church Street, Room 1501, New York, NY 10007. Tel: 212/264-7161.

Norfolk
Director: Kathryne Stokes
U.S. Equal Employment Opportunity Commission, Norfolk Area Office, 252 Monticello Avenue, First Floor, Norfolk, VA 23510. Tel: 804/441-3470.

Oakland
Director: Rolland D. Taylor
U.S. Equal Employment Opportunity Commission, Oakland Local Office, 1333 Broadway, Room 430, Oakland, CA 94612. Tel: 415/273-7588.

Oklahoma
Director: Donald P. Burris
U.S. Equal Employment Opportunity Commission, Oklahoma Area Office, 531 Couch Drive, Oklahoma City, OK 73102. Tel: 405/231-4911.

Philadelphia
Director: Johnny J. Butler
Regional Attorney: Reginald Sydnor (Acting)
U.S. Equal Employment Opportunity Commission, Philadelphia District Office, 1421 Cherry Street, 10th Floor, Philadelphia, PA 19102. Tel: 215/597-9350.

Phoenix
Director: Charles Burtner (Acting)
Regional Attorney: vacant
U.S. Equal Employment Opportunity Commission, Phoenix District Office, 4520 N. Central Avenue, Suite 300, Phoenix, AZ 85012. Tel: 602/261-3882.

Pittsburgh
Director: Eugene V. Nelson
U.S. Equal Employment Opportunity Commission, Pittsburgh Area Office, 1000 Liberty Avenue, Room 2038-A, Pittsburgh, PA 15222. Tel: 412/644-3444.

Raleigh
Director: Richard E. Walz
U.S. Equal Employment Opportunity Commission, Raleigh Area Office, 1309 Annapolis Drive, Suite 500, Raleigh, NC 27608. Tel: 919/856-4064.

Richmond
Director: Gloria Underwood
U.S. Equal Employment Opportunity Commission, Richmond Area Office, 400 North 8th Street, Room 7026, Richmond, VA 23240. Tel: 804/771-2692.

San Antonio
Director: Pedro Esquivel
Regional Attorney: Calvin Washington
U.S. Equal Employment Opportunity Commission, San Antonio District Office, 5410 Fredericksburg Road, Suite 200, San Antonio, TX 78229. Tel: 512/229-4810.

San Diego
Director: LaVonne S. Carman
U.S. Equal Employment Opportunity Commission, San Diego Local Office, 880 Front Street, Room 4S-21, San Diego, CA 92188. Tel: 619/293-6288.

San Francisco
Director: Paula Montanez
Regional Attorney: John de J. Pemberton
U.S. Equal Employment Opportunity Commission, San Francisco District Office, 901 Market Street, Suite 500, San Francisco, CA 94103. Tel: 415/995-5049.

San Jose
Director: Charles Carattini
U.S. Equal Employment Opportunity Commission, San Jose Local Office, 280 South First Street, Room 4150, San Jose, CA 95113. Tel: 408/291-7352.

Savannah
Director: Gloria Barnett-Mentor
U.S. Equal Employment Opportunity Commission, Savannah Local Office, 10 Whitaker Street, Suite B, Savannah, GA 31401. Tel: 912/944-4234.

Seattle
Director: Jeanette M. Leino
Regional Attorney: A. Louis Lucero
U.S. Equal Employment Opportunity Commission, Seattle District Office, 1321 Second Avenue, 7th Floor, Seattle, WA 98101. Tel: 206/442-0968.

St. Louis
Director: Lynn Bruner
Regional Attorney: James Neely
U.S. Equal Employment Opportunity Commission, St. Louis District Office, 625 N. Euclid Street, 5th Floor, St. Louis, MO 63108. Tel: 314/425-6585.

Tampa
Director: James D. Packwood Jr.
U.S. Equal Employment Opportunity Commission, Tampa Area Office, 700 Twiggs Street, Room 302, Tampa, FL 33602. Tel: 813/228-2310.

Washington, D.C. Field Office
Director: Susan B. Reilly
U.S. Equal Employment Opportunity Commission, Washington, D.C. Field Office, 1400 L Street, N.W., Suite 200, Washington, D.C. 20005. Tel: 202/275-7377.

OFFICE OF INSPECTOR GENERAL (Room 3001)

The Inspector General directs a centralized, comprehensive, independent audit and investigations program at EEOC to identify and report program deficiencies, improve the efficiency and effectiveness of operations, and to enhance employee and program integrity through prevention and detection of criminal activity, unethical conduct, and program fraud, waste, and abuse.

(Area Code 202)
Inspector General: William D. Miller III 663-4379

OFFICE OF LEGAL COUNSEL (Room 6002)

The Office of Legal Counsel serves as principal advisor to the Commission on nonenforcement litigation matters; represents the EEOC and staff in defensive litigation and administrative hearings; and carries out the Commission's leadership and coordination role for the Federal Government's EEO enforcement programs.

(Area Code 202)
Legal Counsel: Thomasina Rogers (Acting) 663-4637
Deputy Legal Counsel: Thomasina Rogers 663-4640
Assistant Legal Counsel for Advice and External Litigation Division: Nicholas M. Inzeo 663-4670
Assistant Legal Counsel for Internal Litigation Division I: Richard Roscio 663-4654
Assistant Legal Counsel for Internal Litigation Division II: David G. Liss 663-4667

(Area Code 202)
Coordination and Guidance Services
Associate Legal Counsel: Elizabeth Thornton 663-4638
Associate Legal Counsel for Age Discrimination in Employment Division: Joseph M. Cleary 663-4690
Associate Legal Counsel for Coordination Division: Irene Hill 663-4689
Associate Legal Counsel for Title VII/Equal Pay Act Division: Diana Johnston 663-4679

OFFICE OF PROGRAM OPERATIONS

(Area Code 202)
Determinations Review Program
Director: Michael S. Dougherty 663-4505
Supervisory Attorney Advisor: Howard Kallem 663-4498

(Area Code 202)
Systemic Investigations and Individual Compliance Programs
Director: Ronnie Blumenthal 663-4863

OFFICE OF REVIEW AND APPEALS (Suite 5000)

The Office of Review and Appeals processes final decision appeals of EEO complaints filed by employees of, or applicants for, jobs with the Federal Government and reviews petitions for review of Merit Systems Protection Board appeals decisions of employment discrimination.

To obtain a single copy of a decision, contact the Docket Clerk.

(Area Code 202)
Director: Dolores L. Rozzi 663-4599

Appeals Division "A"
Director: Willie Garrett 663-4599

Appeals Division "B"
Director: Robbie Dix 663-4599

(Area Code 202)
Compliance and Control Division
Director: Richard Reda 663-4599

Review Division
Director: Jay Pagano 663-4599
Docket Clerk 663-4592

EQUAL EMPLOYMENT OPPORTUNITY COMMISSION

DATABASES AND PUBLICATIONS OF INTEREST

Database:

Equal Employment Opportunity Commission Federal Sector Case Decisions. Available on CD-ROM through the PERSONNET Service of Information Handling Services, 15 Inverness Way East, P.O. Box 1154, Englewood, CO 80150. Tel: 800/241-7824. In Colorado, call 303/790-0600 ext 59.

Publications:

Federal Equal Opportunity Reporter. A monthly service reporting the full text of decisions of both the EEOC and the courts on Federal employee EEO appeals. Back decisions dating from 1979 are available at extra expense. Product# 4070. Price: $760.00 per year. Contact: LRP Publications, 747 Dresher Road, P.O. Box 980, Horsham, PA 19044-0980. Tel: 800/341-7874.

Employment Practices Guide. Four volumes, updated biweekly. Contains Federal and state decisions in discrimination cases. Price: $575.00 a year. Contact: Commerce Clearing House, 4025 West Peterson Avenue, Chicago, IL 60646. Tel: 312/583-8500. Or, in Washington, D.C. call 202/626-2200.

Single copies of the following publications are available free of charge from: **U.S. Equal Employment Opportunity Commission,** Office of Communications and Legislative Affairs, 1801 L Street, N.W., Room 9024, Washington, D.C. 20507.

Brochures: Age Discrimination is Against the Law, Equal Work/Equal Pay, Title VII Enforces Job Rights, Filing a Charge, Voluntary Assistance Program, Complaints of Discrimination by Federal Employees or Applicants, Equal Employment Opportunity Guide for Handicapped Federal Employees and Applicants for Federal Jobs, and Employee Appeals of Federal Agency EEO Decisions.

Booklets: The Charging Party: Your Rights and Responsibilities. Laws Enforced by the U.S. Equal Employment Opportunity Commission.

Fact Sheets: Pregnancy, National Origin, Religion, Sexual Harassment.

Regulations: Procedural, Sex, Religion, National Origin, Affirmative Action, Availability of Records, Federal EEO, Equal Pay Act, ADEA (A&B), ADEA Procedures, and ADEA Recordkeeping. To receive a full set of regulations, request publication #35.

EQUAL EMPLOYMENT OPPORTUNITY COMMISSION

KEY LEGAL AUTHORITIES

General Regulations: 29 C.F.R. Parts 1600 et seq. (1989).

Uniform Guidelines on Employee Selection Procedures, 28 C.F.R. 50.14 (1989)--principles issued jointly by the Departments of Justice and Labor, the Equal Employment Opportunity Commission, and the Office of Personnel Management and designed to assist employers, labor organizations, employment agencies, and licensing and certification boards to comply with Federal equal employment opportunity laws.

Title VII of the Civil Rights Act of 1964, as amended, 42 U.S.C. 2000e et seq.--mandates equal employment opportunity by prohibiting discrimination in employment on the basis of race, color, religion, sex, or national origin, and establishes the EEOC, setting forth the duties and powers of the Commission.

Legislative History: 1964 U.S. Code Cong. & Admin. News 2355; 1972 U.S. Code Cong. & Admin. News 2137; 1974 U.S. Code Cong. & Admin. News 7159; 1976 U.S. Code Cong. & Admin. News 690; 1978 U.S. Code Cong. & Admin. News 496; 1980 U.S. Code Cong. & Admin. News 50.

Equal Pay Act, 29 U.S.C. 206(d)--prohibits wage discrimination based on the sex of the employee.

Legislative History: 1963 U.S. Code Cong. & Admin. News 687.

Age Discrimination in Employment Act of 1967, as amended, 29 U.S.C. 621 et seq.--prohibits arbitrary age discrimination in employment against persons between the ages of 40 and 70, and promotes employment of older persons based on their ability rather than age.

Legislative History: 1967 U.S. Code Cong. & Admin. News 2213; 1974 U.S. Code Cong. & Admin. News 2811; 1978 U.S. Code Cong. & Admin. News 504; 1982 U.S. Code Cong. & Admin. News 781; 1984 U.S. Code Cong. & Admin. News 697 & 2974; 1986 U.S. Code Cong. & Admin. News 42 & 5628.

Sec. 501 of the Rehabilitation Act of 1973, as amended, 29 U.S.C. 791--requires Federal agencies to establish and maintain affirmative action plans for hiring, placing, and advancing handicapped individuals.

Legislative History: 1973 U.S. Code Cong. & Admin. News 2076; 1984 U.S. Code Cong. & Admin. News 15; 1986 U.S. Code Cong. & Admin. News 3471.

Sec. 504 of the Rehabilitation Act of 1973, as amended, 29 U.S.C. 794a--makes the remedies, procedures, and rights set forth in the Civil Rights Act of 1964 available to any person aggrieved by any recipient of Federal assistance or Federal provider of such assistance under Sec. 794, which prohibits discrimination against handicapped persons by any program or activity receiving Federal financial assistance or any Federal agency conducting a program or activity.

Legislative History: 1978 U.S. Code Cong. & Admin. News 7312.

Title VI of the Civil Rights Act of 1964, as amended, 42 U.S.C. 2000d et seq.--prohibits discrimination on the basis of race, color, or national origin by any recipient of Federal financial assistance.

Legislative History: 1964 U.S. Code Cong. & Admin. News 2355.

Title IX of the Education Amendments of 1972, 20 U.S.C. 1681 et seq.--prohibits discrimination on the basis of sex by any educational program or activity receiving Federal financial assistance.

Legislative History: 1972 U.S. Code Cong. & Admin. News 2462; 1974 U.S. Code Cong. & Admin. News 6779; 1976 U.S. Code Cong. & Admin. News 4713.

EXPORT-IMPORT BANK OF THE UNITED STATES

811 Vermont Avenue, N.W.
Washington, D.C. 20571

DESCRIPTION: The Export-Import Bank (Eximbank) is the independent U.S. Government agency that facilitates the export financing of American goods and services. The Bank implements a variety of programs to meet the needs of the U.S. exporting community, according to the size of the transaction. These programs take the form of loans or the issuance of guarantees and insurance, so that exporters and private banks can extend appropriate financing without taking undue risks.

(Area Code 202)

President and Chairman: John D. Macomber 566-8144
Procurement Information 566-8111
Public Affairs and Publications 566-8990
Facsimile...566-7524

Freedom of Information Act Office 566-4784
There is a copying charge of 25 cents per page for FOIA requests, as well as a per hour search fee. Searches performed by a professional staff member cost $24.00 per hour, while searches performed by a clerical staff member are $12.00 per hour.

(Area Code 202)

Privacy Act Office 566-8111
The costs for the privacy act requests are identical to those for the FOIA requests.

OFFICE OF THE GENERAL COUNSEL (Room 947)

The Office of the General Counsel performs legal duties and services for and on behalf of the Bank. Responsibilities include advising on issues relating to insurance and banking, claims filed under the Bank's guarantee and insurance programs, international lending, and country risk analysis, as well as issues relating to contracting, procurement, EEO, and labor-management relations.

(Area Code 202)

General Counsel: Hart Fessenden 566-8334
Associate General Counsel: Stephen G. Glazer 566-8864

(Area Code 202)

Associate General Counsel: Fred H. Massey, Jr 566-8891

EXPORT FINANCE GROUP (Room 1115)

(Area Code 202)

Claims and Recoveries Division
Vice President: Stephen D. Proctor 566-8822

COUNTRY RISK ANALYSIS (Room 1137)

(Area Code 202)

Vice President: Daniel Bond 566-8890

EXPORT-IMPORT BANK OF THE UNITED STATES
KEY LEGAL AUTHORITIES

Regulations: 12 C.F.R. Part 400 et seq. (1989).

Export-Import Bank Act of 1945, as amended, 12 U.S.C. 635 et seq.--establishes the Export-Import Bank as a Federal corporation to aid in financing and to facilitate exports and imports and the exchange of commodities and services between the U.S. and foreign countries, agencies, or nationals.

Legislative History: 1961 U.S. Code Cong. & Admin. News 3005; 1968 U.S. Code Cong. & Admin. News 2541; 1977 U.S. Code Cong. & Admin. News 3126; 1978 U.S. Code Cong. & Admin. News 9273; 1983 U.S. Code Cong. & Admin. News 1768; 1986 U.S. Code Cong. & Admin. News 2334, 2472, 4075.

FARM CREDIT ADMINISTRATION

1501 Farm Credit Drive
McLean, VA 22102-5090

DESCRIPTION: The Farm Credit Administration (FCA) is responsible for the regulation and examination of the borrower-owned banks and associations and their service organizations that comprise the cooperative Farm Credit System. These institutions are the Federal land banks that make long-term loans on farm or rural real estate, or real estate connected with a commercial fisherman's operation, through local Federal land bank associations; the Federal intermediate credit banks providing funds to associations and other institutions financing farmers, ranchers, rural homeowners, and commercial fisherman; and the banks for cooperatives that make loans of all kinds to agricultural and aquatic cooperatives. The loan funds provided by these institutions are obtained primarily through the sale of securities to investors in the nation's capital markets.

(Area Code 703)
Chairman: Harold B. Steele 883-4010
Procurement Information 883-4149
Office of Congressional and Public Affairs 883-4056
Small and Disadvantaged Business Utilization Director:
Michael A. Bronson....................................883-4200
Facsimile..734-5784

(Area Code 703)
Freedom of Information Act/Privacy Act Office 883-4056
Requests must be in writing. There are variable copying and per hour search fee charges.
Library 883-4296
This library is located on the first floor and is open to the public Monday through Friday from 8:30 AM until 5:00 PM. Materials cannot be checked out by the public. No photocopying privileges.

OFFICE OF GENERAL COUNSEL (Room 4116)

(Area Code 703)
General Counsel: Anne E. Dewey 883-4020

The Office of General Counsel is divided into two sections:

The **Corporate and Administrative Law Division**, which researches and drafts legal opinions interpreting the Farm Credit Act, its implementing regulations, and other applicable Federal laws; participates in Regulatory Task Forces to provide legal advice during the development of regulations; counsels the Office of Analysis and Supervision and the Office of Examination on a wide variety of matters; and provides advice on Agency administrative matters.

(Area Code 703)
Associate General Counsel for Corporate and Administrative Law Division: Nancy E. Lynch 883-4020

The **Enforcement and Litigation Division**, which represents FCA in enforcement cases and litigation matters when an action has been brought against the Administration or its personnel. This Division also processes administrative claims and requests for FCA official documents, and handles matters related to the supervisory area, such as drafting criminal referral regulations, bank bribery guidelines, and proposed enforcement legislation.

(Area Code 703)
Associate General Counsel for Litigation and Enforcement Division: Gary L. Bohlke 883-4020

PUBLICATIONS OF INTEREST

FCA Bulletin, published monthly since 1986 as a digest and reference guide to regulatory activities affecting farm credit banks and other System institutions, contains summaries of Farm Credit Administration Board actions decisions, policy statements, directives, interpretations, proposed and final regulations, formal enforcement pending litigation involving the Farm Credit Administration, and actions, interpretations, and agency reorganizations. Available free from: Editor, Farm Credit Bulletin, Office of Congressional and Public Affairs, Farm Credit Administration, 1501 Farm Credit Drive, McLean, VA 22102-5090. Tel: 703/883-4056.

FARM CREDIT ADMINISTRATION

KEY LEGAL AUTHORITIES

General Regulations: 12 C.F.R. Parts 600-624 (1989).
Rules of Practice & Procedure: 12 C.F.R. Part 622 (1989).

Farm Credit Act of 1971, as amended, 12 U.S.C. 2000 et seq.--establishes the Farm Credit System, consisting of farm credit banks, farm credit associations, Federal land bank associations, production credit associations, and banks for cooperatives, chartered by the United States to serve the credit needs of farmers and ranchers; and authorizes the Farm Credit Administration to act as the examiner and regulator of the System.
Legislative History: 1971 U.S. Code Cong. & Admin. News 2091.

Agricultural Credit Act of 1987, Pub. L. 100-233, 101 Stat. 1611 (1988)--establishes:

*the Farm Credit System Insurance Corporation under the Farm Credit Administration to provide an insurance program for Farm Credit System obligations similar to the Federal Deposit Insurance Corporation; and requires each system bank to have insurance as a condition of retaining its Federal charter;

*the Farm Credit System Assistance Board to provide assistance to, and protect the stock of borrowers of, Farm Credit System institutions and assist in restoring them to economic viability;

*the Farm Credit System Financial Assistance Corporation to provide capital to institutions of the Farm Credit System experiencing financial difficulty; and

*the Federal Agricultural Mortgage Corporation ("Farmer Mac") to provide a secondary market for trading securities backed by farm real estate loans.

Legislative History: 1987 U.S. Code Cong. & Admin. News 2723.

FARM CREDIT SYSTEM ASSISTANCE BOARD

1301 Pennsylvania Avenue, N.W., Suite 702
Washington, D.C. 20004

DESCRIPTION: The Farm Credit System Assistance Board, a government corporation, was created by the Agricultural Credit Act of 1987 as a successor to the Farm Credit System Capital Corporation. The mission of the Board is to provide assistance and supervise necessary reforms for troubled Farm Credit System institutions.

(Area Code 202)
President and CEO: Eric P. Thor 737-9255
Public Information/Legislative Affairs 737-9255

(Area Code 202)
Freedom of Information/Privacy Act Office 737-9255
Facsimile 737-9295

OFFICE OF GENERAL COUNSEL

There are three attorneys at the Board: the General Counsel, the Deputy General Counsel, and Assistant General Counsel. Their responsibilities focus on corporate, banking, securities, and administrative law, as well as on government contracts. Activities include litigation and interacting with senior officials from Government and the banking industry.

(Area Code 202)
General Counsel: Kenneth L. Peoples 737-9255
Deputy General Counsel: Kathleen Mullarkey 737-9255

(Area Code 202)
Assistant General Counsel: Christine Pembroke 737-9255

FARM CREDIT SYSTEM ASSISTANCE BOARD
KEY LEGAL AUTHORITIES

General Regulations: 12 C.F.R. Parts 600-624 (1989).
Rules of Practice & Procedure: 12 C.F.R. Part 622 (1989).

Farm Credit Act of 1971, as amended, 12 U.S.C. 2000 et seq.--establishes the Farm Credit System, consisting of farm credit banks, farm credit associations, Federal land bank associations, production credit associations, and banks for cooperatives, chartered by the United States to serve the credit needs of farmers and ranchers; and authorizes the Farm Credit Administration to act as the examiner and regulator of the System.
Legislative History: 1971 U.S. Code Cong. & Admin. News **2091.**

Agricultural Credit Act of 1987, Pub. L. 100-233, 101 Stat. 1611 (1988)--establishes:

*the Farm Credit System Insurance Corporation under the Farm Credit Administration to provide an insurance program for Farm Credit System obligations similar to the Federal Deposit Insurance Corporation; and requires each system bank to have insurance as a condition of retaining its Federal charter;

*the Farm Credit System Assistance Board to provide assistance to, and protect the stock of borrowers of, Farm Credit System institutions and assist in restoring them to economic viability;

*the Farm Credit System Financial Assistance Corporation to provide capital to institutions of the Farm Credit System experiencing financial difficulty; and

*the Federal Agricultural Mortgage Corporation ("Farmer Mac") to provide a secondary market for trading securities backed by farm real estate loans.

Legislative History: 1987 U.S. Code Cong. & Admin. News 2723.

FEDERAL COMMUNICATIONS COMMISSION

1919 M Street, N.W.
Washington, D.C. 20554

DESCRIPTION: The Federal Communications Commission (FCC) is an independent regulatory agency tasked with regulating interstate and foreign commerce in communication by wire and radio. The Commission has broad regulatory and licensing authority over communications common carriers (e.g., telephone companies), mass media facilities (e.g., broadcast and cable services) and various private communication systems (e.g., aviation and marine radio communication systems, amateur radio, etc.).

(Area Code 202)

Chairman: Alfred C. Sikes 632-6600
Procurement Information 634-1530
Consumer Assistance 632-7000
Publications Information 632-4178
Dockets 632-7535
Mass Media Bureau, Complaints & Investigations Branch...632-7048
Facsimile 632-7092

Freedom of Information Act Office 632-7143
The first 100 pages copied and the first 2 hours of search time are free for FOIA requests. After that, there is a copying charge of 17 cents per page and a variable per hour search fee.

Privacy Act Office 634-1535
The first 25 pages copied are free for Privacy Act requests. After that, there is a copying charge of 17 cents per page.

Library (Room 639) 632-7100
The library is open to the public from 10:00 AM until 4:00 PM. Materials may not be checked out but copying machines are available. The law library is contained within this library.

Public Reference Rooms
The FCC maintains several public reference room which are open to the public. Materials may not be checked out, but copying machines are available. Unless otherwise noted, the public reference rooms are located in the main building on M Street.

(Area Code 202)

Dockets Reference (Room 239) 632-7569
Open from 9:00 AM until 4:30 PM Monday through Friday.

Mass Media Bureau Reference (Room 239) 632-6485
Open to the public from 9:00 AM until 5:30 PM Monday through Friday.

Common Carrier Bureau Reference Rooms

Domestic Facilities Division 634-1860
2025 M Street, N.W.,Room 6220, Washington, D.C. 20554
Open from 8:30 AM until 12:30 PM and 1:30 PM until 3:00 PM Monday through Thursday.

Mobile Services Division (Room 628) 632-6400
Open from 8:00 AM until 12:00 Noon Monday through Thursday.

OFFICES OF THE COMMISSIONERS (Room 814)

(Area Code 202)

Chairman: Dennis R. Patrick 632-6600
Senior Legal Advisor: Kenneth Robinson 632-6600
Legal Advisor/Common Carrier: Cheryl Tritt 632-6600
Legal Advisor/Mass Media: Lauren J. Belvin 632-6600

Commissioner: Ervin Duggan 632-6996
Senior Legal Advisor: Leonard J. Kennedy 632-6996

Commissioner: James H. Quello 632-7557
Legal Assistant: Robert Corn-Revere 632-7557

(Area Code 202)

Commissioner: Sherrie P. Marshall 632-6446
Senior Legal Advisor: Steve Kamines 632-6446
Legal Advisor/Common Carrier: Diane Cornell 632-6446
Legal Advisor/Mass Media: Peter Ross 632-6446

Commissioner: Andrew Barrett 632-7117
Senior Legal Advisor: Robert E. Branson 632-7117
Legal Advisor/Common Carrier: Cindy Z. Schonhaut 632-7117
Legal Advisor/Mass Media: Byron F. Marchant 632-7117

OFFICE OF GENERAL COUNSEL (Room 614)

The Office of General Counsel serves as chief legal advisor to the Commission and its various bureaus and offices. The General Counsel advises the FCC on legal issues involved in establishing and implementing policy, handles legal questions affecting the Agency's internal operations, coordinates the preparation of its legislative program and represents it in court. Through its Adjudication Division, the Office of General Counsel also assists the Commission in reviewing Review Board decisions and, in specific cases, initial decisions of the Administrative Law Judges, as well as in drafting FCC decisions in adjudicatory cases.

(Area Code 202)

General Counsel: Robert L. Pettit 632-7020
Deputy General Counsel: Renee Licht 632-7020
Associate General Counsel: Marjorie R. Greene 632-7020
Special Counsel: Ruth Milkman 632-7020

Administrative Law Division
Associate General Counsel: Sheldon M. Guttmann 632-6990
Deputy Associate General Counsel/Administrative Law:
Susan H. Steiman 632-6990
Assistant General Counsel/Administrative Law:
Lawrence S. Schaffner 632-6990

Litigation Division

(Area Code 202)

Associate General Counsel/Litigation:
Daniel M. Armstrong 632-7112
Deputy Associate General Counsel/Litigation:
John E. Ingle 632-7112
Assistant General Counsel/Trial & Enforcement:
Jane Mago 632-7112

Adjudication Division
Associate General Counsel: John I. Riffer 632-7220

FEDERAL COMMUNICATIONS COMMISSION

OFFICE OF INSPECTOR GENERAL (Room 752)

The Office of Inspector General conducts, supervises, and coordinates audits and investigations relating to FCC programs and operations. It coordinates and recommends policies for activities designed to promote economy, efficiency, and effectiveness, as well as to prevent and detect fraud and abuse in FCC programs.

(Area Code 202)
Inspector General: James Warwick 632-0471

COMMON CARRIER BUREAU (Room 500)

The Common Carrier Bureau regulates such entities as telephone and telegraph companies, domestic and international satellite operators, mobile communication companies, and microwave operators. This includes regulation of charges, rates of return, mergers, classifications, accounting methods and depreciation rates, construction, acquisition and operation of service facilities, and regulation and radio licensing of common carrier operations.

(Area Code 202)
Chief: Richard M. Firestone 632-6910
Legal Assistants:
Lawrence N. Boone 632-6910
Susan O'Connell 632-6910
Michael Wack 632-6910

Domestic Facilities Division
Chief: James R. Keegan 632-1860
Legal Assistant: Cassandra Thomas 634-1860

Mobile Services Division
Chief: Gregory J. Vogt 632-6400
Legal Branch Chief: Abraham A.Leib 632-6450

(Area Code 202)
Enforcement Division
Chief: Mary Beth Hess 632-4890
Formal Complaints and Investigations Branch Chief:
Gregory A. Weiss 632-4890
Informal Complaints and Public Inquiries Branch Chief:
Kathie A. Kneff 632-7553

Policy and Program Planning Division
Chief: James D. Schichting 632-9342
Special Counsel/Competitive Issues: vacant 632-9342

Tariff Division
Chief: John Cimko, Jr 632-6387
Legal Branch Chief: Ann Stevens 632-6917

MASS MEDIA BUREAU (Room 314)

The Mass Media Bureau licenses commercial and noncommercial radio and television broadcasting stations, direct broadcast satellites, and other electronic mass media. The Bureau is responsible for issuance of new licenses, license renewals, waiver of technical and other rules, compliance with operating standards, grants of construction permits, etc. The Bureau also has some regulatory responsibilities relating to cable television. It has its own hearing and investigative staffs.

(Area Code 202)
Chief: Roy J. Stewart 632-6460
Assistant Chief/Legal: Robert H. Ratcliff 632-6460

Audio Services Division
Chief: Larry Eads 632-6485
Assistant Chief: W. Jan Gay 632-6485
Assistant Chief: Stuart Bedell 632-6485
AM Branch Chief: Thomas N. Albers 254-9570
FM Branch Chief/Legal: Edwin Jorgensen 632-6908

Video Services Division
Chief: Barbara A. Kreisman 632-6993
Assistant Chief: Stephen Sewell 632-6993
Assistant Chief: James Brown 632-6993
Television Branch Chief: Clay Pendarvis 632-6357

(Area Code 202)
Low Power TV Branch/Legal: Mary Fitzgerald 632-3894
Cable TV Branch Chief: Ronald Parver 632-7480

Enforcement Division
Chief: Charles W. Kelley 632-6968
Complaints and Investigations Branch Chief:
Edythe Wise 632-3860
Fairness/Political Programming Branch Chief:
Milton O. Gross 632-7586
Hearing Branch Chief: Charles Dziedzic 632-6402

Policy and Rules Division
Legal Branch Chief:Marilyn Mohrman-Gillis 632-7792
Chief/Legal: Steve Bailey 632-5414

PRIVATE RADIO BUREAU (Room 5002)

2025 M Street, N.W., Washington, D.C., 20554

The Private Radio Bureau regulates special radio communication services. The Bureau licenses individuals, corporations, state and local governments, and other organizations to operate communications systems for their own use. Included are aviation, marine, amateur, industrial and public safety applications of radio.

(Area Code 202)
Chief: Ralph A. Haller 632-6940
Legal Assistant: Kent A. Nakamura 632-0278

Licensing Division: Gary Stanford, Chief ....(717) 337-1311

FIELD OPERATIONS BUREAU (Room 734)

The Field Operations Bureau monitors, inspects, and investigates radio and wire facilities for technical compliance with Federal statutes, Commission rules and international treaties.

(Area Code 202)

Chief: Richard M. Smith 632-6980
Attorney Advisor: Lawrence Clance 632-7591

Enforcement Division
Chief: W. Elliott Ours, Jr 632-7090
Investigations and Inspections Branch Chief: Dan Emrich 632-6345

(Area Code 202)

Management and Legal Assistance Branch Chief: Wayne McKee 632-7059

The Federal Communications Commission has regional offices in Atlanta, Boston, Chicago, Kansas City, MO, San Francisco, and Seattle, and various field offices throughout the United States. Any legal questions in the field are handled by the Attorney Advisor in Washington, D.C.

REVIEW BOARD (Room 230)

2000 L Street, N.W., Washington, D.C. 20554

The Review Board is a four-member board of senior FCC employees and serves as an appellate body to review decisions issued by Administrative Law Judges.

(Area Code 202)

Chairman: Joseph A. Marino 632-7180
Chief for Law: Allan Sacks 632-7180

(Area Code 202)

Deputy Chief for Law: Leland J. Blair 632-7180
Senior Attorney: Charles J. Iseman 632-7180

OFFICE OF ADMINISTRATIVE LAW JUDGES (Room 230)

The Administrative Law Judges hear and conduct all adjudicatory cases designated for evidentiary adjudicatory hearing other than those designated to be heard by the Commission en banc or by one or more members of the Commission and also conduct hearings as the Commission assign them. They exercise such authority as may be assigned by the Commission pursuant to Section 5(d) of the Communications Act as amended.

The decisions of the Administrative Law Judges are published in the FCC Record, which is cited below.

(Area Code 202)

Chief Judge: Joseph Stirmer 632-7680
Deputy Chief Judge: James F. Tierney 632-7215

(Area Code 202)

Administrative Officer: Mary Gosse 632-7682

For rules of procedures see 47 C.F.R. 1.23 (1989)

PUBLICATIONS OF INTEREST

The Daily Digest which lists FCC notices, releases, texts and decisions, is available to the public, on a first-come, first-served basis after 10:00 AM each day. Outside the D.C. area, the Daily Digest must be ordered by commercial distributors at a cost of between $25.00 and $44.00 per month. Two of these distributors are: Berry Best Services, Ltd., 1990 M Street, N.W., Suite 740, Washington, D.C. 20036. Tel: 202/293-4964; and, ITS, Inc., 2100 M. Street, N.W., Suite 240, Washington, D.C. 20037. Tel: 202/857-3800. A list of other distributors can be obtained from the FCC's Office of Public Affairs, 1919 M Street, N.W., Room 200, Washington, D.C. 20554. Tel: 202/632-5050.

FCC Rulemaking Reports provides full-text reporting of the rulemaking procedures of the FCC, plus editorial summaries and the latest rules and changes as they affect the day-to-day operations of private and broadcast radio, television, cable TV, telephone common carriers, cellular radios and manufacturers of equipment for all such businesses. This report is published in three volumes, and is updated every two weeks. Price: $715.00 annually. The report can be obtained from Commerce Clearinghouse, Inc, 4025 West Peterson Avenue, Chicago, IL 60646. Tel: 312/583-8500. Or, in Washington, D.C., call 202/626-2200.

The following publications can be purchased from the **U.S. Government Printing Office.** Stock numbers and prices for annual subscriptions are shown below. Submit requests for these publications to: The Superintendent of Documents, U.S. Government Printing Office, Washington, D.C. 20402. Tel: 202/783-3238.

FCC Record, a biweekly compilation, containing comprehensive information of FCC Decisions, Reports, Public Notices and other documents. Price: $220.00 a year domestic; $275.00 a year foreign; $21.00 a single copy. GPO Stock# 903-008-00000-8.

Manual of Regulations and Procedures for Federal Radio Frequency Management. 1989. Covers the regulation of Federal interstate and foreign telecommunications. Subscription service consists of a basic manual and supplementary material for an indeterminate period. Price: $72.00 domestic; $90.00 foreign. GPO Stock# 903-008-00000-8.

FEDERAL COMMUNICATIONS COMMISSION
KEY LEGAL AUTHORITIES

General Agency Regulations: 47 C.F.R. Parts 0-100 (1989).
Rules of Practice & Procedure: 47 C.F.R. Part 1 (1989).

Communications Act of 1934, as amended, 47 U.S.C. 151-609--created the Commission and established the system of regulation over interstate and international communications by wire and radio (since expanded to cover television and cable communications).
Legislative History: 1954 U.S. Code Cong. & Admin. News 2133; 1964 U.S. Code Cong. & Admin. News 2175 & 2238; 1978 U.S. Code Cong. & Admin. News 109; 1982 U.S. Code Cong. & Admin. News 2237; 1983 U.S. Code Cong. & Admin. News 2219; 1984 U.S. Code Cong. & Admin. News 4655.

Submarine Cable Landing Act, 47 U.S.C. 34-39--establishes licensing requirement for landing or operating submarine cables directly or indirectly connecting the U.S. with any foreign country or any portion of the U.S. with any other portion of the U.S.

Communications Satellite Act of 1962, 47 U.S.C. 701-744--established the Communications Satellite Corporation (ComSat) to represent the U.S. in the global satellite communications network and authorized the Federal Communications Commission to regulate the new entity.
Implementing Regulations: 47 C.F.R. 25.101 et seq. (1988).

FEDERAL DEPOSIT INSURANCE CORPORATION

550 17th Street, N.W.
Washington, D.C. 20429

DESCRIPTION: The Federal Deposit Insurance Corporation (FDIC) is an independent agency which insures deposits in more than 14,000 commercial banks, mutual savings banks, and industrial banks. It is also the primary Federal supervisory authority for insured state-chartered banks that are not members of the Federal Reserve System. When an insured bank fails, the FDIC is usually appointed receiver, liquidates its assets, and winds up its affairs. The FDIC provides assistance to troubled banks by providing financial assistance for mergers with sound banks, by purchasing assets of troubled banks, and by making guarantees against certain losses.

(Area Code 202)

Chairman of the Board of Directors: L. William Seidman 898-6974
Procurement Information 898-3655
Public Information 898-6996
Publications Information 898-6996
Consumer Hot Line:
Washington, D.C. Metro Area 898-3536
Outside Washington, D.C. Metro Area ....(800) 424-5488
Facsimile...347-2773

Freedom of Information Act/Privacy Act Office 898-3813
There is a copying charge of 10 cents per page for FOIA requests. There is also a search and review charge which can range from $7.50 per hour to $14.50 per hour. These prices can vary depending on the type of request. The charge for Privacy Act requests is identical to the charge for FOIA requests.

(Area Code 202)

Library/Law Library (Room 4060) 898-3631
The library is open to the public from 8:30 AM until 5:15 PM on Tuesdays, Wednesdays, and Thursdays by appointment. Material cannot be checked out from this library but the library does have a copying machine.

OFFICE OF THE GENERAL COUNSEL - LEGAL DIVISION (Room 3028)

(Area Code 202)

General Counsel: Alfred J.T. Byrne 898-3680
Facsimile 898-7394

The Legal Division is organized into four branches:

The **Supervision and Legislation Branch** is responsible for providing legal support in the development of legislation and the supervision of FDIC-insured thrifts and banks. The Branch is separated into three sections:

* The **Bank Regulation and Legislation Section** provides legal advice and expertise on the laws and regulations that govern the activities, operations, and structure of open banks and savings associations. This section develops, drafts, and researches the legal authority for FDIC regulations.

* The **Compliance and Enforcement Section** provides advice on whether banks regulated by the FDIC are violating the Federal Deposit Insurance Act and other laws and regulations. In addition, the Section conducts administrative and investigatory actions to ensure compliance with Federal and state banking laws.

* The **Assisted Acquisitions and Transactions Section** is responsible for all legal aspects of assistance transactions under Section 13 of the FDI Act and various other financial transactions involving the Corporation, such as the sale of securities obtained by the Corporation in an assistance transaction.

(Area Code 202)

Deputy General Counsel: Douglas Jones 898-3700
Associate General Counsel Compliance and Enforcement Section: Arthur L. Beamon 898-3707
Assistant General Counsel Bank Regulation and Legislation Section: Roger A. Hood 898-3681
Assistant General Counsel Assisted Acquisitions and Transactions Section: Ross S. Delston 898-3714

The **Litigation Branch** is responsible for litigation matters handled from Washington rather than field locations. The branch's other major area of responsibility relates to claims involving improper conduct of professionals such as directors, officers, attorneys, accountants, and appraisers. The Litigation Branch is composed of three sections:

* The **Trial Litigation Section** is primarily responsible for litigation arising from bank regulations and legislation. FDIC compliance and enforcement efforts, assisted bank transactions and acquisitions, challenges to FDIC statutory and regulatory authority, and challenges to the resolution of major bank or saving and loan holding company system financial problems.

* The **Appellate Litigation Section** is responsible for handling and overseeing all appellate litigation matters in various state and Federal courts of appeal and the United States Supreme Court.

* The **Professional Liability Section** investigates and prosecutes claims arising from improper conduct of directors, officers, appraisers, accountants, and other professionals.

(Area Code 202)

Deputy General Counsel: Mark I. Rosen 898-3795
Associate General Counsel Trial Litigation and Appellate Sections: Dorothy Nichols 898-3791
Associate General Counsel Directors and Offers Liability Section: John V. Thomas 898-7275
Assistant General Counsel Trial Litigation Section: Thomas Schultz 898-7267
Assistant General Counsel Appellate Section: Ann DuRoss 898-3704
Assistant General Counsel Professional Liability
Non-RTC Section:
Cecil Underwood 898-3766
Anne Sobol 906-6204
RTC Section: John Beaty 416-7003

FEDERAL DEPOSIT INSURANCE CORPORATION

The **Financial Institutions Operations and Liquidation Branch,** comprised of five sections, is responsible for legal operations at all FDIC regional offices and field sites that support either RTC or FDIC or old FSLIC matters.

* The **Special Projects Section** identifies legal issues of overriding liquidation duties, provides legal coordination and advice on these matters to the other sections in the Financial Institutions Operations and Liquidations Branch and to DOS, DOL, RTC and DFO. This section is also responsible for the Legal Division's computerized Case Management System.

* The **Operations & Liquidations (Banks/Thrifts) Section** develops and coordinates all legal procedures through which the FCDIC discharges its obligation to liquidate the assets of insolvent insured banks and to liquidate assets from pre-January 1989 FSLIC receiverships and open assistance transactions involving savings associations.

* The **Thrift Agreement Administrative and Oversight Section** performs a broad range of legal work relating to the Corporation's administration and oversight of assistance agreements entered into by the FSLIC prior to the enactment of FIRREA to prevent the default of failing savings associations.

The section's work includes interpreting the provisions of assistance agreements and providing legal review of the initiation and settlement of litigation or claims for which the corporation is indemnifying an acquirer and of the reports submitted by an acquirer pursuant to such agreements.

* The **Operations and Liquidations Section (Resolution Trust Corporation [RTC])** develops and coordinates all legal policies and issues relating to the Resolution Trust Corporation's discharge of its duties as conservator or receiver of insolvent thrifts. This section maintains consistency and provides legal policy for transactions such as purchase and assumption agreements.

* The **Bankruptcy Section** provides Bankruptcy support to DOS, RTC, DOL and DFO. It continues to provide bankruptcy advice to the rest of the Legal Division and other Divisions here in Washington, D.C. and provides training to DOS examiners.

(Area Code 202)

Deputy General Counsel: Thomas A. Rose 416-7573
Associate General Counsel Operations & Liquidations (Banks/Thrifts) Section: Carroll Shifflett 416-7570
Associate General Counsel Operations & Liquidations (RTC): Rex Veal 416-7565
Assistant General Counsel Special Projects Section: James T. Lantelme 416-7064
Assistant General Counsel Thrift Agreement Administrative and Oversight Section: Henry Griffin 416-7052
Assistant General Counsel Bankruptcy Section: Vivian Comer 416-7571

The **Operations Branch** is responsible for administration of the division, including personnel, training and office automation matters; corporate affairs; and coordination of criminal restitution and conflicts between problem institutions. It is divided into three sections.

* The **Corporate Affairs Section** is responsible for providing legal advice on corporate and administrative matters and represents the corporation in administrative proceedings related to EEO complaints, adverse actions, labor relations matters and grievances.

* The **Conflicts and Criminal Restitution Section** spearheads the effort to assist the Justice Department in the investigation and prosecution of criminal conduct in the banking and savings and loan industries. It acts as a national resource for training and materials and has jurisdiction over Congressional inquiries, delegations, a Legal Divison brief bank and other legal issues.

* The **Administration Section** is responsible for planning for all budget and accounting, procurement, human resource development and utilization, information resource management, space and facilities management, and other administrative and management support functions.

(Area Code 202)

Deputy General Counsel: Jack Smith 898-3706
Assistant General Counsel Corporate Affairs Section: Jerry L. Langley 898-3687
Assistant General Counsel Conflict and Criminal Restitution Section: Howard Feinstein 416-7028

OFFICE OF INSPECTOR GENERAL (Room 380)

The Office of Inspector General (OIG) is responsible for conducting, supervising, and coordinating audits, investigations, and other activities designed to promote economy and efficiency and to prevent and detect fraud and abuse in corporate and receivership programs and operations. The Inspector General is appointed by the Chairman of the Board of Directors. In response to the Financial Institutions Reform, Recovery, and Enforcement Act of 1989 appropriate responsibilities of the Inspector General of the former Federal Home Loan Bank Board were incorporated into the FDIC OIG. Besides Headquarters, the OIG has offices within several major liquidation locations.

(Area Code 202)

Inspector General: Robert D. Hoffman 898-6557
Deputy Inspector General: James A. Renick 898-6500

(Area Code 202)

Counsel to Inspector General: Laurence A. Froehlich ...898-6560
Facsimile 898-6552

OFFICE OF THE EXECUTIVE SECRETARY (Room 400)

(Area Code 202)

Ethics Counselor: Kathy Corigliano 898-7272

LIQUIDATION DIVISION (Room 856)

(Area Code 202)

Director: Steven Seelig 898-7371

SUPERVISION DIVISION (Room 6130)

(Area Code 202)

Director: Paul G. Fritts 898-6946

OFFICE OF LEGISLATIVE AFFAIRS (Room 6064)

(Area Code 202)

Legislative Attorneys/Advisors:

Roberta McInerney 898-6991

Scott Baker 898-6988

REGIONAL OFFICES

The FDIC Legal Division's regional offices are as follows: Division of Liquidation offices in Chicago; Dallas; Kansas City, MO; New York; and San Francisco. Division of Supervision offices in Atlanta; Needham, MA; Chicago; Dallas; Kansas City, MO; Memphis; New York; and San Francisco. Division Liquidation/Resolution Trust Corporation (RTC) offices in Atlanta; Kansas City, Mo; Dallas; and Boston.

Division of Liquidation

Chicago
Regional Counsel: Pamela Shea
Federal Deposit Insurance Corporation, 30 South Wacker Dr., 33rd Floor, Chicago, IL 60606. Tel: 312/207-0495.

Dallas
Regional Counsel: Donald B. McKinley
Federal Deposit Insurance Corporation, 1910 Pacific Avenue, 12th Floor, Dallas, TX 75201. Tel: 214/220-3300.

New York
Regional Counsel: Rae Nathan
Federal Deposit Insurance Corporation, 452 Fifth Avenue, 15th Floor, New York, NY 10018. Tel: 212/704-1200.

San Francisco
Regional Counsel: John J. Sullivan
Federal Deposit Insurance Corporation, 25 Ecker Street, Suite 1400, San Francisco, CA 94105. Tel: 415/546-1810.

Division of Supervision

Atlanta
Regional Counsel: John Rubin
Federal Deposit Insurance Corporation, Maquis One Tower, 245 Peachtree Center Ave., Suite 1200, Atlanta, GA 30303. Tel: 404/522-1145.

Chicago
Regional Counsel: William M. Lloyd
Federal Deposit Insurance Corporation, 30 South Wacker Dr., 33rd Floor, Chicago, IL 60606. Tel: 312/207-0495.

Dallas
Regional Counsel: Judith K. Sinclair
Federal Deposit Insurance Corporation, 1910 Pacific Avenue, 12th Floor, Suite 1900, Dallas, TX 75201. Tel: 214/220-3400.

Kansas City, MO
Regional Counsel: Gerald F. Lamberti
Federal Deposit Insurance Corporation, 2345 Grand Avenue, 12th Floor, Kansas City, MO 64108. Tel: 816/234-8000.

Memphis
Regional Counsel: Phillip H. Schwartz
Federal Deposit Insurance Corporation, 5100 Poplar Avenue, Suite 1900, Memphis, TN 38137. Tel: 901/685-1603.

Needham
Regional Counsel: Thomas W. Lawless, Jr.
Federal Deposit Insurance Corporation, 160 Gould Street, Needham, MA 02194. Tel: 617/449-9080.

New York
Regional Counsel: Sheldon J. Reisman
Federal Deposit Insurance Corporation, 452 Fifth Avenue, 15th Floor, New York, NY 10018. Tel: 212/704-1200.

San Francisco
Regional Counsel: vacant
Federal Deposit Insurance Corporation, 25 Ecker Street, Suite 2300, San Francisco, CA 94105. Tel: 415/546-0160.

Resolution Trust Corporation (RTC)

Atlanta
Regional Counsel: Ross P. Kendall
Resolution Trust Corporation, 245 Peachtree Tower Center Avenue NE, Suite 1400, Atlanta, GA 30303. Tel: 404/52-1145.

Dallas
Regional Counsel: Arturo Vera Rojas
Resolution Trust Corporation, 300 N. Ervay Tower I, 17th Floor, Dallas, TX 75201. Tel: 214/953-2358.

Denver
Regional Counsel: Richard T. Aboussie
Resolution Trust Corporation, 1515 Arapahoe Street Tower III, Suite 600, Denver, CO 80202. Tel: 303/820-4242.

Kansas City, MO
Regional Counsel: E. Glion Curtis
Resolution Trust Corporation, 2345 Grand Avenue, 12th Floor, Kansas City, MO 64108. Tel: 816/234-8000.

CONSOLIDATED FIELD OFFICES:

Division of Liquidation (Banks/Thrifts)

Anchorage
Managing Attorney: vacant
Federal Deposit Insurance Corporation, 440 East 36th, Anchorage, AK 99503. Tel: 907/261-7400.

Bossier City
Managing Attorney: Jean Ray
Federal Deposit Insurance Corporation, 1325 Barksdale Blvd., Bossier City, LA 71171. Tel: 318/742-3290.

FEDERAL DEPOSIT INSURANCE CORPORATION

Dallas
Managing Attorney: David Jackson
Federal Deposit Insurance Corporation, 14651 Dallas Parkway, 2d Floor, Dallas, TX 75380. Tel: 214/239-3317.
Managing Attorney: Sharon Davis
Federal Deposit Insurance Corporation, 5080 Spectrum Drive, Suite 400, Dallas, TX 75248. Tel: 214/701-5404.

Denver
Managing Attorney: Jack Karford
Federal Deposit Insurance Corporation, 1125 17th Street, Suite 700, Denver CO 80202. Tel: 303/296-4703 ext. 620.

Houston
Managing Attorney: Rhea Sanderson
Federal Deposit Insurance Corporation, 7324 South West Freeway, Suite 1600, Arena Tower 2, Houston, TX 77074. Tel: 713/270-6565 ext. 670.

Irvine
Managing Attorney: Debra Meyers
Federal Deposit Insurance Corporation, 3347 Michelson Dr., Suite 100, Irvine, CA 92715. Tel: 714/975-7211.

Knoxville
Managing Attorney: David Tranum
Federal Deposit Insurance Corporation, 800 South Gay Street, Knoxville, TN 37901. Tel: 615/544-4501.

Midland
Managing Attorney: vacant
Federal Deposit Insurance Corporation, North Petroleum Bldg, 303 Air Park Drive, Midland, TX 79705. Tel: 915/685-6400.

Monmouth Station, NJ
Managing Attorney: Louis Di Piertro
Federal Deposit Insurance Corporation, 1100 Cornwall Road, Monmouth Junction, NJ 08852. Tel: 212/704-1477.

New York
Managing Attorney: Richard Printz
Federal Deposit Insurance Corporation, 452 5th Avenue, 21st Floor, New York, NY 10018. Tel: 212/704-1200.

Oklahoma City
Managing Attorney: Robert Bracken
Federal Deposit Insurance Corporation, 777 North West Grand Blvd., Suite 400, Oklahoma City, OK 73118. Tel: 405/848-3342.

Orlando
Managing Attorney: Gina Micalizio
Federal Deposit Insurance Corporation, 5778 South Semoran Blvd., Orlando, FL 32812. Tel: 407/273-2230.

Puerto Rico
Managing Attorney: Nancy Pujals
Federal Deposit Insurance Corporation, 1607 Ponce de Leon Avenue, Cobian Plaza Bldg., Upper Mall 17, Santurce, PR 00909. Tel: 809/724-1740.

San Antonio
Managing Attorney: John Creighton
Federal Deposit Insurance Corporation, 1777 NE Loop 410, Suite 1001, San Antonio, TX 78217. Tel: 512/737-3100 ext. 226.

San Jose
Managing Attorneys: Miriam S. Aguiar
Federal Deposit Insurance Corporation, 2870 Zanker Rd., Suite 200, San Jose, CA 95134. Tel: 408/434-0640 ext. 318.

Westmont
Managing Attorney: Robert Kern
Federal Deposit Insurance Corporation, 900 Oakmont Lane, 3d Floor, Westmont, IL 60559. Tel: 312/789-0300 ext.4000.

Division of Liquidation (Resolution Trust Corporation [RTC])

Atlanta
Managing Attorney: Sally Ridenour
Resolution Trust Corporation, Marquis One Tower, Suite 900, 245 Peachtree Center Avenue, Atlanta, GA 30003. Tel: 404/225-5681.

Baton Rouge
Managing Attorney: E. Robert Belluomini
Resolution Trust Corporation, 8225 Florida Blvd, Baton Rouge, LA 70806. Tel: 505/927-5380.

Burnsville, MN
Managing Attorney: David A. Yonke
Resolution Trust Corporation, 501 East Highway 13, Burnsville, MN 55337. Tel: 612/894-0800.

Dallas
Managing Attorney: vacant
Resolution Trust Corporation, 300 North Ervay Tower I, Suite 23, Dallas, TX. 75201. Tel: 214/220-3300.

Houston
Managing Attorney: Charles Barbera
Resolution Trust Corporation, 10000 Memorial Drive, Suite 210, Houston, TX 77024. Tel: 713/683-4924.

Irvine
Managing Attorney: Neil Van Winkle
Resolution Trust Corporation, 1901 Newport Blvd., Irvine, CA 92627. Tel: 714/975-7211.

Kansas City, MO
Managing Attorney: David Swiff
Resolution Trust Corporation, 2345 Grand Avenue, Suite 1500, Kansas City, MO 64108. Tel: 816/531-2212.

Phoenix
Managing Attorney: James M. Barker
Resolution Trust Corporation, Western Savings & Loan, 6001 North 24th Street, Phoenix, AZ 85016. Tel: 602/468-5674.

Rolling Meadows, IL
Managing Attorney: Anna Lynn Simon
Resolution Trust Corporation, 2100 East Golf Road, West Bldg., Suite 300, Rolling Meadows, IL 60008. Tel: 708/806-7750.

San Antonio
Managing Attorney: Sam E. Taylor
Resolution Trust Corporation, 1777 NE Loop 410, Suite 1001, San Antonio, TX 78217. Tel: 512/820-8165.

Tampa
Managing Attorney: Mary Riche
Resolution Trust Corporation, 221 Madison Street, Tampa, FL 33602. Tel: 813/870-5356.

PUBLICATIONS OF INTEREST

Merger Decisions contains approval and denial decisions of bank absorptions. It can be obtained from the Corporate Communications Office, Federal Deposit Insurance Corporation, 550 17th St. NW, Washington, DC 20429. Tel: 202/898-6996. The first copy is free of charge and subsequent copies are $2.00 each.

FDIC Law, Regulations and Related Acts is presented in loose-leaf format in three volumes and includes the FDI Act, regulations and miscellaneous statutes that affect the operations of insured banks and the FDIC. Report bulletins issued at monthly or bi-monthly intervals reflect the text of statutory or regulatory changes that may have occurred and summarize congressional and Federal agency actions.

This three volume set is available by subscription for $175 which includes report bulletins through the end of the year. For information on ordering contact the Corporate Communications Office, Federal Deposit Insurance Corporation, 550 17th Street, N.W., Washington, D.C. 20429. Tel: 202/898-6996.

OVERSIGHT BOARD/Resolution Trust Corporation
1777 F Street, N.W.
Washington, D.C. 20232

DESCRIPTION: The Oversight Board, established by the Financial Institutions Reform, Recovery and Enforcement Act of 1989 (FIRREA), formulates the policy, approves the funding, and provides the general oversight of the Resolution Trust Corporation (RTC). The Oversight Board has established one national and six regional advisory boards to advise it and the RTC on policies and programs for the disposition of real property assets of the nation's failed thrifts. The national board is headquartered in Washington, D.C. and the regional advisory boards are headquartered in New York, Atlanta, Kansas City, MO, Dallas, Denver, and Los Angeles.

(Area Code 202)
Oversight Board President and CEO: Peter Monroe 786-9661
General Counsel: Michael Jungman 786-9666
Deputy General Counsel: Larry Hayes 786-9681

(Area Code 202)
Public Affairs 786-9672
Facsimile 786-9717

RESOLUTION TRUST CORPORATION
801 Seventeenth Street, N.W.
Washington, D.C. 20552

DESCRIPTION: The Resolution Trust Corporation (RTC) is charged with the responsibility for resolving insolvent thrifts and disposing of their assets.

(Area Code 202)
Chairman: L. William Seidman 898-6974

(Area Code 202)
Facsimile 393-5168

OFFICE OF INSPECTOR GENERAL (Room 726)

The Office of Inspector General is responsible for all audits and investigations within RTC. The Office gives technical assistance to RTC staff, analyzes programs, and reviews proposed regulations in order to prevent and detect fraud, waste, and abuse within RTC.

(Area Code 202)
Inspector General: John J. Adair 416-7428

OFFICE OF THE EXECUTIVE DIRECTOR (Room 820)

(Area Code 202)
Executive Director: David C. Cooke 416-7560
RTC Special Counsel: Rex Veal 416-7565

(Area Code 202)
Corporate Communications: 416-7566

FIELD OFFICES

The RTC has four regional offices in Atlanta, Kansas City, MO, Dallas, and Denver which report directly to the Executive Director and oversee Savings and Loan sales, asset sales and contracting operations. The RTC also has 14 consolidated field offices under the direction of the regional offices.

East Region (Atlanta)

Director: William M. Dudley
Resolution Trust Corporation, Marquis One Tower, Suite 1100, 245 Peachtree Center Avenue, NE, Atlanta, GA 30303.
Tel: 404/522-1145; 800/234-3342.

Bayou Consolidated Field Office (Baton Rouge)
Acting Director: James R. Hambric, III (Acting)
Resolution Trust Corporation, 10725 Perkins Road, Baton Rouge, LA 70810. Tel: 504/769-8860.
(Jurisdiction: LA, MI)

Northeast Consolidated Office (Red Hill, PA)
Director: Stephen W. Wood
Resolution Trust Corporation, East Sixth Street, Red Hill, PA 18076. Tel: 215/679-9515.
(Jurisdiction: CT, DE, MA, MD, ME, NH, NJ, NY, OH, PA, RI, VT)

Southeast Consolidated Office (Tampa)
Acting Director: Jimmy R. Caldwell
Resolution Trust Corporation, Freedom Savings & Loan Association, 220 E. Madison Street, Suite 302, Tampa, FL 33602. Tel: 813/870-5000
(Jurisdiction: FL)

Mid-Atlantic Consolidated Office (Atlanta)
Director: William C. Thomas
Resolution Trust Corporation, Colony Square, Building 400, Suite 900, Atlanta GA 30361. Tel: 404/881-4840; 800/628-4362.
(Jurisdiction: AL, DC, GA, KY, NC, SC, TN, VA, WV)

Central Region (Kansas City, MO)

Director: Michael J. Martinelli
Resolution Trust Corporation, Board of Trade Building II, 4900 Main Street, Kansas City, MO 64112. Tel: 816/531-2212; 800/365-3342.

Mid-Central Consolidated Office (Kansas City, MO)
Director: Dennis Cavinaw
Resolution Trust Corporation, Board of Trade Building II, 4900 Main Street, Kansas City, MO 64112. Tel: 816/531-2212; 800/365-3342.
(Jurisdiction: AK, KS, MO)

Lake Central Consolidated Office (Rolling Meadows, IL)
Director: Joseph Minitti
Resolution Trust Corporation, 2100 East Gold Road, West Building, Suite 300, Rolling Meadows, IL 60008.
Tel: 708/806-7750; 800/526-7521.
(Jurisdiction: IL, IN, MI)

North Central Consolidated Office (Burnsville, MN)
Director: Donaldson Wickens
Resolution Trust Corporation, 501 East Highway 13, Burnsville, MN 55337. Tel: 612/894-0800; 1-800/338-8098.
Note: This office will be moving to Egan, MN in Fall, 1990.
(Jurisdiction: IA, MN, ND, NE, SD, WI)

Southwest Region (Dallas)

Director: Carmen J. Sullivan
Resolution Trust Corporation, 300 N. Ervay, 23rd Floor, Dallas, TX. 75201. Tel: 214/953-2300.

Metroplex Consolidated Office (Dallas)
Director: Jim Messec
Resolution Trust Corporation, 300 N. Ervay, 22nd Floor, Dallas, TX 75201. Tel: 214/953-2300.
(Jurisdiction: Northeast TX)

Gulf Coast Consolidated Office (Houston)
Acting Director: Timothy Putman
Resolution Trust Corporation, 10000 Memorial Drive, Houston, TX 77024. Tel: 713/683-3476.
(Jurisdiction: Southeast TX)

Southern Consolidated Office (San Antonio)
Acting Director: James Forrestal
Resolution Trust Corporation, Bexar Savings Association, 1777 NE Loop 410, San Antonio, TX 78217. Tel: 512/820-8164.
(Jurisdiction: West TX)

Northern Consolidated Office (Tulsa)
Director: Virginia Kingsley
Resolution Trust Corporation, 4606 S. Garnett, Tulsa, OK 74146. Tel: 918/627-9000.
(Jurisdiction: OK)

West Region (Denver)

Director: Anthony Scalzi
Resolution Trust Corporation, 1515 Arapahoe Street, Tower 3, Suite 800, Denver, CO 80202. Tel: 303/556-6500.

Central Western Consolidated Office (Phoenix)
Acting Director: Virginia Juedes
Resolution Trust Corporation, 2910 N. 44th Street, Phoenix, AZ 85018. Tel: 602/224-1100.
(Jurisdiction: AZ, NE)

Coastal Consolidated Office (Costa Mesa)
Acting Director: James G. Klingensmith
Resolution Trust Corporation, 1901 Newport Blvd., 3d Floor, East Wing, Costa Mesa, CA 92627. Tel: 714/631-8380 ext.4239.
(Jurisdiction: AL, CA, HI, OR, WA, Guam)

Intermountain Consolidated Office (Denver)
Director: Keith Carson
Resolution Trust Corporation, 1515 Arapahoe Street, Tower 3, Suite 800, Denver, CO 80202. Tel: 303/556-6500.
(Jurisdiction: CO, ID, MT, MN, UT, WY)

FEDERAL DEPOSIT INSURANCE CORPORATION
KEY LEGAL AUTHORITIES

General Regulations: 12 C.F.R. Part 300 et seq. (1989).

Financial Institutions Reform, Recovery, & Enforcement Act of 1989, 12 U.S.C. 1441a et seq.--directs the Federal Deposit Insurance Corporation to be the "exclusive manager" of the Resolution Trust Corporation and to administer the Bank Insurance Fund and the Savings Association Insurance Fund.
Legislative History: 1989 U.S. Code Cong. & Admin. News 86.

Federal Deposit Insurance Act, as amended, 12 U.S.C. 1811 et seq.--created the Federal Deposit Insurance Corporation to insure deposits of all eligible banks and savings associations.
Legislative History: 1950 U.S. Code Cong. Service 3765; 1989 U.S. Code Cong. & Admin. News 86.

Change in Bank Control Act of 1978, 12 U.S.C. 1817(j)--requires 60 days' notice to the appropriate Federal banking agency, and agency approval of any acquisition of control over an insured depository institution.
Legislative History: 1978 U.S. Code Cong. & Admin. News 1421 & 9273.
Implementing Regulations: 12 C.F.R. 5.50 (1990).

Depository Institution Management Interlocks Act, as amended, 12 U.S.C. 3201 et seq.--designed to foster competition by prohibiting a management official of a depository institution or holding company from also serving as a management official of another such entity if the two organizations are: (1) not affiliated, and (2) very large or located in the same area.

Legislative History: 1978 U.S. Code Cong. & Admin. News 9273; 1983 U.S. Code Cong. & Admin. News 1768; 1988 U.S. Code Cong. & Admin. News 3054; 1989 U.S. Code Cong. & Admin. News 86.
Implementing Regulations: 12 C.F.R. Part 26 (1990).

Home Mortgage Disclosure Act of 1975, as amended, 12 U.S.C. 2801 et seq.--provides the public with loan data to determine whether depository institutions are serving the housing needs of the communities in which they are located.
Legislative History: 1975 U.S. Code Cong. & Admin. News 2303.
Implementing Regulations: 12 C.F.R. Part 203 (1990).

Truth in Lending Act of 1968, as amended, 15 U.S.C. 1601 et seq.--promotes the informed use of consumer credit by requiring disclosures about its terms and costs; gives consumers the right to cancel certain credit transactions that involve a lien on a consumer's principal dwelling.
Legislative History: 1968 U.S. Code Cong. & Admin. News 1962; 1981 U.S. Code Cong. & Admin. News 74; 1982 U.S. Code Cong. & Admin. News 3054.
Implementing Regulations: 12 C.F.R. Part 226 (1990).

Equal Credit Opportunity Act of 1974, as amended, 15 U.S.C. 1691 et seq.--promotes the availability of credit to all credit worthy applicants without regard to race, color, religion, national origin, sex, marital status, or age.
Legislative History: 1974 U.S. Code Cong. & Admin. News 6119. 1976 U.S. Code Cong. & Admin. News 403.
Implementing Regulations: 12 C.F.R. Part 202 (1990).

International Lending Supervision Act of 1983, as amended, 12 U.S.C. 3901 et seq.--strengthens the bank regulatory process to insure closer supervision of international loans and authorizes Federal bank regulatory agencies to require banking institutions to maintain special reserves whenever the quality of their foreign loans deteriorates.
Legislative History: 1983 U.S. Code Cong. & Admin. News 1768.
Implementing Regulations: 13 C.F.R. Parts 3 & 20 (1990).

International Banking Act of 1978, as amended, 12 U.S.C. 3101 et seq.--sets out rules governing the international and foreign activities of U.S. banking organizations.
Legislative History: 1978 U.S. Code Cong. & Admin. News 1421.
Implementation Regulations: 12 C.F.R. Part 211 (1990).

Currency & Foreign Transactions Reporting Act, as amended, 31 U.S.C. 5311-5326--designed to combat money laundering by requiring U.S. financial agencies to report certain transactions to the Government.
Legislative History: 1984 U.S. Code Cong. & Admin. News 3182; 1988 U.S. Code Cong. & Admin. News 5937.
Implementing Regulations: 31 C.F.R. Part 103 (1989).

Garn-St. Germain Depository Institutions Act of 1982, as amended, 12 U.S.C. 216 et seq.--provides guidelines for the Federal financial supervisory agencies, including the Department of the Treasury's Office of the Comptroller of the Currency and Office of Thrift Supervision to deal with financially distressed depository institutions.
Legislative History: 1982 U.S. Code Cong. & Admin. News 3054.
Implementing Regulations: 12 C.F.R. Part 33 (1990).

Financial Institutions Regulatory and Interest Rate Control Act of 1978, as amended, 12 U.S.C. 375 et seq.--governs any extension of credit by a member bank, a bank holding company of which the member bank is a subsidiary and any other subsidiary of that bank holding company; implements the reporting requirements concerning extension of credit by a member bank to its executive officers.
Legislative History: 1978 U.S. Code Cong. & Admin. News 9273; 1982 U.S. Code Cong. & Admin. News 3054.
Implementing Regulations: 12 C.F.R. Part 215 (1990).

Depository Institutions Deregulation and Monetary Control Act of 1980, as amended, 12 U.S.C. various sections--authorizes the automatic transfer of funds and negotiable order of withdrawal (NOW) accounts at depository institutions; also authorizes Federally-chartered savings and loan associations to establish remote service units.
Legislative History: 1980 U.S. Code Cong. & Admin. News 236.
Implementing Regulations: 12 C.F.R. Part 204 (1990).

Bank Secrecy Act of 1970, as amended, 12 U.S.C. 1951 et seq.--requires financial recordkeeping and reporting of currency and foreign transactions by banks and businesses where such records would have a high degree of usefulness in criminal, tax or regulatory investigations or proceedings.
Legislative History: 1970 U.S. Code Cong. & Admin. News 4394.
Implementing Regulations: 12 C.F.R. Part 21 (1989)[customs enforcement]; 31 C.F.R. Part 103 (1989)[Comptroller of the Currency].

FEDERAL ELECTION COMMISSION

999 E Street, N.W.
Washington, D.C. 20463

DESCRIPTION: The Federal Election Commission (FEC) is an independent regulatory agency which administers and enforces the provisions of the Federal Election Campaign Act of 1971, as amended, which deals with the financing of Federal election campaigns. The law affects candidates for the U.S. House of Representatives, the U.S. Senate, and the Presidency, and the political committees which support them. The Act provides for: disclosure of the sources and uses of funds for Federal elections; limits on contributions; and public financing of Presidential elections.

(Area Code 202)

Chairman: Lee Ann Elliott 376-5114
Procurement Information 376-5270
Information Services:
  Washington, D.C. Metro area 376-3120
  Outside Washington, D.C. Metro area ....(800) 424-9530
Freedom of Information Act Office 376-3155
Reports Analysis Division 376-2480
Public Disclosure Division 376-3140
Facsimile 376-5280

(Area Code 202)

Law Library (Room 801) 376-5312
The library is open to the public Monday through Friday from 9:00 AM until 4:00 PM. A photo ID is required for access to the main building. Materials may only be checked out through an interlibrary loan system. Copying machines are available. The first 25 pages are free of charge. Additional pages are 5 cents each.

THE COMMISSION

(Area Code 202)

Chairman: Lee Ann Elliott 376-5114
  Executive Assistant: Craig M. Engle 376-5114
Vice Chairman: John W. McGarry 376-5104
  Executive Assistant: Anne L. Head 376-5104
Commissioner: Joan D. Aikens 376-5110
  Executive Assistant: Anton E. Reel III 376-5110
Commissioner: Thomas J. Josefiak 376-5100
  Executive Assistant: Robert A. Dahl 376-5100
Commissioner: Danny Lee McDonald 376-5122
  Executive Assistant: Frances H. Glendening 376-5122
Commissioner: Scott E. Thomas 376-5118
  Executive Assistant: Jeffrey H. Bowman 376-5118

OFFICE OF GENERAL COUNSEL (Room 657)

The Office of the General Counsel directs the FEC's enforcement activities and represents the Commission in any legal actions brought against it. The Office of the General Counsel handles all civil litigation, including several cases which have come before the U.S. Supreme Court. Attorneys in the office conduct legal research; draft regulations and advisory opinions, as well as other legal memoranda interpreting the Federal Election Campaign Act; receive and analyze complaints alleging violations of the Act; and participate in litigation.

The FEC has exclusive jurisdiction over civil enforcement of the Federal Election Campaign Act (FECA) and the Public Financing statutes found in Chapters 95 and 96 of the Internal Revenue Code. Unlike other Government agencies which must look to the Department of Justice for representation in court, the FEC has been given responsibility for litigating its cases at all levels.

(Area Code 202)

General Counsel: Lawrence M. Noble 376-5690
Deputy General Counsel: (vacant) 376-5690
Docket Section Chief: Retha L. Dixon 376-3110

The Office of General Counsel is divided into four functional areas: Enforcement; Litigation; Policy; and Title 26 and Ethics:

Enforcement Area: Enforcement is the largest single function of the OGC. The Associate General Counsel for Enforcement oversees the work of four enforcement teams which shoulder substantial responsibility for the prosecution of the cases assigned to them. The FEC is primarily an investigative agency and settles most cases by negotiation and conciliation rather than through litigation. Accordingly, Commission attorneys negotiate the resolution of their cases directly with counsel for respondents.

(Area Code 202)

Associate General Counsel: Lois G. Lerner 376-8200

Assistant General Counsel for: (Area Code 202)
  Team No 1: George F. Rishel 376-5690
  Team No 2: Jonathan A. Bernstein 376-5690
  Team No 3: Robert W. Bonham III 376-5690
  Team No 4: Lisa E. Klein 376-5690

Litigation Area: Due to the requirement for independence, the FEC is not a client agency of the Department of Justice and is not represented by the Department in legal proceedings. Consequently, the Office of General Counsel is responsible for offensive and defensive litigation involving the FEC in the U.S. District Courts, the U.S. Courts of Appeals, and the U.S. Supreme Court. The Associate General Counsel directly supervises the work of the Appellate Litigation Team. The District Court Litigation Team is headed by an Assistant General Counsel who reports to the Associate General Counsel for Litigation.

The Commission brings enforcement suits in the U.S. District Courts when matters are not satisfactorily resolved through the administrative enforcement process. Defensive litigation involves suits contesting Commission dismissals of administrative complaints filed under the administrative enforcement process; petitions for review of Commission decisions in administration of the Presidential public funding program; an civil suits challenging the constitutionality of FECA provisions.

(Area Code 202)
Associate General Counsel: Richard B. Bader 376-8200
Assistant General Counsel for:
Appellate Court Litigation: (vacant) 376-8200
District Court Litigation: David Fitzgerald 376-8200

Policy Area: Attorneys assigned to the Policy Area issue advisory opinions (Advisory Opinions Team), draft new and revised regulations dealing primarily with campaign finance issues (Regulations Team), and provide the Agency with legal support in those areas which do not directly involve the FECA (Legal Review/Administrative Law Team). For example, attorneys working on Administrative Law issues advise the agency's Freedom of Information Act Officer, its Contracting Officer, and its Personnel Officer. They also provide advice on the Sunshine Act and the Privacy Act, and provide legal support to the agency's Inspector General.

(Area Code 202)
Associate General Counsel: N. Bradley Litchfield 376-5690
Assistant General Counsel for Legal Review/
Administrative Law: Vincent J. Convery, Jr ..376-5690
Assistant General Counsel for Advisory Opinions:
(vacant)....................................376-5690
Assistant General Counsel for Regulations:
Susan E. Propper 376-5690

Title 26 and Ethics: The administration of the public financing programs for Presidential primary and general election candidates and national nominating conventions is one of the FEC's major responsibilities. Staff attorneys are primarily responsible for providing legal guidance to the Commission, the Audit Division, and other staff members on the public financing statutes. In addition, the staff assists the General Counsel in fulfilling his duties as the Commission's Designated Agency Ethics Official and in administering the FEC's ethics programs.

(Area Code 202)
Special Assistant to the Counsel: Kim Bright-Coleman 376-5690
Attorneys:
Lorenzo Holloway 376-5690
Delanie D. Painter 376-5690
Thomas E. Zoeller 376-5690

OFFICE OF INSPECTOR GENERAL (Room 235)

The Office of Inspector General (OIG) provides the Commissioners with an independent and objective evaluation of the FEC's efficiency, effectiveness, and economy in administering the FECA and makes recommendations to improve the economy, effectiveness and efficiency of the FEC. The OIG assists the Commissioners in the prevention and detection of fraud, waste and abuse of FEC financial and other resources, reports to the Commissioners and Congress instances of such occurrences, and takes appropriate steps to ameliorate the problems caused by fraud, waste and abuse.

(Area Code 202)
Inspector General: Lynn A. McFarland 376-2267

PUBLICATIONS OF INTEREST

The following publications can be obtained free of charge. Contact: **Federal Election Commission, Information Services,** 999 E Street, N.W., Washington, D.C. 20463. Tel: 202/376-3120; 800/424-9530.

Federal Election Campaign Laws is a complete compilation of Federal election campaign laws; the Federal Election Campaign Act of 1971, as amended, and as codified in titles 2 and 26 of the United States Code; statutory provisions which are not under the Commission's jurisdiction but are relevant to persons involved with Federal elections; and a subject index to titles 2 and 26 prepared by the FEC.

FEC Regulations contains FEC regulations which appear in title 11 of the Code of Federal Regulations. Subject indexes prepared by FEC staff are included.

FEC Record, a monthly newsletter published as a binder insert, is the primary source of information on Commission activity. It covers reporting, advisory opinions, litigation, legislation, statistics, regulations, compliance, Federal Register notices, FEC procedures and staff, and publications.

Campaign Guides include four separate guides explaining how the law affects, respectively, four different audiences: candidates, parties, corporation/unions and nonconnected PACs. In each guide, election law requirements for the "three R's" (registration, recordkeeping and reporting) are explained and illustrated with examples of completed FEC forms. The guides also discuss fundraising and different ways of supporting Federal candidates.

1) Campaign Guide for Congressional Candidates and Committees, prepared for U.S. Senate and House candidates and their authorized committees, examines the complete cycle of election activity: testing-the-waters; gaining support through volunteer activity, contribution, independent expenditures and party activity; and winding down the campaign.

2) Campaign Guide for Party Committees, written for State and local party organizations which support Federal candidates, deals with such subjects as allocating Federal and non-Federal expenses, coordinated party expenditures and voter drives.

3) Campaign Guide for Corporations and Labor Organizations explains the rules governing corporate and labor activity in connection with Federal elections: separate segregated funds (SSFs); partisan and nonpartisan communications; and election-related use of corporate/labor treasury funds and facilities. This guide also pertains to national banks; incorporated membership organizations, trade associations and cooperatives; and corporations without capital stock.

4) Campaign Guide for Nonconnected Political Committees outlines the rules applicable to committees not established by a candidate, party, corporation or labor organization. It examines contributions and expenditures; political communications and support from a sponsoring organization.

The FEC and the Federal Campaign Finance Law gives a brief overview of the major provisions of the Federal Election Campaign Act and the Commission's role in administering it.

FEDERAL ELECTION COMMISSION

Public Funding of Presidential Elections is written for the general public and gives a brief history of Presidential public funding, describing how the process works. It explains the ways individuals may support publicly funded candidates and the various materials on Presidential campaign finance available from the Commission.

Using FEC Campaign Finance Information explains how to gather information about the financial activity of Federal political committees. It describes the FEC's computer indexes and suggests ways to utilize them.

Filing a Complaint tells how the complaint process works and what role the FEC plays in the process. Anyone may file a complaint if he or she believes an individual or a committee has violated the Federal election law.

Advisory Opinions is a brochure in question-and-answer format explaining how individuals may seek guidance from the FEC by requesting advisory opinions. An advisory opinion is an official Commission response to a question relating to the application of the Federal campaign finance law to a specific factual situation.

FEDERAL ELECTION COMMISSION
KEY LEGAL AUTHORITIES

Regulations: 11 C.F.R. Parts 1-9039 (1988).

Federal Election Campaign Act of 1971, as amended, 2 U.S.C. 431-455--establishes the Federal election campaign regulatory scheme, including spending limits, disclosure of contributions and expenditures; authorizes public financing of presidential campaigns; establishes the Federal Election Commission to regulate Federal election campaigns and administer the Act.

Legislative History: 1972 U.S. Code Cong. & Admin. News 1773; 1974 U.S. Code Cong. & Admin. News 5587; 1976 U.S. Code Cong. & Admin. News 929; 1979 U.S. Code Cong. & Admin. News 2860.

FEDERAL EMERGENCY MANAGEMENT AGENCY

500 C Street, S.W.
Washington, D.C. 20472

DESCRIPTION: The Federal Emergency Management Agency (FEMA) is responsible for emergency planning and implementing and maintaining a national system for managing emergencies ranging from local natural disasters to major national emergencies. FEMA serves as a professional clearing house for ideas, advice, and technical information for emergency management agencies at all levels of government.

(Area Code 202)

Director: Jerry D. Jennings (Acting) 646-4221
Procurement Information 646-3742
Public Information 646-4600
Publications Division 646-3484
Federal Insurance Administration:
Washington, D.C. Metro area 646-2781
Outside Washington, D.C. Metro area ....(800) 838-8820

(Area Code 202)

Freedom of Information Act/Privacy Act Office 646-3840
Facsimile 646-2531

Library (Room 123) 646-3771
The library is open to the public from 8:30 AM until 5:00 PM, Monday through Friday by appointment only. Materials cannot be checked out, but copying machines are available. The first 10 pages copied are free of charge.

OFFICE OF GENERAL COUNSEL (Room 843)

The Office of General Counsel renders legal opinions with respect to: (1) the duties, powers and responsibilities of the Director and other officers and employees, and (2) the application of statutes, rules and regulations, other administrative issuances and judicial precedents to agency operations. The Office also reviews and clears for legal sufficiency all agency documents requiring legal interpretation or opinion; establishes agency policy for and prepares, coordinates, and conducts all agency appearances in litigation or administrative proceedings and hearings; serves as liaison with the Department of Justice; maintains the rules and the litigation docket for the agency and provides liaison with the Federal Register; and provides a wide range of legal services in connection with legislation and regulations.

(Area Code 202)

General Counsel: George W. Watson (Acting) 646-4105

The Office is divided into three divisions:

The **General Law Division** reviews and makes determinations on procurement actions, financial management responsibilities, financial disclosure statements, Ethics in Government Act, freedom of information and privacy issues, and personnel activities. The office conducts administrative litigation; and advises all offices on the application, effect, and compliance with laws related to the administration and management of all functions and authorities of FEMA.

(Area Code 202)

Associate General Counsel for General Law:
Thomas Ainora 646-4093

The **Insurance and Litigation Division** provides legal analysis and opinions to agency officials on activities under the National Flood Insurance Act of 1968, the Flood Disaster Protection Act of 1973, the Urban Property & Reinsurance Act of 1968, the Coastal Barrier Act of 1982, the Earthquake Hazards Reduction Act of 1977. The office conducts the defense of all litigation claims filed under the various laws.

(Area Code 202)

Associate General Counsel for Insurance and Litigation: Susan K. Bank 646-3543

The **Program Law Division** provides legal analysis and opinions to agency officials on programs, functions, and activities under the National Security Act of 1947, the Defense Production Act of 1950, the Federal Civil Defense Act of 1950, the Robert T. Stafford disaster Relief and Emergency Assistance Act, and the Federal Fire Prevention and Control Act of 1971. The office coordinates legislation and testimony of FEMA witnesses and represent FEMA before boards of the Nuclear Regulatory Commission.

(Area Code 202)

Associate General Counsel for Program Law:
H. Joseph Flynn 646-4102

OFFICE OF INSPECTOR GENERAL (Room 824)

The Office of Inspector General (OIG) provides audit and investigative support services for FEMA covering all Agency programs and operations. OIG objectives are to prevent and detect fraud, waste and abuse and to improve economy and efficiency in the administration of FEMA programs and operations. Activities are planned and conducted in response to requirements of laws, regulations, and Congressional and OMB directives; specific requests from the Director and other FEMA management officials; and allegations received from Agency employees and other sources.

(Area Code 202)

Inspector General: Gary J. Barard (Acting) 646-3912
Assistant Inspector General for Investigations
Division: F. G. McGrath 646-3894
Eastern District ....(404) 853-4242
Western District ....(415) 923-7017

FEDERAL EMERGENCY MANAGEMENT AGENCY
KEY LEGAL AUTHORITIES

Regulations: 44 C.F.R. Parts 1-361 (1989).

National Flood Insurance Act of 1968, as amended, 42 U.S.C. 4001-4128--provides flood insurance protection to property owners in flood-prone areas as well as areas prone to mudslides and flood-related erosion.
Legislative History: 1968 U.S.Code Cong. & Admin. News 2873; 1969 U.S.Code Cong. & Admin. News 1524; 1973 U.S.Code Cong. & Admin. News 3217.

Housing and Urban Development Act of 1970, Title VI, 12 U.S.C. 1749bbb et seq.--authorizes FEMA to make crime insurance available at affordable rates in any state in which it is unavailable commercially through the normal insurance market.
Legislative History: 1970 U.S.Code Cong. & Admin. News 5582.

Disaster Relief Act of 1974, as amended, 42 U.S.C. 5121 et seq.--provides continuing Federal assistance to states and localities to alleviate suffering and damage resulting from natural disasters.
Legislative History: 1974 U.S.Code Cong. & Admin. News 3070; 1988 U.S.Code Cong. & Admin. News 6085.

Federal Civil Defense Act of 1950, as amended, 50 U.S.C. App. 2251 et seq.--provides for Federal financial assistance to state and local governments to increase civil defense operational capabilities.
Legislative History: 1950 U.S.Code Cong. & Admin. News 4328.

Defense Production Act of 1950, as amended, 50 U.S.C. App. 2061 et seq.--authorizes diversion of resources to national security needs and the allocation of such resources by the Government when necessary.
Legislative History: 1951 U.S.Code Cong. & Admin. News 1549.

National Security Act of 1947, as amended, 50 U.S.C. 404--directs FEMA to advise the President with respect to the coordination of military, industrial, and civil mobilization.
Legislative History: 1954 U.S.Code Cong. & Admin. News 3991.

Strategic and Critical Materials Stock Piling Act, as amended, 50 U.S.C. 98 et seq.--provides for the acquisition and retention of stocks of certain strategic and critical materials and the development of US sources of these materials in order to decrease foreign dependence in times of national emergency.
Legislative History: 1979 U.S.Code Cong. & Admin. News 793; 1987 U.S.Code Cong. & Admin. News 1018.

Earthquake Hazards Reduction Act of 1977, as amended, 42 U.S.C. 7701-7706--establishes a national earthquake hazards reduction program coordinated by FEMA.
Legislative History: 1977 U.S.Code Cong. & Admin. News 2785.

Exec. Order No. 11988, as amended, "Floodplain Management," 3 C.F.R., 1977 Comp., p. 117.

Exec. Order No. 12148, as amended, "Federal Emergency Management," 3 C.F.R., 1979 Comp., p. 412.

FEDERAL LABOR RELATIONS AUTHORITY

500 C Street, S.W.
Washington, D.C. 20424

DESCRIPTION: The Federal Labor Relations Authority (FLRA) is an independent, neutral, Executive Branch agency which provides leadership in establishing policies and guidance relating to matters under Title VII of the Civil Service Reform Act of 1978. Specifically, it determines the appropriateness of units for labor organization representation; supervises or conducts representation elections; resolves issues relating to bargaining in good faith; conducts hearings and resolves complaints of unfair labor practices; and resolves exceptions to arbitrators' awards. When the agency is engaged in court actions in either the U.S. District Courts or the Circuit Courts of Appeals, it is authorized to use its own attorneys rather than those designated by the Justice Department.

(Area Code 202)
Chairman: Jean McKee 382-0900
Procurement Information 382-0736
Public Information 382-0715
Publications Information 382-0715
Dockets 382-0748
Hotline 382-6004

Freedom of Information Act/Privacy Act Office 382-0781
Standard regulations apply.

Law Library (Room 234) 755-6420
The library is open to the public from 8:15 AM until 4:45 PM Monday through Friday. This is strictly a reference library with copying privileges restricted.

THE AUTHORITY (Room 217)

FLRA has three full-time members, each of whom is appointed by the President. These three members (frequently referred to as the "Authority" to distinguish them from the General Counsel and the Federal Service Impasses Panel) are responsible for the overall direction of the agency and its administration of the Federal labor-relations program. They are independent decision-makers who function primarily in an adjudicative capacity deciding negotiability disputes, appeals from arbitration awards, representation cases, and exceptions to the decisions of Administrative Law Judges in unfair labor practice complaints. The members are assisted by a staff of attorneys and labor relations specialists divided into three areas of subject matter responsibility: negotiability, arbitration, and representation and unfair labor practice cases.

(Area Code 202)
Chairman: Jean McKee 382-0900
Chief Counsel: Susan D. McCluskey 382-0900
Supervisory Attorney-Advisors:
James H. Adams 382-0956
Jean A. Savage 382-0956

Member: Tony Armendariz 382-0800
Chief Counsel: Steven H. Svartz 382-0800
Supervisory Attorney-Advisor: Edward Bachman 382-0926

Member: Pamela Talkin 382-0700
Chief Counsel: Stuart Horn...........................382-0776
Supervisory Attorney-Advisor:
George W. Birch (Acting) 382-0895

OFFICE OF GENERAL COUNSEL (Room 236)

The Office of the General Counsel has direct responsibility for the activities of the nine Regional Offices and for the investigation and prosecution of unfair labor practice complaints. Unfair labor practice complaints are currently the single largest category of cases filed with the Regional Offices and are likely to remain so. The General Counsel's decision to dismiss an unfair labor practice complaint is final and not appealable to the Authority.

(Area Code 202)
General Counsel: Kathleen Day Koch 382-0742
Deputy General Counsel & Director of Operations:
Michael W. Doheny 382-0842

(Area Code 202)
Assistant General Counsel/Appeals:
Michael D. Nossaman 382-0815
Assistant General Counsel/Legal Policy:
David L. Feder 382-0834

OFFICE OF INSPECTOR GENERAL (Room 216)

The Inspector General at the Federal Labor Relations Authority has statutory responsibility 1) to conduct audits and investigations relating to the programs and operations of the FLRA; and 2) to recommend policies to promote economy and efficiency and to prevent fraud, waste, and abuse. The Inspector General keeps the Chairman of the FLRA and the Congress informed of any problems.

(Area Code 202)
Inspector General: Paul D. Miller 382-6002

FEDERAL LABOR RELATIONS AUTHORITY

REGIONAL OFFICES

There are nine Regional Offices (located in Boston, New York, Washington, D.C., Atlanta, Chicago, Dallas, Denver, Los Angeles, and San Francisco; with Sub-Regional Offices in Philadelphia and Cleveland. These offices are responsible for initially investigating and processing all representation and unfair labor practice cases. Approximately 75% of FLRA's entire caseload is finally disposed of by the Regional Offices. Their addresses are listed below.

Washington, D.C.
Regional Director: S. Jesse Reuben
Federal Labor Relations Authority, 1111 -18th Street, N.W., Seventh Floor, P.O. Box 33758, Washington, D.C. 20033-0758. Tel: 202/653-8500.

Atlanta
Regional Director: Brenda M. Robinson
Federal Labor Relations Authority, 1371 Peachtree Street, N.E., Suite 736, Atlanta, GA 30367. Tel: 404/347-2324.

Boston
Regional Director: Edward S. Davidson
Federal Labor Relations Authority, 10 Causeway Street, Room 1017, Boston, MA 02222-1046. Tel: 617/565-7280.

Chicago
Regional Director: LeRoy L. Bradwish
Federal Labor Relations Authority, 175 W. Jackson Blvd, Suite 1359-A, Chicago, IL 60604. Tel: 312/353-6306.

Dallas
Regional Director: Gabriel Perales, Jr.
Federal Labor Relations Authority, 525 Griffin Street, Suite 926, Dallas, TX 75202. Tel: 214/767-4996.

Denver
Regional Director: Marjorie K. Thompson
Federal Labor Relations Authority, 535 16th Street, Suite 310, Denver, CO 80202. Tel: 303/844-5224.

Los Angeles
Regional Director: William E. Washington
Federal Labor Relations Authority, 350 S. Figueroa Street, Room 370, Los Angeles, CA 90071. Tel: 213/894-3805.

New York
Regional Director: James E. Petrucci
Federal Labor Relations Authority, 26 Federal Plaza, Room 3700, New York, NY 10278. Tel: 212/264-4934.

San Francisco
Regional Director: Ronald T. Smith
Federal Labor Relations Authority, 901 Market Street, Ste 220, San Francisco, CA 94103. Tel: 415/744-4000.

Subregional Office/Cleveland
Federal Labor Relations Authority, 1 Cleveland Center, 1375 East 9th Street, Suite 850, Cleveland, OH 44114. Tel: 216/522-2114.

Subregional Office/Philadelphia
Federal Labor Relations Authority, 105 South 7th Street, 5th Floor, Philadelphia, PA 19106. Tel: 215/597-1527.

OFFICE OF THE SOLICITOR (Room 222)

The Office of the Solicitor serves as agency legal advisor, representing FLRA in courts as well as providing legal counsel on such issues as the Freedom of Information Act, Privacy Act, ethics issues, etc.

(Area Code 202)

Solicitor: William E. Persina 382-0781
Deputy Solicitor: William R. Tobey 382-0781
Associate Solicitor: Arthur A. Horowitz 382-0781
Attorney Advisors:

(Area Code 202)

James F. Blanchford 382-0781
Jill A. Griffin 382-0781
Pamela P. Johnson 382-0781
Denise M. Morelli 382-0781

FEDERAL SERVICE IMPASSES PANEL (Room 215)

The Federal Service Impasses Panel is an entity within FLRA which provides assistance in resolving negotiation impasses between agencies and exclusive representatives. If voluntary means of resolving negotiation impasses, including the services of the Federal Mediation and Conciliation Service and other third-party services, are unsuccessful, a party may request the Panel either to consider the dispute or approve the use of outside arbitration. If parties do not arrive at a settlement after assistance by the Panel, it may hold further hearings and take whatever action is necessary to resolve the impasse.

(Area Code 202)

Chairman: Roy M. Brewer 382-0981

(Area Code 202)

Chief Legal Advisor: Donna M. DiTullio 382-0981

FOREIGN SERVICE LABOR RELATIONS BOARD AND FOREIGN SERVICE IMPASSE DISPUTE PANEL

The Foreign Service Labor Relations Board and Foreign Service Impasse Dispute Panel administer a similar but separate labor-management relations statute for Foreign Service employees. FLRA's General Counsel also serves as General Counsel for the Board.

(Area Code 202)

Foreign Service Labor Relations Board (Room 217)
Chairman: Jean McKee 382-0700
General Counsel: Kathleen D. Koch 382-0742

(Area Code 202)

Foreign Service Impasse Disputes Panel (Room 215)
Chairman: Margery F. Gootnick 382-0981

OFFICE OF ADMINISTRATIVE LAW JUDGES (Room 238)

The eight Administrative Law Judges (ALJs) hear unfair labor practice complaints prosecuted by the Office of the General Counsel. They hear cases both in Washington and in the Regions. After the hearing, the ALJ issues a report and recommendation for disposition of the case, which is reviewable by Members of the Authority who can affirm, modify, or reverse the ALJ's recommendation.

(Area Code 202)

Chief Administrative Law Judge: John H. Fenton 382-0851

Administrative Law Judges:

Salvatore J. Arrigo 382-0851
Samuel E. Chaitovitz 382-0851
William B. Devaney 382-0851
Jesse Etelson 382-0851
William Naimark 382-0851
Eli Nash Jr. 382-0851
Garvin L. Oliver 382-0851
Burton S. Sternburg 382-0851

To obtain rules of procedure see 5 C.F.R. 2411.1 et sec. (1990)

DATABASES AND PUBLICATIONS OF INTEREST

Database:

Federal Labor Relations Authority Case Decisions, Federal Service Impasses Panel Decisions, and Administrative Law Judge Decisions. Available on CD-ROM through the PERSONNET Service of Information Handling Services, 15 Inverness Way East, P.O. Box 1154, Englewood, CO 80150. Tel: 800/241-7824. In Colorado, call 303/790-0600 ext 59.

Publications:

FLRA Reports of Case Decisions, FSIP (Federal Service Impasses Panel) Releases and Administrative Law Judge Decisions of the FLRA. The decisions and releases are issued irregularly during a twelve month period. Price: $152.00 domestic; $190.00 foreign. GPO Stock# 863-002-00000-1. Contact: Superintendent of Documents, U.S. Government Printing Office, Washington, D.C. 20402. Tel: 202/783-3238. Note: Single copies may be obtained from the Federal Labor Relations Authority, 500 C Street, S.W., Washington, D.C. 20424.

FLRA (Federal Labor Relations Authority) Publications is published irregularly during a twelve month period with an annual subscription rate of $6.00 domestic; $7.50 foreign. Single copies of the quarterly issue, Report of Case Handling Developments of the Office of General Counsel (FLRA), and the annual issue, Subject Matter Index and Table of Cases (FSIP) vary in price. GPO Stock# 863-001-00000-5. Contact: Superintendent of Documents, U.S. Government Printing Office, Wash., D.C. 20402. Tel: 202/783-3238.

Federal Labor Relations Reporter. A monthly service reporting labor relations decisions for the Federal sector. It includes decisions of the FLRA, FLRA General Counsel, FSIP, Administrative Law Judges, labor arbitrators, and Federal courts. Back volumes dating from 1979 are available at extra expense. Product# 4010. Price: $685.00 per year. Contact: LRP Publications, 747 Dresher Road, P.O. Box 980, Horsham, PA 19044-0980. Tel: 800/341-7874.

FEDERAL LABOR RELATIONS AUTHORITY
KEY LEGAL AUTHORITIES

General Agency Regulations: 5 C.F.R. Parts 2411-2472 (1989).

Rules of Practice & Procedure: 5 C.F.R. Parts 2422-2429 (1989).

Civil Service Reform Act of 1978, Title VII, as amended, 5 U.S.C. 7101-7135--established the FLRA to regulate labor-management relations in the Federal service an authorized labor unions to bargain collectively over personnel policies, practices, procedures, and working conditions within the authority of agency managers; also provides a statutory basis for the establishment of Federal employee union grievance and arbitration procedures, and sets up the Federal Services Impasses Panel to resolve impasses between agencies and unions.

Legislative History: 1978 U.S. Code Cong. & Admin. News 2723.

FEDERAL MARITIME COMMISSION

1100 L Street, N.W.
Washington, D.C. 20573

DESCRIPTION: The Federal Maritime Commission is an independent regulatory agency charged with the administration of the ocean commerce of the U.S., as required by such statutes as the Shipping Acts of 1916 and 1984, the Intercoastal Shipping Act of 1933, and the Merchant Marine Acts of 1920 and 1936.

The responsibilities of the Commission include: monitoring agreements of common carriers engaged in the U.S. foreign commerce; reviewing tariff filings; regulating rates, charges, tariffs, and practices of ocean common carriers in domestic offshore trades of the U.S.; licensing international ocean freight forwarders; issuing passenger vessel certificates; investigating discriminatory rates, charges, and practices of ocean common carriers and freight forwarders; and rendering decisions, issuing orders, and adopting rules and regulations.

(Area Code 202)

Chairman: James J. Carey (Acting) 523-5911
Procurement Information/Administrative Services 523-5900
Public Information/Publications Information 523-5725
Office of Informal Inquiries, Complaints and Informal Dockets 523-5807
Facsimile 523-3782

Freedom of Information Act/Privacy Act Office 523-5725
For FOIA requests, there is a copying charge of 5 cents per page, with a minimum of $3.50. If a staff member does the copying, there is an additional charge of $11.00 per hour. For searches, the charge is $11.00 per hour if done by the clerical staff, and $23.00 per hour if done by the professional staff. A review is $38.00 per hour. Privacy Act requests are 30 cents per page, with no minimum. There is no charge for searches.

(Area Code 202)

Law Library (Room 11139) 523-5762
The law library is open to the public Monday through Friday from 8:30 AM until 5:00 PM. A copying machine is available for a charge of 5 cents per page. Interlibrary loans with area libraries may be arranged.

OFFICES OF THE COMMISSIONERS (Room 12313)

(Area Code 202)

Chairman: James J. Carey (Acting) 523-5911
Counsel to the Chairman: David G. Dye 523-5911
Vice Chairman: James J. Carey 523-5712
Confidential Assistant: Norman A. Caron 523-5712
Commissioner: William D. Hathaway 523-5715
Confidential Assistant: Cynthia Crawford 523-5715
Commissioner: Francis J. Ivancie 523-5721
Confidential Assistant: Dennis Bechara 523-5721
Commissioner: Donald R. Quartel, Jr 523-5723
Confidential Assistant (vacant) 523-5723

OFFICE OF THE GENERAL COUNSEL (Room 12226)

The Office of General Counsel provides legal counsel to the Commission. The Office reviews for legal sufficiency staff recommendations for Commission action; drafts proposed rules and prepares final decisions, orders, and regulations; prepares or presents testimony to Congress on various maritime regulatory matters; and represents the Commission in litigation before courts and other administrative agencies. Although litigation consists largely of representing the Commission on petitions for review of its orders filed with the U.S. Courts of Appeals, the Office also participates in actions for injunctions, enforcement of Commission orders, and actions to collect civil penalties. The Office is also responsible for monitoring international maritime developments and participates as a technical advisor on regulatory matters in bilateral and multilateral maritime discussions.

(Area Code 202)

General Counsel: Robert D. Bourgoin 523-5740
Legislative Counsel: David R. Miles 523-5740

BUREAU OF HEARING COUNSEL (Room 11129)

The Bureau of Hearing Counsel participates as trial counsel in formal adjudicatory investigations and rulemaking proceedings. The Bureau monitors formal proceedings to ensure that major issues affecting the shipping industry and the general public are adequately developed; advises on the development of Commission rules and regulations; provides legal advice during field investigations; reviews enforcement reports; prepares and serves notices of violations of shipping statutes and regulations; acts as prosecutor in formal Commission proceedings; and may participate in court litigation.

(Area Code 202)

Director: Seymour Glanzer 523-5783
Trial Attorneys:
Carolyn Grigg 523-5783
Charles Haslup 523-5783
Vern Hill 523-5783
Peter King 523-5783
Kamau Philbert 523-5783
Aaron Reese 523-5783
Joseph Slunt 523-5783
Martha Smith 523-5783

BUREAU OF DOMESTIC REGULATION (Room 10220)

(Area Code 202)

Director: Robert G. Drew 523-5769

ADMINISTRATIVE LAW JUDGES (Room 12101)

The Administrative Law Judges preside at hearings held after receipt of a complaint or institution of a proceeding on the Commission's own motion, regulate the course of the hearings, and make or recommend decisions.

The decisions of the Administrative Law Judges may be obtained from the Federal Maritime Commission, Office of Administrative Services, Room 10409, 1100 L St. N.W., Washington, D.C. 20573. Tel: 202/523-5900. Single copies are free. An annual subscription is $120.00.

The decisions of the Administrative Law Judges may also be obtained commercially. Shipping Regulation Reporter contains the decisions of the Federal Maritime Commission and the Maritime Administration. Also included are the rules, regulations and statutes related to the maritime industry. It is published every two weeks in looseleaf form by Pike & Fisher, Inc., 4600 East-West Highway, Suite 200, Bethesda, MD 20814. Tel: 301: 654-6262. Price: $1720.00 annually for a first subscription; $1390.00 for a renewal.

(Area Code 202)

Chief Administrative Law Judge: Charles E. Morgan 523-5750
Attorney Advisor: James S. Oneto 523-5749
Administrative Law Judges:
Joseph N. Ingolia 523-5755
Norman D. Kline 523-5754

FEDERAL MARITIME COMMISSION
KEY LEGAL AUTHORITIES

Regulations:

General Agency Regulations: 46 C.F.R. Parts 500-587 (1988).
Rules of Practice & Procedure: 46 C.F.R. Part 502 (1988).

Shipping Act of 1984, 46 U.S.C. App. 1701-1720--confers antitrust immunity on carriers participating in cartels and conferences and authorizes the Commission to seek an injunction against any agreement that unnecessarily raises transportation costs or limits services.
Legislative History: 1984 U.S. Code Cong. & Admin. News 167.

Shipping Act of 1916, as amended, 46 U.S.C. App. 801 et seq.--requires ocean common carriers and intercoastal shippers to file their tariffs for Commission approval; regulates competition among carriers; and authorizes the Commission to grant antitrust immunity for certain agreements among shippers.
Legislative History: 1978 U.S. Code Cong. & Admin. News 3536; 1984 U.S. Code Cong. & Admin. News 595 & 5426.

Merchant Marine Act of 1920, Sec. 12(46), as amended, 46 U.S.C. App. 876--authorizes the Commission to make rules and regulations to implement the Act's provisions designed to diminish the impact on U.S. shippers of unfavorable foreign country rules.
Legislative History: 1981 U.S. Code Cong. & Admin. News 92.

FEDERAL MEDIATION AND CONCILIATION SERVICE

2100 K Street, N.W.
Washington, D.C. 20427

DESCRIPTION: The Federal Mediation and Conciliation Service (FMCS) is an independent Federal agency whose mission is to prevent and minimize labor-management disputes having a significant impact on interstate commerce or national defense throughout the nation, both in the private and public sectors of the economy (excepting the railroad and airline industries). This responsibility is fulfilled by providing mediation assistance in preventing and settling collective bargaining controversies. For this purpose Federal mediators, known as commissioners, are stationed strategically throughout the country. There are approximately 250 Federal mediators located in headquarters, and regional, district, and field offices. The mediators have professional backgrounds in labor relations, with only a very small number holding law degrees.

(Area Code 202)

Director: Bernard E. DeLury 653-5300
Procurement Information 653-5310
Public Affairs Office................................653-5290

(Area Code 202)

Freedom of Information Act/Privacy Act Office 653-5305
Facsimile...653-2002

LEGAL SERVICES OFFICE (Room 712)

The small Office of the Legal Counsel provides a full range of legal services to the entire staff of the National Office, Regional Offices, and field stations. Responsibilities include: rendering legal advice on all matters pertaining to the Service; representing the Service in dealings with other Federal agencies and departments; assisting in the mediation of major labor-management disputes; administering the arbitration services functions of the agency; and handling litigation, internal labor-management relations, conflict of interest matters, and congressional relations.

(Area Code 202)

General Counsel: Theodore M. Chaskelson 653-5305

ARBITRATION SERVICES DIVISION

(Area Code 202)

Director: Jewell L. Myers 653-5280

PUBLICATIONS OF INTEREST

Single copies of the following publications may be obtained free of charge by contacting: **Federal Mediation and Conciliation Service**, Public Affairs, Room 710, 2100 K Street, N.W., Washington, D.C. 20427.

Change and Its Impact on Labor Management Relations (pamphlet)

Mediation in Public Sector Labor Management Disputes (pamphlet)

Mediation in Age Discrimination Disputes (pamphlet)

Arbitration (pamphlet)

America Works: The Report of the President's Advisory Committee on Mediation and Conciliation. (book, 48 pages)

FEDERAL MEDIATION AND CONCILIATION SERVICE

KEY LEGAL AUTHORITIES

Regulations: 29 C.F.R. Parts 1400-1471 (1989).

Labor-Management Relations Act of 1947, Title II, as amended, 29 U.S.C. 171 et seq.--established the Service to assist parties to labor disputes to settle them through conciliation and mediation.
Legislative History: 1947 U.S. Code Cong. Service 1135.

Civil Service Reform Act of 1978, Title VII, 5 U.S.C. 7119-7134--directs FMCS to provide services and assistance to agencies and union representatives in resolving negotiating impasses.
Legislative History: 1978 U.S. Code Cong. & Admin. News 2723.

Federal Insecticide, Fungicide, & Rodenticide Act, Secs. 3(c)(1)(D)(ii) & 3(c)(2)(D)(B)(iii), as amended, 7 U.S.C. 136a--authorizes applicants for registration of a pesticide with the Environmental Protection Agency to have data disputes between applicants and original data submitters arbitrated by the Service.
Legislative History: 1988 U.S. Code Cong. & Admin. News 3474.

FEDERAL MINE SAFETY AND HEALTH REVIEW COMMISSION

1730 K Street, N.W.
Washington, D.C. 20006

DESCRIPTION: The Federal Mine Safety and Health Review Commission is an independent administrative agency that adjudicates cases arising under the Federal Mine Safety and Health Act of 1977.

(Area Code 202)

Chairman: Ford B. Ford 653-5660
Executive Director: Richard Baker 653-5625

THE COMMISSION (Room 606)

Chairman: Ford B. Ford 653-5660
Attorney Advisor: Michael Duffy 653-5660
Commissioner: Richard V. Backley 653-5644
Attorney Advisor: Thomas Piliero 653-5626
Commissioner: Joyce A. Doyle 653-5656
Attorney Advisor: William Moran 653-5656

(Area Code 202)

Commissioner: James A. Lastowka 653-5648
Attorney Advisor: Richard Manning 653-5648
Commissioner: L. Clair Nelson 653-5652
Attorney Advisor: vacant 653-5652

Law Library (Room 621) 653-5459
The law library is open to the public Monday through Friday, from 8:00 AM until 5:00 PM. Materials may not be checked out, but a photocopying machine is available. Copies are 15 cents per page.

LEGAL STAFF (Room 630)

The Commission's legal staff is responsible for conducting in-depth legal research, defining legal and factual issues and problems, preparing legal memoranda regarding issues raised in cases, and drafting Commission decisions.

(Area Code 202)

General Counsel: Joseph Ferrara 653-5610
Deputy General Counsel: Richard Manning (Acting) 653-5610

(Area Code 202)

Dockets Chief: Jean Ellen 653-5629

OFFICE OF ADMINISTRATIVE LAW JUDGES (Room 1000)

Two Skyline Place, 5203 Leesburg Pike, Falls Church, VA 22041

The decisions of the Administrative Law Judges can be purchased from the U.S. Government Printing Office. Stock number and price for annual subscription are shown below. Submit request for this publication to: The Superintendent of Documents, U.S. Government Printing Office, Washington, D.C. 20402. Tel: 202/783-3238.

Federal Mine Safety and Health Review Commission Decisions. Monthly. Price: $69.00 a year domestic; $86.25 a year foreign. GPO Stock# 752-019-00000-2.

To request a single copy of a decision contact: Federal Mine Safety and Health Review Commission, Docket Clerk, 1730 K Street, N.W., Room 630, Washington, D.C. 20006. Tel: 202/653-5629.

(Area Code 703)

Chief Administrative Law Judge: Paul Merlin ....(202) 653-5454
Administrative Law Judges:
James A. Broderick 756-6220
William Fauver 756-6230
George A. Koutras 756-6232
Roy Mauer 756-6215
Gary Mellick 756-6261
Avram Weisberger 756-6225

FEDERAL MINE SAFETY AND HEALTH REVIEW COMMISSION
KEY LEGAL AUTHORITIES

General Agency Regulations: 29 C.F.R. Parts 2700-2706 (1987).
Rules of Practice and Procedure: 29 C.F.R. Part 2700 (1987).

Federal Mine Safety & Health Act of 1977, as amended, 30 U.S.C. 801 et seq.--established mandatory safety and health standards for coal mines and other mines and created the Commission to enforce them.

Legislative History: 1977 U.S. Code Cong. & Admin. News 3401.

FEDERAL RESERVE BOARD

20th & C Streets, N.W.
Washington, D.C. 20551

DESCRIPTION: The Federal Reserve System was created by the Federal Reserve Act of 1913 in order to provide for a safer and more flexible banking and monetary system. The Federal Reserve contributes to the attainment of the nation's economic and financial goals through its ability to influence money and credit in the economy. As the nation's central bank, it attempts to ensure that growth in money and credit over the long run is sufficient to encourage growth in the economy in line with its potential and with reasonable price stability.

Along with other Federal banking agencies, the Federal Reserve supervises the banking system. Its responsibilities for supervising and regulating the activities of depository institutions in the U.S. include: 1) supervision and regulation of state-chartered banks which are members of the Federal Reserve System, all Edge Act and agreement corporations, and all bank holding companies; 2) supervision and regulation of the U.S. activities of foreign banking organizations under the International Banking Act of 1978; 3) regulation of U.S. commercial banking structure through administration of the Bank Holding Company Act of 1956 as amended and, along with other Federal agencies, the Bank Merger Act of 1960 and the Change in Bank Control Act of 1978; and 4) regulation of the foreign activities of all U.S. commercial banking organizations which are members of the Federal Reserve System or which conduct their foreign activities through an Edge corporation.

Congress also assigned to the Federal Reserve regulatory responsibilities for a number of consumer protection statutes, whose coverage often extends well beyond banks to other financial institutions and creditors. Generally, the purpose of these statutes (such as the Truth in Lending Act, the Fair Credit Billing Act, and the Equal Credit Opportunity Act) is to ensure that consumers, including bank customers, are adequately informed and are treated in a fair and nondiscriminatory manner when they engage in financial transactions.

The apex of the Federal Reserve's organization is the Board of Governors in Washington, D.C. The Board consists of seven members appointed by the President and confirmed by the U.S. Senate. The full term of a Board member is fourteen years, and the seven terms are arranged so that one expires every even-numbered year. The Board's primary function is the formulation of monetary policy. In addition, the Board has broad supervisory and regulatory responsibilities over the activities of various banking institutions and the operations of the Federal Reserve Banks.

In order to carry out its responsibilities, the country has been divided into 12 Federal Reserve districts, with Banks in Boston, New York, Philadelphia, Cleveland, Richmond, Atlanta, Chicago, St. Louis, Minneapolis, Kansas City, Dallas, and San Francisco.

(Area Code 202)

Chairman: Alan Greenspan 452-3201
Procurement Information 452-3296
Public Information 452-3204
Publications Information 452-3244
Facsimile 452-3819

Board of Governors

Chairman: Alan Greenspan 452-3201
Vice Chairman: Manuel H. Johnson Jr. 452-3735
Governor Wayne D. Angell 452-3213
Governor Martha R. Seger 452-3217
Governor John P. LaWare 452-3211
Governor Edward W. Kelley Jr. 452-3285
Governor David W. Mullins Jr. 452-3271

(Area Code 202)

Freedom of Information Act/Privacy Act Office 452-3684
There is a copying charge of 8 cents per page for FOIA and Privacy Act Requests. The search fee for both requests can range from $8.50 per hour to $25.90 per hour.

Research Library (Room BC-241) 452-3332
The library is accessible to the public on Thursdays from 9:00 AM until 5:00 PM. Appointments should be made prior to 2:30 on the preceding Wednesday. Materials cannot be checked out, but material may be copied at 6 cents per page. Interlibrary loans of Federal Reserve publications can be arranged through Washington D.C. law libraries.

Law Library (Room B1066) 452-3284
The law library is open from 9:00 AM until 5:00 PM, Monday through Friday. An appointment is necessary. Materials cannot be checked out, but material may be copied at 6 cents per page. There is no charge for making copies of Federal Reserve Board publications. Interlibrary loans of other materials can be arranged under the auspices of the Interlibrary Loan Program.

OFFICE OF THE INSPECTOR GENERAL (Room 1070)

1850 K Street, N.W., Washington, D.C. 20006 (Mailing Address: 20th & C Streets, N.W., Stop 300, Washington, D.C. 20551)

The Inspector General conducts audits, operations reviews, and investigations relating to the Board's programs and operations. Responsibilities include: reviewing existing and proposed laws and regulations concerning their impact on the economy and efficiency of Board programs and operations (as well as in those administered or financed by the Board); and conducting activities to prevent and detect fraud and abuse.

(Area Code 202)

Inspector General: Brent L. Bowen 862-3801

LEGAL DIVISION (Room B1046)

The Legal Division is involved in all aspects of the Federal regulation of the nation's banking system, including the implementation of monetary policy and the supervision and regulation of banks and bank holding companies. In general, the staff is concerned with questions relating to the fields of commercial, corporate, antitrust, administrative, and banking law.

For example, in support of the Board's administration of the Bank Holding Company Act, attorneys analyze proposals for the formation of bank holding companies and the acquisition by bank holding companies of banks and nonbank companies, and are responsible for research, analysis and development of necessary revisions to the Board's regulations implementing the Act as well as monitoring legislative proposals affecting the Board's administration of the Act.

In addition, the legal staff prepares amendments to and interpretations of other Board regulations--such as those dealing with the operations of the nation's payments system and electronic fund transfers, interest rate controls, discounts and advances, and reserve requirements.

Other important areas of responsibility include: (1) analysis, recommendation and the preparation of testimony relating to proposed legislation in the banking and monetary fields; (2) participation in a full range of international banking matters; (3) evaluation of the relationship between banks, savings and loan associations and securities firms; (4) negotiation and preparation of contracts; (5) interpretation of the Freedom of Information, Government in the Sunshine and Privacy Acts; and (6) participation at both the trial and appellate levels in litigation affecting the Board.

(Area Code 202)

General Counsel: J. Virgil Mattingly, Jr 452-3293
Assistant to the General Counsel: Mary Ellen Brown 452-3608
Associate General Counsel (Litigation): Richard Ashton 452-3750
Associate General Counsel (Monetary Affairs):
Oliver I. Ireland 452-3625

(Area Code 202)

Associate General Counsel (International):
Ricki R. Tigert 452-3428
Assistant General Counsel: Scott G. Alvarez 452-3583

DIVISION OF CONSUMER AND COMMUNITY AFFAIRS (Room M4446)

The Division of Consumer and Community Affairs aims at protecting consumers in their financial affairs. The staff of this Division, which currently includes approximately 15 attorneys, monitors banks' compliance with such regulations as Regulation AA (Unfair or Deceptive Acts or Practices), Regulation Z (Truth in Lending), Regulation B (Equal Credit Opportunity), and Regulation E (Electronic Fund Transfers)

(Area Code 202)

Director: Griffith L. Garwood 452-2631
Assistant Director and Consumer Liaison: Delores Smith 452-2412

(Area Code 202)

Assistant Director (Regulations): Ellen Maland 452-3667
Assistant Director (Compliance): Glenn E. Loney 452-3585

PUBLICATIONS OF INTEREST

To order any of the following publications, submit a check (made payable to the **Board of Governors of the Federal Reserve System**) to: Publications Services, MS-138, Board of Governors of the Federal Reserve System, Washington, D.C. 20551. Or, call 202/452-3244.

Federal Reserve Bulletin. Published monthly. Bulletins contain information on financial and business statistics, current banking issues, statements of the Chairman to Congress, and legal developments, such as Board orders, final rules, and amendments to regulations. Price: $25.00 per year in the U.S., Canada, and Mexico; $35.00 elsewhere.

The Federal Reserve Act, and other statutory provisions affecting the Federal Reserve System, as amended through December 1988. 608 pages. Price: $10.00.

Regulations of the Board of Governors of the Federal Reserve System. Includes a copy of each of the 26 regulations. Free of charge.

Federal Reserve Regulatory Service. Looseleaf; updated at least monthly. Four Handbooks:

1) Consumer and Community Affairs Handbook. Price: $75.00 a year.

2) Monetary Policy and Reserve Requirements Handbook. Price: $75.00 a year.

3) Securities Credit Transactions Handbook. Price: $75.00 a year.

4) The Payment System Handbook. Price: $75.00 a year.

Federal Reserve Regulatory Service. 3 vols. Contains all four Handbooks plus substantial additional material. Price: $200.00 a year. The price for subscribers outside the U.S. is $250.00 a year for the Federal Reserve Regulatory Service; $90.00 a year for each Handbook.

FEDERAL RESERVE BOARD
KEY LEGAL AUTHORITIES

Regulations: 12 C.F.R. Parts 200-299 (1990).

Federal Reserve Act, as amended, 12 U.S.C. 221 et seq.--created the Federal Reserve System and enumerated its central banking functions: conducting monetary policy; maintaining the liquidity, safety, and soundness of the banking system, primarily through the loan of reserve funds to banks and other depository institutions for the short term; and assisting the Treasury in carrying out its fiscal duties.

Securities Exchange Act of 1934, as amended, 15 U.S.C. 77b et seq.--empowers the Federal Reserve Board to prescribe minimum margin requirements with respect to securities listed on national exchanges in order to regulate extensions of credit by securities brokers, banks, and other lenders for the purpose of buying or carrying specified securities.

Depository Institutions Deregulation and Monetary Control Act of 1980, as amended, 12 U.S.C. 248 et seq.--extended the Federal Reserve Board's reserve requirements beyond commercial banks that are System members to non-member banks and other depository institutions; extended access to the discount window to all such institutions; eliminated interest rate ceilings on time deposits in phases; and authorized interest-bearing NOW accounts nationwide.
Legislative History: 1980 U.S. Code Cong. & Admin. News 236.

Equal Credit Opportunity Act, as amended, 15 U.S.C. 1691 et seq.--prohibits financial institutions from discriminating on the basis of sex, race, religion, marital status, color, national origin, age, receipt of public assistance, or the exercise of rights under the Consumer Credit Protection Act, and directs the Federal Reserve Board to regulate in this area.
Legislative History: 1974 U.S. Code Cong. & Admin. News 6119; 1976 U.S. Code Cong. & Admin. News 403.

Home Mortgage Disclosure Act, as amended, 12 U.S.C. 2801 et seq.--requires depository institutions to disclose where their mortgage and home improvement loans have been made, so that depositors and others can make informed judgments whether specific institutions are meeting the needs of local communities for housing-related credit.
Legislative History: 1975 U.S. Code Cong. & Admin. News 2303.

Community Reinvestment Act of 1977, as amended, 12 U.S.C. 2901-2905--encourages banks and other institutions to help meet housing and other credit needs in their communities, including low and moderate-income areas, provided such credit is consistent with the safety and soundness of the lenders. Compliance evaluations are conducted during bank examinations, and the extent of compliance is weighed by the System when it considers applications for branches, bank mergers, bank holding company formations, and acquisitions.
Legislative History: 1977 U.S. Code Cong. & Admin. News 2884.

Electronic Funds Transfer Act, as amended, 15 U.S.C. 1693-1693r--established the basic rights, liabilities, and responsibilities of consumers who use electronic money transfer services and of financial institutions who offer these services.
Legislative History: 1978 U.S. Code Cong. & Admin. News 9273.

Depository Institution Management Interlocks Act, as amended, 12 U.S.C. 3201 et seq.--fosters competition by generally prohibiting a management official of a depository institution or holding company from also serving as a management official of another depository or holding company if the two are (1) not affiliated, and (2) very large or are located in the same local area.
Legislative History: 1978 U.S. Code Cong. & Admin. News 9273.

Truth in Lending Act, as amended, 15 U.S.C. 1601 et seq.--requires disclosure of the "finance charge," "annual percentage rate," and other credit costs and terms so consumers can compare credit costs from different sources, and also limits liability on lost or stolen credit cards. In addition to enforcing this Act with respect to state-chartered banks that are members of the Federal Reserve System, the Federal Reserve Board also accepts complaints about policies and practices of any bank or thrift and refers them to the appropriate regulatory agency.
Legislative History: 1968 U.S. Code Cong. & Admin. News 1962; 1974 U.S. Code Cong. & Admin. News 6119; 1976 U.S. Code Cong. & Admin. News 431.

International Lending Supervision Act of 1983, as amended, 12 U.S.C. 3900 et seq.--directs the Federal Reserve Board to consult with financial institution supervisory authorities of other countries in order to adopt consistent and effective supervisory policies and practices with respect to international lending; provides for the maintenance of specific reserves when the quality of an institution's assets are impaired by a foreign borrower's inability to make debt repayments; required the Federal Reserve Board to establish minimum capital requirements for banking institutions; and established regulations for accounting for fees on international loans and for the collection and disclosure of certain international lending data.
Legislative History: 1983 U.S. Code Cong. & Admin. News 1768.

International Banking Act of 1978, as amended, 12 U.S.C. 3101 et seq.--provided for Federal regulation of the U.S. operations of foreign banks and directs the Federal Reserve Board to supervise and regulate these operations in a manner similar to that applicable to U.S. banks.
Legislative History: 1978 U.S. Code Cong. & Admin. News 1421.

Bank Holding Company Act of 1956, as amended, 12 U.S.C. 1841 et seq.--gives the Federal Reserve Board primary responsibility for supervising and regulating activities of bank holding companies in order to control their expenditures and preserve competition in banking and to maintain the separation between banking and commerce.
Legislative History: 1956 U.S. Code Cong. & Admin. News 2482; 1966 U.S. Code Cong. & Admin. News 2385; 1970 U.S. Code Cong. & Admin. News 5519; 1987 U.S. Code Cong. & Admin. News 489.

Bank Merger Act of 1960, as amended, 12 U.S.C. 1828--requires that all proposed bank mergers between insured banks receive prior approval from the Federal bank regulatory agency under whose jurisdiction the surviving bank will fall. The Federal Reserve Board acts on such mergers when the survivor is to be a state member bank. The Act also makes the Federal Reserve the sole authority for approving bank holding company mergers.
Legislative History: 1960 U.S. Code Cong. & Admin. News 1995.

Change in Bank Control Act of 1978, as amended, 12 U.S.C. 1817--gives Federal bank regulatory agencies the authority to disapprove changes in control of insured banks and bank holding companies. The Federal Reserve Board has this authority with respect to bank holding companies and state member banks.
Legislative History: 1978 U.S. Code Cong. & Admin. News 1421, 9273.

Fair Credit Billing Act, as amended, 15 U.S.C. 1666-1666j--established a procedure for the prompt correction of revolving credit account errors and prevents damage to credit ratings while a dispute is being settled.
Legislative History: 1974 U.S. Code Cong. & Admin. News 6119; 1980 U.S. Code Cong. & Admin. News 236.

Fair Credit Reporting Act, as amended, 15 U.S.C. 1681-1681t--established a procedure for correcting credit records and requires that records only be used for legitimate business purposes.
Legislative History: 1970 U.S. Code Cong. & Admin. News 4394.

Consumer Leasing Act, as amended, 15 U.S.C. 1667-1667e--requires disclosure of information to help consumers compare the cost and terms of one lease of consumer goods with another and with the cost of buying cash or credit.
Legislative History: 1976 U.S. Code Cong. & Admin. News 431.

Real Estate Settlement Procedures Act, as amended, 12 U.S.C. 2601-2617--requires the disclosure of information about services and costs involved in real property settlements.
Legislative History: 1974 U.S. Code Cong. & Admin. News 6546.

Federal Trade Commission Improvement Act, as amended, 15 U.S.C. 57a(f)--authorizes the Federal Reserve Board to identify unfair or deceptive acts or practices by banks and to issue regulations prohibiting such acts or practices.
Legislative History: 1980 U.S. Code Cong. & Admin. News 1073.

Bank Secrecy Act, as amended, 12 U.S.C. 1951-1959--requires financial institutions doing business in the U.S. to report large currency transactions and retain certain records; prohibits the use of foreign bank accounts to launder illicit funds or avoid U.S. taxes or statutory restrictions; and directs the Federal Reserve Board to monitor compliance by state member banks and Edge Act corporations.
Legislative History: 1970 U.S. Code Cong. & Admin. News 4394.

Bank Export Services Act, as amended, 12 U.S.C. 1843--authorizes banking organizations to invest a limited proportion of their capital and surplus in export trading companies subject to prior approval by the Federal Reserve Board and to lend money to such companies to finance exports.
Legislative History: 1982 U.S. Code Cong. & Admin. News 2431.

Financial Institution Reform, Recovery, and Enforcement Act, 12 U.S.C. 1841 et seq.--amends the Bank Holding Company Act to permit the Federal Reserve Board to allow bank holding companies to acquire any savings association, not only failed or failing ones.
Legislative History: 1989 U.S. Code Cong. & Admin. News No. 6 (Sep, 1989), p. 86.

FEDERAL RETIREMENT THRIFT INVESTMENT BOARD

805-15th Street, N.W.
Washington, D.C. 20005

DESCRIPTION: The Federal Retirement Thrift Investment Board operates the Thrift Savings Plan for Federal employees. The Thrift Savings Plan is akin to a private sector 401(k) plan.

(Area Code 202)

Chairman: Roger W. Mehle 523-6367
Public Information 523-4511
Facsimile 523-9004

OFFICE OF GENERAL COUNSEL (Suite 500)

The Office of General Counsel provides legal advice to the Board Members, the Executive Director, and other Board officials concerning the Federal Employees' Retirement System Act (FERSA) and the operation of the Board as a Federal agency. Advice on FERSA covers such matters as the Federal income tax impact of various Board actions, ERISA requirements, fiduciary requirements, and the operation of the Thrift Savings Plan (including error correction, withdrawals, purchase of annuities, and loans). Advice on the operation of the Board as a Federal agency covers such matters as protecting the independence of the Board, Federal procurement, civil rights, the Freedom of Information Act, Privacy Act, Sunshine Act, Federal Tort Claims Act, and Government ethics.

(Area Code 202)

General Counsel: Robert Bloom 523-6367
Assistant General Counsel for Administration:
John J. O'Meara 523-6367
Assistant General Counsel for Programs:
James B. Petrick 523-6367

FEDERAL RETIREMENT THRIFT INVESTMENT BOARD
KEY LEGAL AUTHORITIES

Regulations: 5 C.F.R. Parts 1600-1690 (1989).

Federal Employees Retirement System Act of 1986, as amended, 5 U.S.C. 8401 et seq.--established the Federal Employees Retirement System and created the Board to administer the System, including investing and managing contributions.
Legislative History: 1986 U.S. Code Cong. & Admin. News 1405; 1987 U.S. Code Cong. & Admin. News 3217.

FEDERAL TRADE COMMISSION

6th Street and Pennsylvania Avenue, N.W.
Washington, D.C. 20580

DESCRIPTION: The Federal Trade Commission (FTC) is a law enforcement agency charged by Congress with protecting the general public--consumers and business people alike--against anticompetitive behavior and deceptive and unfair practices. Its goal is to ensure that the marketplace is as competitive as possible so consumers receive the widest variety of goods and services at the most competitive price.

The headquarters office in Washington, D.C. consists of the Bureaus of Consumer Protection, Competition, and Economics, as well as the Office of Congressional Relations, the Executive Director, General Counsel, Secretary, and Public Affairs.

(Area Code 202)

Chairman: Janet D. Steiger 326-2100
Office of Consumer and Competition Advocacy Director:
Richard F. Fielding 326-2236
Procurement Information 326-2258
Public Reference Service/Publications 326-2222
Records Branch 326-2523
Helper Service Hotline (ADP Problems & Repairs) 326-3500
Facsimile 326-2050

(Area Code 202)

Freedom of Information Act/Privacy Act Office 326-2402
All questions and requests for information must be in writing. There is a copying charge of 12 cents per page, and the first 100 pages are free.

Library (Room 630) 326-2395
The library is open to the public from 8:30 AM until 5:00 PM Monday through Friday. Materials may not be checked out but copying machines are available at 12 cents per page. The law library is contained within this library.

OFFICE OF COMMISSIONERS (Room 440)

(Area Code 202)

Chairman: Janet D. Steiger 326-2100
Attorney Advisers:
William E. Cohen 326-2110
David Conn 326-2114
Katherine Armstrong 326-2104

Commissioner: Mary L. Azcuenaga 326-2145
Attorney Advisors:
Alexandra P. Buek 326-2145
Gary D. Hailey 326-2145
Joan L. Heim 326-2145
John B. Warden 326-2145

Commissioner: Terry Calvani: 326-2150
Attorney Advisors:
MichaelSibarium.............................326-2150
MichaelWise.................................326-2150
Paul Yale 326-2150

(Area Code 202)

Commissioner: Deborah K. Owen 326-2159
Attorney Advisors:
Philip Eisenstat 326-2159
John Parisi 326-2159
Joyce Plyler 326-2159

Commissioner: Andrew J. Strenio, Jr. 326-2171
Attorney Advisors:
Dave P. Frankel 326-2835
Heather A. Hippsley 326-2835
Rosemary Rosso 326-2835

OFFICE OF GENERAL COUNSEL (Room 568)

The Office of General Counsel renders legal advice to the Commission and its staff on numerous subjects and supervises all litigation except administrative cases. Attorneys entering the office work with attorneys and economists from the three Bureaus and the Regional Offices to resolve legal problems arising in their work; ensure agency compliance with Freedom of Information Act (FOIA), Government in Sunshine Act, and other statutes; and advise the Commissioners on legal problems confronted in antitrust, consumer protection, and administrative law. As attorneys gain experience, they also have the opportunity to assist senior attorneys conducting appropriate litigation in the Federal courts.

(Area Code 202)

General Counsel: James M. Spears 326-2480
Deputy General Counsel: Jay C. Shaffer 326-2557
Counselor to the General Counsel and Federal/State
Liaison Officer: Bruce G. Freedman 326-2464
Assistant to the General Counsel for Confidentiality
Law: Marc L. Winerman 326-2451
Assistant General Counsel for Legal Counsel:
Christian S. White 326-2476

(Area Code 202)

Deputy Assistant General Counsel for Legal Counsel:
William P. Golden 326-2494
Assistant General Counsel for Litigation:
Ernest J. Isenstadt 326-2473
Deputy Assistant General Counsel for Litigation:
Jerold D. Cummins 326-2471

REGIONAL OFFICES

The Federal Trade Commission has ten regional offices whose staffs include approximately 115 attorneys. The principle attorney is the Regional Director of each regional office. The regional offices act as "mini-FTCs." They recommend cases and engage in litigation before administrative law judges and in Federal District Courts, provide local outreach services to consumers and businesspersons, and coordinate activities with local, state, and regional authorities.

The FTC'S regional offices are:

Atlanta
Regional Director: vacant
Assistant Regional Director: Harold Kirtz
Federal Trade Commission, 1718 Peachtreee Street, N.W., Room 1000, Atlanta, GA 30367. Tel: 404/257-4836.

Boston
Regional Director: Phoebe Morse
Assistant Regional Director: Raymond L. Betts
Federal Trade Commission, 10 Causeway Street, Room 1184, Boston, MA 02222-1073. Tel: 617/835-7240.

Chicago
Regional Director: C. Steven Baker
Assistant Regional Director: Thomas J. Russell
Federal Trade Commission, 55 E. Monroe Street, Suite 1437, Chicago, IL 60603. Tel: 312/353-8156.

Cleveland
Regional Director: Mark Kindt
Assistant Regional Director: John Mendenhall
Federal Trade Commission, 668 Euclid Avenue, Suite 520-A, Cleveland, OH 44114. Tel: 216/942-4210.

Dallas
Regional Director: Thomas B. Carter
Assistant Regional Director: Steven Wert
Federal Trade Commission, 100 N. Central Expressway, Suite 500, Dallas, TX 75201. Tel: 214/729-5503.

Denver
Regional Director: Claude C. Wild III
Assistant Regional Director: Janice Charter
Federal Trade Commission, 1405 Curtis Street, Suite 2900, Denver, CO 80202-2393. Tel: 313/564-2271.

Los Angeles
Regional Director: Marcy J. K. Tiffany
Assistant Regional Director: Marjorie Erickson
Federal Trade Commission, 11000 Wilshire Blvd., Los Angeles, CA 90024. Tel: 213/793-7890.

New York
Regional Director: Michael J. Bloom
Assistant Regional Director: Rhonda McLean
Federal Trade Commission, 150 William Street, 13th Floor, New New York, NY 10038. Tel: 212/264-1200.

San Francisco
Regional Director: Jeffrey A. Klurfeld
Assistant Regional Director: Erika Wodinsky
Federal Trade Commission, 901 Market Street, Suite 570, San Francisco, CA 94103. Tel: 415/848-7920.

Seattle
Regional Director: Charles A. Harwood
Assistant Regional Director: Robert Schroeder
Federal Trade Commission, 915 Second Avenue, 2806 Federal Bldg., Seattle, WA 98174. Tel: 206/399-5768.

OFFICE OF INSPECTOR GENERAL (Room 492)

The Office of Inspector General conducts, supervises, and coordinates audits and investigations relating to FTC programs and operations. It coordinates and recommends policies for activities designed to promote economy, efficiency, and effectiveness, as well as to prevent and detect fraud and abuse in FTC programs.

(Area Code 202)
Inspector General: Frederick J. Zirkel 326-2800

BUREAU OF COMPETITION (Room 370)

The Bureau of Competition, which is the FTC's antitrust arm, seeks to prevent business practices that restrain competition. The Bureau operates in two ways. First, it exercises its enforcement responsibility by investigating alleged law violations and, when appropriate, recommending that the Commission take enforcement action. Enforcement action may include a lawsuit in a Federal District Court seeking injunctive relief, litigation before the FTC's administrative law judges (with appeals to the five Commissioners), a consent agreement, or a compliance investigation to see if an FTC order is being violated. Second, the Bureau advocates the merits of a free marketplace by filing briefs with courts and by participating in the intervention program in which the Commission's three operating bureaus present comments to other Government agencies.

(Area Code 202)
Director: Kevin J. Arquit 326-2556
Deputy Director: Mary Lou Steptoe 326-2584

(Area Code 202)
Director for Litigation & Administration:
Barbara Clark 326-2562

(Area Code 202)

Associate Director for International Antitrust:
Edward F. Glynn, Jr 326-2946
Assistant Director for Compliance: Daniel Ducore 326-2526
Premerger Notification Office Chief: John Sipple, Jr 326-2862

Director for Litigation: James C. Egan, Jr 326-2886
Assistant Director for Mergers & Nonmerger Case Development: Steve Newborn 326-2815
Assistant Director for Licensed Occupations:
Michael McNeely 326-2904

(Area Code 202)

Director for Litigation: Ronald B. Rowe 326-2610
Assistant Director for Mergers: Ernest Nagata 326-2714
Assistant Director for Energy & Food:
Marc Schildkraut 326-2622

Director for Litigation & Planning: Walter T. Winslow ..326-2560
Assistant Director for Health Care: Mark Horoschak ..326-2756
Assistant Director for Planning: John Lopatka 326-2884

BUREAU OF CONSUMER PROTECTION (Room 466)

The Bureau of Consumer Protection aims at keeping the marketplace free from unfair, deceptive, or fraudulent practices. The Bureau enforces a variety of consumer protection laws enacted by Congress, as well as trade regulation rules issued by the Commission. Its actions include individual company or industry-wide investigations, administrative or Federal court litigation, rulemaking proceedings, and consumer and business education.

(Area Code 202)

Director: Barry J. Cutler 326-3238
Assistants to the Director:
Nancy Kantrowitz 326-3238
Louise Jung 326-2989
Collot Guerard 326-3338
Deputy Director: Gloria Larson 326-3330

(Area Code 202)

Associate Director for:
Advertising Practices: C. Lee Peeler 326-3090
Credit Practices: L. Jean Noonan 326-3224
Enforcement: William S. Sanger 326-2996
Marketing Practices: Lydia B. Parnes 326-3126
Service Industry Practices 326-3303

OFFICE OF ADMINISTRATIVE LAW JUDGES (Room 102)

The Administrative Law Judges are officials to whom the Commission, in accordance with law, delegates the initial performance of its adjudicative fact-finding functions to be exercised in conformity with Commission decisions and policy directives and with its rules of practice. The Administrative Law Judges also serve as presiding officers assigned to conduct rulemaking proceedings under Section 18(a)(1)(B) of the Federal Trade Commission Act as amended and other rulemaking proceedings as directed. The Chief Administrative Law Judge also serves as the Chief Presiding Officer. Administrative Law Judges are appointed under the authority and subject to the prior approval of the Office of Personnel Management.

The decisions of the Administrative Law Judges can be found in Federal Trade Commission Decisions, Findings, Opinions, and Orders which is listed below in Publications of Interest.

(Area Code 202)

Chief Administrative Law Judge: Montgomery K. Hyun 326-3625
Administrative Officer: Patricia A. Harringer 326-3626

Administrative Law Judges: (Area Code 202)
Lewis F. Parker 326-3632
James P. Timony 326-3635

PUBLICATIONS OF INTEREST

Businessperson's Guide to Federal Warranty Law includes a discussion of the Magnuson-Moss Act and also refers to specific sections of the Act, the rules of the Federal Trade Commission which were adopted under the Act, and the FTC's Warranty Advertising Guides. The publication is free of charge and can be obtained from the FTC, Division of Marketing Practices, 6th Street and Pennsylvania Avenue, N.W., Room 238, Washington, D.C. 20580. Tel: 202/326-3128.

Consumer Guide to the FTC Funeral Rule describes consumers' legal right to information concerning prices and options of funeral services. Available from Consumer Information Center-P, P.O. Box 100, Pueblo, CO 81002. Price: $2.00. Booklet number 109W.

The following publication can be purchased from the **U.S. Government Printing Office**. Stock numbers and prices are shown below. Submit requests for these publications to: The Superintendent of Documents, U.S. Government Printing Office, Washington, D.C. 20402. Tel: 202/783-3238.

Federal Trade Commission Decisions, Findings, Opinions, and Orders is a compilation of the official citations of the Commissions' decisions, findings, opinions, and orders. Volume 108 (July 1-December 31, 1986) Price: $17.00 domestic; $21.25 foreign. GPO Stock# 018-000-00327-9. Volume 109 (January 1-June 30, 1987). Price: $11.00 domestic; $13.75 foreign. GPO Stock# 018-000-00329-5. Volume 110 (July 1, 1987-June 30, 1988) Price: $30.00 domestic; $37.50 foreign. GPO Stock# 018-000-00331-7. Current decisions can be found in the Public Reference Section of the FTC. Tel: 202/326-2222.

FEDERAL TRADE COMMISSION
KEY LEGAL AUTHORITIES

Regulations:

General Agency Regulations: 16 C.F.R. Parts 0-901 (1989).
Rules of Practice and Procedure: 16 C.F.R. Parts 1-4 (1989).
Business Review Procedures (whereby firms can obtain clearance letters with respect to planned activities affecting domestic or foreign commerce): 16 C.F.R. 1.1-1.4 (1989).

Clayton Anti-Trust Act, as amended, 15 U.S.C. 12-27--prohibits mergers and acquisitions that may substantially lessen competition or lead to monopolies.

Federal Trade Commission Act of 1914, as amended, 15 U.S.C. 41-58--created the FTC and declared unlawful all unfair methods of competition and unfair or deceptive acts or practices, as defined by the Commission, as well as false advertising.

Sherman Antitrust Act, as amended, 15 U.S.C. 1-7--makes illegal restraints of trade and the monopolization of trade or commerce.

Export Trade Act, as amended, 15 U.S.C. 61-65--exempts certain business combinations entered into for the sole purpose of export trade from the Sherman Act and the FTC Act, and directs FTC to monitor compliance with these exemptions.
Legislative History: 1976 U.S. Code Cong. & Admin. News 2572.

Wool Products Labeling Act, as amended, 15 U.S.C. 68-68j--declares unlawful the misbranding of wool products and confers enforcement authority on the Commission.
Legislative History: 1984 U.S. Code Cong. & Admin. News 2647.

Fur Products Labeling Act, as amended, 15 U.S.C. 69-69j--declares unlawful the misbranding, false advertising, and false invoicing of furs and fur products.
Legislative History: 1984 U.S. Code Cong. & Admin. News 2647.

Textile Fiber Products Identification Act, as amended, 15 U.S.C. 70-70k--declares unlawful the misbranding and false advertising of the fiber content of textile fiber products.
Legislative History: 1958 U.S. Code Cong. & Admin. News 5165; 1965 U.S. Code Cong. & Admin. News 1589; 1984 U.S. Code Cong. & Admin. News 2647.

Lanham Trademark Act of 1946, as amended, 15 U.S.C. 1051, 1064--empowers the Commission to apply to cancel registration of a trademark under certain circumstances.
Legislative History: 1984 U.S. Code Cong. & Admin. News 5708.

Federal Cigarette Labeling & Advertising Act, as amended, 15 U.S.C. 1331-1339--requires cigarette packages to display health warnings and directs the Commission to enforce the law.
Legislative History: 1965 U.S. Code Cong. & Admin. News 2349; 1970 U.S. Code Cong. & Admin. News 2652; 1973 U.S. Code Cong. & Admin. News 2040; 1984 U.S. Code Cong. & Admin. News 3718; 1985 U.S. Code Cong. & Admin. News 312.

Fair Packaging & Labeling Act, as amended, 15 U.S.C. 1451-1461--makes illegal unfair and deceptive packaging and labeling of certain consumer products.
Legislative History: 1966 U.S. Code Cong. & Admin. News 4069.

Truth in Lending Act, as amended, 15 U.S.C. 1601 et seq.--requires disclosure of credit terms to consumers before (1) a charge account is opened, or (2) a credit transaction is concluded, and also limits liability in the event a credit card is lost or stolen; also designates the Commission as the lead enforcement agency in the Government.
Legislative History: 1968 U.S. Code Cong. & Admin. News 1962; 1974 U.S. Code Cong. & Admin. News 6119; 1976 U.S. Code Cong. & Admin. News 431; 1980 U.S. Code Cong. & Admin. News 236; 1982 U.S. Code Cong. & Admin. News 3054.

Fair Credit Reporting Act, as amended, 15 U.S.C. 1681-1681t--requires that consumer reporting agencies adopt fair and equitable procedures with regard to confidentiality, accuracy, relevancy, and proper utilization of information, and confers general compliance and enforcement authority on the Commission.
Legislative History: 1970 U.S. Code Cong. & Admin. News 4394; 1984 U.S. Code Cong. & Admin. News 2857.

Fair Credit Billing Act, as amended, 15 U.S.C. 1666-1666j--requires prompt correction of revolving credit account errors and prohibits damage to credit ratings while a dispute is being settled.
Legislative History: 1974 U.S. Code Cong. & Admin. News 6119.

Equal Credit Opportunity Act, as amended, 15 U.S.C. 1691 et seq.--prohibits creditors from discriminating on the basis of sex, race, religion, marital status, color, national origin, age, receipt of public assistance, or exercise of rights under the Consumer Credit Protection Act, and grants overall enforcement authority to the Commission.
Legislative History: 1974 U.S. Code Cong. & Admin. News 6119; 1976 U.S. Code Cong. & Admin. News 403; 1984 U.S. Code Cong. & Admin. News 2857.

Fair Debt Collection Practices Act, as amended, 15 U.S.C. 1692-1692o--prohibits abusive debt collection practices and directs the Commission to regulate debt collection practices.
Legislative History: 1977 U.S. Code Cong. & Admin. News 1695.

Electronic Funds Transfer Act, as amended, 15 U.S.C. 1693-1693r--established rights, liabilities, and responsibilities of consumers and financial institutions who participate in electronic funds transfer systems, and confers general enforcement authority on the Commission.
Legislative History: 1978 U.S. Code Cong. & Admin. News 9273.

Consumer Leasing Act of 1976, as amended, 15 U.S.C. 1667-1667e--requires full disclosure of consumer goods lease terms and conditions.
Legislative History: 1976 U.S. Code Cong. & Admin. News 431.

Petroleum Marketing Practices Act, 15 U.S.C. 2801 et seq.--requires disclosure of octane ratings and requirements by refiners and retailers and by manufacturers of new motor vehicles, respectively, and directs the Commission to regulate these practices.
Legislative History: 1978 U.S. Code Cong. & Admin. News 873.

Hobby Protection Act, 15 U.S.C. 2101-2106--requires that political items be marked with their year of manufacture, and that imitation coins and numismatic items be marked "copy;" directs the Commission to enforce the statute.
Legislative History: 1973 U.S. Code Cong. & Admin. News 2719.

Magnuson-Moss Warranty-FTC Improvement Act, as amended, 15 U.S.C. 2301-2312, 45-58--authorizes the FTC to regulate written warranties on consumer products; authorizes trade regulation rules to prohibit unfair or deceptive trade practices industrywide rather than on a case-by-case basis; permits the Commission to represent itself in court; and expands Commission jurisdiction over activities "affecting commerce" as well as "in commerce."

Legislative History: 1974 U.S. Code Cong. & Admin. News 7702.

Hart-Scott-Rodino Antitrust Improvement Act of 1976, 15 U.S.C. 1311note--requires companies to give prior notice to the Commission and the Dept of Justice of intent to merge if one of the companies involved is worth more than $100 million and the other is worth more than $10 million, and if the transaction would affect more than $15 million in stock or assets of 15 percent of the voting securities of the acquired company.
Legislative History: 1976 U.S. Code Cong. & Admin. News 2572.

Comprehensive Smokeless Tobacco Health Education Act, 15 U.S.C. 4401-4408--requires health warning on smokeless tobacco product packages and directs the Commission to enforce this provision.
Legislative History: 1986 U.S. Code Cong. & Admin. News 7.

Energy Policy and Conservation Act, as amended, 42 U.S.C. 6291 et seq.--requires energy efficiency labeling standards for consumer products other than automobiles and directs the Commission to regulate such labeling.
Legislative History: 1975 U.S. Code Cong. & Admin. News 1762; 1987 U.S. Code Cong. & Admin. News 52; 1988 U.S. Code Cong. & Admin. News 784.

GENERAL SERVICES ADMINISTRATION

18th & F Streets, N.W.
Washington, D.C. 20405

DESCRIPTION: The General Services Administration (GSA) is the Federal Government's business agent. GSA operates as a large, diversified corporation, directing and coordinating billions of dollars of purchases, sales, and services from private sector suppliers on behalf of Federal agencies in all branches of the Government and their facilities worldwide. For its clientele, GSA plans and manages the construction, purchase, or lease of office buildings, laboratories, and warehouses; oversees the operation of over 7,000 buildings housing Federal employees, and the employees' safety and protection; buys and delivers almost $3 billion worth of goods and services per year in retail supply operations; negotiates prices and terms for direct business between Federal groups and private industry; operates the Federal civilian telecommunications network (the world's largest special-purpose system); coordinates the repair and redistribution of Federal personal property assets; directs property sales--ranging from land to office equipment--the Government no longer needs; establishes and interprets the rules for Federal travel and negotiates reduced fares and lodging rates for Federal travelers; and manages an 85,000-vehicle motor pool.

(Area Code 202)
Administrator: Richard G. Austin 501-0800
Procurement Information (Business Service Center) 708-5804
Office of Small & Disadvantaged Business Utilization ...501-1021
Office of Ethics and Civil Rights: Special Counsel:
Allie B. Latimer: 501-0765
Office of Contract Review 501-1867
Office of Federal Acquisition 501-0692
Office of GSA Acquisition Policy and Regulations 501-1224
Media Relations 501-1231
Publications Information 501-1235
Fraud Hot Line: D.C. Metro Area 501-1780
Outside D.C. Metro Area ....(800) 424-5210
Facsimile....................566-1376

(Area Code 202)
Freedom of Information Act/Privacy Act Office 501-2696
Questions must be written and specific. There is a search and review fee of $9.00 per hour if done by a non-professional and $18.00 per hour if done by a professional. Reproduction fees are 10 cents per page; however, there is no charge if total amount is $10.00 or less. Non-commercial, educational or scientific requestors receive the first 100 pages free and two hours of search time without cost. Commercial requestors pay full costs.

Law Library (Room 1033) 501-0788
The library is open to the public from 8:00 AM until 4:30 PM Monday through Friday. This is a reference library with no copying or check-out privileges available.

OFFICE OF INSPECTOR GENERAL (Room 5340)

The Office of Counsel to the Inspector General, the in-house legal arm of the Office of Inspector General (OIG), provides legal services covering the full range of programs, activities, and operations of the OIG. All Office of Counsel personnel are located at OIG headquarters in Washington, D.C. The Office of Counsel is responsible for providing independent legal counsel to the Inspector General and all other OIG officials, including assistance with investigations and audits. Attorneys in the office participate with U.S. Attorneys, the Justice Department, and the GSA Office of General Counsel in preparing and conducting legal proceedings relevant to or arising out of OIG programs and operations. Duties include preparing all subpoenas for the OIG, reviewing and preparing OIG comments on existing and proposed legislation and regulations, reviewing cases having civil recovery potential, and participating with the Department of Justice and the GSA General Counsel in litigation arising out of OIG activities.

(Area Code 202)
Inspector General: William R. Barton 501-0450
Counsel to the Inspector General: Joel S. Gallay 501-1932
Facsimile....................786-0119

(Area Code 202)
Office of Investigations
Assistant Inspector General: Lawrence J. Dempsey 501-1397

OFFICE OF GENERAL COUNSEL (Room 4140)

The Office of General Counsel in the General Services Administration (GSA) has attorneys in the headquarters office in Washington, D.C. and in regional offices. These attorneys are involved in diverse areas of law, including:

***Government Procurement Law.** GSA purchases billions of dollars worth of ADP and telecommunications resources, real property, and general supplies annually. Contracts to buy this equipment and billions of dollars of supplies must be drafted and negotiated; audits must be performed; and specifications must be reviewed for legal sufficiency.

***Real Estate Law and Construction Law.** As the nation's largest landlord, real estate developer, and commercial buildings manager, GSA contracts for the building or purchase of hundreds of millions of square feet of office space

annually. GSA also sells or transfers properties valued at millions of dollars. Based on total sales, if GSA were a private corporation it would rank 55th on the Fortune 500 list. The legal work surrounding the construction, sale, and management of these facilities is among the most complex an attorney can handle.

***Litigation.** GSA attorneys handle all phases of construction, procurement, and claims litigation. Most cases are tried before the General Services Board of Contract Appeals. GSA attorneys also serve as co-counsel with attorneys from the Department of Justice in all cases GSA litigates in U.S. District Court, Courts of Appeals, and U.S. Claims Court.

***Utilities Law.** GSA attorneys represent the interests of executive agencies before Federal, state, and local regulatory bodies in proceedings involving electric, gas, water, and telecommunications. This work includes activities such as the development and presentation of complaints against utilities, the development and submission of material in rulemaking and other non-adversarial proceedings, and participation in ratemaking and general investigation proceedings.

***Labor Law.** GSA's involvement in the construction and renovation of Federal buildings inevitably raises many novel and complex labor law issues. These issues include the application of the Davis Bacon, Fair Labor Standards, Taft-Hartley and Walsh-Healy Acts, among others. GSA attorneys also represent the agency in labor negotiations with employee unions.

***EEO and Federal Personnel Law.** Since GSA employs more than 24,000 individuals nationwide, disputes inevitably occur relating to promotions, transfers, and job assignments. The Office of General Counsel represents the agency before the Merit Systems Protection Board in these cases.

***Constitutional Law.** GSA is often a principal party in cases involving the use of Federal facilities and property where significant First Amendment and other constitutional law issues arise. These include the rights of political candidates and private advocacy groups to demonstrate and distribute materials on Federal property. Further, issues of a criminal law nature may arise in connection with GSA's Federal Protective Officers who are charged with the security of Federal buildings.

(Area Code 202)

General Counsel: Robert C. MacKichan, Jr 501-2200
Deputy General Counsel: Frederick P. Hink 501-2200
Special Counsel: Michael J. Wooten 501-2200
Associate General Counsel/Law Division: vacant 501-1460

(Area Code 202)

Associate General Counsel/Personal Property Division:
Vincent Crivella 501-1156
Associate General Counsel/Real Property Division:
Melville H. Valkenburg (Acting) 501-0430

REGIONAL OFFICES

GSA has ten regional offices and the National Capital Regional Office (an office that is separate from the headquarters office).

Business Service Centers are also located in the Regional Offices. They serve as the first point of contact for anyone wishing to do business with the Federal Government. Each center is staffed with experts who will help prospective bidders find out if their products are purchased by GSA, how to introduce a new item for Government purchase, and what bidding opportunities are available. Bid abstracts, government publications regarding Government procurement, and general counseling are also available at the Centers.

Washington, D.C.
National Capital Region, General Services Administration,
7th & D Streets, S.W., Washington, D.C. 20407.
Regional Counsel: Gary Davis ....(202) 472-1804
Business Service Center ....(202) 472-1804

Atlanta
General Services Administration, RBR Federal Building,
75 Spring Street, S.W., Atlanta, GA 30303.
Regional Counsel: Ralph Howard ....(403) 331-0915
Business Service Center ....(403) 331-5103

Auburn, WA
General Services Administration, 15th & C. Streets, S.W.
Auburn, WA 98002.
Assistant Regional Counsel: Richard Moen ......(206) 931-7007
Business Service Center ....(206) 931-7956

Boston
General Services Administration, 10 Causeway Street, Boston, MA 02222.
Attorney Advisor: Robert Kline ....(617) 565-8100
Business Service Center ....(617) 565-8100

Chicago
General Services Administration, 230 South Dearborn Street,
Chicago, IL 60604.
Regional Counsel: Harry Gerdy ....(312) 353-5392
Business Service Center ....(312) 353-5383

Denver
General Services Administration, Denver Federal Center,
Bldg.41, Denver, CO 80225.
Regional Counsel: John Hewins ....(303) 236-7352
Business Service Center ....(303) 236-7408

Fort Worth
General Services Administration, 819 Taylor Street, Fort Worth, TX 76102.
Regional Counsel: Howard Hardegree ....(817) 334-2325
Business Service Center ....(817) 334-3284

Kansas City, MO
General Services Administration, 1500 E. Bannister Road,
Kansas City, MO 64131.
Regional Counsel: Samuel Skare ....(816) 926-7212
Business Service Center ....(816) 926-7203

Los Angeles
General Services Administration, 300 North Los Angeles Street,
Los Angeles, CA 90012.
Business Services Center ....(213) 894-3210
Note: There is no regional counsel in this office.

New York
General Services Administration, 26 Federal Plaza, New York, NY 10278.
Regional Counsel: Barbara Gerwin ....(212) 264-8306
Business Service Center ....(212) 264-1234

GENERAL SERVICES ADMINISTRATION

Philadelphia
General Services Administration, 9th & Market Streets, Philadelphia, PA 19107.
Regional Counsel: Manuel Oasin ....(215) 597-1319
Business Service Center ....(215) 597-9613

San Francisco
General Services Administration, 525 Market Street, San Francisco, CA 94105.
Regional Counsel: Donald Jayne ....(415) 744-5057
Business Service Center ....(415) 974-0523

BOARD OF CONTRACT APPEALS (Room 7022)

The General Services Administration (GSA) Board of Contract Appeals, established pursuant to the Contract Disputes Act of 1978, functions as a trial court and is the final administrative authority in Government contract cases. It also issues findings of fact and recommended decisions in suspension and debarment hearings of Government contractors. The Competition in Contracting Act of 1984 expanded the Board's jurisdiction to hear and decide bid protests involving the procurement of automatic data processing (ADP) equipment and services. Appeals from Board decisions may be taken to the U.S. Court of Appeals for the Federal Circuit.

The GSA Board is the largest of the civilian boards of contract appeals, and resolves disputes not only for GSA but also for the Departments of Treasury, Commerce, and Education, and for numerous other agencies and commissions, including the Merit Systems Protection Board, the Equal Employment Opportunity Commission, and the Federal Communications Commission. The subject matter of cases before the Board includes the design and construction of major Federal buildings, leases, acquisition of computer systems and services, procurement of a wide range of other kinds of personal property and services, and the disposal of excess personal property. In the bid protest area, the Board resolves bid protest disputes on ADP procurements for all agencies of the Federal Government.

The Board is organized into three divisions under the Chief Judge and Chairman.

1) The Judicial Division, which is responsible for the adjudication of actions before the Board.

2) The Office of Board Counsel, whose attorneys (under the direction of the Chief Counsel) provide all legal counsel and services for the Board; liaison on legal matters with other Federal agencies; and legal assistance in preparing, hearing, and deciding cases before the Board, including serving as hearing examiners.

3) The Administrative and Technical Services Division, which provides administrative, technical, and Clerk of the Board services required for Board operation.

Board of Contract Appeals Reporter reports the decisions of the General Services Administration Board of Contract Appeals. The monthly publication also includes rulings of other Boards of Contract Appeals. It can be obtained at an annual cost of $760.00 by Commerce Clearing House Inc., 4025 West Peterson Avenue, Chicago, IL 60646. Tel: 312/583-8500. Or, in Washington, D.C., call 202/626-2200.

(Area Code 202)
Chief Judge and Chairman: Leonard J. Suchanek 501-0720
Vice Chairman/Judicial Division: Vincent A. LaBella ...501-0402
Board Counsel: Thomas Sisti: 501-0890

(Area Code 202)
Clerk: Beatrice Jones 501-0116
Facsimile 786-0664

PUBLICATIONS OF INTEREST

Doing Business with the Federal Government is an information booklet published by GSA explaining government procurement programs in executive branch agencies. Topics discussed include: principles and procedures of government procurement; government procurement programs; government sales of surplus property; and the specifications, standards, and commercial item descriptions. The cost is $2.75 and can be obtained from the Superintendent of Documents, Government Printing Office, Washington, D.C. 20402. Tel: 202/783-3238.

Lists of Parties Excluded from Federal Procurement or Nonprocurement Programs is a monthly GSA publication identifying those parties excluded throughout the United States Government (unless otherwise noted) from receiving Federal contracts or federally approved subcontracts and from certain types of Federal financial and nonfinancial assistance and benefits. The cost is $50.00 annually or $3.75 per copy and can be obtained from the Superintendent of Documents, U.S. Government Printing Office, Washington, D.C. 20402. Tel: 202/783-3238.

Federal Buying Directory is a listing of procurement offices, address, and phone numbers of federal agencies within the D.C. metropolitan area. It is free of charge and can be obtained from the General Services Administration, Office of Small & Disadvantaged Business Utilization, Room 6029, Washington, D.C. 20405. Tel: 202/501-1021.

GSA Subcontracting Directory is an aid to small business and small disadvantaged business concerns seeking subcontracting opportunities with GSA prime contractors. It is free of charge and can be obtained from the General Services Administration, Office of Small & Disadvantaged Business Utilization, Room 6029, Washington, D.C. 20405. Tel: 202/501-1021.

Board of Contract Appeals Bid Protests Decisions is a monthly looseleaf publication of current GSA decisions. It is published at an annual cost of $380.00 by Federal Publications, Inc. 1120 20th Street, N.W., Washington, D.C. 20036. Tel: 202/337-7000.

Catalogue of Federal Domestic Assistance is a Government-wide summary of financial and nonfinancial Federal programs, projects, services, and activities that provide assistance or benefits to the American public administered by departments and establishments of the Federal Government. It describes the type of assistance available and the eligibility requirements for the particular assistance being sought, with guidance on how to apply. It is also intended to improve coordination and communication between the Federal Government and State and local governments. The basic manual and supplementary material which is updated for an indeterminate period costs $38.00 annually and can be obtained from the Superintendent of Documents, U.S. Government Printing Office, Washington, D.C. 20402. Tel: 202/783-3238.

GSA Supply Catalogue contains a listing of items - office products, industrial products, tools, furniture - used throughout the Federal Government which are available from GSA supply distribution facilities. Descriptions, prices, units of issue, and other pertinent information for ordering these items are also included. The basic manual and supplementary material which is updated for an indeterminate period costs $69.00 annually and can be obtained from the Superintendent of Documents, U.S. Government Printing Office, Washington, D.C. 20402. Tel: 202/783-3238.

GENERAL SERVICES ADMINISTRATION
KEY LEGAL AUTHORITIES

Key Agency Regulations:

General Agency Regulations: 41 C.F.R. Part 105 (1989).
GSA Acquisition Regulations: 48 C.F.R. Parts 501-570 (1988).
Silver Sales: 41 C.F.R. Part 56 (1989).
Federal Property Management: 41 C.F.R. Part 101 (1988).
Federal Information Resources Management: 41 C.F.R. Part 201 (1989).
Rules of the GSA Board of Contract Appeals: 48 C.F.R. Part 6101 (1988).

Federal Property and Administrative Services Act of 1949, as amended, 40 U.S.C. 471 et seq.--established the General Services Administration (GSA) and provides a uniform Federal system for procurement of personal property, nonpersonal services, real and personal property, and records management.
Legislative History: 1949 U.S. Code Cong. Service 1475; 1954 U.S. Code Cong. & Admin. News 3883; 1986 U.S. Code Cong. & Admin. News 1833; 1987 U.S. Code Cong. & Admin. News 362; 1988 U.S. Code Cong. & Admin. News 4311 & 5937.

Strategic and Critical Materials Stock Piling Act, as amended, 50 U.S.C. 98 et seq.--provides for the acquisition and retention of certain strategic and critical materials and seeks to lessen reliance on foreign sources of supply in times of national emergency.
Legislative History: 1979 U.S. Code Cong. & Admin. News 793; 1987 U.S. Code Cong. & Admin. News 1018.

Public Buildings Act of 1959, as amended, 40 U.S.C. 601 et seq.--authorizes GSA to construct, operate, maintain, alter, and manage and acquire space necessary to accommodate Federal agencies.
Legislative History: 1959 U.S. Code Cong. & Admin. News 2291; 1988 U.S. Code Cong. & Admin. News 5677.

Federal Information Centers Act, 40 U.S.C. 760--authorizes GSA to establish and administer a nationwide network of Federal information centers for the purpose of providing the public with information about programs and procedures of the Federal Government.
Legislative History: 1979 U.S. Code Cong. & Admin. News 3626.

Federal Urban Land-Use Act, 40 U.S.C. 531-535--prescribes uniform policies and procedures whereby GSA shall acquire, use, and dispose of urban land in order that such transactions shall, to the greatest practicable extent, be consistent with zoning and land use practices and local government planning and development.
Legislative History: 1968 U.S. Code Cong. & Admin. News 4220.

Slum Clearance Housing Act, 40 U.S.C. 421-425--preserves state and local civil and criminal jurisdiction over Federal low-cost housing project property and provides for payments to states and municipalities in lieu of taxes for municipal services provided to such projects.

Mechanics Lien Act, as amended, 40 U.S.C. 270a-270d--prescribes bonds required of any person awarded a contract in excess of $25,000 for construction, alteration, or repair of Federal buildings or public works.
Legislative History: 1966 U.S. Code Cong. & Admin. News 3722; 1978 U.S. Code Cong. & Admin. News 5579.

Protection of Public Property Act, as amended, 40 U.S.C. 318-318d--authorizes GSA to appoint special policemen for public buildings and other areas under GSA jurisdiction and outlines their powers.
Legislative History: 1948 U.S. Code Cong. & Admin. News 1627.

Surplus Real Property Disposal Act, as amended, 40 U.S.C. 304a-304e--authorizes GSA to dispose of excess civilian agency real property outside the District of Columbia by reassignment, auction sale, or lease, or by negotiation if no bids are received.

INTER-AMERICAN FOUNDATION

1515 Wilson Boulevard
Rosslyn, VA 22209

DESCRIPTION: The Inter-American Foundation is an independent Government corporation that supports social and economic development in Latin America and the Caribbean. Approximately one-half of the Foundation's funds come from congressional appropriations and the remainder from the Inter-American Development Bank. Most grants are made to private, grassroots organizations or to larger organizations that work with local groups and provide them with credit, technical assistance, training, and marketing services.

(Area Code 703)

President: Deborah Szekely 841-3810
Facsimile 841-0973
Public Information 841-3800
Publications Office 841-3876

Freedom of Information Act Office 841-3869
All questions must be in writing. There is a copying charge of 40 cents per page for FOIA requests. There is also a variable per hour search fee. Submit requests to the Freedom of Information Act Officer (Melvin Asterken), at the Inter-American Foundation address cited at the beginning of this listing.

(Area Code 703)

Privacy Act Office 841-3812

Library (5th Floor) 841-3860
This library is very small, and it is not open to the public. However, there is a Reading Room available to the public which contains development literature on the Foundation's programs. It is not possible to charge material out from the Reading Room.

OFFICE OF GENERAL COUNSEL

The Office of the General Counsel, provides legal counsel on all phases of the Foundation's activities, including: review and clearance of project proposals and contracts; negotiation of agreements with private, quasi-governmental, regional, and international organizations; interpretation of U.S. legislation and international agreements; and management of the congressional relations and public affairs programs.

(Area Code 703)

General Counsel: Charles M. Berk 841-3812

INTER-AMERICAN FOUNDATION
KEY LEGAL AUTHORITIES

Regulations: 22 C.F.R. Parts 1001-1006 (1989).

Foreign Assistance Act of 1969, as amended, 22 U.S.C. 290f--establishes the Inter-American Foundation as a non-profit corporation to provide support for developmental activities in Latin America and the Caribbean in cooperation with private, regional, and international organizations.

Legislative History: 1969 U.S. Code Cong. & Admin. News 2611.

INTERNATIONAL DEVELOPMENT COOPERATION AGENCY

320 21st Street, N.W.
Washington, D.C. 20523

DESCRIPTION: The International Development Cooperation Agency's (IDCA) function is policy planning, policymaking, and policy coordination on the range of international economic issues affecting developing countries. The Agency's mission is twofold:

* to ensure that development goals are taken fully into accounts in all executive branch decisionmaking on trade, financing and monetary affairs, technology, and other economic policy issues affecting the less developed nations.

* to provide strong direction for U.S. economic policies toward the developing world and a coherent development strategy through the effective use of U.S. bilateral development assistance programs and U.S. participation in multilateral development organizations.

The IDCA Director has a wide range of authorities to assist in the pursuit of the Agency's mission. The Agency for International Development (AID) is a component of IDCA, and its Administrator currently serves as the IDCA Director. The Trade and Development Program (TDP) is an organizational unit within IDCA, and the TDP Director reports to the IDCA Director. The Overseas Private Investment Corporation (OPIC) is a component of IDCA, and the IDCA Director serves as Chairman of the Board of Directors of the Corporation.

(Area Code 202)

Director: Ronald W. Roskens 647-9620

AGENCY FOR INTERNATIONAL DEVELOPMENT

320 21st Street, N.W.
Washington, D.C. 20523

DESCRIPTION: The Agency for International Development (AID) administers the bilateral foreign economic assistance programs of the U.S. Government. It operates from headquarters in Washington, D.C. through field missions and representatives in approximately 80 developing countries in Africa, Asia, Latin America and the Caribbean, and the Near East. AID's purpose is to help people in the developing world acquire knowledge and resources to build the economic, political, and social institutions necessary for a better life. Such assistance covers many diverse areas, including agriculture, rural development, nutrition, family planning, health, education and human resources, energy, and science and technology.

(Area Code 202)

Administrator: Ronald W. Roskens 647-8578
Security Clearance and Records Inquiries .... (703) 875-4050
Office of Small and Disadvantaged Business
  Utilization/Minority Resource Center .... (703) 875-1551
U.S. Foreign Disaster Assistance Operations Office 647-5916
Procurement Information .... (703) 875-1150
Public Inquiries 647-1850
Publications 647-4330
Facsimile 663-1770

Freedom of Information Act/Privacy Act Office 647-1850
Questions must be in writing. There is a copying charge of 20 cents per page, as well as a variable per hour search fee.

Submit requests to the Director, Office of Public Inquires, 04 External Affairs, Rm 2884, at the AID address cited at the beginning of this listing.

Library (Room 105) .... (703) 875-4818
1601 N. Kent St, Rosslyn, VA
The library is open to the public from 10:00 AM until 4:00 PM, Monday through Friday. Only computer printouts and other materials with interlibrary loan capacity can be removed from the library. Ten pages can be copied free of charge. There is a commercial copying center in the building, and material is permitted to be taken there for copying if identification is shown.

INTERNATIONAL DEVELOPMENT COOPERATION AGENCY

OFFICE OF THE INSPECTOR GENERAL (Room 5644)

The Office of Inspector General (OIG) is responsible for conducting audits and investigations relating to programs and operations of the Agency. The OIG is also responsible for preventing and detecting fraud and abuse in Agency programs and operations and for recommending policies for the promotion of economy and efficiency in Agency programs and operations.

(Area Code 703)

Inspector General: Herbert L. Beckington ....(202) 647-7844
Legal Counsel: Robert Perkins 875-4181
Assistant Inspector General for Investigations:
Gene Richardson 875-4100

(Area Code 703)

Assistant Inspector General for Security:
C.M. Flannery 875-4800

OFFICE OF THE GENERAL COUNSEL (Room 6859)

The Office of General Counsel provides legal advice and guidance to AID officials in the areas of legislation and policy, employee and public affairs, central programs, litigation and enforcement, contract and commodity management, private enterprise, as well as programs to be implemented abroad.

(Area Code 202)

General Counsel: Howard M. Fry 647-8548
Deputy General Counsel: John E. Mullin 647-8556
Assistant General Counsel for Africa: Edward Spriggs ...647-9218
Assistant General Counsel for Asia & Near East:
Herbert E. Morris 647-6504
Assistant General Counsel for Central Programs:
Programs: Stephen Tisa 647-8416
Assistant General Counsel for Contract and
Commodity Management: Kenneth E. Fries 647-8332
Assistant General Counsel for Employee and
Public Affairs: Jan Miller 647-8218

(Area Code 202)

Assistant General Counsel for Latin America and
the Caribbean: Thomas Geiger 647-9182
Assistant General Counsel for Legislation and
Policy: Robert M. Lester 647-8371
Assistant General Counsel for Litigation and
Enforcement: Gary Winter 647-8874
Assistant General Counsel for Private Enterprise:
Michael G. Kitay 647-8235
Facsimile 647-8557

OVERSEAS PRIVATE INVESTMENT CORPORATION
1615 M Street, N.W.
Washington, D.C. 20527

DESCRIPTION: Since 1971, the Overseas Private Investment Corporation (OPIC) has served as the key Federal agency for encouraging American business investment in the world's developing nations. Operating as a self-sustaining U.S. Government agency, OPIC promotes economic growth in developing countries by encouraging U.S. private investment in approximately 100 of those nations. OPIC assists American investors in this effort through two principal programs: (1) the insurance of investment against certain political risks; and (2) the financing of U.S.-sponsored enterprises through direct loans and/or loan guarantees. In all instances, the investment projects supported by OPIC must assist in the social and economic development of the host country, and be consistent with the economic interests of the United States.

(Area Code 202)

Chairman: Ronald Roskens 647-9620
President and CEO: Fred M. Zeder II 457-7001
Procurement Information 457-7152
Public Information 457-7200
Facsimile 331-4234

Program Information 457-7010
This is a recorded message in which one can request brochure information concerning OPIC's programs. It is also possible to leave your name and telephone number to have any specific questions concerning OPIC's programs answered. The toll-free number is: 800/424-6742.

(Area Code 202)

Freedom of Information Act Office 457-7093
Questions must be in writing. There is a variable per hour search fee. Submit requests to the Director of Public Affairs, at the OPIC address cited at the beginning of this listing.

Privacy Act Office 457-7082
This line is the Personnel Office, which coordinates Privacy Act questions in conjunction with the Office of General Counsel.

Library 457-7123
The library is open to the public by appointment only from 9:00 AM until 5:00 PM, Monday through Friday. Check-out privileges are reserved for OPIC staff members.

OFFICE OF GENERAL COUNSEL

The Office of the General Counsel includes a Deputy General Counsel, an Assistant General Counsel for Finance, an Assistant General Counsel for Insurance, an Assistant General Counsel for Claims, and a Senior Counsel for Legislative and Administrative Affairs, with the rest being Senior Commercial Counsels. Attorneys perform legal work in the areas of loans, investment guaranties, and political risk insurance. They provide legal advice and assistance to OPIC officials, review pending or proposed actions, and participate as legal counsel in complex contracts, agreements, and claims settlements, including the preparation of all necessary legal instruments.

(Area Code 202)

Vice President and General Counsel: Howard L. Hills ...457-7020
Deputy General Counsel: Jane H. Chalmers 457-7031
Associate General Counsel for Claims:
Robert C. O'Sullivan 457-7029
Associate General Counsel for Investment:
Herbet A. Glaser 457-7015
Associate General Counsel for Finance:
Peter F. Fitzgerald 457-7032
Assistant General Counsel for Legislative and
Administrative Affairs: James R. Offutt 457-7038

(Area Code 202)

Assistant General Counsel:
David Nerkle 457-7021
Kenneth W. Hansen 457-7014
Senior Commercial Counsel:
Ana-Mita Betancourt 457-7018
Vincent Salvatore 457-7021
Linda Wells 457-7026
Facsimile 872-9305

PUBLICATIONS OF INTEREST

To assist American businesses considering overseas ventures, OPIC created the **Investor Information Service (IIS)**. IIS is a publications clearinghouse that provides interested companies and individuals with easy "one-stop-shopping" for basic business, economic, and political information commonly sought when considering investment overseas. The materials, which are gathered into "kit" form, are obtained from various U.S. Government agencies, foreign governments and international organizations. At present, IIS kits are available for more than 100 developing counties and 16 regions.

Each information kit generally contains the following country-specific publications:

* **Background Notes** (from U.S. Department of State) describing a country's land, people, history, government, political conditions, economy and foreign relations.

* **Foreign Economic Trends and Their Implications for the United States** (from U.S. Department of Commerce, International Trade Administration) discussing the economic and financial conditions of a country.

* **Overseas Business Reports** (from U.S. Department of Commerce, International Trade Administration) containing information on a country's trade patterns, industry trends, distribution and sales channels, natural resources, infrastructure, and trade regulations.

* **Post Report** (from U.S. Department of State) containing practical information on living and traveling in a country.

* **Investment Climate Statement** (from the U.S. Embassy in the host country) summarizing those laws, policies, and changes in a country's economic climate that may affect existing or new U.S. direct investment.

* **Foreign Labor Trends** (from Department of Labor) discussing employment trends, union activities, and relations among labor, government and industry.

* **Travel Advisories** (from U.S. Department of State) providing information on travel conditions, restrictions, and document requirements.

* **Map** (from U.S. Department of State) showing transportation networks, economic activities, and land utilization.

* **Foreign Publications** (from foreign government trade and investment authorities) outlining legal codes and discussing business regulations, investment incentives, and other related topics.

Because the number of publications available at any particular time varies from country to country, individual IIS kits differ in size, scope and price. For more information contact: Investor Information Service, Overseas Private Investment Corporation, 1615 M Street, N.W. Washington, D.C. 20527. Telephone orders by credit card can be made by calling 202/457-7010 or 800/424-6742.

TRADE AND DEVELOPMENT PROGRAM
Rosslyn Plaza East, 1621 N. Kent Street
Rosslyn, VA 22209

DESCRIPTION: The mission of the Trade and Development Program (TDP) is to promote economic development in and, simultaneously, export U.S. goods and services to Third World and middle-income developing countries. TDP finances feasibility studies for high priority development projects that will be financed by the World Bank or other international financial institutions or from the host country's own resources. TDP-financed studies are performed only by U.S. firms.

(Area Code 703)

Director: Priscilla Rabb-Ayres 875-4357

(Area Code 703)

General Counsel: Lisa DeSoto 875-4357

INTERNATIONAL DEVELOPMENT COOPERATION AGENCY
KEY LEGAL AUTHORITIES

Agency for International Development Regulations: 22 C.F.R. Parts 200-224 (1989).
Overseas Private Investment Corporation Regulations: 22 C.F.R. Parts 705-711 (1989).
IDCA Acquisition Regulations: 48 C.F.R. Parts 701-753 (1989).

Foreign Assistance Act of 1961, as amended, 22 U.S.C. 2191 et seq., 2381 et seq.--authorizes the President to delegate authority to direct bilateral foreign economic assistance program responsibility; created the Overseas Private Investment Corporation to mobilize and facilitate participation of U.S. private capital and skills in the economic and social development of less-developed friendly countries, by providing insurance, financing, or reinsurance for specific foreign development projects.
Legislative History: 1961 U.S. Code Cong. & Admin. News 2472. 1969 U.S. Code Cong. & Admin. News 2611; 1974 U.S. Code Cong. & Admin. News 4517; 1978 U.S. Code Cong. & Admin. News 618; 1985 U.S. Code Cong. & Admin. News 2572.

Exec. Order 12163 3 C.F.R., 1979 Comp., p. 435--delegates the above authority to the Agency for International Development (AID) through the International Development Cooperation Agency (IDCA).

Agricultural Act of 1949, as amended, 7 U.S.C. 1431--authorizes the donation of surplus U.S. agricultural and other commodities to developing and friendly countries.
Legislative History: 1949 U.S. Code Cong. Service 2407; 1954 U.S. Code Cong. & Admin. News 2509; 1966 U.S. Code Cong. & Admin. News 4410; 1982 U.S. Code Cong. & Admin. News 1641; 1985 U.S. Code Cong. & Admin. News 158, 1103; 1988 U.S. Code Cong. & Admin. News 1547.

Agricultural Trade Development & Assistance Act of 1954, as amended, 7 U.S.C. 1721-1722--authorizes the President to determine the requirements and furnish agricultural commodities to meet famine and other urgent and extraordinary relief requirements abroad; to combat malnutrition, especially in children; and for related purposes.
Legislative History: 1954 U.S. Code Cong. & Admin. News 2509; 1966 U.S. Code Cong. & Admin. News 4410.

INTERNATIONAL TRADE COMMISSION

500 E Street, S.W.
Washington, D.C. 20436

DESCRIPTION: The U.S. International Trade Commission (ITC) is an independent, bi-partisan, quasi-judicial agency with broad powers to investigate all factors relating to the effect of U.S. foreign trade on domestic production, employment, and consumption. Activities include: making recommendations regarding relief for industries seriously injured by increasing imports; determining whether U.S. industries are materially injured by imports that benefit from pricing below fair value or subsidization; directing actions against unfair trade practices, such as patent infringement; and conducting studies on trade and tariff issues and monitoring import levels.

Attorneys at the Commission work in the following offices: Office of the General Counsel, Office of Unfair Import Investigations, Office of Tariff Affairs and Trade Agreements, and the Office of Administrative Law Judges.

(Area Code 202)

Chairman: Anne E. Brunsdale (Acting) 252-1012
Procurement Information 252-1730
Public Affairs 252-1819
Public Information 252-1000
Docket 252-1802
Publications Information 252-1807
Facsimile 252-1798

Freedom of Information Act/Privacy Act Office 252-1802
There is a copying charge of 10 cents per page. There is also a variable per hour search fee. If calling with a question about when the request will be filled, call the number above. If calling about the cost, call 202/252-1000 (Public Information).

(Area Code 202)

Main Library (Room 300) 252-1626
The library is open to the public from 8:00 AM until 5:15 PM, Monday through Friday. Appointments are necessary for use of microfilm.

Law Library (Room 614) 252-1287
The law library is open to the public from 8:30 AM until 5:00 PM, Monday through Friday. Materials can be viewed, but can only be charged out through an interlibrary loan. Photocopying is free, but only a maximum of 50 pages may be copied.

OFFICES OF THE COMMISSIONERS

(Area Code 202)

Office of the Chairman: Anne E. Brunsdale (Acting)
Counsel Robert P. Parker 252-1012

Office of Vice Chairman: Anne E. Brunsdale 252-1012

Office of Commissioner: Don E. Newquist
Legal Assistants:
Mitchell Dale 252-1781
O. Fielding Cochran 252-1781

(Area Code 202)

Office of Commissioner: Seeley G. Lodwick
Attorney-Advisor: Peter P. Scherle 252-1021

Office of Commissioner: David B. Rohr
Attorney-Advisor: John S. Sciortino 252-1041

Office of Commissioner: vacant

OFFICE OF INSPECTOR GENERAL (Room 220)

The Inspector General is responsible for directing and carrying out all audits and investigations relating to Commission programs and operations; and for recommending and commenting on proposed legislation, regulations, and procedures as to their economy, efficiency, and effectiveness.

(Area Code 202)

Inspector General: Jane E. Altehofen 252-2210

(Area Code 202)

Emergency Hotline 252-2217

OFFICE OF GENERAL COUNSEL (Room 707)

The Office of General Counsel provides legal expertise to the Commission in support of its requirements for litigation and special projects. Attorneys in the Office defend and enforce all Commission decisions, determinations, and orders in U.S. courts; analyze highly involved international trade law disputes; prepare litigation strategies; provide legal expertise in support of the Commission's antidumping and countervailing duty investigations, including the preparation of proposed amendments to Commission rules and regulations; provide legal expertise to the Commission while the case is before an Administrative Law Judge; prepare and draft legal briefs and memoranda; and provide advice to foreign governments and international organizations on the administration of U.S. trade laws.

INTERNATIONAL TRADE COMMISSION

(Area Code 202)

General Counsel: Lyn M. Schlitt 252-1061
Assistant General Counsel for Administration and Other Investigations: William W. Gearhart 252-1091
Assistant General Counsel for Antidumping and Countervailing Duties: Charles Nalls 252-1106
Assistant General Counsel for Litigation: James A. Toupin 252-1101
Assistant General Counsel for Section 337 Investigations: N. Timor Yaworski 252-1096
Facsimile 252-1111

OFFICE OF INVESTIGATIONS (Room 615)

(Area Code 202)

Director: William L. Featherstone 252-1161
Supervisory Investigators:
Vera A. Libeau 252-1176
Robert W. Eninger 252-1194
George L. Deyman 252-1197
Robert G. Carpenter 252-1172

OFFICE OF TARIFF AFFAIRS AND TRADE AGREEMENTS (Room 404)

The Office of Tariff Affairs and Trade Agreements works to reduce tariff and nontariff barriers to the international movement of goods and services, represents the interests of domestic industries, and assists in the General Agreement on Tariffs and Trade (GATT) negotiations in Geneva, Switzerland.

(Area Code 202)

Director: Eugene A. Rosengarden 252-1592
Chief of the Legal Division: (vacant) 252-1601
Attorney-Advisors:
Daniel P. Shepherdson 252-1598
Janis L. Summers 252-1605
Leo A. Webb 252-1599
Chief of the Nomenclature Division: David B. Beck 252-1604
Chief of the Trade Agreements Division: (vacant) 252-1614

OFFICE OF UNFAIR IMPORT INVESTIGATIONS (Room 401)

The Office of Unfair Import Practice Investigations, applies U.S. statutory and common law of unfair competition to the importation of articles into the U.S. and their sale. Once a violation is found, the Commission may issue orders excluding the offending articles from entry into the U.S., as well as cease and desist orders. Appeals of Commission orders are heard by the Court of Appeals for the Federal Circuit.

Section 337 investigations require formal evidentiary hearings held in accordance with the Administrative Procedure Act before an Administrative Law Judge. The most common cases involving unfair methods of competition brought before the Commission involve infringements of intellectual property rights including patent, copyright, or trademark. Other investigations involve theft of trade secrets or violation of the antitrust laws.

(Area Code 202)

Director: Lynn Levine 252-1561

Supervisory Attorneys:
T. Spence Chubb 252-1575
Jeffrey A. Whieldon 252-1561

General Attorneys/Investigative Attorneys:
T. Spence Chubb 252-1575
Juan S. Cockburn 252-1572
Daniel Duty 252-1581
James Gould 252-1578
Gary Hnath 252-1571
Deborah J. Kline 252-1576
John Kroeger 252-1573
Thomas Jarvis 252-1568
George Summerfield 252-1582

OFFICE OF TRADE REMEDY ASSISTANCE (Room 317)

The Office of Trade Remedy Assistance provides general information to the public, upon request, and, to the extent feasible, assistance and advice to interested parties concerning the remedies and benefits available under trade laws, and the procedures to be followed and appropriate filing dates in investigations under those trade laws. In coordination with other agencies responsible for administering trade laws, the Office also provides technical assistance to eligible small businesses that seek to obtain remedies and benefits under the trade laws.

(Area Code 202)

Director: Gary Kaplan 252-2200
Paralegal: Mary Abbott 252-2200

Note: There is a toll-free number for anyone calling the Office of Trade Remedy Assistance from outside the Washington, D.C. metro area. The number is (800) 343-9822.

OFFICE OF THE ADMINISTRATIVE LAW JUDGES (Room 213)

The Office of Administrative Law Judges conducts formal proceedings in section 337 investigations, exercises independent judgment, and transmits determinations to the Commission for its consideration in rendering a final decision.

To obtain information on rules of procedure, see Section 210 of the Commission's Rules of Practice and Procedure, 19 C.F.R. part 210.

Copies of decisions of the Administrative Law Judges, as well as Commission decisions, are available for public inspection in Room 112. Individual copies of these decisions can be obtained by contacting the Docket Clerk on 202/252-1802.

	(Area Code 202)
Chief Administrative Law Judge: Janet D. Saxon	252-1691
Attorney-Advisors:	
Thomas S. Fusco	252-1692
John E. McKie	252-1694
Paul A. Newhouse	252-1691
David Paul Shaw	252-1691
Kent R. Stevens	252-1693

PUBLICATIONS OF INTEREST

Citizen's Guide to the Statutory Procedures of the United States International Trade Commission gives a summary of the laws under which the Commission currently conducts investigations and also lists other reports and activities. It can be obtained free of charge from the United States International Trade Commission, Office of Public Affairs, Room 112, Washington, D.C. 20436. Tel: 202/252-1819.

Selected Publications of the U.S. International Trade Commission, through December 1989. Lists reports issued by the International Trade Commission under various sections of the Trade Act of 1974 (e.g., unfair import practices, countervailing duty investigations, antidumping investigations, escape-clause investigations, market disruption), as well as reports issued under the Commission's general investigative powers provided under the Tariff Act of 1930. Reports are organized both by countries (or other geographic areas) and by commodities. USITC Publication #2263. Available free of charge from: Publications, U.S. International Trade Commission, Washington, D.C. 20436. Tel: 202/252-1807.

U.S. Laws and U.S. and EC Trade Agreements Relating to Non-Market Economies. Volumes I and II. Issued March 1990. USITC Publication #2269. Available free of charge from: Publications, U.S. International Trade Commission, Washington, D.C. 20436. Tel: 202/252-1807.

Harmonized Tariff Schedules of the United States Annotated for Statistical Reporting Purposes, Second Edition contains the legal text of the Schedules, as amended and modified, together with annotations prescribing statistical information to be supplied on customs forms. The publication sets forth the changes brought about by the Kennedy Round of Trade negotiations and includes amendments and modifications made on or after August 31, 1963, and before January 1990. This is a subscription service consisting of a basic manual and supplementary material for an indeterminate period and is used in classifying imported merchandise for rate of duty and statistical purposes. The annual cost is $80.00 (priority mail) and $64.00 (non-priority mail). GPO Stock# 949-006-0000-0. Contact: Superintendent of Documents, U.S. Government Printing Office, Washington, D.C. 20402. Tel: 202/783-3238.

INTERNATIONAL TRADE COMMISSION
KEY LEGAL AUTHORITIES

General Agency Regulations: 19 C.F.R. Parts 200-213 (1989).
Rules of Practice and Procedure: 19 C.F.R. 201.4-201.16 (1989).

Revenue Act of 1916, as amended, 19 U.S.C. 1330 & note--establishes the International Trade Commission (renamed from the U.S. Tariff Commission) to examine and investigate U.S. foreign trade factors, the impact of imports, and U.S. and foreign trade barriers.

Agricultural Adjustment Act, as amended, 7 U.S.C. 624--authorizes the International Trade Commission to investigate agricultural commodities and related production imports and to recommend whether the President should exercise his authority to impose a tariff or otherwise restrict such imports.
Legislative History: 1948 U.S. Code Cong. Service 2320.

Tariff Act of 1930, as amended, 19 U.S.C. 1202 et seq.--protects U.S. industries from unfair imports and competition.
Legislative History: 1953 U.S. Code Cong. & Admin. News 2187; 1974 U.S. Code Cong. & Admin. News 7186; 1977 U.S. Code Cong. & Admin. News 1673; 1979 U.S. Code Cong. & Admin. News 30.

Trade Act of 1974, as amended, 19 U.S.C. 2101--provides procedures to safeguard U.S. industry and labor against unfair or injurious import competition and to assist injured companies, workers, and communities adjust to changes wrought by international trade.
Legislative History: 1974 U.S. Code Cong. & Admin. News 7186.

Trade Agreements Act of 1979, as amended, 19 U.S.C. 2501-2504--implements trade agreements negotiated under the Trade Act of 1974 and protects U.S. industry against dumped or subsidized foreign goods.
Legislative History: 1979 U.S. Code Cong. & Admin. News 381.

Trade and Tariff Act of 1984, 19 U.S.C. 1304 et seq.--delineates criteria for Commission injury threat assessments and established the Trade Remedy Assistance Center in the International Trade Commission to provide public information on remedies and benefits available under certain trade laws and technical assistance to small businesses seeking remedies and benefits under the trade remedy laws administered by the Commission.
Legislative History: 1984 U.S. Code Cong. & Admin. News 4910.

Omnibus Trade and Competitiveness Act of 1988, 19 U.S.C. 2901note--improves enforcement of antidumping and countervailing duty laws.
Legislative History: 1988 U.S. Code Cong. & Admin. News 1547.

U.S.-Canada Free Trade Agreement Implementation Act of 1988, 19 U.S.C. 2112note--implements the Agreement, defines its relationship to U.S. law, authorizes the Commission to investigate and recommend that the President grant import relief to U.S. industries adversely affected by the Agreement.
Legislative History: 1988 U.S. Code Cong. & Admin. News 2395.

INTERSTATE COMMERCE COMMISSION

12th Street and Constitution Avenue, N.W.
Washington, D.C. 20423

DESCRIPTION: The Interstate Commerce Commission (ICC) is an independent regulatory agency responsible for regulating the interstate surface transportation system, including railroads, trucking companies, intercity bus lines, and barge lines.

Most of the attorneys work in the Office of Proceedings, with the rest assigned to the Office of the General Counsel, the Office of Compliance and Consumer Assistance, the Office of Public Assistance, the Office of Transportation Analysis, and the personal staffs of the Commissioners.

(Area Code 202)

Chairman: Edward J. Philbin 275-7582
Procurement Information 275-0890
Docket (for General Counsel's Office only) 275-7173
Storage Docket Recall Service 275-7285
Appellate Briefing Unit 275-7208
Fees and New Applications 275-7218
Motor Carrier Insurance Inquiries 275-0783
Tariff Charge-out Control 275-0712
Handles questions concerning tariffs. There is no charge for this information unless a copy is necessary.
Tariff Certification Clerk 275-6891
Public Information/Public Affairs 275-7252
Publications 275-0783
Facsimile 275-9237

Microfilm Unit 275-6803
The Microfilm Unit (Room 1221) provides free microfiche copies of the full records of Commission cases including (as appropriate) applications, complaints, petitions, hearing transcripts, decisions, and protests. The Microfilm Unit can also provide paper copies at ten cents per page. The Microfilm Unit cannot mail out materials (see Certification Unit).

(Area Code 202)

Certification Unit 275-1295
The Certification Unit (Room 1312) will mail out free microfiche copies of the full records of Commission cases. They will send telefax copies of up to ten pages from decisions at no cost. They can also have paper copies made from the microfiche at 60 cents per page ($5.00 minimum), which they will send with a bill.

Freedom of Information Act Office/Privacy Act Office ..275-7076
Questions must be in writing. Costs vary depending on the time spent responding to the request and by whom it is requested. Submit requests to the Freedom of Information Act Officer, Room 3168, at the ICC address cited at the beginning of this listing.

Library (Room 3392) 275-7328
The library is open to the public from 8:30 AM until 5:00 PM, Monday through Friday. However, only ICC employees may remove materials from the library. Photocopying is available. The law library, which has an extensive collection of material dealing with transportation law, is contained within the library,

---

OFFICES OF THE COMMISSIONERS

The Commissioners are responsible for overall ICC management and operations, including the formulation of plans and policies and the identification and resolution of major regulatory problems.

(Area Code 202)

Advisors to Chairman Edward J. Philbin:
Attorney-Advisor: Laura Cooper 275-7582
Economist/Advisor: Howard Face 275-7582

Attorney-Advisors to Vice Chairperson Karen Phillips:
Debra Weiner 275-7054
Paul Joyce 275-7690
Samuel E. Eastman 275-7997

Attorney-Advisor to Commissioner Edward M. Emmett:
William A. Mullins 275-7815
J. Courtney Cunningham 275-7814
Robert A. Voltmann 275-7750

(Area Code 202)

Attorney-Advisors to Commissioner Paul H. Lamboley:
Dixie E. Horton 275-7773
Ted Kalick 275-7419

Attorney-Advisors to Commissioner J.J. Simmons, III:
Van A. Bosco 275-7187
Rickey L. Crawford 275-7086
Thomas T. Vining 275-7813

OFFICE OF THE GENERAL COUNSEL (Room 5211)

The Office of the General Counsel (OGC) defends the agency's orders in court, provides expert legal advice to the Commission, and assists in formulating the Commission's position on pending legislation and the preparation of legislative statements and testimony.

Attorneys in the OGC's Section of Litigation and Legal Counsel brief and argue one or two complex cases a month in the U.S. Courts of Appeals, prepare drafts of briefs for filing in the U.S. Supreme Court, and prepare legal memoranda on difficult issues of administrative and transportation law. Unlike many other Federal agencies, the ICC is authorized by statute to defend its orders in court in its own name and through its own attorneys.

Attorneys for Research and Legislation assist in formulating the ICC's position on pending legislation, prepare legislative statements and testimony, and draft proposed bills for submission to Congress.

(Area Code 202)

General Counsel: Robert S. Burk 275-7312
Deputy General Counsel: Henri F. Rush 275-7312
Associate General Counsel for Litigation and Legal Counsel: Ellen D. Hanson 275-7312

(Area Code 202)

Deputy Associate General Counsel:
Craig M. Keats 275-7602
John J. McCarthy, Jr 275-1857
Facsimile 275-7632

OFFICE OF PROCEEDINGS (Room 2118)

The Office of Proceedings is responsible for preparing decisions in cases brought before the Commission. Attorneys in this Office may also assist Administrative Law Judges during oral hearings and in the preparation of decisions; prepare recommendations concerning petitions and motions; and assist in drafting regulations and preparing notices of rulemaking proceedings. Attorneys in this Office do not handle litigation. The Office has two sections, the Rail Section and the Motor Section.

(Area Code 202)

Director: Jane F. Mackall 275-7513

Motor Section
Principal Attorney: Suzanne O'Malley 275-7292

(Area Code 202)

Rail Section
Principal Attorney: Beryl Gordon (Abandonments & Finance) 275-7245

OFFICE OF COMPLIANCE AND CONSUMER ASSISTANCE (Room 4412)

The Office of Compliance and Consumer Assistance, which includes a Section of Enforcement, monitors the surface transportation industry's compliance with ICC regulations; develops and implements a nationwide investigatory and prosecutorial program for all modes of surface transportation subject to Commission jurisdiction; and receives and resolves complaints from the general public. Administration of the enforcement program includes the initiation of administrative, civil, and criminal cases. This Office also has attorneys in regional and field offices around the country.

(Area Code 202)

Director: Bernard Gaillard 275-7849
Associate Director: William J. Love 275-7849
Associate Director for Policy and Review:
Sidney L. Strickland, Jr 275-7614

Enforcement Section
Deputy Director: Charles E. Wagner 275-7846
Assistant Deputy Director: Stanley M. Braverman 275-7846
Interpretation: John L. Chaney, Jr 275-7842

(Area Code 202)

Trial Attorneys:
Warren I. Cohn 275-7081
Patricia B. Kuhlmann 275-7819
Brenda B. White 275-7590
Special Assistant (Legal): James R. Taylor 275-0807

Operations Section
Deputy Director: Heber P. Hardy 275-7148

OFFICE OF PUBLIC ASSISTANCE (Room 3123)

The Office of Public Assistance is a new office established to assume the functions previously performed by the Office of Special Counsel, the Small Business Assistance Office, and the State/Community Affairs Liaison position formerly in the Office of Legislation and Governmental Affairs. The Office is managed by a Director who is also Special Counsel of the Commission, and a Deputy Director who is also the Small Business Assistance Officer of the Commission. The Office of Public Assistance represents the Commission on all matters of consumer and public interest, except in the area of compliance and enforcement. It ensures that the public interest is fully developed in proceedings before the Commission; that small and minority owned transportation entities, consumer groups, carriers and shippers, and state regulatory officials are advised on the applicability and interpretation of the law; and that the Commission is advised on policy matters related to its small business assistance functions and programs.

(Area Code 202)

Director and Special Counsel: Dan G. King (Acting) 275-7597
Deputy Director and Small Business Assistance Officer:
Dan G. King 275-7597
Attorney Advisors:
Eric Davis 275-7597

(Area Code 202)

Lillian A. Bateman 275-7597
Nancy Beiter 275-7597
J. Carol Brooks 275-7597
Alan D. Rothenberg 275-7597
Rudolph A. Saint-Louis 275-7597
Deputy State/Community Liaison: John Feehan 275-7597

INTERSTATE COMMERCE COMMISSION

OFFICE OF TRANSPORTATION ANALYSIS (Room 3219)

The Office of Transportation Analysis conducts economic and statistical analyses of the transportation industry, provides economic advice to the Commission, and provides liaison with other Government agencies, industries, and public/private organizations on major transportation issues.

(Area Code 202)

Director: Leland L. Gardner (Acting) 275-7684

Energy and Environment Section (Area Code 202)
Chief/Attorney Advisor: Elaine Kaiser 275-0800
Attorney: Harold E. Johnson 275-6874

OFFICE OF HEARINGS (Room 1211)

The Office of Hearings (three Administrative Law Judges): conducts hearings for those cases which require a public hearing because of Commission policy, the Administrative Procedure Act, or due process considerations, and adjudicates those controversies promptly and fairly.

(Area Code 202)

Chief Administrative Law Judge: Paul S. Cross 275-7502
Administrative Law Judges:
Paul J. Clerman 275-7036
Frederick M. Dolan, Jr 275-4387
Case Control Manager: Linda M. Charles 275-7450

BUREAU OF TRAFFIC (Room 4318)

The Bureau of Traffic monitors tariff publication, filing, and interpretation, and suspends any unreasonable or unlawful tariffs before they may become effective.

(Area Code 202)

Director: Neil S. Llewellyn 275-7348

Tariffs Section
Chief: Charles E. Langyher III 275-7739
Tariff Examining Branch Chief: Thomas A. Mongelli ...275-7462

Rates and Informal Cases Section (Area Code 202)
Chief: Lawrence C. Herzig 275-7358
Enforcement and Adjudication Support Branch Chief:
James E. Manning 275-7561
Informal Rate Case Branch Chief: Joel W. King 275-6886

FIELD OFFICES

The ICC now has three regional offices: Philadelphia (Eastern Region), Chicago (Central Region) and San Francisco (Western Region). Each of the regional offices has a number of field offices under its jurisdiction.

Eastern Region (Philadelphia)

Interstate Commerce Commission, 3535 Market Street, Room 16400, Philadelphia, PA 19104. Tel: 215/596-4040.

Office of Compliance and Consumer Assistance
Regional Director: Richard M. Biter
Tel: 215/596-4062.

Compliance and Investigations
Regional Compliance Officer: Glenn A. Eady
Assistant Regional Compliance Officer: Gail Giovannetti
Tel: 215/596-4040

Complaint and Authority Center
Tel: 215/596-4040

Enforcement
Regional Counsel: Michael J. Falk
Trial Attorney: Edward J. Schock
Tel: 215/596-4040.

FIELD OFFICES:

Atlanta
Officer in Charge/Trial Attorney: Edward Arnn
Trial Attorney: Michael N. Nafpliotis
Interstate Commerce Commission, Peachtree Twenty-Fifth Bldg., 1371 Peachtree Street, NE, Room 638, Atlanta, GA 30309.
Tel: 404/347-4371.

Baltimore
Officer in Charge: William L. Hughes
Interstate Commerce Commission, 1025 Fallon Federal Bldg., Charles Center, 31 Hopkins Plaza, Baltimore, MD 21201.
Tel: 301/962-0809 or 301/962-2561.

Boston
Officer in Charge: Richard J. Breen
Trial Attorney: Stuart B. Robbins
Interstate Commerce Commission, Boston Federal Office Bldg., 10 Causeway Street, Room 1015, Boston, MA 02222.
Tel: 617/565-6600.

Charlotte
Officer in Charge: (vacant)
Interstate Commerce Commission, Rm CC-516, Mart Office Bldg., 800 Briar Creek Road, Charlotte, NC 28205. Tel: 704/371-6115.

Cleveland
Officer in Charge: Wesley C. Shapiro
Interstate Commerce Commission, Celebrezze Federal Building, Room 913, 1240 East 9th Street, Cleveland, OH 44119.
Tel: 216/522-4000.

Jacksonville
Officer in Charge: Frank H. Wait, Jr.
Interstate Commerce Commission, 4057 Carmichael Avenue, Suite 233, Jacksonville, FL 32207. Tel: 904/791-2551.

New York
Officer in Charge: Joseph O'Reilly
Interstate Commerce Commission, Jacob K. Javits Federal Bldg., 26 Federal Plaza, Room 1807, New York, NY 10278. Tel: 212/264-1072.

Central Region (Chicago)

Interstate Commerce Commission,, Everett McKinley Dirksen Bldg., 219 South Dearborn Street, Room 1304, Chicago, IL 60604. Tel: 312/353-6204.

Office of Compliance and Consumer Assistance
Regional Director: William Redmond, Jr.
Tel: 312/353-6204.

Compliance and Investigations
Regional Compliance Officer: David V. Armitage
Assistant Regional Compliance Officer: Nathaniel U. Jackson
Tel: 312/353-6204.

Complaint and Authority Center
Tel: 312/353-6204

Enforcement
Regional Counsel: Barbara J. Welsch
Trial Attorneys: Yvonne Anagnost, Joseph P. Bohn
Tel: 312/886-6403.

FIELD OFFICES:

Fort Worth
Office of Compliance and Consumer Assistance
Officer in Charge: Haldon G. West
Trial Attorneys: Simon W. Oderberg, Judith A. Rutledge
Interstate Commerce Commission, 411 West 7th Street, Suite 510, Fort Worth, TX 76102. Tel: 817/334-2837.

Indianapolis
Officer in Charge: Loren Laufman
Interstate Commerce Commission, Federal Bldg & U.S. Courthouse, 46 East Ohio Street, Room 429, Indianapolis, IN 46204. Tel: 317/226-7701.

Kansas City
Officer in Charge: Michael W. Walker
Interstate Commerce Commission, 2111 Federal Building, 911 Walnut Street, Kansas City, MO 64106. Tel: 816/426-5561.

Minneapolis
Officer in Charge: Gail A. Daugherty
Interstate Commerce Commission, Federal Building & U.S. Courthouse, 110 South Fourth Street, Room 475, Minneapolis, MN 55401. Tel: 612/348-1661.

New Orleans
Officer in Charge: (vacant)
Interstate Commerce Commission, T-3015 Federal Building and U.S. Post Office, 701 Loyola Avenue, New Orleans, LA 70113. Tel: 504/589-6101.

Omaha
Officer in Charge: Jarred D. Adkins
Interstate Commerce Commission, Room 728, Federal Office Bldg, 106 South 15th Street, Omaha, NE 68102. Tel: 402/221-4644.

St. Louis
Officer in Charge: Joseph P. Werthmann
Interstate Commerce Commission, 210 North Tucker Boulevard, Room 1161, St. Louis, MO 63101. Tel: 314/425-4103.

Western Region (San Francisco)

Interstate Commerce Commission, 211 Main Street, Suite 500, San Francisco, CA 94105. Tel: 415/744-6520.

Office of Compliance and Consumer Assistance
Regional Director: John H. Kirkemo
Regional Director: James W. Boyd
Tel: 415/744-6520.

Compliance and Investigations
Assistant Regional Compliance Officer: Joanne B. Rudolph
Tel: 415/744-6520.

Complaint and Authority Center
Tel: 415/744-6520.

Enforcement
Regional Counsel: (vacant)
Tel: 415/744-6520.

FIELD OFFICES:

Denver
Officer in Charge: Raymond S. Weddel
Interstate Commerce Commission, Room 440, Federal Office Bldg., Drawer #3549, 1961 Stout Street, Denver, CO 80294. Tel: 303/844-3162.

Los Angeles
Officer in Charge: Philip Yallowitz
Senior Trial Attorney: Yvonne Tanagnost
Interstate Commerce Commission, 360 East 2nd Street, Suite 304, Los Angeles, CA 90012. Tel: 213/894-4008.

Phoenix
Officer in Charge: Billy Martin
Interstate Commerce Commission, 3415 Federal Building, 230 North First Avenue, Phoenix, AZ 85025. Tel: 602/379-3834.

Salt Lake City
Officer in Charge: Patricia Allgier
Interstate Commerce Commission, 2419 Federal Building, 125 State Street, Salt Lake City, UT 84138. Tel: 801/524-5680.

Seattle
Officer in Charge/Regional Counsel: Stephen L. Day
Interstate Commerce Commission, 1894 Federal Building, 915 Second Avenue, Seattle, WA 98174. Tel: 206/442-5421.

PUBLICATIONS OF INTEREST

Copies of ICC decisions and case annotations are available for reference in the ICC Library (Room 3392).

Records of cases and copies of decisions can also be obtained from the ICC's Microfilm Unit and its Certification Unit (see explanation at the beginning of the ICC section).

Dynamic Concepts, Inc. keeps a file of all **ICC decisions** for one year from the date of the decision. They can provide copies at 22 cents per page plus postage and 75 cents for handling. Sales tax of six percent will be added for sales within the District of Columbia. To obtain a copy of a decision, provide Dynamic Concepts with the docket number and, if possible, the service date. Dynamic Concepts, Inc. ICC Building, Room 2229, 12th and Constitution Ave., N.W., Wash., D.C. 20423. Tel: 202/289-4357.

Federal Carriers Reports, published by Commerce Clearing House, cover the Federal regulation of carriers engaged in interstate commerce. Issued every two weeks, subscribers receive four loose-leaf volumes with contents as follows:

INTERSTATE COMMERCE COMMISSION

1) General Guide
2) Transportation Law and Regulation: Interstate Commerce
3) General Orders-Forms-Rulings: ICC and DOT general orders, forms, and rulings concerning the various modes of carriage.
4) Commission and Court Decisions: digests of pertinent new ICC decisions and court decisions.

Annual subscription price is $800.00 per year. Contact: Commerce Clearing House Inc., 4025 West Peterson Avenue, Chicago, IL 60646. (312/583-8500). Or, in Washington, D.C. call 202/626-2200.

The following publication(s) can be purchased from the **U.S. Government Printing Office.** Stock numbers and prices for annual subscriptions are shown below. Submit requests for these publications to: The Superintendent of Documents, U.S. Government Printing Office, Washington, D.C. 20402. Tel: 202/783-3238.

ICC Register: A Daily Summary of Motor Carrier Applications and of Decisions and Notices Issued by the Interstate Commerce Commission. Published daily. Price: $444.00 a year domestic; $555.00 a year foreign. GPO Stock# 726-001-00000-6.

Interstate Commerce Commission Vol 366: Finance Cases, Decisions of the Interstate Commerce Commission of the U. S., October 1981 through June 1983. Price: $24.00 domestic; $30.00 foreign. GPO Stock# 026-000-01245-7.

Volume I: Interstate Commerce Commission, 2d Series. Decisions of the Interstate Commerce Commission, February 1984-May 1986. Price: $34.00. GPO Stock# 026-000-01264-3.

Volume II: Interstate Commerce Commission, 2d Series. Decisions of the Interstate Commerce Commission, August 1984-July 1986. Price: $47.00. GPO Stock# 026-000-01266-0.

Volume III: Interstate Commerce Commission, 2d Series. Decisions of the Interstate Commerce Commission, June 1985-August 1987. Price: $35.00. GPO Stock# 026-000-01272-4.

INTERSTATE COMMERCE COMMISSION
KEY LEGAL AUTHORITIES

General Agency Regulations: 49 C.F.R. Parts 1000-1186 (1988).
Rules of Practice and Procedure: 49 C.F.R. Parts 1100-1104, 1110-1120, 1130-1177 (1988).

Interstate Commerce Act, as amended, 49 U.S.C. 501 et seq., 10301 et seq.--established the Interstate Commerce Commission and sets forth its regulatory authority over operating right, financial structures, rates and practices of brokers, electric railways, express companies, freight forwarders, motor carriers, pipelines, private car companies, rail carriers, and water carriers.

MERIT SYSTEMS PROTECTION BOARD

1120 Vermont Avenue, N.W.
Washington, D.C. 20419

DESCRIPTION: The U.S. Merit Systems Protection Board (MSPB), created pursuant to the Reorganization Plan of 1978 and the Civil Service Reform Act of 1978, is an independent judicial agency charged with guardianship of the Federal merit systems. Its duties include: adjudicating actions brought by the Special Counsel and employee appeals; conducting special studies of the merit systems to determine whether they are free from prohibited personnel practices; analyzing and reporting on significant activities of the Office of Personnel Management (OPM); and reviewing OPM regulations to determine whether they require the commission of prohibited personnel practices.

The Board consists of 11 trial-level regional offices and an appellate forum at Headquarters in Washington, D.C. Since its inception, the Board has decided over 72,500 appeals and petitions for review. Board decisions have withstood the scrutiny of the U.S. Court of Appeals for the Federal Circuit in over 93% of the cases appealed.

(Area Code 202)

Chairman: Daniel R. Levinson 653-7101
Executive Director: Lucretia F. Myers 653-6842
Procurement Information 653-7654
Public Information/Legislative Counsel 653-7175
Office of the Clerk of the Board/Docket 653-7200
Facsimile 653-7130

Freedom of Information Act Office/Privacy Act Office 653-7200
There is a copying charge of 10 cents per page after the first 50 pages. There is also a variable per hour search fee.

Law Library (8th Floor) 653-7132
The library is open to the public from 1:00 PM until 5:00 PM, Monday through Friday.

(Area Code 202)

Offices of the Board

Chairman: Daniel R. Levinson 653-7101
Legal Counsel: Garry M. Ewing 653-7101

Vice Chairman: Maria L. Johnson 653-7103
Legal Assistant: Stephanie M. Conley 653-7113

Member: Jessica L. Parks 653-7105
Legal Assistant: MaryAnn Kane 653-8906

OFFICE OF INSPECTOR GENERAL (Room 968)

The Inspector General plans and directs audits, investigations, and internal control evaluations of Board programs and operations in order to promote economy and efficiency, to prevent and detect fraud and abuse, and to advise the Chairman and Executive Director of any problems and deficiencies detected.

(Area Code 202)

Inspector General: T. Paul Riegert 653-2514

OFFICE OF THE GENERAL COUNSEL (Room 816)

The Office of the General Counsel (OGC) performs four principal functions: litigation, advisory services, case-related services, and management of congressional relations and public affairs.

The Office of the General Counsel represents the Board and its interests in litigation involving its decisions, policies, and practices. The Whistleblower Protection Act substantially increased the Office's litigation responsibilities. Specifically, the Act provides that the Board will be the named respondent in judicial review of its decisions on appeals, unless the review requires the court to address the merits of the underlying personnel actions or a request for attorney fees. Thus, the Board will defend its decisions involving the jurisdictional and procedural matters in the U.S. Court of Appeals for the Federal Circuit.

The Board is the named respondent in most appeals from its decisions issued under its original jurisdiction authority. OGC represents the Board in these cases, including appeals of decisions on complaints brought by the Special Counsel, and requests to review OPM rules or regulations.

The Office of the General Counsel also represents the Board in district courts in other types of cases, and in many of these cases OGC attorneys serve as trial counsel. OGC attorneys represent the Board in actions for extraordinary relief, such as injunction or writs of mandamus, in Federal trial and appellate courts. Moreover, when Board officials are sued for alleged violations of constitutional rights or for alleged discriminatory acts, the Office coordinates the judicial defense of those officials with representatives of the Justice Department.

OGC also monitors the progress of judicial appeals from decisions issued under the Board's appellate jurisdictional authority. These cases are filed in the Court of Appeals for the Federal Circuit or, in cases involving allegations of discrimination, in the various Federal courts.

MERIT SYSTEMS PROTECTION BOARD

In addition to its litigation function, OGC provides legal advice to the Board, and to offices of the Board, on all matters that arise in connection with the operation of MSPB as a Government agency. For example, the Office provides advice on labor relations, personnel disputes, and discrimination complaints. It provides advice on FOIA and Privacy Act matters, and on regulatory, contract, appropriated funds, and ethics issues.

With respect to its case-related services, the OGC gives advice and prepares decisions for the Board in a variety of cases within the Board's jurisdiction. These include stay requests, corrective actions, disciplinary actions, and Hatch Act actions filed by the Special Counsel. They also include cases involving compliance with Board orders and other, often complicated, appellate jurisdiction cases that have been assigned by the Board to OGC.

The Office of the General Counsel also manages legislative policy, congressional relations, and public affairs for the Board.

(Area Code 202)

General Counsel: Llewellyn Fischer 653-7168
Deputy General Counsel and Legislative Counsel:
Mary L. Jennings 653-7162
Deputy Legislative Counsel: Susan Williams 653-8875
Legal Counsel: Michael Doheny 653-8903
Assistant General Counsel: David C. Kane 653-8923
Assistant General Counsel: Martha B. Schneider 653-8920
Attorneys:
Rita Arendal 653-2373

(Area Code 202)

William A. Cardoza 653-8904
Peter Constantine 653-8921
Joyce Friedman 653-8903
Anita Marshall 653-8917
Michael K. Martin 653-8261
Calvin M. Morrow 653-8915
Patricia Price 653-8919
Sara Rearden 653-8922

OFFICE OF THE APPEALS COUNSEL (Room 864)

The Office of Appeals Counsel drafts proposed decisions for the Board based on petitions for review of initial decisions issued in appellate jurisdiction cases, and on cases reopened by the Board.

(Area Code 202)

Director: William DuRoss 653-8888
Assistant to the Director: John J. Murphy 653-8980

Supervisory General Attorneys (Area Code 202)
Ramon V. Gomez 653-7160
Lois S. Schwartz 653-7159
Rose Tyson 653-7158

OFFICE OF THE CLERK OF THE BOARD (Room 802)

The Office of the Clerk processes petitions to the Board, distributes Board opinions and orders, rules on procedural matters relating to adjudication, and makes initial determinations on Freedom of Information Act (FOIA) and Privacy Act Requests.

Adjudicating appeals filed in one of the Board's 11 regional offices is the major function of the Board. Most cases stem from requests by an appellant or an agency in the form of petitions for review of a presiding official's decision. The petitions must be based on specific legal grounds, not mere disagreements with the regional office decision.

Decisions of the Board's Administrative Law Judges in original jurisdiction cases (i.e., cases not involving appeals from agency actions) are recommended decisions to the full Board. Cases under the Board's original jurisdiction include complaints against administrative law judges by their employing agency, and actions brought by the Office of Special Counsel for violations of the Hatch Act and for commission of prohibited personnel practices by supervisors.

(Area Code 202)

Clerk: Robert E. Taylor 653-7262
Legal Counsel: Matthew D. Shannon 653-7262

(Area Code 202)

Case Management Division 653-7200

OFFICE OF THE ADMINISTRATIVE LAW JUDGE (Room 846)

The Office of Administrative Law Judges adjudicates cases within the Board's original jurisdiction, including proposed disciplinary actions against administrative law judges and disciplinary actions filed by the Office of Special Counsel for violations of the Hatch Political Activities Act or for the commission of prohibited personnel practices by supervisors. This office also has jurisdiction over motions to compel discovery and motions for subpoenas filed in the regional offices.

(Area Code 202)

Administrative Law Judge: Edward J. Reidy 653-2258

(Area Code 202)

General Attorney: vacant 653-2258

REGIONAL OFFICES:

Atlanta Regional Office
Chief Administrative Judge: R. J. Payne
Administrative Officer: Bonnie L. Meyo
U.S. Merit Systems Protection Board, 1365 Peachtree Street, N.E., Room 500, Atlanta, GA 30309. Tel: 404/347-3631.
(Jurisdiction: AL, FL, GA, MS, NC, SC)

Boston Regional Office
Chief Administrative Judge: William Carroll
Administrative Officer: Maureen Nash-Cole
U.S. Merit Systems Protection Board, 10 Causeway Street, Rm. 1078, Boston, MA 02222. Tel: 617/565-6650.
(Jurisdiction: CT, ME, MA, NH, RI, VT)

Chicago Regional Office
Chief Administrative Judge: Martin W. Baumgaertner
Administrative Officer: Elizabeth A. Caplis
U.S. Merit Systems Protection Board, 230 South Dearborn Street, Rm 3100, Chicago, IL 60604. Tel: 312/353-2923.
(Jurisdiction: IL, IN, MI, MN, OH, WI)

Dallas Regional Office
Chief Administrative Judge: Paula A. Latshaw
Administrative Officer: Patricia Perry
U.S. Merit Systems Protection Board, 1100 Commerce Street, Room 6F20, Dallas, TX 75242. Tel: 214/767-0555.
(Jurisdiction: AR, LA, OK, TX)

Denver Regional Office
Chief Administrative Judge: Gail E. Skaggs
Administrative Officer: Vicky J. Boiko
U.S. Merit Systems Protection Board, 730 Simms Street, Ste 301, P.O. Box 25025, Denver, CO 80225. Tel: 303/236-2710.
(Jurisdiction: AZ, CO, KS, MT, NE, NV, NM, ND, SD, UT, WY)

New York Regional Office
Chief Administrative Judge: Sean P. Walsh
Administrative Officer: Sonja R. Maxwell
U.S. Merit Systems Protection Board, 26 Federal Plaza, Room 3137A, New York, NY 10278. Tel: 212/264-9372.
(Jurisdiction: NJ [Bergen, Essex, Hudson, Hunterdon, Morris, Passaic, Somerset, Sussex, Union, and Warren Counties], NY, PR, VI)

Philadelphia Regional Office
Chief Administrative Judge: Lonnie L. Crawford
Administrative Officer: Mary H. Wilson
U.S. Merit Systems Protection Board, 2nd & Chestnut Streets, Room 501, Philadelphia, PA 19106. Tel: 215/597-9960.
(Jurisdiction: NJ [Atlantic, Burlington, Camden, Cape May, Cumberland, Gloucester, Mercer, Middlesex, Monmouth, Ocean, and Salem Counties], DE, PA, VA [except areas covered by the Washington, D.C. Regional Office], WV)

St. Louis Regional Office
Chief Administrative Judge: Earl A. Witten
Administrative Officer: Jo Ann Baumstark
U.S. Merit Systems Protection Board, 911 Washington Avenue, Room 615, St. Louis, MO 63101. Tel: 314/425-4295.
(Jurisdiction: IA, KY, MO, TN)

San Francisco Regional Office
Chief Administrative Judge: Denis Marachi
Administrative Officer: Lizabeth B. Yee
U.S. Merit Systems Protection Board, 525 Market Street, Room 2800, San Francisco, CA 94105. Tel: 415/744-3081.
(Jurisdiction: CA)

Seattle Regional Office
Chief Administrative Judge: Carl Berkenwald
Administrative Officer: Dianne D. Suhara
U.S. Merit Systems Protection Board, 915 Second Avenue, Room 1840, Seattle, WA 98174. Tel: 206/442-0394.
(Jurisdiction: AK, HI, ID, OR, WA, and Pacific overseas)

Washington, D.C. Regional Office
Chief Administrative Judge: P. J. Winzer
Administrative Officer: Nancy E. Sopich
U.S. Merit Systems Protection Board, 5203 Leesburg Pike, Room 1109, Falls Church, VA 22041. Tel: 703/756-6250.
(Jurisdiction: VA [Alexandria, Falls Church City, Arlington, Fairfax, Loudon, and Prince William Counties], all overseas areas not otherwise covered)

Note: This Washington, D.C. regional office address in Falls Church, VA, should not be confused with the Board's Headquarters Office on 1120 Vermont Ave, N.W., Washington, D.C. 20419 (cited at the beginning of this listing).

DATABASES AND PUBLICATIONS OF INTEREST

Databases:

Merit Systems Protection Board Case Decisions. Available on CD-ROM through the PERSONNET Service of Information Handling Services, 15 Inverness Way East, P.O. Box 1154, Englewood, CO 80150. Tel: 800-241-7824. In Colorado, call 303/790-0600 ext 59.

Publications:

Federal Merit Systems Reporter. A weekly format reporting the full text of decisions handed down by the U.S. Merit Systems Protection Board and Federal court rulings on appeals from the Board. Back volumes dating from 1979 are available at extra expense. Product# 4050. Price: $685.00. Contact: LRP Publications, 747 Dresher Road, P.O. Box 980, Horsham, PA 19044-0980. Tel: 1-800-341-7874.

Decisions of the Merit Systems Protection Board are available through West Publishing Company, 50 West Kellogg Blvd., P.O. Box 64833, St. Paul, MN 55164. Tel: 612/688-3600. Or, 800/328-9352. West offers several related publications and services:

The Merit System Protection Reporter is a 43 volume hard-bound set that contains the full text of all opinions from 1985 through 1989. Price: $3,229.00. Additional volumes are sold for $77.50 each as published.

Merit System Protection Reporter Advance Sheets are issued biweekly. The price of an annual subscription is $260.00.

West's Merit Protection Board Digest is a two-volume soft bound index to volumes 1-27 of the Merit System Protection Reporter. Price: $170.00.

The following reports and pamphlets available free of charge from: **U.S. Merit Systems Protection Board**, Office of Management Analysis, 1120 Vermont Avenue, N.W., Room 884, Washington, D.C. 20419.

Introduction to MSPB. 1989. (28 pages)
Questions and Answers on Appeals. 1989. (25 pages)
Questions and Answers on Whistleblower Appeals. 1990. (27 pages)
A Study of Cases Decided by the U.S. Merit Systems Protection Board in FY 1989. 1990. (58 pages)

MERIT SYSTEMS PROTECTION BOARD
KEY LEGAL AUTHORITIES

General Agency Regulations: 5 C.F.R. Parts 1200-1207 (1990).
Rules of Practice and Procedure: 5 C.F.R. Parts 1201 & 1203 (1989).

Civil Service Reform Act of 1978, Title II, sec. 202(a), 5 U.S.C. 1201-1209 & 7701-7703--established the Merit Systems Protection Board as an independent Government agency and directed it to ensure that all Federal Government agencies follow Federal merit systems practices and to hear and adjudicate appeals of certain personnel actions taken by Federal agencies.
Legislative History: 1978 U.S. Code Cong. & Admin. News 2723.

Reorganization Plan No. 2 of 1978, Part II, 5 U.S.C. 1101note--redesignated the U.S. Civil Service Commission the Merit Systems Protection Board and transferred certain Commission hearing, adjudication, and appeals functions, as well as enforcement authorities to the Board.

NATIONAL AERONAUTICS AND SPACE ADMINISTRATION

400 Maryland Avenue, S.W.
Washington, D.C. 20546

DESCRIPTION: The National Aeronautics and Space Administration (NASA), established in 1958 as an independent agency, conducts research and development related to space and aeronautics. The principal statutory functions of NASA are to conduct research for the solution of problems of flight within and outside the Earth's atmosphere and develop, construct, test, and operate aeronautical and space vehicles; conduct activities required for the exploration of space with manned and unmanned vehicles; arrange for the most effective utilization of the scientific and engineering resources of the United States with other nations engaged in aeronautical and space activities for peaceful purposes; and to provide for the widest practicable and appropriate dissemination of information concerning NASA's activities and their results.

(Area Code 202)

Administrator: Admiral Richard H. Truly 453-1010
Procurement Information 453-2090
Public Information 453-1000
Publications Information 453-8332
Office of Small & Disadvantaged Business Utilization .. 453-2088
Inspector General's Hot Line
  Washington, D.C. Metro area 755-3402
  Outside Washington, D.C. Metro Area .... (800) 424-9183
Facsimile 755-9235

Freedom of Information Act/Privacy Act Office 453-2939
Requests must be made in writing. There is a copying charge of 10 cents per page, and a variable per hour search fee. Submit requests to the attention of the Freedom of Information Act Officer, Mail code LN, at the NASA address cited at the beginning of this listing.

(Area Code 202)

Law Library (Room F7062) 453-2458
The law library is open to the public from 8:00 AM until 4:30 PM, Monday through Friday. There are no charge-out privileges but photocopying is available for a charge.

Library (Room DBD-3) 453-8545
The library is located at 600 Independence Ave, S.W. It is open to the public from 8:00 AM until 4:30 PM, Monday through Friday. There are no charge-out privileges but photocopying is available for a charge.

OFFICE OF INSPECTOR GENERAL (Room F6075)

The Office of Inspector General (OIG) performs investigations and audits to prevent and detect fraud and abuse and to assist NASA management in promoting economy, efficiency, and effectiveness in its programs and operations. OIG investigators and auditors perform work at NASA Headquarters, eight field offices, the Jet Propulsion Laboratory, and contractor locations. When joint jurisdiction exists, OIG investigators and auditors work with the Federal Bureau of Investigation (FBI), the Defense Contract Audit Agency (DCAA), and other audit and investigative entities.

(Area Code 202)

Inspector General: Bill D. Colvin 453-1220
Deputy Inspector General: Lewis D. Rinker 453-2162

(Area Code 202)

Attorney-Advisor: Francis P. LaRocca Jr 453-1220
Facsimile 472-4086

OFFICE OF GENERAL COUNSEL (Room F7065)

The legal work of the Office of General Counsel falls under three main groupings: **General** (including international); **Contracts**; and **Intellectual Property.** In each category, attorneys represent the agency not only in administrative matters and negotiations, but also in litigation in support of the Department of Justice.

Under the **Associate General Counsel (General)**, attorneys work on environmental problems, Freedom of Information Act (FOIA), Privacy Act questions, and EEO and other personnel matters; draft new legislation and interagency agreements; settle tort claims; assist in the acquisition of real and personal property; and participate in international negotiations.

Under the **Associate General Counsel (Contracts)**, attorneys draft, negotiate, and interpret procurement contracts, research grants, and Federal procurement laws and regulations; advise on labor relations matters; and negotiate launch services agreements with U.S. companies and foreign countries.

Under the **Associate General Counsel (Intellectual Property)**, attorneys handle all phases of intellectual property matters (patents, copyrights, trademarks, and trade secrets); prepare and prosecute patent applications; license NASA technology; investigate and settle patent and copyright infringement actions against NASA; and determine rights to inventions. NASA's patent program is generally considered one of the most active and productive in the entire Federal Government.

NATIONAL AERONAUTICS AND SPACE ADMINISTRATION

(Area Code 202)

General Counsel: Edward A. Frankle 453-2450
Deputy General Counsel: Gary L. Tesch 453-8608
Associate General Counsel for:
Contracts: David P. Forbes 453-2440
General Law: George Reese 453-2465
Intellectual Property: Robert F. Kempf 453-2424
Assistant General Counsel: June W. Edwards 453-2432
Facsimile..755-2371

FIELD OFFICES

Cleveland

Chief Counsel: J. William Sikora
Lewis Research Center (LE-LAW), 21000 Brookpark Road, Cleveland, OH 44135. Tel: 216/433-2318.

Patent Counsel: Gene E. Shook
Lewis Research Center (LE-LAW), 21000 Brookpark Road, Cleveland, OH 44135. Tel: 216/433-5753.

Library: 216/433-5779.

Greenbelt

Chief Counsel: Lawrence F. Watson
Goddard Space Flight Center (140), Greenbelt, MD 20771. Tel: 301/286-9181.

Patent Counsel: Dennis Marchant
Goddard Space Flight Center (204), Greenbelt, MD 20771. Tel: 301/286-7351.

Library: 301/286-4394.

Hampton

Chief Counsel: David F. Caplan
Langley Research Center (278), Langley Station, Hampton, VA 23665. Tel: 804/864-3221.

Patent Counsel: George F. Helfrich
Langley Research Center (279), Langley Station, Hampton, VA 23665. Tel: 804/864-3523.

Library: 804/864-2383.

Houston

Chief Counsel: Henry W. Flagg, Jr.
Lyndon B. Johnson Space Center (AL), Houston, TX 77058. Tel: 713/483-3021.

Patent Counsel: Edward K. Fein
Lyndon B. Johnson Space Center (AL3), Houston, TX 77058. Tel: 713/483-4871.

Library: 713/483-4225.

Kennedy Space Center

Chief Counsel: Edward F. Parry
John F. Kennedy Space Center (CC), Kennedy Space Center, FL 32899. Tel: 407/867-2550.

Patent Counsel: James O. Harrell
John F. Kennedy Space Center (PT-PAT), Kennedy Space Center, FL 32899. Tel: 407/867-2544.
Library: 407/867-3600.

Marshall Space Center

Chief Counsel: Susan McGuire Smith
Law Librarian: Lonia R. Moore
George C. Marshall Space Flight Center (CC01), Marshall Space Flight Center, AL 35812. Tel: 205/544-0012.

Patent Counsel: William J. Sheehan
George C. Marshall Space Flight Center (CC01), Marshall Space Flight Center, AL 35812. Tel: 205/544-0024.

Library: 205/544-4524.

Moffett Field

Chief Counsel: George T. Lenehan
Ames Research Center (Code 200-26), Moffett Field, CA 94035. Tel: 415/604-5055.

Patent Counsel: Darrell Brekke
Ames Research Center (Code 200-11A), Moffett Field, CA 94035. Tel: 415/604-5104.

Library: 415/604-5157.

Pasadena

Chief Counsel: William T. Barr
NASA Resident Office-JPL, 4800 Oak Grove Drive (180-801), Pasadena, CA 91109. Tel: 818/354-2562.

Patent Counsel: Paul F. McCaul
NASA Resident Office-JPL, 4800 Oak Grove Drive (180-801), Pasadena, CA 91109. Tel: 818/354-2700.

Library: 818/354-4200.

Stennis Space Center

Chief Counsel: Kenneth R. Human
John C. Stennis Space Center (CA00), Stennis Space Center, MS 39529. Tel: 601/688-2164.

Patent Counsel: William J. Sheehan
George C. Marshall Space Flight Center (CC01), Marshall Space Flight Center, AL 35812. Tel: 205/544-0024.
NOTE: Although William J. Sheehan is located at Marshall Space Center, his office provides legal support for Stennis Space Center.

Library: 601/688-3245.

BOARD OF CONTRACT APPEALS (Room F5065)

The Administrative Judges of the Board of Contract Appeals conduct hearings, examine witnesses, report the evidence and argument to a designated panel of the Board, and write decisions. Further, the judges may concur in or dissent from decisions of designated panels and, in appeals of $10,000 or less, issue dispositive decisions or orders of dismissal. The Board Chairman, as Chief Administrative Judge, assigns cases to individual judges and to designated panels, issues rules of procedure, and generally manages the Board's activities.

The Board of Contract Appeals Reporter is a bi-weekly publication which reports the decisions of the following Boards of Contract Appeals: Agriculture, Armed Services, Corps of Engineers, Department of Transportation, Energy, General Services Administration, Department of Housing and Urban Development, Interior, Labor, National Aeronautics and Space Administration, U.S. Postal Service, and Veterans Administration. Annual Price $760.00. Contact: Commerce Clearing House, Inc., 4025 West Peterson Avenue, Chicago, IL 60646. Tel: 312/583-8500. Or in Washington, D.C., call 202/626-2200. publication

(Area Code 202)
Chairman: Carroll C. Dicus, Jr 453-2890
Recorder: Teresa Grimes 453-2890

Administrative Judges: (Area Code 202)
Richard M. Bayus 453-2890
Lisa Anderson Todd 453-2890

CONTRACT ADJUSTMENT BOARD (Room F7071)

(Area Code 202)
Chairman: George Reese 453-2465

INVENTIONS AND CONTRIBUTIONS BOARD (Room F5065)

(Area Code 202)
Chairman: Carroll C. Dicus, Jr 453-2890

DATABASES AND PUBLICATIONS OF INTEREST

Databases:

ARIN is an online catalog which provides access to approximately 50,000 titles in the Homer E. Newell Memorial Library as well as 460,000 titles throughout all NASA libraries. Information is provided through AUTHOR, TITLE, SUBJECT, and includes a BIBLIOGRAPHIC RECORD for each title, which describes the item, call number and material location. ARIN can also be accessed in all NASA field locations in their libraries.

Publications:

The following publications can be purchased from the **U.S. Government Printing Office.** Stock numbers and prices for annual subscriptions are shown below. Submit requests for these publications to: The Superintendent of Documents, U.S. Government Printing Office, Washington, D.C. 20402. Tel: 202/783-3238.

NASA FAR Supplement (June 1989). Contains NASA's uniform policies and procedures for procuring supplies and services defined in the Federal Acquisition Regulation. Subscription service consists of a basic manual and changes for an indeterminate period. In looseleaf form, punched for 3-ring binder. Price: $86.00 domestic; $107.50 foreign. GPO Stock# 933-003-00000-1.

NASA Grant and Cooperative Agreement Handbook (October 1983). This handbook prescribes policies and regulations relating to the award and administration of NASA research grants. It represents a significant NASA step in the publication and dissemination of NASA policies and procedures. Subscription service consists of a basic manual, changes, and procurement grant directives issued irregularly for an indeterminate period. Price: $23.00 domestic; $28.75 foreign. GPO Stock# 933-001-00000-8.

Selling to NASA (1986). Prepared to assist potential contractors in the process of doing business with NASA. The procurement process is explained and advice is offered for marketing products. 44 pp. Price: $3.25. GPO Stock# 033-000-00995-0.

NATIONAL AERONAUTICS AND SPACE ADMINISTRATION
KEY LEGAL AUTHORITIES

Regulations:

General Agency Regulations: 14 C.F.R. Parts 1201-1265 (1989).
NASA Procurement Regulations: 41 C.F.R. Chapt. 18 (1989).
NASA Supplement to Federal Acquisition Regulations: 48 C.F.R. Parts 1801-1870 (1988).

National Aeronautics and Space Act of 1958, as amended, 42 U.S.C. 2451-2477--established NASA as the civilian agency to direct aeronautical and space activities of the U.S., except for those determined by the President to be peculiar to or primarily associated with weapons development, military operations, or defense, which are the responsibility of the Department of Defense.

Legislative History: 1958 U.S. Code Cong. & Admin. News 3160; 1976 U.S. Code Cong. & Admin. News 2315; 1980 U.S. Code Cong. & Admin. News 6460; 1985 U.S. Code Cong. & Admin. News 975.

NATIONAL ARCHIVES AND RECORDS ADMINISTRATION

8th and Pennsylvania Avenue, N.W.
Washington, D.C. 20408

DESCRIPTION: The National Archives and Records Administration (NARA) establishes policies and procedures for managing the records of the U.S. Government. It was established in 1984 as an independent agency, succeeding the National Archives and Records Service, which was part of the General Services Administration. NARA maintains the historically valuable records of the U.S. Government dating from the Revolutionary War era to the recent past. It makes original records available for use by researchers, answers written and oral requests for information contained in its holdings, and provides copies of documents for a fee. NARA also manages the Presidential Libraries and Federal Records Centers. It is also responsible for publishing a wide variety of public documents, including slip laws, the U.S. Statutes at Large, the daily Federal Register, the Weekly Compilation of Presidential Documents, the annual Code of Federal Regulations, Public Papers of the Presidents, and U.S. Government Manual, and the Codification of Presidential Proclamations and Executive Orders.

(Area Code 202)

Archivist of the United States: Don Wilson 501-5500
Public Affairs 501-5525
Publications Information 501-5240
Federal Register 523-5240
Statutes at Large 523-5240
Reference Services Branch 501-5402

(Area Code 202)

Use of Records in Archives 501-5400
Public Laws Updates (Recording) 523-6641
This recording of public laws is updated as these laws become available.
Facsimile 501-5505

OFFICE OF GENERAL COUNSEL (Room 305)

The small Office of General Counsel (recently renamed from Legal Services Staff), provides legal advice to the Archivist of the U.S. and other agency officials. Responsibilities include providing legal advice and analysis, preparing legal opinions and legal documents, providing litigation support services, preparing testimony, drafting proposed legislation and regulations, and reviewing claims on behalf of or against the Government. Staff attorneys also provide advice on questions involving the Freedom of Information Act, the Privacy Act, Federal Records Act, and ethics laws and regulations, and serve as legal counsel in litigation arising out of the Presidential Recordings and Materials Preservation Act and other archival and records related activities.

(Area Code 202)

General Counsel: Gary Brooks 501-5535
Attorney-Advisors:
Christopher Runkel 501-5535
Howard Shecter 501-5535
Amy Krupsky 501-5535

OFFICE OF THE FEDERAL REGISTER (Room 8401)

(Area Code 202)

Director: Martha L. Girard 523-5240

(Area Code 202)

Presidential Documents and Legislative Division
Director: Martha L. Girard 523-5240

CARTOGRAPHIC AND ARCHITECTURAL BRANCH

841 South Pickett Street, Alexandria, VA 22304

The Cartographic and Architectural Branch is the world's largest repository of maps, atlases, charts, aerial photographs, architectural and engineering drawings, patents and ships' plans. Its holdings include over 13 million items made or accumulated by 167 U.S. Government agencies. Maps and aerial photographs of virtually every inch of ground in the U.S., even your own neighborhood, are available, and may be examined and purchased by the general public. Foreign maps are also part of the collection. This facility is heavily used by attorneys seeking aerial photographs in the preparation of environmental cases.

Chief: John A. Dwyer ....(703) 756-6700

FEDERAL RECORDS CENTERS

Federal agencies retire certain noncurrent records to Federal Records Centers in accordance with established disposition schedules. The centers provide reference services, including loan or return of records to the agency of origin, prepare authenticated reproductions of documents, and furnish information from records. Federal Records Centers are located in the following cities:

Washington, D.C.
Director: Ferris E. Stovel
Washington National Records Center, 4205 Suitland Rd, Suitland, MD 20409. Tel: 301/763-7000.

Atlanta
Director: Thomas G. Hudson
Federal Records Center, 1557 St. Joseph Avenue, East Point, GA 30344. Tel: 404/763-7476.

Boston
Director: Clifford G. Amsler
Federal Records Center, 380 Trapelo Road, Waltham, MA 02154. Tel: 617/839-7745.

Chicago
Director: Robert Hutchinson
Federal Records Center, 7358 South Pulaski Road, Chicago, IL 60629. Tel: 312/581-7816.

Dayton
Director: Denis Pauskauskas
Federal Records Center, 3150 Springboro Road, Dayton, OH 45439. Tel: 513/225-2878.

Denver
Director: Robert Svenningsen
Federal Records Center, Denver Federal Center, Bldg. 48, P.O. Box 25307, Denver, CO 80225. Tel: 303/236-0804.

Fort Worth
Director: James W. Mouat
Federal Records Center, P.O. Box 6216, Fort Worth, TX 76115. Tel: 817/334-5515.

Kansas City, MO
Director: John J. Allshouse
Federal Records Center, 2312 East Bannister Road, Kansas City, MO 64131. Tel: 816/926-7272.

Los Angeles
Director: Sharon L. Roadway
Federal Records Center, 24000 Avila Road, Laguna Niguel, CA 92677. Tel: 714/643-4220.

New York
Director: Karen Lucas
Federal Records Center, Bldg 22, Military Ocean Terminal, Bayonne, NJ 07002. Tel: 201/823-7161.

Philadelphia
Director: David S. Weber
Federal Records Center, 5000 Wissahickon Avenue, Philadelphia, PA 19144. Tel: 215/951-5588.

St. Louis
Director: David L. Petree
National Personnel Records Center, 9700 Page Blvd, St. Louis, MO 63132. Tel: 314/263-7201.

San Francisco
Director: David D. Drake
Federal Records Center, 1000 Commodore Drive, San Bruno, CA 94066. Tel: 415/876-9003.

Seattle
Director: Steven M. Edwards
Federal Records Center, 6125 Sand Point Way NE, Seattle, WA 98115. Tel: 206/392-6501.

REGIONAL ARCHIVES AND AREAS SERVED

Each regional archives receives records from Federal agency offices in the states listed. Each facility is open one or more Saturdays a month. Please call for more information.

New England Region (Boston)

Director: James K. Owens
National Archives, 380 Trapelo Road., Waltham, MA 02154. Tel: 617/647-8100.
(Receives records from CT, MA, MA, NH, RI, VT)

Northeast Region (New York)

Director: Robert C. Morris
National Archives, Bldg 22, Military Ocean Terminal, Bayonne, NJ 07002-5388. Tel: 201/823-7545.
(Receives records from NJ, NY, PR, VI)

Mid-Atlantic Region (Philadelphia)

Director: Robert J. Plowman
National Archives, 9th & Market Streets, Room 1350, Philadelphia, Pa. 19107. Tel: 215/597-3000.
(Receives records from DE, PA, MD, VA, WV)

Southeast Region (Atlanta)

Director: Gayle P. Peters
National Archives, 1557 St. Joseph Avenue, East Point, GA 30344. Tel: 404/763-7477.
(Receives records from AL, GA, FL, KY, MI, NC, SC, TN)

Great Lakes Region (Chicago)

Director: Peter W. Bunce
National Archives, 7358 South Pulaski Road, Chicago, IL 60629. Tel: 312/581-7816.
(Receives records from IL, IN, MI, MN, OH, WI)

Central Plains Region (Kansas City, MO)

Director: Diana L. Duff
National Archives, 2312 E. Bannister Rd, Kansas City, MO 64131. Tel: 816/926-6272.
(Receives records from IO, KS, MO, NE)

Southwest Region (Fort Worth)

Director: Kent C. Carter
National Archives, 501 W. Felix St., P.O. Box 6216, Fort Worth, TX 76115. Tel: 817/334-5525.
(Receives records from AK, LA, NM, OK, TX)

Rocky Mountain Region (Denver)

Director: Joel D. Barter
National Archives, Denver Federal Center, Bldg. 48, P.O. Box 25307, Denver, CO 80225. Tel: 303/236-0817.
(Receives records from CO, MT, ND, SD, UT, WY)

Pacific Southwest Region (Los Angeles)

Director: Diane S. Nixon
National Archives, 24000 Avila Rd., P.O. Box 6719, Laguna Niguel, CA 92677-6719. Tel: 714/643-4241.
(Receives records from AZ, Southern CA counties of Imperial, Inyo, Kern, Los Angeles, Orange, Riverside, San Bernardino, San Diego, San Luis Obispo, Santa Barbara, and Ventura; and Clark County, NV)

Pacific Sierra Region (San Francisco)

Director: Waverly B. Lowell
National Archives, 1000 Commodore Dr., San Bruno, CA 94066. Tel: 415/876-9009.
(Receives records from Northern CA, HI, NV [except Clark County] and the Pacific Ocean area)

Pacific Northwest Region (Seattle)

Director: Phillip E. Lothyan
National Archives, 6125 Sand Point Way, Seattle, W 98115. Tel: 206/526-6507.
(Receives records from ID, OR, WA)

Alaska Region (Anchorage)

Director: Thomas E. Wiltsey
National Archives, 654 West 3rd Avenue, Anchorage, AK 99501. Tel: 907/ 271-2441.
(Receives records from AK)

PUBLICATIONS AND SOURCES OF INFORMATION

The following publications can be obtained from the **National Archives.** Send check or money order (Payable to the National Archives Trust Fund) to: National Archives Trust Fund, NEPS Dept. 724, P.O. Box 100793, Atlanta, GA 30384. Orders may be placed over the phone or by fax. Tel: 202/724-0084. Fax: 202/523-4357. Please add $3.00 for orders up to $50.00 for shipping and handling.

<u>Select List of Publications of the National Archives and Records Administration</u> can be obtained from Publications Information. This pamphlet lists the various general information leaflets, guides and indexes, microfilm catalogs, and reference information papers that are available through the National Archives and Records Administration. There is no charge for this brochure. Call the number listed above.

<u>Guide to the National Archives of the United States, 1987</u> documents our history from the First Continental Congress and includes the basic records of the three branches of our Federal Government. This comprehensive guide provides a general description of these records within the context of the Government agencies that created them or received them in the course of official business. Item #100009. Price $25.00.

<u>Military Service Records: A Select Catalog of National Archives Microfilm Publications.</u> The National Archives is the official depository for records of military personnel separated from the U.S. Air Force, Army, Coast Guard, Marine Corps, and Navy. Some records date back to the Revolutionary War. Item #200028. Price: $5.00.

<u>Guide to Records in the National Archives Relating to American Indians 1984</u> enables researchers to review descriptions of records that are available in the National Archives and its regional archives. It includes concise information about records that trace the evolution of Federal Indian policy, the effects of national policies on traditional Indian culture, Indian wars and their results, and the role of Native Americans in the development of U.S. society. Item #100004. Price: $25.00.

<u>Federal Court Records: A Select Catalog of National Archives Microfilm Publication, 1987</u>. Item #200043. Price: $2.00.

The **regional catalog series** contains selected National Archives microfilm publications grouped by geographical area. The introduction to each catalog lists the regional archives that serves the region:

<u>New England: A Select List of National Archives Microfilm Publications</u>. Item #200039. Price $2.00.

<u>Chesapeake/Mid-Atlantic: A Select List of National Archives Microfilm Publications</u>. Item #200037. Price $2.00.

<u>The South and Southwest: A Select List of National Archives Microfilm Publications</u>. Item #200035. Price $2.00.

<u>Central States: A Select List of National Archives Microfilm Publications</u>. Item #200036. Price $2.00.

<u>The West: A Select List of National Archives Microfilm Publications</u>. Item #200038. Price $2.00.

The following publications can be purchased from the **U.S. Government Printing Office.** Stock numbers and prices for annual subscriptions are shown below. Submit requests for these publications to: The Superintendent of Documents, U.S. Government Printing Office, Washington, D.C. 20402. Tel: 202/783-3238.

<u>Federal Register</u>. Published daily, Monday through Friday, except Federal Holidays. Provides a uniform system for making available to the public regulations and legal notices issued by Federal agencies. These include Presidential proclamations and Executive orders, Federal agency documents having general applicability and legal effect, documents required to be published by Act of Congress, and other Federal agency documents of public interest. Price (paperback): $340.00 a year domestic; $425.00 a year foreign. GPO Stock# 769-004-00000-9. Note: Subscribers to this service will automatically receive copies of the <u>Federal Register Index</u> (a cumulative monthly itemization of material published in the daily <u>Federal Register</u>), and the <u>Code of Federal Regulations, LSA, List of CFR Sections Affected</u>, at no additional cost.

<u>Code of Federal Regulations, LSA, List of CFR Sections Affected</u>. A monthly listing of amendatory actions published in the <u>Federal Register</u>. Entries indicate type of change. The December issue is the Annual for CFR Titles 1-16; the March issue is the Annual for CFR Titles 17-27; the June issue is the Annual for CFR Titles 28-41; the September issue is the Annual for CFR Titles 42-50. Subscribers to the daily <u>Federal Register</u> will receive this service automatically as part of that subscription. Price: $21.00 a year domestic; $26.25 a year foreign. No single copies sold. GPO Stock# 769-001-00000-0.

Code of Federal Regulations. Revised annually; issued irregularly. Codification of the general and permanent rules published in the Federal Register by the Executive departments and agencies of the Federal Government. Divided into 50 titles representing broad areas subject to Federal regulation. Price (paperback, approximately 175 books): $620.00 a year domestic; $775.00 foreign. Single copies vary in price. GPO Stock# 869-011-00000-2.

Public Laws. Published irregularly. A Public Law, often referred to as a "Slip Law," is the initial publication of a Federal law upon enactment and is printed as soon as possible after approval by the President. Some legislative references appear on each law. Price: $107.00 domestic per session of Congress; $133.75 foreign per session of Congress. GPO Stock# 869-010-00000-6.

The United States Government Manual, 1989/90 is the official handbook of the Federal Government, providing comprehensive information on the agencies of the legislative, judicial, and executive branches. It also includes information on quasi-official agencies, international organizations in which the United States participates, and boards, committees, and commissions. Price: $21.00 domestic, $26.25 foreign. GPO Stock# 060-000-00022-3.

Weekly Compilation of Presidential Documents. Includes transcripts of the President's news conferences, messages to Congress, public speeches and statements, and other presidential materials released by the White House. The Compilation carries a monthly dateline and covers materials released during the preceding week. Each issue carries an index of contents and a cumulative index to prior issues. Separate indices are published quarterly, semiannually, and annually. Other finding aids include lists of laws approved by the President, nominations submitted to the Senate, and a checklist of White House releases. Price: $96.00 a year domestic (priority mail) or $55.00 a year domestic (non-priority mail); $68.75 a year foreign (non-priority mail). Foreign airmail distribution available upon request. GPO Stock#769-007-00000-8.

Codification of Presidential Proclamations and Executive Orders, April 13, 1945 - January 20, 1989. Published by the Office of the Federal Register, National Archives and Records Administration. Provides in one convenient volume proclamations and Executive orders with general applicability and continuing effect. Proclamations and Executive orders issued before April 13, 1945 are included if they were amended or otherwise affected by documents issued during the 1945-1989 period. One of the great benefits of this volume is that it incorporates amendments into the text of each codified proclamation and Executive order. All documents are cited to the Federal Register and Code of Federal Regulations. It also reflects changes made by a document other than a proclamation or Executive order, such as a Public Law or Federal regulation.

The Codification is divided into 50 chapters corresponding to the title designations of the Code of Federal Regulations and the United States Code. There is also a Disposition Table listing all included documents, their amendments and an indication of their current status. Price: $32.00. GPO Stock# 069-000-00018-5.

NATIONAL ARCHIVES AND RECORDS ADMINISTRATION
KEY LEGAL AUTHORITIES

Regulations: 36 C.F.R. Parts 1200-1280 (1989).

National Archives and Records Administration Act of 1984, 44 U.S.C. 2101-2118--established the National Archives and Records Administration as an independent agency (formerly called the National Archives under the General Services Administration) to manage the archival and records management functions of the Federal Government, specifically to inventory, selectively dispose of, and preserve the records of the U.S. Government; to operate the Presidential library system; and to publish legislative, regulatory, and other public documents.

Legislative History: 1984 U.S. Code Cong. & Admin. News 3865.

NATIONAL CAPITAL PLANNING COMMISSION

1325 G Street, N.W.
Washington, D.C. 20576

DESCRIPTION: The National Capital Planning Commission, an independent Federal establishment, is the central planning agency for the Federal Government in the Washington, D.C. metropolitan area. The Commission has three primary functions: comprehensive planning to ensure the orderly development of the Federal Establishment and protection of Federal interests in the National Capital region; a plan and program review function; and preparation of the Federal Capital Improvements Program. The Commission is composed of five appointed and seven ex officio members. Three citizen members, including the Chairman, are appointed by the President and two by the mayor of the District of Columbia.

(Area Code 202)
Chairman: Glen T. Urquhart 724-0173
Vice Chairman: Robert J. Nash 724-0173
Executive Director: Reginald W. Griffith 724-0176
Public Information 724-0174
Facsimile 724-0195
Freedom of Information Act/Privacy Act Office 724-0174

All requests must be writing. If the document requested is processed and available, there will be no charge. The first 100 pages will be copied free of charge; each page after that limit costs 25 cents. There are variable search fees. Submit requests to: Freedom of Information Act Officer, National Capital Planning Commission, address cited at the beginning of this listing.

OFFICE OF GENERAL COUNSEL (Room 1008)

The General Counsel advises the Commission and its staff on statutory powers, duties, and functions of the agency in the fields of planning, land use, urban renewal, historic preservation, and transportation. The office is also responsible for reviewing and preparing reports on pending legislation, congressional testimony, and statutory drafting. In addition, the General Counsel serves as the agency's ethics and Freedom of Information Act officer.

(Area Code 202)
General Counsel: Linda Dodd-Major 724-0187

NATIONAL CAPITAL PLANNING COMMISSION
KEY LEGAL AUTHORITIES

Regulations: 1 C.F.R. Parts 455-457 (1989).

40 U.S.C. 71-74a--created the Commission as the central Federal planning agency of the U.S. Government in the National Capital and to preserve the important historical and natural features thereof, except with respect to the U.S. Capitol building and grounds (which are under the jurisdiction of the Architect of the Capitol).

Legislative History: 1962 U.S. Code Cong. & Admin. News 2617.

NATIONAL CREDIT UNION ADMINISTRATION

1776 G Street, N.W.
Washington, D.C. 20456

DESCRIPTION: The National Credit Union Administration (NCUA) is an independent Executive Branch agency which regulates and insures all Federal credit unions and insures state-chartered credit unions which apply and qualify for share insurance. The Administration also conducts periodic examinations of Federal credit unions to determine their solvency and compliance with laws and regulations.

(Area Code 202)

Chairman of the Board: Roger W. Jepson 682-9600
Executive Director: Donald E. Johnson 682-9600
Procurement Information 682-9700
Publications 682-9700
Public and Congressional Affairs 682-9650
Facsimile 682-9620

Freedom of Information Act Office/Privacy Act Office....682-9700
All requests for FOIA information must be submitted in writing. There is a copying charge of 25 cents per page. There is also a variable per hour search fee. Submit requests to the Freedom of Information Act Officer at the NCUA address cited at the beginning of this listing.

(Area Code 202)

Law Library (Sixth Floor) 682-9630
The Law Library is located within the Office of the General Counsel. It is open to the public by appointment only Monday through Friday from 8:30 AM until 4:30 PM. There are no charge-out privileges. Copies can be made for a charge.

THE BOARD

Chairman: Roger W. Jepson 682-9600
Vice Chairman: Elizabeth F. Burkhart 682-9600
Member: Robert H. Swan 682-9600

OFFICE OF INSPECTOR GENERAL (Seventh Floor)

The Office of Inspector General (OIG) is responsible for conducting and supervising all audits and investigations of NCUA programs and operations. OIG is also responsible for providing leadership and coordination and for recommending policies to promote economy, efficiency, and effectiveness in administering NCUA programs and operations; to prevent and detect fraud, waste, abuse, and mismanagement in NCUA programs and operations; and to prevent, detect, and handle cases involving misconduct.

(Area Code 202)

Inspector General: Joan Perry 682-9730

OFFICE OF GENERAL COUNSEL (Sixth Floor)

The Office of General Counsel is responsible for all legal matters affecting the Administration. Attorneys represent the agency in judicial and administrative adjudications; prepare litigation related briefs, pleadings, and documents; perform legal research; conduct studies on credit union operational matters such as investments, liquidations, and insurance activities; assist in settlement negotiations; prepare advisory opinions and regulations; and draft testimony.

Although the Administration does have six regional offices, all legal matters are handled in the Washington, D.C. headquarters office.

(Area Code 202)

General Counsel: Robert M. Fenner 682-9630
Deputy General Counsel: James J. Engel 682-9630

Assistant General Counsel for: (Area Code 202)
Litigation and Liquidation: Allan H. Meltzer 682-9630
Operations: Hattie Ulan 682-9630

PUBLICATIONS OF INTEREST

NCUA News is published ten times a year and covers activities and actions of the agency, including speeches, meetings, proposed rules and regulations, and legal opinions issued by the agency. It is free of charge. Contact: National Credit Union Administration, Office of Public and Congressional Affairs, 1776 G Street, N.W., Washington, D.C. 20456. Tel: 202/682-9650.

Rules and Regulations Concerning Credit Unions outlines the rules and regulations that are officially codified in 12 C.F.R. Parts 700-796 (1990). Price: $10.00. Send check to National Credit Union Administration, Administrative Offices, 1776 G Street, N.W., Washington, D.C. 20456. Tel: 202/682-9700.

NATIONAL CREDIT UNION ADMINISTRATION

National Credit Union Administration Rules and Regulations (1990). Subscription service consists of a basic manual and changes for an indeterminate period. Looseleaf for updating. Price: $44.00 domestic; $55.00 foreign. GPO Stock# 954-004-00000-7. Contact: Superintendent of Documents, U.S. Government Printing Office, Washington, D.C. 20402. Tel: 202/783-3238.

NATIONAL CREDIT UNION ADMINISTRATION

KEY LEGAL AUTHORITIES

General Agency Regulations: 12 C.F.R. Parts 700-795 (1989).
Rules of Procedure--NCUA Board: 12 C.F.R. Part 791 (1989).
Rules of Practice and Procedure: 12 C.F.R. Part 747 (1989).

Federal Credit Union Act, as amended, 12 U.S.C. 1751 et seq.--established the National Credit Union Administration to regulate and insure the Federal credit union industry and also to insure certain state-chartered credit unions.

Legislative History: 1948 U.S. Code Cong. Service 2172; 1959 U.S. Code Cong. & Admin. News 2784; 1970 U.S. Code Cong. & Admin. News 2479; 1978 U.S. Code Cong. & Admin. News 9273; 1984 U.S. Code Cong. & Admin. News 2809 & 3817; 1987 U.S. Code Cong. & Admin. News 489.

Depository Institutions Management Interlocks Act, as amended, 12 U.S.C. 3201 et seq.--fosters competition by generally prohibiting a management official of a depository institution or depository holding company from also serving as a management official of another such unaffiliated institution or like institution if the like institution is very large and located in the same local area.

Legislative History: 1978 U.S. Code Cong. & Admin. News 9273.

Bank Secrecy Act, as amended, 31 U.S.C. 5311 et seq.--requires financial institutions, including credit unions, to report certain monetary transactions where such reports may have a high degree of usefulness in criminal, tax, or regulatory investigations or proceedings.

Legislative History: 1984 U.S. Code Cong. & Admin. News 3182; 1988 U.S. Code Cong. & Admin. News 5937.

NATIONAL FOUNDATION ON THE ARTS AND HUMANITIES

1100 Pennsylvania Avenue, N.W.
Washington, D.C. 20506

DESCRIPTION: The National Foundation on the Arts and the Humanities is an independent agency which consists of the National Endowment for the Arts, the National Endowment for the Humanities, the Federal Council on the Arts and Humanities, and the Institute of Museum Services.

The Federal Council on the Arts and Humanities and the Institute of Museum Services, do not have in-house staff attorneys.

NATIONAL ENDOWMENT FOR THE ARTS

1100 Pennsylvania Avenue, N.W.
Washington, D.C. 20506

DESCRIPTION: The National Endowment for the Arts fosters professional excellence in the arts in America, nurtures and sustains them, and assists in creating a climate in which they may flourish.

(Area Code 202)
Chairman: John E. Frohnmayer 682-5414
Grants Division 682-5403
Contracts and Procurement Division 682-5482
Public Information 682-5400
Facsimile 682-5798

Freedom of Information Act Office/Privacy Act Office....682-5418
Requests must be made in writing. There are both variable copying and per hour search fees. Submit requests to the attention of the Freedom of Information Act Officer, Room 522, at the National Endowment of the Arts address cited at the beginning of this listing.

(Area Code 202)
Library (Room 213) 682-5485
The library is open to the public by appointment only from 9:00 AM until 5:30 PM, Monday through Friday. There are no check-out privileges. Limited copying is available free of charge.

OFFICE OF GENERAL COUNSEL (Room 522)

(Area Code 202)
General Counsel: Julie Ann R. Davis 682-5418

(Area Code 202)
Deputy General Counsel: Arthur A. Warren 682-5418

NATIONAL ENDOWMENT FOR THE HUMANITIES

1100 Pennsylvania Avenue, N.W.
Washington, D.C. 20506

DESCRIPTION: The National Endowment for the Humanities is an independent grant-making agency which supports research, education, and public programs in the humanities.

(Area Code 202)
Chairman: Lynn V. Cheney 786-0310
Grants Office 786-0494
Public Information 786-0438
Publications and Public Affairs 786-0438
Facsimile: Publications and Public Affairs 786-0240
Administrative Services 786-0243

(Area Code 202)
Freedom of Information Act Office/Privacy Act Office....786-0322
Requests must be made in writing. There is copying charge of 10 cents per page; 20 cents if double-sided. There is also a variable per hour search fee. Submit requests to the Freedom of Information Act Officer, Rm 530, at the National Endowment for the Humanities at the address cited at the beginning of this listing. The first two hours of a search are free.

NATIONAL FOUNDATION ON THE ARTS AND HUMANITIES

(Area Code 202)

Library (Room 216) 786-0244

The library is open to the public by appointment only from 8:30 AM until 5:00 PM, Monday through Friday. There are no charge out privileges but an interlibrary loan is possible. Limited copying is available free of charge.

OFFICE OF THE GENERAL COUNSEL (Room 530)

(Area Code 202)

General Counsel: Rex O. Arney 786-0322

(Area Code 202)

Deputy General Counsel: Stephen J. McCleary 786-0322

NATIONAL FOUNDATION ON THE ARTS AND HUMANITIES
KEY LEGAL AUTHORITIES

Regulations: 45 C.F.R. Parts 1100-1185 (1989).

National Foundation on the Arts and Humanities Act of 1965, as amended, 20 U.S.C. 951 et seq.--established the Foundation to develop and promote a national policy for support of the humanities and arts in the U.S. and for institutions which preserve the cultural heritage of the U.S., and authorizes the awarding of contracts and grants for this purpose.

Legislative History: 1965 U.S. Code Cong. & Admin. News 3186; 1984 U.S. Code Cong. & Admin. News 530.

Arts and Artifacts Indemnity Act, as amended, 20 U.S.C. 971-977--authorizes indemnification against loss or damage for certain art works and artifacts brought into the U.S. or elsewhere for exhibition.

Legislative History: 1975 U.S. Code Cong. & Admin. News 1640; 1985 U.S. Code Cong. & Admin. News 1055.

NATIONAL LABOR RELATIONS BOARD

1717 Pennsylvania Avenue, N.W.
Washington, D.C. 20570

DESCRIPTION: The National Labor Relations Board (NLRB), an independent Federal agency established in 1935, administers the nation's principal labor relations law. This statute, the National Labor Relations Act, generally applies to all interstate commerce except railroads and airlines.

The purpose of the National Labor Relations Act is to serve the public interest by reducing interruptions in commerce caused by industrial strife. It seeks to do this by providing orderly processes for protecting and implementing the respective rights of employees, employers, and unions in their relations with one another.

In its statutory assignment, the NLRB has two primary functions: (1) to determine and implement, through secret-ballot elections, the free democratic choice by employees as to whether they wish to be represented by a union and, if so, by which one; and (2) to prevent and remedy unlawful acts, called unfair labor practices, by either employers or unions.

Each fiscal year the NLRB receives more than 50,000 cases of all kinds. Some two-thirds are unfair labor practice charges. Over the years, charges filed against employers have outnumbered those filed against unions by about two to one. Charges are filed by individual workers, employers, and unions. The total flow of cases of all types filed with the NLRB has sharply increased in the last decade.

The NLRB's **judicial functions** are separate, by law, from its **prosecuting functions.** 1) The five-member Board acts primarily as a quasi-judicial body in deciding cases upon formal records, generally upon review from Regional Directors' or Administrative Law Judges' decisions. 2) The General Counsel is responsible for the investigation and prosecution of charges of violations of the Act, and has general supervision of the Regional Offices.

The NLRB currently has over 730 attorneys, of whom approximately 240 are assigned to the Washington, D.C. office and approximately 490 are located in Regional, Subregional, and Resident Offices in major cities across the country.

(Area Code 202)

Chairman: James M. Stephens 254-9392
Executive Secretary: John C. Truesdale 254-9430
Procurement Information 634-1991
Public Information/Copies of Decisions 632-4950
Docket Information/Office of the Executive Secretary ...254-9430
Publications Information 632-4950
Facsimile..634-4832

Freedom of Information Act/Privacy Act Offices

FOIA: Offices of the Board 254-9430
Questions concerning the Board must be submitted in writing. There is a copying charge of 10 cents per page. There is also a variable per hour search fee. Submit requests to the attention of The Freedom of Information Act Officer, Room 701, at the NLRB address cited at the beginning of this listing.

(Area Code 202)

FOIA: Office of General Counsel 254-9350
Questions concerning the General Counsel must submitted in writing. Fees for copying and per hour searches vary depending upon the information requested, who requests it, and who researches it. Submit requests to the attention of the Freedom of Information Act Officer, Room 1107, at the NLRB address cited at the beginning of this listing.

OFFICES OF THE BOARD (Room 630)

The organization of the Board, so far as case handling is concerned, consists of the offices of the Chairman and the four Board Members, their respective staff counsel, and the Executive Secretary and the Solicitor. Each Board Member has a professional staff consisting of a Chief Counsel, a Deputy Chief Counsel, three assistant Chief Counsel, a small number of senior Counsel, and approximately 10-12 Counsel. This means there are over 100 attorneys serving as staff counsel for the Board as a whole.

A **Chief Counsel** serves in the dual capacity of staff director and legal advisor for his or her respective Board Member. The Executive Secretary, by tradition an attorney, is principally concerned with the administrative management of the Board's judicial affairs--in other words, management of the Board's caseload. The **Solicitor** and his or her staff are legal advisers and consultants to the Board as a whole.

(Area Code 202)

Office of Chairman James M. Stephens
Chief Counsel: Elinor Hadley Stillman.................254-9218
Deputy Chief Counsel: Donald R. Klenk.................254-9061

Office of Member Mary Miller Cracraft
Chief Counsel: Anne G. Purcell........................254-9424
Deputy Chief Counsel: Jonathan R. Scheinbart..........254-9123

Office of Member Dennis M. Devaney
Chief Counsel: Susan Holik............................634-1908
Deputy Chief Counsel: Lester A. Heltzer...............254-9338

(Area Code 202)

Office of Member (vacant)
Chief Counsel: vacant.................................254-9112
Deputy Chief Counsel: Howard D. Johnson...............254-7906

Office of Clifford Oviatt (Acting)
Chief Counsel: Frederick Freilicher...................254-9416
Deputy Chief Counsel: William A. Hill.................254-9414

NATIONAL LABOR RELATIONS BOARD

OFFICE OF GENERAL COUNSEL (Room 1001)

The Office of the General Counsel in Washington, D.C. The attorneys in this office may be assigned to one of several offices, but work in each consists primarily of research, analysis, discussion, and the drafting of memoranda, decisions, briefs, and other documents. These offices are:

* **Division of Advice** which advises Regional Directors concerning the action to be taken on difficult or unusual cases, or those arising in newly developing policy areas;

* **Office of Appeals** which processes appeals to the General Counsel from refusals of Regional Directors to issue complaints;

* **Division of Enforcement Litigation** which represents the Board in U.S. Courts of Appeals by submission of briefs and oral argument; and

* **Legal Research and Policy Planning Branch** which maintains the Board's vital case digest and classification system and prepares research memoranda of all kinds.

(Area Code 202)

General Counsel: Jerry M. Hunter 254-9150
Associate General Counsel: D. Randall Frye 254-9150

Division of Advice (Room 820)
Associate General Counsel: Harold J. Datz 254-9128
Injunction Litigation Branch:
Assistant General Counsel: Richard A. Siegel 254-9294
Legal Research and Policy Planning Branch:
Assistant General Counsel: John W. Hornbeck ..254-9350
Regional Advice Branch:
Assistant General Counsel: Jane C. Clark 254-9450

Division of Enforcement Litigation (Room 1070)
Associate General Counsel: Robert E. Allen 254-9275
Appellate Court Branch:
Deputy Associate General Counsel:
Aileen A. Armstrong 254-9216
Supreme Court Branch:
Deputy Associate General Counsel: Norton Come 254-7364
Contempt Litigation Branch:
Assistant General Counsel: William Wachter ..254-9009
Special Litigation Branch:
Assistant General Counsel: Margery E. Lieber 634-1729
Office of Appeals:
Director: Mary M. Shanklin 254-9316

Division of Operations Management (Room 1030) (Area Code 202)
Associate General Counsel Joseph E. DeSio.............254-9102

District I
Assistant General Counsel: Shirley A. Bednarz 254-9301
(Albany, Boston, Brooklyn, Buffalo, Hartford, New York, Newark)

District II
Assistant General Counsel: John P. Falcone 254-9132
(Cincinnati, Cleveland, Indianapolis, Peoria, Pittsburgh)

District III
Assistant General Counsel: Eugene L. Rosenfeld 254-9016
(Chicago, Detroit, Grand Rapids, Little Rock, Memphis, Milwaukee, Nashville, St. Louis)

District IV
Assistant General Counsel: Nicholas E. Karatinos 254-9241
(Atlanta, Baltimore, Birmingham, Jacksonville, Miami, Philadelphia, Puerto Rico, Tampa, Wash, DC, Winston-Salem)

District V
Assistant General Counsel: vacant 254-6334
(Anchorage, Denver, Des Moines, Ft. Worth, Houston, Kansas City, Minneapolis, New Orleans, Portland, San Antonio, Seattle, Tulsa)

District VI
Assistant General Counsel: B. Allan Benson 254-9336
(Albuquerque, El Paso, Honolulu, Las Vegas, Los Angeles, Oakland, Phoenix, San Diego, San Francisco)

FIELD OFFICES

Field attorneys investigate cases to determine the facts, participate in settlement efforts, draft complaints, prepare the case for trial, and try it before an Administrative Law Judge. In some cases, field attorneys may seek injunctive relief in Federal District Courts. A field attorney may also serve as a Hearing Officer in a contested representation election case; may prepare drafts of decisions for the Regional Director; and may assist in conducting representation elections.

Atlanta
Regional Director: Martin M. Arlook
Regional Attorney: Kenneth Meadow
National Labor Relations Board, Marietta Tower, Ste 2400, 101 Marietta Street, N.W., Atlanta, GA 30323. Tel: 404/331-2896.

Baltimore
Regional Director: Louis J. D'Amico
Regional Attorney: Albert W. Palewicz
Deputy Regional Attorney: Joseph J. Baniszenski
National Labor Relations Board, Candler Building, 4th Floor, 109 Market Place, Baltimore, MD 21202. Tel: 301/962-2822.

Boston
Regional Director: Rosemary Pye
Regional Attorney: Michael F. Walsh
Deputy Regional Attorney: Joel F. Gardiner
National Labor Relations Board, Federal Office Building, 10 Causeway Street, 6th Fl, Boston, MA 02222. Tel: 617/565-6700.

Brooklyn
Regional Director: Alvin P. Blyer
Regional Attorney: Rochelle Kentov
Deputy Regional Attorney: Anthony A. Ambrosia
National Labor Relations Board, 75 Clinton Street, 8th Floor, Brooklyn, NY 11201. Tel: 718/330-7713.

Buffalo
Regional Director: Richard L. Ahearn
Regional Attorney: Sandra L. Dunbar
National Labor Relations Board, Federal Building, Room 901, 111 West Huron Street, Buffalo, NY 14202. Tel: 716/846-4931.

Chicago
Regional Director: Elizabeth Kinney
Regional Attorney: Harvey A. Roth
Deputy Regional Attorney: William G. Kocol
National Labor Relations Board, 200 West Adams Street, Suite 800, Chicago, IL 60606. Tel: 312/353-7570.

Cincinnati
Regional Director: Emil C. Farkas
Regional Attorney: Thomas M. Sheeran
Deputy Regional Attorney: Edward C. Verst
National Labor Relations Board, Federal Building, Room 3003, 550 Main Street, Cincinnati, OH 45202. Tel: 513/684-3686.

Cleveland
Regional Director: Frederick Calatrello
Regional Attorney: John Kollar
National Labor Relations Board, Anthony J. Celebrezze Federal Building, Room 1695, 1240 E. 9th Street, Cleveland, OH 44199. Tel: 216/522-3715.

Denver
Regional Director: W. Bruce Gillis, Jr.
Regional Attorney: Albert A. Metz
National Labor Relations Board, 600 17th Street, 3rd Floor, South Tower, Denver, CO 80202. Tel: 303/844-3551.

Detroit
Regional Director: Bernard Gottfried
Regional Attorney: William C. Schaub
Deputy Regional Attorney: George Alexander
National Labor Relations Board, Federal Building, 477 Michigan Avenue, Room 300, Detroit, MI 48226. Tel: 313/226-3200.

Fort Worth
Regional Director: Michael Dunn
Regional Attorney: Jerome L. Avedon
National Labor Relations Board, Federal Office Bldg, Room 8A24, 819 Taylor Street, Fort Worth, TX 76102. Tel: 817/334-2921.

Hartford
Regional Director: Peter B. Hoffman
Regional Attorney: Jonathan B. Kreisberg
National Labor Relations Board, One Commercial Plaza, 21st Fl, Hartford, CT 06103. Tel: 203/240-3522.

Hato Rey, PR
Regional Director: Mary Zelma Asseo
Regional Attorney: Leonard P. Bernstein
National Labor Relations Board, U.S. Courthouse, Room 591, Carlos E. Chardon Avenue, Hato Rey, Puerto Rico 00918. Tel: 8+809/766-5347.

Indianapolis
Regional Director: William T. Little
Regional Attorney: Ralph R. Tremain
Deputy Regional Attorney: (vacant)
National Labor Relations Board, Federal Bldg, Rm 238, 575 North Pennsylvania Street, Indianapolis, IN 46204. Tel: 317/226-7430.

Kansas City, KS
Regional Director: F. Rozier Sharp
Regional Attorney: Harold E. Jahn
Deputy Regional Attorney: Milford R. Limesand
National Labor Relations Board, 5799 Broadmoor, Room 500, Mission, KS 66202. Tel: 913/236-2777.

Los Angeles
Regional Director: Victoria E. Aguayo
Regional Attorney: James J. McDermott
Deputy Regional Attorney: William M. Pate, Jr.
National Labor Relations Board, 615 South Flower Street, 11th Floor, Los Angeles, CA 90017. Tel: 213/894-5200.
(Jurisdiction: Imperial, Orange, Riverside, San Diego, and part of Los Angeles County.)

Los Angeles
Regional Director: Roger W. Goubeaux
Regional Attorney: Byron B. Kohn
Deputy Regional Attorney: (vacant)
National Labor Relations Board, 11000 Wilshire Boulevard, Room 12100, Los Angeles, CA 90024. Tel: 213/209-7352.
(Jurisdiction: Inyo, Kern, San Bernardino, San Luis Obispo, Santa Barbara, Ventura, and part of Los Angeles County)

Memphis
Regional Director: Gerard P. Fleischut
Regional Attorney: Michael S. Maram
National Labor Relations Board, Mid-Memphis Tower, Suite 800, 1407 Union Avenue, Memphis, TN 38104. Tel: 901/521-2725.

Milwaukee
Regional Director: Joseph A. Szabo
Regional Attorney: Philip E. Bloedorn
National Labor Relations Board, Henry S. Reuss Federal Plaza, 310 W. Wisconsin Avenue, Suite 700, Milwaukee, WI 53203. Tel: 414/291-3861.

Minneapolis
Regional Director: Ronald M. Sharp
Regional Attorney: Herbert S. Dawidoff
National Labor Relations Board, Federal Building, Room 316, 110 South 4th Street, Minneapolis, MN 55401. Tel: 612/348-1757.

Newark
Regional Director: William A. Pascarell
Regional Attorney: Michael J. Lightner
National Labor Relations Board, Peter D. Rodino, Jr. Federal Building, Room 1600, 970 Broad Street, Newark, NJ 07102. Tel: 201/645-2100.

New Orleans
Regional Director: H. Frank Malone
Regional Attorney: Mark Kaplan
National Labor Relations Board, Federal Bldg, 1515 Poydras Street, Room 610, New Orleans, LA 70112. Tel: 504/589-6361.

New York
Regional Director: Daniel Silverman
Regional Attorney: Karen P. Fernbach
National Labor Relations Board, Jacob K. Javits Federal Bldg, 26 Federal Plaza, Room 3614, New York, NY 10278. Tel: 212/264-0300.

Oakland
Regional Director: James S. Scott
Regional Attorney: Paul Eggert
Deputy Regional Attorney: Joseph P. Norelli
National Labor Relations Board, Breuner Building, 2nd Floor, 2201 Broadway, Oakland, CA 94612. Tel: 415/273-7200.

Peoria
Regional Director: Glenn A. Zipp
Regional Attorney: Michael B. Ryan
National Labor Relations Board, Savings Center Tower, 16th Fl, 411 Hamilton Boulevard, Peoria, IL 61602. Tel: 309/671-7080.

Philadelphia
Regional Director: Peter W. Hirsch
Regional Attorney: Leonard Leventhal
Deputy Regional Attorney: Dorothy L. Moore-Duncan
National Labor Relations Board, 1 Independence Mall, 7th Fl, 615 Chestnut Street, Philadelphia, PA 19106. Tel: 215/597-7601.

Phoenix
Regional Director: Roy H. Garner
Regional attorney: Peter N. Maydanis
National Labor Relations Board, 234 North Central Avenue, Suite 440, Phoenix, AZ 85004. Tel: 602/261-3361.

Pittsburgh
Regional Director: Gerald Kobell
Regional Attorney: Stanley R. Zawatski
Deputy Regional Attorney: Janet G. Harner
National Labor Relations Board, William S. Moorhead Federal Building, Room 1501, 1000 Liberty Avenue, Pittsburgh, PA 15222. Tel: 412/644-2977.

St. Louis
Regional Director: Joseph H. Solien
Regional Attorney: Leo D. Dollard
National Labor Relations Board, 210 Tucker Boulevard, North, Room 448, St. Louis, MO 63101. Tel: 314/425-4167.

NATIONAL LABOR RELATIONS BOARD

San Francisco
Regional Director: Robert H. Miller
Regional Attorney: Veronica I. Clements
Deputy Regional Attorney: Alan D. Longman
National Labor Relations Board, 901 Market Street, Room 400, San Francisco, CA 94103. Tel: 415/744-6810.

Seattle
Regional Director:John D. Nelson
Regional Attorney: Walter J. Mercer
Deputy Regional Attorney: Terry C. Densen
National Labor Relations Board, Federal Building, Room 2948, 915 Second Avenue, Seattle, WA 98174. Tel: 206/442-4532.

Tampa
Regional Director: Francis E. Dowd
Regional Attorney: Charles E. Deal
National Labor Relations Board, 700 Twiggs Street, Suite 511, Tampa, FL 33602. Tel: 813/228-2641.

Winston-Salem
Regional Director: Willie L. Clark, Jr.
Regional Attorney: Ronald C. Morgan
National Labor Relations Board, Federal Bldg, U.S. Courthouse, Room 447, 251 North Main Street, Winston-Salem, NC 27101. Tel: 919/631-5201.

OFFICE OF THE INSPECTOR GENERAL (Room 232)

Responsibilities include: conducting audits and investigations relating to NLRB programs and operations; reviewing existing and proposed legislation and regulations with respect to these programs and operations; preventing and detecting fraud and abuse; and recommending policies to promote economy and efficiency in agency programs and operations.

(Area Code 202)
Inspector General: Bernard Levine 254-4880

(Area Code 202)
Counsel to the Inspector General: Carolyn Ladd 254-4880

OFFICE OF REPRESENTATION APPEALS (Room 760)

(Area Code 202)
Director: Berton Subrin 254-9118

OFFICE OF THE SOLICITOR (Room 729)

(Area Code 202)
Solicitor: John E. Higgins, Jr 254-9110

(Area Code 202)
Associate Solicitor: Jeffrey D. Wedekind 254-9110

DIVISION OF ADMINISTRATIVE LAW JUDGES (Room 1122)

1375 K Street, N.W., Washington, D.C. 20005

There are 49 Administrative Law Judges in Washington, D.C., including the Chief Administrative Law Judge, an Associate Chief Administrative Law Judge, and a Deputy Chief Administrative Law Judge. There are also three Branch Offices, one in New York City with 13 Administrative Law Judges; one in Atlanta with nine Administrative Law Judges; and one in San Francisco with 19 Administrative Law Judges. These Administrative Law Judges do not have any staff attorneys, but periodically employ law clerks.

The NLRB has no statutory independent power of enforcement of its orders, but it may seek enforcement in the U.S. Courts of Appeals. Similarly, parties aggrieved by its orders may seek judicial review in the courts.

Upon filing of an unfair labor practice charge with an NLRB Regional Office, members of the professional staff of that office investigate circumstances from which the charge arises in order to determine whether formal proceedings are warranted. Approximately one-third of the unfair labor practice allegations are found, after investigation, to require legal disposition. If a voluntary settlement cannot be reached, then a formal complaint is issued and the case is heard before an Administrative Law Judge. NLRB Administrative Law Judges conduct formal hearings and issue decisions, which may be appealed to the five-member Board; if they are not appealed, the Administrative Law Judges' recommended orders then become orders of the Board.

(Area Code 202)
Chief Administrative Law Judge: Melvin J. Welles 633-0500
Deputy Chief Administrative Law Judge: David Davidson ..633-0500
Associate Chief Administrative Law Judge: John M. Dyer 633-0500
Administrative Officer: Joann McIntosh 633-0508
Facsimile...523-5884

Atlanta Branch Office
National Labor Relations Board, 44 Broad Street, NW, Grant Building, Atlanta, GA 30303
Associate Chief Administrative Law Judge:
William N. Cates ....(404) 331-6652
Facsimile ....(404) 331-2061

New York Branch Office
National Labor Relations Board, 1501 Broadway, Paramount Building, New York, NY 10036
Associate Chief Administrative Law Judge:
Edwin H. Bennett ....(212) 944-2941
Facsimile ....(212) 944-4904

San Francisco Branch Office
National Labor Relations Board, 901 Market Street, Suite 300, San Francisco, CA 94103
Deputy Chief Administrative Law Judge:
Earldean V.S. Robbins ....(415) 744-6800
Facsimile ....(415) 744-7905

PUBLICATIONS OF INTEREST

The following NLRB publications can be purchased from the **U.S. Government Printing Office.** Stock numbers and prices per copy are shown below. Submit requests for these publications to: The Superintendent of Documents, U.S. Government Printing Office, Washington, D.C. 20402.

(1) National Labor Relations Act and Labor Management Relations Act. GPO Stock# 031-000-00255-9. Price: $1.00.

(2) A Guide to Basic Law and Procedures Under the National Labor Relations Act. GPO Stock# 031-000-00273-7. Price: $2.00.

(3) Decisions and Orders of the National Labor Relations Board
(GPO Stock# 031-000-00267-2; Vol. 275: 04/06/85-08/27/85; $48.00)
(GPO Stock# 031-000-00267-1; Vol. 276: 08/28/85-10/29/85; $45.00)
(GPO Stock# 031-000-00272-9; Vol. 277: 10/29/85-01/14/86; $45.00)
(GPO Stock# 031-000-00274-5; Vol. 278: 01/15/86-03/27/86; $45.00)
(GPO Stock# 031-000-00275-3; Vol. 279: 03/28/86-05/30/86; $45.00)
(GPO Stock# 031-000-00276-1; Vol. 280: 05/30/86-08/07/86; $48.00)
(GPO Stock# 031-000-00285-1; Vol. 281: 08/08/86-10/21/86; $47.00)
(GPO Stock# 031-000-00287-7; Vol. 282: 10/22/86-02/23/87; $48.00)
(GPO Stock# 031-000-00288-5; Vol. 283: 02/24/87-05/29/87; $45.00)
(GPO Stock# 031-000-00291-5; Vol. 284: 05/27/87-07/29/87; $50.00)
(GPO Stock# 031-000-00292-3; Vol. 285: 07/30/87-09/29/87; $47.00)
(GPO Stock# 031-000-00293-1; Vol. 286: 09/30/87-12/07/87; $48.00)

(4) Court Decisions Relating to the National Labor Relations Act
(GPO Stock# 031-000-00252-4; Vol. 32: 01/01/80-12/31/80; $37.00)
(GPO Stock# 031-000-00254-1; Vol. 33: 01/01/81-12/31/81; $43.00)
(GPO Stock# 031-000-00258-3; Vol. 34: 01/01/82-12/31/82; $45.00)
(GPO Stock# 031-000-00261-3; Vol. 35: 01/01/83-12/31/83; $41.00)
(GPO Stock# 031-000-00271-1; Vol. 36: 01/01/84-12/31/84; $38.00)
(GPO Stock# 031-000-00277-0; Vol. 37: 01/01/85-12/31/85; $38.00)
(GPO Stock# 031-000-00283-4; Vol. 38: 01/01/86-12/31/86; $38.00)

(5) Weekly Summary of NLRB Cases includes summaries of all published NLRB decisions in unfair labor practice and representation election cases; lists decision of NLRB Administrative Law Judges and directions of elections by NLRB Regional Directors; reprints the General Counsel's Quarterly Report on (1) cases decided upon a request for advice from a Regional Director or an appeal from a Director's dismissal of unfair labor practice charges and (2) cases in which the General Counsel sought and obtained Board authorization to institute injunction proceedings under Section 10(j) of the Act; carries notices of publication of volumes of NLRB decisions and orders; NLRB Annual Report and other agency informational literature. GPO Stock# 731-002-00000-2. Price: $84.00 a year for domestic subscriptions, $105.00 a year for foreign subscriptions.

(6) NLRB Election Report is a monthly report detailing the outcome of secret-ballot voting by employees in NLRB-conducted representation elections in cases closed for each month. It is compiled from results following resolution of postelection objections and/or challenges. Election tallies are listed by unions involved, with employer name and location, and is arranged in two parts, single union elections and multi-union elections. The most current edition is from October 1989. GPO Stock# 731-001-00000-6. Price: $27.00 for 12 issues mailed domestically; $33.75 for foreign subscriptions.

(7) Rules and Regulations and Statements of Procedure of the National Labor Relations Board, Series 8, as amended 3/15/89 contains supplements for an indefinite period. It is in looseleaf form, punched for a three-ring binder (binder not included). GPO Stock# 931-002-00000-7. Price: $13.00 for domestic subscriptions; $16.25 for foreign subscriptions.

(8) National Labor Relations Board Casehandling Manual contains complete, updated General Counsel procedural and operational guidelines to NLRB Regional Offices in processing cases received under the Act in three parts. Part One: "Unfair Labor Practice Proceedings," Part Two: "Representation Proceedings." and Part Three: "Compliance Proceedings and Settlement Agreements." GPO Stock# 931-001-00000-1. Price: $50.00 for domestic subscriptions; $62.50 for foreign subscriptions.

(9) Classified Index of NLRB Decisions and Related Court Decisions (CINDR) is published as a paperback on a quarterly basis, and covers all board, Administrative Law Judges' and NLRB-related court decisions issued during the period covering publication. GPO Stock# 831-003-00000-6. Price: $18.00 (domestic) for four issues; $22.50 foreign.

(10) Classified Index of Dispositions of Unfair Labor Practice Charges by the General Counsel of the National labor Relations Board (CIDUL) is compiled by the Office of General Counsel, published on an irregular basis and cumulated, and is an index of Advice memoranda, Regional Directors' dismissal letters, and Appeals memoranda and dispositions. Last issue dated Dec 1989. GPO Stock# 031-000-00294-0. Price: $27.00 domestic; $33.75 foreign.

(11) Classification Outline with Topical Index of Decisions of the National Labor Relations Board and Related Court Decisions. This is a set consisting of four items: 1) Classified Index of National Labor Relations Board Decisions and Related Court Decisions; 2) Classified Index of Unfair Labor Practice Charges by the General Counsel of the National Labor Relations Board; 3) Classified Index of Decisions of the Regional Directors of the National Labor Relations Board in Representation Proceedings; and 4) National Labor Relations Board Decisions. GPO Stock# 031-000-00281-8. Price for the set: $41.00 domestic; $51.25 foreign.

A number of publications are available, free-of-charge, from the Division of Information at the NLRB. They include: The National Labor Relations Board and You -- Unfair Labor Practices, and The National Labor Relations Board and You -- What It Is? What It Does? Contact: NLRB, Division of Information, Suite 710, 1717 Pennsylvania Avenue, N.W., Washington, D.C. 20570. (202/632-4950).

NATIONAL LABOR RELATIONS BOARD
KEY LEGAL AUTHORITIES

Regulations: 29 C.F.R., Parts 100-103 (1989).

National Labor Relations Act of 1935 (Wagner Act), as amended, 29 U.S.C. 151 et seq.--established the Board to protect the rights of workers and prohibited employers from engaging in certain illegal labor practices.

Labor-Management Relations Act of 1947 (Taft-Hartley Act), 29 U.S.C. 141 et seq.--provided protection to employers in collective bargaining and union organization situations, and prohibited closed shops, strikes against the Government, and also authorized the courts to enjoin strikes and provide an 80-day "cooling-off" period.

Legislative History: 1947 U.S. Code Cong. Service 1135.

Labor-Management Reporting and Disclosure Act of 1959 (Landrum-Griffin Act), 29 U.S.C. 401 et seq.--established a Federal regulatory scheme to monitor union activities and control corruption in the labor movement.

Legislative History: 1959 U.S. Code Cong. & Admin. News 2318.

Postal Reorganization Act of 1970, 39 U.S.C. 1201-1209--empowered the National Labor Relations Board to preside over labor disputes and union representation elections in the U.S. Postal Service.

Legislative History: 1970 U.S. Code Cong. & Admin. News 3649.

NATIONAL MEDIATION BOARD

1425 K Street, N.W., Suite 910
Washington, D.C. 20572

DESCRIPTION: The National Mediation Board, in administering the Railway Labor Act, assists in maintaining a free flow of commerce in the railroad and airline industries by resolving labor/management disputes that could disrupt travel or imperil the economy. Over 97% of the collective bargaining disputes submitted to the Board's mediation assistance are resolved without work stoppages. The Board also handles railroad and airline employee representation disputes and is responsible for financial supervision of the National Railroad Adjustment Board (located in Chicago) which handles rail grievances relating to the interpretation and application of existing contracts.

(Area Code 202)

Chairman: Joshua M. Javits 523-5024
Executive Director: William A. Gill, Jr 523-5920
Procurement and Publication Information 523-5950
Public Information 523-5335
Facsimile 523-1494

THE BOARD
Chairman: Joshua M. Javits 523-5024
Members:
Patrick J. Cleary 523-5268
Walter C. Wallace 523-5428

(Area Code 202)

Freedom of Information Act/Privacy Act Office 523-5996
Requests must be made in writing. There is a copying charge of 20 cents per page. There is also a variable per hour search fee. Submit requests to the attention of the Executive Director, Room 910, at the National Mediation Board address cited at the beginning of this listing.

Research and Information Management (Room 910)..........357-0466
This research office is open to the public from 9:00 AM until 4:30 PM, Monday through Friday, by appointment only. Call this office for an appointment so that a staff member can have the information ready when you come in. Materials may not be checked out but photocopying is possible for a fee.

LEGAL STAFF

The legal staff of the Board consists of the General Counsel and three Hearing Officers. Responsibilities of the General Counsel include defensive litigation, handling Freedom of Information Act and Ethics in Government matters, and providing general legal advice. The Hearing Officers assist in resolving employee representation issues at the appellate or Board level, including Presidential Emergency Boards in the case of railway labor disputes, and perform other related duties.

(Area Code 202)

General Counsel: Ronald M. Etters 523-5944
Hearing Officers:
Mary L. Johnson 523-5939

(Area Code 202)

Joyce Klein 523-5328
Roland Watkins 523-5995

NATIONAL RAILROAD ADJUSTMENT BOARD

175 West Jackson Blvd, Chicago, IL 60604

Staff Director (Grievances): Roy J. Carvatta ....(312) 886-7300

Division I: Train and Yard Service Disputes
Chairman: R.K. Radek ....(312) 886-7303
Vice-Chairman: M.W. Fingerhut ....(312) 886-7303

Division II: Shop Craft Disputes
Chairman: R.A. Johnson ....(312) 886-7303
Vice-Chairman: P.V. Varga ....(312) 886-7303

Division III: Disputes involving Clerical Personnel, Dispatchers, etc.
Chairman: N.R. Miller ....(312) 886-7303
Vice-Chairman: J.E. Yost ....(312) 886-7303

Division IV: Disputes involving Water Transportation etc.
Chairman: R.C. Arthur ....(312) 886-7303
Vice-Chairman: M.C. Lesnik ....(312) 886-7303

NOTE: The Chairman and Vice-Chairman rotate positions at the beginning of the fiscal year in October.

PUBLICATIONS OF INTEREST

The National Mediation Board has three separate subscription services. The subscription period covers the current Fiscal Year (October 1 through September 30). Make check payable to the United States Treasury and mail to: **The National Mediation Board**, Attn: M. C. Maione-Pricci, Washington, D.C. 20572.

(1) **Subscription List No. 1** covers all of the Board's publications. They include: Certifications and Dismissals, Determinations of Craft or Class, Findings Upon Investigations, Annual Report of the National Mediation Board, and Emergency Board Reports. Price: $175.00.

(2) **Subscription List No. 2** covers the following publications: Annual Report of the National Mediation Board, Emergency Board Reports, and Determinations of Craft of Class (bound volume). Price: $50.00.

(3) **Subscription List No. 3** consists of the Representation Manual and any subsequent amendments issued. Price: $35.00 (one time charge).

The following publications are also published by the **National Mediation Board** and can be ordered from the address listed above.

The Railway Labor Act (U.S.Code Provisions). Price: 75 cents.

NMB Determinations is published by Fiscal Year and include Certifications and Dismissals, Determinations of Craft or Class, and Findings of the Board. The following years are available: Volume 1 (FY74) $3.80; Volume 2 (FY75) $2.00; Volume 3 (FY76) $1.95; Volume 4 (FY77) $2.45; Volume 5 (FY78) $4.50; Volume 6 (FY79) $10.00; Volume 7 (FY80) $8.00; Volume 8 (FY81) $9.00; Volume 9 (FY82) $8.00; Volume 10 (FY83) $11.00; Volume 11 (FY84) $8.00; Volume 12 (FY85) $9.00; Volume 3 (FY86) $10.00; Volume 14 (FY87) $11.00; Volume 15 (FY88) $12.00; Volume 16 (FY89) $13.00. Volume 17 (FY90) is in the process of being published.

NATIONAL MEDIATION BOARD
KEY LEGAL AUTHORITIES

Regulations:

General Agency Regulations: 29 C.F.R. Parts 1200-1209 (1989).
Rules of Practice and Procedure: 29 C.F.R. Part 1202 (1989).

Railway Labor Act, as amended, 45 U.S.C. 151-163--established the National Mediation Board to mediate labor disputes between rail and air carriers and their unions.

NATIONAL SCIENCE FOUNDATION

1800 G Street, N.W.
Washington, D.C. 20550

DESCRIPTION: The purposes of the National Science Foundation (NSF) are to increase the nation's base of scientific knowledge and strengthen its ability to conduct research in all areas of science and engineering; to develop and help implement science education programs that can better prepare the nation for meeting the challenges of the future; and to promote international cooperation through science. In its role as a leading Federal supporter of science, NSF also has an important role in national science policy planning.

(Area Code 202)

Chairman: Mary L. Good 357-9582
Director: Erich Bloch 357-7748
Procurement Information 357-7922
Grants/Contracts Information 357-7880
Legislative and Public Affairs 357-9498
Publications Information 357-7668
Facsimile 357-7884

Freedom of Information Act Office 357-9495
All requests for FOIA information must be submitted in writing. There is a copying charge of 10 cents per page. There is also a variable per hour search fee. The first two hours of a search are free, and there is no charge for an amount under $25.00. Submit requests to the attention of the Freedom of Information Act Officer, Room 527, at the address cited at the beginning of this listing.

(Area Code 202)

Privacy Act Office................................357-9520

Library (Room 248)................................357-7811
The library is open to the public from 7:30 AM until 5:00 PM, Monday through Friday. Materials can only be charged out with an interlibrary loan form. A single copy can be made without charge.

OFFICE OF INSPECTOR GENERAL (Room 1241)

The Office of Inspector General is responsible for conducting and supervising all audits and investigations of NSF programs and operations. OIG is also responsible for providing leadership and coordination and for recommending policies to promote economy, efficiency, and effectiveness in administering NSF programs and operations; to prevent and detect fraud, waste, abuse, and mismanagement in NSF programs and operations; and to prevent, detect, and handle cases involving misconduct in science.

(Area Code 202)

Inspector General: Linda Sundro 357-9457

(Area Code 202)

Counsel to Inspector General: Philip Sunshine 357-9457

OFFICE OF GENERAL COUNSEL (Room 501)

The Office of the General Counsel provides legal and policy advice to NSF officials and members of the National Science Board. Attorneys review proposed legislative actions which have an impact on NSF operations and more generally on science policy in the nation. This review would include NSF's own statutes as well as those that deal with such issues as export control, education of foreign students in America, and patents and intellectual property. The principal focus of much of the daily work is on grants for the performance of basic science research, on the procurement of services and goods, and on the full range of administrative laws and regulations which govern any Federal Government operation, including the Freedom of Information Act, Privacy Act, Administrative Procedure Act, EEO, civil service laws, etc. There is a special emphasis on those laws most relevant to national science policy, including antitrust, patent, copyright, and other intellectual property laws.

The Office of the General Counsel, through the Director of the Foundation and the National Science Board, interacts heavily with the Office of Science and Technology Policy in the White House, with the Departments of Commerce and Justice, with Congress, and with the National Academy of Sciences in the development of select science policy issues.

(Area Code 202)

General Counsel: Charles H. Herz 357-9435
Deputy General Counsel: vacant 357-9435
Assistant General Counsels:
Jesse Lasken 357-9435
John Chester 357-9435

(Area Code 202)

Lewis Grotke 357-9435
Lawrence Rudolph 357-9435
D. Matthew Powell 357-9435
Facsimile 357-7521

DATABASES AND PUBLICATIONS OF INTEREST

A copy of Publications of the National Science Foundation can be obtained from Publications Information at NSF. Tel: 202/357-7668.

The following publications are available from the NSF free-of-charge. Write: **National Science Foundation,** Attn: Forms and Publications, 1800 G Street, N.W., Room 232, Washington, D.C. 20550. Tel: 202/357-7861.

National Science Foundation Bulletin is a monthly publication (except for July and August) which includes news about current programs, deadlines, meetings, and new publications. No order number is necessary.

An NSF Strategy for Compliance with Environmental Law in Antarctica (A Report to the Director). NSF 90-4.

Antarctic Conservation Act of 1989, Public Law 95-54. NSF 89-59.

Small Business Guide to Federal R&D Funding Opportunities. NSF 86-28.

The following publication can be purchased from the **U.S. Government Printing Office.** Stock number and price for annual subscription is shown below. Submit requests for this publication to: The Superintendent of Documents, U.S. Government Printing Office, Washington, D.C. 20402. Tel: 202/783-3238.

National Science Foundation Grant Policy Manual. July 1989. A compendium of basic NSF grant policies and procedures for use by the grantee community and by NSF staff. Subscription service consists of a basic manual and supplementary material for an indeterminate period. Price: $21.00 domestic; $26.25 foreign. GPO Stock# 938-001-00000-6.

Research findings and results of studies supported by NSF are generally published in scientific journals or as reports prepared by the grantee institutions for NSF. These technical reports, as well as a few general publications, can be purchased from the National Technical Information Service (NTIS), 5285 Port Royal Rd, Springfield, VA 22161. Call 202/487-4650 for prices and availability.

In the near future, NSF will be providing electronic access to publications, program announcements and award information. The system will be called the **Science and Technology Information System (STIS)** and will support multiple simultaneous users. Access to STIS will be via dial-up connection or remote log-in across **Internet.** Information on progress of the STIS effort will be published in the NSF Bulletin.

NATIONAL SCIENCE FOUNDATION
KEY LEGAL AUTHORITIES

Regulations:

General Agency Regulations: 45 C.F.R. Parts 601-689 (1989).
National Science Foundation Acquisition Regulations: 48 C.F.R. Parts 2501-2532 (1989).
Fellowship Review Panel Procedures: 45 C.F.R. Part 630 (1989).

National Science Foundation Act of 1950, as amended, 42 U.S.C. 1861-1875--established the National Science Foundation to initiate, support, and strengthen basic scientific and engineering research and programs through contracts, grants, loans, and other forms of assistance and to appraise the impact of research upon industrial development and general welfare.

Legislative History: 1950 U.S. Code Cong. Service 2269; 1985 U.S. Code Cong. & Admin. News 754; 1988 U.S. Code Cong. & Admin. News 3749.

Antarctic Conservation Act of 1978, as amended, 16 U.S.C. 2401 et seq.--provides for conservation and protection of Antarctic flora and fauna and authorizes the National Science Foundation to issue permits to obtain and handle Antarctic flora and fauna in a manner otherwise prohibited by the Act.

Legislative History: 1978 U.S. Code Cong. & Admin. News 4666.

NATIONAL TRANSPORTATION SAFETY BOARD

800 Independence Avenue, S.W.
Washington, D.C. 20594

DESCRIPTION: The National Transportation Safety Board (NTSB) is an independent Federal agency consisting of five Board members appointed by the President, two of whom are designated as Chairman and Vice Chairman. The Board's mission is to promote transportation safety by conducting independent investigations of accidents and other safety problems and formulating recommendations for safety improvements. Responsibilities include investigating, determining probable cause, and making safety recommendations on all U.S. civil aviation accidents and certain railroad accidents, pipeline accidents, highway accidents, major marine accidents, and other transportation accidents that are catastrophic in nature.

(Area Code 202)

Chairman: James L. Kolstad 382-6502
Managing Director: Terry L. Baxter 382-6518
Procurement Information 382-6731
Public Information 382-6600
Publications Information 382-6735
Docket...382-6735
Facsimile..382-6609

Freedom of Information Act/Privacy Act Office 382-6700
All requests must be submitted in writing. There is a copying charge of 10 cents per page, but there is no charge for search time. Submit requests to the attention of the Freedom of Information Act Officer, Room 802, at the NTSB address cited at the beginning of this listing.

Public Inquiry Section (Room 805-F)....................382-6735
The Public Inquiry Section is open to the public from 8:30 AM until 5:00 PM, Monday through Friday. Only Federal Government employees may check out materials, but photocopies can be made at a charge of 12 cents per page.

MEMBERS OF THE BOARD

(Area Code 202)

Chairman of the Board: James L. Kolstad 382-6502
Special Assistant: John Moulden 382-6502

Vice Chairman: Susan M. Coughlin 382-6506
Special Assistant: vacant 382-6506

Member: James Eugene Burnett Jr 382-6500
Special Assistant: John A. Hammerschmidt 382-6500

Member: John K. Lauber 382-6504
Special Assistant: Julie Beals 382-6504

Member: Christopher Hart (Designate) 382-6508

OFFICE OF GENERAL COUNSEL (Room 818)

The Office of General Counsel provides advice and assistance on legal aspects of policy matters, legislation, and preparation of Board rules, opinions, and orders; undertakes legal research and renders legal opinions; and represents the Board in court actions to which the NTSB is a party or in which the Board is interested. Actions may be undertaken in the U.S. Court of Appeals on appeals taken by airmen from Board opinions and orders; in both U.S. District Courts and state courts in connection with the enforcement of Board orders and regulations; or before the Merit Systems Protection Board and Equal Employment Opportunity Commission on personnel and employment matters. The Office of General Counsel also prepares opinions and orders for Board approval on all cases appealed to the Board from decisions of Board Administrative Law Judges and from the Commandant of the U.S. Coast Guard; and serves on the Board of Inquiry at public hearings held by the Safety Board in connection with its accident investigations.

(Area Code 202)

General Counsel: Daniel D. Campbell 382-6540
Deputy General Counsel: Ronald Battocchi 382-6540
Associate General Counsel for Adjudications:
David E. Bass 382-6540
Facsimile..382-6819

OFFICE OF ADMINISTRATIVE LAW JUDGES (Suite 505)

1951 Kidwell Drive, Vienna, VA 22182

The Office of Administrative Law Judges provides the initial forum for the review of appeals from the suspension, amendment, revocation, or denial of any operating certificate or license issued by the Secretary of Transportation under the Federal Aviation Act of 1958. Many, but not all appeals involve a formal hearing. When required, hearings are held throughout the U.S. and its possessions. The Judges function as trial judges, regulating the course of the hearings and issuing decisions.

(Area Code 703)

Chief Administrative Law Judge: William E. Fowler, Jr 506-9280
Deputy Chief Judge for Administration:
Jimmy N. Coffman 506-9280
Aviation Appeals Admin/Case Manager: Dina Clayborn 506-8864
Facsimile 506-8865

Circuit I

National Transportation Safety Board, 15000 Aviation Blvd, Federal Building, Lawndale, CA 90261
Administrative Law Judge: Jerrell R. Davis ..... (213) 297-1045
Hearing Assistant: Joyce Donenfeld .... (213) 297-1045
Facsimile .... (213) 297-1920

Circuit II

National Transportation Safety Board, 4760 Oakland Street, Denver, CO 80239
Administrative Law Judge: Patrick G. Geraghty .. (303) 361-0615
Hearing Assistant: Jeannette Wilson .... (303) 361-0615
Facsimile .... (303) 361-0619

Circuit III

National Transportation Safety Board, 1200 Copeland Road, Suite 300, Arlington, TX 76011
Administrative Law Judge: William R. Mullins
(phone number not yet determined)

Circuit IV

National Transportation Safety Board, 1951 Kidwell Drive, Suite 505, Vienna, VA 22182
Administrative Law Judge: William E. Fowler, Jr. (703) 506-9280
Hearing Assistant: June Grayson .... (703) 506-9280
Facsimile .... (703) 506-8865

Circuit V

National Transportation Safety Board, 1951 Kidwell Drive, Suite 505, Vienna, VA 22182
Administrative Law Judge: Joyce Capps .... (703) 506-9280
Hearing Assistant: June Grayson .... (703) 506-9280
Facsimile .... (703) 506-8865

Circuit VI

National Transportation Safety Board, 1951 Kidwell Drive, Suite 505, Vienna, VA 22182
Administrative Law Judge: Jimmy N. Coffman ..... (703) 506-9280
Hearing Assistant: June Grayson .... (703) 506-9280
Facsimile .... (703) 506-8865

PUBLICATIONS OF INTEREST

Database:

Computer Tapes of Aviation Accident Data are continuously updated and are available going back to 1964. They are available from the NTSB Analysis and Data Division. Tel: 202/382-6538. Indicate the specific type of accident data needed and the calendar year, or portion thereof, for which the data is needed. There is no charge if the person requesting the data provides his own computer tape.

Publications:

The following publications can be obtained through either the **National Transportation Safety Board's Public Inquiries Section** or the **National Technical Information Services (NTIS).**

Contact the NTSB for more information at: National Transportation Safety Board, Public Inquiries Section, Room 805-F, 800 Independence Avenue, S.W., Washington, D.C. 20594, or call 202/382-6735.

Contact the National Technical Information Service at: 5285 Port Royal Road, Springfield, VA 22161, or call 703/487-4630 (for annual subscriptions) or 703/487-4650 (for single copies and microfiche). Prepayment is required for all orders.

These publications include:

1. Accident Reports (Major) are detailed narrative reports which contain the facts, conditions, analysis, conclusions, and probable cause of major aviation, railroad, highway, pipeline, and marine accident investigations which are issued for all accidents which resulted in a major investigation. They are available on an irregular basis from NTIS by annual subscription or by single issue. When ordering annual subscriptions, specify the transportation mode and the type of publications (i.e., Aviation Accident Report). When ordering single issues, specify the exact title of the document, the NTSB report number, or the NTIS accession number.

2. News Digest, issued bi-monthly from the NTSB, contains a summary of all major NTSB activities, including the issuance of major safety recommendations and the NTSB position on major transportation issues. It can be ordered, free-of-charge, by either annual subscription or single issue. When ordering annual subscriptions, specify the type of document (i.e., News Digest). When ordering single issues, specify the type of document and the publication number.

3. Public Records and Files are detailed records and files maintained for specified periods of time on all major Board activities, such as accident investigations, safety recommendations, studies and objectives, special investigations, initial decisions of the Administrative Law Judges, and opinions and orders. They are available from the NTSB Public Inquiries Section for a fee. When ordering, indicate, if applicable, the document or file number; or name and title of the record or document; or for accident records, the date and location of the accident records, the date and location of the accident and the operator or carrier involved.

4. Regulations of the NTSB are issued irregularly as procedures change. When ordering them from the NTSB Public Inquiries Section, specify, by number or by title, the part or parts of the regulations needed. Currently issued parts include:

Part 821: Rules of practice in air safety proceedings.
Part 825: Rules of procedure for merchant marine appeals from decisions of the Commandant, U.S. Coast Guard.
Part 831: Aircraft accident/incident investigation procedures.
Part 845: Rules of practice in transportation accident/incident hearings and reports.

5. Initial Decisions of the Administrative Law Judges. Sets forth Administrative Law Judges' findings, conclusions, and decisions in safety enforcement proceedings involving petitions from applicants denied airmen's certificates by the Administrator of the Federal Aviation Administration; and appeals from orders of the Administrator of the Federal Aviation Administration suspending or revoking certificates issued to airmen, aircraft, air agencies, and air carriers for alleged violations of the regulations or for lack of qualifications to hold such certificates. Initial Decisions are issued both individually and in a monthly publication. Individual Initial Decisions are available, for a fee, from the NTSB Public Inquiries Section. When ordering individual decisions, specify the type of document and the docket number. The monthly publication is available, for a fee, from NTIS by annual subscription and single issue.

6. Opinions and Orders. Sets forth decisions of the Board resulting from the review of appeals from decisions of the Commandant of the U.S. Coast Guard involving seamen's certificates or initial decisions of the NTSB Administrative Law Judges involving airmen and/or air safety certificates. Opinions and Orders are issued individually, in a monthly publication, and in bound volumes containing several years of Opinions and Orders. Individual Opinions and Orders are available, for a fee, from the NTSB Public Inquiries Section. The monthly publication is available, for a fee, from the NTIS by annual subscription or a single issue. The bound volumes are available, for a fee, from the NTIS until limited supplies are exhausted.

NATIONAL TRANSPORTATION SAFETY BOARD
KEY LEGAL AUTHORITIES

Regulations:

General Agency Regulations: 49 C.F.R. Parts 800-850 (1989).
Rules of Practice and Procedure:
- **Air Safety Proceedings:** 49 C.F.R. Part 821 (1989).
- **Merchant Marine Appeals from Decisions of the Coast Guard Commandant:** 49 C.F.R. Part 825 (1989).
- **Accident/Incident Investigations:** 49 C.F.R. Part 831 (1989).
- **Transportation Accident Hearings:** 49 C.F.R. Part 845 (1989).

Independent Safety Board Act of 1974, as amended, 49 U.S.C. 1901 et seq.--established the National Transportation Safety Board as an independent agency of the Executive Branch and empowered it to investigate transportation accidents and recommend regulations and other improvements to transportation safety.
Legislative History: 1974 U.S. Code Cong. & Admin. News 7669; 1988 U.S. Code Cong. & Admin. News 1089.

Federal Aviation Act of 1958, as amended, 49 U.S.C. 1301, 1441-1443--directs the Board to investigate aircraft accidents.
Legislative History: 1958 U.S. Code Cong. & Admin. News 3741.

NUCLEAR REGULATORY COMMISSION

Washington, D.C. 20555

DESCRIPTION: The Nuclear Regulatory Commission (NRC) is the independent regulatory agency responsible for the licensing and regulation of civilian nuclear power facilities and materials. Established in 1975, the primary mission of the Commission is to regulate the uses of nuclear energy so as to protect the radiological health and safety of the public, to maintain the safety and security of nuclear materials, to protect the environment, and to ensure compliance with pertinent antitrust laws. To carry out this mission, the NRC has developed a comprehensive program consisting of regulation, licensing, and enforcement.

(Area Code 301)

Chairman: Kenneth M. Carr 492-1759
Procurement Information:
Small Purchases 492-7054
Contracts 492-4210
Public Information (White Flint North Bldg) 492-0240
Publications Information 492-8523
Office of Small and Disadvantaged Business Utilization 492-4667
Facsimile: (White Flint North Building) 492-0262/0264

Freedom of Information Act Office/Privacy Act Office .. 492-8133
Requests must be made in writing. There is a copying charge of 20 cents per page. There is also a variable per hour search fee.

Submit FOIA/Privacy Act requests to the attention of the Director of Information and Publications Services Division, Phillips Bldg, Mailstop P-378, 7920 Norfolk Avenue, Bethesda, MD 20184.

(Area Code 202)

Public Documents Room (Lower Level) 634-3273
2120 L Street, N.W., Washington, D.C. (Mailing address: NRC, Washington, D.C. 20555)
The Public Documents Room is open to the public from 7:45 AM until 4:15 PM, Monday through Friday. There are no charge-out privileges. Photocopies can made for a charge of 10 cents per page.

OFFICES OF THE COMMISSIONERS (17th Floor)

One White Flint North Bldg, 11555 Rockville Pike, Rockville, MD 20852. (Mailing address: NRC, Washington, D.C. 20555)

(Area Code 301)

Legal Assistant to Chairman Kenneth M. Carr:
Karen Cyr 492-1750
Executive/Legal Assistant to Commissioner Forrest J. Remick: Bradley W. Jones 492-1820
Counsel to Commissioner James R. Curtiss:
Joseph R. Gray 492-1875

(Area Code 301)

Legal Assistant to Commissioner Thomas M. Roberts:
James M. Cutchin IV 492-1800
Legal Assistant to Commissioner Kenneth C. Rogers:
Myron Karman 492-1855

OFFICE OF GENERAL COUNSEL (Mailstop 15B18)

One White Flint North Bldg, 11555 Rockville Pike, Rockville, MD 20852. (Mailing address: NRC, Washington, D.C. 20555)

The Office of the General Counsel is located in NRC offices in Washington, D.C. and Bethesda, MD. Its primary responsibilities involve providing legal advice to the agency with respect to all of its activities. Duties include: reviewing and preparing draft Commission decisions; interpreting laws, regulations, and other sources of authority; preparing or concurring in all contractual documents, regulations, orders, licenses, and other legal documents; directing intellectual property work; and representing the NRC in legal matters and in court proceedings.

The Solicitor has primary responsibility for supervising litigation in courts, representing the NRC in Court of Appeals litigation and, in conjunction with the Justice Department, in other Federal courts. Attorneys in this office assist in supervising litigation and advise the Commission in litigation implications of proposed actions.

The Deputy General Counsel for Licensing and Regulation provides advise on all aspects of domestic licensing and regulation, with particular emphasis on adjudication, legislation, rulemaking, and fuel cycle matters. Provides advice on employee-conduct and administrative law issues as well as on the implementation of atomic energy and environmental law.

The Assistant General Counsel for Adjudications and Opinions provides advice on the review of adjudicatory decisions, on the implementation of employee-conduct regulations, and in the development of the Commission's legislative program. Provides legal advice to the Office of Investigations and the Office of Inspector General.

The Assistant General Counsel for Rulemaking and Fuel Cycle provides legal advice with respect to the promulgation and amendment of NRC regulations and guides pertinent to licensing and construction of nuclear facilities, including nuclear power plants, fuel cycle facilities, and the high-level waste repository; represents the NRC staff in public rulemaking hearings; interprets regulations and statutes relevant to NRC activities and provides legal analyses of those authorities impacting the NRC; and provides legal advice and assistance to the NRC on the licensing of the possession and use of nuclear materials on safeguards issues, on "agreement states" issues, and on international authorities of the Agency.

The Deputy General Counsel for Hearings, Enforcement and Administration provides advice on all licensing, inspection, and enforcement activities, with particular emphasis on the conduct of adjudicatory hearings and the implementation of the Commission's enforcement program. Assists in providing legal advice on interagency and international agreements, procurement, intellectual property, security, personnel, and administrative functions.

The Assistant General Counsel for Hearings and Enforcement assists in representing the NRC in public hearings conducted in conjunction with the licensing of nuclear reactors and materials users and facilities; and provides legal advice and assistance on inspection and enforcement matters, representing NRC officials in enforcement proceedings against licensees involving imposition of civil penalties, modifications, suspension, or revocation of licenses.

The Assistant General Counsel for Administration provides advice and assistance to NRC offices involved in interagency and international agreements, procurement, intellectual property, security, personnel, EEO, labor relations, FOIA, and other administrative functions.

The Special Assistant for International Affairs assists in the development of legal policy and advice bearing on export of nuclear materials and facilities, including development of regulations, review of license applications, hearings on export license applications, and other Commission activities involving international activities or considerations.

(Area Code 301)

General Counsel: William C. Parler 492-1743
Solicitor: John F. Cordes 492-1600
Legal/Legislative Information 492-1526
Special Assistant for International Affairs:
Joanna M. Becker 492-1740
Facsimile....................492-0262/0264

Licensing and Regulation
Deputy General Counsel: Martin G. Malsch 492-1740
Assistant General Counsel for Adjudications and Opinions: James A. Fitzgerald 492-1607
Assistant General Counsel for Rulemaking and Fuel Cycle: Stuart A. Treby 492-1636

(Area Code 301)

Hearings, Enforcement and Administration
Deputy General Counsel: Joseph F. Scinto 492-1740
Assistant General Counsel for Administration:
Dennis C. Dambly 492-1550
Assistant General Counsel for Hearings and Enforcement:
Lawrence J. Chandler 492-1681
Deputy Assistant General Counsel for Materials, Antitrust, and Special Proceedings: Joseph Rutberg 492-1532
Deputy Assistant General Counsel for Reactor Licensing:
Edwin J. Reis 492-1578

OFFICE OF THE INSPECTOR GENERAL (Mailstop MNBB-8607)

Maryland National Bank Bldg, 7735 Old Georgetown Rd, Bethesda, MD 20814. (Mailing address: NRC, Washington, D.C. 20555)

The Office of the Inspector General provides policy direction for and conducts, supervises, and coordinates audits and investigations relating to all NRC programs and operations; and reviews existing and proposed legislation and regulations and makes recommendations concerning their impact on the economy and efficiency of NRC programs and operations, and on the prevention and detection of fraud and abuse in such programs and operations. The Inspection Staff reviews specific events relating to the NRC's conduct of its regulatory responsibilities; assesses the NRC staff's response to specific operational situations; identifies lessons learned from those responses; and recommends improved policies or procedures for dealing with similar situations in the future. The Assistant Inspector General for Investigations directs investigative activities concerning NRC programs and operations; prepares reports of possible violations of criminal laws and other irregularities; and maintains liaison with law enforcement agencies and investigative organizations in criminal and other investigative matters.

(Area Code 301)

Inspector General: David C. Williams 492-9093
Assistant Inspector General for Audits:
William Glenn (Acting) 492-7051

(Area Code 301)

Assistant Inspector General for Investigations:
Leo Norton 492-7170

THE ATOMIC SAFETY AND LICENSING BOARD PANEL (Fourth Floor)

East-West Towers West Bldg, 4350 East-West Highway, Bethesda, MD 20814. (Mailing address: NRC, Washington, D.C. 20555)

The Atomic Safety and Licensing Board Panel conducts trial-level public hearings involving applications for nuclear power reactor construction permits, operating licenses, and license amendments; the licensing of nuclear waste disposal facilities; license enforcement proceedings; and other matters. The Panel's judges include not only attorneys but also nuclear reactor engineers, physicists, and environmental scientists. There are currently six attorneys working for this Panel as Administrative Judges and two as Administrative Law Judges. There is also one attorney who serves as Director and Chief Counsel of the Technical and Legal Support Staff. The cases heard generally involve complex litigation with multiple parties.

(Area Code 301)

Chief Administrative Judge/Chairman:
B. Paul Cotter Jr 492-7814
Deputy Chief Administrative Judges:
Robert M. Lazo (Executive) 492-7842
Frederick J. Shon (Technical) 492-7993

(Area Code 301)

Technical and Legal Support Staff Director and Chief Counsel: Sebastian Aloot 492-7787
Assistant Director, Support and Analysis Staff:
Jack G. Whetstone (docket information) 492-7858
Facsimile....................492-7285

THE ATOMIC SAFETY AND LICENSING APPEAL PANEL (Room 529)

East-West Towers West Bldg, 4350 East-West Highway, Bethesda, MD 20814. (Mailing address: NRC, Washington, D.C. 20555)

The Atomic Safety and Licensing Appeal Panel is a quasi-judicial appellate tribunal with technical and legal staff members. In divisions of three, known as Appeal Boards, its members review the decisions of the Atomic Safety and Licensing Boards and the Commission's Administrative Law Judges. There are currently three attorneys serving as Administrative Judges and one serving as Counsel to the Panel.

(Area Code 301)

Chairman: Christine N. Kohl 492-7662
Counsel: Andrea I. Cali 492-7666

(Area Code 301)

Technical Advisor: Stephen M. Goldberg 492-7666
Facsimile....................492-5061

REGIONAL OFFICES

There is only one Regional Attorney in each of the NRC's five regional offices (located in King of Prussia, PA; Atlanta, GA; Glen Ellyn, IL; Arlington, TX; and Walnut Creek, CA).

Region I (King of Prussia, PA)

Regional Administrator: William T. Russell
Regional Counsel: Karla Smith
U.S. Nuclear Regulatory Commission, Region I, 475 Allendale Road, King of Prussia, PA 19406. Tel: 215/337-5000.

Region II (Atlanta, GA)

Regional Administrator: Stewart D. Ebneter
Regional Counsel: Richard J. Goddard
U.S. Nuclear Regulatory Commission, Region II, 101 Marietta Street, Suite 2900, Atlanta, GA 30323. Tel: 404/331-4503.

Region III (Glen Ellyn, IL)

Regional Administrator: A. Bert Davis
Regional Counsel: Bruce A. Berson
U.S. Nuclear Regulatory Commission, Region III, 799 Roosevelt Road, Glen Ellyn, IL 60137. Tel: 312/790-5500.

Region IV (Arlington, TX)

Regional Administrator: Robert D. Martin
Regional Counsel: William A. Brown
U.S. Nuclear Regulatory Commission, Region IV, Parkway Central Plaza Bldg, 611 Ryan Plaza Drive, Suite 1000, Arlington, TX 76011. Tel: 817/860-8100.

Region V (Walnut Creek, CA)

Regional Administrator: John B. Martin
Regional Counsel: Michael B. Blume
U.S. Nuclear Regulatory Commission, Region V, 1450 Maria Lane, Suite 210, Walnut Creek, CA 94596. Tel: 415/943-3700.

PUBLICATIONS OF INTEREST

The following NRC publications can be purchased from the **U.S. Government Printing Office.** Stock numbers and prices for annual subscriptions to each are shown below. Submit requests for these publications to: The Superintendent of Documents, U.S. Government Printing Office, Washington, D.C. 20402. Tel: 202/783-3238.

Regulatory and Technical Reports, NUREG-0304, 15th volume, is a quarterly compilation that consists of bibliographic data and abstracts for the formal regulatory and technical reports issued by the NRC Staff and its contractors. Price: $14.00 per year; $17.50 foreign. Stock# 752-018-00000-6.

Single copies of the Regulatory and Technical Reports are available from the National Technical Information Service (NTIS), 5385 Port Royal Rd, Springfield, VA 22161 (703/487-4650).

Title List of Documents Made Publicly Available, NUREG-0540, is a monthly report that contains descriptions of the information that the NRC receives and generates. It includes: (1) docketed material associated with civilian nuclear power plants and other uses of radioactive materials and (2) nondocketed material that the NRC receives and generates and is relevant to its role as a regulatory agency. These documents are indexed by a Personal Author Index, a Corporate Source Index, and a Report Number Index. Price: $74.00 per year; $92.50 foreign. Stock# 752-025-00000-2.

Microfiche of the docketed information listed in the Title List is available for sale on a subscription basis from NTIS, at the NTIS address cited above.

Nuclear Regulatory Commission Issuances (NUREG-0750), is a monthly publication containing all opinions, decisions, denials, memoranda, and orders of the Commission, the Atomic Safety and Licensing Appeal Board, the Atomic Safety and Licensing Board, the Administrative Law Judge, and program offices. Price: $132.00 a year priority mail; $102.00 non-priority mail; $127.50 foreign. Stock# 752-015-00000-7.

Weekly Information Report. Prepared by the NRC's Office of the Executive Director for Operations, this report summarizes items of interest and actions taken by NRC offices. Also included are a section on items approved by the Commission; a status report of FOIA requests; a list of Requests for Proposals issued, contracts awarded and closed out; and a status report from the Three Mile Island Program Office. Price: $122 a year; $152.50 foreign. Stock# 752-005-00000-1.

Enforcement Actions: Significant Actions Resolved (NUREG-0940). Published quarterly, this publication compiles summaries of significant enforcement actions that were resolved, as well as copies of letters, notices, and orders sent by the NRC to the licensee with respect to the enforcement action. Price: $22.00 a year; $27.50 a year foreign. GPO Stock# 752-006-00000-8.

NRC Information Notices and Bulletins. Issued irregularly. Price: $106.00 a year domestic; $132.50 a year foreign. GPO Stock# 852-008-00000-8.

Nuclear Regulatory Commission Rules and Regulations. 1989. Subscription service consists of a basic manual and supplements issued irregularly for an indeterminate period. Price: $261.00 domestic; $326.25 foreign. GPO Stock# 952-003-00000-3.

Nuclear Regulatory Commission Rules and Regulations for Medical Licensees. 1989. Contains information from "Nuclear Regulatory Commission Rules and Regulations," Parts 19, 20, 30, 32, 33, and 35. Subscription service consists of a basic manual and quarterly supplements for an indeterminate period. In looseleaf form, punched for 3-ring binder. Price: $125.00 domestic; $156.25 foreign. GPO Stock# 952-004-00000-0.

NUCLEAR REGULATORY COMMISSION
KEY LEGAL AUTHORITIES

Regulations:

General Agency Regulations: 10 C.F.R. Parts 0-171 (1989)
Rules of Practice and Procedure: 10 C.F.R. Part 2 (1989)
Security Clearances: 10 C.F.R. Part 10 (1989)
Special Nuclear Materials: 10 C.F.R. Part 11 (1989)

Atomic Energy Act of 1954, as amended, 42 U.S.C. 2011 et seq.--established the Atomic Energy Commission (predecessor agency of the Nuclear Regulatory Commission) to promote and regulate nuclear energy development.
Legislative History: 1954 U.S. Code Cong. & Admin. News 3456.

Energy Reorganization Act of 1974, as amended, 42 U.S.C. 5801 et seq.--abolished the Atomic Energy Commission and transferred all licensing and regulatory functions of the AEC to the newly-created Nuclear Regulatory Commission.
Legislative History: 1974 U.S. Code Cong. & Admin. News 5470.

Nuclear Nonproliferation Act of 1978, as amended, 22 U.S.C. 3201-3282--established the framework for monitoring and controlling the export of nuclear materials, equipment, technology.
Legislative History: 1978 U.S. Code Cong. & Admin. News 326.

Nuclear Waste Policy Act of 1982, as amended, 42 U.S.C. 10101-10126--established Federal responsibility for radioactive waste and spent nuclear fuel disposal.
Legislative History: 1982 U.S. Code Cong. & Admin. News 3792; 1987 U.S. Code Cong. & Admin. News 2313.

Uranium Mill Tailings Radiation Control Act of 1978, as amended, 42 U.S.C. 7901-7942--directs the Nuclear Regulatory Commission to regulate the handling and disposal of uranium processing wastes.
Legislative History: 1978 U.S. Code Cong. & Admin. News 7433.

OCCUPATIONAL SAFETY AND HEALTH REVIEW COMMISSION

1825 K Street, N.W.
Washington, D.C. 20006-1246

DESCRIPTION: The Occupational Safety and Health Review Commission (OSHRC) is an independent quasi-judicial agency established by the Occupational Safety and Health Act of 1970. It adjudicates issues in dispute between the U.S. Department of Labor's Occupational Safety and Health Administration (OSHA) and employers (or their employees) to whom OSHA has issued citations charging a violation of the Act.

Within the Commission there are two levels of adjudication. All cases that require a hearing are assigned to a Review Commission Administrative Law Judge (ALJ) who decides the case. A substantial number of decisions of the judges become final orders of the Commission. There are currently 18 Administrative Law Judges employed by the Review Commission. The Chief Administrative Law Judge and the Deputy Chief Administrative Law judge work out of Commission headquarters in Washington, D.C. The remaining 16 ALJ's are stationed in regional offices located in Atlanta, Boston, Dallas, and Denver (four assigned to each office). For the convenience of parties in each case, judges conduct hearings as close as possible to the site of the alleged safety or health violation.

However, any of the three Commissioners may direct a review of an Administrative Law Judge's decision within 30 days of the filing. When a case is directed for such a review, it is assigned to the Office of the General Counsel. Following the submission of briefs, the case is assigned to an attorney who is responsible for it (including the preparation of legal analyses and drafting of an opinion) until the three Commissioners render a decision affirming, modifying, or vacating the Administrative Law Judge's decision. If no Commissioner directs a review during the 30-day period, the Judge's decision becomes final. All Commission decisions are subject to direct appeal to the U.S. Courts of Appeal.

In addition to handling this case review function, the Office of General Counsel also provides legal advice to the Chairman on administrative matters such as labor relations, procurement, personnel, the Sunshine Act, the Freedom of Information Act, Privacy Act, and Ethics Act. The General Counsel also represents the Commission before other administrative forums, such as the Merit Systems Protection Board, or in the courts through the U.S. Department of Justice.

(Area Code 202)
Chairman: Edwin G. Foulke, Jr 634-7970
Executive Director: Janet S. Williams 634-7940
Procurement Information 634-4006
Public Information 634-7943
Publications Information 634-7943
Docket (Executive Secretary's Office) 634-7950
Facsimile 634-4008

Freedom of Information Act Office/Privacy Act Office ..634-7943
Requests must be submitted in writing. There is a copying charge of 25 cents per page. There is also a variable per hour search fee. Submit requests to the attention of the Freedom of Information Act Officer, Fourth Floor, at the address cited at the beginning of this listing.

(Area Code 202)
Law Library (Room 400) 634-7933
The library is open to the public from 8:30 AM until 4:45 PM, Monday through Friday. There are no charge-out privileges. There is a fee for photocopying unless it concerns a Commission decision.

OFFICES OF THE COMMISSIONERS

(Area Code 202)
Chairman: Edwin G. Foulke Jr 634-7970
Legal Counsel and Special Advisor: David E. Jones ...634-7972

Commissioner: Velma Montoya 634-7946
Counsel: Scott H. Strickler 634-7977

(Area Code 202)
Commissioner: Donald G. Wiseman 634-7946
Counsel: Craig Metz 634-7946

OFFICE OF GENERAL COUNSEL (Room 402-A)

(Area Code 202)
General Counsel: Earl R. Ohman Jr 634-4015

(Area Code 202)
Deputy General Counsel: E. Patrick Moran 634-4015

OFFICE OF CHIEF ADMINISTRATIVE LAW JUDGE (Room 417)

(Area Code 202)
Chief Administrative Law Judge: Paul A. Tenney 634-7980

(Area Code 202)
Deputy Chief Administrative Law Judge: Irving Sommer....634-7980

OCCUPATIONAL SAFETY AND HEALTH REVIEW COMMISSION

REGIONAL OFFICES

There are four regional Administrative Law Judge offices. They are located in Atlanta, Boston, Dallas, and Denver.

Atlanta

Administrative Law Judges:
James D. Burroughs (First Judge), Paul L. Brady, Edwin G. Salyers, and Joe D. Sparks.
Attorney-Advisor: Jeanne Marie Faust
U.S. Occupational Safety and Health Review Commission, 1365 Peachtree St, NE, Rm 240, Atlanta, GA 30309. Tel: 404/347-4197.

Boston

Administrative Law Judges:
Richard DeBenedetto (First Judge), David G. Oringer, Delbert R. Terrill, and one vacancy.
Attorney-Advisor: Janine Hart
U.S. Occupational Safety and Health Review Commission, McCormack Post Office and Courthouse, Rm 420, Boston, MA 02109. Tel: 617/223-9746.

Dallas

Administrative Law Judges:
Stanley M. Schwartz (First Judge), Dee C. Blythe, E. Carter Botkin, and Louis G. LaVecchia.
Attorney-Advisor: Pamela G. Merrifield
U.S. Occupational Safety and Health Review Commission, Federal Building, Room 7B11, 1100 Commerce Street, Dallas, TX 75242. Tel: 214/767-5271.

Denver

Administrative Law Judges:
Sidney J. Goldstein (First Judge), James Barkley, James A. Cronin, and Benjamin R. Loye.
Attorney-Advisor: Christian E. Reid
U.S. Occupational Safety and Health Review Commission, Colonnade Building, Room 250, 1244 North Speer Boulevard, Denver, CO 80204. Tel: 303/844-2281.

PUBLICATIONS OF INTEREST

OSHRC offers a number of publications that can be obtained from the **Occupational Safety and Health Review Commission Information Office**, 1825 K Street, N.W., Washington, D.C. 20006. Tel: 202/634-7943.

The following publications are available free-of-charge:

(1) Individual copies of OSHRC decisions
(2) Simplified Proceedings
(3) Rules of Procedures
(4) A Guide to Procedures of the OSHRC

The Index to Decisions of the OSHRC details company names and OSHRC docket numbers. It is sold based on the number of pages and the years requested. Contact the Commission's Information Office for the price.

OSHRC Reports (copies of OSHRC decisions) are available by subscription on microfiche from the US Government Printing Office. Contact the Superintendent of Documents, U.S. Government Printing Office, Washington, D.C. 20401. Tel: 202/783-3238.

OCCUPATIONAL SAFETY AND HEALTH REVIEW COMMISSION
KEY LEGAL AUTHORITIES

Regulations: 29 C.F.R. Parts 2200-2400 (1989).

Occupational Safety and Health Act of 1970, as amended, 29 U.S.C. 651-678--established the Commission as an independent adjudication agency with jurisdiction over appeals from citations issued by the Department of Labor's Occupational Safety and Health Administration.

Legislative History: 1970 U.S. Code Cong. & Admin. News 5177.

OFFICE OF GOVERNMENT ETHICS

1201 New York Avenue, N.W.
Washington, D.C. 20005-3917

DESCRIPTION: The Office of Government Ethics (OGE) was established in 1978 to provide overall direction of Executive Branch policies related to preventing conflicts of interest on the part of officers and employees of any executive agency.

(Area Code 202)
Director: Donald Campbell (Acting)........................523-5757
Administration Chief: Robert E. Lammon....................523-5757
Education and Liaison Chief: Stuart C. Gilman...........523-5757
Management Information Systems Chief: James V. Parle....523-5757
Monitoring and Compliance Chief: Jack Covaleski.........523-5757
Facsimile..523-6325

(Area Code 202)
Freedom of Information Act/Privacy Act Office..........523-5757

Reading Room (Suite 500)...............................523-5757
The Reading Room is open to the public from 8:00 AM until 4:30 PM, Monday through Friday. There are no charge-out privileges. Photocopies can be made for a charge.

OFFICE OF GENERAL COUNSEL (Suite 500)

The Office of Chief Counsel assists in implementing an advisory opinion system enabling ethics counselors and employees to apply the standards of conduct and conflict of interest laws to situations arising in the Executive Branch. The attorneys provide assistance and oversight to the Designated Agency Ethics Officials to ensure compliance and uniformity in the application of the ethics responsibilities. This includes training, approval of regulations to ensure conformity to the law, and recommendations for corrective action where agencies are not in compliance with OGE directives. The attorneys also review public financial disclosure forms of the President, Vice President, presidential appointees, postal officials, and agency ethics officials.

(Area Code 202)
General Counsel: F. Gary Davis..........................523-5757
Deputy General Counsel: Jane S. Ley.....................523-5757

Attorneys: (Area Code 202)
Sid Smith...523-5757
Leslie Wilcox.......................................523-5757
Laura Powell..523-5757

PUBLICATIONS OF INTEREST

Government Ethics Newsgram is published quarterly. It is available free of charge from the Office of Government Ethics, 1201 New York Avenue, N.W., Washington, D.C. 20005. Tel: 202/523-5757.

The Informal Advisory Letters and Memoranda and Formal Opinions (1989) presents a complete collection of all OGE opinions issued between 1979 and 1988. Beginning with the Summer of 1990, yearly supplements will be issued for the previous year. OGE will notify the Superintendent of Documents at Government Printing Office (GPO) of any individual supplements and their availability. These supplements will be announced in Government Ethics, and will be available from The Superintendent of Documents, U.S. Government Printing Office, Washington, D.C. 20402. Tel: 202/783-3238. Price: $25.00. GPO Stock# 052-003-01172-7.

OFFICE OF GOVERNMENT ETHICS

KEY LEGAL AUTHORITIES

Regulations: 5 C.F.R. Part 738 (1989).

Ethics in Government Act, as amended, 5 U.S.C. App. 4, sec. 201 et seq. & 5 U.S.C. App. 5, sec. 401-408--established standards of conduct for Federal officials and created the Office of Government Ethics within the Civil Service Commission (now the Office of Personnel Management) to monitor and enforce financial disclosure and other provisions of the Act, issue guidelines to agencies on financial disclosure information collection, provide advisory opinions to agencies, and act as the information clearinghouse on government ethics.

Legislative History: 1978 U.S. Code Cong. & Admin. News 4216; 1983 U.S. Code Cong. & Admin. News 1313; 1988 U.S. Code Cong. & Admin. News 4125.

OFFICE OF PERSONNEL MANAGEMENT

1900 E Street, N.W.
Washington, D.C. 20415

DESCRIPTION: The Office of Personnel Management (OPM) was created as an independent establishment under the Civil Service Reform Act of 1978. Many of the functions of the former U.S. Civil Service Commission were transferred to OPM at that time. The Office of Personnel Management administers a merit system for Federal employment, which includes recruiting, examining, training, and promoting people on the basis of their knowledge and skills, regardless of any nonmerit factor such as race, religion, sex, or political influence.

(Area Code 202)
Director: Constance Berry Newman 606-1000
Procurement Information 606-2240
Public Information (Office of Communication) 606-1800
Inspector General's Hot Line 606-2423
Publishing Management 606-1822
Facsimile 606-2573

Freedom of Information Act/Privacy Act Office 606-1860
Requests must be made in writing. There is a copying charge of 13 cents per page; however, the fees are waived if the total is less than $25.00. If a printed document is ordered, the charge is 25 cents per 25 pages. There is also a variable per hour search fee.

Requests should be sent to the appropriate official, depending upon the nature of the information desired, at the OPM address cited at the beginning of this listing. A request must be clearly marked on the envelope as a "Freedom of Information Act Office Request."

* Information about background investigations and related records on individuals should be submitted to the attention of the "Assistant Director for Federal Investigations."

* Questions concerning nationwide examining and testing for employment; promotions; administrative law judges; affirmative employment programs for minorities, women, veterans, and the disabled, should be submitted to the attention of the "Associate Director for Career Entry."

* Questions of ethics and conflict interest matters are sent to the attention of the "Director, Office of Government Ethics."

* Requests for information not specifically mentioned above should be submitted to the Information Systems Plans and Policies Division, Room 6410.

(Area Code 202)
Library (Room 5H27) 606-1381
The library is open to the public by appointment only from 8:30 AM until 4:30 PM, Monday through Friday. Materials may not be checked out and there are no photocopying facilities.

OFFICE OF THE INSPECTOR GENERAL (Room 6H31)

The Office of the Inspector General conducts audits and investigations relating to OPM programs and operations; reviews existing and proposed legislation and regulations; prevents and detects fraud and abuse in OPM's programs and operations; and recommends policies for the promotion of economy and efficiency of programs and operations.

(Area Code 202)
Inspector General: Patrick J. Conklin 606-1200

Assistant Inspector General for Investigations: (Area Code 202)
J. David Cope 606-1200

OFFICE OF GENERAL COUNSEL (Room 7353)

The Office of the General Counsel provides general legal and advisory services to the Director, Deputy Director, operating entities within OPM, and, on a Government-wide basis, to all Federal agencies and components concerning Federal civilian personnel law and related matters. In addition to the General Counsel and Deputy General Counsel, the Office has an Associate General Counsel responsible for litigation matters and Office administration.

(Area Code 202)
General Counsel: Jaime Ramon 606-1700
Deputy General Counsel: James S. Green 606-1700
Facsimile 606-0082

The General Counsel's office has three operating divisions:

The **Administration and Civil Rights Division** has responsibility for legal issues involving staffing, executive personnel, civil rights and EEO, the Freedom of Information Act and Privacy, Reductions-in-Force, examining and recruiting.

Assistant General Counsel for Administration & Civil Rights: Rhoda G. Lawrence 606-1701

The **Compensation Division** has responsibility for pay, leave, FLSA, retirement, health and life insurance and garnishment.

(Area Code 202)
Assistant General Counsel for Compensation: Thomas F. Moyer 606-1980

The **Merit Systems Division** is responsible for adverse actions and other disciplinary matters, labor and employee relations, and tort and property claims.

Principal Assistant General Counsel for Merit Systems: Ann C. Wilson 606-1920

INVESTIGATIONS GROUP (Room 5478)

(Area Code 202)

Associate Director: Frances A. Sclafani 606-1999
Deputy Associate Director: John J. Lafferty 606-1999

(Area Code 202)

Legal Advisor: vacant 606-1999

OFFICE OF ADMINISTRATIVE LAW JUDGES (Room 2433)

The Office of Administrative Law Judges is the examining group for Administrative Law Judges throughout the Federal Government.

(Area Code 202)

Assistant Director: Craig B. Pettibone 606-0810

PUBLICATIONS OF INTEREST

Handbook of OPM Publications, Periodicals, and FPM Issuances is available from the Publishing Management Branch, Administrative Policy Division, Office of Finance and Administrative Services, Administration Group, U.S. Office of Personnel Management, 1990 E Street, N.W., Washington, D.C. 20415. Tel: 202/606-1822.

Requesting OPM Federal Investigations, I.D.# OFI-15. Available from the Investigations Group at OPM, at the following address: U.S. Office of Personnel Management, Investigations Group, 1900 E Street, N.W., Washington, D.C. 20415. Tel: 202/606-1822.

Requests for the following publications should be sent to: **National Technical Information Service**, Department A/Operations Division, 5285 Port Royal Road, Springfield, VA 22161 (703/487-4650).

Guide to Administering Examinations to Handicapped Individuals for Employment Purposes, I.D.# PR-80-16. Stock# PB81-121675.

A Guide for Assessing the Distribution of Minorities and Women in Relevant Labor Markets, I.D.# TM-79-10. Stock# PB80-152655.

Voluntary and Involuntary Separations from the Work Force, I.D.# PR-75-2. Stock# PB-258-241.

The following publications can be purchased from the **U.S. Government Printing Office**. Stock numbers and prices for annual subscriptions are shown below. Submit requests for these publications to: The Superintendent of Documents, U.S. Government Printing Office, Washington, D.C. 20402. Tel: 202/783-3238.

Digest of Significant Classification Decisions and Opinions, I.D.# AR-100. Published semi-annually. Presents decisions and opinions made by OPM which have, in their opinion, Government-wide impact. Price: $2.75 a single copy domestic; $3.44 a single copy foreign; $5.00 a year domestic; $6.25 a year foreign. GPO Stock# 706-0001-00000-0.

The Federal Labor Management and Employee Relations Consultant Newsletter (FLMERC). Published 24 times a year. Presents current information in the field of labor-management and employee relations. Price: $28.00 a year domestic; $35.00 a year foreign. No single copies will be sold. GPO Stock# 706-003-00000-2.

OFFICE OF PERSONNEL MANAGEMENT
KEY LEGAL AUTHORITIES

Regulations: 5 C.F.R. Parts 1-1001 (1989).

Civil Service Reform Act of 1978, as amended, 5 U.S.C. 1101 et seq.--replaced the Civil Service Commission with the Office of Personnel Management and separated out various functions, assigning them to other agencies.

Legislative History: 1978 U.S. Code Cong. & Admin. News 2723.

Uniform Guidelines on Employee Selection Procedures, 28 C.F.R. 50.14 (1989)--principles issued jointly by the Departments of Justice and Labor, the Equal Employment Opportunity Commission, and the Office of Personnel Management and designed to assist employers, labor organizations, employment agencies, and licensing and certification boards to comply with Federal equal employment opportunity laws.

THE OFFICE OF SPECIAL COUNSEL

1120 Vermont Avenue, N.W.
Washington, D.C. 20005

DESCRIPTION: The Office of Special Counsel (OSC) is an independent agency that investigates allegations of prohibited personnel practices and activities prohibited by civil service laws, rules, and regulations. The OSC may prosecute before the Merit Systems Protection Board the officials who are alleged to be in violation of those rules and regulations.

The relationship of the Office of Special Counsel to the Merit Systems Protection Board (MSPB) is similar to that of a prosecutor to a court. The OSC performs as the prosecutor, the MSPB as the court.

The OSC has three primary areas of statutory responsibility which are:

1) providing a secure channel through which information evidencing waste, fraud, mismanagement, abuse of authority, or substantial and specific danger to public health or safety may be disclosed without fear of retaliation and without disclosure of identify except with the employee's consent;

2) receiving and investigating allegations of activities prohibited by civil service law, rule, or regulation, and if warranted, initiating corrective or disciplinary action; and

3) enforcing the Hatch Act which prohibits Federal employees from participating in certain political activities.

(Area Code 202)

Complaints Examining Unit:
Washington, D.C. Metro Area 653-7188
Outside Washington, D.C. Metro Area ....(800) 872-9855
Whistleblower 653-9125
Facsimile 653-5151

(Area Code 202)

Freedom of Information Act Office 663-7122
Questions must be in writing. Costs vary depending upon the material requested and the requestor. Submit requests to the Freedom of Information Act Officer, Room 1100, Office of Special Counsel, address cited above.

THE SPECIAL COUNSEL (Room 1100)

(Area Code 202)

Special Counsel: Mary F. Wieseman 653-7122
Deputy Special Counsel: Erin McDonnell....................653-8971
Associate Special Counsel for Investigation Division:
Robert D. L'Heureux 653-7193

(Area Code 202)

Associate Special Counsel for Prosecution Division:
William E. Reukauf 653-8970
Deputy Associate Special Counsel for Prosecution:
Leonard M. Dribinsky 653-8968
Complaints Examining Unit Chief: Ralph Eddy 653-8944

FIELD OFFICES

The OSC has two small field offices, one in Dallas and one in San Francisco. They are both investigation outposts.

Dallas Field Office
Supervisory Investigator: Harley McIlroy
General Attorney: Anthony Cardillo
Office of Special Counsel, 1100 Commerce Street, Room 7C30, Dallas, TX 75242. Tel: 214/767-8871.

San Francisco Field Office
Supervisory Investigator/Attorney: Jacqueline Martinez
Senior Trial Attorney: Bruce Fong
General Attorney: Joseph Siegelman
Office of Special Counsel, 50 United Nations Plaza, Rm 121, San Francisco, CA 94102. Tel: 415/556-9450.

OFFICE OF SPECIAL COUNSEL
KEY LEGAL AUTHORITIES

Regulations: 5 U.S.C. Parts 1250-1262 (1990).

Civil Service Reform Act of 1978, as amended, 5 U.S.C. 1101, 1204-1209--established the Office of Special Counsel [in the Merit Systems Protection Board] to investigate prohibited personnel practices, recommend corrective actions, or request such actions of the Merit Systems Protection Board.

Legislative History: 1978 U.S. Code Cong. & Admin. News 2723.

PANAMA CANAL COMMISSION

APO Miami 34011-5000

DESCRIPTION: The Panama Canal Commission manages, operates and maintains the Panama Canal, its complimentary works, installations and equipment, and provides for the orderly transit of vessels through the Canal. The Commission is a unique agency supervised by both the U.S. and the Republic of Panama. In the year 2000, responsibility for Canal operations will be turned over to Panama.

Secretary: Michael Rhode Jr ....(202) 634-6441
Facsimile ....(202) 634-6439
Office of Public Affairs (Panama) 011-507-523165
Procurement (Panama) 011-507-524687

OFFICE OF INSPECTOR GENERAL

Inspector General: James A. Mathis (Panama)...011 507-523142

OFFICE OF GENERAL COUNSEL

The Office of General Counsel, located in Balboa, Panama, has a staff of 10 U.S. and Panamanian attorneys. Attorneys provide legal advice to the Commission, represent the agency in administrative proceedings to which it is a party, and defend the agency in vessel-accident suits filed in the U.S. District Court for the Eastern District of Louisiana. Attorneys also assist the U.S. Justice Department in handling non-admiralty cases in which the Commission is involved.

General Counsel: John L. Haines Jr (Panama)........011-507-527511
Deputy General Counsel:
Pat Lindley-Dominguez (Panama) 011-507-527511

PANAMA CANAL COMMISSION
KEY LEGAL AUTHORITIES

Regulations: 35 C.F.R. Parts 3-257 (1989).

Panama Canal Act of 1979, 22 U.S.C. 3601 et seq.--implemented the Panama Canal Treaty of 1977, which replaced the Canal Zone Government and Panama Canal Company with the Panama Canal Commission as the entity maintaining and operating the Panama Canal and related facilities.

Legislative History: 1979 U.S. Code Cong. & Admin. News 1034.

Exec. Order 12215, as amended, 3 C.F.R., 1980 Comp. p. 257--delegates certain administrative functions vested in the President to the Panama Canal Commission.

PEACE CORPS

806 Connecticut Avenue, N.W.
Washington, D.C. 20526

DESCRIPTION: Established in 1961, the purpose of the Peace Corps is to promote world peace and friendship, to promote a better understanding of the American people, and to support projects aimed at meeting the basic needs of those living in the poorest areas of the countries in which the Peace Corps operates. Today, more than 5,000 volunteers serve throughout Latin America, Africa, the Near East, Asia, and the Pacific.

(Area Code 202)
Director: Paul D. Coverdell 606-3970
Media Relations 606-3010
Facsimile 606-3110

Freedom of Information Act/Privacy Act Office 606-3420
Requests must be made in writing. There are variable copying charges and per hour search fees.

(Area Code 202)
Library (Room 5353) 606-3307
The library is open to the public Monday through Friday from 8:30 AM until 5:00 PM. Materials cannot be checked out, but copying machines are available.

OFFICE OF INSPECTOR GENERAL (Room 5108)

The Office of Inspector General conducts, supervises, and coordinates audits and investigations relating to Peace Corps programs. The Office coordinates and recommends policies for activities designed to promote economy, efficiency, and effectiveness, as well as to prevent and detect fraud and abuse in agency programs.

(Area Code 202)
Inspector General: Gerard A. Roy 606-3320

OFFICE OF GENERAL COUNSEL (Room 8300)

The Office of General Counsel provides legal advice and assistance concerning Peace Corps programs and activities. Duties include reviewing policy information and regulations affecting the Peace Corps; acting as liaison with other Federal agencies; drafting legislation and assisting in its presentation to OMB and Congress; assisting in the preparation of interagency agreements; preparing and negotiating all Peace Corps country agreements; and reviewing administrative determinations involving such matters as claims by or against the Peace Corps, conflicts of interest, the Freedom of Information Act/ Privacy Act, and the observance of Peace Corps' policies against involvement in intelligence operations.

(Area Code 202)
General Counsel: John K. Scales 606-3114
Associate General Counsels:
Robert L. Martin 606-3114

(Area Code 202)
C. Kirby Mullen 606-3114
Ronald C. Owens 606-3114
Assistant General Counsel: Daniel J. Bosco 606-3114

PEACE CORPS

KEY LEGAL AUTHORITIES

Regulations: 22 C.F.R. Parts 301-310 (1989).

Peace Corps Act, as amended, 22 U.S.C. 2501-2523--established the Peace Corps to promote world peace and friendship by making available U.S. volunteers to interested countries.

Legislative History: 1961 U.S. Code Cong. & Admin. News 2842; 1981 U.S. Code Cong. & Admin. News 2404.

PENSION BENEFIT GUARANTY CORPORATION

2020 K Street, N.W.
Washington, D.C. 20006

DESCRIPTION: The Pension Benefit Guaranty Corporation (PBGC) is a Government corporation that guarantees benefit payments to participants in certain private pension plans under Title IV of the Employee Retirement Income Security Act of 1974 (ERISA). ERISA is administered by the Department of Labor, the Internal Revenue Service, and PBGC. The law grants new rights and protection to the millions of American workers who depend on pension plans of private industry for retirement income. One of the protections afforded them is the plan termination insurance program established under Title IV of ERISA and administered by PBGC.

(Area Code 202)
Chairman: Elizabeth Hanford Dole 523-8271
Executive Director: James B. Lockhart III 778-8810
Procurement Information 778-8806
Public Information 778-8800
Public Affairs/Publications 778-8840
Case Operations & Assistance Division 778-8829
Facsimile 778-8819

(Area Code 202)
Freedom of Information Act Office/Privacy Act Office....778-8839
Request must be submitted in writing. There is a copying charge of 15 cents per page. There is also a variable per hour search fee.

OFFICE OF INSPECTOR GENERAL (Room 3300)

The Office of Inspector General (OIG) is responsible for establishing policy for and directing the development and operation of an independent audit and investigative program for PBGC; and for enhancing employee and program integrity by prevention and detection of criminal activity, unethical conduct, and program fraud and abuse.

(Area Code 202)
Inspector General: Wayne R. Poll 778-8855

OFFICE OF GENERAL COUNSEL (Room 7200)

The Legal Department provides a full range of legal services for the Corporation. Since PBGC is not represented by the Justice Department, the General Counsel conducts a substantial amount of Federal litigation and all staff attorneys have an opportunity to share in it.

The activity of the Legal Department focuses on the new and rapidly developing area of pension law. In addition to tax and labor, pension law now encompasses, among others, elements of corporate, trust, insurance, and bankruptcy law.

(Area Code 202)
General Counsel: Carol Connor Flowe 778-8820
Associate General Counsel: William G. Beyer 778-8820

Deputy General Counsels: (Area Code 202)
John Falsy 778-8820
Jeanne K. Beck 778-8820

PARTICIPANT AND EMPLOYER APPEALS DEPARTMENT (Room 2500)

(Area Code 202)
Director & Appeals Board Chairman: Charles E. Skopic ..778-8841

PUBLICATIONS OF INTEREST

The following publications can be obtained free of charge by contacting the **Pension Benefit Guaranty Corporation**, Office of Public Affairs, 2020 K Street, N.W., Washington, D.C. 20006. Tel: 202/778-8840.

Employer's Pension Guide is a cooperative project of the Pension and Welfare Benefits Administration of the U.S. Department of Labor, the Internal Revenue Service, and the Pension Benefit Guaranty Corporation to provide a general overview of the responsibilities under Federal law of employers who sponsor single-employer defined benefit pension plans. It describes Federal pension law effective as of 1989.

PENSION BENEFIT GUARANTY CORPORATION

Your Guaranteed Pension answers some of the most frequently asked questions about the Pension Benefit Guaranty Corporation and its termination insurance program for single-employer defined benefit pension plants. The answers apply to pension plan terminations taking place in 1990.

Your Pension serves as a handy explanation of pension plans: what they are, how they operate, and the rights an options of participants. It should not be relied upon for information about a specific pension plan.

PENSION BENEFIT GUARANTY CORPORATION
KEY LEGAL AUTHORITIES

General Agency Regulations: 29 C.F.R. Parts 2601-2677 (1989).
Rules of Practice and Procedure: 29 C.F.R. Part 2606 (1989).

Employee Retirement Income Security Act of 1974, as amended, 29 U.S.C. 1001 et seq.--designed to preserve and protect multiemployer pension plans and other employee benefit plans and established the Pension Benefit Guaranty Corporation.
Legislative History: 1974 U.S. Code Cong. & Admin. News 4639.

PENNSYLVANIA AVENUE DEVELOPMENT CORPORATION

1331 Pennsylvania Avenue, N.W., Suite 1220-North
Washington, D.C. 20004-1703

DESCRIPTION: The Pennsylvania Avenue Development Corporation (PADC) is a wholly owned Government corporation responsible for the redevelopment of Pennsylvania Avenue between the White House and the Capitol.

(Area Code 202)

Chairman: Richard A. Hauser 861-1541
Executive Director: M.J. Brodie 724-9073
Public Information 724-9091
Procurement Information 724-9091
FOIA/Privacy Act 724-9088
Facsimile 724-0246

OFFICE OF GENERAL COUNSEL

The Office of General Counsel conducts research and provides legal advice to the Board of Directors and staff. The legal staff drafts policy statements and rules and regulations; monitors the Corporation's adherence to relevant Federal and local laws and regulations; prepares all legal documents (such as contracts, leases, and agreements to purchase and convey real estate); participates in the negotiation of all development agreements; and represents the Corporation in litigation of administrative matters, such as contract disputes, and assists the U.S. Attorney in litigation of other matters.

(Area Code 202)

Assistant Director and General Counsel:
Robert E. McCally 724-9088
Deputy General Counsel: Madeleine B. Schaller 724-9088
Staff Attorneys:
Janet Bruner 724-9088
Talbot Nicholas 724-9088

PENNSYLVANIA AVENUE DEVELOPMENT CORPORATION
KEY LEGAL AUTHORITIES

Regulations: 36 C.F.R. Parts 901-910 (1989).

Pennsylvania Avenue Development Corporation Act of 1972, as amended, 40 U.S.C. 871 et seq.--established the Pennsylvania Avenue Development Corporation to manage the orderly development, maintenance, and use of Pennsylvania Avenue between the Capitol and White House in a manner suitable to its ceremonial, physical, and historic relationship to the legislative and executive branches of the Federal Government and to governmental buildings, monuments, memorials, and parks in or adjacent to the area.

Legislative History: 1972 U.S. Code Cong. & Admin. News 4721.

POSTAL RATE COMMISSION

1333 H Street, N.W., Suite 300
Washington, D.C. 20268

DESCRIPTION: The Postal Rate Commission is an independent regulatory agency responsible for holding hearings and making recommendations on questions involving postal rates and mail classification. It also conducts proceedings to investigate changes in the nature of mail services proposed by the U.S. Postal Service and hears complaints from mail users regarding postal rates and services.

(Area Code 202)

Chairman: George W. Haley 789-6868
Chief Administrative Officer: Charles L. Clapp 789-6840
General Information 789-6800
Publications Information 789-6840
Docket 789-6845
Facsimile 789-6861

(Area Code 202)

Freedom of Information Act/Privacy Act Office 789-6840
All requests must be in writing. There are variable search charges. Copying charges are 15 cents per page.

Library (Room 300) 789-6877
The library is open to the public from 8:30 AM until 4:30 PM, Monday through Friday. There are no check-out privileges. Copying machines are available at a cost of 15 cents per page. The law library is contained within this library.

OFFICES OF THE COMMISSIONERS

(Area Code 202)

Chairman: George W. Haley 789-6868
Vice Chairman: Henry R. Folsom 789-6801

(Area Code 202)

Commissioner: John W. Crutcher 789-6805
Commissioner: W.H. Trey LeBlanc III 789-6813
Commissioner: Patti B. Tyson 789-6810

OFFICE OF GENERAL COUNSEL

The Office of the General Counsel represents the Commission in any court proceedings that might arise; advises the Commission on pending legislative proposals and rulemaking; assists in the preparation of Congressional testimony; and advises on matters involving appeals of post office closings and consolidations.

(Area Code 202)

General Counsel: David F. Stover 789-6820

(Area Code 202)

Assistant General Counsel: Stephen L. Sharfman 789-6820

OFFICE OF THE CONSUMER ADVOCATE

The Office of the Consumer Advocate represents the interests of the general public in proceedings before the Commission. These appearances involve primarily the preparation of testimony, cross-examination of expert witnesses, brief writing, and oral argument.

(Area Code 202)

Director: Stephen A. Gold 789-6830
Attorneys:
Emmett R. Costich 789-6830

(Area Code 202)

Shelley S. Dreifuss 789-6830
Mark T. Stephens 789-6830

POSTAL RATE COMMISSION

KEY LEGAL AUTHORITIES

General Agency Regulations: 39 C.F.R. Parts 3000-3003 (1989).
Rules of Practice and Procedure: 39 C.F.R. Part 3001 (1989).

Postal Reorganization Act of 1970, as amended, 39 U.S.C. 3601-3604--created the Postal Rate Commission to hold public hearings on postal rates, fees for postal services, and mail classification and to make recommendations with respect to these matters to the U.S. Postal Service.

Legislative History: 1970 U.S. Code Cong. & Admin. News 3649.

UNITED STATES POSTAL SERVICE

475 L'Enfant Plaza, S.W.
Washington, D.C. 20260

DESCRIPTION: While no longer part of the Executive Branch, the Postal Service is a unique hybrid of Federal agency and public business corporation. Its basic mission is to move over 119 billion pieces of mail each year and to provide to the American public a wide range of postal services.

(Area Code 202)

Postmaster General: Anthony M. Frank 268-2500
General Information 268-2020
Procurement Information 268-4141
Media Relations 268-2155
Communications 268-2148
Consumer Advocate 268-2284
Docket 268-2134
Fraud Hot Line: Washington, D.C. Metro Area 484-5480
Outside Washington, D.C. Metro Area .... (800) 654-8896
Facsimile 268-2175

Freedom of Information Act/Privacy Act Office 268-2924

The fee for duplicating any record or publication is 15 cents per page. Research rates are $4.40 per quarter hour if performed by clerical personnel and $5.35 per quarter hour if performed by professionals. Information stored within micrographic systems can be obtained at the same fees except that for the general public the first two hours of search time are free and the first 100 pages of duplications are free.

Library (Room 11800) .... (202) 268-2904
The library is open to the public Monday through Friday from 9:00 AM until 4:00 PM. Materials cannot be checked out, but copying machines are available. The law library is within this library.

OFFICE OF GENERAL COUNSEL - LAW DEPARTMENT (Room 6006)

The Law Department serves as both counselor to and advocate for the Postal Service. It is divided into four major offices, each of which contains several divisions, described below. In addition, the Postal Service has five Regional Counsels' offices which provide legal services to each of the Service's regional organizations. They are headquartered in Windsor, Connecticut (Northeastern Region), Philadelphia (Eastern Region), Chicago (Central Region), Memphis (Southern Region) and San Bruno, California (Western Region). Labor law field offices with small staffs located in each regional headquarters city constitute the Labor Law Division (Field).

(Area Code 202)

General Counsel: Harold J. Hughes 268-2950
Deputy General Counsel: J. Fred Eggleston 268-2952
Facsimile 268-4997

The **Office of Deputy General Counsel** consists of the following two divisions:

General Administrative Law Division attorneys decide administrative appeals under the Freedom of Information and Privacy Acts, and participate, together with attorneys from the Justice Department, in Federal court litigation brought under these two acts, as well as other openness-in-government statutes, such as the Government in the Sunshine Act. The division also implements and renders advice concerning the conflict of interest laws and regulations and is involved in other ethical conduct matters, such as the review of financial disclosure statements filed by postal officials and the advising of postal employees about the restrictions on political activity imposed by the Hatch Act. The division also renders advisory opinions to the public on the Private Express statutes, which restrict the private carriage and delivery of letters.

(Area Code 202)

Assistant General Counsel for General Administrative Law: Charles D. Hawley 268-2971

Legislative Division attorneys prepare and coordinate the Service's legislative program, prepare the official views of the Service on proposed bills in which the Service has an interest, serve as liaison to the Office of Management and Budget for Postal Service participation in the internal Executive Branch reviews of legislation and the preparation of Executive Orders, prepare testimony given by the Postmaster General and other senior postal officials before congressional committees, and, upon request, draft bills and amendments for members of Congress and their staffs. The division also prepares postal regulations, reviews handbooks and manuals, and serves as legal advisor to the Service on regulatory matters.

(Area Code 202)

Assistant General Counsel for Legislation: Stanley F. Mires 268-2958

Office of Labor Law

The Office of Labor Law advises the Postal Service on legal matters involving relations between the Service and its 800,000 employees, most of whom are members of unions. Its attorneys represent the Service in labor and personnel disputes arising in several different forums, including the National Labor Relations Board (representation and unfair labor practice cases), arbitrations arising out of grievances filed under the collective bargaining agreement between the Service and its unions, the Merit Systems Protection Board or in-house hearing officers in disciplinary matters, and the Equal Employment Opportunity Commission. The office is also actively involved in Federal court litigation throughout the country. Attorneys are involved in the full range of employee and labor relations law, including workers' compensation, unfair labor practices, labor contract interpretation, the Fair Labor Standards Act, occupational safety and health, EEO, contract negotiation and administration, and formulation of Postal Service employment regulations.

(Area Code 202)

Associate General Counsel: Stephen E. Alpern 268-3026
Assistant General Counsel for Division A:
Richard Froelke 268-3029
Assistant General Counsel for Division B:
Andrew German 268-3034
Assistant General Counsel for Division C:
Edward F. Ward 268-3051
Assistant General Counsel for Appellate Division:
Jesse L. Butler 268-3058

Office of Contracts and Property Law

The Office of Contracts and Property Law is responsible for a variety of legal questions arising from the acquisition of real property, the construction and operation of postal facilities and the acquisition of supplies, equipment and services. Attorneys in all divisions of the Office of Contracts and Property Law handle contract disputes in formal trial proceedings before the Postal Service Board of Contract Appeals. Assistance is also given to the Department of Justice in litigation in the various Federal courts, including the U.S. Claims Court and the Court of Appeals in the Federal Circuit.

***Construction and Real Property Division** attorneys are involved in every stage of the acquisition of facilities from the purchase or lease of building sites through construction and any litigation which may follow, including the review of purchase or lease agreements and assistance in the negotiation of such contracts. They also advise contracting officers in connection with decisions on claims and disputes arising from the performance of contracts and are involved in legal problems related to property management.

***Procurement Division** attorneys provide counsel in connection with the Service's acquisition of supplies, equipment and services. They develop and review initial solicitations, participate in the resolution of bid protests, advise and help resolve claims and disputes under contracts, represent the Postal Service in the administrative trial of appeals from the contracting officer's decisions, and assist the Justice Department with any ensuing litigation. The division also provides counsel on intellectual property law matters, prosecutes patent and trademark applications in the United States Patent and Trademark Office, secures copyrights, and takes action to protect and enforce these rights.

*The **Transportation Division** advises postal management on all matters relating to the transportation of mail and represents the Service before the Department of Transportation, the Interstate Commerce Commission, and the Federal Maritime Commission in ratemaking cases.

(Area Code 202)

Associate General Counsel: William J. Jones 268-3002
Patent Counsel: Theodore Major 268-3018
Assistant General Counsel for Construction and
Real Property: Norman D. Menegat 268-3006
Assistant General Counsel for Procurement:
Donald D. Anna 268-3012
Assistant General Counsel for Transportation:
Michael J. Vandamm 268-3021

Office of Postal Rates and Mailing Rules

The Office of Postal Rates and Mailing Rules has overall responsibility for litigation involving changes in postal rates and fees, in the creation or alteration of postal services, in the enforcement of existing rates and service provisions, and a variety of matters relating to the provision of postal services, including the closing of post offices.

***Consumer Protection Division** attorneys litigate administrative actions to enforce the postal false representation and lottery statute and a variety of laws declaring particular categories of matter non-mailable.

***Rates Division** attorneys represent the Postal Service in proceedings before the Postal Rate Commission and litigate omnibus rate cases involving changes in practically all postal rates and fees.

***Classification Division** attorneys also appear before the Postal Rate Commission, and handle cases involving new or changed service offerings, in particular those offerings incorporating new technologies.

***Rate Application Division** attorneys represent the Service in matters arising out of the application of rates and classifications. They also advise Postal Service officials on decisions to grant or deny mailing privileges and defend those decisions before administrative law judges and in Federal court.

(Area Code 202)

Associate General Counsel: John L. DeWeerdt 268-2979
Assistant General Counsel for Classification:
Grayson M. Poats 268-2981
Assistant General Counsel for Consumer Protection:
George C. Davis 268-3076
Assistant General Counsel for Rate Application:
(vacant) 268-2985
Assistant General Counsel for Rates:
Daniel J. Foucheaux 268-2989

Office of Field Legal Services

The Office of Field Legal Services includes the Claims Division, which is located at national headquarters, and the field divisions which consist of attorneys who either specialize in labor or have a more general practice.

***The five field labor counsel offices** serve as the de facto trial branch for labor and employment cases arising in the field. Each office is responsible for providing advice and representation to postal management in labor and employment matters. Attorneys in these offices represent postal management in Federal District Court litigation, EEOC administrative hearings, NLRB charges and trials, and arbitrations involving various labor and employment issues.

Attorneys in the office of field counsel having a more general practice work in a wide variety of areas of law affecting postal management but concentrate primarily in the field of Government contract law. In that capacity, they offer advisory services to clients in the facilities, procurement, and transportation areas, and represent those clients before the Postal Service Board of Contract Appeals. They also provide advice on issues such as ethical conduct, mail disputes, environmental law, information access, and other topics, in addition to having responsibility for all real estate closings on property purchased by the Postal Service.

***Claims Division** attorneys adjudicate personal injury and property damage claims filed under the Federal Tort Claims Act against the Postal Service by postal patrons and other non-employees. Although they do not generally represent the Service in court, they are involved in all stages of the litigation, including representing the Service in negotiations and settlement. The division also reviews claims and litigation arising out of money order operations, losses or damage to registered, insured, and C.O.D. mail, and other miscellaneous claims asserted by or against the Postal Service. Division attorneys also coordinate the retention of legal counsel for postal employees prosecuted or sued in their individual capacities for actions taken as employees and officials of the Service.

(Area Code 202)

Associate General Counsel: William P. Bennett 268-2966
Assistant General Counsel for Claims:
Clinton I. Newman 268-3063

REGIONAL OFFICES

Northeast Region (Windsor)

Chief Field Counsel: James H. French
Northeast Region - United States Postal Service, 6 Griffin Road North, Room 7209, Windsor, CT 06006-0120. Tel: 203/285-7127. FAX: 203/285-7088.

Field Counsel: James D. Burroughs
Northeast Region - United States Postal Service, 6 Griffin Road North, Room 7128, Windsor, CT 06006-0170. Tel: 203/285-7128. FAX: 203/285-7088.

Eastern Region (Philadelphia)

Chief Field Counsel: John T. Farrell
Eastern Region - United States Postal Service, P.O. Box 8601, Philadelphia, PA 19197-0170. Tel: 215/496-6011. FAX: 215/496-6134.

Field Counsel: Charles F. Kappler
Eastern Region - United States Postal Service, P.O. Box 8601, Philadelphia, PA 19197-0120. Tel: 215/496-6346. FAX: 215/496-6134.

Southern Region (Memphis)

Chief Field Counsel: Thomas H. Pigford
Southern Region - United States Postal Service, 1407 Union Avenue, Memphis, TN 38166-0170. Tel: 901/722-7491.

Field Counsel: John G. Hollingsworth, Jr.
Southern Region - United States Postal Service, 1407 Union Avenue, Memphis, TN 38166-0120. Tel: 901/722-7355. FAX: 901/722-7491.

Central Region (Chicago)

Chief Field Counsel: Gregg R. Sackrider
Central Region - United States Postal Service, 300 South Riverside Plaza, Suite 1480 South, Chicago, IL 60606-6617. Tel: 312/765-5264. FAX: 312/765-5259.

Field Counsel: Gladys N. Bryer
Central Region - United States Postal Service, 300 South Riverside Plaza, Suite 1480 South, Chicago, IL 60606-6617. Tel: 312/765-5230. FAX: 312/765-5259.

Western Region (San Bruno)

Chief Field Counsel: M. Perry Johnson
Western Region - United States Postal Service, 850 Cherry Avenue, San Bruno, CA 94099-0170. Tel: 415/742-4810. FAX: 415/742-4103.

Field Counsel: William A. Campbell, Jr.
Western Region - United States Postal Service, 850 Cherry Avenue, San Bruno, CA 94099-0120. Tel: 415/742-4824. FAX: 415/742-4103.

JUDICIAL OFFICER DEPARTMENT (ROOM 10902)

The Judicial Officer Department consists of five Administrative Judges and two Administrative Law Judges. The Judges are primarily responsible for adjudicating disputes between the Postal Service and private parties.

The Administrative Judges are selected in accordance with requirements of the Contract Disputes Act of 1978. The majority of their cases involve the adjudication of disputes between contractors and the U.S. Postal Service.

The Administrative Law Judges meet the requirements of the Administrative Procedure Act. Postal Service Administrative Law Judges adjudicate a variety of postal matters, including false advertising through the mail, second-class mailing privileges, and post office box closings.

Copies of individual decisions of the Administrative Law Judges or the Board of Contract Appeals can be obtained from the Recorder. The charge is 15 cents per page. However, if the total charge is less than $3.00 the material is usually sent free of charge. Decisions of the Administrative Law Judges are available for reference in the USPS Law Library.

Board of Contract Appeals Reporter is a bi-weekly publication which reports the decisions of the following Boards of Contract Appeals: Agriculture, Armed Services, Corps of Engineers, Department of Transportation, Energy, General Services Administration, Department of Housing and Urban Development, Interior, Labor, National Aeronautics and Space Administration, U.S. Postal Service, and Department of Veterans Affairs. Annual Price $760.00. Contact: Commerce Clearing House, Inc., 4025 West Peterson Avenue, Chicago, IL 60646. Tel: 312/583-8500. Or in Washington, D.C., call 202/626-2200.

(Area Code 202)

Judicial Officer: James A. Cohen 268-2136
Recorder: Olytha E. Martin 268-2134

Office of Administrative Law Judges
Chief Administrative Law Judge: Quentin E. Grant 268-2136
Administrative Law Judges:
Randolph D. Mason 268-2137
vacant 268-2139

(Area Code 202)

Board of Contract Appeals
Chairman: James A. Cohen 268-2128
Vice Chairman: James D. Finn, Jr. 268-2133
Administrative Judges:
David I. Brochstein 268-3385
James E. Lemert 268-2132
Joan B. Thompson 268-2130

INSPECTION SERVICE (Room 3100)

(Area Code 202)

Chief Postal Inspector: Charles R. Clauson 268-4267

(Area Code 202)

Legal Liaison Branch Manager: Henry J. Bauman 268-4415

UNITED STATES POSTAL SERVICE

EMPLOYEE RELATIONS DEPARTMENT (Room 9431)

(Area Code 202)

Office of Equal Employment Opportunity
Executive Director: Sherry Cagnoli 268-3986

(Area Code 202)

Employee Appeals Division General Manager:
Peter L. Garwood 268-3994

PUBLICATIONS OF INTEREST

The following publications can be purchased from the **U.S. Government Printing Office.** Stock numbers and prices for annual subscriptions are shown below. Submit requests for these publications to: The Superintendent of Documents, U.S. Government Printing Office, Washington, D.C. 20402. (202/783-3238).

Employee and Labor Relations Manual. Published semiannually. Sets forth the personnel policies and regulations governing employment with the U.S. Postal Service. Topics covered include organization management, employment and placement, pay administration, employee benefits, employee relations, safety and health, and labor relations. Price: $18.00 a year domestic; $22.50 a year foreign. GPO Stock# 739-005-00000-1.

U.S. Postal Service Procurement Manual. 1987. This manual establishes uniform policies and procedures relating to procuring facilities, equipment, supplies, and services under the authority of Chapter 4, Title 39, USC, and mail transportation services by contract under Part 5, Title 39, USC. Subscription service consists of a basic manual and supplementary material for an indeterminate period. In looseleaf form, punched for 3-ring binder. Price: $103.00 domestic; $128.75 foreign. GPO Stock# 939-006-00000-1.

UNITED STATES POSTAL SERVICE
KEY LEGAL AUTHORITIES

Regulations: 39 C.F.R. Parts 1-965 (1989).

Postal Reorganization Act of 1970, as amended, 39 U.S.C. 101 et seq.--established the U.S. Postal Service as an independent establishment of the Executive branch.

Legislative History: 1970 U.S. Code Cong. & Admin. News 3649.

RAILROAD RETIREMENT BOARD

844 Rush Street
Chicago, IL 60611

DESCRIPTION: The Railroad Retirement Board administers the Railroad Retirement Act, the Railroad Unemployment Insurance Act, and certain other Federal statutes providing benefits for railroad employees. This relatively small Federal agency has its headquarters offices in Chicago, IL. All of the agency's attorneys, except the Legislative Counsel, are located in Chicago. The Legislative Counsel is located in Washington, D.C.

(Area Code 312)

Chairman: Glen L. Bower 751-4900
Chief Executive Officer: Kenneth P. Boehne 751-4590
Freedom of Information Act/Privacy Act Office 751-4692
Hearings and Appeals Bureau 751-4793
Public Affairs 751-4777
Facsimile..751-4923

Offices of the Board

(Area Code 312)

Chairman: Glen L. Bower 751-4900
Labor Member: Charles J. Chamberlain 751-4905
Management Member: John D. Crawford 751-4910

OFFICE OF INSPECTOR GENERAL

The Office of Inspector General is responsible for conducting audits and investigations relating to programs and operations of the Board. The Office recommends policies for the promotion of economy and efficiency in programs and operations and for the prevention and detection of fraud and abuse in the Board's programs and operations.

(Area Code 312)

Inspector General: William J. Doyle III 751-4690

OFFICE OF THE GENERAL COUNSEL (Room 530)

(Area Code 312)

General Counsel: Dale G. Zimmerman 751-4970
Deputy General Counsel: Steven A. Bartholow 751-4935
Law Library 751-4926

Washington, D.C. Liaison Office
Legislative Counsel: David O. Lucci ....(202) 653-9540
Facsimile ....(202) 653-9538

RAILROAD RETIREMENT BOARD
KEY LEGAL AUTHORITIES

Regulations: 20 C.F.R. Parts 200-399 (1989).

Railroad Retirement Act of 1974, as amended, 45 U.S.C. 231-231v--restructured the Railroad Retirement Act of 1937 to set up a two-tier retirement benefit system for railroad employees consisting of Social Security and Railroad Retirement Act benefits.
Legislative History: 1974 U.S. Code Cong. & Admin. News 5702.

Railroad Unemployment Insurance Act, as amended, 45 U.S.C. 351-368--established an unemployment insurance system for railroad workers.
Legislative History: 1946 U.S. Code Cong. & Admin. News 1316.

Regional Rail Reorganization Act of 1973, as amended, 45 U.S.C. 701 et seq.--reorganized rail service in the Northeast and Midwest and directed the Railroad Retirement Board to establish and maintain a central register of railroad employment.
Legislative History: 1973 U.S. Code Cong. & Admin. News 3242; 1981 U.S. Code Cong. & Admin. News 396.

SECURITIES AND EXCHANGE COMMISSION

450 Fifth Street, N.W.
Washington, D.C. 20549

DESCRIPTION: Under the Securities Exchange Act of 1934, Congress created the Securities and Exchange Commission (SEC). The SEC is an independent, nonpartisan, quasi-judicial regulatory agency. The principal responsibilities of the SEC are the administration and enforcement of Federal securities laws. The Commission regulates the nation's securities markets, stock brokers, investment companies and investment advisers, and prescribes certain requirements, disclosure and otherwise, for companies that issue stock or other securities.

SEC staff, rather than the Department of Justice, conducts all its own civil litigation except for U.S. Supreme Court cases, which are handled in conjunction with the Solicitor General. As an independent regulatory agency, the Commission deals directly with Congress on legislative matters impacting agency programs.

(Area Code 202)
Chairman: Richard C. Breeden 272-2000
Procurement Information 272-7010
Public Reference Branch 272-7450
Publications Information 272-7040
Public Affairs 272-2650
Consumer and Investor Complaints 272-7440
Facsimile 272-7050

Freedom of Information Act/Privacy Act Office 272-7420
Requests must be submitted in writing. Copying (up to 100 pages) and search and review charges are free for news media, scientific, and educational institutions. Investors, broker-dealers, lawyers are charged for search and review time. Searches cost either $16.00 an hour or $28.00 an hour depending on the salary level of the employee handling the request. Copying fee is set by an outside contractor.

(Area Code 202)
Library (Room 1C00) 272-2618
The Library is located in the basement (first level) and is open to the public Monday through Friday from 9:00 AM until 5:30 PM. Material may not be checked out but photocopying is available. The law library is contained within this library.

OFFICES OF THE COMMISSIONERS (Room 6010)

(Area Code 202)
Chairman: Richard C. Breeden 272-2000
Special Counsel:
Barbara Green 272-2014
David Underhill 272-2014
John Kincaid 272-2014
Legislative Counsel: Peter S. Kiernan 272-2500

Commissioner: Edward H. Fleischman 272-2200
Counsel: Ronald Mueller 272-3077
Counsel: Jonathan E. Gottlieb 272-2092

Commissioner: vacant 272-2400
Counsel: vacant 272-2468
Counsel: vacant 272-3085

(Area Code 202)
Commissioner: Mary L. Schapiro 272-2100
Counsel: Daniel O. Hirsch 272-2149
Counsel: Holly H. Smith 272-2091

Commissioner: Phillip R. Locher, Jr 272-2300
Counsel: Daniel Gray 272-3195
Counsel: Steven Young 272-2467

Office of the Executive Director
Counsel: Elizabeth Stein 272-2700

OFFICE OF GENERAL COUNSEL (Room 6063)

The **Office of the General Counsel** is responsible for work encompassing litigation, legislation, and counseling on a broad range of matters arising under Federal securities laws and other Federal laws affecting the operations of administrative agencies.

(Area Code 202)
General Counsel: James R. Doty 272-3171
Assistant General Counsel (Branch 6-Administration and Contracting): Carol K. Scott 272-2474
Solicitor: Paul Gonson 272-2471
Ethics Counsel: Lynn Blatch 272-2437
Facsimile 272-2479

The Office of General Counsel is divided into four operating groups.

The **Appellate Litigation Group** represents the Commission in litigation to which it is a party in Federal Courts of Appeals, and (in conjunction with the Solicitor General) in the U.S. Supreme Court. Attorneys in this group also represent the Commission in proceedings under Chapter 11 of the Federal Bankruptcy Code in cases involving companies with a significant number of public security holders and raising issues of general significance.

(Area Code 202)
Associate General Counsel: Jacob Stillman 272-4802
Assistant General Counsel (Branch 1-Bankruptcy & Appellate Litigation): Katharine Gresham 272-2493
Counsel to Assistant General Counsel: Catherine Broderick 272-2461
Bankruptcy Counsel: Michael A. Berman 272-2493
Special Counsel: Leslie Smith 272-2493
Assistant General Counsel (Branch 2-Appellate Litigation): Eric Summergrad 272-3088
Senior Special Counsel: Brian Bellardo 272-2493
Assistant General Counsel (Branch 3-Appellate Litigation): Lucinda McConathy 272-3088
Special Counsel: Martha McNelly 272-3070

The **Litigation and Administrative Practices Group** represents the Commission, its members, and employees, at the trial and appellate levels, when they are parties to civil litigation arising from the performance of the Commission's official functions, such as enforcement investigations and rulemaking proceedings. Cases often involve issues arising under a variety of Federal administrative statutes, such as the Administrative Procedure Act, the Freedom of Information Act, Privacy Act, and the Right to Financial Privacy Act. This group also handles some of the SEC's enforcement-related appellate litigation.

(Area Code 202)
Associate General Counsel: vacant 272-2476
Senior Litigation Counsel: Richard A. Kirby 272-7374
Assistant General Counsel (Branch 4-Litigation & Administrative Practice: Richard M. Humes ...272-2454
Special Trial Attorney: vacant 272-2454
Special Counsel: vacant 272-2454
Assistant General Counsel (Branch 5-Litigation & Administrative Practice): James Brigagliano 272-2871
Special Trial Attorney: Faith Ruderfer 272-2871
Senior Special Counsel: John E. Birkenheier 272-2871
Senior Litigation Counsel (Branch 10-Rule 2(e) Litigation & Administrative Practice): Susan F. Wyderko 272-2871
Special Counsel: vacant 272-2871

The **Counseling, Legislation and Administration Group** renders legal advice on a variety of Federal securities law and administrative law issues, most of which relate to the SEC's enforcement responsibilities. In addition, this group also prepares congressional testimony and drafts comments on pending legislation affecting the Commission's work. The Counseling Group also occasionally represents the Commission in appellate litigation challenging SEC regulatory actions, particularly those relating to its market regulation responsibilities, and handles a wide range of special research projects.

(Area Code 202)
Associate General Counsel: Phillip D. Parker 272-2469
Counsel to Associate General Counsel: Robert J. Mills 272-2436
Assistant General Counsel (Legislation, Investment Company, & Investment Adviser Regulation: David C. Mahaffey 272-2428
Special Counsel: Thomas M. Selman 272-2428
Assistant General Counsel (Branch 8-Market Regulation, Accounting & Administrative Law): Anne Chafer 272-2422
Special Counsel: Joan A. McCarthy 272-2422
Assistant General Counsel (Branch 9-Enforcement & Disclosure Policy): Diane Sanger 272-2263
Special Counsel: Richard A. Levine 272-2420
Assistant General Counsel (Branch 11-International Litigation & Policy): Thomas L. Riesenberg ..272-3088
Special Counsel: Joseph Franco 272-2892

The **Adjudication Group** prepares draft decisions for the Commission in administrative proceedings that are appealed to the Commission from the decisions of Administrative Law Judges and from the decisions of self-regulatory organizations.

(Area Code 202)
Associate General Counsel: William S. Stern 272-7402
Deputy Associate General Counsel:
Herbert V. Efron 272-7400
R. Moshe Simon 272-7400
Special Counsel: Daniel J. Savitsky 272-7400

OFFICE OF INSPECTOR GENERAL (Room 7010)

The duties and responsibilities of the office of Inspector General are: to provide policy direction for and to conduct, supervise, and coordinate audits, and investigations relating to the programs and operations of the Commission; to review existing and proposed legislation and regulations and make recommendations concerning the impact of such legislation or regulations on the economy and efficiency in the administration of programs and operations and to prevent and detect fraud and abuse in programs and operations.

(Area Code 202)
Inspector General: Walter Stachnik 272-3152

(Area Code 202)
Deputy Inspector General: Nelson Egbert 272-3152

DIVISION OF CORPORATION FINANCE (Room 3000)

The Division of Corporation Finance oversees much of the public disclosure of business and financial information by publicly-held companies. Through its various roles related to the issuance of new securities, this division operates on the leading edge of corporate finance. Attorneys in this division are frequently called upon to render legal interpretations relating to mergers and acquisitions, novel methods of raising capital, and issues relating to international securities offerings.

(Area Code 202)
Director: Linda C. Quinn 272-2800

Office of the Associate Director (Chief Counsel-Legal)

Associate Director and Chief Counsel-Legal:
William E. Morley 272-2573
Deputy Chief Counsel: Abigail Arms 272-2573
Special Counsel:
Cecilia D. Blye 272-2573

(Area Code 202)
Mary Anne Busse 272-2573
John C. Brousseau 272-2573
William H. Carter 272-2573
Mark Green 272-2573
Michael G. Hyatte 272-2573
Anne Krauskopf 272-2573
Felicia Smith 272-2573

(Area Code 202)

Office of Tender Offers

Chief: David A. Sirignano 272-3097
Special Counsel:
Greg Corso 272-3097
Catherine Dixon 272-3097
Jacob L. Fien-Heffman 272-3097
Staff Attorneys:
Mark A. Cleaves 272-3097
Elizabeth Lord 272-3097
John Maguire 272-3097
Richard A. Silfen 272-3097

Office of the Associate Director (Operations)

Associate Director: Ernestine M.R. Zippoy 272-2573
Special Counsel: John S. Bernas 272-2573

Office of Disclosure Policy (Area Code 202)

Chief: Ann D. Wallace 272-7618
Special Counsels:
James R. Budge 272-2589
Richard Konrath 272-2589
Brian L. Lane 272-2589
Elizabeth Murphy 272-2589
Barbara C. Smith 272-2589

Office of the Associate Director (Small Business and International Corporate Finance)

Associate Director: Mary E.T. Beach 272-2585
International Corporate Finance Chief: vacant 272-3246
Special Counsels:
Anita T. Klein 272-3246
Amy N. Kroll 272-3246
Brent Taylor 272-3246
Small Business Policy Chief: Richard K. Wulff 272-2644
Special Counsel: Patricia Jayne 272-2644

DIVISION OF ENFORCEMENT (Room 4000)

The Division of Enforcement is the SEC's chief investigative and enforcement arm. Federal securities laws grant the SEC broad investigatory powers, including the authority to issue subpoenas for testimony and the production of documents. The types of violations investigated include activities such as insider trading, market manipulation, fraudulent accounting practices, and the sale of unregistered securities. These investigations and trials are the day-to-day work of attorneys in the division.

Note: Branch numbers are internal designations for cases assigned to various lawyers.

(Area Code 202)

Director: William R. McLucas 272-2900

Office of Chief Counsel

Chief Counsel: Colleen P. Mahoney 272-2214
Associate Chief Counsel: Gretta J. Powers 272-2188

Office of Chief Litigation Counsel

Chief Litigation Counsel: Thomas C. Newkirk 272-2225
Deputy Chief Litigation Counsel: Barry R. Goldsmith 272-2219

Office of the Associate Director

Associate Director: Joseph Goldstein 272-2216
Market Manipulation Program Chief: Sarah Ackerson 272-3857
Assistant Director: Gary N. Sundick 272-3871
Enforcement Branch Chiefs:
Branch 5: Thomas Lawson 272-3854
Branch 6: Michael Wolk 272-3848
Branch 9: Leonard W. Wang 272-3823
Assistant Director: Rudolf Gerlick 272-3830
Enforcement Branch Chiefs:
Branch 7: Leo F. Orenstein 272-3832
Branch 8: Ellen Ross 272-3831
Assistant Director (Banking & Thrift Fraud):
Juan Marcelino 504-2200
Enforcement Branch Chiefs:
Susan LeBeaux 272-2328
Lani Lee 272-3871

Office of the Associate Director **(Area Code 202)**

Associate Director: Bruce Hiler 272-2224
Assistant Director: Laura Singer 272-2921
Criminal Reference Branch Chief: vacant 272-2935
Organized Crime Branch Chief: Yuri Zelinsky 272-2945
Assistant Director: Herbert Janick 272-2985
Municipal Securities Branch Chief: Eric Schwartz 272-7528
Options and Special Studies Branch Chief:
Daniel A. Nathan 272-7528
Assistant Director for Corporate Finance & Investment:
Julie K. Lutz 272-2344
Corporation Finance Enforcement Branch Chief:
Jonathan I. Golamb 272-2337
Investment Management Enforcement Branch Chief:
William Baker 272-2333

Office of the Associate Director

Associate Director: Harry Weiss 272-2230
Market Surveillance Branch Chief: Richard V. Norell 272-2202
Assistant Director: Jerry A. Isenberg 272-2248
Trading and Markets Branch Chief: Eva Heffernan 272-2258
Changes and Corporate Ownership Branch Chief: vacant 272-2242
Assistant Director for Home Office: Therese Pritchard 272-2291
Enforcement Branch Chiefs:
Branch 1: Eric Seltzer 272-2287
Branch 2: Paul Huey-Burns 272-2204
Assistant Director: Gary Lloyd 272-3111
Enforcement Branch Chiefs:
Branch 3: Catherine M. Cottom 272-3810
Branch 4: L. Hilton Foster Jr. 272-3800
Assistant Director: James Coffman 272-3942
Branch Chief: Antonia Chion 272-3942

DIVISION OF INVESTMENT MANAGEMENT (Room 5093)

The Division of Investment Management is responsible for administering Federal securities laws as they relate to the regulation of and disclosure by investment companies and investment advisers. The division is currently immersed in several projects to consider restructuring the Government's regulation of these areas. Recent developments in financial markets have led to major changes in the investment management industry, changes which present many regulatory and investor protection issues.

(Area Code 202)

Director: vacant 272-2750
Senior Counsel: Angela Goelzer 272-2060

Office of the Associate Director (Compliance and Insurance)

Associate Director: Gene A. Gohlke 272-3038
Special Counsel: Carl M. Rizzo 272-3038
Special Counsel for Insurance Products & Legal Compliance: Heidi Stam 272-2061

Office of the Associate Director (Legal and Disclosure)

Associate Director: Mary S. Podesta 272-2045
Senior Special Counsel:
Stanley B. Judd 272-2079
Anthony A. Vertuno (EDGAR Project) 272-7116
Chief Counsel: Thomas S. Harman 272-2030
Associate Chief Counsel: Nancy Morris 272-2048
Special Counsel:
vacant.......................................272-2030
Elizabeth T. Tsai 272-2030
Assistant Director for Disclosure & Review:
Carolyn B. Lewis 272-2109
Branch Chiefs:
Branch 16: Paul Goldman 272-2071
Branch 17: David Wills 272-2115
Branch 18: Jeremiah deMichaelis 272-2096

(Area Code 202)

Office of Policy and Disclosure Adviser Regulation
Special Counsel: Kenneth J. Berman 272-2107

Office of the Associate Director (Regulation)

Associate Director: vacant 272-2039

Office of Investment Company Regulation
Special Counsel: Houghton R. Hallock Jr 272-3030
Branch Chiefs:
Branch 21: Stephanie L. Monaco 272-3030
Branch 25: Max Berueffy 272-3016
Branch 26: Jeremy Rubenstein 272-3023

Office of Public Utility Regulation
Senior Special Counsel: Sidney L. Cimmet 272-7340
Special Counsel (Exempt Holding Companies):
Joanne Rutkowski 504-2267
Special Counsel (Registered Holding Companies):
Catherine Fisher 272-7676
Branch Chiefs:
Branch 1: Yvonne M. Hunold 272-2676
Branch 2: Barbara T. Heussler 272-7676
Branch 3: Martha C. Baker 272-7699

Office of Regulatory Policy
Special Counsel: Diane C. Blizzard 272-2048

DIVISION OF MARKET REGULATION (Room 5000)

The Division of Market Regulation is responsible for regulating the nation's securities markets and the activities of investment bankers, stock brokers, and other market professionals. A new attorney, under the guidance of senior colleagues, will often be called upon to recommend solutions to difficult policy questions that require the application of legal and economic reasoning based upon a comprehensive understanding of how securities are traded and how the capital markets operate.

(Area Code 202)

Director: Richard G. Ketchum 272-3000
Special Counsel: Barbara N. Ferrara 272-2407

Office of Inspections and Financial Responsibility

Associate Director: Mark D. Fitterman 272-2830
Principal Senior Special Counsel: Harry Melamed 272-2382
Assistant Director for Compliance and Financial Responsibility: Michael A. Macchiaroli 272-2904
Assistant Director for Market Operations and Surveillance: Julio A. Mojica 272-7497
Assistant Director for Self-Regulatory Inspections:
Joseph Furey 272-7471
Special Counsel:
Michael Dorsey 272-2792
Robert Love 272-3064

Office of Legal Policy and Trading Practices

Associate Director: Larry E. Bergmann 272-2836
Senior Special Counsel:
M. Blair Corkran Jr 272-7490
Karen Burgess 272-7494
Chief Counsel: Robert L.D. Colby 272-7487
Special Counsel: Edward Pittman 272-7492
Legal Interpretations Branch Chief: Susan Walters ..272-7488
Assistant Director for Trading Practices:
Nancy J. Sano 272-7493
Special Counsel: Ivette Lopez 272-7491

(Area Code 202)

Office of Self-Regulatory Oversight and Market Structure

Associate Director: Brandon Becker 272-2866
Senior Special Counsel: Anthony Ain 272-2905
Assistant Director for Exchange and Options:
Howard Kramer 272-2889
Special Counsel: Sharon Lawson 272-2406
Exchange Regulations Branch Chief: Mary Revell 272-2910
Options Regulations Branch Chief: Thomas Gira 272-2893
Assistant Director for National Market System and OTC Regulation: Kathryn Natale 272-2405
Special Counsel: Gordon Fuller 272-2414
National Market System Branch Chief:
Christine Sakach 272-2857
OTC Regulation Branch Chief: Katherine A. England ...272-2378
Assistant Director for Securities Processing Regulation: Jonathan Kallman 272-2402
Special Counsel: Sandra Sciole 272-7379
Clearing Agency Regulation Branch Chief:
Judith Poppalardo 272-7470
Transfer Agent Regulation Branch Chief:
Ester Saverson 272-2775
Special Counsel for Automation & International Markets:
Eugene Lopez 272-2828

SECURITIES AND EXCHANGE COMMISSION

OFFICE OF INTERNATIONAL AFFAIRS (Room 4027)

(Area Code 202)
Director: Michael Mann 272-2306
Senior Counsels:
Lise Lustgarten 272-2306
Elizabeth Jacobs 272-2306

OFFICE OF ADMINISTRATIVE LAW JUDGES (Room 7200)

The decisions of the Administrative Law Judges are kept in bound volumes in the SEC Library. Copies of specific decisions can be obtained by contacting the SEC Public Reference Desk at the address and phone number cited at the beginning of this section.

(Area Code 202)
Chief Administrative Law Judge: Warren E. Blair 272-7636
Administrative Law Judges:
Brenda P. Murray 272-7636
Max O. Regensteiner 272-7636
Jerome K. Soffer 272-7636

OFFICE OF CONSUMER AFFAIRS & INFORMATION SERVICES (Room 2115)

(Area Code 202)
Counsel: Richard Pullano 272-7432

OFFICE OF ELECTRONIC DATA GATHERING ANALYSIS AND RETRIEVAL MANAGEMENT (EDGAR) (Room 1150)

(Area Code 202)
Special Counsel: vacant 272-3808

OFFICE OF THE CHIEF ACCOUNTANT (Room 4197)

(Area Code 202)
Chief Counsel: Robert E. Burns 272-2130

REGIONAL OFFICES

The SEC's regional offices, located in Atlanta, Boston, Chicago, Denver, Fort Worth, Los Angeles, Miami, New York, Philadelphia, and Seattle, serve as field representatives of the Commission in the administration and enforcement of the various statutes. Enforcement attorneys at these offices, like their counterparts in Washington, investigate possible securities law violations and, where appropriate, bring actions against the perpetrators. They may also work closely with U.S. Attorneys' Offices when a violation seems to warrant criminal prosecution, or with state securities commissions.

In addition, regional and branch office personnel also handle a number of functions which the SEC has found can be performed more efficiently from decentralized locations. Such activities include: examining registered broker-dealers, investment companies, and investment advisers; reviewing filings from small businesses which want to issue securities; and appearing on the Commission's behalf in bankruptcy proceedings in Federal district court.

Atlanta Regional Office

U.S. Securities and Exchange Commission, 1375 Peachtree Street, N.E., Ste 788, Atlanta, GA 30367.

(Area Code 404)
Regional Administrator: Richard P. Wessel 257-2524
Regional Counsel: Joseph L. Grant 257-2025
Regional Trial Counsel: Nancy J. Van Sant 257-2775
Assistant Regional Administrator (Enforcement):
Ronald L. Crawford 257-2050
Assistant Regional Administrator (Regulation):
James E. Long 257-2075
(Jurisdiction: AL, FL, GA, MS, NC, PR, SC, TN, VI, and part of LA)

Miami Branch Office

U.S. Securities and Exchange Commission, Dupont Plaza Center 300 Biscayne Blvd Way, Ste 500, Miami, FL 33131.

(Area Code 305)
Associate Regional Administrator: Charles C. Harper ..350-4851
Securities Compliance Specialist: (Area Code 305)
Charles D. Hochmuth 350-4866
Assistant Regional Administrator (Enforcement):
William P. Hicks 350-7456
Chief, Branch of Regulation: John D. Mahoney 350-7453

Boston Regional Office

U.S. Securities and Exchange Commission, John W. McCormack Post Office and Courthouse Bldg., 90 Devonshire Street, Suite 700, Boston, MA 02109.

(Area Code 617)
Regional Administrator: Douglas Scarff 223-9948
Regional Trial Counsel: D. Robert Cervera 223-9946
Assistant Regional Administrator (Enforcement):
Dennis Suprenent 223-9944
Assistant Regional Administrator (Regulation):
Peter F. Flynn 223-9924
(Jurisdiction: CT, MA, ME, NH, RI, VT)

Chicago Regional Office

U.S. Securities and Exchange Commission, Everett M. Dirksen Bldg, Room 1204, 219 South Dearborn Street, Chicago, IL 60604.
(Area Code 312)
Regional Administrator: William D. Goldsberry 353-9338
Senior Trial Counsel: Edward G. Kohler 353-7418
Senior Trial Counsel: Mary H. Weiss 353-7410
Assistant Regional Administrator (Office of Regulation No. 1): Joan M. Fleming 353-7402
Senior Supervisory Securities Compliance Examiner: Michael J. O'Rourke 353-7436
Assistant Regional Administrator (Office of Regulation No. 2): Philip D. Hausken 886-3956
Assistant Regional Administrator (Enforcement No. 1): Joyce A. Glynn 353-7651
Assistant Regional Administrator (Enforcement No. 2): Mary E. Keefe 353-5453
(Jurisdiction: IA, IL, IN, KY, MI, MN, MO, OH, WI)

Denver Regional Office

U.S. Securities and Exchange Commission, 410 Seventeenth Street, Ste 700, Denver, CO 80202.
(Area Code 313)
Regional Administrator: Robert H. Davenport 564-3149
Regional Trial Counsel: Robert M. Fusfeld 564-3129
Regional Trial Counsel: Thomas D. Carter 564-3105
Assistant Regional Administrator (Enforcement): Fred L. Chavez 564-3384
Assistant Regional Administrator (Enforcement): Edward A. Lewkowski 564-3083
Assistant Regional Administrator (Regulation): James E. Birchby 564-3182
Special Counsel (Regulation): Weldon H. Schwartz 564-3201
(Jurisdiction: CO, ND, NE, NM, SD, UT, WY)

Salt Lake Branch Office

U.S. Securities and Exchange Commission, U.S. Post Office & Court House, 350 S. Main Street, #505, Salt Lake City, UT 84101.
(Area Code 801)
Assistant Regional Administrator: Donald M. Hoerl ..588-6745
Branch Chief, Enforcement: Jennifer J. Ausenbaugh ..588-6742
Branch Chief, Regulation: Floyd G. Hastings 588-6739

Fort Worth Regional Office

U.S. Securities and Exchange Commission, 411 West Seventh Street, Eighth Floor, Fort Worth, TX 76102.
(Area Code 817)
Regional Administrator: T. Christopher Browne 334-3821
Regional Trial Counsel: Stephen Webster 334-3821
Assistant Regional Administrator (Enforcement): Hugh M. Wright 334-3821
Assistant Regional Administrator (Regulation): Mary Lou Felsman 334-3821
(Jurisdiction: AR, KS, OK, TX, and part of LA)

Houston Branch Office

U.S. Securities and Exchange Commission, 7500 San Felipe Street, Ste 550, Houston, TX 77063.
(Area Code 713)
Assistant Regional Administrator: Joseph C. Matta ...526-8725

Los Angeles Regional Office

U.S. Securities and Exchange Commission, 5757 Wilshire Blvd, Ste 500 East, Los Angeles, CA 90036-3648.
(Area Code 213)
Regional Administrator: James L. Sanders 793-3807

(Area Code 213)
Regional Trial Counsel: Robert D. Laframenta 793-3960
Assistant Regional Administrator (Enforcement No 1): Lori A. Richards 793-3962
Assistant Regional Administrator (Enforcement No. 2): Elaine M. Cacheris 793-3964
Assistant Regional Administrator (Regulation): Rosalind R. Tyson 793-3950
Special Counsel: P. Christine Vento 793-3950
(Jurisdiction: AZ, CA, HI, NV, Guam)

San Francisco Branch Office

U.S. Securities and Exchange Commission, 901 Market Street, San Francisco, CA 94103.
(Area Code 415)
Associate Regional Administrator: Cer Gladwyn Goins 484-3140
Senior Trial Counsel: Denise O'Brien 484-3140
Assistant Regional Administrator (Enforcement): vacant..................................484-3140
Chief, Branch of Regulation: Richard A. Castro 484-3140

New York Regional Office

U.S. Securities and Exchange Commission, 75 Park Place, 14th Floor, New York, NY 10007.
(Area Code 212)
Regional Administrator: Lawrence Iason 264-1636
Regional Counsel: Dorothy Heyl 264-1618
Office of the Associate Regional Administrator-Enforcement:
Associate Regional Administrator: Carmen J. Lawrence 264-1630
Office of the Associate Regional Administrator-Investment Management and Corporate Reorganization:
Associate Regional Administrator: Richard D. Marshall 264-1647
Chief Counsel (Corporate Reorganization): Nathan M. Fuchs 264-9517
Office of the Associate Regional Administrator-Broker/Dealer and Corporation Finance:
Associate Regional Administrator: Martin A. Kuperberg 264-1634
Securities Compliance Specialist: Martin Stein 264-8503
Branch Chief, Broker/Dealer, Enforcement and Interpretations: Jeffrey Plotkin 264-2694
Branch Chief, Small Issues: Donald Rinehart ..264-5260
(Jurisdiction: NJ, NY)

Philadelphia Regional Office

U.S. Securities and Exchange Commission, Curtis Center, Ste 1005 East, 601 Walnut Street, Philadelphia, PA 19106-3322.
(Area Code 215)
Regional Administrator: James C. Kennedy 597-3106
Regional Trial Counsel: David S. Horowitz 597-2950
Associate Regional Administrator (Enforcement): Thomas H. Monahan 597-2905
Special Litigation Counsel: Merri Jo Gillette-Meadows 597-2936
Assistant Regional Administrator (Regulation): Herbert F. Brooks, Jr. 272-7806
Special Counsel: Theodore S. Bloch 597-4040
(Jurisdiction: DC, DE, MD, PA, VA, WV)

Seattle Regional Office

U.S. Securities and Exchange Commission, 3040 Jackson Federal Bldg, 915 Second Avenue, Seattle, WA 98174.
(Area Code 206)
Regional Administrator: Jack H. Bookey 399-7990

(Area Code 206)
Regional Trial Counsel: Lawrence L. Kiser 399-2035
Assistant Regional Administrator (Enforcement):
Nobuo Kawasaki 399-2020
Special Counsel: Barbara E. Barnhart 399-2033
Special Counsel: N. Michael Hansen 399-2039

(Area Code 206)
Assistant Regional Counsel (Regulation):
Rosyln M. Houtman 399-2013
Special Counsel: George N. Prince 399-2011
(Jurisdiction: AK, ID, MT, OR, WA)

DATABASES AND PUBLICATIONS OF INTEREST

Forms required to make filings with the Commission can be obtained by writing or calling the SEC Publications Section, Forms and Publications Division. Tel: 212/272-7460.

The open meetings of the Commission are recorded and can be obtained by calling 202/272-3130. The cost is $2.95 per cassette.

SEC News Digest is a daily summary of important SEC developments including listings of registrations, acquisitions and filings received by the Commission. Time, date and place of Commission hearings open to the public are listed. These hearings can also be found in the Federal Register. SEC News Digest can be seen at the SEC's Public Reference Desk, Room 1024, every day after 1:00 PM or in the SEC Library the following day. It can be ordered by subscription under the title, SEC Today, from the Washington Service Bureau, 1225 Connecticut Ave. NW, Washington, DC 20036. Tel: 202/833-9200 ($490.00 annually). On-line NEXUX subscribers can order SEC News Digest (SEC-NEW) from Mead Data Central-NEXUS, 1050 Connecticut Ave., N.W., Suite 1090, Washington D.C. 20036. Tel: 202/785-3550.

SEC Docket is a weekly publication of the full text of all SEC releases which pertain to the laws administered by the SEC. The publication also includes financial reporting releases, staff accounting bulletins and litigation releases. SEC Docket can be seen in the SEC Library or ordered by subscription from Commerce Clearing House, Inc., 4025 W. Peterson, Chicago IL 60646. Tel: 312/583-8500 or from Soreg Inc., Appeals Handbook Division Dept. 111, Eighth Avenue, New York, NY 10011. Tel: 212/741-6600.

The following publications can be purchased from the **U.S. Government Printing Office.** Stock numbers and prices for annual subscriptions are shown below. Submit requests for these publications to: The Superintendent of Documents, U.S. Government Printing Office, Washington, D.C. 20402. Tel: 202/783-3238.

Official Summary of Security Transactions and Holdings. A monthly publication made up of securities holdings figures showing owners, relationships to issues, amounts of securities bought or sold by each owner, their individual holdings at the end of the reported month, and types of securities. Price: $69.00 a year domestic; $86.25 a year foreign. GPO Stock# 746-001-00000-2. This publication is also kept in the SEC Library.

Decisions and Reports of the Commission pursuant to the various securities laws is presently published in two volumes: Vol. 47 (Nov. 1978-June 1984). Price: $44.00 domestic; $55.00 foreign. Vol. 48 (July 1984-June 1988). Price: $43.00 domestic; $53.75 foreign. Current decisions and reports are first published as releases which can be found in the SEC Docket.

The following publications are free of charge and can be obtained by writing to: **U.S. Securities & Exchange Commission,** Publications Section, Printing Branch Stop C-9, Washington, D.C. 20549.

Arbitration Procedures. A discussion of procedures for disputes with brokerage firms involving financial claims.

Information on Bounties. Information on bounties the SEC is authorized to award to persons who provide information leading to the recovery of a civil penalty from an inside trader.

SECURITIES AND EXCHANGE COMMISSION
KEY LEGAL AUTHORITIES

General Agency Regulations: 17 C.F.R. Parts 200-301 (1989).
Rules of Practice & Procedure: 17 C.F.R. Parts 201-202 (1989).

Securities Act of 1933, as amended, 15 U.S.C. 77a-77aa--purpose is to provide information upon which investors may make an informed and realistic evaluation of the worth of offered securities by:

*requiring public offerings of securities sold in interstate commerce or through the mails to be registered with the Commission;

*directing that registration statements must contain pertinent financial and other data about both the issuer and the offering and any controlling person of the issuer; and

*making it unlawful to sell such securities unless a registration statement is in effect.

The Act also contains anti-fraud provisions applicable to the sale of securities whether or not registered.

Securities Exchange Act of 1934, as amended, 15 U.S.C. 77b et seq.--established the Commission and:

*requires that companies whose securities are listed upon national securities exchanges, and certain companies whose securities are traded in the over-the-counter markets, to file registration applications and annual and other reports containing financial and other data prescribed by the Commission for the information of investors;

*makes unlawful the solicitation of proxies, authorizations, or consents from the holders of listed securities in contravention of Commission rules providing for disclosure of information relevant to matters subject to solicitation;

*requires disclosure of holdings and transactions by officers, directors, and holders of 10 percent of equity securities of listed companies; and

*provides for registration with, and regulation by, the Commission of national securities exchanges, over-the-counter brokers and dealers, and national associations of such dealers.

Public Utility Holding Company Act of 1935, as amended, 15 U.S.C. 79-79z-6--authorizes the Commission to regulate the purchase and sale of securities, properties, and other assets by electric and gas utility holding company system firms, their intra-system transactions, and service and management arrangements, and limits system operations to physically integrated and coordinated properties.

Trust Indenture Act of 1939, as amended, 15 U.S.C. 77aaa-77bbbb--safeguards the interests of purchasers of publicly-offered debt securities issued under trust indentures by requiring the inclusion of certain protective provisions and the exclusion of certain types of exculpatory clauses in such indentures; and requires that indenture trustees be "independent" by prohibiting certain potential conflicts of interest.

Investment Company Act of 1940, as amended, 15 U.S.C. 80a-1-80a-64--requires investment companies to register with the Commission;
*directs the Commission to regulate their activities in order to protect investors;
*prohibits certain investment company transactions unless exempted by the Commission;
*authorizes the Commission to:
-prepare reports to security holders on the fairness of reorganization, merger, or consolidation plans;
-seek an injunction against the consummation of plans deemed grossly unfair to security holders;
-enjoin management acts and practices involving gross misconduct or gross abuse of trust; and
-disqualify from office the responsible officials.

Investment Advisers Act of 1940, as amended, 15 U.S.C. 80b-1-80b-21--requires paid investment advisers to register with the Commission with respect to security transactions; makes unlawful fraudulent and deceitful business practices; and requires disclosure of any interests advisers may have in the transactions they execute for their clients.

Bankruptcy Code, Chapts. 9 and 11, as amended, 11 U.S.C. 901 & 1109(a)--provides for Commission participation as a statutory party in reorganization cases involving a judgment of debts of a municipality administered in the Federal courts.
Legislative History: 1978 U.S. Code Cong. & Admin. News 5787.

Securities Investor Protection Act of 1970, as amended, 15 U.S.C. 78aaa-78fff-4--established the Securities Investor Protection Corporation (SIPC) to provide protection for investors if their broker-dealer encounters financial troubles; requires all SIPC rules and determinations to be approved by the Commission; established an insurance fund consisting of assessments of brokers and dealers to make public customers whole up to statutory limits; and establishes financial responsibility requirements for broker-dealers.
Legislative History: 1970 U.S. Code Cong. & Admin. News 5254.

SELECTIVE SERVICE SYSTEM

1023 31st Street, N.W.
Washington, D.C. 20435

DESCRIPTION: The purpose of the Selective Service System is to be prepared to supply to the Armed Forces manpower adequate to ensure the security of the United States. Responsibilities include policies and procedures for registration and compliance programs, mobilization systems, and the operation of Civilian Review Boards.

(Area Code 202)
Director: Samuel Kenric Lessey Jr 724-0817
Procurement Information 724-0795
Public Affairs/Publications 724-0790
General Information 724-0820
Registration Information .... (800) 621-5388
Inspector General: Donna L. Bahls 724-1053
Facsimile 724-1792

Freedom of Information Act/Privacy Act Office 724-0843
Requests for FOIA information must be in writing. Search fees are based on the salary of the person doing the search. Copying charges are 10 cents per page, with charges for the first 100 pages waived. There is no charge for privacy act requests.

(Area Code 202)
Library (4th Floor Conference Room) 724-0851
The library is open by appointment, 8:00 AM until 4:30 PM, Monday through Friday. A building escort is required. Materials cannot be checked out, but may be copied at no charge.

OFFICE OF GENERAL COUNSEL (Fifth Floor)

The Office of the General Counsel consists of two attorneys: the General Counsel/Counselor, and the Deputy General Counsel. The Office of the General Counsel provides legal opinions, advice, and services; handles litigation involving the Agency; prepares and coordinates proposed legislation; ensures the legality of Agency regulations; and manages the passive compliance program. As Counselor, the General Counsel also serves the Director and Deputy Director as confidential advisor and consultant on all matters relating to Agency mission and activities.

(Area Code 202)
General Counsel: Henry N. Williams 724-1167

(Area Code 202)
Assistant General Counsel: Paul J. Knapp 724-1167

PUBLICATIONS OF INTEREST

The Selective Service System publishes Fact Sheets on various topics, some of which include: "Aliens and Dual Nationals" (registration and liability for service), "Who Must Register" (an explanation of Section 3 of the Military Selective Service Act), "State Legislation" (the Solomon Amendment to the Defense Authorization Act of 1983 and student financial aid), "Sources of Information on Selective Service" (a selected bibliography), and "Background of Selective Service" (an explanation of the purposes and a description of the agency). All of the Fact Sheets are free of charge and can be obtained from the Selective Service System, Office of Public Affairs, 1023 31st Street, N.W., Washington, D.C. 20435. Tel: 202/724-0790.

The Selective Service System: Information for Registrants discusses the law requiring 18 year-old males to register. What would happen if the draft were started again, and how to request reclassification or postponement of induction into the armed forces. Available from Consumer Information Center-P, P.O. Box 100, Pueblo, CO 81002. Free. If you order two or more free publications, include a check for $1.00 payable to Superintendent of Documents. Booklet number 567W.

SELECTIVE SERVICE SYSTEM
KEY LEGAL AUTHORITIES

Regulations: 32 C.F.R. Parts 1602-1699 (1989).

Military Selective Service Act, as amended, 50 U.S.C. App. 451 et seq.--the basic U.S. conscription law authorizing a military registration system and providing authority to activate the National Guard and Reserve components whenever Congress determines that they are needed for national security.

Legislative History: 1948 U.S. Code Cong. & Admin. News 1989; 1951 U.S. Code Cong. & Admin. News 1472; 1967 U.S. Code Cong. & Admin. News 1308; 1971 U.S. Code Cong. & Admin. News 1439; 1979 U.S. Code Cong. & Admin. News 1818; 1981 U.S. Code Cong. & Admin. News 1781.

Presidential Proclamation No. 4771, "Registration Under the Selective Service Act," 3 C.F.R., 1980 Comp., p. 82--requires males who have attained their 18th birthday to register with the Selective Service System at U.S. post offices.

SMALL BUSINESS ADMINISTRATION

1441 L Street, N.W.
Washington, D.C. 20416*

* **NOTE:** The offices will move to 3rd and D Street S.W., Washington, D.C. beginning October 30, 1990. The move is expected to be completed by March 1991.

DESCRIPTION: The Small Business Administration (SBA) counsels, assists, and protects the interests of small business; ensures that small business concerns receive a fair portion of Government contracts and subcontracts; makes loans to small business concerns, state and local development companies, and the victims of floods or other catastrophes, or of certain types of economic injury; and license, regulate, and make loans to small business investment companies.

(Area Code 202)

Administrator: Susan S. Engeleiter 653-6605
Procurement Information 653-6635
Procurement Assistance for Small Businesses 653-6635
Public Information 653-6365
Docket 653-6500
Inspector General's Hot Line 653-7557
Information Hotlines:
  Washington, D.C. Metro area 653-7561
  Outside D.C. Metro area .... (800) 368-5855
Facsimile 254-6429

Freedom of Information Act/Privacy Act Office 653-6460
Initial requests for Freedom of Information or Privacy Act can be made directly to this office and will then be given to the office under which the request falls. Copying fees are 10 cents per page. Search fees are $18.00 per hour professional staff; $9.00 per hour clerical staff. Computer time is actual cost. Address requests to Small Business Administration, FOIA, Room 305, 2100 K St. N.W., Washington, D.C. 20416.

(Area Code 202)

Law Library (Room 714) 653-6462
The law library is open Monday through Friday from 8:30 AM until 5:00 PM by appointment only. Materials may be photocopied for 10 cents per page (the first 10 pages are free). The library will also loan materials through the Interlibrary Loan Program. Size appeal decisions are located in the public reading room (Room 300) at 2100 K Street, N.W., Washington, D.C. 20416. Hours are 8:30 AM until 5:00 PM, Monday through Friday.

OFFICE OF INSPECTOR GENERAL (Room 1018)

The responsibilities of the Office of Inspector General include: conducting and supervising audits and investigations; making recommendations to promote economy and efficiency in SBA operations; preventing and detecting fraud and abuse in SBA programs and operations; and informing Congress and the Administrator of SBA of problems in agency operations and the status of any necessary corrective actions.

The **Counsel Division** of the Office of Inspector General includes two attorneys: the Deputy Inspector General and Counsel to the Inspector General, and an attorney-advisor. The Division provides independent legal advice and assistance on complex and sensitive matters in support of the activities of the office, including: reviewing and evaluating proposed legislation and regulations to determine their impact on agency programs; responding to Freedom of Information Act (FOIA) and Privacy Act requests; identifying and analyzing complex issues of criminal, civil, and administrative law, as well as identifying remedial and enforcement actions; and representing the office in civil, criminal, and administrative proceedings before Federal/state courts and administrative tribunals.

(Area Code 202)

Inspector General: Charles R. Gillum 653-6597
Counsel to the Inspector General: Daniel B. Peyser 653-9207

(Area Code 202)

Assistant Counsel: Michelle Whalen 653-6370
FOIA/Privacy Act .... (703) 235-3890

OFFICE OF GENERAL COUNSEL (Room 700)

The Office of General Counsel provides legal counsel, legal opinions, and legal representation for the agency. The office prepares drafts of legislation and agency regulations; comments on proposed legislation; and provides technical direction to SBA attorneys assigned to regional, district, and branch offices. The office does not provide legal advice to small businesses or to other members of the public.

Attorneys in the field offices handle over 10,000 claims cases annually. Although such cases are the immediate responsibility of the Department of Justice and various U.S. Attorneys, almost half the claims cases are handled directly by SBA attorneys, 55 of whom in the headquarters and field offices have been designated "Special Assistant U.S. Attorneys" by the Department of Justice.

SMALL BUSINESS ADMINISTRATION

(Area Code 202)

General Counsel: Sally Bruester Narey 653-6642
Deputy General Counsel: Martin D. Teckler 653-6644

Office of Finance and Legislation
Associate General Counsel: Martin D. Teckler 653-6644
Chief Counsel for:
Business Loans: Harry D. Kempler 653-6757
Investment: Howard S. Cooper 653-6561
Legislation: Patricia R. Forbes 653-6573

Office of General Law (Area Code 202)
Associate General Counsel: David R. Kohler 653-6660
Chief Counsel for:
Administrative Law: Mona K. Mitnick 653-6762
Procurement and Grants: David Gray 653-6699

Office of Litigation
Associate General Counsel: Eric S. Benderson 653-6509
Chief Counsel for:
Claims and Investment Company Liquidation:
Claire Schenk ....(314) 279-4790
Enforcement: vacant 653-6487
Special Litigation: Gary Fox 653-6438

REGIONAL OFFICES

REGION I (BOSTON)

Regional Counsel: Francis Conley, Jr.
Assistant Regional Counsel: Mary L. Russell
U.S. Small Business Administration, 60 Batterymarch St, 10th Fl, Boston, MA 02110. Tel: 617/451-2044.

District Offices are located in Augusta, Boston, Concord, Hartford, Montpelier, and Providence:

Augusta District Office
District Counsel: Harlan J. Choate
Attorney Adviser: Mark O'Brien
U.S. Small Business Administration, Federal Building, Room 512, 40 Western Avenue, Augusta, ME 04330. Tel: 207/622-8378.

Boston District Office
District Counsel: Philip A. Vitiello
Attorney Advisers: Horace J. Cammack, Jr., Christina Robinson Davis, and Catherine Morgan
U.S. Small Business Administration, 10 Causeway Street, Room 265, Boston, MA 02222. Tel: 617/565-5630.

Concord District Office
District Counsel: Pilar B. Pinili-Silva
U.S. Small Business Administration, P.O. Box 1257, Concord, NH 03301. Tel: 603/225-1400.

Hartford District Office
District Counsel: Harold Pitt
Attorney Adviser: Kenneth Hayden
U.S. Small Business Administration, 330 Main Street, 2nd Fl, Hartford, CT 06106. Tel: 203/240-4664.

Montpelier District Office
District Counsel: Kirby S. Scarborough
U.S. Small Business Administration, 87 State Street, Room 205, P.O. Box 605, Montpelier, VT 05602. Tel: 802/828-4474.

Providence District Office
District Counsel: Allen E. Hanson
Attorney Adviser: Robert Welch
U.S. Small Business Administration, 380 Westminster Mall, 5th Fl, Providence, RI 02903. Tel: 401/528-4575.

REGION II (NEW YORK)

Regional Counsel: John Matthews
Assistant Regional Counsel: Joseph A. Hallock
U.S. Small Business Administration, 26 Federal Plaza, Room 31-08, New York, NY 10278. Tel: 212/264-2845.

District Offices are located in Buffalo, Newark, New York, Puerto Rico/Virgin Islands, and Syracuse; with Branch Offices in Elmira, NY and Melville, NY.

Buffalo District Office
District Counsel: Molly Beth Gaughan
U.S. Small Business Administration, Federal Bldg, Room 1311, 111 West Huron Street, Buffalo, NY 14202. Tel: 716/846-4690.

Newark District Office
District Counsel: David Elbaum
Attorney Advisers: J. Harold. Brooks and Linda P. Rodriguez
U.S. Small Business Administration, Military Park Bldg, 60 Park Place, 4th Fl, Newark, NJ 07102. Tel: 201/645-2427.

New York District Office
District Counsel: Thomas Loftus
Attorney Advisers: Kevin Barry, Ernesto Rosado Rivera, and William B. Young
U.S. Small Business Administration, 26 Federal Plaza, Room 3100, New York, NY 10278. Tel: 212/264-3487.

Puerto Rico and Virgin Islands District Office
District Counsel: Jerome E. Smith
Attorney Adviser: Ines M. Equia
U.S. Small Business Administration, Federico Degatau Federal Bldg, Room 691, Carlos Chardon Avenue, Hato Rey, PR 00918. Tel: 809/766-5222.

Syracuse District Office
District Counsel: Gordon T. MacArthur
Attorney Adviser: Nancy Caple
U.S. Small Business Administration, Federal Bldg, Room 1071, 100 South Clinton St, Syracuse, NY 13260. Tel: 315/423-5363.

Elmira Branch Office
Branch Counsel: Ann R. Teeter
U.S. Small Business Administration, Elmira Savings Bank Bldg, 4th Fl, 333 East Water St, Elmira, NY 14901. Tel: 607/734-6130.

Melville Branch Office
Branch Counsel: Bertram F. Schulman
U.S. Small Business Administration, 35 Pinelawn Road, Room 102E, Melville, NY 11747. Tel: 516/454-0755.

REGION III (PHILADELPHIA)

Regional Counsel: Robert C. Hall
Assistant Regional Counsel: Richard W. Burcik
U.S. Small Business Administration, 475 Allendale Road, Suite 201, King of Prussia, PA 19406. Tel: 215/962-3753.

District Offices are located in Baltimore, Clarksburg, WV, Philadelphia, Pittsburgh, Richmond, and Washington, D.C.

Baltimore District Office
District Counsel: Diane L. Jansson
Attorney Adviser: Nicole E. Porter
U.S. Small Business Administration, Equitable Bldg, 3rd Floor, 10 N. Calvert Street, Baltimore, MD 21202. Tel: 301/962-2474.

Clarksburg District Office
District Counsel: Stephen M. Glass
U.S. Small Business Administration, 168 W. Main Street, 5th Fl, Clarksburg, WV 26301. Tel: 304/623-5631.

Philadelphia District Office
District Counsel: John R. Abbott
Attorney Advisers: Paul E. Beck, Patricia K. Younce, William Gery, and Nadine Prater
U.S. Small Business Administration, 475 Allendale Road, Suite 201, King of Prussia, PA 19406. Tel: 215/962-3810.

Pittsburgh District Office
District Counsel: Mary M. Merman
Attorney Adviser: John F. Wohlin
U.S. Small Business Administration, 960 Penn Avenue, 5th Floor, Pittsburgh, PA 15222. Tel: 412/644-2785.

Richmond District Office
District Counsel: Stran L. Trout
Attorney Adviser: Sally Y. Wood
U.S. Small Business Administration, Federal Building, Room 3015, P.O. Box 10126, 400 North Eighth St, Richmond, VA 23240. Tel: 804/771-2948.

Washington District Office
District Counsel: vacant
Attorney Advisers: Leslie Forrest, Jon Haitsuka, and Stuart M. Shalloway
U.S. Small Business Administration, 1111-18th St, N.W., 6th Fl, P.O. Box 19993, Washington, D.C. 20036. Tel: 202/634-4398.

REGION IV (ATLANTA)

Regional Counsel: William B. Grace
Attorney Adviser: Joe E. Brown
U.S. Small Business Administration, 1375 Peachtree Street, N.E., 5th Floor, Atlanta, GA 30367. Tel: 404/347-4533.

District Offices are located in Atlanta, Birmingham, Charlotte, Columbia, Jackson, Jacksonville, Louisville, Miami, and Nashville; with a Branch Office in Gulfport, MS.

Atlanta District Office
District Counsel: Adrienne Rodgers
Attorney Advisers: Linda Dunham, George E. Schaeffer, Judith Levinson, Alice McQuade, John Byrnes, and Carol Duvic
U.S. Small Business Administration, 1720 Peachtree Road, N.W. 6th Floor, Atlanta, GA 30309. Tel: 404/347-4434.

Birmingham District Office
District Counsel: William A. Howell
Attorney Advisers: John Bancroft and E.H. (Zeke) Bixler
U.S. Small Business Administration, 2121 8th Avenue North, Suite 200, Birmingham, AL 35203. Tel: 205/731-1336.

Charlotte District Office
District Counsel: Bynum Rudisill
Attorney Advisers: Cheryl Sloan and Edward Leach
U.S. Small Business Administration, 222 South Church Street, Room 300, Charlotte, NC 28202. Tel: 704/371-6596.

Columbia District Office
District Counsel: Patricia Melvin
Attorney Advisers: Sandra Burr and Sheri McAllister
U.S. Small Business Administration, P.O. Box 2786, 1835 Assembly Street, Rm 358, Columbia, SC 29202. Tel: 803/765-5903.

Jackson District Office
District Counsel: William B. Thompson Jr.
Attorney Adviser: Katherine McLeod
U.S. Small Business Administration, Federal Building, 101 West Capitol St, Suite 322, Jackson, MS 39269. Tel: 601/965-4367.

Jacksonville District Office
District Counsel: Larry E. Denney
Attorney Advisers: Susan Irwin and Lisa M. Stotesbery
U.S. Small Business Administration, 7825 Baymeadows Way, Suite 100-B, Jacksonville, FL 32256. Tel: 904/443-1990.

Louisville District Office
District Counsel: Linda Creek
Attorney Advisers: Susan Leavenworth, Deborah Harrod, and Donna Jane Yenowine
U.S. Small Business Administration, Federal Office Building, Rm 188, 600 Martin Luther King Jr Place, Louisville, KY 40202. Tel: 502/582-5961.

Miami District Office
District Counsel: Susan P. Rosenfeld
Attorney Advisers: Richard Braverman, Audrey Goldman, and Linda Cook
U.S. Small Business Administration, 1320 South Dixie Highway, Suite 501, Coral Gables, FL 33136. Tel: 305/536-5521.

Nashville District Office
District Counsel: Richard Cummings
Attorney Adviser: David W. Higgs
U.S. Small Business Administration, 50 Vantage Way, Suite 201, Nashville, TN 37228. Tel: 615/736-5091.

Gulfport Branch Office
Branch Counsel: Phil R. Dunnaway
U.S. Small Business Administration, One Hancock Plaza, Suite 1001, Gulfport, MS 39501. Tel: 601/863-4449.

REGION V (CHICAGO)

Regional Counsel: Haten El-Gabri (Acting)
Assistant Regional Counsel: Timothy G. Treanor
U.S. Small Business Administration, 230 S. Dearborn Street, Room 510, Chicago, IL 60604. Tel: 312/353-0355.

District Offices are located in Chicago, Cleveland, Columbus, Detroit, Indianapolis, Madison, and Minneapolis; with Branch Offices in Milwaukee, and Springfield, IL.

Chicago District Office
District Counsel: Judith L. Irle
Attorney Advisers: Mary Cvengros, Jody R. Adler & Stacy E. Streur
U.S. Small Business Administration, 219 S. Dearborn Street, Room 437, Chicago, IL 60604. Tel: 312/353-3951.

Cleveland District Office
District Counsel: Richard A. Lukich
Attorney Adviser: Paul J. Kukuca
U.S. Small Business Administration, AJC Federal Building, Room 317, 1240 East Ninth St, Cleveland, OH 44199.
Tel: 216/522-4172.

Columbus District Office
District Counsel: Louis Stevenson
Attorney Advisers: Larry Brake and Jody M. Oster
U.S. Small Business Administration, Federal Building-U.S. Courthouse, 85 Marconi Blvd, Room 512, Columbus, OH 43215. Tel: 614/469-7312.

Detroit District Office
District Counsel: Edward S. Witzke
Attorney Advisers: Lawrence Z. Pazol, Richard Pasiak, and Mark T. Sophiea
U.S. Small Business Administration, 515 Patrick V. McNamara Bldg, 477 Michigan Ave, Detroit, MI 48226. Tel: 313/226-6075.

Indianapolis District Office
District Counsel: Donald R. Keppler (Acting)
Attorney Advisers: Robert A. Ledgerwood and Francine Protogere
U.S. Small Business Administration, Minton-Capehart Federal Bldg, Room 578, 575 North Pennsylvania Street, Indianapolis, IN 46204. Tel: 317/226-7281.

Madison District Office
District Counsel: Thomas C. Eckerle
Attorney Adviser: Michael G. Hitt
U.S. Small Business Administration, 212 East Washington Avenue, Room 213, Madison, WI 53703. Tel: 608/264-5510.

Minneapolis District Office
District Counsel: Royce G. Nelligan (Acting)
Attorney Adviser: Debra K. Luther
U.S. Small Business Administration, 610-C Butler Square, 100 North 6th Street, Minneapolis, MN 55403. Tel: 612/370-2328.

Milwaukee Branch Office
Branch Counsel: Bradley G. Trimble
U.S. Small Business Administration, Henry S. Reuss Federal Plaza, 310 West Wisconsin Avenue, Suite 400, Milwaukee, WI 53203. Tel: 414/291-4090.

Springfield Branch Office
Branch Counsel: Thomas L. Jackson
U.S. Small Business Administration, Illinois Financial Center-South, 511 W. Capitol Street, 3rd Floor, Springfield, IL 62704. Tel: 217/492-4416.

REGION VI (DALLAS)

Regional Counsel: Francis M. Flato
Attorney Adviser: Frances H. Goodwin
U.S. Small Business Administration, 8625 King George Drive, Building C, Dallas, TX 75235. Tel: 214/767-7626.

District Offices are located in Albuquerque, Dallas, El Paso, Harlingen, Houston, Little Rock, Lubbock, New Orleans, Oklahoma City, and San Antonio; with a Branch Office in Corpus Christi.

Albuquerque District Office
District Counsel: vacant
Attorney Advisers: John D. Dalton and Ron E. Andazola
U.S. Small Business Administration, 5000 Marble N.E., Ste 320, Patio Plaza Building, Albuquerque, NM 87110. Tel: 505/262-6031.

Dallas District Office
District Counsel: Ron Weisenberger
Attorney Advisers: Andrew Baka and Thomas Moroney
U.S. Small Business Administration, 1100 Commerce Street, Room 3C36, Dallas, TX 75242. Tel: 214/767-9474.

El Paso District Office
District Counsel: Jan Donovan
Attorney Adviser: Theresa Espinoza
U.S. Small Business Administration, 10737 Gateway West, Suite 320, El Paso, TX 79935. Tel: 915/540-5572.

Houston District Office
District Counsel: Najla Tanous
Attorney Adviser: William A. Wirth
U.S. Small Business Administration, 2525 Murworth, Suite 112, Houston, TX 77054. Tel: 713/660-4418.

Little Rock District Office
District Counsel: Michael Price
Attorney Adviser: Dee Davenport Ball
U.S. Small Business Administration, 320 West Capitol Avenue, Suite 601, Little Rock, AR 72201. Tel: 501/378-6156.

Lower Rio Grande Valley District Office
District Counsel: Suzanne Novisky
U.S. Small Business Administration, 222 E. Van Buren, Suite 500, Harlingen, TX 78550. Tel: 512/427-8533.

Lubbock District Office
District Counsel: John D. Walz
Attorney Adviser: Elizabeth L. Clark
U.S. Small Business Administration, Regency Plaza, 1611 10th Street, Suite 200, Lubbock, TX 79401. Tel: 806/743-7462.

New Orleans District Office
District Counsel: Alan J. Wells
Attorney Advisers: Thomas L. Chanove, Jr., Paul Arrington, and Mary P. Gattuso
U.S. Small Business Administration, Ford-Fisk Bldg, 1661 Canal Street, Suite 2000, New Orleans, LA 70112. Tel: 504/589-2031.

Oklahoma City District Office
District Counsel: Tsu Kreidler
Attorney Advisers: John O'Toole and Rosa Lee Morris
U.S. Small Business Administration, 200 N.W. 5th Street, Suite 670, Federal Bldg, Oklahoma City, OK 73102. Tel: 405/231-5053.

San Antonio District Office
District Counsel: G. Ted Ressler
Attorney Adviser: Verne E. Powell
U.S. Small Business Administration, North Star Executive Center, 7400 Blanco Road, Suite 200, San Antonio, TX 78216. Tel: 512/229-4510.

Corpus Christi Branch Office
Branch Counsel: Donald J. Pichinson
U.S. Small Business Administration, 400 Mann Street, Suite 403, Corpus Christi, TX 78401. Tel: 512/888-3302.

REGION VII (KANSAS CITY, MO)

Regional Counsel: Robert Gangwere
U.S. Small Business Administration, 911 Walnut Street, 13th Fl, Kansas City, MO 64106. Tel: 816/426-2658.

District Offices are located in Cedar Rapids, Des Moines, Kansas City, MO, Omaha, St. Louis, and Wichita; with a Branch Office in Springfield, MO.

Cedar Rapids District Office
District Counsel: Harvey E. Sumner
Attorney Adviser: Christa Brusen-Gomez
U.S. Small Business Administration, 373 Collins Road, N.E., Room 100, Cedar Rapids, IA 52402. Tel: 319/399-2571.

Des Moines District Office
District Counsel: Debora A. Anderson
Attorney Advisers: Christy Grundberg and William C. Purdy
U.S. Small Business Administration, 210 Walnut Street, Com-Room 749, Des Moines, IA 50309. Tel: 515/284-4563.

Kansas City District Office
District Counsel: Michael Donnigan
Attorney Advisers: George J. Capra and James P. Landis
U.S. Small Business Administration, 1103 Grand Avenue, 6th Floor, Kansas City, MO 64106. Tel: 816/374-6752.

Omaha District Office
District Counsel: Stephen M. Cramer
Attorney Adviser: Michael T. McAdams
U.S. Small Business Administration, 11145 Mill Valley Road, Omaha, NE 68154. Tel: 402/221-4691.

St. Louis District Office
District Counsel: Ivan I. Schenbert
Attorney Advisers: Lonnie Whittaker and Maria C. Sanchez
U.S. Small Business Administration, 815 Olive Street, Room 242, St. Louis, MO 63101. Tel: 314/539-6600.

Wichita District Office
District Counsel: Ronald L. Nieto
Attorney Adviser: Linda C. McMasters
U.S. Small Business Administration, Main Place Building, 110 East Waterman Street, Wichita, KS 67202. Tel: 316/269-6191.

Springfield Branch Office
Branch Counsel: John H. Reed
U.S. Small Business Administration, 620 South Glenstone, Room 110, Springfield, MO 65802. Tel: 417/864-7670.

REGION VIII (DENVER)

Regional Counsel: George E. DeRoos
U.S. Small Business Administration, 999 18th Street, Suite 701, Denver, CO 80202. Tel: 303/294-7115.

District Offices are located in Casper, Denver, Fargo, Helena, Salt Lake City, and Sioux Falls.

Casper District Office
District Counsel: Mahlon L. Sorensen
U.S. Small Business Administration, Federal Bldg, Room 4001, 100 East B Street, P.O. Box 2839, Casper, WY 82602. Tel: 307/261-5761.

Denver District Office
District Counsel: Robert C. Kelly
Attorney Advisers: Ralph E. Layman, Douglas Vasquez, and Robert Holt
U.S. Small Business Administration, 721 19th Street, P.O. Box 660, Denver, CO 80201. Tel: 303/844-2607.

Fargo District Office
District Counsel: Jack Duis
U.S. Small Business Administration, Federal Office Building, Room 218, P.O. Box 3086, 657 Second Avenue, North, Fargo, ND 58108. Tel: 701/239-5131.

Helena District Office
District Counsel: Donald MacPherson
Attorney Advisers: John O'Keefe and Steve Lobdell
U.S. Small Business Administration, 301 South Park, Room 528, Federal Office Building, Drawer 10054, Helena, MT 59626. Tel: 406/449-5381.

Salt Lake City District Office
District Counsel: William F. Hanson
Attorney Adviser: Nick Newbold
U.S. Small Business Administration, Wallace F. Bennett Federal Building, 125 South State Street, Room 2237, Salt Lake City, UT 84138. Tel: 801/524-3203.

Sioux Falls District Office
District Counsel: E. George Peterson
Attorney Adviser: Jon K. Haverly
U.S. Small Business Administration, Security Building, Suite 101, 101 S. Main Ave, Sioux Falls, SD 57102. Tel: 605/330-4231.

REGION IX (SAN FRANCISCO)

Regional Counsel: Dale N. Retting
Assistant Regional Counsel: Constance M. Kobayashi
U.S. Small Business Administration, 450 Golden Gate Avenue, Box 36044, San Francisco, CA 94102. Tel: 415/556-7780.

District Offices are located in Fresno, Honolulu, Las Vegas, Los Angeles, Phoenix, San Diego, San Francisco, and Santa Ana; with a Branch Office in Sacramento.

Fresno District Office
District Counsel: John J. McGarry
Attorney Adviser: Jeffrey W. Eisinger
U.S. Small Business Administration, 2719 N. Air Fresno Drive, Fresno, CA 93727. Tel: 209/487-5189.

Honolulu District Office
District Counsel: Ann M. Nakagawa
Attorney Advisers: Ron R. Ashlock and Huddy T. Lucas
U.S. Small Business Administration, P.O. Box 50207, 300 Ala Moana, Room 2213, Honolulu, HI 96850. Tel: 808/541-2992.

Las Vegas District Office
District Counsel: Susan Gorrow
U.S. Small Business Administration, 301 East Stewart, Box 7527-Downtown Station, Las Vegas, NV 89125. Tel: 702/388-6611.

Los Angeles District Office
District Counsel: Alberto G. Alvarado
Attorney Advisers: Terry R. Gibson, Kent S. Robinson, Tina M. Toy, David T. Uyekawa, Joel K. Meese, and Lorraine Conn
U.S. Small Business Administration, 330 N. Brand Boulevard, Suite 1200, Glendale, CA 91203. Tel: 213/894-2956.

Phoenix District Office
District Counsel: Nina J. Rivera
Attorney Advisers: Brent C. Applegren and Alan Rabkin
U.S. Small Business Administration, 2005 N. Central Avenue, 5th Floor, Phoenix, AZ 85004. Tel: 602/379-3737.

San Diego District Office
District Counsel: Terrill K. Ashker
Attorney Adviser: Mark S. Raynes
U.S. Small Business Administration, Federal Building, Suite 4-S-29, 880 Front Street, San Diego, CA 92188. Tel: 619/557-7263.

San Francisco District Office
District Counsel: Dana Sohm
Attorney Advisers: Sara M. Purcell and Douglas L. Sanders
U.S. Small Business Administration, 211 Main Street, 4th Floor, San Francisco, CA 94105. Tel: 415/744-6779.

Santa Ana District Office
District Counsel: Dace Pavlovskis
Attorney Adviser: Roy Y. Nakano
U.S. Small Business Administration, 901 W. Civic Center Drive, Suite 160, Santa Ana, CA 92703. Tel: 714/836-2494.

Sacramento Branch Office
Branch Counsel: Michele L. Waldinger
Attorney Adviser: Michael Bayuk
U.S. Small Business Administration, 660 J Street, Suite 215, Sacramento, CA 95814. Tel: 916/551-1434.

REGION X (SEATTLE)

Regional Counsel: Marsha L. Beck
Assistant Regional Counsel: John L. Loesch
U.S. Small Business Administration, 2615 4th Avenue, Room 440, Seattle, WA 98121. Tel: 206/442-7276.

District Offices are located in Anchorage, Boise, Portland, Seattle, and Spokane.

Anchorage District Office
District Counsel: Jon M. DeVore
Attorney Adviser: Karlee A. Gaskill
U.S. Small Business Administration, Room A36, Federal Building Annex, 222 W. 8th Avenue, #67, Anchorage, AK 99513. Tel: 907/271-4815.

Boise District Office
District Counsel: Michael G. Morfitt
U.S. Small Business Administration 1020 Main Street, Suite 290, Boise, ID 83702. Tel: 208/334-1156.

Portland District Office
District Counsel: Peter A. Plumridge
Attorney Adviser: Celeste Kaptur
U. S. Small Business Administration, 222 S.W. Columbia Street, Portland, OR 97201. Tel: 503/326-5226.

Seattle District Office
District Counsel: David F. Morado
Attorney Adviser: Patricia M. Cavanaugh
U.S. Small Business Administration, 915 Second Avenue, Federal Building, Room 1792, Seattle, WA 98174. Tel: 206/442-5534.

Spokane District Office
District Counsel: Patricia L. Johnson
U.S. Small Business Administration, Farm Credit Building, 10th Fl East, W. 601 First Ave, Spokane, WA 99204. Tel: 509/353-2825.

CHIEF COUNSEL FOR ADVOCACY (Room 1012)

The Chief Counsel for Advocacy, along with the Deputy Chief Counsel, serve as the representatives for small business and advance the interests of small business before Federal agencies and Congress. The Chief Counsel participates in regulatory proceedings, contributes to interagency and White House task forces, and testifies before Congress. Among other things, the Office of Advocacy has played an important role in small business tax policy, regulatory relief, and the reauthorization of small business research and attorney fees laws. The attorneys working on issues advocacy who report to the Chief Counsel for Advocacy are located in the Office of Interagency Affairs. They specialize in key issues such as health care, pensions, transportation, environment, procurement, tax, foreign trade, competition, finance, and antitrust. Staff members gather and analyze information from both individual small businesses and trade associations. This information is then shared with regulatory agencies and Congress to assist in their rulemaking and legislative decisions.

(Area Code 202)

Chief Counsel: Mark S. Hayward (Acting) 653-6533

Office of Interagency Affairs
Assistant Chief Counsel for:
Agriculture: Barry Pinellas 634-6115
Entrepreneurial Policy: Patricia McBride ...634-6115
Environment: Kevin L. Bromberg 634-6115

(Area Code 202)

Finance: vacant 634-7613
Labor Policy: Barney Singer 634-6115
Patents: Mark Hankins 634-6115
Pension and Employee Benefit Policy:
Hazel Witte 634-6115
Regulation: vacant 634-6115
Tax: Dan Mastromarco 634-6115
Transportation and Trade: Richard Ramlall ..634-6115

OFFICE OF HEARINGS AND APPEALS (Room 300)

The Office of Hearings and Appeals, located at Washington, D.C. headquarters, has five Administrative Judges, one Administrative Law Judge, and a few attorneys. It handles matters such as appeals involving size and standard industrial classifications (SIC appeals), cases arising under the Administrative Procedure Act, formal employee grievances, and resolution of the Freedom of Information Act and Privacy Act questions.

Online WESTLAW or LEXIS users can access the decisions of the Office of Hearings and Appeals. Copies of a specific decision can be obtained from the Office of Hearings and Appeals, U.S. Small Business Administration, 1441 L Street, N.W., Room 300, Washington, D.C. 20416. Tel: 202/653-7735.

(Area Code 202)

Assistant Administrator: John H. Barnett 653-7735
Chief Administrative Law Judge: Benjamin G. Usher 653-7732
Administrative Law Judges:
Gloria E. Blazsik 653-7732
Michael S. Cole 653-7732
Jane E. Phillips 653-7732

(Area Code 202)

Joseph K. Riotto 653-7732
Elwin H. White 653-7732
Size Appeals Staff Paralegal Specialist:
Mary Ann Smith 653-6500
FOIA/Privacy Act 653-6460

PUBLICATIONS OF INTEREST

The following publications can be obtained by sending a check or money order made payable to the **U.S. Small Business Administration.** Send to SBA-Publications, P.O. Box 30, Denver, CO 80201-0030.

Selecting the Legal Structure for Your Business discusses the various legal structures that a small business can use in setting up its operations. It briefly identifies the types of legal structures and lists the advantages and disadvantages of each. Price: 50 cents.

Curtailing Crime - Inside and Out discusses positive steps that can be taken to curb crime. They include safeguards against employee dishonesty and ways to control shoplifting. In addition, this publication includes measures to outwit bad check passing and ways to prevent burglary and robbery. Price: $1.00.

A Small Business Guide to Computer Security helps small businesses understand the nature of computer security risks and offers timely advice on how to control them. Price: $1.00.

Market Overseas with U.S. Government Help offers ideas on programs available to help small businesses break into the world of exporting. Price: $1.00.

Introduction to Patents offers some basic facts about patents to help clarify your rights. It discusses the relationships among a business, an inventor and the Patent and Trademark Office to ensure protection of your product and to avoid or win infringement suits. Price: 50 cents.

SMALL BUSINESS ADMINISTRATION
KEY LEGAL AUTHORITIES

General Regulations: 13 C.F.R. Parts 101-145 (1989).
Rules of Practice and Procedure: 13 C.F.R. Parts 103 & 134 (1989).

Small Business Act, as amended, 15 U.S.C. 631 et seq.--established the Small Business Administration and authorized assistance, government set-aside, and disaster loan programs for small business.
Legislative History: 1958 U.S. Code Cong. & Admin. News 3071; 1980 U.S. Code Cong. & Admin. News 2340; 1984 U.S. Code Cong. & Admin. News 614.

Small Business Investment Act of 1958, as amended, 15 U.S.C. 661 et seq.--authorizes the creation of Small Business Investment Companies (SBICs), which are designed to provide financing for small businesses, and directs the Small Business Administration to regulate SBICs.
Legislative History: 1958 U.S. Code Cong. & Admin. News 3678; 1965 U.S. Code Cong. & Admin. News 2614; 1966 U.S. Code Cong. & Admin. News 4199; 1976 U.S. Code Cong. & Admin. News 1166.

Domestic Volunteer Service Act of 1973, as amended, 42 U.S.C. 2991 et seq.--establishes the Service Core of Retired Executives (SCORE) and the Active Corps of Executives (ACE), which are designed to provide consulting advice to small businesses, and directs the Small Business Administration to administer these programs.
Legislative History: 1973 U.S. Code Cong. & Admin. News 2155.

Exec. Order No. 12138, as amended, 3 C.F.R., 1979 Comp., p. 393, "Creating a National Women's Business Enterprise Policy and Prescribing Arrangements for Developing, Coordinating, and Implementing a National Program for Women's Business Enterprise."

THE SMITHSONIAN INSTITUTION

Arts and Industries Building, 900 Jefferson Drive, S.W.
Washington, D.C. 20560

DESCRIPTION: The Smithsonian Institution is an independent trust establishment which performs fundamental research; publishes the results of studies, explorations, and investigations; preserves for study and reference over 100 million items of scientific, cultural, and historical interest; maintains exhibits representative of the arts, American history, technology, aeronautics and space exploration, and natural history; participates in the international exchange of learned publications; and engages in programs of education and national and international cooperative research and training. The Institution is supported by its trust endowments and gifts, grants and contracts, and funds appropriated to it by Congress.

Some of the Smithsonian's well-known activities include the Arthur M. Sackler Gallery, the Freer Gallery of Art, the Hirshhorn Museum and Sculpture Garden, the National Air and Space Museum, the National Museum of American Art, the National Museum of American History, the National Museum of Natural History, the National Portrait Gallery, the National Zoo, the John F. Kennedy Center for the Performing Arts, the National Gallery of Art, and the Woodrow Wilson International Center for Scholars.

Area Code (202)

Secretary: Robert McC. Adams 357-1846
Procurement Information 287-3331
Public Affairs 357-2700
Fraud Hot Line 287-3676
Facsimile 786-2515

(Area Code 202)

Freedom of Information Act/Privacy Act Office 357-2627
Although the Freedom of Information Act and Privacy Act guidelines do not apply to the Smithsonian Institution, the Public Affairs office may be contacted for general information.

OFFICE OF THE GENERAL COUNSEL (Room H-400)

Smithsonian Institution Building (The Castle) 1000 Jefferson Dr, S.W., Washington, D.C.

The Office of the General Counsel advises on legal matters involved in the administration of the Institution; coordinates and oversees the conduct of litigation and other adversarial proceedings to which the Institution is a party; reviews administrative claims arising out of Smithsonian operations; and generally monitors all aspects of Smithsonian administration for legal implications vis-a-vis developments in the law.

As the legal arm of the Institution, the Office of the General Counsel is responsible for ensuring the legal soundness of Smithsonian operations. Areas of legal responsibility include:

* the fiduciary obligations and responsibilities of the U.S. in accepting the Smithson trust and the powers granted the Institution by its enabling charter;
* the trustee duty and relationship inherent in the administration of Smithsonian programs;
* fiscal policies and procedures required for Federally appropriated funds as well as trust principles applicable to the Institution's endowment funds;
* employment policies and procedures involving the civil service laws, civil rights laws, labor laws, and standards of conduct;
* national and international legal requirements, procedures, and ramifications pertinent to scientific field studies and research, and to the importation and exportation of exhibitions, art works, and cultural property;
* the impact on Smithsonian activities of environmental and endangered species laws;
* contract awards and agreements, and claims and disputes arising therefrom;
* collections acquisition management regarding purchases, gifts, loans, and bequests;
* Federal and state taxes, and intellectual property rights arising out of publishing, performing arts, and collection acquisition activities; and
* real and personal property transactions.

These matters require the full spectrum of legal activities, from drafting a routine legal document to negotiating contracts, agreements, or settlements involving large sums, performing expensive legal research, formulating Institution-wide legal procedures, and conducting pre-trial investigative and discovery proceedings for pending litigation.

Area Code (202)

General Counsel: Peter G. Powers 357-2583
Associate General Counsel: George S. Robinson 357-2583
Associate General Counsel: Alan D. Ullberg 357-2583

John F. Kennedy Center for the Performing Arts
General Counsel: Harry C. McPherson Jr 371-6026

(Area Code 202)

National Gallery of Art
Secretary and General Counsel: Philip Jessup Jr 842-6363
Associate General Counsel: Elizabeth A. Croog 842-6363

OFFICE OF INSPECTOR GENERAL (Room 7600)

The mission of the Office of Inspector General (OIG) is to provide policy direction for and to conduct, supervise, and coordinate audits and investigations relating the to programs and operations of the Smithsonian; to promote economy, efficiency and effectiveness; and to prevent and detect fraud and abuse. While other units of the Smithsonian may conduct a variety of investigations appropriate to their programmatic responsibilities, the Inspector General (IG) may enter into and/or take charge of any Smithsonian investigation when in his or her judgment it falls within the IG's investigative responsibilities. The IG reports all violations of Federal criminal law to the Attorney General.

(Area Code 202)

Inspector General: Thomas D. Blair 287-3326
Assistant Inspector General for Audits:
Jerry L. Chandler (Acting) 287-3326

(Area Code 202)

Assistant Inspector General for Investigations:
Richard H. Cook (Acting) 287-3017
Facsimile 287-3017

SMITHSONIAN INSTITUTION
KEY LEGAL AUTHORITIES

General Agency Regulations: 36 C.F.R. Parts 504-530 (1989).

Preservation of American Antiquities: 43 C.F.R. Part 3 (1989).

Acts, Aug. 10, 1846, c. 178, secs. 1 et seq., 9 Stat. 102, 20 U.S.C. 41-67--established the Smithsonian Institution to increase and diffuse knowledge among men and to administer the James Smithson bequest.

Smithsonian Institution Special Policing Act, 40 U.S.C. 193n-193x--governs policing of Smithsonian buildings and grounds and prohibits certain activities thereon.
Legislative History: 1951 U.S. Code Cong. & Admin. News 2433; 1964 U.S. Code Cong. & Admin. News 2650.

Anthropological Research Act, 20 U.S.C. 69-70--authorizes the Smithsonian Institution to undertake independently, and cooperate in, Native American anthropological research and excavate and preserve archeological remains.

National Gallery of Art Act, as amended, 20 U.S.C. 71 et seq.--established the National Gallery of Art under the Smithsonian Institution in order to house a national collection of fine arts.

National Portrait Gallery Act, as amended, 20 U.S.C. 75a-75g--established the National Portrait Gallery under the Smithsonian Institution to function as a free public museum for the exhibition and study of portraiture and statuary depicting men and women who have made significant contributions to U.S. history, development, and culture.
Legislative History: 1962 U.S. Code Cong. & Admin. News 1601.

20 U.S.C. 76h-76q--established the John F. Kennedy Center for the Performing Arts under the Smithsonian Institution.

20 U.S.C. 76aa-76ee--established the Joseph H. Hirshhorn Museum and Sculpture Garden to be administered by the Smithsonian Institution.

20 U.S.C. 77-77d--established the National Air and Space Museum under the Smithsonian Institution.
Legislative History: 1966 U.S. Code Cong. & Admin. News 2540.

20 U.S.C. 78-78a--parallels the Anthropological Research Act for paleontological research.
Legislative History: 1949 U.S. Code Cong. Service 1927.

20 U.S.C. 79-79e--gives the Smithsonian Institution control over scientific studies in the Canal Zone Biological Area.
Legislative History: 1965 U.S. Code Cong. & Admin. News 3665.

NOTE: Authority to administer various other museums et al. may be found in 20 U.S.C. 41 et seq.

TENNESSEE VALLEY AUTHORITY

400 West Summit Hill Drive
Knoxville, TN 37902

DESCRIPTION: The Tennessee Valley Authority (TVA) is an independent corporate agency of the Federal Government which was created by Congress in 1933 for the purpose of conserving and developing the natural and human resources of the Tennessee River basin. In addition to operating the nation's largest electric power system, TVA conducts a multitude of innovative programs for social, economic, agricultural, environmental, and energy development.

(Area Code 615)

Chairman: Marvin T. Runyon 632-3554
Purchasing Information (Chattanooga) 751-2624
Small and Disadvantaged Business Utilization Office ... 751-6267
Freedom of Information Act/Privacy Act Office 632-6000
Publications/Public Information 632-6000
Library 632-3464

Washington, D.C. Office .... (202) 479-4412
Inspector General's Hot Line:
  Knoxville Area 632-3550
  Tennessee (except Knoxville) .... (800) 423-3071
  Continental U.S., HI, AK .... (800) 323-3835
Facsimile 632-6634

OFFICE OF THE INSPECTOR GENERAL

The Office of Inspector General (OIG) is responsible for reporting to the TVA Board of Directors and Congress on the overall efficiency, effectiveness, and economy of all TVA programs and operations; on TVA efforts to prevent and detect waste, fraud, and abuse; and on investigations of employee concerns. The Inspector General's function is advisory and no management decisions are made by the incumbent. Once findings have been reported or recommendations have been made, TVA management must decide on any corrective actions.

(Area Code 615)

Inspector General: Norman A. Zigrossi 632-4765
Counsel to the Inspector General: James B. Hall 632-4329
Assistant Inspector General (Investigative Operations):
  James H. Yelvington 632-7720

(Area Code 615)

Fraud Investigations Manager: George T. Prosser 632-3956
General Investigations Manager: Robert G. Carter 632-3325
Internal Investigations Manager: Ron W. Taylor 632-3414
Nuclear Investigations Manager: G. Donald Hickman 632-3979

OFFICE OF THE VICE PRESIDENT AND GENERAL COUNSEL

The Office of the General Counsel handles all of the agency's legal work and has exclusive control over its litigation. Because TVA is both a Federal agency and a largely self-financed corporation, attorneys are called upon to practice in many diverse fields.

Since TVA has independent litigating authority, its trial docket consists of several hundred cases pending before Federal and state courts of all levels, as well as proceedings before the NRC, EPA, ICC, MSPB, and other administrative bodies. Cases include matters involving admiralty, antitrust, RICO, bankruptcy, EEO/affirmative action, constitutional law, eminent domain, environmental laws and regulations, permits, licenses, procurement contracts, personnel, the Freedom of Information Act, labor relations, personal injury and property damage, patents, and power contracts and rates. Litigation involving significant legal issues and/or millions of dollars is commonplace.

The Office of General Counsel also analyzes all proposed Federal legislation and legislation in six Tennessee Valley states to determine possible effects on TVA programs, prepares testimony on pending legislation, and prepares legislation for introduction in Congress.

As attorneys representing the largest nuclear electric generating system in the U.S., members of the Office of the General Counsel handle all legal aspects of NRC licensing, environmental impact statements, and other legal issues arising during the construction and operation of nuclear power plants.

Because TVA generally acts as its own architect-engineer and general contractor on construction projects, the legal staff is called upon to handle a wide variety of work in procurement and contract administration. The legal staff also participates in the administration of the thousands of contracts which TVA has in effect at any given time, and in the negotiation and settlement of any claims which arise under them. In addition, mineral law is a major area of work in connection with TVA's holding of extensive coal and uranium reserves in the TVA area and in the Far West.

Other areas of current interest in which the Office of General Counsel is active include urban planning, land use planning, navigation, minority economic development, and outdoor recreation.

(Area Code 615)

Vice President and General Counsel:
Edward S. Christenbury 632-2241
Deputy General Counsel: James E. Fox 632-4151
Associate General Counsel (General and Contracts):
William L. Osteen Jr 632-4142
Assistant General Counsel for:
General and Complex Litigation: Edwin W. Small 632-3021

(Area Code 615)

Legislation, Budget, and Congressional Relations:
Lynn G. Morehous 632-3081
General Litigation and Claims: Robert C. Glinski 632-2577
EEO, Labor, and Special Assignments Litigation:
Justin M. Schwamm Sr 632-2061
Nuclear: Douglas R. Nichols 632-6627
Personnel and General: Maureen H. Dunn 632-4131
Power: John L. Dugger 632-4591

TENNESSEE VALLEY AUTHORITY
KEY LEGAL AUTHORITIES

Regulations: 18 C.F.R. Parts 1300-1313 (1989).

Tennessee Valley Authority Act of 1933, as amended, 16 U.S.C. 831-831dd--established the Tennessee Valley Authority (TVA) to maintain and operate U.S. properties in Muscle Shoals, Alabama, improve navigation on the Tennessee River, and for flood control in the Tennessee and Mississippi River basins.

Archeological Resources Protection Act of 1979, as amended, 16 U.S.C. 470aa-470ll--provides uniform procedures to be followed by all Federal land managers in providing protection for archeological resources located on public and Indian lands of the U.S.
Legislative History: 1979 U.S. Code Cong. & Admin. News 1709; 1988 U.S. Code Cong. & Admin. News 3983.

UNITED STATES INFORMATION AGENCY

301 Fourth Street, S.W.
Washington, D.C. 20547

DESCRIPTION: The United States Information Agency (USIA) is responsible for the U.S. Government's overseas information and cultural programs, including the Voice of America and the Fulbright scholarship program. The Agency, which is known overseas as the U.S. Information Service (USIS), conducts U.S. overseas informational, educational, and cultural affairs programs. It engages in a wide variety of communication activities--from academic and cultural exchange to press, radio, TV, film, seminar, library, and cultural center programs abroad. The purpose of these activities is to strengthen foreign understanding and support for U.S. policies and actions; counter attempts to distort U.S. policies and objectives; promote and administer educational and cultural exchange programs to bring about greater understanding between the people of the United States and the peoples of the world; assist in the development of a comprehensive policy on the free flow of information and international communications; and conduct negotiations on information, educational, and cultural exchanges with other governments.

(Area Code 202)

Director: Bruce S. Gelb 619-4742
Procurement Information 485-6414
Public Liaison 619-4355
Publications Information 619-4257
Inspector General's Hot Line 401-7202
Facsimile....................................554-0836

Freedom of Information Act/Privacy Act Office 619-5499
Requests must be in writing. Search fees are $20.00 and $36.00 per hour for supervisory personnel, and $10.00 per hour for clerical personnel. Printing charges are 15 cents per page. By congressional mandate, program materials cannot be distributed in the United States. Printing charges for Privacy Act requests are 15 cents per page.

(Area Code 202)

Library (Room 135) 619-5947
The library is open Monday through Friday from 8:15 AM until 5:00 PM. Permission from the Public Liaison is needed in order to use the library. There is no charge for copying materials. Loans may be arranged through the Interlibrary Loan Program.

OFFICE OF INSPECTOR GENERAL (Room 1100)

The Office of Inspector General (OIG) conducts, supervises, and coordinates audits, program reviews and evaluations, and investigative inquiries relating to programs and operations of the Agency. In addition, the Inspector General recommends policies to promote economy, efficiency, and effectiveness, and to prevent and detect fraud and abuse in the administration of the Agency's programs and operations. The Inspector General also reports to the Attorney General suspected violations of Federal criminal law and operates the OIG Hotline for receiving employee complaints.

(Area Code 202)

Inspector General: J. Richard Berman (Acting) 401-7931

OFFICE OF THE GENERAL COUNSEL (Room 700)

The Office of the General Counsel serves USIA both domestically and internationally in a number of ways. In addition to twelve attorneys (a General Counsel, a Deputy General Counsel, and ten Assistant General Counsels), it also encompasses a Freedom of Information Act/Privacy Act Unit and an Exchange Visitor Facilitative Staff, and provides copyright clearance services.

The legal work is extremely varied in nature, including such matters as personnel and labor relations, procurement, litigation, administrative rulemaking, taxation, ethics, cultural property, international educational and cultural exchange, and telecommunications.

The Exchange Visitor Facilitative Staff occupies a highly visible role within the Office. It designates programs as promoting international educational and cultural exchange, thereby authorizing them direct access to the J-1 visa, and it provides the Immigration and Naturalization Service with recommendations as to whether to waive the two-year home residency requirement applicable to most foreigners temporarily in the United States on such a visa.

(Area Code 202)

General Counsel: Alberto J. Mora 619-4979
Deputy General Counsel: R. Wallace Stuart 619-4979
Assistant General Counsels:
- Louisa Alvarez 619-6829
- Carlyle M. Dunaway 619-6829
- Carol B. Epstein 619-6827

(Area Code 202)

- Jacqueline P. Higgs 619-6827
- Merry A. Lynn 619-6829
- Lorie J. Nirenberg 619-6975
- Peter J. Ritenburg 619-6827
- Richard H. Swan 619-5078
- Richard S. Werksman 619-6975

Copyright Office Rights Clearance Specialist: (Area Code 202)
Constance Jordan 619-6501
Exchange Visitor Program Services Director:
Mary D. Hitt 401-7809
Program Designation Branch Chief: Ann St. Denis 401-7809

(Area Code 202)
Waiver Review Officers:
Jean L. Perelli 401-7962
M. Jean Peters 401-7962
Margaret A. Wilson 401-7962

UNITED STATES INFORMATION AGENCY
KEY LEGAL AUTHORITIES

Regulations:

General Agency Regulations: 22 C.F.R. Parts 500-530 (1989).
USIA Acquisition Regulations: 48 C.F.R. Parts 1901-1953 (1988).

U.S. Information and Educational Exchange Act of 1948, as amended, 22 U.S.C. 1431-1442--established the U.S. Information Agency (USIA) to promote a better understanding of the U.S. in other countries and increase mutual understanding.
Legislative History: 1948 U.S.Code Cong. Service 1011; 1961 U.S. Code Cong. & Admin. News 2759; 1982 U.S. Code Cong. & Admin. News 651.

Mutual Education and Cultural Exchange Act of 1961, as amended, 8 U.S.C. 1101, 1104, 1182, 1258 and 22 U.S.C. 2451-2460--authorizes educational and cultural exchanges under USIA administration.
Legislative History: 1961 U.S. Code Cong. & Admin. News 2759.

National Endowment for Democracy Act, 22 U.S.C. 4411 et seq.--established the National Endowment as a private, non-profit corporation to encourage free and democratic institutions throughout the world through private sector initiatives; strengthen democratic election processes abroad; and run exchange programs under USIA grants.
Legislative History: 1983 U.S. Code Cong. & Admin. News 1484.

Beirut Agreement of 1948, 17 U.S.T. 1578 (T.I.A.S. 6116)--as implemented by Pub.L. 89-634 (1966) and Exec. Order 11311, designates the U.S. Information Agency to administer U.S. compliance with and obligations under the agreement for the free flow of audio-visual materials across national boundaries.

Legislative Branch

UNITED STATES CONGRESS

(Area Code 202)

Capitol Hill Operators:
House....................................225-3121
Senate....................................224-3121

Federal Register, Statutes Unit 523-5230
(Public Law and statutory references, Executive Orders, etc)

Federal Register, Public Laws Update Service 523-6641
(Information on Public Laws recently signed, prior to inclusion by the Statutes Unit)

Federal Register, General Information and Finding Aids 523-5227
(Assistance on locating information in the Federal Register and citations for the Code of Federal Regulations) The office will copy up to 10 pages of material and send it to you with a bill (35 cents per page). They will also identify the Federal Depository Library nearest you so you can go use the material there.

Legislative Information (LEGIS) 225-1772
(Provides status of House and Senate legislation, including floor action, amendments, etc.) **LEGIS** can be accessed only by those who work for Congress. All others have to contact one of their Senators or their Representative to have him/her access the information on their behalf.

U.S. Senate:

Democratic Cloakroom (schedule for floor action)........224-4691
Taped recording on floor action.......................224-8541

(Area Code 202)

Republican Cloakroom (schedule for floor action) 224-6391
Taped recording on floor action.......................224-8601

Senate Document Room (Room SH-B04) 224-7860
Copies of bills, reports, documents, Public Laws, etc., can be picked up in person or copies can be sent to you following a written request (please enclose a self-addressed mailing label).

U.S. House of Representatives:

Democratic Cloakroom (schedule for floor action).......225-7330
Taped recording on floor action.......................225-7400
Taped recording on legislative program...............225-1600

Republican Cloakroom (schedule for floor action).......225-7350
Taped recording on floor action.......................225-7430
Taped recording on legislative program 225-2020

House Document Room (Room H-226 Capitol) 225-3456
Copies of bills, reports, documents, Public Laws, etc., can be picked up in person or copies can be sent to you following a written request (please enclose a self-addressed mailing label).

House Library (Room B-18 Cannon House Office Building) 225-0462
The library is open to the public from 9:00 AM until 5:30 PM, Monday through Friday, for research/reference work only, primarily research on legislative histories and bills.

STATE DELEGATIONS

ALABAMA

Zip Codes:
U.S. Senate..20510
U.S. House of Representative 20515

Note: When a Senate or House staff does not include a Legislative Director, we have listed here the name of a Legislative Assistant (generally the first one listed alphabetically.)

(Area Code 202)

U.S. SENATE

Howell T. Heflin (D-AL)
SH-728 Hart Senate Office Building.....................224-4124
FAX...224-3149
Chief Policy Adviser/Legislative Director: Mansel Long

Richard C. Shelby (D-AL) (Area Code 202)
SH-313 Hart Senate Office Building.....................224-5744
FAX...224-3416
Administrative Assistant/Legislative Director:
Thomas N. Meriwether

U.S. House of Representatives
(Listed by Congressional District)

1. Sonny Callahan (R-AL)
1232 Longworth House Office Building..................225-4931
FAX...225-0562
Legislative Director: Nancy Tippins

(Area Code 202)

2. William L. Dickinson (R-AL)
2406 Rayburn House Office Building......................225-2901
Chief Legislative Assistant: Bill Stiers

3. Glen Browder (D-AL)
1630 Longworth House Office Building..................225-3261
FAX..225-9020
Legislative Assistant: David Plunkett

4. Tom Bevill (D-AL)
2302 Rayburn House Office Building 225-4876
Administrative Assistant/Legislative Assistant:
Don Smith

5. Ronnie G. Flippo (D-AL)
2334 Rayburn House Office Building 225-4801
FAX..225-4392
Administrative Assistant/Legislative Director:
Frank Toohey

6. Ben Erdreich (D-AL)
439 Cannon House Office Building 225-4921
Legislative Director: Laurie Harrison

7. Claude Harris (D-AL)
1009 Longworth House Office Building 225-2665
FAX..225-0175
Legislative Director: Kathy Smith

ALASKA

Zip Codes:
U.S. Senate...20510
U.S. House of Representative 20515

Note: When a Senate or House staff does not include a Legislative Director, we have listed here the name of a Legislative Assistant (generally the first one listed alphabetically.)

(Area Code 202)

U.S. Senate

Ted Stevens (R-AK)
SH-522 Hart Senate Office Building......................224-3004
Legislative Director: Svend Brandt-Erichsen

Frank Murkowski (R-AK)
SH-709 Hart Senate Office Building......................224-6665
Legislative Director: Gregg Renkes

U.S. House of Representatives
(listed by Congressional District)

1. Don Young (R-AK)
2331 Rayburn House Office Building......................225-5765
Legislative Assistant: Eric Namrow

ARIZONA

Zip Codes:
U.S. Senate...20510
U.S. House of Representative 20515

Note: When a Senate or House staff does not include a Legislative Director, we have listed here the name of a Legislative Assistant (generally the first one listed alphabetically.)

(Area Code 202)

U.S. Senate

Dennis DeConcini (D-AZ)
SH-328 Hart Senate Office Building......................224-4521
FAX..224-3464
Legislative Director: Mary Hawkins

John McCain (R-AZ)
SR-111 Russell Senate Office Building.................224-2235
Administrative Assistant/Legislative Director:
Christopher Koch
Legislative Counsel: Marta Aguirre

U.S. House of Representatives
(Listed by Congressional District)

1. John J. Rhodes III (R-AZ)
412 Cannon House Office Building........................225-2635
FAX..225-0985
Legislative Director: Jim Huska

2. Morris K. Udall (D-AZ)
235 Cannon House Office Building........................225-4065
Legislative Director: Anne Scott

3. Bob Stump (R-AZ)
211 Cannon House Office Building........................225-4576
FAX..225-6328
Administrative Assistant: Lisa Jackson

4. Jon Kyl (R-AZ)
313 Cannon House Office Building.......................225-3361
FAX..225-1143
Senior Legislative Assistant: Tim Glazewski

5. Jim Kolbe (R-AZ)
410 Cannon House Office Building........................225-2542
FAX..225-0378
Legislative Director: Stefanie Reiser

ARKANSAS

Zip Codes:
U.S. Senate 20510
U.S. House of Representative 20515

Note: When a Senate or House staff does not include a Legislative Director, we have listed here the name of a Legislative Assistant (generally the first one listed alphabetically.)

(Area Code 202)

U.S. Senate

Dale Bumpers (D-AR)
SD-229 Dirksen Senate Office Building 224-4843
Legislative Director: Paula Casey

David Pryor (D-AR)
SR-267 Russell Senate Office Building 224-2353
Legislative Director: Ed Quick

U.S. House of Representatives
(Listed by Congressional District)

1. Bill Alexander (D-AR) (Area Code 202)
233 Cannon House Office Building 225-4076
FAX 225-6182
Legislative Director: Dorothy Thomas

2. Tommy F. Robinson (R-AR)
1541 Longworth House Office Building 225-2506
FAX 225-9273
Legislative Director: David Huebler

3. John Paul Hammerschmidt (R-AR)
2110 Rayburn House Office Building 225-4301
Legislative Assistant: Randi Fredholm

4. Beryl F. Anthony Jr (D-AR)
1117 Longworth House Office Building 225-3772
FAX 225-3646
Administrative Assistant/Legislative Assistant: Mark Lowman

CALIFORNIA

Zip Codes:
U.S. Senate 20510
U.S. House of Representative 20515

Note: When a Senate or House staff does not include a Legislative Director, we have listed here the name of a Legislative Assistant (generally the first one listed alphabetically.)

(Area Code 202)

U.S. Senate

Alan Cranston (D-CA)
SH-112 Hart Senate Office Building 224-3553
Legislative Counsel: Susanne Martinez

Pete Wilson (R-CA)
SH-720 Hart Senate Office Building 224-3841
Legislative Director: Alexander S. Mathews
Legislative Assistant/Counsel: Ira H. Goldman

U.S. House of Representatives
(Listed by Congressional District)

1. Douglas H. Bosco (D-CA)
225 Cannon House Office Building 225-3311
FAX 225-5577
Legislative Director: Jason Liles

2. Wally Herger (R-CA)
1108 Longworth House Office Building 225-3076
Legislative Director: Roger Mahan

3. Robert T. Matsui (D-CA)
2419 Rayburn House Office Building 225-7163
FAX 225-0566
Legislative Assistant: Azar Kattan

4. Vic Fazio (D-CA)
2113 Rayburn House Office Building 225-5716
FAX 225-0354
Legislative Director: Roger Gwinn

5. Nancy Pelosi (D-CA)
1005 Longworth House Office Building 225-4965
FAX 225-8259
Legislative Director: Carolyn Bartholomew

6. Barbara Boxer (D-CA)
307 Cannon House Office Building 225-5161
Legislative Assistant: Josh Kardon

7. George Miller (D-CA)
2228 Rayburn House Office Building 225-2095
Administrative Assistant/Legislative Director:
John Lawrence

8. Ronald V. Dellums (D-CA)
2136 Rayburn House Office Building 225-2661
FAX 225-9817
Legislative Director: George Withers
Special Counsel: Robert Brauer

9. Fortney H. "Pete" Stark (D-CA)
1125 Longworth House Office Building 225-5065
Legislative Assistant: Perry Plumart
Tax Attorney: Anne Raffaelli

10. Don Edwards (D-CA)
2307 Rayburn House Office Building 225-3072
Legislative Director: Marie McGlone

11. Tom Lantos (D-CA)
1526 Longworth House Office Building 225-3531
Legislative Assistant: Alexandra Arriaga

12. Tom Campbell (R-CA) (Area Code 202)
516 Cannon House Office Building........................225-5411
FAX...225-5944
Legislative Director: Tom Gann

13. Norman Y. Mineta (D-CA)
2350 Rayburn House Office Building......................225-2631
Legislative Director: Suzanne Sullivan

14. Norman D. Shumway (R-CA)
1203 Longworth House Office Building....................225-2511
FAX...225-5444
Legislative Assistant: Paul Anderson

15. Gary A. Condit (D-CA)
1729 Longworth House Office Building....................225-6131
FAX...225-0819
Legislative Director: Dee Dee Moosekian

16. Leon E. Panetta (D-CA)
339 Cannon House Office Building........................225-2861
Legislative Aide: Emily Beizer

17. Charles Pashayan Jr (R-CA)
203 Cannon House Office Building........................225-3341
FAX...225-9308
Legislative Assistant: Chris Mardesich

18. Richard H. Lehman (D-CA)
1319 Longworth House Office Building....................225-4540
Legislative Director: Melanie Beller

19. Robert J. Lagomarsino (R-CA)
2332 Rayburn House Office Building......................225-3601
Legislative Director: Matthew A. Reynolds

20. William M. Thomas (R-CA)
2402 Rayburn House Office Building......................225-2915
Legislative Director: Bob Winters

21. Elton Gallegly (R-CA)
107 Cannon House Office Building........................225-5811
Legislative Director: Ed Cook

22. Carlos J. Moorhead (R-CA)
2346 Rayburn House Office Building......................225-4176
FAX...226-1279
Legislative Assistant: Dave Joergenson

23. Anthony C. Beilenson (D-CA)
1025 Longworth House Office Building....................225-5911
Legislative Assistant: Kaye Edwards Davis

24. Henry A. Waxman (D-CA)
2418 Rayburn House Office Building......................225-3976
FAX...225-4099
Legislative Assistant: Patricia Delgado

25. Edward R. Roybal (D-CA)
2211 Rayburn House Office Building......................225-6235
FAX...226-1251
Legislative Assistant: Irene Bueno

26. Howard L. Berman (D-CA)
137 Cannon House Office Building........................225-4695
Legislative Director: Bari Schwartz

27. Mel Levine (D-CA)
132 Cannon House Office Building........................225-6451
FAX...225-6975
Legislative Assistant: Jon Cowan

28. Julian C. Dixon (D-CA)
2400 Rayburn House Office Building......................225-7084
FAX...225-4091
Legislative Director: Gwen Brown

29. Augustus F. Hawkins (D-CA) (Area Code 202)
2371 Rayburn House Office Building......................225-2201
FAX...225-7854
Legislative Assistant: Gail Perry

30. Matthew G. Martinez (D-CA)
240 Cannon House Office Building........................225-5464
FAX...225-5467
Administrative Assistant/Legislative Director:
Maxine Grant

31. Mervyn M. Dymally (D-CA)
1717 Longworth House Office Building....................225-5425
FAX...225-6847
Legislative Director: Marwan Burgan
Counsel: Marvajo Camp

32. Glenn M. Anderson (D-CA)
2329 Rayburn House Office Building......................225-6676
FAX...225-1597
Legislative Director: Steve Johnson

33. David Dreier (R-CA)
411 Cannon House Office Building........................225-2305
Legislative Director: Vince Randazzo

34. Esteban Edward Torres (D-CA)
1740 Longworth House Office Building....................225-5256
FAX...225-9711
Legislative Coordinator: Nancy Alcalde

35. Jerry Lewis (R-CA)
2312 Rayburn House Office Building......................225-5861
FAX...225-6498
Legislative Director: Doc Syers

36. George E. Brown Jr (D-CA)
2188 Rayburn House Office Building......................225-6161
Legislative Assistant: Bill Grady

37. Al McCandless (R-CA)
435 Cannon House Office Building........................225-5330
FAX...226-1040
Legislative Director: William P. Binzel

38. Robert K. Dornan (R-CA)
301 Cannon House Office Building........................225-2965
FAX...225-3694
Senior Legislative Assistant: Jerry Gideon

39. William E. Dannemeyer (R-CA)
2351 Rayburn House Office Building......................225-4111
Legislative Assistant: Mark Benhard
Legislative Counsel: Mike Franc

40. C. Christopher Cox (R-CA)
510 Cannon House Office Building........................225-5611
FAX...225-9177
Legislative Director: Jan Fujiwara

41. Bill Lowery (R-CA)
2433 Rayburn House Office Building......................225-3201
Legislative Assistant: Jean Gingras

42. Dana Rohrabacher (R-CA)
1017 Longworth House Office Building....................225-2415
FAX...225-0145
Administrative Assistant/Legislative Director:
Richard T. Dykema

43. Ron Packard (R-CA)
434 Cannon House Office Building........................225-3906
FAX...225-0134
Legislative Director: Alana Evert

44. Jim Bates (D-CA) (Area Code 202)
224 Cannon House Office Building........................225-5452
FAX..225-2558
Legislative Director: Kristine Edmunds

45. Duncan L. Hunter (R-CA) (Area Code 202)
133 Cannon House Office Building........................225-5672
FAX..225-0235
Legislative Director: Victoria Middleton

COLORADO

Zip Codes:
U.S. Senate...20510
U.S. House of Representative 20515

Note: When a Senate or House staff does not include a Legislative Director, we have listed here the name of a Legislative Assistant (generally the first one listed alphabetically.)

(Area Code 202)

U.S. Senate

William L. Armstrong (R-CO)
SH-528 Hart Senate Office Building......................224-5941
Legislative Director: David Jensen

Timothy E. Wirth (D-CO)
SR-380 Russell Senate Office Building...................224-5852
Legislative Director: Rochelle Dornatt

U.S. House of Representatives
(Listed by Congressional District)

1. Patricia Schroeder (D-CO)
2208 Rayburn House Office Building......................225-4431
FAX..225-5842
Senior Legislative Assistant: Andrea Pamfilis-Camp

2. David E. Skaggs (D-CO)
1709 Longworth House Office Building....................225-2161
Senior Legislative Assistant: Jonathan Lindgren

3. Ben Nighthorse Campbell (D-CO)
1724 Longworth House Office Building....................225-4761
Legislative Director: Dan McAuliffe

4. Hank Brown (R-CO)
1424 Longworth House Office Building....................225-4676
FAX..225-8630
Chief Legislative Assistant: Roxie Burris

5. Joel Hefley (R-CO)
222 Cannon House Office Building........................225-4422
FAX..225-1942
Legislative Assistant: David Emerick

6. Dan Schaefer (R-CO)
1317 Longworth House Office Building....................225-7882
FAX..225-7885
Legislative Director: David Eck

CONNECTICUT

Zip Codes:
U.S. Senate...20510
U.S. House of Representative 20515

Note: When a Senate or House staff does not include a Legislative Director, we have listed here the name of a Legislative Assistant (generally the first one listed alphabetically.)

(Area Code 202)

U.S. Senate

Christopher J. Dodd (D-CT)
SR-444 Russell Senate Office Building...................224-2823
Legislative Director: Peter Kinzler

Joseph I. Lieberman (D-CT)
SH-502 Hart Senate Office Building......................224-4041
FAX..224-9750
Legislative Director/Chief Counsel: William B. Bonvillian

U.S. House of Representatives
(Listed by Congressional District)

1. Barbara B. Kennelly (D-CT)
204 Cannon House Office Building........................225-2265
FAX..225-1031
Legislative Assistant: Patricia Kery

2. Sam Gejdenson (D-CT)
1410 Longworth House Office Building....................225-2076
FAX..225-4977
Administrative Assistant/Legislative Director:
Perry Pockros

3. Bruce A. Morrison (D-CT)
330 Cannon House Office Building........................225-3661
Legislative Director: Lori Valencia Greene

4. Christopher Shays (R-CT)
1531 Longworth House Office Building....................225-5541
FAX..225-9629
Legislative Director: Betsy Wright Hawkings

5. John G. Rowland (R-CT)
329 Cannon House Office Building........................225-3822
FAX..225-5085
Legislative Director: Hugh H. Marthinsen

6. Nancy L. Johnson (R-CT)
119 Cannon House Office Building........................225-4476
FAX..225-4488
Legislative Director: Ronald Lefrancois

DELAWARE

Zip Codes:
U.S. Senate..20510
U.S. House of Representative 20515

Note: When a Senate or House staff does not include a Legislative Director, we have listed here the name of a Legislative Assistant (generally the first one listed alphabetically.)

(Area Code 202)

U.S. Senate

William V. Roth, Jr (R-DE)
SH-104 Hart Senate Office Building......................224-2441
Legislative Assistant: Nancy Anderson
Tax Counsel: Mark Mullet

Joseph R. Biden Jr (D-DE) (Area Code 202)
SR-221 Russell Senate Office Building...................224-5042
Legislative Director: Liz Tankersley

U.S. House of Representatives
(Listed by Congressional District)

1. Thomas R. Carper (D-DE)
131 Cannon House Office Building........................225-4165
FAX...225-1912
Legislative Director: Christophe Tulou

FLORIDA

Zip Codes:
U.S. Senate..20510
U.S. House of Representative 20515

Note: When a Senate or House staff does not include a Legislative Director, we have listed here the name of a Legislative Assistant (generally the first one listed alphabetically.)

(Area Code 202)

U.S. Senate

Bob Graham (D-FL)
SD-241 Dirksen Senate Office Building...................224-3041
Legislative Director: Leslie Woolley

Connie Mack (R-FL)
SH-517 Hart Senate Office Building......................224-5274
FAX...224-9365
Legislative Director: Robert N. Mottice

U.S. House of Representatives
(Listed by Congressional District)

1. Earl Hutto (D-FL)
2435 Rayburn House Office Building......................225-4136
FAX...225-5785
Legislative Director: DeLisa Harmon

2. Bill Grant (R-FL)
1330 Longworth House Office Building....................225-5235
FAX 225-1586
Legislative Director: Steven Cohen

3. Charles E. Bennett (D-FL)
2107 Rayburn House Office Building......................225-2501
FAX 225-9635
Chief Legislative Assistant: James Pearthree

4. Craig T. James (R-FL)
1408 Longworth House Office Building....................225-4035
FAX...225-1727
Legislative Director: Kevin Harvey

5. Bill McCollum (R-FL)
2453 Rayburn House Office Building 225-2176
Legislative Director: Don Morrissey

6. Cliff Stearns (R-FL)
1207 Longworth House Office Building....................225-5744
Legislative Director: Pam Stillson

7. Sam M. Gibbons (D-FL)
2204 Rayburn House Office Building......................225-3376
Legislative Director: Flora Sullivan

8. C.W. Bill Young (R-FL)
2407 Rayburn House Office Building......................225-5961
Legislative Director: Harry Glenn

9. Michael Bilirakis (R-FL)
1530 Longworth House Office Building....................225-5755
FAX...225-4085
Legislative Assistant: Pattie DeLoatche

10. Andy Ireland (R-FL)
2416 Rayburn House Office Building......................225-5015
Legislative Director: Elizabeth Mehl

11. Bill Nelson (D-FL)
2404 Rayburn House Office Building......................225-3671
FAX..225-9039
Senior Legislative Assistant: Marilyn Rosenthal

12. Tom Lewis (R-FL)
1216 Longworth House Office Building....................225-5792
FAX...225-1860
Legislative Director: Mary Jane Rose

13. Porter J. Goss (R-FL)
509 Cannon House Office Building........................225-2536
Legislative Assistant: Kelleen Jackson

14. Harry Johnston (D-FL)
1517 Longworth House Office Building....................225-3001
FAX...225-8791
Legislative Director: Cheryl Federline

15. E. Clay Shaw Jr (R-FL) (Area Code 202)
2338 Rayburn Office Building............................225-3026
FAX..225-8398
Legislative Director: Scott Spear

16. Lawrence J. Smith (D-FL)
113 Cannon House Office Building........................225-7931
FAX..225-9816
Legislative Director: Bob Dobek

17. William Lehman (D-FL)
2347 Rayburn House Office Building......................225-4211
FAX..225-6208
Legislative Assistant: Nadine Berg

18. Ileana Ros-Lehtinen (R-FL) (Area Code 202)
1022 Longworth House Office Building....................225-3931
Legislative Director: Mauricio J. Tamargo

19. Dante B. Fascell (D-FL)
2354 Rayburn House Office Building......................225-4506
Legislative Assistant: Marcia A. Schmitz

GEORGIA

Zip Codes:
U.S. Senate...20510
U.S. House of Representative 20515

Note: When a Senate or House staff does not include a Legislative Director, we have listed here the name of a Legislative Assistant (generally the first one listed alphabetically.)

(Area Code)

U.S. Senate

Sam Nunn (D-GA)
SD-303 Dirksen Senate Office Building..................224-3521
FAX..224-0072
Legislative Director: Julie Abbot
Legislative Assistant/House Counsel: Rob Hall

Wyche Fowler Jr (D-GA)
SR-204 Russell Senate Office Building..................224-3643
FAX..224-8227
Chief of Staff/Legislative Director: Bill Johnstone
Chief Counsel: Bob Redding

U.S. House of Representatives
(Listed by Congressional District)

1. Lindsay Thomas (D-GA)
431 Cannon House Office Building......................225-5831
Legislative Director: Karen Long

2. Charles F. Hatcher (D-GA)
405 Cannon House Office Building........................225-3631
FAX..225-1117
Legislative Director: Joel Bush

3. Richard Ray (D-GA)
425 Cannon House Office Building........................225-5901
Legislative Director: Lee Culpepper

4. Ben Jones (D-GA)
514 Cannon House Office Building........................225-4272
FAX..225-8675
Legislative Director: John Ahmann

5. John Lewis (D-GA)
501 Cannon House Office Building........................225-3801
FAX..225-0351
Legislative Director: Julius Hall

6. Newt Gingrich (R-GA)
2438 Rayburn House Office Building......................225-4501
FAX 225-4656
Legislative Director: Greg Wright

7. George Darden (D-GA)
228 Cannon House Office Building........................225-2931
Legislative Director: Richard Patrick

8. J. Roy Rowland (D-GA)
423 Cannon House Office Building........................225-6531
Legislative Director: Kathy Hennemuth

9. Ed Jenkins (D-GA)
2427 Rayburn House Office Building......................225-5211
Legislative Assistant: Joel Grist

10. Doug Barnard Jr (D-GA)
2227 Rayburn House Office Building......................225-4101
FAX..225-1873
Legislative Assistant: Paula Barnett
Banking Counsel: Jeff Tassey

HAWAII

Zip Codes:
U.S. Senate...20510
U.S. House of Representative 20515

Note: When a Senate or House staff does not include a Legislative Director, we have listed here the name of a Legislative Assistant (generally the first one listed alphabetically.)

U.S. Senate

(Area Code 202)

Daniel K. Inouye (D-HI)
SH-722 Hart Senate Office Building......................224-3934
FAX..224-6747
Senior Legislative Assistant: Phyliss Minn

Daniel K. Akaka (D-HI)
SH-109 Hart Senate Office Building......................224-6361
Legislative Director: Patrick McGarey

U.S. House of Representatives

(Listed by Congressional District)

(Area Code 202)

1. Patricia Saiki (R-HI)
1609 Longworth House Office Building....................225-2726
FAX..225-4580
Legislative Director: David M. Young

2. The second Congressional District, formerly held by Daniel K. Akaka, is now vacant, pending a special September 1990 election to determine who will serve out the remainder of Akaka's term.

IDAHO

Zip Codes:
U.S. Senate..20510
U.S. House of Representative 20515

Note: When a Senate or House staff does not include a Legislative Director, we have listed here the name of a Legislative Assistant (generally the first one listed alphabetically.)

U.S. Senate

(Area Code 202)

James A. McClure (R-ID)
SH-309 Hart Senate Office Building......................224-2752
Legislative Director: Jack Gerard

Steven D. Symms (R-ID)
SH-509 Hart Senate Office Building......................224-6142
FAX..224-5893
Legislative Director: Taylor Bowlden

U.S. House of Representatives

(Listed by Congressional District)

1. Larry E. Craig (R-ID)
1034 Longworth House Office Building....................225-6611
FAX..226-1213
Senior Legislative Assistant: Norm Semanko

2. Richard H. Stallings (D-ID)
1221 Longworth House Office Building....................225-5531
FAX..225-2393
Legislative Director: Cheryl Canova

ILLINOIS

Zip Codes:
U.S. Senate..20510
U.S. House of Representative 20515

Note: When a Senate or House staff does not include a Legislative Director, we have listed here the name of a Legislative Assistant (generally the first one listed alphabetically.)

U.S. Senate

(Area Code 202)

Alan J. Dixon (D-IL)
SH-331 Hart Senate Office Building......................224-2854
FAX..224-5581
Legislative Director: William Mattea

Paul Simon (D-IL)
SD-462 Dirksen Senate Office Building...................224-2152
Legislative Director: Vicki Otten

U.S. House of Representatives

(Listed by Congressional District)

1. Charles A. Hayes (D-IL)
1028 Longworth House Office Building....................225-4372
FAX..225-7571
Legislative Director: S. Howard Woodson III

2. Gus Savage (D-IL)
1121 Longworth House Office Building....................225-0773
FAX..225-8608
Legislative Director: Donovan Dunkley

3. Marty Russo (D-IL)
2233 Rayburn House Office Building......................225-5736
FAX..225-0295
Legislative Assistant: Mike Kelliher

4. George E. Sangmeister (D-IL)
1607 Longworth House Office Building....................225-3635
Legislative Director: Jody Lenkoski

5. William O. Lipinski (D-IL)
1032 Longworth House Office Building....................225-5701
FAX..225-1012
Legislative Assistant: Marc Howard

6. Henry J. Hyde (R-IL)
2262 Rayburn House Office Building......................225-4561
FAX..226-1240
Chief of Staff/Legislative Director: Judy Wolverton

7. Cardiss Collins (D-IL)
2264 Rayburn House Office Building......................225-5006
FAX..225-8396
Legislative Director: Sarah Matthews
Legislative Counsel: Brad Kane

8. Dan Rostenkowski (D-IL) (Area Code 202)
2111 Rayburn House Office Building....................225-4061
FAX....................225-4064
Legislative Assistant: Tom Sneeringer

9. Sidney R. Yates (D-IL)
2234 Rayburn House Office Building....................225-2111
FAX....................225-3493
Legislative Assistant: Donald Fisher

10. John Edward Porter (R-IL)
1501 Longworth House Office Building....................225-4835
FAX....................225-0157
Legislative Director: Robert C. Gustaffon

11. Frank Annunzio (D-IL)
2303 Rayburn House Office Building....................225-6661
Legislative Assistant: David Lovett

12. Philip M. Crane (R-IL)
1035 Longworth House Office Building....................225-3711
Legislative Director: Kirt Johnson

13. Harris W. Fawell (R-IL)
318 Cannon House Office Building....................225-3515
FAX....................225-9420
Legislative Director: Tracy Wurzel

14. J. Dennis Hastert (R-IL)
515 Cannon House Office Building....................225-2976
FAX....................225-0697
Senior Legislative Assistant: Marc Wheat

15. Edward R. Madigan (R-IL)
2109 Rayburn House Office Building....................225-2371
Counsel/Legislative Director: Mark Dungan

16. Lynn M. Martin (R-IL) (Area Code 202)
1214 Longworth House Office Building....................225-5676
Legislative Director: John Anelli

17. Lane Evans (D-IL)
328 Cannon House Office Building....................225-5905
FAX....................225-5396
Legislative Director: Randy Slovic

18. Robert H. Michel (R-IL)
2112 Rayburn House Office Building....................225-6201
FAX....................225-9461
Legislative Director: David Kehl

19. Terry L. Bruce (D-IL)
419 Cannon House Office Building....................225-5001
FAX....................225-9810
Legislative Directors: Joan Mooney and Michael Bushman

20. Richard J. Durbin (D-IL)
129 Cannon House Office Building....................225-5271
Legislative Assistant: Tom Faletti

21. Jerry F. Costello (D-IL)
315 Cannon House Office Building....................225-5661
FAX....................225-0285
Legislative Assistant: Eric Fairfield

22. Glenn Poshard (D-IL)
506 Cannon House Office Building....................225-5201
FAX....................225-1541
Legislative Director: Stephen Ball

INDIANA

Zip Codes:
U.S. Senate....................20510
U.S. House of Representative....................20515

Note: When a Senate or House staff does not include a Legislative Director, we have listed here the name of a Legislative Assistant (generally the first one listed alphabetically.)

(Area Code 202)

U.S. Senate

Richard G. Lugar (R-IN)
SH-306 Hart Senate Office Building....................224-4814
Legislative Director: Ellen Whitt

Dan Coats (R-IN)
SR-407 Russell Senate Office Building....................224-5623
Legislative Director: Mark Souder
Legislative Director: Eric Thoemmes
Counsel: G. Thomas Long

U.S. House of Representatives
(Listed by Congressional District)

1. Peter J. Visclosky (D-IN)
420 Cannon House Office Building....................225-2461
FAX....................225-2493
Legislative Director: Robert Falb

2. Philip R. Sharp (D-IN)
2217 Rayburn House Office Building....................225-3021
Legislative Director: Tom Wanley

3. John P. Hiler (R-IN)
407 Cannon House Office Building....................225-3915
FAX....................225-6798
Legislative Assistant/Counsel: Joseph Seidel

4. Jill Long (D-IN)
1632 Longworth House Office Building....................225-4436
FAX....................225-8810
Legislative Director: Bartholomew Chilton

5. Jim Jontz (D-IN)
1039 Longworth House Office Building....................225-5037
FAX....................225-5870
Legislative Director: Tom Buis

6. Dan Burton (R-IN)
120 Cannon House Office Building....................225-2276
FAX....................225-0016
Legislative Assistant: Scott Feeney

7. John T. Myers (R-IN)
2372 Rayburn House Office Building....................225-5805
FAX....................225-1649
Chief Legislative Assistant: Ray Little

8. Frank McCloskey (D-IN)
127 Cannon House Office Building....................225-4636
FAX....................225-4688
Legislative Director: Paul Weber

9. Lee H. Hamilton (D-IN) (Area Code 202)
2187 Rayburn House Office Building......................225-5315
FAX..225-1101
Legislative Assistant: Jonathan Friedman

10. Andrew Jacobs Jr (D-IN) (Area Code 202)
2313 Rayburn House Office Building......................225-4011
Administrative Assistant/Legislative Assistant:
David Wildes

IOWA

Zip Codes:
U.S. Senate...20510
U.S. House of Representative 20515

Note: When a Senate or House staff does not include a Legislative Director, we have listed here the name of a Legislative Assistant (generally the first one listed alphabetically.)

(Area Code 202)

U.S. Senate

Charles E. Grassley (R-IA)
SH-135 Hart Senate Office Building......................224-3744
FAX..224-0473
Legislative Director: Ken Cunningham

Tom Harkin (D-IA)
SH-316 Hart Senate Office Building......................224-3254
FAX..224-7431
Legislative Director: Kay Casstevens

U.S. House of Representatives
(Listed by Congressional District)

1. Jim Leach (R-IA)
1514 Longworth House Office Building....................225-6576
FAX..226-1278
Legislative Assistant: Mary Andrus

2. Thomas J. Tauke (R-IA)
2244 Rayburn House Office Building......................225-2911
FAX..225-9129
Legislative Director: Ed Senn

3. David R. Nagle (D-IA)
214 Cannon House Office Building........................225-3301
FAX..225-9104
Legislative Director: Jean Hessburg

4. Neal Smith (D-IA)
2373 Rayburn House Office Building......................225-4426
Administrative Assistant: Tom Dawson

5. Jim Lightfoot (R-IA)
1222 Longworth House Office Building....................225-3806
FAX..225-6973
Legislative Director: Christine Smith Cohen

6. Fred Grandy (R-IA)
418 Cannon House Office Building........................225-5476
Legislative Director: Mike Neruda

KANSAS

Zip Codes:
U.S. Senate...20510
U.S. House of Representative 20515

Note: When a Senate or House staff does not include a Legislative Director, we have listed here the name of a Legislative Assistant (generally the first one listed alphabetically.)

(Area Code 202)

U.S. Senate

Robert Dole (R-KS)
SH-141 Hart Senate Office Building......................224-6521
FAX..224-8952
Administrative Assistant/Legislative Director:
James Kevin Wholey

Nancy Landon Kassebaum (R-KS)
SR-302 Russell Senate Office Building...................224-4774
Legislative Director: Liz Wehr
General Counsel: Dan Bolen
Legislative Counsel: Ted Verheggen

U.S. HOUSE OF REPRESENTATIVES
(Listed by Congressional District)

1. Pat Roberts (R-KS)
110 Longworth House Office Building.....................225-2715
FAX..225-5375
Legislative Assistant: Sarah Coleman

2. Jim Slattery (D-KS)
1440 Longworth House Office Building....................225-6601
Legislative Assistant: Roger Claassen

3. Jan Meyers (R-KS)
1507 Longworth House Office Building....................225-2865
FAX..225-0554
Legislative Director: Sandra Chalmers

4. Dan Glickman (D-KS)
1212 Longworth House Office Building....................225-6216
FAX..225-5398
Legislative Director/Counsel: Kevin O'Leary

5. Bob Whittaker (R-KS) (Area Code 202)
2436 Rayburn House Office Building......................225-3911
FAX..225-9415
Legislative Assistant: Steve Ahnen

KENTUCKY

Zip Codes:
U.S. Senate...20510
U.S. House of Representative 20515

Note: When a Senate or House staff does not include a Legislative Director, we have listed here the name of a Legislative Assistant (generally the first one listed alphabetically.)

(Area Code 202)

U.S. Senate

Wendell H. Ford (D-KY)
SR-173A Russell Senate Office Building..................224-4343
Administrative Assistant/Legislative Director:
James T. Fleming
Legislative Counsel: Kennie Gill

Mitch McConnell (R-KY)
SR-120 Russell Senate Office Building...................224-2541
FAX..224-2499
Administrative Assistant/Legislative Director:
Niels C. Holch

U.S. House of Representatives
(Listed by Congressional District)

1. Carroll Hubbard Jr (D-KY)
2267 Rayburn House Office Building......................225-3115
FAX..225-1622
Legislative Director: Maureen Fletcher

2. William H. Natcher (D-KY)
2333 Rayburn House Office Building......................225-3501
Staff Associate: Diane Rihely

3. Romano L. Mazzoli (D-KY)
2246 Rayburn House Office Building......................225-5401
Legislative Director: Lisa Gallagher

4. Jim Bunning (R-KY)
116 Cannon House Office Building........................225-3465
FAX..225-0003
Legislative Director: Richard Robinson

5. Harold Rogers (R-KY)
343 Cannon House Office Building........................225-4601
FAX..225-0940
Legislative Director: Sue Ann Losey

6. Larry J. Hopkins (R-KY)
2437 Rayburn House Office Building......................225-4706
FAX..225-1413
Legislative Assistant: Sally Jefferson

7. Carl C. Perkins (D-KY)
1004 Longworth House Office Building....................225-4935
Legislative Assistant: Treeby Williamson

LOUISIANA

Zip Codes:
U.S. Senate...20510
U.S. House of Representative 20515

Note: When a Senate or House staff does not include a Legislative Director, we have listed here the name of a Legislative Assistant (generally the first one listed alphabetically.)

(Area Code 202)

U.S. Senate

J. Bennett Johnston (D-LA)
SH-136 Hart Senate Office Building......................224-5824
Legislative Director: Laura Hudson

John B. Breaux (D-LA)
SH-516 Hart Senate Office Building......................224-4623
Legislative Director: Paul Carothers

U.S. House of Representatives
(Listed by Congressional District)

1. Bob Livingston (R-LA)
2412 Rayburn House Office Building......................225-3015
FAX..225-0739
Legislative Assistant: Paul Cambon

2. Lindy Boggs (D-LA)
2353 Rayburn House Office Building......................225-6636
Legislative Director: Jan Schoonmaker

3. W.J. "Billy" Tauzin (D-LA)
2342 Rayburn House Office Building......................225-4031
Administrative Assistant/Legislative Director:
Elizabeth Megginson

4. Jim McCrery (R-LA)
429 Cannon House Office Building........................225-2777
Legislative Assistant: Alec Alexander

5. Jerry Huckaby (D-LA)
2182 Rayburn House Office Building......................225-2376
FAX..225-2387
Legislative Assistant: Carol Connors

6. Richard Baker (R-LA)
404 Cannon House Office Building........................225-3901
Administrative Assistant/Counsel: Tim Leighton
Legislative Assistant: Dorena Bertussi

7. Jimmy Hayes (D-LA) (Area Code 202)
503 Cannon House Office Building........................225-2031
Chief of Staff/Legislative Director: Rhod Shaw

8. Clyde C. Holloway (R-LA) (Area Code 202)
1206 Longworth House Office Building....................225-4926
FAX...225-6252
Legislative Director: Cal Odom

MAINE

Zip Codes:
U.S. Senate...20510
U.S. House of Representative 20515

Note: When a Senate or House staff does not include a Legislative Director, we have listed here the name of a Legislative Assistant (generally the first one listed alphabetically.)

(Area Code 202)

U.S. Senate

William S. Cohen (R-ME)
SH-322 Hart Senate Office Building......................224-2523
Legislative Director: Robert P. Savitt

George J. Mitchell (D-ME)
SR-176 Russell Senate Office Building...................224-5344
Legislative Counsel: Robert Rozen

U.S. House of Representatives
(Listed by Congressional District)

1. Joseph E. Brennan (D-ME)
1428 Longworth House Office Building....................225-6116
FAX...225-9065
Legislative Director: E.H. Michalek

2. Olympia J. Snowe (R-ME)
2464 Rayburn House Office Building......................225-6306
Legislative Assistant: Jane Calderwood

MARYLAND

Zip Codes:
U.S. Senate...20510
U.S. House of Representative 20515

Note: When a Senate or House staff does not include a Legislative Director, we have listed here the name of a Legislative Assistant (generally the first one listed alphabetically.)

(Area Code 202)

U.S. Senate

Paul S. Sarbanes (D-MD)
SD-332 Dirksen Senate Office Building...................224-4524
Legislative Director: Julie Kehrli
Legislative Counsel: Fred Millhiser

Barbara A. Mikulski (D-MD)
SH-320 Hart Senate Office Building......................224-4654
FAX...224-8858
Legislative Director: Glenn Roberts

U.S. House of Representatives
(Listed by Congressional District)

1. Roy P. Dyson (D-MD)
326 Cannon House Office Building........................225-5311
FAX...225-0254
Legislative Director: Todd A. Skipper

2. Helen Delich Bentley (R-MD)
1610 Longworth House Office Building....................225-3061
FAX...225-4251
Legislative Director: Chris Griffin

3. Benjamin L. Cardin (D-MD)
507 Cannon House Office Building........................225-4016
Legislative Assistant: Sean Cavanaugh

4. Tom McMillen (D-MD)
327 Cannon House Office Building........................225-8090
Legislative Assistant: Trip Carey

5. Steny H. Hoyer (D-MD)
1513 Longworth House Office Building....................225-4131
Legislative Director: John Berry

6. Beverly B. Byron (D-MD)
2430 Rayburn House Office Building......................225-2721
FAX...225-6159
Legislative Director: Sara Morningstar

7. Kweisi Mfume (D-MD)
128 Cannon House Office Building........................225-4741
Administrative Assistant/Legislative Director:
Tammy Hawley

8. Constance A. Morella (R-MD)
1024 Longworth House Office Building....................225-5341
Legislative Director: Cindy Hall

MASSACHUSETTS

Zip Codes:
U.S. Senate 20510
U.S. House of Representative 20515

Note: When a Senate or House staff does not include a Legislative Director, we have listed here the name of a Legislative Assistant (generally the first one listed alphabetically.)

(Area Code 202)

U.S. Senate

Edward M. Kennedy (D-MA)
SR-315 Russell Senate Office Building..................224-4543
FAX..224-2417
Chief Legislative Assistant: Carey Parker

John F. Kerry (D-MA)
SR-421 Russell Senate Office Building..................224-2742
FAX..224-8525
Legislative Director: Timothy Barnicle

U.S. House of Representatives
(Listed by Congressional District)

1. Silvio O. Conte (R-MA)
2300 Rayburn House Office Building.....................225-5335
Legislative Director: Ed Gresser

2. Richard E. Neal (D-MA)
437 Cannon House Office Building.......................225-5601
FAX..225-8112
Administrative Assistant/Legislative Director:
Morgan Broman

3. Joseph D. Early (D-MA)
2349 Rayburn House Office Building.....................225-6101
FAX..225-3181
Legislative Assistant: Patrick Lane

(Area Code 202)

4. Barney Frank (D-MA)
1030 Longworth House Office Building...................225-5931
Legislative Assistant: Pam Gogol

5. Chester G. Atkins (D-MA)
504 Cannon House Office Building.......................225-3411
Legislative Director: Dalena Wright

6. Nicholas Mavroules (D-MA)
2432 Rayburn House Office Building.....................225-8020
FAX..225-8023
Legislative Director: Grace Pearson Waters

7. Edward J. Markey (D-MA)
2133 Rayburn House Office Building.....................225-2836
Legislative Director: David Nemtzow

8. Joseph P. Kennedy II (D-MA)
1208 Longworth House Office Building...................225-5111
FAX..225-9322
Legislative Assistant: Wendell Bugg

9. John Joseph Moakley (D-MA)
221 Cannon House Office Building.......................225-8273
FAX..225-7804
Legislative Assistant: Jim McGovern

10. Gerry E. Studds (D-MA)
237 Cannon House Office Building.......................225-3111
Chief Legislative Assistant: Eileen O'Brien

11. Brian Donnelly (D-MA)
2229 Rayburn House Office Building.....................225-3215
Legislative Director: Tom Barker

MICHIGAN

Zip Codes:
U.S. Senate 20510
U.S. House of Representative 20515

Note: When a Senate or House staff does not include a Legislative Director, we have listed here the name of a Legislative Assistant (generally the first one listed alphabetically.)

(Area Code 202)

U.S. Senate

Donald W. Riegle Jr (D-MI)
SD-105 Dirksen Senate Office Building..................224-4822
Administrative Assistant/Legislative Director:
David Krawitz

Carl Levin (D-MI)
SR-459 Russell Senate Office Building..................224-6221
Legislative Director: Chuck Cutolo

U.S. House of Representatives
(Listed by Congressional District)

1. John Conyers Jr (D-MI)
2426 Rayburn House Office Building.....................225-5126
FAX..225-0072
Legislative Assistant: Agnieska Fryszman

2. Carl D. Pursell (R-MI)
1414 Longworth House Office Building...................225-4401
Legislative Director: Troy Zimmerman
Legislative Counsel: Kevin J. Kraushaar

3. Howard Wolpe (D-MI)
1535 Longworth House Office Building...................225-5011
FAX..225-8602
Legislative Director: Kate English

4. Fred Upton (R-MI)
1713 Longworth House Office Building...................225-3761
FAX..225-4986
Legislative Director: Patrick Knudsen

5. Paul B. Henry (R-MI)
215 Cannon House Office Building.......................225-3831
Legislative Assistant: Bob Filka

6. Bob Carr (D-MI) **(Area Code 202)**
2439 Rayburn House Office Building....................225-4872
FAX....................225-1260
Legislative Director: Mark Miller

7. Dale E. Kildee (D-MI)
2239 Rayburn House Office Building....................225-3611
Legislative Director: Christopher Mansour

8. Bob Traxler (D-MI)
2366 Rayburn House Office Building....................225-2806
FAX....................225-3046
Legislative Director: William Gilmartin

9. Guy Vander Jagt (R-MI)
2409 Rayburn House Office Building....................225-3511
Legislative Assistant: Lori Harju

10. Bill Schuette (R-MI)
415 Cannon House Office Building....................225-3561
FAX....................225-6971
Legislative Director: Heather Bremer

11. Robert W. Davis (R-MI)
2417 Rayburn House Office Building....................225-4735
FAX....................225-3588
Legislative Director: Cindy Lovett

12. David E. Bonior (D-MI) **(Area Code 202)**
2242 Rayburn House Office Building....................225-2106
FAX....................226-1169
Legislative Director: Ann Dye

13. George W. Crockett Jr (D-MI)
2235 Rayburn House Office Building....................225-2261
Legislative Assistant: Tony Carter

14. Dennis M. Hertel (D-MI)
2442 Rayburn House Office Building....................225-6276
Legislative Counsel: Brian O'Malley

15. William D. Ford (D-MI)
239 Cannon House Office Building....................225-6261
Legislative Director: Ross Eisenbrey

16. John D. Dingell (D-MI)
2221 Rayburn House Office Building....................225-4071
FAX....................225-7426
Legislative Counsel: Walter Sanders

17. Sander M. Levin (D-MI)
323 Cannon House Office Building....................225-4961
Legislative Director: John Griffen

18. William S. Broomfield (R-MI)
2306 Rayburn House Office Building....................225-6135
FAX....................225-1807
Legislative Assistant: Paul Russinoff

MINNESOTA

Zip Codes:
U.S. Senate....................20510
U.S. House of Representative....................20515

Note: When a Senate or House staff does not include a Legislative Director, we have listed here the name of a Legislative Assistant (generally the first one listed alphabetically.)

(Area Code 202)

U.S. Senate

Dave Durenberger (R-MN)
SR-154 Russell Senate Office Building....................224-3244
Legislative Director: Steve Moore

Rudy Boschwitz (R-MN)
SH-506 Hart Senate Office Building....................224-5641
Legislative Director: Hillel Weinberg

U.S. House of Representatives
(Listed by Congressional District)

1. Timothy J. Penny (D-MN)
436 Cannon House Office Building....................225-2472
FAX....................225-0051
Legislative Director: Joe Theissen

2. Vin Weber (R-MN)
106 Cannon House Office Building....................225-2331
FAX....................225-0987
Legislative Director: Todd Johnson

3. Bill Frenzel (R-MN)
1026 Longworth House Office Building....................225-2871
FAX....................225-6351
Legislative Assistant: Michelle Harris

4. Bruce F. Vento (D-MN)
2304 Rayburn House Office Building....................225-6631
FAX....................225-1968
Legislative Assistant: Steve Francisco

5. Martin Olav Sabo (D-MN)
2201 Rayburn House Office Building....................225-4755
Legislative Director: Eileen Baumgartner

6. Gerry Sikorski (D-MN)
403 Cannon House Office Building....................225-2271
FAX....................225-4347
Legislative Director: Rick Jauert

7. Arlan Stangeland (R-MN)
2245 Rayburn House Office Building....................225-2165
FAX....................225-1593
Legislative Assistant: Jim Hagedorn

8. James L. Oberstar (D-MN)
2209 Rayburn House Office Building....................225-6211
FAX....................225-0699
Legislative Assistant: Alan Becicka

MISSISSIPPI

Zip Codes:
U.S. Senate....................20510
U.S. House of Representative....................20515

Note: When a Senate or House staff does not include a Legislative Director, we have listed here the name of a Legislative Assistant (generally the first one listed alphabetically.)

(Area Code 202)

U.S. Senate

Thad Cochran (R-MS)
SR-326 Russell Senate Office Building....................224-5054
Legislative Director: Jack Hoggard

Trent Lott (R-MS)
SR-487 Russell Senate Office Building....................224-6253
FAX....................224-2262
Legislative Director: Laura Ann Smith

U.S. House of Representatives
(Listed by Congressional District)

1. Jamie L. Whitten (D-MS)
2314 Rayburn House Office Building....................225-4306
FAX....................225-4328
Administrative Assistant: Hal DeCell

2. Mike Espy (D-MS) (Area Code 202)
216 Cannon House Office Building....................225-5876
FAX....................225-5898
Legislative Assistant: Mike Alexander

3. G.V. "Sonny" Montgomery (D-MS)
2184 Rayburn House Office Building....................225-5031
Legislative Director: Kyle Steward

4. Mike Parker (D-MS)
1725 Longworth House Office Building....................225-5865
FAX....................225-5886
Administrative Assistant/Legislative Director: Arthur D. Rhodes

5. Gene Taylor (D-MS)
1429 Longworth House Office Building....................225-5772
FAX....................226-7074
Legislative Director: Cindy Newman

MISSOURI

Zip Codes:
U.S. Senate....................20510
U.S. House of Representative....................20515

Note: When a Senate or House staff does not include a Legislative Director, we have listed here the name of a Legislative Assistant (generally the first one listed alphabetically.)

(Area Code 202)

U.S. Senate

John C. Danforth (R-MO)
SR-249 Russell Senate Office Building....................224-6154
Legislative Director: Jon Chambers

Christopher Bond (R-MO)
SR-293 Russell Senate Office Building....................224-5721
Legislative Director: Julie Dammann
Legislative Counsel: Brent Franzel

U.S. House of Representatives
(Listed by Congressional District)

1. William L. Clay (D-MO)
2470 Rayburn House Office Building....................225-2406
FAX....................225-1783
Legislative Assistant: Michele Bogdanovich

2. Jack Buechner (R-MO)
502 Cannon House Office Building....................225-2561
FAX....................225-1378
Legislative Director: Thom Stohler

3. Richard A. Gephardt (D-MO)
1432 Longworth House Office Building....................225-2671
FAX....................225-7452
Legislative Director: Jim Hawley

4. Ike Skelton (D-MO)
2134 Rayburn House Office Building....................225-2876
Legislative Director: Amy Blankenship

5. Alan Wheat (D-MO)
1210 Longworth House Office Building....................225-4535
Legislative Director: Jan Hoefer Kamp

6. E. Thomas Coleman (R-MO)
2468 Rayburn House Office Building....................225-7041
Legislative Director: Christopher Jacobs

7. Mel Hancock (R-MO)
511 Cannon House Office Building....................225-6536
FAX....................225-7700
Legislative Assistant: Duncan Haggart

8. Bill Emerson (R-MO)
438 Cannon House Office Building....................225-4404
FAX....................225-9621
Senior Legislative Assistant: Perry Anne Buchanan

9. Harold L. Volkmer (D-MO)
2411 Rayburn House Office Building....................225-2956
FAX....................225-7834
Chief Legislative Assistant: Cherry Schloman

MONTANA

Zip Codes:
U.S. Senate 20510
U.S. House of Representative 20515

Note: When a Senate or House staff does not include a Legislative Director, we have listed here the name of a Legislative Assistant (generally the first one listed alphabetically.)

(Area Code 202)

U.S. Senate

Max Baucus (D-MT)
SH-706 Hart Senate Office Building...................... 224-2651
Legislative Director: Mike Evans

Conrad Burns (R-MT)
SD-183 Dirksen Senate Office Building.................. 224-2644

(Area Code 202)
FAX... 224-8594
Senior Legislative Assistant: Tom Fulton

U.S. House of Representatives
(Listed by Congressional District)

1. Pat Williams (D-MT)
2457 Rayburn House Office Building...................... 225-3211
FAX... 225-1257
Administrative Assistant/Legislative Director:
Jon Weintraub

2. Ron Marlenee (R-MT)
2465 Rayburn House Office Building...................... 225-1555
FAX... 225-1558
Legislative Director: Philip Eskeland

NEBRASKA

Zip Codes:
U.S. Senate 20510
U.S. House of Representative 20515

Note: When a Senate or House staff does not include a Legislative Director, we have listed here the name of a Legislative Assistant (generally the first one listed alphabetically.)

(Area Code 202)

U.S. Senate

J. James Exon (D-NE)
SH-330 Hart Senate Office Building...................... 224-4224
Legislative Assistant: Robyn Henderson

J. Robert Kerrey (D-NE)
SH-302 Hart Senate Office Building...................... 224-6551
FAX... 224-7645
Legislative Director: Sheila Murphy

U.S. House of Representatives
(Listed by Congressional District)

1. Doug Bereuter (R-NE)
2446 Rayburn House Office Building...................... 225-4806
FAX... 226-1148
Legislative Assistant: Wrexie Agan

2. Peter Hoagland (D-NE)
1415 Longworth House Office Building.................... 225-4155
Legislative Assistant: Phil Kiekhaefer

3. Virginia Smith (R-NE)
2202 Rayburn House Office Building...................... 225-6435
FAX... 225-0207
Senior Legislative Assistant: Jeri Finke

NEVADA

Zip Codes:
U.S. Senate 20510
U.S. House of Representative 20515

Note: When a Senate or House staff does not include a Legislative Director, we have listed here the name of a Legislative Assistant (generally the first one listed alphabetically.)

(Area Code 202)

U.S. Senate

Harry Reid (D-NV)
SH-324 Hart Senate Office Building...................... 224-3542
FAX 224-7327
Legislative Director: Wayne Mehl

Richard H. Bryan (D-NV)
SR-364 Russell Senate Office Building.................. 224-6244
FAX 224-1867
Senior Legislative Assistant: Andrew Vermilye

U.S. House of Representatives
(Listed by Congressional District)

1. James H. Bilbray (D-NV)
319 Cannon House Office Building........................ 225-5965
FAX... 225-8808
Legislative Director: Mike Talisnik

2. Barbara Vucanovich (R-NV)
206 Cannon House Office Building........................ 225-6155
FAX... 225-2319
Legislative Director: James Kameen

NEW HAMPSHIRE

Zip Codes:
U.S. Senate 20510
U.S. House of Representative 20515

Note: When a Senate or House staff does not include a Legislative Director, we have listed here the name of a Legislative Assistant (generally the first one listed alphabetically.)

(Area Code 202)

U.S. Senate

Gordon J. Humphrey (R-NH)
SH-531 Hart Senate Office Building 224-2841
FAX 224-1353
Legislative Assistant: John Balbach

Warren B. Rudman (R-NH) (Area Code 202)
SH-530 Hart Senate Office Building 224-3324
Legislative Director: Thomas C. Polgar
Counsel: James Farrell

U.S. House of Representatives
(Listed by Congressional District)

1. Robert C. Smith (R-NH)
115 Cannon House Office Building 225-5456
Legislative Director: Jim Krey

2. Chuck Douglas (R-NH)
1338 Longworth House Office Building 225-5206
FAX 225-0046
Legislative Director: Paul Guppy

NEW JERSEY

Zip Codes:
U.S. Senate 20510
U.S. House of Representative 20515

Note: When a Senate or House staff does not include a Legislative Director, we have listed here the name of a Legislative Assistant (generally the first one listed alphabetically.)

(Area Code 202)

U.S. Senate

Bill Bradley (D-NJ)
SH-731 Hart Senate Office Building 224-3224
FAX 224-8567
Legislative Director: Ken Apfel
Legislative Assistant/Counsel: Gina Despres

Frank R. Lautenberg (D-NJ)
SH-717 Hart Senate Office Building 224-4744
FAX 224-9707
Legislative Director: Mitch Ostrer

U.S. House of Representatives
(Listed by Congressional District)

1. The first Congressional District, formerly held by James J. Florio, is vacant pending the November 1990 election.

2. William J. Hughes (D-NJ)
341 Cannon House Office Building 225-6572
FAX 226-1108
Legislative Assistant: Marci Bortman

3. Frank Pallone Jr (D-NJ)
213 Cannon House Office Building 225-4671
FAX 225-9665
Administrative Assistant/Legislative Director:
Seth Maiman

4. Christopher H. Smith (R-NJ)
2440 Rayburn House Office Building 225-3765
FAX 225-7768
Legislative Director: Mary McDermott

5. Marge Roukema (R-NJ)
303 Cannon House Office Building 225-4465
FAX 225-9048
Legislative Director: Vince Morelli

6. Bernard J. Dwyer (D-NJ)
2428 Rayburn House Office Building 225-6301
FAX 225-1553
Legislative Assistant: Brenda Brockman

7. Matthew J. Rinaldo (R-NJ)
2469 Rayburn House Office Building 225-5361
Legislative Director: Barbara Gay

8. Robert A. Roe (D-NJ)
2243 Rayburn House Office Building 225-5751
FAX 225-3071
Legislative Assistant: Raphael I. Panitz

9. Robert G. Torricelli (D-NJ)
317 Cannon House Office Building 225-5061
FAX 225-0843
Legislative Director: Lewis Warshauer

10. Donald M. Payne (D-NJ)
417 Cannon House Office Building 225-3436
FAX 225-4160
Legislative Director: Kerry B. McKenney
Legislative Assistant/Counsel: Paige Cottingham

11. Dean A. Gallo (R-NJ)
1318 Longworth House Office Building 225-5034
Legislative Director: Donna Mullins

12. Jim Courter (R-NJ)
2422 Rayburn House Office Building 225-5801
FAX 225-9181
Legislative Assistant: Dave Anderson

13. H. James Saxton (R-NJ)
324 Cannon House Office Building 225-4765
FAX 225-0778
Legislative Director: Jeff DeKorte

14. Frank J. Guarini (D-NJ)
2458 Rayburn House Office Building 225-2765
FAX 225-7023
Legislative Director: Marcia Fusilli
Counsel: Brent Budowsky

NEW MEXICO

Zip Codes:
U.S. Senate....................20510
U.S. House of Representative....................20515

Note: When a Senate or House staff does not include a Legislative Director, we have listed here the name of a Legislative Assistant (generally the first one listed alphabetically.)

(Area Code 202)

U.S. Senate

Pete V. Domenici (R-NM)
SD-434 Dirksen Senate Office Building....................224-6621
FAX....................224-7371
Legislative Director: Denise Greenlaw Ramonas

Jeff Bingaman (D-NM)
SH-524 Hart Senate Office Building....................224-5521
Legislative Director: Ed McGaffigan

U.S. House of Representatives
(Listed by Congressional District)

1. Steven H. Schiff (R-NM) **(Area Code 202)**
1520 Longworth House Office Building....................225-6316
FAX....................225-4975
Legislative Director: Mary Martinek

2. Joe Skeen (R-NM)
1007 Longworth House Office Building....................225-2365
FAX....................225-9599
Legislative Director: John Sneed

3. Bill Richardson (D-NM)
332 Cannon House Office Building....................225-6190
Legislative Director: Tara Federici

NEW YORK

Zip Codes:
U.S. Senate....................20510
U.S. House of Representative....................20515

Note: When a Senate or House staff does not include a Legislative Director, we have listed here the name of a Legislative Assistant (generally the first one listed alphabetically.)

(Area Code 202)

U.S. Senate

Daniel P. Moynihan (D-NY)
SR-464 Russell Senate Office Building....................224-4451
Legislative Director: Andrew Samet

Alfonse M. D'Amato (R-NY)
SH-520 Hart Senate Office Building....................224-6542
FAX....................224-5871
Legislative Director/General Counsel: Philip Bechtel

U.S. House of Representatives
(Listed by Congressional District)

1. George J. Hochbrueckner (D-NY)
124 Cannon House Office Building....................225-3826
FAX....................225-0776
Senior Legislative Assistant: Victoria Holt

2. Thomas J. Downey (D-NY)
2232 Rayburn House Office Building....................225-3335
FAX....................226-1275
Legislative Director: Jeff Moore

3. Robert J. Mrazek (D-NY)
306 Cannon House Office Building....................225-5956
FAX....................225-7215
Legislative Assistant: Ann Bennett

4. Norman F. Lent (R-NY)
2408 Rayburn House Office Building....................225-7896
FAX....................225-0357
Administrative Assistant/Legislative Director:
Michael Scrivner

5. Raymond J. McGrath (R-NY)
205 Cannon House Office Building....................225-5516
FAX....................225-3626
Administrative Assistant/Counsel: Arthur DeCelle
Legislative Assistant: John Falardeau

6. Floyd H. Flake (D-NY)
1427 Longworth House Office Building....................225-3461
FAX....................226-4169
Legislative Director: Gloria Bryant

7. Gary L. Ackerman (D-NY)
238 Cannon House Office Building....................225-2601
Legislative Assistant: Carol Cayo

8. James H. Scheuer (D-NY)
2466 Rayburn House Office Building....................225-5471
FAX....................225-9695
Legislative Assistant: Lisa Jordan

9. Thomas J. Manton (D-NY)
331 Cannon House Office Building....................225-3965
Legislative Assistant: Jim Mathews

10. Charles E. Schumer (D-NY)
126 Cannon House Office Building....................225-6616
FAX....................225-4183
Legislative Director: Tom Freedman

11. Edolphus Towns (D-NY)
1726 Longworth House Office Building....................225-5936
FAX....................225-1018
Legislative Assistant: Cherri Branson

12. Major R. Owens (D-NY)
114 Cannon House Office Building....................225-6231
Legislative Director: Braden Goetz

13. Stephen J. Solarz (D-NY)
1536 Longworth House Office Building....................225-2361
FAX....................225-9469
Legislative Assistant: David Lachmann

(Area Code 202)

14. Susan Molinari (R-NY)
1723 Longworth House Office Building 225-3371
Legislative Assistant: Lisa Bellucci

15. Bill Green (R-NY)
2301 Rayburn House Office Building......................225-2436
FAX...225-0840
Legislative Director: Jeff Lawrence

16. Charles B. Rangel (D-NY)
2252 Rayburn House Office Building......................225-4365
FAX...225-0816
Legislative Assistant: Emile Milne
Tax Counsel: Jon Sheiner

17. Ted Weiss (D-NY)
2467 Rayburn House Office Building......................225-5635
FAX...225-6923
Legislative Assistant: Randy Farmer

18. Jose E. Serrano (D-NY)
1107 Longworth House Office Building 225-4361
Legislative Assistant: Achieng Akumu

19. Eliot L. Engel (D-NY)
1407 Longworth House Office Building....................225-2464
Senior Legislative Assistant: John Mills

20. Nita M. Lowey (D-NY)
1313 Longworth House Office Building....................225-6506
FAX...225-0546
Legislative Director: Mark Isaac

21. Hamilton Fish Jr (R-NY)
2269 Rayburn House Office Building......................225-5441
FAX...225-0962
Legislative Director: Deborah Reilly

22. Benjamin A. Gilman (R-NY)
2185 Rayburn House Office Building......................225-3776
Legislative Director: Thad Bereday

23. Michael R. McNulty (D-NY)
1431 Longworth House Office Building....................225-5076
Legislative Director: Pete Rose

24. Gerald B. Solomon (R-NY)
2265 Rayburn House Office Building......................225-5614
FAX...225-1168
Legislative Director: Mark Gage

(Area Code 202)

25. Sherwood L. Boehlert (R-NY)
1127 Longworth House Office Building....................225-3665
FAX...225-1891
Senior Legislative Assistant: Paul Mackert

26. David O'B. Martin (R-NY)
442 Cannon House Office Building........................225-4611
Legislative Assistant: Judith Brewer

27. James T. Walsh (R-NY)
1238 Longworth House Office Building....................225-3701
FAX...225-4042
Senior Legislative Assistant: Martha Carmen

28. Matthew F. McHugh (D-NY)
2335 Rayburn House Office Building......................225-6335
Legislative Assistant: Gary Bombardier

29. Frank Horton (R-NY)
2108 Rayburn House Office Building......................225-4916
FAX...225-5909
Legislative Director: Phil Boyle

30. Louise M. Slaughter (D-NY)
1707 Longworth House Office Building....................225-3615
FAX...225-7822
Legislative Director: Tom Bantle

31. L. William Paxon (R-NY)
1711 Longworth House Office Building....................225-5265
FAX...225-5910
Legislative Director: Christopher Dawe

32. John J. LaFalce (D-NY)
2367 Rayburn House Office Building......................225-3231
FAX...225-8693
Legislative Assistant: Ellen Bayer

33. Henry J. Nowak (D-NY)
2240 Rayburn House Office Building......................225-3306
FAX...225-3523
Legislative Director: Helen Burton

34. Amo Houghton (R-NY)
1217 Longworth House Office Building....................225-3161
FAX...225-5574
Legislative Director: Marijo Gorney

NORTH CAROLINA

Zip Codes:
U.S. Senate...20510
U.S. House of Representative 20515

Note: When a Senate or House staff does not include a Legislative Director, we have listed here the name of a Legislative Assistant (generally the first one listed alphabetically.)

(Area Code 202)

U.S. Senate

Jesse Helms (R-NC)
SD-403 Dirksen Senate Office Building...................224-6342
FAX...224-1376
Chief Legislative Assistant: Andy Hartsfield

Terry Sanford (D-NC)
SH-716 Hart Senate Office Building......................224-3154
FAX...224-7406
Legislative Director: Jennifer Hillman
Legislative Assistants/Counsel: Richard Blanks, Barbara Larkin

U.S. House of Representatives
(Listed by Congressional District)

1. Walter B. Jones (D-NC)
241 Cannon House Office Building........................225-3101
Legislative Assistant: Bob Peele

2. Tim Valentine (D-NC)
1510 Longworth House Office Building....................225-4531
FAX...225-1539
Legislative Assistant: Jack Blaylock Jr

3. H. Martin Lancaster (D-NC)
1417 Longworth House Office Building....................225-3415
FAX...225-0666
Legislative Director: Charles R. Rawls

4. David E. Price (D-NC)
1224 Longworth House Office Building....................225-1784
FAX...225-6314
Legislative Director: Paul Feldman

(Area Code 202)

5. Stephen L. Neal (D-NC)
2463 Rayburn House Office Building.......................225-2071
FAX...225-4060
Legislative Director: Corky Collins

6. Howard Coble (R-NC)
430 Cannon House Office Building.........................225-3065
FAX...225-8611
Legislative Director: Blaine Merritt

7. Charlie Rose (D-NC)
2230 Rayburn House Office Building.......................225-2731
FAX...225-2470
Legislative Director: Keith Pitts

8. W.G. Hefner (D-NC)
2161 Rayburn House Office Building.......................225-3715

(Area Code 202)

FAX...225-4036
Legislative Director: Irene Schecter

9. Alex McMillan (R-NC)
401 Cannon House Office Building.........................225-1976
Chief Counsel: Donna Alexander
Legislative Assistant: Polly Hubbell

10. Cass Ballenger (R-NC)
218 Cannon House Office Building.........................225-2576
FAX...225-0316
Legislative Director: Ashley McArthur

11. James McClure Clarke (D-NC)
217 Cannon House Office Building.........................225-6401
FAX...225-0519
Legislative Assistant: Steve Seiberling

NORTH DAKOTA

Zip Codes:
U.S. Senate...20510
U.S. House of Representative 20515

Note: When a Senate or House staff does not include a Legislative Director, we have listed here the name of a Legislative Assistant (generally the first one listed alphabetically.)

(Area Code 202)

U.S. Senate

Quentin N. Burdick (D-ND)
SH-511 Hart Senate Office Building.......................224-2551
Legislative Assistant: Shelley Feist

Kent Conrad (D-ND)
SD-361 Dirksen Senate Office Building....................224-2043
Legislative Director: Mary Eccles

U.S. House of Representatives
(Listed by Congressional District)

1. Byron L. Dorgan (D-ND)
109 Cannon House Office Building.........................225-2611
Legislative Assistant: Allen Huffman

OHIO

Zip Codes:
U.S. Senate...20510
U.S. House of Representative 20515

Note: When a Senate or House staff does not include a Legislative Director, we have listed here the name of a Legislative Assistant (generally the first one listed alphabetically.)

(Area Code 202)

U.S. Senate

John Glenn (D-OH)
SH-503 Hart Senate Office Building.......................224-3353
Legislative Director: Kenneth Dameron
Legislative Counsel: Linda Parson

Howard M. Metzenbaum (D-OH)
SR-140 Russell Senate Office Building....................224-2315
Legislative Director: Joel Johnson

U.S. House of Representatives
(Listed by Congressional District)

1. Thomas A. Luken (D-OH)
2368 Rayburn House Office Building.......................225-2216
FAX...225-2293
Legislative Assistant: Valerie Greene

2. Willis D. Gradison Jr (R-OH)
2311 Rayburn House Office Building.......................225-3164
Legislative Assistant: Bonnie Brown

3. Tony P. Hall (D-OH)
2162 Rayburn House Office Building.......................225-6465
FAX 225-6766
Legislative Assistant: Gail Amidzich

4. Michael G. Oxley (R-OH)
1131 Longworth House Office Building.....................225-2676
Legislative Assistant: Brian Hicks

5. Paul E. Gillmor (R-OH)
1008 Longworth House Office Building.....................225-6405
Legislative Director: Fred Eames

6. Bob McEwen (R-OH) (Area Code 202)
2431 Rayburn House Office Building....................225-5705
FAX..225-0224
Legislative Director: Mary Mertz

7. Michael DeWine (R-OH)
1705 Longworth House Office Building....................225-4324
FAX..225-1984
Legislative Director: Ted Hollingsworth

8. Donald E. Lukens (R-OH)
117 Cannon House Office Building........................225-6205
FAX..225-0704
Legislative Director: James Dornan

9. Marcy Kaptur (D-OH)
1228 Longworth House Office Building....................225-4146
FAX..225-7711
Legislative Director: Bobbi Jeanquart

10. Clarence E. Miller (R-OH)
2308 Rayburn House Office Building......................225-5131
FAX..225-5132
Legislative Assistant: Bob Clark

11. Dennis E. Eckart (D-OH)
1111 Longworth House Office Building....................225-6331
Legislative Assistant: Sara Franko

12. John R. Kasich (R-OH)
1133 Longworth House Office Building....................225-5355
Legislative Assistant: Greg Hampton

13. Don J. Pease (D-OH)
2410 Rayburn House Office Building......................225-3401
Legislative Director: Brent Fogt

14. Thomas C. Sawyer (D-OH)
1518 Longworth House Office Building....................225-5231
FAX..225-5278
Legislative Director: Sara Platt-Davis

15. Chalmers P. Wylie (R-OH) (Area Code 202)
2310 Rayburn House Office Building......................225-2015
FAX..225-7548
Legislative Assistant: Ted Williams

16. Ralph Regula (R-OH)
2207 Rayburn House Office Building......................225-3876
FAX..225-3059
Legislative Counsel: Mark Benedict

17. James A. Traficant Jr (D-OH)
312 Cannon House Office Building........................225-5261
FAX..225-3719
Legislative Director: Christopher Whitehead

18. Douglas Applegate (D-OH)
2183 Rayburn House Office Building......................225-6265
FAX..225-3087
Legislative Assistant: Anne Grady

19. Edward F. Feighan (D-OH)
1124 Longworth House Office Building....................225-5731
FAX..226-1230
Counsel: Leah Gurowitz
Legislative Assistant: Jennifer Duke

20. Mary Rose Oakar (D-OH)
2231 Rayburn House Office Building......................225-5871
FAX..225-0663
Legislative Assistant: Scott Frey

21. Louis Stokes (D-OH)
2365 Rayburn House Office Building......................225-7032
FAX..225-1339
Legislative Assistant: Leslie Atkinson

OKLAHOMA

Zip Codes:
U.S. Senate..20510
U.S. House of Representative 20515

Note: When a Senate or House staff does not include a Legislative Director, we have listed here the name of a Legislative Assistant (generally the first one listed alphabetically.)

(Area Code 202)

U.S. Senate

David L. Boren (D-OK)
SR-453 Russell Senate Office Building...................224-4721
Chief Legislative Assistant: Cody Graves

Don Nickles (R-OK)
SH-713 Hart Senate Office Building......................224-5754
Legislative Director: Les Brorsen

U.S. House of Representatives
(Listed by Congressional District)

1. James M. Inhofe (R-OK)
408 Cannon House Office Building........................225-2211
FAX..225-9187
Legislative Director: Ruth Van Mark

2. Mike Synar (D-OK)
2441 Rayburn House Office Building......................225-2701
FAX..225-2796
Legislative Director: Kim Koontz

3. Wes Watkins (D-OK)
2348 Rayburn House Office Building......................225-4565
FAX..225-9029
Legislative Director: Jeanette Hanna

4. Dave McCurdy (D-OK)
2344 Rayburn House Office Building......................225-6165
Legislative Director: Stephanie Reed

5. Mickey Edwards (R-OK)
2330 Rayburn House Office Building......................225-2132
Legislative Assistant: Doug Hatcher

6. Glenn English (D-OK)
2206 Rayburn House Office Building......................225-5565
Legislative Assistant: Chris Bohanon

OREGON

Zip Codes:
U.S. Senate 20510
U.S. House of Representative 20515

Note: When a Senate or House staff does not include a Legislative Director, we have listed here the name of a Legislative Assistant (generally the first one listed alphabetically.)

(Area Code 202)

U.S. Senate

Mark O. Hatfield (R-OR)
SH-711 Hart Senate Office Building 224-3753
Legislative Director/Counsel: Jim Fitzhenry

Bob Packwood (R-OR)
SR-259 Russell Senate Office Building 224-5244
Legislative Director/Counsel: Jim Fitzhenry

U.S. House of Representatives
(Listed by Congressional District)

1. Les AuCoin (D-OR) (Area Code 202)
2159 Rayburn House Office Building 225-0855
FAX 225-2707
Legislative Assistant: Marie Mentor

2. Robert F. Smith (R-OR)
118 Cannon House Office Building 225-6730
FAX 225-3129
Legislative Director: Pete Thomson

3. Ron Wyden (D-OR)
2452 Rayburn House Office Building 225-4811
Legislative Director/Counsel: Ken Rosenbaum

4. Peter A. DeFazio (D-OR)
1233 Longworth House Office Building 225-6416
Legislative Assistant: Brad DeVries

5. Denny Smith (R-OR)
1213 Longworth House Office Building 225-5711
FAX 225-9477
Legislative Assistant: Mike Champness

PENNSYLVANIA

Zip Codes:
U.S. Senate 20510
U.S. House of Representative 20515

Note: When a Senate or House staff does not include a Legislative Director, we have listed here the name of a Legislative Assistant (generally the first one listed alphabetically.)

(Area Code 202)

U.S. Senate

John Heinz (R-PA)
SR-277 Russell Senate Office Building 224-6324
Legislative Director: Richard Bryers

Arlen Specter (R-PA)
SH-303 Hart Senate Office Building 224-4254
Legislative Director: Michael Russell
Counsel: Hans Hageman

U.S. House of Representatives
(Listed by Congressional District)

1. Thomas M. Foglietta (D-PA)
231 Cannon House Office Building 225-4731
FAX 225-0088
Legislative Director: Keith Morrison

2. William H. Gray III (D-PA)
2454 Rayburn House Office Building 225-4001
Chief of Staff/Legislative Director: Alan C. Bowser

3. Robert A. Borski (D-PA)
314 Cannon House Office Building 225-8251
FAX 225-4628
Legislative Assistant: Peter Madaus

4. Joe Kolter (D-PA)
212 Cannon House Office Building 225-2565
FAX 225-0526
Legislative Assistant: Bob Powers

5. Richard T. Schulze (R-PA)
2369 Rayburn House Office Building 225-5761
Legislative Assistant: Kathryn Lowell

6. Gus Yatron (D-PA)
2205 Rayburn House Office Building 225-5546
FAX 225-5548
Legislative Assistant: Dale Morris

7. Curt Weldon (R-PA)
316 Cannon House Office Building 225-2011
FAX 225-8137
Legislative Director: Nancy Lifset

8. Peter H. Kostmayer (D-PA)
123 Cannon House Office Building 225-4276
FAX 225-5060
Legislative Assistant: Peter Buckey

9. Bud Shuster (R-PA)
2268 Rayburn House Office Building 225-2431
Legislative Director: Tim Hugo

10. Joseph M. McDade (R-PA)
2370 Rayburn House Office Building 225-3731
FAX 225-9594
Legislative Director: John Enright

11. Paul E. Kanjorski (D-PA)
424 Cannon House Office Building 225-6511
Legislative Director: Mike Radway

12. John P. Murtha (D-PA)
2423 Rayburn House Office Building 225-2065
Executive Assistant/Legislative Assistant: William Allen

13. Lawrence Coughlin (R-PA)
2309 Rayburn House Office Building 225-6111
Legislative Director: Bill Klein
Counsel: Kenneth Kraft

(Area Code 202)

14. William J. Coyne (D-PA)
2455 Rayburn House Office Building......................225-2301
Legislative Assistant: Grace Hailer

15. Don Ritter (R-PA)
2447 Rayburn House Office Building......................225-6411
FAX..225-5248
Legislative Director: Jean Perih

16. Robert S. Walker (R-PA)
2445 Rayburn House Office Building......................225-2411
FAX..225-2484
Legislative Director: Deirdre Cavanaugh

17. George W. Gekas (R-PA)
1519 Longworth House Office Building....................225-4315
FAX..225-8440
Administrative Assistant/Legislative Director:
Allan Cagnoli

18. Doug Walgren (D-PA)
2241 Rayburn House Office Building......................225-2135
FAX..225-7747
Legislative Assistant: David Allnut

(Area Code 202)

19. William F. Goodling (R-PA)
2263 Rayburn House Office Building......................225-5836
Legislative Assistant: Karen Baker

20. Joseph M. Gaydos (D-PA)
2186 Rayburn House Office Building......................225-4631
Administrative Assistant: Barbara Pogue

21. Tom Ridge (R-PA)
1714 Longworth House Office Building....................225-5406
FAX..225-1081
Legislative Assistant: Mary Whalen

22. Austin J. Murphy (D-PA)
2210 Rayburn House Office Building 225-4665
FAX..225-4772
Legislative Director: Ron Ungvarsky

23. William F. Clinger Jr (R-PA)
2160 Rayburn House Office Building......................225-5121
FAX..225-4681
Legislative Director: Tammy Lindenberg

RHODE ISLAND

Zip Codes:
U.S. Senate..20510
U.S. House of Representative 20515

Note: When a Senate or House staff does not include a Legislative Director, we have listed here the name of a Legislative Assistant (generally the first one listed alphabetically.)

(Area Code 202)

U.S. Senate

Claiborne Pell (D-RI)
SR-335 Russell Senate Office Building...................224-4642
Legislative Director: Bill Young

John H. Chafee (R-RI)
SD-567 Dirksen Senate Office Building...................224-2921
Legislative Director/Counsel: Christine C. Ferguson

U.S. House of Representatives
(Listed by Congressional District)

1. Ron Machtley (R-RI)
1123 Longworth House Office Building....................225-4911
Administrative Assistant/Legislative Director:
Tim Meyer

2. Claudine Schneider (R-RI)
1512 Longworth House Office Building....................225-2735
Legislative Director: David Stonner

SOUTH CAROLINA

Zip Codes:
U.S. Senate..20510
U.S. House of Representative 20515

Note: When a Senate or House staff does not include a Legislative Director, we have listed here the name of a Legislative Assistant (generally the first one listed alphabetically.)

(Area Code 202)

U.S. Senate

Strom Thurmond (R-SC)
SR-217 Russell Senate Office Building...................224-5972
FAX..224-1300
Legislative Director: Cindi Blackburn

Ernest F. Hollings (D-SC)
SR-125 Russell Senate Office Building...................224-6121
Legislative Director: David Rudd

U.S. House of Representatives
(Listed by Congressional District)

1. Arthur Ravenel Jr (R-SC)
508 Cannon House Office Building........................225-3176
FAX..225-4340
Legislative Director: Rebecca Page

2. Floyd Spence (R-SC)
2405 Rayburn House Office Building......................225-2452
FAX..225-2455
Legislative Director: Marilyn King

3. Butler Derrick (D-SC)
201 Cannon House Office Building........................225-5301
Legislative Assistant: Wren Ivester

(Area Code 202)

4. Elizabeth J. Patterson (D-SC)
1641 Longworth House Office Building....................225-6030
FAX...225-7664
Legislative Director: Eric Spitler

5. John M. Spratt Jr (D-SC)
1533 Longworth House Office Building....................225-5501
FAX...225-0464
Legislative Director: Bob DeGrasse

6. Robin M. Tallon (D-SC)
432 Cannon House Office Building........................225-3315
FAX...225-2857
Legislative Director: Margaret Conrad

SOUTH DAKOTA

Zip Codes:
U.S. Senate 20510
U.S. House of Representative 20515

Note: When a Senate or House staff does not include a Legislative Director, we have listed here the name of a Legislative Assistant (generally the first one listed alphabetically.)

(Area Code 202)

U.S. Senate

Larry Pressler (R-SD)
SH-133 Hart Senate Office Building......................224-5842
FAX...224-1630
Legislative Director: Douglas L. Miller

Thomas A. Daschle (D-SD)
SH-317 Hart Senate Office Building......................224-2321
FAX...224-2047
Legislative Director: Laura Petrou

U.S. House of Representatives
(Listed by Congressional District)

1. Tim Johnson (D-SD)
513 Cannon House Office Building........................225-2801
FAX...225-2427
Legislative Director: Mark Rubin

TENNESSEE

Zip Codes:
U.S. Senate 20510
U.S. House of Representative 20515

Note: When a Senate or House staff does not include a Legislative Director, we have listed here the name of a Legislative Assistant (generally the first one listed alphabetically.)

(Area Code 202)

U.S. Senate

Jim Sasser (D-TN)
SR-363 Russell Senate Office Building...................224-3344
FAX...224-9590
Legislative Director: Jeff Lane

Albert Gore Jr (D-TN)
SR-393 Russell Senate Office Building...................224-4944
Legislative Director: Carol Browner

U.S. House of Representatives
(Listed by Congressional District)

1. James H. Quillen (R-TN)
102 Cannon House Office Building........................225-6356
FAX...225-7812
Legislative Assistant: Sheryl Bonifer

2. John J. Duncan Jr (R-TN)
416 Cannon House Office Building........................225-5435
FAX...225-6440
Legislative Director: Jim Coon

3. Marilyn Lloyd (D-TN)
2266 Rayburn House Office Building......................225-3271
FAX...225-6974
Legislative Director: Patty Flaherty

4. Jim Cooper (D-TN)
125 Cannon House Office Building........................225-6831
FAX...225-4520
Legislative Director: Thomas J. Fields

5. Bob Clement (D-TN)
325 Cannon House Office Building........................225-4311
Legislative Director: Jay Hansen

6. Bart Gordon (D-TN)
103 Cannon House Office Building........................225-4231
FAX 225-6887
Legislative Director: Harrison Wadsworth

7. Don Sundquist (R-TN)
230 Cannon House Office Building........................225-2811
FAX...225-2814
Legislative Director: Kimberley Best

8. John Tanner (D-TN)
512 Cannon House Office Building........................225-4714
FAX...225-1765
Legislative Director: Vickie L. Walling

9. Harold E. Ford (D-TN)
2305 Rayburn House Office Building......................225-3265
Legislative Director: Seth Berger
Tax Counsel: Vanessa Brooks

TEXAS

Zip Codes:
U.S. Senate..20510
U.S. House of Representative 20515

Note: When a Senate or House staff does not include a Legislative Director, we have listed here the name of a Legislative Assistant (generally the first one listed alphabetically.)

(Area Code 202)

U.S. Senate

Lloyd Bentsen (D-TX)
SH-703 Hart Senate Office Building......................224-5922
Legislative Director: Blaine Bull
Legal Counsel: Robert Mallett

Phil Gramm (R-TX)
SR-370 Russell Senate Office Building...................224-2934
Legislative Director: Richard Ribbentrop

U.S. House of Representatives
(Listed by Congressional District)

1. Jim Chapman (D-TX)
236 Cannon House Office Building........................225-3035
FAX...225-7265
Legislative Director: Karen Troutman

2. Charles Wilson (D-TX)
2256 Rayburn House Office Building......................225-2401
FAX...225-1764
Legislative Director: P.L. Murphy

3. Steve Bartlett (R-TX)
1113 Longworth House Office Building....................225-4201
Legislative Assistant: Deborah Winters

4. Ralph M. Hall (D-TX)
2236 Rayburn House Office Building......................225-6673
FAX...225-3332
Legislative Assistant: William Cargill

5. John Bryant (D-TX)
208 Cannon House Office Building........................225-2231
Legislative Director: Barbara Crapa

6. Joe Barton (R-TX)
1225 Longworth House Office Building....................225-2002
FAX...225-3052
Legislative Director: Jeff MacKinnon

7. Bill Archer (R-TX)
1236 Longworth House Office Building....................225-2571
FAX...225-4381
Legislative Director: Donna Steele Flynn

8. Jack Fields (R-TX)
108 Cannon House Office Building........................225-4901
Legislative Director: Gail Giblin

9. Jack Brooks (D-TX)
2449 Rayburn House Office Building......................225-6565
FAX...225-1584
Legislative Director: Joan Kelly

10. J.J. Pickle (D-TX)
242 Cannon House Office Building........................225-4865
Legislative Assistant: Dave Mason

11. Marvin Leath (D-TX)
336 Cannon House Office Building........................225-6105
FAX...225-0350
Legislative Aide: Cathline Domingues

12. Preston M. Geren (D-TX) (Area Code 202)
1730 Longworth House Office Building....................225-5071
FAX...225-2786
Legislative Director: Lionel Collins Jr.

13. Bill Sarpalius (D-TX)
1223 Longworth House Office Building....................225-3706
FAX...225-6142
Legislative Director: Joel Brandenberger

14. Greg Laughlin (D-TX)
414 Cannon House Office Building........................225-2831
Legislative Assistant: Normalinda Gonzalez

15. E. "Kika" de la Garza (D-TX)
1401 Longworth House Office Building....................225-2531
FAX...225-2533
Legislative Assistant: Anton Papich

16. Ronald D. Coleman (D-TX)
440 Cannon House Office Building........................225-4831
Senior Legislative Assistant: John Ferriter

17. Charles W. Stenholm (D-TX)
1226 Longworth House Office Building....................225-6605
FAX...225-2234
Legislative Director: Rebecca Tice
Counsel/Legislative Assistant: Damon Tobias

18. Craig A. Washington (D-TX)
1631 Longworth House Office Building....................225-3816
Legislative Director: James Williams
Legal Counsel: Sidney Braquet

19. Larry Combest (R-TX)
1527 Longworth House Office Building....................225-4005
Legislative Assistant: Rob Lehman

20. Henry B. Gonzalez (D-TX)
2413 Rayburn House Office Building......................225-3236
FAX...225-1915
Legislative Director: Jennifer Cell Sada

21. Lamar Smith (R-TX)
422 Cannon House Office Building........................225-4236
Legislative Assistant: Jennifer Cromwell

22. Tom DeLay (R-TX)
308 Cannon House Office Building........................225-5951
Legislative Assistant: Lori Farber

23. Albert G. Bustamante (D-TX)
1116 Longworth House Office Building....................225-4511
Legislative Assistant: Gene Fisher

24. Martin Frost (D-TX)
2459 Rayburn House Office Building......................225-3605
FAX...225-4951
Legislative Director: Matthew Angle

25. Michael A. Andrews (D-TX)
322 Cannon House Office Building........................225-7508
Tax Counsel/Legislative Director: Nancy Powers Perry

26. Dick Armey (R-TX)
130 Cannon House Office Building........................225-7772
FAX...225-7614
Legislative Director: Brian Gunderson

27. Solomon P. Ortiz (D-TX)
1524 Longworth House Office Building....................225-7742
FAX...226-1134
Legislative Director: Sheila Clarke

UTAH

Zip Codes:
U.S. Senate 20510
U.S. House of Representative 20515

Note: When a Senate or House staff does not include a Legislative Director, we have listed here the name of a Legislative Assistant (generally the first one listed alphabetically.)

(Area Code 202)

U.S. Senate

Jake Garn (R-UT)
SD-505 Dirksen Senate Office Building.................. 224-5444
Legislative Director: Joanne Snow-Neumann

Orrin G. Hatch (R-UT)
SR-135 Russell Senate Office Building.................. 224-5251
Legislative Director: Wendy Higginbotham

U.S. House of Representatives

(Listed by Congressional District)

(Area Code 202)

1. James V. Hansen (R-UT)
2421 Rayburn House Office Building..................... 225-0453
FAX.. 225-5857
Legislative Assistant: Rick Guldan

2. Wayne Owens (D-UT)
1728 Longworth House Office Building................... 225-3011
FAX.. 225-3524
Legislative Director: Scott Kearin

3. Howard C. Nielson (R-UT)
1122 Longworth House Office Building................... 225-7751
FAX.. 226-1223
Chief of Staff/Counsel: L. Reid Ivins
Senior Legislative Assistant: JayneAnne Rex

VERMONT

Zip Codes:
U.S. Senate 20510
U.S. House of Representative 20515

Note: When a Senate or House staff does not include a Legislative Director, we have listed here the name of a Legislative Assistant (generally the first one listed alphabetically.)

(Area Code 202)

U.S. Senate

Patrick J. Leahy (D-VT)
SR-433 Russell Senate Office Building.................. 224-4242
Legislative Director: Luke Albee

James M. Jeffords (R-VT)
SD-530 Dirksen Senate Office Building.................. 224-5141
Legislative Director: Mark Powden
Legislative Counsel: Peter Caldwell

U.S. House of Representatives

(Listed by Congressional District)

1. Peter Smith (R-VT)
1020 Longworth House Office Building................... 225-4115
FAX.. 225-6790
Legislative Director: James Bressor

VIRGINIA

Zip Codes:
U.S. Senate 20510
U.S. House of Representative 20515

Note: When a Senate or House staff does not include a Legislative Director, we have listed here the name of a Legislative Assistant (generally the first one listed alphabetically.)

(Area Code 202)

U.S. Senate

John Warner (R-VA)
SR-225 Russell Senate Office Building.................. 224-2023
FAX.. 224-6295
Legislative Counsel: Claudia McMurray
Legislative Assistant: Mike Brown

Charles S. Robb (D-VA)
SR-493 Russell Senate Office Building.................. 224-4024
FAX.. 224-8689
Legislative Director: Kerry A. Walsh Skelly

U.S. House of Representatives

(Listed by Congressional District)

1. Herbert H. Bateman (R-VA)
1230 Longworth House Office Building................... 225-4261
FAX.. 225-4382
Legislative Director: John Rayfield

2. Owen B. Pickett (D-VA)
1204 Longworth House Office Building................... 225-4215
Legislative Director: Albert A. Oetken

3. Thomas J. Bliley Jr (R-VA) (Area Code 202)
2448 Rayburn House Office Building......................225-2815
Legislative Director: Jim Derderian

4. Norman Sisisky (D-VA)
426 Cannon House Office Building........................225-6365
FAX...226-1170
Legislative Director: Perry Floyd

5. Lewis F. Payne Jr (D-VA)
1118 Longworth House Office Building....................225-4711
FAX...226-1147
Legislative Director: Terry C. Hoye

6. Jim Olin (D-VA)
1314 Longworth House Office Building....................225-5431
FAX...225-9623
Legislative Director: Dian Copelin

7. D. French Slaughter Jr (R-VA) (Area Code 202)
1404 Longworth House Office Building....................225-6561
Senior Legislative Assistant: Greg Erken

8. Stan Parris (R-VA)
2434 Rayburn House Office Building......................225-4376
FAX...225-0017
Legislative Director: Mark Robertson

9. Rick Boucher (D-VA)
428 Cannon House Office Building........................225-3861
Legislative Director: Larry Clinton

10. Frank R. Wolf (R-VA)
104 Cannon House Office Building........................225-5136
FAX...225-0437
Legislative Director: Janet Shaffron

WASHINGTON

Zip Codes:
U.S. Senate...20510
U.S. House of Representative 20515

Note: When a Senate or House staff does not include a Legislative Director, we have listed here the name of a Legislative Assistant (generally the first one listed alphabetically.)

(Area Code 202)

U.S. Senate

Brock Adams (D-WA)
SH-513 Hart Senate Office Building......................224-2621
FAX...224-0238
Legislative Director: Sam Spina
Special Counsel: Tom Keefe

Slade Gorton (R-WA)
SH-730 Hart Senate Office Building......................224-3441
Senior Legislative Assistants: Terri Claffey, Jeff Roe, Robert Soofer, and J. Vander Stoep

U.S. House of Representatives
(Listed by Congressional District)

1. John Miller (R-WA)
1406 Longworth House Office Building....................225-6311
Legislative Director: Charles Broches

2. Al Swift (D-WA)
1502 Longworth House Office Building....................225-2605
Legislative Director: Scott Cooper

3. Jolene Unsoeld (D-WA)
1508 Longworth House Office Building....................225-3536
FAX...225-9095
Administrative Assistant/Legislative Director: Dan Evans

4. Sid Morrison (R-WA)
1434 Longworth House Office Building....................225-5816
FAX...225-9293
Legislative Assistant: Allison Biggs

5. Thomas S. Foley (D-WA)
1201 Longworth House Office Building....................225-2006
Legislative Assistant: Nick Ashmore

6. Norman D. Dicks (D-WA)
2429 Rayburn House Office Building......................225-5916
Legislative Director: Ted Bristol

7. Jim McDermott (D-WA)
1529 Longworth House Office Building....................225-3106
Administrative Assistant/Legislative Director: Charles M. Williams

8. Rod Chandler (R-WA)
223 Cannon House Office Building........................225-7761
FAX...225-7762
Legislative Director: Ed Gilroy
Legislative Counsel: Chris Dachi and Damian King

WEST VIRGINIA

Zip Codes:
U.S. Senate...20510
U.S. House of Representative 20515

Note: When a Senate or House staff does not include a Legislative Director, we have listed here the name of a Legislative Assistant (generally the first one listed alphabetically.)

(Area Code 202)

U.S. Senate

Robert C. Byrd (D-WV)
SH-311 Hart Senate Office Building......................224-3954
FAX...224-8070
Legislative Director: Jan Heininger

John D. Rockefeller IV (D-WV) (Area Code 202)
SH-724 Hart Senate Office Building......................224-6472
Legislative Director: Tamera Stanton
General Counsel/Legislative Assistant: Paul Joffe

U.S. House of Representatives
(Listed by Congressional District)

1. Alan B. Mollohan (D-WV)
229 Cannon House Office Building........................225-4172
FAX..225-7564
Legislative Director: David Herring

2. Harley O. Staggers Jr (D-WV) (Area Code 202)
1504 Longworth House Office Building....................225-4331
FAX..225-2962
Legislative Assistant: Annelise Hafer

3. Bob Wise (D-WV)
1421 Longworth House Office Building....................225-2711
FAX..225-7856
Legislative Director: Sonia Daugherty

4. Nick Joe Rahall II (D-WV)
2104 Rayburn House Office Building......................225-3452
FAX..225-9061
Legislative Assistant: Michael Goulding

WISCONSIN

Zip Codes:
U.S. Senate..20510
U.S. House of Representative 20515

Note: When a Senate or House staff does not include a Legislative Director, we have listed here the name of a Legislative Assistant (generally the first one listed alphabetically.)

(Area Code 202)

U.S. Senate

Robert W. Kasten Jr (R-WI)
SH-110 Hart Senate Office Building......................224-5323
Legislative Director: Jim Morhard
General Counsel/Legislative Assistant: David N. Meeker

Herbert Kohl (D-WI)
SH-702 Hart Senate Office Building......................224-5653
Chief of Staff/Legislative Director: Bob Seltzer
Counsel: Jon Leibowitz

U.S. House of Representatives
(Listed by Congressional District)

1. Les Aspin (D-WI)
2336 Rayburn House Office Building......................225-3031
Administrative Assistant/Legislative Director:
Ted Bornstein

2. Robert W. Kastenmeier (D-WI)
2328 Rayburn House Office Building......................225-2906
Legislative Assistant: Stuart Applebaum

3. Steve Gunderson (R-WI)
227 Cannon House Office Building........................225-5506
Legislative Director: Brad Cameron

4. Gerald D. Kleczka (D-WI)
226 Cannon House Office Building........................225-4572
Legislative Director: Ron Bookbinder

5. Jim Moody (D-WI)
1019 Longworth House Office Building....................225-3571
FAX..225-1396
Legislative Director: Nick Meyers

6. Thomas E. Petri (R-WI)
2443 Rayburn House Office Building......................225-2476
Administrative Assistant/Legislative Director:
Joe Flader

7. David Obey (D-WI)
2462 Rayburn House Office Building......................225-3365
FAX..225-0561
Legislative Director: Paul G. Carver

8. Toby Roth (R-WI)
2352 Rayburn House Office Building......................225-5665
Legislative Director: Edmund Rice

9. Jim Sensenbrenner Jr (R-WI)
2444 Rayburn House Office Building......................225-5101
Legislative Director: Paul Zanowski

WYOMING

Zip Codes:
U.S. Senate..20510
U.S. House of Representative 20515

Note: When a Senate or House staff does not include a Legislative Director, we have listed here the name of a Legislative Assistant (generally the first one listed alphabetically.)

(Area Code 202)

U.S. Senate

Malcolm Wallop (R-WY)
SR-237 Russell Senate Office Building...................224-6441
FAX..224-3230
Legislative Director: Lynn Bragg

Alan K. Simpson (R-WY)
SD-261 Dirksen Senate Office Building...................224-3424
FAX..224-1315
Legislative Director: Tom Bauer

U.S. House of Representatives
(Listed by Congressional District)

1. Craig Thomas (R-WY)
1721 Longworth House Office Building....................225-2311
FAX..225-0726
Legislative Director: Steve McMillan

DISTRICT OF COLUMBIA

Zip Codes:
U.S. Senate 20510
U.S. House of Representative 20515

Note: When a Delegate's staff does not include a Legislative Director, we have listed here the name of a Legislative Assistant (generally the first one listed alphabetically.)

(Area Code 202)

1. Walter E. Fauntroy (D-District of Columbia)
2135 Rayburn House Office Building 225-8050
Legislative Director: Stephen Horblitt

PUERTO RICO

Zip Codes:
U.S. Senate 20510
U.S. House of Representative 20515

Note: When a Delegate's staff does not include a Legislative Director, we have listed here the name of a Legislative Assistant (generally the first one listed alphabetically.)

(Area Code 202)

1. Jaime B. Fuster (D-PR)
427 Cannon House Office Building 225-2615
FAX 225-1959
Legislative Assistant: Jim Cohen

AMERICAN SAMOA

Zip Codes:
U.S. Senate 20510
U.S. House of Representative 20515

Note: When a Delegate's staff does not include a Legislative Director, we have listed here the name of a Legislative Assistant (generally the first one listed alphabetically.)

(Area Code 202)

1. Eni F.H. Faleomavaega (D-American Samoa)
413 Cannon House Office Building 225-8577
FAX 225-8757
Legislative Director: Martin Yerick

GUAM

Zip Codes:
U.S. Senate 20510
U.S. House of Representative 20515

Note: When a Delegate's staff does not include a Legislative Director, we have listed here the name of a Legislative Assistant (generally the first one listed alphabetically.)

(Area Code 202)

1. Ben Blaz (R-Guam)
1130 Longworth House Office Building 225-1188
FAX 225-0086
Legislative Director: Ben Bibb

VIRGIN ISLANDS

Zip Codes:
U.S. Senate 20510
U.S. House of Representative 20515

Note: When a Delegate's staff does not include a Legislative Director, we have listed here the name of a Legislative Assistant (generally the first one listed alphabetically.)

(Area Code 202)

1. Ron de Lugo (D-VI)
2238 Rayburn House Office Building 225-1790
FAX 225-9392
Administrative Assistant/Legislative Director: Sheila Ross

COMMITTEES OF THE U.S. SENATE AND THE U.S. HOUSE OF REPRESENTATIVES

DESCRIPTION: Standing, Select, and Special committees and subcommittees of the U.S. Senate and House of Representatives do most of the substantive legal work of the Congress pertaining to pending legislation. Oversight of Executive Branch departments and agencies also generates some legal work, as do requests by agencies for interpretations of legislation and legislative history, and committee investigations.

Titles of staff members vary by committee, but most committees have: a Staff Director or Staff Director/ Chief Counsel (the most powerful person on the staff); a General Counsel; a Chief Clerk; other Professional Staff Members; a Minority Staff Director; and a Minority Counsel.

Currently, committee chairmen in both the Senate and the House of Representatives are all Democrats and ranking minority members are all Republicans.

Unless otherwise specified, the majority and minority staff members identified under each committee may be contacted through the main committee telephone number.

COMMITTEES OF THE U.S. SENATE

COMMITTEE ON AGRICULTURE, NUTRITION, AND FORESTRY
(Area Code 202)

SR-328A Russell Senate Office Building 224-2035

Jurisdiction: Agricultural economics and research; agricultural extension services and experiment stations; agricultural production, marketing, and stabilization of prices; agricultural commodities; animal industry and diseases; crop insurance and soil conservation; farm credit and farm security; food from fresh waters; food stamp programs; forestry and forest reserves and wilderness areas other than those created from the public domain; home economics; human nutrition; inspection of livestock, meat, and agricultural products; pests and pesticides; plant industry, soils, and agricultural engineering; rural development, rural electrification, and watersheds; and school nutrition programs.

Majority Chief Counsel: Jim Cubie.......................224-5207
Minority Counsel: Brent Baglien.........................224-6901

COMMITTEE ON APPROPRIATIONS

S-128 Capitol Building.................................224-3471

Jurisdiction: Appropriation of the revenue for the support of the Government; rescission of appropriations contained in appropriation Acts; the amount of new spending authority which is to be effective for a fiscal year.

Majority Staff Director: James H. English...............224-7200
Minority Staff Director: J. Keith Kennedy...............224-7335

COMMITTEE ON ARMED SERVICES

SR-228 Russell Senate Office Building.................224-3871

Jurisdiction: Aeronautical and space activities associated with the development of weapons systems or military operations; common defense; Department of Defense, the Department of the Army, the Department of the Navy, and the Department of the Air Force; maintenance and operation of the Panama Canal, including administration, sanitation, and government of the Canal Zone; military research and development; national security aspects of nuclear energy; Naval petroleum reserves, except those in Alaska; pay, promotion, retirement, and other benefits and privileges of members of the Armed Forces, including overseas education of civilian and military dependents; selective service system; strategic and critical materials necessary for the common defense.

Majority General Counsel: Andrew S. Effron
Minority Staff Director/Counsel: Patrick A. Tucker

COMMITTEE ON BANKING, HOUSING, AND URBAN AFFAIRS
(Area Code 202)

SD-534 Dirksen Senate Office Building.................224-7391
FAX...224-5137

Jurisdiction: Banks, banking, and financial institutions; control of prices of commodities, rents, and services; deposit insurance; economic stabilization and defense production; export and foreign trade promotion; export controls; Federal monetary policy, including the Federal Reserve System; financial aid to commerce and industry; issuance and redemption of notes; money and credit, including currency and coinage; nursing home construction; public and private housing (including veterans' housing); renegotiation of Government contracts; urban development and urban mass transit. The committee will also study and review, on a comprehensive basis, matters relating to international economic policy as it affects U.S. monetary affairs, credit, and financial institutions; economic growth, urban affairs, and credit.

Majority Staff Director/Chief Counsel: Steven B. Harris
Majority Senior Counsel/International Affairs Adviser: Patrick A. Mulloy
Minority General Counsel: Raymond Natter

COMMITTEE ON THE BUDGET

SD-621 Dirksen Senate Office Building.................224-0642

Jurisdiction: This committee reports the matters required to be reported by it under titles III and IV of the Congressional Budget Act of 1974; makes continuing studies of the effect on budget outlays of relevant existing and proposed legislation; requests and evaluates continuing studies of tax expenditures, devises methods of coordinating tax expenditures, policies, and programs with direct budget outlays, and reports the results of such studies to the Senate on a recurring basis; and reviews the work of the Congressional Budget Office.

(Area Code 202)

Majority Staff Director: John Hilley....................224-0553
Assistant Director/Counsel for Financial Affairs:
Gordon Stoddard..224-9547
Minority Staff Director: G. William Hoagland 224-0769

COMMITTEE ON COMMERCE, SCIENCE, AND TRANSPORTATION

SD-508 Dirksen Senate Office Building..................224-5115

Jurisdiction: The Coast Guard; coastal zone management; communications; highway safety; inland waterways, except construction; interstate commerce; marine and ocean navigation, safety, and transportation, including navigational aspects of deepwater ports; marine fisheries; merchant marine and navigation; nonmilitary aeronautical and space sciences; oceans, weather, and atmospheric activities; Panama Canal and interoceanic canals generally; regulation of consumer products and services, including testing related to toxic substances, other than pesticides, and except for credit, financial services, and housing; regulation of interstate common carriers, including railroads, buses, trucks, vessels, pipelines, and civil aviation; science, engineering, and technology research and development and policy; sports; standards and measurement; transportation; transportation and commerce aspects of Outer Continental Shelf lands.

Majority Chief Counsel/Staff Director: Kevin G. Curtin..224-0427
Minority Chief Counsel/Staff Director:
Walter B. McCormick Jr 224-5183

COMMITTEE ON ENERGY AND NATURAL RESOURCES

SD-364 Dirksen Senate Office Building..................224-4971

Jurisdiction: Coal production, distribution, and utilization; energy policy; energy regulation and conservation; energy related aspects of deepwater ports; energy research and development; extraction of minerals from oceans and Outer Continental Shelf lands; hydroelectric power, irrigation, and reclamation; mining education and research; mining, mineral lands, mining claims, and mineral conservation; national parks, recreation areas, wilderness area, wild and scenic rivers, historical sites, military parks and battlefields, and preservation of prehistoric ruins and objects of interest on the public domain; naval petroleum reserves in Alaska; nonmilitary development of nuclear energy; oil and gas production and distribution; public lands and forests, including farming and grazing thereon, and mineral extraction therefrom; solar energy systems; and territorial possessions of the U.S., including trusteeships.

Majority Chief Counsel: Mike Harvey.....................224-4971
Minority Chief Counsel: Gary Ellsworth..................224-1017

COMMITTEE ON ENVIRONMENT AND PUBLIC WORKS

SD-458 Dirksen Senate Office Building..................224-6176

Jurisdiction: Air pollution; construction and maintenance of highways; environmental aspects of Outer Continental Shelf lands; environmental policy; environmental research and development; fisheries and wildlife; flood control and improvements of rivers and harbors, including environmental aspects of deepwater ports; noise pollution; nonmilitary environmental regulation and control of nuclear energy; ocean dumping; public buildings and improved grounds of the U.S., including Federal buildings in the District of Columbia; public works, bridges, and dams; regional economic development; solid waste disposal and recycling; water pollution; and water resources.

Majority Counsel for Environmental Protection:
Katharine Kimball.......................................224-3339
Majority Counsel for Public Works/Transportation:
Mike Weiss 224-8216
Minority Chief Counsel: Steven Shimberg 224-6228

COMMITTEE ON FINANCE

(Area Code 202)

SD-205 Dirksen Senate Office Building..................224-4515
FAX...224-3014

Jurisdiction: Bonded debt of the U.S., except as provided in the Congressional Budget Act of 1974; customs, collection districts, and ports of entry and delivery; deposit of public moneys; general revenue sharing; health programs under the Social Security Act and health programs financed by a specific tax or trust fund; national social security; reciprocal trade agreements; revenue measures generally, except as provided in the Congressional Budget Act of 1974; revenue measures relating to the insular possessions; tariffs and import quotas; and transportation of dutiable goods.

Majority Staff Director/Chief Counsel: Van McMurtry.....224-4515
Majority Chief Tax Counsel: Samuel Sessions.............224-4515
Majority Chief International Trade Counsel:
Robert D. Kyle 224-4515
Minority Deputy Chief of Staff/Chief Tax Counsel:
Lindy Paull 224-5315
Minority Tax Counsel: Richard A. Grafmeyer,
T. Nina Oviedo, and Mark Prater 224-5315
Minority Chief Trade Counsel: Brad Figel................224-5315

COMMITTEE ON FOREIGN RELATIONS

SD-446 Dirksen Senate Office Building..................224-4651

Jurisdiction: Acquisition of land and buildings for embassies and legations in foreign countries; boundaries of the U.S.; diplomatic service; foreign economic, military, technical, and humanitarian assistance; foreign loans; international activities of the American National Red Cross and the International Committee of the Red Cross; international aspects of nuclear energy, including nuclear transfer policy; international conferences and congresses; international law as it relates to foreign policy; International Monetary Fund and other international organizations established primarily for international monetary purposes; intervention abroad and declarations of war; measures to foster commercial intercourse with foreign nations and safeguard American business interests abroad; national security and international aspects of trusteeships of the U.S.; oceans and international environmental and scientific affairs as they relate to foreign policy; protection of U.S. citizens abroad and expatriation; relations of the U.S. with foreign nationals generally; treaties and executive agreements, except reciprocal trade agreements; the United Nations and its affiliated organizations; the World Bank group, the regional development banks, and other international organizations established primarily for development assistance purposes.

Majority Chief Counsel: Michael T. Epstein 224-9032
Minority Chief Counsel: Robert A. Friedlander...........224-3941

COMMITTEE ON GOVERNMENTAL AFFAIRS

SD-340 Dirksen Senate Office Building..................224-4751

Jurisdiction: Archives of the U.S.; budget and accounting measures, other than appropriations, except as provided in the Congressional Budget Act of 1974; census and collection of statistics, including economic and social statistics; congressional organization, except for any part of the matter that amends the rules or orders of the Senate; Federal Civil Service; government information; intergovernmental relations; municipal affairs of the District of Columbia (except appropriations); organization and management of U.S. nuclear export policy; organization and reorganization of the executive branch of the Government; the Postal Service; status of officers and employees of the U.S., including their classification, compensation, and benefits.

Majority General Counsel: Steve Ryan 224-4751
Minority Counsel: John Mercer...........................224-2627

COMMITTEE ON THE JUDICIARY

(Area Code 202)

SD-224 Dirksen Senate Office Building................224-5225

Jurisdiction: Apportionment of Representatives; bankruptcy, mutiny, espionage, and counterfeiting; civil liberties; constitutional amendments; Federal courts and judges; government information; holidays and celebrations; immigration and naturalization; interstate compacts generally; judicial proceedings, civil and criminal, generally; local courts in the territories and possessions; measures relating to claims against the U.S.; national penitentiaries; the Patent Office; patents, copyrights, and trademarks; protection of trade and commerce against unlawful restraints and monopolies; revision and codification of the statutes of the U.S.; and state and territorial boundary lines.

Majority Chief Counsel: Ron Klain......................224-5225
Minority Chief Counsel: Terry Wooten...................224-9494

COMMITTEE ON LABOR AND HUMAN RESOURCES

SD-428 Dirksen Senate Office Building.................224-5375

Jurisdiction: Measures relating to education, labor, health, and public welfare; aging; agricultural colleges; arts and humanities; biomedical research and development; child labor; convict labor and the entry of goods made by convicts into interstate commerce; domestic activities of the American National Red Cross; equal employment opportunity; Gallaudet College, Howard University, and Saint Elizabeth's Hospital; handicapped individuals; labor standards and labor statistics; mediation and arbitration of labor disputes; occupational safety and health, including the welfare of miners; private pension plans; public health; railway labor and retirement; regulation of foreign laborers; student loans; and wages and hours of labor.

Majority Staff Director/Chief Counsel: Nick Littlefield 224-5465
Minority Chief Labor Counsel: Sharon Prost.............224-3491

COMMITTEE ON RULES AND ADMINISTRATION

SR-305 Russell Senate Office Building.................224-6352

Jurisdiction: Administration of the Senate Office Buildings and the Senate wing of the Capitol; congressional organization relative to rules and procedures, and Senate rules and regulations; corrupt practices; credentials and qualifications of members of the Senate, contested elections, and acceptance of incompatible offices; Federal elections generally, including the election of the President, Vice President, and Members of Congress; the Government Printing Office and printing of the Congressional Record; meetings of Congress and attendance of Members; payment of money out of the contingent fund of the Senate; Presidential succession; purchase of books and manuscripts and erection of monuments to the memory of individuals; Senate Library and statuary, art and pictures in the Capitol and Senate Office Buildings; services in the Senate including the Senate restaurant; the U.S. Capitol and congressional office buildings, the Library of Congress, the Smithsonian Institution, and the Botanic Gardens.

Majority Chief Counsel: John L. Sousa..................224-5648
Minority Counsel: Charles S. Konigsberg and
Mark Mackie...224-8923

COMMITTEE ON SMALL BUSINESS

SR-428A Russell Senate Office Building................224-5175

Jurisdiction: All proposed legislation, messages, petitions, and other matters relating to the Small Business Administration; and the research and investigation of all problems of American small business enterprises.

Majority Staff Director/Chief Counsel: John W. Ball.....224-5175
Majority Counsel for Procurement Policy:
William B. Montalto.................................224-8490

(Area Code 202)

Majority Counsel for Taxes: Charles E. Ludlam..........224-3095
Minority Staff Director/Chief Counsel: Peter Coyle......224-8494

COMMITTEE ON VETERANS' AFFAIRS

SR-414 Russell Senate Office Building.................224-9126

Jurisdiction: Compensation of veterans; life insurance issued by the Government on account of service in the Armed Forces; national cemeteries; pensions of all wars of the U.S., general and special; readjustment of servicemen to civil life; soldiers' and sailors' civil relief; veterans' hospitals, medical care, and treatment of veterans; veterans' measures generally; and vocational rehabilitation and education of veterans.

Majority Chief Counsel/Staff Director: Jonathan R.
Steinberg...224-6202
Minority Chief Counsel/Staff Director: Alan C. Ptak.....224-2074

SELECT COMMITTEE ON ETHICS

SH-220 Hart Senate Office Building....................224-2981

Jurisdiction: To administer, interpret, and enforce the Senate's Code of Official Conduct; to investigate allegations of improper conduct and recommend disciplinary action; to recommend additional rules or regulations; and to investigate allegations of unauthorized disclosures of information from the Select Committee on Intelligence.

Staff Director/Chief Counsel: Wilson Abney

SELECT COMMITTEE ON INDIAN AFFAIRS

SH-838 Hart Senate Office Building....................224-2251
FAX...224-2309

Jurisdiction: To study matters pertaining to problems and opportunities of Indians, including Indian land management and trust responsibilities, Indian education, health, special services, and loan programs, and Indian claims against the U.S.

Majority Chief Counsel: Patricia Zell
Minority Counsel/Staff Director: Eric Eberhard

SELECT COMMITTEE ON INTELLIGENCE

SH-211 Hart Senate Office Building....................224-1700

Jurisdiction: To oversee and study intelligence activities and programs of the U.S. Government; to submit to the Senate appropriate legislative proposals; to assure that appropriate departments and agencies provide informed and timely intelligence necessary for the executive and legislative branches to make sound decisions affecting the security and vital interests of the Nation; and assure that intelligence activities are in conformity with the Constitution and laws of the U.S.

General Counsel: L. Britt Snider

SPECIAL COMMITTEE ON AGING

SD-G31 Dirksen Senate Office Building.................224-5364

Jurisdiction: To study matters pertaining to problems and opportunities of older people, including the problems and opportunities of maintaining health, of assuring adequate income, of finding employment, of engaging in productive and rewarding activity, of securing proper housing, and, when necessary, of obtaining care or assistance.

Majority Staff Director: Portia Mittelman...............224-5364
Minority Staff Director: Jeffrey R. Lewis...............224-1467

COMMITTEES OF THE U.S. HOUSE OF REPRESENTATIVES

COMMITTEE ON AGRICULTURE (Area Code 202)

1301 Longworth House Office Building.................225-2171
FAX...225-8510

Jurisdiction: Agriculture generally; agricultural and industrial chemistry; agricultural colleges and experiment stations; agricultural economics; agricultural production and marketing and stabilization of prices of agricultural products, and commodities; animal industry and animal diseases; crop insurance and soil conservation; dairy industry; entomology and plant quarantine; extension of farm credit; forestry and forest reserves (other than those created from the public domain); human nutrition and home economics; inspection of livestock and meat products; rural electrification; and commodities exchanges.

Majority Counsel: Daniel E. Brinza
Minority Counsel: John E. Hogan

COMMITTEE ON APPROPRIATIONS

H-218 Capitol Building 225-2771

Jurisdiction: Appropriation of revenue for the support of the Government; rescissions of appropriations contained in the appropriation Acts; transfers of unexpended balances; and the amount of new spending authority which is to be effective for a fiscal year.

Majority Staff Director: Frederick G. Mohrman...........225-2771
Minority Staff Director: James W. Kulikowski............225-3481

COMMITTEE ON ARMED SERVICES

2120 Rayburn House Office Building....................225-4151
FAX...225-9077

Jurisdiction: Common defense generally; the Department of Defense generally, including the Departments of the Army, Navy, and Air Force; the conservation, development, and use of naval petroleum and oil shale reserves; the pay, promotion, retirement, and other benefits and privileges of members of the armed forces; scientific research and development in support of the armed services; selective service; soldiers' and sailors' homes; strategic and critical materials necessary for the common defense; and military applications of nuclear energy. The committee has a special oversight function with respect to international arms control and disarmament, and military dependents' education.

General Counsel: Colleen A. Preston.....................225-4223

COMMITTEE ON BANKING, FINANCE AND URBAN AFFAIRS

2129 Rayburn House Office Building 225-4247

Jurisdiction: Banks and banking, including deposit insurance and Federal monetary policy; money and credit, including currency and the issuance of notes, gold and silver, and valuation of the dollar; urban development; public and private housing; economic stabilization, defense production, renegotiation, and control of the price of commodities, rents, and services; international finance; financial aid to commerce and industry (other than transportation); and international financial and monetary organizations.

Majority General Counsel: Barbara Timmer................225-3548
Minority Staff Director/General Counsel: Tony Cole......225-7502

COMMITTEE ON THE BUDGET (Area Code 202)

214 House Office Building Annex I......................226-7200

Jurisdiction: To report the matters required under titles III and IV of the Congressional Budget Act of 1974; to make continuing studies of the effect on budget outlays of relevant existing and proposed legislation; to request and evaluate continuing studies of tax expenditures, and devise methods of coordinating tax expenditures, policies, and programs with direct budget outlays; and to review the work of the Congressional Budget Office.

Majority Chief Counsel: Martha Foley....................225-7233
Minority Counsel: Karen Buttaro.........................226-7270

COMMITTEE ON THE DISTRICT OF COLUMBIA

1310 Longworth House Office Building..................225-4457

Jurisdiction: All measures relating to the municipal affairs of the District of Columbia in general (other than appropriations therefore), including: insurance, executors wills, and divorce; municipal code and amendments to the criminal and corporation laws; municipal and juvenile courts; public health and safety; taxes and tax sales.

Majority Senior Staff Counsel: Harley Daniels, Dale MacIver, E. Faye Williams....................................225-4457
Minority Counsel: vacant................................225-7158

COMMITTEE ON EDUCATION AND LABOR

2181 Rayburn House Office Building....................225-4527
FAX 225-9070

Jurisdiction: Measures relating to education or labor generally; child labor; Columbia Institution for the Deaf, Dumb, and Blind; Howard Hospital; Freedmen's Hospital; convict labor and the entry of goods made by convicts into interstate commerce; labor standards and statistics; mediation and arbitration of labor disputes; regulation or prevention of importation of foreign laborers under contract; food programs for children in schools; U.S. Employees' Compensation Commission; vocational rehabilitation; wages and hours of labor; welfare of miners; work incentive programs. The committee has special oversight functions with respect to domestic educational programs and institutions, and programs of student assistance, which are within the jurisdiction of other committees.

Majority General Counsel: Richard E. Johnson............225-6808
Majority Counsel for Civil Rights and Labor Standards: Reginald C. Govan.......................................225-3388
Majority Counsel for Elementary and Secondary Education, Postsecondary Education, Select Education: John F. Jennings...225-4944
Majority Counsel for Labor Relations, Health and Safety: Karen S. Vagley...225-9328
Minority Counsel for Education: Jo-Marie St. Martin 225-1743
Minority Counsel for Labor: Randel Johnson 225-3725

COMMITTEE ON ENERGY AND COMMERCE

2125 Rayburn House Office Building 225-2927
FAX 225-2525

Jurisdiction: Interstate and foreign commerce generally; national energy policy generally; measures relating to the conservation of energy resources and to the commercial applications of energy technology; measures relating to the generation and marketing of power (except by Federal regional power marketing authorities), and to the reliability and interstate transmission of, and rate-making for, all power; interstate energy compacts; measures relating to general management of the Department of Energy and the Federal Energy Regulatory Commission; inland waterways; railroads; interstate and foreign communications; securities and exchanges; consumer affairs and consumer protection; travel and tourism; public health and quarantine; biomedical research and development. The committee has the same jurisdiction with respect to the regulation of nuclear facilities and use of nuclear energy as it has with respect to the regulation of nonnuclear facilities and the use of nonnuclear energy.

(Area Code 202)

Majority Counsel: David B. Finnegan, Richard Frandsen, Alan Roth, Donald Shriber, and Consuela Washington 225-2927
Minority Chief Counsel/Staff Director: MargaretA. Durbin....225-3641

COMMITTEE ON FOREIGN AFFAIRS

2170 Rayburn House Office Building....225-5021

Jurisdiction: Relations of the U.S. with foreign nations generally; acquisition of land and buildings for embassies and legations in foreign countries; establishment of boundary lines between the U.S. and foreign nations; foreign loans; international conferences; intervention abroad and declaration of war; measures relating to the diplomatic service; measures to encourage commercial dealings with foreign nations and safeguard American business interests abroad; neutrality; protection of American citizens abroad and expatriation; the American National Red Cross; United Nations organizations; export controls; international commodity agreements; trading with the enemy; and international education. The committee has special oversight functions with respect to customs administration, intelligence activities relating to foreign policy, international financial and monetary organizations, and international fishing agreements.

Majority Chief Counsel: R. Spencer Oliver....225-5021
Minority Chief Counsel: Daniel P. Finn....225-6735

COMMITTEE ON GOVERNMENT OPERATIONS

2157 Rayburn House Office Building....225-5051
FAX....225-4784

Jurisdiction: Budget and accounting measures, other than appropriations; the overall economy and efficiency of Government operations and activities, including Federal procurement; reorganization in the Executive Branch of the Government; intergovernmental relationships between the U.S. and states/- municipalities and general revenue sharing; and national archives.

Majority Deputy General Counsel: Ronald A. Stroman....225-5051
Majority Legislative Counsel: Thomas A. Trimboli....225-5051
Minority Counsel: Jared Burden, Ilene G. Rosenthal....225-5074

COMMITTEE ON HOUSE ADMINISTRATION

H-326Capitol Building....225-2061
FAX....225-4345

Jurisdiction: Appropriations from the contingent fund; employment of persons by the House; matters relating to the Library of Congress and the House Library, to the purchase of works of art for the Capitol, the Botanic Gardens, and erection of monuments to the memory of individuals; matters relating to the Smithsonian Institution and the incorporation of similar institutions; matters relating to the printing and correction of the Congressional Record; measures relating to assignment of office space for Members and committees; measures relating to the disposition of useless executive papers; measures relating to the election of President, Vice President, or Members of Congress, corrupt practices, contested elections, credentials and qualifications, and Federal elections generally; measures relating to the raising, reporting, and use of campaign contributions for candidates for office of Representative in the House of Representatives; and measures relating to the compensation, retirement, and other benefits of the Members, officers, and employees of the Congress.

(Area Code 202)

Majority Chief Counsel: Charles T. Howell....225-2061
Minority Elections Counsel: Roman Buhler....225-8281

COMMITTEE ON INTERIOR AND INSULAR AFFAIRS

1324 Longworth House Office Building....225-2761

Jurisdiction: Forest reserves and national parks created from public domain; forfeiture of land grants and alien ownership; Geological Survey; interstate compacts relating to apportionment of waters for irrigation purposes; irrigation and reclamation; measures relating to the care and management of Indians; measures relating generally to the insular possessions of the U.S., except those affecting the revenue and appropriations; military parks and battlefields, national cemeteries administered by the Secretary of the Interior, and parks within the District of Columbia; mineral land laws and claims; mineral resources of the public lands; mining interests generally; mining schools and experimental stations; petroleum conservation on the public lands and conservation of the radium supply in the U.S.; preservation of prehistoric ruins and objects of interests on the public domain; public lands generally, including entry, easements, and grazing thereon; relations of the U.S. with Indians and Indian tribes; and regulation of the domestic nuclear energy industry. The Committee has special oversight functions with respect to all programs affecting Indians and nonmilitary nuclear energy and research and development, including the disposal of nuclear waste.

Majority Staff Director/Counsel: Stanley Scoville....225-2761
Minority Chief Counsel: Richard A. Agnew....225-6065

COMMITTEE ON THE JUDICIARY

2138 Rayburn House Office Building....225-3951
FAX....225-1958

Jurisdiction: Judicial proceedings, civil and criminal generally; apportionment of Representatives; bankruptcy, mutiny, espionage, and counterfeiting; civil liberties; constitutional amendments; Federal courts and judges; immigration and naturalization; interstate compacts generally; local courts in the Territories and possessions; measures relating to claims against the U.S.; meetings of Congress, attendance of Members and their acceptance of incompatible offices; national penitentiaries; the Patent Office; patents, copyrights, and trademarks; Presidential succession; protection of trade and commerce against unlawful restraints and monopolies; revision and codification of the statutes of the U.S.; state and territorial boundary lines; and Communist and other subversive activities affecting the internal security of the U.S.

Majority General Counsel: William M. Jones....225-3951
Minority Chief Counsel: Alan F. Coffey Jr....225-6906

COMMITTEE ON MERCHANT MARINE AND FISHERIES

1334 Longworth House Office Building....225-4047

Jurisdiction: Merchant marine generally; oceanography and marine affairs, including coastal zone management; the Coast Guard, including lifesaving service, lighthouses, lightships, and ocean derelicts; fisheries and wildlife; measures relating to the regulation of common carriers by water (except matters subject to the jurisdiction of the Interstate Commerce Commission) and to the inspection of merchant marine vessels, lights and signals, lifesaving equipment, and fire protection on such vessels; merchant marine officers and seamen; navigation and the laws relating thereto, including pilotage; Panama Canal and the maintenance and operation of the Panama Canal, and interoceanic canals generally; registering and licensing of vessels and small boats; rules and international arrangements to prevent collisions at sea; U.S. Coast Guard and Merchant Marine Academies; and international fishing agreements.

(Area Code 202)

Majority Chief Counsel: Edmund B. Welch................225-4047
Minority Chief Counsel: Duncan C. Smith III............225-2650

COMMITTEE ON POST OFFICE AND CIVIL SERVICE

309 Cannon House Office Building......................225-4054

Jurisdiction: Census and the collection of statistics generally; all Federal Civil Service, including intergovernmental personnel; Postal-savings banks; the Postal Service generally, including the railway mail service and measures relating to ocean mail; status of officers and employees of the U.S., including their compensation, classification, and retirement; the Hatch Act; holidays and celebrations; and population and demography.

Majority General Counsel: Robert E. Lockhart...........225-4054
Minority General Counsel: Dan Blair....................226-7536

COMMITTEE ON PUBLIC WORKS AND TRANSPORTATION

2165 Rayburn House Office Building....................225-4472

Jurisdiction: Flood control and improvement of rivers and harbors; measures relating to the Capitol Building and the Senate and House Office Buildings; measures relating to the construction or maintenance of roads and post roads, other than appropriations therefor; measures relating to the construction, maintenance, and care of the buildings and grounds of the Botanic Gardens, the Library of Congress, and the Smithsonian Institution; measures relating to the purchase of sites and construction of post offices, customhouses, Federal courthouses, and Government buildings within the District of Columbia; oil and other pollution of navigable waters; public buildings and occupied or improved grounds of the U.S. generally; public works for the benefit of navigation, including bridges and dams (other than international bridges and dams); water power; transportation, including civil aviation except railroads, railroad labor and pensions; roads and the safety thereof; water transportation subject to the jurisdiction of the Interstate Commerce Commission; and related transportation regulatory agencies, except the Interstate Commerce Commission as it relates to railroads, the Federal Railroad Administration, and Amtrak.

Majority Chief Counsel: Sante J. Esposito..............225-4472
Minority Chief Counsel/Staff Director: Jack Schenendorf 225-9446

COMMITTEE ON RULES

H-312 Capitol Building................................225-9486
FAX...225-5373

Jurisdiction: The rules and joint rules (other than rules or joint rules relating to the Code of Official Conduct), and order of business of the House; emergency waivers of the required reporting date for bills and resolutions authorizing new budget authority; and recesses and final adjournments of Congress.

Majority Staff Director: John J. Dooling................225-9486
Minority Chief Counsel: William D. Crosby Jr...........225-9191

COMMITTEE ON SCIENCE, SPACE, AND TECHNOLOGY

(Area Code 202)

2321 Rayburn House Office Building....................225-6371

Jurisdiction: Astronautical research and development; Bureau of Standards; National Aeronautics and Space Administration; National Science Foundation; outer space, including exploration and control thereof; science scholarships; scientific research and development; civil aviation research and development; environmental research and development; all energy research and development, and all Federally owned or operated nonmilitary energy laboratories; and the National Weather Service.

Majority Chief of Staff: Robert C. Ketcham.............225-1774
Minority General Counsel: Barry Beringer................225-8500

COMMITTEE ON SMALL BUSINESS

2361 Rayburn House Office Building....................225-5821

JURISDICTION: Assistance to and protection of small business, including financial aid. Participation of small-business enterprises in Federal procurement and Government contracts.

Majority General Counsel: Thomas G. Powers.............225-0117
Majority Senior Trade Counsel: Jeanne Roslanowick.......225-5821
Minority Staff Director: J. Drew Hiatt..................225-4038

COMMITTEE ON STANDARDS OF OFFICIAL CONDUCT

HT-2 Capitol Building.................................225-7103
FAX...225-7392

Jurisdiction: Measures relating to the Code of Official Conduct.

Chief Counsel: Ralph L. Lotkin..........................225-7103

COMMITTEE ON VETERANS' AFFAIRS

335 Cannon House Office Building......................225-3527
FAX...225-5486

Jurisdiction: Veterans' measures generally; cemeteries of the U.S. in which veterans or any war or conflict are or may be buried, whether in the U.S. or abroad, except cemeteries administered by the Secretary of the Interior; compensation, vocational rehabilitation, and education of veterans; life insurance issued by the Government on account of service in the Armed Forces; pensions of all the wars of the U.S.; readjustment of servicemen to civil life; soldiers' and sailors' civil relief; and veterans' hospitals, medical care, and treatment of veterans.

Majority Chief Counsel/Staff Director: Mack G. Fleming..225-3527
Minority Staff Director/Counsel: Carl Commenator........225-9756

COMMITTEE ON WAYS AND MEANS

1102 Longworth House Office Building..................225-3625

Jurisdiction: Customs, collection districts, and ports of entry and delivery; reciprocal trade agreements; revenue measures generally; the bonded debt of the U.S.; the deposit of public moneys; transportation of dutiable goods; tax exempt foundations and charitable trusts; and national social security, except 1) health care and facilities programs that are supported from general revenues as opposed to payroll deductions, and 2) work incentive programs.

Majority Chief Counsel/Staff Director: Robert Leonard..225-3625
Majority Chief Tax Counsel: Janice Mays 225-3625
Minority Counsel for Budget & Debt: Margaret Hostetler..225-4021
Minority Counsel for Tax: James D. Clark...............225-4021

SELECT COMMITTEE ON AGING

(Area Code 202)

712 House Office Building Annex I......................226-3375

Jurisdiction: Problems of older Americans, including income maintenance, housing, health, welfare, employment, education, recreation, and participation in family and community life; to study the means of encouraging the development of public and private programs and policies to assist older Americans in taking full part in national life and encourage the utilization of their knowledge, skills, and abilities to contribute to a better life for all Americans; and to review recommendations made by the President or by the White House Conference on Aging relating to programs or policies affecting older Americans.

Majority General Counsel: Paul S. Ceja..................226-3375
Minority Counsel: Andrea Levario........................226-3393

SELECT COMMITTEE ON CHILDREN, YOUTH, AND FAMILIES

H2-385 House Office Building Annex II.................226-7660

Jurisdiction: To study and review the problems of children, youth, and families, including income maintenance, health (including medical and child development research), nutrition, education, welfare, employment, and recreation; to study the means of encouraging the development of public and private programs and policies to assist American children and youth in taking a full part in national life and becoming productive citizens; and to develop policies to encourage the coordination of both governmental and private programs designed to address the problems of childhood and adolescence.

Majority Staff Director: Karabelle Pizzigati............226-7660
Minority Staff Director: Dennis G. Smith................226-7692

SELECT COMMITTEE ON HUNGER

H2-505 House Office Building Annex II..................226-5470
FAX..226-0034

Jurisdiction: To study and review the problems of hunger and malnutrition, including these issues addressed in reports of the Presidential Commission on World Hunger and the Independent Commission on International Development Issues, including the U.S. development and economic assistance program, world food security, trade relations between the U.S. and less developed countries, food production and distribution, corporate and agribusiness efforts to further international development, policies of multilateral development banks and international development institutions, and food assistance programs in the U.S.

(Area Code 202)

Majority Staff Director: Martin S. Rendon..............226-5470
Minority Staff Director: Robert L. Jackson.............226-5460

PERMANENT SELECT COMMITTEE ON INTELLIGENCE

H-405 Capitol Building.................................225-4121

Jurisdiction: The CIA and the Director of the CIA; intelligence and intelligence-related activities of all other departments and agencies; the direct and indirect authorizations for the CIA and the Director of the CIA, the Defense Intelligence Agency, the National Security Agency, and all intelligence and intelligence-related activities of other agencies and subdivisions of the Department of Defense, the Department of State, and the FBI, including all activities of the Intelligence Division.

Associate Counsel: Thomas R. Smeeton....................225-4121

SELECT COMMITTEE ON NARCOTICS ABUSE AND CONTROL

H2-234 House Office Building Annex II..................226-3040
FAX..225-0094

Jurisdiction: Oversight and review of the problems of narcotics, drug, and polydrug abuse and control, including the abuse and control of opium and its derivatives, other narcotic drugs, psychotropics, and other controlled substances; domestic and international trafficking, manufacturing, and distribution; treatment, prevention, and rehabilitation; narcotics-related violations of the Internal Revenue Code; international treaties and agreements relating to the control of narcotics and drug abuse; problems of narcotics and drug abuse and control in the U.S. Armed Forces; and problems of narcotics and drug abuse and control in industry.

Majority Counsel: George R. Gilbert and Michael J. Kelley..226-3040
Minority Staff Director: Nancy Hobbs....................225-3779

JOINT COMMITTEES OF THE U.S. CONGRESS

JOINT ECONOMIC COMMITTEE

SD-G01 Dirksen Senate Office Building.................224-5171
FAX..224-0240

Jurisdiction: The committee conducts a continuing study of matters relating to the Economic Report made by the President and studies means of promoting the national policy on employment.

Majority General Counsel: Richard F. Kaufman...........224-5171
Minority Staff Director: Joe Cobb.......................224-0374

JOINT COMMITTEE ON THE LIBRARY

103 House Office Building Annex I.....................226-7633

Jurisdiction: The committee considers proposals concerning the management and expansion of the Library of Congress, the development and maintenance of the Botanic Gardens, the receipt of gifts for the benefit of the Library, and certain matters relating to placing statues and other works of art in the Capitol.

Staff Director: Hilary Lieber...........................226-7633

JOINT COMMITTEE ON PRINTING (Area Code 202)

SH-818 Hart Senate Office Building....................224-5241
FAX...224-1176

Jurisdiction: The committee adopts measures necessary to remedy inefficiencies or waste in the public printing, binding, and distribution of Government publications, and has control of the arrangement and style of the Congressional Record.

General Counsel: Anthony J. Zagami......................224-5241

JOINT COMMITTEE ON TAXATION (Area Code 202)

1015 Longworth House Office Building..................225-3621
FAX...225-0832

Jurisdiction: The Committee investigates the operation and effects of the Federal system of internal revenue taxation. It acts as a technical support staff to the House Ways and Means Committee and the Senate Finance Committee.

Associate Chief of Staff/Law: Mary M. Schmitt...........226-3270
Special Counsel: Laurie Matthews........................225-3780
Senior Legislation Counsel: H. Benjamin Hartley.........225-7377
Harold E. Hirsch.....................................225-6641
Melvin C. Thomas.....................................225-7377
Senior Refund Counsel: Roland Ford......................556-4424

OTHER CONGRESSIONAL ORGANIZATIONS

SENATE LEGISLATIVE COUNSEL

SD-668 Dirksen Senate Office Building.................224-6461

Jurisdiction: This non-partisan office assists in drafting legislation for U.S. Senators and Senate committees, and provides advice and counsel on legislation and the interpretation of legislation.

Senate Legislative Counsel: Douglas B. Hester
Deputy Legislative Counsel: Hugh C. Evans
Senior Counsel: Francis L. Burk Jr, James W. Fransen and Robert C. Louthian Jr

SENATE LEGAL COUNSEL

SH-642 Hart Senate Office Building....................224-4435

Jurisdiction: This non-partisan office represents U.S. Senators, staff members, committees, and officers in legal matters, including litigation, involving their official duties. Assists committees in investigations, including the issuance of subpoenas.

Senate Legal Counsel: Michael Davidson
Deputy Counsel: Ken U. Benjamin Jr
Assistant Counsel: Morgan J. Frankel and Claire M. Sylvia

HOUSE OFFICE OF THE LEGISLATIVE COUNSEL

136 Cannon House Office Building......................225-6060

Jurisdiction: This non-partisan office assists in drafting legislation for U.S. House of Representatives and its committees, and provides advice and counsel on legislation and the interpretation of legislation.

Legislative Counsel: David E. Meade
Deputy Legislative Counsel: Roger Young

HOUSE OFFICE OF THE LAW REVISION COUNSEL

H2-304 House Office Building Annex II.................226-2411

Jurisdiction: This non-partisan office is responsible for the preparation and publication of the U.S. Code.

Law Revision Counsel: Edward F. Willett Jr
Deputy Law Revision Counsel: Lawrence A. Monaco Jr

GENERAL COUNSEL TO THE CLERK OF THE HOUSE

H-105 Capitol Building................................225-9700

Jurisdiction: This non-partisan office represents Members of the House of Representatives, staff members, committees, and officers in legal matters, including litigation, involving their official duties. Assists committees in investigations, including the issuance of subpoenas.

General Counsel: Steven R. Ross

U.S. CONGRESS

PUBLICATIONS OF INTEREST

The following publications can be purchased from the **U.S. Government Printing Office.** Stock numbers and prices for annual subscriptions are shown below. Submit requests for these publications to: The Superintendent of Documents, U.S. Government Printing Office, Washington, D.C. 20402. Tel: 202/783-3238.

Calendars of the United States House of Representatives and History of Legislation. Published weekly when Congress is in session. Price: $159.00 a year domestic; no foreign distribution. GPO Stock# 752-001-00000-6.

Congressional Record. Published daily when Congress is in session, this is a verbatim report on congressional debates and other proceedings. Each issue includes a Daily Digest that summarizes the proceedings for that day in each House and before each of their committees and subcommittees. Price (paperback): $225.00 a year domestic; $281.25 foreign. A special six-month subscription to the Record is available for one-half the yearly price. GPO Stock# 752-002-00000-2.

PUBLICATIONS

Major Legislation of the Congress. Published irregularly. Provides summaries of topical congressional issues and major legislation introduced in response to those issues. Subscription service consists of approximately ten irregular issues per Congress (two-year period). Price: $19.00 domestic; $23.75 foreign. GPO Stock# 830-002-00000-6.

Public Bills, Resolutions, and Amendments. Published irregularly. Price: $4,898.00 domestic per session of Congress; $6,122.50 foreign per session of Congress. GPO Stock# 852-011-00000-9.

Reports on Public Bills. Published irregularly. Price: $1,323.00 domestic per session of Congress; $1,653.75 foreign per session of Congress. GPO Stock# 852-009-00000-4.

Public Laws. Published irregularly. A Public Law, often referred to as a "Slip Law," is the initial publication of a Federal law upon enactment and is printed as soon as possible after approval by the President. Some legislative references appear on each law. Price: $107.00 domestic per session of Congress; $133.75 foreign per session of Congress. GPO Stock# 869-010-00000-6.

ARCHITECT OF THE CAPITOL

U.S. Capitol
Washington, D.C. 20515-8000

DESCRIPTION: As an agent of Congress, the Architect of the Capitol is responsible for the structural and mechanical care of the U.S. Capitol Building, the Library of Congress, and the U.S. Supreme Court Building; maintenance and improvement of the Capitol grounds; and the operation of the Senate and House restaurants.

(Area Code 202)
Architect of the Capitol: George M. White 225-1200

(Area Code 202)
Facsimile 225-3167

OFFICE OF GENERAL COUNSEL (Room H2-265, HOB Annex #2)

The Office of the General Counsel is a small legal office which provides advice and services in three broad areas: internal administrative functions; activities for which the Architect has legal responsibility; and litigation activities. In the first category, the Office of the General Counsel (OGC) advises on procurement, fiscal, budgetary, and personnel matters. In the second category, the OGC prepares draft legislation affecting the Office; provides advice on issues arising from the Architect's statutory responsibility for superintendence of the buildings and grounds of the Legislative Complex, including claims arising under the Federal Tort Claims Act; and provides legal review of contracts for the procurement of materials, supplies, and services. In the third area, the OGC's Litigation Division provides advice and support with respect to litigation brought or defended by the Architect of the Capitol, particularly with respect to litigation arising out of construction contracts in which the Architect of the Capitol serves as Contracting Officer.

Additionally, the OGC represents the Architect in congressional and administrative hearings and, when necessary, arranges for representation of the Agency in judicial proceedings by attorneys from the Department of Justice.

(Area Code 202)
General Counsel: Ben C. Wimberly 225-1210
Deputy General Counsel: Charles K. Tyler 225-3991

(Area Code 202)
Attorney Advisor: Alan Jackson 225-9697

ARCHITECT OF THE CAPITOL
KEY LEGAL AUTHORITIES

40 U.S.C. 161 et seq.--confers responsibility for the upkeep, repair, improvement, alteration, and additions to the Capitol buildings and grounds on the Architect of the Capitol.

CONGRESSIONAL BUDGET OFFICE

Washington, D.C. 20515

DESCRIPTION: The mission of the Congressional Budget Office (CBO) is to provide Congress with relevant information and analyses with respect to Federal budget issues, to include economic forecasts, projected costs, "scorekeeping" of legislative progress against fiscal targets, development of taxing and spending options affecting the deficit, and similar matters.

(Area Code 202)
Director: Robert D. Reischauer 226-2700
Public Information 226-2600
Publications 226-2809

Freedom of Information/Privacy Act Office 226-2633
Requests may be in writing or by telephone. There is no search or copying fee.

(Area Code 202)
Library (Room 472) 226-2635
The library is open to the public Monday through Friday from 9:00 AM until 5:30 PM. Materials may not be checked out but copying machines are available.

OFFICE OF GENERAL COUNSEL (Room 408E)

The General Counsel and a single staff attorney handle CBO's legal work, which consists of: 1) the typical subjects in any small bureaucracy--contracts, conflicts of interest, interpreting legislation bearing directly on the work of the CBO, etc; and 2) reviewing the analytic products of non-lawyers to ensure consistency and correctness in a legal sense.

(Area Code 202)
General Counsel: Alfred B. Fitt 226-2633

(Area Code 202)
Associate General Counsel: Gail Del Blazo 226-2886

CONGRESSIONAL BUDGET OFFICE

KEY LEGAL AUTHORITIES

Congressional Budget and Impoundment Control Act of 1974, 2 U.S.C. 601 et seq.--established the Congressional Budget Office to assist the Budget and Appropriation Committees of Congress, the House Ways and Means Committee, the Senate Finance Committee, and other committees and members of Congress, by providing information with respect to the budget, appropriation bills, and other bills authorizing or providing budget authority or tax expenditures; information on revenues, receipts, estimated future revenues and receipts, and changing revenue conditions.

Legislative History: 1974 U.S. Code Cong. & Admin. News 3462.

COPYRIGHT ROYALTY TRIBUNAL

1111 20th Street, N.W., Suite 450
Washington, D.C. 20036

DESCRIPTION: The Copyright Royalty Tribunal establishes four copyright royalty rates and distributes two copyright royalty funds. To accomplish these tasks, the Commissioners of the Tribunal sit en banc at administrative hearings.

(Area Code 202)

Chairman: J.C. Argetsinger 653-5175
Publications 653-5175
Facsimile 653-5183
FOIA/Privacy Act Office 653-5175

(Area Code 202)

Library 653-5175
The library is open to the public Monday through Friday from 9:00 AM until 5:00 PM. Copying machines are available. The cost is 20 cents per page.

OFFICE OF GENERAL COUNSEL

The General Counsel advises the Commissioners on hearing procedures, objections and motions; drafts all interlocutory orders and final hearing decisions; monitors all legislation which may affect the Tribunal; and advises the agency on the applicability of laws such as the Administrative Procedure Act, Freedom of Information Act, Sunshine Act, and the Privacy Act. If and when agency decisions are appealed in court, the General Counsel works with the Department of Justice on the appeal.

(Area Code 202)

General Counsel: Robert Cassler 635-5175

COPYRIGHT ROYALTY TRIBUNAL
KEY LEGAL AUTHORITIES

General Agency Regulations: 37 C.F.R. Parts 301-308 (1989).
Rules of Practice & Procedure: 37 C.F.R., Part 301 (1989).

Copyright Act, as amended, 17 U.S.C. 801 et seq.--established the Copyright Royalty Tribunal to adjust reasonable copyright royalty rates and set terms and payment rates in order to maximize the availability of creative works to the public, afford the copyright owner a fair return and the copyright user a fair income, and for other purposes.

Legislative History: 1976 U.S. Code Cong. & Admin. News 5659.

LIBRARY OF CONGRESS

First and Independence Avenue, S.E.
Washington, D.C. 20540

DESCRIPTION: The Library of Congress is the Nation's Library. Its services extend not only to Members and committees of the Congress, but to the Executive and Judicial Branches of government, to libraries throughout the Nation and the world and to the scholars, researchers, artists, and scientists who use its resources. Collections of the Library include more than 86 million items covering virtually every subject in formats that vary from papyrus to optical disk.

There are currently around 100 attorneys working for the Library of Congress, most of whom work in the Congressional Research Service, with the rest divided among the Copyright Office, the Law Library, the Office of the General Counsel, and the Human Resources Office.

(Area Code 202)
Librarian of Congress: James H. Billington 707-5205
Law Library 707-5065
Congressional Research Service 707-5700

(Area Code 202)
General Reference Assistance/Reference Services 707-5522
Copyright Information 479-0700
Copyright Application Forms/Hotline 707-9100

OFFICE OF GENERAL COUNSEL (Room LM-601)

The Office of the General Counsel, in the Office of the Librarian of Congress, consists of five attorneys. The work of these attorneys involves contracts for the procurement of supplies and services; negotiating conditions for gifts to the Library or deposit instruments; handling tax questions, particularly those involving gifts to the Library; handling litigation, including Title VII discrimination cases; writing regulations; and providing advice on a myriad of legal questions relating to Library operations.

(Area Code 202)
General Counsel: John J. Kominski 707-6316
Assistant General Counsel: Lana Kay Jones 707-6316
Assistant General Counsel: Robert A. Lincoln 707-6316

Office of Counsel for Human Resources
The attorneys in the Human Resources Office, which is within the Office of the Associate Librarian for Management, provide legal advice and assistance on questions relating to personnel and EEO law, labor relations, and internal grievances and appeals.

(Area Code 202)
Counsel: Peter J. Watters 707-6197
Assistant Counsels:
Frank Mach 707-6197
Christa McClure 707-6197

CONGRESSIONAL RESEARCH SERVICE (Room LM-205)

The Congressional Research Service (CRS) is the department within the Library which works exclusively as a reference and research arm for the U.S. Congress. (Persons outside of Congress must go through their Congressman to use this service.) The Service provides a variety of in-depth policy analysis and research on every subject of interest to Congress, including background analyses; scientific, economic, and legislative analyses; legal research; and legislative histories. Its professional staff includes attorneys, economists, engineers, political scientists, defense and foreign affairs analysts, and physical and behavioral scientists. Although attorneys work throughout CRS, most are employed in the American Law Division, which responds to congressional requests for legal research and analysis covering such diverse subjects as criminal code reform, abortion, child custody, judicial reform, securities law reform taxation, antitrust, congressional ethics, campaign financing, and the legislative veto.

The Division also maintains the automated Bill Digest File for the SCORPIO system, publishes the Digest of Public General Bills and Resolutions, and prepares the Constitution Annotated. Most attorneys are called "Legislative Attorneys" but other titles, such as "Congressional Research Review Specialists," are also used. "Senior Specialist" positions, which are distributed throughout the Service, are filled by nationally recognized experts in certain subject areas, such as American public law, constitutional law, election law, American government, conservation and energy, environmental policy, taxation and fiscal policy, national defense, national security, and international affairs.

(Area Code 202)
Director: Joseph E. Ross 707-5775
Legal Adviser: Douglas A. Warshof 707-2345
American Law Division Chief: Richard C. Ehlke 707-6006
Constitution Annotated Editor: John Killian 707-6006

(Area Code 202)
Digest of Public General Bills and Resolutions Editor:
Terry G. Guertin 707-6996
Congressional Reference Division Chief:
Catherine Ann Jones 707-5741

LAW LIBRARY (Room LM-240)

The Law Library is open to the public Monday through Friday from 8:30 AM until 9:30 PM, Saturday from 8:30 AM until 5:00 PM, and Sunday from 1:00 PM until 5:00 PM. Copying machines are available.

The Law Library serves primarily as the foreign law research arm of Congress, but its reference and legal specialists also provide American law reference and foreign law research and reference to other branches of Government and to the public. Its collections now constitute the world's largest and most comprehensive in foreign, international and comparative law. The Law Library's unique staff, recruited from over 30 foreign countries and competent in approximately 50 languages, is conversant with almost every known legal system. Its five research divisions consist of American-British, European, Far Eastern, Hispanic, and the Near Eastern and African Law Division. Although there are attorneys working in the Law Library who are specialists in American law, most are "Foreign Law Specialists" who have professional legal training and experience in the foreign jurisdiction for which they have research responsibility. These Foreign Law Specialists also have foreign language skills.

(Area Code 202)

Law Librarian: Charles Doyle (Acting) 707-5065
Law Library Reading Room 707-5080

American-British Law Division
Chief: Robert Nay (Acting) 707-5077

European Law Division
Chief: Ivan Sipkov 707-5088

(Area Code 202)

Far Eastern Division
Chief: Tao-tai Hsia 707-5085

Hispanic Law Division
Chief: Rubens Medina 707-5070

Near Eastern and African Law Division
Chief: Zuhair E. Jwaideh 707-5073

COPYRIGHT OFFICE (Room LM-403)

The Copyright Office is responsible for performing all duties relating to the registration of copyrights, pursuant to the provisions of Title 17 U.S.C. The **Office of the Register of Copyrights** includes a legal and administrative staff. There is an Office of the General Counsel (not to be confused with the Office of General Counsel for the Library as a whole, which is part of the Office of the Librarian) whose attorneys work in four main areas. First, promulgating and amending Copyright Office regulations. Second, preparing testimony for the Register to deliver and furnishing technical assistance to congressional committees having jurisdiction over copyright and intellectual property matters. Third, working with Justice Department attorneys in cases where the Register of Copyrights is either a plaintiff or defendant. Fourth, providing legal guidance to operating divisions of the Copyright Office. In addition to "Copyright Attorneys," the Office also has "Copyright Examiners" (in the Examining Division), many of whom have law degrees. Copyright Examiners examine claims to copyright received in the Section, determine if there has been compliance with the copyright law, and conduct legal or factual research to resolve difficult questions that arise during the examination process.

(Area Code 202)

Register of Copyrights: Ralph Oman 707-8350
Associate Register for Legal Affairs/General Counsel:
Dorothy Schrader 707-8380
Assistant General Counsel: Richard W. Glasgow 707-8380
Information and Reference Division 707-2100

Freedom of Information Act Office 707-8394
While the Library of Congress is not covered under FOIA, the Copyright Office is covered under the Copyright Act. There is a copying charge of 40 cents per page. For more information contact: Supervisory Copyright Information Specialist in the Information and Reference Division of the Copyright Office (Room 401).

DATABASES AND PUBLICATIONS OF INTEREST

Databases:

LOCIS (Library of Congress Information System) contains a database **SCORPIO** which is available to the general public for use within the Library of Congress itself.

SCORPIO (Subject-Content-Oriented Retriever For Processing Information Online) contains the following files: 1) **BIBL (Bibliographic Citation File):** selected articles and government publications since 1976 on public policy and current events topics of interest to Congress. 2) **LCCC:** books cataloged or recataloged and written in English since 1968 and other non-English titles with varying dates. 3) **CG-CURRENT CG:** Legislative information files from the current back to the 93rd Congress (1973); status and digests of public bills and resolutions introduced in Congress. 4) **NRCM (National Referral Master File):** list of organizations doing research or providing information and willing to answer questions from the public. 5) **COHM/COHD:** copyright registrations and documents since 1978. 6) **PREMARC:** books, serials, maps, music earlier than those in LCCC. Records briefer and unedited. Contact: General Reference Assistance, Library of Congress, First and Independence Avenue, S.E., Washington, D.C. 20540. Tel: 202/707-5522.

Publications:

The following publications can be purchased from the **U.S. Government Printing Office.** Stock numbers and prices for annual subscriptions are shown below. Submit requests for these publications to: The Superintendent of Documents, U.S. Government Printing Office, Washington, D.C. 20402. Tel: 202/783-3238.

Compendium of Copyright Office Practices (Compendium II). 1984. A general guide to the operating problems and practices for the staff of the Copyright Office, with individual cases that represent common fact situations. Also known as Compendium II. Subscription service consists of a basic manual and two semiannual supplements for an indeterminate period. Price: $51.00 domestic; $63.75 foreign. GPO Stock# 930-001-00000-7.

Congressional Research Service Review. Contains articles of interest to the U.S. Congress, legislative staff members, congressional committees, other offices of the Legislative Branch, others in Government, and the general public. Ten issues a year. Price: $9.50 domestic; $11.88 foreign. GPO Stock# 730-009-00000-3.

LIBRARY OF CONGRESS

The Constitution of the United States of America, Library of Congress, Congressional Research Service, 1987. This 800-plus page annotated volume is supplemented biennially with pocket supplements. Each article, section, and clause of the Constitution is immediately followed by analysis and commentary, including a discussion of the most important Supreme Court interpretive decisions. The volume also includes tables of proposed amendments pending before the states, proposed amendments not ratified by the states, and acts of Congress held unconstitutional in whole or in part by the Supreme Court. Price: $70.00. GPO Stock# 052-071-00674-5.

LIBRARY OF CONGRESS

KEY LEGAL AUTHORITIES:

2 U.S.C. 131-176--established the Library of Congress and delineated its functions.

Legislative History: 1957 U.S. Code Cong. & Admin. News 1948; 1966 U.S. Code Cong. & Admin. News 2585; 1970 U.S. Code Cong. & Admin. News 3270; 1972 U.S. Code Cong. & Admin. News 2364; 1976 U.S. Code Cong. & Admin. News 5659.

Copyright Act, as amended, 17 U.S.C. 801 et seq.--established the Copyright Office and set forth the subject matter and scope of copyright protection, ownership, transfer, and duration, as well as copyright procedures, what constitutes an infringement, and remedies for infringements.

Legislative History: 1976 U.S. Code Cong. & Admin. News 5659.

Implementing Regulations: 37 C.F.R. Parts 201-211 (1989).

GENERAL ACCOUNTING OFFICE

441 G Street, N.W.
Washington, D.C. 20548

DESCRIPTION: The General Accounting Office (GAO), headed by the Comptroller General of the United States, was created by the Congress as an independent, non-partisan agency to assist in congressional oversight of the Executive Branch of Government. The GAO's major responsibilities are carried out principally through auditing and evaluating Federal programs, functions and financial operations.

(Area Code 202)

Comptroller General: Charles A. Bowsher 275-5481
Office of Public Information 275-2812
Publications 275-6241
Facsimile 275-4021

(Area Code 202)

Freedom of Information Act/Privacy Act Office 275-6172
While GAO is not subject to FOIA and the Privacy Act, GAO's disclosure policy follows the spirit of the Act consistent with its duties, functions and responsibility to the Congress.

Library (Room 7056) 275-2585
The library is open Monday through Friday from 8:00 AM until 4:45 PM. A photo ID is required. Copying machines are available.

OFFICE OF GENERAL COUNSEL (Room 7064)

The Office of General Counsel (OGC) employs more than 160 attorneys, all located at GAO headquarters in Washington, D.C. OGC is divided into seven divisions: Accounting and Financial Management Division; General Government Division; Human Resources and Program Evaluation Methodology Division; Legal Services Division; National Security, International Affairs, and Information Management Division; Procurement Law Division; and Resources, Community, and Economic Development Division. Division attorneys advise GAO evaluators in reviews of Federal programs, provide legal opinions to Congress and federal agencies, testify before congressional committees, brief Members of Congress and congressional staff, draft legislation, render bid protest decisions and advise GAO senior management.

(Area Code 202)

General Counsel: James F. Hinchman 275-5205
Deputy General Counsel: vacant 275-5201
Senior Associate General Counsel for Opinions and Decisions: Seymour Efros 275-5208
Associate General Counsel for Operations: Kathleen E. Wannisky 275-6198
Assistant General Counsel for Operations: Alan Zuckerman 275-6198
Office of Special Investigations Director: Pat Noble .. 275-5500

The **Accounting and Financial Management Division** provides legal advice and assistance to GAO evaluators in such areas as budget systems and practices, federal agency accounting and financial management, and audit oversight and policy. Division attorneys provide legal opinions to congressional committees and federal agencies regarding the legality of specific uses of public funds. Division attorneys also provide legal support in the fulfillment of the Comptroller General's authority with respect to the Impoundment Control Act and the certification of payments from the Judgment Fund.

(Area Code 202)

Associate General Counsel for Accounting and Financial Management: Gary Kepplinger 275-0424

The **General Government Division** provides legal advice and assistance to GAO evaluators, Members of Congress, congressional committees, congressional staff and federal agencies in such areas as tax policy and administration, administration of justice, financial services regulation, federal sector management, and federal personnel. Division attorneys also decide a wide range of cases relating to the compensation, leave, travel, and transportation entitlement of Government civilian personnel.

(Area Code 202)

Senior Associate General Counsel for General Government Matters: Henry Wray 275-5156

The **Human Resources and Program Evaluation Methodology Division** provides legal advice and assistance to GAO evaluators, Members of Congress, congressional committees, congressional staff and federal agencies in such areas as health delivery and quality of care, health financing, employment and training programs, education, income security, and intergovernmental and management issues.

(Area Code 202)

Associate General Counsel for Human Resources and Program Evaluation Methodology: Barry Bedrick 275-5881

The **Legal Services Division** provides legal support for the day-to-day operations of the GAO, including all matters relating to GAO employees, operations of the GAO building, GAO procurement, use of GAO appropriations, access to GAO records, ethics, and internal GAO investigations. Division attorneys frequently represent GAO in administrative and judicial litigation, and they also advise GAO's Office of Special Investigations which conducts investigations within the government.

(Area Code 202)

Associate General Counsel for Legal Services: Joan Hollenbach (Acting) 275-6404

The **National Security, International Affairs, and Information Management Division** provides legal advice and assistance to GAO evaluators, Members of Congress, congressional committees, congressional staff and federal agencies in such areas as national security, defense acquisition, military personnel, international relations, foreign economic assistance, and automated information systems management. Division attorneys also decide a wide range of cases relating to the compensation, leave, travel, and transportation entitlement of members of the military.

(Area Code 202)

Associate General Counsel for National Security, International Affairs, and Information Management: Robert Hunter 275-6071

GENERAL ACCOUNTING OFFICE

The **Procurement Law Division** provides an objective, independent, and impartial forum for the resolution of bid protests concerning the award of federal contracts. Division attorneys also may become involved in other procurement related activities such as analyzing and preparing GAO comments on proposed procurement legislation, and advising other GAO divisions on government contract matters.

(Area Code 202)

Senior Associate General Counsel for Procurement Law: Robert Murphy 275-6071

The **Resources, Community, and Economic Development Division** provides legal advice and assistance to GAO evaluators, Members of Congress, congressional committees, congressional staff and federal agencies in such areas as energy, national resources, agriculture, environment, housing, community development, and transportation.

(Area Code 202)

Senior Associate General Counsel for Resources, Community and Economic Development: Richard Pierson ...275-6263

PERSONNEL APPEALS BOARD

Academy Bldg, 2nd Floor, 441 G Street, N.W.
Washington, D.C. 20548

Under the GAO Personnel Act of 1980, the General Accounting Office was allowed to create its own personnel system independent of administrative, adjudicatory, and oversight agencies in the Executive Branch. This Act also created the Personnel Appeals Board (PAB) and the Board's Office of General Counsel.

The **Personnel Appeals Board** has substantially the same adjudicatory responsibilities at GAO as the Federal Labor Relations Authority, the Merit Systems Protection Board (MSPB), and the Equal Employment Opportunity Commission have in the Executive Branch. The Board also has responsibility for oversight of the EEO program at the General Accounting Office.

The decisions of the Personnel Appeals Board can be obtained by contacting the Board at the above address. Tel: 202/275-6137. Publication of a compilation of cumulative Personnel Appeals Board decisions (1981089) is in progress and should be available from the same address in September, 1990.

(Area Code 202)

Chairman: Jessie James Jr 275-6137

(Area Code 202)

Facsimile: 275-8842

OFFICE OF GENERAL COUNSEL (1st Floor)

The PAB General Counsel's responsibilities are similar to, though somewhat broader than, those of the MSPB Special Counsel. The Board and its General Counsel have jurisdiction over employee cases at GAO, including adverse actions, performance-based actions, EEO complaints, prohibited personnel practices, negotiability determinations, unit determinations, and other related labor-management issues.

(Area Code 202)

General Counsel: Carl D. Moore 275-1663

(Area Code 202)

Deputy General Counsel: Janice Willis 275-1663

PUBLICATIONS OF INTEREST

Decisions of the Comptroller General of the United States. Published monthly. Each issue contains decisions of the Comptroller General on financial matters arising in the Federal Service.

Price: $18.00 a year domestic; $22.50 a year foreign. GPO Stock# 720-001-00000-4.

GENERAL ACCOUNTING OFFICE
KEY LEGAL AUTHORITIES

Regulations:

General Agency Regulations: 4 C.F.R. Parts 2-93 (1989).
Bid Protest Regulations: 4 C.F.R. Part 21 (1989).
Claims Against the U.S.: 4 C.F.R. Part 31 (1989).
Federal Claims Collection Standards: 4 C.F.R. Part 101 et seq. (1989)[issued jointly with the U.S. Department of Justice].

31 U.S.C. 701-783--the GAO enabling statute, setting forth the agency's duties and powers.
Legislative History: 1988 U.S. Code Cong. & Admin. News 2167.

31 U.S.C. 3551-3556--outlines the Federal procurement protest system and directs the Comptroller General to decide such protests.
Legislative History: 1984 U.S. Code Cong. & Admin. News 697; 1985 U.S. Code Cong. & Admin. News 472.

31 U.S.C. 3701-3731--covers claims of and against the United States and authorizes the Comptroller General to settle such claims.
Legislative History: 1983 U.S. Code Cong. & Admin. News 4301; 1984 U.S. Code Cong. & Admin. News 3.

GOVERNMENT PRINTING OFFICE

North Capitol and H Streets, N.W.
Washington, D.C. 20401

DESCRIPTION: The Government Printing Office (GPO) executes orders for printing and binding placed by Congress and the departments and establishments of the Federal Government. Through mail orders and Government bookstores, GPO sells approximately 14,000 different publications that originate in various Government agencies, and administers the depository library program through which selected Government publications are made available in libraries throughout the country. The head of GPO is the Public Printer, who is appointed by the President.

(Area Code 202)
Public Printer: William W. Houck 275-2034
Assistant Public Printer (Superintendent of Documents):
Donald E. Fossedal 275-3345
Public Affairs 275-3204

(Area Code 202)
Publications 783-3238
Freedom of Information Act/Privacy Act Office 275-2757
GPO Order Desk 783-3238
Facsimile 275-7507

OFFICE OF GENERAL COUNSEL (Room C8124)

The Office of the General Counsel, with six attorneys, serves as legal advisor to the Public Printer and provides legal services in support of GPO operations and activities. The office reviews selected procurement contracts, represents the agency on disputed contracts and claims, and represents the GPO on procurement matters before the General Accounting Office, the GPO Board of Contract Appeals, and other Boards of Contract Appeals. The Office also reviews all laws and proposed legislation affecting GPO; reviews and makes recommendations on equal employment complaints; reviews the legality and impact of various labor-management proposals; and reviews for legal sufficiency all agreements and Memorandums of Understanding to which GPO is a party. Attorneys in the office also represent the GPO before the Equal Employment Opportunity Commission, the Merit Systems Protection Board, and other administrative tribunals; and assist the U.S. Department of Justice in court cases involving the GPO and/or its officials.

(Area Code 202)
General Counsel: Grant G. Moy Jr 275-2757
Deputy General Counsel: Drew Spalding 275-2757

(Area Code 202)
Associate General Counsel for Procurement and Contracts:
Kerry L. Miller 275-2826

GOVERNMENT PRINTING OFFICE BOOKSTORES

Washington, DC
U.S. Government Printing Office, 710 No. Capitol Street, N.W., Washington, DC 20401 ....(202) 275-2091
U.S. Government Printing Office, 1510 H Street, N.W., Washington, DC 20005 ....(202) 653-5075

Atlanta
U.S. Government Printing Office, 100 Federal Building, 275 Peachtree Street, N.E., Atlanta, GA 30343 ..(404) 331-6947

Birmingham
U.S. Government Printing Office, O'Neill Building, 2021 3rd Avenue, Birmingham, AL 35203 ....(205) 731-1056

Boston
U.S. Government Printing Office, 179 Thomas P. O'Neill Jr. Federal Building, 10 Causeway Street, Boston, MA 02222 ....(617) 565-6680

Chicago
U.S. Government Printing Office, 1365 Everett McKinley Dirksen Federal Building, 219 South Dearborn Street, Chicago, IL 60604 ....(312) 353-5133

Cleveland
U.S. Government Printing Office, 1653 Anthony J. Celebrezze Federal Building, 1240 E. Ninth Street, Cleveland, OH 44199 ....(216) 522-4922

Columbus, OH
U.S. Government Printing Office, 207 Federal Building, 200 North High Street, Columbus, OH 43215 ....(614) 469-6956

Dallas
U.S. Government Printing Office, 1C46 Earle Cabell Federal Building & U.S. Courthouse, 1100 Commerce Street, Dallas, TX 75242 ....(214) 767-0076

Denver
U.S. Government Printing Office, 117 Byron G. Rogers Federal Building & U.S. Courthouse, 1961 Stout Street, Denver, CO 80294 ....(303) 844-3964

Detroit
U.S. Government Printing Office, 160 Patrick V. McNamara Federal Building, 477 Michigan Avenue, Detroit, MI 48226 ....(313) 226-7816

Houston
U.S. Government Printing Office, Texas Crude Building, 801 Travis Street, Houston, TX 77002 (713) 653-3100

Jacksonville
U.S. Government Printing Office, 158 Federal Building, 400 W. Bay Street, Jacksonville, FL 32202 ....(904) 791-3801

GOVERNMENT PRINTING OFFICE

Kansas City
U.S. Government Printing Office, 120 Bannister Mall, 5600 E. Bannister Road, Kansas City, MO 64137 (816) 765-2256

Laurel, MD
U.S. Government Printing Office, 8660 Cherry Lane, Laurel, MD 20707 ....(301) 953-7974

Los Angeles
U.S. Government Printing Office, ARCO Plaza, C-Level, 505 So. Flower Street, Los Angeles, CA 90071 ...(213) 894-5841

Milwaukee
U.S. Government Printing Office, 190 Federal Building & U.S. Courthouse, 517 E. Wisconsin Avenue, Milwaukee, WI 53202 ....(414) 291-1304

New York
U.S. Government Printing Office, 110 Jacob K. Javits Federal Building, 26 Federal Plaza, New York, NY 10278 ....(212) 264-3825

Philadelphia
U.S. Government Printing Office, Robert Morris Building, 100 North 17th Street, Philadelphia, PA 19103 ....(215) 597-0677

Pittsburgh
U.S. Government Printing Office, 118 William S. Moorhead Federal Office Building, 1000 Liberty Avenue, Pittsburgh, PA 15222 ....(412) 644-2721

Portland, OR
U.S. Government Printing Office, 1305 S.W. First Avenue, Portland, OR 97201 ....(503) 221-6217

Pueblo, CO
U.S. Government Printing Office, World Savings Building, 720 North Main Street, Pueblo, CO 81003 ....(719) 544-3142

San Francisco
U.S. Government Printing Office, 1023 Phillip Burton Federal Building & U.S. Courthouse, 450 Golden Gate Avenue, San Francisco, CA 94102 ....(415) 566-0643

Seattle, WA
U.S. Government Printing Office, 194 Henry M. Jackson Federal Building, 915 Second Avenue, Seattle, WA 98174 ....(206) 442-4270

PUBLICATIONS OF INTEREST

The U.S. Government publishes thousands of documents, all of which may be ordered directly from the **Superintendent of Documents, U.S. Government Printing Office**, Washington, D.C. 20402. Tel: 202/783-3238, or from any of the regional GPO bookstores. Orders may be paid by check (made out to the Superintendent of Documents) or charged to a Visa or Master Card. It is important to cite the exact title of the publication being ordered and, if possible, the GPO stock number. Phone orders are accepted Monday through Friday from 7:30 AM to 4:00 PM.

To obtain a current list of GPO publications, customers can subscribe to the Monthly Catalog of United States Government Publications (information on all publications issued on a monthly basis). The annual rate is $167.00 or $26.00 per single copy.

Government Periodicals and Subscription Services, issued quarterly, provides information on publications sold by subscription, including the Federal Register and the Congressional Record. Single issues are free of charge.

U.S. Government Books, issued three times a year, contains information on over 1,000 new and frequently ordered GPO publications. Single issues are free of charge.

Certain Government publications sold by the Superintendent of Documents and produced in electronic format are available in magnetic tape form. **Publication tapes** may be purchased on an individual tape basis or as a subscription service. Included among the individual publication tapes available are: the Budget of the United States; the Congressional Directory; the Statistical Abstract; the Government Manual; the Congressional Record; and the Federal Register. Prices for individual tapes are $125.00 per tape except for the Federal Register and the Congressional Record which are $175 per tape. (Prices are per tape not per title. A title may consist of multiple tapes.)

Subscription services currently available on tape are: the Congressional Record; the Code of Federal Regulations; the Federal Communications Commission Records; the Federal Register; the Monthly Catalog of United States Government Publications; and Daily Bills. For price information call 202/783-3238.

GOVERNMENT PRINTING OFFICE
KEY LEGAL AUTHORITIES

44 U.S.C. 301-517--established the Government Printing Office and set forth its functions, powers, and administrative provisions.

Legislative History: 1968 U.S. Code Cong. & Admin. News 4438; 1976 U.S. Code Cong. & Admin. News 5659.

OFFICE OF TECHNOLOGY ASSESSMENT

U.S. Congress
Washington, D.C. 20510-8025

DESCRIPTION: The Office of Technology Assessment (OTA) is a nonpartisan analytical support agency that serves the U.S. Congress by providing objective analyses of major public policy issues related to scientific and technological change. OTA works directly with and for the committees of Congress, providing them with detailed analyses of technological issues and responding to specific questions based on those analyses. A 12-member bipartisan congressional Technology Assessment Board, composed of six Senators and six Representatives, governs OTA. A multidisciplinary staff plans, directs, and drafts all assessments.

The staff is organized into nine program areas: energy and materials; international security and commerce; industry, technology, and employment; food and renewable resources; health; biological applications; communication and information technologies; oceans and environment; and science, education, and transportation.

(Area Code 202)
Director: John H. Gibbons 224-3695
Publications 224-8996
FOIA/Privacy Act 228-6104

(Area Code 202)
Library/Information Center 228-6150
The information center is open Monday through Friday from 8:30 AM until 5:30 PM by appointment only. Copying machines are available.

OFFICE OF GENERAL COUNSEL (5th Floor)

In addition to the General Counsel, there are approximately ten attorneys working for OTA. However, these attorneys are not handling traditional legal responsibilities but are working as staff analysts.

(Area Code 202)
General Counsel: Holly L. Gwin 228-6104

OFFICE OF TECHNOLOGY ASSESSMENT
KEY LEGAL AUTHORITIES

Technology Assessment Act of 1972, as amended, 2 U.S.C. 471-481--established the Office of Technology Assessment to provide early indications of the probably beneficial and adverse impacts of technology applications and to develop information on these and related issues to assist Congress.

Legislative History: 1972 U.S. Code Cong. & Admin. News 3568.

Judicial Branch

SUPREME COURT OF THE UNITED STATES
1 First Street, N.E.
Washington, D.C. 20543

DESCRIPTION: Sections 1 and 2, Article III of the Constitution of the United States establish the Supreme Court as follows:

Section 1. The judicial Power of the United States, shall be vested in one supreme Court, and in such inferior Courts as the Congress may from time to time ordain and establish. The Judges, both of the supreme and inferior Courts, shall hold their Offices during good Behaviour, and shall, at stated Times, receive for their Services, a Compensation, which shall not be diminished during their Continuance in Office.

Section 2. The judicial Power shall extend to all Cases, in Law and Equity, arising under this Constitution, the Laws of the United States, and Treaties made, or which shall be made, under their Authority;--to all Cases affecting Ambassadors, other public Ministers and Consuls;--to all Cases of admiralty and maritime Jurisdiction;--to Controversies to which the United States shall be a Party;--to Controversies between two or more States; between a State and Citizens of another State;--between Citizens of different States;--between Citizens of the same State claiming Lands under Grants of different States, and between a State, or the Citizens thereof, and foreign States, Citizens or Subjects.

In all Cases affecting Ambassadors, other public Ministers and Consuls, and those in which a State shall be Party, the supreme Court shall have original jurisdiction. In all the other Cases before mentioned, the supreme Court shall have appellate jurisdiction, both as to Law and Fact, with such Exceptions, and under such Regulations as the Congress shall make.

The Trial of all Crimes, except in Cases of Impeachment, shall be by Jury; and such Trial shall be held in the State where the said Crimes shall have been committed; but when not committed within any State, the Trial shall be at such Place or Places as the Congress may by Law have directed.

***

Attorneys work for the Supreme Court in a number of capacities in addition to the well-known ones such as Law Clerks to the Justices. Attorneys can be found in the following offices:

Clerk's Office. The Clerk's Office consists of the Clerk of the Supreme Court, several Deputy Clerks, and approximately 25 Assistant Clerks. The office supervises the execution of the many judicial functions of the Court, including: administering dockets and argument calendars; receiving and recording all motions, petitions, jurisdictional statements, briefs and other documents filed on the various dockets; distributing these various papers to the Justices; collecting filing fees and assessing costs; preparing and maintaining the Court's order list and Journal, upon which are entered all the Court's orders and judgments; preparing formal judgments and mandates; notifying counsel and lower courts of all formal actions, including written opinions; supervising the printing of briefs and appendices after review has been granted in **in forma pauperis** cases; requesting and securing the certified record from the lower court upon the grant of review or other direction of the Court; supervising the admission of attorneys to the Supreme Court Bar, as well as the imposition of disciplinary measures; and rendering procedural advice to counsel and litigants in need of assistance with respect to the Court's rules and procedures.

Reporter of Decisions. The Reporter of Decisions formally edits the opinions of the Court after release and supervises their publication in the official United States Reports. The Reporter and his staff of 10 check all citations in the Justices' opinions after they have been delivered, corrects all typographical or other formal errors, and helps draft the headnotes that appear on the opinions on their release.

Legal Officers. These relatively new additions to the Court's staff work directly with the Court and with individual Justices on a variety of problems resulting from the dockets. They also act as in-house counsel with respect to legal problems arising from the operation of the Supreme Court Building. Appointments are restricted to attorneys with prior legal experience. Terms are for a minimum of four years. Specifically, Legal Officers analyze motions presented to the Court; provide assistance, upon request, to any individual Justice in the discharge of his Circuit responsibilities; and undertake special projects assigned by the Court. Legal Officers also advise the Clerk, the administrative staff, and the Justices' law clerks in procedural or other matters unique to the Supreme Court.

Law Clerks. Law Clerks are typically selected by each Justice from among recent law school graduates with superior academic records, particularly individuals with previous experience clerking for a lower court judge. The customary term of service is one term, although some may stay longer. Each Justice is entitled to four Law Clerks. The Chief Justice, in addition, has a special assistant who serves as a Senior Law Clerk with a wide range of responsibilities. Law Clerk duties vary with each individual Justice, but virtually all engage in legal research and analysis for the preparation of opinions; and reading and reduction to memoranda of petitions, jurisdictional statements, motions, and briefs. A recent development is the pooling of Law Clerks from several Justices' chambers, in order to equitably divide the workload at the screening stage of petitions for certiorari and jurisdictional statements.

SUPREME COURT OF THE UNITED STATES

(Area Code 202)

Basic telephone number for the Supreme Court 479-3000

Chief Justice: William H. Rehnquist

Associate Justices:

William J. Brennan, Jr.	John Paul Stevens
Byron R. White	Sandra Day O'Connor
Thurgood Marshall	Antonin Scalia
Harry A. Blackmun	Anthony Kennedy

NOTE: The resignation of Associate Justice William J. Brennan, Jr. was effective as of July 20, 1990.

Administrative Assistant to the Chief Justice:
Laurence H. Averill, Jr 479-3400
Clerk: Joseph F. Spaniol Jr. 479-3011

(Area Code 202)

Librarian: Shelly Dowling 479-3175
Staff Counsel: Richard Schickele 479-3000
Reporter of Decisions: Frank Wagner 479-3390
Public Information Officer: Toni House 479-3211
Opinion Information 479-3360
Bar Admissions 479-3017

Library (Third Floor) 479-3175
The library is open to members of the Supreme Court Bar and to U.S. Government attorneys. The librarians have a list of members of the Supreme Court Bar; U.S. Government attorneys will be asked to show their Federal identification. The library is for reference purposes only and does not circulate documents. It is open from 9:00 AM until 4:15 PM Monday through Friday.

DECISIONS OF THE COURT

The following publications can be purchased from the **U.S. Government Printing Office.** Stock numbers and prices for annual subscriptions are shown below. Submit requests for these publications to: The Superintendent of Documents, U.S. Government Printing Office, Washington, D.C. 20402. (202/783-3238).

Supreme Court of the United States. Individual Slip Opinions. 1989 Term. Published irregularly. All the Court's opinions as announced from the bench. Price: $163.00 domestic per court term; $203.75 foreign per court term. GPO Stock# 828-003-00000-3.

Preliminary Prints. "Advance Sheets." 1987 Term. Published irregularly. Official United States Reports containing all the opinions with syllabi, names of counsel, indices, tables of cases, and other editorial additions. Price: $47.00 domestic per court term; $58.75 foreign/court term. GPO Stock# 828-002-00000-7.

United States Reports. Volume 481 (1987 Term--the most recent bound volume available). Price: $37.00 per volume. Initially issued separately as slip opinions (see above) and then subsequently published in advance sheets ("Preliminary Prints") with a fact summary, syllabi, and index prepared by the Court's Reporter of Decisions (see above). After the end of the Court's term each year, the advance sheets are replaced by bound volumes (usually 3-4 per term). GPO Stock# 028-001-00451-2.

The United States Reports also includes opinions of the Supreme Court since its inception. Before 1827, these decisions were published by private reporters. Until 1874, the reports were cited by the name of the reporter, as follows:

Dallas	(4 volumes, now vols. 1-4 U.S.)(1789-1800)
Cranch	(9 volumes, now vols. 5-13 U.S.)(1801-1815)
Wheaton	(12 volumes, now vols. 14-25 U.S.)(1816-1827)
Peters	(16 volumes, now vols. 26-41 U.S.)(1828-1842)
Howard	(24 volumes, now vols. 42-65 U.S.)(1843-1860)
Black	(2 volumes, now vols. 66-67 U.S.)(1861-1862)
Wallace	(23 volumes, now vols. 68-90 U.S.)(1863-1874)

In addition to the above official reports of decisions, there are also four unofficial decisional reporters published by private publishing companies. These reports are available in most law libraries and also directly from the publishers. They are:

United States Supreme Court Reports, Lawyers' Edition. Published by the Lawyers' Cooperative Publishing Company and the Bancroft-Whitney Company. The "Lawyers' Edition" covers the entire series from 1 Dallas to date and also contains many decisions not reported in the early official volumes. The publishers prepare their own case summaries and headnotes which precede the opinions. For selected important cases, there is also an appendix to each volume which contains summaries of attorneys' briefs submitted to the Court and annotations written by the publishers' editorial staff. The annotations consist largely of articles and essays about legal issues raised by the cases. Current decisions of the Court are issued biweekly as advance sheets during each term. These advance sheets do not contain annotations. Contact: Lawyers Co-operative Publishing Company, 50 Broad Street East, Rochester, NY 14694. Tel: 716/546-5530. Or, 800/828-6266.

Supreme Court Reporter. Published by West Publishing Company. Begins with volume 106 (1882) and is current to date. The publisher adds its own headnotes and editorial features. Decisions are first issued as advance sheets biweekly during the Court's term. The Reporter also contains, as adopted, all Federal court rules and amendments, except local rules of the Federal District Courts. Contact: West Publishing Company, 50 West Kellogg Blvd., P.O. Box 64833, St. Paul, MN 55164. Tel: 612/688-3600. Or, 800/328-9352.

United States Law Week. Looseleaf. Weekly. Published by the Bureau of National Affairs, Inc. Includes the following features: opinions of the Court; a Summary of Orders, which indicates cases acted upon and lower court holdings that the Supreme Court has agreed to review, along with the questions presented for review; a Journal of Proceedings, which contains the minutes of all Court sessions the previous week; Cases Docketed, which includes citations to lower court opinions and also the general subject matter of the case; a Summary of Cases Recently Filed; Arguments Before the Court, a summary of oral arguments in the most important cases each week; a Table of Cases and Case Status Report, which is issued every three to four weeks; and a Topical Index, which is issued seven times a year. Contact: Bureau of National Affairs, 9435 Key West Ave., Rockville, MD 20850. Tel: 301/258-1033. Or, 800/372-1033.

Supreme Court Bulletin. Looseleaf. Mailed to subscribers on decision day. Published by Commerce Clearing House, Inc. Incudes current opinions of the Court, and index to docket numbers, the status of pending cases, and a tentative calendar of scheduled arguments. Contact: Commerce Clearing House, 4025 West Peterson Avenue, Chicago, IL 60646. Tel: 312/583-8500. Or, in Washington, D.C., call 202/626-2200.

The latter two reports are most useful for staying current with the Supreme Court, while the other three reports are of most value in researching older decisions.

RULES OF PRACTICE AND PROCEDURE

The Supreme Court has promulgated rules of practice and procedure to be followed by litigants and parties petitioning the court for relief. These rules may be found in the Appendix to Title 28 of the United States Code.

FEDERAL COURT RULES

The Supreme Court is also authorized to prescribe rules for the U.S. Courts of Appeal, the U.S. District Courts, and certain specialized Federal courts established under Article III of the Constitution, as well as certain special proceedings in the Federal courts, such as bankruptcy, admiralty, and copyright proceedings. Federal court rules promulgated by the Supreme Court are for the general guidance of the lower Federal courts. Note: Most admiralty cases since 1966 fall under the Federal Rules of Civil Procedure. However, certain special admiralty rules come into play if the only constitutional or statutory ground of jurisdiction is the admiralty ground or, if more than one jurisdictional ground may be invoked, the admiralty ground is the one designated in the complaint. Admiralty rules are not codified in one place, but are scattered throughout the U.S. Code.

In addition, special local conditions and circumstances have led each lower court to issue its own special rules not inconsistent with the general rules set forth by the Supreme Court. These local rules apply only to the issuing court and are primarily concerned with rules for filing motions, brief preparations, and procedural rules of an operational nature.

Generally, court rules control court operations and the conduct of litigants appearing before the courts. they are designed to establish uniform procedures, render efficient their business functions, and provide parties with information and instructions on matters pertaining to judicial proceedings.

Federal court rules consist of: (1) rules of general applicability, such as the Federal Rules of Civil Procedure; (2) the Federal Rules of Appellate Procedure; (3) individual rules of Federal courts; and (4) forms used by litigants.

Rules of court not inconsistent with legislative enactments have the force and effect of statutes.

Publication of Court Rules. Rules of general applicability may be found in the appendixes to Titles 11, 18, and 28 of the United States Code. The U.S. Code Annotated and the U.S. Code Service also publish Federal court rules of general applicability and annotate them to both case law and Opinions of the Attorney General.

Each Circuit Court of Appeals and many Federal District Courts publish their own local rules in pamphlet form, available from the appropriate clerk's office.

DATABASES AND PUBLICATIONS OF INTEREST

DATABASE:

Project Hermes. Project Hermes is an electronic dissemination service for opinions of the Supreme Court. The service, which first transmitted Supreme Court decisions on June 21, 1990, will operate for a two-year trial period. Opinions are electronically transmitted to subscribers simultaneously with their being announced by the Court. The organizations initially selected to disseminate this data are:

*Associated Press
*Bureau of National Affairs
*Case Western Reserve University
*Commerce Clearing House
*Mead Data Central
*National Clearinghouse for Legal Services
*Supreme Court Opinion Network (SCON)
*United Press International
*U.S. Department of Justice
*UUNet Communications Services
*VERALEX, The Thompson Group
*West Publishing Company

PUBLICATION:

West's Federal Rules Decisions. Issued monthly. Price: $52.00 per year. Contains decisions of the Federal courts construing rules of practice and procedure, and articles on Federal rules. Available from West Publishing Company, 50 West Kellogg Blvd, P.O. Box 64833, St. Paul, MN 55164-0526.

UNITED STATES COURTS OF APPEALS

DESCRIPTION: The United States Courts of Appeals are intermediate appellate courts that consider all appeals in cases originally decided by the U.S. District Courts. They review all final decisions and certain interlocutory decisions of the District Courts, except in the very few cases where the law provides for a direct review by the U.S. Supreme Court. Courts of Appeals are also empowered to review and enforce orders of many Federal administrative bodies. Their decisions are final except as they are subject to discretionary review or appeal in the Supreme Court.

The United States is divided geographically into 12 judicial circuits, including the District of Columbia. Each circuit has a Court of Appeals, and each of the 50 states is assigned to one of these circuits. There is also a Court of Appeals for the Federal Circuit, which has nationwide jurisdiction defined by subject matter (see below). There are 156 judges currently serving on the Courts of Appeals. Each court has from six to 28 judges, and normally hears cases in three-judge panels.

UNITED STATES COURTS OF APPEALS

The support staff of the U.S. Courts of Appeals include numerous attorneys. They are employed in varying capacities and occupy both legal and law-related positions. Following is a description of the typical positions in which attorneys may be found. Although the job titles may vary from one court to another for some of these positions, the responsibilities described are generally consistent from court to court.

Circuit Executive: This position, created by Congress in 1971, is designed to exercise administrative control of the nonjudicial activities of the Court of Appeals. Circuit Executives often have law degrees as well as substantial administrative experience and training.

Assistant to the Circuit Executive: This position assists with financial and case management, including statistical compilation and evaluation; special research projects; space and facilities; and performing other duties as assigned by the Circuit Executive.

Clerk: The clerk is the judicial counterpart of the Circuit Executive, and functions as the administrator of all the judicial activities of the court, including, docketing, relations with attorneys appearing before the court, paperwork management, etc.

Deputy Clerk: This position assists the clerk in managing the judicial functions of the court. In courts with more than one deputy clerk, each deputy is generally responsible for one functional area of judicial administration, such as initial processing of new cases before the court.

Senior Case Manager: This position screens appellate cases at early stages for possible early disposition, expedition, or placement on the settlement conference calendar.

Director, Office of Staff Attorneys: The Director is responsible for supervising the staff attorneys. The work of the office generally includes conducting pre-briefing conferences; coordinating the court's motions practice; preparing case memoranda; drafting dispositions; and evaluating incoming cases.

Supervisory Staff Attorney/Chief Staff Counsel: This position is responsible for training new staff law clerks. Incumbents also serve as a resource on substantive issues and edit legal memoranda. There are currently 21 such positions (including both the Circuit and District Courts).

Staff Attorney: The primary function of the Staff Attorney is to assist the court in disposing of substantive motions, including motions for summary affirmance or reversal, dismissal, transfer, appointment of counsel, and emergency applications for stay or injunction pending appeal. Staff Attorneys prepare memoranda analyzing the issues presented and recommend an appropriate disposition of the motion. In addition, they assist in screening cases for hearing on the merits, prepare recommendations on summary dispositions, and manage civil appeals.

Motions Attorney: These attorneys represent the court in civil appeals and assist the court with substantive motion practice, including petitions for mandamus, petitions to appeal in forma pauperis, applications for certificates of probable cause, etc. In some circuits, Motions Attorneys also assist judges of the Bankruptcy Appellate Panel in legal and administrative matters, with an emphasis on the processing, evaluation, and disposition of substantive and procedural motions.

Law Clerk: Judicial Law Clerks are normally hired for two-year terms commencing in the summer. Clerks assist the court and its judges in the prompt disposition of appeals. Primary assignments involve the preparation of proposed opinions and supporting memoranda for pro se appeals and appeals screened for summary disposition.

Pro Se Clerk: These one-year or two-year term positions are held by recent law school graduates who prepare bench memoranda in civil and criminal appeals in which at least one party is proceeding pro se. They also provide information to pro se litigants. Most of the work involves issues of constitutional law, particularly in the criminal and civil rights areas.

DECISIONS OF THE COURTS

There have never been any official published reports of opinions of the U.S. Courts of Appeals. The standard unofficial source of these decisions is the Federal Reporter and Federal Reporter, Second Series, which are components of the West Publishing Company's National Reporter System. The Federal Reporter and the current Federal Reporter, Second Series have been published continuously since 1880. The West Publishing Company has also collected all available decisions of the lower Federal courts from 1789 to 1880 and reprinted them in Federal Cases. Contact: West Publishing Company, 50 West Kellogg Blvd., P.O. Box 64833, St. Paul, MN 55164. Tel: 612/688-3600. Or, 800/328-9352.

RULES OF PRACTICE AND PROCEDURE

Federal Rules of Appellate Procedure. Promulgated by the U.S. Supreme Court for use in appellate proceedings in Federal Circuit Courts of Appeals. The text of the rules may be found in the Appendix to Title 28 of the United States Code.

Rules of Evidence for United States Courts and Magistrates ("Federal Rules of Evidence"). Congress enacted these rules in 1974 in order to provide a uniform evidentiary code for all U.S. courts. The text of the rules may be found in the Appendix to Title 28 of the United States Code.

Federal Rules of Evidence, 1989. Senate Judiciary Committee. Available from Superintendent of Documents, U.S. Government Printing Office, Washington, D.C. 20402. Price: $1.50. GPO Stock# 052-070-06591-5.

ELECTRONIC BULLETIN BOARDS

Several circuit courts have instituted ACES (Appeals Court Electronic Services), which was developed by the Federal Judicial Center, the research and development arm of the Federal Judiciary. ACES is an electronic bulletin board for the electronic dissemination of appellate court information. This service allows public users with a microcomputer and terminal emulation software and hardware to view and transfer electronically published slip opinions, court oral argument calendars, court rules, notices and reports, and press releases. Access to ACES is free and does not require prior registration. The following courts have implemented ACES or plan to implement it by the end of 1990:

*The Third Circuit Court of Appeals (Philadelphia)
*The Fourth Circuit Court of Appeals (Richmond)
*The Sixth Circuit Court of Appeals (Cincinnati)
*The Ninth Circuit Court of Appeals (San Francisco)
*The Tenth Circuit Court of Appeals (Denver)

Other courts are also planning to implement ACES in the near future.

PACER (Public Access to Court Electronic Records) is a dial-in service from any personal computer that permits the retrieval of complete official electronic case histories and docket reports in less than a minute. This service is free-of-charge and is available 24 hours a day. Cases may be searched by participant name or case number. At the appellate level, the system is only available in the Fourth and Sixth Circuits.

Public Access Terminals are available in several courthouses on a walk-up basis. These terminals allow the public to obtain docket information without waiting for a clerk to become available.

U.S. COURTS OF APPEALS ADDRESSES

U.S. Court of Appeals for the District of Columbia Circuit:
U.S. Courthouse, 3rd & Constitution Avenue, N.W., Washington, D.C. 20001

Chief Judge: Patricia M. Wald ....(202) 535-3366
Circuit Executive: Linda Finkelstein ....(202) 535-3340
Clerk: Constance L. Dupre ....(202) 535-3308
Chief Staff Counsel: Mark J. Langer ....(202) 535-3328

Library (Room 3518) ....(202) 535-3400
Very limited access is available to the library at the U.S. Court of Appeals for the District of Columbia Circuit between the hours of 9:00 AM and 4:00 PM. Members of any bar may use the library for reference purposes. There is no access to the stacks. The first 50 pages of photocopying are free.

Publications:

Opinions. Opinions of the Court are issued on Tuesdays and Fridays of each week. An annual subscription may be purchased for $250.00 by sending a check with your organization's name and address to the Clerk of the Court. The subscription year is from July 1 through June 30. Part-year subscriptions are not prorated.

U.S. Court of Appeals for the First Circuit:
John W. McCormack Post Office and Courthouse, Boston, MA 02109

Chief Judge: Levin H. Campbell ....(617) 223-9002
Circuit Executive: Vincent Flanagan ....(617) 223-9049
Clerk: Francis P. Scigliano ....(617) 223-9057
Senior Staff Attorney: Kathy McGill Lanza ....(617) 223-9030
Librarian: Karen Moss ....(617) 223-9044

Another library location within the Circuit:
300 Recinto Sur, Room 399C, San Juan, PR 00901 (809) 729-6761

U.S. Court of Appeals for the Second Circuit:
U.S. Courthouse, Foley Square, New York, NY 10007

Chief Judge: James L. Oakes ....(802) 254-5000
Circuit Executive: Steven Flanders ....(212) 791-0982
Clerk: Elaine B. Goldsmith ....(212) 791-0103
Senior Staff Attorney: Eileen Shapiro ....(212) 791-1054
Librarian: Margaret J. Evans ....(212) 791-1052

Other library locations within the Circuit:
225 Cadman Plaza East, Brooklyn, NY 11201 ....(212) 330-7483
U.S. Courthouse, 450 Main St, Hartford, CT 06103 ....(203) 722-2565
141 Church Street, New Haven, CT 06510 ....(203) 773-2346
Uniondale Ave & Hempstead Turnpike, Uniondale, NY 11553 ....(516) 485-6410

Community Defender Organization:
Executive Director and Attorney-in-Chief:
Archibald R. Murray, The Legal Aid Society, 15 Park Row, New York, NY 10038 .....(212) 577-3313
Attorney-in-Charge: Phyllis Bamberger, Federal Defender Services Unit, 52 Duane Street, New York, NY 10007 ....(212) 285-2842

U.S. Court of Appeals for the Third Circuit:
U.S. Courthouse, Independence Mall West, 601 Market Street, Philadelphia, PA 19106

Chief Judge: A. Leon Higginbotham, Jr ....(215) 597-9157
Circuit Executive: John P. Hehman ....(215) 597-0718
Clerk: Sally Mrvos ....(215) 597-2995
Senior Staff Attorney: P. Douglas Sisk ....(215) 597-2378
Librarian: Jean L. Willis ....(215) 597-2009

Other library locations within the Circuit:
Lockbox 43, 844 King St, Wilmington, DE 19801 (302) 573-6178
425 U.S. Post Office & Courthouse, Newark, NJ 07101 ....(201) 645-3034
512 U.S. Post Office & Courthouse, Pittsburgh, PA 15219 ....(412) 644-6485
402 U.S. Courthouse, 402 East State Street, Trenton, NJ 08605 ....(609) 989-2345

U.S. Court of Appeals for the Fourth Circuit:
10th and Main Streets, Richmond, VA 23219

Chief Judge: Sam J. Ervin III ....(704) 438-4222
Circuit Executive: Samuel W. Phillips ....(804) 771-2184
Clerk: John Greacen ....(804) 771-2213
Senior Staff Attorney: Arlen Coyle ....(804) 771-2348
Librarian: Peter A. Frey ....(804) 771-2219
ACES (Appeals Court Electronic Services).........(804) 771-2028

Other library locations within the Circuit:
101 West Lombard Street, Baltimore, MD 21201 (301) 962-0997
319 U.S. Courthouse, 600 Granby Street, Norfolk, VA 23510 ....(804) 441-3814
4400 U.S. Courthouse & Federal Building, 500 Quarrier Street, Charleston, WV 25301 (304) 347-5295

U.S. Court of Appeals for the Fifth Circuit:
U.S. Courthouse, 600 Camp Street, New Orleans, LA 70130

Chief Judge: Charles Clark ....(601) 353-0911
Circuit Executive: Lydia Comberrel ....(504) 589-2730
Clerk: Gilbert F. Ganucheau ....(504) 589-6514
Senior Staff Attorney: Anthony J. Bonfanti ......(504) 589-6935
Librarian: Kay E. Duley ....(504) 589-6510

Other library locations within the Circuit:
10017 U.S. Courthouse, 515 Rusk Avenue, Houston, TX 77002 ....(713) 221-9696
10th and East Elizabeth Streets, U.S. Courthouse, P.O. Box 1873, Brownsville, TX 78520 ..(512) 548-2509
130 Federal Building, Baton Rouge, LA 70801 ...(504) 389-0595
725 Washington Loop, Rm 212, Biloxi, MS 39530 ..(601) 435-9108
705 Jefferson St, Rm 170, Lafayette, LA 70501 ..(318) 264-6878

U.S. Court of Appeals for the Sixth Circuit:
U.S. Post Office and Courthouse Building, 5th & Walnut Streets, Cincinnati, OH 45202

Chief Judge: Gilbert S. Merritt ....(615) 736-5957
Circuit Executive: James A. Higgins ....(513) 684-3161
Clerk: Leonard Green ....(513) 684-2953
Senior Staff Attorney: Kenneth A. Howe, Jr. .....(513) 684-2953
Librarian: Kathy J. Walker ....(513) 684-2678
ACES (Appeals Court Electronic Services) ....(513) 684-2842

Other library locations within the Circuit:
722 Federal Building, Detroit, MI 48226 ....(313) 226-6986
A-810 U.S. Courthouse, Nashville, TN 37203 ....(615) 736-7492
U.S. Courthouse, Cleveland, OH 44114 ....(216) 522-4250
Federal Building, Grand Rapids, MI 49502 ......(616) 456-2363
1125 Federal Building, 167 North Main Street, Memphis, TN 38103 ....(901) 521-4170

U.S. Court of Appeals for the Seventh Circuit:
219 South Dearborn Street, Chicago, IL 60604

Chief Judge: William J. Bauer ....(312) 435-5810
Circuit Executive: Collins T. Fitzpatrick ....(312) 435-5803
Clerk: Thomas F. Strubbe ....(312) 435-5850
Senior Staff Attorney: Donald J. Wall ....(312) 435-5805
Librarian: Janet Wishinsky ....(312) 435-5660

Other library locations within the Circuit:
464 U.S. Courthouse, 517 East Wisconsin Avenue, Milwaukee, WI 53202 ....(414) 291-1698
U.S. Courthouse, Room 550, 120 North Henry Street, Madison, WI 53703 ....(608) 246-5448
46 East Ohio Street, Room 116, Indianapolis, IN 46204 ....(317) 226-2092
316 U.S. Courthouse, 204 S. Main Street, South Bend, IN 46601 ....(219) 236-8767

U.S. Court of Appeals for the Eighth Circuit:
U.S. Court & Custom House, 1114 Market St, St. Louis, MO 63101

Chief Judge: Donald P. Lay ....(612) 290-3838
Circuit Executive: June L. Boadwine
St. Paul, MN ....(612) 290-3311
St. Louis, MO ....(314) 539-6219
Clerk: Robert D. St. Vrain
St. Paul, MN ....(612) 290-3636
St. Louis, MO ....(314) 539-3609
Senior Staff Attorney: Sheila Greenbaum ....(314) 539-3620
Librarian: Ann T. Fessenden ....(314) 539-2930

Other library locations within the Circuit:
Post Office and Courthouse, 600 West Capitol, Room 220, Little Rock, AR 72201 ....(510) 378-5039
543 Federal Court Building, 316 North Robert Street, St. Paul, MN 55101 ....(612) 290-3177
215 North 17th Street, Omaha, NE 68102 ....(402) 221-4768
306 U.S. Courthouse, Des Moines, IA 50309 .....(515) 284-6228
805 U.S. Courthouse, 811 Grand Avenue, Kansas City, MO 64106 ....(816) 426-2937
560 U.S. Courthouse, 110 S. Fourth Street, Minneapolis, MN 55401 ....(612) 348-1829
657 Second Avenue North, Rm 247, Fargo, ND 58102(701) 239-5175

U.S. Court of Appeals for the Ninth Circuit:
P.O. Box 547, San Francisco, CA 94101

Chief Judge: Alfred T. Goodwin ....(818) 405-7100
Circuit Executive: Gregory B. Walters ....(415) 556-7340
Clerk: Cathy Catterson Hensen ....(415) 556-7340
Senior Staff Attorney: Dinah L. Shelton ....(415) 556-7361
Librarian: Francis Gates ....(415) 556-6129
ACES (Appeals Court Electronic Services) ....(415) 556-8620

Other library locations within the Circuit:
1702 U.S. Post Office & Courthouse, 312 North Spring Street, Los Angeles, CA 90012 ..(213) 688-3636
125 South Grand Avenue, P.O. Box 91510, Pasadena, CA 91109 ....(818) 405-7020
907 U.S. Courthouse, Seattle, WA 98104 ....(206) 442-4475
P.O. Box 36060, San Francisco, CA 94102 ....(415) 556-7979
U.S. Courthouse, 940 Front Street, San Diego, CA 92189 ....(619) 557-5066
213 Gus J. Solomon U.S. Courthouse, 620 S.W. Main Street, Portland, OR 97205 ....(503) 326-6042
104 Pioneer Courthouse, 555 S.W. Yamhill Street, Portland, OR 97204 ....(503) 326-2142
6434 U.S. Courthouse & Federal Building, 230 N. 1st Avenue, Phoenix, AZ 85025 ....(602) 261-3879
220 U.S. Courthouse, 55 East Broadway, Tucson, AZ 85701 ....(602) 792-6552
3311 U.S. Courthouse, 650 Capitol Mall, Sacramento, CA 95814 ....(916) 440-2246
P.O. Box 50128, Honolulu, HI 96850 ....(808) 541-1797

Bankruptcy Appellate Panel of the Ninth Circuit, 315 Park Place Building, Room 407, 1200 Sixth Avenue, Seattle, WA 98101
Presiding Judge: Sidney C. Violinn ....(206) 442-1624
Clerk: Jed G. Weintraub (in Pasadena) ....(818) 405-7906

U.S. Court of Appeals for the Tenth Circuit:
U.S. Courthouse, 1929 Stout Street, Denver, CO 80294

Chief Judge: William J. Holloway Jr ....(405) 231-5575
Circuit Executive: Eugene J. Murret ....(303) 844-6031
Clerk: Robert Hoecker ....(303) 844-3157
Senior Staff Attorney: John K. Kleinheksel ......(303) 844-5306
Librarian: J. Terry Hemming ....(303) 844-3591

Other library locations within the Circuit:
2314 Federal Building, Cheyenne, WY 82003 ....(307) 328-2752
5114 U.S. Courthouse, Oklahoma City, OK 73102 ....(405) 231-4866

4-520 U.S. Courthouse, Tulsa, OK 74103 ....(918) 581-7498
259 U.S. Courthouse, 350 S. Main Street, Salt Lake City, UT 84101 ....(801) 524-3505
P.O. Box 2066, Albuquerque, NM 87103 ....(505) 766-8489

U.S. Court of Appeals for the Eleventh Circuit:

56 Forsyth Street, N.W., Atlanta, GA 30303

Chief Judge: Gerald B. Tjoflat ....(904) 791-3416
Circuit Executive: Norman E. Zoller ....(404) 331-5724
Clerk: Miguel J. Cortez Jr ....(404) 331-6187
Senior Staff Attorney: Karen C. Wilbanks ....(404) 331-5775
Librarian: Elaine Fenton ....(404) 331-2510

Other library locations within the Circuit:
2356 U.S. Courthouse, 75 Spring Street, S.W., Atlanta, GA 30303 ....(404) 331-6496
P.O. Box 539, Jacksonville, FL 32201 ....(904) 791-2281
15 Lee Street, PO Box 1589, Montgomery, AL 36102 ....(205) 832-7210
Federal Courthouse Square, 301 North Miami Avenue, Miami, FL 33128 ....(305) 536-5146

UNITED STATES COURT OF APPEALS FOR THE FEDERAL CIRCUIT

717 Madison Place, N.W.
Washington, D.C. 20439

DESCRIPTION: The U.S. Court of Appeals for the Federal Circuit (CFAC), established in 1982 under the Federal Courts Improvement Act, was formed by the merger of the U.S. Court of Customs and Patent Appeals and the appellate division of the U.S. Court of Claims. The Court's geographic jurisdiction is nationwide. Its subject matter jurisdiction rests essentially in the fields of international trade, government contracts, patents, claims for money from the Government, and Federal personnel. It hears appeals from the U.S. Court of International Trade, the U.S. Claims Court, all Federal District Courts (in patent and Little Tucker Act cases), the Boards of the Patent and Trademark Office, the U.S. International Trade Commission, the Merit Systems Protection Board, and the Boards of Contract Appeals.

The U.S. Court of Appeals for the Federal Circuit consists of 12 judges. Upon reaching age 70, judges may elect to take senior status and continue serving. At present, there are six senior judges who continue to assist the Court in meeting its workload.

Appeals are normally heard by three-judge panels, but the Court is unique in its authorization to sit in panels of five, seven, or nine judges as well as en banc. Larger panels are assigned to hear appeals that are especially complex or sensitive or that raise new and important issues. Any decision of the Federal Circuit may be reviewed by the U.S. Supreme Court on petition for writ of certiorari. Sessions are held monthly throughout the year in Washington, D.C. Additional sessions are periodically scheduled in other cities. The Chief Justice of the United States serves as the Court's Circuit Justice.

Each judge usually engages two law clerks, one or both of whom can be engaged for two years. Historically, one or both of the law clerks selected by a judge generally has had a technical degree (engineering, science, or technology) as well as a law degree.

Other attorneys at the Court include three Technical Assistants (a Senior Technical Assistant, a Deputy Senior Technical Assistant, and a Technical Assistant) and a Motions Staff Attorney.

The Technical Assistants assist in reviewing panel approved opinions intended for publication to avoid conflicts in holdings; assist in reviewing briefs and preparing Evaluation Reports; assist in advising judges and law clerks on legal or technical matters; conduct technological and legal research; and prepare research memoranda as requested.

The Motions Staff Attorney assists judges and panels in resolving motions that require action by a judge or panel of judges, and performs other duties at the direction of the Chief Judge.

(Area Code 202)

Chief Judge: Helen W. Nies 633-6562
Clerk: Francis X. Gindhart 633-6550
Motions Staff Attorney: Eleanor Thayer 633-6087
Senior Technical Assistant: Melvin L. Halpern 633-6564
Technical Assistant: Janet Stockhausen 633-6564
Technical Assistant: MaryAnn Lastova 633-6564
Librarian: Patricia M. McDermott 633-5871

Library (Room 218) **633-5871**
The library is available for reference to members of the U.S. Claims Court Bar and members of the U.S. Court of Appeals Bar. It is open Monday through Friday from 9:00 AM until 5:00 PM. Photo copies are 15 cents per page.

TEMPORARY EMERGENCY COURT OF APPEALS

DECISIONS OF THE COURT

United States Court of Appeals for the Federal Circuit, V 6, Trade Cases. (Judiciary) 1989. 200 pp. Price: $13.00. GPO Stock# 028-002-00048-3. Contact: The Superintendent of Documents, United States Government Printing Office, Washington, D.C. 20402. Tel: 202/783-3238.

Federal Reporter, Second Series. Published by West Publishing Company. Contains current and past decisions of the Federal Circuit and, beginning with volume 34 of the Second Series, decisions of the former U.S. Court of Patent Appeals, which was abolished in 1982. Contact: West Publishing Company, 50 West Kellogg Blvd., P.O. Box 64833, St. Paul, MN 55164. Tel: 612/688-3600. Or, 800/328-9352.

Opinions. Slip opinions of the Court are published by the Patent Resources Institute and by BNA Plus. Contact: Patent Resources Institute, Inc., 2000 Pennsylvania Avenue, N.W., Suite 3450, Wash., D.C. 20037. Tel: 202/452-4323. Or, 800/452-7773.

PRI Opinions is a weekly periodical of all published and unpublished patent, trademark and copyright opinions of the U.S. Court of Appeals for the Federal Circuit, which the Court issued during the five business-day period preceding the publication date. PRI Opinions also includes other CAFC opinions likely to be of interest to members of the intellectual property law bar. All slip opinions released for publication by the U.S. Patent and Trademark Office or by applicant's attorneys are also included. Annual subscription: (October 1 - September 30): $235.00. Patent Resources Institute, Inc., 2000 Pennsylvania Avenue, N.W., Suite 3450, Washington, D.C. 20006. Tel: 202/223-1175.

BNA Plus CAFC Opinions. BNA Plus provides a weekly subscription service for U.S. Court of Appeals for the Federal Circuit decisions. Opinions are mailed on Tuesday of the week after they are issued by the Court. BNA Plus offers subscriptions to all published CAFC decisions and to all unpublished patent and trademark decisions. They will also screen and deliver only those decisions pertinent to specific interests. For pricing and order information contact BNA Plus, 1231 25th Street, Washington, D.C. 20037. Tel: Washington, DC Metro area: 202/452-4323; Outside Washington, DC Metro area: 800/452-7773.

RULES OF PRACTICE AND PROCEDURE

Federal Rules of Appellate Procedure. Promulgated by the U.S. Supreme Court for use in appellate proceedings in Federal Circuit Courts of Appeals. Appeals to the Federal Circuit are also governed by the Federal Rules of Appellate Procedure with such modifications and additions as are dictated by the special nature of the Court's jurisdiction. The text of the rules may be found in the Appendix to Title 28 of the United States Code.

Rules of the U.S. Court of Appeals for the Federal Circuit. The local rules peculiar to the Federal Circuit and necessitated by the special nature of the Court's jurisdiction. The text of the rules may be found in the Appendix to Title 28 of the United States Code.

TEMPORARY EMERGENCY COURT OF APPEALS

1130 U.S. Courthouse, 3rd and Constitution Avenue, N.W.
Washington, D.C. 20001

DESCRIPTION: The Temporary Emergency Court of Appeals has nationwide jurisdiction with regard to cases arising under the Economic Stabilization Act of 1970 [12 U.S.C. Sec 1904 note] and the Emergency Petroleum Allocation Act of 1973 [15 U.S.C. Sec 754a].

Chief Judge: Reynaldo G. Garza.(Brownsville, TX) (512) 548-2592

Clerk: Cynthia Dykes ....(202) 535-3390

DECISIONS OF THE COURT

Opinions. Opinions of the Court are published as issued. Individual opinions may be purchased for $2.00. A six-month subscription may be purchased for $25.00 by sending a check with your organization's name and address to the Court.

Federal Reporter, Second Series. Published by West Publishing Company. Contains the decisions of the Court. Contact: West Publishing Company, 50 West Kellogg Blvd., P.O. Box 64833, St. Paul, MN 55164. Tel: 612/688-3600. Or, 800/328-9352.

RULES OF PRACTICE AND PROCEDURE

General Rules of the Temporary Emergency Court of Appeals of the United States. The text of these rules may be found in the Appendix to Title 28 of the United States Code.

UNITED STATES CLAIMS COURT
717 Madison Place, N.W.
Washington, D.C. 20005

DESCRIPTION: The United States Claims Court succeeds to the original jurisdiction formerly exercised by the Court of Claims. The Court has jurisdiction to render money judgments upon any claim against the U.S. founded either upon the Constitution, or any act of Congress, or any regulation or an executive department, or upon any express or implied contract with the U.S., or for liquidated or unliquidated damages in cases not sounding in tort.

As collateral to any such judgment, the Court may issue orders directing the restoration to office or status and the correction of applicable records. As part of its jurisdiction over contract claims, the Court has the authority, if the claim is filed before a contract is awarded, to grant declaratory judgments and such equitable relief including, but not limited to, injunctive relief. In addition to its authority to entertain money judgment claims under the Contract Disputes Act of 1978, it also has jurisdiction to render judgment upon any claim by or against, or dispute with, a contractor arising under that Act.

The court also has jurisdiction over other specific types of claims against the U.S., including the rendering of judgment for reasonable and entire compensation in cases where the U.S., in its governmental capacity, had manufactured or used an invention covered by a patent or had infringed any work protected by copyright without license of its owner.

Further, the National Childhood Vaccine Injury Act of 1986 vests jurisdiction in the Court over compensation claims by individuals who have been injured by certain vaccines. Under the Act, whose effective date was October 1, 1988, the Court is required to appoint Special Masters who will require testimony and documents needed to prepare proposed findings of fact and conclusions of law. For cases filed after December 18, 1989, if neither party files a motion for review within 30 days, the Special Master's decision is the basis for the Court's judgment on the case. Depending on caseload, up to 10 Special Masters may be needed to handle this new responsibility.

Jurisdiction of the Court is nationwide, and jurisdiction over the parties is obtained when suit is filed and process is served on the U.S. through the Attorney General. Trials for the purpose of taking testimony and receiving exhibits are conducted before judges of the Court, and are conducted at locations most convenient for the claimants and their witnesses.

Judgments of the Court are final and conclusive on both the claimant and the U.S., subject to an appeal to the U.S. Court of Appeals for the Federal Circuit.

The Court is composed of 16 judges, one of whom is the Chief Judge. There are 17 law clerks: each judge has one law clerk except for the Chief Judge, who has two. One other attorney on the Court's staff is the Chief of Staff, who is the Court Administrator.

(Area Code 202)

Chief Judge: Loren A. Smith 633-7267
Clerk: Frank T. Peartree 633-7257
Chief of Staff: John F. Edwards 633-7252
Chief Special Master: Gary Golkiewicz .... (703) 235-4386
Docket 633-7261
Copies of Opinions: 633-7230

Library (Room 218) **633-5871**
The library is available for reference to members of the U.S. Claims Court Bar and members of the U.S. Court of Appeals Bar. It is open Monday through Friday from 9:00 AM until 5:00 PM. Photocopies are 15 cents per page.

DECISIONS OF THE COURT

United States Claims Court Reporter. Published by West Publishing Company. 1983-date. Contains decisions of the Claims Court and also includes reprints of opinions reviewing U.S. Claims Court decisions originally published in the Federal Reporter (see above) and Supreme Court Reporter (see above). Contact: West Publishing Company, 50 West Kellogg Blvd., P.O. Box 64833, St. Paul, MN 55164. Tel: 612/688-3600. Or, 800/328-9352.

Index to Opinions. The monthly index to opinions of the United States Claims Court is available for a $10.00 annual subscription. Individual opinions cost $1.00 each. To obtain publications write to the Clerk of the Court.

For cases decided in the predecessor U.S. Court of Claims, which was abolished in 1982, see Cases Decided in the Court of Claims, 1863-1982, vols. 1-231. Consult a law library since this serial publication is now out of print and no longer available for purchase.

RULES OF PRACTICE AND PROCEDURE

Rules of the U.S. Claims Court. the text of these rules may be found in the Appendix to Title 28 of the United States Code.

UNITED STATES COURT OF INTERNATIONAL TRADE

1 Federal Plaza
New York, NY 10007

DESCRIPTION: The U.S. Court of International Trade has jurisdiction over any civil action against the United States arising from Federal laws governing import transactions. This includes classification and valuation cases as well as authority to review certain Federal agency determinations involving antidumping and countervailing duty matters. In addition, it has exclusive jurisdiction of civil actions to review determinations as to the eligibility of workers, firms, and communities for adjustment assistance under the Trade Act of 1974. Civil actions commenced by the United States to recover custom duties, to recover on a customs bond, or certain civil penalties alleging fraud or negligence are also within the exclusive jurisdiction of the court. Appeals from final decisions of the court may be taken to the U.S. Court of Appeals for the Federal Circuit and, ultimately, to the U.S. Supreme Court.

The geographic jurisdiction of the court is nationwide. The court is also authorized to hold hearings in foreign countries. The chambers of the judges, the courtrooms, and offices of the court are located in New York City at the Courthouse of the U.S. Court of International Trade.

The court is composed of a chief judge and eight active judges, not more than five of whom may belong to any one political party. There is also a small number of senior judges who have retired from the court but may be called upon as needed.

The attorneys on the court staff are the Clerk, the Assistant Clerk, and the individual judge's law clerks. Most judges have two law clerks, who are either working for an individual judge on a permanent, career basis or for a one- or two-year term.

(Area Code 212)

Chief Judge: Edward D. Re 264-2900
Clerk: Joseph E. Lombardi 264-2814
Assistant Clerk: Leo M. Gordon 264-7090

Library (Eighth Floor) 264-2816
The library is open for reference to judges, attorneys, and Federal employees Monday through Friday from 9:00 AM until 4:30 PM. Photocopying is available at 50 cents per page.

DECISIONS OF THE COURT

The following publications can be purchased from the **U.S. Government Printing Office**. Stock numbers and prices for annual subscriptions are shown below. Submit requests for these publications to: The Superintendent of Documents, U.S. Government Printing Office, Washington, D.C. 20402. Tel: 202/783-3238.

United States Court of International Trade Reports: Cases Adjudged in the United States Court of International Trade. All volumes are out of print except Volume 10. Volume 12 is forthcoming:

Volume 10, January - December, 1986. Price: $33.00 domestic, $41.25 foreign. GPO Stock# 028-003-00058-7.

Volume 12 is scheduled for release at the end of 1990. Its price has not yet been decided. GPO Stock# 028-003-00060-9.

Federal Supplement. Published by West Publishing Company. Contains the decisions of the Court. Beginning with volume 135, the Federal Supplement also contains the decisions of the predecessor United States Customs Court. Contact: West Publishing Company, 50 West Kellogg Blvd., P.O. Box 64833, St. Paul, MN 55164. Tel: 612/688-3600. Or, 800/328-9352.

RULES OF PRACTICE AND PROCEDURE

Rules of the U.S. Court of International Trade. the text of these rules may be found in the Appendix to Title 28 of the United States Code.

Rules Service Company, 7658 Standish Place, Ste 106, Rockville, MD 20855. Tel: 301/424-9402. Looseleaf. Updated when necessary. Price: $42.00 for subscription plus binder.

PUBLICATIONS OF INTEREST

Lawyers Information Bulletin: A Newsletter from the Clerk's Office. Published twice a year. Volume 6, No. 1 was published in May 1990. To have your name added to the mailing list contact the Assistant Clerk of the Court.

JUDICIAL PANEL ON MULTIDISTRICT LITIGATION
1120 Vermont Avenue, N.W.
Washington, D.C. 20005

DESCRIPTION: Created in 1968, the Judicial Panel on Multidistrict Litigation is authorized to temporarily transfer to a single district those civil actions pending in different districts which involve one or more common questions of fact. Transfers are made by the Panel for the convenience of parties and witnesses, and to promote the just and efficient coordination of pretrial proceedings.

The Panel's authority is not encumbered by venue restrictions and extends only to civil actions and transfers for pretrial. Typical subject matter areas of Panel involvement are antitrust, securities, air disaster and other common disasters, patent, copyright, trademark, and products liability. Various other types of litigation, such as contracts and employment practices, have been before the Panel as well. Antitrust enforcement actions commenced by the United States are exempt from the Panel's power, as are Government enforcement actions under Federal securities laws.

The Panel consists of seven Federal circuit and district judges, no two of whom may be from the same circuit. All appointments are made by the Chief Justice of the United States, who also selects one of the judges to serve as Chairman. The judges devote approximately one day a month to hearings on multidistrict matters. These hearings are held as ordered by the Panel and convene wherever necessary in the judgment of the Chairman. Concurrence of four members is required in any action to be taken.

Chairman: Hon. Andrew A. Caffrey (Boston, MA) ...(617) 223-2929
Executive Attorney: Robert A. Cahn ....(202) 653-6090
Clerk of the Panel: Patricia D. Howard ....(202) 653-6090

RULINGS OF THE PANEL

Federal Supplement. Contains key rulings of the Judicial Panel. Published by West Publishing Company. Contact: West Publishing Company, 50 West Kellogg Blvd., P.O. Box 64833, St. Paul, MN 55164. Tel: 612/688-3600. Or, 800/328-9352.

UNITED STATES SENTENCING COMMISSION
1331 Pennsylvania Avenue, N.W., Suite 1400
Washington, D.C. 20004

DESCRIPTION: The Commission was created by the Sentencing Reform provisions of the Comprehensive Crime Control Act, Pub. L. No. 98-473 (1984) and its authority and duties are set out in Chapter 58 of Title 28, United States Code. Procedures for implementing guideline sentencing are prescribed in chapter 227 of Title 28.

The Commission's primary function is to promulgate sentencing policies and practices for the Federal courts that include guidelines prescribing the appropriate form and severity of punishment for offenders convicted of Federal crimes.

(Area Code 202)
Chairman: William W. Wilkins, Jr. 626-8502
General Counsel: John R. Steer 626-8500
Library 626-8500
The library is open to the public by appointment on Tuesday through Thursday from 9:00 AM until 5:00 PM.

UNITED STATES COURT OF MILITARY APPEALS
450 E Street, N.W.
Washington, D.C. 20442-0001

DESCRIPTION: Subject only to certiorari review by the U.S. Supreme Court in a limited number of cases, the United States Court of Military Appeals, a judicially independent tribunal located in the Department of Defense for administrative purposes only, is the civilian court of final review for criminal convictions obtained by courts-martial in all four military services and the Coast Guard.

The work of the Court involves reviewing pleadings and court-martial trial records and making recommendations on their disposition to the Court. Considerable research is also done on current military justice policies, as the Court is required by law to make yearly progress reports and recommendations for improvements to Congress.

UNITED STATES TAX COURT

(Area Code 202)
Chief Judge: Robinson O. Everett 272-1463
Clerk: Thomas F. Granahan 272-1448
Central Legal Staff Director: William N. Early 272-1454

(Area Code 202)
Docket Room 272-1452
Library 272-1466

DECISIONS OF THE COURT

Decisions of the Court are available through West Publishing Company, Dept M-2, P.O. Box 64833, St. Paul, MN 55164-1804. Tel: 800/328-9352. West offers several related publications and services:

The Military Justice Reporter is a 29 volume hard-bound set that contains the full text of all opinions from 1978 through 1989. Price: $1297.25. Additional volumes are sold for $60.00 each.

Military Justice Reporter Advance Sheets are issued biweekly. Advance sheets are free with a subscription to the Military Justice Reporter. An annual subscription to the Advance Sheets may be purchased separately for $95.00.

West's Military Justice Digest is a two-volume soft bound index to volumes 1-27 of the Military Justice Reporter. Price: $44.50.

Courts-Martial Reports. These volumes include decisions of the Court from its inception in 1951 to 1975. It was published by the Lawyer's Cooperative Publishing Company.

PUBLICATIONS OF INTEREST

Annual Report. The Annual Report discusses the current state of military justice in the United States. In addition to a section on the Court of Military Appeals, it also contains reports from the Judge Advocates General of the Army, Navy, and Air Force, and a report from the Chief Counsel of the Coast Guard. A limited number of copies are available from the Clerk of the Court at no charge. Contact: Clerk, U.S. Court of Military Appeals, 450 E Street, N.W., Washington, D.C. 20442.

UNITED STATES TAX COURT
400 Second Street, N.W.
Washington, D.C. 20217

DESCRIPTION: The United States Tax Court is really an administrative tribunal established under Article I of the Constitution (as opposed to a true court established under Article III). It was originally established as the Board of Tax Appeals in 1924, and became the U.S. Tax Court in 1942.

Most of the Court's work involves the trial and adjudication of controversies involving deficiencies in income, estate, and gift taxes. The Court also has jurisdiction to determine deficiencies in certain excise taxes and in windfall profit tax; to redetermine liabilities of certain transferees and fiduciaries; to issue declaratory judgments in the areas of qualification of retirement plans, exemption of charitable organizations, and the status of certain Governmental obligations; and to decide certain cases involving disclosure of tax information by the Commissioner of Internal Revenue. Its decisions, except under the small tax case procedure, are subject to review by the regional Courts of Appeals and the U.S. Supreme Court. In small tax cases, the decisions of the Court are final.

The Court is comprised of 19 Judges who are appointed by the President to serve for terms of 15 years. Its strength is augmented by Senior Judges who are recalled by the Chief Judge to perform further judicial duties and by 17 Special Trial Judges who are appointed by the Chief Judge.

The Court is organized into divisions, each of which is headed by a Judge. Administrative functions of the Court are handled by the Offices of the Clerk of the Court and the Court Administrator.

The offices of the Court and all of its Judges and Special Trial Judges are located in Washington, D.C. The Court conducts trial sessions at various places within the U.S. and maintains a field office in Los Angeles, CA. Each trial session is conducted by a single Judge or Special Trial Judge. A trial in the Tax Court is conducted as a civil action, without a jury. Taxpayers are permitted to represent themselves if they so desire.

(Area Code 202)
Chief Judge: Arthur L. Nims III 376-2700
Clerk: Charles S. Casazza 376-2754

(Area Code 202)
Court Administrator: Paul Nejelski 376-2751

DECISIONS OF THE COURT

U.S. Tax Court Reports. Published monthly. Each issue is a consolidation of the decisions for a month. Price: $26.00 a year domestic; $32.50 a year foreign. GPO Stock# 728-001-00000-3. This publication can be purchased from the Superintendent of Documents, U.S. Government Printing Office, Washington, D.C. 20402. Tel: 202/783-3238.

Memorandum Opinions of the U.S. Tax Court. Published weekly in looseleaf form and in a bound volume at the end of each year. The bulk of the Tax Court's work is reflected in memorandum opinions which are not published in the U.S. Tax Court Reports. The Tax Court only prints a few copies of such decisions. They are otherwise only available through commercial sources. Contact: Prentice-Hall, Inc., 910 Sylvan Avenue, Englewood Cliffs, NJ 07632. Tel: 800/562-0245. Or, in Washington, D.C., call 202/293-0707.

RULES OF PRACTICE AND PROCEDURE

The following publication(s) can be purchased from the **U.S. Government Printing Office.** Stock numbers and prices for annual subscriptions are shown below. Submit requests for these publications to: The Superintendent of Documents, U.S. Government Printing Office, Washington, D.C. 20402. Tel: 202/783-3238.

United States Tax Court Rules of Practice and Procedure. On June 5, 1990, Chief Judge Arthur L. Nimms, III issued a completely revised and republished set of Rules of Practice and Procedure. The new Rules are effective July 1, 1990. Many of the changes in the Rules from prior editions are designed to carry out the Tax Court's responsibilities under the Taxpayer's Bill of Rights. Other changes deal with such subjects as expert witnesses, arbitration, and counsel's conflict of interest. The rules are now gender neutral. Copies of the Court's Rules of Practice and Procedures, as amended, may be obtained for $9.00 per copy by writing to the Court's Administrative Office (Room 150) at 400 Second Street, N.W., Washington, D.C. 20217. A check or money order made payable to the "Clerk, United States Tax Court" should accompany each such written request.

Rules of Practice and Procedure of the United States Tax Court: Effective July 1, 1990, with Additions and Amendments through January 12, 1990. Price: $9.00 domestic, $11.25 foreign. GPO Stock# 028-005-00163-2.

U.S. Tax Court Reports, Volumes 60, 64, 68, 71, 77, 79, 81, 82, 85, 87, and 90. Volume 60 contains the original rules of the Court. The other volumes contain all of the amendments issued since the original rules were promulgated. For price and ordering information, see the entry for the Tax Court Reports above.

UNITED STATES COURT OF VETERANS APPEALS

1625 K Street, N.W., Suite 400
Washington, D.C. 20006

DESCRIPTION: Created by an act of Congress in November 1988, the United States Court of Veterans Appeals began operations in October 1989. The Court has exclusive jurisdiction to review decisions of the Board of Veterans' Appeals. Only the claimant may seek review of a decision of the Board, and the Court is empowered to affirm, modify, reverse, or remand a decision of the Board as appropriate. The legislation creating the Court provides for a limited review of the Court's judgments by the U.S. Court of Appeals for the Federal Circuit. Cases handled by the Court will cover all types of veterans' benefits, such as loan eligibility and educational benefits, but the major issues will concern disability benefits. Although located in Washington, D.C., the United States Court of Veterans Appeals is a national court and may sit anywhere in the U.S.

(Area Code 202)
Chief Judge: Frank Q. Nebeker 254-6605
Clerk: Melanie G. Dorsey 254-6600

(Area Code 202)
Senior Staff Attorney: Col. Michael Carmichael 254-6619

DECISIONS OF THE COURT

A few copies of each decision are available from the Office of the Clerk of the Court. In addition, there are four commercial sources of the decisions of the Court of Veterans Appeals:

Daily Washington Law Reporter. Daily. Includes all of the decisions of the Court and semi-annual indexes. Price: $147.60 per year. Available from: Daily Washington Law Reporter, 1625 I Street, N.W., Washington, D.C. 20006. Tel: 202/331-1700.

U.S. Law Week. Weekly. Selected decisions published by the Bureau of National Affairs, 9435 Key West Ave., Rockville, MD 20850. Tel: 301/258-1033. Or, 800/372-1033.

Veterans Disability Law Reporter. Contact Steven Babitsky, Box 590, Falmouth, MA 02540. Tel: 508/540-3101.

Veterans Law Reporter. Contact Keith Snyder, Veterans Education Project, P.O. Box 42130, Washington, D.C. 20015. Tel: 202/547-8387.

RULES OF PRACTICE AND PROCEDURE

The Court does not publish an official version of its rules. Contact one of the following commercial sources:

National Veterans Legal Services Project, Attn: Ronald B. Abrams, 2001 S Street, N.W., Washington, D.C. 20009-1125. Tel: 202/265-8305. Price: Free to veterans; $5.00 to members of the public, including attorneys representing veterans.

Rules Service Company, 7658 Standish Place, Ste 106, Rockville, MD 20855. Tel: 301/424-9402. Looseleaf. Updated when necessary. Price: $20.00 for subscription plus binder.

Veterans Education Project, Attn: Keith Snyder, P.O. Box 42130, Washington, D.C. 20015. Tel: 202/547-8387.

Federal Rules Decisions. Published by West Publishing Company, 50 West Kellogg Blvd., P.O. Box 64833, St. Paul, MN 55164. Tel: 612/688-3600. Or, 800/328-9352.

UNITED STATES DISTRICT COURTS

DESCRIPTION: The 94 United States District Courts are the Federal general jurisdiction trial courts. There is at least one in each state, but some of the larger states have as many as four District Courts. Cases decided by the District Courts are reviewable on appeal by the appropriate United States Court of Appeals, except that injunctive orders issued by special, three-judge District Courts and certain decisions holding acts of Congress unconstitutional may be appealed directly to the U.S. Supreme Court.

The support staff of the U.S. District Courts also include many attorneys serving in a number of different capacities. As with the Courts of Appeals, job titles tend to vary from court to court. The following descriptions, however, are representative of ones found frequently in the District Court system:

District Court Executive: Since 1979, this position has emerged in the larger District Courts as part of a pilot program. Like the Circuit Executive, the District Court Executive is the chief administrative officer of the court, responsible for nonjudicial administrative matters.

Clerk of Court: The Clerk serves as the court administrator and chief operating officer, managing the administrative activities of the clerk's office, and overseeing the performance of the statutory duties of that office, including case processing, records management, financial management, facilities management, and personnel management. In some jurisdictions, this position may be called Clerk of Court/Court Executive Officer.

U.S. Magistrate: Magistrates hear cases involving petty offenses committed on Federal property, issue search and arrest warrants, determine bail for Federal defendants, try misdemeanors, hear civil cases upon consent of the parties, and conduct other initial proceedings to expedite the disposition of the civil and criminal caseloads for the District Courts. Magistrates are appointed by majority vote of the District Court judges. They must be members in good standing of the bar of the highest court of the state in which they will serve, and must have at least five years of active law practice experience. Full-time magistrates are appointed for a term of eight years and may not engage in the private practice of law during their tenure. Part-time magistrates serve four-year terms and may engage in any outside activities that do not conflict with their duties.

Since the office of U.S. Magistrate was created by Congress in 1969, the geographic scope and duties of the position have been constantly evolving. As a general rule, U.S. Magistrates can be found in the largest District Courts.

Law Clerk to U.S. Magistrate: Law Clerks to U.S. Magistrates serve from one-year to two-year appointments. They research and the draft recommendations and orders in prisoner litigation as well as civil and criminal cases.

Probation Officer: Probation officers prepare presentence investigation reports for the court and other reports for Federal and state agencies; supervise persons on probation, parole, and mandatory release; handle juvenile and youth offenders; prepare case records as required by the court; and participate in community-sponsored programs in law enforcement and correctional fields.

Law Clerks: As a rule, most of the active judges of the U.S. District Courts are authorized two law clerks. Appointments are for up to two-year terms. Law Clerks assist District Judges in organizing their case loads and drafting decisions.

Pro Se Law Clerk: This position, found in districts with significant prisoner litigation, provides legal advice and assistance in connection with prisoner petitions and complaints; drafts recommendations and orders for the court's signature; reviews the docket of pending litigation; and provides advice to judges, magistrates, and other court personnel.

Bankruptcy Judge: Each U.S. District Court contains a Bankruptcy Court unit and a number of Bankruptcy Judges specified by statute. Unlike Circuit and District Court Judges, Bankruptcy Judges are not appointed by the President with the advice and consent of the Senate. Rather, they are hired by the responsible Circuit Court of Appeals after a merit selection panel or the circuit council develops a list of nominees, and serve for 14-year terms.

Bankruptcy Clerk: Bankruptcy Clerks make recommendations to the judges regarding court policies and procedures; manage the business of the courts, including case management, records maintenance, statistical reporting, work flow, manual processing of bankruptcy cases, and adversary proceedings; participate in personnel management; conduct studies of court operations and case flow; prepare statistical and narrative reports; direct the fiscal and accounting functions and controls of the court; and coordinate with other courts, the U.S. Trustee, members of the bar, and others having business with the court. The Bankruptcy Clerk is accountable for bankruptcy fees and costs.

Deputy Clerk-Estate Administration: The **Deputy Clerk-Estate Administration** serves as chief liaison on all matters related to trustee qualification, selection, performance, and discipline; develops and monitors trustee qualifications to serve in specific areas; oversees performance of both panel and non-panel trustees, debtor-in-possession, and all other appointees serving in all cases; develops procedures for and conducts meetings of creditors; provides technical assistance; and develops and implements trustee training.

Deputy-in-Charge: This position involves managing a divisional bankruptcy office, administering all bankruptcy cases filed in the division, and performing personnel, fiscal, and facilities management.

Bankruptcy Administrator: This position has been recently developed to meet the statutorily defined estate administration oversight and trustee supervision requirements specified in the transition provisions of the 1986 Bankruptcy Act. Bankruptcy Administrators are not part of the staffs of Bankruptcy Judges or Bankruptcy Clerks. Rather, they are independent, nonjudicial officers of the Judiciary, under the supervision of the appointing Courts of Appeals. Their primary function is to supervise trustees and estates, and includes: (1) establishing, maintaining, and supervising panels of private trustees in Chapter 7 cases; (2) supervising the performance of Chapter 11 and 12 trustees; (3) monitoring the activities of debtors in possession and creditors' committees in Chapter 11 cases; and (4) supervising the performance of Chapter 13 trustees. Bankruptcy Administrators are appointed for five-year terms. Six administrator programs are now fully operational.

Law Clerk to Bankruptcy Judge: Law Clerks assist Bankruptcy Judges in organizing their case loads and drafting decisions.

FEDERAL PUBLIC DEFENDERS/FEDERAL COMMUNITY DEFENDER ORGANIZATIONS

Federal Public Defender Organizations and Community Defender Organizations provide legal representation in particular judicial districts, under the Criminal Justice Act [18 U.S.C. 3006A(g)(2)(A)] for any person who is financially unable to obtain adequate counsel, and who:

*is charged with a felony or Class A misdemeanor;
*is a juvenile alleged to have committed an act of juvenile delinquency as defined in 18 U.S.C. 5031;
*is charged with a violation of probation;
*is under arrest, when such representation is required by law;
*is charged with a violation of supervised release or faces modification, reduction or enlargement of a condition, or extension or revocation of a term of supervised release;
*is subject to a mental condition hearing under 18 U.S.C. 313;
*is in custody as a material witness;
*is entitled to appointment of counsel under the Sixth Amendment; or
*faces loss of liberty in a case, and Federal law requires appointment of counsel.

In addition, Defender Organizations may also provide legal representation in other cases when the U.S. court or magistrate determines that the interests of justice so require.

Defender Organizations may be established in a district or part of a district in which at least 200 persons annually require the appointment of counsel. In some instances, this threshold requirement is achieved by aggregating the numbers of persons required to be represented in two adjacent districts or parts of districts in order to establish eligibility.

Federal Public Defenders are appointed by the Circuit Court of Appeals for a term of four years. Staff attorney employment levels are also fixed by the Court of Appeals and are Federal judiciary employees.

Community Defender Organizations are non-profit defense counsel services established and administered by any group authorized by the U.S. District Court's representation plan to provide representation. They furnish attorneys to represent indigent persons and receive payments from the Government for their services. Their employees are not considered Federal employees.

DECISIONS OF THE COURTS

Federal Supplement. Published by the West Publishing Company. There have never been any official published reports of the opinions of the Federal District Courts. The standard unofficial source of the most important selected decisions of the District Courts is the Federal Supplement, which is part of West's National Reporter System. The Federal Supplement includes selected cases from 1932 to date. For cases decided from 1880 to 1932, see West's Federal Reporter. For cases decided between 1789 and 1880, see West's Federal Cases. The Federal Supplement also includes selected decisions of the U.S. Court of International Trade, the Special Court, Regional Rail Reorganization Act, and selected rulings of the Judicial Panel on Multidistrict Litigation. Contact: West Publishing Company, 50 West Kellogg Blvd., P.O. Box 64833, St. Paul, MN 55164. Tel: 612/688-3600. Or, 800/328-9352.

Bankruptcy Reporter. There are no official published reports of decisions of the Bankruptcy Divisions of the U.S. District Courts. The standard commercial source is the Bankruptcy Reporter, which is part of West's National Reporter System. Contact West Publishing Company at the address listed above.

UNITED STATES DISTRICT COURTS

RULES OF PRACTICE AND PROCEDURE

Federal Rules of Civil Procedure. Promulgated by the U.S. Supreme Court for use in the Federal District Courts. The text of the Rules may be found in the Appendix to Title 28 of the United States Code.

Rules of Civil Procedure for the United States District Courts, with Forms, 1989. Senate Judiciary Committee. Available from the Superintendent of Documents, U.S. Government Printing Office, Washington, DC 20402. Price: $3.75. GPO Stock# 052-070-06589-3.

Federal Rules of Criminal Procedure. Promulgated by the U.S. Supreme Court for use in the Federal District Courts. The text of the Rules may be found in the Appendix to Title 18 of the United States Code.

Rules of Criminal Procedure for the United States District Courts, with Forms, 1989. Senate Judiciary Committee. Price: $2.25. Available from the Superintendent of Documents, U.S. Government Printing Office, Washington, D.C. 20402. GPO Stock# 052-070-06619-9.

Rules of Evidence for United States Courts and Magistrates ("Federal Rules of Evidence"). Congress enacted these rules in 1974 in order to provide a uniform evidentiary code for all U.S. courts. The text of the rules may be found in the Appendix to Title 28 of the United States Code.

Federal Rules of Evidence, 1989. Senate Judiciary Committee. Available from Superintendent of Documents, U.S. Government Printing Office, Washington, D.C. 20402. Price: $1.50. GPO Stock# 052-070-06591-5.

In addition, many District Courts have promulgated local rules not inconsistent with the rules of general applicability indicated above, which are applicable only to their particular proceedings. District Courts often publish these in pamphlet form and make them available through the offices of the clerks of the courts.

Rules of Evidence for United States Courts and Magistrates ("Federal Rules of Evidence"). Congress enacted these rules in 1974 in order to provide a uniform evidentiary code for all U.S. courts. The text of the rules may be found in the Appendix to Title 28 of the United States Code.

Bankruptcy Rules and Official Forms Under Chapters 1-13 of the Bankruptcy Act ("Rules of Bankruptcy Procedure"). The text of these rules may be found in the Appendix to Title 11 of the United States Code.

ELECTRONIC BULLETIN BOARDS

Thirteen U.S. District Courts and Bankruptcy Divisions have instituted PACER (Public Access to Court Electronic Records), which was developed by the Federal Judicial Center, the research and development arm of the Federal Judiciary. PACER is a dial-in service from any personal computer that permits the retrieval of official electronic case histories and court dockets in less than a minute. The system can provide lists of cases, searched by name, as well as a comprehensive summary of any case, including case and party information. There is currently no charge for accessing PACER, although the Bankruptcy Divisions are considering instituting fees in the future. To register for PACER, contact the clerk of the appropriate court. U.S. District Courts currently offering PACER are:

*Arizona
*District of Columbia
*Georgia-Northern District
*Texas-Western District
*Utah

Bankruptcy Divisions currently offering PACER are:

*California-Southern District
*Kansas
*Maine
*New Hampshire
*Oregon
*Rhode Island
*Massachusetts
*Texas-Western District

(VCIS) Voice Case Information System allows public access via a Touch-Tone telephone to information in Bankruptcy Division databases. A computer-generated voice reads case information to callers in response to inquiries entered on the telephone keyboard. VCIS is currently operational in 25 courts and by the end of 1992 should be available in virtually all Bankruptcy Divisions. There is no charge for this service. Current VCIS telephone numbers are indicated in the lists for each court below.

*Arkansas (Eastern & Western)
*California-Southern
*Illinois-Central
*Florida-Southern
*Kansas
*Louisiana-Eastern
*Maine
*Massachusetts
*Michigan-Western
*Mississippi-Northern
*Missouri-Western
*New Hampshire
*New Jersey
*New York-Eastern
*New York-Western
*Oklahoma-Eastern
*Oregon
*Pennsylvania-Eastern
*Rhode Island
*South Carolina
*Texas-Eastern
*Texas-Western
*Virginia-Eastern
*Washington-Western
*West Virginia-Southern

Public Access Terminals are available in several courthouses on a walk-up basis. These terminals allow the public to obtain docket information without waiting for a clerk to become available.

U.S. DISTRICT COURT ADDRESSES

U.S. District Court-Northern District of Alabama

U.S. Courthouse, 1729-5th Ave North, Birmingham, AL 35203

Chief Judge: Sam C. Pointer, Jr. ....(205) 731-1709
District Clerk: Charles T. Cliver ....(205) 731-1025
Divisional Office:
U.S. Post Office & Courthouse,
101 Holmes Avenue, N.E.,
Huntsville, AL 35801 ....(205) 534-6495
Chief Bankruptcy Judge: George S. Wright ....(205) 752-0426
Bankruptcy Clerk: William C. Redden ....(205) 731-1615
Bankruptcy Administrator: Benjamin G. Cohen .....(205) 731-1705
Chief Probation Officer: Jerone A. Savage ....(205) 731-1746
Death Penalty Resource Center/Community Defender
Organization: Alabama Capital Representation Resource
Center, 444 Clay St, Montgomery, AL 36104 .....(205) 269-1803

U.S. District Court-Middle District of Alabama

P.O. Box 711, Montgomery, AL 36101

Chief Judge: Truman M. Hobbs ....(205) 223-7128
District Clerk: Thomas C. Caver ....(205) 223-7308
Chief Bankruptcy Judge: Rodney R. Steele ....(205) 223-7278
Bankruptcy Clerk: James M. Jones ....(205) 223-7250
Bankruptcy Administrator:
Dwight H. Williams, Jr. ....(205) 223-7355
Chief Probation Officer: Henry Rawls, Jr. ....(205) 223-7301
Death Penalty Resource Center/Community Defender
Organization: Alabama Capital Representation Resource
Center, 444 Clay St, Montgomery, AL 36104 .....(205) 269-1803

U.S. District Court-Southern District of Alabama

113 St. Joseph St, Mobile, AL 36602

Chief Judge: Alex T. Howard Jr ....(205) 690-3133
District Clerk: John V. O'Brien ....(205) 690-2371
Chief Bankruptcy Judge: Gordon B. Kahn ....(205) 694-3625
Bankruptcy Clerk: Geraldine S. Lester ....(205) 690-2391
Bankruptcy Administrator:
Travis M. Bedsole, Jr. ....(205) 690-4133
Chief Probation Officer: William W. Wynne Jr ....(205) 690-2386
Death Penalty Resource Center/Community Defender
Organization: Alabama Capital Representation Resource
Center, 444 Clay St, Montgomery, AL 36104 .....(205) 269-1803

U.S. District Court-Alaska

222 West 7th Ave, Anchorage, AK 99513

Chief Judge: H. Russel Holland ....(907) 271-5621
District Clerk: Phyllis Rhodes ....(907) 271-5568
Divisional Offices:
101-12th Avenue, Box 1, Fairbanks, AK 99701 ..(907) 452-3163
Box 349, Juneau, AK 99802 ....(907) 586-7458
415 Main Street, Room 400,
Ketchikan, AK 99901 ....(907) 225-3195
Chief Bankruptcy Judge: Herbert A. Ross ....(907) 271-2361
Bankruptcy Clerk: Wayne W. Wolfe ....(907) 271-2655
Chief Probation Officer: Norman E. Mugleston ....(907) 271-5492

U.S. District Court-Arizona

U.S. Courthouse and Federal Building, 230 North 1st Avenue, Phoenix, AZ 85025

Chief Judge: Richard M. Bilby ....(602) 629-6536
District Clerk: Richard H. Weare ....(602) 261-3341
Divisional Office:
55 E. Broadway, Tucson, AZ 85701 ....(602) 629-6575
PACER (Public Access to Court Electronic Records):
District Court ....(602) 261-3547
Chief Bankruptcy Judge: Robert G. Mooreman ......(602) 379-3870
Bankruptcy Clerk: Kevin E. O'Brien ....(602) 379-6965
Chief Probation Officer: Robert J. Thomas ....(602) 261-3214
Federal Public Defender:
Frederic F. Kay, 97 East Congress, Suite 130,
Tucson, AZ 85701 ....(602) 629-6521
Divisional Office:
320 N. Central Avenue, Suite 200, Phoenix, AZ
85004 ....(602) 261-3561

U.S. District Court-Eastern District of Arkansas

P.O. Box 869, Little Rock, AR 72203-0869

Chief Judge: Garnett Thomas Eisele ....(501) 378-5960
District Clerk: Carl R. Brents ....(501) 378-5353
Divisional Offices:
312 Federal Building, Jonesboro, AR 72401 .....(501) 972-4610
P.O. Box 8307, Pine Bluff, AR 71611 ....(501) 536-1190
Chief Bankruptcy Judge: Robert F. Fussell ....(501) 378-6357
Bankruptcy Clerk: Peggy A. Carroll ....(501) 378-6357
VCIS (Voice Case Information System):
Bankruptcy Court ....(501) 378-5770
Chief Probation Officer: Charles H. Gray ....(501) 378-5745

U.S. District Court-Western District of Arkansas

P.O. Box 1523, Fort Smith, AR 72902

Chief Judge: H. Franklin Waters ....(501) 442-7251
District Clerk: Christopher R. Johnson ....(501) 783-6833
Divisional Offices:
P.O. Box 1566, El Dorado, AR 71730 ....(501) 862-1202
Federal Building & U.S. Courthouse, Room 523,
Fayetteville, AR 72701 ....(501) 521-6980
P.O. Drawer I, Hot Springs, AR 71901 ....(501) 623-6411
P.O. Box 2746, Texarkana, AR 75501 ....(501) 773-3381
Chief Bankruptcy Judge: Robert F. Fussell ....(501) 378-6357
VCIS (Voice Case Information System):
Bankruptcy Court ....(501) 378-5770
Bankruptcy Clerk: Peggy A. Carroll ....(501) 378-6357
Chief Probation Officer: Lee R. Owen ....(501) 783-8050

U.S. District Court-Northern District of California

P.O. Box 36060, 450 Golden Gate Avenue, San Francisco, CA 94102

Chief Judge: William A. Ingram ....(408) 291-7595
District Clerk: Richard W. Wieking ....(415) 556-3031

Divisional Office:
4050 U.S. Courthouse, 280 South First Street, San Jose, CA 95113 ....(408) 291-7783
Chief Bankruptcy Judge: Lloyd King ....(415) 556-2257
Bankruptcy Clerk: Paul C. Karney, Jr. ....(415) 556-2250
Chief Probation Officer: Loren Buddress ....(415) 556-0200
Federal Public Defender: Barry J. Portman ....(415) 556-7712
Divisional Office:
188 U.S. Courthouse, 280 South First Street, San Jose, CA 95113 ....(408) 291-7753
Death Penalty Resource Center/Community Defender Organization: Michael G. Millman, Director, California Appellate Project, 345 Franklin St, San Francisco, CA 94102 ....(415) 626-5600

U.S. District Court-Eastern District of California

U.S. Courthouse, 650 Capitol Mall, Sacramento, CA 95814

Chief Judge: Robert E. Coyle ....(916) 551-2825
District Clerk: James R. Grindstaff ....(916) 551-2615
Divisional Office:
5408 U.S. Courthouse, 1130 O Street, Fresno, CA 93721 ....(209) 487-5083
Chief Bankruptcy Judge: Loren S. Dahl ....(916) 551-2662
Bankruptcy Clerk: Richard G. Heltzel ....(916) 551-2662
Chief Probation Officer: Charles E. Varnon ......(916) 551-2641
Federal Public Defender:
Arthur W. Ruthenbeck, 801 K St, Suite 1024, Sacramento, CA 95814 ....(916) 551-1067
Divisional Office:
1313 P Street, Suite 104, Fresno, CA 93721 ....(209) 487-5561
Death Penalty Resource Center/Community Defender Organization: Michael G. Millman, Director, California Appellate Project, 345 Franklin St, San Francisco, CA 94102 ....(415) 626-5600

U.S. District Court-Central District of California

312 North Spring Street, Los Angeles, CA 90012

Chief Judge: Manuel L. Real ....(213) 894-5267
District Court Executive: George C. Ryker ....(213) 894-7034
District Clerk: Leonard A. Brosnan ....(213) 894-3535
Chief Bankruptcy Judge: William J. Lasarow ......(213) 894-4073
Bankruptcy Clerk: Jack L. Wagner ....(714) 836-2993
Chief Probation Officer: Robert M. Latta ....(213) 894-3600
Federal Public Defender: Peter Horstman ....(213) 894-2854
Divisional Office:
201 U.S. Courthouse, 751 W. Santa Ana Boulevard, Santa Ana, CA 92701 ....(714) 836-2252
Death Penalty Resource Center/Community Defender Organization: Michael G. Millman, Director, California Appellate Project, 345 Franklin St, San Francisco, CA 94102 ....(415) 626-5600

U.S. District Court-Southern District of California

940 Front Street, San Diego, CA 92189

Chief Judge: Gordon Thompson, Jr. ....(619) 557-6480
District Clerk: William W. Luddy ....(619) 557-5600
Chief Bankruptcy Judge: James W. Meyers ....(619) 557-5622
Bankruptcy Clerk: Barry K. Lander ....(619) 557-5620
VCIS (Voice Case Information System):
Bankruptcy Court ....(619) 557-6521
Chief Probation Officer: Mark W. Fisher ....(619) 293-6650
Community Defender Organization:
Judy Clarke, Executive Director, Federal Defenders of San Diego Inc, Central Savings Tower, 225 Broadway, Suite 500 San Diego, CA 92101 ....(619) 234-8467
Death Penalty Resource Center/Community Defender Organization: Michael G. Millman, Director, California Appellate Project, 345 Franklin St, San Francisco, CA 94102 ....(415) 626-5600

U.S. District Court-Colorado

1929 Stout Street, U.S. Courthouse, Denver, CO 80924

Chief Judge: Sherman G. Finesilver ....(303) 844-4151
District Clerk: James R. Manspeaker ....(303) 844-3433
Chief Bankruptcy Judge: Charles E. Matheson .....(303) 844-2294
Bankruptcy Clerk: Bradford L. Bolton ....(303) 844-4045
Chief Probation Officer: Richard P. Miklic ......(303) 844-4155
Federal Public Defender: Michael G. Katz, PO Box 689, Denver, CO 80202 ....(303) 844-4545

U.S. District Court-Connecticut

141 Church Street, New Haven, CT 06510

Chief Judge: Ellen B. Burns ....(203) 773-2105
District Clerk: Kevin F. Rowe ....(203) 773-2140
Divisional Offices:
915 Lafayette Boulevard, Bridgeport, CT 06604 ....(203) 579-5861
450 Main Street, Hartford, CT 06103 ....(203) 240-3200
Chief Bankruptcy Judge: Robert L. Krechevsky ....(203) 240-3679
Bankruptcy Clerk: Thomas H. Abraham ....(203) 240-3675
Chief Probation Officer:
Maria Rodrigues McBride ....(203) 773-2100
Federal Public Defender:
Thomas G. Dennis, 450 Main Street, Room 710, Hartford, CT 06103 ....(203) 240-3357
Divisional Office:
234 Church Street, Suite 1001, New Haven, CT 06510 ....(203) 773-2148

U.S. District Court-Delaware

844 King Street, Lockbox 18, Wilmington, DE 19801

Chief Judge: Joseph J. Longobardi ....(302) 573-6151
District Clerk: John R. McAllister, Jr. ....(302) 573-6170
Bankruptcy Judge: Helen S. Balick ....(302) 573-6174
Bankruptcy Clerk: Carolyn C. Raniszewski ....(302) 573-6174
Chief Probation Officer: Barry W. Polsky ....(302) 573-6179

U.S. District Court-District of Columbia

U.S. Courthouse, 3rd and Constitution Avenue, N.W., Washington, D.C. 20001

Chief Judge: Aubrey E. Robinson, Jr. ....(202) 535-3470
District Clerk: James F. Davey ....(202) 535-3594
PACER (Public Access to Court Electronic Records):
District Court ....(202) 535-3508
Bankruptcy Judge: S. Martin Teel, Jr. ....(202) 535-7595
Bankruptcy Clerk: Martin L. Bloom ....(202) 535-3042
Chief Probation Officer: Eugene Wesley, Jr. .....(202) 535-3200
Admission to the Bar ....(202) 535-3513
Courts Calendar ....(202) 535-3535
Dockets - Civil ....(202) 535-3564
Dockets - Criminal ....(202) 535-3503

U.S. District Court-Northern District of Florida

110 East Park Avenue, Tallahassee, FL 32301

Chief Judge: William H. Stafford, Jr. ....(904) 681-7550
District Clerk: Marvin S. Waits ....(904) 681-7165
Divisional Office:
P.O. Box 990, Pensacola, FL 32502 ....(904) 435-8440
Bankruptcy Judge: Lewis M. Killian, Jr. ....(904) 681-7510
Bankruptcy Clerk: Larry A. Pace ....(904) 681-7500
Chief Probation Officer: Kenneth B. Anderson ....(904) 681-7185
Federal Public Defender:
Robert J. Vossler, 2067 Federal Building, 227 N. Bronough Street, Tallahassee, FL 32301 ....(904) 681-7439
Divisional Office:
17 S. Palafox Street, Suite 394, Pensacola, FL 32501 ....(904) 432-1418
Death Penalty Resource Center/Community Defender Organization: Robert Wesley, Executive Director, Volunteer Lawyer's Resource Center of Florida, Inc., Suite A, 805 North Gadsen, Tallahassee, FL 32303-6313 ....(904) 681-6499

U.S. District Court-Middle District of Florida

P.O. Box 53558, Jacksonville, FL 32201-3558

Chief Judge: Susan Black ....(813) 228-2912
District Clerk: David L. Edwards ....(813) 791-2854
Divisional Offices:
611 U.S. Courthouse, 80 N. Hughey Avenue, Orlando, FL 32801 ....(407) 648-6366
105 U.S. Courthouse, Tampa, FL 33602 ....(813) 228-2105
U.S. Courthouse, First & Lee Street, Ft. Myers, FL 33901 ....(813) 332-3655
Chief Bankruptcy Judge: Alexander L. Paskay .....(813) 228-2261
Bankruptcy Clerk: Carl R. Stewart ....(813) 228-2139
Chief Probation Officer: Dan W. Stowers ....(813) 228-2901
Federal Public Defender:
H. Jay Stevens, 417 U.S. Courthouse, 80 N. Hughey Avenue, Orlando, FL 32801 ....(407) 648-6338
Divisional Offices:
P.O. Box 4998, Jacksonville, FL 32201 ..(904) 791-3039
500 Zack Street, Room 204, Tampa, FL 33602 ....(813) 228-2715
Death Penalty Resource Center/Community Defender Organization: Robert Wesley, Executive Director, Volunteer Lawyer's Resource Center of Florida, Inc, Suite A, 805 North Gadsen, Tallahassee, FL 32303-6313 (904) 681-6499

U.S. District Court-Southern District of Florida

301 North Miami Avenue, Miami, FL 33128-7788

Chief Judge: James Lawrence King ....(305) 536-5000
District Court Executive: Keenan G. Casady ......(305) 536-6968
District Clerk: Robert M. March ....(305) 536-4131
Divisional Offices:
299 E. Broward Boulevard, Ft. Lauderdale, FL 33301 ....(305) 527-7075
701 Clematis Street, West Palm Beach, FL 33401 ....(407) 655-8710
Chief Bankruptcy Judge: Thomas C. Britton ....(305) 536-4111
Bankruptcy Clerk: Karen Eddy ....(305) 536-5216
VCIS (Voice Case Information System):
Bankruptcy Court ....(305) 536-5979
Chief Probation Officer: Carlos K. Juenke ....(305) 536-5334
Federal Public Defender:
Theodore J. Sakowitz ....(305) 536-6900
Divisional Offices:
299 E. Broward Boulevard, Ft. Lauderdale, FL 33301 ....(305) 527-7293
Harvey Building, 224 Datura Street, Suite 601, West Palm Beach, FL 33401 ....(407) 833-6288
Death Penalty Resource Center/Community Defender Organization: Robert Wesley, Executive Director, Volunteer Lawyer's Resource Center of Florida, Inc, Suite A, 805 North Gadsen, Tallahassee, FL 32303-6313 (904) 681-6499

U.S. District Court-Northern District of Georgia

U.S. Courthouse, 75 Spring Street, S.W., Atlanta, GA 30335

Chief Judge: William C. O'Kelley ....(404) 331-4346
District Court Executive: John Shope ....(404) 331-2922
District Clerk: Luther D. Thomas ....(404) 331-6496
Divisional Offices:
201 Federal Building, Gainesville, GA 30501 ..(404) 534-5954
P.O. Box 939, Newnan, GA 30264 ....(404) 253-8847
P.O. Box 1186, Rome, GA 30161 ....(404) 291-5629
PACER (Public Access to Court Electronic Records):
District Court ....(404) 331-3496
Chief Bankruptcy Judge: A. David Kahn ....(404) 331-4466
Bankruptcy Clerk: Michael W. Dobbins ....(404) 331-6490
Chief Probation Officer: Daniel D. Rector ....(404) 331-6441
Community Defender Organization:
Stephanie Kearns, Executive Director, Federal Defender Program Inc, Suite 3310, 101 Marietta Tower, Atlanta, GA 30303 ....(404) 688-7530
Death Penalty Resource Center/Community Defender Organization: Mark E. Olive, Executive Director, Georgia Resource Center, 920 Ponce de Leon Ave, NE, Atlanta, GA 30306 ....(404) 898-2060

U.S. District Court-Middle District of Georgia

P.O. Box 128, Macon, GA 31202

Chief Judge: Wilbur D. Owens, Jr. ....(912) 752-3491
District Clerk: Gregory J. Leonard ....(912) 752-3497
Divisional Offices:
P.O. Box 1906, Albany, GA 31702 ....(912) 430-8431
P.O. Box 124, Columbus, GA 31902 ....(404) 649-7816
P.O. Box 68, Valdosta GA 31601 ....(912) 226-3651

Chief Bankruptcy Judge:
Robert F. Hershner, Jr. ....(912) 752-3505
Bankruptcy Clerk: William E. Tanner ....(912) 752-3506
Chief Probation Officer:
Daniel C. Lanford, Jr. ....(912) 752-8106
Death Penalty Resource Center/Community Defender Organization: Mark E. Olive, Executive Director, Georgia Resource Center, 920 Ponce de Leon Ave, NE, Atlanta, GA 30306 ....(404) 898-2060

U.S. District Court-Southern District of Georgia

P.O. Box 8286, Savannah, GA 31412

Chief Judge: B. Avant Edenfield ....(912) 265-1800
District Clerk: Henry R. Crumley, Jr. ....(912) 944-4281
Divisional Offices:
P.O. Box 1130, Augusta, GA 30903 ....(404) 722-2074
P.O. Box 1636, Brunswick, GA 31521 ....(912) 265-1758
Chief Bankruptcy Judge: Lamar W. Davis, Jr. .....(912) 944-4110
Bankruptcy Clerk: Mary C. Becton ....(912) 944-4100

Chief Probation Officer: Tommaso D. Rendino .....(912) 944-4355
Death Penalty Resource Center/Community Defender Organization: Mark E. Olive, Executive Director, Georgia Resource Center, 920 Ponce de Leon Ave, NE, Atlanta, GA 30306 ....(404) 898-2060

U.S. District Court-Guam
6th Floor, Pacific News Building, 238 O'Hara Street, Agana, GU 96910

Senior Judge: Cristobal C. Duenas ....(671) 472-7292
District Clerk: Mary Lou Michels ....(671) 472-7411
Chief Probation Officer: Frank Michael Cruz .....(671) 472-7369

U.S. District Court-Hawaii
P.O. Box 50129, Honolulu, HI 96850

Chief Judge: Harold M. Fong ....(808) 541-1807
District Clerk: Walter A.Y.H. Chinn ....(808) 541-1300
Bankruptcy Judge: Jon J. Chinen ....(808) 541-1793
Bankruptcy Clerk: Dorothy K. Ippongi ....(808) 541-1791
Chief Probation Officer: Elizabeth Taylor ...... (808) 541-1283
Federal Public Defender: Michael R. Levine ......(808) 541-2521

U.S. District Court-Idaho
550 West Fort Street, Box 039, Boise, ID 83724

Chief Judge: Harold L. Ryan ....(208) 334-9111
District Clerk: Gerold L. Clapp ....(208) 334-1361
Chief Bankruptcy Judge: Alfred C. Hagan ....(208) 334-9341
Chief Probation Officer: Terrence A. Nummel .....(208) 334-1630

U.S. District Court-Northern District of Illinois
219 South Dearborn Street, Chicago, IL 60604

Chief Judge: James B. Moran ....(312) 435-5600
District Clerk: H. Stuart Cunningham ....(312) 435-5670
Divisional Office:
211 South Court Street, Room 252, Rockford, IL 61101 ....(815) 987-4355
Chief Bankruptcy Judge: John D. Schwartz ....(312) 435-5652
Bankruptcy Clerk: Wayne E. Nelson ....(312) 435-5587
Chief Probation Officer: William T. Foster ......(312) 435-5700
Community Defender Organization:
Terrence F. MacCarthy, Executive Director .....(312) 435-5580

U.S. District Court-Central District of Illinois
P.O. Box 315, Springfield, IL 62705

Chief Judge: Harold Albert Baker ....(217) 431-4800
District Clerk: John M. Waters ....(217) 492-4020
Divisional Offices:
P.O. Box 786, Danville, IL 61832 ....(217) 431-4805
174 Federal Building, 100 N.E. Monroe, Peoria, IL 61602 ....(309) 671-7117
Room 40, Post Office Building, Rock Island, IL 61201 ....(309) 793-5778
Chief Bankruptcy Judge: Larry L. Lessen ....(217) 492-4566
Bankruptcy Clerk: Hardin W. Hawes ....(217) 492-4550
VCIS (Voice Case Information System):
Bankruptcy Court ....(217) 492-4550
VCIS (Voice Case Information System):
Bankruptcy Court (for in-state calls) 1-900-827-9005
Chief Probation Officer: John P. Meyer ....(217) 431-4810
Federal Public Defender:
David R. Freeman, 835 U.S. Courthouse, 1114 Market Street, St. Louis, MO 63101 ....(314) 539-6186

U.S. District Court-Southern District of Illinois
P.O. Box 249, 750 Missouri Avenue, East St. Louis, IL 62202

Chief Judge: James L. Foreman ....(618) 482-9425
District Clerk: Stuart J. O'Hare ....(618) 482-9371
Divisional Offices:
501 Belle Street, Alton, IL 62002 ....(618) 463-6402
P.O. Box 677, 301 W. Main Street, Benton, IL 62812 ....(618) 435-2109
Chief Bankruptcy Judge: Kenneth J. Meyers ....(618) 482-9365
Bankruptcy Clerk: Thomas J. Mackin ....(618) 482-9365
Chief Probation Officer: J. Bruce Chambers ......(618) 435-2509
Federal Public Defender:
David R. Freeman, 835 U.S. Courthouse, 1114 Market Street, St. Louis, MO 63101 ....(314) 539-6186

U.S. District Court-Northern District of Indiana
Federal Building, 204 South Main Street, South Bend, IN 46601

Chief Judge: Allen Sharp ....(219) 236-8266
District Clerk: Richard E. Timmons ....(219) 236-8260
Divisional Offices:
1108 Federal Building, 1300 S. Harrison Street, Fort Wayne, IN 46802 ....(219) 424-7360
507 State Street, Hammond, IN 46320 ....(219) 937-5235
P.O. Box 1498, Federal Building, Lafayette, IN 47902 ....(317) 742-0512
Chief Bankruptcy Judge: Kent Lindquist ....(219) 981-3332
Bankruptcy Clerk: Sharon A. James ....(219) 236-8247
Chief Probation Officer: Paul E. Panther ....(219) 937-5234

U.S. District Court-Southern District of Indiana
U.S. Courthouse, 46 East Ohio Street, Indianapolis, IN 46204

Chief Judge: Gene E. Brooks ....(812) 465-6431
District Clerk: John A. O'Neal ....(317) 226-6670
Divisional Offices:
304 Federal Building, 101 N.W. 7th Street, Evansville, IN 47708 ....(812) 465-6426
210 Federal Building, New Albany, IN 47150 ....(812) 948-5238
210 Federal Building, Terre Haute, IN 47808 ...(812) 234-9484
Chief Bankruptcy Judge: Robert L. Bayt ....(317) 226-6717
Bankruptcy Clerk: Dennis E. Burton ....(317) 226-6710
Chief Probation Officer: Frank DeVon Hall, Jr. ..(317) 226-6751

U.S. District Court-Northern District of Iowa
Federal Building and U.S. Courthouse, 101 First Street, S.E., Cedar Rapids, IA 52401

Chief Judge: Donald E. O'Brien ....(712) 233-3317
District Clerk: William J. Kanak ....(319) 399-2566
Divisional Office:
301 Federal Building, 320 Sixth Street, Sioux City, IA 51101 ....(712) 233-3240
Chief Bankruptcy Judge: Michael J. Melloy ....(319) 362-9786

Bankruptcy Clerk: Barbara A. Everly ....(319) 362-9696
Chief Probation Officer: Michael Ebinger ....(319) 399-2468

U.S. District Court-Southern District of Iowa

U.S. Courthouse, East 1st and Walnut Streets, Des Moines, IA 50309

Chief Judge: Harold D. Vietor ....(515) 284-6237
District Clerk: James R. Rosenbaum ....(515) 284-6248
Divisional Offices:
P.O. Box 307, Council Bluffs, IA 51502 ....(712) 325-5517
P.O. Box 256, Davenport, IA 52805 ....(319) 322-3223
Chief Bankruptcy Judge: Lee M. Jackwig ....(515) 284-6229
Bankruptcy Clerk: Mary M. Weibel ....(515) 284-6230
Chief Probation Officer: Edwin G. Ailts ....(515) 284-6207

U.S. District Court-Kansas

U.S. Courthouse, 401 North Market Street, Wichita, KS 67202

Chief Judge: Earl E. O'Connor ....(913) 236-3710
District Clerk: Ralph DeLoach ....(316) 269-6491
Divisional Offices:
151 U.S. Courthouse, 812 North 7th Street, Kansas City, KS ....(913) 236-3719
490 Federal Building, 444 S.E. Quincy Street, Topeka, KS 66683 ....(913) 295-2610
Chief Bankruptcy Judge: Benjamin E. Franklin ....(913) 236-3726
Bankruptcy Clerk: Russell L. Brenner ....(316) 269-6486
VCIS (Voice Case Information System):
Bankruptcy Court ....(316) 269-6668
VCIS (Voice Case Information System):
Bankruptcy Court (for in-state calls) ....(800) 827-9028
Chief Probation Officer: Perry D. Mathis ....(913) 236-3717
Federal Public Defender:
Charles D. Anderson ....(316) 269-6455
Divisional Offices:
408 U.S. Courthouse, 812 North 7th Street, Kansas City, KS 66101 ....(913) 236-3712
365 U.S. Courthouse, 444 S.E. Quincy Street, Topeka, KS 66683 ....(913) 295-2595

U.S. District Court-Eastern District of Kentucky

P.O. Box 741, Lexington, KY 40586

Chief Judge: Eugene E. Siler, Jr. ....(606) 878-6822
District Clerk: Leslie G. Whitmer ....(606) 233-2503
Divisional Offices:
1405 Greenup Avenue, Ashland, KY 41101 ....(606) 329-2465
P.O. Box 1073, Covington, KY 41012 ....(606) 292-3167
P.O. Box 1040, Frankfort, KY 40602 ....(502) 223-5225
P.O. Box 689, London, KY 40741 ....(606) 864-5137
203 Federal Building, 102 Main Street, Pikeville, KY 41501 ....(606) 437-6160
Bankruptcy Judge: Joe Lee ....(606) 233-2814
Bankruptcy Clerk: Betty L. Jennette ....(606) 233-2608
Chief Probation Officer: Charles S. Webb ....(606) 233-2646
Death Penalty Resource Center/Community Defender Organization: Randall Wheeler, Director, Kentucky Capital Litigation Resource Center, Department of Public Advocacy, 1264 Louisville Road, Perimeter Park West, Frankfort, KY 40601 ....(502) 564-8006

U.S. District Court-Western District of Kentucky

U.S. Courthouse, 601 West Broadway, Louisville, KY 40202

Chief Judge: Edward H. Johnstone ....(502) 443-8273
District Clerk: Jesse W. Grider ....(502) 582-5156
Divisional Offices:
213 Federal Building, 242 East Main Street, Bowling Green, KY 42101 ....(502) 781-1110
P.O. Box 538, Owensboro, KY 42302 ....(502) 683-0221
322 Federal Building, 5th & Broadway, Paducah, KY 42001 ....(502) 443-1347
Chief Bankruptcy Judge: J. Wendell Roberts .....(502) 582-5514
Bankruptcy Clerk: Jeffry Apperson ....(502) 582-5145
Chief Probation Officer:
Louis S. Sutherland, Jr. ....(502) 582-5161
Death Penalty Resource Center/Community Defender Organization: Randall Wheeler, Director, Kentucky Capital Litigation Resource Center, Department of Public Advocacy, 1264 Louisville Road, Perimeter Park West, Frankfort, KY 40601 ....(502) 564-8006

U.S. District Court-Eastern District of Louisiana

U.S. Courthouse, 500 Camp Street, New Orleans, LA 70130

Chief Judge: Frederick J.R. Heebe ....(504) 589-6504
District Clerk: Loretta G. Whyte ....(504) 589-2946
Chief Bankruptcy Judge: Thomas M. Brahney III ..(504) 589-6506
Bankruptcy Clerk: Frank J. Mathius ....(504) 589-6506
VCIS (Voice Case Information System):
Bankruptcy Court ....(504) 589-3951
Chief Probation Officer: Gerald J. Bonnaffons ..(504) 589-6317
Federal Public Defender:
John T. Mulvehill ....(504) 589-2468
Death Penalty Resource Center/Community Defender Organization: Rebecca Hudsmith, Executive Director, 348 Baronne, Suite 420, New Orleans, LA 70112 (504) 522-0578

U.S. District Court-Middle District of Louisiana

P.O. Box 2630, Baton Rouge, LA 70821

Chief Judge: John V. Parker ....(504) 389-0535
District Clerk: C. Lee Dupuis ....(504) 389-0321
Chief Bankruptcy Judge: Louis M. Phillips ......(504) 389-0371
Bankruptcy Clerk: Dora A. Erfurt ....(504) 389-0211
Chief Probation Officer: Robert K. Sibille .....(504) 389-0494
Death Penalty Resource Center/Community Defender Organization: Rebecca Hudsmith, Executive Director, 348 Baronne, Suite 420, New Orleans, LA 70112 ....(504) 522-0578

U.S. District Court-Western District of Louisiana

500 Fannin Street, Shreveport, LA 71101-3091

Chief Judge: Tom Stagg ....(318) 226-5260
District Clerk: Robert H. Shemwell ....(318) 226-5273
Divisional Offices:
P.O. Box 1269, Alexandria, LA 71309 ....(318) 473-7415
113 Federal Building, 705 Jefferson Street, Lafayette, LA 70501 ....(318) 232-2106

P.O. Box 393, Lake Charles, LA 70601 ....(318) 376-7246
306 Federal Building, Union and Vine Streets, Opelousas, LA 70570 ....(318) 948-8594
Chief Bankruptcy Judge: Stephen V. Callaway .....(318) 226-5269
Bankruptcy Clerk: J. Barry Dunford ....(318) 226-5267
Chief Probation Officer: William R. Sayes ....(318) 264-6615
Death Penalty Resource Center/Community Defender Organization: Rebecca Hudsmith, Executive Director, 348 Baronne, Suite 420, New Orleans, LA 70112 ....(504) 522-0578

U.S. District Court-Maine

P.O. Box 7505 DTS, Portland, ME 04112

Chief Judge: Gene Carter ....(207) 780-3662
District Clerk: William S. Brownell ....(207) 780-3357
Divisional Office:
P.O. Box 1007, Bangor, ME 04401 ....(207) 945-0357
Chief Bankruptcy Judge: Frederick A. Johnson ....(207) 780-3653
Bankruptcy Clerk: Samuel A. Wilkinson ....(207) 780-3482
PACER (Public Access to Court Electronic Records):
Bankruptcy Court ....(207) 780-3482
VCIS (Voice Case Information System):
Bankruptcy Court ....(207) 780-3755
Chief Probation Officer: Henry N. Milburn ....(207) 780-3358

U.S. District Court-Maryland

101 West Lombard Street, Baltimore, MD 21201

Chief Judge: Alexander Harvey II ....(301) 962-4655
District Clerk: James A. Haas ....(301) 962-2600
Chief Bankruptcy Judge: Paul Mannes ....(301) 443-7023
Bankruptcy Clerk: Michael Kostishak ....(301) 962-2688
Chief Probation Officer: David E. Johnson ....(301) 962-4785
Federal Public Defender:
Fred W. Bennett, Equitable Bank Center, Tower II, Suite 401, 100 South Charles St, Baltimore, MD 21201 ....(301) 962-3962

U.S. District Court-Massachusetts

John W. McCormack Post Office and Courthouse, Boston, MA 02109

Chief Judge: Frenk H. Freedman ....(413) 785-0006
District Clerk: Robert J. Smith, Jr. ....(617) 223-9152
Divisional Office:
1550 Main Street, Springfield, MA 01103 ....(413) 785-0214
Chief Bankruptcy Judge: James N. Gabriel ....(617) 565-6052
Bankruptcy Clerk: Robert L. Bingham ....(617) 565-6050
PACER (Public Access to Court Electronic Records):
Bankruptcy Court ....(617) 565-6093
VCIS (Voice Case Information System):
Bankruptcy Court ....(617) 565-6025
Chief Probation Officer:
Thomas J. Weadock, Jr. ....(617) 223-9188
Federal Public Defender:
Owen S. Walker, 195 State St, Boston, MA 02109 (617) 565-8335

U.S. District Court-Eastern District of Michigan

U.S. Courthouse, 231 West Lafayette Blvd, Detroit, MI 48226

Chief Judge: Julian A. Cook, Jr. ....(313) 226-3860
District Court Executive: John P. Mayer ....(313) 226-2120
District Clerk: David R. Sherwood ....(313) 226-7200
Divisional Offices:
200 E. Liberty Street, Ann Arbor, MI 48107 ....(313) 668-2380
219 Federal Building, 1000 Washington Avenue, Bay City, MI 48706 ....(517) 892-6571
140 Federal Building, 600 Church Street, Flint, MI 48502 ....(313) 766-5021
Chief Bankruptcy Judge: Arthur J. Spector ....(517) 892-8521
Bankruptcy Clerk: Mary G. Turpin ....(313) 226-7064
Chief Probation Officer: Raymond L. Frank ....(313) 961-7445
Community Defender Organization:
Paul D. Borman, Chief Federal Defender, Legal Aid and Defender Association of Detroit, 2255 Penobscot Building, 645 Griswold Street, Detroit, MI 48226 ....(313) 961-4159

U.S. District Court-Western District of Michigan

Federal Building, 110 Michigan St, N.W., Grand Rapids, MI 49503

Chief Judge: Douglas W. Hillman ....(616) 456-2523
District Clerk: C. Duke Hynek ....(616) 456-2381
Divisional Offices:
B-35 Federal Building, 410 West Michigan Avenue, Kalamazoo, MI 49005 ....(616) 349-2922
229 Federal Building, P.O. Box 698, Marquette, MI 49855 ....(906) 226-2021
315 W. Allergan, Lansing, MI 48933 ....(517) 377-1559
Chief Bankruptcy Judge: Laurence E. Howard ......(616) 456-2233
Bankruptcy Clerk: Mark Van Allsburg ....(616) 456-2693
VCIS (Voice Case Information System):
Bankruptcy Court ....(616) 456-2072
Chief Probation Officer: Robert L. Brent ....(616) 456-2384

U.S. District Court-Minnesota

Federal Building, 316 North Robert Street, St. Paul, MN 55101

Chief Judge: Donald D. Alsop ....(612) 290-3000
District Clerk: Francis E. Dosal ....(612) 290-3212
Divisional Offices:
417 U.S. Courthouse, 515 W. First Street, Duluth, MN 55802 ....(218) 720-5250
514 U.S. Courthouse, 110 S. 4th Street, Minneapolis, MN 55401 ....(612) 348-1821
Chief Bankruptcy Judge: Robert J. Kressel ....(612) 348-1850
Bankruptcy Clerk: Timothy R. Walbridge ....(612) 348-1853
Chief Probation Officer: Glenn Baskfield ....(612) 348-1980
Federal Public Defender:
Daniel M. Scott, 174 U.S. Courthouse, 110 S. 4th Street, Minneapolis, MN 55401 ....(612) 348-1755

U.S. District Court-Northern District of Mississippi

P.O. Box 727, Oxford, MS 38655

Chief Judge: L.T. Senter, Jr. ....(601) 369-8307
District Clerk: Norman L. Gillespie ....(601) 234-1971
Divisional Offices:
P.O. Box 704, Aberdeen, MS 39730 ....(601) 369-4952
P.O. Box 190, Clarksdale, MS 38614 ....(601) 624-6208
P.O. Box 190, Greenville, MS 38701 ....(601) 335-1651
Bankruptcy Judge: David W. Houston III ....(601) 369-2624
Bankruptcy Clerk: Joseph E. Wroten ....(601) 369-2596
VCIS (Voice Case Information System):
Bankruptcy Court ....(601) 369-8147
Chief Probation Officer: Johnny Dean Still, Jr. ..(601) 234-2761
Death Penalty Resource Center/Community Defender Organization: James W. Craig, Executive Director, P.O. Box 510, Jackson, MS 39205 ....(601) 352-0784

U.S. District Court-Southern District of Mississippi

245 East Capitol Street, Jackson, MS 39201

Chief Judge: William H. Barbour, Jr. ....(601) 960-4545
District Clerk: (vacant) ....(601) 960-4439
Divisional Offices:
P.O. Box 369, Biloxi, MS 39533 ....(601) 432-8623
P.O. Box 511, Hattiesburg, MS 39401 ....(601) 583-2433
P.O. Box 1186, Meridian, MS 39301 ....(601) 693-2883
Chief Bankruptcy Judge: Edward Ellington ....(601) 965-5304
Bankruptcy Clerk: Mollie C. Jones ....(601) 965-5301
Chief Probation Officer: (vacant) ....(601) 432-5003
Death Penalty Resource Center/Community Defender Organization: James W. Craig, Executive Director, P.O. Box 510, Jackson, MS 39205 ....(601) 352-0784

U.S. District Court-Eastern District of Missouri

1114 Market Street, U.S. Court & Custom Bldg, St. Louis, MO 63101

Chief Judge: Edward L. Fillipine ....(314) 539-3603
District Clerk: Eyvon Mendenhall ....(314) 539-6056
Divisional Office:
339 Broadway, Cape Girardeau, MO 63701 ....(314) 335-8538
Chief Bankruptcy Judge: James J. Barta ....(314) 539-6430
Bankruptcy Clerk: Frank E. Goodroe ....(314) 539-2222
Chief Probation Officer: Jerome F. Lawrenz ......(314) 539-2585
Federal Public Defender: David R. Freeman ....(314) 539-6186
Death Penalty Resource Center/Community Defender Organization: Sean O'Brien, Director, Missouri Capital Punishment Resource Center, 500 East 52nd St, P.O. Box 22609, Kansas City, MO 644113-2609 ...(816) 276-2383

U.S. District Court-Western District of Missouri

U.S. Courthouse, 811 Grand Avenue, Kansas City, MO 64106

Chief Judge: Scott O. Wright ....(816) 221-6271
District Clerk: Robert F. Connor ....(816) 426-2811
Divisional Offices:
310 U.S. Courthouse, 131 West High Street, Jefferson City, MO 65102 ....(314) 636-6124
206 U.S. Courthouse, 302 Joplin Street, Joplin, MO 64801 ....(417) 623-6536
222 John Q. Hammons Parkway, Springfield, MO 65806 ....(417) 865-7719
229 U.S. Courthouse, 201 S. 8th Street, St. Joseph, MO 64501 ....(816) 279-2428
Chief Bankruptcy Judge: Frank W. Koger ....(816) 426-2180
VCIS (Voice Case Information System):
Bankruptcy Court ....(816) 842-7985
Chief Probation Officer: Lewis D. Frazier ....(816) 426-3921
Federal Public Defender:
Raymond C. Conrad, 911 Walnut, 12th Floor, Kansas City, MO 64106 ....(816) 426-5851
Divisional Office:
1949 East Sunshine, Suite 3-104, Springfield, MO 65804 ....(417) 881-4090
Death Penalty Resource Center/Community Defender Organization: Sean O'Brien, Director, Missouri Capital Punishment Resource Center, 500 East 52nd St, P.O. Box 22609, Kansas City, MO 644113-2609 ..(816) 276-2383

U.S. District Court-Montana

Federal Bldg, 316 North 26th Street, Billings, MT 59101

Chief Judge: Paul G. Hatfield ....(406) 657-6503
District Clerk: Louis Aleksich, Jr. ....(406) 657-6366
Divisional Offices:
Federal Building, Butte, MT 59701 ....(406) 782-0432
P.O. Box 2186, Great Falls, MT 59403 ....(406) 727-1922
P.O. Box 8537, Missoula, MT 59807 ....(406) 329-3598
Bankruptcy Judge: John L. Peterson ....(406) 782-3338
Bankruptcy Clerk: Bernard McCarthy ....(406) 782-3354
Chief Probation Officer: Herbert K. Anderson ....(406) 657-6287

U.S. District Court-Nebraska

P.O. Box 129 DTS, Omaha, NE 68101

Chief Judge: Lyle E. Strom ....(402) 221-3421
District Clerk: Norbert H. Ebel ....(402) 221-4761
Divisional Office:
593 Federal Building, 1100 Centennial Mall North, Lincoln, NE 68508 ....(402) 437-5225
Chief Bankruptcy Judge: Timothy J. Mahoney ......(402) 221-3155
Bankruptcy Clerk: Judith M. Napier ....(402) 221-4687
Chief Probation Officer: Burton L. Matthies .....(402) 221-4785

U.S. District Court-Nevada

300 Las Vegas Blvd South, Las Vegas, NV 89101

Chief Judge: Edward C. Reed, Jr. ....(702) 784-5754
District Clerk: Carol C. FitzGerald ....(702) 388-6351
Divisional Office:
5003 U.S. Courthouse, 300 Booth Street, Reno, NV 89509 ....(702) 784-5515
Chief Bankruptcy Judge: Robert C. Jones ....(702) 388-6505
Bankruptcy Clerk: Patricia Gray-Edwards ....(702) 385-6257
Chief Probation Officer: Fred C. Pierce ....(702) 388-6428
Federal Public Defender:
Frances A. Forsman, Phoenix Building, 330 South 3rd Street, Suite 1050, Las Vegas, NV 89101.(702) 388-5677
Divisional Office:
4109 U.S. Courthouse, 300 Booth Street, Reno, NV 89509 ....(702) 784-5626

U.S. District Court-New Hampshire

P.O. Box 1498, Concord, NH 03301

Chief Judge: Shane Devine ....(603) 225-1491
District Clerk: James R. Starr ....(603) 225-1423
Chief Bankruptcy Judge: James E. Yacos ....(603) 666-7532
Bankruptcy Clerk: George A. Vannah ....(603) 666-7532
PACER (Public Access to Court Electronic Records):
Bankruptcy Court ....(603) 666-7783
VCIS (Voice Case Information System):
Bankruptcy Court ....(603) 666-7424
Chief Probation Officer: David M. Sawyer ....(603) 225-1515

U.S. District Court-New Jersey

U.S. Post Office and Courthouse, P.O. Box 419, Newark, NJ 07102

Chief Judge: John F. Gerry ....(609) 757-5020
District Clerk: William T. Walsh ....(201) 645-3730

Divisional Offices:
P.O. Box 2797, Camden, NJ 08101 ....(609) 757-5021
402 E. State Street, P.O. Box 515, Trenton, NJ 08603 ....(609) 989-2068
Chief Bankruptcy Judge: Vincent J. Commisa ......(201) 645-2630
Bankruptcy Clerk: James Waldron ....(201) 645-2630
VCIS (Voice Case Information System):
Bankruptcy Court ....(201) 645-3098
Chief Probation Officer: David A. Mason ....(201) 645-6161
Federal Public Defender:
John F. McMahon, 976 Broad Street, Newark, NJ 07101 ....(201) 645-6347
Divisional Offices:
330 Market Street, Camden, NJ 08102 ....(609) 757-5341
402 E. State Street, Room 110, Trenton, NJ 08615 ....(609) 989-2160

U.S. District Court-New Mexico

P.O. Box 689, Albuquerque, NM 87103

Chief Judge: Juan G. Burciaga ....(505) 988-6341
District Clerk: Jesse Casaus ....(505) 766-2851
Divisional Offices:
C-309 Federal Building, 200 E. Griggs Avenue, Las Cruces, NM 88001 ....(505) 523-8220
P.O. Box 2384, Santa Fe, NM 87501 ....(505) 988-6481
Chief Bankruptcy Judge: Mark B. McFeeley ....(505) 766-1873
Bankruptcy Clerk: Jack L. Smith ....(505) 766-2051
Chief Probation Officer: Daniel Perez ....(505) 766-2237
Federal Public Defender:
Tova M. Indritz, P.O. Box 306, Albuquerque, NM 87103 ....(505) 766-3293
Divisional Office:
118 South Downtown Mall, Las Cruces, NM 88001 ....(505) 523-8366

U.S. District Court-Northern District of New York

P.O. Box 1037, Albany, NY 12201

Chief Judge: Neal P. McCurn ....(315) 423-5432
District Clerk: Joseph R. Scully ....(518) 472-5651
Divisional Offices:
Federal Building, 15 Henry Street, Binghamton, NY 13901 ....(607) 773-2893
100 S. Clinton Street, Syracuse, NY 13260 .....(315) 423-5549
Alexander Pirnie Federal Bldg, 10 Broad St, Utica, NY 13501 ....(315) 793-8151
Chief Bankruptcy Judge: Justin J. Mahoney ....(518) 472-4226
Bankruptcy Clerk: Richard G. Zeh, Jr. ....(518) 472-4226
Chief Probation Officer: Frank T. Waterson ......(518) 472-3618

U.S. District Court-Southern District of New York:

U.S. Courthouse, Foley Square, New York, NY 10007

Chief Judge: Charles L. Brieant ....(914) 683-9597
District Court Executive: Clifford P. Kirsch ....(212) 791-9349
District Clerk: Raymond F. Burghardt ....(212) 791-0108
Chief Bankruptcy Judge: Burton R. Lifland ....(212) 791-9616
Bankruptcy Clerk: Cecelia M. Lewis ....(212) 791-2247
Chief Probation Officer: Eunice R. Holt Jones ..(212) 791-0218
Community Defender Organization:
Archibald R. Murray, Executive Director and Attorney-in-Chief, The Legal Aid Society, 15 Park Row, New York, NY 10038 ....(212) 577-3313
Jack Lipson, Chief of Operations, Federal Defender Services Unit, The Legal Aid Society, 52 Duane Street, New York, NY 10007 ......(212) 285-2838
John J. Byrnes, Attorney-in-Charge, 158 Grand Street, Rm 7-1st Floor, White Plains, NY 10601 ...(914) 428-7214

U.S. District Court-Eastern District of New York

225 Cadman Plaza East, Brooklyn, NY 11201

Chief Judge: Thomas C. Platt, Jr. ....(718) 330-7575
District Court Executive: S. Bruce Barton ....(516) 485-6508
District Clerk: Robert C. Heinemann ....(718) 330-2105
Divisional Offices:
300 Rabro Drive, Hauppauge, NY 11788 ....(516) 582-1100
Uniondale Avenue at Hempstead Turnpike, Uniondale, NY 11553 ....(516) 485-6500
Chief Bankruptcy Judge: Conrad B. Duberstein ....(718) 330-2188
Bankruptcy Clerk: Carol Robinson ....(718) 330-2188
VCIS (Voice Case Information System):
Bankruptcy Court ....(718) 852-5726
Chief Probation Officer: Ralph K. Kistner ....(718) 330-2626
Community Defender Organization:
Archibald R. Murray, Executive Director and Attorney-in-Chief, The Legal Aid Society, 15 Park Row, New York, NY 10038 ....(212) 577-3313
Thomas ConCannon, Attorney-in-Charge, Legal Aid Society, 50 Court Street, Room 1103, Brooklyn, NY 11201 ....(718) 330-1200

U.S. District Court-Western District of New York

U.S. Courthouse, 68 Court Street, Buffalo, NY 14202

Chief Judge: Michael A. Telesca ....(716) 263-5785
District Clerk: Michael J. Kaplan ....(716) 846-4211
Divisional Office:
282 U.S. Courthouse, 100 State Street, Rochester, NY 14614 ....(716) 263-6263
Chief Bankruptcy Judge: Beryl E. McGuire ....(716) 846-4206
VCIS (Voice Case Information System):
Bankruptcy Court ....(716) 846-5311
Bankruptcy Clerk: Martin H. Oogjen III ....(716) 846-4130
Chief Probation Officer: Daniel J. McMorrow .....(716) 846-4241

U.S. District Court-Eastern District of North Carolina

P.O. Box 25670, Raleigh, NC 27611

Chief Judge: W. Earl Britt ....(919) 856-4050
District Clerk: J. Rich Leonard ....(919) 856-4370
Divisional Offices:
P.O. Box 43, Fayetteville, NC 28302 ....(919) 483-9509
P.O. Box 1336, New Bern, NC 28560 ....(919) 638-8534
P.O. Box 338, Wilmington, NC 28401 ....(919) 343-4663
Chief Bankruptcy Judge: Thomas M. Moore ....(919) 291-6413
Bankruptcy Clerk: Peggy B. Deans ....(919) 273-0248
Bankruptcy Administrator: June L. Farmer ....(919) 237-6455
Chief Probation Officer: John W. Sisson ....(919) 856-4660
Federal Public Defender:
Willie E. Martin, 300 Montague Building, 128 East Hargett Street, P.O. Box 25967, Raleigh, NC 27611-5967 ....(919) 856-4236
Death Penalty Resource Center/Community Defender Organization: Robert S. Mahler, Director, North Carolina Death Penalty Resource Center, P.O. Box 1070, Raleigh, NC 27602 ....(919) 733-9490

U.S. District Court-Middle District of North Carolina
P.O. Box V-1, Greensboro, NC 27402

Chief Judge: Richard C. Erwin ....(919) 761-3007
District Clerk: J.P. Creekmore ....(919) 333-5347
Chief Bankruptcy Judge: James B. Wolfe, Jr. .....(919) 333-5729
Bankruptcy Clerk: William L. Schwenn ....(919) 333-5647
Bankruptcy Administrator: Michael D. West ......(919) 333-5421
Chief Probation Officer: Melvin C. Smith ....(919) 333-5341
Death Penalty Resource Center/Community Defender Organization: Robert S. Mahler, Director, North Carolina Death Penalty Resource Center, P.O. Box 1070, Raleigh, NC 27602 ....(919) 733-9490

U.S. District Court-Western District of North Carolina
U.S. Courthouse, 100 Otis Street, Asheville, NC 28801-2611

Chief Judge: Robert D. Potter ....(704) 371-6343
District Clerk: Thomas McGraw ....(704) 259-0648
Divisional Offices:
204 Charles R. Jonas Federal Building, 401 W. Trade Street, Charlotte, NC 48202 ....(704) 371-6200
P.O. Box 466, Statesville, NC 28677 ....(704) 873-7112
Chief Bankruptcy Judge: Marvin R. Wooten ....(704) 371-6218
Bankruptcy Clerk: Warren L. Tadlock ....(704) 371-6103
Bankruptcy Administrator:
Linda J. Wright Simpson ....(704) 371-6894
Chief Probation Officer: S. Thomas Noell, Jr. ...(704) 371-6102
Death Penalty Resource Center/Community Defender Organization: Robert S. Mahler, Director, North Carolina Death Penalty Resource Center, P.O. Box 1070, Raleigh, NC 27602 ....(919) 733-9490

U.S. District Court-North Dakota
P.O. Box 1193, Bismarck, ND 58502

Chief Judge: Patrick A. Conmy ....(701) 250-4445
District Clerk: Edward J. Klecker ....(701) 250-4295
Divisional Office:
P.O. Box 870, Fargo, ND 58107 ....(701) 239-5377
Chief Bankruptcy Judge: William A. Hill ....(701) 239-5631
Bankruptcy Clerk: Ellen A. Johanson ....(701) 239-5120
Chief Probation Officer: W. Dan Broome ....(701) 239-5123

U.S. District Court-Northern Mariana Islands
P.O. Box 687, Saipan, Northern Mariana Islands 96950

Judge: Alex R. Munson
Clerk: Hedwig V. Hofschneider ....(670) 934-7131
Note: Messages may be left with the Circuit Executive Office in San Francisco. Tel: 415/556-7340.

U.S. District Court-Northern District of Ohio:
U.S. Courthouse, 201 Superior Avenue, N.E., Cleveland, OH 44114

Chief Judge: Thomas D. Lambros ....(216) 522-2080
District Clerk: James S. Gallas ....(216) 522-4359
Divisional Offices:
568 Federal Building & U.S. Courthouse, Two S. Main Street, Akron, OH 44308 ....(216) 375-5705
108 U.S. Courthouse, 1716 Spielbusch Avenue, Toledo, OH 43624 ....(419) 259-6411
329 U.S. Courthouse, City Hall Annex, 9 West Front St, Youngstown, OH 44503 ....(216) 746-3351
Chief Bankruptcy Judge: James H. Williams ....(216) 489-4430
Bankruptcy Clerk: Beth A. Dick ....(216) 942-7555
Chief Probation Officer: Keith A. Koenning ......(216) 522-2200
Federal Public Defender:
Edward F. Marek, 75 Public Square, Suite 410, Cleveland, OH 44113 ....(216) 522-4856

U.S. District Court-Southern District of Ohio
U.S. Courthouse, 85 Marconi Boulevard, Columbus, OH 43215

Chief Judge: Carl B. Rubin ....(513) 684-3297
District Clerk: Kenneth J. Murphy ....(614) 469-6945
Divisional Offices:
326 Courthouse & Post Office Building, 5th & Walnut Streets, Cincinnati, OH 45202 ....(513) 684-2777
PO Box 970, Mid-City Station, Dayton, OH 45402 ....(513) 225-2896
Chief Bankruptcy Judge: Burton Perlman ....(513) 684-2342
Bankruptcy Clerk: Michael D. Webb ....(614) 469-2087
Chief Probation Officer: Gerald J. Wright ....(513) 684-2978

U.S. District Court-Northern District of Oklahoma
U.S. Courthouse, 333 West 4th Street, Tulsa, OK 74103

Chief Judge: H. Dale Cook ....(918) 581-7616
District Clerk: Jack C. Silver ....(918) 581-7796
Chief Bankruptcy Judge: Mickey D. Wilson ....(918) 581-7184
Bankruptcy Clerk: Dorothy A. Evans ....(918) 581-7183
Chief Probation Officer: Rodney Baker ....(918) 581-7187
Federal Public Defender:
David E. Booth, 215 Dean A. McGee Avenue, Suite 524, Oklahoma City, OK 73102 ....(405) 231-5725
Divisional Office:
222 S. Houston, Suite C, Tulsa, OK 74127 .....(918) 581-7656

U.S. District Court-Eastern District of Oklahoma
P.O. Box 607, Muskogee, OK 74401

Chief Judge: Frank H. Seay ....(918) 687-2437
District Clerk: William B. Guthrie ....(918) 687-2471
Chief Bankruptcy Judge: James E. Ryan ....(918) 758-0366
Bankruptcy Clerk: D. Sue Ashley ....(918) 758-0126
VCIS (Voice Case Information System):
Bankruptcy Court ....(918) 756-8617
Chief Probation Officer: John R. Bowden ....(918) 687-2366
Federal Public Defender:
David E. Booth, 215 Dean A. McGee Avenue, Suite 524, Oklahoma City, OK 73102 ....(405) 231-5725
Divisional Office:
222 S. Houston, Suite C, Tulsa, OK 74127 .....(918) 581-7656
Death Penalty Resource Center/Community Defender Organization: Ms. Mandy Welch, Director, Capital Post Conviction Project of the Oklahoma Appellate Public Defender System, 1660 Cross Center Drive, Norman, OK 73019 ....(405) 325-3128

U.S. District Court-Western District of Oklahoma

U.S. Courthouse, 200 N.W. 4th Street, Oklahoma City, OK 73102

Chief Judge: Ralph G. Thompson ....(405) 231-5153
District Clerk: Robert D. Dennis ....(405) 231-4792
Chief Bankruptcy Judge: Richard L. Bohanon .....(405) 231-5141
Bankruptcy Clerk: Walter W. Mounts ....(405) 231-5143
Chief Probation Officer: Travis R. Windham ......(405) 231-5055
Federal Public Defender:
David E. Booth, 215 Dean A. McGee Avenue, Suite 524, Oklahoma City, OK 73102 ....(405) 231-5725
Divisional Office:
222 S. Houston, Suite C, Tulsa, OK 74127 ......(918) 581-7656
Death Penalty Resource Center/Community Defender Organization: Ms. Mandy Welch, Director, Capital Post Conviction Project of the Oklahoma Appellate Public Defender System, 1660 Cross Center Drive, Norman, OK 73019 ....(405) 325-3128

U.S. District Court-Oregon

U.S. Courthouse, 620 S.W. Main Street, Portland, OR 97205

Chief Judge: Owen M. Panner ....(503) 326-4190
District Clerk: Donald Cinnamond ....(503) 326-2202
Divisional Office:
102 U.S. Courthouse, 211 East 7th Street, Eugene, OR 97401 ....(503) 687-6423
Chief Bankruptcy Judge: Henry L. Hess, Jr. ......(503) 326-4186
Bankruptcy Clerk: Terence H. Dunn ....(503) 326-2231
VCIS (Voice Case Information System):
Bankruptcy Court ....(503) 326-2249
Chief Probation Officer: Frank S. Gilbert ....(503) 326-2117
Federal Public Defender:
Steven T. Wax, 615 W. Broadway, Suite 200, Portland, OR 97205 ....(503) 326-2123
Divisional Office:
44 W. Broadway, Suite 406, Eugene, OR 97401 ..(503) 687-6937

U.S. District Court-Eastern District of Pennsylvania

U.S. Courthouse, Independence Mall West, 601 Market Street, Philadelphia, PA 19106

Chief Judge: Louis Charles Bechtle ....(215) 597-0436
District Clerk: Michael E. Kunz ....(215) 597-7704
Chief Bankruptcy Judge: Thomas M. Twardowski ....(215) 320-5093
VCIS (Voice Case Information System):
Bankruptcy Court ....(215) 597-2244
Chief Probation Officer: Albert J. Christy ......(215) 597-7950
Community Defender Organization:
Maureen Kearney Rowley, Federal Court Division of the Defender Association of Philadelphia, Cast Iron Building, Suite 500S, 718 Arch Street, Philadelphia, PA 19106 ....(215) 925-9220

U.S. District Court-Middle District of Pennsylvania

P.O. Box 1148, Scranton, PA 18501

Chief Judge: Richard P. Conaboy ....(717) 344-8537
District Clerk: Donald R. Berry ....(717) 347-5623
Divisional Offices:
P.O. Box 983, Harrisburg, PA 17108 ....(717) 782-4445
203 Federal Building, 197 S. Main Street, Wilkes-Barre, PA 18701 ....(717) 823-8034
P.O. Box 608, Williamsport, PA 17701 ....(717) 323-6380
Chief Bankruptcy Judge: Thomas C. Gibbons ....(717) 826-6336
Bankruptcy Clerk: Margaret A. Smith ....(717) 826-6450
Chief Probation Officer: Joseph P. Donahue ......(717) 342-8171
Federal Public Defender:
James V. Wade, 100 Chestnut Street, Suite 306, Harrisburg, PA 17101 ....(717) 782-2237
Divisional Office:
401 Adams Avenue, 404 Scranton Center, Scranton, PA 18510 ....(717) 343-6285

U.S. District Court-Western District of Pennsylvania

P.O. Box 1805, Pittsburgh, PA 15230

Chief Judge: Maurice B. Cohill Jr ....(412) 644-6482
District Clerk: Catherine C. Martrano ....(412) 644-3528
Divisional Office:
P.O. Box 1820, Erie, PA 16507 ....(814) 453-4829
Chief Bankruptcy Judge: Joseph L. Cosetti ....(412) 644-4710
Bankruptcy Clerk: Theodore S. Hopkins ....(412) 644-2700
Chief Probation Officer: Nicholas P. Muller .....(412) 644-2907
Federal Public Defender:
George E. Schumacher, 415 Convention Tower, 960 Penn Avenue, Pittsburgh, PA 15222 .....(412) 644-6565
Divisional Office:
P.O. Box 1776, Erie, PA 16507 ....(814) 455-8089

U.S. District Court-Puerto Rico

P.O. Box 3671, San Juan, PR 00904

Chief Judge: Juan M. Perez-Gimenez ....(809) 729-6740
District Clerk: Juan M. Masini-Soler ....(809) 729-6701
Chief Bankruptcy Judge: Enique S. Lamoutte .....(809) 766-5615
Bankruptcy Clerk: Frances Rios de Moran ....(809) 766-5123
Chief Probation Officer:
Isidoro Mojica-Vazquez ....(809) 766-5596
Federal Public Defender:
Gerardo Ortiz Del Rivero, P.O. Box 3832, San Juan, PR 00904 ....(809) 729-6775

U.S. District Court-Rhode Island

Federal Building and U.S. Courthouse, Providence, RI 02903

Chief Judge: Francis J. Boyle ....(401) 528-5155
District Clerk: Frederick R. DeCesaris ....(401) 528-5100
Bankruptcy Judge: Arthur N. Votolato, Jr. ....(401) 528-4487
Bankruptcy Clerk: James M. Lynch ....(401) 528-4477
PACER (Public Access to Court Electronic Records):
Bankruptcy Court ....(401) 528-4465
VCIS (Voice Case Information System):
Bankruptcy Court ....(401) 528-4476
Chief Probation Officer: Donald J. Blackburn ....(401) 528-5162

U.S. District Court-South Carolina

P.O. Box 867, Columbia, SC 29202

Chief Judge: Falcon B. Hawkins ....(803) 724-4685
District Clerk: Ann A. Birch ....(803) 765-5816
Divisional Offices:
P.O. Box 835, Charleston, SC 29402 ....(803) 724-4225
P.O. Box 2317, Florence, SC 29503 ....(803) 662-1223
P.O. Box 10768, Greenville, SC 29603 ....(803) 233-2781
Chief Bankruptcy Judge: J. Bratton Davis ....(803) 765-5973
Bankruptcy Clerk: Brenda A. Schueler ....(803) 765-5211

VCIS (Voice Case Information System):
Bankruptcy Court ....(803) 765-5211
Chief Probation Officer: James W. Duckett, Jr. ..(803) 765-3300
Federal Public Defender:
Parks N. Small, 1835 Assembly Street, Room 146, Columbia, SC 29201 ....(803) 765-5147
Death Penalty Resource Center/Community Defender Organization: John H. Blume, Executive Director, P.O. Box 11311, Columbia, SC 29211 ....(803) 765-0650

U.S. District Court-South Dakota

U.S. Courthouse and Federal Building, 400 South Phillips Avenue, Sioux Falls, SD 57102

Chief Judge: Donald J. Porter ....(605) 224-0476
District Clerk: William F. Clayton ....(605) 338-5566
Divisional Offices:
302 Federal Building, 515 Ninth Street, Rapid City, SD 57701 ....(605) 342-3066
405 U.S. Courthouse, Pierre, SD 57501 ....(605) 224-5849
Chief Bankruptcy Judge: Irvin N. Hoyt ....(605) 224-0560
Bankruptcy Clerk: Patricia Merritt ....(605) 330-4541
Chief Probation Officer: Jack R. Saylor ....(605) 336-0721

U.S. District Court-Eastern District of Tennessee

P.O. Box 2348, Knoxville, TN 37901

Chief Judge: Thomas G. Hull ....(615) 638-1305
District Clerk: Murry Hawkins ....(615) 673-4227
Divisional Offices:
P.O. Box 591, Chattanooga, TN 37401 ....(615) 752-5200
101 Summer Street West, Greeneville, TN 37743 ....(615) 639-3105
Chief Bankruptcy Judge: Ralph H. Kelley ....(615) 752-5168
Bankruptcy Clerk: Ralph T. Brown ....(615) 752-5163
Chief Probation Officer: Rosalind Andrews ....(615) 673-4248
Community Defender Organization:
William P. Redick Jr, Executive Director, 1225 17th Avenue So, Nashville, TN 37212 ....(615) 327-8791

U.S. District Court-Middle District of Tennessee

U.S. Courthouse, 801 Broadway, Nashville, TN 37203

Chief Judge: Thomas A. Wiseman, Jr. ....(615) 736-7013
District Clerk: Juliet Griffin ....(615) 736-5728
Divisional Office:
228 U.S. Courthouse, 9 East Broad St, Cookeville, TN 38501 ....(615) 526-3269
Chief Bankruptcy Judge: George C. Paine II ......(615) 736-5587
Bankruptcy Clerk: Lloyd C. Ray, Jr. ....(615) 736-5590
Chief Probation Officer: Don E. Savage ....(615) 736-5771
Federal Public Defender:
Henry A. Martin, 808 Broadway, Nashville, TN 37203 ....(615) 736-5047
Community Defender Organization:
William P. Redick Jr, Executive Director, 1225 17th Avenue So, Nashville, TN 37212 ....(615) 327-8791

U.S. District Court-Western District of Tennessee

Federal Building, 167 North Main Street, Memphis, TN 38103

Chief Judge: Odell Horton ....(901) 521-4268
District Clerk: J. Franklin Reid ....(901) 521-3317
Divisional Office:
206 Federal Bldg, 109 S. Highland Ave, Jackson, TN 38301 ....(901) 427-6586
Chief Bankruptcy Judge: David S. Kennedy ....(901) 521-3202
Bankruptcy Clerk: Toni Campbell Parker ....(901) 521-3202
Chief Probation Officer: Eugene G. Shaw ....(901) 521-3256
Federal Public Defender:
Edward C. Duke, 1116 Federal Building, Memphis, TN 38103 ....(901) 521-3895
Community Defender Organization:
William P. Redick Jr, Executive Director, 1225 17th Avenue So, Nashville, TN 37212 ....(615) 327-8791

U.S. District Court-Northern District of Texas

U.S. Courthouse, 1100 Commerce Street, Dallas, TX 75242

Chief Judge: Barefoot Sanders ....(214) 767-8528
District Clerk: Nancy Doherty ....(214) 767-0787
Divisional Offices:
P.O. Box 1218, Abilene, TX 79604 ....(915) 677-6311
P.O. Box F-13240, Amarillo, TX 79189 ....(806) 376-2352
202 U.S. Courthouse, Ft. Worth, TX 76102 ......(817) 334-3132
C-221 U.S. Courthouse, 1205 Texas Avenue, Lubbock, TX 79401 ....(806) 743-7624
202 Federal Building, 33 E. Twohig Street, San Angelo, TX 79603 ....(915) 655-4506
P.O. Box 1234, Wichita Falls, TX 76307 ....(817) 767-1902
Chief Bankruptcy Judge: Robert C. McGuire ....(214) 767-0816
Bankruptcy Clerk: Michael W. Youdin ....(214) 767-0814
Chief Probation Officer: Al Havenstrite ....(214) 767-0704
Federal Public Defender:
Ira R. Kirkendoll, Room 14A20, U.S. Courthouse, 1100 Commerce St, Dallas, TX 75242 ....(214) 767-2746
Death Penalty Resource Center/Community Defender Organization: Robert G. McGlasson, Director, Texas Appellate Practice & Education Resource Center, 511 West 7th St, Austin, TX 78701 ....(512) 320-8300

U.S. District Court-Southern District of Texas

P.O. Box 61010, Houston, TX 77208

Chief Judge: James De Anda ....(713) 221-9594
District Clerk: Jesse E. Clark ....(713) 221-9505
Divisional Offices:
P.O. Box 2299, Brownsville, TX 78520 ....(512) 548-2500
521 Starr Street, Corpus Christi, TX 78401 ...(512) 888-3142
P.O. Box 2300, Galveston, TX 77553 ....(409) 766-3530
P.O. Box 597, Laredo, TX 78042 ....(512) 723-3542
P.O. Box 5059, McAllen, TX 78501 ....(512) 631-2205
P.O. Box 1541, Victoria, TX 77902 ....(512) 575-3512
Chief Bankruptcy Judge:
Randolph F. Wheless, Jr. ....(713) 221-9784
Chief Probation Officer: Louis G. Brewster ......(713) 226-2744
Federal Public Defender:
Roland E. Dahlin II, P.O. Box 61508, Houston, TX 77208 ....(713) 220-2194
Divisional Offices:
P.O. Box 2163, Brownsville, TX 78522 ....(512) 548-2573
P.O. Box 1562, Laredo, TX 78042 ....(512) 726-2218
Texas Commerce Bank Building, 1701 W. Highway 83, Suite 905, McAllen, TX 78501 ....(512) 630-2995
Death Penalty Resource Center/Community Defender Organization: Robert G. McGlasson, Director, Texas Appellate Practice & Education Resource Center, 511 West 7th St, Austin, TX 78701 ....(512) 320-8300

U.S. District Court-Eastern District of Texas
Federal Bldg and U.S. Courthouse, 211 West Ferguson Street, Tyler, TX 75702

Chief Judge: Robert M. Parker ....(214) 597-9387
District Clerk: Murray L. Harris ....(214) 592-8195
Divisional Offices:
320 U.S. Courthouse, 300 Willow Street, Beaumont, TX 77701 ....(409) 839-2645
P.O. Box 1499, Marshall, TX 75672 ....(214) 935-2912
216 Federal Building, 101 E. Pecan Street, Sherman, TX 75090 ....(214) 892-2921
P.O. Box 2667, Texarkana, TX 75501 ....(214) 794-8561
Chief Bankruptcy Judge: C. Houston Abel ....(214) 597-8432
Bankruptcy Clerk: James D. Tokoph ....(214) 592-1212
VCIS (Voice Case Information System):
Bankruptcy Court ....(214) 592-6119
Chief Probation Officer: Wade E. French ....(214) 597-3727
Death Penalty Resource Center/Community Defender Organization: Robert G. McGlasson, Director, Texas Appellate Practice & Education Resource Center, 511 West 7th St, Austin, TX 78701 ....(512) 320-8300

U.S. District Court-Western District of Texas
Hemisfair Plaza, 655 East Durango Boulevard, San Antonio, TX 78206

Chief Judge: Lucius D. Bunton III ....(915) 683-9457
District Clerk: Charles W. Vagner ....(512) 229-6550
Divisional Offices:
200 West 8th Street, Austin, TX 78701 ....(512) 482-5896
P.O. Box 1349, Del Rio, TX 78840 ....(512) 775-2021
108 U.S. Courthouse, El Paso, TX 79901 ....(915) 534-6725
P.O. Box 10708, Midland, TX 79702 ....(915) 683-2001
P.O. Box 191, Pecos, TX 79772 ....(915) 445-4228
P.O. Box 608, Waco, TX 76703 ....(817) 756-0307
PACER (Public Access to Court Electronic Records):
District Court ....(512) 229-4149
Chief Bankruptcy Judge: Larry E. Kelly ....(512) 482-5875
PACER (Public Access to Court Electronic Records):
Bankruptcy Court ....(512) 229-5211
VCIS (Voice Case Information System):
Bankruptcy Court ....(512) 229-4023
Chief Probation Officer:
Harvey H. Whitehill, Jr. ....(512) 229-6590
Federal Public Defender:
Lucien B. Campbell, B-207 Federal Building, Hemisfair Plaza, 727 E. Durango Boulevard, San Antonio, TX 78206 ....(512) 229-6700
Divisional Office:
Federal Building, Suite D-401, 700 E. San Antonio, El Paso, TX 79901 ....(915) 534-6525
Death Penalty Resource Center/Community Defender Organization: Robert G. McGlasson, Director, Texas Appellate Practice & Education Resource Center, 511 West 7th St, Austin, TX 78701 ....(512) 320-8300

U.S. District Court-Utah
U.S. Courthouse, 350 South Main Street, Salt Lake City, UT 84101

Chief Judge: Bruce S. Jenkins ....(801) 524-5167
District Clerk: Markus B. Zimmer ....(801) 524-5160
PACER (Public Access to Court Electronic Records):
District Court ....(801) 524-5662
Chief Bankruptcy Judge: Glen E. Clark ....(801) 524-6549
Bankruptcy Clerk: William C. Stillgebauer ....(801) 524-5157
Chief Probation Officer: Terry F. Callahan .....(801) 524-5176

U.S. District Court-Vermont
P.O. Box 945, Burlington, VT 05402

Chief Judge: Franklin S. Billings, Jr. ....(802) 773-0241
District Clerk: Leonard W. Lafayette ....(802) 951-6301
Divisional Office:
P.O. Box 607, Rutland, VT 05701 ....(802) 773-0245
Bankruptcy Judge: Francis G. Conrad ....(802) 773-0219
Bankruptcy Clerk: Thomas J. Hart ....(802) 773-0219
Chief Probation Officer: James M. Dean ....(802) 951-6304

U.S. District Court-Virgin Islands
P.O. Box 720, Charlotte Amalie, St. Thomas, U.S. VI 00801

Chief Judge: (vacant) ....(809) 744-0640
District Clerk: Orinn Arnold ....(809) 774-0640
Divisional Office:
P.O. Box 3439, Christiansted, St. Croix, VI 00820 ....(809) 773-1130
Chief Probation Officer: Lionel A. Todman ....(809) 774-4821
Federal Public Defender:
Robert L. Tucker, P.O. Box 3450, Christiansted, St. Croix, VI 00820 ....(809) 773-3585
Divisional Office:
P.O. Box 720, Charlotte Amalie, St. Thomas, VI 00801 ....(809) 774-4449

U.S. District Court-Eastern District of Virginia
P.O. Box 21449, 200 South Washington Street, Alexandria, VA 22320

Chief Judge: Albert V. Bryan, Jr. ....(703) 549-5050
District Clerk: Doris R. Casey ....(703) 557-5127
Divisional Offices:
P.O. Box 494, Newport News, VA 23607 ....(804) 244-0539
193 U.S. Courthouse, 600 Granby Street, Norfolk, VA 23510 ....(804) 441-6677
P.O. Box 2-AD, Richmond, VA 23205 ....(804) 782-2611
Chief Bankruptcy Judge:
Martin V.B. Bostetter, Jr. ....(703) 557-3867
Bankruptcy Clerk: Robert M. Wily, Jr. ....(804) 771-2878
VCIS (Voice Case Information System):
Bankruptcy Court ....(804) 771-2736
Chief Probation Officer: George Becouvarakis ....(804) 441-6673

U.S. District Court-Western District of Virginia
P.O. Box 1234, Roanoke, VA 24006

Chief Judge: James C. Turk ....(703) 982-6216
District Clerk: Joyce F. Witt ....(703) 982-6224
Divisional Offices:
P.O. Box 398, Abingdon, VA 24210 ....(703) 628-5116
P.O. Box 490, Big Stone Gap, VA 24219 ....(703) 523-3557
255 W. Main Street, Room 304, Charlottesville, VA 22901 ....(804) 296-9284
P.O. Box 52, Danville, VA 24540 ....(703) 793-7147
P.O. Box 1207, Harrisonburg, VA 22801 ....(703) 434-3181
P.O. Box 744, Lynchburg, VA 24505 ....(804) 847-5722
Chief Bankruptcy Judge: H. Clyde Pearson ....(703) 982-6391
Bankruptcy Clerk: John W.L. Craig II ....(703) 982-6391
Chief Probation Officer:
Brice E. Johnston, Jr. ....(703) 982-6281

U.S. District Court-Eastern District of Washington

P.O. Box 1493, Spokane, WA 99210

Chief Judge: Justin L. Quackenbush ....(509) 353-2180
District Clerk: James R. Larsen ....(509) 353-2150
Chief Bankruptcy Judge: John M. Klobucher ......(509) 353-2110
Bankruptcy Clerk: Theodore S. McGregor ....(509) 353-2404
Chief Probation Officer: Robert D. Banta ....(509) 353-2382

U.S. District Court-Western District of Washington

U.S. Courthouse, 1010 Fifth Avenue, Seattle, WA 98104

Chief Judge: Barbara J. Rothstein ....(206) 442-2740
District Clerk: Bruce Rifkin ....(206) 442-5598
Divisional Office:
P.O. Box 1935, Tacoma, WA 98401 ....(206) 593-6313
Chief Bankruptcy Judge: Samuel J. Steiner ....(206) 442-1628
Bankruptcy Clerk: Lewis P. Stephenson ....(206) 442-2751
VCIS (Voice Case Information System):
Bankruptcy Court ....(206) 442-8543
Chief Probation Officer: Robert B. Lee ....(206) 442-7435
Federal Public Defender:
Thomas W. Hillier II, 1111 Third Avenue, Suite 380,
Seattle, WA 98101 ....(206) 442-1100
Divisional Office:
800 A Street, Room 205, Anchorage, AK 99501 ..(907) 271-2277

U.S. District Court-Northern District of West Virginia

P.O. Box 1518, Elkins, WV 26241

Chief Judge: Robert Earl Maxwell ....(304) 636-5198
District Clerk: Wally A. Edgell ....(304) 636-1445
Divisional Offices:
P.O. Box 2857, Clarksburg, WV 26302 ....(304) 622-8513
P.O. Box 471, Wheeling, WV 26003 ....(304) 232-0011
Chief Bankruptcy Judge: L. Edward Friend II .....(304) 233-1655
Bankruptcy Clerk: Michael D. Sturm ....(304) 233-1655
Chief Probation Officer: James F. Ancell ....(304) 636-7277

U.S. District Court-Southern District of West Virginia

P.O. Box 2546, Charleston, WV 25329

Chief Judge: Charles H. Haden II ....(304) 420-6480
District Clerk: Ronald D. Lawson ....(304) 342-5154
Divisional Offices:
Federal Station, Box 4128, Bluefield, WV 27702 (304) 327-9798
P.O. Box 1570, Huntington, WV 25716 ....(304) 529-5588
P.O. Box 1526, Parkersburg, WV 26102 ....(304) 420-6490
1002 Federal Building, Woodlawn & Neville Streets,
Beckley, WV 25801 ....(304) 253-7481
Chief Bankruptcy Judge: Ronald G. Pearson ....(304) 347-5291
Bankruptcy Clerk: Samuel L. Kay ....(304) 347-5114
VCIS (Voice Case Information System):
Bankruptcy Court ....(304) 347-5337
Chief Probation Officer: James D. Wilmoth ......(304) 347-5110
Federal Public Defender:
Ira R. Kirkendoll, 2307 Federal Building, 500
Quarrier Street, Charleston WV 25301 ...(304) 343-9551

U.S. District Court-Eastern District of Wisconsin

U.S. Courthouse, 517 East Wisconsin Avenue, Milwaukee, WI 53202

Chief Judge: Robert W. Warren ....(414) 297-1475
District Clerk: Sofron B. Nedilsky ....(414) 297-3372
Chief Bankruptcy Judge:
Charles N. Clevert, Jr. ....(414) 297-1586
Bankruptcy Clerk: Betty J. Small ....(414) 297-3293
Chief Probation Officer: Trudi A. Schmitt ....(414) 297-1425

U.S. District Court-Western District of Wisconsin

P.O. Box 432, Madison, WI 53701

Chief Judge: Barbara B. Crabb ....(608) 264-5447
District Clerk: Joseph W. Skupniewitz ....(608) 264-5156
Chief Bankruptcy Judge: Robert D. Martin ....(608) 264-5188
Bankruptcy Clerk: Ann B. Manley ....(608) 264-5178
Chief Probation Officer: Jack B. Verhagen ....(608) 264-5175

U.S. District Court-Wyoming

P.O. Box 727, Cheyenne, WY 82001

Chief Judge: Clarence A. Brimmer ....(307) 634-6072
District Clerk: William C. Beaman ....(307) 772-2145
Chief Bankruptcy Judge: Harold L. Mai ....(307) 772-2114
Bankruptcy Clerk: Joyce W. Harris ....(307) 772-2191
Chief Probation Officer: Robert E. Bonham ....(307) 772-2317

PUBLICATIONS OF INTEREST

The following publication(s) can be purchased from the **U.S. Government Printing Office.** Stock numbers and prices for annual subscriptions are shown below. Submit requests for these publications to: The Superintendent of Documents, U.S. Government Printing Office, Washington, D.C. 20402. (202/783-3238).

Rules of Civil Procedure for the United States District Courts, with Forms, 1989. Price: $3.75 domestic, $4.69 foreign. GPO Stock# 052-070-06589-3.

Rules of Criminal Procedure for the United States District Courts, December 1, 1989. Price: $2.25 domestic, $2.81 foreign. GPO Stock# 052-070-06619-9.

ADMINISTRATIVE OFFICE OF THE U.S. COURTS
811 Vermont Avenue, N.W.
Washington, D.C. 20544

DESCRIPTION: Under the direction of the Judicial Conference of the U.S, which is headed by the Chief Justice of the Supreme Court, the Administrative Office of the U.S. Courts provides program management and administrative services and support to all of the U.S. Courts except the Supreme Court. The programs administered include the Federal Bankruptcy Court System, the Magistrates System, the Federal Probation System, and the Federal Public Defender System. The Administrative Office also provides support in financial management, including budget administration fund accounting and financial accounting auditing, personnel management, statistical reporting and analysis, procurement, space and facilities management, and library management. In addition, the agency provides legal advice and counsel to the courts.

The Administrative Office receives reports from and exercises some degree of supervision over the clerical staffs of the courts, the probation officers, bankruptcy judges, U.S. Magistrates, reporters and other court personnel; audits and disburses money for the operation of the courts; compiles and publishes statistics on the volume and distribution of the business of the courts; supplies a professional secretariat and legal and statistical services to committees of the Judicial Conference of the U.S.; and conducts studies of courts procedures under the direction of and for the Judicial Conference, and for other interested groups including committees of the Congress.

(Area Code 202)

Director: L. Ralph Mecham 633-6097
General Counsel: William R. Burchill, Jr. 633-6127
Deputy General Counsel: Robert K. Loesche 633-6127
Bankruptcy Division Chief: Francis F. Szczebak 633-6231
Contracts and Services Division Chief:
Ralph J. Simmons 633-6117
Court Administration Division Chief:
Duane R. Lee 633-6478
Defender Services Division Chief:
Theodore J. Lidz 633-6051
Magistrates Division Chief: John Thomas Jones 633-6251
Probation Division Chief: Donald L. Chamlee 633-6226
Statistical Analysis and Reports Division 633-6094
Legislative and Public Affairs Office 633-6040
Legal Research and Library Services Chief:
Pat Thomas 633-6314

Library 633-6104
The library is open for reference by appointment only.

PUBLICATIONS OF INTEREST

Report of the Proceedings of the Judicial Conference of the United States and Annual Report of the Director of the Administrative Office of the U.S. Courts. Published annually. Available for reference at the Administrative Office of the U.S. Courts in Washington, D.C. and at Federal court libraries nationwide.

The Third Branch. A monthly newsletter that deals with various issues of interest and importance to the Federal court system. 12 pages. Available free of charge. To get on the mailing list, contact: Legislative and Public Affairs, Administrative Office of the U.S. Courts, 811 Vermont Avenue, N.W., Washington, D.C. 20544.

The following publications can be purchased from the **U.S. Government Printing Office.** Stock numbers and prices for annual subscriptions are shown below. Submit requests for these publications to: The Superintendent of Documents, U.S. Government Printing Office, Washington, D.C. 20402. (202/783-3238).

U.S. Court Directory. Published twice a year, this directory contains the names, addresses, and phone numbers of Federal court personnel nationwide. Latest edition published Spring 1990. Price: $21.00. GPO Stock# 028-004-00076-1.

Federal Probation: A Journal of Correctional Philosophy and Practice. A quarterly publication containing articles relating to preventive and correctional activities in delinquency and crime. Price: $5.00 a year domestic; $6.25 a year foreign. GPO Stock# 727-001-00000-0.

FEDERAL JUDICIAL CENTER
1520 H Street, N.W.
Washington, D.C. 20005

DESCRIPTION: The Federal Judicial Center is designed to improve judicial administration in the courts of the U.S. To that end, it: conducts research on the operation of the courts; coordinates similar research being undertaken by other entities; and is responsible for programs of continuing education and training for judges and personnel of the Judicial Branch of the Government.

The 23 staff attorneys provide research and support to Federal judges and court personnel nationwide, and participate in the many orientation and continuing education/training programs developed and administered by the Center. They also assist in developing educational and training materials, drafting monographs and other publications on issues of interest to the Center's constituencies, and disseminating information on court innovations to the Federal judiciary.

(Area Code 202)

Director: John C. Godbold 633-6311
Continuing Education and Training Division:
Director: Daniel L. Skoler 633-6332
Legal Services Training Branch:
Chief: Charles S. Arberg 633-6032

(Area Code 202)

Inter-Judicial Affairs & Information Services
Division Director: Alice L. O'Donnell 633-6347
Information Specialist: Leonard E. Klein 633-6365

PUBLICATIONS OF INTEREST

The Federal Judicial Center has published over 220 documents since its creation in 1967. Its free 1990 catalog lists 148 of these as still being available. The Center's publications include reports of research and analysis done by or for the Center, as well as products of Center seminars and workshops conducted for various third branch personnel. These publications are available from the Center's Information Services Office. Some, however, are available only to certain groups within the Federal judiciary; these are clearly noted in the catalog. Most of the publications published by the Center are free. When requesting publications, enclose a self-addressed mailing label to expedite receipt of the requested material. Some of the recent publications of the Center include:

Trends in Asbestos Litigation. Thomas E. Willging, 1987, 138 pages.

Settlement Strategies for Federal District Judges. D. Marie Provine, 1986, 103 pages.

Patent Law and Practice. Herbert F. Schwartz, 1988, 119 pages.

Major Issues in Immigration Law. David A. Martin, 1987, 147 pages.

Major Issues in the Federal Law Of Employment Discrimination. George Rutherglen, 1987, 150 pages.

Handbook on Jury Use in the Federal District Courts. Jody George, Deirdre Golash, and Russell Wheeler, 1989, 93 pages.

Unpublished Dispositions: Problems of Access and Use in the Courts of Appeals. Donna Stienstra, 1985, 75 pages.

Federal Judicial Center Annual Report 1989. The Annual Report describes the organization and activities of the Federal Judicial Center. It also contains a list of publications released in 1989 or scheduled for release early in 1990. 29 pages.

Other Legal Offices

LEGAL SERVICES CORPORATION

400 Virginia Avenue, S.W.
Washington, D.C. 20024-2751

DESCRIPTION: The Legal Services Corporation is a private, non-profit corporation established in 1974 for the purpose of providing financial support for legal assistance in non-criminal matters to persons unable to afford legal assistance. Executive direction for the Corporation is provided by an eleven-member Board of Directors, all of whom are appointed by the President. The staff of the headquarters office is located in Washington, D.C. attorneys. Most of these attorneys are in the Office of General Counsel, the Office of Field Services, and the Office of Monitoring, Audit and Compliance. However, attorneys can also be found in the Office of the President, and in the Office of Policy Development and Communications.

(Area Code 202)
President: (vacant) 863-1839
Vice-President: Timothy B. Shea 863-1839

(Area Code 202)
General Information 863-1820
Facsimile 863-1859

OFFICE OF GENERAL COUNSEL

The Office of the General Counsel provides legal and policy advice to the Board of Directors and Corporate officers. Responsibilities include reviewing and preparing memoranda, briefs, contracts, and reports; negotiating and drafting contracts, leases, and other legal instruments; and representing the Corporation in administrative hearings and civil litigation.

(Area Code 202)
General Counsel: Timothy B. Shea 863-1823
Deputy General Counsel: Victor Fortuno 863-1823
Senior Litigation Counsel: John Pensinger, Sr 863-1823
Senior Counsel, Operations and Regulations:
Suzanne Glasow 863-1823

(Area Code 202)
Assistant General Counsel: Carolyn Kennedy 863-1823
Staff Attorneys:
Laurie Tarantowicz 863-1823
J. Kelly Martin 863-1823

OFFICE OF INSPECTOR GENERAL

The Office of Inspector General provides policy direction for and conducts, supervises, and coordinates audits and investigations relating to recipient programs of the Legal Services Corporation. Responsibilities include recommending policies for, and conducting or coordinating the following: other activities carried out or financed by Legal Services Corporation for the purpose of promoting economy and efficiency in the administration of, or preventing and detecting fraud and abuse in, its programs and operations; and relationships between the Legal Services Corporation and other Federal agencies, state and local governmental agencies, and nongovernmental entities.

(Area Code 202)
Inspector General: David Wilkinson....863-1821
Chief Deputy Inspector General: Sam Blesie....863-1821

(Area Code 202)
Deputy Inspector General: Dean Reuter....863-1821

OFFICE OF FIELD SERVICES

The Office of Field Services reviews, analyzes, and develops regulations and guidelines for program oversight; establishes standards of performance for recipients of Corporation funds; and monitors the performance of Legal Services programs.

(Area Code 202)
Director: Ellen J. Smead....863-1837
Associate Director: Charles Moses....863-1837

(Area Code 202)
Grants and Budget Division
Manager: Phyllis Doriot 863-1837

OFFICE OF MONITORING, AUDIT AND COMPLIANCE

The Office of Monitoring, Audit and Compliance designs and implements systems to monitor and audit program activities, ensuring compliance with Corporate guidelines and regulations.

LEGAL SERVICES CORPORATION

(Area Code 202)

Director: Emilia DiSanto 863-1853

Audit Division
Manager: Patricia Batie 863-4086

Compliance Division
Manager: Susan Sparks 863-1835

(Area Code 202)

Monitoring Division
Manager: Susan Sparks 863-1835

Review and Analysis Division
Manager: Susan Sparks 863-1835

OFFICE OF POLICY DEVELOPMENT AND COMMUNICATIONS

The Office of Policy Development and Communications develops and implements operational policies and practices for the Division of Policy Development.

(Area Code 202)

Director: Ken Boehm....................................863-1839

OFFICE OF HUMAN RESOURCES/EQUAL OPPORTUNITY

(Area Code 202)

Director: Alice Dickerson..............................863-1847

(Area Code 202)

Equal Opportunity Administrator: Shelia Williams........863-1847

MONITORING OFFICES

These offices oversee the grantee programs and the allocation of resources within these programs.

Northeast (Headquarters) Regional Office

Manager: Susan Sparks
Legal Services Corporation, Monitoring Division, 400 Virginia Avenue, S.W., Washington, D.C. 20024. Tel: 202/863-1835.

Southern Regional Office

Regional Office Administrator: Robert Millen
Legal Services Corporation, Southern Regional Office, 615 Peachtree Street, N.E., Suite 916, Atlanta, GA 30308. Tel: 404/347-7647.

Mid-West Regional Office

Regional Officer: (vacant)
Legal Services Corporation, Mid-West Regional Office, 53 West Jackson Blvd, Suite 1005, Chicago, IL 60604. Tel: 312/353-0350.

Rocky Mountain Regional Office

Regional Officer: (vacant)
Legal Services Corporation, Rocky Mountain Regional Office, 1380 Lawrence Street, Suite 850, Denver, CO 80204. Tel: 303/844-4290.

Pacific Regional Office

Regional Office Administrator: Jack Walker
Legal Services Corporation, Pacific Regional Office, 1330 Broadway, Suite 1444, Oakland, CA 94612. Tel: 415/273-6415.

Native American Unit

Manager: (vacant)
Legal Services Corporation, Native American Unit, 1380 Lawrence Street, Suite 850, Denver, CO 80204. Tel: 303/844-4205.

LEGAL SERVICES PROGRAM NATIONAL SUPPORT CENTERS

The Legal Services Corporation has 16 national support centers which provide a variety of specialized services to promote quality representation of the poor on issues of substantial complexity. The subject areas covered by the centers include the most important areas of legal services practice, as well as the special legal needs of certain client populations.

Center staffs have in-depth knowledge of the particular program areas in which they specialize, and are experienced in the interpretation of regulations, statutory provisions, and judicial decisions applicable to the programs in the centers' areas of concern. They maintain extensive libraries containing materials necessary for effective representation in the centers' specialties that are not generally available to the field.

Professional staff members are experienced in litigation, administrative agency, and legislative procedures, which are often so complex that the general practitioner is precluded from presenting a client's case effectively without assistance. Center litigation expertise is especially useful on matters of strategy or technique unique to the particular substantive law or client group in which the center specializes. The number of attorneys working at each center varies from 1-11, depending on the size of the staff.

Since its beginning, national support has been one of many important means by which the Legal Services Corporation has sought to fulfill Congress's purpose to make high quality and economical legal assistance available to the poor.

The 16 national support centers are:

NATIONAL CONSUMER LAW CENTER, INC.

Executive Director: Willard P. Ogburn
11 Beacon Street, Suite 821, Boston, MA 02108.
Tel: 617/523-8010.

Washington Office:
Contact Person: Charles E. Hill
Congressional House, 236 Massachusetts Avenue, N.E., Washington, D.C. 20002. Tel: 202/543-6060.

The National Consumer Law Center, whose principal office is in Boston, works in both the consumer and energy areas. Subjects covered include bankruptcy, banking practices, class actions, collection agencies, credit cards, debt collection, deceptive trade practices, garnishment, health and hospital collections, health spas, installment contracts, insurance, repossession, small claims courts, student loans, Truth-in-Lending, used cars, vocational schools, energy assistance programs, HUD utility issues, Lifeline programs, utility rate increases, and utility service termination.

NATIONAL LEGAL CENTER FOR MEDICALLY DEPENDENT AND DISABLED, INC.

Director: James Bopp, Jr.
P.O. Box 1586, Terre Haute, IN 46808-1586. Tel: 317/632-6245.

The National Legal Center provides support, technical assistance, and training to legal services and pro bono attorneys representing critically ill infants, adults, and persons with disabilities who are at risk from discrimination in the delivery of beneficial medical treatment. Treatment decisions for persons who are disabled or medically dependent involve interdisciplinary issues requiring specialized knowledge and experience.

NATIONAL ECONOMIC DEVELOPMENT AND LAW CENTER

Director: James W. Head
1950 Addison Street, Suite 200, Berkeley, CA 94704.
Tel: 415/548-2600.

Washington Office:
Contact Person: Perry Stewart
1815 H Street, N.W., Suite 700, Washington, D.C. 20006.
Tel: 202/659-0040.

The National Economic Development and Law Center provides assistance to legal services employees, eligible client organizations/individuals, and private bar members who are working with eligible client organizations/individuals engaged in some aspect of community and economic development. The Center receives funds from the Legal Services Corporation and the Ford Foundation, as well as a number of smaller grants and contracts. The concept of community and economic development encompasses a wide range of activities and programs, including: a tenant's group organizing to secure Community Development Block Grant funds to undertake housing rehabilitation; senior citizens developing cottage industry ventures; poor people forming and operating a credit union; farmworkers developing an agricultural co-op; or a tribe of Native Americans developing a shopping center. Community economic development programs aim at total community upgrading rather than individual financial gain.

CENTER FOR LAW AND EDUCATION, INC.

Executive Director: Paul Newman
955 Massachusetts Avenue, Suite 3-A, Cambridge, MA 02139.
Tel: 617/876-6611.

Washington Office:
Contact Person: Paul Weckstein
236 Massachusetts Avenue, N.E., Suite 504, Washington, D.C. 20002. Tel: 202/546-5300.

The Center for Law and Education provides support services on education issues to advocates working on behalf of low-income students and parents. Primary areas of Center attention include: special education, school discipline, vocational education, Chapter I (compensatory education), limited English proficiency/bilingual education, higher education, testing/tracking, and the educational rights of homeless children. The problem of racial discrimination in schools is addressed frequently as it arises in the context of the priority areas listed above.

NATIONAL EMPLOYMENT LAW PROJECT, INC.

Director: Barbara A. Morris
475 Riverside Drive, Suite 240, New York, NY 10115.
Tel: 212/870-2121.

The National Employment Law Project (NELP) provides a variety of litigation and support services to all local legal services programs, as well as to eligible pro bono private attorneys. Current priority areas for the Project include: unemployment compensation, employment discrimination, wrongful discharge, employment testing, wages/hours, and public employment.

NATIONAL CENTER ON WOMEN AND FAMILY LAW, INC.

Director: Laurie Woods
799 Broadway, Room 402, New York, NY 10003. Tel: 212/674-8200.

The National Center on Women and Family Law (NCOWFL) is the national legal services support center on poor women's issues in family law. It provides legal expertise, information, and legal assistance to legal services and pro bono attorneys handling cases dealing with issues such as civil and criminal protection for battered women, battered women and custody/visitation, child custody/support, child support enforcement, division of property, incest and custody/visitation, interstate custody disputes, parental kidnapping, paternity, and mediation of family law disputes.

FOOD RESEARCH AND ACTION CENTER

Director: Robert J. Fersh
1319 F Street, N.W., Suite 500, Washington, D.C. 20004.
Tel: 202/393-5060.

Since 1970, The Food Research and Action Center (FRAC) has served as a nonpartisan center seeking lasting solutions to hunger, malnutrition, and poverty in America. Major areas of concentration involve the Federal food programs, and women, infants and children (WIC) programs. In addition, FRAC also engages in litigation, assists community and religious groups concerned about hunger, provides targeted research on nutrition and health issues affecting lower income people, and offers legal advice and technical assistance to Legal Services offices throughout the country.

NATIONAL HEALTH LAW PROGRAM, INC.

Director: Laurence M. Lavin
2639 South La Cienega Boulevard, Los Angeles, CA 90034.
Tel: 213/204-6010.

Washington Office:
Contact Person: Judith Waxman
2025 M Street, N.W., Suite 400, Washington, D.C. 20036.
Tel: 202/887-5310.

Since 1969, the National Health Law Program (NHeLP) has represented the poor, minorities, and the aged in their quest for equity and non-discrimination in Federal, state, local, and private health care programs. NHeLP attorneys work with a wide range of health care issues affecting the poor, primarily assisting local legal services attorneys and non-legal services attorneys who are representing eligible clients. Areas of concentration include: civil rights (segregation or denial of access in health care facilities, bilingual services, AIDS); health care financing reform; Hill-Burton (administrative complaint monitoring, emergency room access, collection defense, nursing home access of Medicaid eligibles); maternal and child health; Medicaid/Medicare; private insurance (policy coverage issues, COBRA continuation); and public hospitals (reimbursements, cutbacks, closures).

NATIONAL HOUSING LAW PROJECT

Program Director: Frances E. Werner
1950 Addison Street, Suite 200, Berkeley, CA 94704.
Tel: 415/548-9400.

Washington Office:
Contact Person: Antoinette McLeod
122 C Street, N.W., Suite 875, Washington, D.C. 20002-2109.
Tel: 202/783-5140.

The National Housing Law Project (NHLP) provides back-up and assistance to local legal services attorneys and paralegals on issues related to publicly assisted and private housing, community development, and other housing-related issues. Typical requests for assistance involve private landlord/tenant problems, Section 8 issues, public housing problems, and FHA subsidized and multifamily housing matters.

NATIONAL CENTER FOR IMMIGRANTS' RIGHTS

Director: Katharine Krause
Legal Aid Foundation of Los Angeles, 1550 West Eighth Street, Los Angeles, CA 90017. Tel: 213/487-2531.

The National Center for Immigrants Rights (NCIR) provides backup assistance to legal serves programs and other nonprofit agencies on issues involving immigration law and aliens' rights. The NCIR staff specializes in areas relating to visa processing, legalization, defenses to deportation, and aliens' eligibility for public benefit programs. Other areas of expertise include constitutional challenges to actions of the Immigration and Naturalization Service (INS) and specific responses to INS misconduct.

NATIONAL CENTER FOR YOUTH LAW

Director: John Francis O'Toole
114 Sansome Street, Suite 900, San Francisco, CA 94104-3820.
Tel: 415/543-3307.

The National Center for Youth Law (NCYL) was established in 1970 to provide specialized assistance to local legal services programs. The Center's attorneys are familiar with a wide range of substantive areas of law that affect the well-being of poor children and adolescents. Particular areas of expertise include foster care; children's and adolescents' health; public benefits for children; access to housing for families with children; abuse, neglect, and termination of parental rights; and the special problems of children and adolescents who live in institutions.

MIGRANT LEGAL ACTION PROGRAM, INC.

Director: Roger C. Rosenthal
2001 S Street, N.W., Suite 310, Washington, D.C. 20009.
Tel: 202/462-7744.

Since 1970, the Migrant Legal Action Program (MLAP) has provided legal representation to migrant and seasonal farmworkers, the poorest group of working people in America. Subject matter priorities include: the Migrant and Seasonal Agricultural Worker Protection Act, the Fair Labor Standards Act, pesticides and occupational safety, the H-2A Foreign Worker Program, income transfer programs and taxes, employment rights, migrant education, migrant housing, and assistance to eligible organizations.

INDIAN LAW SUPPORT CENTER

Director: Steven C. Moore
Native American Rights Fund, 1506 Broadway, Boulder, CO 80302.
Tel: 303/447-8760.

Washington Office:
Directing Attorney: Henry Sokbeson
Native American Rights Fund, 1712 N Street, N.W., Washington, D.C. 20036. Tel: 202/785-4166.

Alaska Office:
Directing Attorney: Lawrence Aschenbrenner
Native American Rights Fund, 310 K Street, Suite 708, Anchorage, AK 99501. Tel: 907/276-0680.

The Native American Rights Fund (NARF) operates the Indian Law Support Center (ILSC) which provides backup legal assistance to legal services programs serving Indians on reservations, in rural communities, and in urban areas throughout the country. Because these two organizations are so interrelated, they share the same priorities, which are: preserving Indian tribal existence, including Indian religion, Indian customs, and treaties; protecting Indian tribal resources, including enforcing Federal trust responsibilities; assisting in the protection of human rights of Indian people, including education, health, and prison reform; ensuring accountability for Indian people on the part of tribal, Federal, state, and local governments; and working for the development of Indian law.

NATIONAL SENIOR CITIZENS LAW CENTER

Executive Director: Burton Fretz
2025 M Street, N.W., Suite 400, Washington, D.C. 20036.
Tel: 202/887-5280.

Los Angeles Office:
Deputy Director: Neal Dudovitz
1052 West 6th Street, Suite 700, Los Angeles, CA 90017.
Tel: 213/482-3550.

The National Senior Citizens Law Center (NSCLC) was established in 1972 to help older Americans live their lives in dignity and freedom from poverty. NSCLC attorneys are conversant on a broad range of legal areas and practice matters that affect the security and welfare of older persons of limited income. Subjects covered include: Social Security and SSI; Medicare/Medicaid; nursing home residents' rights; alternatives to institutionalization; private pensions; public pensions; age discrimination and mandatory retirement; Older Americans Act services; and protective services.

NATIONAL VETERANS LEGAL SERVICES PROJECT, INC.

Co-Director: Barton F. Stichman
Co-Director: David F. Addlestone
2001 S Street, N.W., Suite 702, Washington, D.C. 20009.
Tel: 202/265-8305.

The National Veterans Legal Services Project (NVLSP) was established in 1981 following a Legal Services Corporation study on access and legal problems of veterans and other groups. Staff members are familiar with a wide range of substantive areas of law that affect veterans and their dependents. Particular areas of expertise include the service-connected disability benefit system, non-service connected disability benefits, and other programs administered by the Department of Veterans Affairs; VA application and appellate procedures; VA advocacy; government collection or recoupment of alleged overpayments of VA benefits; foreclosure of VA-guaranteed homes; military charge upgrading; and correction of military and VA records.

CENTER ON SOCIAL WELFARE POLICY AND LAW

Director: Henry A. Freedman
95 Madison Avenue, Room 701, New York, NY 10016.
Tel: 212/679-3709.

Washington Office:
Contact Person: Adele Blong
1029 Vermont Avenue, N.W., Suite 850, Washington, D.C. 20005.
Tel: 202/347-5615.

The Center on Social Welfare Policy and Law, located in New York City and Washington, D.C., was founded in 1965 to work on issues relating to government benefit programs for the poor. The Center focuses on means-tested cash public assistance programs and is the only national legal organization that deals exclusively with these programs: Aid to Families with Dependent Children (AFDC), Supplemental Security Income (SSI), and state and local general assistance programs, including state programs supplementing SSI benefits.

NATIONAL CLEARINGHOUSE FOR LEGAL SERVICES, INC.

Program Director: Michael Leonard
407 South Dearborn, Suite 400, Chicago, IL 60605.
Tel: 312/939-3830.

The National Clearinghouse for Legal Services, Inc., provides informational support services in a timely and complete manner to legal services case handling staff and others representing the poor. Its objective is to promote the concept of "equal access to justice for all" by helping such representatives be more efficient and effective in their representation of the poor. This goal is accomplished by offering a wide variety of legal information services to legal services programs funded by the Legal Services Corporation and through the Administration on Aging and to others, including private bar involvement programs and law schools, which directly represent and advise low-income persons.

LEGAL SERVICES GRANTEE PROGRAMS

The approximately 325 Legal Services grantee programs, located throughout the continental U.S., Guam, Micronesia, Puerto Rico, and the Virgin Islands, currently employ thousands of attorneys. Staff attorneys in these programs provide legal services to eligible clients in such areas as consumer, housing, employment, public benefits, disability benefits, education, and health law; environmental law; domestic relations and family law; veterans rights; juvenile and senior citizens law; migrant farmworker problems and immigration law; and Native American issues. Individual programs usually emphasize selected poverty law areas in response to the legal needs of the client community they serve. In addition to handling individual caseloads, staff attorneys may also participate in community education, legislative/administrative advocacy, and complex litigation.

PUBLICATIONS OF INTEREST

The following publications can be purchased from **The National Clearinghouse for Legal Services.** Submit requests for these publications to: The National Clearinghouse for Legal Services, 407 South Dearborn, Suite 400, Chicago, IL 60605. Tel: 312/939-3830.

The Clearinghouse Review. This monthly (except for a combined August/September issue) legal journal deals with articles and case developments in poverty law. Price: There is no charge for any attorney or paralegal who is part of a Legal Services program (it must be ordered through the program, not individually). The cost for a subscription is $75.00 a year for everyone else. Single copies cost $6.00 each.

Federal Register Highlights newsletter. Published twice a month. It summarizes final and proposed rules and other items in the Federal Register that affect the poor. Price: $50.00 a year. No single copies sold.

Annotated Bibliography of Federal Legal Databases and Publications

ANNOTATED BIBLIOGRAPHY OF FEDERAL LEGAL DATABASES AND PUBLICATIONS

TOPICS

EXECUTIVE BRANCH

General Government
General Government: Federal Records
Advisory Opinions of the U.S. Department of Justice
Agriculture
Alcohol, Tobacco and Firearms
Antitrust
Banking
Business and Commerce: General
Business and Commerce: International Trade
Civil Rights/Equal Rights
Communications
Consumer Protection
Contracts/Procurement
Criminal Justice
Customs
Decisions of Administrative Adjudicative Bodies
Decisions of Boards of Contract Appeals
Defense/Military
Domestic Relations
Elections
Energy/Nuclear Energy
Environment
Ethics
Freedom of Information/Privacy
Health and Medicine
Housing
Immigration
Interior and Natural Resources
International Relations/Foreign Affairs
Labor
Legal Services
Parole/Probation
Patents, Trademarks, and Copyrights
Pensions
Personnel Management
Safety and Health
Science, Space and Technology
Securities/Commodities
Social Security/Medicare
Taxes
Transportation
U.S. Attorneys
Veterans

LEGISLATIVE BRANCH

JUDICIAL BRANCH

EXECUTIVE BRANCH

GENERAL GOVERNMENT

Directory of U.S. Government Depository Libraries. Addresses for more than 1,400 U.S. libraries that maintain or have access to Federal government documents. 1989. Available from Consumer Information Center-P, P.O. Box 100, Pueblo, CO 81002. Free. If you order two or more free publications, include a check for $1.00 payable to Superintendent of Documents. Booklet number 570W.

* * * * * * * * * * * *

The U.S. Government publishes thousands of documents, all of which may be ordered directly from the **Superintendent of Documents, U.S. Government Printing Office (GPO), Washington, D.C.**, or from any of the regional GPO bookstores. Orders may be paid by check (made out to the Superintendent of Documents) or charged to a Visa or Master Card. GPO stock numbers and prices are shown below. Submit requests for these publications to: The Superintendent of Documents, U.S. Government Printing Office, Washington, D.C. 20402. Phone orders are accepted Monday through Friday from 7:30 AM to 4:00 PM. Tel: 202/783-3238.

To obtain a current list of GPO publications, customers can subscribe to the Monthly Catalog of United States Government Publications (information on all publications issued on a monthly basis). The annual rate is $167.00 or $26.00 per single copy.

Government Periodicals and Subscription Services, issued quarterly, provides information on publications sold by subscription, including the Federal Register and the Congressional Record. Single issues are free of charge.

U.S. Government Books, issued three times a year, contains information on over 1,000 new and frequently ordered GPO publications. Single issues are free of charge.

Certain Government publications sold by the Superintendent of Documents and produced in electronic format are available in magnetic tape form. **Publication tapes** may be purchased on an individual tape basis or as a subscription service. Included among the individual publication tapes available are: the Budget of the United States; the Congressional Directory; the Statistical Abstract; the Government Manual; the Congressional Record; and the Federal Register. Prices for individual tapes are $125.00 per tape except for the Federal Register and the Congressional Record which are $175 per tape. (Prices are per tape not per title. A title may consist of multiple tapes.)

Subscription services currently available on tape are: the Congressional Record; the Code of Federal Regulations; the Federal Communications Commission Records; the Federal Register; the Monthly Catalog of United States Government Publications; and Daily Bills. For price information call 202/783-3238.

Federal Register. Published daily, Monday through Friday, except Federal holidays. Provides a uniform system for making available to the public regulations and legal notices issued by Federal agencies. These include Presidential proclamations and Executive Orders, Federal agency documents having general applicability and legal effect, documents required to be published by Act of Congress, and other Federal agency documents of public interest. Price (paperback): $340.00 a year domestic; $425.00 a year foreign. GPO Stock# 769-004-00000-9. Note: Subscribers to this service will automatically receive copies of the Federal Register Index (a cumulative monthly itemization of material published in the daily Federal Register), and the Code of Federal Regulations, LSA, List of CFR Sections Affected, at no additional cost.

Code of Federal Regulations, LSA, List of CFR Sections Affected. A monthly listing of amendatory actions published in the Federal Register. Entries indicate type of change. The December issue is the Annual for CFR Titles 1-16; the March issue is the Annual for CFR Titles 17-27; the June issue is the Annual for CFR Titles 28-41; the September issue is the Annual for CFR Titles 42-50. Subscribers to the daily Federal Register will receive this service automatically as part of that subscription. Price: $21.00 a year domestic; $26.25 a year foreign. No single copies sold. GPO Stock# 769-001-00000-0.

Code of Federal Regulations. Revised annually; issued irregularly. Codification of the general and permanent rules published in the Federal Register by the Executive departments and agencies of the Federal Government. Divided into 50 titles representing broad areas subject to Federal regulation. Price (paperback, approximately 175 books): $620.00 a year domestic; $775.00 foreign. Single copies vary in price. GPO Stock# 869-011-00000-2.

Public Laws. Published irregularly. A Public Law, often referred to as a "Slip Law," is the initial publication of a Federal law upon enactment and is printed as soon as possible after approval by the President. Some legislative references appear on each law. Price: $107.00 domestic per session of Congress; $133.75 foreign per session. GPO Stock# 869-010-00000-6.

United States Code (U.S.C.). The United States Code is arranged in 50 subject-matter titles. A new edition of the complete set of titles is published every six years, with cumulative supplements, published in separate volumes, issued during the intervening years. The U.S. Code represents a codification of all sections of the Revised Statutes and Statutes at Large in force. The entire United States Code is not prima facie evidence of the law for legal purposes. Rather, it is being submitted to Congress for enactment into positive law title by title, as revised by the Office of Law Revision Counsel of the U.S. House of Representatives. To date, 25 titles have been so enacted into positive law. It is important when citing the United States Code to determine (as indicated in the introductory material at the beginning of each title) if the title in question has been enacted into positive law. If not, the comparable sections of the Statutes at Large should also be cited, since those titles not enacted are not considered prima facie evidence of the law.

The 1988 edition of the United States Code, containing the general and permanent laws of the United States, in force on January 3, 1989, are:

Volume 1, Title 1 to Title 6. Contains Title 1, General Provisions; Title 2, The Congress; Title 3, The President; Title 4, Flag and Seal, Seat of Government, and the States; Title 5, Government Organization and Employees; and Title 6, Surety Bonds (Repealed). Price: $47.00. GPO Stock# 052-001-00310-1.

Volume 2, Title 7 to Title 9. Contains Title 7, Agriculture; Title 8, Aliens and Nationality; and Title 9, Arbitration. Price: $46.00. GPO Stock# 052-001-00311-0.

Volume 3, Title 10. Contains Title 10, Armed Forces. Price: $49.00. GPO Stock# 052-001-00312-8.

Volume 4, Title 11 to Title 12. Contains Title 11, Bankruptcy; and Title 12, Banks and Banking. Price: $47.00. GPO Stock# 052-001-00313-6.

Volume 5, Title 13 to Title 15. Contains 13, Census; Title 14, Coast Guard; and Title 15, Commerce and Trade. Price: $47.00. GPO Stock# 052-001-00314-4.

Volume 6, Title 16. Contains Title 16, Conservation. Price: $53.00. GPO Stock# 052-001-00315-2.

Volume 7, Title 17 to Tile 19. Contains Title 17, Copyrights; Title 18, Crimes and Criminal Procedure; and Title 19, Custom Duties. Price: $51.00. GPO Stock# 052-001-00316-1.

Volume 8, Title 20 to Title 21. Contains Title 20, Education, and Title 21, Food and Drugs. Price: $50.00. GPO Stock# 052-001-00317-9.

Volume 9, Title 22 to Title 25. Contains Title 22, Foreign Relations and Intercourse; Title 23, Highways; Title 24, Hospitals and Asylums; and Title 25, Indians. Price: $57.00. GPO Stock# 052-001-00318-7.

United States Statutes at Large. Annual. Published by the Office of the Federal Register, National Archives and Records Administration. The Statutes at Large serve as the official legal evidence of Federal laws, concurrent resolutions, Presidential proclamations, and proposed and ratified amendments to the Constitution in all U.S. Federal and state courts. It is sold in sets only.

Volume 99, Parts 1-2. Price: $70.00. GPO Stock# 069-000-00010-0.

Volume 100, Parts 1-5. Price: $132.00. GPO Stock# 069-000-00024-0.

The United States Government Manual, 1989/90 is the official handbook of the Federal Government, providing comprehensive information on the agencies of the legislative, judicial, and executive branches. It also includes information on quasi-official agencies, international organizations in which the United States participates, and boards, committees, and commissions. Price: $21.00 domestic, $26.25 foreign. GPO Stock# 060-000-00022-3.

Weekly Compilation of Presidential Documents. Includes transcripts of the President's news conferences, messages to Congress, public speeches and statements, and other Presidential materials released by the White House. The Compilation carries a monthly dateline and covers materials released during the preceding week. Each issue carries an index of contents and a cumulative index to prior issues. Separate indices are published quarterly, semiannually, and annually. Other finding aids include lists of laws approved by the President, nominations submitted to the Senate, and a checklist of White House releases. Price: $96.00 a year domestic (priority mail) or $55.00 a year domestic (non-priority mail); $68.75 a year foreign (non-priority mail). Foreign airmail distribution available upon request. GPO Stock# 769-007-00000-8.

Codification of Presidential Proclamations and Executive Orders, April 13, 1945 - January 20, 1989. Published by the Office of the Federal Register, National Archives and Records Administration. Provides in one convenient volume proclamations and Executive Orders with general applicability and continuing effect. Proclamations and Executive Orders issued before April 13, 1945 are included if they were amended or otherwise affected by documents issued during the 1945-1989 period. One of the great benefits of this volume is that it incorporates amendments into the text of each codified proclamation and Executive order. All documents are cited to the Federal Register and Code of Federal Regulations. It also reflects changes made by a document other than a proclamation or Executive Order, such as a Public Law or Federal regulation. The Codification is divided into 50 chapters corresponding to the title designations of the Code of Federal Regulations and the United States Code. There is also a Disposition Table listing all included documents with their amendments and an indication of their current status. Price: $32.00. GPO Stock# 069-000-00018-5.

* * * * * * * * * * * *

United States Code Annotated (U.S.C.A.). Published by West Publishing Company. The U.S.C.A. is very similar to the United States Code Service (see below). Like the United States Code, it has the same, 50 subject-matter title format. The entire set is kept updated by an annual, cumulative, pocket part supplement in the back of each volume or separate, soft-cover volume when the amount of new material requires it. Pamphlets are also issued during the year in order to keep the pocket parts up to date. Each code section is annotated by the inclusion of court decisions which have cited or interpreted the section, Code of Federal Regulations citations when appropriate, amendments to the section, Executive orders, reorganization plans, and citations to the relevant legislative history as reproduced in the United States Code Congressional & Administrative News (see below). The notes following each code section also refer to other West publications where additional cases and discussion may be found. For price and ordering information, contact: West Publishing Company, 50 West Kellogg Blvd, P.O. Box 64833, St. Paul, MN 55164. Tel: 800/328-9352 or 612/688-3600 in Minnesota.

United States Code Service, Lawyer's Edition (U.S.C.S.). Published by Lawyers Co-operative Publishing Company. The U.S.C.S. is one of the two primary commercial compilations of the United States Code. It contains detailed annotations for each code section, including case notes, amendments, references to implementing regulations, Executive orders and reorganization plans, cross-references to relevant code sections, and includes a multi-volume index and a multi-volume U.S. Code Guide. It follows the United States Code title arrangement and is published by Lawyers' Cooperative Publishing Company in conjunction with the Bancroft-Whitney Company. There is an annual supplement; quarterly supplements which update the cumulative Later Case service (annual supplement); and monthly supplements which are an advance service and update the Later Case service (quarterly supplements). Price: $2,340.00 for a complete set of books and three years of upkeep and all supplements, or $65.00 a month for three years for upkeep and all supplements ("level-charge" program). Discount and variable price information is available from local representatives. Contact Lawyers Co-operative Publishing Company, 50 Broad Street East, Rochester, NY 14694, for the name and telephone number of local representative. Tel: 800/828-6266.

* * * * * * * * * * * *

Administrative Conference of the U.S.

Administrative Conference News is a newsletter published quarterly highlighting activities of the Administrative Conference of the U.S. To obtain a free copy of this publication, contact: Administrative Conference of the United States, Office of the Chairman, 2120 L Street, N.W., Suite 500, Washington, D.C. 20037. Tel: 202/254-7020.

1989 Annual Report. The Annual Report reviews research and implementation activities of the Conference. Conference initiatives in 1989 include: alternative means of dispute resolution, Government ethics, Banking regulation, agency actions, medical benefit programs, immigration issues, biotechnology regulation, and research activities. At the end of 1989 approximately 30 research projects were underway. These included studies on the choice of forum in Government contract litigation, FAA sanctions and enforcement procedures, the role of Inspectors General in carrying out their responsibilities of internal oversight, judicial remands of cases to administrative agencies, oversight and regulation of Government-Sponsored Enterprises and pro bono practice by Government attorneys. To obtain a free copy of this publication, contact the Office of the Chairman at the above address.

GENERAL GOVERNMENT: FEDERAL RECORDS

Your Right to Federal Records. How to use the Freedom of Information Act and Privacy Act to obtain records from the Federal Government. 1989. Available from Consumer Information Center-P, P.O. Box 100, Pueblo, CO 81002. Price: 50 cents. Booklet number 462W.

National Archives

The following publications can be obtained from the **National Archives.** Send check or money order (Payable to the National Archives Trust Fund) to: National Archives Trust Fund, NEPS Dept. 724, P.O. Box 100793, Atlanta, GA 30384. Orders may be placed over the phone or by FAX. Tel: 202/724-0084. FAX: 202/523-4357. Please add $3.00 for orders up to $50.00 for shipping and handling.

Federal Court Records: A Select Catalog of National Archives Microfilm Publication, 1987. Item #200043. Price: $2.00.

Guide to the National Archives of the United States, 1987 documents our history from the First Continental Congress and includes the basic records of the three branches of our Federal Government. This comprehensive guide provides a general description of these records within the context of the Government agencies that created them or received them in the course of official business. Item #100009. Price $25.00.

Guide to Records in the National Archives Relating to American Indians 1984 enables researchers to review descriptions of records that are available in the National Archives and its regional archives. It includes concise information about records that trace the evolution of Federal Indian policy, the effects of national policies on traditional Indian culture, Indian wars and their results, and the role of Native Americans in the development of U.S. society. Item #100004. Price: $25.00.

Military Service Records: A Select Catalog of National Archives Microfilm Publications. The National Archives is the official depository for records of military personnel separated from the U.S. Air Force, Army, Coast Guard, Marine Corps, and Navy. Some records date back to the Revolutionary War. Item #200028. Price: $5.00.

Select List of Publications of the National Archives and Records Administration can be obtained from Publications Information. This pamphlet lists the various general information leaflets, guides and indexes, microfilm catalogs, and reference information papers that are available through the National Archives and Records Administration. There is no charge for this brochure. Call the number listed above.

The **regional catalog series** contains selected National Archives microfilm publications grouped by geographical area. The introduction to each catalog lists the regional archives that serves the region:

New England: A Select List of National Archives Microfilm Publications. Item #200039. Price $2.00.
Chesapeake/Mid-Atlantic: A Select List of National Archives Microfilm Publications. Item #200037. Price $2.00.
The South and Southwest: A Select List of National Archives Microfilm Publications. Item #200035. Price $2.00.
Central States: A Select List of National Archives Microfilm Publications. Item #200036. Price $2.00.
The West: A Select List of National Archives Microfilm Publications. Item #200038. Price $2.00.

ADVISORY OPINIONS OF THE U.S. DEPARTMENT OF JUSTICE

Although the following publications are out of print, they are available in many law libraries as well as in all Federal Depository Libraries.

The Opinions of the Attorneys General. 1789-1974. 42 volumes. Only selected opinions are included. These are merely advisory statements addressing statutory interpretations or general legal problems faced by executive departments and agencies. They are not mandatory orders, although Attorneys General have asserted their binding effect. Thus, although executive department officials are not bound to follow them, they are in fact generally followed. Attorney General opinions have also had a significant influence on judicial decisionmaking. Consequently, they have great value as guides to executive and administrative rulings and requirements and serve as valuable precedents. The bound volumes include headnotes, indexes, and tables. Over time, fewer and fewer opinions have been published. In the last volume, for example, fewer than ten percent of the opinions issued by the Attorney General in the period from 1961 to 1974 have been included. Opinions for the period from 1974 to 1986 have been compiled by the Department of Justice, but have not yet been published.

Opinions of the Office of Legal Counsel of the U.S. Department of Justice. 6 volumes, covering 1977-1982. Selected memorandum opinions advising the President, the Attorney General, and other executive officers of the Federal Government with respect to their official duties. Volumes 4-6 also include selected formal opinions of the Attorney General.

AGRICULTURE

U.S. Department of Agriculture

How to Get Information from the United States Department of Agriculture. USDA Office of Public Affairs, Office of Programs and Planning, April 1990. Lists sources of information in the Department and its agencies. Contains brief descriptions of the responsibilities of each office and agency. Also includes the names of the various Freedom of Information Act officers. Free. To obtain copies call 202/447-7454.

* * * * * * * * * * * *

The following publications can be purchased from the **U.S. Government Printing Office.** Stock numbers and prices for annual subscriptions are shown below. Submit requests for these publications to: The Superintendent of Documents, U.S. Government Printing Office, Washington, D.C. 20402. Tel: 202/783-3238.

Inspection System Guide. The subscription service consists of a basic looseleaf manual and eight supplements over a three year period. Price: $39.00 domestic; $48.75 foreign. GPO Stock# 901-006-00000-8.

Meat and Poultry Inspection Regulations (1986). Consolidated reprint. Contains regulations for slaughter and processing of livestock and poultry, as well as for certain voluntary services and humane slaughter. Subscription service consists of a basic manual and monthly changes for an indeterminate period. In looseleaf form, punched for binder. Price: $133.00 domestic; $166.25 foreign. GPO Stock# 901-005-00000-1.

* * * * * * * * * * * *

Federal and State Regulations of Food Product Safety and Quality: A Selected, Partially Annotated Bibliography. USDA Economic Research Service, September, 1988. Available from National Technical Information Service (NTIS), 5285 Port Royal Road, Springfield, VA 22161. Tel: 703/487-4650 or 800/336-4700. Price: $15.00. NTIS Order Number PB90187345.

Databases:

The National Agricultural Library (NAL) provides reference-research services to Government staff and the public. U.S. citizens who have made full use of their local, state, and/or university resources can receive services up to the threshold level without charge. The threshold level is defined as one hour of staff time or $25.00 in computer time. Services beyond the threshold are provided for a fee.

The following databases associated with the **U.S. Department of Agriculture** are available to the public:

Agriculture Buyer Alert Program. This is a network that provides product publicity to assist American suppliers in introducing their agricultural products to foreign markets. For access information, call either 202/447-7103, or Telex 7400232 Buyer UC. FAX: 202/472-4374.

Agricultural Economics. This is a subfile of the **AGRICOLA** database, and covers literature of the US and Canada pertaining to agricultural marketing, agricultural policies and programs, as well as other agricultural information. One can access **AGRICOLA** through such commercial vendors as BRS and DIALOG or one can perform searches in person at the National Agriculture Library in Beltsville or at the South Building of the USDA in Washington, D.C. For further information call 202/344-4479.

Agricultural Research Results Database contains over 1500 one-page narratives of recent research discoveries that are ready for distribution to farms, ranches, and rural communities. The subject matter covers animal and plant production and protection. Database reports are available nine to 18 months before information becomes available through literature publications. To obtain complete access to this database one must subscribe to the Dialcom database However, if one wants a specific piece of information one may get it through the USDA or land grant universities. For further information, contact: Dr. Janet Poley, Extension Services, U.S. Department of Agriculture, 14th and Independence St NW, Room 3329 South, Washington, D.C. 20250. Or call Dr. Poley at 202/447-8155.

Information Services Agricultural Market News Service (MARKET NEWS) is a nationwide network for the gathering and reporting of up-to-the-minute information on the supply, demand, prices, and movement of agricultural products. To access **MARKET NEWS** contact: Telenet Communications Corporation, 12490 Sunrise Valley Drive, Reston, VA 22096. Tel: 703/689-5700 or 800/835-3638.

ALCOHOL, TOBACCO AND FIREARMS

The following publications can be ordered from the **U.S. Treasury Department, Bureau of Alcohol, Tobacco and Firearms, Distribution Center**, 7943 Angus Court, Springfield, VA 22153. Tel: 703/455-7801. All of these publications are free of charge when ordered in small quantities.

Laws and Regulations Under the Federal Alcohol Administration Act, Title 27, U.S. Code of Federal Regulations. Publication# 5100.8.
Liquor Laws and Regulations for Retail Dealers. Publication# 5170.2.
Your Guide to Federal Firearms Regulations. Publication# 5300.4.
ATF: Explosives Laws and Regulations. Publication # 5400.7.
Rulings and Procedures Relating to Alcohol, Tobacco and Wagering Matters. Publication # 5600.1.
International Traffic in Arms Regulations (ITAR): Title 22, Code of Federal Regulations, Parts 121-130. Publication# SD-P-3310.1
Selling to the Department of the Treasury. Publication# TD-P-70-06C.

* * * * * * * * * * * *

Bureau of Alcohol, Tobacco and Firearms Quarterly Bulletin. Announces all new laws, regulations, codes, and rulings or changes relating to alcohol, tobacco, and firearms. Order from: The Superintendent of Documents, U.S. Government Printing Office, Washington, D.C. 20402. Tel: 202/783-3238. Price: $13.00 domestic; $16.25 foreign. GPO Stock# 748-001-00000-0.

ANTITRUST

Antitrust Enforcement and the Consumer. Explains how laws governing competition in business are enforced and how consumers can benefit. 1987. Available from Consumer Information Center-P, P.O. Box 100, Pueblo, CO 81002. Free. If you order two or more free publications, include a check for $1.00 payable to Superintendent of Documents. Booklet number 550W.

* * * * * * * * * * * *

Justice Department

Antitrust Division Manual is a guide to the operating policies and procedures of the Antitrust Division of the Department of Justice with a discussion of conducting investigations and litigation that the Division has employed in the past. Order from: The Superintendent of Documents, U.S. Government Printing Office, Washington, D.C. 20402. Tel: 202/783-3238. Price for basic manual with supplements: $40.00 domestic; $50.00 foreign. Issued irregularly for an indeterminate period. GPO Stock# 927-001-00000-4.

BANKING

Comptroller of the Currency, U.S. Treasury Department

The following publications are issued by the **Comptroller of the Currency.** To order, cite the title(s) of the publication(s) which you want, include a check payable to Comptroller of the Currency for the total cost, and submit to: Comptroller of the Currency, P.O. Box 70004, Chicago, IL 60673-0004.

The Director's Book. Provides general guidance to directors of national banks. It outlines the responsibilities of the board and addresses in broad terms the duties and liabilities of the individual director. Price: $2.00.

Banking Bulletins and Circulars. Contains issuances sent to all national banks. Circulars provide information of continuing concern regarding OCC policies and guidelines. Bulletins inform readers of pending regulatory changes and other general information. Annual subscription price: $100.00.

Examining Bulletins and Circulars. Contains advice and instructions to OCC's staff of national bank examiners. They provide insight into how examiners are being told to evaluate the banks they supervise. Annual subscription price: $100.00.

Interpretations. Monthly. Provides legal staff interpretations, trust interpretative letters, and investment securities letters. This monthly package represents the informal views of the Comptroller's staff concerning the applications of banking law to contemplated activities or transactions. Annual subscription price: $125.00.

Weekly Bulletin. Reports on all corporate decisions by the Office nationwide each week. Applications, approvals or denials, and consummations are noted for new banks, mergers, consolidations, and purchases and assumptions that result in national banks. Annual subscription price: $250.00.

Quarterly Journal. The journal of record for the most significant actions and policies of the Office of the Comptroller of the Currency. Published in March, June, September, and December. Annual subscription price: $60.00.

Comptroller's Manual for Corporate Activities. Makes available in one place OCC policies and procedures for processing applications for forming a new national bank. It includes sample documents required from applicants as well as pertinent laws, rulings, and regulations. Price: $90.00.

Comptroller's Manual for National Banks. A looseleaf legal reference containing laws applicable to national banks with sections dealing with regulations and interpretative rulings issued by the OCC. Price: $90.00.

Comptroller's Handbook for Consumer Examinations. A looseleaf publication intended to assist the examiner in understanding those selected portions of consumer laws and regulations pertinent to an examination of a national bank. Examination procedures are also included in this volume. Price: $90.00.

Comptroller's Handbook for National Bank Examiners. A looseleaf publication containing policies and procedures for the commercial examination of national banks. Price: $90.00.

Comptroller's Handbook for National Trust Examiners. A looseleaf publication presenting policies and procedures for the examination of the fiduciary activities of national banks. Price: $90.00.

Comptroller's Handbook for Compliance. Contains all the procedures used in compliance examinations. A handbook intended for use by examiners as a supervisory tool in performing compliance examinations and by bankers as a self-assessment tool for analyzing bank compliance systems. Price: $25.00.

Fair Housing Home Loan Data System. Published for lending departments and officials of national banks, this booklet contains the final regulation for the Fair Housing Home Loan Data System, instruction forms, and examples. Price: $1.50.

Money Laundering: A Banker's Guide to Avoiding Problems. No charge.

* * * * * * * * * * * *

Farm Credit Administration

FCA Bulletin, published monthly since 1986 as a digest and reference guide to regulatory activities affecting farm credit banks and other System institutions, contains summaries of Farm Credit Administration Board actions decisions, policy statements, directives, interpretations, proposed and final regulations, formal enforcement pending litigation involving the Far Credit Administration, and actions, interpretations, and agency reorganizations. Available free from: Editor, FCA Bulletin, Office of Congressional and Public Affairs, Farm Credit Administration, 1501 Farm Credit Drive, McLean, VA 22102-5090. Tel: 703/883-4056.

* * * * * * * * * * * *

Federal Deposit Insurance Corporation

Merger Decisions, Federal Deposit Insurance Corporation: contains approval and denial decisions of bank absorptions. It can be obtained from the Corporate Communications Office, Federal Deposit Insurance Corporation, 550 17th St. N.W., Washington, D.C. 20429. Tel: 202/898-6996. The first copy is free of charge and subsequent copies are $2.00 each.

FDIC Law, Regulations and Related Acts is presented in looseleaf format in three volumes and includes the FDI Act, regulations and miscellaneous statutes that affect the operations of insured banks and the FDIC. Report bulletins issued at monthly or bi-monthly intervals reflect the text of statutory or regulatory changes that may have occurred and summarize congressional and Federal agency actions. The three volume set is available by subscription for $175 which includes report bulletins through the end of the year. For information on ordering contact the Corporate Communications Office as listed above.

* * * * * * * * * * * *

Federal Reserve

To order any of the following publications, submit a check (made payable to the **Board of Governors of the Federal Reserve System**) to: Publications Services, MS-138, Board of Governors of the Federal Reserve System, Washington, D.C. 20551. Or, call 202/452-3244.

The Federal Reserve Act, and other statutory provisions affecting the Federal Reserve System, as amended through December 1988. 608 pp. Price: $10.00.

Federal Reserve Bulletin. Published monthly. Bulletins contain information on financial and business statistics, current banking issues, statements of the Chairman to Congress, and legal developments, such as Board orders, final rules, and amendments to regulations. Price: $25.00 per year in the U.S., Canada, and Mexico; $35.00 elsewhere.

Federal Reserve Regulatory Service. Looseleaf; updated at least monthly. Four Handbooks:

1) Consumer and Community Affairs Handbook. Price: $75.00 a year.

2) Monetary Policy and Reserve Requirements Handbook. Price: $75.00 a year.

3) Securities Credit Transactions Handbook. Price: $75.00 a year.

4) The Payment System Handbook. Price: $75.00 a year.

Federal Reserve Regulatory Service. 3 vols. Contains all four Handbooks plus substantial additional material. Price: $200.00 a year. The price for subscribers outside the U.S. is $250.00 a year for the Federal Reserve Regulatory Service; $90.00 a year for each Handbook.

Regulations of the Board of Governors of the Federal Reserve System. Includes a copy of each of the 26 regulations. Free of charge.

* * * * * * * * * * * *

National Credit Union Administration

NCUA News is published ten times a year by the National Credit Union Administration and covers activities and actions of the agency, including speeches, meetings, proposed rules and regulations, and legal opinions issued by the agency. It is free of charge. Contact: National Credit Union Administration, Office of Public and Congressional Affairs, 1776 G Street, N.W., Washington, D.C. 20456. Tel: 202/682-9650.

Rules and Regulations Concerning Credit Unions outlines the rules and regulations that are officially codified in 12 C.F.R. Parts 700-796 (1990). Price: $10.00. Send check to National Credit Union Administration, Administrative Offices, 1776 G Street, N.W., Washington, D.C. 20456. Tel: 202/682-9700.

National Credit Union Administration Rules and Regulations. 1990. Subscription service consists of a basic manual and changes for an indeterminate period. Looseleaf for updating. Price: $44.00 domestic; $55.00 foreign. GPO Stock# 954-004-00000-7. Contact: The Superintendent of Documents, U.S. Government Printing Office, Washington, D.C. 20402. Tel: 202/783-3238.

* * * * * * * * * * * *

Office of Thrift Supervision, U.S. Treasury Department

To order any of the following publications, submit a check (made payable to the Office of Thrift Supervision), to: Controller, **Office of Thrift Supervision,** 1700 G Street, N.W., Washington, D.C. 20552. Tel: 202/906-6155.

Application Processing Handbook. Contains guidance on how to process and analyze thrift and holding company applications. Price: $50.00 for regulated institutions; $75.00 for others.

Bank Secrecy Act. Preventive and corrective actions for violations of Treasury Department and Office of Thrift Supervision regulations. Price: $3.00.

Compliance Activities Handbook. Addresses compliance examination matters related to consumer protection laws and regulations, such as the Truth in Lending Act, and those related to the public interest, such as the Community Reinvestment Act and Bank Secrecy Act. Also contains examination objectives, procedures, and checklists for performing compliance reviews. Price: $50.00 for regulated institutions; $75.00 for others.

Compliance: A Self-Assessment Guide. Assists thrift institutions develop or improve internal policies and programs to ensure compliance with consumer and public interest laws. It covers consumer protection laws and regulations and several other statutes, including the Bank Secrecy Act and Bank Protection Act. Price: $20.00.

Director Information Guidelines. This pamphlet helps thrift directors meet their responsibilities in overseeing the management of their institutions by providing guidelines for evaluating information received in monthly board meetings. Price: $3.00.

Holding Companies Handbook. Addresses areas of particular interest when reviewing holding company operations. It focuses on methods to identify risks to thrift institutions of holding company activities. Price: $50.00 for regulated institutions; $75.00 for others.

Legal Alert Memo Subscription Series. Issued periodically by the Chief Counsel of the Office of Thrift Supervision, this series provides national guidance on significant legal issues such as securities disclosure requirements, mergers and acquisitions, transactions with affiliates, and management interlocks. Basic subscription price: $200.00. Copies of all back issues can be purchased for $35.00.

Trust Activities Handbook. Assists in the examination of thrift institutions and their subsidiaries that engage in trust activities. It summarizes requirements and other laws and regulations applicable to trust activities of regulated institutions. Price: $50.00 for regulated stitutions; $75.00 for others.

* * * * * * * * * * * *

U.S. Secret Service, U.S. Treasury Department

Know Your Money: U.S. Department of the Treasury, United States Secret Service. 20-page booklet designed to help individuals detect counterfeit currency and guard against forgery loss. Order from: U.S. Department of the Treasury, United States Secret Service, 1800 G Street, N.W., Room 805, Washington, D.C. 20225. Free of charge.

BUSINESS AND COMMERCE: GENERAL

U.S. Department of Commerce

The following publications can be purchased from the **U.S. Government Printing Office.** Stock numbers and prices for annual subscriptions are shown below. Submit requests for these publications to: The Superintendent of Documents, U.S. Government Printing Office, Washington, D.C. 20402. Tel: 202/783-3238.

Commerce Business Daily is a daily (Monday-Friday) synopsis of U.S. Government proposed procurement, sales, and contract awards of particular value to firms interested in bidding on U.S. Government purchases, surplus property offered for sale, or in seeking subcontract opportunities from prime contractors. It includes information received daily from military and civilian procurement offices. Price: domestic - $208.00 per year (non-priority mail); $261.00 (priority mail); foreign - $260.00 (plus additional cost based on International Postal Zone-sent airmail). A special six-month introductory rate is available at one-half the yearly price. GPO Stock# 703-013-00000-7.

Commerce Publications Update is a biweekly bulletin highlighting all of the latest Commerce publications. Price: $21.00 per year. GPO Stock# 703-014-00000-3.

* * * * * * * * * * * *

U.S. Small Business Administration

The following **Small Business Administration** publications can be obtained by sending a check or money order made payable to the U.S. Small Business Administration. Send to SBA-Publications, P.O. Box 30, Denver, CO 80201-0030.

Curtailing Crime - Inside and Out discusses positive steps that can be taken to curb crime. They include safeguards against employee dishonesty and ways to control shoplifting. In addition, this publication includes measures to outwit bad check passing and ways to prevent burglary and robbery. Price: $1.00.

Selecting the Legal Structure for Your Business discusses the various legal structures that a small business can use in setting up its operations. It briefly identifies the types of legal structures and lists the advantages and disadvantages of each. Price: 50 cents.

A Small Business Guide to Computer Security helps small businesses understand the nature of computer security risks and offers timely advice on how to control them. Price: $1.00.

BUSINESS AND COMMERCE: INTERNATIONAL TRADE

U.S. Department of Commerce

The following publications can be purchased from the **U.S. Government Printing Office.** Stock number and prices for annual subscriptions are shown below. Submit requests for these publications to: The Superintendent of Documents, U.S. Government Printing Office, Washington, D.C. 20402. Tel: 202/783-3238.

Business America, The Magazine of International Trade. A biweekly publication designed to help American exporters penetrate overseas markets by providing them with timely information on opportunities for trade and methods of doing business in foreign countries. Includes news of congressional and government actions affecting trade, economic and market reports gathered by the Foreign Commercial Service, and other trade news gathered by the International Trade Administration and other agencies as well as foreign governments. Price: $49.00 domestic; $61.25 foreign. GPO Stock# 703-011-00000-4.

Export Administration Regulations. 1989 is a compilation of official regulations and policies governing the export licensing of commodities and technical data. The subscription service consists of a basic manual with supplementary material issued as Export Administration Bulletins for approximately one year. The cost is $87.00 domestic; $108.75 foreign. GPO Stock# 903-014-00000-8.

Foreign Economic Trends contains information on the implications of foreign trade for the United States and covers most countries in the world. Price: $55.00 domestic; $68.75 foreign. GPO Stock# 803-006-00000-8.

Key Officers of Foreign Service Posts: Guide for Business Representatives. Published three times a year. Lists key officers at Foreign Service posts: the Chiefs and Deputy Chiefs of Missions; the senior officers of the political, economic, commercial, and consular sections of the post; and the agricultural attache. It also lists all embassies, legations, and consulates general. Annual subscription price: $5.00 domestic; $6.25 foreign. Single copy price: $1.75 domestic; $2.19 foreign. GPO Stock# 744-006-00000-7.

Overseas Business Reports contains information on the economic outlook, industry trends, trade regulations, distribution and sales channels, transportation, credit and other aspects of business in various countries. It is published at irregular intervals at an annual cost of $14.00 domestic; foreign $17.50 GPO Stock# 803-007-00000-4.

U.S.-Canada Free Trade Agreement summarizes the 1988 trade agreement, including details of its effect on agriculture, auto trade, cultural industries, financial services and trade remedies. It can be obtained free of charge by writing the Office of Canada, International Trade Administration, 14th and Constitution Avenue, N.W., Washington, D.C. 20230. The full text can be obtained at a cost of $32.00. GPO Stock# 052-071-00826-8.

* * * * * * * * * * * *

International Trade Commission

Citizen's Guide to the Statutory Procedures of the United States International Trade Commission gives a summary of the laws under which the Commission currently conducts investigations and also lists other reports and activities. It can be obtained free of charge from the United States International Trade Commission, Office of Public Affairs, Room 112, Washington, D.C. 20436. Tel: 202/252-1819.

Harmonized Tariff Schedules of the United States Annotated for Statistical Reporting Purposes, Second Edition contains the legal text of the Schedules, as amended and modified, together with annotations prescribing statistical information to be supplied on customs forms. The publication sets forth the changes brought about by the Kennedy Round of Trade negotiations and includes amendments and modifications made on or after August 31, 1963, and before January 1990. This is a subscription service consisting of a basic manual and supplementary material for an indeterminate period and is used in classifying imported merchandise for rate of duty and statistical purposes. The annual cost is $80.00 (priority mail) and $64.00 (non-priority mail). GPO Stock# 949-006-0000-0. Contact: Superintendent of Documents, U.S. Government Printing Office, Washington, D.C. 20402. Tel: 202/783-3238.

Selected Publications of the U.S. International Trade Commission, through December 1989. Lists reports issued by the International Trade Commission under various sections of the Trade Act of 1974 (e.g., unfair import practices, countervailing duty investigations, antidumping investigations, escape-clause investigations, market disruption), as well as reports issued under the Commission's general investigative powers provided under the Tariff Act of 1930. Reports are organized both by countries (or other geographic areas) and by commodities. USITC Publication #2263. Available free of charge from: Publications, U.S. International Trade Commission, Washington, D.C. 20436. Tel: 202/252-1807.

U.S. Laws and U.S. and EC Trade Agreements Relating to Non-Market Economies. Volumes I and II. Issued March 1990. USITC Publication #2269. Available free of charge from: Publications, U.S. International Trade Commission, Washington, D.C. 20436. Tel: 202/252-1807.

Database:

Antidumping Central Records Information Management System (CRIMS) is an internal database index of the International Trade Administration prepared for judicial review of duty cases. Public documents in an individual case can be reviewed in the Public Reading Room (B099) of the Department of Commerce, 14th and Constitution Ave., N.W. Washington, D.C. 20230, Monday through Friday from 8:30 AM until 5:00 PM.

* * * * * * * * * * * *

Overseas Private Investment Corporation

To assist American businesses considering overseas ventures, OPIC created the **Investor Information Service (IIS).** IIS is a publications clearinghouse that provides interested companies and individuals with easy "one-stop-shopping" for basic business, economic, and political information commonly sought when considering investment overseas. The materials, which are gathered into "kit" form, are obtained from various U.S. Government agencies, foreign governments and international organizations. At present, IIS kits are available for more than 100 developing counties and 16 regions.

Each information kit generally contains the following country-specific publications:

***Background Notes** (from U.S. Department of State) describing a country's land, people, history, government, political conditions, economy and foreign relations.

***Foreign Economic Trends and Their Implications for the United States** (from U.S. Department of Commerce, International Trade Administration) discussing the economic and financial conditions of a country.

***Overseas Business Reports** (from U.S. Department of Commerce, International Trade Administration) containing information on a country's trade patterns, industry trends, distribution and sales channels, natural resources, infrastructure, and trade regulations.

***Post Report** (from U.S. Department of State) containing practical information on living and traveling in a country.

***Investment Climate Statement** (from the U.S. Embassy in the host country) summarizing those laws, policies, and changes in a country's economic climate that may affect existing or new U.S. direct investment.

***Foreign Labor Trends** (from Department of Labor) discussing employment trends, union activities, and relations among labor, government and industry.

***Travel Advisories** (from U.S. Department of State) providing information on travel conditions, restrictions, and document requirements.

***Map** (from U.S. Department of State) showing transportation networks, economic activities, and land utilization.

***Foreign Publications** (from foreign government trade and investment authorities) outlining legal codes and discussing business regulations, investment incentives, and other related topics.

Because the number of publications available at any particular time varies from country to country, individual IIS kits differ in size, scope and price. For more information contact: Investor Information Service, Overseas Private Investment Corporation, 1615 M Street, N.W. Washington, D.C. 20527. Telephone orders by credit card can be made by calling 202/457-7010 or 800/424-6742.

* * * * * * * * * * * *

U.S. Department of State

US-Canada Free Trade Agreement. July 1989, Public Information Series, 23 pp. Available free of charge from the Bureau of Public Affairs, Room 6805, U.S. Department of State, Washington, D.C. 20520-6810.

The following gists are available for free from the **Bureau of Public Affairs,** Room 6805, U.S. Department of State, Washington, D.C. 20520-6810. Gists are two-page summaries of foreign policy issues, including a concise background review on current facts and history and a brief summary of U.S. policy.

GATT and Multilateral Trade Negotiations. June 1989.
Generalized System of Preferences. June 1989.
Trade Protection. June 1989.
US Trade Policy. June 1989.
US Export Controls and China. November 1989.
US Exports: Foreign Policy Controls. April 1989.

* * * * * * * * * * * *

U.S. Small Business Administration

Market Overseas with U.S. Government Help offers ideas on programs available to help small businesses break into the world of exporting. Price: $1.00. This publication can be obtained by sending a check or money order made payable to the U.S. Small Business Administration. Send to SBA-Publications, P.O. Box 30, Denver, CO 80201-0030.

CIVIL RIGHTS/EQUAL RIGHTS

A Working Woman's Guide to Her Job Rights 1988 is a comprehensive booklet covering freedom from discrimination and harassment, maternity leave, minimum wage, pension and retirement benefits, and more. Available from Consumer Information Center-P, P.O. Box 100, Pueblo, CO 81002. Price: $2.00. Booklet number 109W.

* * * * * * * * * * * *

U.S. Architectural and Transportation Barriers Compliance Board

The following publications are available free of charge. Requests must be in writing addressed to: **U.S. Architectural and Transportation Barriers Compliance Board**, Suite 501, 1111 18th Street, N.W., Washington, D.C. 20036.

Access America is a quarterly journal containing news of pending legislation and regulatory actions, staff changes, Board meetings, court decisions, related actions by other agencies, new publications, and a research and technical assistance section. Also available in cassette and large type.

Access America: The Architectural Barriers Act and You describes the Access Board and how to file complaints about inaccessible federally funded buildings and facilities. Also available in braille, large type, cassette and floppy disk.

Laws Concerning the ATBCB contains the Architectural Barriers Act of 1968 (Public Law 90-480) and sections 502 (which established the ATBCB), 506, and 507 of the Rehabilitation Act of 1973. Also available in braille and large type.

Uniform Federal Accessibility Standards) (UFAS) discusses design, construction and alteration standards for access to federally funded facilities (based on the ATBCB Minimum Guidelines and Requirements for Accessible Design). Also available in cassette.

* * * * * * * * * * * *

U.S. Commission on Civil Rights

Catalogue of Publications is an annotated list of the publications available from the Commission on Civil Rights. These include: clearinghouse publications, statutory and interim reports, staff reports, hearings, consultations, conferences and state advisory committee reports.

The publications listed below are a selection from the catalogue. The Catalogue of Publications and the following publications are free of charge and may be obtained from the **Clearinghouse Division, U.S. Commission on Civil Rights**, 1121 Vermont Ave., N.W., Washington, D.C. 20425. Tel: 202/376-8110. If available, stock numbers are listed after each publication.

Federal Enforcement of Equal Employment Requirements (1987) describes the responsibilities and policies of the Equal Employment Opportunity Commission, the Employment Litigation Section of the Justice Department's Civil Rights Division, and the Labor Department's Office of Federal Contract Compliance Programs during the Reagan Administration. CHP 93. 40 pp. No. 005-902-00041-0.

The Immigration Reform and Control Act: Assessing the Evaluation Process (1989) examines the reports by the General Accounting Office on the extent of discrimination and the burden on employers under the employer sanctions provisions of the Immigration Reform and Control Act of 1986. Concludes that the law has caused at least a pattern of discrimination. Recommends that Congress extend the evaluation period and clarify certain provisions in the law. Contains other findings and recommendations. 46 pp.

Medical Discrimination Against Children with Disabilities (1989) looks at the nature and extent of the practice of withholding medical treatment and nourishment from children born with disabilities. Among areas discussed are the role of quality of life judgments, economic considerations, infant care review committees, the relationship between parents and physicians, and enforcement of the Child Abuse Amendments of 1984. Concludes that denials of treatment continue and makes recommendations to alleviate the situation. 513 pp. No. 005-901-00058-8.

* * * * * * * * * * * *

U.S. Equal Employment Opportunity Commission

Single copies of the following publications are available free of charge from: **U.S. Equal Employment Opportunity Commission**, Office of Communications and Legislative Affairs, 1801 L Street, N.W., Room 9024, Washington, D.C. 20507.

Brochures: Age Discrimination is Against the Law, Equal Work/Equal Pay, Title VII Enforces Job Rights, Filing a Charge, Voluntary Assistance Program, Complaints of Discrimination by Federal Employees or Applicants, Equal Employment Opportunity Guide for Handicapped Federal Employees and Applicants for Federal Jobs, and Employee Appeals of Federal Agency EEO Decisions.

Booklets: The Charging Party: Your Rights and Responsibilities. Laws Enforced by the U.S. Equal Employment Opportunity Commission.

Fact Sheets: Pregnancy, National Origin, Religion, Sexual Harassment.

Regulations: Procedural, Sex, Religion, National Origin, Affirmative Action, Availability of Records, Federal EEO, Equal Pay Act, ADEA (A&B), ADEA Procedures, and ADEA Recordkeeping. To receive a full set of regulations, request publication #35.

* * * * * * * * * * * *

Employment Practices Guide. Four volumes, updated biweekly. Contains Federal and state decisions in discrimination cases. Price: $575.00 a year. Contact: Commerce Clearing House, 4025 West Peterson Avenue, Chicago, IL 60646. Tel: 312/583-8500. Or, in Washington, D.C. call 202/626-2200.

Federal Equal Opportunity Reporter. A monthly service reporting the full text of decisions of both the EEOC and the courts on Federal employee EEO appeals. Back decisions dating from 1979 are available at extra expense. Product# 4070. Price: $760.00 per year. Contact: LRP Publications, 747 Dresher Road, P.O. Box 980, Horsham, PA 19044-0980. Tel: 800/341-7874.

Database:

Equal Employment Opportunity Commission Federal Sector Case Decisions. Available on CD-ROM through the PERSONNET Service of Information Handling Services, 15 Inverness Way East, P.O. Box 1154, Englewood, CO 80150. Tel: 800/241-7824. In Colorado, call 303/790-0600 ext 59.

* * * * * * * * * * * *

U.S. Office of Personnel Management

Guide to Administering Examinations to Handicapped Individuals for Employment Purposes, compiled by the Office of Personnel Management, can be obtained from the National Technical Information Service, Department A/Operations Division, 5285 Port Royal Road, Springfield, VA 22161. Tel: 703/487-4650. I.D.# PR-80-16. Stock# PB81-121675.

A Guide for Assessing the Distribution of Minorities and Women in Relevant Labor Markets, compiled by the Office of Personnel Management, can be obtained from the National Technical Information Service, Department A/Operations Division, 5285 Port Royal Road, Springfield, VA 22161. Tel: 703/487-4650. I.D.# TM-79-10. Stock# PB80-152655.

COMMUNICATIONS

Federal Communications Commission

The Daily Digest of the Federal Communications Commission lists FCC notices, releases, texts and decisions. It is available to the public, on a first-come, first-served basis after 10:00 AM each day. Outside the D.C. area, the Daily Digest must be ordered by commercial distributors at a cost of between $25.00 and $44.00

per month. Two of these distributors are: Berry Best Services, Ltd., 1990 M Street, N.W., Suite 740, Washington, D.C. 20036. Tel: 202/293-4964; and, ITS, Inc., 2100 M. Street, N.W., Suite 240, Washington, D.C. 20037. Tel: 202/857-3800. A list of other distributors can be obtained from the FCC's Office of Public Affairs, 1919 M Street, N.W., Room 200, Washington, D.C. 20554. Tel: 202/632-5050.

* * * * * * * * * * * *

The following publications can be purchased from the **U.S. Government Printing Office**. Stock numbers and prices for annual subscriptions are shown below. Submit requests for these publications to: The Superintendent of Documents, U.S. Government Printing Office, Washington, D.C. 20402. Tel: 202/783-3238.

FCC Record, a biweekly compilation, containing comprehensive information of FCC Decisions, Reports, Public Notices and other documents. Price: $220.00 a year domestic; $275.00 a year foreign; $21.00 a single copy. GPO Stock# 903-008-00000-8.

Manual of Regulations and Procedures for Federal Radio Frequency Management. 1989. Covers the regulation of Federal interstate and foreign telecommunications. Subscription service consists of a basic manual and supplementary material for an indeterminate period. Price: $72.00 domestic; $90.00 foreign. GPO Stock# 903-008-00000-8.

* * * * * * * * * * * *

FCC Rulemaking Reports provides full-text reporting of the rulemaking procedures of the FCC, plus editorial summaries and the latest rules and changes as they affect the day-to-day operations of private and broadcast radio, television, cable TV, telephone common carriers, cellular radios and manufacturers of equipment for all such businesses. This report is published in three volumes, and is updated every two weeks. Price: $715.00 annually. The report can be obtained from Commerce Clearinghouse, Inc, 4025 West Peterson Avenue, Chicago, IL 60646. Tel: 312/583-8500. Or, in Washington, D.C., call 202/626-2200.

CONSUMER PROTECTION

Antitrust Enforcement and the Consumer. Explains how laws governing competition in business are enforced and how consumers can benefit. 1987. Available from Consumer Information Center-P, P.O. Box 100, Pueblo, CO 81002. Free. If you order two or more free publications, include a check for $1.00 payable to Superintendent of Documents. Booklet number 550W.

Consumers Resource Handbook. Extensive listing of contacts to assist with consumer problems. Includes corporate consumer representatives, private dispute resolution programs, automobile manufacturers, and Federal, state, county and city agencies with consumer responsibilities. also provides information on avoiding purchasing problems and how to write an effective complaint letter. 1990. Available from Consumer Information Center-P, P.O. Box 100, Pueblo, CO 81002. Free. If you order two or more free publications, include a check for $1.00 payable to Superintendent of Documents. Booklet number 569W.

* * * * * * * * * * * *

Federal Trade Commission

Businessperson's Guide to Federal Warranty Law includes a discussion of the Magnuson-Moss Act and also refers to specific sections of the Act, the rules of the Federal Trade Commission which were adopted under the Act, and the FTC's Warranty Advertising Guides. The publication is free of charge and can be obtained from the FTC, Division of Marketing Practices, 6th Street and Pennsylvania Avenue, N.W., Room 238, Washington, D.C. 20580. Tel: 202/326-3128.

Consumer Guide to the FTC Funeral Rule describes consumers' legal right to information concerning prices and options of funeral services. Available from Consumer Information Center-P, P.O. Box 100, Pueblo, CO 81002. Price: $2.00. Booklet number 109W.

Federal Trade Commission Decisions, Findings, Opinions, and Orders is a compilation of the official citations of the Commissions' decisions, findings, opinions, and orders. Volume 108 (July 1-December 31, 1986) Price: $17.00 domestic; $21.25 foreign. GPO Stock# 018-000-00327-9. Volume 109 (January 1-June 30, 1987). Price: $11.00 domestic; $13.75 foreign. GPO Stock# 018-000-00329-5. Volume 110 (July 1, 1987-June 30, 1988) Price: $30.00 domestic; $37.50 foreign. GPO Stock# 018-000-00331-7. Contact: The Superintendent of Documents, U.S. Government Printing Office, Washington, D.C. 20402. Tel: 202/783-3238.

Note: Current decisions can be found in the Public Reference Section of the FTC. Tel: 202/326-2222.

* * * * * * * * * * * *

U.S. Consumer Product Safety Commission

Compilation of Laws. September 1989; 122 pp. Single copies can be requested by writing: Office of Information and Public Affairs, U.S. Consumer Product Safety Commission, Washington, D.C. 20207.

CONTRACTS/PROCUREMENT

The following publications are free of charge and can be obtained from the **General Services Administration**, Office of Small & Disadvantaged Business Utilization, Room 6029, Washington, D.C. 20405. Tel: 202/501-1021.

Federal Buying Directory is a listing of procurement offices, address, and phone numbers of Federal agencies within the D.C. metropolitan area.

GSA Subcontracting Directory is an aid to small business and small disadvantaged business concerns seeking subcontracting opportunities with GSA prime contractors.

* * * * * * * * * * * *

The following publications can be purchased from the **U.S. Government Printing Office**. Stock numbers and prices for annual subscriptions are shown below. Submit requests for these publications to: The Superintendent of Documents, U.S. Government Printing Office, Washington, D.C. 20402. Tel: 202/783-3238.

Air Force Federal Acquisition Regulations Supplement. October 1988. A supplement to the Federal Acquisition Regulation for use in acquiring supplies and services for the Air Force. Subscription service consists of a basic manual and supplementary material for an indeterminate period. In looseleaf form, punched for 3-ring binder. Price: $92.00 domestic; $115.00 foreign. GPO Stock# 908-013-00000-0.

Army Federal Acquisition Regulations Supplement. April 1988. This Army supplement to the Federal Acquisition Regulation is a subscription service consisting of a basic manual and changes for an indeterminate period. Price: $100.00 domestic; $125.00 foreign. GPO Stock# 908-020-00000-6.

Catalogue of Federal Domestic Assistance is a Government-wide summary of financial and nonfinancial Federal programs, projects, services, and activities that provide assistance or benefits to the American public administered by departments and establishments of the Federal Government. It describes the type of assistance available and the eligibility requirements for the particular assistance being sought, with guidance on how to apply. It is also intended to improve coordination and communication between the Federal Government and State and local governments. The basic manual and supplementary material is updated for an indeterminate period. Price: $38.00 domestic; $47.50 foreign. GPO Stock# 922-002-00000-8.

Companies Participating in the Department of Defense Subcontracting Program. Quarterly. This publication summarizes information submitted by DOD prime contractors required to submit reports on subcontracting to small and small disadvantaged businesses. Approximately 900 companies, listed alphabetically and indicating their location, date of latest Government subcontracting surveillance review, net value of subcontract awards, and amount/percent of awards. The report has a section for each military department and the Defense Logistics Agency. Annual subscription price: $15.00 domestic; $18.75 foreign. GPO Stock# 708-066-00000-1.

Department of Energy Acquisition Regulation. Supplements the Federal Acquisition Regulation for procuring supplies and services for the U.S. Department of Energy. Subscription service consists of a basic manual and supplemental material for an indeterminate period. Latest update published March 1990. In looseleaf form, punched for 3-ring binder. Price: $67.00 domestic; $83.75 foreign. GPO Stock# 961-002-00000-1.

DOD Federal Acquisition Regulation Supplement (Department of Defense) 1988. Contains guidelines on the provisions, clauses, and cost principles authorized for DOD contracts, as well as the procedures and actions necessary for awarding and administering the contracts. Subscription service consists of a basic manual and changes for an indeterminate period. In looseleaf form, punched for 3-ring binder. Price: $102.00 domestic; $127.50 foreign. GPO Stock# 908-011-00000-7.

Doing Business with the Federal Government is an information booklet published by the General Services Administration (GSA) explaining Government procurement programs in Executive Branch agencies. Topics discussed include: principles and procedures of Government procurement; Government procurement programs; Government sales of surplus property; and the specifications, standards, and commercial item descriptions. Price: $2.75. GPO Stock# 022-003-01162-5.

Federal Acquisition Regulation. 1989. Consolidated reprint. The Federal Acquisition Regulation (FAR) is the primary regulation used by Federal Executive agencies requesting supplies and services. It provides coordination, simplicity, and uniformity in the Federal acquisition process. The DOD, NASA, and Air Force Federal acquisition supplements must be read in conjunction with the FAR for their acquisitions. Subscription service consists of a basic manual and supplementary material issued for an indeterminate period. Price: $81.00 domestic; $101.25 foreign. GPO Stock# 922-006-00000-8.

Federal Information Resources Management Regulation. Procurement and contracting regulations for ADP and telecommunications equipment and services to be used in conjunction with general procurement and contracting regulations in the Federal Acquisition Regulation. Subscription service consists of a basic manual and supplementary material for an indeterminate period. In looseleaf form, punched for 3-ring binder. Price: $105.00 domestic; $131.25 foreign. GPO Stock# 922-007-00000-4.

GSA Supply Catalogue contains a listing of items--office products, industrial products, tools, furniture--used throughout the Federal Government which are available from GSA supply distribution facilities. Descriptions, prices, units of issue, and other pertinent information for ordering these items are also included. The basic manual and supplementary material is updated for an indeterminate period. Price: $69.00 domestic; $86.25 foreign. GPO Stock# 922-003-00000-9

Guide to Doing Business with the Department of State. May 1990. Price: $1.75 domestic; $2.19 foreign. GPO Stock# 044-000-02287-7.

How to Buy Surplus Personal Property from the United States Department of Defense. A pamphlet providing information necessary to purchase personal property from the Department of Defense, bidder's lists, and types of property sold. Price: $1.50. GPO Stock# 008-007-03288-7.

Lists of Parties Excluded from Federal Procurement or Nonprocurement Programs is a monthly GSA publication identifying those parties excluded throughout the United States Government (unless otherwise noted) from receiving Federal contracts or federally approved subcontracts and from certain types of Federal financial and nonfinancial assistance and benefits. The cost is $40.00 domestic; $50.00 foreign. GPO Stock# 722-002-00000-8.

NASA FAR Supplement (National Aeronautics and Space Administration), June 1989. Contains NASA's uniform policies and procedures for procuring supplies and services defined in the Federal Acquisition Regulation. Subscription service consists of a basic manual and changes for an indeterminate period. In looseleaf form, punched for 3-ring binder. Price: $86.00 domestic; $107.50 foreign. GPO Stock# 933-003-00000-1.

NASA Grant and Cooperative Agreement Handbook. October 1983. This handbook prescribes policies and regulations relating to the award and administration of NASA research grants. It represents a significant NASA step in the publication and dissemination of NASA policies and procedures. Subscription service consists of a basic manual, changes, and procurement grant directives issued irregularly for an indeterminate period. Price: $23.00 domestic; $28.75 foreign. GPO Stock# 933-001-00000-8.

Selling to NASA. 1986. Prepared to assist potential contractors in the process of doing business with NASA. The procurement process is explained and advice is offered for marketing products. 44 pp. Price: $3.25. GPO Stock# 033-000-00995-0.

U.S. Postal Service Procurement Manual. 1987. This manual establishes uniform policies and procedures relating to procuring facilities, equipment, supplies, and services under the authority of Chapter 4, Title 39, USC, and mail transportation services by contract under Part 5, Title 39, USC. Subscription service consists of a basic manual and supplementary material for an indeterminate period. In looseleaf form, punched for 3-ring binder. Price: $103.00 domestic; $128.75 foreign. GPO Stock# 939-006-00000-1.

* * * * * * * * * * * *

National Science Foundation

National Science Foundation Grant Policy Manual. July 1989. A compendium of basic NSF grant policies and procedures for use by the grantee community and by NSF staff. Subscription service consists of a basic manual and supplementary material for an indeterminate period. Price: $21.00 domestic; $26.25 foreign. GPO Stock# 938-001-00000-6. Contact: The Superintendent of Documents, U.S. Government Printing Office, Washington, D.C. 220402. Tel: 202/783-3238.

Small Business Guide to Federal R&D Funding Opportunities, National Science Foundation. Publication #NSF 86-28. Available free of charge from: National Science Foundation, Attn: Forms and Publications, 1800 G Street, N.W., Room 232, Washington, D.C. 20550. Tel: 202/357-7861.

CRIMINAL JUSTICE

U.S. Department of Justice

The following publications can be purchased from the **U.S. Government Printing Office.** Stock numbers and prices for annual subscriptions are shown below. Submit requests for these publications to: The Superintendent of Documents, U.S. Government Printing Office, Washington, D.C. 20402. Tel: 202/783-3238.

FBI Law Enforcement Bulletin. A monthly journal of articles covering all aspects of law enforcement with principal emphasis on management, training, and law. Price: $14.00 a year domestic; $17.50 a year foreign. GPO Stock# 727-006-00000-1.

Sentencing Guidelines Manual, Amendments is a Department of Justice sentencing guidelines manual including amendments which took effect June 15, 1988. Price: $26.00 domestic; $32.50 foreign. GPO Stock# 052-070-00600-8.

U.S. Attorney's Manual. Subscription service for each volume consists of a basic manual and supplementary material for an indeterminate period. In looseleaf form, punched for 3-ring binder.

Volumes I and II, Titles I Through 8. October 1988. Subscription service consists of a two-volume basic manual (Volume I, Titles 1 through 3 and Volume II, Titles 4 through 8), cumulative semiannual updates, and blue sheets for an indeterminate period. Price: $485.00 domestic; $606.25 foreign. GPO Stock# 927-004-00000-3.

Volume III, Title 9, Criminal Division. Price: $434.00 domestic; $542.50 foreign. GPO Stock# 927-005-00000-0.

Volume IV, Indices. This volume is a general index which covers Titles 1 through 9. It has a comprehensive USC and CFR reference table, and also includes a prior approval listing for the Department of Justice. Price: $18.00 domestic; $22.50 foreign. GPO Stock# 927-007-00000-2.

* * * * * * * * * * * *

The National Criminal Justice Reference Service (NCJRS) is an international clearinghouse of the latest criminal justice research. Its services include the following:

*** Publications:** By registering with NCJRS you will receive a bi-monthly publication, NIJ REPORTS. There are other publications regularly sent to registered users such as: a Research in Brief series, AIDS Bulletin and Research in Action series.

For more information or to order any NCJRS products or services call 800/851-3420 or 301/251-5500 in Maryland and the Metropolitan Washington D.C. Area. Or, write: National Institute of Justice/-NCJRS, Box 6000, Dept. AFA, Rockville, MD 20850. Registration with NCJRS is free. If you call the above number for a registration form, you will be put on their mailing list.

Databases:

***Database of Criminal Justice Information:** A computerized clearinghouse of 90,000 criminal justice related information sources. It features summaries of books, reports, and articles --government and non-government, published and non-published-- as well as audiovisual materials.

***Reference and Referral Services.** Highly trained criminal justice information specialists have direct online access to the NCJRS database on such topics as law enforcement, drugs and crime, courts, juvenile justice, statistics, and victims of crime. Topical searches cost $17.50. A topical bibliography on a specific subject costs $5.00. Information specialists will also do a custom search tailored to a need for $48.00. If the service does not have the information you need, specialized librarians will refer you to another source. Documents in the data base are accessible by interlibrary loan or by visiting the NCJRS Reading Library at 1600 Research Blvd, Rockville, MD. Hours are Monday through Friday, 8:30 AM to 5:00 PM. You may also access this database by using the DIALOG service.

***Specialized Data Bases.** These data bases are also available by calling the toll-free 800 number above: **Federal Criminal Justice Research Data Base, Criminal Justice Calendar Data Base, Juvenile Justice Automated Conference Calendar.**

CUSTOMS

U.S. Customs Service, U.S. Treasury Department

Single copies of the following publications can be obtained free of charge from: **U.S. Customs Service**, P.O. Box 7407, Washington, D.C. 20044.

Importing into the United States. March 1990. 88 pp. Topics addressed include entry of goods, assessment of duty, classification and value, marking, fraud, and foreign trade zones. Appendix contains copies of a pro forma invoice, carrier's certificate, corporate surety power of attorney, Customs bond, and entry summary.

U.S. Import Requirements. Pamphlet.
U.S. Customs: International Mail Imports. Pamphlet.
Tariff Classification of Prospective Imports. Pamphlet.
Foreign Trade Zones: U.S. Customs Procedures and Requirements. Pamphlet.

The following publications can be purchased from the **U.S. Government Printing Office.** Stock numbers and prices for annual subscriptions are shown below. Submit requests for these publications to: The Superintendent of Documents, U.S. Government Printing Office, Washington, D.C. 20402. Tel: 202/783-3238.

Customs Bulletin and Decisions. A weekly publication containing regulations, rulings, decisions, and notices concerning Customs and related matters in the U.S. Court of Appeals for the Federal Circuit and the U.S. Court of International Trade. Price: $114.00 domestic; $142.50 foreign. GPO Stock# 748-002-00000-6.

Customs Regulations of the United States. 1989. Contains regulations made and published for the purpose of carrying out customs laws administered by the U.S. Customs Service. A subscription service consisting of a basic manual and supplementary material for an indeterminate period. In looseleaf form, punched for 3-ring binder. Price: $40.00 domestic; $50.00 foreign. GPO Stock# 948-006-00000-6.

DECISIONS OF ADMINISTRATIVE ADJUDICATIVE BODIES

U.S. Department of Agriculture

Decisions of the Administrative Law Judges and the Judicial Officer are published in Agriculture Decisions, which also contains selected court opinions on issues related to agricultural law from a variety of courts. Although this journal is published monthly, the schedule is running late and the office is currently working on ALJ decisions from 1988. To get on the mailing list for this free publication, contact: Hearing Clerk Unit, Office of Administrative Law Judges, U.S. Department of Agriculture, Room 1081 South Agriculture Building, Washington, D.C. 20250. Tel: 202/447-4443.

To obtain a copy of current decisions, contact the Hearing Clerk's Office at 202/447-4443 or write to: Hearing Clerk Unit, Office of Administrative Law Judges, U.S. Department of Agriculture, Room 1081 South Agriculture Building, Washington, D.C. 20250.

* * * * * * * * * * * *

U.S. Department of Commerce, U.S. Patent and Trademark Office

The decisions of the Board of Patent Appeals and Interferences are reported in either full text or digest in U.S. Patents Quarterly. The weekly publication can be obtained from the Bureau of National Affairs, 9435 Key West Avenue, Rockville, MD 20850. Tel: 301/258-1033. Or 800/372-1033. The annual cost is $1,020.00.

The decisions of the Trademark Trial and Appeals Board can be found in U.S. Patents Quarterly. The weekly publication can be obtained from the Bureau of National Affairs, 9435 Key West Avenue, Rockville, MD 20850. Tel: 301/258-1033. Or 800/372-1033. The annual cost is $1,020.00.

* * * * * * * * * * * *

U.S. Department of Energy

Decisions of the Office of Hearings and Appeals are also available from Commerce Clearing House in a weekly looseleaf service entitled Federal Energy Guidelines. This publication also includes regulations, interpretations, related court decisions etc. Price: $790.00 a year. Contact: Commerce Clearing House, 4025 West Peterson Avenue, Chicago, IL 60646. Tel: 312/583-8500. Or, in Washington, D.C. call 202/626-2200.

* * * * * * * * * * * *

U.S. Department of Housing and Urban Development

Decisions of the Administrative Law Judges are not published; however, requests for a printed copy of the decision rendered in a specific case can be obtained by calling the Docket Clerk, Tel: 202/708-2540. Excerpts of the decisions of the Administrative Law Judges in cases involving the Fair Housing Amendments Act of 1988 can be found in Fair Housing-Fair Lending, a monthly updated publication of Prentice Hall, Law and Business Division, 270 Sylvan Avenue, Englewood Cliffs, NJ 07632. Tel: 800/223-0231. The annual subscription, with monthly report bulletins, costs $390.00.

* * * * * * * * * * * *

U.S. Department of the Interior

Decisions of the Department of the Interior contains significant decisions by the U.S. Department of the Interior on appeals, claims, and acts. It is published monthly and placed in bound volumes at the end of the year. Contact: The Superintendent of Documents, U.S. Government Printing Office, Washington, D.C. 20402. Tel: 202/783-3238.

Volume 95 (1988). Annual price: $14.00 domestic; $17.50 foreign. GPO Stock# 724-010-00000-8.
Volume 96 (1989). Annual price: $11.00 domestic; $13.75 foreign. GPO Stock# 724-011-00000-4.
Volume 97 (1990). Annual price: $11.00 domestic; $13.75 foreign. GPO Stock #724-013-00000-7.

The decisions of the Administrative Law Judges, mainly those involving surface mining cases, can be obtained by subscription from the Office of Hearings, 4015 Wilson Blvd., Arlington, VA 22203. Tel: 703/235-3799. Annual price: $45.00. If you have a request for a specific case, you can call the office at the above number for a copy of that record.

The decisions of the Administrative Law Judges of the Board of Land Appeals can be obtained by subscription from the Office of Hearings, 4015 Wilson Blvd., Arlington, VA 22203. Tel: 703/235-3799. Annual price: $475.00. If you have a request for a specific case, you can call the office at the above number for a copy of that record. Online WESTLAW users can also access these decisions.

The decisions of the Board of Indian Appeals can be obtained by subscription from the Office of Hearings, 4015 Wilson Blvd., Arlington, VA 22203. Tel: 703/235-3799. Annual price: $75.00. If you have a request for a specific case you can call the office at the above number for a record of that case. Online WESTLAW users can also access the decisions of the Board.

Surface Mining Law Summary is a looseleaf publication, updated periodically. It contains decisions of the Administrative Law Judges of the Board of Land Appeals and decisions of the Administrative Law Judges of the Hearings Division in selected surface mining cases. Annual price: $375.00. Contact: Surface Mining Law Summary, Inc., P.O. Box 281, Corbin, KY 40701. Tel: 606/528-9481.

* * * * * * * * * * * *

U.S. Department of Justice

Interim Decisions of the Department of Justice contains selected precedential Board of Immigration Appeals decisions which are binding on all Immigration and Naturalization Offices. Published at irregular intervals. Price: $65.00 domestic; $81.25 foreign. GPO Stock# 827-002-00000-3. Contact: The Superintendent of Documents, U.S. Government Printing Office, Washington, D.C. 20402. Tel: 202/783-3238.

* * * * * * * * * * * *

U.S. Department of Labor

Decisions of the Office of Administrative Law Judges and Office of Administrative Appeals. Published bimonthly. Price $28.00 a year domestic; $35.00 a year foreign. GPO Stock# 729-011-00000-2. Contact: The Superintendent of Documents, U.S. Government Printing Office, Washington, D.C. 20402. Tel: 202/783-3238.

Digest and Decisions of ECAB (Employees' Compensation Appeals Board), Vol. 38 covers October 1, 1986 through September 30, 1987 with index digest supplement. Price $37.00 domestic; $46.25 foreign. GPO Stock# 029-009-00033-3. Contact: The Superintendent of Documents, U.S. Government Printing Office, Washington, D.C. 20402. Tel: 202/783-3238.

* * * * * * * * * * * *

U.S. Department of Transportation, U.S. Coast Guard

Decisions: The decisions of the Administrative Law Judge and any appeals of decisions can be obtained by contacting the Office of the Commandant (G-LMI), Maritime and International Law Division, U.S. Coast Guard, 2100 Second Street, S.W., Washington, D.C. 20593.

* * * * * * * * * * * * *

Commodity Futures Trading Commission

Decisions of the Commodity Futures Trading Commission: Decisions rendered by the Commission, the Administrative Law Judges, and the Judgment Officers can be obtained by contacting the Office of Proceedings, 2033 K Street, N.W., Washington, D.C. 20581. Tel: 202/254-5008. There is a $12.00 reproduction service charge and 15 cents per page copying fee.

* * * * * * * * * * * *

Federal Communications Commission

FCC Record, a biweekly compilation, containing comprehensive information on FCC Decisions, Reports, Public Notices and other documents. Price: $220.00 a year domestic; $275.00 a year foreign; $21.00 a single copy. GPO Stock# 903-008-00000-8. Contact: The Superintendent of Documents, U.S. Government Printing Office, Washington, D.C. 20402. Tel: 202/783-3238.

* * * * * * * * * * * *

Federal Labor Relations Authority

FLRA (Federal Labor Relations Authority) Reports of Case Decisions, FSIP (Federal Service Impasses Panel) Releases and Administrative Law Judge Decisions of the FLRA. The decisions and releases are issued irregularly during a twelve month period.

Price: $152.00 domestic; $190.00 foreign. GPO Stock# 863-002-00000-1. Note: Single copies may be obtained from The Federal Labor Relations Authority, 500 C Street, S.W., Washington, D.C. 20424.

* * * * * * * * * * * *

Federal Maritime Commission

Decisions: The decisions of the Administrative Law Judges may be obtained from the Federal Maritime Commission, Office of Administrative Services, Room 10409, 1100 L St. N.W., Washington, D.C. 20573. Tel: 202/523-5900. Single copies are free. An annual subscription is $120.00.

The decisions of the Administrative Law Judges may also be obtained commercially. Shipping Regulation Reporter contains the decisions of the Federal Maritime Commission and the Maritime Administration. Also included are the rules, regulations and statutes related to the maritime industry. It is published every two weeks in looseleaf form by Pike & Fisher, Inc., 4600 East-West Highway, Suite 200, Bethesda, MD 20814. Tel: 301: 654-6262. Price: $1720.00 annually for a first subscription; $1390.00 for a renewal.

* * * * * * * * * * * *

Federal Mine Safety and Health Review Commission

Federal Mine Safety and Health Review Commission Decisions. Monthly. Price: $69.00 a year domestic; $86.25 a year foreign. GPO Stock# 752-019-00000-2. Contact: The Superintendent of Documents, U.S. Government Printing Office, Washington, D.C. 20402. Tel: 202/783-3238.

* * * * * * * * * * * *

National Transportation Safety Board

Initial Decisions of the Administrative Law Judges. Sets forth Administrative Law Judges' findings, conclusions, and decisions in safety enforcement proceedings involving petitions from applicants denied airmen's certificates by the Administrator of the Federal Aviation Administration; and appeals from orders of the Administrator of the Federal Aviation Administration suspending or revoking certificates issued to airmen, aircraft, air agencies, and air carriers for alleged violations of the regulations or for lack of qualifications to hold such certificates. Initial Decisions are issued both individually and in a monthly publication. Individual Initial Decisions are available, for a fee, from: The National Transportation Safety Board, Public Inquiries Section, Room 805-F, 800 Independence Avenue, S.W., Washington, D.C. 20594. Tel: 202/382-6735. When ordering individual decisions, specify the type of document and the docket number. The monthly publication is available, for a fee, from: The National Technical Information Service (NTIS), 5285 Port Royal Road, Springfield, VA 22161. Tel: 703/487-4630 (for annual subscriptions) or 703/487-4650 (for single copies and microfiche). Prepayment is required for all orders.

* * * * * * * * * * * *

Nuclear Regulatory Commission

Nuclear Regulatory Commission Issuances (NUREG-0750), is a monthly publication containing all opinions, decisions, denials, memoranda, and orders of the Commission, the Atomic Safety and Licensing Appeal Board, the Atomic Safety and Licensing Board, the Administrative Law Judge, and program offices. Price: $132.00 a year priority mail; $102.00 non-priority mail; $127.50 foreign. Stock# 752-015-00000-7. Contact: The Superintendent of Documents, U.S. Government Printing Office, Washington, D.C. 20402. Tel: 202/783-3238.

* * * * * * * * * * * *

General Accounting Office

Decisions of the Comptroller General of the United States. Published monthly. Each issue contains decisions of the Comptroller General on financial matters arising in the Federal Service. Price: $18.00 a year domestic; $22.50 a year foreign. GPO Stock# 720-001-00000-4.

DECISIONS OF BOARDS OF CONTRACT APPEALS

General Services Administration

Board of Contract Appeals Bid Protests Decisions is a monthly looseleaf publication of current GSA decisions. It is published at an annual cost of $380.00 by Federal Publications, Inc. 1120 20th Street, N.W., Washington, D.C. 20036. Tel: 202/337-7000.

* * * * * * * * * * * *

The Board of Contract Appeals Reporter is a bi-weekly publication which reports the decisions of the following Boards of Contract Appeals: Agriculture, Armed Services, Corps of Engineers, Department of Transportation, Energy, General Services Administration, Department of Housing and Urban Development, Interior, Labor, National Aeronautics and Space Administration, U.S. Postal Service, and Department of Veterans Affairs. Annual Price $760.00. Contact: Commerce Clearing House, Inc., 4025 West Peterson Avenue, Chicago, IL 60646. Tel: 312/583-8500. Or in Washington, D.C., call 202/626-2200.

DEFENSE/MILITARY

U.S. Department of Defense

Department of Defense Directives can be obtained from U.S. Naval Publications and Forms Center, 5801 Tabor Avenue, Attn: Code 301, Philadelphia, PA 19120.

The following publications can be purchased from the **U.S. Government Printing Office.** Stock numbers and prices for annual subscriptions are shown below. Submit requests for these publications to: The Superintendent of Documents, U.S. Government Printing Office, Washington, D.C. 20402. Tel: 202/783-3238.

Air Force Law Review. Published semiannually by the Office of the Judge Advocate General of the Air Force, this Review provides a means for exchange of ideas and information. It contains a survey of important legislative, administrative, and judicial developments in military and related law fields. Price: $5.00 domestic; $6.25 foreign. GPO Stock# 708-005-00000-2.

The Army Lawyer. Published monthly by the Judge Advocate General's School for the official use of Army lawyers in the performance of their legal responsibilities. The publication covers current issues in criminal law, Government procurement law, tort law, labor and employment law, and international law. Price: $13.00 domestic; $16.25 foreign. GPO Stock# 708-011-00000-2.

Military Law Review. Quarterly. Designed as a medium for the military lawyer, active and reserve, to share the product of his/her experience and research with fellow lawyers. Price: $12.00 domestic; $15.00 foreign. GPO Stock# 708-038-0000-8.

Manual for Courts-Martial. 1984. This procedural and practice manual implements the Uniform Code of Military Justice (10 U.S.C. 801-940) and applies to all of the military services. It also contains the Military Rules of Evidence. Price: $13.00 domestic; $16.25 foreign. GPO Stock# 008-000-00403-0.

The Reporter. Published quarterly. A legal journal which provides a forum for the exchange of information pertinent to the practice of law in the military as well as the civilian community. Each issue contains three to six articles on current topics of interest in the law and sections devoted to military justice, claims, and tort litigation and preventive law. Price: $9.00 domestic; $11.25 foreign. GPO Stock# 708-047-00000-7.

* * * * * * * * * * * *

Selective Service System

The Selective Service System publishes Fact Sheets on various topics, some of which include: "Aliens and Dual Nationals" (registration and liability for service), "Who Must Register" (an explanation of Section 3 of the Military Selective Service Act), "State Legislation" (the Solomon Amendment to the Defense Authorization Act of 1983 and student financial aid), "Sources of Information on Selective Service" (a selected bibliography), and "Background of Selective Service" (an explanation of the purposes and a description of the agency). All of the Fact Sheets are free of charge and can be obtained from the Selective Service System, Office of Public Affairs, 1023 31st Street, N.W., Washington, D.C. 20435. Tel: 202/724-0790.

The Selective Service System: Information for Registrants discusses the law requiring 18 year-old males to register. What would happen if the draft were started again, and how to request reclassification or postponement of induction into the armed forces. Available from Consumer Information Center-P, P.O. Box 100, Pueblo, CO 81002. Free. If you order two or more free publications, include a check for $1.00 payable to Superintendent of Documents. Booklet number 567W.

DOMESTIC RELATIONS

Department of Health and Human Services

Handbook of Child Support Enforcement. Contains suggestions for resolving enforcement child support problems. Lists the basic steps to follow to obtain child support enforcement services. 1985. Available from Consumer Information Center-P, P.O. Box 100, Pueblo, CO 81002. Free. If you order two or more free publications, include a check for $1.00 payable to Superintendent of Documents. Booklet number 505W.

Wage Withholding for Child Support--An Employer's Guide for Small Businesses. As of November 1990, employers have legal responsibilities for enforcing child support. This booklet provides an overview of the law. It also lists telephone numbers of State Child Support Agency Wage Withholding Offices. Available from Consumer Information Center-P, P.O. Box 100, Pueblo, CO 81002. Free. If you order two or more free publications, include a check for $1.00 payable to Superintendent of Documents. Booklet number 502W.

* * * * * * * * * * * *

U.S. Department of State

International Parental Child Abduction. Available free from U.S. Department of State, ATTN: Consuelo Pachon, Office of Citizen's Consular Services, Room 4817, Washington, D.C. 20520-4818. Tel: 202/647-3666. Publication #9794.

ELECTIONS

U.S. Commission on Civil Rights

A Citizen's Guide to Understanding the Voting Rights Act (1984) explains the provisions of the 1965 Voting Rights Act as amended, including preclearance, minority language protections, and Federal observers, and how individuals and groups may make complaints and comments. Appendices include the text of the act, lists of jurisdictions covered, various sample letters, and source materials. CHP 84. 91 pp. No. 005-902-00038-0. This publication is free of charge and may be obtained from the Clearinghouse Division, U.S. Commission on Civil Rights, 1121 Vermont Ave., N.W., Washington, D.C. 20425. Tel: 202/376-8110.

* * * * * * * * * * * *

Federal Election Commission

The following publications can be obtained free of charge. Contact: **Federal Election Commission,** Information Services, 999 E Street, N.W., Washington, D.C. 20463. Tel: 202/376-3120; 800/424-9530.

Advisory Opinions is a brochure in question-and-answer format explaining how individuals may seek guidance from the FEC by requesting advisory opinions. An advisory opinion is an official Commission response to a question relating to the application of the Federal campaign finance law to a specific factual situation.

Campaign Guides include four separate guides explaining how the law affects, respectively, four different audiences: candidates, parties, corporation/unions and nonconnected PACs. In each guide, election law requirements for the "three R's" (registration, recordkeeping and reporting) are explained and illustrated with examples of completed FEC forms. The guides also discuss fundraising and different ways of supporting Federal candidates.

1) Campaign Guide for Congressional Candidates and Committees, prepared for U.S. Senate and House candidates and their authorized committees, examines the complete cycle of election activity: testing-the-waters; gaining support through volunteer activity, contribution, independent expenditures and party activity; and winding down the campaign.

2) Campaign Guide for Party Committees, written for State and local party organizations which support Federal candidates, deals with such subjects as allocating Federal and non-Federal expenses, coordinated party expenditures and voter drives.

3) Campaign Guide for Corporations and Labor Organizations explains the rules governing corporate and labor activity in connection with Federal elections: separate segregated funds (SSFs); partisan and nonpartisan communications; and election-related use of corporate/labor treasury funds and facilities. This guide also pertains to national banks; incorporated membership organizations, trade associations and cooperatives; and corporations without capital stock.

4) Campaign Guide for Nonconnected Political Committees outlines the rules applicable to committees not established by a candidate, party, corporation or labor organization. It examines contributions and expenditures; political communications and support from a sponsoring organization.

Federal Election Campaign Laws is a complete compilation of Federal election campaign laws; the Federal Election Campaign Act of 1971, as amended, and as codified in titles 2 and 26 of the United States Code; statutory provisions which are not under the Commission's jurisdiction but are relevant to persons involved with Federal elections; and a subject index to titles 2 and 26 prepared by the FEC.

The FEC and the Federal Campaign Finance Law gives a brief overview of the major provisions of the Federal Election Campaign Act and the Commission's role in administering it.

FEC Record, a monthly newsletter published as a binder insert, is the primary source of information on Commission activity. It covers reporting, advisory opinions, litigation, legislation, statistics, regulations, compliance, Federal Register notices, FEC procedures and staff, and publications.

FEC Regulations contains FEC regulations which appear in title 11 of the Code of Federal Regulations. Subject indexes prepared by FEC staff are included.

Filing a Complaint tells how the complaint process works and what role the FEC plays in the process. Anyone may file a complaint if he or she believes an individual or a committee has violated the Federal election law.

Public Funding of Presidential Elections is written for the general public and gives a brief history of Presidential public funding, describing how the process works. It explains the ways individuals may support publicly funded candidates and the various materials on Presidential campaign finance available from the Commission.

Using FEC Campaign Finance Information explains how to gather information about the financial activity of Federal political committees. It describes the FEC's computer indexes and suggests ways to utilize them.

ENERGY/NUCLEAR ENERGY

U.S. Department of Energy, Federal Energy Regulatory Commission

Copies of specific orders and other items. To obtain a copy of a specific order, notice, filing, etc., submit a written request to: Reference and Information Center, Federal Energy Regulatory Commission, Room 3308, 941 N. Capitol Street, N.E., Washington, D.C. 20426. Tel: 202/208-1371.

Service List. To get on a mailing list ("Service List") to receive copies of all material issued concerning a particular docket number, submit a written request to: The Secretary of the Commission, Federal Energy Regulatory Commission, 825 N. Capitol Street, N.E., Room 3110, Washington, D.C. 20426. Tel: 202/208-0400.

Database

CIPS (Commission Issuance Posting System). This is a database containing copies of all Commission formal issuances, including opinions, orders, initial decisions, and the Commission agenda, as well as proposed, interim, and final rulings. All available free of charge to anyone with a computer and a modem. For further information, call 202/208-2474.

* * * * * * * * * * * *

U.S. Nuclear Regulatory Commission

The following publications of the Nuclear Regulatory Commission (NRC) can be purchased from the **U.S. Government Printing Office.** Stock numbers and prices for annual subscriptions to each are shown below. Submit requests for these publications to: The Superintendent of Documents, U.S. Government Printing Office, Washington, D.C. 20402. Tel: 202/783-3238.

Enforcement Actions: Significant Actions Resolved (NUREG-0940). Published quarterly, this publication compiles summaries of significant enforcement actions that were resolved, as well as copies of letters, notices, and orders sent by the NRC to the licensee with respect to the enforcement action. Price: $22.00 a year domestic; $27.50 a year foreign. GPO Stock# 752-006-00000-8.

NRC Information Notices and Bulletins. Issued irregularly. Price: $106.00 a year domestic; $132.50 a year foreign. GPO Stock# 852-008-00000-8.

Nuclear Regulatory Commission Issuances (NUREG-0750), is a monthly publication containing all opinions, decisions, denials, memoranda, and orders of the Commission, the Atomic Safety and Licensing Appeal Board, the Atomic Safety and Licensing Board, the Administrative Law Judge, and program offices. Price: $132.00 a year priority mail; $102.00 non-priority mail; $127.50 foreign. Stock# 752-015-00000-7.

Nuclear Regulatory Commission Rules and Regulations. 1989. Subscription service consists of a basic manual and supplements issued irregularly for an indeterminate period. Price: $261.00 domestic; $326.25 foreign. GPO Stock# 952-003-00000-3.

Nuclear Regulatory Commission Rules and Regulations for Medical Licensees. 1989. Contains information from "Nuclear Regulatory Commission Rules and Regulations," Parts 19, 20, 30, 32, 33, and 35. Subscription service consists of a basic manual and quarterly supplements for an indeterminate period. In looseleaf form, punched for 3-ring binder. Price: $125.00 domestic; $156.25 foreign. GPO Stock# 952-004-00000-0.

Regulatory and Technical Reports, NUREG-0304, 15th volume, is a quarterly compilation that consists of bibliographic data and abstracts for the formal regulatory and technical reports issued by the NRC Staff and its contractors. Price: $14.00 per year; $17.50 foreign. Stock# 752-018-00000-6. Single copies of the Regulatory and Technical Reports are available from the National Technical Information Service (NTIS), 5385 Port Royal Road, Springfield, VA 22161. Tel: 703/487-4650.

Title List of Documents Made Publicly Available, NUREG-0540, is a monthly report that contains descriptions of the information that the NRC receives and generates. It includes: (1) docketed material associated with civilian nuclear power plants and other uses of radioactive materials and (2) nondocketed material that the NRC receives and generates and is relevant to its role as a regulatory agency. These documents are indexed by a Personal Author Index, a Corporate Source Index, and a Report Number Index. Price: $74.00 per year; $92.50 foreign. Stock# 752-025-00000-2. Microfiche of the docketed information listed in the Title List is available for sale on a subscription basis from NTIS, at the NTIS address cited above.

Weekly Information Report. Prepared by the NRC's Office of the Executive Director for Operations, this report summarizes items of interest and actions taken by NRC offices. Also included are a section on items approved by the Commission; a status report of FOIA requests; a list of Requests for Proposals issued, contracts awarded and closed out; and a status report from the Three Mile Island Program Office. Price: $122 a year; $152.50 foreign. Stock# 752-005-00000-1.

ENVIRONMENT

U.S. Department of Commerce, National Oceanic and Atmospheric Administration (NOAA)

Weather Records in Private Litigation is part of NOAA's Environmental Information Summaries C-1 containing information on how to obtain certified copies of weather reports. It is published irregularly with the last one dated January 1988. It can be obtained free of charge from the National Climatic Data Center, Federal Building, Asheville, NC 28801-2696. Tel: 704/259-0682.

* * * * * * * * * * * *

U.S. Environmental Protection Agency

EPA Regulatory Agenda provides scientific information on the status of regulations that are under development, revision, and review at EPA. It can be obtained free of charge by contacting EPA, Regulation Development Branch, 401 M Street, S.W., 415 W. Tower, Washington, D.C. 20460. Tel: 202/382-5475.

Guide to EPA Libraries and Information Services is available from National Technical Information Service (NTIS), 5285 Port Royal Road, Springfield, VA 22161. Tel: 703/487-4650 or 800/336-4700. Price: $23.00. NTIS Order Number PB89144786/HDM. NTIS charges $3.00 per total order for shipping and handling.

Databases:

The **Integrated Risk Information System (IRIS)**, developed by the U.S. Environmental Protection Agency, contains summary information related to human health risk assessment. Updated monthly, **IRIS** is the Agency's primary vehicle for communication of chronic health hazard information that represents EPA consensus positions following comprehensive review by intra-Agency work groups. **IRIS** contains chemical-specific information in summary format for over 400 chemicals and provides a description of the basis for the hazard assessment and a discussion of the uncertainties in that assessment. **IRIS** can be accessed via several methods: telecommunications link with a commercial carrier (BT Tymnet); through the National Library of Medicine's TOXNET system; and, on diskettes from the National Technical Information Service (NTIS), Tel: 703/487-4650 or 800/336-4700. For further information, contact IRIS User Support, ECAO/EPA (MS114), 26 West Martin Luther King Drive, Cincinnati, OH 45268.

Road Maps to Information Sources on Section 313 Chemicals provides support data on EPA's preliminary exposure and risk assessment activities of the TRI (Toxic Release Inventory) Section 313 chemicals. The database contains references to EPA hazard and risk assessment review documents and online databases concerning toxicity and risk assessment; covers major Federal regulations and regulatory levels on the chemicals; provides State information on air and drinking water levels and standards; and summarizes toxicity information available on the Section 313 chemicals. The present information is from the summer of 1989. EPA hopes to update this annually. This database is available from NTIS, 5285 Port Royal Road, Springfield, VA 22161. Tel: 703/487-4650 or 800/336-4700. Price for database: $180.00. NTIS Order Number PB90-501487. Price for user's manual: $17.00 (paperback), $8.00 (microfiche). NTIS Order Number PB90-174855. NTIS charges $3.00 per total order for shipping and handling.

* * * * * * * * * * * *

U.S. Army Corps of Engineers

Database:

CELDS (Computer-aided Environmental Legislative Data System) is part of the Environmental Technical Information System (ETIS) database maintained by the U.S. Army Corps of Engineers. CELDS is a collection of abstracted Federal and State environmental regulations covering seventeen subject areas such as air quality, pesticides, radiation, toxic substances and hazardous waste. Database information is continuously updated. Subscription service is available to those users desiring online access to ETIS programs. The fees are $200.00 (one-time subscription fee); $20.00 per hour (telecommunications charge, if applicable); $20.00 (annual maintenance fee); $90.00 per hour (connect time, billed monthly); and $15.00 (one time charge per additional log-in). The ETIS office offers individual assistance for CELDS information retrieval. ETIS staff searches cost $90.00/hour (computer connect time, prorated per minute); $25.00 per hour (staff time, prorated per quarter hour); $1.00/page (FAX); and ten cents a page (Xeroxing). For information, contact Environmental Technical Information System, University of Illinois at Urbana-Champaign, 1003 W. Nevada St., Urbana, IL 61801. Tel: 217/333-1369.

ETHICS

Office of Government Ethics

Government Ethics Newsgram is published quarterly. It is free of charge and can be obtained from the Office of Government Ethics, 1201 New York Avenue, N.W., Suite 500, Washington, D.C. 20005. Tel: 202/523-5757.

The Informal Advisory Letters and Memoranda and Formal Opinions (1989) presents a complete collection of all OGE opinions issued between 1979 and 1988. Beginning with the Summer of 1990, yearly supplements will be issued for the previous year. OGE will notify the Superintendent of Documents at Government Printing Office (GPO) of any individual supplements and their availability. These supplements will be announced in Government Ethics, and will be available from GPO. Contact: The Superintendent of Documents, U.S. Government Printing Office, Washington, D.C. 20402. Tel: 202/783-3238. Price: $25.00. GPO Stock# 052-003-01172-7.

FREEDOM OF INFORMATION/PRIVACY

The following publications can be purchased from the **U.S. Government Printing Office.** Stock numbers and prices for annual subscriptions are shown below. Submit requests for these publications to: The Superintendent of Documents, U.S. Government Printing Office, Washington, D.C. 20402. Tel: 202/783-3238.

A Citizen's Guide on Using the Freedom of Information Act and the Privacy Act of 1974 to Request Government Records gives instructions on how to make a FOIA request and a Privacy Act request for access to information. Price: $1.75 domestic; $2.19 foreign. GPO Stock# 052-071-00865-9.

FOIA (Freedom of Information Act) Update contains updated news articles pertaining to the Freedom of Information Act. Published quarterly. Price: $5.00 per year domestic; $6.25 foreign. GPO Stock# 727-002-00000-6.

* * * * * * * * * * * *

Your Right to Federal Records. How to use the Freedom of Information Act and Privacy Act to obtain records from the Federal Government. 1989. Available from Consumer Information Center-P, P.O. Box 100, Pueblo, CO 81002. Price: 50 cents. Booklet number 462W.

* * * * * * * * * * * *

U.S. Department of Justice

Although the following publication is out of print, it is available in many law libraries as well as in all Federal Depository Libraries.

Freedom of Information Case List, 1989 Edition is a compilation of published and nonpublished judicial decisions addressing access issues under the Freedom of Information Act, 5 U.S.C. 552, as amended. This publication also contains full texts of these statutes, a revised list of related law review articles, and a "Short Guide to the Freedom of Information Act."

HEALTH AND MEDICINE

U.S. Environmental Protection Agency

Databases:

The **Integrated Risk Information System (IRIS)**, developed by the U.S. Environmental Protection Agency, contains summary information related to human health risk assessment. Updated monthly, **IRIS** is the Agency's primary vehicle for communication of chronic health hazard information that represents EPA consensus positions following comprehensive review by intra-Agency work groups. **IRIS** contains chemical-specific information in summary format for over 400 chemicals and provides a description of the basis for the hazard assessment and a discussion of the uncertainties in that assessment. **IRIS** can be accessed via several methods: telecommunications link with a commercial carrier (BT Tymnet); through the National Library of Medicine's TOXNET system; and, on diskettes from the National Technical Information Service (NTIS), Tel: 703/487-4650 or 800/336-4700. For further information, contact IRIS User Support, ECAO/EPA (MS114), 26 West Martin Luther King Drive, Cincinnati, OH 45268.

Road Maps to Information Sources on Section 313 Chemicals provides support data on EPA's preliminary exposure and risk assessment activities of the TRI (Toxic Release Inventory) Section 313 chemicals. The database contains references to EPA hazard and risk assessment review documents and online databases concerning toxicity and risk assessment; covers major Federal regulations and regulatory levels on the chemicals; provides State information on air and drinking water levels and standards; and summarizes toxicity information available on the Section 313 chemicals. The present information is from the summer of 1989. EPA hopes to update this annually. This database is available from NTIS, 5285 Port Royal Road, Springfield, VA 22161. Tel: 703/487-4650 or 800/336-4700. Price for database: $180.00. NTIS Order Number PB90-501487. Price for user's manual: $17.00 (paperback), $8.00 (microfiche). NTIS Order Number PB90-174855. NTIS charges $3.00 per total order for shipping and handling.

* * * * * * * * * * * *

U.S. Department of Health and Human Services

The following publications can be purchased from the **U.S. Government Printing Office.** Stock numbers and prices for annual subscriptions are shown below. Submit requests for these publications to: The Superintendent of Documents, U.S. Government Printing Office, Washington, D.C. 20402. Tel: 202/783-3238.

Approved Drug Products with Therapeutic Equivalence Evaluations (1990). Lists current marketed prescription drug products that have been approved on the basis of their safety and effectiveness by the Food and Drug Administration. Subscription service consists of a basic manual and supplemental material for an indeterminate period. Price: $91.00 domestic; $113.75 foreign. GPO Stock# 917-016-00000-3.

FDA Consumer. Contains information written especially for consumers about Food and Drug Administration regulatory and scientific decisions, and about the safe use of products regulated by FDA. Published ten times a year. Price: $12.00 domestic; $15.00 foreign. GPO Stock# 717-009-00000-2.

FDA Enforcement Report. This weekly publication of the Food and Drug Administration contains information on prosecutions, seizures, injunctions, and recalls. Price: $51.00 domestic; $63.75 foreign. GPO Stock# 717-010-00000-1.

Federal Food, Drug, and Cosmetics Act as Amended and Related Laws. Price: $7.50 domestic; $9.38 foreign. GPO Stock# 017-012-00347-8.

Requirements of Laws and Regulations Enforced by Food and Drug Administration. Price: $2.75 domestic; $3.44 foreign. GPO Stock# 017-012-00343-5.

* * * * * * * * * * * *

Food and Drug Interactions. This four-page booklet describes how some commonly used drugs affect nutritional needs. It also discusses how foods affect drug actions and how to avoid ill effects. 1988. Available from Consumer Information Center-P, P.O. Box 100, Pueblo, CO 81002. Free. If you order two or more free publications, include a check for $1.00 payable to Superintendent of Documents. Booklet number 549W.

* * * * * * * * * * * *

Deciding to Forego Life-Sustaining Treatment: Ethical, Medical, and Legal Issues in Treatment Decisions. President's Commission for the Study of Ethical Problems in Medicine and Biomedical and Behavioral Research, 1983. Available from National Technical Information Service, Springfield, VA 22161. Price: $11.00 plus $3.00 for handling. Document no. PB 83226836.

Databases and Bulletin Boards:

Departmental Appeals Board, Electronic Bulletin Board. The Departmental Appeals Board Electronic Bulletin Board is a computerized database that provides summaries of Departmental Appeals Board decisions, the full text of the decisions, and related index materials. It can be accessed through any microcomputer using a 1200 baud modem. There is no fee for use of the Bulletin Board, but usage is limited to one hour per day per user. For information call 202/474-0008.

Food and Drug Administration, Electronic Bulletin Board. The FDA Electronic Bulletin Board provides the full texts of announcements the moment that they are released. The bulletin board It offers FDA news releases, recalls, FDA Federal Register summaries, the FDA Drug Bulletin, selected stories from the FDA Consumer magazine, congressional testimony, speeches delivered by FDA officials, and a special section on AIDS. It is designed for users with little computer experience and is available 24 hours a day, 7 days a week. To obtain FDA's free packet of information about the bulletin board, contact: U.S. Food and Drug Administration, 5600 Fishers Lane, Rockville, MD 20857. Tel: 301/443-3285.

The bulletin board can be accessed through BT TYMNET. For pricing or equipment information, contact: BT TYMNET Customer Support, 6120 Executive Boulevard, Suite 500, Rockville, MD 20852. Tel: 301/770-4280. Pricing information is also available from BT TYMNET at 800/872-7654.

Food and Drug Administration, Adverse Reaction Database. The FDA Adverse Reaction Database includes all adverse reactions to prescription drugs that are reported to FDA. The database was started in 1970 and contains over 100,000 records. Search requests must be submitted in writing and should include the trade name, generic name, and manufacturer of the drug. Reports list adverse reactions that are not normally found in the product insert. They also include summaries of case reports that show each specific case, the case accession number, and the adverse reactions encountered in the case. These reports cost $50.00 per drug. A second type of report is available describing specific cases in detail. The case reports should be requested by accession number. The cost of case reports is 50 cents per page plus staff search time, which is billed at $10.00 per hour or $20.00 per hour depending on the level of staff required to complete the search. Allow at least two to three weeks per search. Search charges are billed once per month. Contact: U.S. Food and Drug Administration, Division of Epidemiology and Surveillance, 5600 Fishers Lane (HFD737), Room 15B23, Rockville, MD 20857. Tel: 301/443-6260.

Food and Drug Administration, Product Defects Database. The FDA's Product Defects Database was started in 1974 and includes product defect information that has been reported to FDA. Only drugs produced in the U.S. are covered. Search requests must be submitted in writing and should include the trade name, generic name, and manufacturer of the drug. It is helpful to include the type of defect when known. Searches are performed on a cost reimbursement basis. Typical searches cost $10.00 to $60.00. All incidents meeting the search criteria are included in the search reports. A typical incident will be described in one to five lines. Allow at least two to three weeks per search. Search charges are billed once per month. Contact: U.S. Food and Drug Administration, Division of Epidemiology and Surveillance, 5600 Fishers Lane (HFD737), Room 15B23, Rockville, MD 20857. Tel: 301/443-6260.

BIOETHICSLINE. This is a National Library of Medicine (NLM) online bibliographic database focused on questions of ethics and public policy. Its scope spans the literature of the health sciences, law, religion, philosophy, social sciences, and the popular media. For example, the database contains citations on such topics as euthanasia, organ donation and transplantation, the allocation of health care resources, patients' rights, codes of professional ethics, in vitro fertilization and other reproductive technologies, genetic intervention, abortion, behavior control and mental health therapies, and human experimentation. Published each year since 1975, BIOETHICSLINE currently contains approximately 30,000 records and is updated bimonthly. It is growing at the rate of approximately 2,400 records per year. The database is produced by the Information Retrieval Project at the Kennedy Institute of Ethics, Georgetown University, Washington, D.C. 20057. Tel: 202/625-8709 in the Washington, D.C. metropolitan area or 800/MED-ETHX outside the Washington, D.C. metropolitan area. The National Center for Bioethics will conduct searches of BIOETHICSLINE at no charge.

BIOETHICSLINE is also available through the National Library of Medicine's MEDLAR system. NLM charges about $24.00 per computer connect hour during prime time (10:00 AM to 5:00 PM, Eastern time) and about $17.00 per hour at all other times. NLM also charges 25 cents for each page printed offline. A hard copy version of the database is published annually as the Bibliography of Bioethics. Volume 16, available November 1990, is $45.00 in the U.S. and Canada; $50.00 elsewhere.

HOUSING

U.S. Department of Housing and Urban Development

Fair Housing-Fair Lending is an annual subscription with monthly report bulletins covering Federal and state equal housing opportunity law as represented in statutes, regulations, guidelines and court decisions. An annual subscription costs $390.00 and can be obtained from Prentice-Hall, Inc., Law and Business Division, 270 Sylvan Avenue, Englewood Cliffs, NJ 07632. Tel: 201/894-8484. Or, 800/447-1717.

Databases:

HUD USER is a research information service sponsored by HUD's Office of Policy Development and Research. This system consists of research-oriented materials on such topics as affordable housing, building technology, community development, services for the elderly and handicapped, and neighborhood rehabilitation and conservation. The following services are offered:

*__HUD USER ONLINE:__ BRS has the rights to approximately 145 bibliographic and full-text databases. The basic on-line connect cost varies depending on which database is used. For more information contact: BRS, 8000 West Park Drive, McLean, VA 22102. Tel: 800/289-4277 or 703/442-0900.

*__Document Delivery:__ Printed copies of recently published reports may be obtained for $3.00 if the materials are currently in stock. Those reports not in stock may be obtained at a higher cost. For information, contact: **HUD USER,** P.O. Box 6091, Rockville, MD 20850. Or, call 800/245-2691.

*__Recent Research Results:__ This free bulletin features information on HUD's policies, programs, publications and research activities. Call 800/245-2691 to order.

*__HUD USER__ Standard Searches: Reports on key topics in housing and urban development are available for $10.00 and custom searches are available for $20.00. Call 800/245-2691 for information.

*Copies of non-copyrighted documents from **HUD USER ONLINE** are available in microfiche, contact: **HUD USER,** P.O. Box 6091, Rockville, MD 20850. Or, call 800/245-2691.

IMMIGRATION

U.S. Commission on Civil Rights

The Immigration Reform and Control Act: Assessing the Evaluation Process (1989) examines the reports by the General Accounting Office on the extent of discrimination and the burden on employers under the employer sanctions provisions of the Immigration Reform and Control Act of 1986. Concludes that the law has caused at least a pattern of discrimination. Recommends that Congress extend the evaluation period and clarify certain provisions in the law. Contains other findings and recommendations. 46 pp. Available free of charge from the **Clearinghouse Division, U.S. Commission on Civil Rights,** 1121 Vermont Ave., N.W., Washington, D.C. 20425. Tel: 202/376-8110.

* * * * * * * * * * * *

U.S. Department of Justice

The following publications can be purchased from the **U.S. Government Printing Office.** Stock numbers and prices for annual subscriptions are shown below. Submit requests for these publications to: The Superintendent of Documents, U.S. Government Printing Office, Washington, D.C. 20402. Tel: 202/783-3238.

Immigration and Naturalization Service Operating Instructions, Regulations, and Interpretations contains definitions, regulations and interpretation of the INS. Updated irregularly. Price: $196.00 domestic; $245.00 foreign. GPO Stock# 927-002-00000-1.

Interim Decisions of the Department of Justice contains selected precedential Board of Immigration Appeals decisions which are binding on all Immigration and Naturalization Offices. Published at irregular intervals. Price: $65.00 domestic; $81.25 foreign. GPO Stock# 827-002-00000-3.

United States Immigration Laws: General Information is a pamphlet containing information on emigration and immigration law. Price: $1.00 domestic; $1.25 foreign. GPO Stock# 027-002-00377-2.

* * * * * * * * * * * *

U.S. Department of Labor

Instructions for Filing Applications for Alien Employment Certification for Permanent Employment in the United States. Published in one volume. Price $2.25. GPO Stock# 029-014-01796-5. Contact: The Superintendent of Documents, U.S. Government Printing Office, Washington, D.C. 20402. Tel: 202/783-3238.

INTERIOR AND NATURAL RESOURCES

Appalachian Regional Commission

Appalachia is a quarterly magazine highlighting the activities and projects of the Commission with special emphasis on the activities of the people in the region. To obtain a free copy, contact: The Appalachian Regional Commission, 1666 Connecticut Avenue, N.W., Washington, D.C. 20235. Tel: 202/673-7968.

* * * * * * * * * * * *

U.S. Department of the Interior

The following publications can be purchased from the **U.S. Government Printing Office.** Stock numbers and prices for annual subscriptions are shown below. Submit requests for these publications to: The Superintendent of Documents, U.S. Government Printing Office, Washington, D.C. 20402. Tel: 202/783-3238.

Decisions of the Department of the Interior contains significant decisions by the U.S. Department of the Interior on appeals, claims, and acts. It is published monthly and placed in bound volumes at the end of the year.

Volume 95 (1988). Annual price: $14.00 domestic; $17.50 foreign. GPO Stock# 724-010-00000-8.
Volume 96 (1989). Annual price: $11.00 domestic; $13.75 foreign. GPO Stock# 724-011-00000-4.
Volume 97 (1990). Annual price: $11.00 domestic; $13.75 foreign. GPO Stock #724-013-00000-7.

* * * * * * * * * * * *

Index Digest is the computer printout of published and unpublished headnotes of the Board of Land Appeals, the Board of Indian Appeals, and the Board of Contract Appeals, and the published Solicitor's opinions. It is published quarterly and bound in paperback at the end of each year. After five years, it is bound in hardback. Annual price: $65.00. Contact the U.S. Department of the Interior, Office of Hearings, 4015 Wilson Boulevard, Arlington, VA 22203. Tel: 703/235-3799.

* * * * * * * * * * * *

Surface Mining Law Summary is a looseleaf publication, updated periodically. It contains decisions of the Administrative Law Judges of the Board of Land Appeals and decisions of the Administrative Law Judges of the Hearings Division in selected surface mining cases. Annual price: $375.00. Contact: Surface Mining Law Summary, Inc., P.O. Box 281, Corbin, KY 40701. Tel: 606/528-9481.

INTERNATIONAL RELATIONS/FOREIGN AFFAIRS

The following publications can be purchased from the **U.S. Government Printing Office**. Stock numbers and prices for annual subscriptions are shown below. Submit requests for these publications to: The Superintendent of Documents, U.S. Government Printing Office, Washington, D.C. 20402. Tel: 202/783-3238.

American Foreign Policy Series. The annual volume of the series contains official statements that set forth the goals and objectives of U.S. foreign policy. The series includes texts of major official messages, addresses, statements, interviews, press conferences and briefings, reports, congressional testimony and communications by the White House, the Department of State, and other Federal agencies or officials involved in the foreign policy process. Each volume is divided into geographic and topical chapters, and then chronologically within chapters. Editorial annotations, maps, lists of names and abbreviations, and a comprehensive index by document numbers are also included.

Each volume is compiled by the professional staff in the Office of the Historian and is intended to make available in the year following the events "the best contemporary collection of public expressions of U.S. foreign policy by U.S. Government officials." Each volume is individually priced. A typical volume is American Foreign Policy: Current Documents, 1988. Price $31.00 domestic; $38.75 foreign. GPO Stock# 044-000-02256-7.

Digest of U.S. Practice in International Law and Digest of International Law. 1990. This document contains a bibliography of Government publications on international law. Free. GPO Stock# 021-185-00006-0.

Diplomatic List. This is a quarterly list of foreign diplomatic representatives in Washington, D.C., and their addresses. Annual subscription price: $7.50 domestic; $9.38 foreign. GPO Stock# 744-004-00000-4.

Foreign Consular Offices in the United States. Contains a complete and official listing of the foreign consular offices in the United States, together with their jurisdictions and recognized consular officers. Price: $4.00 domestic; $5.00 foreign. GPO Stock# 044-000-02283-4.

Foreign Relations Series. This series presents the documentary record of U.S. foreign policy. The series is prepared by a staff of professional historians in the Office of the Historian, Department of State. The principles that guide the selection of documents and the editing of the series are set forth in the prefaces of the volumes. Although based largely upon Department of State records, volumes also include significant Presidential and White House documents, as well as important records of other agencies and foreign governments. Nearly all the material printed was originally classified. The volumes are priced individually.

For example, the most recent volume is Foreign Relations of the United States, 1955-1957, Volume XVI, Suez Crisis, July 26-December 31, 1956. This volume represents the comprehensive official historical documentary record of U.S. diplomacy in the events surrounding the Suez crisis. Its 1,344 pages were gathered from the White House, the Department of State, the Dwight D. Eisenhower Presidential Library, and other Government agencies. Nearly all the documents selected were declassified for this publication. Price: $41.00 domestic; $51.25 foreign. GPO Stock# 044-000-02251-6.

Standardized Regulations (Government Civilians, Foreign Areas). Published 13 times a year. Presents information on standardized regulations pertaining to civilian employees working in foreign areas. Also announces changes and updates to current regulations as well as new regulations. Price: $36.00 domestic; $45.00 foreign. GPO Stock# 744-009-00000-6.

Treaties in Force. Annual. Published by the U.S. Department of State. This compilation lists all treaties and international agreements by country and subject. Price: $20.00 for January 1, 1989 edition (a new January 1, 1990 edition will soon be available). GPO Stock# 044-000-02257-5.

Treaties and Other International Acts Series (TIAS). This compilation, which begins with Treaty No. 1501, contains all treaties proclaimed during the calendar year to which the United States is a party, as well as all international agreements other than treaties to which the United States is a party, which have been signed, proclaimed, or subjected to any other final formality during the calendar year. TIAS consists of literal prints of single copies of the original treaties and international agreements, published in pamphlet form. Ultimately, the pamphlets are compiled and published in bound volume sets under the title United States Treaties and Other International Agreements (see below). Price: $89.00 domestic; $111.25 foreign. GPO Stock# 844-001-00000-2.

United States Treaties and Other International Agreements (UST). Contains the full text of U.S. treaties and agreements. The first ten volumes are out of print. Through Volume 35, the treaties and agreements have been prepared for publication in chronological order. Beginning with Volume 36, the most frequently requested treaties and agreements will be given priority for publication. The volumes are priced individually. The most recently published volumes are:

Volume 34, Part 3, 1982. (Published 1988). Price: $48.00 domestic; $60.00 foreign. GPO Stock# 044-000-02214-1.

Volume 34, Part 4. 1982. (To be published late in 1990). No price available. GPO Stock# 044-000-02215-0.

* * * * * * * * * * * *

Twenty-seventh Semiannual Report--Implementation of Helsinki Final Act, April 1, 1989 - September 30, 1989. February 1989. Special Report No. 183, 58 pp. Available free of charge from the **Bureau of Public Affairs**, Room 6805, U.S. Department of State, Washington, D.C. 20520-6810.

LABOR

Handy Reference Guide to the Fair Labor Standards Act 1987 is a publication for employees and employers covering Federal laws on minimum wage, overtime pay, child labor, and more. It is available from Consumer Information Center-P, P.O. Box 100, Pueblo, CO 81002. Price: 50 cents. Booklet number 401W.

* * * * * * * * * * * * *

Federal Labor Relations Authority

The following publications can be purchased from the **U.S. Government Printing Office**. Stock numbers and prices for annual subscriptions are shown below. Submit requests for these publications to: The Superintendent of Documents, U.S. Government Printing Office, Washington, D.C. 20402. Tel: 202/783-3238.

FLRA (Federal Labor Relations Authority) Reports of Case Decisions, FSIP (Federal Service Impasses Panel) Releases and Administrative Law Judge Decisions of the FLRA. The decisions and releases are issued irregularly during a twelve month period. Price: $152.00 domestic; $190.00 foreign. GPO Stock# 863-002-00000-1. Note: Single copies may be obtained from The Federal Labor Relations Authority, 500 C Street, S.W., Washington, D.C. 20424.

FLRA (Federal Labor Relations Authority) Publications is published irregularly during a twelve month period with an annual subscription rate of $6.00 domestic; $7.50 foreign. Single copies of the quarterly issue, Report of Case Handling Developments of the Office of General Counsel (FLRA), and the annual issue, Subject Matter Index and Table of Cases (FSIP) vary in price. GPO Stock# 863-001-00000-5.

* * * * * * * * * * * *

Federal Labor Relations Reporter. A monthly service reporting labor relations decisions for the Federal sector. It includes decisions of the FLRA, FLRA General Counsel, FSIP, Administrative Law Judges, labor arbitrators, and Federal courts. Back volumes dating from 1979 are available at extra expense. Product# 4010. Price: $685.00 per year. Contact: LRP Publications, 747 Dresher Road, P.O. Box 980, Horsham, PA 19044-0980. Tel: 800/341-7874.

Database:

Federal Labor Relations Authority Case Decisions, Federal Service Impasses Panel Decisions, and Administrative Law Judge Decisions. Available on CD-ROM through the PERSONNET Service of Information Handling Services, 15 Inverness Way East, P.O. Box 1154, Englewood, CO 80150. Tel: 800/241-7824. In Colorado, call 303/790-0600 ext 59.

* * * * * * * * * * * *

Federal Mediation and Conciliation Service

Single copies of the following publications may be obtained free of charge by contacting: **Federal Mediation and Conciliation Service**, Public Affairs, Room 710, 2100 K Street, N.W., Washington, D.C. 20427.

Change and Its Impact on Labor Management Relations (pamphlet)

Mediation in Public Sector Labor Management Disputes (pamphlet)

Mediation in Age Discrimination Disputes (pamphlet)

Arbitration (pamphlet)

America Works: The Report of the President's Advisory Committee on Mediation and Conciliation. (book, 48 pp.).

* * * * * * * * * * * *

U.S. Department of Labor

OFCCP Federal Contract Compliance Manual is in the process of being updated. It is an eight volume manual. Updated chapters 2-7 can be obtained free of charge by contacting the Office of Policy, Planning and Review Division, Office of Federal Contract Compliance Programs, U.S. Department of Labor, 200 Constitution Ave., N.W., Washington, D.C. 20210. Tel: 202/523-9434. Chapter 8 will be published shortly.

U.S. Department of Labor Highlights summarizes the major programs within each agency of the Department. Each agency is covered separately in a two page summary. A single copy is free and can be obtained by contacting the U.S. Department of Labor, Office of Public Affairs, Room S1032, 200 Constitution Ave., N.W., Washington, D.C. 20210. Tel: 202/523-7343.

Decisions of the Office of Administrative Law Judges and Office of Administrative Appeals. Published bimonthly. Price: $28.00 a year domestic; $35.00 a year foreign. GPO Stock# 729-011-00000-2.

Database:

Labor News is a 24 hour electronic bulletin board maintained by the Department of Labor containing the full text of each day's press releases. Speeches given by the Secretary of Labor are also included. A 30 day index of the preceding 30 days is available. Potential users can obtain further information on the bulletin board by contacting the Department of Labor, Office of Public Affairs, Room S1032, 200 Constitution Ave., N.W., Washington, D.C. 20210. Tel: 202/523-7343.

* * * * * * * * * * * *

National Labor Relations Board

The following National Labor Relations Board (NLRB) publications can be purchased from the **U.S. Government Printing Office.** Stock numbers and prices per copy are shown below. Contact: The Superintendent of Documents, U.S. Government Printing Office, Washington, D.C. 20402. Tel: 202/783-3238.

(1) National Labor Relations Act and Labor Management Relations Act. GPO Stock# 031-000-00255-9. Price: $1.00.

(2) A Guide to Basic Law and Procedures Under the National Labor Relations Act. GPO Stock# 031-000-00273-7. Price: $2.00.

(3) Decisions and Orders of the National Labor Relations Board
(GPO Stock# 031-000-00267-2; Vol. 275: 04/06/85-08/27/85; $48.00)
(GPO Stock# 031-000-00267-1; Vol. 276: 08/28/85-10/29/85; $45.00)
(GPO Stock# 031-000-00272-9; Vol. 277: 10/29/85-01/14/86; $45.00)
(GPO Stock# 031-000-00274-5; Vol. 278: 01/15/86-03/27/86; $45.00)
(GPO Stock# 031-000-00275-3; Vol. 279: 03/28/86-05/30/86; $45.00)
(GPO Stock# 031-000-00276-1; Vol. 280: 05/30/86-08/07/86; $48.00)
(GPO Stock# 031-000-00285-1; Vol. 281: 08/08/86-10/21/86; $47.00)
(GPO Stock# 031-000-00287-7; Vol. 282: 10/22/86-02/23/87; $48.00)
(GPO Stock# 031-000-00288-5; Vol. 283: 02/24/87-05/29/87; $45.00)
(GPO Stock# 031-000-00291-5; Vol. 284: 05/27/87-07/29/87; $50.00)
(GPO Stock# 031-000-00292-3; Vol. 285: 07/30/87-09/29/87; $47.00)
(GPO Stock# 031-000-00293-1; Vol. 286: 09/30/87-12/07/87; $48.00)

(4) Court Decisions Relating to the National Labor Relations Act
(GPO Stock# 031-000-00252-4; Vol. 32: 01/01/80-12/31/80; $37.00)
(GPO Stock# 031-000-00254-1; Vol. 33: 01/01/81-12/31/81; $43.00)
(GPO Stock# 031-000-00258-3; Vol. 34: 01/01/82-12/31/82; $45.00)
(GPO Stock# 031-000-00261-3; Vol. 35: 01/01/83-12/31/83; $41.00)
(GPO Stock# 031-000-00271-1; Vol. 36: 01/01/84-12/31/84; $38.00)
(GPO Stock# 031-000-00277-0; Vol. 37: 01/01/85-12/31/85; $38.00)
(GPO Stock# 031-000-00283-4; Vol. 38: 01/01/86-12/31/86; $38.00)

(5) Weekly Summary of NLRB Cases includes summaries of all published NLRB decisions in unfair labor practice and representation election cases; lists decision of NLRB Administrative Law Judges and directions of elections by NLRB Regional Directors; reprints the General Counsel's Quarterly Report on (1) cases decided upon a request for advice from a Regional Director or an appeal from a Director's dismissal of unfair labor practice charges and (2) cases in which the General Counsel sought and obtained Board authorization to institute injunction proceedings under Section 10(j) of the Act; carries notices of publication of volumes of NLRB decisions and orders; NLRB Annual Report and other agency informational literature. GPO Stock# 731-002-00000-2. Price: $84.00 a year for domestic subscriptions, $105.00 a year for foreign subscriptions.

(6) NLRB Election Report is a monthly report detailing the outcome of secret-ballot voting by employees in NLRB-conducted representation elections in cases closed for each month. It is compiled from results following resolution of postelection objections and/or challenges. Election tallies are listed by unions involved, with employer name and location, and is arranged in two parts, single union elections and multi-union elections. The most current edition is from October 1989. GPO Stock# 731-001-00000-6. Price: $27.00 for 12 issues mailed domestically; $33.75 for foreign subscriptions.

(7) Rules and Regulations and Statements of Procedure of the National Labor Relations Board, Series 8, as amended 3/15/89 contains supplements for an indefinite period. It is in looseleaf form, punched for a three-ring binder (binder not included). GPO Stock# 931-002-00000-7. Price: $13.00 for domestic subscriptions; $16.25 for foreign subscriptions.

(8) National Labor Relations Board Casehandling Manual contains complete, updated General Counsel procedural and operational guidelines to NLRB Regional Offices in processing cases received under the Act in three parts. Part One: "Unfair Labor Practice Proceedings," Part Two: "Representation Proceedings." and Part Three: "Compliance Proceedings and Settlement Agreements." GPO Stock# 931-001-00000-1. Price: $50.00 for domestic subscriptions; $62.50 for foreign subscriptions.

(9) Classified Index of NLRB Decisions and Related Court Decisions (CINDR) is published as a paperback on a quarterly basis, and covers all board, Administrative Law Judges' and NLRB-related court decisions issued during the period covering publication. GPO Stock# 831-003-00000-6. Price: $18.00 (domestic) for four issues; $22.50 foreign.

(10) Classified Index of Dispositions of Unfair Labor Practice Charges by the General Counsel of the National labor Relations Board (CIDUL) is compiled by the Office of General Counsel, published on an irregular basis and cumulated, and is an index of Advice memoranda, Regional Directors' dismissal letters, and Appeals memoranda and dispositions. Last issue dated Dec 1989. GPO Stock# 031-000-00294-0. Price: $27.00 domestic; $33.75 foreign.

(11) Classification Outline with Topical Index of Decisions of the National Labor Relations Board and Related Court Decisions. This is a set consisting of four items: 1) Classified Index of National Labor Relations Board Decisions and Related Court Decisions; 2) Classified Index of Unfair Labor Practice Charges by the General Counsel of the National Labor Relations Board; 3) Classified Index of Decisions of the Regional Directors of the National Labor Relations Board in Representation Proceedings; and 4) National Labor Relations Board Decisions. GPO Stock# 031-000-00281-8. Price for the set: $41.00 domestic; $51.25 foreign.

* * * * * * * * * * * *

A number of publications are available, free-of-charge, from the Division of Information at the NLRB. They include: The National Labor Relations Board and You--Unfair Labor Practices, and The National Labor Relations Board and You--What It Is? What It Does? Contact: National Labor Relations Board, Division of Information, Suite 710, 1717 Pennsylvania Avenue, N.W., Washington, D.C. 20570. Tel: 202/632-4950.

* * * * * * * * * * * *

National Mediation Board

The **National Mediation Board** has three separate subscription services. The subscription period covers the current Fiscal Year (October 1 through September 30). Make check payable to the United States Treasury and mail to: The National Mediation Board, Attn: M. C. Maione-Pricci, Washington, D.C. 20572.

(1) **Subscription List No. 1** covers all of the Board's publications. They include: Certifications and Dismissals, Determinations of Craft or Class, Findings Upon Investigations, Annual Report of the National Mediation Board, and Emergency Board Reports. Price: $175.00.

(2) **Subscription List No. 2** covers the following publications: Annual Report of the National Mediation Board, Emergency Board Reports, and Determinations of Craft of Class (bound volume). Price: $50.00.

(3) **Subscription List No. 3** consists of the Representation Manual and any subsequent amendments issued. Price: $35.00 (one time charge).

* * * * * * * * * * * *

The following publications are also published by the National Mediation Board and can be ordered from the address listed above.

The Railway Labor Act (U.S. Code Provisions). Price: 75 cents.

NMB Determinations is published by Fiscal Year and include Certifications and Dismissals, Determinations of Craft or Class, and Findings of the Board. The following years are available: Volume 1 (FY74) $3.80; Volume 2 (FY75) $2.00; Volume 3 (FY76) $1.95; Volume 4 (FY77) $2.45; Volume 5 (FY78) $4.50; Volume 6 (FY79) $10.00; Volume 7 (FY80) $8.00; Volume 8 (FY81) $9.00; Volume 9 (FY82) $8.00; Volume 10 (FY83) $11.00; Volume 11 (FY84) $8.00; Volume 12 (FY85) $9.00; Volume 3 (FY86) $10.00; Volume 14 (FY87) $11.00; Volume 15 (FY88) $12.00; Volume 16 (FY89) $13.00. Volume 17 (FY90) is in the process of being published.

* * * * * * * * * * * *

U.S. Office of Personnel Management

The Federal Labor Management and Employee Relations Consultant Newsletter (FLMERC). Published 24 times a year. Presents current information in the field of labor-management and employee relations. Price: $28.00 a year domestic; $35.00 a year foreign. No single copies will be sold. GPO Stock# 706-003-00000-2. Contact: The Superintendent of Documents, U.S. Government Printing Office, Washington, D.C. 20402. Tel: 202/783-3238.

* * * * * * * * * * * *

U.S. Postal Service

Employee and Labor Relations Manual, U.S. Postal Service. Published semiannually. Sets forth the personnel policies and regulations governing employment with the U.S. Postal Service. Topics covered include organization management, employment and placement, pay administration, employee benefits, employee relations, safety and health, and labor relations. Price: $18.00 a year domestic; $22.50 a year foreign. GPO Stock# 739-005-00000-1. Contact: The Superintendent of Documents, U.S. Government Printing Office, Washington, D.C. 20402. Tel: 202/783-3238.

LEGAL SERVICES

Legal Services Corporation

The following publications can be purchased from **The National Clearinghouse for Legal Services.** Submit requests for these publications to: The National Clearinghouse for Legal Services, 407 South Dearborn, Suite 400, Chicago, IL 60605. Tel: 312/939-3830.

The Clearinghouse Review. This monthly (except for a combined August/September issue) legal journal deals with articles and case developments in poverty law. Price: There is no charge for any attorney or paralegal who is part of a Legal Services program (it must be ordered through the program, not individually). The cost for a subscription is $75.00 a year for everyone else. Single copies cost $6.00 each.

Federal Register Highlights newsletter. Published twice a month. It summarizes final and proposed rules and other items in the Federal Register that affect the poor. Price: $50.00 a year. No single copies sold.

PAROLE/PROBATION

Federal Probation: A Journal of Correctional Philosophy and Practice contains articles relating to preventive and correctional activities in delinquency and crime. Published quarterly. Price: $5.00 per year domestic; $6.25 foreign. GPO Stock# 727-001-00000-0. Contact: The Superintendent of Documents, U.S. Government Printing Office, Washington, D.C. 20402. Tel: 202/783-3238.

Database:

DRAM (Decision Recording and Monitoring System) is an in-house database not available to the public but a hard copy of specifically requested information is available; e.g. parole risk statistics, lengths of sentence vis-a-vis an offense committed. Call or write the U.S. Parole Commission, 5550 Friendship Boulevard, Chevy Chase, MD 20815. Tel: 301/492-5980.

PATENTS, TRADEMARKS, AND COPYRIGHTS

U.S. Department of Commerce, Patent and Trademark Office

Facts About Trademarks contains information about the advantages and procedures of filing a trademark application, including blank application forms. It can be obtained free of charge by contacting the Office of Public Information, U.S. Patent and Trademark Office, 2121 Crystal Drive, Crystal Park 2, Arlington, VA 22202. Tel: 703/557-5168.

* * * * * * * * * * * *

The following publications can be purchased from the **U.S. Government Printing Office.** Stock numbers and prices for annual subscriptions are shown below. Submit requests for these publications to: The Superintendent of Documents, U.S. Government Printing Office, Washington, D.C. 20402. Tel: 202/783-3238.

General Information Concerning Patents contains information on patents including the workings of the Patent and Trademark Office, what applicants must do, and definitions of patents, copyrights, and trademarks. The cost is $2.00. GPO Stock# 003-004-00641-2.

Manual of Classification (Patent Office), December 1988 lists the numbers and descriptive titles of the Patent Office classes and subclasses, as well as the Design Classes. Subscription service consists of a two-volume basic manual, the index to Classification of Patents, and semiannual replacement pages for the manual for an indeterminate period. The cost is $66.00 domestic; $82.50 foreign. GPO Stock# 903-006-00000-5.

Manual of Patent Examining Procedure, 1988, is a consolidated reprint providing information on practices and procedures related to the prosecution of patent applications before the U.S. Patent and Trademark Office. Subscription service consists of a basic manual and supplementary material for an indeterminate period. The cost is $78.00 domestic; $97.50 foreign. GPO Stock# 903-007-00000-1.

Trademark Manual of Examining Procedure, 1987, provides trademark examiners in the Patent Office, trademark applicants, and attorneys for applicants with a reference work on the practices and procedures related to the prosecution of applications to register marks in the Patent Office. Subscription service consists of a basic manual and semiannual changes for an indeterminate period. The cost is $14.00 domestic; $17.50 foreign. GPO Stock# 903-010-00000-2.

Official Gazette of the U.S. Patent and Trademark Office: Patents is published weekly and contains the Patents, Patent Office Notices, and Designs issued each week. The annual indexes are not included as part of the subscription service but are sold separately. Subscribers will be notified when the indexes are published. The cost is $593.00 a year domestic (priority mail) or $449.00 a year (non-priority mail); $561.25 a year foreign. Foreign airmail distribution available upon request, plus an additional cost based upon International Postal Zone. GPO Stock# 703-033-00000-8.

Official Gazette of the U.S. Patent and Trademark Office: Trademarks is published weekly and contains Trademarks, Trademark Notices, Marks Published for Opposition, Trademark Registrations Issued, and Index of Registrants. The cost is $312.00 a year domestic; $390.00 a year foreign. GPO Stock# 703-034-00000-4.

Patent and Trademark Office Notices is published weekly. The cost is $82.00 a year domestic (priority mail) or $59.00 a year (non-priority mail); $73.75 a year foreign. Foreign airmail distribution available upon request, plus an additional cost based upon International Postal Zone. GPO Stock# 703-035-00000-1.

* * * * * * * * * * * *

U.S. Patents Quarterly, 2d Series publishes the full text of decisions involving patent, trademark, copyright, and unfair competition law. Weekly Advance Sheets contain both digest and texts of pertinent decisions from: U.S. Supreme Court, U.S. Court of Appeals for the Federal Circuit, U.S. Courts of Appeals, U.S. Claims Courts, U.S. District Courts, Commissioner of Patents and Trademarks, Patent and Trademark Office Board of Patent Appeals and Interferences, Patent and Trademark Office Trademark Trial and Appeal Board, U.S. Tax Court, U.S. International Trade Commission, and state courts. Price: $1,020.00 annually. Contact: Bureau of National Affairs, 9435 Key West Avenue, Rockville, MD 20850. Tel: 301/258-1033. Or, 800/372-1033.

* * * * * * * * * * * *

Databases:

The following databases are available from the Department of Commerce. These records can be obtained from the addresses listed below.

Technology Assessment and Forecast (TAF) Program is a database containing more than 27 million documents which make up the categorized U.S. patent file. Patent information is disseminated to users through the following various methods:

1) **Publications** are prepared on topics of general interest. The **Patent Profiles** series includes surveys of U.S. patenting activity in biotechnology, solar energy, and microelectronics. The ten **Technology Assessment and Forecast Reports** include reviews of technology areas having the most new patents or the most foreign inventors, explanations of information available by studying patents; comparisons of the patenting activity of major corporations; and analyses of the inventions patented in selected technology. The TAF Program also publishes reports on design patents, industrial robots, and annual statistics of industrial patent activity. The costs vary from $6.50 to $95.00 according to report. A complete list of publications and costs can be obtained from the National Technical Information Service, 5285 Port Royal Road, Springfield, VA 22161. Tel: 703/487-4650.

2) **Custom Patent Reports** are generated from the TAF data cost base and prepared in response to specific requests. These include: Technology Profile Report which has four parts: a) patenting activity percentages and time-series distribution by general assignment category and origin of patents; b) a ranked listing of organizations, and counts of patents granted by both year of application filing and year of grant; c) lists of organizations alphabetically with patent numbers and titles; and d) names and addresses of the inventors of patents assigned to individuals or unassigned at time of issue, including patent numbers and titles. **Organizational Profile Report** profiles patent activity, usually of a specified organization, with specific patent numbers and titles. **Multi-Corporate Patent Activity Profile** profiles the activity of up to eight organizations simultaneously, facilitating comparisons between organizations but giving no patent numbers or titles. **Enterprise Patenting Report** shows the number of patents per year for a parent company and its patenting subsidiaries.

These **Custom Patent Reports** are provided on a cost reimbursable basis with costs varying from as low as $50.00 to several thousand dollars. For more information contact the Office of Documentation Information, U.S. Patent and Trademark Office, CM2-304, Washington, D.C. 20231. Tel: 703/557-0433.

3) **Statistical Reports can be obtained which** cover all patents in the data base and show yearly levels of patenting distributed by state or country of origin, category of ownership and/or technology class within the U.S. Patent Classification (USPC) System. These reports are free of charge from the Office of Documentation Information, U.S. Patent and Trademark Office, CM2-304, Washington, D.C. 20231. Tel: 703/557-5652.

* * * * * * * * * * * *

The **Office of Electronic Data Conversion and Dissemination** within the Patent and Trademark Office disseminates a variety of information in electronic form. An example of the 1990 patent products are:

1) **Patent Full Text File** contains the full text of each patent issued. Some of the data included are: patent number, series code and application number, type of patent, filing date, title, abstract, assignee name and address at time of issue, attorney, agent, or firm/legal representative, related U.S. patent documents, classification information, field of search, U.S. and foreign references, priority data, and claims. Each weekly update contains approximately 2,000 patents. The annual charge for this weekly service is $8,980.00 and can be obtained from the Office of Electronic Data Conversion and Dissemination, U.S. Patent and Trademark Office, Crystal Park 2, Suite 1100B, Washington, D.C. 20231. Tel: 703/557-6154.

This file is commercially available through Mead Data Central's LEXPAT. Tel: 800/543-6862.

2) **Patent Attorney Roster File** contains records for attorneys and/or agents who are registered to practice before the Patent and Trademark Office. It provides their names and addresses and contains approximately 12,500 names and is often used for mass mailings. Its costs is $300.00 and is issued on demand. It can be ordered through the Office of Electronic Data Conversion and Dissemination, U.S. Patent and Trademark Office, Crystal Park 2, Suite 1100B, Washington, D.C. 20231. Tel: 703/557-6154.

3) **Patent Master Classification File (MCF)** contains the classes and subclasses of technology that all patents are assigned by the Patent Examining Corps. It is broken into approximately 120,000 categories. The MCF is completely updated each time it is issued, relating all issued patents since 1790 to their current classification. MCF can be obtained at an annual cost of $510.00 from the Office of Electronic Data Conversion and Dissemination, U.S. Patent and Trademark Office, Crystal Park 2, Suite 1100B, Washington, D.C. 20231. Tel: 703/557-6154.

Commercial availability: IFI/Plenum and DIALOG (Tel: 800/334-2564); Derwent, Inc. (Tel: 800/421-7229); and NERAC (Tel: 203/486-4533). The public, through the Patent Depository Libraries (PDL), may search the MCF by using the CD-ROM system provided to each PDL by the Patent and Trademark Office.

4) **Trademark Weekly Text File** contains the text data of pending and registered trademarks. Some of the fields include: word mark, serial number, registration number, filing date, and TTAB (Trademark Trial and Appeal Board) data. This weekly file can be obtained at an annual cost of $4,850 from the Office of Electronic Data Conversion and Dissemination, U.S. Patent and Trademark Office, Crystal Park 2, Ste 1100B, Wash., D.C. 20231. Tel: 703/557-6154.

This file is commercially available from The Trademark Register through Bell Atlantic Gateway Operator 2606 (Tel: 800/638-6363) and Maxwell Online's U.S. Trademark Watch (Tel: 800/456-7248).

5) **Trademark Image File** contains the images of pending and registered trademarks and the corresponding serial/registration number. The retrospective file is available from the present to April 1, 1987 and contains approximately 500 images per each weekly update. This weekly file costs $3,945.00 annually and can be obtained from the Office of Electronic Data Conversion and Dissemination. U.S. Patent and Trademark Office, Crystal Park 2, Suite 1100B, Washington, D.C. 20231. Tel: 703/557-6154.

This file is commercially available through Thomson and Thomson or through DIALOG. Tel: 800/227-7229.

* * * * * * * * * * * *

U.S. Small Business Administration

Introduction to Patents offers some basic facts about patents to help clarify your rights. It discusses the relationships among a business, an inventor and the Patent and Trademark Office to ensure protection of your product and to avoid or win infringement suits. Price: 50 cents. This publication can be obtained by sending a check or money order made payable to the U.S. Small Business Administration. Send to SBA-Publications, P.O. Box 30, Denver, CO 80201-0030.

PENSIONS

Pension Benefit Guaranty Corporation

The following publications can be obtained free of charge by contacting the **Pension Benefit Guaranty Corporation**, Office of Public Affairs, 2020 K Street, N.W., Washington, D.C. 20006. Tel: 202/778-8840.

Employer's Pension Guide is a cooperative project of the Pen sion and Welfare Benefits Administration of the U.S. Department of Labor, the Internal Revenue Service, and the Pension Benefit Guaranty Corporation to provide a general overview of the responsibilities under Federal law of employers who sponsor single-employer defined benefit pension plans. It describes Federal pension law effective as of 1989.

Your Guaranteed Pension answers some of the most frequently asked questions about the Pension Benefit Guaranty Corporation and its termination insurance program for single-employer defined benefit pension plants. The answers apply to pension plan terminations taking place in 1990.

Your Pension serves as a handy explanation of pension plans: what they are, how they operate, and the rights an options of participants. It should not be relied upon for information about a specific pension plan.

PERSONNEL MANAGEMENT

U.S. Office of Personnel Management

Handbook of OPM Publications, Periodicals, and FPM Issuances is available from the Publishing Management Branch, Administrative Policy Division, Office of Finance and Administrative Services, Administration Group, U.S. Office of Personnel Management, 1990 E Street, N.W., Washington, D.C. 20415. Tel: 202/606-1822.

Requesting OPM Federal Investigations, I.D.# OFI-15. Available from the Investigations Group at OPM, at the following address: U.S. Office of Personnel Management, Investigations Group, 1900 E Street, N.W., Washington, D.C. 20415. Tel: 202/606-1822.

* * * * * * * * * * * *

Requests for the following publications should be sent to: **National Technical Information Service**, Department A/Operations Division, 5285 Port Royal Road, Springfield, VA 22161 (703/487-4650).

Guide to Administering Examinations to Handicapped Individuals for Employment Purposes, I.D.# PR-80-16. Stock# PB81-121675.

A Guide for Assessing the Distribution of Minorities and Women in Relevant Labor Markets, I.D.# TM-79-10. Stock# PB80-152655.

Voluntary and Involuntary Separations from the Work Force, I.D.# PR-75-2. Stock# PB-258-241.

* * * * * * * * * * * *

The following publications can be purchased from the **U.S. Government Printing Office**. Stock numbers and prices for annual subscriptions are shown below. Submit requests for these publications to: The Superintendent of Documents, U.S. Government Printing Office, Washington, D.C. 20402. Tel: 202/783-3238.

Digest of Significant Classification Decisions and Opinions, I.D.# AR-100. Published semi-annually. Presents decisions and opinions made by OPM which have, in their opinion, Government-wide impact. Price: $2.75 a single copy domestic; $3.44 a single copy foreign; $5.00 a year domestic; $6.25 a year foreign. GPO Stock# 706-0001-00000-0.

The Federal Labor Management and Employee Relations Consultant Newsletter (FLMERC). Published 24 times a year. Presents current information in the field of labor-management and employee relations. Price: $28.00 a year domestic; $35.00 a year foreign. No single copies will be sold. GPO Stock# 706-003-00000-2.

* * * * * * * * * * * *

Merit Systems Protection Board

The following reports and pamphlets available free of charge from: **U.S. Merit Systems Protection Board**, Office of Management Analysis, 1120 Vermont Avenue, N.W., Room 884, Washington, D.C. 20419.

Introduction to MSPB. 1989. (28 pp.)
Questions and Answers on Appeals. 1989. (25 pp.)
Questions and Answers on Whistleblower Appeals. 1990. (27 pp.)
A Study of Cases Decided by the U.S. Merit Systems Protection Board in FY 1989. 1990. (58 pp.)

* * * * * * * * * * * *

Federal Merit Systems Reporter. A weekly format reporting the full text of decisions handed down by the U.S. Merit Systems Protection Board and Federal court rulings on appeals from the Board. Back volumes dating from 1979 are available at extra expense. Product# 4050. Price: $685.00. Contact: LRP Publications, 747 Dresher Road, P.O. Box 980, Horsham, PA 19044-0980. Tel: 800/341-7874.

* * * * * * * * * * * * *

Decisions of the Merit Systems Protection Board are available through West Publishing Company, P.O. Box 64833, St. Paul, MN 55164-1804. Tel: 612/688-3600. Or, 800/328-9352. West offers several related publications and services:

The Merit System Protection Reporter is a 43 volume hard-bound set that contains the full text of all opinions from 1985 through 1989. Price: $3,229.00. Additional volumes are sold for $77.50 each as published.

Merit System Protection Reporter Advance Sheets are issued biweekly. The price of an annual subscription is $260.00.

West's Merit Protection Board Digest is a two-volume soft bound index to volumes 1-27 of the Merit System Protection Reporter. Price: $170.00.

Database:

Merit Systems Protection Board Case Decisions. Available on CD-ROM through the PERSONNET Service of Information Handling Services, 15 Inverness Way East, P.O. Box 1154, Englewood, CO 80150. Tel: 800/241-7824. In Colorado, call 303/790-0600 ext 59.

SAFETY AND HEALTH

U.S. Department of Labor

The following publications can be purchased from the **U.S. Government Printing Office.** Stock numbers and prices for annual subscriptions are shown below. Submit requests for these publications to: The Superintendent of Documents, U.S. Government Printing Office, Washington, D.C. 20402. Tel: 202/783-3238.

OSHA Standards and Regulations. Published in six volumes, each covering a different subject. Subscription service of each volume includes changes for an indeterminate period. Looseleaf for updating.

Volume I-General Industry Standards and Interpretations. Price: $98.00 domestic; $122.50 foreign. GPO Stock# 929-005-00000-7.

Volume II-Maritime Standards and Interpretations. Price: $29.00 domestic; $36.25 foreign. GPO Stock# 929-006-00000-3.

Volume III-Construction Industry Standards and Interpretations. Price: $29.00 domestic; $36.25 foreign. GPO Stock# 929-007-00000-0.

Volume IV-Other Regulations and Procedures. Price: $55.00 domestic; $68.75 foreign. GPO Stock# 929-008-00000-6.

Volume V-Field Operations Manual. Price: $54.00 domestic; $67.50 foreign. GPO Stock# 929-004-00000-1.

Volume VI-Industrial Hygiene Technical Manual. Price: $51.00 domestic; $63.75 foreign. GPO Stock# 929-009-00000-2.

* * * * * * * * * * * *

Federal Mine Safety and Health Review Commission

Federal Mine Safety and Health Review Commission Decisions. Monthly. Price: $69.00 a year domestic; $86.25 a year foreign. GPO Stock# 752-019-00000-2.

* * * * * * * * * * * *

Occupational Safety and Health Review Commission

The **Occupational Safety and Health Review Commission** (OSHRC) offers a number of publications that can be obtained free of charge from the Occupational Safety and Health Review Commission Information Office, 1825 K Street, N.W., Washington, D.C. 20006. Tel: 202/634-7943).

(1) Individual copies of OSHRC decisions
(2) Simplified Proceedings
(3) Rules of Procedures
(4) A Guide to Procedures of the OSHRC

The Index to Decisions of the OSHRC details company names and OSHRC docket numbers. It is sold based on the number of pages and the years requested. Contact the Commission's Information Office, at the above address, for the price.

Occupational Safety and Health Review Commission Decisions. Published monthly. Price: $13.00 a year domestic; $16.25 a year foreign. GPO Stock# 752-007-00000-4. Contact: The Superintendent of Documents, U.S. Government Printing Office, Washington, D.C. 20402. Tel: 202/783-3238.

SCIENCE, SPACE AND TECHNOLOGY

National Aeronautics and Space Administration

Database:

ARIN is an online catalog of the **National Aeronautics and Space Administration (NASA)** which provides access to approximately 50,000 titles in the Homer E. Newell Memorial Library as well as 460,000 titles throughout all NASA libraries. Information is provided through AUTHOR, TITLE, SUBJECT, and includes a BIBLIOGRAPHIC RECORD for each title, which describes the item, call number and material location. **ARIN** can be accessed in NASA's Library, Room DBD-3, 400 Maryland Ave., S.W., Washington, D.C. 20546. The staff will accept reference requests. Tel: 202/453-8545. **ARIN can also be accessed in all NASA field locations in their libraries.**

* * * * * * * * * * * *

National Science Foundation

A copy of Publications of the National Science Foundation can be obtained from Publications Information at the National Science Foundation (NSF). Tel: 202/357-7668.

The following publications are available from the NSF free of charge. Write: **National Science Foundation**, Attn: Forms and Publications, 1800 G Street, N.W., Room 232, Washington, D.C. 20550. Tel: 202/357-7861.

National Science Foundation Bulletin is a monthly publication (except for July and August) which includes news about current programs, deadlines, meetings, and new publications. No order number is necessary.

An NSF Strategy for Compliance with Environmental Law in Antarctica (A Report to the Director). NSF 90-4.

Antarctic Conservation Act of 1989, Public Law 95-54. NSF 89-59.

Research findings and results of studies supported by NSF are generally published in scientific journals or as reports prepared by the grantee institutions for NSF. These technical reports, as well as a few general publications, can be purchased from the National Technical Information Service (NTIS), 5285 Port Royal Road, Springfield, VA 22161. Call 202/487-4650 for prices and availability.

Database

STIS: In the near future, NSF will be providing electronic access to publications, program announcements and award information. The system will be called the **Science and Technology Information System (STIS)** and will support multiple simultaneous users. Access to STIS will be via dial-up connection or remote log-in across **Internet.** Information on progress of the STIS effort will be published in the NSF Bulletin.

SECURITIES/COMMODITIES

Commodity Futures Trading Commission

Decisions of the Commodity Futures Trading Commission: Decisions rendered by the Commission, the Administrative Law Judges, and the Judgment Officers can be obtained by contacting the Office of Proceedings, 2033 K Street, N.W., Washington, D.C. 20581. Tel: 202/254-5008. There is a $12.00 reproduction service charge and 15 cents per page copying fee.

Commodities Futures Law Report contains semi-monthly reports on the latest court decisions and regulatory activity of the Commodity Futures Trading Commission. New regulations and interpretations covering controls and standards as issued by CFTC are reported promptly upon release. Reparation procedures for resolving complaints against registrants, as well as significant decisions from the CFTC are included. Price: $600.00 a year includes 2 vols. and semi-monthly reports. Contact: Commerce Clearing House, Inc., 4025 West Peterson Avenue, Chicago, IL 60646. Tel: 312/583-8500, Or in Wash., D.C., call 202/626-2200.

* * * * * * * * * * * *

U.S. Securities and Exchange Commission

Forms required to make filings with the Commission can be obtained by writing or calling the SEC Publications Section, Forms and Publications Division. Tel: 202/272-7460.

The open meetings of the Commission are recorded and can be obtained by calling 202/272-3130. The cost is $2.95 per cassette.

* * * * * * * * * * * *

The following publications are free of charge and can be obtained by writing to: **U.S. Securities and Exchange Commission,** Publications Section, Printing Branch Stop C-9, Wash, D.C. 20549.

Arbitration Procedures. A discussion of procedures for disputes with brokerage firms involving financial claims.

Information on Bounties. Information on bounties the SEC is authorized to award to persons who provide information leading to the recovery of a civil penalty from an inside trader.

* * * * * * * * * * * *

The following publications can be purchased from the **U.S. Government Printing Office.** Stock numbers and prices for annual subscriptions are shown below. Submit requests for these publications to: The Superintendent of Documents, U.S. Government Printing Office, Washington, D.C. 20402. Tel: 202/783-3238.

Official Summary of Security Transactions and Holdings. A monthly publication made up of securities holdings figures showing owners, relationships to issues, amounts of securities bought or sold by each owner, their individual holdings at the end of the reported month, and types of securities. Price: $69.00 a year domestic; $86.25 a year foreign. GPO Stock# 746-001-00000-2. This publication is also kept in the SEC Library.

Decisions and Reports of the Commission pursuant to the various securities laws. Volume 48 (July 1984-June 1988). Price: $43.00 domestic; $53.75 foreign. GPO Stock# 046-000-00144-3. Current decisions and reports are first published as releases which can be found in the SEC Docket.

* * * * * * * * * * * *

SEC News Digest is a daily summary of important SEC developments including listings of registrations, acquisitions and filings received by the Commission. Time, date and place of Commission hearings open to the public are listed. These hearings can also be found in the Federal Register. SEC News Digest can be seen at the SEC's Public Reference Desk, Room 1024, everyday after 1:00 PM. or in the SEC Library the following day.

It can be ordered by subscription under the title, SEC Today, from the Washington Service Bureau, 1225 Connecticut Avenue, N.W., Washington, D.C. 20036. Tel: 202/833-9200 ($490.00 annually).

On-line NEXUS subscribers can order SEC News Digest (SEC-NEW) from Mead Data Central-NEXUS, 1050 Connecticut Avenue, N.W., Suite 1090, Washington D.C. 20036. Tel: 202/785-3550.

SEC Docket is a weekly publication of the full text of all SEC releases which pertain to the laws administered by the SEC. The publication also includes financial reporting releases, staff accounting bulletins and litigation releases. SEC Docket can be seen in the SEC Library or ordered by subscription from Commerce Clearing House, Inc., 4025 West Peterson Avenue, Chicago IL 60646. Tel: 312/583-8500; in Washington, D.C. call 202/626-2200; Or, from Soreg Inc., Appeals Handbook Division Dept. 111, Eighth Avenue, New York, NY 10011. Tel: 212/741-6600.

SOCIAL SECURITY/MEDICARE

U.S. Department of Health and Human Services

The following publications can be purchased from the **U.S. Government Printing Office.** Stock numbers and prices for annual subscriptions are shown below. Submit requests for these publications to: The Superintendent of Documents, U.S. Government Printing Office, Washington, D.C. 20402. Tel: 202/783-3238.

Compilation of the Social Security Laws, Including the Social Security Act, as Amended, and Related Enactments, Through January 1, 1989, Volume I. Contains an index of the Social Security Act as well as selected provisions of the Act and the Internal Revenue Code. Price: $31.00 domestic; $38.75 foreign. GPO Stock# 052-070-06583-4.

Compilation of the Social Security Laws, Including the Social Security Act, as Amended, and Related Enactments, Through January 1, 1989, Volume II. Includes applicable provisions of the Internal Revenue Code as well as other relevant public laws which effect the operating procedures of the Social Security Act. Price: $30.00 domestic; $37.50 foreign. GPO Stock# 052-070-06584-2.

Social Security Handbook (1988). Rulings are published as needed and consolidated annually. A cumulative manual is published every 5 years. This handbook contains rulings as amended through December 31, 1987. Price: $13.00 domestic; $16.25 foreign. GPO Stock# 017-070-00437-7.

Social Security and Acquiescence Rulings. Published irregularly. Contains interpretations and decisions of the Social Security Administration, as well as rulings of the U.S. Courts of Appeals that are in disagreement with the Administration's decisions, changes in Title II of the Social Security Act and related regulations, and items of general interest. Service consists of approximately 25 Social Security Rulings and eight Acquiescence Rulings. Price: $35.00 a year domestic; $43.75 a year foreign. GPO Stock# 817-003-00000-1.

These irregular issues are combined annually into the Social Security Rulings Cumulative Bulletin, which is not included in the subscription service but is sold as a separate publication at various prices.

Social Security Rulings on Federal Old Age, Survivors, Disability, Supplemental Income, and Black Lung Benefits. Cumulative edition 1988. Contains precedential decisions based on case decisions, policy statements, decisions of administrative law judges, and the Appeals Council. Price: $6.00 domestic; $7.50 foreign. GPO Stock# 017-070-00445-8.

Medicare Coverage Issues Manual. HFCA Publication #6. 1990. Consolidated reprint. Contains the appendices previously issued in Medicare Hospital Manual, HFCA #10; Medicare Intermediary Manual, Part A, Claims Process, Part 3, HFCA #13-3; and Medicare Carriers Manual, Part B, Claims Process, Part 3, HFCA #14-3. Subscription service consists of a basic manual and transmittals issued for an indeterminate period. Price: $115.00 domestic; $143.75 foreign. GPO Stock# 917-012-00000-8.

Medicare Provider Reimbursement Manual. HFCA Publication #15-1. 1990. Consolidated reprint. Provides guidelines and policies to implement Medicare regulations which set forth principles for determining the reasonable cost of provider services. Subscription service consists of a basic manual and supplementary material issued for an indeterminate period. In looseleaf form, punched for 3-ring binder. Price: $91.00 domestic; $113.75 foreign. GPO Stock# 917-007-00000-4.

TAXES

Internal Revenue Service, U.S. Treasury Department

The following publication can be purchased from the **U.S. Government Printing Office.** Stock numbers and prices for annual subscriptions are shown below. Submit requests for these publications to: The Superintendent of Documents, U.S. Government Printing Office, Washington, D.C. 20402. Tel: 202/783-3238.

Internal Revenue Bulletin. A weekly publication containing official IRS rulings, Treasury Decisions, Executive Orders, legislation, and court decisions pertaining to internal revenue matters. Price: $104.00 a year domestic; $130.00 a year foreign. GPO Stock# 748-004-00000-9.

Twice a year the weekly issues of the Internal Revenue Bulletin are consolidated into Cumulative Bulletins. These cumulative bulletins are not included as part of the subscription, but are sold as separate publications. Price: 1989-2: $40.00. GPO Stock# 048-004-02292-3; 1989-1: $44.00. GPO Stock# 048-004-02286-9.

Bulletin Index-Digest System. Contains the Finding List and Digests for all permanent tax matters published in the Internal Revenue Bulletin. Each subscription service consists of a basic manual and cumulative supplements for an indeterminate period.

Service #1. Income Taxes 1953-1988. Publication No. 641. Price: $42.00 domestic; $52.50 foreign. GPO Stock# 948-001-00000-4.

Service #2. Estate and Gift Taxes, 1953-1988. Publication No. 642. Price: $19.00 domestic; $23.75 foreign. GPO Stock# 948-002-00000-1.

Service No. 3. Employment Taxes, 1953-1988. Publication No. 643. Price: $19.00 domestic; $23.75 foreign. GPO Stock# 948-003-00000-7.

Service No. 4. Excise Taxes, 1953-1988. Publication No. 644. Price: $19.00 domestic; $23.75 foreign. GPO Stock #948-004-00000-3.

Cumulative List of Organizations Described in Section 170(c) of the Internal Revenue Code of 1986. Revised to September 1989. Publication No. 78. Lists contributions of organizations which are deductible under Section 170(c) of the Internal Revenue Code of 1986. Subscription service includes the revised edition containing the names of exempt organizations, through September 1989, and three cumulative quarterly supplements. Price: $41.00 domestic; $51.25 foreign. GPO Stock# 948-009-00000-5.

* * * * * * * * * * * *

Catalog of Federal Tax Forms, Form Letters, Notices, and Taxpayer Information Publications. To request a free copy contact: Internal Revenue Service, Forms Distribution Center, P.O. Box 25866, Richmond, VA 23289. Tel: 800/829-FORM.

* * * * * * * * * * * *

CCH Standard Federal Tax Reporter. Looseleaf. This multi-volume set consists of:

*Code Volumes, which print, in Internal Revenue Code section order, all provisions of the Code, and include tables and annotations cross-referencing and explaining Code sections;

*Index Volume, with a topical index, tax calendar, and rate tables, checklists, tax planning materials, the IRS Tax Shelter Examination Handbook, a glossary of tax terms, and sections covering tax treaties, tax return preparers, and bond and annuity tables;

*Compilation Volumes, in Code section order, containing the full text of the Code, final and temporary regulations, digest-annotations to letter rulings, revenue rulings, revenue procedures, and court decisions, as well as some legislative histories, plus editorial explanation;

*New Matters Volume, which has a topical index of recent developments and a legal periodicals section containing an order list of IRS publications and digests of current tax articles, information on pending tax bills before Congress, and an Illustrative Cases section;

*U.S. Tax Cases Advance Sheets Volume, which contains Treasury Department proposed regulations, tax decisions of the U.S. District Courts, U.S. Claims Court, U.S. Courts of Appeals, and the U.S. Supreme Court; and

*Citator Volumes, which list all decisions alphabetically and can be used to determine if subsequent decisions have affected earlier volumes.

Price: $1,435 for a one-year subscription; $1,305 per year for a two-year subscription. Order from Commerce Clearing House, Inc., 4025 West Peterson Avenue, Chicago, IL 60646. Tel: 312/583-8500 Or, in Washington, D.C., call 202/626-2200.

* * * * * * * * * * * *

Prentice-Hall Federal Taxes 2d. Looseleaf. This multivolume set consists of:

*Code Volumes, which reproduce, in Code section order, all Internal Revenue Code provisions, with a brief history of each provision, Code and cross-reference tables, annotations, an effective-date table, proposed regulations, a Code section index for these regulations, and a topical index;

*Index Volume, which has topical and transactions indexes to all of the materials in the Compilation Volumes (below), a Federal Tax Calendar, checklists, lists of tax forms, tax and bond tables, a Tax Elections Checklist, Tables of Rulings and of Cases, and an Index to Tax Articles;

*Compilation Volumes, which contain, in Code section order, the full text of the Code, final, temporary and proposed regulations, digest-annotations to revenue rulings and procedures and to letter rulings and court decisions, plus extensive editorial material explaining tax issues and questions, as well as information about U.S. income tax treaties;

*Current Matters Volume, which cross-references new items to Compilation Volumes items and contains a List of Current Decisions, gives information about appeals and selected pending tax legislation, and also includes several useful indexes;

*American Federal Tax Reports 2d (AFTR2d) Decisions Advance Sheets Volume, which includes decisions by the U.S. District Courts, U.S. Claims Court, U.S. Courts of Appeals, and the U.S. Supreme Court; and

*Citator Volumes, which list all decisions alphabetically and can be used to determine the effect of later decisions upon earlier ones.

Prices: 1) Income Tax Set (16 volumes, two semi-annual AFTR2d bound volumes, a Topical Index, and weekly reports): $1,150 per year; 2) Income and Excise Tax Set (17 volumes, two semi-annual AFTR2d bound volumes, a Topical Index, and weekly reports): $1,271 per year; 3) Income and Estate and Gift Tax Set (18 volumes, two semi-annual AFTR2d bound volumes, a Topical Index, and weekly reports): $1,456 per year; 4) Income, Excise and Estate and Gift Tax Set (19 volumes, two semi-annual AFTR2d bound volumes, a Topical Index, and weekly reports): $1,562 per year.

Order from: Prentice-Hall, Inc., 910 Sylvan Avenue, Englewood Cliffs, NJ 07632. Tel: 800/562-0245. Or, in Washington, D.C., call 202/293-0707.

* * * * * * * * * * * *

Tax Notes. Weekly report of tax developments, including congressional action, court opinions, IRS and Treasury Department actions, General Accounting Office reports, international tax news, a calendar, digests of tax articles, and special reports. Price: $995 per year from Tax Analysts, 6830 North Fairfax Drive, Arlington, VA 22213. Tel: 703/532-1850 or 800/336-0439.

* * * * * * * * * * * *

Federal Tax Coordinator 2d. Looseleaf. Weekly. Discusses all areas of taxation, using a subject-matter approach, with numerous citations and cross-references to related topics in other chapters; also includes analyses of matters not yet resolved, planning checklists, tax tables, and tax calendars, and also contains a Weekly Alert as part of the subscription. The text of U.S. tax treaties and annotations and proposed regulations and their preambles are also included. Price: $1,476 per year. Order from Research Institute of America, Inc., 90 Fifth Avenue, New York, NY 10011. Tel: 800/431-9025 or in Wash., D.C., call 202/628-6050.

* * * * * * * * * * * *

Internal Memorandums of the IRS. Weekly. Contains the strategic thinking behind IRS' decisions. Price: $378 per year from Prentice-Hall, Inc., 910 Sylvan Avenue, Englewood Cliffs, NJ 07632. Tel: 800/562-0245. Or, in Washington, D.C., call 202/293-0707.

* * * * * * * * * * * *

U.S. Savings Bonds Division, U.S. Treasury Department

Legal Aspects. Contains a discussion of U.S. Savings Bonds and tax liability; of particular interest to executors in estate administration. Available free of charge from the Public Affairs Office, U.S. Savings Bonds Division, 1111 20th Street, N.W., Washington, D.C. 20226. Tel: 202/634-5377.

TRANSPORTATION

U.S. Department of Transportation

The following publication can be purchased from the **U.S. Government Printing Office.** Stock numbers and prices for annual subscriptions are shown below. Submit requests for these publications to: The Superintendent of Documents, U.S. Government Printing Office, Washington, D.C. 20402. Tel: 202/783-3238.

Federal Aviation Regulations. This is a subscription service in which there are several parts, all priced individually. For example, Part 1 consists of Definitions and Abbreviations. Price: $30.00 domestic; $37.50 foreign. GPO Stock# 950-006-00000-5. Part 11 deals with General Rule-Making Procedures. Price: $27.00 domestic; $33.75 foreign. GPO Stock# 950-007-00000-1. Part 13 deals with Investigation and Enforcement Procedures. Price: $34.00 domestic; $42.50 foreign. GPO Stock# 950-008-00000-8. Subscription service for each part consists of a basic manual and supplementary changes for an indeterminate period. Contact the Government Printing Office for a full description of all the parts.

Federal Motor Vehicle Safety Standards and Regulations with Amendments and Interpretations. 1989. Consolidated reprint. Contains three sections: procedural rules and regulations; standards; and rulings and additional regulations. Subscription service consists of a basic manual and periodic amendments for an indeterminate period. Looseleaf for updating, punched for 3-ring binder. Price: $134.00 domestic; $167.50 foreign. GPO Stock# 950-031-00000-0.

Navigation and Vessel Inspection Circulars. 1990. Published irregularly. Provides information relating to navigation, regulation of ships by the U.S., and vessel inspection. Subscription service consists of approximately ten publications issued irregularly. Price: $14.00 domestic; $17.50 foreign. GPO Stock# 850-001-00000-6.

* * * * * * * * * * * *

Accident, Incident Bulletin is an annual statistical overview summarizing reportable railroad accidents/incidents. It can be obtained free of charge from Federal Railroad Administration, Office of Public Affairs, 400 Seventh Street, S.W., Washington, D.C. 20590. Tel: 202/366-0881.

* * * * * * * * * * * *

Aviation Law Reports covers Federal aviation laws, regulations, decisions, plus air liabilities. This four-volume publication is updated semi-annually. Price: $1,375.00 per year. The publication can be ordered from Commerce Clearing House, Inc., 4025 West Peterson Avenue, Chicago, IL 60646. Tel: 312/583-8500. Or, in Washington, D.C., call 202/626-2200.

Databases:

The **Auto Safety Hotline** is a toll-free telephone service operated by the National Highway Traffic Safety Administration (NHTSA) which provides callers with information on motor vehicle safety recalls and safety defect investigations. New car crash test results, and other safety topics are sent by mail. Consumer complaints about possible safety defects are also accepted. The number outside the Washington, D.C. metro area is 800/424-9393. Callers inside the Washington, D.C. metro area should use 202/366-0123. Hotline operators are on duty Monday through Friday from 8:00 AM to 4:00 PM.

The **Office of Defects Investigation** (ODI) conducts investigations of alleged safety related defect trends in motor vehicles. Currently, there are nearly 2200 ODI investigation files available for public viewing in the Technical Reference Division (TRD), including 137 active files. Current files are maintained in a paper format. TRD maintains a complete collection of manual indexes to active investigations. This collection is found in the **Monthly Defect Investigation Report** which can be obtained by sending a written request to: National Traffic Safety Administration, General Services Division (NAD-51), 400 Seventh Street, S.W., Room 6123, Washington, D.C. 20590.

The Office of Defect Investigation (ODI) maintains the following computer files: The **Recall File** contains records of all vehicle and vehicle equipment, including tires, safety defect and noncompliance recalls since 1966. The **Letter File** contains records of complaints submitted by vehicle owners from 1981 to present. The **Service Bulletin File** contains records of service bulletins submitted by manufacturers. The **Active Investigation File** contains records of investigations initiated by the Office of Defect Investigations since mid-1985. The **New Car Assessment Program (NCAP) File** contains records of vehicles that have been crash tested in the NCAP.

To access the files of the Office of Defect Investigation, contact the Technical Reference Division, National Highway Traffic Safety Administration, 400 7th Street, S.W., Washington, D.C. 20590. Tel: 202/366-2768. There is a search fee.

Technical Service Bulletins are maintained by the **Technical Reference Division (TRD)** dating from 1968 to present. These bulletins describe the instructions motor vehicle manufacturers provide their dealer repair services. The Office of Defect Investigation (ODI) has selected certain bulletins for their automated data files. (Information on the automated data files is listed below.) The bulletins are designated in the following categories: technical, informational, warranty, product improvement, part and recall. TRD maintains the selected safety related bulletins in a microfiche format, with the addition of an optical disk system for retrieving bulletins from 1986 to present. For information, contact National Highway Traffic Safety Administration, Technical Reference Division, 400 7th Street, S.W., Washington, D.C. 20590. Tel: 202/366-2768.

Compliance Test Reports are the results of the testing, inspection and investigation of foreign and domestic vehicles and equipment manufacturers. A **monthly compliance report news release** is issued which lists investigations opened, closed and pending during the month, identifies compliance test reports accepted and indicates how individual reports may be obtained. These releases may be requested from the Office of Public and Consumer Affairs (NOA-40), National Highway Traffic Safety Administration, 400 7th Street, S.W., Washington, D.C. 20590.

Automated Search Files, maintained by the Technical Reference Division, include Defect Investigation files, Compliance Test Reports, Technical Service Bulletins, and consumer complaints and recall campaigns as taken from the Hotline. A search of these files, with the exception of the Compliance Test Reports, will result in a computer printout, if information is available. A statement is sent with the search results which indicates the total cost and how the payment is to be paid. The cost of an average search of the above files is between $20 to $30. Information on the automated search files can be obtained by writing or calling the National Highway Traffic Safety Administration, Technical Reference Division, 400 7th Street, S.W., Washington, D.C. 20590. Tel: 202/366-2768.

* * * * * * * * * * * *

Docket Files contain information and data relating to rulemaking actions, including notices of proposed rulemaking, comments received in response to notices, petitions for rulemaking or reconsideration, denials of petitions for rulemaking or reconsideration, the final rules and the technical materials used by the standards writer. This is the public record of rulemaking activities for motor vehicle and highway safety standards. Details of these rulemaking procedures may be found in 49 CFR, Chapter V, Part 551-557 (1989). For information, contact the Technical Reference Division, National Highway Traffic Safety Administration, 400 7th Street, S.W., Washington, D.C. 20590. Tel: 202/366-4949. There is a search fee.

* * * * * * * * * * * *

TRIS, a computerized information file maintained and operated by the Transportation Research Board of the National Research Council (a private organization), contains information on various aspects of highway and automobile safety, accidents and litigation. Online DIALOG users can access TRIS or Online Search Specialists at the Transportation Research Board will conduct searches for a fee. For more information, call or write the Transportation Research Board, National Research Council, 2101 Constitution Ave., N.W., Wash., D.C. 20418. Tel: 202/334-3251.

* * * * * * * * * * * *

Urban Mass Transportation Administration (UMTA): All of UMTA's reports are kept by the Department of Commerce's National Technical Information Service (NTIS) and entered on DIALOG. Information regarding these documents can be obtained from NTIS, 5285 Port Royal Road, Springfield, VA 22161. Rush sales: Tel: 800/336-4700. Regular sales: Tel: 703/487-4650. To identify a document: Tel: 703/487-4783.

Online DIALOG users can access UMTA documents on **TRIS (Transportation Research Information Services)** which is maintained by the Transportation Research Board (TRB) of the National Research Council, which is a private organization. TRB will conduct searches for a fee. Contact the Transportation Research Board, National Research Council, 2101 Constitution Ave., N.W., Washington, D.C. 20418. Tel: 202/334-3251.

* * * * * * * * * * * *

National Transportation Safety Board

The following publications can be obtained through either the **National Transportation Safety Board's Public Inquiries Section** or the **National Technical Information Services (NTIS).**

Contact the NTSB for more information at: **National Transportation Safety Board, Public Inquiries Section,** Room 805-F, 800 Independence Avenue, S.W., Washington, D.C. 20594, or call 202/382-6735.

Contact the **National Technical Information Service** at: 5285 Port Royal Road, Springfield, VA 22161, or call 703/487-4630 (for annual subscriptions) or 703/487-4650 (for single copies and microfiche). Prepayment is required for all orders.

These publications include:

1. Accident Reports (Major) are detailed narrative reports which contain the facts, conditions, analysis, conclusions, and probable cause of major aviation, railroad, highway, pipeline, and marine accident investigations which are issued for all accidents which resulted in a major investigation. They are available on an irregular basis from NTIS by annual subscription or by single issue. When ordering annual subscriptions, specify the transportation mode and the type of publications (i.e., Aviation Accident Report). When ordering single issues, specify the exact title of the document, the NTSB report number, or the NTIS accession number.

2. News Digest, issued bi-monthly from the NTSB, contains a summary of all major NTSB activities, including the issuance of major safety recommendations and the NTSB position on major transportation issues. It can be ordered, free-of-charge, by either annual subscription or single issue. When ordering annual subscriptions, specify the type of document (i.e., News Digest). When ordering single issues, specify the type of document and the publication number.

3. Public Records and Files are detailed records and files maintained for specified periods of time on all major Board activities, such as accident investigations, safety recommendations, studies and objectives, special investigations, initial decisions of the Administrative Law Judges, and opinions and orders. They are available from the NTSB Public Inquiries Section for a fee. When ordering, indicate, if applicable, the document or file number; or name and title of the record or document; or for accident records, the date and location of the accident records, the date and location of the accident and the operator or carrier involved.

4. Regulations of the NTSB are issued irregularly as procedures change. When ordering them from the NTSB Public Inquiries Section, specify, by number or by title, the part or parts of the regulations needed. Currently issued parts include:

Part 821: Rules of practice in air safety proceedings.
Part 825: Rules of procedure for merchant marine appeals from decisions of the Commandant, U.S. Coast Guard.
Part 831: Aircraft accident/incident investigation procedures.
Part 845: Rules of practice in transportation accident/incident hearings and reports.

5. Initial Decisions of the Administrative Law Judges. Sets forth Administrative Law Judges' findings, conclusions, and decisions in safety enforcement proceedings involving petitions from applicants denied airmen's certificates by the Administrator of the Federal Aviation Administration; and appeals from orders of the Administrator of the Federal Aviation Administration suspending or revoking certificates issued to airmen, aircraft, air agencies, and air carriers for alleged violations of the regulations or for lack of qualifications to hold such certificates. Initial Decisions are issued both individually and in a monthly publication. Individual Initial Decisions are available, for a fee, from the NTSB Public Inquiries Section. When ordering individual decisions, specify the type of document and the docket number. The monthly publication is available, for a fee, from NTIS by annual subscription and single issue.

6. Opinions and Orders. Sets forth decisions of the Board resulting from the review of appeals from decisions of the Commandant of the U.S. Coast Guard involving seamen's certificates or initial decisions of the NTSB Administrative Law Judges involving airmen and/or air safety certificates. Opinions and Orders are issued individually, in a monthly publication, and in bound volumes containing several years of Opinions and Orders. Individual Opinions and Orders are available, for a fee, from the NTSB

Public Inquiries Section. The monthly publication is available, for a fee, from the NTIS by annual subscription or a single issue. The bound volumes are available, for a fee, from the NTIS until limited supplies are exhausted.

Database:

Computer Tapes of Aviation Accident Data, prepared by the National Transportation Safety Board (NTSB), are continuously updated and are available back to 1964. They are available from the NTSB Analysis and Data Division. Tel: 202/382-6538. Indicate the specific type of accident data needed and the calendar year, or portion thereof, for which the data is needed. There is no charge if the person requesting the data provides his own computer tape.

* * * * * * * * * * * *

Interstate Commerce Commission

Copies of ICC decisions and case annotations are available for reference in the ICC Library (Room 3392).

Records of cases and copies of decisions can also be obtained from the ICC's Microfilm Unit and its Certification Unit (see explanation at the beginning of the ICC section).

Dynamic Concepts, Inc. keeps a file of all **ICC decisions** for one year from the date of the decision. They can provide copies at 22 cents per page plus postage and 75 cents for handling. Sales tax of six percent will be added for sales within the District of Columbia. To obtain a copy of a decision, provide Dynamic Concepts with the docket number and, if possible, the service date. Dynamic Concepts, Inc. ICC Building, Room 2229, 12th and Constitution Ave., N.W., Wash., D.C. 20423. Tel: 202/289-4357.

* * * * * * * * * * * *

The following publications can be purchased from the **U.S. Government Printing Office.** Stock numbers and prices for annual subscriptions are shown below. Submit requests for these publications to: The Superintendent of Documents, U.S. Government Printing Office, Washington, D.C. 20402. Tel: 202/783-3238.

ICC Register: A Daily Summary of Motor Carrier Applications and of Decisions and Notices Issued by the Interstate Commerce Commission. Published daily. Price: $444.00 a year domestic; $555.00 a year foreign. GPO Stock# 726-001-00000-6.

Interstate Commerce Commission Vol 366: Finance Cases, Decisions of the Interstate Commerce Commission of the U. S., October 1981 through June 1983. Price: $24.00 domestic; $30.00 foreign. GPO Stock# 026-000-01245-7.

Volume I: Interstate Commerce Commission, 2d Series. Decisions of the Interstate Commerce Commission, February 1984-May 1986. Price: $34.00. GPO Stock# 026-000-01264-3.

Volume II: Interstate Commerce Commission, 2d Series. Decisions of the Interstate Commerce Commission, August 1984-July 1986. Price: $47.00. GPO Stock# 026-000-01266-0.

Volume III: Interstate Commerce Commission, 2d Series. Decisions of the Interstate Commerce Commission, June 1985-August 1987. Price: $35.00. GPO Stock# 026-000-01272-4.

* * * * * * * * * * * *

Federal Carriers Reports, published by Commerce Clearing House, cover the Federal regulation of carriers engaged in interstate commerce. Issued every two weeks, subscribers receive four looseleaf volumes with contents as follows:

1) General Guide
2) Transportation Law and Regulation: Interstate Commerce
3) General Orders-Forms-Rulings: ICC and DOT general orders, forms, and rulings concerning the various modes of carriage.
4) Commission and Court Decisions: digests of pertinent new ICC decisions and court decisions.

Annual subscription price is $800.00 per year. Contact: Commerce Clearing House Inc., 4025 West Peterson Avenue, Chicago, IL 60646. Tel: 312/583-8500, Or, in Washington, D.C., call 202/626-2200.

U.S. ATTORNEYS

U.S. Attorney's Manual. Subscription service for each volume consists of a basic manual and supplementary material for an indeterminate period. In looseleaf form, punched for 3-ring binder. GPO stock numbers and prices are shown below. Contact: The Superintendent of Documents, U.S. Government Printing Office, Washington, D.C. 20402. Tel: 202/783-3238.

Volumes I and II, Titles I Through 8. October 1988. Subscription service consists of a two-volume basic manual (Volume I, Titles 1 through 3 and Volume II, Titles 4 through 8), cumulative semiannual updates, and blue sheets for an indeterminate period. Price: $485.00 domestic; $606.25 foreign. GPO Stock# 927-004-00000-3.

Volume III, Title 9, Criminal Division. Price: $434.00 domestic; $542.50 foreign. GPO Stock# 927-005-00000-0.

Volume IV, Indices. This volume is a general index which covers Titles 1 through 9. It has a comprehensive USC and CFR reference table, and also includes a prior approval listing for the Department of Justice. Price: $18.00 domestic; $22.50 foreign. GPO Stock# 927-007-00000-2.

VETERANS

U.S. Department of Veterans Affairs

Federal Benefits for Veterans and Dependents 1989 discusses medical, educational, loan, insurance, compensation, pension, and other programs and benefits administered by the Veterans Administration and other agencies. It lists VA facilities nationwide. It is available from Consumer Information Center-P, P.O. Box 100, Pueblo, CO 81002. Price: $2.75. Booklet number 116W.

United States Code, Title 38, Veteran's Benefits contains the exact text of laws in the field of veterans' affairs which come within the jurisdiction of the House Committee on Veterans' Affairs. Subscription service consists of a basic manual and one change per Congress (two-year period). In looseleaf form, punched for 3-ring binder. Price: $25.00 domestic; $31.25 foreign. GPO Stock# 952-002-00000-7. Contact: The Superintendent of Documents, U.S. Government Printing Office, Washington, D.C. 20402. Tel: 202/783-3238.

LEGISLATIVE BRANCH

U.S. CONGRESS

The following publications can be purchased from the **U.S. Government Printing Office.** Stock numbers and prices for annual subscriptions are shown below. Submit requests for these publications to: The Superintendent of Documents, U.S. Government Printing Office, Washington, D.C. 20402. Tel: 202/783-3238.

Calendars of the United States House of Representatives and History of Legislation. Published weekly when Congress is in session. Price: $159.00 a year domestic; no foreign distribution. GPO Stock# 752-001-00000-6.

Congressional Record. Published daily when Congress is in session, this is a verbatim report on congressional debates and other proceedings. Each issue includes a Daily Digest that summarizes the proceedings for that day in each House and before each of their committees and subcommittees. Price (paperback): $225.00

a year domestic; $281.25 foreign. A special six-month subscription to the Record is available for one-half the yearly price. GPO Stock# 752-002-00000-2.

Major Legislation of the Congress. Published irregularly. Provides summaries of topical congressional issues and major legislation introduced in response to those issues. Subscription service consists of approximately ten irregular issues per Congress (two-year period). Price: $19.00 domestic; $23.75 foreign. GPO Stock# 830-002-00000-6.

Public Bills, Resolutions, and Amendments. Published irregularly. Price: $4,898.00 domestic per session of Congress; $6,122.50 foreign per session of Congress. GPO Stock# 852-011-00000-9.

Reports on Public Bills. Published irregularly. Price: $1,323.00 domestic per session of Congress; $1,653.75 foreign per session of Congress. GPO Stock# 852-009-00000-4.

Public Laws. Published irregularly. A Public Law, often referred to as a "Slip Law," is the initial publication of a Federal law upon enactment and is printed as soon as possible after approval by the President. Some legislative references appear on each law. Price: $107.00 domestic per session of Congress; $133.75 foreign per session of Congress. GPO Stock# 869-010-00000-6.

Library of Congress

The following publications can be purchased from the **U.S. Government Printing Office.** Stock numbers and prices for annual subscriptions are shown below. Submit requests for these publications to: The Superintendent of Documents, U.S. Government Printing Office, Washington, D.C. 20402. Tel: 202/783-3238.

Compendium of Copyright Office Practices (Compendium II). 1984. A general guide to the operating problems and practices for the staff of the Copyright Office, with individual cases that represent common fact situations. Also known as Compendium II. Subscription service consists of a basic manual and two semiannual supplements for an indeterminate period. Price: $51.00 domestic; $63.75 foreign. GPO Stock# 930-001-00000-7.

Congressional Research Service Review. Contains articles of interest to the U.S. Congress, legislative staff members, congressional committees, other offices of the Legislative Branch, others in Government, and the general public. Ten issues a year. Price: $9.50 domestic; $11.88 foreign. GPO Stock# 730-009-00000-3.

The Constitution of the United States of America, Library of Congress, Congressional Research Service, 1987. This 800-plus page annotated volume is supplemented biennially with pocket supplements. Each article, section, and clause of the Constitution is immediately followed by analysis and commentary, including a discussion of the most important Supreme Court interpretive decisions. The volume also includes tables of proposed amendments pending before the states, proposed amendments not ratified by the states, and acts of Congress held unconstitutional in whole or in part by the Supreme Court. Price: $70.00. GPO Stock# 052-071-00674-5.

Databases:

LOCIS (Library of Congress Information System) contains a database **SCORPIO** which is available to the general public for use within the Library of Congress itself.

SCORPIO (Subject-Content-Oriented Retriever For Processing Information Online) contains the following files: 1) **BIBL (Bibliographic Citation File):** selected articles and government publications since 1976 on public policy and current events topics of interest to Congress. 2) **LCCC:** books cataloged or recataloged and written in English since 1968 and other non-English titles with varying dates. 3) **CG-CURRENT CG:** Legislative information files from the current back to the 93rd Congress (1973); status and digests of public bills and resolutions introduced in Congress. 4) **NRCM (National Referral Master File):** list of organizations doing research or providing information and willing to answer questions from the public. 5) **COHM/COHD:** copyright registrations and documents since 1978. 6) **PREMARC:** books, serials, maps, music earlier than those in LCCC. Records briefer and unedited. Contact: General Reference Assistance, Library of Congress, First and Independence Avenue, S.E., Washington, D.C. 20540. Tel: 202/707-5522.

* * * * * * * * * * * *

United States Congressional Code and Administrative News. Published by West Publishing Company. Monthly. Contains new Public Laws and legislative histories (selected Senate and House committee reports and conference committee reports on bills that have become law). Published first in monthly soft-cover pamphlets and subsequently in bound volumes. Price: $170.00 per year from West Publishing Company, 50 West Kellogg Boulevard, P.O. Box 64833, St. Paul, MN 55164. Tel: 800/328-9352 or 612/688-3600 in Minnesota

---

JUDICIAL BRANCH

U.S. Supreme Court

Decisions of the Court

The following publications can be purchased from the **U.S. Government Printing Office.** Stock numbers and prices for annual subscriptions are shown below. Submit requests for these publications to: The Superintendent of Documents, U.S. Government Printing Office, Washington, D.C. 20402. Tel: 202/783-3238.

Supreme Court of the United States. Individual Slip Opinions. 1989 Term. Published irregularly. All the Court's opinions as announced from the bench. Price: $163.00 domestic per court term; $203.75 foreign per court term. GPO Stock# 828-003-00000-3.

Preliminary Prints. "Advance Sheets." 1987 Term. Published irregularly. Official United States Reports containing all the opinions with syllabi, names of counsel, indices, tables of cases, and other editorial additions. Price: $47.00 domestic per court term; $58.75 foreign/court term. GPO Stock# 828-002-00000-7.

United States Reports. Volume 481 (1987 Term--the most recent bound volume available). Price: $37.00 per volume. Initially issued separately as slip opinions (see above) and then subsequently published in advance sheets ("Preliminary Prints") with a fact summary, syllabi, and index prepared by the Court's Reporter of Decisions (see above). After the end of the Court's term each year, the advance sheets are replaced by bound volumes (usually 3-4 per term). GPO Stock# 028-001-00451-2.

The United States Reports also includes opinions of the Supreme Court since its inception. Before 1827, these decisions were published by private reporters. Until 1874, the reports were cited by the name of the reporter, as follows:

Dallas	(4 volumes, now vols. 1-4 U.S.)	(1789-1800)
Cranch	(9 volumes, now vols. 5-13 U.S.)	(1801-1815)
Wheaton	(12 volumes, now vols. 14-25 U.S.)	(1816-1827)
Peters	(16 volumes, now vols. 26-41 U.S.)	(1828-1842)
Howard	(24 volumes, now vols. 42-65 U.S.)	(1843-1860)
Black	(2 volumes, now vols. 66-67 U.S.)	(1861-1862)
Wallace	(23 volumes, now vols. 68-90 U.S.)	(1863-1874)

* * * * * * * * * * * * *

In addition to the above official reports of decisions, there are also four unofficial decisional reporters published by private publishing companies. These reports are available in most law libraries and also directly from the publishers. They are:

ANNOTATED BIBLIOGRAPHY

United States Supreme Court Reports, Lawyers' Edition. Published by the Lawyers Co-operative Publishing Company and the Bancroft-Whitney Company. The "Lawyers' Edition" covers the entire series from 1 Dallas to date and also contains many decisions not reported in the early official volumes. The publishers prepare their own case summaries and headnotes which precede the opinions. For selected important cases, there is also an appendix to each volume which contains summaries of attorneys' briefs submitted to the Court and annotations written by the publishers' editorial staff. The annotations consist largely of articles and essays about legal issues raised by the cases. Current decisions of the Court are issued biweekly as advance sheets during each term. These advance sheets do not contain annotations. Contact: Lawyers Co-operative Publishing Company, 50 Broad Street East, Rochester, NY, 14694. Tel: 716/546-5530. Or, 800/828-6266.

Supreme Court Reporter. Published by West Publishing Company. Begins with volume 106 (1882) and is current to date. The publisher adds its own headnotes and editorial features. Decisions are first issued as advance sheets biweekly during the Court's term. The Reporter also contains, as adopted, all Federal court rules and amendments, except local rules of the Federal District Courts. Contact: West Publishing Company, 50 West Kellogg Boulevard, P.O. Box 64833, St. Paul, MN 55164. Tel: 612/688-3600. Or, 800/328-9352.

United States Law Week. Looseleaf. Weekly. Published by the Bureau of National Affairs, Inc. Includes the following features: opinions of the Court; a Summary of Orders, which indicates cases acted upon and lower court holdings that the Supreme Court has agreed to review, along with the questions presented for review; a Journal of Proceedings, which contains the minutes of all Court sessions the previous week; Cases Docketed, which includes citations to lower court opinions and also the general subject matter of the case; a Summary of Cases Recently Filed; Arguments Before the Court, a summary of oral arguments in the most important cases each week; a Table of Cases and Case Status Report, which is issued every three to four weeks; and a Topical Index, which is issued seven times a year. Contact: Bureau of National Affairs, 9435 Key West Avenue, Rockville, MD 20850. Tel: 301/258-1033. Or, 800/372-1033.

Supreme Court Bulletin. Looseleaf. Mailed to subscribers on decision day. Published by Commerce Clearing House, Inc. Incudes current opinions of the Court, and index to docket numbers, the status of pending cases, and a tentative calendar of scheduled arguments. Contact: Commerce Clearing House, 4025 West Peterson Avenue, Chicago, IL 60646. Tel: 312/583-8500, Or, in Washington, D.C., call 202/626-2200.

* * * * * * * * * * * * *

Rules of Practice and Procedure

The Supreme Court has promulgated rules of practice and procedure to be followed by litigants and parties petitioning the court for relief. These rules may be found in the Appendix to Title 28 of the United States Code.

The Supreme Court is also authorized to prescribe rules for **the U.S. Courts of Appeal, the U.S. District Courts, and certain specialized Federal courts** established under Article III of the Constitution, as well as certain special proceedings in the Federal courts, such as bankruptcy, admiralty, and copyright proceedings. Federal court rules promulgated by the Supreme Court are for the general guidance of the lower Federal courts. Note: Most admiralty cases since 1966 fall under the Federal Rules of Civil Procedure. However, certain special admiralty rules come into play if the only constitutional or statutory ground of jurisdiction is the admiralty ground or, if more than one jurisdictional ground may be invoked, the admiralty ground is the one designated in the complaint. Admiralty rules are not codified in one place, but are scattered throughout the U.S. Code.

In addition, special local conditions and circumstances have led each lower court to issue its own special rules not inconsistent with the general rules set forth by the Supreme Court. These local rules apply only to the issuing court and are primarily concerned with rules for filing motions, brief preparations, and procedural rules of an operational nature.

Generally, court rules control court operations and the conduct of litigants appearing before the courts. they are designed to establish uniform procedures, render efficient their business functions, and provide parties with information and instructions on matters pertaining to judicial proceedings.

Federal court rules consist of: (1) rules of general applicability, such as the Federal Rules of Civil Procedure; (2) the Federal Rules of Appellate Procedure; (3) individual rules of Federal courts; and (4) forms used by litigants.

Rules of court not inconsistent with legislative enactments have the force and effect of statutes.

Publication of Court Rules. Rules of general applicability may be found in the appendixes to Titles 11, 18, and 28 of the United States Code. The U.S. Code Annotated and the U.S. Code Service also publish Federal court rules of general applicability and annotate them to both case law and Opinions of the Attorney General.

Each Circuit Court of Appeals and many Federal District Courts publish their own local rules in pamphlet form, available from the appropriate clerk's office.

West's Federal Rules Decisions. Issued monthly. Price: $52.00 per year. Contains decisions of the Federal courts construing rules of practice and procedure, and articles on Federal rules. Contact: West Publishing Company, 50 West Kellogg Boulevard, P.O. Box 64833, St. Paul, MN 55164. Tel: 612/688-3600. Or, 800/328-9352.

Database:

Project Hermes. Project Hermes is an electronic dissemination service for opinions of the Supreme Court. The service, which first transmitted Supreme Court decisions on June 21, 1990, will operate for a two-year trial period. Opinions are electronically transmitted to subscribers simultaneously with their being announced by the Court. The organizations initially selected to disseminate this data are:

*Associated Press
*Bureau of National Affairs
*Case Western Reserve University
*Commerce Clearing House
*Mead Data Central
*National Clearinghouse for Legal Services
*Supreme Court Opinion Network (SCON)
*United Press International
*U.S. Department of Justice
*UUNet Communications Services
*VERALEX, The Thompson Group
*West Publishing Company

U.S. Courts of Appeals

Decisions of the Courts

There have never been any official published reports of opinions of the U.S. Courts of Appeals. The standard unofficial source of these decisions is the Federal Reporter and Federal Reporter, Second Series, which are components of the West Publishing Company's National Reporter System. The Federal Reporter and the current Federal Reporter, Second Series have been published continuously since 1880. The Company has also collected all available decisions of the lower Federal courts from 1789 to 1880 and reprinted them in Federal Cases. Contact: West Publishing Company, 50 West Kellogg Boulevard, P.O. Box 64833, St. Paul, MN 55164. Tel: 612/688-3600. Or, 800/328-9352.

Rules of Practice and Procedure

Federal Rules of Appellate Procedure. Promulgated by the U.S. Supreme Court for use in appellate proceedings in Federal Circuit Courts of Appeals. The text of the rules may be found in the Appendix to Title 28 of the United States Code.

Rules of Evidence for United States Courts and Magistrates ("Federal Rules of Evidence"). Congress enacted these rules in 1974 in order to provide a uniform evidentiary code for all U.S. courts. The text of the rules may be found in the Appendix to Title 28 of the United States Code.

Federal Rules of Evidence, 1989. Senate Judiciary Committee. Available from Superintendent of Documents, U.S. Government Printing Office, Washington, D.C. 20402. Price: $1.50. GPO Stock# 052-070-06591-5.

Electronic Bulletin Boards

Several circuit courts have instituted ACES (Appeals Court Electronic Services), which was developed by the Federal Judicial Center, the research and development arm of the Federal Judiciary. ACES is an electronic bulletin board for the electronic dissemination of appellate court information. This service allows public users with a microcomputer and terminal emulation software and hardware to view and transfer electronically published slip opinions, court oral argument calendars, court rules, notices and reports, and press releases. Access to ACES is free and does not require prior registration. The following courts have implemented ACES or plan to implement it by the end of 1990:

*The Third Circuit Court of Appeals (Philadelphia)
*The Fourth Circuit Court of Appeals (Richmond)
*The Sixth Circuit Court of Appeals (Cincinnati)
*The Ninth Circuit Court of Appeals (San Francisco)
*The Tenth Circuit Court of Appeals (Denver)

Other courts are also planning to implement ACES in the near future.

PACER (Public Access to Court Electronic Records) is a dial-in service from any personal computer that permits the retrieval of complete official electronic case histories and docket reports in less than a minute. This service is free-of-charge and is available 24 hours a day. Cases may be searched by participant name or case number. At the appellate level, the system is only available in the Fourth and Sixth Circuits.

Public Access Terminals are available in several courthouses on a walk-up basis. These terminals allow the public to obtain docket information without waiting for a clerk to become available.

U.S. Court of Appeals for the District of Columbia Circuit

Opinions. Opinions of the Court are issued on Tuesdays and Fridays of each week. An annual subscription may be purchased for $250.00 by sending a check with your organization's name and address to the Clerk of the Court. The subscription year is from July 1 through June 30. Part-year subscriptions are not prorated. Contact: U.S. Court of Appeals for the District of Columbia Circuit, U.S. Courthouse, 3rd & Constitution Avenue, N.W., Washington, D.C. 20001.

U.S. Court of Appeals for the Federal Circuit

Decisions of the Court

Federal Reporter, Second Series. Published by West Publishing Company. Contains current and past decisions of the Federal Circuit and, beginning with volume 34 of the Second Series, decisions of the former U.S. Court of Patent Appeals, which was abolished in 1982. Contact: West Publishing Company, 50 West Kellogg Boulevard, P.O. Box 64833, St. Paul, MN 55164. Tel: 612/688-3600. Or, 800/328-9352.

Opinions. Slip opinions of the Court are published by the Patent Resources Institute and by BNA Plus. Contact: Patent Resources Institute, Inc., 2000 Pennsylvania Avenue, N.W., Suite 3450, Washington, D.C. 20006. Tel: 202/223-1175. Or, BNA Plus, 1231 25th Street, Washington, D.C. 20037. Tel: 202/452-4323. Or, 800/452-7773.

PRI Opinions is a weekly periodical of all published and unpublished patent, trademark and copyright opinions of the U.S. Court of Appeals for the Federal Circuit, which the Court issued during the five business-day period preceding the publication date. PRI Opinions also includes other CAFC opinions likely to be of interest to members of the intellectual property law bar. All slip opinions released for publication by the U.S. Patent and Trademark Office or by applicant's attorneys are also included. Annual subscription: (October 1 - September 30): $235.00. Contact: Patent Resources Institute, Inc., 2000 Pennsylvania Avenue, N.W., Suite 3450, Washington, D.C. 20006. Tel: 202/223-1175.

BNA Plus CAFC Opinions. BNA Plus provides a weekly subscription service for U.S. Court of Appeals for the Federal Circuit decisions. Opinions are mailed on Tuesday of the week after they are issued by the Court. BNA Plus offers subscriptions to all published CAFC decisions and to all unpublished patent and trademark decisions. They will also screen and deliver only those decisions pertinent to specific interests. For pricing and order information contact BNA Plus, 1231 25th Street, Washington, D.C. 20037. Tel: 202/452-4323. Or, 800/452-7773.

United States Court of Appeals for the Federal Circuit, V 6, Trade Cases. (Judiciary) 1989. 200 pp. Price: $13.00. GPO Stock# 028-002-00048-3. Contact: The Superintendent of Documents, U.S. Government Printing Office, Washington, D.C. 20402. Tel: 202/783-3238.

Rules of Practice and Procedure

Federal Rules of Appellate Procedure. Promulgated by the U.S. Supreme Court for use in appellate proceedings in Federal Circuit Courts of Appeals. Appeals to the Federal Circuit are also governed by the Federal Rules of Appellate Procedure with such modifications and additions as are dictated by the special nature of the Court's jurisdiction. The text of the rules may be found in the Appendix to Title 28 of the United States Code.

Rules of the U.S. Court of Appeals for the Federal Circuit. The local rules peculiar to the Federal Circuit and necessitated by the special nature of the Court's jurisdiction. The text of the rules may be found in the Appendix to Title 28 of the United States Code.

Temporary Emergency Court of Appeals

Decisions of the Court

Opinions. Opinions of the Court are published as issued. Individual opinions may be purchased for $2.00. A six-month subscription may be purchased for $25.00 by sending a check with your organization's name and address to the Court. Contact: Temporary Emergency Court of Appeals, 1130 U.S. Courthouse, 3rd and Constitution Avenue, N.W., Washington, D.C. 20001.

Federal Reporter, Second Series. Published by West Publishing Company. Contains the decisions of the Court. Contact: West Publishing Company, 50 West Kellogg Boulevard, P.O. Box 64833, St. Paul, MN 55164. Tel: 612/688-3600. Or, 800/328-9352.

Rules of Practice and Procedure

General Rules of the Temporary Emergency Court of Appeals of the United States. The text of these rules may be found in the Appendix to Title 28 of the United States Code.

U.S. Claims Court

Decisions of the Court

United States Claims Court Reporter. Published by West Publishing Company 1983-date. Contains decisions of the Claims Court and also includes reprints of opinions reviewing U.S. Claims Court decisions originally published in the Federal Reporter and Supreme Court Reporter. Contact: West Publishing Company, 50 West Kellogg Boulevard, P.O. Box 64833, St. Paul, MN 55164. Tel: 612/688-3600. Or, 800/328-9352.

Index to Opinions. The monthly index to opinions of the United States Claims Court is available for a $10.00 annual subscription. Individual opinions cost $1.00 each. To obtain publications write to the Clerk of the Court. Contact: United State Claims Court, 717 Madison Place, N.W., Washington, D.C. 20005.

For cases decided in the predecessor U.S. Court of Claims, which was abolished in 1982, see Cases Decided in the Court of Claims, 1863-1982, vols. 1-231. Consult a law library since this serial publication is now out of print and no longer available for purchase.

Rules of Practice and Procedure

Rules of the U.S. Claims Court. the text of these rules may be found in the Appendix to Title 28 of the United States Code.

U.S. Court of International Trade

Lawyers Information Bulletin: A Newsletter from the Clerk's Office. Published twice a year. Volume 6, No. 1 was published in May 1990. To have your name added to the mailing list contact the Assistant Clerk of the Court, United States Court of International Trade, 1 Federal Plaza, New York, NY 10007.

* * * * * * * * * * * *

Decisions of the Court

The following publications can be purchased from the **U.S. Government Printing Office.** Stock numbers and prices for annual subscriptions are shown below. Submit requests for these publications to: The Superintendent of Documents, U.S. Government Printing Office, Washington, D.C. 20402. Tel: 202/783-3238.

United States Court of International Trade Reports: Cases Adjudged in the United States Court of International Trade. All volumes are out of print except Volume 10. Volume 12 is forthcoming:

Volume 10, January - December, 1986. Price: $33.00 domestic, $41.25 foreign. GPO Stock# 028-003-00058-7.

Volume 12 is scheduled for release at the end of 1990. Its price has not yet been decided. GPO Stock# 028-003-00060-9.

* * * * * * * * * * * *

Federal Supplement. Published by West Publishing Company. Contains the decisions of the Court. Beginning with volume 135, the Federal Supplement also contains the decisions of the predecessor United States Customs Court. Contact: West Publishing Company, 50 West Kellogg Boulevard, P.O. Box 64833, St. Paul, MN 55164. Tel: 612/688-3600. Or, 800/328-9352.

Rules of Practice and Procedure

Rules of the U.S. Court of International Trade. the text of these rules may be found in the Appendix to Title 28 of the United States Code.

Rules Service Company, 7658 Standish Place, Ste 106, Rockville, MD 20855. Tel: 301/424-9402. Looseleaf. Updated when necessary. Price: $42.00 for subscription plus binder.

Judicial Panel on Multidistrict Litigation

Rulings of the Panel

Federal Supplement. Contains key rulings of the Judicial Panel. Published by West Publishing Company. Contact: West Publishing Company, 50 West Kellogg Boulevard, P.O. Box 64833, St. Paul, MN 55164. Tel: 612/688-3600. Or, 800/328-9352.

U.S. Court of Military Appeals

Annual Report. The Annual Report discusses the current state of military justice in the United States. In addition to a section on the Court of Military Appeals, it also contains reports from the Judge Advocates General of the Army, Navy, and Air Force, and a report from the Chief Counsel of the Coast Guard. A limited number of copies are available from the Clerk of the Court at no charge. Contact: U.S. Court of Military Appeals, 450 E Street, N.W., Washington, D.C. 20442.

* * * * * * * * * * * *

Decisions of the Court

Decisions of the Court are available through West Publishing Company, P.O. Box 64833, St. Paul, MN 55164. Tel: 612/688-3600 or 800/328-9352. West offers several related publications and services:

The Military Justice Reporter is a 29 volume hard-bound set that contains the full text of all opinions from 1978 through 1989. Price: $1297.25. Additional volumes are sold for $60.00 each.

Military Justice Reporter Advance Sheets are issued biweekly. Advance sheets are free with a subscription to the Military

Justice Reporter. An annual subscription to the Advance Sheets may be purchased separately for $95.00.

West's Military Justice Digest is a two-volume soft bound index to volumes 1-27 of the Military Justice Reporter. Price: $44.50.

* * * * * * * * * * * *

Courts-Martial Reports. These volumes include decisions of the Court from its inception in 1951 to 1975. It was published by the Lawyers Cooperative Publishing Company, 50 Broad Street East, Rochester, NY 14696. Tel: 716/546-5530. Or, 800/828-6266.

U.S. Tax Court

Decisions of the Court

U.S. Tax Court Reports. Published monthly. Each issue is a consolidation of the decisions for a month. Contact: The Superintendent of Documents, U.S. Government Printing Office, Washington, D.C. 20402. Tel: 202/783-3238. Price: $26.00 a year domestic; $32.50 a year foreign. GPO Stock# 728-001-00000-3.

Tax Court Memorandum Decisions. Published weekly in looseleaf form and in a bound volume at the end of each year. The bulk of the Tax Court's work is reflected in memorandum opinions which are not published in the U.S. Tax Court Reports. The Tax Court only prints a few copies of such decisions. They are otherwise only available through commercial sources. Contact: Prentice-Hall, Inc., 910 Sylvan Avenue, Englewood Cliffs, NJ 07632. Tel: 800/562-0245. Or, in Washington, D.C, call 202/293-0707.

Rules of Practice and Procedure

Rules of Practice and Procedure of the United States Tax Court: Effective July 1, 1990, with Additions and Amendments through January 12, 1990. Contact: The Superintendent of Documents, U.S. Government Printing Office, Washington, D.C. 20402. Tel: 202/783-3238.Price: $9.00 domestic; $11.25 foreign. GPO Stock# 028-005-00163-2.

United States Tax Court Rules of Practice and Procedure. On June 5, 1990, Chief Judge Arthur L. Nimms, III issued a completely revised and republished set of Rules of Practice and Procedure. The new Rules are effective July 1, 1990. Many of the changes in the Rules from prior editions are designed to carry out the Tax Court's responsibilities under the Taxpayer's Bill of Rights. Other changes deal with such subjects as expert witnesses, arbitration, and counsel's conflict of interest. The rules are now gender neutral. Copies of the Court's Rules of Practice and Procedures, as amended, may be obtained for $9.00 per copy by writing to the Court's Administrative Office (Room 150) at 400 Second Street, N.W., Washington, D.C. 20217. A check or money order made payable to the "Clerk, United States Tax Court" should accompany each such written request.

U.S. Tax Court Reports, Volumes 60, 64, 68, 71, 77, 79, 81, 82, 85, 87, and 90. Volume 60 contains the original rules of the Court. The other volumes contain all of the amendments issued since the original rules were promulgated. For price and ordering information, see the entry for the Tax Court Reports above.

U.S. Court of Veterans Appeals

Decisions of the Court

A few copies of each decision are available from the Office of the Clerk of the Court, 1625 K Street, N.W. Suite 400, Washington, D.C. 20006. In addition, there are four commercial sources of the decisions of the Court of Veterans Appeals:

Daily Washington Law Reporter. Daily. Includes all of the decisions of the Court and semi-annual indexes. Price: $147.60 per year. Available from: Daily Washington Law Reporter, 1625 I Street, N.W., Washington, D.C. 20006. Tel: 202/331-1700.

U.S. Law Week. Weekly. Selected decisions published by the Bureau of National Affairs, Inc., 9435 Key West Avenue, Rockville, MD 20850. Tel: 301/258-1033. Or, 800/372-1033.

Veterans Disability Law Reporter. Contact Steven Babitsky, Box 590, Falmouth, MA 02540. Tel: 508/540-3101.

Veterans Law Reporter. Contact Keith Snyder, Veterans Education Project, P.O. Box 42130, Wash., D.C. 20015. Tel: 202/547-8387.

Rules of Practice and Procedure

The Court does not publish an official version of its rules. Contact one of the following commercial sources:

National Veterans Legal Services Project, Attn: Ronald B. Abrams, 2001 S Street, N.W., Washington, D.C. 20009-1125. Tel: 202/265-8305. Price: Free to veterans; $5.00 to members of the public, including attorneys representing veterans.

Rules Service Company, 7658 Standish Place, Ste 106, Rockville, MD 20855. Tel: 301/424-9402. Looseleaf. Updated when necessary. Price: $20.00 for subscription plus binder.

Veterans Education Project, Attn: Keith Snyder, P.O. Box 42130, Washington, D.C. 20015. Tel: 202/547-8387.

Federal Rules Decisions. Published by West Publishing Company, 50 West Kellogg Boulevard, P.O. Box 64833, St. Paul, MN 55164. Tel: 612/688-3600. Or, 800/328-9352.

U.S. District Courts

Decisions of the Court

Federal Supplement. Published by the West Publishing Company. There have never been any official published reports of the opinions of the Federal District Courts. The standard unofficial source of the most important selected decisions of the District Courts is the Federal Supplement, which is part of West's National Reporter System. The Federal Supplement includes selected cases from 1932 to date. For cases decided from 1880 to 1932, see West's Federal Reporter. For cases decided between 1789 and 1880, see West's Federal Cases. The Federal Supplement also includes selected decisions of the U.S. Court of International Trade, the Special Court, Regional Rail Reorganization Act, and selected rulings of the Judicial Panel on Multidistrict Litigation. Contact: West Publishing Company, 50 West Kellogg Boulevard, P.O. Box 64833, St. Paul, MN 55164. Tel: 612/688-3600. Or, 800/328-9352.

Bankruptcy Reporter. There are no official published reports of decisions of the Bankruptcy Divisions of the U.S. District Courts. The standard commercial source is the Bankruptcy Reporter, which is part of West's National Reporter System. Contact West Publishing Company at the address listed above.

Rules of Practice and Procedure

Federal Rules of Civil Procedure. Promulgated by the U.S. Supreme Court for use in the Federal District Courts. The text of the Rules may be found in the Appendix to Title 28 of the United States Code.

Federal Rules of Criminal Procedure. Promulgated by the U.S. Supreme Court for use in the Federal District Courts. The text of the Rules may be found in the Appendix to Title 18 of the United States Code.

Rules of Evidence for United States Courts and Magistrates ("Federal Rules of Evidence"). Congress enacted these rules in 1974 in order to provide a uniform evidentiary code for all U.S. courts. The text of the rules may be found in the Appendix to Title 28 of the United States Code.

Rules of Evidence for United States Courts and Magistrates ("Federal Rules of Evidence"). Congress enacted these rules in 1974 in order to provide a uniform evidentiary code for all U.S. courts. The text of the rules may be found in the Appendix to Title 28 of the United States Code.

Bankruptcy Rules and Official Forms Under Chapters 1-13 of the Bankruptcy Act ("Rules of Bankruptcy Procedure"). The text of these rules may be found in the Appendix to Title 11 of the United States Code.

* * * * * * * * * * * *

The following publication can be purchased from the **U.S. Government Printing Office**. Stock numbers and prices for annual subscriptions are shown below. Submit requests for these publications to: The Superintendent of Documents, U.S. Government Printing Office, Washington, D.C. 20402. Tel: 202/783-3238.

Rules of Civil Procedure for the United States District Courts, with Forms, 1989. Senate Judiciary Committee. Price: $3.75. GPO Stock# 052-070-06589-3.

ANNOTATED BIBLIOGRAPHY

Rules of Criminal Procedure for the United States District Courts, with Forms, 1989. Senate Judiciary Committee. Price: $2.25. GPO Stock# 052-070-06619-9.

Federal Rules of Evidence, 1989. Senate Judiciary Committee. Price: $1.50. GPO Stock# 052-070-06591-5.

* * * * * * * * * * * *

In addition, many District Courts have promulgated local rules not inconsistent with the rules of general applicability indicated above, which are applicable only to their particular proceedings. District Courts often publish these in pamphlet form and make them available through the offices of the clerks of the courts.

* * * * * * * * * * * *

Electronic Bulletin Boards

Thirteen U.S. District Courts and Bankruptcy Divisions have instituted PACER (Public Access to Court Electronic Records), which was developed by the Federal Judicial Center, the research and development arm of the Federal Judiciary. PACER is a dial-in service from any personal computer that permits the retrieval of official electronic case histories and court dockets in less than a minute. The system can provide lists of cases, searched by name, as well as a comprehensive summary of any case, including case and party information. There is currently no charge for accessing PACER, although the Bankruptcy Divisions are considering instituting fees in the future. To register for PACER, contact the clerk of the appropriate court. U.S. District Courts currently offering PACER are:

*Arizona
*District of Columbia
*Georgia-Northern District
*Texas-Western District
*Utah

Bankruptcy Divisions currently offering PACER are:

*California-Southern District
*Kansas
*Maine
*New Hampshire
*Oregon
*Rhode Island
*Massachusetts
*Texas-Western District

(VCIS) Voice Case Information System allows public access via a Touch-Tone telephone to information in Bankruptcy Division databases. A computer-generated voice reads case information to callers in response to inquiries entered on the telephone keyboard. VCIS is currently operational in 25 courts and by the end of 1992 should be available in virtually all Bankruptcy Divisions. There is no charge for this service. Current VCIS telephone numbers are indicated in the individual sections of this Directory for each court below:

*Arkansas (Eastern & Western)
*California-Southern
*Illinois-Central
*Florida-Southern
*Kansas
*Louisiana-Eastern
*Maine
*Massachusetts
*Michigan-Western
*Mississippi-Northern
*Missouri-Western
*New Hampshire
*New Jersey
*New York-Eastern
*New York-Western
*Oklahoma-Eastern
*Oregon
*Pennsylvania-Eastern
*Rhode Island
*South Carolina
*Texas-Eastern
*Texas-Western
*Virginia-Eastern
*Washington-Western
*West Virginia-Southern

Public Access Terminals are available in several courthouses on a walk-up basis. These terminals allow the public to obtain docket information without waiting for a clerk to become available.

Administrative Office of the U.S. Courts

Report of the Proceedings of the Judicial Conference of the United States and Annual Report of the Director of the Administrative Office of the U.S. Courts. Published annually. Available for reference at the Administrative Office of the U.S. Courts in Washington, D.C. and at Federal court libraries nationwide. Contact: Administrative Office of the U.S. Courts, 811 Vermont Avenue, N.W., Washington, D.C. 20544.

The Third Branch. A monthly newsletter that deals with various issues of interest and importance to the Federal court system. 12 pp. Available free of charge. To get on the mailing list, contact: Legislative and Public Affairs, Administrative Office of the U.S. Courts, 811 Vermont Avenue, N.W., Washington, D.C. 20544.

* * * * * * * * * * * *

The following publications can be purchased from the **U.S. Government Printing Office.** Stock numbers and prices for annual subscriptions are shown below. Submit requests for these publications to: The Superintendent of Documents, U.S. Government Printing Office, Washington, D.C. 20402. Tel: 202/783-3238.

U.S. Court Directory. Published twice a year, this directory contains the names, addresses, and phone numbers of Federal court personnel nationwide. Latest edition published Spring 1990. Price: $21.00. GPO Stock# 028-004-00076-1.

Federal Probation: A Journal of Correctional Philosophy and Practice. A quarterly publication containing articles relating to preventive and correctional activities in delinquency and crime. Price: $5.00 a year domestic; $6.25 a year foreign. GPO Stock# 727-001-00000-0.

Federal Judicial Center

The Federal Judicial Center has published over 220 documents since its creation in 1967. Its free 1990 catalog lists 148 of these as still being available. The Center's publications include reports of research and analysis done by or for the Center, as well as products of Center seminars and workshops conducted for various third branch personnel. These publications are available from the Center's Information Services Office. Some, however, are available only to certain groups within the Federal judiciary; these are clearly noted in the catalog. Most of the publications published by the Center are free. When requesting publications, enclose a self-addressed mailing label to expedite receipt of the requested material. Contact: Federal Judicial Center, Information Services Office, 1520 H Street, N.W., Washington, D.C. 20005.

Some of the recent publications of the Center include:

Trends in Asbestos Litigation. Thomas E. Willging, 1987, 138 pp.

Settlement Strategies for Federal District Judges. D. Marie Provine, 1986, 103 pp.

Patent Law and Practice. Herbert F. Schwartz, 1988, 119 pp.

Major Issues in Immigration Law. David A. Martin, 1987, 147 pp.

Major Issues in the Federal Law Of Employment Discrimination. George Rutherglen, 1987, 150 pp.

Handbook on Jury Use in the Federal District Courts. Jody George, Deirdre Golash, and Russell Wheeler, 1989, 93 pp.

Unpublished Dispositions: Problems of Access and Use in the Courts of Appeals. Donna Stienstra, 1985, 75 pp.

Federal Judicial Center Annual Report 1989. The Annual Report describes the organization and activities of the Federal Judicial Center. It also contains a list of publications released in 1989 or scheduled for release early in 1990. 29 pp.

Commercial Online Databases and Document Retrieval Services

COMMERCIAL ONLINE DATABASES WITH U.S. GOVERNMENT INFORMATION

Access to information regarding the Federal Government is of great importance to any attorney. While the Federal Government does maintain a number of database systems which can be useful to attorneys, many of these databases are unavailable to the public. This fact, coupled with the increasing demand for information, has contributed to the growth of a great number of commercial online databases which provide Federal information (and some which provide access to those otherwise unavailable Government databases).

In this section we have attempted to describe these services so that the reader might know which services will meet his informational needs. Basically, there are two types of services presented herein: self-contained online database services, such as WESTLAW or WASHINGTON ON-LINE, and services which are not themselves databases but which provide access to a number of other databases. Examples of this type of service are the BRS Search Service and DIALOG.

Note: Unless otherwise specified, all that is needed to access these database services are a computer, a modem, and a phone line.

BRS SEARCH SERVICE

This service has over 150 information sources that answer questions on business, finance, medicine, biomedical research, education, engineering, and other areas. These sources encompass both unique databases serving special information needs and standard bibliographic databases (titles and article summaries) used by information specialists around the world. The BRS Search Service databases include Legal Resource Index, Federal Register Abstracts, Congressional Register Abstracts, Newsearch, Government Printing Office Monthly Catalog, and Index to U.S. Government Periodicals.

CUSTOMIZED SERVICES:

* **AfterDark Service:** This service can be used after 6:00 PM and is menu driven and user friendly. There are 110 databases available. There is a $75 start-up fee and a minimum monthly charge of $12 for this service.

* **SDI:** This feature permits you to enter a search strategy that will be processed automatically on a monthly basis.

AVAILABILITY: Available at all times except from 4:00 AM to 6:00 AM Monday through Saturday and 2:00 AM to 9:00 AM Sunday (EST).

COST: There are three payment options:

* **Open Access Plan.** No prepayments or monthly minimums. The customer pays a $75 annual password fee and then pays as he uses the service.

* **Annual Commitment Advance Purchase Plan:** The customer makes an annual prepayment of at least $1000 (nonrefundable) and then receives a discount when using the service. For example, a prepayment of $1000 gives the customer a discount of $6 per hour.

* **Annual Commitment Monthly Installment Plan:** The customer pays at least $250 per month and then receives an hourly discount. For example, a monthly payment of $250 entitles the customer to a discount of $6 per hour. Under this option, the customer will receive a refund during the first two months in which the service charges are less than the minimum pre-paid.

FOR FURTHER INFORMATION: Contact: BRS Information Technologies, 8000 Westpark Drive, McLean, VA 22102. Tel: 800/955-0906.

DIALCOM

This service offers access to various information sources, including: FEDNEWS, a public affairs database published by several key government agencies; FAR Online, which provides access to the Federal Acquisition Regulation database, as well as 29 other Federal procurement databases; Dow Jones News/Retrieval, a comprehensive library of financial information, business news, and stock quotes; and BNA Online, which provides business analyses and tax news through six online publications, as well as regulatory news and other highlights from the U.S. Securities and Exchange Commission. Dialcom also provides links to other public databases such as DIALOG.

CUSTOMIZED SERVICES:

* **Bulletin Boards:** Allows subscribers to maintain custom bulletin boards for their organization.

***UpFront:** A communication software package providing customized access to Dialcom's electronic mail, telex, and postal delivery messaging services.

AVAILABILITY: 24-hour service.

COST: For non-Federal users: $25 monthly minimum; $19 per hour in prime-time hours (8:00 AM - 6:00 PM EST, Monday - Friday), $10.50 per hour in non-prime time hours. In addition, individual databases have additional hourly fees which will be added on to these basic rates.

FOR FURTHER INFORMATION: Contact: BT Tymnet Inc., 6120 Executive Boulevard, Rockville, MD 20852. Tel: 800/872-7654.

DIALOG

Organized from an extensive collection of bibliographies, corporate directories, newswire services, technical reports, patents, trademarks and journal abstracts, **DIALOG** includes more than 200 million records in over 380 databases. The complete text of over 450 journals and newspapers, as well as current news and press releases, is also available. **DIALOG** allows lawyers to obtain background information, research people and companies, prepare for litigation, research the status of patents, trademarks, and the latest tax issues, and investigate corporate takeovers. Databases include The Library of Congress, National Technical Information Service, U.S. Department of Energy, Congressional Record Abstracts, LABORLAW, Legal Resource Index, Federal Index, Federal Register Abstracts, Government Printing Office Publication Reference File, MEDLINE, National Institute of Occupational Safety and Health (NIOSH), TRADESMARKSCAN-FEDERAL, Database of Databases, World Patent Index, Tax Notes Today, and National Criminal Justice Research Statistics.

CUSTOMIZED SERVICES

* **DIALOGLINK** software, DIALOG's custom communication software.
* specialized training seminars for government and legal research, business, chemistry, and patent searches.
* introductory and advanced hands-on seminars.
* **DIALOG** will print and mail information to subscribers via first class mail.
* **DIALMAIL:** an electronic communications system, which sends electronic messages, memos, or complete reports from one computer to another. In addition, **DIALOG** output can be sent directly to any electronic mail system linked to MCI Mail.
* **DIALORDER:** enables the user to order the complete texts of articles found in abstracts or references.
* 24-hour customer support "Hotline."
* **CHRONOLOG:** a monthly newsletter which offers regular updates about databases, new DIALOG features, announcements of new information sources, and training seminars.
* **TRADEMARKSCAN FEDERAL:** conducts a search and identifies trademarks of interest. You will get an image of the trademark on your PC, as well as the textual record of the trademark. The database contains information on all trademarks registered or pending at the U.S. Patent and Trademark Office.

AVAILABILITY: 24-hour service, except Sundays from 3:00 AM to 1:00 PM (EST).

COST: $35 annual service fee. There is a $45 start up fee to cover a starter tutorial kit; no minimum usage requirements. A typical on-line search takes about 15 minutes and averages about $2 per minute.

FOR FURTHER INFORMATION: Contact: Dialog Information Services, Inc., 3460 Hillview Avenue, Palo Alto, CA 94304. Tel: 800/334-2564 or 415/858-3785 in California.

DISCLOSURE, INC.

The Disclosure database contains financial, management and directory information extracted from reports that all public companies file with U.S. Securities and Exchange Commission. This service provides users with detailed profiles of more than 12,000 public companies whose securities are traded in the United States.

CUSTOMIZED SERVICES

* **Spectrum:** this service provides the Subscriber with extensive ownership information (including institutional holdings, 5% owners, and insiders). This service is an additional $2000 per year. Thirty day free trial period.

AVAILABILITY: The **Disclosure** database is available either through online vendors or directly from Disclosure in the form of **Compact Disclosure. Compact Disclosure** features a searchable database containing financial and textual data provided in a CD-ROM product. **Compact Disclosure** contains the full database plus **Zacks Earnings Estimates** and additional stock ownership information. Purchasers of **Compact Disclosure** receive a compact disc player, which can be hooked up to any IBM compatible computer. Subscribers receive monthly updated disks which contain the **Disclosure** database. **LaserDisclosure,** an image-based system providing users with exact reproductions of original SEC filings, is also available.

COST: $6,000 per year (includes the lease of disk player; $5,500 if a disk player is not required); $9,000 for foreign subscriptions.

FOR FURTHER INFORMATION: Contact: Disclosure, Inc., 5161 River Road, Bethesda, MD 20816 or 161 William Street, New York, NY 10038. Tel: 800/843-7747 or 212/581-1414.

DOW JONES NEWS/RETRIEVAL

This online news and information service provides the user with access to the full-text of **The Wall Street Journal, Barrons,** information about Supreme Court decisions, up-to-the-minute filings at the Securities and Exchange Commission, SEC actions, mergers, acquisitions, divestitures, anti-trust actions, product liability matters, stock prices and repurchases, as well as U.S. Government (including Federal regulatory agencyd) news.

AVAILABILITY: 24-hour service.

COST: There is a $29.95 start-up fee for the standard membership. During prime time hours (6:00 AM. to 6:00 PM EST), there is a per-minute charge of from 70 cents to $2.90, depending on baud output and the type of information sought. During non-prime time hours, the per-minute charge ranges from 14 cents to $1.80.

FOR FURTHER INFORMATION: Contact: Dow Jones and Company, P.O. Box 300, Princeton, NJ 08543. Tel: 800/225-3170, ext. 2201.

ELECTRONIC LEGISLATIVE SEARCH SYSTEM (ELSS)

This comprehensive service tracks current Federal and state legislation and allows monitoring of the status of the bills in its database. The ELSS database consists of summary notices of new bill introductions and their corresponding legislative histories. This information is available for current regular and special legislative sessions of the U.S. Congress and the 50 state legislatures on over 2500 different subjects.

CUSTOMIZED SERVICES

* **PROFILE:** this service allows legislative tracking on selected subject areas and jurisdictions. The database forms their profile and provides Electronic Nightly Action Reports (NAR).
* **PROFILE PLUS:** with this service the subscriber receives introductory notices, action reports, and mailed paper copy of bill texts, amendments, and copies for all bills in the profile.

AVAILABILITY: 24-hour service.

COST: There is an initial $500 subscription fee (one-time only) and a $2,500 minimum annual usage commitment. If a customer uses the service three hours or less per month, the charge for an immediate search is $235 per hour; $150 for an overnight search. As usage per month increases, the charges for immediate and overnight searches decrease.

FOR FURTHER INFORMATION: Contact: Commerce Clearing House, Inc., 2700 Lake Cook Road, Riverwoods, IL 60015. Attn: ELSS Department. Tel: 708/940-4600, ext. 2330.

LEGI-SLATE

This congressional service offers on-line reports, including subject indexing of all bills introduced in Congress since 1979, as well as current bills and bill status. Bill status is updated daily. The Congressional Record, committee reports, hearing schedules, new bills, verbatim transcripts of committee hearings and news reports are updated daily. LEGI-SLATE's Federal Register service is searchable by date, agency, enabling Public Law, and Code of Federal Regulations citation. Updates are daily with that day's announcements available in full text. A subsidiary of LEGI-SLATE, **Current USC**, is a full text service of the United States Code, updated as each new public law is approved by the President, usually within 24 hours.

AVAILABILITY: 24-hour service.

COST: $20 for each hour connected; $15 per hour communications fee; ($10 outside within the greater Washington, D.C. area). There are also Information Charges for the aggregate hours of use. For example the first 5 hours per month carry a $175 per hour charge, and the next 20 hours per month cost $170 per hour.

FOR FURTHER INFORMATION: Contact LEGI-SLATE, 111 Massachusetts Avenue, N.W., Washington, D.C. 20001. Tel: 800/877-6999 or 202/898-2300 in Washington, D.C.

LEXIS

This online, full-text database is a legal research service containing the following libraries and services.

* **Federal and state archives** containing case law, codes, and regulations.
* **29 specialized libraries** covering virtually every field of practice including tax, securities, banking, environmental, and insurance law.
* **United States Supreme Court briefs.**
* **Supreme Court decisions** (full texts) within three hours of being announced by the Court.
* **Legislative histories.**
* **Federal Register** and **Code of Federal Regulations.**
* **Auto-Cite,** which provides instant access to more than 3.5 million Federal and state case law citations and more than 1 million references to 12,000 American Law Reports (ALR) annotations.
* **Shepard's Citation Service.**

A subscriber to LEXIS also receives NEXIS and its related services. **NEXIS** is a full-text research service which includes information on pending cases, trials in progress, and recently released decisions. This service also includes a file of all Federal contracts. The service uses more than 650 sources. In addition, the following NEXIS services are available:

* **Lexis Financial Information Service,** which offers business and financial news, SEC filings, brokerage house research reports, private company market share information, and real-time stock quotes from all North American exchanges.
* **LEXPAT,** which contains the full text of more than 1 million patents issued since 1975. New patents are usually added within three days of issuance.
* **NAARS,** which provides accounting materials and annual reports from more than 4200 companies and government entities.
* **MEDIS,** which offers the full text of more than 40 current medical journals and textbooks, as well as **MEDLINE**, a bibliographic database produced by the National Library of Medicine, and various libraries with medical, drug and poison, pharmaceutical, cancer, and health care administration information.

AVAILABILITY: 24-hour service, except from 2:00 AM to 2:15 AM (EST) Monday through Saturday and from 10:00 PM Saturday to 6:00 AM Sunday (EST).

COST: $125 per month subscription fee; $22 per hour connect time charge; and $13 per hour telecommunications charge. There is also a charge for each search, which ranges from $6-51 per hour; and $2.50 per citation for Shepard's or Auto-Cite. There is also a small printing charge calculated on a per-line or per-screen basis, and various one-time charges upon signing up, as well as optional equipment rental charges.

FOR FURTHER INFORMATION: Contact: Mead Data Central, 9393 Springboro Pike, P.O. Box 933, Dayton, OH 45401. Tel: 800/227-4908 or 513/865-6800 in Ohio.

ONLINE RESOURCES

This service allows customers to receive information from thousands of domestic and international databases without actually having to subscribe to them. Instead, the user telephones the service with a research request and ONLINE RESOURCES will search the extensive databases to which it subscribes to find the relevant information. This information retrieval service provides access to nearly every commercial database, including LEXIS, DISCLOSURE, BRS Search Service, Orbit Search Service, WESTLAW, DIALOG, and Dow Jones News.

COST: The subscriber pays the database fee plus a $100 per hour research fee. Deposit or advance accounts are available.

FOR FURTHER INFORMATION: Contact: On-Line Resources, Inc. 1121 North Irving Street, Second Floor, Arlington, VA 22201. Tel: 800/678-9393, or 703/358-9600 in Virginia.

ORBIT SEARCH SERVICE

This is an international online information retrieval service which gathers its information from many of the world's best known and most experienced information indexing and abstracting services, including government agencies, professional and academic societies, and private information companies. **ORBIT** contains 100 databases, including Federal Register, National Technical Information Service (U.S. Department of Commerce), LABORDOC, COLD (Cold Regions Research and Engineering Laboratory of the U.S. Army Corps of Engineers), CLAIMS (over 2 million U.S. Patents; chemical patents since 1950), CLAIMS Classification (dictionary index to U.S. Patent and Trademark Office's classification codes), Congressional Record, and POWER (Energy Library, U.S. Department of Energy, USPA (U.S. Patents), INPADOC (International Patent Documentation Center 1968-present), WPI (World Patent Index 1963-present).

CUSTOMIZED SERVICES:

* customized training sessions.
* **Selective Dissemination of Information Service (SDI):** generates and mails to customers the results of stored searches each time their selected files are updated.

* **ORBDOC Online Ordering Service:** allows users to order copies of full text sources.
* **Searchlight:** a monthly newsletter through which ORBIT users are constantly kept up to date with information about the newest databases, system features and search techniques.
* international access.

AVAILABILITY: 24-hour service, except 9:45 PM - 10:15 PM (EST), Monday - Friday, and 9:45 PM - 10:00 AM (EST) Saturday.

COST: $40 per year for USERID (this is the user's password). If the service is used during a particular month the user will be charged a minimum of $15; if charges are over $15 then the user will be charged that amount. The databases are accessed through Telenet or Tymnet, which have a $13 per hour fee. Once on a database, there is an additional hourly research fee, which can range from $35 to $300, depending on which database is used.

FOR FURTHER INFORMATION: Contact ORBIT Search Service, 8000 Westpark Drive, McLean, VA 22102. Tel: 800/456-7248 or 703/442-0900 in Virginia.

VERALEX 2

VERALEX 2 contains both the VERALEX And LEXIS databases. VERALEX can be used to access both AUTO-CITE and SHOWME. AUTO-CITE provides current information regarding published court opinions, cases, IRS Revenue Rulings and Revenue Procedures, as well as American Law Reports (ALR) and U.S. Supreme Court Reports, Lawyers Edition 2d annotation that discusses the requested document. Auto-Cite also gives the prior and subsequent history of the case as it travels through the courts. **SHOWME** is a full-text document retrieval service which brings the user Federal and state cases, plus IRS materials. One can also get the full text of ALR annotations and information from Federal Tax Coordinator, Second Edition. With LEXIS the user has access to virtually every case that courts release for publication. LEXIS also includes the following: NEXIS, which provides information about government activities, pending litigation, and business actions; LEXPAT, which includes the full text of utility, plant, and design patents issued by the U.S. Patent and Trademark Office; and NAARS, which contains annual reports from thousands of publicly traded companies. (Note: through VERALEX 2 the subscriber does not receive access to LEXIS' Shepard's Citation service). VUSTAT is a full text service of the United States Code Service and the Internal Revenue Code, as well as selected state statutes.

AVAILABILITY: 24-hour service (some down-time on weekends).

COST: $25 monthly minimum, or a usage fee, whichever is higher; plus $40 per hour connect time charges; plus $45 per hour plus request fees; LEXIS $35 per hour plus library charges.

FOR FURTHER INFORMATION: Contact: Veralex, Inc., 1 Graves Street, Rochester, NY 14692. Tel: 800/828-6373.

WASHINGTON ON-LINE

This service offers comprehensive access to Federal legislative information, including:

* **Bill Tracking:** legislative histories, complete calendar, keyword search of official summaries, Bill-File capabilities, and committee and floor votes.
* **Text Tracking:** including keyword search of the full text of every bill moving through the U.S. Congress.

AVAILABILITY: 24-hour service.

COST: Option 1: $500 start-up fee and an unlimited access fee of $4,500. Option 2: $750 start-up fee and a computer-connect time per hour of $100.

FOR FURTHER INFORMATION: Tel: 916/447-1886 (Sacramento, CA).

WESTLAW

WESTLAW can be used to research substantive law as well as procedural and evidentiary issues. Its comprehensive law database contains a wide variety of case law, statutory, regulatory and administrative law materials. The United States Code, Code of Federal Regulations, U.S. Supreme Court decisions, and Federal Courts of Appeals Rulings are among the 2,000 databases available on WESTLAW. WESTLAW also contains state statutes, case law from all 50 states, a broad range of topical databases, and more than 300 legal texts and periodicals.

CUSTOMIZED SERVICES:

* **Insta-Cite:** a current source of case histories, with direct history from 1938 to present for state cases, 1754 to present for Federal cases, and precedential history from 1972.
* **Shepard's Citations** for complete case commentary.
* **Shepard's PreView** for updating Shepards.
* **WESTLAW as a Citator** to find the most current citing cases.
* **EXPERTNET, FSD, and TASA:** these databases can help the user find medical, scientific, and technical expert witnesses.
* **EZ ACCESS:** the new menu-driven approach to using WESTLAW that simplifies many common research tasks for first-time and occasional users.

AVAILABILITY: 24-hour service except from 11:00 PM Saturday to 7:00 AM Sunday (EST).

COST: WESTLAW pricing plans are based on anticipated usage. Contact vendor for specific pricing information.

FOR FURTHER INFORMATION: Contact: West Publishing Company, 58 West Kellogg Blvd., P.O. Box 65779, St. Paul, MN 55164. Tel: 800/328-0109.

COMMERCIAL DOCUMENT RETRIEVAL SERVICES WITH U.S. GOVERNMENT INFORMATION

Another means of obtaining Federal Government information is through hard-copy document retrieval services. These services can provide users with a wide variety of information about the Federal Government. Whereas the database services are used on a continuing subscription basis, these services are used intermittently, whenever a specific document or piece of information is required.

CHARLES E. SIMON & COMPANY

This service offers research, retrieval, and watch services for most Federal departments and agencies, including: Securities and Exchange Commission, Office of Thrift Supervision, Federal Reserve Board, Federal Deposit Insurance Corporation, Office of the Comptroller of the Currency, Federal Communications Commission, Federal Energy Regulatory Commission, Federal Trade Commission, Interstate Commerce Commission, Department of Transportation, Department of Labor, U.S. District Courts, U.S. Courts of Appeals, U.S. Supreme Court, Library of Congress, and the Congressional Record.

COST: To start search: $25 ($60 to begin a rush search). Per hour research fee: $60. Photocopying charges: 55 cents per page.

FOR FURTHER INFORMATION: Contact: Charles E. Simon & Company, 1300 New York Avenue, NW, Suite 205E, Washington, D.C. 20005. Tel: 202/289-5300.

CONGRESSIONAL DOCUMENTS ON DEMAND

This service offers access to any congressional document published since 1970 and any statistical document published by a Federal department or agency since 1970. Full text is available in microfiche or paper copy. The databases are available through DIALOG.

COST: $100 per hour search fee, plus telecommunications cost for total time connected.

FOR FURTHER INFORMATION: Contact: Congressional Information Service, 4520 East-West Highway, Bethesda, MD 20814. Attn: Online Department. Tel: 301/654-1550.

FEDERAL DOCUMENT RETRIEVAL

This service provides information in the following areas:

* **CONGRESS:** bills, reports, hearings, public laws, legislative histories from current and past sessions, and committee prints;

* **WHITE HOUSE:** executive orders, reports, and presidential proclamations;

* **FEDERAL AGENCIES:** opinion letters, proposed and final rules, comment files, annual reports, and staff studies from any agency of the Federal Government;

* **COURTS:** pleadings, decisions, briefs from any court in the United States.

* **Miscellaneous Services:** Patents, trademarks, copyrights, Freedom of Information requests; and Government Printing Office, National Technical Information Service, and General Accounting Office publications. This service also provides extensive information on the Securities and Exchange Commission through eight Disclosure Information Centers.

COST: To start a search: $15 ($40 to begin a rush search). Per hour research fee: $40. 45 cents per page photocopying charges. Delivery charges are additional.

FOR FURTHER INFORMATION: Contact: Federal Documents Retrieval, Inc., 810 First Street, NE, Suite 700, Washington D.C. 20002. Tel: 800/874-4337 or 202/789-2233 in Washington, D.C. For SEC documents call 800/638-8241 or 202/347-2819 in Washngton, D.C.

WASHINGTON DOCUMENT SERVICE (WDS)

This service monitors and retrieves documents in all areas of Federal activity, including: court filings and rulings, energy regulations, Senate and House bills and reports, environmental rulings, patent and trademark searches, Treasury Department actions, bank regulatory agency releases, and merger and acquisitions activity. This service also focuses on the Securities Exchange Commission. In addition to document retrieval of SEC filings, WDS provides information on the following: litigation and securities violation checks, insider holdings, institutional holdings, and No Action Letters. WDS also monitors the following banking agencies on a daily basis: Office of Thrift Supervision, Resolution Trust Corporation, Federal Reserve Board, Federal Deposit Insurance Corporation, and Comptroller of the Currency.

SPECIFIC SERVICES:

* **Daily Banking Update Service:** index of all notices, proposed regulations, press releases, and filings with Federal bank regulatory agencies. These are sent per subscriber's request.

* **Hot-Document Service:** list of important documents filed daily in all Government agencies. List is faxed daily to all subscribers.

* **Freedom of Information Act Requests:** WDS will submit confidential FOIA requests on behalf of customers in its own name.

* **Courts:** WDS manages a nationwide network to provide copies of complaints, consent orders, briefs, opinions, and judgments filed in any court in the United States.

COST: Service charge: $40. Per hour research fee: $50 (payment by the quarter hour). Photocopying charges: 45 cents per page. Additional delivery charges at cost.

FOR FURTHER INFORMATION: Contact: Washington Document Service, 450 Fifth Street, NW, Washington, D.C. 20001. Tel: 800/366-3305 or 202/628-5200 in Washington, D.C.

WASHINGTON SERVICE BUREAU

This service can obtain any document from any Federal department or agency, Congress, and all Federal Courts (as well as some state courts)

COMMERCIAL DOCUMENT RETRIEVAL SERVICES

SPECIFIC SERVICES:

* **SEC Daily Release Service:** rulemakings, complaints, consents, decisions, orders, speeches press releases, reports.

* **FERC Daily Release Service:** full text of documents with a daily summary sheet.

* **FCC Daily Release Service:** FCC Daily Digest summary, plus full-text back-up of all releases, docket items, notices, and reports on FCC actions.

* **Banking Daily Release Service:** full text of rule changes, regulations, notices, and releases issued by all Federal bank regulatory agencies.

* **Watch Services:** up-to-the-minute developments regarding any agency, subject, or company.

PUBLICATIONS:

* **SEC Today:** includes the SEC News Digest, feature articles, and most current lists of daily SEC filings.

* **Federal Immigration Law Update:** weekly summaries of statutes, regulations, operating guidelines, court and administrative decisions.

* **ERISA Update:** a monthly loose-leaf reporter providing full text and abstracts of releases from the Department of Labor and the Pension Benefit Guaranty Corporation; includes full text and abstracts of advisory opinions, information letters, and opinion letters.

* **ERISA Citator:** a monthly compilation of Employee Retirement Income Security Act (ERISA) citations.

* **Significant SEC Filings Reporter:** indices and abstracts of significant and unusual proxies, registration statements, and Williams Act filings.

* **Ethics In Government Reporter:** monthly loose leaf reporter covering ethics law; especially related to government contractors.

* **SEC No-Action Letters Index and Summaries:** includes weekly abstracts of every no-action letter released by SEC and monthly supplements with topical and alphabetical indices.

* **The Bank Digest:** provides daily summaries of releases from all banking related activities at the SEC, Congress and the Federal Courts.

COST: To begin searches: $65 for same-day service; $50 for 24-hour service. Per hour research fee: $75. Photocopying charges 65 cents per page.

FOR FURTHER INFORMATION: Contact: Washington Service Bureau, 655 Fifteenth Street, NW, Suite 275, Washington, D.C. 20005. Tel: 800/828-5354 or 202/833-9200 in Washington, D.C.

Topical Index

TOPICAL INDEX

ADMINISTRATIVE LAW JUDGE/ADJUDICATIVE OFFICES

ADMINISTRATIVE PROCEDURE/REGULATORY AFFAIRS

ADMIRALTY/MARITIME

TOPICAL INDEX

CORPORATIONS

CORRECTIONS

CRIME VICTIMS

CRIMINAL LAW

Department and Agency Index

DEPARTMENT AND AGENCY INDEX

EXECUTIVE BRANCH-EXECUTIVE OFFICE OF THE PRESIDENT AND CABINET DEPARTMENTS

LEGISLATIVE **BRANCH**